The World's Leading Autograph Pricing Authority

The SANDERS
Price Guide
to
Autographs

Sixth Edition

The SANDERS Price Guide to Autographs

Sixth Edition

Dr. Richard Saffro

Jim Smith, Don Shaw

Helen Sanders and Ralph Roberts

Alexander Books
abooks.com

Publisher Alexander Books: Ralph Roberts

Price Guide Publisher: Dr. Richard Saffro

Cover Design: Ralph Roberts
Editors: Ralph Roberts, Pat Roberts, Richard Saffro, Jim Smith, Don Shaw

Interior Design and Electronic Page Assembly: **WorldComm**® and Ralph Roberts

Printed in Canada

10 9 8 7 6 5 4 3 2 1
Sixth Edition

Trade Paper version: ISBN 1-57090-213-5
Limited Hardback version: ISBN 1-57090-214-3

Library of Congress Number: 2003108532

While every effort has been made to ensure the accuracy of the information in this book, the authors and publisher accept no responsibility for inaccuracries or omissions, and the authors and publisher will in no event be liable for any loss of profit or any other damage, including but not limited to special, incidental, consequential, or any other damages. Be sure to read Chapter 14 "How to Use This Price Guide" in this book for how our pricing works and how to use those prices.

The opinions expressed in this book are solely those of the authors and are not necessarily those of Alexander Books.

Trademarks
Names of products mentioned in this book known to be or that are suspected of being trademarks or service marks are capitalized. Use of a product or service name in this book should not be regarded as affecting the validity of any trademark or service mark.

Alexander Books—a division of Creativity, Inc.—is a full-service publisher located at 65 Macedonia Road, Alexander NC 28701. Phone (828) 252-9515 or (828) 255-8719 fax or e-mail **sales@abooks.com**. Dealer inquiries welcome.

Internet web sites: **abooks.com, sigs.net, sanderspriceguide.com**

Contents

Preface 9
    Acknowledgements 10
    A Note From Helen Sanders and Ralph Roberts 12

1 Authenticating Autographs John Reznikoff   **15**
    Knowing Right from Wrong 15
    A Start in Uncovering Forgeries 16
    Autograph Organizations and Other Sources 17
    Making Comparisons 18
    Giveaways 21
    The Forger's Art 22

2 Quality and Content Steven S. Raab   **25**
    An Introduction to the Concept 25
    Defining Quality in Letters, Manuscripts and Documents 26
    Assessing Content and Importance 26
    Gradations of Autograph Values 28
    How This Applies to Signed Photographs 30
    The Impact of Condition on Prices 32
    Learn to Protect Yourself 33
    Thoughts on the Autograph Marketplace Today 34

3 The Double Edged Sword Stuart Lutz   **37**
    The Good 37
    The Bad 38
    The Improved 41
    The Suggestions 42
    Points To Remember 43
    Protect Yourself 44
    Educate Yourself 45
    Conclusions 46

4 Investment Daniel Brams   **47**

    Appreciation Potential 47
    Rare Documents 48
    Limited Availability 49
    Affordability 51

5 Buying Autographs at Auction George Hollingsworth   **53**

    Auction Rules 53

6 Presidential Autographs Mike Minor and Larry Vzralik   **57**

    Collecting Presidential Pieces 58
    More Than One 59
    Signed Photographs 60
    Executive Mansion or White House Cards 60
    Signed White House Vignettes 61
    Presidential Bank Checks 61
    Letters With Content 61
    Presidential Rarities or Oddities and Bad Handwriting 66
    Books Signed by Presidents 66
    Presidential Franks 69
    Material Signed by Both a President and First Lady 72

7 HOLLYWOOD AUTOGRAPHS Tom Kramer   **75**

    Real or Fake? 77
    Finding the Treasures 80
    Tracking Down the Possible 81

8 Autographed First Edition Books Tim Miller   **85**

    Major Shifts 85
    A Good Time To Be Collecting 86
    Value Increases 87
    Making Points 89

9 The Manuscript Society Edward C. Oetting and David R. Smith   **91**

10 UACC Paul K. Carr   **93**

11 PADA Sheldon L. Tarakan   **95**

12   IACC–DA Stephen Koschal   **97**

13 International Groups Ralph Roberts   **99**
    Autograph Collectors Club of India 99
    The Autograph Club of Great Britain 100
    Club der Autogrammsammler (German) 100

14 How to Use This Price Guide Dr. Richard Saffro   **103**
    Pricing Categories 104
    Additional information 106

15 Prices   **107**
    A 107
    B 130
    C 187
    D 231
    E 260
    F 271
    G 293
    H 320
    I 359
    J 363
    K 375
    L 395
    M 421
    N 467
    O 477
    P 484
    Q 510
    R 511
    S 536
    T 582
    U 600
    V 602
    W 610
    X 638
    Y 638
    Z 641

16 Facsimiles

A 649
B 651
C 657
D 661
E 663
F 664
G 666
H 669
I 672
J 672
K 673
L 675
M 679
N 682
O 683
P 683
Q 686
R 686
S 689
T 693
U 694
V 694
W 695
Y 698
Z 698
BONUS: Dream Autographs 699

Autograph Dealers   702

Dealer Index 702

Preface

Dr. Richard Saffro

Margaret Bourke-White. Michael Mocogni. What is a name really worth? In some cases, they are worth far more than their stated value. I found that to be true. As it happened, these names brought me to my new role as owner of this publication.

In early 2002, I was looking to purchase a Margaret Bourke-White signature to accompany an historic World War II photograph she had taken for *Life Magazine*. The picture captured the liberation of Buchenwald, and it is considered one of the greatest photographs of the twentieth century. A cherished patient of mine, Michael Mocogni, survived the Holocaust and appears in this famous work. Michael had given me an inscribed copy of this photo and I wanted Margaret Bourke-White's signature to accompany his.

I found the Margaret Bourke-White signature and purchased it from the Autograph House of George and Helen Sanders. The Sanders were the publishers of the guide book that I relied upon for pricing autographs. Realizing that I was using an outdated 5th edition of **The Sanders Price Guide to Autographs**, I inquired about their upcoming 6th edition. I learned that there were no immediate plans to print a 6th edition; in fact, the guide book was looking for a new owner.

Together with Jim Smith and Don Shaw, I purchased the rights to **The Sanders Price Guide to Autographs**. We each bring a different expertise and knowledge to the world of autographs. Collectively we have spent hundreds of hours revising and editing the prices in the guide. We have employed the talents of some of the most respected men in the autograph industry to author important topics of concern to the autograph collector. These topics include Authenticating Autographs, Quality and Content of Autographs, Autograph Auctions, eBay, and Autographs as an Investment. I am indebted to these men for their erudite contributions.

In this 6th edition, we have chosen to include articles on three additional autograph categories: Presidents of the United States, Hollywood autographs, and signed books. All future editions of the Sanders guide will continue to explore a broad spectrum of topics of interest to collectors. We hope that you find this 6th edition of **The Sanders Price Guide to Autographs** to be the preeminent source of autograph information and accurate pricing.

While I'm grateful to Ms. Bourke-White for the serendipitous role she played in my involvement with this Guide, my true thanks goes to the person who first ignited my passion for autograph collecting: my Dad. Yale Saffro was both an artist and a collector. Using pen and ink or scratchboard, he drew pictures of celebrities, politicians, artists, athletes, and musicians. He then mailed out the drawings with a personalized letter asking the subjects for their signature. His collection grew to over 7500 signed drawings. The cover of this book features his fine art work as a tribute to him as my mentor, my hero.

—Dick Saffro

Acknowledgements

The 6th Edition of **The Sanders Price Guide to Autographs** is the result of the committed efforts of many individuals providing time and expertise to assure that the highest standard of publication was attained. Our most valuable asset is our time. Many individuals provided their time and creativity to refine and expand upon the heritage, which **The Sanders Price Guide to Autographs** has developed since its inception in 1988. A special thank you goes to Helen Sanders and Ralph Roberts, who provided the opportunity and shared their expertise and experience to make this 6th Edition possible. The thrill and excitement of autograph collecting is further enhanced when those providing the acquisition experience are ones of integrity and trust. The publishers of the 6th Edition want to express their gratitude and acknowledge the contributions made by the following individuals and companies who have provided their resources and knowledge in the production of this guide.

Abraham Lincoln Bookshop
Alexander Autographs
American Historical Guild

American Memorabilia
Autograph Pros
Jack Bacon
Catherine Barnes Historical Autographs
Dave Beach
Benedikt & Salmon
Jim Berland
John Blair
Edward N. Bomsey Autographs
Daniel Brams
Collectibles Insurance Agency
Custer Battlefield Museum
Jerry Docteur
EAC Galleries
Early American History Auctions
A. Lovell Elliott
Elmer's Nostalgia
Estoric.com
David Frohman
Brian and Maria Green
Roger Gross Ltd. Musical Autographs
Marc Held
Heroes & Legends
George Hollingsworth
Steve Hoskins
Howard Hurwitz
IACC/IADA
Chuck Jasiak
Kaller and Associates
Keya Galleries
Tom Kramer
Lewis Leigh, Jr.
Stuart Lutz
Manuscript Society
Mike Masters
Mastronet
Tim Miller
Mike Minor and Larry Vrzalik

Mitchell Marketing LLC
Todd Mueller Autographs
Lenamarie Natale
Dick Newell
PADA
R&R Enterprises
Steven S. Raab
Larry Rafferty
John Reznikoff
John Rogers
Fred Senese
Showcase Portfolio
Signature House
Signatures in Time
R.M. Smythe
Sterncastle Collectibles
Christophe Stickel Autographs
Gerald A.J. Stodolski, Inc.
UACC
Visible Ink Incorporated
Scott Winslow

A Note From Helen Sanders and Ralph Roberts

Events move on. The three of us—George and Helen Sanders, and Ralph Roberts—conceived this price guide to autographs concept in 1986. We went on to author and publish five editions of the general autograph guide and three of the sports guide, plus a book on collecting autographs. We're not through publishing books about autographs by any means but, with George's passing in 1998 and the burden of pricing growing ever greater, we realized the need for new leadership. Which brings us to the team of Dr. Richard Saffro, Jim Smith, and Don Shaw—all longtime experts in autographs. This sixth edition with its thousands of new names and comprehensive updating results from their hard work in expanding **The Sanders Price Guides** and taking them to this next exciting level.

Helen remains as a consultant and Ralph, as he always has, continues to maintain the now-gargantuan database of prices, edit, and typeset **The Sanders Price Guide to Autographs**.

The **SANDERS**

Price Guide

to

Autographs

6

Sixth Edition

Section 1:

INFORMATION

Being an illuminating collection of informative articles by carefully selected experts.

The late George Sanders—one of the founders of this price guide—with Frank Sinatra at a Hollywood gala. George's early interest in collecting autographs and his long career of obtaining in-person signatures allowed him to become an expert on autograph authenticity and, during a 50-year-plus tenure as an autograph expert was the basis for this guide's expertise—a tradition we continue.

Chapter 1

Authenticating Autographs

by John Reznikoff

Knowing Right from Wrong

The single question I have heard more than any other in my career is "how do you know it's real?" This has been a question that paradoxically has paralleled my career over the last twenty-three years. As one could ascertain by the plethora of writing on this subject, this is no easy question to answer. The answers have for some launched careers, for others sunk them. This topic has put many an offender in jail, made some rich and some poor and even on one occasion that I am aware of, ended the lives of several individuals. For the purposes here, I will attempt to initiate the uninitiated, and reduce the learning curve for those who are involved but can use a little help. However, I will only be able to partially answer this question here.

I started in this business at the age of eighteen while attending Fordham University. This was a time well before the Internet, even fax machines and cell phones. As technology has advanced so has the trade of the forger. We are constantly battling new innovations in this field with the technology itself as well as some good old homespun detective work. It was in the late 70s and into the 80s that my journey had begun. I started selling mostly free-franks and civil war soldier's letters, which for the most part needed very little authentication. The signatures on envelopes in lieu of postage, pretty much spoke for themselves and the accompanying postmarks made authenticating pretty simple. My background in stamps, including expertising at the prestigious Philatelic Foundation in New York made it rather easy to determine whether or not the envelope and postmarks were authentic. If this were true and the envelope in question lacked stamps or equivalent postmarks than it would be fairly safe to determine that the signature, say that of a President, was authentic. Likewise letters written by Civil War soldiers, particularly those that were in period stamped envelopes, could relatively easily be deemed authentic on their face value. Then came the harder stuff.

A Start in Uncovering Forgeries

Fortunately there is a magnificent body of published material that is useful to the neophyte as well as the advanced dealer in uncovering most forgeries. The first thing you will need is a decent library. For under the cost of a routine John F. Kennedy as senator, one can have quite an arsenal to help defend against the purchase of non-authentic material. I have over 3000 volumes in my library. Add to that another 5000+ auction and retail catalogs and a large collection of actual forgeries and other non-authentic autographs (the basis of this collection was formed by the late Charles Hamilton from whom I purchased the same) and it's no wonder I need about 1000 square feet to house my references. You don't however! The most important thing in a library is exemplars, that being the commonly used forensic term for examples of a known authentic autograph. These can be gleaned from auction and retail catalogs alike but always at the risk that the exemplars are not correct. Some are better than others and to avoid lawsuits, I'll keep that discussion to an in-person one.

Other than auction catalogs, a great source and perhaps a more reliable one, are the reference books which I have mentioned previously. A complete bibliography of these sources would fill many pages, and for the purposes of this article, I'll only mention a few of my favorites. If I've left anybody out, I apologize in advance. I highly recommend every book written by the late, great, dean of autographs, Charles Hamilton. Top among these books in my perspective is *American Autographs, Volumes One and Two*, considered by many to be the most important reference book extant on the subject. Expect to use a lot of your budget, as it would be difficult to find them for under $300. Almost as important is Hamilton's *Great Fakes and Famous Forgers*, as well as *Collecting Autographs and Manuscripts*, which is a portable paperback containing over 1,400 "exemplars" or facsimiles. Although very specialized, don't even consider buying a Kennedy autograph without having *The Robot That Helped to Make a President.* Equally informative would be the books and catalogs of Kenneth W. Rendell, especially *Forging History, The Detection of Fake Letters and Documents.* This book has an extensive selected bibliography from which to choose other books that might fit your specialty. Of course, all the Sanders catalogs, back to Volume 1, have many reliable facsimiles to help with your authenticating. I would also recommend all the books by Mark Allen Baker and Paul Carr. If Civil War is your concentration, try *War Between the States, Autographs and Biographical Sketches* by Jim Hayes, and *Autographs of the Confederacy* by Michael Reese II. Also recommended in the Presidential/ Americana area are *From the President's Pen* by Vrzalik and Minor, *From the White House Inkwell* by John M. Taylor, *American Literary Autographs* by Cahoon, Lang and Ryskemp. A real sleeper is *History of the 'Free Franking' of Mail in the United States* by Edward Stern. This book not only illustrates just about every American that ever free franked an envelope, but also shows a nearly complete collection of presidential checks, autograph letters signed, photographs signed, as well as campaign ribbons. The books and catalogs of Todd Axelrod provide excellent reference, especially *The Handbook of Historical Documents.* In the specialty area of signed photographs, M. Wesley Marins' *Sincerely Yours* has no peer. As far as entertainment autographs, try Christianson's *Celebrity Autographs.*

Autograph Organizations and Other Sources

The various autograph organizations have contributed greatly to the field as far as published material. The Manuscript Society has a number of publications which would be worthy of any library. *The Pen and Quill,* which is a publication of the UACC, has published prolifically for many years. Perhaps the most outstanding body of work have been the signature studies conducted and published by the IADA/IACC.

Don't try to complete this list all at once, because you'll undoubtedly end up overpaying. The Internet has made the acquisition of references quite a bit easier. A search of any of the book sites, including Amazon, Half.com, and the ABAA and ABE sites, will help you locate many of these reference works that are second hand and reasonably priced. The various organizations usually have sufficient stock of many of their publications to offer to you. If you exhibit to a dealer that you are a serious collector, they will often help you to build your library and find you the books that fit your specialty.

Making Comparisons

Now that you've accumulated thousands of exemplars from which to judge prospective purchases, how do you make the comparison? Comparisons can be made in many ways, but perhaps the most logical, easiest method is to hold the questioned document in one hand and a known exemplar in the other and make a determination whether the questioned document would fit within the parameters of variation that could exist with the known exemplar. This is an incredible over-simplification, and it takes years, if not decades, to develop an eye for such things. It's been my experience that some people, no matter how much time they spend at it, never develop that "eye."

Another very useful method is the creation of transparencies. I have used these often in court testimony and not only is this a useful way of authenticating items, but its also very dramatic and demonstrative. Transparencies can be bought at any office supply store, and simply placed in a standard copier machine to create the tool that you'll need. The transparency allows you to place known exemplars directly next to a questioned document, or if needed, over the questioned document. If for example, a modern presidential signature matches up with the transparency of a known autopen, you'll know not to buy it. Again, this is an oversimplification, and it takes years to get the most use out of such an examination.

Another excellent method of examination is one that I call "cut-ups" for short. When questioned documents are compared in this analytic manner, the variations become much more immediately apparent. Take the questioned document and make a copy. Make another copy at a 200% enlargement. Then take a known exemplar and do the same. You may need multiple copies for this analysis, because what you will be doing is taking a scissor and cutting the copy letter by letter or word by word, and making a comparative flow chart. Known and questioned can be placed side by side on a blank piece of paper (use a glue stick) for a striking exposé. I have used this method in expert testimony with startling results. A great illustration of this method is presented in Kenneth W. Rendell's previously mentioned book, *Forging History, The Detection of Fake Letters and Documents*. On pages 77-82, Rendell does an excellent cut-up of a known Washington letter versus a forgery by Robert Spring. Spring's forgeries are quite well executed and I have seen them offered at auctions both live and on the Internet. I illustrate several examples here. (Illus. 1).

Another method of examination involves magnification. There are a host of products available on the market that can give you enlargements that range from 2x to several hundred x. For purposes of autographs authentication, I suggest anywhere between 2x and 30x, depending on your own preferences and what it is that you're trying to achieve. Magnification can often reveal ink which is not contemporary, overwriting, hesitation, tracing, and a host of other anomalies that are most often associated with forgeries. You could spend five- or twenty thousand dollars on a magnification device. At the high end is the video-spectral comparator. This is an instrument designed to detect the different optical properties of a questioned item. This is a non-destructive test and does not alter the appearance or condition of the item. It is often used to examine documents for the presence of fraudulent alterations and identify the presence of different inks. Inks that come from different writing instruments can react differently when illuminated with ultraviolet and infrared light. The differences can be easily detected with a video-spectral comparator. This same device can be used to "bring back" erased writing and to reveal original information that has been somehow erased or overwritten. (Illus. 2).

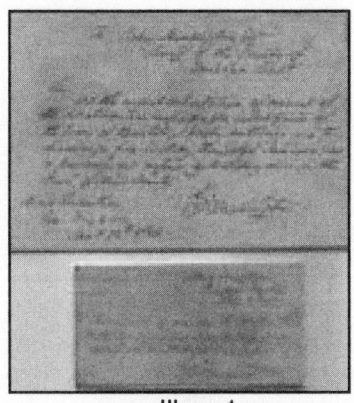

Illus. 1

If you don't want to spend twenty thousand on such a machine, and I certainly don't recommend that expense unless you're a full-time court appointed forensic expert, a simple ultraviolet light can be very effective.

Illustration 2 is a fascinating forgery, executed by Henry Woodhouse. A chapter in Hamilton's book, *Great Fakes and Famous Forgers*, is devoted to this scoundrel. All the signatures on this otherwise genuine philatelic cover, are forgeries, and the ultraviolet light does much to expose them. There is evidence of practice which is shown under ultraviolet examination, especially of the Roosevelt signature. This

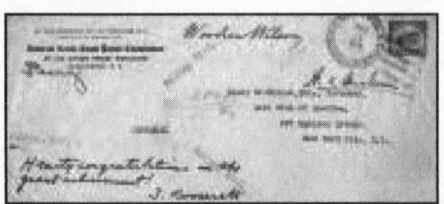

item if it were genuine would be worth $2,000-$3,000, but, instead, we have what would have been a $300 philatelic item that has been defaced by forgery. Illustration 3 and 4 show an excellent and interesting Joseph Cosey forgery.

Illus. 2

There are many attributes of this letter that expose it as a forgery, and an ultraviolet examination is one of them. Cosey is dealt with in Hamilton's book, as well. Another one of my mentors, the late Robert A. Siegel, actually bought items from Cosey in his lifetime. As he explained to me, Cosey

was a drinker, and would often trade his items for a bottle of booze. This particular item bears several Cosey trademarks. One being the apparent docketing of N.W. Edwards, the other a convincing authentication of that docketing by a seemingly credible source. Under ultraviolet light, the outer folded address leaf exhibits evidence of a previous washed out address. It also shows that several of the hand stamps were executed in this same ink. It would be unlikely that these markings which should have been applied many miles apart would contain exactly the same ink. This item if genuine, could have commanded as much as $100,000. Cosey was also excellent at forging the autograph of Edgar Allan Poe, Illustration 5 shows three Poe letters that would command $20,000-$50,000 each if they were authentic.

Note the docketing on the December 7, 1847 letter, which says "N.J. Howard..." A careful look at the handwriting of this docketing shows that it is exactly the same handwriting on the previously mentioned Lincoln letter (see Illustration 3 and 4). Isn't it interesting that both

Illus.3 & 4

Lincoln's and Poe's correspondence while having different names, were the same person?

Ultraviolet light is more of a second line of defense for things that appear genuine but have attributes that require caution. Some non-authentic items can be avoided simply by having the proper reference at hand. Secretarial signatures top the hit list. Items signed by secretaries are abundant and a general knowledge of who used secretaries should be acquired by every serious collector and dealer. Every day on eBay I see such items offered by either inexperienced dealers or those who would take advantage of inexperienced buyers. John F. Kennedy's secretaries were probably the most prolific of any president. Illustration 6 and 7 show typical Kennedy secretarial signatures executed by his secretary, Evelyn Lincoln.

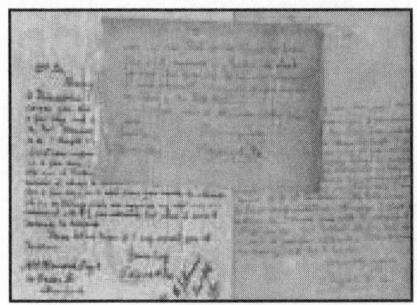
Illus. 5

These items would sell for a minimum of several thousand each if they were authentic. The inauguration cover even comes with a convincing White House letter of Evelyn Lincoln, attesting to its authenticity. I have seen Evelyn Lincoln transmit authentic JFK signatures, but in most cases, she is the one who penned his name. It is interesting to note that under ultraviolet light the ink of Evelyn Lincoln's signature matches exactly that of the signature on the envelope. Illustration 8 shows another famous secretarial signature, that of Richard Nixon, most likely executed by the infamous Rosemary Woods.

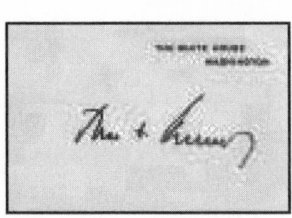

Giveaways

One of the giveaways that this signature is indeed secretarial is what I call the tall 'd.' The final "d" of "Richard" extends in height above that of the first "R". Measurement can be an excellent tool to determine whether an autograph is authentic or not. While it is true that signatures may vary in size, depending on the object that is signed, day-to-day signatures, particularly those on routine items, rarely change significantly. You can measure width, height, spacing between letters, spacing between words, spacing from the border of the document that's signed, and spacing between lines of writing, to help

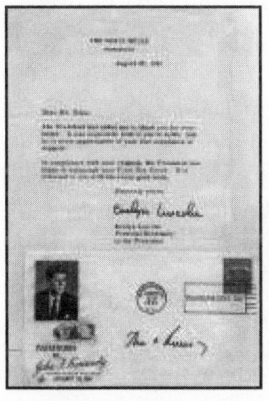
Illus. 6 & 7

AUTHENTICATING AUTOGRAPHS   21

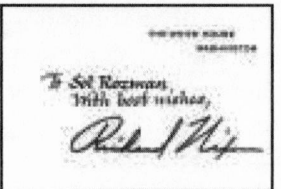

Illus. 8

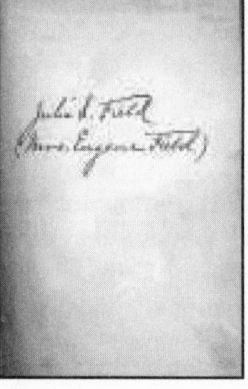

Illus. 9

you determine if what you have is the real McCoy. Illustration 9 shows a TR signed book that would fool a good many—collector and dealer alike. One criterion for branding a forgery is the space between the first and last names, which is quite variant to what one normally sees. This book, incidentally, was from the library of Mrs. Eugene Field, another great tip-off that it's a forgery. Field's son, Eugene II, was a notorious old-time forger and even forged the works of his own father. Incidentally, the ink of the ownership attribution fluoresces exactly the same as that of Roosevelt's purported signature. Hmmm......?

The Forger's Art

As I have said before, modern forgers have really advanced the art. This, combined with deceptive or inexperienced sellers that proliferate on the Internet, has made collecting in the 21st Century a veritable minefield. In the 80s and 90s, forgers were able to use technological advancements to fool many great experts. Perhaps the most notorious forger of the last several decades was Mark Hofmann, who was responsible for possibly, by today's values, tens of millions of dollars worth of spurious autographs. He was also responsible for the deaths of several people killed so that they would not uncover his scheme. Hofmann was able to prevent telltale signs of forgery of new ink on old paper by immersing the paper in an ammonia hydrochloride bath. One of the ways this was discovered was by its blue fluorescence. Hofmann plied his trade in the 80s yet forgers and technology in the 90s and the new millennium have really raised the bar. Many of the non-authentic autographs on the market today come from foreign countries. As the market has grown for genuine autographs from regions that were formerly fairly inaccessible from a trade standpoint, like Cuba and Russia, so has the proliferation of non-authentic items. In the last half-dozen years, I have seen countless books signed by

Stalin, Lenin, Castro, or Che Guevara, that are highly suspect. There's always a story behind them, like "my grandfather was a KGB agent," or "my great uncle fought in the Cuban Revolution." The better the

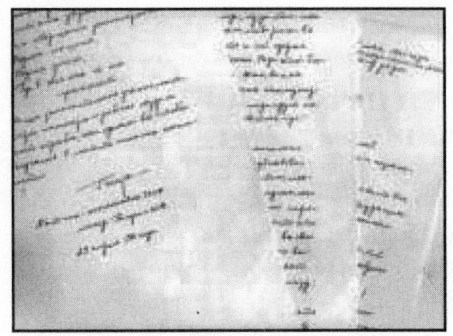

story, the more I am critical of the autograph. The fact that these forgeries are usually in a foreign language makes it even harder to authenticate. To most buyers, Russian is a language that is unidentifiable scribbles. Thus we are easy targets for the foreign forger. Illustration 10 shows a purported multi-page Gagarin with amazing content about his momentous first space flight. Dozens of these letters have recently surfaced, and many have passed through the auction rooms. Before the recent flour-

Illus. 10

ish of these letters, unquestionably authentic examples have sold from $25,000 to well into the six figures. I have done cut-ups and significant analysis of these letters and based on my work, would not authenticate them. Similar highly valuable pieces of space pioneer Konstantin Tsiolkovsky have also surfaced. Caveat emptor.

Perhaps the most dangerous high-tech forgeries in today's world are items that are printed as opposed to a human hand adding writing or signature to a piece of paper. This is not a new story, just one that keeps getting better. In the 40s, Einstein sent out numerous letters which looked hand-typed and were "signed" in blue ink. See Illustration 11.

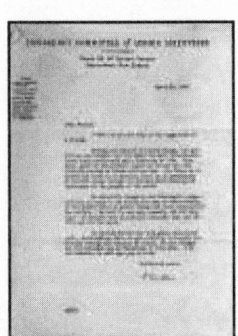

These are actually deceptively printed signatures, and make what would have been a $5,000+ letter virtually worthless. These cannot be authenticated from a scan, for example, if they were at auction on eBay.

Illustration No. 12 shows a Patrick Henry document complete with toning and what I will call three-dimensionality. It is a very dangerous printed facsimile which behind

Illus. 11

a frame (or in a scan) would fool 99.9% of interested parties. I have in my collection similar items that actually have the paper flaws printed right on them. Included are some magnificent George Washington facsimiles. Illustration No. 13 shows a beautiful Horatio Nelson handwritten and franked outer address leaf; too bad it's a

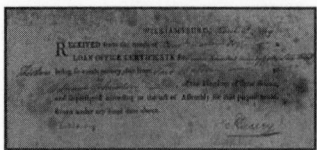

Illus. 12

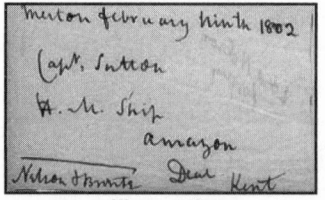

Illus. 13

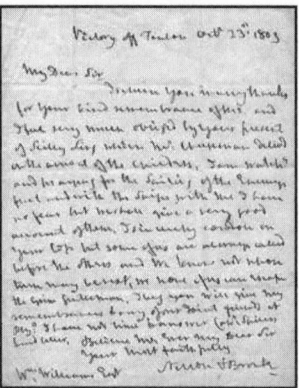

Illus. 14

forgery. If you were to make a transparency or use the cut-up method, you would see that it does not match the writing on this fabulous content letter, Illustration No. 14. Here's a surprise—not only is Illustration 14 a wonderful content letter, that would favorably match known authentic examples, but it is a printed facsimile as well. It too has an outer folder address leaf and all the earmarks of authenticity, except for the inconsistency of pressure and ink that is left by the human hand that is writing. Again, this would be undetectable on a scan when proving authenticity.

One of the highest art forms of forgery that I have seen most recently is laser printer application of a signature onto an otherwise authentic article. What comes to mind is a Babe Ruth photo that recently came across my desk that had a very believable and even convincingly somewhat uneven application of a signature. It was not detected until the exact same inscription popped up on another photograph. A transparency of the inscription proved the items to be unquestionably fake, as no one can duplicate a signature, moreover an inscription, exactly the same.

The Sanders Price Guide is one of the most valuable reference tools an autograph dealer or collector can have. To know the value of an item is very important in determining whether or not a purchase should be made. However, as we all know, value becomes moot if the autograph cannot be authenticated and determined to be real or forged.

—John Reznikoff, University Archives,
universityarchives.com

University Archives has been buying and selling rare documents since 1979. They have emerged as a leading document and manscript firm, with divisions and affiliates in five states, and a worldwide reputation. While University specializes in American history, they also buy and sell valuable letters, documents, manuscripts, and family correspondences in all fields including Presidents, World Government, Sports, Entertainment, Literature, Civil War, Revolutionary War, Science, African-American History, and Women in History.

Chapter 2

Quality and Content

by Steven S. Raab

Recently we had two letters of Franklin D. Roosevelt in our catalog and on our RaabAutographs.com web site. One was listed for $700 and the other for $10,000. I received an email from a new collector who found our name in a price guide and then visited the web site. He observed that the lower priced letter seemed consistent with price guide value, but asked how I could possibly justify the higher price of the other letter. His question was an important one, as it went to the very heart of understanding what matters most in collecting autographs and manuscripts.

An Introduction to the Concept

It also took me back to 1986 when I first got started in this exciting field. At that time, I was like a kid in a candy store, buying without discrimination whatever caught my eye and fit my budget. Over lunch a respected dealer gave me some unsolicited advice. "Buy fewer things," he told me, "but make them the highest quality you can afford." He did not elaborate further, and left me pondering. I began a search for the meaning of quality that has defined my relationship to autographs, and taken me through analysis of dealer and auction catalogs by the hundreds, innumerable purchases at auction and by direct sale from dealers and private sellers, and conversations galore with knowledgible individuals over the entire span of years. In so doing I learned many lessons that, I am convinced, are of value to others as well as myself.

Defining Quality in Letters, Manuscripts and Documents

Quality, I have determined, depends directly upon the autograph's content or intrinsic importance (by this latter term I mean that it has importance in and of itself). If you understand these two concepts, you will be armed with the tools you need to navigate successfully in autograph waters. And considering the price of autographs today, they are tools you can ill afford to be without. Yet despite the fact that this knowledge is central to the autograph field, there are very few sources in which collectors can find it gathered together in one place and avoid the necessity of laboriously digging it out for themselves. The editors of this price guide have asked me to tackle the job of creating such a resource, with the intention of fulfilling this pressing need.

Autographs come in six basic formats: letters, manuscripts, documents, signed photographs, signed books and signatures. The first three are of greatest significance in our search for quality, so we will concentrate on them. We will begin with some practical definitions. These are not meant to be dictionary definitions, but to explain how the words are commonly used in an autograph context. Letters are communications between people, whether handwritten or typed. They will usually address someone by name, such as "Dear Mrs. Jones." Manuscripts are descriptive narratives or other original handwritten or typed materials not intended as inter-personal communications. Classroom notes and diaries would be good examples. Documents are signed forms or official papers, such as your driver's license. We will also deal here to a lesser extent with two of the other formats, signed photographs and signed books. Signatures are outside of our sphere, as even if valuable, they lack content or intrinsic importance.

Assessing Content and Importance

The content of a letter or manuscript, put simply, consists of what it says. But it is also the creative product of the human mind, and is frequently illuminating. The content means everything to value, so determining its quality is crucial. How can you measure something as subjective as quality? Here are the rules I use. A good content letter is one in which the writer either tells you something of great interest or significance about himself or a primary field of his endeavor, or provides valuable descriptions or information about an important event. A few examples will illustrate what I mean. A letter of George Washington saying he is too busy to accept an invitation to dinner may be expensive, but says nothing anyone benefits by knowing, so it does not have good content. One of him about running his plantation at Mount Vernon would be interesting because it is germane to his life, but since Washington is best remembered for his leadership as general and president (and not as a farmer), it would be considered of just medium quality. One of him from 1780 ordering his chief spy in the Revolutionary War, Benjamin Tallmadge, to obtain information on enemy troop dispositions, has good content, as it is historically significant and directly relates to his performance as commander of the Continental Army.

A letter of a Civil War soldier writing home about camp life may contain anecdotes but is routine and lacks content, while one containing details about the Battle of Antietam is exciting and has good content (and may even shed new light on the event). When Albert Einstein writes a letter about what compelled him to a life in science, that's content. When Grover Cleveland pens a letter describing the nature of the presidency, that's content. And not all good content letters are expensive, as these principles hold true regardless of likely price. For example, when Robert Ballard relates his emotions on first seeing the Titanic, that content is just as good in its sphere as Washington's war date letter is in his. Good content is equally key in manuscripts.

When a Revolutionary War soldier writes a journal relating his experiences and telling that he saw Washington on horseback directing his troops at Monmouth, that's content. When Orville Wright makes notes on his early aviation experiments, that's content. And when George Gershwin composes a musical manuscript, that's the most creative content imaginable. As with letters, good content does not mean the same thing as expensive. A signature of Mozart would be very expensive but have no content, while a diary from Woodstock might have great content and not be costly.

Turning now to intrinsic importance, the vast majority of the letters and manuscripts that are that important will also have good content, and thus not require a separate analysis to establish importance. For example, even U.S. Gen. Anthony MacAuliffe's famous and historic one word reply—"Nuts" —to a German demand for surrender at the Battle of the Bulge has good content, as it is a creative show of determination. However, there are exceptions where routine letters have had a big impact on history. A brief letter inviting President McKinley to visit the Pan American Exposition would have little content, but would be intrinsically important, as he was assassinated there. Similarly, a note from Charles Bartlett inviting Senator John F. Kennedy to dinner at his house in 1951 would have no content, but since that was where he met his wife Jacqueline, would certainly be important. Thus importance may exist in the absence of content.

Although they may recite crucial facts (as does the ultimate document, the Declaration of Independence), documents do not really have content in the same way as letters or manuscripts. However, they can, and do, have intrinsic importance. Such documents are often mementos of a key moment in history or were the cause or result of a memorable event. Meriwether Lewis' signed pay receipt for the Lewis and Clark Expedition is intrinsically important. Abraham Lincoln's appointment of George Meade to command the Union Army is intrinsically important. Al Capone's prison intake form is intrinsically important. Thomas Edison's patent papers for his invention of the phonograph are intrinsically important. And as with content, intrinsic importance and expensive are not synonyms. A receipt signed by Benjamin Franklin may be expensive but lacks any claim to importance, while Calvin Coolidge's appointment of Dwight Morrow to head the Aviation Board (which first set U.S. aviation policy) would be important and yet not cost very much.

Gradations of Autograph Values

Not every autograph can be as significant as the items mentioned above, which is just as well, as few collectors could afford such expensive examples. Fortunately, however, within each of our three main categories, there are numerous readily identifiable gradations with correspondingly different price levels (all relating to content and importance). These are not, however, the same distinctions found in price guides. Price guides base their categories on whether an item is an autograph letter signed, typed letter signed, signed photograph or signature, and these categories bear minimal relevance to us in our quest for content and importance. As an example of how this is true, in price guides, an ALS of a person is considered to be worth more than a TLS. Yet, without doubt, a good content TLS will beat a routine ALS most every time. Moreover, the guides premise their values on typical or average prices asked or paid, and since what is average or typical is almost by definition routine, the listings cannot really take into account our primary concerns of content and importance. Were the guides to try, their categories and price charts would have to be expanded to consider all the factors dealt with in this article (thus quadrupling the size of the book and making it more complex to use).

To illustrate our point about price gradations, let's assess letters of British Prime Minister Winston Churchill. A TLS thanking a man for sending him an article on motoring might be worth $1,300, as it is not interesting and shows us nothing about him. Perhaps a typical TLS in a price guide would be just a bit better (it might be a cover letter sending someone a copy of one of his books), and be worth about $2,000. A letter to the Canadian House of Commons saying farewell at the end of his illustrious career has significantly better content and would sell for about $4,500. We are now well past the price guide level but only starting our climb. A letter defending his controversial role in World War I could well fetch $10,000 to $15,000. We once had a TLS of his as World War II Prime Minister revealing this fearless man's fear; not for his personal safety, but that the Americans would be angered with Britain (and perhaps accelerate the schedule for D-Day and launch before the Allied armed forces were ready). It sold for $30,000. Imagine how inclusion of such a letter would skew the average (and thus the price guide value) for a Churchill TLS! It is also important to note that neither of these latter values would have been appreciably higher if the letter had been an ALS.

It is likewise for manuscripts. A Theodore Roosevelt TLS refusing a speaking invitation would be worth less than $500; if as President and on White House letterhead, make that $700. A better letter from him extolling the importance of libraries to education would sell for $3,000. Somewhere in this range might lie a price guide value of $1,500. However, a letter of Roosevelt branding Woodrow Wilson the worst president ever would be worth at least $6,000, and one describing in detail his formative experiences as a cowboy could easily fetch $10,000. Stepping up the ladder, we had a portion of the speech he gave to his Bull Moose loyalists in June 1912, urging them on to the fight. It was about a quarter of the original typed manuscript with his handwritten revisions, and was not signed. This would challenge a price guide, as it is neither a TLS nor ALS; where would it fit in? Yet it is clearly of historic importance, and even in an incomplete state, brought $20,000. As another example, a Civil War soldier's routine diary would be worth $1,500. If there were some good descriptions of action, that would climb to $3,500. We recently sold a diary with sensational battle content for almost $10,000, and have an important five-volume war date journal which served as the basis of a published book and might well bring ten times that amount.

The same principle holds true for documents. A receipt signed by John Hancock would bring at most $3,000. An appointment of a justice of the peace, signed by him as Governor of Massachusetts, is more interesting and might fetch $10,000-15,000. This is likely where a price guide would let matters stand, but our analysis continues. Military appointments Hancock signed as President of the Continental Congress, many dated in the magic year of 1776, are a definite step up, and where they commission an officer who made a notable contribution to the Revolutionary War effort, can be intrinsically important as well. They would be worth between $7,500 and $12,000, depending mainly on how prominent the appointee was. Some years ago, Hancock's appointment of Benedict Arnold as major general came on the market. Today such a key document would be worth at least $50,000. The importance of the document thus accounts for the spread between $3,000 and $50,000.

Here's another instance. A Franklin Pierce document signed as President ordering the Secretary of State to affix the great seal of the United States to a pardon for Joe Doaks, who had stolen a loaf of bread, would be hard pressed to command $700. Yet his original appointment of Francis Scott Key's son Philip as U.S. Attorney for the District of Columbia, which led to a scandal and resulted in the younger Key's murder on a public street in Washington, sold readily for $2,500. Again, importance was the difference.

How This Applies to Signed Photographs

Many people collect signed photographs, and even here our concepts of content and intrinsic importance hold true. We always start with the perhaps surprising proposition that photographs inscribed to a named individual are best. One reason this is preferable is that the more handwriting there is on the photograph, the more certain the determination of authenticity. However, the added writing is also laden with possibilities for content. Perhaps the inscription will reveal something important about the writer, as when Harry Truman signs the famous photograph showing him holding the *Chicago Tribune* with its premature headline "Dewey Defeats Truman," adding that this was a memorable moment. It may also illustrate something interesting about the relationship between the signer and the recipient, as in a photograph we once had which was inscribed by Warren Harding to his corrupt Veteran's Bureau administrator, Charles Forbes. It was full of expressions of trust and praise, emotions that showed Harding's view of the men's relationship, but which were repaid by Forbes with betrayal. Signed photographs with such inscriptions have good content and may even rise to the level of importance; they are two to four times as valuable as similar uninscribed pictures. By the way, these same rules apply to inscriptions in signed books.

With signed photographs, what they show can be as important as what they say, as it is a form of content. A signed portrait photograph of Franklin D. Roosevelt as Governor of New York would be worth $900 or so, while one as President might sell for $1,500. These would be consistent with typical guide values. However, if the photograph pictures FDR with his cabinet (and if the other cabinet members have also signed), the value would rise to at least $5,000. A signed photograph of him delivering his first inaugural address or war message to Congress would easily jump to $10,000 or even $15,000, if you could find one. The Truman photograph mentioned above is another case in point. A signed portrait shot of HST in older age would sell for $500, one as President for $1,000, a signed photograph with his cabinet for $3,500, and the terrific "Dewey Defeats Truman" signed picture in the range of $5,000. This is the kind of distinction it is hard to make with a price guide.

The analogous criteria in the case of a book would be the importance of the book within the context of the author's work. Thus, a copy of *The White Company* signed by Arthur Conan Doyle would be lucky to fetch $800, but one of *The Adventures of Sherlock Holmes* should sell for at least $5,000. A signed copy of F. Scott Fitzgerald's *The Great Gatsby* might be worth $10,000, while one of *All the Sad Young Men* could bring $2,500.

QUALITY AND CONTENT   31

The Impact of Condition on Prices

Another important factor affecting the value of autographs, even those of high quality, is condition. Here again, price guides are unable to efficiently deal with this issue because condition requires an item-by-item analysis and does not lend itself to categorization. Here are some examples. A good content letter of George Washington written during the Revolutionary War would be exciting to own. In fine condition, it might be worth a cool $50,000. If it has faded a little, and the content is not compelling, that number might be $40,000. Now add a pervasive water stain and it may drop to $20,000. With a small piece missing that causes the loss of a few key words, it might fetch $15,000. As the Bard said, "What a falling off was there!" And not even content could prevent the fall.

It should be noted that there are three exceptions to the rule on the role of condition: uniqueness, extraordinary importance and true rarity. If the Washington letter in our example was addressed to the Continental Congress and accepted its offer of the supreme command of the American army, then it would be both unique and extraordinarily important. Few would care if it were discolored. A faded but one-of-a-kind letter of Robert E. Lee to George Meade that crossed the battle lines at Gettysburg would be an example of uniqueness, as no other such letters exist. What excitement just to hold it! An example of extraordinary importance without uniqueness would be a fair condition letter of William Henry Harrison issuing his first orders as a general in the War of 1812. Two identical signed copies containing the orders were sent out, one of which is now in private hands and the other in a state historical society. As for true rarity, I am not referring to autographs that are merely uncommon and nice to find, like Civil War date ALS's of Stonewall Jackson. I mean autographs like those of Columbus or Shakespeare, where just finding one would be a news-making event. Of course, not all exceptions need to be expensive ones. A letter of evolution teacher John Scopes describing his defense lawyer, Clarence Darrow, at the famed Monkey Trial, would be so unusual to come across, and so historically significant, that condition would be a much reduced factor.

Learn to Protect Yourself

Here's something else you need to know. Sadly, it is not uncommon to find sellers of autographs who are not satisfied with the lily they have and try to gild it. They will praise the most routine letter as having good (if not great) content, label as important the most mundane manuscript, and say a stained document is in super fine condition. Logically, we know that a letter simply turning down a speaking invitation cannot be considered interesting, much less have good content. Presidents signed untold thousands of documents appointing postmasters, and one naming John Doe the postmaster of Podunk cannot be important regardless of how it is labeled. And a manuscript that is torn and stained is simply not in fine condition. Some sellers utterly lack self-restraint and slant or mischaracterize almost everything they offer in this way. Skepticism must therefore be the starting point in assessing what you are told.

It is true, however, that not all calls about content and importance are clear-cut. For instance, if Alexander Graham Bell makes a passing reference to the telephone in a letter about his desk, does the letter have good content? If it states in passing that he bought a green desk ten years after inventing the telephone, then I would say no. If he wrote that while seated at his old green desk, he had a flash of inspiration that led to his discovering the telephone, then I would maintain yes. What do you think?

Of course, beauty is in the eye of the beholder, and a letter tedious to one man may be music to another's ears. Still, the basic truths discussed here do not vary, and now that your eyes are open, you can read autograph descriptions more critically and distinguish whether the claims made for a piece are accurate and make sense within its context. Be smart and you won't get bamboozled.

You should also take care to avoid fads. When actor River Phoenix died in 1993, the cost of his autograph sky-rocketed. The price guides, quite naturally, reflected this reality. However, his fame did not stand the test of time, and within a few years the value had plummeted. No price guide could tell you that buying his autograph high would be a poor investment. You have to be aware of what really matters in the long run and determine this kind of thing for yourself. Sometimes the decision is not as easy as in the above case. When Princess Diana died, her autographs (mainly Christmas cards) increased in value from about $800 to as much as $10,000. Interest in her was no fad, yet the price was clearly being influenced by the tragedy and intense emotion that followed it. The market ultimately stabilized the value at about $2,500.

Thoughts on the Autograph Marketplace Today

The last dozen years have seen substantial growth in interest in the autograph field, and at the same time more and more good content and important autographs have disappeared from the private market-place into institutions. These factors alone cause scarcity and affect price. And unlike years past, when letters and manuscripts of recent notables provided a constant source of new material, there is no longer a reliable, corresponding replenishment of supply. This is because, as I told *The Wall Street Journal* for an article it published in February 2003, emails, faxes, cell phones and the like have reduced the volume of postally-mailed letters to a trickle, and of this pittance, a growing number are signed mechanically by autopen or printer. When to this dismal picture is added the fact that manuscripts are usually created today in computers, and more and more forms have preprinted signatures, it seems clear that there will be precious few authentic personally-signed autographs to collect that were created from the year 2000 forward. This will put (in fact already is putting) pressure on the supply of remaining autographs of the past, and finding quality autographs has become much more difficult. In fact, the difference between the substantial number of important items readily available when I started as a dealer in 1989, and the shrunken number on the market now, is striking. So if quality is what motivates you, although fine things are still out there waiting to be found, you will need to become something of a treasure hunter, and be willing to be both patient and persistent.

Some of the desirable autographs I have used as examples here are expensive and out of the financial reach of many interested collectors. Yet I do not want to leave the impression that it is impractical if not impossible for such collectors to build superb collections. Fortunately, there is one very inexpensive commodity that is often directly exchangeable for cash: knowledge. The more you know about an autograph, the greater the chance you will know more than others in the marketplace and get a bargain. Here's how this works. Earlier I mentioned a Theodore Roosevelt manuscript speech. I bought this at public auction from a seller who knew that it was quite interesting, and billed it as such. However, I recognized the text as being part of a famous speech T.R. delivered to his Bull Moose supporters to start his 1912 campaign, while the auctioneer (and apparently his other customers) did not. I got the manuscript at a low price as a result. And if I can benefit financially in this way, so can you. It is a form of building your own value and creating your own prices, compliments of this price guide.

This autograph price guide is a tool, and a crucial one, for getting your bearings in the field. It illustrates the values of the autographs of thousands of noted people, and in so doing enables us to see the comparative relationships between them. It also shows the basic categories of autographs, and we learn that typically a handwritten letter, flowing right from the mind of a great person into his pen, is more valuable than one typed out by a secretary for signature. But even as we understand a price guide's utility, its limitations are evident. After all, wouldn't you rather have an important typed letter signed of any notable than a routine handwritten one of that person? We would. So this knowledge brings us full circle, and we see plainly the central role quality and content play in determining autograph values.

—*Steven S. Raab, www.RaabAutographs.com*

Founded in 1989, Steven S. Raab Autographs deals in autographs, manuscripts, documents and signed photographs. The firm specializes in American historical autographs, but its stock is strong in other fields of interest, such as science, literature, the fine arts, military, aviation and space, foreign notables, vintage entertainment, and important celebrities in all walks of life. It publishes illustrated catalogs about 4 times per year.

Steven Raab began collecting autographs and historical memorabilia in 1959, when he was a child. He made his career in law and initially started this business as a hobby, working on weekends. It rapidly grew and became a successful enterprise requiring full time attention. Seeing a chance to make a life-long passion into a vocation, he closed his law office to devote his time to Steven S. Raab Autographs. His wife Susan discontinued her business baking gourmet desserts for fine restaurants and joined the enterprise in 1993. She has become a noted desktop publisher in the autograph field.

Dr. Richard Saffro—publisher of this edition of **The Sanders Price Guide to Autographs**—relaxes in his Arizona home in November, 2002. This was early in the process. After personally editing the million-plus-pieces-of-data database that provides the information for the 550-page pricing section of this massive tome, he was not quite so relaxed. But he was secure in the knowledge that this edition is by far the most accurate and comprehensive one to date.

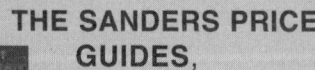
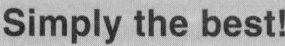

Chapter 3

The Double Edged Sword

by Stuart Lutz

eBay is the greatest change to the autograph field in decades, perhaps since the rise of dealer catalogs a century ago. In less than ten years, eBay has supplanted traditional houses, like Christie's and Sotheby's, as the largest auctioneer of autograph material in the world.

As with all change, there have been positive and negative developments with eBay's rise, and the adjustment has not always been smooth. In this article, I will examine the good and bad changes wrought by eBay, as well as review some of the internal improvements the company has made, and make some suggestions to protect yourself from autograph forgeries and fraud.

The Good

eBay has been a terrific buying and selling tool for me, a full-time historic document and manuscript dealer. I believe a lot of fellow full-time autograph dealers would concur with that statement. I have bought tremendous pieces on eBay, such as a wonderful archive of letters by author James Thurber, a book from the library of James Boswell, and a manuscript draft of the Panama Canal treaty between Panama, Columbia and the United States. Before eBay, my chances of finding these gems were remote.

Similarly, I have sold letters and manuscripts to new clients I never knew existed before the advent of eBay, nor would I have had any way to know of them if not for the Internet. Today, I have an array of clients across the country who buy manuscripts mentioning whale oil, letters from western Rhode Island towns, and correspondence signed by the poet William Carlos Williams. Likewise, there are a number of potential customers who see something I offer on eBay. Though it is not quite what they want, they send me an e-mail and ask me to find particular pieces for them; this frequently leads to later sales. Many of these eBay collectors have never joined the traditional Manuscript Society, Universal Autograph Collectors Club (UACC) or International Autograph Collectors Club (IACC), so I would not have had any way to sell to them.

For the autograph buying public, eBay has continually upgraded itself to make purchasing easier. The company has recently installed the "Buy It Now" feature, allowing a consumer to win automatically a piece by paying a higher price. eBay also e-mails "Saved Searches" daily, giving buyers an update of new pieces they seek.

Finally, the mere existence of eBay has created many new autograph collectors. Before eBay, average people never realized that they could, with the click of a mouse button, own something signed by Albert Einstein, Andrew Jackson or Ty Cobb. And growing the collector pool is definitely an asset for the business.

The Bad

The obvious downside of eBay is the proliferation of non-genuine pieces on eBay. I will divide this section into a discussion of the sale of non-intentional forgeries and intentional forgeries sold on eBay.

With non-intentional forgeries, I am discussing casual autograph sellers or general antiques dealers who sell secretarial, facsimile and Autopen material as genuine because they lack the expertise to distinguish genuine material from non-authentic pieces. Ten years ago, if Mrs. Jones cleaned out her Aunt Gertie's house and found a letter from John Kennedy with Autopen pattern #3 on it, she would

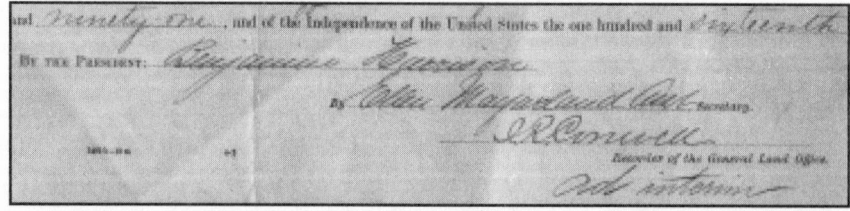

A typical land grant signed by a Presidential secretary, not President Benjamin Harrison. Note the signature of the secretary on the line below the President's name.

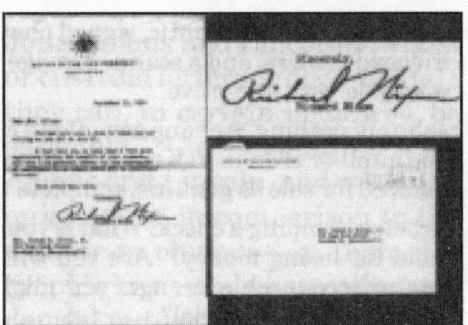

A Richard Nixon Autopenned letter as Vice President that sold for $300 on Ebay.

probably have called an autograph dealer to sell it. The dealer would have researched the letter using Charles Hamilton's *The Robot That Helped To Make A President*, seen it was a mechanical signature, and declined to purchase it. A decade ago, that would have marked the end of the Kennedy letter, for there was no forum to sell the letter, other than a garage sale. Today, if Mrs. Jones finds that same Kennedy Autopenned letter to dear Aunt Gertie, she can sell it on eBay. She can see that similar but genuine Kennedy presidential letters sell for over $1,000 on eBay, and she can ask a similar price, even though the Autopenned letter is nearly worthless (it has been my experience that when I inform casual autograph sellers that they are selling an Autopenned letter, and even propose to e-mail them the identical pattern from a reference book, they almost universally decline my offer. To me, this is no better than knowingly selling an outright forgery).

Non-intentional forgeries come in a variety of types in addition to the aforementioned Autopen patterns. There are pre-printed facsimiles, like Lincoln's Gettysburg Address or his letter to Mrs. Bixby concerning the death of her five sons in the Civil War. Facsimiles are not limited to letters, for Mark Twain included a blurb "This is the authorized Uniform Edition of all my books" in some of his volumes, and I have seen these sold as having a genuine signature for over $700. Likewise, President Ulysses Grant's *Memoirs* were published after his death, and the deceptive inscription "These volumes are dedicated to the American soldier and sailor" is a printed facsimile. There are also secretarial signatures, such as Presidential land grants (Andrew Jackson was the last President to sign land grants, and he quit halfway through his term, meaning not all Jackson land grants are genuine. All the land grants "signed" by Presidents Polk, Lincoln and Grant are *not* autographed by the President).

I have also seen some very creative marketing of genuine material by casual autograph sellers. For example, I once saw a genuine presidential military commission advertised as "triple signed." The naïve or sleazy seller thought that the handwritten engrossment of the commission, in which the secretary also handwrote the President's name twice at the top of the document, counted as genuine autographs (a

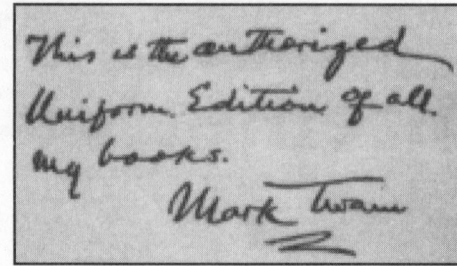

A facsimile inscription in some Mark Twain books. I have seen these books, advertised as genuinely signed by Twain, sell for over $700 on Ebay.

simple comparison between the genuine signature at the bottom and the engrossment of the names should have informed him that there was only one authentic autograph on it). Another time, I saw a Richard Nixon secretarial letter offered as "guaranteed old," though the warrantee did not cover the letter as being genuine. Finally, I have seen casual sellers exaggerate the rarity of pieces. Harry Truman, as ex-President, mailed out hundreds of letters a year. Yet I see some sellers list routine Harry Truman typed letters signed from the 1960s are "very rare," when in fact, they are plentiful (but Harry Truman handwritten and signed letters as President are rare).

Finally, with regards to non-intentional forgeries, I am shocked at the number of worthless Certificates of Authenticity (COAs) that accompany Autopenned, secretarial or facsimile material.

I believe that autographs are the easiest field to create spurious pieces for eBay, and many crooks have taken advantage of this simplicity. All it takes to create a fake is a pen, a blank album page or photograph (or bat or baseball or football), and three to four seconds. A good forger can crank out tens of thousands of dollars of bad merchandise a day. Faking autographs is certainly far easier than creating forgeries with furniture, glass or nearly any other known collecting field. As a result, eBay is an orchard for forgers selling intentionally spurious pieces, and the counterfeits come in all sizes and shapes, from Presidents Washington and Lincoln, to the modern athletes.

Recently, I was alerted by a friend in the business to view a first day cover "signed" by Albert Einstein and Niels Bohr. As soon as I saw the final selling price of $200, I knew, based on the price (even before seeing a scan of it) that it had to be fake since there was no way all the Einstein collectors searching eBay would allow a genuine autograph to sell for only $200. When eBay was still in diapers several years ago, when few people were checking eBay daily, a savvy collector could swipe a genuine Einstein or Babe Ruth signature or letter for nearly nothing. But with the advent of eBay's Saved Searches e-mails, every time an Einstein or Babe Ruth is listed, hundreds of people are notified. If the Einstein first day cover was genuine, there is no way a knowledgeable collector is going to let one sell for $200. This sadly proves the old adage that if the price is too good to be true...

The same personal computers that link to eBay have created a new class of forgeries, the high quality color copy. Today, an unscrupulous person can purchase a genuine Abraham Lincoln or Charles Lindbergh letter, use his scanner and color printer to duplicate it, and then sell it on eBay as genuine. To a person seeing it on the Internet, the handwriting would appear authentic. Once the collector receives it, there is no way to determine it is a color copy, except by using a magnifying glass.

The Improved

To keep the bad points from overwhelming the good aspects of eBay, eBay has cleaned up its act with regards to autographs over the past few years. It no longer takes its former laissez-faire approach, but has taken steps to kick known forgers off of eBay and to cooperate with law enforcement in the investigation of forgeries.

First, eBay has improved itself by disallowing certificates of

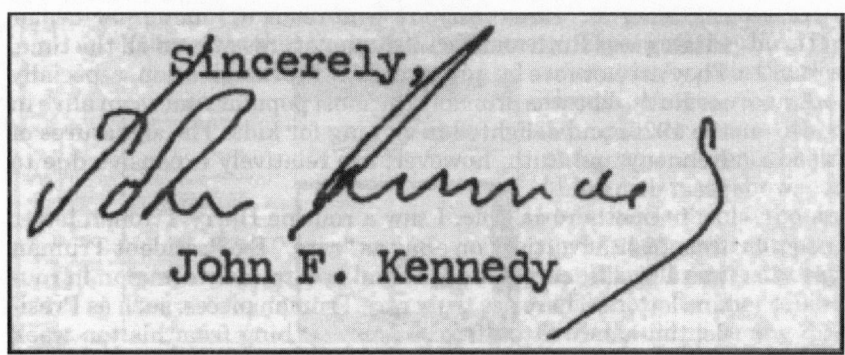

A John Kennedy Autopenned letter as Senator offered as genuine on Ebay.

authenticity from such unscruplous individuals and companies. Refer to www.pages.ebay.com/help/community/png-autograph.html.

Second, according to its own Website, "eBay reserves the right, in its sole discretion, to remove any autographed item listed on its site and refund the associated listing fee, if eBay believes that the listing of the item is inconsistent with eBay's goal of providing a safe trading environment, or if in its sole discretion eBay believes that the sale of the item might create liability for the buyer, the seller, or any third party.

Third, the F.B.I.'s well-publicized Operation Bullpen has shut down a number of sports memorabilia forgers who were peddling their fake wares on eBay. In its raids, the government seized over $10 million of fraudulent material.

Fourth, eBay has continued to improve its bidding practices, such as eliminating shill bidding, stopping bidders who put in ridiculously high bids to scare off other bidders before revoking the high bid just before the auction ends, and improving feedback to include responses from both parties.

The Suggestions

Despite eBay's steps, it is still an autograph minefield, and buyers must be wary of bad material. In addition, collectors should

A pre-printed Franklin D. Roosevelt letter. Note the lack of greeting on the letter, a clue that it is not genuine.

educate themselves so they can spot questionable material. In this final section, I will discuss what collectors should remember, how they can protect themselves, and how they can educate themselves.

Points To Remember

- A high feedback rating is no sign that material is genuine. The peddler who was selling the fake Einstein and Bohr first day cover had a tremendous rating. Feedback means that the deal was completed to the satisfaction of both parties, not that the material is necessarily authentic.
- There is a difference between a full-time autograph dealer, who knows what he or she is selling and guarantees it in writing, and a casual autograph seller or general antiques dealer, who occasionally brokers autographs and manuscripts, and may not be have the reference library to tell if something is an Autopen or not.
- Certificates Of Authenticity (COAs) mean nothing unless backed up by a lifetime guarantee for a full refund of the complete purchase price in writing if ever proven not to be genuine.

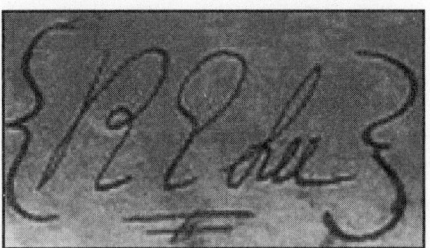

A questionable Robert E. Lee that sold on Ebay for over $2,000.

- Letters that begin "Dear Friend" or have no specific greeting are almost always facsimiles.
- Bidding on pieces that don't have a scan is risky.
- Beware of dealers who constantly have excessively rare pieces (especially at give-away prices). If a dealer had, on a weekly or monthly basis, a Button Gwinnett signature, an Edgar Allan Poe letter and a Christy Matthewson single signed baseball, that should raise suspicions.
- I am cautious about dealers who opt to use the "Private Auction" feature on eBay. I've seen many forged pieces sold that way, since there is no way for an expert to alert a customer about authenticity problems.
- If a dealer claims a piece is rare, do a search on eBay for similar pieces. If the aforementioned Harry Truman TLS from the 1960s is advertised by the dealer as "rare" and you find eight similar ones

on eBay at the same time, how rare can it really be?
- I am often wary of clipped signatures and signed album pages, for they can be skillfully forged by the hundreds.
- If you want to buy a genuine Presidential piece, try a Presidential commission with the attractive engravings. Presidents were required to sign each one, and there are thousands of them. It is probably the safest way to buy an Abraham Lincoln, for example. Do not, however, purchase Presidential land grants signed by the commander in chief after Andrew Jackson, for they are secretarial. Likewise, cancelled checks should also be generally safer than clipped signatures. Recently, the check archives of Thomas Edison and Lucille Ball have been located, and a collector should feel confident when purchasing one of their checks.

Protect Yourself

Many of the most prestigious autograph and manuscript organizations list their members on their websites. Some unscrupulous dealers falsely claim they are members of these groups. Feel free to research dealers by using these sites:

- The Manuscript Society: http://www.manuscript.org/dealers.html
- The Universal Autograph Collector's Club (UACC) Registered Dealers: http://www.uacc.org/registered.htm
- The Professional Autograph Dealer's Association (PADA): http://www.padaweb.org/
- The Antiquarian Booksellers Association of America (ABAA): http://www.abaa.org/
- The International Autograph Dealers Alliance (IADA): http://www.iacc-da.com/
- The Ephemera Society: http://www.ephemerasociety.org/

Realize that attaining membership in the UACC Registered Dealer program, PADA, the ABAA and the IADA is difficult. New dealers often need to find three sponsors to support their membership and have to fill out an application stating their qualifications, education, years in business, size of their reference library and other credentials.

* If you suspect something on eBay may be Autopen, use the Internet to help you find out. There are a number of Websites

dedicated to showing Autopens, and they include:
- http://www.geocities.com/~sbeck/
- http://www.geocities.com/szarelli/fakes/fakes_phonies_frauds.htm

Educate Yourself

Purchase autograph reference books, and many of the out-of-print ones can be bought on eBay. Some of the best ones I use on a regular basis include:

Charles Hamilton - *Collecting Autographs And Manuscripts* (the best and most comprehensive basic autograph reference book), *The Illustrated Letter* (chronicling letters with drawings in them), *The Signature Of America, American Autographs* (but good luck finding a copy), and *Great Forgers And Famous Fakes* (proving that counterfeits started long before eBay).

Ken Rendell - *History Comes To Life* and *Forging History*.

Joe Nickell - *Pen, Ink & Evidence* (a more technical book on the history of writing).

Ray Rawlins – *The Stein And Day Book Of World Autographs*.

Mark Allen Baker – *Collecting Autographs* and *Advanced Autograph Collecting*.

Ron Seagrave – *Civil War Autographs And Manuscripts*.

Michael Reese II – *Autographs Of The Confederacy*.

Mary Benjamin – *Autographs: A Key To Collecting* (another good general book).

Larry Vrzalik and Michael Minor – *From the President's Pen*.

John M. Taylor – *From The White House Inkwell*. Also, Taylor edited the infinitely useful *Autograph Collector's Checklist*, published by the Manuscript Society.

Go to autograph shows and book fairs held around the country. Hold material in your hand, meet dealers and pick up some catalogs. Notice how the iron gall ink used two hundred years ago "rusts" to an auburn color, so that if you see a Thomas Jefferson or George Washington signature in jet black ink, that is a tip that it is likely a forgery. See how Babe Ruth and Humphrey Bogart never signed with a Sharpie marker or ballpoint pen. Also, seeing autographs and manuscripts in person is a three dimensional experience, whereas looking at them on a computer screen in only a two dimensional encounter.

Conclusions

The bottom line in purchasing autographs on eBay is authenticity and responsibility. Just as you buy clothes or electronics from a store where you can take it back if it proves not be to be adequate, you also want to buy your autographs from a responsible and knowledgeable party. With this said, I confess that 90% of the manuscripts I purchase on eBay are from other dealers because I know the material is genuine and, in the very rare case it is not, I can return it to the dealer for a full refund. Only on unusual occasions do I purchase letters from people who claim to have uncovered correspondences in their attic.

Happy hunting on eBay!

—Stuart Lutz, Stuart Lutz Historic Documents, Inc.,
www.historydocs.com

Stuart Lutz Historic Documents strives to bring you the finest in historic documents, autographs, letters, and manuscripts. They specialize in the correspondence of "household famous" people, such as the Presidents, Civil War notables, writers, scientists, entertainers, musicians, Founding Fathers, business leaders, and aviators. They also sell great content letters signed by eyewitnesses now lost to history's dust. All material is guaranteed genuine, and thecompany is a member in good standing of all the major trade organizations.

His company prides itself on fine customer service, including proactive notification of material when it arrives, and prompt shipment of pieces.

Chapter 4

Investment

by Daniel Brams

Significant autographed material, such as a fine Lincoln letter or a Washington Society of Cincinnati Certificate inspire us to contemplate the historical significance of this tangible part of our world and truly challenges the imagination. But this is the real world and one must contemplate the investment potential of any significant historical document in much the same way that one contemplates the tangible value of stocks, bonds, gold, artwork, rare coins and the like. After all, to the extent that you consider the purchase of a significant historical document as an investment vehicle, one must contemplate much of the same criteria that applies to any investment. With that in mind, this article will consider the basic investment "criteria" applicable to the purchase of autographed material and memorabilia.

Appreciation Potential

First and foremost, one must ask, "What is the prospect for appreciation in value?" Obviously, the prospect for appreciation in value has something to do with the prices that exist in the marketplace. In other words, "How affordable is the investment?" Finally, to the extent that you determine that the autographed material is affordable and, therefore, there is a great prospect for appreciation, one must ask, "How liquid is the investment?" This article will examine the factors in determining how the historical autograph market stacks up as an "investment" relative to other potential investment vehicles available in the market today.

Like everything else in a free market system, supply and demand determine price. First we look at "supply." This medium is generally referred to as "ephemera." The contemporary definition of "ephemera" is something short lived or transitory. Because these items were generally not meant to last through the ages, many autographic pieces simply do not survive. Either they are kept in a highly acidic environment over the years or they are ravaged by insects or moisture. The odds are that a piece of paper will not survive for 200 or more years in "investment grade" condition. Further, many of the more important investment grade autograph material has found its way into museums or permanent collections. More recently, with the advent of e-mail and fax machines, much of the material that would have otherwise been memorialized in writing is relegated to electronic storage. Based upon the foregoing, it is no wonder that the supply of important autographed material is severely limited.

Rare Documents

Notwithstanding the very limited availability of important autograph material, the demand has continued to escalate. *The Wall Street Journal* ran a headline stating, "The Rare Document Field Sees Prices Spiral As A New Breed of Collector Signs On." It has been estimated that ten years ago, there were less than 5,000 autograph collectors in the United States. Today, the number is projected to be 500,000. As demand for quality material rises, the supply has begun to dry up. The impact of such keen demand on such limited supply of manuscripts is sending prices through the roof. Malcolm Forbes was quoted as saying "Autographed materials are the most undervalued of all areas of collecting, especially when you consider what people are paying for even second-rate paintings." Indeed, Malcolm Forbes put his money where his mouth was by becoming one of the most avid collectors of historical autographed material in history.

Abraham Lincoln and George Washington only signed so many letters and documents during their lifetimes and that finite supply has been eroded through time. As more autograph collectors stream into the market, fewer and fewer letters, documents and other signed pieces become available year after year as the supply is absorbed into individual collections.

Various newspapers and magazines have featured stories touting autographs as sound investments including *The Los Angeles Times, The*

New York Times, USA Today, Forbes, Business Week, U.S. News and World Report, Newsweek, Esquire and *The Robb Report*, to name a few.

Back in October of 1980, *Money Magazine* ran an article called "Investments Score Card." In that article, *Money Magazine* compared the Dow Jones Industrial (then up 5.06%), long term corporate bonds, (then up 32.6%), commodities, such as pork bellies (then up 23%), east coast Florida condominiums (then up 40.4%), with a typical autograph portfolio (then up 92%). Since 1980, the value of a well placed autograph portfolio has risen even more dramatically with recognition by the public that autograph collecting could be so lucrative. Of course, these other "investments" have not fared so well.

In analyzing the potential for appreciation, one must consider many factors including: (1) the amount of material this is available; (2) total amount of current collectors pursing that material; (3) the possibility of new material available to meet increased demand; (4) awareness of collectors as to marketability; (5) projected impact of new collectors on current price levels; and (6) the maturity level of autograph collecting on the growth curve. In virtually every area, one must conclude that the prospect for appreciation is overwhelming.

Limited Availability

It is well known that this material was not meant to survive and, as such, the availability of investment grade material is severely limited. While prices rose at a steady but a conservative level for many years, the total number of collectors has exploded, thereby creating upside price pressure. With the advent of the internet, market awareness and availability have grown in a way that could never have been anticipated. Thus, the autograph world finds itself very early in the growth curve. This is especially so in light of the fact that new material is being produced at an astonishingly limited rate with the advent of electronic data storage. As the amount of collectors dramatically increases every year, additional pressure will be placed on prices.

As to other investment vehicles, gold is produced at a rate of approximately 40,000,000 ounces annually. It is estimated that there are approximately 6,000,000 purchasers of gold in the world right now. Corporate Stock can be authorized and issued at the discretion of the Board of Directors. On the date of this article, there were 1.69 billion shares outstanding in IBM. Contrast this with only 500,000 active autograph collectors in the United States and one can easily conclude that this market is in its infancy. Indeed, given the lack of supply and the consistently increased demand, impact on price levels should be dramatic. Autographed material has been sold at public auctions and, as such, the prices for this material have been independently recorded in a litany of different publications.

Perhaps the best such publication is *American Book Prices Current*, an annual publication of prices realized for autograph material sold in major auctions world wide. In 1968, a John Hancock signature sold for $65. In 1983, the signature sold for $1,950. In 1970, a signature of Abraham Lincoln sold for $230. In 1993, the same signature went for $4,500. A Thomas Edison signature went for $40 in 1975, whereas, a similiar signature sold in 1993 for an average price of $750. In like manner, a military commission signed by Abraham Lincoln sold in 1968 for $300, today the same commission could be expected to sell for many multiples of the 1968 price. Still, Lincoln material is accessible to the average collector, but not for long.

On May 14, 1992, a John Adams hand written letter was estimated in the Christies' catalog to sell for $7,500. When the auction was over, the letter realized a bid of $12,000. In that same auction, Christies estimated a hand-written letter from George Washington to go somewhere between $35,000–$50,000. The price realized at auction was $137,500. Christies estimated that an autographed letter signed by Robert E. Lee would go for between $5,000–$7,000 and, when the auction was over, it realized $52,800. It is not unusual to see autographed material selling for mulitples of its pre-sale estimate. This is precisely because more and more collectors continue to "discover" this material and compete for the very limited supply thereby forcing prices up.

These prices are not limited to such venerable characters as Lincoln and Washington. At a recent Sotheby's auction, a *Winnie-the-Pooh* signed first edition presentation copy with a pre-auction estimate of $8,000–$12,000 realized a hammer price of $52,000 including the buyer's premium. A *Wizard of Oz* book signed by the cast members sold at auction in July 2000 for $49,306. This represents a multiple of almost 500% from the starting bid.

Perhaps the most incredible increase results from the fascination with "pop culture" by the baby boomers. Ten years ago, a simple set of Beatles signatures routinely sold for $1,500. In a February, 2003 sale, a signed album page went for $7,538, an increase in excess of 500% in only a few short years. In like manner, a typical Babe Ruth signed photograph sold in February, 1996 for $1,500. A similar photo recently realized a hammer price of $3,757. A Marilyn Monroe signed photograph typically sold in 1970 for $1,500. In the early 1990s, the same photograph fetched $3,200. In January, 2002, a Beaton photo of Marilyn sold at auction for $13,906. A Walt Disney signed photograph routinely sold in 1985 for $1,200. In December, 1995, a Disney photo sold for $2,300. In January of 1996, a similar photograph sold for $5,970; and in February of 2000, a Disney photo sold for $10,928 against a minimum bid of $2,500.

Does this mean that every item of autographed material is destined to be worth mind boggling multiples of its original purchase price? Hardly. However, there is no reason to believe that desirable material in fine condition will not continue to enjoy wonderful upside potential as the supply of these pieces decreases and the demand becomes ever greater.

Affordability

Fortunately, investment grade historical documents are available in virtually every price range and, therefore, accessible to any level of investor. While it is possible to purchase a document signed by Abraham Lincoln in excess of $1,000,000, it is equally possible to purchase fine Lincoln material for $10,000 and less. As Malcolm Forbes observed, autographs are affordable because they have been undervalued. It should therefore be no surprise that the demand for quality material is growing at an unprecedented level. However, we perceive this time to be a window of opportunity. As the demand grows and the supply shrinks, the price will appreciate to a market level and the market will no longer be undervalued. According to *The Wall Street Journal*, "No one disputes that historical documents are often undervalued when compared to art, coins, and collectibles."

However, the concept of "affordability" should be an objective one, taking into account the autograph market from a historical perspective. In 1970, an Abraham Lincoln signature might have seemed expensive at $230. What a bargain it was in retrospect. Collectors gasped in 1990 when a set of Beatles signatures fetched $1,500, a pittance compared to $7,500 for a signed album page today. This material was not perceived as "affordable" back then, but in retrospect, it was a bargain.

On the other hand, what may appear to be "a bargain" may not turn out that way in retrospect. Over the years we have seen certain material actually decline in value on a temporary or permanent basis. Immediately after Diana's death, there was intense demand for material autographed by her. In the intervening years, Diana signed material has declined in value compared to the lofty prices paid just subsequent to her death. It is almost a certain bet that autographed material purchased in the heat of a current day event will not be a good "investment." Rather, a studied and disciplined approach to the purchase of "investment material" is necessary.

—Daniel Brams, Treasures Autograph Gallery,
www.papertreasures.com

Since 1988, Daniel Brams, President of The Brams Collection, Inc. has traveled throughout the world to identify , authenticate and acquire the finest and most desirable autographed material on the market. The Brams Collection incorporates every facet of the autograph market including American history, world history, military, space and aviation, art and literature, music, business, entertainment, notables and the notorious. The common thread in the collection is meticulous authenticity. Mr. Brams is the attorney for the International Autograph Collector's Club/Dealers Alliance and a member of its Ethics Committee. He is a long time member of the Manuscript Society and The Universal Autograph Collector's Club.

Chapter 5

Buying Autographs at Auction

by George Hollingsworth

At some time in the remote past of our hobby, it might have been possible to build a fine collection without buying autographs at auction, but this is certainly not true in the present day. The past decade bore witness to a phenomenal increase in the number of autograph auction houses, as well as the size and sophistication of their catalogs. The rapid growth of internet auctions has further helped to increase collector awareness and familiarity with auctions, and at this point in our hobby's history, the vast majority of autographs that are on the market are being offered through the major autograph auction houses.

While some collectors are initially intimidated by the auction experience, buying at auction offers several benefits. Not only can one purchase material at bargain prices, but it can also be a lot of fun. Like anything new, many people express misgivings about participating in auctions, because they are afraid that they may bid poorly, or purchase an item that is not what it is purported to be. As in any other endeavor, a little caution is a wise thing. While no transaction is completely without risk, I have found that if one has properly prepared for a sale, there is simply no reason that they should be reluctant to bid with the greatest of confidence. With a little common sense and preparation, buying at auction can be an extremely enjoyable and worthwhile experience.

Auction Rules

Following a few simple rules of thumb can go a long way towards insuring successful bidding in an auction. First and foremost among these rules, is to KNOW WHO YOU ARE DEALING WITH. The importance of dealing with reputable houses cannot be overestimated, especially for anyone who is not very knowledgeable about autographs. For those not aspiring to pursue a career in authenticating and selling autographs, it is more realistic and certainly less time consuming to cultivate a positive and ongoing professional relationship with the staffs of the reputable autograph auction houses. A good place to start would be checking out the auction houses with advertisements in this publication. These advertisers have been screened by the publisher for their honesty and level of expertise. Ask fellow collectors to relate their experiences with the various houses, and if no one has heard of them, or there is a pattern of unresolved complaints, take your business elsewhere.

A great way to meet fellow collectors and gain information about the various houses is to attend a convention, such as those of the U.A.C.C. or Manuscript Society. These conventions are usually well attended, and many houses send representatives there, both to promote their auctions, and to seek consignments. I have found that these representatives are usually more than willing to answer any questions I may have.

Always be aware of the policies of each house you interact with, including their guarantees and return policies, which are usually found on the inside cover or first few pages of their catalogs. Most reputable houses guarantee the authenticity of the items they sell for at least five years, with many houses offering a lifetime guarantee on authenticity. However, because of the degree to which condition is subject to interpretation by the individual viewer, there is usually a limited period in which an item may be returned for condition problems. While the better auction houses are usually willing to go to great lengths to please their clients, they really shouldn't be expected to make special concessions above and beyond their written guarantees. It might be boring, but it is certainly worthwhile to read the fine print in the front of the catalog well BEFORE the auction. This is especially true if this is your first experience with a given house. If you are like most of us, you will probably go your entire life without experiencing major problems with any of the houses, but knowing the rules beforehand makes the possibility of a problem less likely.

If possible, research the items you wish to bid on well before the sale. It is always best to personally preview auction items. I have found that nothing can replace seeing the actual item, and reviewing it first-hand. If you were to purchase a new automobile you wouldn't dream of doing so sight unseen, yet auction previews are almost always poorly attended. However, if you are unable to attend in person, there is still much you can do to be a more informed bidder. Read catalog descriptions carefully, and study the illustrations of items when they are available. If you have a computer, it is a good idea to check the auction house's website for illustrations. The ease and relative cheapness of illustrating items on the internet has led many houses to illustrate many, if not most, of their auction lots on the web. If you still have unanswered questions, contact the auction house for answers.

In almost every instance, I have found that the auction house staff is extremely knowledgeable about their products, and happy to answer any of my questions. The auction house staff is more pressed for time as the auction date nears, and therefore, if you need to contact the house regarding a specific item, try to do so well before the final auction date. By doing everything you can to get an accurate description of items in the sale, you will avoid the risk of potential dissatisfaction.

Subscribe to the catalogs of several of the major auction houses. It is a good idea to keep both the catalogs and prices realized for future reference. The catalogs of the better houses are excellently written and illustrated, and are an excellent resource for authentic examples of signatures. Over time, they will also provide vast amounts of information about the current values of a wide variety of signed material in nearly every format. After a few auctions you will have accumulated a small library of valuable reference material which, when used in conjunction with references such as this price guide, will allow you to make informed bids based on the selling price of similar items and current market trends.

If you are bidding on a number of items in a particular auction, it is likely that you will be outbid on some of them. It is therefore a good idea to prepare "contingency bids" on some items. These are to be executed in the event that you are outbid on one or more of the items you initially chose. This is especially the case if there are a number of similar items, such as a clipped signature, being offered in the same sale. When several nearly identical items are offered at the same sale, the first item offered will often sell for more than those that follow it. If you need an example of this particular item for your collection, it is therefore wise to prepare bids on several of them.

The most important rule in any auction is to maintain "BIDDER DISCIPLINE." This means that once you have done all the preliminary research necessary for arriving at your bids, you should stick with your initial bidding strategy. You should never allow yourself to bid on impulse or emotion, and always stay with your predetermined bids. Until you are absolutely familiar with the values of the items you are bidding on, you should make it an ironclad rule to only bid on items which you have researched prior to the sale. Even the most seasoned bidders have to resist the impulses to bid more than they intended to, and to avoid placing bids on items they didn't initially want. If the price of an item has risen above what you were initially prepared to pay, then you should let it go to the higher bidder. In no case should you allow yourself to be taken in by "Auction Fever." I repeat, if for any reason you don't have a chance to do your homework on a particular lot in a sale, it is absolutely essential that you be prepared to let it go. From experience, I can testify that this is the toughest of all bidding principles to consistently adhere to. None of us like to see something we want get away from us, making buyer discipline all the more essential. No one has unlimited resources, and all of us have experienced regret at not having bid a little more for a certain piece. However, I have found that the anguish that I have felt from letting things go, is far less than that received from the dreaded phenomenon known as "buyer's remorse." Try to remember that bidding without adequate research is a lot like going on a blind date. You might get lucky, but more often than not, you will end up with an unpleasant surprise.

While the aforementioned rules may seem to be simple, and easy to remember, they are far more difficult to consistently follow. Maintaining a disciplined approach to buying at auction becomes far easier with practice, and bears long-term benefits. Over time, these principles will become a matter of habit, and the knowledge that you are spending your money wisely will ease many potential worries and greatly contribute to the pleasure you get from what is already a very enjoyable pastime.

—George Hollingsworth

George Hollingsworth was the senior Vice President at Alexander Autographs for several years. He is currently an independent dealer, specializing in building collections for clients.

Chapter 6

Presidential Autographs

by Mike Minor and Larry Vrzalik

Collecting autographs is as old as recorded history and far older than handwriting as we know it today. Written records were prized from the dawn of recorded history, long before the alphabet came out of the East. Cuneiform letters were contemporarily prized and collected in libraries by the Assyrians, Egyptians and others. The Athenians highly prized and closely guarded the original manuscripts of the classical Greek writers and only under the threat of force did they reluctantly surrender them to the great library at Alexandria. Ptolemy Philadelphus refused to supply wheat to Athens unless he was allowed to borrow the original manuscripts of Aeschylus, Euripides, Homer and Sophocles. Ptolemy told the Athenians he wanted to have copies made; however, he kept the originals and returned the copies.

From earliest times prominent individuals have collected autographs, particularly of their leaders, Cicero and Pliny avidly collected autographs and Pliny complained that letters of Julius Caesar were scarce even during his lifetime.

In general terms, all other factors being equal, the most expensive presidential autographs are Washington, Jefferson, John Adams and Lincoln. Although signatures (on small cards or cut from letters or documents) are the least expensive format they can, in certain instances, be among the most difficult to assemble. "Cut" signatures of Washington, Jefferson, John Adams and Lincoln, and some of the other early presidents, are quite scarce in comparison to their letters or documents. The answer is obvious—in their day few people collected autographs; however, when collectors did write and request a presidential autograph, the president responded in most instances with a full autograph letter signed!

Also, most people had the great good sense not to clip a presidential signature off a document or letter. Thus, it is far easier, albeit more costly, to find a complete Washington or Lincoln letter than a cut signature. Nevertheless, with patience, a collection of presidential signatures can be assembled and if properly and archivally matted with portraits or engravings such a collection can be very handsome, dramatic and even spectacularly presented. What could be more impressive than to have the walls of a library or other great room lined with a complete collection of presidential signatures matted with their portraits!

Autograph collecting as we know it today began circa 1500 following the invention of the printing press and the replacement of vellum with paper. Education and the art of handwriting became more and more common and widespread, allowing the communication of thoughts and ideas which, simultaneously, precipitated the serious collecting of letters and documents of the famous.

Collecting Presidential Pieces

The ultimate presidential item is a fine content presidential Autograph Letter Signed—a letter written by a president as president and entirely in his handwriting, followed by letters or documents signed while in office. Generally speaking presidential A.Ls.S. are the most costly, particularly if they have good or historic content. Ironically, presidential A.Ls.S. of modern presidents, or A.Ls.S. of any date, are, with few exceptions, infinitely rarer than those of earlier presidents such as Washington and Lincoln. The reason, of course, is because Washington and Lincoln hand wrote most of their letters. However, after the invention of the typewriter, handwritten presidential letters became more and more scarce. For this reason, a routine presidential A.L.S. of Bill Clinton would be worth as much and probably more than a routine Washington presidential A.L.S.

Several of our presidents were generals and military heroes before becoming president. Their military date letters are usually more desirable and valuable than their later presidential letters. Among this group are Washington, Jackson, Grant and Eisenhower.

Th Jefferson presents his compliments to mr Otis & thanks him for the information respecting mr Austin. he did not know that the father was living. the son is the person meant in the nomination & he prays mr Otis to insert the word "jun^r" after the name.

Dec. 3. 04.

Third person presidential ALS (Autograph Letter Signed) of Thomas Jefferson evidencing his idiosyncrasy of not beginning his sentences with capital letters.

Presidential documents are another area of collecting. There are many types of presidential documents which include the land grant, ships papers or "sea letters," seal authorizations, military appointments, civil appointments, particularly postmaster appointments, pardons and executive orders. The most common types of presidential documents are land grants and military commissions. Land grants through the first term of Andrew Jackson were personally signed by the president, but secretarially signed thereafter.

More Than One

Some presidential documents contain the signatures of two presidents because the co-signing cabinet officer later became president. These documents are highly desirable. Some of the combinations are: Washington and Jefferson, Jefferson and Madison, Madison and Monroe, Monroe and J.Q. Adams, Jackson and Van Buren, Polk and Buchanan, Pierce and Jefferson Davis (as Secretary of War), Theodore Roosevelt and Taft, Wilson and Franklin D. Roosevelt (as Assistant Secretary of the Navy), Harding and Hoover, and Coolidge and Hoover.

Signed Photographs

Another exciting area of collecting is presidential signed photographs, although a complete collection is impossible to assemble as the first photographs were not made until the 1840s. The first president to be photographed was John Quincy Adams in old age, although no signed photograph of him is known to exist. However, there are signed 8vo engravings of him. There is also reputedly a signed engraving of Washington. Andrew Jackson was photographed shortly before his death in 1845 but there are no signed photographs of him. The earliest president of whom signed photographs in the technical sense are known is Martin Van Buren in old age. There are no known SPs of W. H. Harrison, Tyler, Polk, or Taylor. There are signed photographs of Pierce and every succeeding president. As one might suspect, signed photographs of the early presidents are rare and costly. Those of Lincoln are the most expensive. A nice signed photograph of Lincoln and his son, which he signed "A Lincoln and son" sold for over $100,000 several years ago.

The signed photographs of some of the later 19th century presidents are inexplicably rare and costly, e.g., Benjamin Harrison and Arthur. Of the 20th century presidents JFK is quite rare in authentically signed SPs, as most are secretarially or autopen signed. Nevertheless, a collection of presidential signed photographs is worth far more than its weight in gold but is not for the fainthearted or the impatient.

Executive Mansion or White House Cards

Signed Executive Mansion or White House cards are another area of collecting. Again, a complete collection is not possible but they make an extremely attractive and desirable collection. This format was introduced by U. S. Grant of whom only one example is known. Practically speaking, they are theoretically obtainable for every president from and after Rutherford B. Hayes. These attractive cards are approximately 2.50 x 3.50 and have either "Executive Mansion, Washington" or "The White House, Washington," embossed on them in blue. Theodore Roosevelt changed the official name of the presidential residence from the "Executive Mansion" to "The White House" in 1901. Truman is scarce but obtainable in this format. Starting with Eisenhower they become increasingly rare. No authentically signed JFK, LBJ or Clinton White House cards are known to the authors. Those for the other presidents, starting with Nixon, are extremely rare. Starting with Carter, White House cards have a vignette of the White House superimposed on the body of the card. The Carter cards have a green vignette. Reagan continued this custom but changed the vignette color to blue, as they have remained.

Signed White House Vignettes

Another attractive and highly collectible presidential item is the signed White House vignette which was introduced by Chester Arthur; however, they are not obtainable for all the presidents following Arthur. Nevertheless, they make an attractive assemblage.

Some collectors specialize in presidential letters on certain topics, e.g. health, religion, finances, etc. Such collections make fascinating reading.

Presidential Bank Checks

Another interesting area of specialization is collecting presidential bank checks. While bank checks of Washington, Jefferson and Lincoln are obtainable, they are rare and expensive; however, for some of the later presidents, e.g., LBJ, they are unobtainable. Still, such a collection is highly interesting and gives great insight into our Chief Executives.

Letters With Content

Good content presidential letters of any date—pre or post presidential, are desirable. Personally we would prefer having a letter of good or historic content of non-presidential date than a presidential ALS sending an autograph!

Not all presidents were good letter writers. And, like everyone, not all presidents were good spellers or had legible handwriting. It was Grover Cleveland who said "it takes a poor mind to only be able to think of one way to spell a word!" Jackson and Truman are well known for their inventive spelling.

In our opinion the best letter writers of the presidential series, in chronological order, were: Washington, whose letters are not only beautifully written but beautifully phrased; John Adams, who could

FIRST PRESIDENT 1789-1797

John Adams
SECOND PRESIDENT 1797-1801

THIRD PRESIDENT 1801-1809

FOURTH PRESIDENT 1809-1817

FIFTH PRESIDENT 1817-1825

SIXTH PRESIDENT 1825-1829

SEVENTH PRESIDENT 1829-1837

EIGHTH PRESIDENT 1837-1841

NINTH PRESIDENT 1841

John Tyler
TENTH PRESIDENT 1841-1845

ELEVENTH PRESIDENT 1845-1849

TWELFTH PRESIDENT 1849-1850

THIRTEENTH PRESIDENT 1850-1853

FOURTEENTH PRESIDENT 1853-1857

FIFTEENTH PRESIDENT 1857-1861

SIXTEENTH PRESIDENT 1861-1865

SEVENTEENTH PRESIDENT 1865-1869

EIGHTEENTH PRESIDENT 1869-1877

NINETEENTH PRESIDENT 1877-1881

TWENTIETH PRESIDENT 1881

TWENTY-FIRST PRESIDENT 1881-1885

22D PRESIDENT 1885-1889, 24TH PRESIDENT 1893-1897

TWENTY-THIRD PRESIDENT 1889-1893

TWENTY-FIFTH PRESIDENT 1897-1901

TWENTY-SIXTH PRESIDENT 1901-1909

TWENTY-SEVENTH PRESIDENT 1909-1913

TWENTY-EIGHTH PRESIDENT 1913-1921

TWENTY-NINTH PRESIDENT 1921-1923

THIRTIETH PRESIDENT 1923-1929

THIRTY-FIRST PRESIDENT 1929-1933

THIRTY-SECOND PRESIDENT 1933-1945

THIRTY-THIRD PRESIDENT 1945-1953

THIRTY-FOURTH PRESIDENT 1953-1961

THIRTY-FIFTH PRESIDENT 1961-1963

THIRTY-SIXTH PRESIDENT 1963-1969

THIRTY-SEVENTH PRESIDENT 1969-1974

THIRTY-EIGHTH PRESIDENT 1974-1977

THIRTY-NINTH PRESIDENT 1977-1981

FORTIETH PRESIDENT 1981-1989

FORTY-FIRST PRESIDENT 1989-1993

FORTY-SECOND PRESIDENT 1993-2001

FORTY-THIRD PRESIDENT 2001-

PRESIDENTIAL AUTOGRAPHS 63

and often did write scathing and highly opinionated letters about the burning issues of the day; Jefferson, although they were a bit formal and stilted; Jackson, who was a notoriously poor speller, but wrote pithy and interesting letters; W. H. Harrison, who could but usually did not write interesting letters; Tyler, Fillmore and Lincoln, whose letters are usually short but often beautifully phrased; Andrew Johnson, Cleveland, Theodore Roosevelt, Taft, Wilson, FDR, Truman, Reagan, Bush and Clinton.

Harding's letters, like his speeches, were known for their rambling but flowery tenor. "His speeches left the impression of pompous phrases moving over the landscape in search of an idea. Sometimes these meandering words would actually capture a straggling thought and bear it triumphantly, a prisoner in their midst, until it died of servitude and overwork"—former Wilson Secretary of the Treasury, William Gibbs McAdoo.

In terms of presidential letters, Truman is in a category by himself. His letter to music critic Paul Hume, who had written an unfavorable review of Margaret's debut as a professional singer, is perhaps the most controversial letter ever written by a sitting president. In much more graphic detail Truman told the critic if he ever met him he would give him a black eye and a bloody nose and "...you'll need a supporter below!" Truman began his letter to Hume by telling him he had read his "lousy review" in the newspaper, and went on to tell Hume that he was an "eight ulcer man on a four ulcer job," and then quite colorfully commented on his ancestry. The country was divided between being aghast that a president would stoop to writing such a shocking letter to being supportive of a father defending his daughter. Critics coined the slogan "To err is Truman!" Truman never apologized nor showed any discernible sign of remorse.

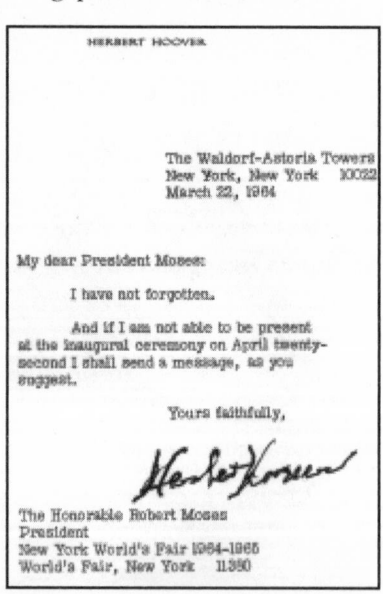

One of Hoover's last letters, signed shortly before his death.

SPIEGEL GROVE, FREMONT, O.
2 JULY, 1889.

The friends who have sent telegraphic messages, letters, floral tributes and newspaper articles, tokens of their regard for Mrs. Hayes, and of sympathy with me and my family, are so numerous that I can not, by the use of the pen alone, within the time it ought to be done, suitably express to all of them my gratitude and thanks.

I therefore beg them to excuse me for sending in this form my assurance of the fullest appreciation of their kindness, and of my lasting and heartfelt obligation to each of them.

Above, printed acknowledgement of sympathy letter on the death of his wife, Lucy, on the bottom of which President Rutherford B. Hayes has written an ALS. Right is a rare full signature of Hayes.

Presidential Rarities or Oddities and Bad Handwriting

Another interesting area of collecting, and one which the coauthor, Michael Minor, collects, is "Presidential Rarities or Oddities," some of which are illustrated in this chapter.

In terms of penmanship, perhaps Washington had the most attractive handwriting. Lincoln's penmanship was plain and usually legible although, with the stress of war many of his presidential notes and directives are difficult to decipher. Jefferson's handwriting is tiny and characterized by his idiosyncrasy of not making capital letters. His signature is so much larger than his handwriting that, at first glance, it appears to have been written by another. John Quincy Adams wrote a plain but attractive hand which changed little throughout his life. Taylor's writing was bold, plain and attractive. He preferred a broad nibbed pen which made his letters quite distinctive and attractive. Truman, LBJ, Ford, Carter, Reagan and Clinton all wrote or write legible and attractive hands.

John F. Kennedy's handwriting is almost undecipherable and his signature varied the most. He has the distinction of having the worst handwriting of all the presidents. Martin Van Buren is a close second and worthy of "honorable mention" in the "Hall of Fame of Illegible Handwriting" is George Bush, Senior.

The two fanciest or most florid signatures of all the presidents are those of James K. Polk and James Buchanan. Attractive, too, are the signatures of Washington, Jefferson, John Adams, Taylor, Taft and Wilson.

Books Signed by Presidents

Another area of collecting is that of books signed by the presidents. These include presidential memoirs and other books owned or authored by the presidents. Not all our presidents have written their memoirs, particularly many of the 19th century ones. Most of the 20th century presidents have. Some of the presidents, e.g., Wilson, Hoover, Nixon, Ford and Carter have written a number of books, all of which are desirable to find signed. Another category of books are those owned by a president and from their personal library. Such books are extremely rare, expensive, and highly desirable in several instances—Washington, Jefferson and Lincoln. Books from Jefferson's

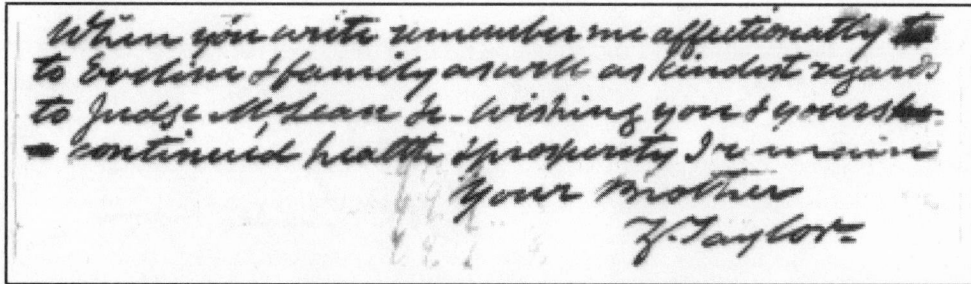

The United States To Zachary Taylor 1st Lieut — in th. Seventh — regiment of Infantry Dr.

For his pay from the 1st of April 1810 to the 31st August 1810. 5 months — days, at Thirty dollars per month, ... $150 00

For his forage from the to the month days, at dollars per month, ...

For his subsistence, per account herewith, ... 61 20

$211 20

I CERTIFY ON HONOR, That the foregoing account is accurate and just, and that I have not received compensation from the United States, for any part of the time above charged.

Zachary Taylor 1st Lieut 7th Regt. U.S. Infl

Very rare full signature of Zachary Taylor on pay voucher as a young army officer. Perhaps unique.

Conclusion of a typical Taylor ALS. Note the signature of "Z. Taylor."

PRESIDENTIAL AUTOGRAPHS 67

Rare full signature of Franklin Delano Roosevelt.

THE WHITE HOUSE

Mr. William T. Marshall
Hotel Willard
Washington, D.C.

Illegal presidential free frank of F.D.R. on a White House envelope. F.D.R. did not have the franking privilege as president. Only a few are known to exist.

I recall with understanding the occasions of which you write and assure you that it is heart-warming to receive word from service associations.

Again many thanks for your kind offer, and with best wishes,

Sincerely,

Rare signature of Eisenhower as "Ike Eisenhower."

Rare in-person full signature of Nixon. Nixon never used his middle name or initial in his signature. Probably written in full at the request of a shrewd collector.

library incorporate a code used by Jefferson incorporating letters from words in which he encoded his initials.

Many presidents had their own personalized book plates, e.g., Washington and many others wrote their names inside their books, or both. Books from Buchanan's library are quite desirable because he bequeathed his library to his favorite niece, Harriet Lane, who was his White House hostess, and who wrote her name "Harriet Lane Johnston" below Buchanan's signature, further authenticating the volume. As a point of interest, the autographic material of Harriet Lane, one of our youngest, loveliest and most popular First Ladies, is much scarcer than the material of her presidential uncle. It was for the lovely young Harriet Lane that the popular pre-civil war ballad "Listen to the Mockingbird" was written and dedicated.

FDR collected bibelots, or miniature books, which he bequeathed to his children along with his famous stamp collection. The remainder of Roosevelt's vast library is housed in his presidential library at Hyde Park, New York. The FDR bibelots are all signed, usually on the first free blank end paper, or inside the front cover. Beneath his signature he usually wrote "Hyde Park"—however, inside those bibelots he obtained during his presidency he wrote "The White House" below his signature.

There are many presidential book rarities as well as many easily obtainable volumes, e.g., most of those authored and signed by Hoover, Nixon, Carter and Ford. However, in 1912 Hoover and his wife translated an early mining treatise Agricola's *De Re Metallica*, first published in 1556. These rare volumes also contain Hoover's scarce early signature "H.C. Hoover." As a member of the Warren Commission, Gerald Ford wrote a book about Lee Harvey Oswald entitled *Portrait of the Assassin*. Signed copies are quite rare.

The young JFK wrote a memorial tribute to his brother who was killed in WWII entitled *We Remember Joe,* and his master's thesis *Why England Slept*. Later, when he was in the Senate, he also authored the Pulitzer Prize winning book *Profiles in Courage*. All three volumes are scarce and highly desirable. Most copies of *Profiles in Courage* bear secretarial inscriptions. Rare and probably unobtainable is a privately printed memorial tribute Theodore Roosevelt wrote after the death in childbirth of his first wife, Alice Lee, in which he wrote "...the light has gone out of my life forever..." He gave his infant daughter, Alice, into the care of his sister and went west. The rest, as they say, is history!

Presidential Franks

A fascinating area of presidential autographs is Presidential Franking signatures. Every president from Washington through Grant was granted permission by Congress to "frank" their mail whereby it would go through the postal system free. Franks were normally written in the upper right corner of the envelope, with the word "Free"

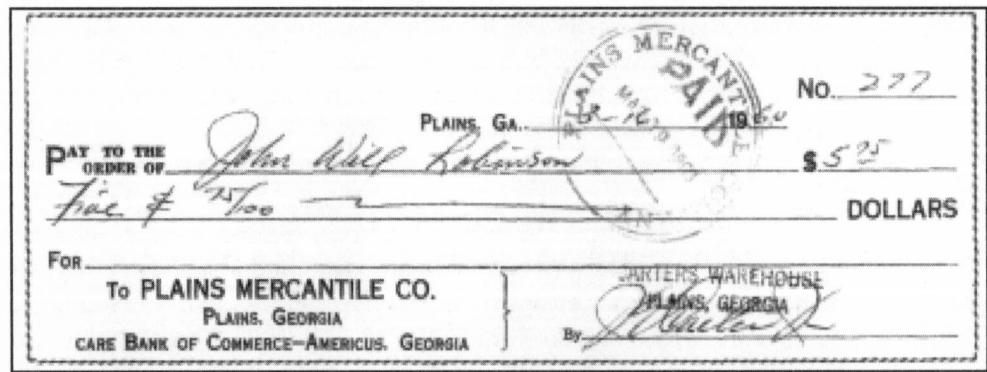

Rare, early signature of Jimmy Carter signed as "J.E. Carter, Jr."

Edith Kermit Roosevelt
Feby. 5th 1909.

For Mike Minor ~ with warm wishes
of a former occupant of this Great house
Betty Ford   Lady Bird Johnson
Bess Truman   Gerald R. Ford   Mamie Doud Eisenhower

White House Vignettes. Top vignette is signed by First Lady Edith Kermit Roosevelt. bottom vignette is signed by Lady Bird Johnson, Betty Ford, Bess Truman, Mamie Doud Eisenhower, and Gerald R. Ford.

written beneath the "franking signature." However, many variations were used by the early presidents—for example, while president, Washington signed his franks in the third person "President U. S." or "Pres. U. S." Jefferson's presidential franking signature is unique among presidents: "Free. Th. Jefferson Pr. U. S." The franks of John Adams, Madison, Monroe, John Quincy Adams, Van Buren and Buchanan are plentiful from pre and post presidential periods, particularly as Secretary of State, but quite rare of presidential date. However, the presidential franks of Zachary Taylor, James Knox Polk and Andrew Johnson are extremely rare, and Johnson in particular, whose son franked his mail for him. Only one example of William Henry Harrision's presidential frank is known.

All the presidents following Grant are rare in franking signatures and some are simply unobtainable. Garfield franked many letters as a Congressman but none as President. Grover Cleveland, Woodrow Wilson, Benjamin Harrison, William McKinley and Franklin D. Roosevelt never had the frank. Although Harrison and McKinley both served in Congress their terms were during periods when postage stamps or penalty envelopes were used for government mail.

In 1891 the free frank was again given to Congress following its abolition in 1877 resulting from abuses of the franking privilege. In 1895 the frank was extended to the Vice President as President of the Senate. Both Theodore Roosevelt and Calvin Coolidge had the right to frank their Vice Presidential mail. However, this privilege was withdrawn when they became president. In 1958 former Presidents Hoover and Truman were given the frank, as has every former president since.

Many of the early presidents illegally franked mail for their wives; Washington not only wrote and signed letters for Martha, who was uncomfortable at best wielding a pen, but he franked them for her as well. Among the presidents who illegally franked their wife's mail were John Adams, Madison, Pierce and Lincoln. One president, Millard Fillmore, otherwise known as a paragon of virtue, illegally franked personal and business letters for his law firm when he served in Congress.

With the exceptions of Julia Gardiner Tyler, Caroline Fillmore and Eliza Johnson, all widowed First Ladies have been granted the franking privilege by special acts of Congress. Several of the First Lady franks are among the rarest and most eagerly sought of both philatelic and

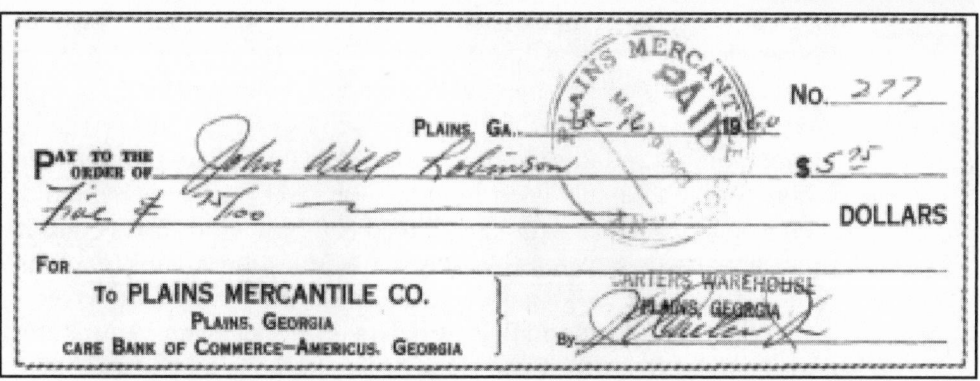

Rare, early signature of Jimmy Carter signed as "J.E. Carter, Jr."

autographic material. For example, only three Martha Washington franks are known and none of Margaret Taylor. Scarce, too, are the franks of Louisa C. Adams, Anna Harrison, Sarah Polk and Ida McKinley. Paradoxically, although Florence Harding lived only ten months after President Harding's death, her franks are somewhat common. The more recent First Ladies who lived or served in the 20th century are obtainable, if not common. However, collectors should be aware that most of the 20th century ex-presidents and First Ladies who had the franking privilege were also allowed to use printed or facsimile signatures, which are of very nominal value and, generally speaking, only those covers which were done for collectors are authentically signed.

Material Signed by Both a President and First Lady

Another interesting area of collecting which kills two birds with one stone is collecting material signed by both a president and his wife. Not only is such material highly desirable it also gives collectors a specimen of the First Lady who wields great influence on the president. We believe collecting First Lady material is one of the most underrated areas in autographs today. One can find a thousand letters of George Washington to every one of Martha. The autographic material of some First Ladies is virtually unobtainable e.g. Martha Jefferson, Elizabeth Monroe, Rachel Jackson, Margaret Taylor, Abigail Fillmore, Eliza Johnson, Ellen Arthur, Ida McKinly and Ellen Wilson. Some First Ladies are so rare no examples from their pens are known to exist such as Hannah Van Buren, Letitia Tyler and Alice Lee Roosevelt. Old or young, homely or lovely, First Ladies have had great influence with their presidential husbands. Some presidential couples were openly powerful political teams such as FDR and his peripatetic Eleanor, Jimmy and Rosalynn Carter and Bill and Hillary Clinton. Many others wielded equally great influence on their husbands behind the scenes. James K. Polk said his beloved Sarah, who also served as his presidential secretary, was his only confidant. John Adams frequently turned for advice to Abigail, who often did not wait to be asked!

Collecting presidential material is an educational, stimulating and exciting pursuit. We highly recommend it to you.

—Mike Minor and Larry Vrzalik, Lone Star Autographs,
www.lonestarautographs.com

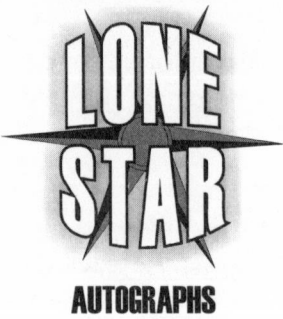

Michael Minor and Larry F. Vrzalik are leading autograph experts and partners in Lone Star Autographs, a rare document company established in 1982 in the great state of Texas. They are authors of *From The President's Pen* and *Geronimo: The Story of His Life,* which contains a monograph about his rare autograph and those of other western Americana figures. Minor and Vrzalik have also written numerous historical articles. They may be reached at: Lone Star Autographs, P. O. Box 10, Kaufman, Texas 75142 (Telephone): 972/932-6050 (Telefax): 972/932-6607;

Email: **mail@lonestarautographs.com**
Website: **www.lonestarautographs.com**

Chapter 7

HOLLYWOOD AUTOGRAPHS

by Tom Kramer

From a contemporary standpoint, it seems difficult to conceive that not much more than three decades ago, Hollywood autographs were treated by most dealers with something bordering on faint contempt, like an impoverished relative whom one felt obligated to invite to the family banquet but sequestered at the far end of the table, where her presence would not offend the finer sensibilities of more distinguished guests. Today, Hollywood autographs have become one of the most explosively popular areas of collecting in the entire autograph hobby, with eager collectors bidding up the prices at auction of such film icons as Marilyn Monroe, James Dean and Jean Harlow to levels that would have been unthinkable as recently as the 1990s.

The reasons for this astonishing growth in interest in movie-related autographs are not difficult to discern. After a calamitous falloff in movie attendance that started in the 1950s as a direct result of the introduction of television, audiences began to return again to theaters in the 1970s, spurred by an exciting new generation of filmmakers that included Robert Altman, Francis Ford Coppola, Martin Scorsese and Steven Spielberg, and those audiences continue to grow today, with blockbuster films breaking old box office records on a virtually yearly basis. Further, the unprecedented expansion of modern media empires, huge conglomerates that own movie studios, television stations and publishing houses, has facilitated the promotion of the cult of celebrity, not only in the United States but around the globe. We are bombarded today with images of film and other entertainment celebrities—in movies, newspapers, magazines, talk shows, tabloid television, a seemingly endless parade of award shows—all in the service of selling tickets, but creating, as well, a fascination with actors and actresses and a desire to collect memorabilia connected with them.

The other side of the commercial coin is that movies have attained intellectual cache, as well, and are now celebrated as an art form—*the* art form, in fact, of the 20th and 21st centuries. Film studies flourish in universities, scholarly studies of the "golden age" of film-making vie for shelf space with biographies of legendary actors and directors, and the easy availability of cinema classics on cable television, video cassettes and DVDs creates new, if more limited, audiences for the great films of the past.

Thus, interest in collecting Hollywood autographs is today at an all-time high. But if interest has never been greater, the same is true of the problems that face experienced and novice collectors alike as forgeries, abetted by ever more sophisticated computer technology and the spreading popularity of Internet auctions, flood the market in increasing volume. For today's Hollywood collector, the goal of building an authentic autograph collection requires that enthusiasm be tempered by knowledge, caution, and plain common sense.

The problem of forged Hollywood autographs is almost as old as the movie industry, itself. In the early days of silent film, the performers in front of the camera were anonymous, receiving virtually no billing. As studios became established, however, and moviegoers began to recognize the faces of actors and actresses who appeared in film after film, curiosity quickly grew about the identities of these unknown players, who soon began to receive billing either at the start of the film or in title cards when they made their first appearance in the film. From billing came stardom, and from stardom, fandom.

Virtually from the beginning, movies were a medium of mass entertainment, and the new stars of the silent screen found them-selves, probably to their own astonishment, virtually deluged with fan letters requesting autographed photos. Unable to personally fill such an overwhelming demand for autographs, the stars responded with a combination of authentically signed portraits, photos with pre-printed or stamped signatures, and hand-signed but forged auto-graphs, more politely termed secretarials. And, as the Hollywood studio system solidified in the early 1920s, hundreds of secretaries found employment signing photos for both the bigger and lesser stars of the period, a practice that was to continue throughout the 1930s, 40s and beyond.

Real or Fake?

Clearly, then, the first task faced by any serious collector of Hollywood autographs is learning to distinguish secretarial from authentic signatures. And to begin, one can conveniently divide the secretaries into two broad categories: those who made no effort to imitate the signature of the star they were signing for, and those who did attempt to make the signature look genuine. As an example of the former, we can look at Bette Davis. During her career at Warner Brothers, Davis employed her sister as her secretary, and the overwhelming majority of "autographed" Bette Davis photos from this period in fact bear the handwriting of her sister. Comparing a "Bette Davis" autograph signed by her sister (Example 1) with an authentic Davis signature circa 1940 (Example 2), one can see that the signatures bear virtually no resemblance to each other. If one knows what a real Bette Davis signature should look like—and this is a big if—there is no way to confuse it with her sister's version. Other celebrity relatives

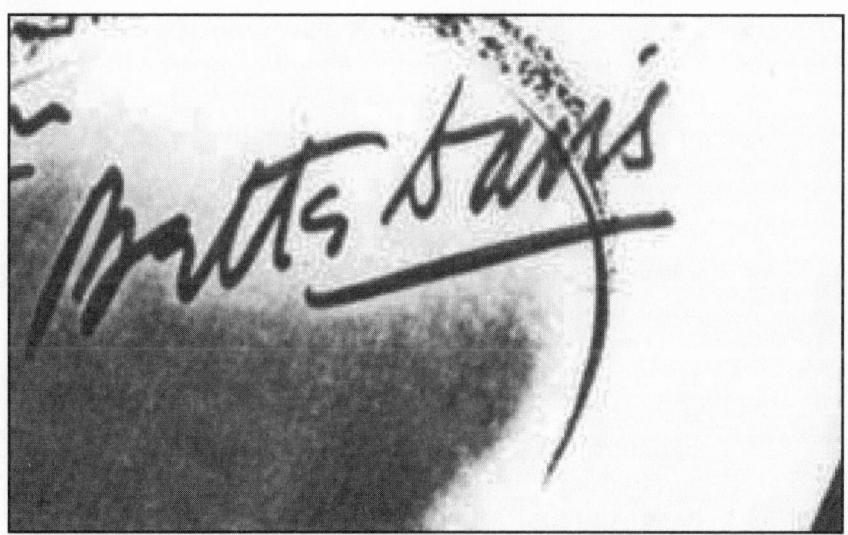

Example 1

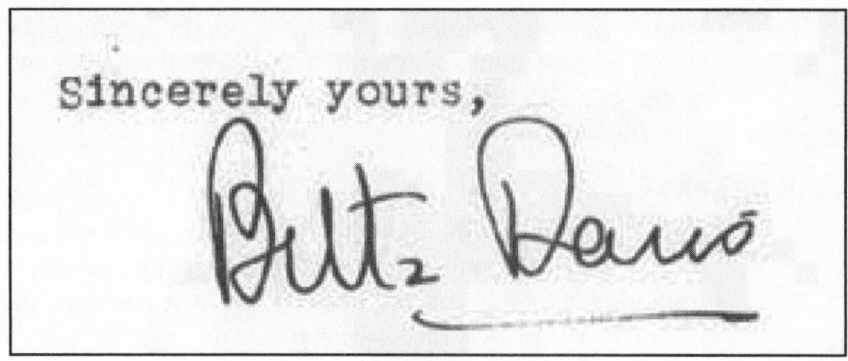

Example 2

who frequently took on secretarial duties included Harold Lloyd's father, who produced a deceptively authentic-looking but somewhat more florid version of his son's signature; the wives of Bela Lugosi, Boris Karloff and Randolph Scott; Shirley Temple's mother, who signed easily spottable autographs in childish block lettering; and the ever-popular "Mama" Jean Harlow.

Things get considerably more complicated when dealing with a secretary who practiced forging a star's signature until she/he achieved a near perfect match. Examples 3 and 4 below illustrate two Gary Cooper signatures and inscriptions. Example 4 is authentic, while Example 3 was penned by one of the better of Cooper's many secretaries. If one compares the signatures alone, they appear to be almost identical; and even an expert could probably be forgiven for mistaking the secretarial signature for the real thing. However, once one looks beyond the signature and examines the inscriptions, it becomes quite apparent that these were written by two different people, with completely different formations of similar letters ("T" and "J") and a decidedly more graceful, feminine flow to Example 3.

This quick comparison also reveals what one might describe as the Achilles heel of Hollywood's secretaries. No matter how accomplished many of them became in imitating a particular star's signature, they never devoted the time to getting the rest of the handwriting correct. Armed with a sample of a given actor's handwriting, a knowledgeable collector looking at an inscribed photo is virtually always in a good position to distinguish an authentic signatures from a secretarial. There are, of course, collectors who insist on acquiring only uninscribed photos; but, as demonstrated above, this can be a fairly risky business.

Happily, finding authentic examples of Hollywood autographs is today only a click of a mouse away. R&R Enterprises, one of the country's largest autograph auction houses, has an extensive illustrated database of items sold in past auctions on their website, www.rrauction.com, which can serve as an excellent study source for collectors. Many other member dealers of such organizations as the Professional Autograph Dealers Association (padaweb.org), the Universal Autograph Collectors Club (uacc.org) and the International Autograph Dealers Alliance (iacc-da.com) also maintain web sites where collectors can examine handwriting samples. Where possible, collectors should actually print copies of these exemplars and start their own autograph reference files. A number of Hollywood autograph facsimile guides have been published over the past two decades. While these are now out of print, copies do surface from time to time and are always worth acquiring.

Example 3

Valuable signature studies also appear periodically in *Pen and Quill*, the publication of the UACC, and *Autograph Collector* magazine.

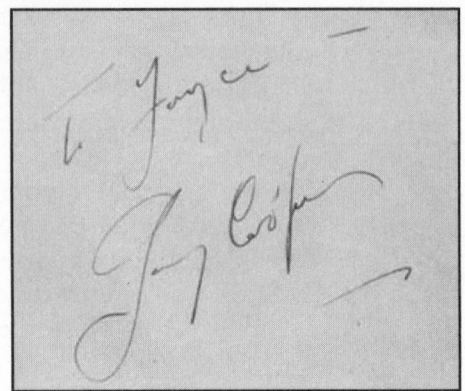

Example 4

Finding the Treasures

And, for collectors of vintage Hollywood autographs, the good news is that once one gets past the secretarials, there is a veritable treasure trove of authentic material to be discovered. A signed photo of Judy Garland from *The Wizard of Oz*—Vivien Leigh as Scarlett O'Hara—Rudolph Valentino as the Son of the Sheik—Gloria Swanson as Norma Desmond—Boris Karloff as the Frankenstein Monster—Charles Laughton as Captain Bligh—Basil Rathbone as Sherlock Holmes—these are a small handful of the superb images that have turned up in recent memory. If few stars attended to their fan mail with the dogged determination of Joan Crawford, most replied with sufficient regularity to make a collector's desire to obtain any particular autograph a feasible possibility.

There are, of course, notable exceptions. The great Jean Harlow, dead at age 26, rarely signed for anyone but personal friends. The same is true for the much-forged Katharine Hepburn, who, however, enjoyed a very lengthy career and appears to have had *many* friends. Autographed photos of Hepburn, though not abundant, do show up on the market. The very private Lon Chaney, Sr., rarely signed photos, while Louise Brooks, an actress whose autograph is very much in demand today, was actually considered of quite minor importance while under contract to Paramount and never took her own career seriously enough to bother with fan mail. Signed photos of the Marx Brothers and the original Three Stooges are also quite scarce and command prices in the $2,500-3,000 range. In a class all by herself is Greta Garbo, who seemed to have had a positive aversion to signing her name. There are probably less than fifteen authentically signed Garbo photos known at this time, and signed album pages are similarly difficult to find.

Tracking Down the Possible

Once one has resigned oneself to the fact that certain names will probably never be possible to track down, however, one can build a rewarding Hollywood autograph collection that reflects one's own particular film enthusiasms (or obsessions). There are some collectors whose tastes are both wide and eclectic, and who collect autographs from both silent and sound films, from the great stars to character actors, with directors, film composers, and studio executives thrown in for good measure. Most collectors, however, are more theme-oriented. They may collect only horror film actors, comedians, Western stars, or film noir. One collector of recent memory was fixated on "the young and tragic"—actresses who met a youthful, untimely end. He quickly discovered, however, that young and tragic, in autographic terms, was synonymous with rare and expensive. Other collectors have built beautiful collections of signed images by Hollywood photographers George Hurrell and Clarence Sinclair Bull. Yet another collected nothing but vintage 11x14 images. The viewing of several hundred of these photos at a single sitting was a breathtaking experience. In sum, building a quality vintage Hollywood autograph collection can be a hobby, a passion, an aesthetic experience and a good investment at the same time.

Collectors of contemporary Hollywood autographs face a very different set of circumstances. Today's top stars receive as much fan mail and autograph requests as the stars of yesteryear—perhaps more—but they no longer, for the most part, respond. Since actors today are no longer tied to a single studio, there are no longer studio-employed secretaries to do the signing for them. Instead, they either employ personal secretaries to deal with autograph requests or send their fan mail out to agencies that for a fee send out secretarially signed or pre-printed photos.

Virtually the only way to get authentically signed autograph photos of current stars, then, is to get them in-person oneself or to purchase them from legitimate in-person dealers. In-person dealers work either individually or with assistants (assistants can aid in getting additional photos signed or can fan out to various locations in a city if several celebrities will be appearing in different places at the same time) and often develop an elaborate series of contacts who feed them information about the comings and goings of autograph-worthy performers – what talk shows they will be appearing on, what hotels they are staying at, even what flights they may be arriving on. Confronting celebrities this way to obtain their autographs can be, in the words of one reputable in-person dealer, "obnoxious," but it is also the only reliable way of making certain one is getting an authentic signature. Occasionally dealers are also able to arrange exclusive private signings for a fee. In-person collecting frequently requires a fair amount of travel and a lot of waiting without any guarantee that a given celebrity will actually agree to sign. And the dealers who do the chasing around town expect to be paid a price commensurate with the effort they have expended.

Today, the main sales venue for contemporary Hollywood/celebrity autographs is the Internet, and, more specifically, the Internet auction site, eBay. Nowhere is the frenzied interest in Hollywood autographs as evident as on the pages of eBay, where dozens of new collectors from all over the world seem to pop up on a weekly basis.

For the knowledgeable Hollywood collector, eBay can be a valuable resource, provided one has time and patience. The best thing about eBay is that it attracts book dealers, antique dealers, miscellaneous collectibles dealers and others who do not primarily deal in autographs but may occasionally have some in stock that they are looking to turn over quickly. Almost all of this is autographic material that without the Internet would not be made available to collectors. Some of this material is of surprisingly high quality and offered at very reasonable opening bids. It is always advisable, though, to read the descriptions of the autographs and contact the seller if there are any questions regarding condition.

More generally, though, with regard to the authenticity of most material on eBay, and more specifically with regard to contemporary Hollywood autographs, eBay is something between a free-for-all and a jungle. It is definitely not for amateurs. Unsuspecting collectors who believe in the implicit goodness of human nature will find eBay the ideal place to have their faith shattered. Because virtually anyone can post anything on eBay, and eBay's owners post a disclaimer regarding the authenticity of autographs offered for sale, the site has attracted a ravenous horde of forgers, shysters and assorted low-lifes who tend to overwhelm the smaller number of trustworthy dealers offering authentic material. Perhaps nothing is as illustrative of the general trustworthiness of autograph offerings on eBay as the near daily appearances of "very rare" Marlon Brando photos from *The Godfather*, usually priced in the area of $19.95, usually accompanied by the all-important Certificate of Authenticity. Hundreds of these "very rare" autographed photos are offered there every year, year after year. None of them, of course, are genuine. All over the country, it would appear, courtesy of the Internet, collections are proudly being built with pristine $2 album pages signed by Montgomery Clift or Spencer Tracy, and cast photos of *Chicago* signed by three for $10. As eBay management graciously warns at the bottom of each web page, *caveat emptor*—buyer beware.

So, secretaries to the left... forgers to the right... It appears that the Hollywood autograph collector is besieged by bad material on all sides. How, finally, is the collector to steer an intrepid path through the morass of inauthentic material to build a Hollywood collection that will be both enjoyable and rewarding? Here, in closing, are a handful of tips to help make you a more knowledgeable collector:

1. Remember, even Joan Crawford used a secretary. Start using some of the resources mentioned in this article to become your own autograph authority. Familiarize yourself with the handwriting of the stars whose autographs you are interested in by collecting and comparing facsimile exemplars. And don't merely give the writing a cursory glance—really *look* at it and compare samples. If your samples differ from one another, there may be secretarials among them and this should be a spur to even further research. If you're not certain, show your samples to a reputable dealer. Autograph authentication is not rocket science, but it does require some effort– effort that will be repaid many-fold every time you avoid purchasing a forged signature.

2. Everyone, the best dealers included, makes mistakes. There are mistakes in all the facsimile guides and on the web sites recommended above, as well. One of the best ways to avoid getting burned is to purchase from dealers who offer a lifetime money back guarantee of authenticity. Member dealers of the various autograph organizations mentioned in this article offer this guaranty and will honor it. If you are purchasing at auction, read the fine print. Many

auction houses allow only a limited period in which to return lots purchased from them.

3. An autograph is either authentic or it isn't. Do not be fooled by certificates of authenticity. They are not worth the paper they're printed on. End of discussion.

4. When bidding on eBay, do not be unduly swayed by a seller's positive feedback numbers. Positive feedback indicates nothing more than that the purchaser was happy with his or her purchase. It does not necessarily prove that what was purchased was genuine.

5. If it seems to good to be true, it probably is.

6. In Hollywood autographs, there are very few things that can truly be described as one-of-a-kind. If something you'd like for your collection seems over-priced, walk away from it. You're likely to find something of similar quality at a more favorable price later on. And you can use the money you've saved to purchase an additional item!

Knowledge, caution, and plain common sense—the essential tools for the Hollywood autograph enthusiast. Meanwhile—the stars await! Get out there and start collecting!

—Tom Kramer

Tom Kramer has been a film buff since the age of 12 and a Hollywood autograph collector for 16 years. His company, Golden Age Autographs, now in its twelfth year, is one of the hobby's largest dealerships specializing in vintage Hollywood autographs. His study on the autographs of Bette Davis was published in 2001. Further information can be obtained by visiting his illustrated online catalog at **goldenageautographs.com**, or by e-mail at silentsaregolden@hotmail.com, or by phone at 212-866-5626.

Chapter 8

Autographed First Edition Books

by Tim Miller

Are you intrigued by autograph collecting? Do you already have some rare treasures, or are you hoping you may have found one? You have come to the right place.

The Sander's Price Guide to Autographs has been helping autograph collectors evaluate, enhance, and market your investment in this hobby for many years. I have gone from collector to proprietor, and I still find this guide to be a very valuable resource.

For the past five centuries, regular people like you and I have enjoyed the pleasure of collecting autographs of both the well known and the not-so-well-known. The hobby began when 16th century German students maintained albums of correspondence from family, friends and noblemen. It wasn't until the late 18th century that autograph collecting, in its modern sense, had evolved into a worldwide past time for millions of people from all socioeconomic levels of humanity. While the number of collectors continued to expand, the hobby went through a natural transition to focus on the most popular figures in human culture – those in power and those in vogue. The subjects of our affection were primarily from the fields of politics, religion, sports, current-events and literature.

Major Shifts

There have been major shifts in the perceived worth of autographs, with many people investing small fortunes in the hobby. The educated consumer of autographs is becoming more and more discriminating, the result being that the quality of the autograph is now highly important. Details are significant—such as whether it is a full signature, or just the family name and first initial (the famous A. Lincoln versus Abraham Lincoln variation), and if the autograph has a good provenance or history that is verifiable and/or special. Important content, like historical references or the mention of well-known persons included in a note, means increased value for an autographed piece. A signature from a United States President is usually more valuable if the signature can be dated to the time the President was in office. The phrase "Signed as President" is used to distinguish this and we tend to value these at a premium price.

Value of an autograph also increases if that autograph is on a desirable medium. Let me explain. Two identical, authentic signatures could have very different marketplace prices if one of them happens to be on a preferred medium. For example, collectors and investors alike place a higher value on mediums—like signed documents or fully handwritten notes that are also signed. An autograph on a piece of plain paper is usually called a simple "cut" signature. If we have a full page of paper with a handwritten note mentioning Gettysburg and a full signature from Abraham Lincoln, then that piece is worth far more than a cut signature of President Lincoln.

A Good Time To Be Collecting

This is an exciting time to be an autograph collector. Many of our most prominent people are recording their thoughts for posterity and then signing their works. The medium that has generated huge interest (and prices) among collectors recently is signed books. The collecting of books was a recognized hobby long before autograph collecting became popular, but it wasn't until the invention of the printing press that those other than the very wealthy could afford to own even a small library. Then, in the 19th century, the idea of having authors autograph their books struck gold and now is one of the most popular and most rewarding forms of autograph collecting. Signed books is the medium through which I first became hooked on the love of select, special autographs, and how I phased away from my full-time profession as Chief Operating Officer of United Publishing into my current multi-million dollar business.

The area of signed books is the fastest-growing segment of the autograph collectibles hobby. After carefully watching the autograph and book markets for two decades, I observed a very intriguing trend that is quite significant in this time of economic instability. When the stock market went up during the booming years of the late 1990s, signed book values climbed, as did most collectibles during that era. However, as the United States economy and collectibles in general began to move toward a recession, the price and value of most signed books continued to go up. The rationale behind this apparent paradox is simple: when the market goes up, more people have more money available to invest in long-term collectibles that they really enjoy. When the market goes down, people look for other investment potential and restrict their spending to areas that they really enjoy (i.e. long-term collectibles).

Investors and collectors have been speculating and investing in collectibles of all types for decades. While many collectibles, such as baseball cards and beanie babies, have large followings, they have provided a market with some peaks, but many pits. However, many collectible books have enjoyed relatively upward-spiraling increases in value over a long time, and they reward investors with hours of reading pleasure.

Value Increases

While there are never guarantees, collectors have seen some of their signed "first edition" books increase in market price from two thousand to twenty-five thousand dollars in a decade or so. One example of this is a First Edition, First Printing of *Old Man and the Sea* by Ernest Hemingway. Of the modern signed "first printings," the most popular are *flatsigned*—meaning they are signed directly on the title-page of the book (not on a bookplate or sticker) and not personalized ("To Billie Sue" or "To Bobby Joe"). Even more precisely and within the very hot area of collecting signed books, I have seen flatsigned, first printing books become the most highly sought after autograph collectibles of the 20th and 21st centuries. With that demand, the value and price of these autograph collectibles has increased accordingly.

How do you define the phrase *true first printing* as it relates to book collecting terminology? A first printing comes from the first batch or print-run of that title. All the copies of a book printed from the first setting of type by the printer are first editions. This definition is easy to understand when applied to the days when type was set by hand. When a book had been printed, the individual pieces of type were physically removed from the press and used on another job.

Now, however, type is set on computers, and an entire book can be stored in a single file and reprinted without being reset. Today, books that go back for reprint many times typically use that same computer setting of type, making them all technically *first editions*, but not necessarily first printings. A *printing* is a single run from the printing press. In other words, if a publisher's first order on a new title is to print 15,000 copies; then, several months later, they order another 10,000 copies to be printed without making any change, the result is *a first and second printing of the first edition*.

To most book collectors, only the *first printing* is considered desirable, and when experts use the term "first edition" without qualification, it would be the first group of 15,000 (*first edition, first printing*), in my example, to which they refer. The term *impression* is used by British dealers and publishers, and is synonymous with the more American word *printing*. When professional/ethical book collectors or dealers use the term "first edition," they are almost always referring to the *first printing of the first edition*.

So, have you got all that now? Well...it's not quite that easy. It is actually possible for copies of a book from a single printing to differ from one another. There are two terms that are used to describe such an occurrence: *state* or *issue*.

A separate *state* (or *issue*) of a printing is created when a change is made during the press run, but all the books are still published simultaneously. For example, if someone discovered a typographical error in the text, after 2,000 copies were printed of our first printing of 15,000, the press might be stopped, the error corrected, and the remaining 13,000 copies printed. All the books would then be sent to the publisher for distribution. This scenario would create *a first and second state of the first edition*.

One of the most famous, multiple states of a first printing is from John Steinbeck's *Of Mice and Men*. After the book had already gone to press, the word "pendula" on page 7 was changed to "loosely," but the presses kept rolling and only a few thousand were ever released with the original word, "pendula." For a collector, the *first state* would be much more desirable. This would hold true even if the first state consisted of 13,000 copies and the second state only 2,000. That's because the collector nearly always prefers the earliest version of a book, even if it is not the rarest.

Dust jackets too can have different states. Some 20th century books from John Steinbeck were available in several different binding colors, due to the binder having used leftovers from previously bound works. In some cases, variants of a book have been noted, but bibliographers have been unable to determine which variant came first. In such instances, books often will be described with the notation "no known priority," which means there is no way to determine whether or not the issue described is the true first. This is often the case for the firsts of Zane Grey.

Making Points

The differences between the various states/issues of an edition are called *points of issue*, or just *points*, and are described in bibliographies and some book price guides. As with many collectibles, there are important subtleties, so only truly knowledgeable booksellers can help you avoid costly mistakes.

There are two things to be very mindful of when purchasing an autographed book for both collecting and/or investment: condition of the book and popularity of the title. As with most collectibles, books in MINT/NEAR MINT condition command a premium price in the market. It is especially true of what we call "hyper-modern" books, that condition plays an incredibly important role in determining value. By hyper-modern, we mean in the last twenty years or so, since there are so many more people who have been carefully storing their treasured copies as they come off the bookstore shelf. For more rare books, it isn't unusual to find just GOOD condition copies of titles in demand by such legends as Hemingway or Salinger that still command prices of over a thousand dollars.

For best values, always pay close attention to new authors and their new books. If you are able to get a MINT *hardcover signed first printing* for $50 or less, what have you got to lose? At worst, you have another interesting and collectible, autographed book for your library! There is no doubt some of today's newcomers will be the literary giants of our future!

How does someone best predict which autographed books will go up in value? One of the most certain signs that an autographed book will significantly go up in value is when that particular book and/or author wins a prominent award. This may be a national book award like the Shamus or a worldwide award like the Pulitzer Prize.

Other signs of particular interest, when buying books for long-term investment potential, would be those that have already held their own during decades of collecting. Examples are books by Hemingway, Steinbeck, Fitzgerald and Faulkner. Those books will experience less volatility in the marketplace since they have withstood the test of time. More recent books are much more likely to have large price swings.

We cannot know for certain if our investment in autographs or autographed books will provide us a fortune when we retire. However, we can certainly improve our chances by being smart collectors. Always remember to collect what YOU enjoy! That way you will always have a wonderful collection whether book values go up or down.

Just like all other autograph collectors, I still get a real thrill when I see and hold that long-desired signature of that famous person who I have always admired. Today's newsmakers and yesterday's heroes all continue to help us have a wonderful hobby and for some, a satisfying career. For me, I am fortunate enough to have both. My best wishes to you on your collecting adventures!

—*Tim Miller, www.FLATSIGNED.com*

The term FLATSIGNED® was coined by Tim Miller to describe the most desirable type of collectible book. FLATSIGNED® means "Signed by the author, directly on the title page without being inscribed to some stranger." Tim has been collecting books all his life and began his large collection in its current form over 10 years ago.

Chapter 9

The Manuscript Society

by Edward C. Oetting and David R. Smith

THE MANUSCRIPT SOCIETY (www.manuscript.org), founded in 1948 as the National Society of Autograph Collectors, has grown to an international membership of approximately 1,500 encompassing the spectrum of private collectors, manuscript professionals (curators, archivists, and librarians), and dealers. Many historical societies, museums, special collections and academic libraries are valued institutional members as well.

The Society publishes, as a benefit to members, two quarterly publications, *Manuscripts* and *The Manuscript Society News*. The quarterly journal *Manuscripts* has an established reputation for excellent scholarly and collector articles reflecting the diverse interests of the field of autographs and manuscripts. . *The Manuscript Society News* features information on the whole contemporary world of manuscripts and autographs, as well as news about the Society and its members.

In addition to our publications, the Society holds a four day annual meeting in a community offering premier manuscript resources and repositories. Major North American and European cities have alternated with smaller communities as venues in order to provide a varied view of the manuscript resources available. The 2003 and 2004 annual meetings will be in Washington, DC and Chicago, Illinois respectively.

The Manuscript Society welcomes new members. The annual individual or institutional membership fee is $45. Contributing memberships at $100, sustaining memberships at $250, benefactor memberships at $500, and patron memberships at $1000 help in furthering Society interests. Memberships are on a calendar year basis; new members joining after July 1 may pay half the annual rate.

Your dues support the following: our publication program; scholarships for individuals interested in the use of manuscripts (e.g. Richie Maass Memorial Grant); the defense of individuals in appropriate replevin suits; and the expenses of managing the Society's programs and activities.

Please join us in appreciating and promoting the use, care and collecting of manuscripts and autographs.

To join The Manuscript Society contact:

Edward C. Oetting
Executive Director
The Manuscript Society
1960 E. Fairmont Dr.,
Tempe, AZ 85282-2844

web: **www.manuscript.org**
email: **manuscrip@cox.net**

Chapter 10

UACC

(Universal Autograph Collectors Club)

by Paul K. Carr, UACC President

The Universal Autograph Collectors Club (UACC) is the world's largest organization for autograph collectors with over 1800 members in the United States, Canada, and more than 25 other countries. Founded in 1965, the UACC is a nonprofit educational organization whose purpose is to inform members and the public about all aspects of autograph collecting through its publications, shows, and seminars.

By joining the UACC, you will receive our renowned 64-page bimonthly journal, *The Pen and Quill,* which features articles and news on autographs in all areas, including U.S. presidents, authors, scientists, aviators, astronauts, royalty, entertainers, athletes, military leaders, Nobel Prize winners, and explorers, to name a few. Studies of authentic, secretarial, Autopen, rubber-stamped, facsimile, and forged signatures help collectors to make informed decisions when purchasing autographic material. Celebrity addresses are published in each issue to assist collectors who enjoy writing for autographs. The UACC also sponsors annual literary awards in addition to paying for articles published in *The Pen and Quill.*

You may also have your name and address published as a new member in *The Pen and Quill.* By so doing, you will receive free autograph catalogues from our dealer members and auction houses. Or you can place a free classified ad in *The Pen and Quill* to list your wants, sell your extra material, or just communicate with other members about your common interests.

All members are required to abide by a strict Code of Ethics and violations of that Code are enforced by the UACC Ethics Board. By dealing with other UACC members, you can be assured that the Ethics Board will assist you in any dispute involving another member who has violated the Code of Ethics. Members who refuse to abide by an Ethics Board decision are subject to sanctions, including expulsion, with notice to members published in *The Pen and Quill.*

The UACC also offers its members the opportunity to purchase uncommon autographic material and reference works at affordable prices through the "UACC Warehouse" page in *The Pen and Quill.*

The UACC sponsors autograph shows in major U.S. cities and London, England featuring educational displays, autograph dealers who abide by the UACC Code of Ethics, and celebrity guests. Seminars are occasionally held in conjunction with the shows to educate our members and the public on all aspects of collecting and preservation, and identification of non-authentic (bogus or forged) material.

George Sanders, when he was U.A.C.C. Regional Director, with current Treasurer Al Wittnebert.

Finally, the UACC sponsors mail auctions through *The Pen and Quill* as well as through the internet via the UACC web site. These auctions are another avenue to assist our members who buy and sell autographs.

To learn more about the UACC, send your request for a brochure and membership application to **UACC, Dept. SPG, PO Box 6181, Washington, DC 20044-6181**. You can also get membership information and an application by visiting our Internet web site at **www.uacc.org**. We hope you will join our universe of fellow collectors soon.

Chapter 11

PADA

(Professional Autograph Dealers Association)

by Sheldon L. Tarakan

The Professional Autograph Dealers Association, Inc. (PADA) was organized in 1995 by many of the nation's leading dealers in historic autograph material. Concerned by the proliferation of new "dealers" lacking expertise, experience, integrity, and fiscal responsibility, PADA's purpose is to raise the standards of the autograph profession by requiring members to adhere to a strict code of ethics when conducting business with collectors, institutions, the general public, and other colleagues.

PADA seeks to encourage interest in and appreciation of the field of autograph collecting. It strives to promote high standards of business ethics, professionalism, and service in the trade. PADA aims to establish a marketplace for autographs in which collectors can buy and sell with confidence, and receive accurate and informed advice from its members.

Membership in PADA is *limited* to dealers who have demonstrated expertise and integrity in buying and selling autographs. All applicants for membership in PADA are carefully screened, and all members must adhere to PADA's strict code of ethics, including its complete guarantee of authenticity. As a result, whether you are buying, selling, or seeking an appraisal of autographs, PADA is your guarantee of quality, service, and integrity.

In addition to a track record of integrity, all members must provide a life-time guarantee of authenticity on the material they sell. Prospective members undergo a rigorous screening process, during which their business history is carefully reviewed and comments by current PADA members are solicited.

PADA members are in all parts of the United States. It is anticipated that as the organization grows, foreign dealers will also join. The present membership includes many leading dealers whose specialties include American and world history, science, literature, music, art, and the performing arts. Dealers who handle primarily contemporary sports and entertainment personalities are ineligible for membership in PADA.

PADA dealers represent a significant market for purchasing autographs, whether single items or entire collections. They can buy autographs outright, offering you a fair price and immediate payment. If you prefer, a PADA dealer can act as your agent for selling material or can take items on consignment, after fully discussing the terms with you. A PADA dealer can also suggest other options for selling your autographs or donating them to an institution.

Believing that PADA fills a strong need in the autograph community, the organization anticipates rapid growth, both in membership and stature. Current plans include trade shows, supporting an internet website, and publications designed to increase knowledge of autographs for collectors and dealers.

For additional information about PADA, check out our extensive website at **www.padaweb.org** or write or phone the current president of PADA:

Professional Autograph Dealers Association
Sheldon L. Tarakan
Visible Ink Incorporated
P.O. Box 474
Roslyn Heights, NY 11577

Phone: 516.621.2445
Fax: 516.908-7945

Chapter 12

IACC–DA

(INTERNATIONAL AUTOGRAPH COLLECTORS CLUB
& DEALERS ALLIANCE)

by Stephen Koschal, Executive Director

The IACC-DA was the first autograph organization to combine a collectors club and dealer alliance under the same flag. This innovation was immediately accepted by the autograph community. We remain unique as we are exclusively devoted to the collecting of autographs.

The IACC-DA is also devoted to keeping our hobby clean and educating our members. In the past the IACC-DA has published numerous signature studies written by some of the most knowledgeable collectors/dealers in the world. Our Gerald R. Ford Signature Study was praised by President Ford and he requested additional copies for the Ford Library. Other studies published are about, Robert Kennedy, Neil Armstrong, Bill Clinton and New Light on the Eugene "Pinny" Field II and Harry Dayton Sickles Forgery Case. A Study of the signature of Richard Nixon is in the works. All signature studies are available on the club website.

The IACC-DA endorses professional autograph events and complimentary educational courses are conducted at select shows. Each person attending receives a Certificate of Completion signed by the instructor, who will be one of the most knowledgeable in his or her field. Other IACC-DA innovations include the creation of the IACC-DA Scholarship Fund for collectors in economically depressed areas who can't afford to join a club and the first autograph authentication service by an organization.

Members have access to one of the finest reference libraries. Used by researchers, librarians and institutions, as well as the finest autograph professionals in the world.

Our dealer members are the finest in the world, they did not simply join but applied for membership. Their credentials were carefully examined before being admitted as a dealer. By looking for our logo (the most recognized autograph symbol in the world) you can be assured of prompt and fair service, quality material at competitive prices from dealers who must adhere to the strictest ethical codes of conduct in the industry. You are invited to share in this rich tradition by becoming a member of an organization who leads the industry.

Join today by logging onto **www.iacc-da.com**.

Chapter 13

International Groups

by Ralph Roberts

The world has grown much smaller with the advent of the worldwide web. The editors of **The Sanders Price Guide to Autographs** work hard to add value for collectors not just in the United States but for all of our collecting friends all across this shrinking planet. You'll see this in our greatly expanded pricing section—which now includes thousands of names of interest to those in Europe and elsewhere. And in this chapter we present you with a few autograph collectors clubs that might be of interest. If your club is not listed, send information to me (ralph@abooks.com) and we'll get it in the next edition.

Autograph Collectors Club of India

Nitin Kalra reports: "...An organisation–The Autograph Collectors Club of India, (ACCI) based in Calcutta is helping a lot of people to carry on with this age-old hobby.

"The Club currently has a membership of over 100 people from across India and even a few from the neighbouring countries. Members of the ACCI have taken autographs of almost all major celebrities of the world. In fact the Secretary of the Club, Mr. Santosh Kumar Lahoti, features in the *Limca Book of Records* since 1994 for his personal autograph collection, which exceeds 1200."

The Club, Nitin continues, provides a forum where collectors from all over come and share their experiences and do some activities for the promotion of the good and aspirant hobby. The ACCI members constantly interact with one another via a quarterly journal called

Autograph News, and an exhibition of autographs collected by members is held every year. Celebrities are also invited to come and deliver speeches about the hobby, thus giving the members an opportunity to take autographs from them. Membership to the ACCI is open to all interested in the hobby on payment of a nominal membership fees.

The Autograph Collectors Club of India,
Shree Sadan, P. K. Tagore Street, Calcutta – 700006
Email: sklahoti@hotmail.com

The Autograph Club of Great Britain

Mr. Robert Gregson reports that The "A.C.O.G.B" is a "free for all" club based on exchanging views, and ideas from all autograph collectors in the UK and internationally. The club itself has been running for five years now. Money is raised for charity by holding memorabilia auctions from time to time.

All we ask is, if you use this site, please provide us with regular feedback such as your successes and failures, or other information see site for general idea.

For additional information, the website is **www.angelfire.com/ journal2/acogb/**.

Club der Autogrammsammler (German)

This German autograph collecting club is over 1500 members, the largest in Europe. (The word *Autogramm* means "autograph" in German). For addition information, contact:

Club der Autogrammsammler e.V.
z. Hd. Herrn Thomas Münch
Postfach 27 05 02
50511 Köln
e-Mail: info@autogramm-post.de

Their website is: **http://www.autogramm-post.de/**

The SANDERS Price Guide to Autographs

6

Sixth Edition

Section 2:

PRICES

We've added thousands of new names and did a comprehensive update of all prices. Following are almost 600 pages, the greatest autograph price reference extant.

Autograph price guide founder, George Sanders, interviews President John F. Kennedy. George collected hundreds of in-person autographs during his long career in entertainment and journalism.

Chapter 14

How to Use This Price Guide

by Dr. Richard Saffro

The Sanders Price Guide to Autographs was conceived by George Sanders, Helen Sanders, and Ralph Roberts, and first compiled in the late 1980s. Prices were initially derived from retail sales figures, primarily from trustworthy catalogs. Where appropriate, these prices were adjusted by expert opinion. Prices were continually updated for the subsequent editions. Both prices and names were manually inserted by Helen Sanders. Multiple inserted prices would eventually create an arithmetic average for any specific item. Often, there would be only one price available on a specific item, and therefore the price would remain stable from one edition to the next. This was the pricing format for the first five editions of the **The Sanders Price Guide to Autographs**.

Over the past few years, the autograph industry has undergone significant changes. There are now far fewer retail autograph catalogs printed, and much of the autograph commerce is done via auctions, and the Internet. It was therefore a decision by the editors of the 6th edition of **The Sanders Price Guide to Autographs**, that we now also include reliable auction house prices into the database. It is our feeling that the auction prices accurately reflect autograph price values. These auction prices are then averaged into the ongoing database, to create what we believe are the most accurate prices.

The Internet also provides us with some pricing data. There are reputable auctions houses that use both standard catalogs, as well as cataloging on the Internet. Where appropriate, we use some of this available data. We do not use individual pricing from eBay. We choose not to incorporate eBay pricing into our database because of our inability to authenticate the autographed items.

As a result of our efforts to integrate auction prices into our database, in many instances, the prices in the guide book may be lower, or higher, than the preceding editions. Autograph pricing should reflect the active and vibrant autograph market. We have made every effort to be fair.

The Sanders Price Guide to Autographs is intended to be a guide book to prices. This fact cannot be overstated. The prices do reflect an average of multiple entries over time, and therefore the price on any particular autographed item, theoretically could be significantly higher or lower than the average price in the guide. Individuals who use **The Sanders Price Guide to Autographs** have to understand this concept. For example, it is impossible that every Abraham Lincoln ALS has the same value. Certainly, those with significant historical content are worth many times the stated average price in the guide.

When using **The Sanders Price Guide to Autographs,** you must always take into account the content, date, and condition of the item. If the content is unique and historical; if the date is important; or if the condition is exemplary, the price on that autographed item would likely be higher than the price stated in the guide. This is a judgment call that needs to be made by the buyer and the seller.

When purchasing autographed material from reputable dealers, their prices can sometimes be higher, or lower than the prices in the **The Sanders Price Guide to Autographs**. When buying material from reputable dealers, you may be willing to pay more, knowing that the material is unequivocally genuine, and that in most cases, you are receiving their lifetime guarantee of authenticity.

The prices in **The Sanders Price Guide to Autographs** reflect pricing of material with average content, and average condition.

Pricing Categories

The Sanders Price Guide to Autographs, 6th edition, continues to use the same pricing format as the preceding editions. There are four autograph price categories. The definitions of these categories are as follows:

- **SIG** (signature). This represents the price of the signature only. It is most often a signature on a piece of paper, a postcard, an album page, or cut from a document or letter. If a date is included with the autograph, this could increase the value of the item. For example, a U.S. Grant signature may be priced at $400.00, but if it is accompanied by a Civil War date, the item becomes far more desirable, and therefore, more valuable.

- **LS/DS** (letter signed or document signed). An LS, or letter signed, could be a hand written letter by one individual and signed by another. This was a common practice, particularly in the 18th and 19th century. Many of George Washington's letters were written by his aide-de-camp, and then signed by George Washington. A DS, or document signed, is often a partially printed document, with the signature within the document, or more commonly, at the end of the document. Examples of a DS include signed Hollywood contracts, signed checks, Land Grants, and Military Commissions. Admittedly, this LS/DS category is the most variable of the categories. For example, the price for a routine White House letter signed by Harry Truman is difficult to equate with a Harry Truman White House signed document. In future editions of **The Sanders Price Guide to Autographs**, we will make an attempt to separate the LS category from the DS category.

- **ALS** (autographed letter signed). An ALS is a letter, written and signed by the same individual.

- **SP** (signed photograph). An SP is a photograph signed by an individual, or a group of individuals. The SP is often inscribed to a person, and then signed. This inscription can either increase or decrease the value of the autographed item. For example, a Thomas Edison inscribed photograph to Henry Ford, would be a more desirable and therefore a more valuable item, than if Edison inscribed the photograph to an average citizen.

In the COMMENTS category, the symbol **AMusQs** or **AMQS**, represents a signed autographed musical quotation. The symbol **WD** refers to war date.

Additional information

Next to each autograph entry, there is a column called CAT-EGORY. This best represents the field of endeavor of the individual listed. In many instances, the individual is notable in more than one category, but every effort was made to make the most appropriate match. In future editions, a HISTORY category will be added.

Quick Explanation of Headings

NAME	Name of a person or group
DATE	Birth and/or death dates
CATEGORY	Artist, entertainer, writer, etc.
SIG	Signature
LS/DS	A signed letter or other document.
ALS	Autograph Letter Signed, i.e. written entirely in the hand of the celebrity
SP	Signed photograph
Comment	Additional information
*	Signed art instead of photograph
WD	War Date

Chapter 15

Prices

Editor's Note: The prices here are general autograph prices; i.e. all categories except sports-related. For Sports names, please refer to **The Sanders Price Guide to Sports Autographs**. Order at 1-800-472-0438.

A

NAME	DATE	CATEGORY	SIG	LS/DS	ALS	SP	COMMENTS
Aaliyah		Entertainment	15		40	72	lt. Actress
Aalto, Hugo Alvar	1899-1976	Architect	62	138		125	Finnish Architect-Designer
Abagnale, Frank		Celebrity	10			15	motivational speaker
Abba		Entertainment	42			78	Swedish Superstar Pop Group (4)
Abbado, Claudio		Entertainment	15			50	Symph. & Opera Conductor
Abbe, Cleveland	1838-1916	Science	15		50	35	Co-Founder US Weather Service 1869
Abbett, Leon	1836-1894	Govenor	10	30	40		
Abbey, Edwin Austin		Artist	15	30	50		Am.Portraitist, Illustrator
Abbot, Charles Greeley	1873-1973	Science	12	42		29	Am. Astrophysicist
Abbott & Costello		Entertainment	475	1066		980	Radio, Film, TV Comedy Team. SP p/c 700
Abbott, Bessie		Entertainment	25			45	Opera
Abbott, Brig. Gen. Oscar B.	1890-1969	Military	30				World War II U.S. general
Abbott, Bud	1895-1974	Entertainment	110	230	365	450	Radio, Film, TV Comedian
Abbott, George	1887-1995	Entertainment	25	35	54	92	Producer/Director/Playwright
Abbott, Henry Larcom	1831-1927	Civil War	30	45	82		Union Gen. Sig/Rank 45
Abbott, Henry Livermore	1842-1864	Civil War	108	210			Union Gen. Sig/Rank 125. Killed at Wilderness
Abbott, John S.C.	1805-1877	Author	12		40		
Abbott, John		Entertainment	6			12	
Abbott, Lyman	1835-1922	Clergy	20	38	45	75	Congregational Minister-Author
Abdnor, James		Congress	5	15		10	Senator SD
Abdul, Paula		Entertainment	18		50	60	Singer-Dancer
Abdullah II, King		Royalty				75	4th ruler of Jordan. Son of King Hussein
Abe, General Nobuyki	1875-1953	Military	25				World War II Japanese general
Abeken, Heinrich	1809-1872	Clergy			40		German Theologian
Abel, I.W.		Labor	10	25	40	25	Pres. United Steel Workers
Abel, Rudolph Ivanovich		Military		252			Soviet spy
Abel, Walter	1898-1987	Entertainment	15	32	30	63	Vint. Char. Actor-Leading Man
Abelson, Alan		Celebrity	10			15	financial expert
Abercrombie, John Joseph (WD)	1798-1877	Civil War	55	102	188		Union Gen. ALS '64 525
Abercrombie, John Joseph	1798-1877	Civil War	44	62	93		Union general

NAME	DATE	CATEGORY	SIG	LS/DS	ALS	SP	COMMENTS
Abercrombie, Leslie P.	1879-1957	Architect		35			Specialist in town planning
Abercrombie, Neil A		Congress	10			15	Member U.S. Congress
Aberdeen, Lord, 4th Earl	1784-1860	Head of State	35	45	78		Br. Prime Minister
Abernathy, Ralph D.	1926-1990	Clergy	38	75	125	67	Civil Rights Leader. Deputy to Martin Luther King
Abernathy, Robert		Celebrity	10			15	political celebrity
Abernathy, Thomas Gerstle		Congress	5	10		10	Congressman MS
Abernethy, John	1764-1831	Science	45	65	185		Br. Surgeon. Devised External Iliac Artery Surgery
Abitbol, William		Political	10			15	Member European Parliament
Abraham, Brig. Gen. Clyde R.	1883-1955	Military	30				World War II U.S. general
Abraham, F. Murray		Entertainment	11	22	35	34	AA Winner. 'Amadeus'
Abraham, Gen. of Infantry Erich	1895-1971	Military	25				World War II German general
Abrams, Creighton W.	1912-1974	Military	20	30	45	70	Gen. WW II Tank Commander
Abrams, Elliott		Diplomat	10	20		25	State Dept.
Abril, Victoria		Entertainment	10			20	actress
Abruzzo, Ben A.		Aviation	32			80	
Abt, Franz	1819-1885	Composer	75		200		
Abzug, Bella		Politician	14	15	46	20	Lawyer, Congresswoman NY. Deceased
AC/DC		Entertainment	45	100		115	Rock Group. Signed by All. Color Poster S 150
Acevedo-Vila, Anibal		Congress	10			15	Member U.S. Congress
Acheson, Dean	1893-1971	Cabinet	25	82	95	93	Sec'y State for Truman. Implemented Marshall Plan
Acheson, George R.		Military	5		20	15	
Ackerman, Gary L. A		Congress	10			15	Member U.S. Congress
Ackland, Joss		Entertainment	10			20	Actor
Ackte, Aino	1876-1944	Opera	15			40	Finnish born soprano
Acland, Arthur Wm.	1805-1877	SEE Hood, Arth.W.					
Acosta, Bert		Aviation	40	60	135	95	
Acquanetta, Burna		Entertainment	10			35	Actress. Pin-up 45
Acton, Loren		Astronaut	8		35	25	
Acuff, Roy		Country Music	16		35	42	Grand Ole Opry Star. Deceased
Adachi, Lt. Gen. Hatazo	1890-1947	Military	27				World War II Japanese general
Adair, Allen		Military	20		55	65	Br. Gen. Operation Mkt. Garden
Adair, John		Governor	40	125	185		Early Gov. KY
Adair, Maj. Gen. Sir Allan Henry S.	1897-1988	Military	25				World War II British general
Adair, Red		Celebrity	20	35	55	30	Oil Well Fires
Adam 12 (Cast Of)		Entertainment	20			45	Kent McCord, Martin Milner
Adam, Adolphe-Charles	1803-1856	Composer	40	125	297	108	Opera & Ballet (Giselle). 'O Holy Night'
Adam, Gordon J.		Political	10			15	Member European Parliament
Adam, Juliette	1836-1936	Author		30	45		
Adam, Paul	1862-1920	Author	15		40		French historical novels
Adam, Sir General Ronald Forbes	1885-1983	Military	25				World War II British general
Adamic, Louis	1899-1951	Author	15	58	110	45	Am. Novelist. Born Yugoslavia
Adamowski, Timothee		Composer	10			25	AMusQS 45
Adams, Abigail		First Lady	750	2200	6500		
Adams, Alva		Governor	5		15	10	Gov. CO
Adams, Alvin	1804-1877	Business	20		50		Formed Adams Express Co.

NAME	DATE	CATEGORY	SIG	LS/DS	ALS	SP	COMMENTS
Adams, Andrew		Revolutionary War	115	388	440		Continental Congress
Adams, Andy	1859-1935	Author			30		American cowboy and author
Adams, Ansel	1902-1984	Artist	108	212	277	275	Photographer, TLS/Content 450
Adams, Brig. Gen. Claude M.	1895-1958	Military	30				World War II U.S. general
Adams, Brig. Gen. Clayton S.	1890-1965	Military	30				World War II U.S. general
Adams, Brooke		Entertainment	6	8	16	15	Actress. Pin-up 40
Adams, Bryan		Entertainment	20			50	Rock
Adams, Charles F.	1866-1954	Cabinet	15	30	55		Sec. of Navy
Adams, Charles Follen	1842-1918	Author			40		American poet
Adams, Charles Francis	1807-1886	Author/ Diplomat	40	150	195		Civil War Ambassador to Eng.
Adams, Charles Francis	1835-1915	Civil War	15	40	75		Union Brevet Brig. General
Adams, Charles R.	1834-1900	Opera	20		60		America's greatest tenor
Adams, Clara		Aviation	45	35		70	Pioneer Zeppelin Flyer. 1st
Adams, Daniel W.	1821-1872	Civil War	180	324	1117		CSA Gen. Sig/Rank 250, War Dte. DS 400
Adams, Don		Entertainment	6	8	14	28	Actor.'Get Smart'. Voice Artist
Adams, Edie		Entertainment	5	10	20	17	Singer-Actress/Ernie Kovac's Widow
Adams, Edwin	1834-1877	Entertainment	15			45	Vintage Stage Actor
Adams, General Paul D.W.	1906-1987	Military	30				World War II U.S. general
Adams, Gerry		Head of State	60	75			Leader Sinn Fein, IRA
Adams, Hannah	1755-1831	Author			350		Historian.May be 1st Fem. Am. Professional Writer
Adams, Harriet		Author	35	45	65		
Adams, Helen		Celebrity	10			15	
Adams, Henry Brooks	1838-1918	Author	110	395	450		Am. Historian, Philosopher, Critic. Als/cont 2800
Adams, Herbert	1858-1945	Sculptor	15		40		Busts in the American Hall of Fame
Adams, James S.		Business	10	35	45	25	
Adams, James Truslow	1878-1949	Author	20		45		Historian, 1922 Pulitzer Prize
Adams, Joe E.		Entertainment	5			25	Comedian
Adams, Joey Lauren		Entertainment	6			30	Actress. Pin-Up 48
Adams, Joey		Entertainment	4	8	9	10	Comedian
Adams, John (as President)		Presidents	1500	7983	20320		LS content 39,500. ALS content 20000-
Adams, John Couch	1812-1892	Astronomer	32	45	118		Discoverer of Neptune
Adams, J Q. & Monroe, J		Presidents		2850			Signed By Both Presidents
Adams, John Quincy (as Pres)		Presidents		900	3525		6th President of USA, ALS w/cont 11950
Adams, John Quincy	1767-1848	President	335	1219	1803	6030	Engr.S 2990-12,500.ALS/Cont.25,000. FF345- 450
Adams, John	1735-1826	President	1419	4082	10232		FF 2500,as Pres.3200. LS 15000
Adams, John	1778-1854	Congress	25		40		Early MOC. NY
Adams, John	1825-1864	Civil War	263	609			CSA Gen. KIA (War Date) DS 2350, S 400-495
Adams, John, & Marshall, John		President		7688			President and Secretary of State
Adams, Julie		Entertainment	8	18	20	20	Actress. Westerns, Horror Sci-Fi SP 30
Adams, Louisa Catherine	1775-1852	First Lady	293	604	1138		Wife of John Q. Adams. Only Foreign Born 1st Lady
Adams, Maj. Gen. Emory S.	1881-1967	Military	30				World War II U.S. general
Adams, Mason		Entertainment	8			15	Character Actor. Films, TV, Radio. Familiar Voice
Adams, Maud (current)		Entertainment	8	8	16	25	Actress. Pin-up 40
Adams, Maude	1872-1953	Entertainment	42	50	85	125	Am. Stage Actress. 'Peter Pan'
Adams, Nick		Entertainment	175	285		362	Actor. 'The Rebel'. Died Young

NAME	DATE	CATEGORY	SIG	LS/DS	ALS	SP	COMMENTS
Adams, Patch		Celebrity	10			15	motivational speaker, medical expert
Adams, Samuel	1722-1803	Revolutionary War	612	1814	3812		Signer Decl. of Indepen. AMsS 9500
Adams, Sherman	1899-1966	Governor	20	75	110	45	Eisenhower Asst., Gov. NH
Adams, Stanley		Composer	15	25	45	25	Lyricist
Adams, Stephen	1807-1857	Senate	10		35		US Senator Mississippi
Adams, Suzanne		Entertainment	60			295	Opera. Great Coloratura Soprano. SP Pc S 150
Adams, William T. (Oliver Optic)	1822-1897	Author	20	25	60	55	Various Popular Series Books For Boys
Adams, William Wirt (WD)		Civil War	365		1368		CSA General
Adams, William Wirt	1819-1888	Civil War	272	602	618		CSA Gen.
Adamson, James C.		Astronaut	5	15		20	
Adamson, William C.		Congress	7	20		30	19th Cent. Congressman GA
Adcock, Maj. Gen. Clarence L.	1895-1967	Military	30				World War II U.S. general
Addams, Charles*		Cartoonist	68		116	348	Addams Family, Signed drawing 248
Addams, Dawn		Entertainment	5			15	Actress
Addams, Jane	1860-1935	Am. Social Worker	65	201	209	322	Social Reformer, Nobel Peace
Addington, Henry	1757-1844	Head of State	35	75	100	63	Sidmouth, 1st Viscount. Prime Minister. Eng.
Addinsell, Richard	1940-1977	Composer	12	30	150	35	Br.' Warsaw Concerto'
Addis, Don*		Cartoonist	10			35	
Addison, Brig Leonard Joseph L.	1902-1975	Military	25				World War II British general
Addison, Chris		Celebrity	10			15	comedian
Addison, Joseph	1672-1719	Author	93	200	340		Br. Poet, Essayist, Playwright
Addison, Maj. Gen. George Henry	1876-1964	Military	28				World War II British general
Ade, George	1866-1944	Author	25	75	150	65	Am. Humorist, Dramatist. AQS 50
Ade, Jerry		Entertainment	10			20	actor
Adelaide, Queen England	1792-1849	Royalty	55	140	152		Queen of William IV. Adelaide, Australia Namesake
Adelman, Ken		Celebrity	10			15	political celebrity
Adenauer, Konrad (der Alte)	1876-1967	Head of State	38	60	85	98	1st Chan. Fed. Rep. of Germany
Ader, Rose		Entertainment	28			85	Opera
Aderholt, Robert B. A.		Congress	10			15	Member U.S. Congress
Adjani, Isabelle		Entertainment	20			75	Opera
Adler, Alfred	1870-1937	Science	110	560	1255	195	Psychiatrist. ALS/Content 2,000
Adler, Buddy		Entertainment	10			25	Film Producer
Adler, Cyrus	1863-1940	Celebrity	25	40	100		American Jewish Leader
Adler, Felix B.		Entertainment	20			45	Professional Clown
Adler, Hermann	1839-1911	Clergy	20		75		British Chief Rabbi
Adler, Jerry		Entertainment				40	Hesh Rabkin, Soprano's
Adler, Kurt A.	1905-1997	Science	20		45		Psychiatrist, son of Alfrred Adler
Adler, Larry	1914-	Entertainment	20			35	Harmonica Virtuoso. AMusQS 75
Adler, Luther	1903-1984	Entertainment	10	20	25	30	Vintage Actor-Stage & Film
Adler, Maj. Gen. Julius O.	1892-1955	Military	30				World War II U.S. general
Adler, Max		Business	15	26	40	35	Pres. Sears, Roebuck. Philanthropy
Adler, Richard		Composer	15	30	55	35	AMusQS 35-135
Adler, Stella		Entertainment	20	15	25	30	Drama Teacher & Coach
Adolph I	1817-1905	Royalty	50	200			Ruler of Luxembourg
Adonis, Joe		Criminal	180	589			Original name: Guiseppe Antonio Doto Adonis

NAME	DATE	CATEGORY	SIG	LS/DS	ALS	SP	COMMENTS
Adoree, Renee		Entertainment	30	45		80	Vintage Film Star. Early Talkies.
Adrian, Edgar Lord	1889-1977	Science	30	45	135	65	Nobel Physiology
Adrian, Iris		Entertainment	9	15	15	22	Character Actress. 30's-40's Deceased
Aebi, Tania		Celebrity	10			15	motivational speaker
Aerosmith (All)		Entertainment	75	250		167	Rock Superstars
Afanasyev, Viktor		Cosmonaut	20			40	Soyuz TM-11 and 18
Affleck, Ben		Entertainment	15			53	Actor 'Good Will Hunting'
Affre, Auguste	1858-1931	Opera	15		50		French opera singer
Aga Khan III, Sultan	1877-1957	Royalty	68	199	275	184	Sultan Sir Mohammed Shah.
Aga Khan IV		Royalty	15	40	85	35	
Agar, John		Entertainment	4	10	13	22	Actor. Westerns. Shirley Temple's 1st Husband
Agassiz, Alexander	1835-1910	Science	20		95		Son of Louis. Naturalist
Agassiz, Jean Louis	1807-1873	Science	50	87	289	631	Swiss-Am. Zoologist, Biologist
Agnew, Spiro	1918-1996	Vice President	54	115	224	77	VP-Resigned. Special Bumper Sticker S. 150
Agnus, Felix	1839-1925	Civil War	30	55			165th NY. Union Gen'l. War Date ALS 250
Aguilera, Christina		Entertainment				50	
Aguinaldo, Emilio		Head of State	75	112	146	140	Filipino Leader Against Spain
Agutter, Jenny		Entertainment	5	6	12	25	British Emmy Winner. Pin-up 55
Ahern, Brig. Gen. Leo J.	1886-1974	Military	30				World War II U.S. general
Ahern, Nuala		Political	10			15	Member European Parliament
Aherne, Brian	1902-1986	Entertainment	15	15	23	48	British Leading Man. Films from 1924
Aherne, Caroline		Celebrity	10			15	comedienne
Ahidjo, Ahmadou	1924-1989	Head of State	15		40	40	Cameroon
Ahlfors, Lars V., Dr.		Science	10	25		25	
Ahtisaari, Martii		Political				50	President of Finland
Aiello, Danny		Entertainment	8	16	25	28	Pleasant Character Actor. Stage-Films-TV
Aiken, Alfred L.	1870-1946	Banker	10		25		Pres. Several Banks. Helped Organize Fed. Reserve
Aiken, Conrad	1889-1973	Author	25	96	98	60	Am.Novelist, Poet. Pulitzer
Aiken, George D.		Senate	20	25		30	Senator & Gov. VT
Aiken, John W.		Political	20			30	Socialist Pres. Cand.1936
Aiken, Kimberly		Celebrity	10			15	motivational speaker
Aiken, Susan		Entertainment	5	6	9	18	Miss America
Aiken, William	1806-1887	Governor	10	15	30	75	Gov. & Congressman SC
Aikenhead, Brig.David Francis	1895-1955	Military	25				World War II British general
Ailey, Alvin	1931-1990	Entertainment	100			150	Am. Dancer, Choreogr. Founder Am. Dance Theatre
Ainardi, Sylviane H.		Political	10			15	Member European Parliament
Ainger, Alfred		Clergy	10	15	30	25	
Air, Donna		Celebrity	10			15	celebrity model
Airey, Lt. Gen. Sir Terence Sidney	1900-1983	Military	25				World War II British general
Airy, George B.	1801-1892	Science	42	130	265		Br. Royal Astronomer
Aitken, Robert Grant		Science	12	20	45		Astronomer
Aitken, Robert Ingersoll		Artist	30	75	170		Am. Sculptor Military Statues
Aitken, Robert	1734-1802	Printer	87	180	360		1st English Bible Printed in Am
Aizlewood, Maj. Gen. John Adam	1895-1990	Military	25				World War II British general
Akaka, Daniel		Senate	10			15	United States Senate (D - HI)

NAME	DATE	CATEGORY	SIG	LS/DS	ALS	SP	COMMENTS
Akbar, Taufik		Astronaut	5			20	Indonesia
Akerman, Amos T.	1821-1880	Cabinet	20	40	65		U.S. Attorney General
Akerman, Maj Gen Wm Philip J.	1888-1972	Military	25				World War II British general
Akers Peter		Clergy	35	45	60		
Akers, Elizabeth		Author	5		20	15	
Akers, Tom		Astronaut	10			18	
Akhmatova, Anna	1888-1966	Author		575			Russian Lyric Poet. Russia's Greatest. AMS 2800
Akihito & Machiko (Both)		Royalty	440				Emperor & Empress of Japan
Akihito, Emperor of Japan		Royalty	475	380	650	572	
Akin, Maj. Gen. Spencer B.	1889-1973	Military	30				World War II U.S. general
Akin, Susan		Entertainment	5	6	9	18	Miss America
Akin, W. Todd A		Congress	10			15	Member U.S. Congress
Akin, Warren	1811-1877	Civil War	62	81	116		CSA Congress. Whig Candidate for Gov. GA
Akins, Claude		Entertainment	9	12	18	25	Character Actor. Deceased
Akins, Zoe		Author	10	25	50	20	Poet, Playwright. Pulitzer
Akroyd, Dan		Entertainment	10	35	55	45	Comedian-Actor
Aksyonov, Vladimir		Cosmonaut	20			40	Soyuz T-2 mission
Al Fayed, Mohammed		Business	40	95			Billionaire Owner of Harrod's. Father of Dodi
Al Sharpton, Rev.		Celebrity	10			15	motivational speaker
Alabama (signed by all 4)		Country Music	30			85	
Alard, Nelly		Entertainment	4			10	
Alaurent, Maj. Gen. Auguste	1883-1970	Military	20				World War II French general
Alavanos, Alexandros		Political	10			15	Member European Parliament
Albanese, Licia		Entertainment	35	45	60	75	It. Soprano. Opera, Concert
Albani, Emma, Dame	1847-1930	Entertainment	55	60	118	190	Canadian Soprano. Opera. AMusQS 40, SP Pc 85
Albee, Edward	1928-	Author	15	84	95	82	Am. Dramatist. Pulitzer. 'Virginia Wolfe'
Alberghetti, Anna Maria		Entertainment	10			40	Singer-Actress. Pin-Up 35
Albert I (Belgium)		Royalty	25	166	260	150	
Albert III (Rainier-Monaco)		Royalty	95	200	435	135	
Albert Russell Wynn		Senate	10			15	Member U.S. Congress
Albert Victor, Duke of Athlone		Royalty	150		1250	550	Eldest Son Edward VII
Albert, Carl		Congress	10	15	20	25	Speaker of the House. OK
Albert, Don		Entertainment	25			50	Trumpet & Bandleader
Albert, Eddie		Entertainment	9	35	38	27	Actor.'Green Acres'. 100's Versatile Roles
Albert, Edward		Entertainment	10			20	Actor Son of Eddie
Albert, Ernest	1857-1946	Artist	20		55		American painter and designer
Albert, Marv		Entertainment	5	5	8	12	TV Host. Sports Ann'cer
Albert, Prince	1819-1861	Royalty	165	406	467		Consort of Queen Victoria
Albert, Stephen		Entertainment	20			35	Pulitzer, AMusQS 75
Albertson, Frank		Entertainment	15	20		30	
Albertson, Jack	1910-1981	Entertainment	25	30	46	46	Actor. Oscar Winner
Albertson, Joseph A.		Business	8	10	20	20	Fndr. Large Am. Grocery Chain
Albom, Mitch		Author	4	6	8	8	'Tuesdays With Morrie'
Alboni, Marietta	1823-1894	Opera	25		75		Italian Operatic Contralto
Albright, Charles (C.W.)		Congress	15	20	35		Union Col. CW, Congressman PA

NAME	DATE	CATEGORY	SIG	LS/DS	ALS	SP	COMMENTS
Albright, Lola		Entertainment	10	10	20	20	Early TV Series Star
Albright, Madeleine		Statesman	20			40	1st woman Secretary of State
Albright, William F.	1891-1971	Science	15	35	60		American Archaelogist
Albritton, Louise		Entertainment	15	15	30	30	Promising Actress. Early Death
Albury, Charles Donald, Capt.		Aviation	20	45	60	55	
Alcock, J. & Brown A..W.		Aviation	465			985	Signed by Both Pioneer Aviators
Alcock, John William	1892-1919	Aviation	295	495	685	600	Pioneer Aviator/A.W. Brown
Alcorn, James Lusk	1816-1894	Civil War	78	216	315		CSA Gen. U.S. Sen. & Postwar Gov. MS
Alcott, Amos Bronson	1799-1888	Author	40	85	135		Social, Civil, Education Reform
Alcott, Louisa May	1832-1888	Author	218	290	445		1 pg AMsS 3500
Alda, Alan		Entertainment	12	15	30	28	TV-Film Star. 'M*A*S*H' SP 40
Alda, Frances	1883-1952	Entertainment	65			85	Opera. New Zealand Born Soprano
Alda, Robert	1914-1986	Entertainment	10	15	15	25	Stage-TV-Film Actor. Father of Alan
Aldasoro, Eduardo		Aviation	15		55	40	
Aldasoro, J. Pablo		Aviation	15		55	35	
Alden, James		Civil War	68	117	190		Union Naval Capt.
Alden, James	1810-1877	Civil War	25	40	95		American Rear Admiral
Alderton, Terry		Celebrity	10			15	comedian
Aldington, Richard	1892-1962	Author	25	125	170	35	Br. Poet, Novelist,Biographer
Aldred, Joel		Aviation-WWII	18	38	50	65	Canadian ACE WW II
Aldred, Norman		Entertainment	12	25	48	55	Radio Personality
Aldred, Stephanie		Entertainment	5			20	Actress
Aldrich, Bess Streeter	1881-1954	Author	5	15	35	40	Am. Novelist,Short Story Writer
Aldrich, Louis	1843-1901	Entertainment	15			50	Vintage Actor
Aldrich, Nelson W.		Senate	10	15		20	Senator NY
Aldrich, Richard	1902-1986	Entertainment	10	30	45		Broadway Producer
Aldrich, Thomas Bailey	1836-1907	Author	33	30	70	225	Novels, Poetry, Editor
Aldridge, Kay	1917-1995	Entertainment	6			30	40's Serial Star. Perils of Nyoka
Aldrin, Edwin 'Buzz'		Astronaut	79	495	675	270	2nd Moonwalker. LS/cont 1000-2000,ALS cont.4500
Aleichem, Shalom	1859-1916	Author			2757		Rus.Born Jewish Writer-Humorist
Aleizandre, Vincent	1898-1984	Author	25		80		Spanish Poet, Nobel Prize
Alekan, Henry		Celebrity	10			15	film industry
Aler, John		Entertainment	10			32	
Alexander I	1777-1825	Royalty	110	450	895		Czar or Russia. Helped defeat Napolean
Alexander I	1876-1903	Royalty	75	250			King of Serbia, murdered
Alexander II	1818-1888	Royalty	120	450	900		Assassinated
Alexander III (Pope)		Clergy		45000			Very Rare
Alexander III	1845-1894	Royalty	275	436	468		Czar of Russia. Cabinet SP/Czarina 2500
Alexander VII	1599-1667	Clergy		437			Pope from 1659-1667
Alexander, Albert, Sir		Statesman	20	85			Br.M.P
Alexander, Barton S.	1819-1878	Civil War	54	80	115		Union Gen. War Dte. S 90, DS 125
Alexander, Ben	1911-1969	Entertainment	55	50		195	Jack Webb Sidekick 'Dragnet'. Deceased
Alexander, Brig. Gen. Clyde C.	1892-1965	Military	30				World War II U.S. general
Alexander, Cecil Frances		Clergy	10	20	25	35	
Alexander, Clifford, Jr.	1933-	Cabinet	10		25	25	Sec'y Army under Carter. Chmn. EEOC

NAME	DATE	CATEGORY	SIG	LS/DS	ALS	SP	COMMENTS
Alexander, Edward Porter (WD)		Civil War	550	925	3075		CSA General. War Dte. ALS/Cont. 6500
Alexander, Edward Porter	1835-1910	Civil War	217	700	1062		CSA General.
Alexander, George		Entertainment	5	8	15	15	
Alexander, Harold R.L., Sir	1891-1969	Military	75	90	163	110	Alexander of Tunis, WW II
Alexander, Henry		Business	3	7	15	10	
Alexander, J. B.		Governor	10	25		20	Guam
Alexander, Jane		Entertainment	7	10	14	20	Actress, Stage-Film-TV. Arts Activist
Alexander, Jason		Entertainment	20	50		50	Multi-Talented Actor-Singer. 'Seinfeld'. Emmy
Alexander, Jay, Dr.		Science	10			20	Prominent Cardiologist
Alexander, John		Entertainment	20			40	Played T.Roosevelt. 'Arsenic & Old Lace'
Alexander, John	1856-1915	Artist	25		80		American painter, portraitist
Alexander, Joshua Wallis	1853-1936	Cabinet	15	40		25	Sec'y Commerce, Congress MO
Alexander, Lamar		Senate	10			15	United States Senate (R - TN)
Alexander, Maj. Gen. Ronald O.	1888-1949	Military	20				World War II Canadian general
Alexander, Robert		Revolutionary War	30	65			
Alexander, Rodney A		Congress	10			15	Member U.S. Congress
Alexander, Sasha		Entertainment				35	
Alexander, William (Lord Stirling)		Military-Rev. War	250	725	1388		Gen. in Continental Army
Alexander, William, Archbishop		Clergy	20	30	40	35	
Alexanderson, Ernst F. W.	1878-1975	Science	60	115	195		Father of Television
Alexandra	1844-1925	Royalty	125		302	430	Dan. Queen of Edw.VII (Eng.)Coronation SP 1500
Alexandra	1872-1918	Royalty	150	235	675	800	Czarina. ALS/Content 5,000. Assassinated
Alexis, Kim		Entertainment	12			28	Actress. Pin-Up 40
Alfano, Franco		Composer					AMusQS 285
Alfieri, Carlo		Entertainment	10		35	35	Opera
Alfieri, Maj. Gen. Frederick John	1892-1961	Military	25				World War II British general
Alfono, Heradio		Aviation	15			35	
Alfonso II	1533-1597	Royalty		2750			Alfonso d'Este, Duke Ferrara.
Alfonso V	1396-1458	Royalty		3250			Aragon, Naples & Sicily.'Magnanimo'
Alfonso XII	1857-1885	Royalty	150	450	850		King of Spain 1874-85
Alfonso XIII	1886-1941	Royalty	140	500	625	500	King of Spain, desposed by Franco
Alfonso, Kristian		Entertainment	5			15	
Alfonte, Brig. Gen. James R.	1886-1951	Military	30				World War II U.S. general
Alford, Henry		Clergy	5	20	30	25	
Alfred, Prince		Royalty	25	35	75		2nd Son of Queen Victoria
Alfven, Hannes		Science	20	30	45	30	Nobel Physics
Alger, Horatio	1832-1899	Author	135	215	340	245	Popular Books For Boys
Alger, Russell Alexander	1836-1907	Civil War,Cabinet	50	60	85	92	Union Gen., Gov. MI, Sec'y War
Algren, Nelson		Author	25	60	185	50	Am.Novelist. Naturalistic Novels
Ali Khan, R. (Prince)		Royalty	15		90	45	
Alice in Chains		Entertainment	35			95	Music. 4 Member Rock Group
Alice, Mary		Entertainment	8			16	Afr-Am Actress. 'Sparkle'
Alice, Princess		Royalty	15		65		2nd Daughter of Queen Victoria
Alicia, Ana		Entertainment	5	6	15	15	
Alieu, Geydar		Head of State	30	110			Pres. Of Azerbaijan

NAME	DATE	CATEGORY	SIG	LS/DS	ALS	SP	COMMENTS
All in the Family (Cast)		Entertainment	45			154	4 Leading Characters
Allan, Brent Dr.		Science	10			15	Physician, author, scientist
Allan, Buddy		Country Music	4	10		10	Singer. Buck Owens' son
Allan, Maj. Gen. Terry de la M.	1888-1969	Military	30				World War II U.S. general
Allan, Robert		Business	17				
Allard, General Jean-Victor	1913-1996	Military	24				World War II Canadian general
Allard, Wayne		Senate	10			15	United States Senate (R - CO)
Allen, Adrienne		Entertainment	5	10	20	25	
Allen, Amos L.	1837-1911	Congress	10			40	Repr. ME
Allen, Andrew		Astronaut	7	10		20	
Allen, Barbara Jo (Vera Vague)		Entertainment	22			35	Comedienne AKA Vera Vague. Radio-Films-Early TV
Allen, Betty		Entertainment	10			22	Afr-Am Dancer, Teacher, Choreographer
Allen, Brig. Gen. Frank A. Jr.	1896-1979	Military	30				World War II U.S. general
Allen, Brig. Gen. Wayne R.	1899-1975	Military	30				World War II U.S. general
Allen, Brig. Gen.	1888-1963	Military	30				World War II U.S. general
Allen, Charles L.		Clergy	10	35	50	35	
Allen, Debbie		Entertainment	10	8	20	25	Actress-Dancer-Singer-Choreographer-Dir.-Producer
Allen, Deborah		Country Music	4			15	Singer-Songwriter
Allen, Elizabeth	1908-	Entertainment	20	9	15	35	Br. Actress. Leading Lady.'Berkely Square'
Allen, Ethan	1738-1789	Military-Rev. War	650	1850	3200		Col. Green Mounain Boys. ALS/Cont. 21,000
Allen, Florence E.	1884-1966	Woman Suffrage	30	75	125		American Jurist and Feminist
Allen, Frank A., Jr.		Military	10	25	45		
Allen, Fred	1894-1956	Entertainment	50	65	110	87	Popular Radio Comedian/Portland Hoffa
Allen, General Roderick R.	1894-1970	Military	30				World War II U.S. general
Allen, George		Senate	10			15	United States Senate (R - VA)
Allen, Ginger Lynn		Model	5			25	Pin-up 35
Allen, Gracie	1902-1964	Entertainment	50	73	75	225	Usually Signed with Husband, George Burns
Allen, Grant		Author	5	15	30	10	
Allen, Henry J.		Congress	5	20			Senator, Kansas
Allen, Henry T.		Military	25	70	125	50	General WW I
Allen, Henry Watkins (WD)	1820-1866	Civil War	235	395	1055		CSA Gen. 1820-66
Allen, Henry Watkins	1820-1866	Civil War	165	685			Confederate general
Allen, Horatio	1802-1890	Business-Engineer	65		115		Designed & Ran 1st Locomotive on Am. RR.
Allen, Ira (Brother of Ethan)		Military-Rev. War					Rev. War Date LS 15,000
Allen, Irwin		Entertainment	12			35	Director Disaster Films. Deceased
Allen, Joan		Entertainment	6			40	Actress. Oscar Nominee. 'Pleasantville'
Allen, Joseph P.		Astronaut	10			25	
Allen, Karen		Entertainment	5	8	14	18	Actress, 'Raiders of Lost Ark' SP 35
Allen, Macon B.	1816-1894	Legal	195	865			Paved Way for All Blacks To Become Lawyers
Allen, Maj. Gen. Arthur Samuel	1894-1959	Military	20				World War II Australian general
Allen, Maj. Gen. Leven C.	1894-1979	Military	30				World War II U.S. general
Allen, Maj. Gen. Robert Hall	1886-1981	Military	25				World War II British general
Allen, Marty		Entertainment	10	10	12	16	Bushy Haired Comedian
Allen, Paul		Business	8			25	Microsoft Co-Founder
Allen, Peter		Composer	35			125	

NAME	DATE	CATEGORY	SIG	LS/DS	ALS	SP	COMMENTS
Allen, Rex		Entertainment	8	10	15	22	Singer-Actor. Western Star
Allen, Robert (WD)		Civil War	44	60	95		Union Gen. (1811-86)
Allen, Robert F.		Business	5			10	Pres., CEO Carrier Corp.
Allen, Robert	1811-1886	Civil War	33	60	91		Union general
Allen, Rosalie		Country Music	10			45	Singer. 'The Prairie Star'
Allen, Steve		Entertainment	10	15	25	42	Composer, Pianist, TV-Radio Host
Allen, Steve, Dr.		Celebrity	10			15	medical expert
Allen, Thomas H. A.		Congress	10			15	Member U.S. Congress
Allen, Thomas S.	1825-1905	Civil War	40	70	110		Union Brevet Brig. General
Allen, Tim		Entertainment	17			63	Comic Star of 'Home Improvement'
Allen, Valerie		Entertainment	4	4	9	10	Actress. 2nd Leads, 50's Films
Allen, Viola		Entertainment	15	20	35	25	Vintage Stage Star 1898
Allen, William M.		Business	15	40	55	30	
Allen, William Wirt	1835-1894	Civil War	184	519	712		CSA Gen., War Dte DS 510, ALS 1,275, LS 775
Allen, Woody	1935-	Entertainment	34	21	35	34	Actor, Comedian, Playwright, AA Director
Allenby, Edmund	1861-1936	Military	66	95	170	348	1st Viscount. Br.Fld Marshal, ALS/Cont.750
Allende Gossens, Salvador		Head of State	35	113	285	70	1st Marxist Pres. Chile
Alley, Kirstie		Entertainment	7	10	12	28	Actress-Comedian. Pin-Up 45
Allfrey, Lt. Gen. Sir Chas. Walter	1895-1964	Military	25				World War II British general
Allgood, Sara		Entertainment	10		35	50	Vintage Screen Character Actress
Allin, Brig. Gen. George R.	1880-1956	Military	30				World War II U.S. general
Allingham, Margery	1904-1966	Author	40	65	155	70	Br. Mystery Writer
Allingham, William		Author			100		Irish Poet
Allison, Alexander		Civil War	218	352			Artist, publisher
Allison, Fran		Entertainment	20	30	45	75	Early TV Children's Show.'Kukla, Fran & Ollie'
Allison, May	1890-1989	Entertainment	15			40	
Allison, Mose		Composer	15			30	Jazz Pianist-Vocalist
Allison, William B.	1829-1908	Senate	5	15	25	15	Senator IA
Allizard, Adolphe		Entertainment	12		35	45	Opera. Bass
Allman Brothers		Music		978			
Allman, Greg		Entertainment	20			65	Rock Star. 'Allman Brothers'
Allmendinger, Gen. of Inf. Karl	1891-1965	Military	27				World War II German general
Allred, Gloria		Entertainment	10			30	Feminist Att'y. Brown vs O.J. Simpson
Allred, James V.	1899-1959	Governor	15	30	45		Gov. of TX 1935-39
Allston, Washington	1779-1843	Artist	275	400	862		Pioneered Romantic Landscapes. Author
Allyson, June	1917-	Entertainment	6	9	14	26	MGM Star. 2nd Career in TV Commercials
Alma-Tadema, Lawrence	1836-1912	Artist	20	65	135		Br. Painter of Roman Scenes
Almeida Garrett, Teresa		Political	10			15	Member European Parliament
Almodovar, Pedro		Celebrity	10			15	film industry
Almond, Lt. Gen. Edward M.	1892-1979	Military	30		50		World War II U.S. general
Almonte, Juan Nepomuceno	1804-1869	Military	50	200	305		Mex. General, Politician
Almy, John J.	1815-1895	Civil War					Union Adm. ALS/Content 1900
Alonzo, Maria Conchita		Entertainment	10	15	25	23	Actress. Pin-Up 40
Alpert, Herb		Entertainment	9	12	15	30	Big Band Leader-Trumpet. 'Tijuana Brass'
Alphand, Nicole H.		Celebrity	6			10	

NAME	DATE	CATEGORY	SIG	LS/DS	ALS	SP	COMMENTS
Al-Said, Sultan		Astronaut	10			35	Saudi Arabia
Alsop, Joseph		Author	5	15	25	10	Journalist, Synd. Columnist
Alsop, Stewart		Author	10	25	35	15	Journalist, Synd. Columnist
Alston, Brig. Llewilyn Arthur Aug.	1890-1968	Military	25				World War II British general
Alston-Roberts-West, Sir Michael	1905 -1978	Military	25				World War II British general
Alt, Carol		Entertainment	8	12	18	28	Actress. Pin-up 45
Altchewsky, Ivan		Entertainment				250	Opera (Rare)
Altgeld, John P.		Governor	10	40			Gov. IL
Altieri, Albert (Johnny)		Celebrity	4			10	Philip Morris Trademark
Alting von Geusau, Maj. Gen. J. T.	1881-1940	Military	20				World War II Dutch general
Altman, Benjamin	1840-1913	Merchant	45	125			'Altman's' NY Dry-Goods Co. Philanthropist. Art
Altman, Robert		Entertainment	5	8	18	30	Movie Director
Altmayer, General Marie-Robert	1875-1959	Military	20				World War II French general
Altmayer, Lt. Gen. Felix-René	1882-1976	Military	20				World War II French general
Alvarez, Albert R.	1861-1933	Opera	20		60		French Operatic tenor
Alvarez, Luis W., Dr.		Science	15	35	85	30	Nobel Physics
Alvarez, Roma		Entertainment	3	3	6	10	
Alvary, Lorenzo		Entertainment	10	12	25	25	
Alvord, Benjamin	1813-1884	Civil War	25	54	75		Union General. Mex. War Vet., Civ.War in OR Terr.
Aly Khan, Prince		Royalty	75				
Alyn, Kirk	1910-	Entertainment	12	18	30	32	Original Superman in Movie Serials
Alyssandrakis, Konstantinos		Political	10			15	Member European Parliament
Ama, Shola		Music	10			15	performing musical artist
Amara, Lucine		Entertainment	15		55	45	Opera
Amato, Pasquale		Entertainment	25			125	It. Baritone. Opera
Amatt, John		Celebrity	10			15	motivational speaker
Ambler, Eric Clifford		Author	50	150			Br.Novelist
Ambrose, Bert	1896-1971	Entertainment	15			45	Notable Br. Bandleader
Ambrose, Brigadier Robert Denis	1896-1974	Military	25				World War II British general
Ambrose, Lauren		Entertainment				40	Claire Fisher, Six Feet Under
Ambrose, Stephen	d. 2003	Author	20	35	45	32	Band of Brothers
Ameche, Don	1908-1993	Entertainment	22	35	45	55	Versatile Oscar Winner. Deceased
Ameche, Jim	1914-1983	Entertainment	10	25		30	Look-alike brother. Radio's 'Jack Armstrongaa..'
Ameling, Elly		Entertainment	15			70	Famed Lieder Singer
Ament, Jeff		Entertainment	6			38	Music. Guitar 'Pearl Jam'
American Beauty (cast)		Entertainment				85	Spacey/ Bening
American Pie (cast)		Entertainment				175	Cast of 5
American President, The (cast)		Entertainment				135	Bening, Douglas
Ames, Adelbert	1835-1933	Civil War	53	75	116		Union Gen., MOH Bull Run.Last Surviving Gen'l.
Ames, Ed	1927-	Entertainment	8	16		20	Singer-Actor of Ames Bros. Group
Ames, Fisher	1758-1808	Statesman	110		500		Organized Federalist Party
Ames, Joseph S.	1864-1943	Science	15		30		Pres. of Johns Hopkins, Physicist
Ames, Leon		Entertainment	10	12	15	30	'Life With Father' etc. Star. TV-Films. Deceased
Ames, Nancy		Entertainment	4	6	8	12	Singer-Actress
Ames, Oakes	1804-1873	Financier	100	410	1900		Founder Union Pac. RR. Rare RR DS 2250

NAME	DATE	CATEGORY	SIG	LS/DS	ALS	SP	COMMENTS
Ames, Oliver		Business.	135	1350	2500		Union Pacific RR. Rare RR DS 2550
Amherst, Jeffrey Lord	1717-97	Rev. War	455	1114	1433		Gov.Gen.Br.No.Br.Gen.
Amick, Madchin		Entertainment	4			18	Actress
Amin Dada, Idi		Heads of State	50	275		425	Dictator of Uganda
Amis, Kingsley		Author	15	30	65	25	
Amis, Suzy		Entertainment	4			18	
Ammen, Daniel	1820-1898	Civil War	37	75	107	175	Union General
Ammen, Jacob	1806-1894	Civil War	20	40	75		Union Gen.
Ammons, John		Author	8			12	Baptist history
Amos & Andy (Corell & Gosden)		Entertainment	233	90		250	Signed by Both
Amos, Tori		Entertainment	10			60	Actress
Amos, Wally 'Famous'		Business	4	10	20	10	Afro-Am. Cookie King
Amoute, John		Entertainment	10			20	actor
Amparan, Belen		Entertainment	10			35	Opera
Ampere, Andre Marie	1775-1836	Science	175	420	1613		Fr. Physicist, Mathematician
Amsden, Ben		Aviation	12	22	38	35	Navy ACE WW II
Amsterdam, Morey		Entertainment	8			30	Comedian-Actor.'Dick Van Dyke Show' Deceased
Amundsen, Roald	1872-1928	Explorer	108	210	450	405	Norwegian Polar Explorer
Analyze This (cast)		Entertainment				95	DeNrio/Crystal
Anami, General Korechika	1887-1945	Military	25				World War II Japanese general
Anastos, Ernie		Celebrity	10			15	media/TV personality
Anaya, Pedro Maria		Political		518			19th century President of Mexico
Ancerl, Karel		Entertainment	3	6	8	6	
Ancona, Mario		Entertainment			65	150	Singer. London Premiere 'Pagliacci' 1893
Ancona, Sydenham E.		Senate/ Congress	15		45		Civil War Congressman PA
Anders, Allison		Celebrity	10			15	film industry
Anders, Luana		Entertainment	17	20		30	Actress.'Song of the South', Deceased
Anders, Merry		Entertainment	5			10	
Anders, Pamela		Entertainment	20			35	
Anders, Peter		Entertainment	25			75	Opera
Anders, William A.		Astronaut	87	375	950	326	
Andersen, Brig. Gen. Wilhelm A.	b. 1894	Military	30				World War II U.S. general
Andersen, Hans Christian	1805-1875	Author	350	650	1468	1818	AQS on CDV 1450-3200, AQS 1725-3500
Anderson , Clive		Celebrity	10			15	television presenter
Anderson, Barbara	1945-	Entertainment	10	15		30	Actress. TV on 'Ironside'
Anderson, Bill		Country Music	4			12	'Whisperin' Bill'
Anderson, 'Bloody' Bill		Civil War					Lt. Quantrill's Raiders. Rare CDV 'in death' 2500
Anderson, Brad*		Cartoonist	15		35	25	'Marmaduke'
Anderson, Brigadier Sir Duncan	1901-1980	Military	25				World War II British general
Anderson, 'Bronco Billy'		Entertainment	105	175	200	375	
Anderson, C.E. Bud		Aviation	12	28	45	40	WW II ACE
Anderson, Carl David		Science	20	35		70	Nobel Physics 1936
Anderson, Carl T.*		Cartoonist	15	45		60	'Henry'
Anderson, Carol Grace		Author	8			12	motivational, gift books
Anderson, Clifford		Civil War	50	95	130		CSA Congress

NAME	DATE	CATEGORY	SIG	LS/DS	ALS	SP	COMMENTS
Anderson, Clinton		Cabinet	15	20		25	Sec'y Agriculture. Senator NM
Anderson, Dr. Wayne Scott		Medical	5			10	Diet expert, 'Take Shape for Life'
Anderson, Dusty		Entertainment	10			25	Actress, Artist. Top 40's Model. Films from '44
Anderson, Eddie Rochester	1905-1977	Entertainment	43		210	208	Actor-Comedian 'Rochester'/ Jack Benny. GWTW
Anderson, Elizabeth G.,Dr.	1836-1917	Science	55	175	210		1st Eng. Hospital for Women
Anderson, Gen. Sir Kenneth A. N.	1891-1959	Military	25				World War II British general
Anderson, George Burgwyn	1831-1862	Civil War	280	528			CSA Gen. War Dte DS 625. Wounded Antietam-Died
Anderson, George T. Tige	1824-1901	Civil War	97	162	349	450	CSA Gen. War Dte.Sig/Rank 395
Anderson, George W.		Military	10	30	40	25	
Anderson, Gillian		Entertainment	14			61	X Files. SP With Duchevny 85-95
Anderson, Harry		Entertainment	15	20	28	30	Actor-Comedian-Magician. 'Night Court' SP 30
Anderson, Henry James		Educator	12				
Anderson, Jack		Author	3	7	15	15	Outspoken Syndicated Newspaper Columnist
Anderson, James Patton (WD)	1822-1872	Civil War	311	690			CSA General
Anderson, James Patton	1822-1872	Civil War	92	243	506		CSA Gen.
Anderson, John B.		Military	5	10	20		
Anderson, John Jr.		Governor	12	15		15	Governor KS
Anderson, John		Country Music	4			15	Black Sheep #1
Anderson, Joseph R.(WD)		Civil War	260	705	1140		CSA General
Anderson, Joseph Reid	1813-1892	Civil War	76	260	828		CSA Gen.
Anderson, Joseph	1757-1837	Revolutionary War	68	235	390		Early Senator TN
Anderson, Judith, Dame		Entertainment	25	35	45	56	Powerful Legitimate Theatre & Film Actress
Anderson, June		Entertainment	5			25	Opera
Anderson, Ken	1909-1993	Entertainment	10			35	Disney Animator, Art Director, Architect from 1934
Anderson, Kevin		Entertainment	10			20	actor
Anderson, Laurie		Entertainment	8	15		20	
Anderson, Leroy		Composer	25	75	195	45	AMusMsS 325
Anderson, Les 'Carrot-top'		Country Music	10	12		15	Top Instrumentalist With Spade Cooley
Anderson, Loni	1946-	Entertainment	8	12	18	26	Actress. Pin-Up 38
Anderson, Louie		Entertainment	5			20	Stand-up & TV Comic
Anderson, Lt. Gen. Sir D. F.	1885-1967	Military	28				World War II British general
Anderson, Lynn		Country Music	4			18	Country Singer Superstar
Anderson, Maj. Gen. Alexander E.	1889-1942	Military	30				World War II U.S. general
Anderson, Maj. Gen. Alexander V.	1895-1963	Military	25				World War II British general
Anderson, Maj. Gen. John B.	1891-1976	Military	30				World War II U.S. general
Anderson, Maj. Gen. Jonathan W.	1890-1967	Military	30				World War II U.S. general
Anderson, Maj. Gen. Thomas V.	1881-1972	Military	20				World War II Canadian general
Anderson, Maj. Gen. Warren M.	1894-1973	Military	20				World War II Australian general
Anderson, Marian	1902-1993	Entertainment	114	136	238	350	1st Afro-Am Singer to Perform at Met. '58
Anderson, Martin B.		Clergy	8	15	25		
Anderson, Mary (American)	1859-1942	Entertainment	15	40	50	100	Actress
Anderson, Mary (English)		Entertainment	10	20	30	30	
Anderson, Maxwell	1888-1959	Author	30	70	135	50	Am. Dramatist. Pulitzer. 'Winterset'.
Anderson, Melissa Sue		Entertainment	8	35		29	Actress. 'Little House on the Prairie' SP 35
Anderson, Michael, Jr.		Entertainment	8			20	Producer

NAME	DATE	CATEGORY	SIG	LS/DS	ALS	SP	COMMENTS
Anderson, O.A.		Aviation	10	25	40	30	General
Anderson, Pamela Lee		Entertainment	10			46	Actress. SP Nude 75
Anderson, Philip W.		Science	45		95	50	Nobel Physics
Anderson, Poul		Author	10	35	45		Science fiction, Hugo and Nebula award winner
Anderson, Richard Dean		Entertainment	6	9	18	30	Actor. 'McGyver' Star
Anderson, Richard Heron (WD)		Civil War	255	508			CSA Gen. Ft. Sumpter Vet.
Anderson, Richard Heron	1821-1879	Civil War	80	145	293		CSA Gen., Present at Ft. Sumpter Bombardment
Anderson, Richard	1926-	Entertainment	5	5	15	15	Actor. 2nd Leads. Versatile Supporting Player
Anderson, Robert B.		Cabinet	10	17	35	20	Sec'y Treasury
Anderson, Robert Houstoun (WD)	1835-1888	Civil War	215	561			CSA General
Anderson, Robert Houstoun	1835-1888	Civil War	125	400	462		CSA Gen.
Anderson, Robert	1805-1871	Civil War	167	330	744	1555	Cmdr. Ft. Sumter, Wardte ALS3500-17,250
Anderson, Robert	1917-	Author	10	20	45	25	Playwright, Screenwriter. 'Tea and Sympathy'
Anderson, Roy A.		Business	5	15	20	10	
Anderson, Samuel Read	1804-1883	Civil War	152	362	865		CSA Gen. Sig/Rank 200, War Dte. ALS 1500
Anderson, Samuel		Military	40	130	220		Early Congressman PA 1827
Anderson, Sherwood	1876-1941	Author	35	95	153	45	Novelist, Journalist, Poet
Anderson, Terry		Journalist	10			25	Radio Host. Longest held Am. Hostage Lebanon
Anderson, Tim		Entertainment	5			20	Actor
Anderson, William B.		Military	15	35		50	Cmdr. N/S Nautilus
Anderson, Willie Y.		Aviation	10	25	35	30	WW II ACE
Anderson-Gunter, Jeffrey		Entertainment	10			20	actor
Andersson, Jan		Political	10			15	Member European Parliament
Anderton, Sophie		Celebrity	10			15	celebrity model
Andes, Keith	1910-	Entertainment	5	6		10	Actor. Radio-Stage-Films. Leads & Supporting Roles
Andino, Tiburcio C.	1876-1943	Head of State	25	70			President of Honduras 1933-49
Ando, General Rikichi	1884-1946	Military	25				World War II Japanese general
Andre, John	1750-1780	Revolutionary War	1200	3500	7875		Br. Officer. Hanged as Spy
Andreasen, Ole		Political	10			15	Member European Parliament
Andreissen, Frans		Celebrity	10			15	political celebrity
Andreotti, Guilio		Head of State	10	20	35	20	It. Journalist, Prime Minister
Andress, Ursula		Entertainment	12	16	22	35	Actress. Voluptuous Pin-Up 45
Andrew, A. Piatt		Senate/Congress	5	10		10	MOC MA
Andrew, Brigadier Basil J.	1894-1941	Military	20				World War II Australian general
Andrew, Brigadier Leslie Wilton	1897-1969	Military	20				World War II New Zealand general
Andrew, John A.	1818-1883	Governor	45	65	120		Civil War Gov. MA
Andrews Sisters (All Three)		Entertainment	150			456	40's Close Harmony Trio. Radio, Records, Films
Andrews, Arkansas Slim		Entertainment	4	5	10	10	
Andrews, Chris. C.	1829-1922	Civil War	30	70	195		Union Gen. ALS '64 265
Andrews, Dana	1909-1992	Entertainment	12	35		47	Actor. Popular 40's Leading Man. 'Laura'
Andrews, Edward	1914-1985	Entertainment	15			50	Character Actor of Stage, Film, TV
Andrews, George Leonard	1828-1899	Civil War	35	58	86		Union Gen. Sig/Rank 50, War Dte. DS 95
Andrews, Harry	1911-	Entertainment	10			30	Br. Character Actor. Key Supporting Part.
Andrews, Julie	1935-	Entertainment	18	24	25	58	SP 'Sound of Music' 125. 'Mary Poppins' 50
Andrews, Landaff W.	1803-1887	Congress	10		20		MOC KY

NAME	DATE	CATEGORY	SIG	LS/DS	ALS	SP	COMMENTS
Andrews, Maxine	1918-1995	Entertainment	15	20	20	25	Singer. (One of Andrews Sisters)
Andrews, Niall		Political	10			15	Member European Parliament
Andrews, Patti	1920-	Entertainment	10			25	Lead Singer of Andrews Sisters
Andrews, Robert E. A		Congress	10			15	Member U.S. Congress
Andrews, Roy Chapman	1884-1960	Science	75		135	125	Naturalist, Explorer, Author
Andrews, Stanley O.		Aviaiton	10	30		30	WW II Ace
Andrews, V.C.		Author	4			10	Novelist
Andrews, William Frederick		Business	4	10		10	CEO Scoville, Inc.
Andria, Generoso		Political	10			15	Member European Parliament
Andric, Ivo (1892-1975)		Author	30		120		Yugoslav Poet, 1961 Nobrl Prize
Andrieux, Francois	1759-1833	Author	20		65		French poet and playwright
Andriola, Alfred*		Cartoonist	5			30	Kerry Drake
Andros, Edmund, Sir		Revolutionary War			7500		Only Reported Amount Shown
Andrus, Cecil D.		Cabinet	5	10	35	15	Sec'y Interior
Andrus, Maj. Gen. Clift	1880-1968	Military	30				World War II U.S. general
Anduran, Lucienne		Entertainment	10			35	Fr. Operatic Mezzo-Sopr.
Anfinsen, Christian		Science	15	25	45	20	Nobel Chemistry
Angel, Heather		Entertainment	8	12	18	42	Br. Leading Lady of 30's-40's
Angel, Jonathan		Entertainment	10			20	actor
Angel, Simone		Celebrity	10			15	television presenter
Angel, Vanessa		Entertainment	5			15	Actress TV's Wierd Science
Angeli, Pier	1932-1971	Entertainment	76	120	195	188	Actress. Died Very Young. Rare Autograph
Angelici, Marthe		Entertainment	20			75	Corsican Lyric Sopr.
Angelilli, Roberta		Political	10			15	Member European Parliament
Angelis, Gen of Art Maximillian de	1889-1974	Military	27				World War II German general
Angell, Norman, Sir		Author	25	60	95	65	Nobel Peace Prize
Angelou, Maya		Author	25	35	40	35	Black Am. Poet
Angelyne		Celebrity	10			20	
Anglesea, Marquis of		Military	15	35	60		
Angus, Brigadier Tom Hardy	1899-1984	Military	25				World War II British general
Angus, Joseph		Clergy	10	20	25		
Animals, The (5)		Entertainment	50			150	Rock HOF
Aniston, Jennifer		Entertainment	18			60	Actress. 'Friends' etc.
Anka, Paul		Composer	12	15	20	25	
Ankcorn, Brig. Gen. Charles M.	1893-1955	Military	30				World War II U.S. general
Ankers, Evelyn		Entertainment	15	30	60	40	
Ankin, Michael, Dr		Science	10			20	Prominent Pulmonologist
Ann Contogiannis, Mary		Celebrity	10			15	medical expert
Ann Geyer, Georgie		Celebrity	10			15	media/TV personality
Anna Ivanovna (Rus)	1693-1740	Royalty	244	662	1750		Czarina of Russia. Niece of Peter the Great
Annabella	1909-1997	Entertainment	18	17	28	37	Fr. Actress. Major European Star. M. Tyrone Power
Annaloro, Antonio		Entertainment	10		35	40	It. Tenor, Opera
Annan, Kofi		Celebrity	20			35	political celebrity, head of UN
Anne of Austria	1601-1666	Royalty			231		Queen of France
Anne Worley, Jo		Entertainment	10			20	actress

NAME	DATE	CATEGORY	SIG	LS/DS	ALS	SP	COMMENTS
Anne, Princess		Royalty	95	250		140	Daughter of Elizabeth II
Anne, Queen	1665-1714	Royalty	365	2155	4500		Queen of Great Britain & Ireland
Annenberg, Walter H.		Business	10	25	40	35	Publisher
Annesley, H.N.		Law Enforcement	5	10		15	Northern Ireland
Annigoni, Pietro		Artist		150			Portrait painter
Annison, Michael		Celebrity	10			15	financial expert
Ann-Margret		Entertainment	8	10	18	33	Actress. AA. Pin-Up 65
Annseau, Fernand		Entertainment	20			75	Opera
Anouilh, Jean		Author	32	87	157	82	Fr. Dramatist, Screenwriter
Ansara, Michael		Entertainment	6	8	15	22	actor
Anselmi, Giuseppe	1876-1929	Entertainment	45			162	Opera. Idolized Handsome Tenor Star
Anselmo, Tony		Entertainment	10				Actor-Animator. Voice of Donald Duck after 1980
Ansermet, Ernest	1883-1969	Entertainment	100			200	Swiss Conductor. SPc 75
Anson, George		Military	40		150		English General Waterloo
Anstis, Toby		Celebrity	10			15	television presenter
Ant, Adam		Entertainment	30			75	Punk Rock
Anthony, Henry B.		Congress	10	15	35		Editor, Gov., Senator RI
Anthony, HRH		Royalty	30	100			King of Saxony
Anthony, Lysette		Entertainment	5			20	Actress. Pin-Up 45
Anthony, Ray		Entertainment	6	10	13	12	Big Band Leader
Anthony, Robert N.		Science	10			20	Nobel
Anthony, Susan B.	1820-1906	Woman Suffrage	306	933	1880	1300	Reformer, Women's Rights. ALS/Cont 3500
Antokolski, Mark Matveyevich		Artist	30	65	155		Russ. Sculp. 1843-1902
Anton, Susan		Entertainment	6	8	10	27	Actress
Antonelli, Giacomo	1806-1876	Clergy	40	120			Roman Catholic Cardinal
Antonelli, Laura		Entertainment	16	18	45	132	Actress
Antonioni, Michelangelo		Entertainment	15			88	Film Director
Antrup, Wilhelm		Aviation	25			75	German WW II Ace
Anwar, Gabrielle	1969-	Entertainment	15			42	Br. Actress. Pin-Up 65
Aoki, Lt. Gen. Jusei	d. 1944	Military	25				World War II Japanese general
Aoti, Rocky		Business	6	15	30	15	Benihana Japanese Resaurants
Aparicio Sánchez, Pedro		Political	10			15	Member European Parliament
Apgar, Virginai	1909-1974	Science	20	45			Physicain, Blue baby test
Apollinaire, Guillaume	1880-1918	Author	140	400	1575		Avant Garde Poet, Art Critic
Apollo 1		Astronaut	1500			4885	Chaffee, White, Grissom
Apollo 10		Astronauts		450		895	Young, Cernan, Stafford
Apollo 11		Astronaut	835	1250		2058	Armstrong, Aldrin, Collins
Apollo 12		Astronaut	350	120		207	Bean, Conrad, Gordon
Apollo 13 (Cast Of Movie)		Entertainment				250	Bacon, Hanks, Paxton
Apollo 14		Astronaut				695	Mitchell ,Shepard Roosa
Apollo 15		Astronaut		450		403	Scott, Worden, Irwin.
Apollo 16		Astronaut				841	Young, Mattingly, Duke.
Apollo 17		Astronauts				401	Schmidt, Cernan, Evans
Apollo 7		Astronauts		350		475	1st US 3 Man Flight.Eisele,Cunningham,Schirra
Apollo 8		Astronauts				722	Lovell, Anders, Borman

NAME	DATE	CATEGORY	SIG	LS/DS	ALS	SP	COMMENTS
Apollo 9		Astronaut	225			745	McDivitt, Scott, Schweickart
Apollo XIII (Crew Of)		Astronauts				1158	Lovell, Swigert, Haise
Apollo/Soyuz Mission		Astronaut	175			400	All 5
Apollonia		Entertainment	20			42	Purple Rain
Appell, Paul	1855-1930	Science	30	60			French mathematician
Apple, Fiona		Entertainment	10			43	Rock Star
Appleby, Ray		Entertainment	3	3	5	5	
Applegate, Christina		Entertainment	15	32		47	Actress-Model
Appleton, Brig. Gen. John A.	1892-1966	Military	30				World War II U.S. general
Appleton, Brig. Gilbert Leonard	1894-1970	Military	25				World War II British general
Appleton, Daniel	1785-1849	Publisher	12				Appleton's Cyclopaedia
Appleton, Edward, Sir		Science	25	35		55	Nobel Physics
Appleton, John F.	1839-1870	Civil War	40		70		Union Brevet Brig. General
Appleton, Nathan	1779-1861	Business	40		95		American Textile Manufacturer
Appleyard, Maj. Gen. Kenelm C.	1894-1967	Military	25				World War II British general
Apt, Jay		Astronaut	6	15		25	
Aquino, Corazon		Head of State	20			45	Pres. Philippines
Arafat, Yassir		Head of State	72	195		138	PLO Leader. Nobel Peace Prize
Aragones, Sergio		Cartoonist	10			25	Long association with Mad Magazine, signed draw265
Araiza, Francesco		Entertainment	5			30	Opera, Concert, Mexican Tenor
Araki, General Sadao Baron	1877-1967	Military	25				World War II Japanese general
Arambula, Roman*		Cartoonist	40			200	Mickey Mouse
Arangi-Lombardi, Giannina		Entertainment				200	Opera
Arau, Alfonso		Celebrity	10			15	film industry
Araujo, Arturo		Head of State	15	40		30	Salvador
Arber, Werner		Science	20	35		30	Nobel Medicine
Arbos, E. Fernandez		Composer	20				AmusQS 350
Arbour, Louise		Celebrity				25	Chief Prosecutor UN Int War Crimes Tribunal
Arbuckle, Maclyn		Entertainment	15	15	30	25	
Arbuckle, Roscoe 'Fatty'	1887-1933	Entertainment	372	400	750	938	Comic-Actor. Involved In Major Scandal
Arbuthnott, Maj. Gen. Robt Keith V	1900-1980	Military	28				World War II British general
Arcedeckne-Butler, Maj Gen St.J	1896-1959	Military	25				World War II British general
Archbold, John	1848-1916	Financier	650	1900	2000		A Founder Standard Oil. TLS Std.Oil Lttrhd. 4400
Archer, Anne		Entertainment	8	12	15	30	Actress. Pin-Up 60-Uncommon
Archer, James J.		Civil War	244	578	735		CSA Gen.
Archer, Jeffrey		Author	5	15		15	Novelist
Archer, Jules		Author	7			10	
Archer, William S.	1789-1855	Congress	12				Sen. & Repr. VA
Archi, Attila		Entertainment	10	15	40	45	Opera
Archibald, Maj. Gen. Sidney C.M.	1890-1973	Military	25				World War II British general
Archipenko, Alexander	1887-1964	Artist	90		246		Rus. Painter-Sculptor
Ardant du Picq, Maj. Gen. C-P-M	1879-1940	Military	20				World War II French general
Arden, Elizabeth		Business	30	65	145	100	Founder & Owner Eliz. Arden Co.
Arden, Eve	1908-1990	Entertainment	15	25	40	45	Actress. 'Our Miss Brooks'
Arden, Nicke		Entertainment	3	3	5	5	

NAME	DATE	CATEGORY	SIG	LS/DS	ALS	SP	COMMENTS
Arditi, Luigi	1822-1903	Entertainment	30		80		Italian Violinist
Arena, Angelina		Entertainment	5		30	25	Australian Soprano
Arens, Moshe		Diplomat-Author		80		20	Israeli
Argentia, Imperia	1889-1962	Entertainment	25			45	Argentine Dancer-Actress. Star 30's Span.Spk Films
Argento, Dominick		Composer	10	30	65	20	Pulitzer, AMusQS 175
Argyll, 8th Duke	1823-1900	Statesman	20	45			Geo. Dougl. Campbell. P.M.Gen'l, Sec'y State India
Argyll, 9th Duke	1845-1914	Head of State	30	40	55		John D. Campbell. Gov-General Canada
Arias Sanchez, Oscar		Head of State	35		65	50	Nobel Peace, Pres.Costa Rica
Arias, Harmodio		Head of State	25	50		30	
Arias, Oscar		Celebrity	10			15	political celebrity
Aric, Sigmund, Dr		Celebrity	10			15	health and fitness expert
Arie, Raffaele		Entertainment	5			25	Bulgarian Basso
Ariyoshi, George R.		Governor	15			25	Governor Hawaii
Arkell, Bartlett		Business	5	27	45	15	
Arkell, W.J. (Judge Publ)		Business	5	15	30	10	
Arkin, Adam		Entertainment	4	7		24	Actor. 'Chicago Hope'SP 22
Arkin, Alan		Entertainment	5	8	15	33	Character Actor
Arkwright, Maj Gen Robt. Henry B.	1903-1971	Military	25				World War II British general
Arledge. John		Entertainment	5			20	2nd Leads 40's
Arlen, Harold	1905-1986	Composer	112	138	180	210	'Over the Rainbow'. AMusQS up to 1,600
Arlen, Michael	1895-1956	Author					English novelist, Signed book 100
Arlen, Richard		Entertainment	25	30	70	65	Early Talkies Star of 'Wings'
Arletty		Entertainment	25			75	Fr. Actress
Arliss, Florence		Entertainment	15	30	40	35	
Arliss, George	1868-1946	Entertainment	59	45	112	76	Br. Actor. Early Academy Award for 'Disraeli'
Arlosoroff, Chaim	1899-1933	Celebrity	100				Assassinated Zionist leader
Armand, Charles	1762-1822	Artist			2185		French Painter
Armand, Elizabeth		Celebrity			150		Mistress of Lenin
Armani, Giorgio		Designer	10			35	
Armapour, Kristiana		Celebrity	10			15	media/TV personality
Armendariz, Pedro		Entertainment	30	35	45	65	
Armetta, Henry		Entertainment	25	30	50	29	
Armey, Dick		Congress	5	20		45	Majority Leader
Armistead, Lewis Addison	1817-1863	Civil War	8875	26000			CSA Gen. (rare)
Armitage, General Sir Charles C.	1881-1973	Military	25				World War II British general
Armour, Philip D.	1832-1901	Business	162	1238	1750	658	Meat Packing. Armour & Co.
Arms, Brig. Gen. Thomas S.	1893-1970	Military	30				World War II U.S. general
Arms, Russ(ell)		Entertainment	3	5	7	12	Singer-Actor. Radio's 'Your Hit Parade'
Armstead, Henry Hugh		Artist	10	20	35		Br. Sculptor.Albert Memorial
Armstrong, Bess		Entertainment	5			30	actress
Armstrong, Brig. Gen. Clare H.	1894-1969	Military	30				World War II U.S. general
Armstrong, Brig. Gen. Donald	1889-1984	Military	30				World War II U.S. general
Armstrong, Charlotte	1905-1969	Author	20	55			American mystery writer
Armstrong, Edw. R., Dr.		Science	30	75	150		Inventor Seadrome
Armstrong, Edwin H.	1890-1954	Science	75	250			Invented FM Broadcasting System TLS/cont 2000

NAME	DATE	CATEGORY	SIG	LS/DS	ALS	SP	COMMENTS
Armstrong, Frank Crawford	1835-1909	Civil War	342	400	1035		CSA Gen.
Armstrong, Garner Ted		Clergy	3			10	Evangelist
Armstrong, Harry	1879-1951	Composer	85	184	195		'Sweet Adeline' AMusQS 365-650
Armstrong, John	1725-1795	Rev. War	75	150	275		American Brig. General
Armstrong, John	1758-1843	Cabinet	45	125	872		Sec'y War.Cont. Congr.,War of 1812
Armstrong, Louis	1900-1971	Entertainment	172	406	710	480	'Satchmo'. Immortal. Jazz Trumpet. SP p/c 350
Armstrong, Martin		Author	5	10	15	10	
Armstrong, Neil A.	1930-	Astronaut	208	892	4133	614	1st Moonwalker. ALS cont 9500,LS cont 1250-5000
Armstrong, Pamela		Celebrity	10			15	newsreader
Armstrong, Robert		Entertainment	55	60	75	350	Actor King Kong
Armstrong, Robert		Military	175	725			Gen. TN Vols, Indian Fighter. Jackson aide-de-camp
Armstrong, Samuel Chapman		Civil War	55	120	350		Union Off. Cmdr. Black Regiment
Armstrong, William, Dr.		Science	20	50	110	40	Inventor
Arnaud, Yvonne	1892-1958	Entertainment	15			40	Fr. Film, Stage actress & pianist. Active in Eng.
Arnaz, Desi	1915-1986	Entertainment	50	78	133	216	Actor-Singer-Prod.DS (Last Will & Testament) 750
Arnaz, Desi, Jr.		Entertainment	4			15	Rock Group. Dino, Desi, Billy
Arnaz, Luci		Entertainment	4	8	10	16	Actress Daughter of Lucy & Desi
Arness, James		Entertainment	16	12	18	58	Actor. 'Gunsmoke'
Arnett, Peter		TV News	5			28	CNN News
Arngrim, Alison		Entertainment	6	8	15	10	
Arnheim, Gus		Bandleader				45	
Arnim, Achim von	1781-1831	Author-Poet			1200		German Romantic Poet/novelist 1781-1831
Arnim, Col-Gen Hans-Jürgen von	1889-1962	Military	25				World War II German general
Arno, Peter		Cartoonist	15	30	75	25	Drew for The New Yorker
Arno, Sig		Entertainment	10			25	
Arnold, Abraham	1837-1901	Civil War	40		90		Union Officer, MOH
Arnold, Archibald		Military	20	62	102		
Arnold, Benedict	1741-1801	Revolutionary War	1300	2920	5397		Am. Army Officer. Traitor
Arnold, Brig. Gen. Calvert Hinton	1894-1963	Military	30				World War II U.S. general
Arnold, Eddy		Country Music	8	48		28	Country Music Hall of Fame
Arnold, Edward	1890-1956	Entertainment	30	40		90	Longtime Versatile Character Actor
Arnold, Edwin, Sir	1832-1904	Author	50	90	150	80	Br. Poet, Journalist
Arnold, Fredric		Aviation	20	35		50	ACE, WWII P-38
Arnold, Henry 'Hap'	1886-1950	Military	55	328	450	325	Air Force Gen. WW II
Arnold, Jonathan	1741-1793	Rev. War	50	125			American patriot
Arnold, Lemuel	1792-1852	Governor	20		50		Gov. RI
Arnold, Leslie P.		Aviation	10	295		30	Pioneer Pilot. '24 Round the World Flight
Arnold, Lewis Golding	1817-1871	Civil War	50	97	205		Union Gen.
Arnold, Lt. Gen. William H.	1901-1976	Military	30				World War II U.S. general
Arnold, Maj. Gen. Allan C.	1893-1962	Military	25				World War II British general
Arnold, Maj. Gen. Archibald V.	1889-1973	Military	30				World War II U.S. general
Arnold, Maj. Gen. William R.	1881-1965	Military	30				World War II U.S. general
Arnold, Matthew	1822-1888	Author	60	90	160		Br. Poet, Critic
Arnold, Richard	1828-1882	Civil War	43	113			Union Gen.
Arnold, Tom		Entertainment	5			31	Comic Actor

NAME	DATE	CATEGORY	SIG	LS/DS	ALS	SP	COMMENTS
Arnoldson, Sigrid	1861-1943	Entertainment	30			100	Swedish Operatic Soprano
Arnot, Bob Dr.		Celebrity	10			20	media/TV personality
Arnot, William		Clergy	10	20	25		
Arnt, Charles		Entertainment	10			25	
Arntzen, Heinrich		Aviation		60			Br.. Ace WW I
Aronson, Judi		Entertainment	5			20	Actress.
Arp, Jean		Artist	75		275		Fr. DaDa Artist, Sculptor
Arquette, Alexis		Entertainment	15				
Arquette, Cliff		Entertainment	16	20		50	'Charlie Weaver'
Arquette, David		Entertainment	5			22	Actor. 'Scream' SP 35
Arquette, Patricia		Entertainment	8			32	Actress.
Arquette, Rosanna		Entertainment	15	15		41	Actress
Arrau, Claudio	1903-1991	Entertainment		45		135	Chilean Pianist. 3x5 SP 120
Arrhenuis, Svante A.	1859-1927	Science	95	295	725		Nobel Chemistry 1903
Arrington, A. H.		Civil War	92	130			CSA Congress
Arriola, Gus*		Cartoonist	5			25	Gordo
Arrow, Kenneth J.		Economist	35	55			Nobel Economics
Arrowsmith, Brig. Gen. John C.	1894-1985	Military	30				World War II U.S. general
Artbuthnot, Marriott		Rev. War			483		Vice-Admiral of the White
Arthur, Beatrice	1926-	Entertainment	9	12	22	22	Stage-Screen-TV Actress. 'Maude', 'Golden Girls'
Arthur, Chester A. (As President)		President	335	919	3155		WH Card S 450-500
Arthur, Chester A.	1829-1886	President	333	708	1121	625	ALS as Actg Pres 2,500. LS '62 650, signed book 1265
Arthur, Chester A.& Ellen Arthur		Pres. & 1st Lady		2500			Rare as Pair
Arthur, Chester,& Lincoln, Robt. T.		President/Sec War		1000			DS by both
Arthur, Duke of Connought	1850-1942	Head of State	10	18	25		Governor General of Canada
Arthur, Ellen Lewis		First Lady	600	1000	1200		
Arthur, George K.		Entertainer	6		15	10	Comedian, Producer
Arthur, Jean	1905-1991	Entertainment	125	150	325	198	Somewhat reclusive. Retired Early. 'Shane' Last
Arthur, Julia		Entertainment	15			25	Pioneer Film Star
Arthur, Timothy Shay		Temperance Author	20	45			Am. 10 Nights In A Barroom
Artot, Desiree		Entertainment	35		150	70	Opera, Concert
Artsebarsky, Anatoly		Cosmonaut	20			45	Soyuz TM-14
Artyukhin, Yuri		Cosmonaut	25			55	Soyuz 14
Arundell of Wardour		Military			225		Fought for Charles I in Civil War. Henry 3rd Baron
Arundell, Brigadier Sir Robt. D. H.	1904-1989	Military	25				World War II British general
Arvidsson, Per-arne		Political	10			15	Member European Parliament
Arvin, Newton		Author	18	40	85		
Asaphiev, Boris	1884-1949	Composer	40		220		Russian Composer
Asboth, Alexander S.	1811-1868	Civil War	50	178	219		Union Gen. ALS '64 330
Asbury, Francis, Bishop		Clergy	175	290	625		
Asbury, Richard		Aviation	20			45	WW II Ace
Asch, Sholem	1880-1957	Author	15	45			Polish Novelist and Playwright
Aschenbrener, Robert		Aviation	20			50	WW II Ace
Asgeirsson, Asgeir	1894-	Head of State	25				4x Premier of Iceland
Ash, Leslie		Celebrity	10			15	celebrity model

NAME	DATE	CATEGORY	SIG	LS/DS	ALS	SP	COMMENTS
Ash, Mary Kay							SEE Kay, Mary
Ash, Roy L.		Business	10	20	50	35	
Ashanti		Entertainment	15			45	Singer
Ashby, Hal		Entertainment	8	8	15	15	
Ashby, Turner (WD)		Civil War	470	1212	1782		CSA General
Ashby, Turner	1828-1862	Civil War	364	716	1250	750	CSA Gen.
Ashcroft, Dame Peggy	1907-1991	Entertainment	75	25	35	65	
Ashcroft, Richard		Entertainment	8			40	Music. Lead Singer 'The Verve'
Ashe, John		Revolutionary War	75	225	450		NC General
Ashe, Thomas	1812-1887	Civil War	72	144			Member Conf. Congress
Ashe, William Shepperd		Senate/Congress	35	90			CW Blockade Runner
Ashford and Simpson		Entertainment	15			40	
Ashley, Alfred	1835-1913	Author	15			50	Br. Poet Laureate after Tennyson
Ashley, Edward		Entertainment	15			35	
Ashley, Elizabeth		Entertainment	6	8	15	18	Actress. Pin-UP 32
Ashley, John		Entertainment	5			15	
Ashley, William		Celebrity	200	750			Pioneer. Route for Oregon Trail
Ashmun, George	1804-1870	Congress	15	35	60		Advisor to A. Lincoln
Ashton, Frederick	1904-1988	Entertainment	20		60		English Ballet Dancer
Ashton, Lt. Gen. Ernest Charles	1873-1957	Military	20				World War II Canadian general
Ashurst, Henry	1874-1962	Congress	25			75	First Arizona senator
Ashworth, Brig. Harold Kenneth	1903-1978	Military	25				World War II British general
Ashworth, Ernie		Country Music	10			25	'Talk Back Trembling Lips'
Ashworth, Frederick		Aviation	1030			50	Bock's Car, Nagasaki
Asimov, Isaac	1920-1992	Author	45	160		100	Rus-Am Biochemist.Sci-Fi Writer
Askew, Reubin		Governor	12			15	Governor FL
Asmus, Barry		Celebrity	10			15	financial expert
Asner, Ed		Entertainment	4	4	12	35	Actor. 'Lou Grant'
Aspin, Les		Cabinet	5			20	Clinton Sec'y Defense
Asquith, Herbert H.	1852-1928	Head of State	35	75	135	150	Prime Minister. Earl of Oxford
Assad, Bashar		Political				100	Syrian President
Assad, Hafez		Head of State	15	40	105	65	Syria
Assante, Armand		Entertainment	5	8	15	27	Actor. Leading Man
Astaire, Adele		Entertainment	30			75	Dancer Sister of Fred Astaire
Astaire, Fred	1899-1987	Entertainment	81	135	238	272	Dancing Star. Actor-Singer. SP/G.Rogers 775-1750
Astaire, Fred, and Rogers, Ginger		Entertainment				419	
Asther, Nils	b. 1897	Entertainment	25	35	65	160	
Astin, John		Entertainment	6	8	12	25	
Astley, Rick		Entertainment	4			10	Singer
Aston, Francis W.		Science	35	80	155		Nobel Chemistry 1922
Astor, Brooke		Author	5	15		10	
Astor, John J.	1886-1971	Publisher	15	40	65	35	1st Baron of Hever.Politician.Owner of 'The Times'
Astor, John Jacob III		Business	300	850	1050		Grandson of Founder
Astor, John Jacob IV	1864-1912	Business	600	1900	2400		Died On the Titanic. RARE
Astor, John Jacob Jr.		Business	300	750	950	325	Union Gen., Financier

NAME	DATE	CATEGORY	SIG	LS/DS	ALS	SP	COMMENTS
Astor, John Jacob Mrs.		Business	35	100	195		
Astor, John Jacob	1763-1848	Business	433	1772	5675		Fur Trader-Capitalist, Financier. LS/Cont. 9500
Astor, Mary	1906-1987	Entertainment	35	70		135	AA
Astor, Nancy (Viscountess)	1879-1964	Celebrity	40	95	120	100	1st Woman To Sit As Br. M.P. American-Born
Astor, Vincent		Business	8	20	45	20	
Astor, Waldorf	1879-1952	Politics	15	35	80	55	Br. M.P., Publisher Observer
Astor, William Backhouse	1792-1875	Business	375	838	1500		Administered Astor Estate. Son of Founder
Astor, William Waldorf	1848-1919	Business	65	200	350		Journalist-Capitalist-Financier
Asturias, Miquel Angel	1899-1974	Author	50	135	285		Guatamala. Nobel Literature
Ataturk, Kemel	1881-1938	Head of State		150			President of Turkey
Atcher, Bob		Country Western	7			25	'National Barn Dance' Star
Atchison, David Rice	1807-1866	President for 1 Day	340	700	976		Pres.for a day.ALS/Cont 4500
Ates, Roscoe		Entertainment	25	30	60	65	
Athenagoras, Archbishop		Clergy	25	40	55	50	
Atherton, Chas. G.	1804-1853	Congress	20	30			Senator NH
Atherton, Gertrude	1857-1948	Author	30	55	150	75	Am. Novelist
Athlone, Earl, Prince Alex.of Teck		Head of State	15	25	40		Governor-General of Canada
Atholl, Katharine, Duch. of	1874-1960	Political	65				Br. Anti-Nazi.1st Woman Cabinet Member
Atkins, Chet		Country Music	5	14		22	Guitar Legend
Atkins, Christopher		Entertainment	6	8	15	21	Actor. 'Blue Lagoon'. Pin-Up 30
Atkins, Gaius Glenn		Clergy	15	30	45		
Atkins, John DeWitt	1825-1908	Civil War	57	162			Member Conf. Congress
Atkins, Robert		Political	10			15	Member European Parliament
Atkins, Robert	1930-2003	Science	15	25	50	30	Cardiologist, Atkins diet
Atkins, Smith D.	1835-1913	Civil War	25		150		Union Gen. 2nd Illinois. ALS Re Chickamauga 750
Atkins, Tom		Entertainment	10			20	actor
Atkinson, Brooks	1894-1984	Author	15	35		30	Theater Drama Critic, Columnist N.Y. Times
Atkinson, Holly G.		Celebrity	10			15	medical expert
Atkinson, Joseph H.		Military	10	25	30		
Atkinson, Rowan		Entrtainment	5			22	Br. Actor-Comic
Atkinson-Wood, Helen		Entertainment	10			20	Actress
Atlantov, Vladimir		Entertainment	20		75	55	Opera. Rus. Tenor
Atlas, Charles		Business	15	30	35	35	Mail Order Phys. Culture
Attenborough, David, Sir		Celebrity	10			15	naturalist
Attenborough, Richard		Entertainment	20	30	30	34	AA Br. Actor-Director
Attenborough, Sir David		Science	20	70			
Atterbury, William W.	1866-1935	Military	15	50			Gen. WW I, Pres. Penn. RR
Attlee, Clement	1883-1967	Head of State	48	140	250	75	Prime Minister. 1st Earl
Attwooll, Elspeth		Political	10			15	Member European Parliament
Atwill, Lionel	1885-1946	Entertainment	100			250	
Auber, Daniel Francois	1782-1871	Composer	110		160		Father of Fr.Opera, AMusQS 350
Auberjonois, Rene		Entertainment	6	8	14	25	Char. Actor 'Star Trek', 'Deep Space Nine'
Aubert, Lenore		Entertainment	5	8	15	20	
Aubrey, M. E.		Clergy	10	15	20		
Aubry, Cecile		Entertainment	15			20	Fr. Actress

NAME	DATE	CATEGORY	SIG	LS/DS	ALS	SP	COMMENTS
Auchincloss, Janet L.		Business	3	5	10	5	
Auchincloss, Louis		Author	15	35	75	30	U.S. Novelist, Short Story
Auchinleck, Claude J.E., Sir		Military	45	75		95	Br. Fld. Marshal WW II
Auckland, Baron (Geo.Eden)		Head of State	40	50	100		Gov-Gen India
Audemars, Edmund		Aviation	27			48	
Auden, W(ystan) H(ugh)	1907-1993	Author	135	250	372	700	Br.-Am. Poet, Pulitzer
Audran, Edmond		Composer	45	85	175		Fr. Operettas
Audran, Marius		Entertainment	12		75		Opera. Tenor
Audubon, John J.	1785-1851	Artist	785	1658	2981		Ornithologist, Naturalist. 'Birds of America'
Auel, Jean M.		Author	6	10	25	25	Novelist
Auer, Leopold		Entertainment	25	35		40	Hungarian Violinist
Auer, Mischa	1905-1967	Entertainment	30	30	45	35	
Aug, Stephen		Celebrity	10			15	financial expert
Auger, Arleen		Entertainment	25			55	Opera. Am Soprano
Auger, Christopher C.		Civil War	43	117	182		Union General
Augereau, P.F.C. de Castiglione		Military	100	218	525		Marshal of Napoleon
Augsburg, Alex. S.,Prince	1663-1737	Royalty		328			Prince Bishop of Augsburg Count Palatine of Rhine
Augur, Brig. Gen. Wayland B.	1894-1982	Military	30				World War II U.S. general
Augusta, Queen of Prussia	1811-1890	Royalty		135			Consort William I. Empress of Ger.
Augustus I, Duke of Saxony		Royalty	2000				1526-1586
Augustus III		Royalty	145	325	425		King Poland
Auld, Georgie		Entertainment	5	6	15	10	
Auleb, Gen. of Infantry Helge	1887-1964	Military	25				World War II German general
Aumont, Jean Pierre	1909-	Entertainment	20	25	40	95	
Aurand, Lt. Gen. Henry S.	1894-1980	Military	30				World War II U.S. general
Auric, Georges	1899-1983	Composer	85				Fr. Member 'The Six'. AMusQS 250-395
Auriol, Jacqueline		Aviation	15	35	70	45	
Auriol, Vincent	1884-1966	Head of State	45	60	85		1st Pres. 4th Republ. France
Auroi, Danielle		Political	10			15	Member European Parliament
Ausensi, Maurel		Entertainment	15			50	Opera, Sp. Baritone
Auslander, Joseph		Author	25	125		50	Poet. Harvard Lecturer Poetry
Aust, Abner		Aviation	10			20	US Ace
Austen, Jane	1775-1817	Author	625	2250	7500		Br. Novelist.'Pride & Prejudice'.Addr. Panel 1995
Austin, Bobby		Country Music	10			20	
Austin, Charlotte		Entertainment	4			15	
Austin, Horace		Governor	10			15	Governor MN
Austin, Karen		Entertainment	10	6	12	15	
Austin, Moses	1761-1821	Pioneer	425	1800	3372		Orig. Founder of TX. Mine Owner, Merchant
Austin, Stephen F.	1793-1836	Texas Colonizer	800	1875	6500		Historical DS 6500,7500
Austin, Teri		Entertainment	5	8	10	10	
Austin, Warren R.		Senate	5	10		20	Senator VT
Autry, Gene	1907-1998	Entertainment	25	75	75	142	Singing Cowboy, Businessman. Deceased
Avallone, Michael		Author	5	15		10	
Avalon, Al		Entertainment	5			20	TV and film
Avalon, Frankie		Entertainment	6	10	15	34	Singer-Actor

NAME	DATE	CATEGORY	SIG	LS/DS	ALS	SP	COMMENTS
Avebury, John Lubbock		Science	20		150		1834-1913. Naturalist.Paleolithic
Avedon, Richard		Artist	40	95	275	170	Photographer. Book S 375
Average White Band		Entertainment	15			25	Rock
Averell, William Woods	1832-1900	Civil War	62	81	117		Union Gen. ALS '62 360
Averoff, Ioannis		Political	10			15	Member European Parliament
Avery, Brig. Gen. Ray L.	1884-1965	Military	30				World War II U.S. general
Avery, James		Entertainment	4			15	
Avery, John, Jr.		Revolutionary War	40	77			
Avery, Margaret		Entertainment	3	3	6	10	
Avery, Milton	1893-1965	Artist	35	50		45	Am. Figure Painter 30-40's. Later Landscapes
Avery, Sewell L.		Business	35	55	105	40	CEO Montgomery Ward
Avery, Tex*		Cartoonist	25			400	Animator. (*Original Cell)
Avery, William W.		Civil War	93	157			CSA Congress
Aviés Perea, Marfa Antonia		Political	10			15	Member European Parliament
Avila, Kay		Celebrity	10			15	TV Chef
Avildsen, John G.		Entertainment	5			20	Film Director
Avril Anson, Dr		Celebrity	10			15	'Edwardian Country Mansion'
Awdry, Wilbert, Rev.		Clergy-Author	50		175		Railway Series of Children's Books
Axelrod, Julius		Science	35	60	95	35	Nobel Medicine
Axtell, George		Aviation	12	25	45	35	Marine ACE
Axton, Hoyt		Country Music	5	12		20	Singer-Songwriter
Ayckbourn, Alan		Author	10	15	30	25	Br. Prolific Playwright
Ayer, Lewis Malone	1821-1895	Civil War	54	130			Member Conf. Congress
Aykroyd, Dan		Entertainment	8	12	15	26	Comic Actor.'Saturday Night Live'.'Ghostbusters'
Aymes, Lt. Gen. Henri-Marie-Jos.	1882-1964	Military	20				World War II French general
Ayres, Agnes		Entertainment	60	75	150	125	Silent Film Star
Ayres, Brig. Gen. Leonard P.	1879-1946	Military	30				World War II U.S. general
Ayres, Lew		Entertainment	8	22	28	25	Actor. Oscar Winner. Original 'Dr. Kildare'
Ayres, Pam		Celebrity	10			15	comedienne
Ayres, Romeyn B. (WD)		Civil War	70	135	440		Union Gen.
Ayres, Romeyn Beck	1825-1888	Civil War	38	68	104		Union Gen.
Ayub Khan, General		Head of State	20	35	75	100	Afghan Prince. General
Ayuso González, Marfa Del Pilar		Political	10			15	Member European Parliament
Azaria, Hank		Entertainment	10			20	actor
Azenberg, Emanuel		Entertainment	10			20	actor
Aznavour, Charles		Entertainment	10			35	

B Jazzie		Music	10			15	DJ
B52's		Entertainment	40			75	Rock Group
Baade, Maj. Gen. Paul W.	1889-1959	Military	30				World War II U.S. general
Babbage, Charles	1792-1871	Science-Math.	88	245	724		Br. Pioneer of Modern Computers. Inventor

NAME	DATE	CATEGORY	SIG	LS/DS	ALS	SP	COMMENTS
Babbitt, Bruce		Cabinet	10	20		15	Gov. AZ
Babbitt, Harry		Entertainment	10			20	Band Vocalist, Radio
Babbitt, Milton		Composer	25		70	30	AMusQS 150
Babcock, Alfred, Dr.	1805-1871	Congress					Repr. NY
Babcock, Barbara		Entertainment	4	4	9	10	
Babcock, Brig. Gen. Franklin	1885-1972	Military	30				World War II U.S. general
Babcock, Joseph W.		Senate/Congress	5		30		Congressman WI
Babcock, Orville E. (WD)		Civil War	40	50	104		Union Gen.LS as Grant ADC 385
Babcock, Orville E.	1845-1884	Civil War	30	103	162		Union Gen.
Babcock, Tim		Governor	12	20	25	15	Governor MT
Babcock, Verne C.		Aviation	16			40	
Babilé, Jean		Entertainment	30	45		70	Ballet
Babson, Roger	1875-1967	Economist	75				Predicted 1919 Crash. Founded Babson Coll.
Baby Peggy		Entertainment	5	6	15	15	
Babyface		Entertainment	6			42	Young Singer-Songwriter
Baca, Joe B		Congress	10			15	Member U.S. Congress
Bacall, Lauren	1924-	Entertainment	20	55	60	37	Sophisticated, Throaty. Successful on Stage & Film
Bacardi Maso, Facundo	1815-1886	Business					Founder Bacardi Rum & Emilio B. 2 DS 1250
Baccaloni, Salvatore		Entertainment	20	25	40	45	Opera, Concert, Films
Bach, Barbara		Entertainment	10	12	15	25	
Bach, Catherine		Entertainment	6	8	15	20	
Bach, Johann Sebastian		Composer	2500	6760	11000		
Bach, Richard		Author	25	100	175		
Bach, Sebastian		Entertainment	20			50	Rock
Bacharach, Burt		Composer	13	25	40	25	
Bacharach, Fabian		Artist	50	100	150	75	
Bache, Alexander D.		Science	25	50	110	40	1st Pres. Nat'l Acad. Science
Bache, Harold L.		Business	15	45	110	65	US Stockbroker. J.S.Bache & Co.
Bache, Jules S.		Financier	350	1100	1400		Founder J. S. Bache & Co.
Bacheller, Irving		Author	25	60	65	75	Am. Novelist, Editor
Bachman, Nathan L.		Congress	10				Senator, TN
Bachus, Spencer B		Congress	10			15	Member U.S. Congress
Back, George, Sir	1796-1878	Explorer	35	105	175		Arctic Navigator
Back, Maj. Gen. George I.	1894-1972	Military	30				World War II U.S. general
Backhaus, Wilhelm	1884-1969	Entertainment	46		65	100	Ger. Concert Pianist
Backhouse, Brig Edw. Henry W.	1895-1973	Military	25				World War II British general
Backhouse, James		Clergy	20	35	50		
Backstreet Boys (5)			55			155	Rock Group (5)
Backus, Jim	1913-1989	Entertainment	20	25	35	53	Actor, Mr. Magoo, SP with Natalie Schafer 138
Baclanova, Olga		Entertainment	10			25	
Bacon, Edmund		Celebrity	10			15	
Bacon, Francis, Sir		Author	1500	3650	6500		Br. Philosopher, Statesman
Bacon, Frank		Entertainment	10	12	20	15	
Bacon, Kevin		Entertainment	9	10	20	45	Actor
Bacon, Leonard		Clergy	10	15	20	25	

NAME	DATE	CATEGORY	SIG	LS/DS	ALS	SP	COMMENTS
Bacon, Lloyd		Entertainment	12			20	Film Director
Bacon, Peggy		Artist	35	65	150		
Bacon, Richard		Celebrity	10			15	television presenter
Bacon, Robert		Senate/Congress	15	25		30	Congressman NY. Military
Bacon, Walter W.		Governor	10		25	15	Governor DE
Badal, Robert John		Entertainment	10			15	Drummer, percussionist VooDoos
Badawi, Zeinab		Celebrity	10			15	newsreader
Baddeley, Hermione		Entertainment	12	15	22	30	
Baddiel, David		Celebrity	10			15	comedian
Badeau, Adam (WD)		Civil War	50		275		Union Gen.
Badeau, Adam	1831-1895	Civil War	44	96	147		Union General
Baden-Powell, Robert, Sir	1857-1941	Military	146	434	484	858	Br. Gen., Defender Mafeking, Founder of Boy Scouts
Bader, Douglas, Sir		Aviation	45	178	205	75	Br. Ace
Bader, General of Artillery Paul	1883-1971	Military	25				World War II German general
Badger, Brig. Gen. George M.	1897-1970	Military	30				World War II U.S. general
Badger, Charles J.	b. 1853	Military	20	45	70	40	U.S. Navy Adm.
Badger, George E.	1795-1866	Cabinet	15	62	80		Sec'y Navy, Sen. NC. Jurist
Badger, Oscar C.	1890-1958	Military	30	45		50	Adm. USN WW II
Badham, John		Entertainment	10			20	Film Director
Badham, W.L.		Aviation	25	50	75	55	Bi-plane , WW I
Badler, Jane		Entertainment	5	8	20	25	
Badoglio, Pietro		Head of State	30		135	55	It. Gen.,succeeded Mussolini
Badura-Skoda, Paul		Entertainment	10			65	Pianist. SP Pc 25
Baehr, Brig. Gen. Carl A.	1885-1959	Military	25				World War II U.S. general
Baekeland, L. H. Dr.	1863-1944	Science-Inventor	35	60	140		Invented Bakelite. (Synthetic Resin) 1st Plastic
Baer, Arthur Bugs *	1886-1959	Journalist	10			40	Syndicated Columnist, Cartoonist
Baer, Brig. Gen. Joseph A.	1878-1958	Military	30				World War II U.S. general
Baer, George F.		Business	10	25	45	30	Pres. Reading Railroad
Baer, John		Entertainment	5	6	15	15	Actor
Baer, Max, Jr.		Entertainment	35	70	85	50	Actor-Son of Boxer.'Beverly Hillbillies', 'Jethro'
Baer, Parley		Entertainment	5	15	22		Familiar Character actor from 50's. 'Young Lions'
Baez, Joan	1941-	Entertainment	10	20	20	30	Folksinger, Political Activist
Bagby, Arthur	1833-1921	Civil War	122		483		Conf. Gen.
Bagian, James P.		Astronaut	5	10		20	
Baglioni, Bruna		Entertainment	10		45	35	Opera
Bagnold, Brigadier Ralph Alger	1896-1990	Military	25				World War II British general
Bagnold, Enid	1889-1981	Author		75	185	75	Novelist, Plays. 'National Velvet', 'Chalk Garden'
Bagot, Charles, Sir	1781-1843	Statesman		45	125		Br. Diplomat.. Gov.-Gen. Canada
Bailey, Bill		Celebrity	10			15	Comedian
Bailey, Buster		Entertainment	30			75	Jazz Clarinet, Sax
Bailey, Carl E.		Governor	10	15			Governor AR
Bailey, Damion 'DaDa'		Author	8			12	African-American poet
Bailey, David		Celebrity	10			15	Photographer
Bailey, F. Lee		Legal	15	25	45	25	Noted Trial Attorney
Bailey, G.W.		Entertainment	10			20	Actor

NAME	DATE	CATEGORY	SIG	LS/DS	ALS	SP	COMMENTS
Bailey, Jack		Entertainment	5	5	6	15	Early Radio-TV M.C. 'Breakfast Club
Bailey, James Anthony	1847-1906	Circus	250	812	1100		Barnum & Bailey Circus
Bailey, Jim		Entertainment	10			20	Actor
Bailey, Joseph	1825-1867	Civil War	90	232	245		Union Gen. ALS '64 1265
Bailey, Louise H		Author	8			12	Regional history
Bailey, Mildred C.		Military	25			202	Brigadier General
Bailey, Pearl	1918-1990	Entertainment	16	32	50	50	Singer-Actress
Bailey, Razzie		Country Music	5			20	
Bailey, Temple		Author	30	45	110		
Bailey, Theodorus	1805-1877	Civil War	49	105	146		Union Naval Officer. Sig/Rank 70, DS 160
Bailey, Walter R.		Business	10	35	45	20	
Baillie, Joanna	1762-1851	Author	40	65	120		Successful Scottish Dramatist, Poet
Baillie, John		Clergy	35	75	110	50	
Baillon, Maj Gen Joseph Aloysius	1895-1951	Military	28				World War II British general
Bailly, Jean-Sylvain	1736-1793	Astronomer	40	95	160		& Fr. Politician. Guillotined
Bain, Barbara		Entertainment	15	15	32	37	Actress. 'Mission Impossible'. Original TV Series
Bain, Conrad		Entertainment	5			10	Actor. 'Mork & Mindy' TV Series
Bainbridge, William	1774-1833	Military	150	238	650		US Naval Officer War 1812
Baines, Ed		Celebrity	10			15	TV Chef
Bainter, Fay	1892-1968	Entertainment	58	80	120	125	Actress. Vintage. Stage, Films. AA Winner
Baio, Scott	1961-	Entertainment	8	17	15	24	Actor. Juvenile 'Happy Days', 'ChaChi'
Bair, Hilbert L.		Aviation	10			45	US Ace. WW I
Baird, Absalom	1824-1905	Civil War	33	71	110		Union Gen. ALS '64 200. S/Rank 70
Baird, Brian B		Congress	10			15	Member U.S. Congress
Baird, Brig. Gen. Harry H.	1893-1969	Military	30				World War II U.S. general
Baird, General Sir Douglas	1877-1963	Military	25				World War II British general
Baird, John Logie		Science	100	160	250	600	1st TV Picture of Moving Object
Baird, Maj. Gen. Henry W.	1881-1963	Military	30				World War II U.S. general
Baird, Robert		Author			52		
Bairnsfather, Bruce	1888-1959	Cartoonist	15	30	110	25	Br. WW I 'Old Bill' Cartoons
Bakaleinikoff, Constantin	1898-1966	Composer	200				Russian Music Dir. RKO Studios
Baker, Alpheus	1828-1891	Civil War	168	375	717		CSA Gen. Sig/Rank 310
Baker, Anita		Entertainment	22			35	Singer
Baker, Art	1898-1966	Entertainment	10	15		20	Early Radio-TV M.C. Master of The Art!
Baker, Benny	1907-1994	Entertainment	8		15	25	Chubby, Baby-faced Character Comedian. Actor
Baker, Blanche	1956-	Entertainment	8	8	15	20	Actress-Daughter of Carroll Baker.
Baker, Bob		Entertainment	50	70		100	Singing Cowboy 1930's
Baker, Bonnie Wee		Entertainment	10	8	15	20	Big Band Vocalist With That Wee Small Voice
Baker, Brig. Gen. Frayne	1891-1968	Military	30				World War II U.S. general
Baker, Brig. Euston Edw. Francis	1895-1981	Military	25				World War II British general
Baker, Carroll	b. 1931	Entertainment	15	25	40	25	Actress. AAN 'Baby Doll'.Now Plays Character Roles
Baker, Charles S.		Senate/Congress	5	10		10	Congressman NY.
Baker, Chauncey		Military	10		25	20	General WW I
Baker, Cheryl		Celebrity	10			15	television presenter
Baker, Danny		Celebrity	10			15	television presenter

NAME	DATE	CATEGORY	SIG	LS/DS	ALS	SP	COMMENTS
Baker, Diane	1938-	Entertainment	10			20	Actress. Leading Lady. Now Mature Leads
Baker, Edward D.	1811-1861	Civil War	185	572	850		Union Gen. RARE. 2nd Gen. Killed. Sig/Rank 465
Baker, Ellen		Astronaut	5			25	
Baker, George*	1915-1975	Cartoonist	40	250		281	'Sad Sack'. Orig. Sketch S 350
Baker, Howard Henry, Jr.		Senate	10		25	25	Senator TN. WH Chief of Staff
Baker, James A., III		Cabinet	10	25		40	Bush Sec'y State
Baker, James McNair		Civil War	52	117			Member Conf. Congress
Baker, Janet, Dame		Entertainment	10	15		35	Opera. Br. Mezzo Soprano
Baker, Jehu	1822-1903	Congress	10		25		Repr. IL
Baker, Josephine	1906-1975	Entertainment	172	210	383	990	Highest Paid Entertainer in Eur. '20's. SPPc 425
Baker, Kenny		Entertainment	6			43	Actor. 'R2D2'
Baker, Kenny	1912-1985	Entertainment	15	15	25	50	Singer-Actor. Jack Benny Show Vocalist. Films
Baker, La Fayette Curry	1826-1868	Civil War	136	185	316		Union Gen. Interesting Background! Sig/Rank 325
Baker, Laurence S.	1830-1907	Civil War	114	189	405		CSA Gen. Sig/Rank 205, War Dte. DS 400+
Baker, LaVerne		Entertainment	28			55	Jazz Vocalist
Baker, Lt Gen Sir Wm. Henry G.	1888-1964	Military	25				World War II British general
Baker, Lucien		Senate	7		30		Senator KS
Baker, Maj. Gen. Walter C.	1877-1957	Military	30				World War II U.S. general
Baker, Mark		Entertainment	5	10		30	Opera
Baker, Michael		Astronaut	5	10		20	
Baker, Newton D.	1837-1937	Cabinet	15	84	93	78	Wilson Sec'y War
Baker, Phil	1896-1963	Entertainment	7			25	Early radio comic. Few Films
Baker, Richard H. B		Congress	10			15	Member U.S. Congress
Baker, Royal N.		Aviation	25		90	50	Air Ace Korea, WW II
Baker, Samuel W., Sir	1821-1893	Explorer	40	75	150		Br. Located Sources of Nile
Baker, Tom		Entertainment	10			20	Actor
Bakewell, William		Entertainment	15			40	'Gone With The Wind' (Cast Member)
Bakker, Jim		Clergy	20	25	35	40	Built Empire. Convicted & Imprisoned. Now Released
Bako, Brigitte		Entertainment	3			10	Actress. Movies
Bakopoulos, Emmanouil		Political	10			15	Member European Parliament
Bakshi, Ralph		Celebrity		230			Producer. Lord of the Rings
Bakst, Leon	1866-1924	Artist	95		650		Rus. Painter, Scenic Designer
Bakula, Scott		Entertainment	20			38	'Quantum Leap' etc
Bakunin, Mikhail	1814-1876	Anarchist	215		1625		Russian Revolutionist
Balaban Bob		Entertainment	15			25	actor
Balakirev, Mily	1837-1910	Composer			865		Russian
Balanchine, George	1904-1983	Entertainment	155		250	287	Ballet-Choreographer
Balbo, Italo	1896-1940	Aviation	125	160	200	195	It. Air Marshal-Pioneer. Valuable Postals Available
Balch, Emily Greene	1867-1961	Sociologist	35	35	60	75	Nobel Economist, Reformer, Pacifist
Balchen, Bernt		Aviation	30	45	75	52	
Balchin, Brigadier Nigel Marlin	1908-1970	Military	25				World War II British general
Balck, Hermann		Military	25			75	Ger. Panzer General
Baldridge, Howard Malcolm		Congress	10	15		15	MOC NE
Baldridge, Malcolm	1922-1987	Cabinet	30	145		45	Sec'y Comm. Reagan.
Baldwin, Abraham	1754-1807	Statesman		3375			Signer Constitution, Rare

NAME	DATE	CATEGORY	SIG	LS/DS	ALS	SP	COMMENTS
Baldwin, Alec	1958-	Entertainment	20	75		45	Handsome Leading Man in Current Hit Films
Baldwin, Brig. Gen. Geoffrey P.	1892-1951	Military	30				World War II U.S. general
Baldwin, Faith	1893-1978	Author	35	25	60	45	Popular Novelist & Screenwriter
Baldwin, Frank D.		Author		115			
Baldwin, Henry	1780-1844	Supreme Court	87	140	230		
Baldwin, James	1924-1987	Author	62	426	500	252	Afr-Am. Novelist, Essayist. ALS/Content 975
Baldwin, John Brown		Civil War	57	117			Member Conf. Congress
Baldwin, Judy		Entertainment	4	3	6	10	
Baldwin, Loammi	b 1744	Rev. War		253			
Baldwin, Raymond E.		Governor	10	20		20	Governor, Senator CT
Baldwin, Roger Sherman		Senate	35		50		Early Gov.1844, Senator CT 1847
Baldwin, Roger		Political	20	25			Civil Libertarian. Founder ACLU
Baldwin, Stanley	1867-1947	Head of State	58	100	125	125	3 Term Br. Prime Minister. Edw. VIII Abdication
Baldwin, Stephen		Entertainment	15			45	Actor
Baldwin, Tammy B		Congress	10			15	Member U.S. Congress
Baldwin, William Edwin	1827-1864	Civil War	287	618	2975		CSA General. Sig/Rank 420, War Dte. ALS 2975
Baldwin, William		Entertainment	15			42	Actor
Bale, Christian		Entertainment	10			20	actor
Balerno of Currie, Brig A. D. B-S	1898-1984	Military	25				World War II British general. Baron
Balewa, A. T., Sir		Head of State	10	35	85	25	Nigeria
Balfe, Michael William		Composer	22	55	125		
Balfe, Richard A.		Political	10			15	Member European Parliament
Balfour, Arthur J.	1848-1930	Head of State	68	101	168	90	Br. Prime Minister. 1st Earl.'Balfour Declaration'
Balfour, Howard		Aviation	25		75		Br. Ace WW I
Balistier, Elliot		Editor	4	15			Liberty Magazine
Balk, Fairuza		Entertainment				35	
Ball, Alan		Entertainment				40	Director/Writer Six Feet Under
Ball, Albert	1896-1917	Aviation	125	225	330	275	Brit. RAF ACE WW I. Shot Down 43 Enemy Planes
Ball, Harvey		Celebrity	15	20	25	25	Creator of Smiley face., Illustrated face 50
Ball, Joseph H.		Congress	12			75	Senator
Ball, Lucille (Lucy)	1911-1989	Entertainment	98	167		290	5 x 7 SP (Lucy) 125
Ballance Jr., Frank W. B		Congress	10			15	Member U.S. Congress
Ballard, Hank		Entertainment	25			75	Rock Pioneer. Uncommon
Ballard, Kaye		Entertainment	10			20	actress
Ballard, Robert, Dr.		Science	16	40	85	25	Oceanographer. Found Titanic
Ballenger, Cass B		Congress	10			15	Member U.S. Congress
Ballentine, Maj Gen John S.	1897-1965	Military	25				World War II British general
Ballew, Smith		Entertainment	15	20		40	Actor
Ballinger, Richard A.		Cabinet	10	25	50	25	Sec'y Interior 1909
Ballmer, Steven A.		Business				20	CEO Microsoft
Ballou, Charles		Military	30	110			General WW I
Balmer, Brig. Gen. Jesmond D.	1895-1979	Military	30				World War II U.S. general
Balsam, Martin	1919-1996	Entertainment	20	25	35	48	Actor. AA Winner. Supporting Actor
Baltas, Alexandros		Political	10			15	Member European Parliament
Baltimore, David, Dr.		Science	15	25	40	35	Nobel Medicine. Controversial Research Scientist

NAME	DATE	CATEGORY	SIG	LS/DS	ALS	SP	COMMENTS
Balzac, Honoré de	1799-1850	Author	600	1506	1828		Fr. Novelist
Bampton, Rose	1909-1997	Entertainment	20	35	45	40	Opera, Concert. Metropolitan
Bananarama		Entertainment	32			70	(4)
Bancroft, Anne	1931-	Entertainment	9	8	15	30	Actress. Stage-Films. AA. 'Miracle Worker'
Bancroft, Cameron		Entertainment	10			20	actor
Bancroft, Edward	1744-1821	Author			1750		Also Inventor-& Spy for British During Am. Rev.
Bancroft, George	1800-1891	Cabinet-Author	35	85	125	135	Polk Sec'y Navy, Historian, Diplomat
Bancroft, George	1882-1956	Entertainment	20	45	63	85	Vintage Actor
Band, The		Entertainment	75			110	Rock HOF. DS 150
Bandaranike, S.W.R.D		Head of State	10	25	45	30	Prime Minister Sri Lanka
Banderas, Antonio		Entertainment	20			56	Latin Actor
Bandy, Moe		Country Music	7			15	Honky Tonk Artist
Bangles, The (All)		Entertainment	40			85	Rock
Bangs, John Kedrick		Author	8	45		20	Humor Editor Harper's Magazine
Banisadr, A.		Head of State	35	45	80	55	Iran. Exiled
Bank, Brig. Gen. Carl C.	1889-1979	Military	30				World War II U.S. general
Bank, C. D.		Cabinet	10	25			
Bankhead, Tallulah	1902-1968	Entertainment	112	115	200	295	Deep Voiced Actress. Orig. Wilding Photo. SP 600
Bankhead, Wm. B.	1874-1940	Congress	10	40			Speaker of the House
Banks, Billy		Entertainment	80			250	Jazz
Banks, Jeff		Celebrity	10			15	Designer
Banks, Joseph, Sir	1743-1820	Science-Explorer	40	130	533		Br. Naturalist, Botanist. Sailed/Capt.Cook
Banks, Leslie	1890-1952	Entertainment	20			40	Distinguished, Sophisticated Br.Stage-Screen Actor
Banks, Maj. Gen. Sir D. T. MacD.	1891-1975	Military	25				World War II British general
Banks, Michael A.		Author	4	10	25	10	Science fiction, computer book author
Banks, Morwenna		Celebrity	10			15	comedienne
Banks, Nathaniel P. (WD)		Civil War	150	498	505		Union Gen.
Banks, Nathaniel P.	1816-1894	Civil War	52	105	168		Gov. MA, MOC, Union Gen.
Banks, Tyra		Entertainment	10			43	Model/actress
Banky, Vilma	1902-1991	Entertainment	50	75	200	212	Silent Star. Co-Star with Valentino. Early Vamp
Bannantyne, Maj. Gen. Neil Chas.	1880-1970	Military	25				World War II British general
Banner, John	1910-1973	Entertainment	75	150		150	Actor. 'Hogan's Heroes' as 'Sgt. Schultz'
Banning, Henry Blackstone		Civil War	30	65			Union Gen., Congressman OH
Banning, Margaret C.		Author	5	12	25	10	
Banotti, Mary Elizabeth		Political	10			15	Member European Parliament
Banting, Frederick G.	1891-1941	Science	378	908	1650	943	Discoverd Insulin with Best. Nobel 1923
Bantock, Granville		Composer	40			125	Br. Composer
Bar=n Crespo, Enrique		Political	10			15	Member European Parliament
Bara, Theda	1890-1955	Entertainment	135		300	256	'The Vamp'. Silent Screen Star.
Barak, Ehud		Political	25	40	50	50	Former PM of Israel
Baraka, Imamu A.(LeRoi Jones)		Author	35	60	85	45	Afr-Am Playwright, Poet, Novelist, Essayist
Barbara, Agatha		Head of State	10			20	Pres. of Malta
Barbarigo, St. Gregorio L.	1625-1697	Clergy		3500			Saint. Canonized 1960
Barbarin, Paul		Entertainment	25		65		Bandleader, Drummer
Barbe, Maj. Gen. Paul	1881-1940	Military	20				World War II French general

NAME	DATE	CATEGORY	SIG	LS/DS	ALS	SP	COMMENTS
Barbeau, Adrienne	1945-	Entertainment	5	15	15	20	Actress
Barbee, John Henry		Entertainment	35				Blues Vocalist
Barbejacque, Prince		Entertainment	4	3	10	10	
Barbe-Marbois, Francois de	1745-1837	Napoleon Cabinet	45	75	250		As Napoleon's Min. of Finance-Louisiana Purchase
Barber, Brig. Gen. Henry A. Jr.	1896-1956	Military	30				World War II U.S. general
Barber, Charles E.	1842-1917	Artist			2300		
Barber, Lt. Gen. Sir Colin Muir	1897-1964	Military	25				World War II British general
Barber, Rex T.		Aviation	15	35	75	40	Am. ACE WW II, Downed Yamamoto
Barber, Samuel	1910-1981	Composer	65	210	312	131	Opera, Songs, String Music. AMusQS/Photo 1250
Barber, William		Military	25			70	Marine MOH Korea
Barbera, Joe*		Cartoonist	40			140	Flintstones, Yogi Bear. (Of Hanna-Barbera)
Barbier, George	1865-1945	Entertainment	10	15	25	25	Vintage Character Actor
Barbieri, Fedora		Entertainment	25			75	Opera, Concert
Barbieri, Paula		Celebrity	10			15	model
Barbirolli, John, Sir	1899-1970	Entertainment	38	35	60	150	Br. Conductor
Barbour, Dave		Composer	15			40	Jazz Guitar
Barbour, James	1775-1842	Cabinet, Congress	50		155		Sec'y War, Gov. & Senator VA. US Minister Gr.Brit.
Barbour, William Warren		Senate	10	35		15	Senator NJ
Barckhausen, Gen of Art Franz	1882-1956	Military	25				World War II German general
Barclay, Brigadier Cyril Nelson	1896-1979	Military	25				World War II British general
Barclay, Thomas		Revolutionary War	25	55			Adj.-Gen'l Nova Scotia
Barclay, William		Clergy	40	75	95	75	
Barcroft, Roy		Entertainment	50			150	
Bard, Ralph A.		Cabinet	15	25		25	FDR. Sec'y Navy
Bardeen, John		Science	30	50	105	63	Nobel. Signed Bio Card 55, inventor transistor, U of I
Bardot, Brigitte		Entertainment	25	25	45	47	French actress. Internat'l Sex Symbol
Bardshar, F.A.		Military	15	25	45	40	Navy ACE, WW II
Barere de Vieuzac, Bertrand	1755-1841	Fr. Revolution	40	120	150		'The Anacreon of the Guillotine'. Exiled
Baretti, Giuseppe	1719-1789	Author	35	80	155		Friend of Burke, Johnson. Italian Critic
Bari, Lynn		Entertainment	5	8	15	20	Actress. Deep Voiced 'Other Woman' Roles
Baring, Alexander	1774-1848	Banking	130		750		Formalized Webster-Ashburton Treaty
Baring, Francis, Sir	1796-1866	Business	35	50	110		1st Lord of Admiralty. ALS/Cont.1975
Baring, Thomas G.	1826-1904	Head of State	15	25	55		English Earl. Viceroy of India
Baring-Gould, Sabine	1834-1929	Author-Divine	25	120	185	65	'Onward Christian Soldiers' AMS 2400
Barkely, Bob		Aviation	10			25	WW II Ace
Barker, Bob		Entertainment	4	6	15	23	'The Price is Right' TV Game Show Host
Barker, Brig. Gen. Harold R.	1891-1965	Military	30				World War II U.S. general
Barker, Brig. Lewis Ernest S.	1895-1981	Military	20				World War II Australian general
Barker, Clive		Author	15	25		25	Br. Horror Novelist
Barker, General Sir Evelyn Hugh	1894-1983	Military	25				World War II British general
Barker, Joel		Celebrity	10			15	motivational speaker
Barker, Lex	1919-1973	Entertainment	65	138	160	175	Actor. Ex Husband Lana Turner & Ex 'Tarzan'
Barker, Linda		Celebrity	10			15	home/gardening expert
Barker, Lt Gen Michael George H.	1884-1960	Military	25				World War II British general
Barker, Maj. Gen. Ray W.	1889-1974	Military	30				World War II U.S. general

NAME	DATE	CATEGORY	SIG	LS/DS	ALS	SP	COMMENTS
Barker, William George		Aviation	125	225	350	295	Canadian ACE, WW I
Barker-Benfield, Brig. Karl Vere	1892-1969	Military	25				World War II British general
Barkhorn, Gerhard		Aviation	65	185		246	Ger. ACE, #2 Worldwide
Barkin, Ellen	1955-	Entertainment	15			49	Actress
Barkley, Alben W.	1877-1956	Vice President	27	70	175	65	Truman VP. Oldest V.P. & Only One To Marry In Off.
Barks, Carl*		Cartoonist	30			197	Donald Duck, Scrooge
Barksdale, Ethelbert		Civil War	38	60	89		CSA Congress
Barksdale, William (WD)		Civil War	908				CSA General. Wounded Gettysburg 7/2/63. Died 7/3
Barksdale, William	1821-1863	Civil War	626		1220		CSA General. KIA Gettysburg '63
Bar-Lev, Chaim		Military	20	65		50	Israeli Military Leader
Barlow, Francis C.	1834-1896	Civil War	79	90	301	1150	Union Gen.
Barlow, Gary		Music	10			15	performing musical artist
Barlow, Howard		Conductor	40			50	Popular Radio/TV Conductor
Barlow, Jane		Author	5	15	25		
Barlow, Joel		Diplomat	40	120	245		Author, Chaplain Rev. War
Barlow, Thelma		Entertainment	10			20	Actress
Barnabee, Henry Clay		Entertainment	6	15	25	15	Operatic Comedian
Barnaby, Ralph S.		Aviation	27			35	
Barnard, Christian, Dr.		Science	40	85	95	70	Heart Specialist
Barnard, Daniel D.	1797-1861	Congress	12		85		MOC. NY, Minister Prussia
Barnard, Frederick A.P.	1809-1889	Educator	75	165	275		Barnard College. For Women's Ed. Pres. Columbia U.
Barnard, George Grey	1863-1938	Artist	25		85		Sculptor. Works in Metr. Mus. Art, The Cloisters
Barnard, John Gross	1815-1882	Civil War	28	92	143		Union Gen. Sig/Rank 45, War Dte. ALS 165
Barne, Michael		Celebrity	12	35	90	40	
Barnes, Binnie	1905-	Entertainment	15	12	15	25	Vintage Br. Actress. Leading Lady & Light Comedy
Barnes, Brig. Gen. Harold A.	1887-1953	Military	30				World War II U.S. general
Barnes, Carol		Celebrity	10			15	newsreader
Barnes, Demus		Senate/Congress	5	15	25		Congressman NY. Writer
Barnes, Djuna		Author	45	110	260	85	Am. Novelist-Short Story Writer
Barnes, Fred		Celebrity	10			15	media/TV personality
Barnes, James	1801-1869	Civil War	170	186	248		Union Gen. Very Scarce
Barnes, Joanna		Entertainment	5	6	15	15	Actress
Barnes, Joseph K.	1817-1883	Civil War	179	410	550		Union Surgeon Gen. Attended Lincoln at Deathbed
Barnes, Julius H.	1873-1939	Business		20		20	Corporation Off'l. Pres. US Chamber of Commerce
Barnes, Maj. Gen. Gladeon M.	1887-1961	Military	30				World War II U.S. general
Barnes, Maj. Gen. Julian F.	1889-1961	Military	30				World War II U.S. general
Barnes, Priscilla		Entertainment	8	10	20	23	Actress.
Barnet, Charlie		Entertainment	15			30	Big Band Leader-Tenor Sax
Barnet, Isaac		Political		25			Mayor Cincinnati
Barnet, Will		Artist				104	
Barnett, Brig. Gen. James W.	1892-1983	Military	30				World War II U.S. general
Barnett, Maj. Gen. Allison J.	1892-1971	Military	30				World War II U.S. general
Barnett, Ross R.		Governor	10		25	15	Governor MS
Barnette, Vince		Entertainment	15	20	35	46	Vintage Character Actor
Barneveld, Jan Van Olden		Dutch Statesman		2000			Father of Dutch Independence

NAME	DATE	CATEGORY	SIG	LS/DS	ALS	SP	COMMENTS
Barney, Natalie	1876-1972	Author	110	315	412		Am. Poet, Translator, Parisian Hostess
Barnhart, George 'Eddie'		Aviation	20	35		50	
Barnum, Henry Alanson	1833-1892	Civil War	52	110	145		Union Gen. ALS '64 190, Sig/Rank 70
Barnum, Malvern H.		Military	10		35	25	General WW I
Barnum, Phineas T.	1810-1891	Business-Circus	160	623	731	1179	ALS/Content 1,100-1,500-2,000-3800
Barnwell, Robert Woodward		Civil War	64	117			CSA Congress
Baronova, Irina		Entertainment	20			58	Rus.-Br. Ballerina
Barr, Candy		Entertainment	10			37	Stripper. Prison for Shooting Husband
Barr, Doug		Entertainment	3	3	6	8	
Barr, Joseph Walker		Cabinet	5	15	30	15	Sec'y Treasury, Congressman IN
Barr, Maj. Gen. David G.	1895-1970	Military	30				World War II U.S. general
Barr, Roseanne		Entertainment	20	25	50	35	
Barranco, Maria		Entertainment	10			20	actress
Barras, Paul-Francois-Jean		Fr. Revolution	85	250			Jacobin Club. Exiled From Paris
Barrault, Jean-Louis		Entertainment	40			125	
Barré, Lt. Gen. Louis-Georges	1886-1970	Military	20				World War II French general
Barrera, Rick		Celebrity	10			15	motivational speaker
Barrett, Brig. Gen. Charles J.	1900-1963	Military	30				World War II U.S. general
Barrett, J. Gresham B		Congress	10			15	Member U.S. Congress
Barrett, John		Military	20		50		WW I Victoria Cross
Barrett, Lawrence	1838-1891	Civil War	20			45	Union Officer, Actor
Barrett, Majel		Entertainment	10			30	Star Trek
Barrett, Rona		Entertainment	6	8	15	15	
Barrett, S. M.		Author	8			12	journalist, interviewed Geronimo
Barrett, Wilson	1847-1904	Entertainment	15		90	65	Br. Playwright, Actor, Manager
Barrie, Barbara		Entertainment	10	6	12	15	Successful Broadway & Film Actress
Barrie, Chris		Entertainment	10			20	Actor
Barrie, James M., Sir	1860-1937	Author	82	265	273	280	Playwright, Novelist. 'Peter Pan' etc.
Barrie, Mona		Entertainment	15	15	35	30	
Barrie, Wendy		Entertainment	20	25	30	45	
Barrier, Edgar		Entertainment	4	7	10	15	
Barringer, Daniel M.	1806-1873	Congress	12				Repr. NC, Minister Spain
Barringer, Rufus	1821-1895	Civil War	110	308	380		CSA Gen.
Barrington, Shute		Clergy	10	15	25	20	
Barrios, Justo R.	1835-1885	Head of State	40	112			Pres. Guatemala. Killed in Battle
Barron, Blue		Bandleader	25			10	
Barron, Brig. Gen. William A. Jr.	1892-1964	Military	30				World War II U.S. general
Barron, Clarence		Business	25			40	Editor, Publisher Barron's
Barron, Maj Gen Frederick Wilmot	1880-1963	Military	25				World War II British general
Barrow, Clyde	1909-1934	Criminal			5688	12650	Bonnie & Clyde
Barrow, Edward G.		Business	100	147		150	Gen'l Mgr. NY Yankees
Barrow, John, Sir	1764-1848	Statesman	60	170	325		Explorer, Traveller, Author
Barrow, Robert H.		Military	10	30	50	20	
Barrowclough, Maj. Gen. H.	1894-1972	Military	20				World War II New Zealand general
Barrows, Lewis O.		Governor	12		25	15	Governor ME

NAME	DATE	CATEGORY	SIG	LS/DS	ALS	SP	COMMENTS
Barrows, Sydney Biddle		Celebrity	10			30	Mayflower Madame
Barry, Charles, Sir	1795-1860	Architect	45	55	138		Br. Houses of Parliament, Westminster Palace
Barry, Dan		Astronaut	7			22	
Barry, Dan*		Cartoonist	10			100	Flash Gordon
Barry, Dave		Author	10			20	Creator Dave's World
Barry, Don 'Red'		Entertainment	22	35	45	58	
Barry, Gene		Entertainment	15	10	15	25	Actor. Westerns, Straight Leads. Films-TV
Barry, John Decatur	1839-1867	Civil War	206	350	490		CSA Gen.
Barry, John Wolfe, Sir		Celebrity	8	15	35	20	
Barry, John		Revolutionary War	1150	2000			Ir. Born US Naval Officer
Barry, Marion		Politician	6	8	15	15	Mayor Washington, D.C.
Barry, Sy*		Cartoonist	14			50	'Phantom'
Barry, Thomas		Military	35		150		General WW I
Barry, Wesley		Entertainment	8	12	25	20	
Barry, William Taylor		Civil War	87				CSA Cong.
Barry, Wm. Farquhar	1818-1879	Civil War	58	146	155		Union Gen. War Dte. S 85
Barrymore, Diana		Entertainment	30	35	45	42	
Barrymore, Drew	1975-	Entertainment	20			50	Actress
Barrymore, Ethel	1898-1954	Entertainment	99	185		221	Stage Star Prior to Films.'The Corn is Green' etc.
Barrymore, John	1882-1942	Entertainment	192	287	300	505	'The Great Profile'. Academy Award.
Barrymore, Lionel	1878-1954	Entertainment	82	244		170	Member 1st Family of Am. Theatre. Oscar 1931
Barrymore, Maurice	1847-1905	Entertainment	35			90	Founding Member of American Familty of Actors
Barstow, Maj. Gen. A.	1888-1942	Military	25				World War II British general
Bartato, Elisabeth		Entertainment	15			40	Opera
Bartel, Jean	1925-	Entertainment	15			55	Miss America '43, Actress. Set new image.
Barth, Brig. Gen. Henry Jr.	1903-1943	Military	30				World War II U.S. general
Barth, John		Author	30	40	85	35	Am. Novelist
Barth, Karl		Clergy	40	95	125	75	
Barthelmess, Richard		Entertainment	20	30	75	70	Vintage Actor.
Bartholdi, Fred. Auguste	1834-1904	Artist	259	432	599	975	Statue of Liberty Print S 700- 1395
Bartholomew, Freddie		Entertainment	30	35	45	73	Brit. Child Actor of 30's-40's
Bartholomew, Gen Sir Wm. Henry	1877-1962	Military	28				World War II British general
Bartle, Joyce		Entertainment	5	6	10	10	
Bartlett, Bonnie		Entertainment	5	6	10	10	
Bartlett, Joseph Jackson	1834-1893	Civil War	70	117			Union Gen.
Bartlett, Josiah	1729-1795	Revolutionary War	215	595	908		Signer.ALS/Cont.3250- 8000, FF 950-1050
Bartlett, Paul Wayland		Artist	10	15	30		US Sculptor
Bartlett, Robert Abram		Explorer	50	120	175		Cmdr. Ship on Peary Arctic Exp.
Bartlett, Roscoe G. B		Congress	10			15	Member U.S. Congress
Bartlett, Thomas		Clergy	15	20	35		
Bartlett, William F.		Civil War	50	96	155		Union Gen.
Bartoe, John David		Astronaut	7	20		30	
Bartok, Bela	1881-1945	Composer	300	770	1312	1708	Hung.Pianist-Comp.AmusQS 1800-2750
Bartok, Eva		Entertainment	5			15	Actress
Bartoli, Cecilia		Entertainment	5			32	It. Mezzo. Opera

NAME	DATE	CATEGORY	SIG	LS/DS	ALS	SP	COMMENTS
Bartolotta, Vince Jr.		Celebrity	5	7	10	15	Prominent lawyer
Bartolozzi, Paolo		Political	10			15	Member European Parliament
Barton, Bruce	1836-1967	Business	10	35	40	30	Advertising Exec.. BBD&O. Writer, Rep. NY
Barton, Clara	1821-1912	Humanitarian	170	481	568	771	Founder & 1st Pres. Am. Red Cross.ALS/Cont.1250
Barton, Derek H. R., Sir		Science	20	30	40	25	Nobel Chemistry
Barton, Diana		Entertainment	10			20	actress
Barton, James		Entertainment	40			70	
Barton, Joe B		Congress	10			15	Member U.S. Congress
Barton, Maj. Gen. Raymond O.	1889-1963	Military	30				World War II U.S. general
Barton, Seth Maxwell (WD)	1829-1900	Civil War	205		935		CSA General
Barton, Seth Maxwell	1829-1900	Civil War	104	281	308		CSA Gen.
Bartow, Francis Stebbins	1816-1861	Civil War	91	236	360		CSA Congress
Barty, Billy		Entertainment	10	18	20	20	Diminuative Character Actor
Baruch, Bernard M.	1870-1965	Statesman	35	132	179	169	Financier, Pres. Advisor
Barun, Ken		Celebrity	10			15	motivational speaker
Baryshnikov, Mikail		Entertainment	62	85	130	161	Rus-Born Ballet Star
Barzun, Jacques		Author	7	12	25	15	
Barzynski, Brig. Gen. Joseph E.	1884-1972	Military	30				World War II U.S. general
Basch, Peter		Entertainment	10			20	actor
Basehart, Richard		Entertainment	6	10	20	15	
Basie, William 'Count'	1904-1984	Composer	72	200		165	Big Band Leader-Pianist
Basile, Frank M.		Celebrity	10			15	
Basinger, Kim		Entertainment	12	20	25	41	Actress. Oscar Winner
Baskett, James		Entertainment	200			600	
Baskin, Leonard	1922-	Artist	25				Sculptor & Graphic Artist
Basov, Nickolay		Science	20	45		30	Rus. Nobel Physicist
Basquette, Lina		Entertainment	15			25	1920's Star
Basquiat, Jean-Michel	1960-1988	Artist	500				rare in any form
Bass, Charles F. B		Congress	10			15	Member U.S. Congress
Basset, Maj Gen Richard Aug. M.	1891-1954	Military	25				World War II British general
Bassett, Angela		Entertainment	16			44	Singer
Bassett, Charles A.		Astronaut	40			65	
Bassett, Leslie		Composer	15	30	65		Pulitzer, AMusQS 100
Bassett, Richard		Revolutionary War	375	800			Signer Constitution
Bassey, Shirley		Entertainment	10			35	actress
Bassi, Amedeo		Entertainment	35			150	Favorite Tenor of Toscanini
Bastin, Brigadier David Terence	1904-1982	Military	25				World War II British general
Bastin, Maj Gen Geo. Edw. R.	1902-1960	Military	25				World War II British general
Bastion, Brig. Gen. Joseph E.	1883-1971	Military	25				World War II U.S. general
Bastos, Regina		Political	10			15	Member European Parliament
Bastyan, Lt Gen Sir Edrick M.	1903-1980	Military	25				World War II British general
Bate, William B. (WD)		Civil War	140	208	1045		CSA Gen., Senator, Gov. TN (Listed ALS/Content)
Bate, William Brimage	1826-1905	Civil War-Senate	70	122	175		CSA General-Also Gov. Tenn.
Bateman, Jason		Entertainment	15			30	
Bateman, Justine		Entertainment	15	15	25	25	

NAME	DATE	CATEGORY	SIG	LS/DS	ALS	SP	COMMENTS
Bateman, Maj Gen Donald R. E. R	1907-1969	Military	25				World War II British general
Bates, Alan		Entertainment	5			30	Br. Actor
Bates, Arthur Laban		Senate/Congress	5	10		20	Congressman PA
Bates, Blanche		Entertainment	15	25	40	45	
Bates, Clayton 'Peg-Leg'	1907-1998	Entertainment	20			45	Famous One-Legged Tap Dancer. Vaud.-TV-Films
Bates, Edward	1793-1869	Cabinet	40	135	365	450	Lincoln Att'y Gen. War Date ALS/Cont. 895
Bates, John C.		Military	25		110		American General
Bates, Joshua H.	1817-1908	Civil War			184		Union General
Bates, Katharine Lee	1859-1929	Author	75	248	369	308	AMsS 'Am. The Beautiful' 51,750, Printed 2000
Bates, Kathy		Entertainment	20			57	Actress, Oscar Winner
Bates, Sanford		Law Enforcement	10	35			Commissioner of Prisons
Bates. Florence		Entertainment	10			25	
Bathazar, Getty		Entertainment	15			35	'The Young Riders' SP 80
Bathori, Jane	1876-1970	Entertainment			75	125	Opera. Legendary Fr. Soprano
Bathurst, Brig. Gen. Robert M.	1893-1964	Military	30				World War II U.S. general
Bathurst, Henry		Clergy	15	25	40	30	
Batista, Fulgencio	1901-1973	Head of State	165	221	475	145	Cuban Pres. 1940-44, 1952-59. Dictator
Batiuk, Tom*		Cartoonist	5			25	Funky Winkerbean
Batman (original cast)		Entertainment				45	West / Ward
Battaglia, Franco		Entertainment	15			50	Opera, Concert
Battaille, Charles	1822-1872	Entertainmment	10		50		Opera
Battelle, John		Celebrity	10			15	media/TV personality
Batten, Hugh		Aviation	10	25	40	30	Navy ACE, WW II
Batten, Jean	1909-1982	Aviation	45	85		90	Pioneer NZ Aviatrix
Battenberg, Louis	1854-1921	Military	10		50		British Adm of the Fleet 1919
Battle, Cullen Andrews	1829-1905	Civil War	280	405			Confederate general
Battle, Kathleen		Entertainment	20	40		52	Opera, Concert
Battley, Brig. Gen. Joseph F.	1893-1970	Military	30				World War II U.S. general
Battu, Marie	1838-1888	Entertainment	15		75		Opera. Sang in World Premiere of L'Africaine
Batz, Willhelm		Aviation	35			95	Ger. ACE, #7 Worldwide
Baucus, Bob		Aviation	10	20	35	25	
Baucus, Max		Senate	10			15	United States Senate (D - MT)
Baudelaire, Charles-Pierre	1821-1867	Author	335	2250	2370		Fr. Modernist Poet, Symbolist, Critic
Baudouin, King (Belg)		Royalty	35	100	250	125	King of Belgium
Baudry, Patrick		Astronaut	12	25		25	
Bauduc, Ray		Entertainment	10			25	Big Band Bassist
Bauer, Harold		Entertainment	38	60	75	70	Br. Piano Virtuoso
Bauer, Jaime Lyn		Entertainment	6	8	10	28	
Bauer, Michelle		Entertainment	10			125	B-Film Star. Signed Lip Print. 15.
Bauer, Steven		Entertainment	6	8	15	20	
Baulieu, Etienne		Science	20		45	40	Inventor RU486 Abortion Pill
Baum, Kurt		Entertainment				40	Operatic Tenor
Baum, L. Frank		Author	2114	2783	6528		The Wizard of Oz books
Baum, Vicki		Author	20				Novelist. Grand Hotel
Baum, William W., Cardinal		Clergy	35	55	70	50	

NAME	DATE	CATEGORY	SIG	LS/DS	ALS	SP	COMMENTS
Baumer, Steven		Entertainment	10	15	20	25	
Baur, Hans		Aviation	30	45	90	125	Hitler's Personal Pilot
Baur, Harry		Entertainment	30			150	Fr. Star Executed by Nazis
Bautista Ojeda, Carlos		Political	10			15	Member European Parliament
Bauvais, Garcelle		Entertainment				40	Models, Inc.
Bavier, Frances	1902-1989	Entertainment	55	60	95	200	Aunt Bee on the Andy Griffith Show
Bax, Arnold		Composer	70				AMusQS 200
Baxley, Barbara		Entertainment	4	4	10	10	
Baxter, Anne		Entertainment	20	38	40	46	AA
Baxter, Henry		Civil War	57	128	160		Union Gen.
Baxter, James P. III		Author	5	15	30	10	
Baxter, Keith		Entertainment	3	3	6	10	
Baxter, Les		Bandleader	26		40		Arranger, Composer
Baxter, Percival P.		Governor	12		25		Governor ME
Baxter, Warner	1892-1951	Entertainment	86	50	155	148	Early Leading Man & Oscar Winner
Baxter-Birney, Meredith		Entertainment	6	8	15	15	
Bay, Michael		Celebrity	10			15	film industry
Bayard, George Dashiell (WD)	1835-1862	Civil War	295		1222		Union Gen.
Bayard, George Dashiell	1835-1862	Civil War	135	170	694		Union Gen., KIA Fredericksburg
Bayard, John B.	1738-1807	Revolutionary War	40	151	168		Continental Congress, Rev.War Col.
Bayard, Richard Henry		Senate	20	40	85		Senator DE
Bayard, Thomas F., Sr.		Cabinet	25	35	80		Sec'y State, Senator DE
Bayard, William		Revolutionary War	85	220	450		
Bayh, Birch		Senate	10	25		20	Senator IN
Bayh, Evan		Senate	10			15	United States Senate (D - IN)
Bayley, Maj. Gen. Kenneth	1903-1967	Military	25				World War II British general
Baylis, Brig. Gen. James E.	1884-1964	Military	30				World War II U.S. general
Bayne, Barbara		Entertainment	20			55	
Bayne, Beverly		Entertainment	9	10	20	20	
Bayne-Jardine, Maj Gen Christian	1888-1959	Military	25				World War II British general
Bayne-Jones, Brig Gen Stanhope	1888-1970	Military	30				World War II U.S. general
Bayona De Perogordo, Juan José		Political	10			15	Member European Parliament
Baywatch (cast)		Entertainment				125	Original cast of 5
Beach Boys (4)		Entertainment	195			425	Alb. Cover. S by 5 Living Members 395. SP 650
Beach, Amy M.	1867-1944	Composer	45		462	200	1st Am. Woman Composer of Note. AMQS 175
Beach, Brig. Gen. George C. Jr.	1888-1948	Military	30				World War II U.S. general
Beach, Michael		Entertainment	10			20	actor
Beach, Rex	1877-	Author	20	35	95	35	Am. Novelist
Beacham, Stephanie		Entertainment	10	6	15	20	Actress
Beadle, George Wells, Dr.		Science	20	30	45	40	Nobel Medicine
Beadle, Jeremy		Celebrity	10			15	television presenter
Beak, Maj Gen Daniel M. Wm	1891-1967	Military	25				World War II British general
Beakley, Wallace M.		Military	5	15	25		
Beal, George Lafayette	1825-1896	Civil War	42	123	156	270	Union Gen.ALS '64 440
Beal, John		Entertainment	15	15	25	25	

NAME	DATE	CATEGORY	SIG	LS/DS	ALS	SP	COMMENTS
Beale, Richard Lee T. (WD)		Civil War	150		550		CSA General
Beale, Richard Lee Turberville	1819-1893	Civil War	78	105	251		CSA General
Beall, Lloyd J.		Civil War		1093	2415		
Beall, William N.R.(WD)		Civil War	175	325	772	883	CSA General
Beals, Jennifer		Entertainment	20	20	40	30	
Beament, Brig. Arthur Warwick	1898-1966	Military	20				World War II Canadian general
Bean, Alan L.		Astronaut	20	60	80	72	Moonwalker Astro.ADS re Apollo 12 975
Bean, L.L.	1872-1967	Inventor-Business				300	Unique Business Empire
Bean, Orson	1928-	Entertainment	5			22	Actor-Comedian
Bean, Roy, Judge		Frontier Judge	3950	4500			The Law West of the Pecos
Bean, Sean		Entertainment	10			20	actor
Beane, Hilary		Entertainment	5	10	15	10	
Beanland, Maj. Gen. Douglas	1893-1963	Military	25				World War II British general
Beard, Charles A.	1874-1948	Author	5	28	65		Am. Historian,Teacher, Political Scientist
Beard, Daniel C.	1850-1941	Author	105	300	352	140	Founder Boy Scouts of America. Author, Teacher
Beard, Maj. Gen. Edmund Chas.	1894-1974	Military	25				World War II British general
Beard. Stymie		Entertainment	75			175	Little Rascals
Bearden, Romare	1914-1988	Artist	45	225	475	200	Afro-Am. Artist. Principally Blk.-Am. Life Collage
Beardshaw, Chris		Celebrity	10			15	home/gardening expert
Beardslee, Lester Anthony		Military	30		100		Admiral Spanish American War
Beardsley, Aubrey	1872-1898	Artist	175	375	1712	2300	Br. Illustrator. Art Nouveau
Beardsley, Samuel	1790-1860	Congress	10				Repr. NY, Assoc. Judge NY Supr. Ct.
Beart, Emmanuelle		Entertainment	10			20	actress
Beasly, Maj. Gen. Rex W.	1892-1961	Military	30				World War II U.S. general
Beastie Boys (3)		Entertainment	40			95	Rock Group (3)
Beatles (all four) on one piece		Entertainment	4960			5304	Set of 4 Separate Sigs. 2,650
Beaton, Cecil	1904-1980	Photographer	40	155	202	375	Br.Portraitist. Theatrical Designer
Beatrice, Princess		Royalty	25	60	115	120	Youngest Daughter Q. Victoria
Beatrix, Queen		Royalty	100		450		Netherlands
Beattie, Brig. Joseph Hamilton	1903-1985	Military	25				World War II British general
Beatty, Clyde	1903-1965	Business-Circus	50	95	175	142	Animal Trainer. Circus Performer-Owner
Beatty, David, Adm.	1871-1926	Military	32	75	90	100	Br. Admiral WW I
Beatty, Ned		Entertainment	7	10	15	30	Actor
Beatty, Samuel	1820-1885	Civil War	36	59	79		Union Gen.
Beatty, Warren	1937-	Entertainment	25	30		58	Actor, Oscar 1981 for 'Reds' Dir.
Beatty. John		Civil War	36	69	100		Union General
Beauharnais, Eugene de	1781-1824	Royalty	45	250	265		Son of Josephine, Adopted by Napoleon
Beauharnais, Hortense de	1783-1837	Royalty	50		435		Wife of Louis Bonaparte
Beauman, Maj. Gen. Archibald B.	1888-1977	Military	252				World War II British general
Beaumarchais, Caron de	1732-1799	Author	150	1413			Fr. Playwright. Aided Am. Colonies In Rev. War
Beaumont, Hugh		Entertainment	75			150	
Beaumont, Kathryn		Entertainment				65	Voice of Alice in Wonderland, Peter Pan
Beauprez, Bob B		Congress	10			15	Member U.S. Congress
Beauregard, Pierre G.T. (WD)	1818-1893	Civil War	403	1550	1756	3500	CSA Gen. Fired on Fort Sumpter
Beauregard, Pierre G.T.	1818-1893	Civil War	274	739	749	1333	CSA Gen.Stock Cert. S 3950

NAME	DATE	CATEGORY	SIG	LS/DS	ALS	SP	COMMENTS
Beauvais, Garcelle		Entertainment	5			40	Actress, Models, Inc.
Beauvoir, Simone de	1908-1986	Author	95	60	512		Fr. Novelist. Philosopher. Existentialist
Beaux, Cecilia	1863-1942	Artist	55	58	65		Am. Portrait Painter
Beaver, James A.		Civil War-Gov.	30	55	110		Union Gen., Gov. PA
Beaverbrook, Max, Lord							SEE MAXWELL. WM.
Beavers, Louise		Entertainment	60			150	Popular Afr.-Am. Film Actress
Beavis, Maj. Gen. Leslie E.	1895-1975	Military	20				World War II Australian general
Beazley, Christopher J.p.		Political	10			15	Member European Parliament
Bebear, Jean-pierre		Political	10			15	Member European Parliament
Becerra, Xavier B		Congress	10			15	Member U.S. Congress
Bechet, Sidney	1897-1959	Entertainment	120	260	422	300	Jazz Clarinetist-Saxaphonist
Bechi, Gino		Entertainment	25			55	Opera
Beck		Music	20			55	Rock
Beck, C.C*		Cartoonist	10			100	Captain Marvel
Beck, Dave	1894-1993	Labor Leader	20	30	50	50	Union Exec. Sent to Prison for Union Fraud
Beck, James M.	1861-1936	Congress		25			Repr. PA
Beck, Jeff		Entertainment	20			45	Rock Guitarist
Beck, John		Entertainment	3	3	6	8	
Beck, Ken		Author	8			12	trivia books
Beck, Maj. Gen. Edward Archibald	1880-1974	Military	25				World War II British general
Beckel, Bob		Celebrity	10			15	media/TV personality
Becker, Barbara		Entertainment	3	3	6	8	
Becker, General of Artillery Karl	1879-1940	Military	25				World War II German general
Beckett, Maj Gen Clifford Thom.	1891-1972	Military	25				World War II British general
Beckett, Samuel	1906-1989	Author	132	250	426	335	Irish Playwright. Nobel Lit. 'Waiting for Godot'
Beckett, Scotty		Entertainment	15			92	Child Actor
Beckinsale, Kate		Entertainment	4			32	
Beckman, Arnold	1900-	Inventor	18				Beckman Instruments. pH testing meter etc.
Beckwith, Edward G.		Civil War	45				Union General
Beckwith, Geo. Sir	1753-1823	Revolutionary War		390			Br. Gen. in the American War
Beckwith, J. Carroll		Artist	35	80	145		
Beckwith-Smith, Maj. Gen. Merton	1890-1942	Military	25				World War II British general
Beckworth, Tamara		Celebrity	10			15	celebrity model
Becquerel, Edmond	1820-1891	Science			1450		Fr. Physicist MsS 3500
Becquerel, Henri	1852-1908	Science	175	450	520		Nobel Curies' Radioactivity., AMS 10,000
Bedard, Irene		Entertainment	10			20	actress
Beddington, Maj Gen William R.	1893-1975	Military	25				World War II British general
Beddoe, Don		Entertainment	8			20	
Bedelia, Bonnie		Entertainment	3	4	10	10	
Bedford, Brian		Entertainment	5	12		20	Actor
Bedford, Brigadier Davis Evan	1898-1978	Military	25				World War II British general
Bedford, Gunning, Jr.		Revolutionary War	285	700			Signer of Constitution. Scarce
Bedford, Gunning, Sr.		Revolutionary War	175	325			Cousin of above, Scarce
Bedwell, Randall		Author	8			12	regional histories/publisher
Bee Gees (3)		Entertainment	40			200	Barry, Robin, Maurice Gibb. 'Stayin' Alive'

NAME	DATE	CATEGORY	SIG	LS/DS	ALS	SP	COMMENTS
Bee, Barnard E.	1824-1861	Civil War	1252	2100	2515	3000	CSA Gen., Sec'y War Rep. Texas
Bee, Carlos		Senate/Congress	10	20		20	Congressman TX
Bee, Hamilton Prioleau (WD)	1822-1897	Civil War	265				CSA General
Bee, Hamilton Prioleau	1822-1897	Civil War	90	168	425		CSA Gen.
Bee, Molly		Country Music	6			20	
Beebe, Charles William	1877-1962	Explorer	30	60	212	75	Bathysphere.Naturalist.Author, Scientist
Beebe, Maj. Gen. Lewis C.	1891-1951	Military	30				World War II U.S. general
Beebe, Marshall		Aviation	18	35	55	42	ACE, WW II
Beech, Olive Ann		Aviation	20	45		50	Beechcraft Airplane Mfg.
Beecham, Stephanie		Entertainment	10			20	Actress
Beecham, Thomas, Sir	1879-1961	Conductor	68	195		262	Flamboyant Br. Conductor. 3x5 Half-Tone SP 120
Beecher, Henry Ward	1813-1887	Clergy	60	120	170	407	Abolition, Temperance Activist, Orator
Beecher, Lyman		Clergy	40	55	65	45	Early Anti Slavery
Beehner, John F.		Author	8			12	Biblical principles of business
Beems, Patricia		Entertainment	3	3	6	8	
Beene, Geoffrey		Business	10	25		25	Fashion Designer
Beerbohm, Max, Sir Henry	1872-1956	Author	55	135	162	75	Humorist, Caricaturist
Beerbohm-Tree, Herbert		Entertainment	20			45	Classical Actor
Beery, Noah Jr.		Entertainment	15	20	25	35	
Beery, Noah	1884-1946	Entertainment	78		250	175	
Beery, Wallace	1885-1949	Entertainment	132	195	350	252	Vintage Oscar Winner. 'The Champ'
Beeson, Jack	1921-	Composer	15	30	63	25	AMusQS 35
Beethoven, Ludwig van		Composer	7800	17500	65000		
Beggs, James		Astronaut	8			30	
Begin, Menachem	1914-1992	Head of State	68	125	210	125	P.M. Israel. Nobel Peace Prize. ALS/Content 1295
Begley, Ed, Jr.		Entertainment	4	7	9	38	Actor
Begley, Ed, Sr.		Entertainment	25	45	70	75	Actor
Behan, Brendan F.		Author	160	400	645		Ir. Author-Playwright
Behlendorff, Gen. of Artillery Hans	1889-1961	Military	25				World War II German general
Behr, Dani		Celebrity	10			15	television presenter
Behr, Henrich von, Baron		Military	10			30	
Behrman, S. N.		Author	15	25	60	25	Am. Playwright, Screenplays
Beichel, Rudolph		Science	20			55	Rocket Pioneer/von Braun
Beiderbecke, Bix		Entertainment	3822				Jazz Musician
Beiderlinden, Maj Gen. William A.	1895-1981	Military	30				World War II U.S. general
Beightler, Maj Gen Robert S.	1892-1978	Military	30				World War II U.S. general
Beinhorn, Elly		Aviation	10	22	40	30	Ger. Aviation Pioneer
Beisswenger, Hans		Military	45			184	Luftwaffe Ace
Beith, Ian Hay (John)		Author	10	30	60	20	Br. Novelist, Playwright
Beke, Charles Tilstone		Explorer	20	50	125		Br. Geographer. Nile Source
Bekhterev, Vladimir	1857-1927	Science		1750	2500		Russ. Neuropathologist/Pavlov
Bekins, Milo		Business	35	45	160	125	Bekins Van & Storage Co.
Bel Geddes, Barbara		Entertainment	10			25	Dallas. NY Drama Critic Award
Bel Geddes, Norman		Artist	20	50	155	75	Scenic Designer Theater
Bela, Magyar		Astronaut	10			25	Hungary

NAME	DATE	CATEGORY	SIG	LS/DS	ALS	SP	COMMENTS
Belafonte, Harry		Entertainment	10	15		45	
Belafonte, Shari		Entertainment	5	6	15	25	
Belasco, David		Entertainment	35	30	70	95	Theatrical Producer
Belaunde, Fernando T.		Head of State	10	20	50	25	
Belcher, Edward, Sir		Military-Navy	15	35	60		Arctic Exped.for J. Franklin
Belcher, Jonathan	1681-1757	Colonial America	210	362	650		Gov. MA, NH, NJ. Instrumental as Fndr. Princeton
Belder, Bastiaan		Political	10			15	Member European Parliament
Belita		Entertainment	15	25	45	45	
Belknap, George		Civil War	45		60		Union Naval Officer. C.W. Cabinet
Belknap, Reginald R.	1871-1959	Military	50	150			U.S. Admiral. Invented Collapsible Submarine Net
Belknap, William W.		Civil War,Cabinet	48	85	112	350	Union General, Sec'y War(Grant) Impeached
Bell, Alexander Graham	1847-1922	Science	901	1251	3163	2958	Inventor of Telephone, ALS/TLS cont 1500-10000
Bell, Brig. Gen. Marcus B.	1893-1981	Military	30				World War II U.S. general
Bell, Caspar Wistar	1819-1898	Civil War	64				Member of the Confederate Congress
Bell, Catherine		Entertainment	6			40	Actress. Pin-Up 55
Bell, Charles H.	1798-1875	Civil War	50	100	145		Union Naval Captain, Admiral
Bell, Charles, Sir	1774-1842	Science	150		475		Scottish Surgeon-Anatomist.Nervous Systm Authority
Bell, Chris B		Congress	10			15	Member U.S. Congress
Bell, Digby		Entertainment	12			20	Vintage Actor
Bell, Eric Temple (John Taine)		Author	30		130	55	Scot., Math Books, Sci-Fi
Bell, Griffin		Cabinet	10			25	Att'y General
Bell, Henry H.	1808-1868	Civil War	60	150			Rear Adm under Farragut
Bell, Herbert A.		Business	15	20	75	50	
Bell, Hiram Parks	1827-1907	Civil War	57	117			Member of the Confederate Congress
Bell, John		Cabinet	46	145			W.H. Harrison, Tyler Sec'y War
Bell, Lauralee		Entertainment	10	12		20	Soaps Actress
Bell, Martin		Celebrity	10			15	newsreader
Bell, Peter Hansborough		Governor		195			Gov. TX 1849-53
Bell, Rex		Entertainment	50			125	
Bell, Terrel H.		Cabinet	5	15	26	15	Sec'y Education
Bell, Tyree Harris	1815-1902	Civil War	65	155	239		CSA Gen.
Bell, Vanessa		Artist	100				Br. Artist-Sister of Virginia Woolf
Bellamy Bros.		Country Music	7			20	Howard & David
Bellamy, Brigadier Robert Hugh	1910-1972	Military	25				World War II British general
Bellamy, David, Prof.		Celebrity	10			15	naturalist
Bellamy, Edward	1850-1898	Author	25	75	150		Novelist
Bellamy, Elizabeth W.		Author	3	9	18		
Bellamy, Madge		Entertainment	10	15	40	35	
Bellamy, Ralph	1904-1991	Entertainment	14	20	28	46	Actor-Leading Man & Character-Films, Stage
Bellanca, Giuseppe M.		Aviation	40	85	160	125	Bellanca Aircraft Designer-Mfg.
Belle, Lulu		Entertainment	10			20	C & W
Beller, Kathleen		Entertainment	6	8	15	15	
Belleri, Marguerite		Entertainment	5		30	25	Metropolitan Opera 1917-20
Bellew, John Chippendall		Clergy	10	20	25	20	
Belli, Melvin		Law	10	15	35	20	Trial Attorney

NAME	DATE	CATEGORY	SIG	LS/DS	ALS	SP	COMMENTS
Belliard, A.D. (Count)	1769-1832	Military	25	55	175		Fr. Gen. under Napoleon
Bellincioni, Gemma		Entertainment	118		195	175	It. Soprano.Sang Premiere of 'Cavalleria Rusticana
Bellini, Vincenzo	1801-1835	Composer	557		5025		It. Opera. 'Norma', 'La Sonnambula'
Bellmer, Hans	1902-1975	Artist	55	160	500		Ger. Surrealist Painter, Engraver, Photographer
Bellmon, Henry Louis		Senate	15	20		20	Senator OK, Gov. OK
Belloc, Hilaire	1870-1953	Author	40	85	128	50	Versatile Novelist, Poet,Critic
Belloc-Lowndes, Marie		Author	15	40	110	30	Br.Author of Historical Works
Bellon, Leoncadia		Entertainment	16			45	Opera, Film
Bellonte, Maurice		Aviation	75	145	270	345	
Bellow, Saul	1915-	Author	35	106	275	73	Nobel Literature 1976. Novelist
Bellows, George	1882-1925	Artist	95	225	375		Urban Scenes, Sports, Landscape
Bellows, Henry W.	1814-1882	Clergy	20	40	55		Founder Antioch College. Unitariarn Clergyman
Bellson, Louis		Entertainment	25		55	70	Jazz Drummer
Bellwood, Pamela		Entertainment	6	9	15	26	
Belmont, August	1816-1890	Business	212	875	1275	683	Banker, Diplomat, Belmont Park Stk.Cert. S 2500
Belmont, August, Jr.		Business	45	120			
Belmont, August, Mrs.		Socialite	15	25	40		
Belsham, Thomas		Clergy	15	20	35	30	
Belushi, James		Entertainment	10	15	20	30	
Belushi, John	1949-1982	Entertainment	250			712	Comedian. 'Second City', 'Sat. Nite Live'
Bemelmans, Ludwig		Author	45	105	255	50	Writer-Illustrator. Novelist
Benacerraf, Baruj		Science	27	55		40	Nobel Medicine-Physiology
Benatar, Pat		Entertainment	20			70	
Benavidez, Roy		Military	10	25	40	20	
Benchley, Peter		Author	15	25	50	20	Sketch of Jaws S 15-35
Benchley, Robert		Author	35	80	195	75	Am. Drama Critic, Humorist
Bendix, William	1906-1964	Entertainment	35	30	60	121	
Benederet, Bea		Entertainment	40			100	
Benedict XV, Pope		Clergy	125	325	450	550	
Benedict, Dick		Entertainment	15	20	25	30	
Benedict, Julius, Sir		Composer	15			25	Br. Pianist
Benedict, Maj. Gen. Jay L.	1882-1953	Military	30				World War II U.S. general
Benedict, William		Entertainment	25			60	
Beneke, Tex		Entertainment	30			105	Sax for Glenn Miller. Big Band
Benes, Eduard	1884-1948	Head of State	85	90	145	200	P.M. & President Czech.
Benet, Stephen Vincent	1898-1943	Author	80	172	200	150	Poet, Novelist. Pulitzer (2)
Ben-Gurion, David	1886-1973	Head of State	128	842	1852	478	1st Prime Minister of Israel. LS-ANS/Cont. 5500
Benham, George W. (WD)		Civil War	120	225	389		Union Gen.
Benham, Henry W.	1813-1884	Civil War	55	85	150		Union Gen.
Benighi, Roberto		Entertainment	6			39	Actor. Films
Bening, Annette		Entertainment	8	25	45	47	Actress
Benjamin, Judah P.	1811-1884	Civil War	322	538	858		CSA Gen. & Sec'y of State
Benjamin, Judah P.(WD)		Civil War	448	1871	2750		CSA Sec'y of State
Benjamin, Park	1809-1864	Author		40			American Journalist
Benjamin, Richard		Entertainment	8			42	Actor-Director

NAME	DATE	CATEGORY	SIG	LS/DS	ALS	SP	COMMENTS
Bennett, Arnold		Author	40	175			Br. Novelist
Bennett, Bruce (Herman Brix)		Entertainment	12	24	30	35	Early Tarzan. Athlete as Herman Brix
Bennett, Constance		Entertainment	30	60	120	81	Glamour Leading Lady of 30's-40's
Bennett, Floyd		Aviation	115	370	750	500	Pilot with Byrd over North Pole
Bennett, James Gordon	1841-1918	Publisher	45	138	150		Financed Stanley-Livingstone African Expedition
Bennett, Joan	1910-1990	Entertainment	16	18	35	66	Actress. Leading Lady Sister of Constance
Bennett, Johnstone		Entertainment	15			35	Actress with Mansfield
Bennett, Julie		Entertainment	3	3	6	10	
Bennett, Lerone Jr.		Celebrity	10			15	motivational speaker
Bennett, Lt. Gen. Henry G.	1887-1962	Military	30				World War II Australian general
Bennett, Richard		Entertainment	15			35	Stage & Silent Films
Bennett, Robert Russell		Composer	40		250	95	Great Broadway Composer. Academy Award
Bennett, Robert		Legal	15			35	Power Att'y for Pres. Clinton vs Paula Jones
Bennett, Robert		Senate	10			15	United States Senate (R - UT)
Bennett, Samuel F.		Composer	30	75	150		In the Sweet Bye & Bye., AQS 920
Bennett, Spencer Gordon		Entertainment	10			25	
Bennett, Tony	b. 1926	Entertainment	5	12	20	35	Top Recording & Club Singer
Bennett, Wallace F.		Senate	5	10	20	15	Senator UT
Bennett, William J.		Author-Cabinet	20	60	75	55	Book of Virtues.Sec'y Ed.
Bennett, Wm. Andrew		Head of State	4	10	15	10	
Benning, Henry Lewis	1814-1875	Civil War	175	317	472		CSA Gen., Statesman. Fort Benning, GA So Named
Benny, Jack	1894-1974	Entertainment	68	235		184	Great Radio-TV Comedian
Benois, Alexander		Artist	45	195	425		Rus. Designed Sets, Costumes
Benoit, Francois (Circa 1804)		Merchant		500			Famous Fur Trader
Benoy, Brigadier James Francis	1896-1972	Military	25				World War II British general
Benoy, Maj. Gen. John Meredith	1896-1977	Military	25				World War II British general
Benson, Arthur Christopher	1862-1925	Celebrity			75		'MAN OF LETTERS'
Benson, Edward Frederic	1867-1940	Author	20	40	112		Satirical, Macabre Novels. Scholar
Benson, Edward W., Archbishop		Clergy	20	35	55	35	
Benson, Egbert		Revolutionary War	40	75	170		Continental Congress
Benson, Elmer A.		Governor	5	12	20	15	Governor & Senator MN
Benson, Ezra Taft	1899-1994	Cabinet	12	25	55	40	Sec'y Agriculture, Pres. Mormon Church
Benson, Frank Robert, Sir		Entertainment	15	20	35	20	Vintage Br. Actor
Benson, George		Entertainment	15			25	Music
Benson, Jodi		Entertainment	10			35	Actress. Disney Voice
Benson, Maj. Gen. Edward Riou	1903-1985	Military	25				World War II British general
Benson, Richard Meux		Clergy	35	55	65	75	
Benson, Robbie		Entertainment	15	16	20	22	Juvenile & Adult Actor. Disney Voice Over
Benson, William S.		Military	10	20	35	25	Adm. USN WW I
Bent, James Theodore	1852-1897	Explorer	10	10	35	25	Br.Archaeologist. Greece, Asia Minor, Abyssinia
Bent, Maj Gen Adrianus R. v. den	1883-1957	Military	20				World War II Dutch general
Benteen, Frederick W.		Civil War/ Military		2833	3700	4250	Involved in the Battle of Big Horn 1876
Bentham, Jeremy	1748-1832	Jurist-Philosopher	120		1300		Br. Writer etc.
Benton, Barbi		Entertainment	5	6	15	20	
Benton, Debra		Celebrity	10			15	motivational speaker

NAME	DATE	CATEGORY	SIG	LS/DS	ALS	SP	COMMENTS
Benton, Robert		Entertainment	10			20	AA Director. 'Kramer vs Kramer', 'Bonnie & Clyde'
Benton, Samuel	1820-1864	Civil War	412	675			CSA Gen. Died Battle of Atlanta 1864
Benton, Thomas Hart	1782-1858	Senate/Congress	84	110	137		30-Year Senator From Missouri
Benton, Thomas Hart	1889-1975	Artist	100	250	765		ALS/Content 1,350
Benton, William Plummer	1828-1867	Civil War	95	166			Union Gen. Rare
Benton, William	1900-1973	Senate	10	30	65	20	Publisher, Statesman, Businessman, Sen. CT
Bentsen, Lloyd		Senate-Cabinet	10	30		20	Senator TX, Sec'y Treas.
Ben-Ur, Aviva		Author	8			12	Sephardic history
Ben-Yehuda, Eliezer		Author	35	175	425		Jewish Scholar
Benzali, Daniel		Entertainment	10			20	actor
Benzell, Mimi		Entertainment	15			35	Opera
Ben-Zvi, Itzhak	1884-1963	Head of State	135	170	250	160	2nd President Israel
Beradino, John	1917-1996	Entertainment	25			40	Actor 'Our Gang' comedies, Baseball Player
Berdan, Hiram	1824-1893	Civil War		506	646		Union General
Berdyaev, Nikolai	1874-1948	Philosopher	75	100	145	175	Russ. Orth. Layman, Marxist. Critic of Both
Berend, Rolf		Political	10			15	Member European Parliament
Berenger, Tom		Entertainment	10			48	Actor
Berenguer Fuster, Luis		Political	10			15	Member European Parliament
Berenschot, Lt. Gen. Gerardus J.	1887-1941	Military	20				World War II Dutch general
Berenson, Marisa		Entertainment	10	12	15	25	Model-Actress. Willowy Member International Jet Set
Berenstain, Stan*		Cartoonist	20			75	'Berenstain Bear'
Beres, Pervenche		Political	10			15	Member European Parliament
Beresford, Bruce		Celebrity	10			15	film industry
Beresford, Charles, Lord	1846-1919	Military	15	35	100	80	Br. Admiral. Bombardment Alexandria. Khartoum Exped
Beresford, Maj Gen Sir G. de la P.	1884-1965	Military	25				World War II British general
Bereuter, Doug B		Congress	10			15	Member U.S. Congress
Berfson, Henri-Louis		Author	30	80	155		
Berg, Alban	1885-1935	Composer	135	660	1502		Austrian. Atonal Music. Orchestral, Songs
Berg, Gertrude		Entertainment	18	15	25	35	Vintage Actress. Stage & Radio's Longtime Serial
Berg, Moe	1902-1972	Celebrity	225				Lawyer, Mathematician, Spy
Berg, Paul		Science	27	35	65	40	Nobel Chemistry
Berg, Peter		Entertainment	6			30	Actor-Director
Berganza, Teresa		Entertainment	9			48	Opera
Bergdorf, Gary		Entertainment	10			35	'Radar'. Mash
Bergen, Candice		Entertainment	12	20	25	43	Actress. Films. Emmy Awards
Bergen, Edgar	1903-1978	Entertainment	55	80	125	162	Am. Ventriloquist-Comedian-Actor. Special AA
Bergen, Frances		Entertainment	5	6	10	10	
Bergen, Polly	1930-	Entertainment	9	10	18	26	Actress, Singer, Films, TV. Cosmetics Mfg.
Berger, Erna		Entertainment	10			30	Opera
Berger, Gottlob		Military	40	120	200	75	
Berger, Maria		Political	10			15	Member European Parliament
Berger, Senta		Entertainment	10	15	35	30	Actress. Leading Lady of Am. & International Films
Bergere, Lee		Entertainment	5	4	9	15	
Bergeron, Marion		Beauty Queen	15			75	Miss America 1934
Berggrav, Eivind Josef		Clergy		50			Bishop of Norway. World Council of Churches

NAME	DATE	CATEGORY	SIG	LS/DS	ALS	SP	COMMENTS
Bergh, Henry	1811-1888	Reformer	85		400		Founder ASPCA
Bergin, Brig. Gen. William E.	1892-1978	Military	30				World War II U.S. general
Bergin, Patrick		Entertainment	10			20	actor
Bergland, Bob		Cabinet	5	10	20	15	Sec'y Agriculture, Congress MN
Bergman, Ingmar		Entertainment	32	40	50	175	Swe. Film Director
Bergman, Ingrid	1913-1982	Entertainment	119	212	272	327	3x Academy Award Winner. SPc 250-325
Bergman, Sandahl		Entertainment	10	8	15	20	
Bergman, Stephen J.		Celebrity	10			15	medical expert
Bergner, Elizabeth	1898-1968	Entertainment	20	35	60	30	Pol-Born Actress. Made Reputation/Max Reinhardt
Bergonzi, Carlo		Entertainment	30			65	Opera
Bergson, Henri	1859-1941	Author	40	125			Philosopher. Nobel Literature 1928. Educator
Bergstein, Milton		Celebrity	10			15	financial expert
Beria, Lavrenty Pavlovich	1899-1953	Military		563	2645		Head of Soviet Secret police
Berio, Luciano		Composer	20	30	75		
Beriot, Charles Auguste de		Composer	40		175		Violinist Virtuoso. Visual Artist
Berjerac, Jacques		Entertainment	15			30	Fr. Actor of Am. Films.40's-50'2
Berkeley, Busby		Entertainment	59	155	275	295	Dance Choreographer-Director
Berkley, Elizabeth		Entertainment	10			33	'Showgirls' ,actress
Berkley, Shelley B		Congress	10			15	Member U.S. Congress
Berkoff, Steven		Entertainment	10			20	actor
Berkowitz, Bob		Celebrity	10			15	media/TV personality
Berkowitz, David		Criminal	85	90	250		Son of Sam, Serial Murderer
Berlato, Sergio		Political	10			15	Member European Parliament
Berle, Adolph	1895-1971	Economist	15	35			Am. Member of FDR's Original 'Brain Trust'
Berle, Milton		Entertainment	15	30	35	72	Comedian. Successful Vaudeville,Radio,'MR. TV'
Berlier, Jean Baptiste	1843-1911	Science	15	30	45		Fr.Engineer. Paris Underground RR System
Berlier, Theophile, Count		Fr. Revolution	50	150	295		
Berlik, Jan		Entertainment	25			50	Czech. Operatic Tenor
Berlin, Gen. of Artillery Wilhelm	1889-1987	Military	25				World War II German general
Berlin, Irving	1888-1990	Composer	138	650	1038	1310	AMusQS 2,300. Many TLS's & ALS's Signed Irving
Berlioz, Hector	1803-1869	Composer	245	1225	1430		Distinguished Fr. Composer. AMusQS 3,900-8,500
Berlitz, Charles		Business	15	25		35	Language Educator
Berman, Eugene	1899-1972	Artist	40	105	195		Rus.-Born Painter-Designer
Berman, Howard L. B		Congress	10			15	Member U.S. Congress
Berman, Pandro S.		Entertainment	20	40		50	Film Producer. 1977 Irving Thalberg Memorial Award
Berman, Shelley		Entertainment	5	3	6	10	Comedian
Bernacchi, Antonio		Entertainment			2500		Classical Singer (Castrato) for Handel
Bernadotte, Jean-Baptiste		Royalty	120	296	650		Charles XIV John. Marshal of Nap.
Bernard, Claude	1813-1878	Science	145		602		Fr. Fndr. Experimental Medicine
Bernard, Crystal		Entertainment	13			40	Actress. 'Wings'
Bernard, Francis, Sir	1712-1779	Colonial Governor	175	522	750		Col.Gov. Mass. Bay Colony
Bernard, John Henry, Archbishop		Clergy	95	45	50	40	
Bernard, Lt. Gen. Denis Kirwan	1882-1956	Military	25				World War II British general
Bernard, Simon	1779-1839	Military	50	125			Fr. Military Eng'r. Nap.at Waterloo. US Gen. 1816
Berndt, Walter*		Cartoonist	10			50	'Smitty'

NAME	DATE	CATEGORY	SIG	LS/DS	ALS	SP	COMMENTS
Berners-Lee, Tim		Science	10			30	Creator of the worldwide web
Bernhard, Sandra		Entertainment	10	6		15	Comedienne.
Bernhardt, Sarah	1844-1923	Entertainment	114	275	373	850	'The Divine Sarah'. Great French Actress
Bernie, Ben		Entertainment	20		25	25	Big Band Leader-M.C.-Comedian.
Bernié, Jean-Louis		Political	10			15	Member European Parliament
Berniquiet, Maj. Gen. André	1878-1940	Military	20				World War II French general
Bernsen, Corbin		Entertainment	15	20	40	40	Actor. 'L.A. Law' etc.
Bernstein, Elmer		Composer	25	40	125	50	Am. Composer-Conductor. ALS/Cont 600
Bernstein, Leonard	1918-1990	Composer	124	299	681	203	AMusMsS 1,600, 4,500. 3x5 SP 120, AMsS 1450-2990
Bernstorff, John H., Graf von		Diplomat	30		100		German Ambass. To US. Member Ger. Reistag
Berosini, Josephine		Entertainment	5	10	25	30	
Berrien, J. Macpherson	1781-1856	Cabinet	30	55	105		Jackson Att'y General
Berrigan, Daniel, Fr.		Clergy	30	30	65	40	Controversial Political Priest
Berry, Brig. Gen. Robert W.	1902-1960	Military	30				World War II U.S. general
Berry, Chuck		Entertainment	50	275		156	Rock. Alb. S 115
Berry, Halle		Entertainment	15			61	Actress, AA
Berry, Hiram G. (WD)	1824-1863	Civil War	475	909			Killed in Action
Berry, Hiram G.	1824-1863	Civil War	388	783			Union Gen. Killed in Action
Berry, Jim*		Cartoonist	10			35	'Berry's World'
Berry, Ken		Entertainment	5	6	15	30	Actor. 'F Troop', 'Mama's Family'
Berry, Lucien		Military	15	50		55	General WW I
Berry, Marion B		Congress	10			15	Member U.S. Congress
Berry, Mary		Celebrity	10			15	TV Chef
Berry, Nick		Entertainment	10			20	Actor
Berry, Richard	1936-1997	Entertainment	30			60	Composer 'Louie, Louie'
Berry, Sidney M.		Clergy	10	15	25		
Berry, Tom		Governor	5			25	Gov. SD
Berry, William H.		Civil War	20				6th Missouri Survivor
Berryman, Clifford*		Artist	55	75	95	150	'Created The 'Teddy Bear'
Berryman, John	1914-1972	Author	75	300			'64 Pulitzer for Poetry. Short Stories
Berryman, Lt. Gen. Frank Horton	1894-1981	Military	20				World War II Australian general
Bertelson, Richard L.		Aviation	10	25	38	30	Navy ACE, WW II
Berthier, L. Alexandre	1753-1815	Napoleonic Wars	75	143	258		Marshal of Napoleon
Berthold, Rudolf		Aviation	200	350	650	475	ACE, WW I, The Iron Knight
Berthollet, Claude-Louis, Count	1748-1822	Science	60	150	330		Fr. Chemist. Senator of Napoleon
Berthu, Georges		Political	10			15	Member European Parliament
Bertinelli, Valerie		Entertainment	10	12	25	25	Actress. TV-Films
Bertinotti, Fausto		Political	10			15	Member European Parliament
Bertolucci, Bernardo	1940-	Entertainment	15			35	Film Director. 'Last Tango in Paris'
Bertram, Laura		Entertainment	10			20	actress
Bertrand, Henri G.	1773-1844	Military	70	120	305		Count Bertrand. General. Chamberlain to Napoleon
Berwick, Duke (J. Fitzjames)	1670-1734	Fr. Military	150	400			Gen. of Louis XIV, Marshal Fr.
Berzelius, Jons Jacob	1779-1848	Science	75	165	475		Swe. Chemist. Chemical Symbols
Besant, Annie Wood	1847-1933	Clergy	50	245	398		Br. Radical Free-Thinker.
Besant, Walter	1836-1901	Author	35	125	130	125	Br. Novelist. AMsS 9000

NAME	DATE	CATEGORY	SIG	LS/DS	ALS	SP	COMMENTS
Besch, Bibi		Entertainment	5	4	15	20	
Beser, Jacob		Aviation	50	100		63	Both Atomic Missions
Besnard, Albert	1849-1934	Artist		65			French post-impressionist artist
Bess, Gordon*		Cartoonist	5			25	'Redeye'
Bessell, Brig. Gen. William W. Jr.	1901-1977	Military	30				World War II U.S. general
Bessell, Ted		Entertainment	10	20		25	Boyfriend in 'That Girl'
Bessell-Browne, Brigadier Alfred	1877-1947	Military	20				World War II Australian general
Bessemer, Henry, Sir	1813-1898	Metallurgist-Inventor	35	60	200	95	Invented Blast Furnace For Producing Steel
Besser, Joe		Entertainment	33	40	75	75	One of 'The Three Stooges'
Bessieres, Bertrand		Fr. Revolution	55	100			
Bessieres, Jean-Baptiste	1766-1813	Fr. Military	175	337			Marshal of France under Napoleon
Besson, Gen Antoine-Marie-B.	1876-1969	Military	20				World War II French general
Besson, General Frank S. Jr.	1910-1985	Military	30				World War II U.S. general
Best, Charles H.	1899-1978	Science	107	188	290	125	Discovered Insulin/Banting
Best, Edna	1900-1974	Entertainment	35	42	32	50	Brit. Character Actress. Films & Stage
Best, James	1926-	Entertainment	7	10	15	20	Actor 'Dukes of Hazzard'
Best, Lt. Gen. Petrus W.	1881-1960	Military	20				World War II Dutch general
Best, Pete		Entertainment	32			112	Pre Ringo. Beatles Drummer
Best, Willie	1916-1962	Entertainment	50			150	Vintage Afro-Am. Film Actor
Bestor, Don		Bandleader	15			30	Jack Benny's 1st Bandleader
Beswick, Martine		Entertainment	5	6	15	15	
Betham-Edwards, Matilda		Author	5	10	22		
Bethe, Hans, Dr.		Science	35	55		45	Nobel Physics
Bethea, Maj. Gen. James A.	1887-1984	Military	30				World War II U.S. general
Bethouart, General Marie-Emil	1890-1982	Military	20				World War II French general
Bethune, Mary McLeod	1875-1955	Educator	125	325	500	175	Black Teacher, Activist. TLS/Cont. 895
Betjeman, John, Sir	1906-1984	Author	40	111	135	50	Br. Poet Laureate
Bett, William Rose	1886-1956	Author	15	35	65	40	Poet, Editor. Pulitzer
Bettelheim, Bruno		Science	35	65		150	Psychiatrist researched Autism
Bettger, Lyle	1915-	Entertainment	8			20	Actor. Films. 50's. Eventually Western Heavy Roles
Betts, Brig. Gen. Edward C.	1890-1946	Military	30				World War II U.S. general
Betts, Brig. Gen. Thomas J.	1894-1977	Military	30				World War II U.S. general
Betz, Carl	1920-1978	Entertainment	40			100	Actor. 50's. Husband 'Donna Reed Show'
Beugnot, J.C., Count		Fr. Military	85	160			
Beverage, John		Civil War	30	85			Union Gen., Gov. IL
Beveridge, Albert J.	1862-1927	Congress	5	20	35		US Sen., Historian. Organizer of Progressive Party
Beveridge, Don		Celebrity	10			15	motivational speaker
Bevin, Ernest	1881-1951	Statesman	25	55	125	45	Br. Powerful Union Leader. NATO Treaty
Bewick, Thomas	1753-1828	Artist	105	275	625		Br. Illustrator, Wood Engraver
Bexley, Don 'Bubba'		Entertainment	7	15	30	35	Actor-Comedian 'Sanford & Son'
Bey, Turhan	1920-	Entertainment	15	20	35	30	Actor. Exotic & Mysterious Roles in 40's Films
Beyer, Gen. of Infantry Eugen	1882-1940	Military	25				World War II German general
Beyer, Gen. of Infantry Franz	1892-1968	Military	25				World War II German general
Beyette, Brig. Gen. Hubert W.	1891-1968	Military	30				World War II U.S. general
Beysen, Ward		Political	10			15	Member European Parliament

NAME	DATE	CATEGORY	SIG	LS/DS	ALS	SP	COMMENTS
Bhutto, Benazir		Celebrity	10			15	political celebrity
Bhutto, Zulfikar Ali	1928-1979	Head of State	35	102	175	200	Pakistan, Pres. & Prime Minister. Coup. Executed
Biaggi, Mario		Senate/Congress	5	15		15	Congressman NY. NY Police MOH
Biagi, Simon		Celebrity	10			15	weather presenter
Bialik, Chaim N.	1873-1934	Author	65	225	425	115	Jewish Poet
Bias, Lonise Dr.		Celebrity	10			15	motivational speaker
Biasini, Piero		Entertainment	10			35	Opera
Bibb, George M.	1776-1859	Cabinet	30	45	80		Early Sec'y Treas.,Senator KY
Bibb, Wm. Wyatt	1781-1820	Governor	25	45			Gov. GA
Bickelhaupt, Brig. Gen. Carroll O.	1888-1954	Military	30				World War II U.S. general
Bickersteth, Edward H., Bishop		Clergy	15	25	35	35	
Bickford, Charles	1889-1967	Entertainment	30	45	65	100	Actor. Burlesque 1914-Broadway 1919-Films 1929
Biddle, Clement Carroll	1784-1855	Military	25	40	75		Col. of 1st Inf. PA. 1812. Political Science
Biddle, Clement	1740-1814	Revolutionary War	176	478	714		Revolutionary Officer, Merchant, War Hero
Biddle, Francis	1886-1968	Cabinet	20	35	75		Att'y General. Judge Intern'l Tribunal-Nurnberg
Biddle, George		Artist	25	85	210		
Biddle, Nicholas	1786-1844	Business	138	310	505		Pres. U.S. Bank, Financier
Biden, Joseph		Senate	10			15	United States Senate (D - DE)
Bidwell, Daniel Davidson	1819-1864	Civil War	280		1128		Union Gen. ALS '63 1595, KIA 1864
Bidwell, John	1819-1900	Western Pioneer	55	160	220		Calif. Pioneer, Pres. Candidate-Prohibition Ticket
Biehn, Michael		Entertainment	10	10	20	35	Actor
Bieler, Gen. of Infantry Bruno	1888-1966	Military	25				World War II German general
Bierbauer, Charles		Celebrity	10			15	media/TV personality
Bierce, Ambrose	1842-1914	Author	275	360	698		Journalist,Short Stories. Literary ALS 1250-2750
Bieri, Ramon		Entertainment	10			35	
Bierstadt, Albert	1830-1902	Artist	140	220	512		Of the Hudson River School. Landscapes
Biery, James S.		Senate/Congress	10	15		25	Congressman PA
Big Bopper		Entertainment	950				Rock. Killed In Plane Crash
Big Man, Chief Max		Native American	30			60	Chief
Bigard, Barney		Entertainment	70			150	Jazz Clarinet, Ten. Sax
Bigelow, Erastus B.	1814-1879	Business-Inventor	100	290	595		Power Looms for Carpet Weaving
Bigelow, John	1817-1911	Publisher	5	20	55	25	Editor& Co-Owner NY Evening Post. Diplomat
Bigelow, Poultney	1855-1954	Journalist	5		22		Traveller, Author. Son of John
Bigge, Arthur, Sir		Military	10	30	65		
Bigger, Margaret		Author	8			12	humor books
Biggers, Earl Derr		Author	150	210	382	350	Am. Novelist,Mystery Writer.Created 'Charlie Chan'
Biggert, Judy B		Congress	10			15	Member U.S. Congress
Biggs, Asa		Civil War	35	70			CSA Judge, US Senator NC
Biggs, Matthew		Celebrity	10			15	home/gardening expert
Biggs, Ronnie		Criminal	25			95	Train Robber. His Book Signed 100
Bigliardo, Roberto Felice		Political	10			15	Member European Parliament
Bikel, Theodore	1924-	Entertainment	5	20		35	Vienna-Born Character Actor-Singer
Bilbo, Theodore G.	1877-1947	Senate	20	30		25	Senator MS, Gov. MS. Demagogue, Racist
Bilirakis, Michael B		Congress	10			15	Member U.S. Congress
Bill, Max	1908-1994	Artist	10	25	40	35	Swiss Painter & Sculptor. Pc Repro Sculpture S 60

NAME	DATE	CATEGORY	SIG	LS/DS	ALS	SP	COMMENTS
Bill, Tony		Entertainment	10			20	Actor, Film Director, Producer-'The Sting'
Billings, John		Civil War	45	117	250		Union Surgeon
Billings, Josh	1818-1885	Author	25	80	165	73	American Humorist. (H.W.Shaw)
Billingsley, Barbara		Entertainment	5	10	15	20	Actress.'Leave It To Beaver'
Billingsley, Peter		Entertainment	4			12	'Xmas Story' SP 30
Billington, E.		Entertainment	55		250		Opera. Internationally Famous Prima Donna.
Billington, Jill		Celebrity	10			15	home/gardening expert
Billo, James D.		Aviation	10	25	40	30	Navy ACE, WW II
Billotte, Gen. Gaston-Henri-Gus.	1875-1940	Military	20				World War II French general
Billotte, Maj Gen Pierre-Arm.-Gas.	1906-1992	Military	20				World War II French general
Billroth, Theodor	1829-1894	Science	45	225	295		Ger. Surgeon. Use of Antisepsis
Binci, Mario		Entertainment	15			45	Opera
Bineau, Gen Henri-Marie-Aug.	1873-1944	Military	20				World War II French general
Bing, Herman	1889-1947	Entertainment	20			40	Actor. Ger. Born. Form Circus Clown, Vaudevilian
Bing, Rudolph	1903-1997	Entertainment	15	35	46	35	Longtime Metropolitan Opera Director
Bingaman, Jeff		Senate	10			15	United States Senate (D - NM)
Bingham, Amelia		Entertainment	6	10	15	25	
Bingham, Henry		Civil War	55		110		Union Gen., MOH Wilderness
Bingham, John A.		Congress	30	35	90		MOC. OH, Lincoln Judge Adv.
Bingham, Judson David	1831-1909	Civil War	45	140	185		Union General
Bingham, Traci		Entertainment	10			46	Actress. Pin-Up 55
Bingham, William	1752-1804	Revolutionary War	120	315	340		Continental Congr.Sen.PA. Fndr.1st Bank in Country
Binney, Thomas		Clergy	20	30	45	35	
Binnig, Gerd, Dr.		Science	20	60		45	Nobel Physics
Binns, Edward		Entertainment	5	4	9	10	Actor. Familiar Face in Many Supporting Roles
Binoche, Juliette		Entertainment	17			60	Actress. 'English Patient'
Biot, Jean Baptiste	1774-1862	Science	100		575		Fr. Mathematician, Physicist, Astronomer
Birch, Thora		Entertainment	6			45	Talented Young Actress
Bird & John Fortune, John		Celebrity	10			15	comedian
Bird, Billie		Entertainment	7			15	Character actress
Bird, Lt. Gen. Sir Clarence August	1885-1986	Military	25				World War II British general
Birdsall, Jesse		Entertainment	10			20	Actor
Birdseye, Clarence	1886-1956	Business	100	340	500	262	Frozen Foods.Prolific Inventor. Over 300 Patents
Birdwood, William R., Sir	1865-1951	Military	45	145			Br. Fld. Marshal, WW I
Birendra, Bir B.		Head of State	10	15		25	Prime Minister Nepal
Birge, Henry Warner	1825-1888	Civil War	46	124	230		Union general
Birkhead, Lt. Gen. Claude V.	1880-1950	Military	30				World War II U.S. general
Birks, Brig. Gen. Hammond D.	1896-1973	Military	30				World War II U.S. general
Birks, Maj. Gen. Horace Leslie	1897-1985	Military	25				World War II British general
Birney, David Bell	1825-1864	Civil War	243	383	572		Union Gen. ANS '63 990. Sig/Rank 365
Birney, David		Entertainment	5	6	15	20	Actor
Birney, William	1819-1907	Civil War	40	89	116		Union General Sig/Rank 80
Bisbee, Horatio, Jr.		Civil War	25	45	105		Union Officer & MOC
Bishop Jr., Sanford D. B		Congress	10			15	Member U.S. Congress
Bishop, Barry		Celebrity	7	14			

NAME	DATE	CATEGORY	SIG	LS/DS	ALS	SP	COMMENTS
Bishop, Elizabeth	1911-1979	Author	35	125			Am. Poet. Pulitzer Prize '55
Bishop, J. Michael, Dr.		Science	25	40		35	Nobel Medicine
Bishop, Jim		Author	15	35	50	20	Journalist. Best Selling Novels. 'The Daya..' Book
Bishop, Joey	1918-	Entertainment	9	12	15	22	Comedian member of Sinatra 'Rat Pack' group
Bishop, Julie		Entertainment	6	8	15	15	Actress
Bishop, Maj Gen Sir Wm. H. Alex.	1897-1984	Military	25				World War II British general
Bishop, Rob B		Congress	10			15	Member U.S. Congress
Bishop, Stephen		Entertainment	5			15	Rock Star
Bishop, Timothy H. B		Congress	10			15	Member U.S. Congress
Bishop, Wm. 'Billy'	1894-1956	Aviation	150	225	325	170	ACE, WW I, 72 Kills
Bismark, Prince Otto von	1815-1898	Royalty	250	600	745	920	The Iron Chancellor
Bispham, David		Entertainment	60	80	110	120	Opera
Bissell, Brig. Gen. John T.B.	1893-1976	Military	30				World War II U.S. general
Bissell, Clayton L.		Aviation	25	40	100		
Bissell, Emily P.	1861-1948	Humanitarian	125				Introduced U.S Xmas Seals
Bissell, Whit	1919-	Entertainment	10		15	20	Character Actor in Films from Mid-40's
Bissell, William H.		Governor	10	28	60		Governor IL, MOC
Bisset, Jacqueline	1944-	Entertainment	12	20	30	33	Brit. Actress. Leading Roles Since 70's
Bissett, Josie		Entertainment	12			53	Actress, 'Melrose Place'
Bissit, J.E.		Br. Navy	10	25		20	Commander HMS Queen Eliz.
Bitter, Karl Theodore	1867-1915	Artist	25	75	155	100	Am. Sculptor
Bittrich, Wilhelm		Military	27	70	135	60	
Bixby, Bill	1934-1993	Entertainment	10	58	40	68	Actor. Premature Death
Bixby, Brig. Gen. Ernest A.	1899-1965	Military	30				World War II U.S. general
Bizet, Georges	1838-1875	Composer	425	890	1791		Fr. Composer. 'Carmen', L'Arlesienne Suite
Bjerknes, Jacob A.B.	1887-1975	Science	35				Discovered Origin of Cyclones
Bjoerling, Jussi	1911-1960	Entertainment	500	650	1000	925	Great 20th Cent. Swedish Tenor. Died Early
Bjornson, Bjornstjerne	1832-1910	Author	50	65	345		3rd Nobel for Literature
Bjornstad, Alfred		Military	10	20	35		General WW I
Blacher, Boris		Composer	40				Rus-Ger. Classical & Experimental Music
Black, Alexander		Author	5	10	20	10	
Black, Brig. Gen. Frederick H.	1894-1986	Military	30				World War II U.S. general
Black, Brig. Gen. Garland C.	1894-1951	Military	30				World War II U.S. general
Black, Cilla		Celebrity	10			15	television presenter
Black, Clint		Entertainment	20			48	Country-Western
Black, Eugene R.		Business	5	20	30	15	
Black, Frank, Dr.		Conductor	10			35	NBC Dir. of Music in '40's
Black, Hugo	1886-1971	Supreme Court	40	120	285	95	Justice 1937-71.Bill of Rights, Constitution Champ
Black, Jack		Entertainment				35	Actor, comedian
Black, Jeremiah		Cabinet	30	60	115		Att'y General (Buchanan)
Black, John Charles	1835-1915	Civil War	50	125	169		Union General, MOH
Black, Karen		Entertainment	10	12	15	20	Actress. Memorable in 'Easy Rider','5 Easy Pieces'
Black, Richard B.		Military	10	25	45		
Black, William		Military	20			45	General WW I
Blackburn, Brig. Arthur Seaforth	1892-1960	Military	20				World War II Australian general

NAME	DATE	CATEGORY	SIG	LS/DS	ALS	SP	COMMENTS
Blackburn, John T.		Aviation	15	24	40	35	ACE, WW II
Blackburn, Luke P.		Governor	15	35			Governor KY
Blackburn, Marsha B		Congress	10			15	Member U.S. Congress
Blackeley, Brig. Travers Robert	1899-1982	Military	25				World War II British general
Blackett, Patrick M.		Science	20	35	50	30	Nobel Physics. Cosmic Rays
Blackman, Honor		Entertainment	8	15	25	27	Br. Actress. 'James Bond'. Leading Lady
Blackmer, Sidney	1895-1973	Entertainment	10	15	20	35	Actor. Stage (Tony Award) Films. Character Actor
Blackmon, Fred L.		Senate/Congress	10	20		15	MOC AL
Blackmore, Brig. Gen. Philip G.	1890-1974	Military	30				World War II U.S. general
Blackmore, Richard D.		Author	15	40	95		Br. Novelist. 'Lorna Doone'
Blackmun, Harry A.		Supreme Court	45	225	270	75	
Blackstone, Harry		Entertainment	138	375	475	193	Magician. Self Sketch Signed 375
Blackstone, Harry, Jr		Entertainment	22	30	35	40	Magician
Blackton, J.Stuart & Smith, A. E.		Entertainment			45		Co-Fndrs Vitagraph Films. Inventor
Blackwell, Alice Stone	1857-1950	Reformer	147		195		Woman's Suffrage. Editor
Blackwell, Elizabeth		Medical	125		650		1st Woman to Receive M.D. Degree in Modern Times
Blackwell, Mr.		Business	5	10		15	Fashion Critic
Blackwell, Otis		Composer	25	85	175		
Blackwell, Roger		Celebrity	10			15	financial expert
Blackwood, Richard		Celebrity	10			15	television presenter
Blades, Ruben		Entertainment	10			20	actor
Blaha, John E.		Astronaut	10	10		20	
Blaine, James G.	1830-1893	Cabinet	46	73	184	188	U.S.Sen. ME,Garfield Sec'y St., Pres. Candidate
Blaine, Vivian	1921-1995	Entertainment	14	12	15	25	Actress-Singer. 'Guys & Doll', 'State Fair'
Blair, Austin	1814-1894	Civil War	20		55		CW Governor of MI
Blair, Charles		Aviation	45			60	
Blair, Eric (See Orwell, George)							Pen-name of George Orwell
Blair, Francis P., Jr.	1821-1875	Civil War	41	91	156		Union General, U.S.Sen. MO. Sig/Rank 75
Blair, Frank		Journalist	10	15	20	35	Radio-TV News Anchor & Correspondent(Deceased)
Blair, Jacob B.		Civil War	25		70		Virginia MOC Who Remained Loyal to Union
Blair, Janet		Entertainment	10	10	20	25	Actress-Singer. 'My Sister Eileen'.
Blair, John L., Dr.		Historian	10			25	American Historian and Collector
Blair, John		Supreme Court	150	775	1200		Signer of Constitution
Blair, John	1802-1899	Business	150	750	950		Helped Charter Union Pacific RR.Built 1st 100 Mile
Blair, Linda		Entertainment	8	10	20	26	Young Actress in 'The Exorcist'
Blair, Montgomery		Legal	82	286	500		Counsel to Dred Scott
Blak, Freddy		Political	10			15	Member European Parliament
Blake, Amanda	1927-1989	Entertainment	60	90	115	120	Veteran 'Gunsmoke' Actress. 'Miss Kitty'
Blake, Bud*		Cartoonist	5			55	'Tiger'. S Original Three Panel Strip 125
Blake, Eubie	1883-1983	Composer	67	166	190	175	Songwriter & Ragtime Pianist. AMusQS 385-650
Blake, Eugene Carson		Clergy	50	95	150	70	
Blake, Madge		Entertainment	100			250	Actress. 'Aunt Harriet' on TV's 'Batman' Series
Blake, Robert (Bobby)		Entertainment	6	8	10	37	'Our Gang' to 'In Cold Blood' & TV's Baretta'
Blake, Robin K.		Celebrity	10			15	medical expert
Blake, Susan		Celebrity	10			15	media/TV personality

NAME	DATE	CATEGORY	SIG	LS/DS	ALS	SP	COMMENTS
Blake, William		Artist					Content ALS 30,000
Blakeley, Maj. Gen. Harold W.	1893-1966	Military	30				World War II U.S. general
Blakelock, Brig. Gen. David H.	1895-1975	Military	30				World War II U.S. general
Blakely, Susan		Entertainment	6	8	15	20	Actress
Blakely, Troy		Entertainment	10			20	actor
Blakeslee, Don		Aviation	10	25	40	30	ACE, WW II
Blakiston-Houston, Maj Gen John	1881-1959	Military	25				World War II British general
Blamey, Field Marshal Thomas A.	1884-1951	Military	20				World War II Australian general
Blanc, Louis	1811-1882	Author	20	40	100		Fr. Socialist, Journalist, Politician, Historian
Blanc, Mel	1908-1989	Entertainment	65	128	135	132	Voice of Bugs Bunny etc.
Blanchard, Albert Gallatin (WD)	1810-1891	Civil War	195	1595			CSA General
Blanchard, Albert Gallatin	1810-1891	Civil War	124	247			CSA Gen.
Blanchard, Gen Geo.-Maur.-Jean	1877-1954	Military	20				World War II French general
Blanchard, Ken		Celebrity	10			15	motivational speaker
Blanchard, Marjorie		Celebrity	10			15	motivational speaker
Blanchard, Nina		Entertainment	4			8	
Blanchard, Rachel		Entertainment	7			30	Actress. TV's 'Clueless'. Pin-Up 55
Blanchett, Cate		Entertainment	8			55	Actress. Golden Globe Award
Bland, Richard P.	1835-1899	Congress	15				Repr. MO, Defeated by W.J.. Bryan for Pres.
Bland, Schuyler Otis		Senate/Congress	5	15	25		MOC VA
Bland, William T.		Senate/Congress	5	15	20		MOC MO
Blandford, Mark Harden	1826-1902	Civil War	48	100	188		CSA Congress
Blandick, Clara	1880-1962	Entertainment	579			650	'Aunt Em' in Oz. Rarest of the Oz Signatures
Blane, Ralph		Composer	5			40	AMusMsS 36
Blane, Sally		Entertainment	6	8	15	15	
Blanks, Mary Lynn		Entertainment	3	3	6	6	
Blanton, Leonard Ray		Governor	10			15	Governor TN, MOC TN
Blanton, Thomas L.		Senate/Congress	10	20		20	Senator TX, MOC TX
Blaschka, Rudolph		Artist	10	35	75		Bohemian Artist in Glass
Blasco-Ibanez, Vicente		Author	100			450	Sp. Novelist. Self Exiled
Blaskowitz, Col-Gen Johannes	1883-1948	Military	25			242	World War II German general
Blaslev, Lisabeth		Entertainment	10			25	Opera
Blass, Bill	d. 2002	Business	10	15		35	Fashion Designer
Blatchford, Samuel		Supreme Court	58	135	190		Supreme Court in 1882
Blatty, William Peter	1928-	Author	15	32	45	25	The Exorcist, AA . TsS 150
Blaxland, Lt. Gen. Alan Bruce	1892-1962	Military	25				World War II British general
Bledsoe, Brig. Gen. William P.	1892-1972	Military	30				World War II U.S. general
Bledsoe, Tempest		Entertainment	15	35		30	
Bleeth, Yasmine		Entertainment	12			44	'Baywatch',actress
Bleiberg, Robert		Celebrity	10			15	financial expert
Blenker, Louis (Ludwig)	1812-1863	Civil War	99	218			Union Gen LS '61 800
Blennerhassett, Harman		Revolutionary War	115	190	253		Funds, Refuge-Burr Conspiracy
Bleriot, Louis	1872-1936	Aviation	250	380	475	750	1st To Fly English Channel
Bless, Frederick		Aviation	10	22	38	32	ACE, Korea
Blesse, Brig. Gen. Frederick A.	1888-1954	Military	30				World War II U.S. general

NAME	DATE	CATEGORY	SIG	LS/DS	ALS	SP	COMMENTS
Blessed, Brian		Entertainment	10			20	Actor
Bletcher, Billy		Entertainment	50			200	
Blethyn, Brenda		Entertainment	6			42	
Bligh, William, Capt.		Military	1458	7967	11875		Br. Adm. Capt. HMS Bounty
Blind, Karl (1826-1907)		Author			30		
Bliss, Arthur, Sir		Composer	25		109		Brit. Opera, Orch. works
Bliss, Brig. Gen. Raymond W.	1888-1965	Military	30				World War II U.S. general
Bliss, Cornelius		Cabinet	10	25	55	40	Sec'y Interior
Bliss, George Jr.		Civil War	8	15	25		MOC OH
Bliss, J. S.		Civil War	5	10	20		
Bliss, Tasker H.		Military	15	25	50	25	US Gen.1st Cmdr. War College
Bliss, William Wallace S.		Military	130	292	500		Pvt. Sec'y, Chief of Staff to Gen'l Zachary Taylor
Bliss, Zenas R.		Civil War	42	110	160		Union Officer
Blitstein, Mark David		Science	10			20	Gastroenterologist, Chief medicine LFH
Blitzer, Wolf		Journalist	10		15	25	TV News
Blitzstein, Marc		Composer	80	82	412		Opera. Brilliant US Composer
Blixen, Karen (Isak Dinesen)		Author	110	500		200	Danish Novelist Out of Africa
Bloch, Ernest	1880-1959	Composer	80		382	288	Swiss-Am. Composer, Teacher
Bloch, Ernst		Author	55	140	425	90	Ger. Philosopher.
Bloch, Felix		Science	25	40	100	75	Nobel Physics
Bloch, Konrad, Dr.		Science	20	30	45	30	Nobel Medicine
Bloch, Raymond		Composer	10	20	35	30	
Bloch, Robert		Author	20	50	60	40	Novelist. TMsS 450
Block, Brigadier Allen Prichard	1899-1973	Military	25				World War II British general
Block, Gen. of Infantry Johannes	1894-1945	Military	25				World War II German general
Block, Henry W.		Business	20	45		65	H & R Block. Founder with Brother
Block, Herb*		Cartoonist	15			100	Herblock-political
Block, John R.		Cabinet	5	10	15	10	
Block, Joseph L.		Business	4	6	9	6	
Block, Martin		Entertainment	5			15	Early radio deejay
Block, Richard		Business	20	35	90	25	H & R Block
Blocker, Dan	1928-1972	Entertainment	170	450		365	'Hoss' On Long Running 'Bonanza'
Blodget, Samuel Jr.		Revolutionary War	285	750	1540		Inventor, Soldier, Judge
Bloembergen, Nicolaas Dr.		Science	20	35	40	30	Nobel Physics
Blokland, Johannes (hans)		Political	10			15	Member European Parliament
Blomberg, Werner Von		Military	35	75	165	224	Ger. Fld. Marshal WW II
Blomfield, Ezekial		Clergy	35	45	60		
Blomfield, Maj. Gen. Valentine	1898-1980	Military	25				World War II British general
Blondell, Joan		Entertainment	35	40	65	67	Oscar Winner
Blondie		Music	15			80	female vocalist
Blondin, Charles	1824-1897	Entertainment	30	60	175	60	Tightrope walker Niagara Falls
Blood, Brig. Wm Edmund Roberts	1897-1976	Military	28				World War II British general
Blood, Maj. Gen. Kenneth T.	1888-1979	Military	30				World War II U.S. general
Blood, Robert O.		Governor	5		25		Governor NH
Blood, Sweat and Tears		Entertainment	35			80	

NAME	DATE	CATEGORY	SIG	LS/DS	ALS	SP	COMMENTS
Bloodworth-Thomason, Linda		Celebrity	10			15	film industry
Bloom, Adam		Celebrity	10			15	comedian
Bloom, Claire		Entertainment	6	8	15	25	
Bloom, David	d. 2003	Entertainment	10			30	TV News reporter
Bloom, Lindsay		Entertainment	8	9	12	15	
Bloom, Orlando		Entertainment				65	Actor
Bloomer, Amelia		Reformer	275	350			Pioneer Dress & Social Reformer
Bloomfield, Joseph		Revolutionary War	30	95	120		Officer, Attorney, Gov. NJ
Bloomfield-Zeisler, Fannie		Entertainment	25			75	Concert Pianist
Blore, Eric		Entertainment	20	25	65	60	
Blossom Rock		Entertainment	40			75	
Blough, Roger		Business	5	15	25	15	
Blount, Brig. Gen. Roy E.	1889-1969	Military	30				World War II U.S. general
Blount, James H.		Civil War	47	40			CSA Officer, MOC GA
Blount, William		Senate	320	900			Continental Congr. Senator TN
Blount, Winton M.		Cabinet	5	15	25	10	P.M. General
Bloustein, Edward J.		Celebrity	5	12	20	10	
Blowers, Sean		Entertainment	10			20	Actor
Blucher, Gebhard L. von		Military	200	557	2200		Pruss. Fld. Marshal vs Napoleon
Blue, Ben	1901-1975	Entertainment	26	30	60	55	
Blue, Monte	1880-1963	Entertainment	19	25	45	75	Griffith Great Silent Star
Bluemel, Brig. Gen. Clifford	1885-1973	Military	30				World War II U.S. general
Bluford, Guion S. Jr.		Astronaut	10			31	1st Afro-American Astronaut
Blum, Leon (Fr)		Head of State	25	40	110	35	Pres. France WW II
Blum, Norbert		Statesman	5			10	German Minister & Statesman
Blumberg, Baruch S.		Science	20	30	55	25	Nobel Medicine
Blumenauer, Earl B		Congress	10			15	Member U.S. Congress
Blumenfeld, Felix		Composer		150		300	Russ. Conductor, Teacher
Blumenthal, Heston		Celebrity	10			15	Chef
Blumenthal, Jacques		Composer	40		350		And Pianist
Blumenthal, W. Michael		Cabinet	5	10	15	10	
Blumentritt, Gen. of Inf. Günther	1892-1967	Military	25				World War II German general
Blunden, Edmund	1896-1974	Poet	55		238		Poet, Critic, Biographer. AMsS 200- 750
Blunt, Anthony	1907-1983	Military		127			British Military Intel.
Blunt, Asa P.		Military	35		200		General
Blunt, James G., Dr.		Civil War	45	75			Union General
Blunt, John Henry		Clergy	15	25	35	25	
Blunt, Roy B		Congress	10			15	Member U.S. Congress
Bly, Julian		Celebrity	10			15	Designer
Blyden, Larry		Entertainment	3	3	6	6	
Blyth, Ann		Entertainment	10		15	18	Actress-Singer
Blythe, Betty	1893-1972	Entertainment	35		75	175	Silent Star. Beautiful 'Vamp' of Early Movies
Blyukher, Vasily		Military		285			Russian General
Boardman, Eleanor	1898-1991	Entertainment	15	15	40	45	Vintage Silent Film Actress. 'The Squaw Man'
Boardman, Russell		Aviation	25	55	95	80	

NAME	DATE	CATEGORY	SIG	LS/DS	ALS	SP	COMMENTS
Boardman, Stan		Celebrity	10			15	comedian
Boase, Lt. Gen. Allan J.	1894-1964	Military	20				World War II Australian general
Boatner, Maj. Gen. Haydon L.	1900-1977	Military	30				World War II U.S. general
Boatwright, Brig. Gen. Walter P.	1886-1957	Military	30				World War II U.S. general
Bob & Ray		Entertainment	25			65	
Bob, Tim		Entertainment	6			25	Music. Bass Guitar 'Rage Against the Machine'
Bobbitt, John Wayne		Media Celebrity	10			20	Victim of Angry Wife
Bobkins, Addie		Entertainment	5	6	9	8	
Bobko, Karol J.		Astronaut	7			15	
Bochco, Steven		Entertainment	10	15		20	TV Emmy Award Producer
Bochner, Lloyd		Entertainment	4	4	9	15	
Bock, Feodor von		Military	100	295		150	Ger. Gen. WW II. Failed
Bock, Jerry		Composer	40	50	70	80	Fiddler.... AMusQS 250
Böckmann, Gen. of Inf. Herbert	1886-1974	Military	25				World War II German general
Bocock, Thomas S.		Civil War	34				CSA Speaker of the House
Bodenschatz, Karl		Aviation	30	75	150	95	
Bodger & Badger		Celebrity	10			15	childrenªs presenter
Bodrato, Guido		Political	10			15	Member European Parliament
Bodwell, Joseph R.		Governor	8	12		10	Gov. ME
Body, Maj. Gen. Kenneth Marten	1883-1973	Military	25				World War II British general
Boe, Nils A.		Governor	10	15			Governor SD
Boege, Gen. of Inf. Ehrenfried	1889-1965	Military	25				World War II German general
Boehlert, Sherwood B		Congress	10			15	Member U.S. Congress
Boehme, Gen Mtn Troops Franz	1885-1947	Military	25				World War II German general
Boehner, John A. B		Congress	10			15	Member U.S. Congress
Boeing, William E.	1881-1956	Business	150	425	1600	800	Signed stock cert. 2850
Boerhaave, Herman	1668-1738	Science		2188			Dutch Physician, Medical Educator
Boesch, Ruthilde		Entertainment	5	10		20	Opera
Bogard, Dirk		Entertainment	10		30	25	
Bogart, Humphrey	1899-1957	Entertainment	771	1567	1750	2362	Academy Award. 'African Queen'
Bogdonavich, Peter		Entertainment	10	30		20	Controversial Film Director
Böge, Reimer		Political	10			15	Member European Parliament
Boggs, Charles		Civil War	54	108	136		Union Adm.
Boggs, Hale		Senate/Congress	10	25			MOC LA
Boggs, Lindy (Mrs. H. Boggs)		Congress	10	15		15	MOC LA
Boggs, William R. (WD)		Civil War	170		495		CSA General
Boggs, William R.	1829-1911	Civil War	73	195	315		CSA General
Bogguss, Suzy		Country Music	5			20	Pin-Up 30
Bogosian, Eric		Entertainment	10			20	actor
Bohay, Heidi		Entertainment	5	6	15	10	
Bohlen, Henry	1810-1862	Civil War	117				Union general
Bohm, Karl		Entertainment	15		75	85	Conductor. Dir. Vienna State Opera
Bohn, Brig. Gen. John J.	1889-1983	Military	30				World War II U.S. general
Bohnen, Carl		Artist	20	35			
Bohr, Aage Niels	1922-	Science	25			55	Nobel Physics 1975

NAME	DATE	CATEGORY	SIG	LS/DS	ALS	SP	COMMENTS
Bohr, Niels H.D.	1885-1962	Science	500	1135		2240	Danish Physicist. Nobel 1922. Development A Bomb
Bohrod, Aaron (Bohrad)	1907-1992	Artist		46			American Artist
Boht, Jean		Entertainment	10			20	Actress
Boichut, Gen Edmund-Just-Victor	1864-1941	Military	20				World War II French general
Boisrond-Canal		Haitian Statesman	30	95			
Boito, Arrigo		Composer	45	110	325		& Verdi Librettist. AMusQS 750
Bok, Edward W.		Author-Business	30	55	140	95	Editor, Curtis Publishing, Pulitzer
Bokor, Margit		Entertainment	10			30	Hung. Soprano
Boland, Brig. Sir Edward Rowan	1898-1972	Military	25				World War II British general
Boland, Frederick		Celebrity	5	15	40	10	
Boland, Mary		Entertainment	15	75		70	
Bolcom, William		Composer	15	25	65		Pulitzer, AMusQS 75
Bolden, Charles F. Jr.		Astronaut	6			25	
Boles, Charles E. (Black Bart)		History	920				notorious stagecoach robber
Boles, John		Entertainment	20	35	45	40	
Bolet, Jorge		Entertainment	20			120	Pianist
Bolger, James		Head of State	10			20	P.M. New Zealand
Bolger, Ray and Haley, Jack		Entertainment		1500			SP (OZ) 595
Bolger, Ray	1904-1987	Entertainment	80	65	196	162	Wizard of OZ. SP as Scarecrow 250-500
Bolingbroke, Henry (St.John)		Author	35	150	398		1st Viscount, Politician, Writer
Bolivar, Simon		Head of State	385	2382	4975		Statesman, Revolutionary Leader
Boll, Heinrich	1917-1985	Author	32	30	95	30	Nobel Lit., Novelist, Poet
Bolling, Lt. Gen. Alexander R.	1895-1964	Military	30				World War II U.S. general
Bolling, Tiffany		Entertainment	10	12	15	20	
Bols, Maj. Gen. Erich Louis	1904-1985	Military	25				World War II British general
Bolt, John		Aviation	12	30	50	35	ACE, WW II & Korea
Bolte, General Charles L.	1895-1989	Military	30				World War II U.S. general
Bolton, Frances Payne		Senate/Congress	10	25			MOC OH
Bolton, Guy		Author	15	100			Playwright
Bolton, James		Inventor	25	75	142		Sewing Machine Inventor
Bolton, Michael		Entertainment	125			35	Singer, Composer
Bolton-Jones, Hugh		Artist	10	25	45		Am. Landscape Painter
Bombeck, Erma		Author	5	18	50	10	Humorous Columnist
Bomford, George		Military Engineer	65	200			Invented Howitzer Bomb Cannon
Bomford, James Voty		Civil War	37	80	116		
Bonaduce, Danny		Entertainment	10			25	
Bonaparte, Caroline		Royalty	35	95	275		Marie-Annonciade
Bonaparte, Charles	1851-1921	Cabinet	30	70			Sec'y Navy, Att'y Gen. Gr.Nephew Napol.
Bonaparte, Elisa (Maria Ana)		Royalty	400		365		Oldest Sister of Napoeon
Bonaparte, Eugene Napoleon		Royalty	75	200	435		Adopted by Napoleon
Bonaparte, Jerome Napoleon	1822-1891	Royalty	60	119	240		Son of King of Westphalia
Bonaparte, Joseph	1768-1844	Royalty	120	317	343		Elder Brother of Napoleon. King of Two Sicilies
Bonaparte, Josephine	1763-1814	Royalty		3500			Empress of France
Bonaparte, Letizia		Royalty		1500	2700		Mother of Napoleon
Bonaparte, Louis	1778-1846	Head of State	91	328			Bro. of Napolean I., King of Holland 1806-1810

NAME	DATE	CATEGORY	SIG	LS/DS	ALS	SP	COMMENTS
Bonaparte, Louis-Napoleon	1914-1997	Royalty	70				Called 'Le Prince Napoleon' from 1926 Till Death
Bonaparte, Lucien	1775-1849	Royalty	60	105	139		Brother. Opposed Nap., Exiled
Bonaparte, Marie Louise		Royalty	195	815	2795		Wife of Napoleon
Bonaparte, Mathilde	1820-1904	Royalty	50		150		Daughter of King Jerome
Bonaparte, Napoleon		Royalty					SEE Napoleon I
Bonaparte, Pauline	1780-1825	Royalty			275		Princess Of Italy
Bonar, Horatius		Clergy	15	20	25		
Bonci, Alessandro		Entertainment	35			115	Opera
Bond, Butch		Entertainment				46	Little Rascals
Bond, Carrie Jacobs		Composer	35	55	70	70	Am. Composer Art Songs
Bond, Charles		Aviation	10	28	40	30	ACE, WW II, Flying Tigers
Bond, Christopher Kit		Senate	5	10		10	Senator MO
Bond, Ford		Entertainment	10			15	Early Network Radio Ann'cer
Bond, Johnny		Country Music	10			20	
Bond, Julian		Politician	10	20	50	20	Afro-Am. Civil Rights Activist. Poet
Bond, Lt. Gen. Sir Lionel Vivian	1884-1961	Military	25				World War II British general
Bond, Maj Gen Richard Lawrence	1890-1979	Military	25				World War II British general
Bond, Tommy 'Butch'		Entertainment	18			22	'Our Gang' Comedy. Bad Boy
Bond, Ward	1903-1960	Entertainment	88	80	95	179	GWTW, Wagon Train. Serious Western Player
Bond, William C.		Science	45	190	350		Am. Astronomer. Harvard Observ.
Bonde, Jens-peter		Political	10			15	Member European Parliament
Bondi, Beulah		Entertainment	15	15	30	38	
Bondi, Renee		Celebrity	10			15	motivational speaker
Bondur, Roberta		Astronaut	10			20	Canadian Astro
Boner, Edmond	1500-1569	Clergy	650				Appealed to Pope for Henry VIII
Bonerz, Peter		Entertainment	3	3	6	6	
Bonesteel, Charles H.		Military	11	35	58		
Bonesteel, Maj. Gen. Charles H.	1885-1964	Military	30				World War II U.S. general
Bonet, Lisa	1967-	Entertainment	25			30	Actress
Bong, Richard		Aviation	975	1600	2500	1800	ACE, WW II, Top U.S. Ace
Bongo, Albert B.		Head of State	100			425	President of Gabon. Elected '72, '79,'86,'93
Bonham, Joe 'Bonzo'		Entertainment	75			125	
Bonham, Milledge L.	1813-1890	Civil War	98	244	262		CSA General
Bonham, Milledge L.(WD)		Civil War	185	332	454		CSA General
Bonham-Carter, Gen. Sir Charles	1876-1955	Military	28				World War II British general
Bonham-Carter, Helena		Entertainment	10			20	Actress
Bonheur, Rosa	1822-1899	Artist	110	155	235		Fr. Horse Fair & Rural Scenes
Bonilla, Henry B		Congress	10			15	Member U.S. Congress
Bonino, Emma		Political	10			15	Member European Parliament
Boninsegna, Celestina		Entertainment	150			850	Legendary Soprano. Vintage
Bonjovi, John		Entertainment	10			55	Rock
Bonnard, Pierre	1867-1947	Artist	119	280	812		Fr.Post-impressionist, Illustrator, Graphic Artist
Bonnat, Leon		Artist			76		French Academic painter
Bonner, Jo B	1833-1922	Congress	10			15	Member U.S. Congress
Bonneville, Benj. L. E. de	1795-1878	Military	225	600	897		Pioneer Explorer NW Territory

NAME	DATE	CATEGORY	SIG	LS/DS	ALS	SP	COMMENTS
Bonney, Barbara		Entertainment	15			35	Opera
Bono		Music	25			65	Lead singer U-2
Bono, Mary B		Congress	10			15	Member U.S. Congress
Bono, Sonny	d. 1998	Entertainment	30			65	Mayor Palm Springs, Congressman. 'Sonny & Cher'
Bonstelle, Jessie		Entertainment	25		40		Stage Actress, Producer, Teacher
Bontemps, Arna		Author	25	175			Am. Novels, Non-Fiction, Poetry
Bonvalot, Gabriel		Celebrity				155	
Bonynge, Richard		Conductor	15			50	Dame Joan Sutherland's Conductor Husband
Book of Love (4)		Entertainment	15			35	Rock Group
Book, Sorrell		Entertainment	5	6	8	10	Actress
Boone, Pickens, T.		Celebrity	10			15	financial expert
Boone, Brig. Gen. Milton O.	1891-1985	Military	30				World War II U.S. general
Boone, Daniel	1734-1820	Revolutionary War	1575	7719	21500		Am. Pioneer Cumberland Gap, AMS 25,000
Boone, Debbie		Entertainment	5	15		20	Singer
Boone, Don MSW,		Author	8			12	series of motivational books
Boone, Laura,		Author	8			12	series of motivational books
Boone, Pat		Entertainment	4	15	16	26	Singer-Actor
Boone, Randy		Entertainment	4			15	Actor. 'The Virginian' Co-Star
Boone, Richard		Entertainment	80	100	120	145	Actor. 'Palladin'
Boone, Squire		Revolutionary War			1150		NC Farmer. Father of Daniel
Boorda, Jeremy M.		Military	30		95		Adm. US Navy
Boorman, John		Celebrity	10			15	film industry
Boorstin, Daniel J.		Author	25				The Creators
Boosler, Elayne		Entertainment	10		30	20	Stand-up Comedienne
Booth, Adrian		Entertainment	5			20	Vintage Actress
Booth, Ballington		Clergy	25	75	165		Co-Cmdr. Salvation Army
Booth, Bromwell		Clergy	25	50	75		
Booth, Edwin	1833-1893	Entertainment	108		196	250	Great 19th Century Actor. Brother of John Wilkes
Booth, Evangeline	1865-1950	Reformer	35	108	345	95	Salvation Army General
Booth, Ewing	1870-1949	Military	20			50	WW I General. Pershing Chief of Staff
Booth, Graham H.		Political	10			15	Member European Parliament
Booth, John Wilkes	1838-1865	Civil War	3200	6500	11000	10000	Assassin of Lincoln. AMsS 35,000.
Booth, Junius Brutus, Jr.	1821-1883	Entertainment	50	105			Actor Brother of John Wilkes
Booth, Maude	1865-1948	Reformer	45	100	225		Fndr. Vols. of Am. & PTA, Signed book 100
Booth, Newell S., Bishop		Clergy	20	35	50	50	
Booth, Newton		Senator	15	25	60		Governor CA, Senator CA
Booth, Shirley	1907-1992	Entertainment	30	50		50	Starred on Broadway.Oscar for'Come Back Littlea'
Booth, William Bramwell		Clergy	40	75	100	65	Eldest Son & Organizer
Booth, William	1829-1912	Clergy	95	216	350	327	Founder & Gen'l Salvation Army
Boothe, Powers		Entertainment	5	6	15	15	
Boozer, Brenda		Entertainment	4	5	10	10	
Boozman, John B		Congress	10			15	Member U.S. Congress
Bor, Tadeusz		Military	15	45	75		
Borah, William E.		Senate	20	30		45	Senator ID
Borch, F.J.		Business	4	10		10	Pres. General Electric

NAME	DATE	CATEGORY	SIG	LS/DS	ALS	SP	COMMENTS
Borchers, Adolf		Aviation	10	15	30	25	
Bordaberry, Juan M		Head of State	7	15	25	10	Uraguay
Bordallo, Madeleine Z. B		Congress	10			15	Member U.S. Congress
Bordelon, Guy		Aviation	8	20	35	25	ACE, Korea
Borden, Brig. Gen. William A.	1890-1967	Military	30				World War II U.S. general
Borden, Lizzy		Celebrity			9110		Alleged Ax Murderess
Borden, Olive		Entertainment	30	35	45	150	
Borden, Robert L.	1854-1937	Head of State	35				P.M. Canada 1911-20
Bordes, Armonia		Political	10			15	Member European Parliament
Bordogni, Giulio-Marco		Entertainment			40		Opera. Tenor. Teacher
Bordoni, Irene		Entertainment	15	15	35	30	
Boreanaz, David		Entertainment	6			48	Actor 'Buffy'
Boreman, Arthur I.	1823-1896	Political	46				1st Govenor of West Virginia
Borge, Victor	1909-2000	Entertainment	15	30	35	55	Pianist-Comedian. Concert Stage & Recordings
Borges, Jorge Luis	1899-1986	Author	75	350			Argentinian.Fiction, Poetry
Borghese, Camillo		Head of State					SEE Paul V, Pope
Borghese, Pauline Bonaparte		Royalty	110		575		Sister of Napoleon
Borghezio, Mario		Political	10			15	Member European Parliament
Borgia, Francis, Saint	1510-1572	Clergy	1850	2600			Roman Catholic Saint
Borglum, Gutzon	1867-1941	Artist	225	375	397	504	Creator Mt. Rushmore Sculptures. Sketch S 950
Borglum, Lincoln		Artist	25	60	85		Son of Gutzon. Sculptor
Borglum, Solon		Artist	15		45		
Borgnine, Ernest		Entertainment	6	10	12	25	Actor. Oscar Winner
Bori, Lucrezia	1887-1960	Entertainment	40	95		90	Opera. Sp. Lyric Soprano. SP 9x13 (Violetta)200
Boring, Wayne*		Cartoonist	30			400	Superman
Boris III		Royalty	120			185	King & Dictator Bulgaria
Boris, Lt. Gen. Pierre-Louis-André	1878-1946	Military	20				World War II French general
Bork, Robert A.		Jurist	5	20		30	
Borkh, Inge		Entertainment	10			25	Opera. Salome
Borland, Carol	1914-1997	Entertainment	25			80	Actress. Vintage Horror Films.
Borlaug, Norman, Dr.		Science	20	35	80	30	Nobel Peace Prize
Borman, F. & Lovell, J.		Astronaut	35			75	Signed by Both
Borman, Frank		Astronaut	22	30		67	
Bormann, Martin	1900-1945	Military	350	788	1500	850	Nazi Private Sec'y to Hitler
Born, Max	1882-1970	Science	175	375	575		Nobel, Ger.-Br. Physicist., Archive 13,800
Borne, Hermann von Dem.		Military	20	45	90		
Borno, Louis		Head of State	15	75			Pres. Haiti
Borodin, Alexander		Composer	250	450	1100		Rus. Composer & Prof. Chemistry
Borowski, Felix		Composer	15	40	100	50	
Borso, Umberto		Entertainment	15			45	It. Tenor
Bortone, Adriana Poli		Political	10			15	Member European Parliament
Bortz, Walter		Celebrity	10			15	medical expert
Borzage, Frank		Entertainment	40			150	Film Director-Producer
Bosanquet, Helen D.		Author	8	15	22		
Bösch, Herbert		Political	10			15	Member European Parliament

NAME	DATE	CATEGORY	SIG	LS/DS	ALS	SP	COMMENTS
Bose, Jagadis, Sir		Science	27	40	150		Indian Physicist
Bose, Lucia	1931-	Entertainment	17			35	Span. Actress. Films from 1950
Boselli, Enrico		Political	10			15	Member European Parliament
Boshell, Louise		Entertainment	6	8	15	15	
Bosley, Tom		Entertainment	5	13	20	12	
Bosson, Barbara		Entertainment	5	5	10	20	
Bostic, Earl		Bandleader	15				Jazz Saxaphonist
Bostwick, Barry		Entertainment	6	8	15	20	
Bostwick, George		Aviation	10	25	40	30	ACE, WW II
Boswell, Connie		Entertainment	10	10	25	10	
Boswell, James		Author	750		4545		Biographer of Sam'l Johnson
Boswell, Leonard L. B		Congress	10			15	Member U.S. Congress
Bosworth, Hobart	1867-1970	Entertainment	25	30	40	65	Films Actor from 1909-43
Boteler, Alexander Robinson	1815-1892	Civil War	84	184	442		Member of Confederate Congress
Botha, Louis		Head of State	52	75	95		S. Afr. Soldier, Statesman
Botta, Lucca	1882-1917	Entertainment	75			225	Enrico Caruso Protégé. early death by brain tumor
Bottesini, G.		Entertainment	50				Double-Bass Virtuoso, Conductor. AMusQS 200
Bottolfsen, C.A.		Governor	12		25	15	Governor ID
Bottome, Margaret		Author	15	45	100	25	Lecturer
Bottoms, Joseph		Entertainment	4	4	9	12	
Bottoms, Sam		Entertainment	6	8	15	12	
Bottoms, Timothy		Entertainment	7			15	
Bouchard, Lucien		Celebrity	10			15	political celebrity
Boucher, Maj Gen Sir Chas. Ham.	1898-1951	Military	25				World War II British general
Boucher, Rick B		Congress	10			15	Member U.S. Congress
Boucicault, Dion		Entertainment	20	35	50	40	19th Cent. Am. Actor-Playwright
Bouck, William C.	1786-1859	Governor	15	25	50		Gov. NY.Supervised Part Construction of Erie Canal
Boudin, Eugene-Louis		Artist	105	280	431		Fr. Sea & Beach Scenes
Boudinot, Brig. Gen. Truman E.	1895-1945	Military	30				World War II U.S. general
Boudinot, Elias Cornelius	1835-1890	Civil War	68	130	190		Member of Confederate Congress
Boudinot, Elias	1740-1821	Revolutionary War	240	460	765		Washington's Att'y Gen. & Close Friend
Boudinot, Elias	1835-1890	History	95	420	1210		Cherokee Leader. Murdered
Boudjenah, Yasmine		Political	10			15	Member European Parliament
Bouffet, Maj. Gen. Jean-Gabriel	1882-1940	Military	20				World War II French general
Boughton, Rutland	b. 1876	Composer					Opera, Etc. AMusQS 125
Bouguereau, Adolphe Wm.	1825-1895	Artist			110		Fr. Painter.Mostly Religious & Mythological Themes
Boulanger, Nadia		Composer			142	375	Fr. Conductor, Teacher
Boulard, Georges		Aviation	15		60	35	
Boulez, Pierre		Composer	40	45	75	100	Fr. Composer-Conductor-Pianist.AMusQS 325
Boullanger, George	1837-1891	Military	100				Gen'l & Politician.'Man on Horseback'. Suicide
Boulle, Pierre	1912-1994	Author	15	15	40	115	'Bridge Over the River Kwai'
Boult, Adrian, Sir		Conductor	18	45	100	75	Esteemed Br. Conductor
Boumediene-thiery, Alima		Political	10			15	Member European Parliament
Bouquet, Carole		Celebrity	10			15	model
Bourbon-Parma, Zita	1892-1989	Royalty				450	Last Austrian Empress

NAME	DATE	CATEGORY	SIG	LS/DS	ALS	SP	COMMENTS
Bourchier, John	1499-1561	Royalty			775		3rd Earl of Bath Lady Jane Grey Trial Commissioner
Bourguiba, Habib		Head of State	15	40	100	25	Pres. Tunisia
Bourke-White, Margaret	1904-1971	Artist	78	160	195		Special SP 770. Photo Essays Life Mag.
Bourlanges, Jean-louis		Political	10			15	Member European Parliament
Bourmont, Louis A.V.	1773-1846	Fr. Military		80	160		General under Napoleon
Bourn, Benjamin	1755-1808	Political			98		US Congressman from RI
Bourne, Francis, Cardinal		Clergy	35	45	60	40	
Bourne, Gen Sir Alan Geo. Barwys	1882-1967	Military	25				World War II British general
Bourret, General Victor	1877-1949	Military	20				World War II French general
Bourrienne, L.A.F. de		Fr. Revolution	45	60	120		Pvt. Sec'y to Napoleon
Bouton, Chas. Marie		Artist	110	165	400		
Boutwell, George S.	1818-1905	Cabinet	20	45	150	97	Grant Sec'y Treasury. Political Leader. TLS 250
Bouwman, Theodorus J.J.		Political	10			15	Member European Parliament
Bow, Clara	1905-1965	Entertainment	145	191	330	495	The 'It' Girl. Silent Film Star
Bowden, Doris		Entertainment	5	3	6	20	
Bowditch, Nathaniel	1773-1838	Science	100	230	610		Astronomer, Mathematician
Bowdoin, James		Rev. War					Rev. War, Gov. Mass. ALS content 9500
Bowe, David Robert		Political	10			15	Member European Parliament
Bowe, Rosemarie		Entertainment	4	4	9	10	
Bowen, Brig. Gen. Charles F.	1889-1977	Military	30				World War II U.S. general
Bowen, Elizabeth		Author	25	75	170	30	Ir.-Br. Psychological Novelist
Bowen, George F., Sir		Head of State	10	25	35		Governor Australia, New Zealand
Bowen, Ira Sprague		Science	10	25	35	15	Dir. Mt. Wilson-Palomar Obs.
Bowen, James	1808-1886	Civil War	45	84	133		Union general
Bowen, Jim		Celebrity	10			15	television presenter
Bowen, John Stevens (WD)		Civil War	175	260	1265		CSA Gen. Early Prisoner
Bowen, John Stevens	1830-1863	Civil War	112	248	528		CSA General.
Bowen, Louise de Koven		Social Reformer	12	20			Pres. Hull House
Bowen, Maj. Gen. Frank S. Jr.	1905-1976	Military	30				World War II U.S. general
Bowen, Maj. Gen. William Oswald	1898-1961	Military	25				World War II British general
Bowen, Otis		Cabinet	5	10			Sec'y Health & Human Services
Bowen, Thomas Meed		Civil War	45				Union General, Senator CO
Bower, Antoinette		Entertainment	3	3	6	8	
Bower, Lt. Gen. Sir Roger Herbert	1903-1990	Military	25				World War II British general
Bowerbank, Maj. Gen. Fred T.	1880-1960	Military	20				World War II New Zealand general
Bowerman, Brig. John Francis	1893-1983	Military	25				World War II British general
Bowers, George M.		Senate/Congress	10	20		10	MOC WV
Bowes, Major Edward		Entertainment	12	15	19	25	
Bowie, David		Entertainment	30	95		76	Rock
Bowie, George Washington	1835-1882	Civil War	90	525			Union General
Bowie, James (Jim)		Military		15000			Co-Cmdr. Alamo. Bowie Knife
Bowie, Sydney J.		Senate/Congress	10	20	35		MOC AL
Bowis, John		Political	10			15	Member European Parliament
Bowker, Judi		Entertainment	10	8	15	22	
Bowler, Metcalf		Jurist	50	135	250		Opponent of The Stamp Act 1765

NAME	DATE	CATEGORY	SIG	LS/DS	ALS	SP	COMMENTS
Bowles, Chester		Governor	10	25	85	40	Diplomat, Advertising Exec.
Bowlin, James B.		Senate/Congress	15	30	45		MOC MO
Bowman, Brig. Gen. Harwood C.	1895-1962	Military	30				World War II U.S. general
Bowman, Lee		Entertainment	10	20	25	25	
Bowman, Maj. Gen. Frank O.	1896-1978	Military	30				World War II U.S. general
Bowser, Charles	-1998	Entertainment	20			45	Silent Film Character Actor."The Price She Paid"
Boxcar Willie		Country Western	6	12		15	Singer
Boxer, Barbara		Senate	10			15	United States Senate (D - CA)
Boxleitner, Bruce		Entertainment	8	9	19	35	
Boy George		Entertainment	15	30	45	50	
Boyce, Max		Celebrity	10			15	comedian
Boyce, William Waters	1818-1890	Civil War	45				Member of Confederate Congress
Boyce, William	1711-1779	Composer		633			
Boyd, Alan S.		Cabinet	4			10	Sec'y Trans., CEO Amtrak
Boyd, Allen B		Congress	10			15	Member U.S. Congress
Boyd, Belle		Western Outlaw	1025	8937		9650	Confederate Spy
Boyd, Brig. Gen. Leonard R.	1891-1977	Military	30				World War II U.S. general
Boyd, Joseph Fulton		Civil War	32	72			Union General
Boyd, Linn	1800-1859	Congress	20	30	55		Repr. KY, Speaker of House
Boyd, Stephen		Entertainment	25	37	70	70	Actor
Boyd, William 'Bill'	1895-1972	Entertainment	179			272	Silent Screen Matinee Idol & 'Hopalong Cassidy'
Boye, Brig. Gen. Frederic W.	1891-1970	Military	30				World War II U.S. general
Boyer, Charles	1897-1978	Entertainment	46	58	75	132	Fr. Actor.Hollywood Screen Lover
Boyer, Jean-Pierre		Head of State	35	125			Pres. Haiti
Boyer, Richard L.		Author	12			22	Edgar Allen Poe award winner
Boyes, John		Author	20			45	African adventure
Boyesen, Hjalmar H.		Author	15	35	70	20	
Boyington, Gregory 'Pappy	1912-1988	Aviation	101	165	282	152	ACE WW II Marine, #4 US, CMH
Boykin, Edward M.		Author	8			12	author, Civil War
Boykin, Richard Manning		Author	8			12	Civil War
Boyle, Jeremiah Tilford	1818-1871	Civil War	48	110	150		Union general
Boyle, John J.		Artist	5	10	20		
Boyle, Kay	1903-1993	Author	25	75	175	40	Am. Short Story Writer, Novels. Expatriot
Boyle, Lara Flynn		Entertainment	20			50	
Boyle, Peter		Entertainment	8	10	15	36	Favorite Character Actor
Boynton, Henry Van Ness		Civil War	50	100	169		Union Officer & MOH winner
Boze, Marie		Entertainment	15			50	Vintage Actress 1879
Braakensiek, Annalise		Celebrity	10			15	celebrity model
Brabazon-Moore, John T.		Aviation	25	60	85	50	1st Licensed. WW I Pilot
Bracco, Lorraine		Entertainment				49	Dr. Melfi, Soprano's
Bracken, Eddie		Entertainment	5	6	9	10	
Brackett, Charles		Entertainment	20			70	Producer. 2 Oscars as Screenwriter
Bradbourn, Philip Charles		Political	10			15	Member European Parliament
Bradbury, James Ware		Senate/Congress	20	25	40		Senator ME 1847
Bradbury, Norris E.		Science	15		25		

NAME	DATE	CATEGORY	SIG	LS/DS	ALS	SP	COMMENTS
Bradbury, Ray		Author	30	100	275	70	Am. Sci-Fi Writer, signed drawing 241
Bradford, Alexander Blackburn	1798-1873	Civil War	54	122	190		Member of Confederate Congress
Bradford, Augustus W.	1805-1881	Civil War		85			Unionist Gov. MD
Bradford, Barbara P.		Author	5			10	
Bradford, Brig. Gen. Karl S.	1889-1972	Military	30				World War II U.S. general
Bradford, Brig. Gen. William B.	1896-1965	Military	30				World War II U.S. general
Bradford, Gamaliel		Author	8			12	Civil War, history
Bradford, William	1729-1808	Senate	125	350	590		Sen. RI 1793
Bradford, William	1755-1856	Cabinet	100	164			G. Washington Att'y Gen'l
Brading, Brig. Norman Baldwin	1896-1990	Military	25				World War II British general
Bradlee, Ben		Editor	18	30		45	Ed. Washington Post
Bradley, Benjamin Franklin	1825-1897	Civil War		117			Member of Confederate Congress
Bradley, Bill		Senate/Congress	5	10		20	Sen. NJ., Pro. Basketball
Bradley, Ed		Entertainment	5	15	25	15	TV News. '60 Minutes'
Bradley, James		Military	11	35	58		
Bradley, Jeb B		Congress	10			15	Member U.S. Congress
Bradley, John H.		Military	88	130	212	438	Iwo Jima Flag Raiser FDC 200 S. Only Navy Man
Bradley, Joseph P.		Supreme Court	39	100	200		
Bradley, Kathleen		Entertainment	4			10	Price is Right Model
Bradley, Luther Prentice	1822-1910	Civil War	38				Union general
Bradley, Maj. Gen. James L.	1891-1957	Military	30				World War II U.S. general
Bradley, Maj. Gen. Joseph S.	1900-1961	Military	30				World War II U.S. general
Bradley, Omar N. (General)	1893-1981	Military	95	131	250	178	5 Star General WW II. ALS/Cont.2000, TLS.1000
Bradley, Owen	1915-1998	Entertainment	20			35	Country Music Record Producer. Musician
Bradley, Steve		Celebrity	10			15	home/gardening expert
Bradley, Tom	1917-1998	Political	10	27	35	29	Ex Poiceman. Mayor Los Angeles.
Bradna, Olympe		Entertainment	10	75		25	
Bradshaw, Maj. Gen. Aaron Jr.	1894-1976	Military	30				World War II U.S. general
Bradshaw, Maj Gen Wm P. Arthur	1897-1966	Military	25				World War II British general
Bradshaw, Terry		Celebrity	10			25	motivational speaker
Bradshaw, Tiny		Bandleader	10				
Bradstreet, John		Colonial	60	140	354		Br. Soldier. Ticonderoga
Brady Bunch The		Entertainment				230	
Brady, Alice	1892-1939	Entertainment	90		95	112	Academy Award Winner
Brady, Charles, Jr.		Astronaut	5			18	
Brady, James B. 'Diamond Jim'		Business	375	1250	1338	1100	Financier. TLS 3800. RR DS 6500
Brady, James S.		Political	43	65		75	Injured in Reagan assassination attempt
Brady, Kevin B		Congress	10			15	Member U.S. Congress
Brady, Mathew B.	1823-1896	Photographer	363	1275	2600		Presidential & Civil War Photos, signed photo 15000+
Brady, Pat	1914-1972	Entertainment	100			250	
Brady, Ray		Celebrity	10			15	media/TV personality
Brady, Robert A. B		Congress	10			15	Member U.S. Congress
Brady, Scott		Entertainment	15	15	25	40	Actor. Sometimes Western Heavy/John Wayne
Brady, William A.		Entertainment	35			65	
Braeden, Eric		Entertainment	10			20	actor

NAME	DATE	CATEGORY	SIG	LS/DS	ALS	SP	COMMENTS
Braga, Gaetano		Composer				312	Cello Music. 8 Operas
Braga, Sonia		Entertainment	10	15	30	33	Sexy Brazilian Leading Lady
Bragdon, Maj. Gen. John S.	1893-1964	Military	30				World War II U.S. general
Bragg, Braxton (WD)	1817-1876	Civil War	498	1030	2305	3000	CSA General
Bragg, Braxton	1817-1876	Civil War	410	599	1039	900	CSA General
Bragg, Edward Stuyvesant	1827-1912	Civil War	46	113	140		Union Gen., Statesman, MOC
Bragg, Thomas	1818-1872	Civil War	171	250			CSA Att'y General
Bragg, Wm. Henry, Sir	1862-1942	Science	50	95			Nobel Physics with son Wm. L. in 1915
Bragg, Wm. Lawrence, Sir	1890-1971	Science	50	85			Nobel Physics with father W.H.
Braham, John (Abraham)	1774-1856	Entertainment	25		100		Supreme Br. Opera, Concert Performer
Brahms, Johannes	1833-1897	Composer	1000	1550	3220	4350	Major 19th Cent. Composer. AMusQS 2,750-12,500
Brailowsky, Alexander		Entertainment	50			85	Concert Pianist.. Chopin Specialist
Brainard, David		Explorer	40		125		Arctic Explorer/G.B.Grinnell
Braithwaite, Kent		Author	8			12	mystery novelist
Braithwaite, Wm. Stanley		Author	35	120	235	175	
Bramesfeld, Heinrich		Military	15		25	40	Ger. Capt. of See. RK Winner
Bramley, Tessa		Celebrity	10			15	TV Chef
Branagh, Kenneth		Entertainment	20			50	Br. Actor-Director-Dramatist
Branch, Anthoney Martin	1823-1867	Civil War			134		Member of Confederate Congress
Branch, John	1782-1863	Cabinet	30	75	148		Sec'y Navy, Gov. NC, Gov. FL
Branch, Lawrence O'Brien (WD)	1820-1862	Civil War	707		1592		CSA Gen. KIA 1862, Antietam
Branch, Lawrence O'Brien	1820-1862	Civil War	289	619	1388		CSA General
Brand, Christopher Q., Sir		Aviation	75	150	300	200	ACE, WW I, Only night Ace
Brand, Harry		Entertainment	5			20	Motion Picture Producer
Brand, Jo		Celebrity	10			15	comedienne
Brand, Max	1892-1944	Author	50			100	Novelist. 'Destry Rides Again', 'Dr. Kildare'
Brand, Neville	1921-1992	Entertainment	75	250		150	Dependable Heavy Through Many Years
Brand, Vance D.		Astronaut	20	55		205	Apollo Soyuz
Brandauer, Klaus Maria	1944-	Entertainment	20	15	30	45	Austrian Actor-Director. 'Out of Africa'
Brandegee, Augustus		Senate/Congress	15	35	200		MOC. CT. Civil War Member
Brandeis, Louis D.	1856-1941	Supreme Court	127	341	502	1275	1st Jewish Supr. Ct. Judge. Important ALS 2200
Brandenstein, Daniel		Astronaut	5			15	
Brander, Maj Gen Maxwell S.	1884-1973	Military	25				World War II British general
Brandis, Jonathan		Entertainment				35	
Brando, Marlon	1924-	Entertainment	120	230	365	652	Reclusive Oscar Winning Actor.
Brandon, Barbara		Celebrity	10			15	motivational speaker
Brandon, Henry	1912-1990	Entertainment	5			10	Am. Character Actor. Reliable Menace for 30 Years
Brandon, Michael	1945-	Entertainment	8			15	Actor. Leading Man
Brandon, William Lindsay	1801-1890	Civil War	103	216			Confederate general
Brandt, Karl	1899-1975	Military	127				Hitler's personal physician
Brandt, Marianne		Entertainment	25		80	75	Opera
Brandt, Willy	1913-1992	Head of State	25	112	210	90	Germ. Chancellor. Nobel Peace Prize
Brandy		Entertainer	20			75	Singer-Actress 'Cinderella'
Brangwyn, Frank	1867-1956	Artist	25		125		Br. Painter-Decorator
Branigan, Laura		Entertainment	10			35	Singer

NAME	DATE	CATEGORY	SIG	LS/DS	ALS	SP	COMMENTS
Branly, Edouard	1844-1940	Science	105	180	264	475	Fr. Physicist. Inventor Radio Wave Detector
Brann, Louis J.		Governor	5	15		10	Gov. ME
Brann, Maj. Gen. Donald W.	1895-1945	Military	30				World War II U.S. general
Brannan, Charles F.		Cabinet	10	15		15	Sec'y Agriculture
Brannan, John Milton	1819-1892	Civil War	36	75	110		Union general
Brant, Joseph (Thayendanegea)		Indian Chief	888	4600	7500		1742-1807. Mohawk Who Fought With British
Brantley, William Felix	1830-1870	Civil War	109	210	320		Confederate general
Branzell, Karin	1891-1974	Entertainment	40			155	Opera. Celebrated in Wagnerian Roles
Braque, Georges	1882-1963	Artist	685	675	1345		Fr. Developed Cubism with Picasso. SB 975
Bratt, Benjamin		Entertainment				35	Actor
Brattain, Walter		Science	35	50	110	50	Nobel Physics. Transistor
Bratton, John, Dr.	1831-1898	Civil War	98	218	412		CSA Gen. Physician. Wounded, Captured
Brauchitsch, Heinrich Von	b. 1881	Military				242	German general WWII
Brauchitsch, Walther von	1881-1948	Military	75	184	225	299	World War II German general
Brauer, Bruno Oswald		military				127	German general
Braun, Brig. Gen. Gustav J. Jr.	1895-1945	Military	30				World War II U.S. general
Braun, Eva	1912-1945	WWII Nazi	1000		2750		Hitler's Mistress-Wife
Braun, Magnus von		Science	15			40	Rocket Pioneer/Brother Wernher
Braun, Wernher von	1912-1977	Science	171	450	1422	390	Ger-Am Rocket Pioneer. Planned Apollo Program
Brautigan, Richard		Author	45	150			Counter-Culture Classic
Braxton, Carter	1736-1797	Revolutionary War	275	550	1718		Signer Decl. of Indepen.
Braxton, Toni		Entertainment	7			38	Actress. Pin-Up 65
Brayman, Mason	1813-1895	Civil War	35	101			Union General, Gov. Idaho
Brayton, Charles Ray		Civil War	58	65	100		Union General
Brazzi, Rossano	1916-1995	Entertainment	10	9	25	48	Romantic Italian Actor
Brearley, David	1745-1790	Revolutionary War	375	403	875		Continental Congress
Breathed, Berke*		Cartoonist	20			175	'Bloom County'
Breaux, John		Senate	10			15	United States Senate (D - LA)
Brécard, Gen. Charles-Théodore	1867-1952	Military	20				World War II French general
Brecht, Bertolt	1898-1956	Author	400	1192	3100		Important 20th Cent. Ger.-Jewish Playwright, Poet
Breckinridge, John Cabell	1821-1875	Civil War & VP US	344	659	865	633	CSA Gen., Sec'y War. Sig/Rank 525, ALS 1585
Breckinridge, Robert Jefferson		Civil War	38	81			Member of Confederate Congress
Breckinridge, Wm. C.	1837-	Civil War	110	228	275		CSA Officer
Breeding, J. Floyd		Senate/Congress	5	15		10	MOCKS
Breen, Bobby		Entertainment	8	15	30	20	Child Singer. Radio & Films
Breese, Lou		Entertainment	20	40	45	70	Big band leader
Breese, Vance		Aviation	30	115		63	Aviator & Aircraft Designer
Breith, Gen. Panz Hermann	1892-1964	Military	25				World War II German general
Bremer, Lucille		Entertainment	10			25	Astaire Dancing Partner MGM Musical
Bremner, Rory		Celebrity	10			15	impressionist
Brendel, El	1890-1964	Entertainment	15	35		42	Stage & Film Comedy Roles
Breneman, Tom		Entertainment	15	15	30	20	Popular Radio Host
Brennan, Eileen		Entertainment	4	4	10	15	Character Actress. Accident Slowed Career
Brennan, Francis J., Cardinal		Clergy	30	45	55	50	
Brennan, Walter	1894-1974	Entertainment	100	125	262	200	3 Time Oscar Winner

NAME	DATE	CATEGORY	SIG	LS/DS	ALS	SP	COMMENTS
Brennan, William J.		Supreme Court	62	91	155	92	Important 20th Cent. Justice. 1200+ Opinions
Brennecke, Kurt		Military	15	35	60	35	
Brenneman, Amy		Entertainment	10			35	actress
Brenner, Victor D.	1871-1924	Artist	322	345	675		Designer Lincoln Penny -V.D.B.
Brent, Charles H., Bishop		Clergy	25	40	55	40	
Brent, Evelyn		Entertainment	15	20	25	40	Vintage Leading Lady
Brent, George Wm.		Civil War	100	210	300		
Brent, George		Entertainment	25	35	35	60	Vintage Leading Man.
Brent, Joseph Lancaster	1826-	Civil War	110	163	396		CSA Colonel. Sig/Rank Brig. Gen. 225
Brent, Robert		Military	35	100	165		
Brereton, Lewis Hyde	1890-1967	Aviation	55	150		300	Am.Cmdr. 1st Allied Airborne Army WW II
Bres, Edward S.		Military	10	30	50		
Breslau, Sophie		Entertainment	35			90	Opera
Breslin, Jimmy		Celebrities	5	15	40	15	Journalist, Novelist
Bresnahan, Brig. Gen. T. F.	1892-1971	Military	30				World War II U.S. general
Bresser-Gianoli, Clotilde		Entertainment	20			55	Opera
Breton, Andre	1896-1966	Author	68	175	400		Fr. Poet, Essayist, Critic, Editor.ALS/Cont. 1000
Brett, Brig. Gen. Sereno E.	1891-1952	Military	30				World War II U.S. general
Brett, Brigadier Rupert John	1890-1963	Military	25				World War II British general
Brett, George H.	1886-	Military	45	125		45	Air Corps Gen. WW II
Brett, Jeremy	1935-1995	Entertainment	20			195	Portrayed Sherlock Holmes. SP Pc 95
Breu, Paul		Aviation	10			25	Ger. Bomber Pilot. RK
Breuer, Marcel		Architect	20	60	125	150	Bauhaus School/Gropius
Brevard, Theodore Washington	1835-1882	Civil War	74	166			Confederate general
Brewer, David J.		Supreme Court	85	123	160		
Brewer, Maj. Gen. Carlos	1890-1976	Military	30				World War II U.S. general
Brewer, Teresa		Entertainment	5	3	10	15	Big Band Singer. Recording Artist
Brewerton, Henry		Civil War			125		Union Gen. Corps of Engineers
Brewster, Benjamin		Cabinet	10	35	50		Chester A. Arthur Att'y General.
Brewster, David, Sir	1781-1868	Science	35	55	198		Physicist. Invented Kaleidoscope
Brewster, Kingman Jr		Educator	5	15	25	15	Diplomat
Brewster, Ralph Owen		Senate	10	25	40	30	Senator, MOC ME
Breyer, Hiltrud		Political	10			15	Member European Parliament
Breyer, Stephen		Supreme Court	20			40	
Brezhnev, Leonid I.		Head of State	375	644		400	Soviet Communist Party Leader
Brian, Mary		Entertainment	5	7	15	20	Vintage Actress. Ingenue
Brice, Benjamin W.		Civil War	15	45			Union Paymaster General
Brice, Fanny	1891-1951	Entertainment	102	138	300	328	Vintage Stage, Radio, Films. Top Comedienne-Singer
Brickell, Edie		Entertainment	8			30	
Bricker, Brig. Gen. Edwin D.	1875-1967	Military	30				World War II U.S. general
Bricker, John W.		Senate	15	30		20	Gov. Ohio
Brickman, Brigadier Ivan Pringle	1891-1980	Military	25				World War II British general
Brico, Antonia, Dr.		Conductor	15			75	Eccentric Female Conductor
Bridgeford, Lt. Gen. William	1894-1971	Military	20				World War II Australian general
Bridgeman, Maj. Gen. Robert	1896-1982	Military	25				World War II British general

NAME	DATE	CATEGORY	SIG	LS/DS	ALS	SP	COMMENTS
Bridgers, Robert Rufus	1819-1888	Civil War	51		117		Member of Confederate Congress
Bridges, Beau		Entertainment	15	20	30	33	Actor. Like Lloyd and Jeff—Versatile Parts
Bridges, H. Styles		Senate	7	15		10	Senator NH
Bridges, Harry		Labor Leader	70	180		140	Pres. Longshoreman Union. Powerful
Bridges, Jeff		Entertainment	15	18	22	30	Actor. Versatile Leading Man. Variety of Parts
Bridges, Lloyd	1913-1998	Entertainment	28	40	45	47	Actor. Much loved for TV series 'Seahunt'
Bridges, Robert	1844-1930	Author	15		65		Poet Laureate England
Bridges, Roy D. Jr.		Astronaut	10			25	
Bridges, Todd		Entertainment	15	20		30	Troubled child actor. 'Different Strokes'
Bridgman, Laura D.	1829-1889	Celebrity	30	55	80		1st Blind, Deaf, Mute Systematically Educated
Bridoux, Lt Gen Eugène-Marie-L.	1888-1955	Military	20				World War II French general
Bridy, Pat*		Cartoonist	10		25		'Rose is Rose'
Brie, André		Political	10			15	Member European Parliament
Brienza, Giuseppe		Political	10			15	Member European Parliament
Briesen, Gen. of Infantry Kurt von	1883-1941	Military	25				World War II German general
Brigdeman, Brig. Geoffrey John O	1898-1974	Military	25				World War II British general
Briggs, Austin*		Cartoonist	25			200	'Flash Gordon'
Briggs, Brig. Gen. Raymond W.	1878-1959	Military	30				World War II U.S. general
Briggs, Brigadier Rawdon	1892-1969	Military	25				World War II British general
Briggs, Charles F.		Author	15	40	125		Editor NY Times
Briggs, Clare A.*	1875-1930	Cartoonist	15			50	'Mr. & Mrs.'
Briggs, Henry Shaw	1824-1887	Civil War	33		190	250	Union Gen. Wounded 'Seven Pines'. War Dte ALS 340
Briggs, James E.		Military	10	25	50	20	
Briggs, Johnny		Entertainment	10			20	Actor
Briggs, Le Baron Russell	1855-1934	Educator	5		20		Legendary Harvard Professor
Briggs, Maj. Gen. Raymond	1895-1985	Military	25				World War II British general
Briggs, Roxanne Dawson		Entertainment	15			35	Actress, Star Trek
Brigham, Louis S.		Business	10	35	45	20	
Bright, John	1811-1889	Statesman	35	50	155		Radical Br. Orator.(Corn Laws)
Bright, Richard	1789-1858	Science			525		Physician
Brightman, Sarah		Entertainment	22			50	Star of Andrew Lloyd Weber's Musicals. Ex Wife
Brigitte, Simone		Entertainment	5			20	Model-Actress
Brimley, Wilford		Entertainment	5			20	Character Actor. Films/TV
Brimmer, Andrew F.		Government	10	15		15	Afro-Am. Gov. Fed. Res. Board
Brind, Gen. Sir John Edward S.	1878-1954	Military	25				World War II British general
Brinegar, Paul		Entertainment	10	15	20	25	
Brink, Brig. Gen. Francis G.	1893-1952	Military	30				World War II U.S. general
Brinkley, Christie		Entertainment	10	25	30	56	Model
Brinkley, David	-2003	Journalist	10			25	TV News Anchor-Commentator
Brinson, Samuel Mitchell		Senate/Congress	10	20	45		MOC NC
Brisbane, Arthur		Author	15	35	100	30	Influential Editorial Writer
Brisbin, James Sanks	1837-1892	Civil War	38		129		Cmdr. Afr-Am. Cavalry.Abolitionist.ALS/Cont. 775
Brisebois, Danielle		Entertainment	4	3	6	9	Actress
Brissette, Tiffany		Entertainment	5			10	Child Actress
Brisson, Carl		Entertainment	15	15	25	20	Danish Actor. Stage-Screen

NAME	DATE	CATEGORY	SIG	LS/DS	ALS	SP	COMMENTS
Bristol, Henry Platt		Business	275	850	1075		Founder Bristol-Myers
Bristol, Mark		Military	20	25		25	Admiral WW I
Bristow, Benjamin Helm	1832-1896	Cabinet	25	65	120		Civil War Commanded 25th KY
Bristow, Lonnie R.		Celebrity	10			15	medical expert
Britt, Mai		Entertainment	10			25	Actress
Britt, Maurice L., Capt.	1912-1984	Military	25	35			WW II Hero CMH & Football Star
Brittain, Delia Tipton		Author	8			12	Southern mountain history
Brittany, Morgan		Entertainment	10	15	25	25	Actress
Britten, Benjamin	1913-1976	Composer	158	344	554	296	Br. Conductor. 'Peter Grimes'. AMusQS 990-1600
Britten, Brigadier Charles Richard	1894-1984	Military	25				World War II British general
Brittingham, Brig. Gen. James F.	1894-1983	Military	30				World War II U.S. general
Britton, Pamela		Entertainment	10			15	Actress
Britton, Barbara		Entertainment	9	8	15	25	Actress-Model. Leading Lady.
Britton, Sherry		Entertainment	5	6	15	10	
Brittorous, Maj Gen Francis G. R.	1896-1974	Military	25				World War II British general
Brix, Herman		Entertainment	10	12	15	20	SEE Bruce Bennett
Broad, Lt Gen Sir Charles Noel F.	1882-1976	Military	25				World War II British general
Broadbent, Jim		Entertainment	15			40	AA winner
Broadhead, James Overton		Law	25		65		Att'y Friend of Lincoln
Broca, Paul	1824-1880	Science	125		746		Fr. Pathologist, Surgeon, Anthropologist
Brocard, Maj Gen Georges-L-M	1886-1947	Military	20				World War II French general
Broccoli, Cubby		Entertainment	10	20	20	25	Film director
Brochler, Jan		Entertainment	10			35	Opera, Dutch Baritone
Brock, Brig. Gen. Ronald C.	1895-1984	Military	30				World War II U.S. general
Brock, Thomas, Sir	1847-1922	Artist	10		35		Brit. Sculptor. Statues of Longfellow, Q. Victoria
Brock, William G. Sen.		Business	20	70	125	40	
Brock, William		Clergy	15	25	40	25	
Brockenbrough, John White	1806-1877	Civil War	64		134		Member of Confederate Congress
Brod, Max	1884-1968	Author	90		675		Czech-born Austrian Writer. Biographer. Kafka Ed.
Broder, David		Celebrity	10			15	media/TV personality
Broderick, Helen		Entertainment	25			70	Vintage Character Actress.
Broderick, Matthew		Entertainment	12	22	20	38	Actor. Films-TV-Stage
Brodhead, Daniel	1736-1809	Revolutionary War	200	650			Legendary Am.Officer.Talented Negotiator.Renegade
Brodhead, James E.		Entertainment	5	6	15	15	
Brodhead, Richard		Senator	15	35	75		Senator from PA
Brodie, Benjamin C.Sir	1783-1880	Science	35	65	138		Br. Orthopedic Surgeon
Brodie, Steve	1856-1901	Entertainment	100				World Champion. Jumped off Brooklyn Bridge
Brodie, Steve	1919-1993	Entertainment	5			25	Actor. Major Film Player in Major Productions
Brodsky, Joseph		Author	10	15	25	30	Poet. Nobel Laureate
Brodsky, Michael A., M. D.		Science	5	7	10	20	Cardiac Electrophysiologist UCI.
Brody, Adrien		Actor	15			35	AA winner, 'Pianist'
Brody, Lane		Entertainment	4			10	
Broglie, Duke A-C-L-V		Statesman	135	270	540		Fr. Politician. Author
Broglie, Louis Victor de	1892-1987	Science	62	200	342	595	Nobel Physics. Theory of Quantum Mechanics
Broglin, Winnie W.		Author	8			12	church history

NAME	DATE	CATEGORY	SIG	LS/DS	ALS	SP	COMMENTS
Brok, Elmar		Political	10			15	Member European Parliament
Brokaw, Meredith		Celebrity	10			15	motivational speaker
Broke, Sir Philip V.I.		Military			345		
Brokow, Tom		Journalist	15	12	25	65	TV News Anchor-Commentator-Author
Brolin, James		Entertainment	15	20	30	33	Actor. 'Marcus Welby', 'Hotel' TV Series
Bromberg, J. Edward		Entertainment	30			65	Character Actor. Major Films
Bromfield, John		Entertainment	10			25	Handsome Leading Man. Films
Bromfield, Louis	1896-1950	Author	35	125	175	65	Am. Novelist. Pulitzer. 'Mrs. Parkington'
Bronk, Detlev W.	1897-1975	Science	15	25	40	25	Pres.Nat'l Adademy of Sci. Physiologist, Neurology
Bronson, Betty		Entertainment	35			75	Vintage
Bronson, Charles	1921-	Entertainment	12	23	25	45	Major Action Star 70's. Watch for Secretarials.
Bronson, David	1800-1863	Congress	25				Repr. ME, Collector of Customs
Bronson, Wilfred S.		Artist					signed drawing 130
Bronte, Charlotte		Author			8250		Br. Novelist. Jane Eyre
Brook, Alexander		Artist	25	40	75		
Brook, Clive	1887-1974	Entertainment	45	55	75	95	Br.Actor. 1st Talky 'Sherlock Holmes'
Brook, Kelly		Celebrity	10			15	celebrity model
Brooke, Alan, Fld Marshal, Sir		Military	40	110	205	87	Cmdr. Br.II Corps WW II,Dunkirk
Brooke, Edward W.		Senate	10	15		25	Afr.-Am. Rep. Senator MA
Brooke, Hillary		Entertainment	10	15	25	25	Actress. Blonde-Sophisticated Other Woman
Brooke, John M.	1826-1906	Civil War			370		Commander Confed. Navy
Brooke, John Rutter	1838-1926	Civil War	47	85	282		Union Gen. Sig/Rank. Wounded at Gettysburg
Brooke, Rupert	1887-1915	Author	540	575	1890		Br. Poet. Died in WW at 28
Brooke, Walter	1813-1869	Civil War		118			Member of Confederate Congress
Brooke-Popham, Robert		Military	30	65	95	50	Br. Air Chief Marshal WW II
Brookes, Bruno		Music	10			15	DJ
Brookhart, Smith W.		Senate	10	15		15	Senator IA
Brooks & Dunn		Country Music	8			45	Kic and Ronnie
Brooks ,Chas. Wm. Shirley	1816-1874	Author	15		55		Humorist, Editor of 'Punch'
Brooks, A. Raymond		Aviation	35	60	85	75	Bi-Plane ACE, WW I
Brooks, Albert		Entertainment	10			10	Actor
Brooks, Angie		Stateswoman	15				Pres. U.N. Assembly
Brooks, Arthur		Aviation	15		30	35	
Brooks, Avery		Entertainment	20			63	Star Trek
Brooks, Dick*		Cartoonist	5			35	Jackson Twins
Brooks, Foster		Entertainment	5	6	15	10	Character Actor. Everybody's Favorite 'Drunk'
Brooks, Fred Emerson		Author	10	15	35		Poet
Brooks, Garth		Country Western	20		35	65	Mega Grammy Winner,signed guitar 450
Brooks, Gwendolyn	1917	Author	20	66		25	Afro-Am. Poet. Pulitzer. FDC S 35
Brooks, James L.		Entertainment	10			20	
Brooks, Jason		Entertainment	10			20	actor
Brooks, John		Military	55	139	275		Am. Revolution Gen., Gov. MA
Brooks, Leslie		Entertainment	10	12	15	15	Actress-Dancer.
Brooks, Louise	1906-1985	Entertainment	165	320	425	595	One of the Screen's Great Beauties. Rare
Brooks, Lt. Gen. Edward H.	1893-1978	Military	30				World War II U.S. general

NAME	DATE	CATEGORY	SIG	LS/DS	ALS	SP	COMMENTS
Brooks, Mel		Entertainment	10	20	25	32	Actor-Comic- Director AA
Brooks, Peter H.		Clergy	15	25	35		
Brooks, Phillips	1835-93	Clergy-Author	82	120	130	125	Episcopal Bishop. 'O Little Town of Bethlehem'.
Brooks, Rand		Entertainment	15	15	40	45	'GWTW' 'Chas. Hamilton'. Scarlett's 1st Husband
Brooks, Randi		Entertainment	5	8	15	15	
Brooks, Richard		Entertainment	20	30		60	AA Film Director
Brooks, Wm. Thos. H.	1821-1870	Civil War	45	85	148		Union Gen. ALS '64 245
Broom, Jacob		Revolutionary War	350	900	2000		Continental Congress
Broomall, John M.		Senate/Congress	10	15	40		MOC DE 1863. CW Officer
Broome, Michael		Celebrity	10			15	motivational speaker
Brophy, Ed		Entertainment	25			40	Character Actor. Rotund Cigar-Smoking
Brophy, Kevin		Entertainment	4	3	6	10	
Brophy, Theodore F.		Business	4	5		10	CEO GTE
Brosnan, Pierce		Entertainment	25	40	45	55	Newest James Bond. SP 65
Brosset, Brig Gen Diego-Chas-J.	1898-1944	Military	20				World War II French general
Brothers, Joyce		Science	5	10	25	15	Early TV Psychiatrist. Frequent Consulting Guest
Brough, Candi & Randi		Entertainment	10			25	
Brough, Fanny		Entertainment	4	4	9	10	Vintage Actress
Brough, Lionel		Entertainment	4	4	9	10	Vintage Actor
Brougham, Henry, Lord	1778-1868	Statesman	82	115	250		Designed One Horse Brougham. Author,Scholar
Brougham, John	1814-1880	Entertainment	20			45	Am. Actor-Playwright-Mgr. 'London Assurance:
Brougher, Brig. Gen. William E.	1889-1965	Military	30				World War II U.S. general
Broughton, Joseph M.		Senate/Congress	5	12		10	Senator/MOC NC
Broun, Heywood	1888-1939	Author	10	35	70	20	Journalist, Novelist, Columnist
Brouncker, William	1620-1684	Scientist		65			
Browder, Earl	1891-1973	Political	15	35	65	25	US Communist Party Leader
Brower, Jordan		Celebrity				30	
Brown, A. Roy		Aviation WW I	288				Can. Ace. Downed Richtofen
Brown, Aaron V.	1795-1859	Cabinet	45	125			PMG, Repr.& Sen. TN
Brown, Albert Gallatin		Governor	60	60	95		CSA Senator, Gov. Miss., Member of CSA Congress
Brown, Alice		Author	15	35	100	60	Prolific Novelist, Poet
Brown, Arthur Whitten	1886-1948	Aviation	292	410	575	575	Alcock & Brown 1st Nonstop Flight Over Atlantic
Brown, Benjamin Gratz	1826-1885	Congress	15		25		Sen. MO
Brown, Blair		Entertainment	10	8	15	20	Actress.
Brown, Bo		Cartoonist	5			20	Magazine Cartoonist
Brown, Bothwell		Entertainment	10	15	25	25	Vintage Actor
Brown, Brig. Gen. Ames T.	1890-1961	Military	30				World War II U.S. general
Brown, Brig. Gen. Charles C.	1890-1970	Military	30				World War II U.S. general
Brown, Brig. Gen. Homer C.	1893-1950	Military	30				World War II U.S. general
Brown, Brig. Gen. Thoburn K.	1888-1958	Military	30				World War II U.S. general
Brown, Brig. Gen. Wyburn D.	1899-1981	Military	30				World War II U.S. general
Brown, Brigadier Alan Ward	1909-1971	Military	25				World War II British general
Brown, Bryan		Entertainment	10			20	actor
Brown, Catherine		Celebrity	10			15	Scottish Chef
Brown, Charles Brockden	1771-1810	Author	975		6500		Father of the American Novel

NAME	DATE	CATEGORY	SIG	LS/DS	ALS	SP	COMMENTS
Brown, Charles		Entertainment	15			50	Blues Singer. Rock/Roll HOF
Brown, Clarence		Entertainment	10			25	
Brown, Corrine B		Congress	10			15	Member U.S. Congress
Brown, Curtis, Jr.		Astronaut	8			25	
Brown, Danielle		Entertainment	10			20	Actress
Brown, David		Astronaut	100			225	Columbia Tragedy
Brown, David		Entertainment	10			20	Producer. Oscar Winner
Brown, Down Town Julie		Entertainment	5			15	TV Host-Singer
Brown, Edmund G. 'Jerry'		Governor	10	25		15	Governor CA, Pres. Candidate. Mayor Oakland, CA
Brown, Edmund G. 'Pat'	1905-1996	Governor	20	25		25	Governor CA. Liberal Civil Rights Champion
Brown, Edward N.		Business	12			15	RR Exec.
Brown, Egbert Benson	1816-1902	Civil War	38	72	128		Union general
Brown, Faith		Celebrity	10			15	comedienne
Brown, Ford Madox	1821-1893	Artist	45		105		Br. Historical Painter
Brown, George Stan		Entertainment	6			15	Afr.-Am Actor
Brown, Harold, Dr.		Science-Cabinet	10	20		15	Sec'y Defense
Brown, Harry Joe		Entertainment	20	40	65	25	Film Producer, Director
Brown, Helen Gurley		Author	5	10	20	20	Editor, Publisher
Brown, Henry B.		Supreme Court	62	175	250		
Brown, Henry E. B., Jr.		Congress	10			15	Member U.S. Congress
Brown, Henry W.		Aviation	12	25	45	30	ACE, WW II
Brown, Herbert C., Dr.		Science	25	30	45	35	Nobel Chemistry
Brown, Jacob	1775-1828	Military	50	135	219		Important Gen'l War of 1812
Brown, James		Entertainment	30			65	Rock. Alb. S 70
Brown, James		Entertainment	5			20	Actor
Brown, Jim Ed		Country Music	5			15	
Brown, Joe E.	1892-1973	Entertainment	30	50	72	91	Vintage Film Comedian
Brown, John Calvin	1827-1889	Civil War	126	205	350		CSA Gen. Sig/Rank 240. Gov. TN 1871-75
Brown, John George		Artist	10	30	45		
Brown, John Y.		Business	10	25	51	20	
Brown, John	1800-1859	Civil War	1138	2080	6516	6910	Fanatical Abolitionist-Hung for treason
Brown, Johnny Mack		Entertainment	50	75		125	Cowboy Actor
Brown, Joseph Emerson		Civil War	48	80	169		Civil War Gov. Georgia
Brown, Julie		Entertainment	10			20	actress
Brown, Les		Entertainment	15			30	Big Band Leader. Many Years/Bob Hope. Radio
Brown, Lt. Gen. Sir John	1880-1958	Military	25				World War II British general
Brown, Lt. John		Revolutionary War	72	175	400		
Brown, Lytle	1872-1951	Military	35			95	U.S. Army Gen'l. Sp-Am.War. Battle San Juan Hill
Brown, Maj. Gen. Albert E.	1889-1984	Military	30				World War II U.S. general
Brown, Maj. Gen. Lloyd D.	1892-1950	Military	30				World War II U.S. general
Brown, Maj. Gen. Philip E.	1896-1978	Military	30				World War II U.S. general
Brown, Mark N.		Astronaut	6			23	
Brown, Marty		Country Music	4			15	Traditional Country Sound
Brown, Moses		Revolutionary War	45		265		Naval Commander
Brown, Nicholas	1729-1791	Revolutionary War	35	110	195		Businessman. Supplied Army. Brown University

NAME	DATE	CATEGORY	SIG	LS/DS	ALS	SP	COMMENTS
Brown, Norma		Military	10	20	30	15	
Brown, Norman		Entertainment	4			10	
Brown, Phil		Entertainment	5			20	Actor. 'Star Wars'. Uncle Owen
Brown, Phyllis George		Entertainment	5	8	20	15	
Brown, Prentiss M.		Senate	10	25		15	Senator MI
Brown, Preston		Military	32	35		45	General WW I. Chief of Staff
Brown, Reno		Entertainment	15			50	Actress. Early Westerns
Brown, Robert		Military	30		75	125	General WW I
Brown, Robert	1773-1858	Science	135		775		Scot. Botanist. Living Cells Nucleus
Brown, Ron		Cabinet	32	40		68	Sec'y Commerce Clinton Cabinet.Tragic Plane Crash
Brown, Ruth		Entertainment	20			45	Rock & Roll HOF
Brown, Sam J.		Aviation	20	40	55	45	ACE, WW II
Brown, Sherrod B		Congress	10			15	Member U.S. Congress
Brown, T. Graham		Country Music	5			18	Country/Soul/Rock Sound
Brown, Tom		Entertainment	10	15	25	25	Actor. Many Youthful Parts
Brown, Tony		Celebrity	10			15	motivational speaker
Brown, William Wallace		Congress	10	15	30		Repr. PA. CW Officer
Brown, William		Celebrity	10			15	political celebrity
Brownback, Sam		Senate	10			15	United States Senate (R - KS)
Browne, Brig. Gen. Frederick W.	1875-1960	Military	30				World War II U.S. general
Browne, Brig. Dominick Andrew S.	1904-1982	Military	25				World War II British general
Browne, Charles Farrar							SEE Ward, Artemus
Browne, Chris*		Cartoonist	20			75	'Hagar'
Browne, Coral		Entertainment	10	15	20	25	
Browne, Dik*		Cartoonist	20			60	Hi & Lois, Hagar
Browne, Hablot Knight		Artist	25	90	150		Watercolor. Illustrator of Dickens
Browne, Jackson		Entertainment	20	35		55	Rock
Browne, Leslie		Entertainment	5	7	12	10	
Browne, Maj. Gen. Beverly Wood	d. 1948	Military	24				World War II Canadian general
Browne, William Montague	1827-1883	Civil War	76	176			Confederate general
Brownell, Francis E.		Civil War	368				CMOH
Brownell, Herbert Jr.	1904-1996	Cabinet	15	20	40	80	Att'y Gen., Eisenhower Adm.'Time' Cover S. 35
Browning, Brig. Gen. Albert J.	1899-1948	Military	30				World War II U.S. general
Browning, Eliz. Barrett		Author	325	1085	4250	3167	Br. Poet
Browning, George		Business	195	580			Browning Arms Mfg.
Browning, John B.		Business	50	160		75	Pres. Browning Arms Co.
Browning, John Moses	1855-1926	Inventor-Business	195	310	575	1650	Inventor-Designer of Fire Arms. Browning Automatic
Browning, Orville H.	1806-1881	Cabinet	25	125			Sec'y of Interior, Sen.IL
Browning, Ricou		Entertainment	12			35	Creature, Olympic Swimmer
Browning, Robert	1812-1889	Author	248	470	865	1150	Br. Poet. AMsS 3250, 3400. AQS 1075
Browning, Tod		Entertainment	75			250	
Brownjohn, General Sir N.	1897-1973	Military	25				World War II British general
Brownlee, John		Entertainment	10		45	30	Opera, Australian/Am. Baritone
Brownlow, William G.	1848-1902	Journalist		242			
Brown-Sequard, Chas. E.	1817-1894	Science			482		Fr. Physician. Father of Endocrinology

NAME	DATE	CATEGORY	SIG	LS/DS	ALS	SP	COMMENTS
Brown-Waite, Ginny B		Congress	10			15	Member U.S. Congress
Brubeck, Dave		Entertainment	15	35	45	50	Jazz Great. Pianist, Composer
Bruce, Andrew D.		Military	35	175		90	Gen. 77th Infantry Div. So. Pacific. WW II
Bruce, Blanche K.	1841-1898	Senator	90	160	220		Born a Slave. 1st Afro-Am.Full Term Senator
Bruce, Brigadier Sir John	1905-1975	Military	25				World War II British general
Bruce, Carol		Entertainment	8	10	15	30	Blues-Jazz Vocalist. Content ALS 95
Bruce, David		Entertainment	10			20	
Bruce, Ed		Country Music	5			15	Singer/Songwriter
Bruce, Eli Metcalfe	1828-1866	Civil War	57	102			Member of Confederate Congress
Bruce, Horatio Wasington	1830-1903	Civil War	48		138		Member of Confederate Congress
Bruce, Lenny	1926-1966	Entertainment	470	575	1150	1075	Controversial ComedianALS/Typescript Archive 5750
Bruce, Maj Gen Geo. McIllree. S.	1896-1966	Military	25				World War II British general
Bruce, Maj. Gen. John Geoffrey	1896-1972	Military	25				World War II British general
Bruce, Nigel	1895-1953	Entertainment	150	175	300	388	Noted for Dr. Watson. Caricature S 250
Bruce, Thos. (7th Earl Elgin)	1766-1841	Diplomat	50	190	340		Conveyed Elgin Marbles. Greece to British Museum
Bruce, Virginia		Entertainment	15			25	Actress. Late 30's-40's Sophisticated Leading Lady
Bruce, Wallace		Author	35		120		
Bruce, Wm. Cabell	1860-1946	Congress	5	15	30	10	Sen. MD, Author
Bruch, Max	1838-1920	Composer	95	200	280	256	Ger. Opera,AMusQS 950-1,100-2,500
Bruckner, Josef Anton	1824-1896	Composer	1600	2750	5500	2500	Aus. 10 Symphonies.
Brummel, Geo. B. 'Beau'	1778-1840	Celebrity	95	220	850		Br. Man of Fashion, Friend of Prince Regent
Brummer, Renate		Astronaut	10			25	Germany
Bruna Rasa, Lina		Entertainment	65			300	Opera. Great Verismo Soprano. Mascagni Favorite
Brune, G.M.A.	1763-1815	Napoleonic Wars	85	350	450		Marshal of Nap. Assassinated
Brunel, Marc Isambard, Sir	1769-1849	Science	75	181	323		Fr.-Br.Inventor, Engineer
Brunetta, Renato		Political	10			15	Member European Parliament
Bruning, Heinrich	1885-1971	Head of State			100	425	Ger. Chancellor. Fled to U.S. '34
Brunner, Emil		Clergy	45	75	110	50	
Brunskill, Brigadier Geo.	1891-1982	Military	25				World War II British general
Brunskill, Maj. Gen. Gerald	1894-1964	Military	25				World War II British general
Bruscantini, Sesto		Entertainment	15			45	Opera
Brush, Maj. Gen. Rapp	1889-1958	Military	30				World War II U.S. general
Bruson, Renato		Entertainment	10			30	Opera
Bruton, Brig. Gen. Philip G.	1891-1960	Military	30				World War II U.S. general
Bry, Ellen		Entertainment	5	3	6	10	Actress
Bryan, Charles W.		Governor	12	25			Governor NE
Bryan, George		Revolutionary War	120	350	750		Jurist. Proposed Abolition 1777
Bryan, Goode	1811-1885	Civil War	172		539		CSA Gen. Sig/Rank 300. Poor Health, Resigned '64
Bryan, Jane		Entertainment	5	10	20	15	Actress. 40's Warner Bros. Leading Lady
Bryan, Lt. Gen. Blackshear M.	1900-1977	Military	30				World War II U.S. general
Bryan, William E.		Aviation	14	22	42	32	ACE, WW II
Bryan, William Jennings	1860-1925	Cabinet	88	308	419	535	Pres. Nominee 3 Times. Sec'y State. TLS/Cont.1150
Bryant, Alys McKey		Aviation	35	60	140	75	
Bryant, Anita		Entertainment	5	8	10	10	Controversial Singer
Bryant, Ed		Congress	5			15	Tennessee

NAME	DATE	CATEGORY	SIG	LS/DS	ALS	SP	COMMENTS
Bryant, William Cullen	1794-1878	Author	65	325	502	750	Am. Poet, ALS/Content 1,750
Bryden, Maj. Gen. William	1880-1972	Military	30				World War II U.S. general
Brynner, Yul	1915-1985	Entertainment	50	55	75	151	Academy Award for 'King & I' 1952
Bryson, Ann		Entertainment	10			20	Actress
Brzezinski, Zbigniew		Celebrity	10			15	political celebrity
Buber, Martin		Clergy	75	175	289	90	
Buchan, Brigadier David Adye	1890-1950	Military	25				World War II British general
Buchan, John, Lord	1875-1940	Author	25	236			Gov. Gen. Canada, Novelist
Buchanan, Brig. Gen. Kenneth	1892-1967	Military	30				World War II U.S. general
Buchanan, Brig. Edgar James B.	1892-1979	Military	25				World War II British general
Buchanan, Edgar	1902-1979	Entertainment	52	40	55	75	Jovial-Rugged AM. Character Actor. 1939-71
Buchanan, Franklin	1800-1874	Civil War	160	348	495		CSA Admiral
Buchanan, James (as Pres)		Presidents	425	1118	1850		15th President of USA
Buchanan, James	1791-1868	President	343	675	889	2583	Special SP 12,500, FF 350-450, ALS cont 2000-5000
Buchanan, James M.		Economics	35	45	85	40	Nobel Economics
Buchanan, Patrick		Political	12	15		28	Political Commentator. Presidential Candidate
Buchanan, Robert C. 'Old Buck'	1811-1878	Civil War	47	128	210		Union general
Buchanon, Neil		Celebrity	10			15	children's presenter
Buchel, August	1813-1864	Civil War		92			1st Texas Calvary
Bucher, Brig. Gen. Oliver B.	1890-1962	Military	30				World War II U.S. general
Bucher, Gen Sir Francis Robert R.	1895-1980	Military	25				World War II British general
Bucher, Lloyd M.		Military	32	90	150	90	Captured Capt. of USS Pueblo
Buchli, James F.		Astronaut	5	15		25	
Buchman, Franklin		Clergy	20	35	65		
Buchwald, Art		Author	10	15	25	15	Syndicated Humor Columnist
Buck, Clayton Douglass		Senate	11	15	25	20	Senator-Governor DE
Buck, Dudley	1839-1909	Composer	10				Organist
Buck, Frank	1884-1950	Big Game Hunter	50	80	198	105	'Bring 'Em Back Alive'.Author, Lecturer
Buck, Paul H.		Author	4	10	15	5	
Buck, Pearl S.	1892-1973	Author	40	122	247	42	Am. Novelist. Nobel, Pulitzer,. AMS 1000
Buckingham, Catharinus Putnam	1808-1888	Civil War	42	114	138		Union Gen. LS '62 745
Buckingham, George V.	1592-1628	Royalty	100		700		1st Duke of..
Buckingham, George V.	1628-1687	Royalty			700		2nd Duke of Buckingham, Politician
Buckingham, William A.		Governor	27	55	83	75	Civil War Gov. CT. & US Sen.
Buckland, Ralph Pomeroy (WD)	1812-1892	Civil War	130		250		Union Gen.
Buckle, Henry Thomas		Author	5	10	25		
Buckle, Maj Gen Denys Herbert V.	1902-1994	Military	28				World War II British general
Buckley, James		Senate/Congress	6	15		10	
Buckley, Maj. Gen. John	1883-1972	Military	25				World War II British general
Buckley, Maj. Gen. Sir Hugh Clive	1880-1962	Military	25				World War II British general
Buckley, William F., Jr.		Author	7	15	45	20	National Revue, Conservative Journalist
Bucknall, Lt. Gen. Gerard Corfield	1894-1980	Military	25				World War II British general
Buckner, Lt. Gen. Simon B.	1886-1945	Military	30				World War II U.S. general
Buckner, Simon Bolivar (WD)		Civil War	450	2500	4608		CSA General
Buckner, Simon Bolivar	1823-1914	Civil War	203	363	482	295	CSA Gen.

NAME	DATE	CATEGORY	SIG	LS/DS	ALS	SP	COMMENTS
Buckstone, John B.	1802-1879	Entertainment	15		25	35	Br. Actor, Comedian, Playwright
Buczacki, Stefan		Celebrity	10			15	home/gardening expert
Budd, Julie		Entertainment	3	3	6	6	
Buechler, Brig. Gen. Theodore E.	1893-1980	Military	30				World War II U.S. general
Buell, Don Carlos	1818-1898	Civil War	90	105	162	250	Union Gen. ADS '62 400
Buell, Nathaniel		Revolutionary War	25	225			His Reg't Secured Ft Ticonderoga. Lt. Col.
Buerk, Michael		Celebrity	10			15	newsreader
Buffalo Bill Jr.		Entertainment	25			50	
Buffett, Jimmy		Entertainment	10			35	Rock
Buffey, Brigadier William	1899-1984	Military	28				World War II British general
Buffington, Thomas Mitchell		Old West	350	550			Chief of Cherokee Nations
Buffy the Vampire Slayer (cast)		Entertainment				200	cast of 7
Buford, Abraham	1820-1884	Civil War	188	356	1144		CSA Gen.
Buford, John	1826-1863	Civil War	300	1582	4715		Union Gen., signed engraving 2415, KIA Gettysburg
Buford, Napoleon Bonaparte	1807-1883	Civil War	58	152	232		Union Gen. ALS '62 320
Bugliosi, Vince		Legal	16				Manson Trial Att'y
Buhari, Mohammed		Head of State	15	50	130	25	
Buick, David D.		Business	170	900	1250	275	Buick Motor Co.
Buitenweg, Kathalijne Maria		Political	10			15	Member European Parliament
Bujold, Genevieve		Entertainment	6	8	15	20	
Bukowski, Charles	1920-1994	Author	70			100	Am. Avant-Garde Writer. BS 750, AMsS 95, s.drw 550
Bulfinch, Charles		Architect	130	375	850		Fanueil Hall, Completed Construction of Capitol
Bulfinch, Thomas		Author	20	45	100		Bulfinch's Mythology
Bulganin, Nicholai	1895-1975	Military		155			Soviet military and political leader
Bulkley, John D.		Military	35	65		35	Adm. USN WW II
Bull, John S.		Astronaut	15			25	
Bull, Lt. Gen. Harold R.	1893-1976	Military	30				World War II U.S. general
Bull, Ole B.		Composer	15		125	125	Nor. Violin Virtuoso
Bull, Robert, Dr.		Celebrity	10			15	health and fitness expert
Bull, William	1710-1791	Rev War	110	310	750		Colonial Governor SC
Bull, William, II		Governor	60		240		Governor SC 1760
Bullard, Joe		Author	8			12	Florida castles
Bullard, Robert Lee		Military	20	75	130	100	General WW I
Bullard, William		Military	15	35			Admiral WW I
Bullene, Maj. Gen. Egbert F.	1895-1958	Military	30				World War II U.S. general
Bullen-Smith, Maj Gen Charles D.	1898-1970	Military	25				World War II British general
Buller, Redvers, Sir		Military	40	110	250	175	Cmdr-in-Chief South Africa
Bullet Boys (4)		Entertainment	10			40	
Bullitt, William P.		Diplomat	10	20		25	Ambassador To USSR
Bullmann, Hans Udo		Political	10			15	Member European Parliament
Bulloch, Terrence		Aviation	20			35	Br. Aviator WWII
Bullock, Brigadier Humpry	1899-1959	Military	25				World War II British general
Bullock, Robert	1828-1905	Civil War	80				Confederate general
Bullock, Sandra		Entertainment	15			46	Actress. Popular Star. Pin-up SP 95
Bullock, Seth		Lawman	200	500			Stock Cert. Signed 975

NAME	DATE	CATEGORY	SIG	LS/DS	ALS	SP	COMMENTS
Bullock, Walter		Author	3	4	7	5	
Bulow, Bernhard H.M.K. von		Head of State	15	35	90	40	Prussian Imperial Chancellor
Bulow, Claus von		Celebrity	15	25		20	Danish Count. Accused Murderer
Bulow, Hans von	1830-1894	Conductor	45	120	285		Germ. Conductor, Pianist. ALS/Content 500
Bultmann, Rudolph		Clergy	70	90	165	80	
Bulwer, Elizabeth		Author			25		
Bulwer, Wm. Henry Lytton	1801-1872	Diplomat	15	40	75		Clayton-Bulwer Treaty. US & Eng
Bulwer-Lytton, Edward		Author	60	220	460		
Bumbry, Grace		Entertainment	10	20		55	Opera. SP 5x7 30
Bumgarner, Wiley		Author	8			12	religion
Bumpers, Dale		Governor	12	15		20	Senator AR
Bunce, Francis M.		Military	25	55	125	65	Admiral Spanish-American War
Bunche, Ralph J.	1904-1971	Diplomat	55	101	225	117	Afro-Am. Diplomat. Nobel Peace Prize
Bundy, McGeorge		Law	15	35	45	18	Director FBI
Bundy, Omar		Military	35	90		55	General WW I
Bundy, Ted		Criminal		800	1000		Infamous Convicted Mass Murderer
Bunin, Ivan	1870-1953	Poet			322		Russian poet
Bunner, Henry C.	1855-1896	Journalist	70	82	135		Editor Puck Magazine. Story-writer
Bunning, Jim		Political	15			35	Congress from KY
Bunny, John		Entertainment	100	130	160	200	Vintage Film Comedian
Bunsen, Christian K.J., Baron		Diplomat	15	45	115		Prussian Theologian, Scholar
Bunsen, Robert W.	1811-1899	Science	175	485	858	1380	Ger. Chemist, Bunsen Burner
Bunting, Mary		Celebrity	10	28		15	
Bunting, William M.		Clergy	45	100	150		
Buntline, Ned (Pseud)	1823-1886	Author	140	185	370	835	(E.Z.C. Judson) Novelist, Adventurer, Dime Novels.
Bunzel, John		Celebrity	10			15	political celebrity
Buono, Victor		Entertainment	30			100	
Burbank, Luther	1849-1926	Science	108	258	295	140	Pioneer, Experimental Botanist. Original Plants-Veg
Burbridge, Stephen Gano	1831-1894	Civil War	45	91	175		Union general
Burch, Maj Gen Frederick W.	1893-1977	Military	28				World War II British general
Burden, Paul		Celebrity	10			15	newsreader
Burden, Ross		Celebrity	10			15	TV Chef
Burder, George		Clergy	10	15	20	15	
Burdette, Robert J.		Author	20	55	135	80	
Burge, V.L.		Aviation	18			35	
Burger, Warren E.		Supreme Court	50	115	195	125	Chief Justice
Burgess, Anthony	b. 1917	Author	40	55		150	Br. Novelist.Clockwork Orange
Burgess, Michael C. B		Congress	10			15	Member U.S. Congress
Burgess, Thomas, Bishop		Clergy	15	25	35		
Burgess, Thornton W.		Author	30	100	225		Peter Rabbit
Burghley, Wm. Cecil, Lord	1520-1593	Statesman	585	1725			Elizabeth I, Tudor Statesman. LS/Essex 1550
Burghoff, Gary	1940-	Entertainment	10	35		27	Actor. 'Radar' on Long Running 'Mash'
Burgin, Maj. Gen. Henry T.	1882-1958	Military	30				World War II U.S. general
Burgoyne, John	1722-1792	Revolutionary War	1100	2850	3562		Br. Gen. vs Am. Colonies
Burke, Arleigh	1901-1996	Military	35	55	110	100	Adm. USN WW II

NAME	DATE	CATEGORY	SIG	LS/DS	ALS	SP	COMMENTS
Burke, Billie (Ziegfield)	1885-1970	Entertainment	121	168	185	180	Wizard of Oz. Four Figures as 'Glinda the Good'
Burke, Chris		Entertainment	10			20	actor
Burke, Delta		Entertainment	10	20	25	24	Actress. 'Designing Women'
Burke, Edmund		Senate/Congress	5	12	20		U.S. MOC NH
Burke, Edmund	1729-1797	Author			2450		Irish Born Br. Statesman, Author, Orator
Burke, Edward A.		Political	35	45		150	Dominated LA Politics 1880's. Embezzled over 1M
Burke, Paul		Entertainment	5	6	15	15	
Burke, Selma		Artist	10	20	52	40	
Burke, Yvonne B.		Congress	10			20	Afro-Am 3 Term Repr CA
Burleigh, Harry Thacker		Composer	25		150		Singer. Spingarn Med. AMusQS 200-300
Burleigh, Walter A.	1820-1896	Congress	10				Delegate from Dakota Terr.
Burleson, Albert S.		Cabinet	10	25	35		P.M. General, MOC TX
Burleson, Omar Truman		Senate/Congress	5	15		10	MOC TX
Burmester, Willy		Entertainment	90		275		Ger. Violinist. AMusQS 350
Burne-Jones, Edward	1833-1898	Artist	125	235	452		Pre-Raphaelite Painter, Designer
Burnell, Brig. Gen. Nathaniel A.	1897-1976	Military	30				World War II U.S. general
Burnell, Brig. Gen. Ray L.	1891-1968	Military	30				World War II U.S. general
Burnet, David G.	1788-1870	Head of State	275	331	1200		1st Pres. Republic TX
Burnet, William	1688-1728	Colonial	145	465			Br. Gov. NY & NJ
Burnett, Carol	1933-	Entertainment	9	17	20	35	Comedienne. TV multi award winner
Burnett, Frances Hodgson	1849-1924	Author	58	145	285		'Little Lord Fauntleroy'
Burnett, Leo		Business	5	10	25	10	Advertising
Burnett, Peter H.		Governor	200		550		California Pioneer & 1st Gov.
Burnette, Michelle		Author	8			12	Civil war book
Burnette, Smiley		Entertainment	40	50		75	
Burnette, Talmadge L.		Author	8			12	regional history, nostalgia
Burney, Cecil, Sir		Military	15	35			Br. Adm. WW I
Burnham, Hiram	1814-1864	Civil War	52	195			Union Gen.
Burns, Bob		Entertainment	25	25	45	45	Bazooka
Burns, Brig. Lionel Bryan Douglas	1895-1966	Military	25				World War II British general
Burns, Conrad		Senate	10			15	United States Senate (R - MT)
Burns, Ed		Celebrity	10			15	film industry
Burns, Edmund		Entertainment	30			75	Silent Screen Star
Burns, Edward		Entertainment	8			41	Actor. 'Saving Private Ryan'
Burns, Geo. & Gracie Allen		Entertainment	275	375		319	Comedy team, husband and wife
Burns, George	1896-1996	Entertainment	25	40	50	51	Vaudeville-Radio-TV-Film Comedian
Burns, Gordon		Celebrity	10			15	television presenter
Burns, James MacGregor		Author	20	30			Educator, Political Science
Burns, John A.		Governor	12	15		20	Hawaii
Burns, John	1791-1872	Civil War	267			960	Vet. War 1812. Vol. Gettysburg
Burns, Ken		Entertainment	5			15	Documentary Film Maker
Burns, Lt Gen Eedson Louis M.	1897-1985	Military	20				World War II Canadian general
Burns, Maj. Gen. James H.	1885-1972	Military	30				World War II U.S. general
Burns, Max B		Congress	10			15	Member U.S. Congress
Burns, Robert	1759-1796	Author	600	1883	4283		Scottish Poet, Early Poem Draft 13500

NAME	DATE	CATEGORY	SIG	LS/DS	ALS	SP	COMMENTS
Burns, William Chalmers		Clergy	25	40	50	35	
Burns, William J.		Business	35	58	175		Chief FBI 1921-24, Det. Agency
Burns, William Wallace	1825-1892	Civil War	46	93	126	150	Union General
Burnside, Ambrose E. (WD)	1824-1881	Civil War	145	390	570	760	Union Gen. ALS 2,500
Burnside, Ambrose E.	1824-1881	Civil War	102	217	242	797	ALS war date 2,500
Burpee, David		Business	25	35	70	35	Burpee Seed Co.
Burpee, Jonathan		Business	10	25	50	20	Burpee Seed Co.
Burr, Aaron	1756-1836	Vice President	330	620	942		ALS's/Content 7,000-12,000+.Rev.War ALS 5800
Burr, Raymond	1917-1993	Entertainment	20	25	30	65	
Burr, Richard B		Congress	10			15	Member U.S. Congress
Burress, Lt. Gen. Withers A.	1894-1977	Military	30				World War II U.S. general
Burritt, Elihu	1810-1879	Author-Linguist	20		120		Pacifist. Known as '..Learned Blacksmith'.AQS 150
Burroughs, Edgar Rice	1875-1950	Author	242	335	452	625	Tarzan. TLS/Cont 1900
Burroughs, John		Governor	10		25	15	Governor NM
Burroughs, John	1837-1921	Author	50	100	200	525	Am. Naturalist, Philosopher
Burroughs, Sherman Everett		Senate/Congress	5	15	25	10	MOC NH
Burroughs, William	1914-1997	Author	75	350			Am. Writer. Influence Beat Writers of 50's
Burrows, Abe		Author	10	15	25	25	Playwright, Pulitzer
Burrows, Brigadier Frederick A.	1897-1973	Military	20				World War II Australian general
Burrows, Brigadier James T.	1901-1991	Military	20				World War II New Zealand general
Burrows, J. C.		Senate	10		25		Senator MI
Burrows, Lt. Gen. Montagu Brocas	1894-1967	Military	25				World War II British general
Burrows, Malandra		Entertainment	10			20	Actress
Burrus, Daniel		Celebrity	10			15	financial expert
Bursch, Daniel		Astronaut	7			18	
Burstyn, Ellen		Entertainment	8	8	15	38	Versatile Leading Lady-Character Leads
Bursum, Holm Olaf		Senate	5	15	25		Senator NM
Burt, Brig. Gen. Ernest H.	1892-1984	Military	30				World War II U.S. general
Burton, Charlotte		Entertainment	8	10	12	15	
Burton, Dan B		Congress	10			15	Member U.S. Congress
Burton, Harold H.	1888-1964	Supreme Court	33	170	325	90	
Burton, Isabel, Lady		Author	25	85	180		
Burton, LeVar		Entertainment	7	10	10	25	Actor. 'Roots' etc.
Burton, Richard F., Sir	1821-1890	Explorer	150	285	1503		Orientalist, Linguist, Author
Burton, Richard		Entertainment	88	172		252	Actor. Important DS 950
Burton, Theodore E.		Senate/Congress	7	10	30		Senator, MOC OH
Burton, Tim		Entertainment	15			45	Film Director, Actor
Busbee, Brig. Gen. Charles M.	1893-1970	Military	30				World War II U.S. general
Busby, George Henry		Governor	10	15			Governor GA
Buscalia, Leo		Author	15	25	40	25	Educator, Author, Lecturer
Buscemi, Steve		Entertainment	10			45	Actor
Busch, Adolphus	1839-1913	Business	300	3500	4000		Founder Anheuser-Busch.TLS 5800
Busch, August A.		Business	250	1850	2500		Anheuser-Busch Brewery
Busch, Field Marshal Ernst	1885-1945	Military	27				World War II German general
Busch, Fritz		Entertainment	45		135	250	Ger. Conductor

NAME	DATE	CATEGORY	SIG	LS/DS	ALS	SP	COMMENTS
Busch, Niven		Author	12		25	25	Dramatist, Screenwriter
Busch, Wilhelm	1832-1908	Artist			1400		Painter & Poet.
Busell, Darcey		Entertainment	15			40	Ballet
Busey, Gary	1944-	Entertainment	8	12	15	29	Actor. Versatile leading man & heavy
Bush		Entertainment	45			150	Music. 4 Member Rock Group
Bush, Barbara		First Lady	53	60	72	95	Christmas Cd. Signed by Both 600
Bush, George (As President)		President	160	610	1550	336	WH Cd. S 500, President'l Cd. 950.SP Oath 1295
Bush, George W. (as President)		Presidents	146	383		449	
Bush, George W.		Political/ President	86	260	631	288	Baseball Exec., TX Gov.
Bush, George	1924-	President	108	207	817	289	Signed Vice Presidential Card 195
Bush, Irving T.		Business		35			Owned Largest Shipping Terminal
Bush, Laura		First Lady	40	75	120	75	Gracious First Lady of George W. Bush
Bush, Owen		Entertainment	5			10	Character Actor
Bush, Prescott		Senate	25	75		90	Senator CT Father, Grandfather of George & Geo.W.
Bush, Vannevar	1890-1974	Science	60	180	255	125	Pioneer In Analog Computers.Atom Bomb
Bushill-matthews, Philip		Political	10			15	Member European Parliament
Bushkin, Joe		Entertainment	6	8	10	12	
Bushman, Francis X.	1883-1966	Entertainment	40	75	110	100	Silent Star of Ben Hur etc.
Bushmiller, Ernie*		Cartoonist	20			125	Nancy
Bushnell, David	1742-1824	Science	250	690	1250		Invented 1st Submarine
Bushnell, Horace	1802-1876	Clergy	25	35	45		New Engl.Congregational Minister
Bushyhead, D.W.		Celebrity	200		1500		
Busk, Niels		Political	10			15	Member European Parliament
Busoni, Ferruccio	1866-1924	Music			210		Classical musician, AMQS 330
Busoni, Ferruccio	1899-1924	Composer	120		316	425	It-born Pianist, AMusQS 175-450-650
Busse, Gen. of Infantry Theodor	1897-1986	Military	25				World War II German general
Busse, Henry		Entertainment	20			50	Big Band Leader
Bussey, Cyrus	1833-1915	Civil War	40	110	140		Union general
Bustamante, Jose Luis		Celebrity	9	35	60		
Busteed, Richard	1822-1898	Civil War	48	118	210		Union general
Butcher, Brig. Gen. Edwin	1879-1950	Military	30				World War II U.S. general
Butcher, Susan		Ididorod	5	10		15	Dog Breeder
Bute, John Stuart		Royalty	85	130			Earl of Bute
Butel, Yves		Political	10			15	Member European Parliament
Butenandt, Adolf F.J.		Science	20	30	45	25	Nobel Chemistry
Buthelezi, Gatsha Mangosuthu		Head of State	20			35	Chief of Zulu Nation
Butler, Benjamin F.	1795-1858	Cabinet	30	75	150		PMG for Jackson
Butler, Benjamin F.	1818-1893	Civil War	60	110	184		Union Gen., LS '62 2750. DS '63 700
Butler, Brig. Gen. Frederic B.	1896-1987	Military	30				World War II U.S. general
Butler, Carl & Pearl		Country Music	15			30	
Butler, Daws		Entertainment	15	15	20	40	
Butler, Dean		Entertainment	5	8	12	15	
Butler, Ellis Parker	1869-1937	Author	10	60	92	40	Pigs is Pigs
Butler, John		Clergy	10	15	20	20	
Butler, John		Revolutionary War	75	185	375		Am. Loyalist.Butler's Rangers

NAME	DATE	CATEGORY	SIG	LS/DS	ALS	SP	COMMENTS
Butler, Maj. Gen. Stephen Seymor	1880-1964	Military	28				World War II British general
Butler, Matthew C. (WD)	1836-1909	Civil War	155	345	675		CSA General
Butler, Matthew C.	1836-1909	Civil War	70	142	285		CSA General, US Sen. SC
Butler, Nicholas Murray		Educator	15	35	90	30	Nobel Peace Prize. Educator
Butler, Pierce	1744-1822	Revolutionary War	60	180	310		Signer of Constitution
Butler, Pierce	1866-1939	Supreme Court	40	90	200	45	Jurist 1922-39
Butler, Samuel	1835-1902	Author	20	60	125		Br. Author, Artist, Musician
Butler, Smedley D.		Military	15	35	75	35	Marine Corps Gen/2 CMH
Butler, Thomas S.		Senate/Congress	5	15			MOC PA
Butler, Walter	1752-1781	Revolutionary War		550	675		Captured,escaped. Butler's Rangers
Butler, William Orlando		Military	50	210			Hero Battle of New Orleans
Butler, Yancy		Entertainment	10			25	Actress. Mann & Machine, Hard Target, Drop Zone
Butler, Zebulon		Military	70	200			Col. Revolutionary War
Butt, Clara	1873-1936	Entertainment	35			150	Opera
Buttafuco, Joey		Celebrity	12				
Butterfield, Billy		Entertainment	25			45	Jazz Trumpet, Bandleader
Butterfield, Daniel (WD)		Civil War	150	270	360	745	Union General .Composed TAPS
Butterfield, Daniel	1831-1901	Civil War	82	250	308		Union Gen. Composed 'Taps'
Butterworth, Charles		Entertainment					
Buttons, Red	1919-	Entertainment	15	18	20	45	Academy Award in Sayonara
Buttram, Pat		Entertainment	20	95		45	Gene Autry Movie Sidekick
Buttrick, George A.		Clergy	25	45	75	45	
Buttrick, John		Rev. War		1208			Hero of Lexington/Concord
Butts, Alfred M.		Inventor	35	50			Scrabble
Butz, Earl L.		Cabinet	6	18	30	15	Sec'y Agriculture
Buxton, Brigadier St John Dudley	1891-1981	Military	25				World War II British general
Buyer, Steve B		Congress	10			15	Member U.S. Congress
Buzzell, Brig. Gen. Reginald W.	1894-1959	Military	30				World War II U.S. general
Buzzi, Ruth		Entertainment	3	6	10	15	
Buzzini, Brian		Celebrity	10			15	model
Byers, Lt. Gen. Clovis E.	1899-1973	Military	30				World War II U.S. general
Byers, Samuel Hawkins		Author	25	40	60		Union Soldier-Author
Byington, Spring		Entertainment	20			55	
Bykovsky, Valeri		Astronaut				40	Russian Cosmonaut
Bylsma, Frederick W., Ph.D.		Science	10	15	20	20	Renowned Neuropsychologist
Byner, John		Entertainment	3	3	6	8	
Byng, Geo. Viscount Torrington		Military	55	75			Br. Adm.Destroyed Sp.Fleet 1719
Byrd, Charlie		Entertainment	15			25	Jazz Guitar
Byrd, Harry F. Byrd, Sr.		Governor	25				Gov. VA
Byrd, Harry F., Jr.		Senate	10	25		25	Senator VA
Byrd, Jerry		Country Music	10			20	
Byrd, Ralph		Entertainment	100	150		350	
Byrd, Richard E.	1888-1957	Aviation-Explorer	60	173	309	293	Adm. USN, Polar Expl. TLS/Cont. 575
Byrd, Robert C.		Senate	15	30	50	25	Senator WV
Byrds, The (Entire Group)		Entertainment					Rock. Alb S 120

NAME	DATE	CATEGORY	SIG	LS/DS	ALS	SP	COMMENTS
Byrne, Bobby		Entertainment	20			70	Big band leader
Byrne, Gabriel		Entertainment	4			15	Actor, Films
Byrne, Jane		Politician	5	10	28	10	Mayor
Byrnes, Edd		Entertainment	5			15	
Byrnes, James F.		Supreme Court	30	125	235	55	
Byrns, Joseph Wellington		Senate/Congress	15	25		20	MOC TN
Byron, Arthur		Entertainment	15	15	20	35	
Byron, Geo. Gordon, Lord	1788-1824	Author	1441	2750	7125		Inflluential, Romantic Br. Poet
Byron, Jean		Entertainment	5			15	
Byron, Maj. Gen. Joseph W.	1892-1951	Military	30				World War II U.S. general

C

NAME	DATE	CATEGORY	SIG	LS/DS	ALS	SP	COMMENTS
Caan, James		Entertainment	8	7	15	25	'Godfather' SP 30
Cabana, Robert D.		Astronaut	6			20	
Cabell, Earle		Mayor	10				Dallas JFK Assassination TLS 475
Cabell, James Branch	1879-1958	Author	30	120	165		Hugely famous author in early 20th century
Cabell, William L.	1827-1911	Civil War	193	460			CSA General
Cable, George Washington	1844-1925	Author	30	48	101	50	CSA Soldier, Short Story Writer
Cabot, Bruce	1904-1972	Entertainment	50	55	90	150	John Wayne Sidekick
Cabot, George	1751-1823	Congress		45	100		Sen. MA.Ratified US Constitution
Cabot, Sebastian		Entertainment	25	30	90	75	
Cabot-Zinn, John		Celebrity	10			15	medical expert
Caceres, Andreas A.		Head of State	10	25	65	20	Peru
Cadbury, George		Business	35		170	50	Cadbury Chocolate Mfg.
Cadbury, Richard		Business	30	45	160	50	Cadbury Chocolate Mfg.
Cade, Robert, Dr.		Business	10	15		10	Inventor of Gatorade
Cadell, Lt Gen Chas. Alexander E	1888-1951	Military	25				World War II British general
Cadman, Chas. Wakefield		Composer	47	147	223	138	AMusQS 195
Cadman, S. Parkes		Clergy	20	35	50	35	
Cadmus, Paul		Artist	35	110	120		Repro. S 75
Cadoux-Hudson, Maj. Gen. P.	1894-1980	Military	25				World War II British general
Cadwalader, George	1806-1879	Civil War	50	124	170		Union Gen. LS '63 385
Cadwalader, Lambert		Revolutionary War	55	140	335		Continental Congress
Cady, Daniel		Congress	20	35	50		MOC NY 1815
Caesar, Irving	1895-1996	Composer	25	55	125	51	Lyricist (Tea for Two) Collaborator/Gershwin etc.
Caesar, Sid	1922-	Entertainment	5	8	18	37	Comedian. Classic early TV
Caffey, Brig. Gen. Benjamin F. Jr.	1893-1972	Military	30				World War II U.S. general
Caffyn, Brigadier Sir Edward Roy	1904-1990	Military	25				World War II British general
Cage, John M.	1912-1992	Composer	75	110	195	165	AMusQS 125-250. AMsS 3750
Cage, Nicholas	1964-	Entertainment	21	38		48	AA Actor
Cagney, James	1899-1987	Entertainment	80	95	124	206	AA Actor. Dancer, Singer
Cagney, Jeanne		Entertainment				20	Jimmy Cagney's Actress Sister

NAME	DATE	CATEGORY	SIG	LS/DS	ALS	SP	COMMENTS
Cahier, Madame Charles		Entertainment	25			90	Early Opera
Cahn, Sammy	1913-1993	Composer	15	76	125	60	AMusQS 250
Caillault, Lt. Gen. Henri-Léon	1880-1952	Military	20				World War II French general
Caille, Brig. Gen. André-Lucien	1881-1940	Military	20				World War II French general
Cain, Dean		Entertainment	10			40	Superman
Cain, James		Author	40	55	90		Novelist. Hard Boiled Fiction
Caine, John T.	1829-1911	Congressman				50	Democratic Rep. From Utah. Newspaper Editor
Caine, Michael	1933-	Entertainment	9	12	24	50	Brit. AA winning actor.
Caine, Thos. Hall, Sir	1853-1931	Author	20	45	74	60	Br. Novelist, Dramatist
Calandral, Joe		Entertainment	6			25	Music. Bass Guitar 'Monster Magnet'
Calavano, Phil		Entertainment	6			25	Music. 'Monster Magnet'
Calder, A. Stirling	1870-1945	Artist			65		Sculptor. Father of Alexander Calder
Calder, Alexander (Sandy)	1898-1976	Artist	108	225	524	283	Sculptor, Mobiles. ALS/Cont. 1000, 1500
Calder, William M.	1869-1945	Congress		20			Sen..NY
Calderio, Frank		Astronaut	5			20	
Calderon, A. W. Gen.		Head of State	5	15	35	10	
Caldicott, Helen		Celebrity	10			15	political celebrity
Caldwell, Erskine	1903-1986	Author	40	88	162	88	'Tobacco Road', 'God's Little Acre'
Caldwell, George A.	1814-1866	Congress	10				Repr. KY, Officer Mexican War
Caldwell, John Curtis	1833-1912	Civil War	42	82		250	Union Gen.
Caldwell, Sarah		Conductor	15			20	1st Woman Conductor NY Met.
Caldwell, Taylor		Author	35	150	225	150	Novelist
Caldwell, Zoe		Entertainment	5	10	15	15	
Calhern, Louis		Entertainment	30	25	45	45	Eminent Stage-Film Actor
Calhoun, Alice		Entertainment	15	15	35	30	
Calhoun, Eleanor		Entertainment	3	3	6	8	
Calhoun, John C.	1782-1850	Vice President	181	308	439	375	Andrew Jackson VP. Statesman, Sec'y War
Calhoun, Rory		Entertainment	6	28	11	26	Handsome Cowboy, Leading Man
Calhoun, William Barron		Congress	10	15	35		Repr. MA 1835
Calhoun, William M.		Senate/Congress	5	10			
Calkin, Dick*		Cartoonist	75			500	Buck Rogers
Callaghan, James	1912-	Head of State	35	75	140	50	Br. Prime Minister
Callaghan, Maj. Gen. Cecil A.	1890-1967	Military	30				World War II Australian general
Callagher, Maj. Gen. Philip E.	1897-1976	Military	30				World War II U.S. general
Callahan, Laurence K.		Aviation	10	20	45	30	
Callanan, Martin		Political	10			15	Member European Parliament
Callas, Charlie		Entertainment	3	5	8	12	
Callas, Maria Meneghini	1923-1977	Entertainment	357	420	592	1264	Opera, Concert. Small format SP 525-850-950-1075
Callcott, Maria Lady	1785-1842	Author			100		
Calleia, Frank		Entertainment	19	25	45	45	
Calleia, Joseph		Entertainment	25			55	
Callendar, Lt. Gen. Colin	1897-1979	Military	28				World War II British general
Callender, Brig. Gen. George R.	1884-1973	Military	30				World War II U.S. general
Calley, William		Military	20	35	45	40	My Lai, Viet Nam
Callies, Gen. Jean-Jules Alexis	1896-1989	Military	20				World War II French general

NAME	DATE	CATEGORY	SIG	LS/DS	ALS	SP	COMMENTS
Calloway, Cab	1907-1995	Entertainment	40	55	70	136	Afro-Am. Big Band Leader. Jazz Musician
Calloway, Joe		Celebrity	10			15	motivational speaker
Calve, Emma		Entertainment	55	90	105	217	Opera
Calvert, Brigadier J. Michael	1913-1998	Military	25				World War II British general
Calvert, Ken C		Congress	10			15	Member U.S. Congress
Calvert, Louis		Entertainment	5	6	15	15	
Calvert, Phyllis		Entertainment	5	15		15	
Calvet, Corinne	1925-	Entertainment	8	12	15	19	Fr. Actress. 50's Genre. Pin-Up 28
Calvin, John		Clergy	5500	7500	10000		
Calvin, Melvin, Dr.		Science	25	35	55	20	Nobel Chemistry
Camacho, Manuel Avila		Head of State	35		80	40	Pres. Mexico
Camargo, Alberto		Head of State	10	18	35	20	Columbia
Cambaceres, J.J.R.(Parma)		Napoleonic Wars	115	160			Prince & Duke
Cambell, James		Cabinet	35	80	120		Pierce P.M. General
Cambern, Donn		Entertainment	10			20	Actor Mayberry
Cambon, Jules		Diplomat	20	25	35		Fr. Ambassador to US
Cambridge, G.O.		Clergy	10	20	25		
Cambridge, Godfrey		Entertainment	25	20		60	Afr-Am Comedian, Activist
Cameron, Betsy		Author	5	10	20	10	
Cameron, Brig. Sir James	1900-1965	Military	25				World War II British general
Cameron, Candace		Entertainment	10			20	actress
Cameron, George	1861-1944	Military	20		45		General WW I
Cameron, James D.	1833-1918	Cabinet	30	35	45		Senator PA. Sec'y War
Cameron, James		Entertainment		25		48	Titanic
Cameron, Kenneth		Astronaut	5			15	
Cameron, Kirk		Entertainment	8	15		20	'Growing Pains' Star
Cameron, Lt. Gen. Sir A.	1898-1986	Military	25				World War II British general
Cameron, Matt		Entertainment	6			25	Music. Drummer 'Soundgarden'
Cameron, Robert Alexander	1828-1894	Civil War	42	92			Union Gen. ALS '62 175
Cameron, Rod	1910-1983	Entertainment	15			50	Actor. Rugged Star of Westerns & 'B' Films
Cameron, Simon (WD)		Cabinet	130	195	265	300	
Cameron, Simon	1800-1889	Cabinet	63	135	150	295	Lincoln Sec'y War, Financier
Camisón Asensio, Felipe		Political	10			15	Member European Parliament
Camm, Brig. Gen. Frank	1895-1976	Military	30				World War II U.S. general
Cammaerts, Emile		Author	10	20	40	15	Belgian Poet-Writer
Cammermeyer, Margarethe, Col.		Celebrity	10			15	motivational speaker
Camp, Brig. Gen. Thomas J.	1886-1973	Military	30				World War II U.S. general
Camp, Colleen		Entertainment	6	10	14	18	Pin-Up 35
Camp, Dave C		Congress	10			15	Member U.S. Congress
Campanella, Joseph		Entertainment	3	3	6	6	
Campanini, Italo		Entertainment	58	80	175		
Campbell, Alexander William	1828-1893	Civil War	80	175	250		Confederate general
Campbell, Archibald		Revolutionary War	95	275			Br. General.
Campbell, Archie		Country Music	8			25	
Campbell, Beatrice Stella	1865-1940	Entertainment	25	40	45	105	Mrs. Patrick Campbell. Actress

NAME	DATE	CATEGORY	SIG	LS/DS	ALS	SP	COMMENTS
Campbell, Ben		Senate	10			15	United States Senate (R - CO)
Campbell, Brig. Gen. Arthur G.	1884-1957	Military	30				World War II U.S. general
Campbell, Brig. Gen. Boniface	1895-1988	Military	30				World War II U.S. general
Campbell, Brig. Gen. William A.	1887-1971	Military	30				World War II U.S. general
Campbell, Brig. Gen. William F.	1892-1964	Military	30				World War II U.S. general
Campbell, Brig. Alex. Donald P.	1894-1974	Military	25				World War II British general
Campbell, Brig. Edmund George	1893-1972	Military	25				World War II British general
Campbell, Charles Thomas	1823-1895	Civil War	40	90	129		Union General
Campbell, Colin, Sir	1792-1863	Military	16	45	75		Br. Gen. Vs U.S., War 1812
Campbell, Douglas		Aviation	38	65	80	125	ACE, WW I, Bi-plane Ace
Campbell, E. Simms*		Cartoonist	20			150	1st Black Mag. Cartoonist
Campbell, Ernest T.		Clergy	20	30	40	30	
Campbell, Geo.J.		Statesman	25	60	130		Author. Br. Cabinet 8th Duke Argyll
Campbell, George W.	1769-1848	Cabinet	55	160	310		Sec'y Treas. Senator TN 1803
Campbell, Glen		Entertainment	5	10	15	20	Singer-Guitarist. 'Wichita Lineman' Alb. S 30
Campbell, Jack M.		Governor	10	20			Governor NM
Campbell, Jacob M.	1821-1888	Civil War			45		Col. Union army
Campbell, James E.		Governor	15	25	30		Governor OH, MOC
Campbell, John A.		Supreme Court	100	210	375		
Campbell, John Hull	1800-1868	Congress	6				Repr. PA
Campbell, John		Revolutionary War	62	175	290		Br. General
Campbell, Josiah Adams	1830-1917	Civil War	54				Member of Confederate Congress
Campbell, Lt. Gen. Levin H. Jr.	1886-1976	Military	30				World War II U.S. general
Campbell, Maj. Gen. Douglas	1889-1980	Military	25				World War II British general
Campbell, Maj. Gen. Robin H.	1894-1964	Military	25				World War II British general
Campbell, Malcolm	1885-1948	Sportsman	50	225			Br Auto. & Hydroplane racer-designer
Campbell, Mary		Entertainment			50		Miss America 1922-23
Campbell, Naomi		Model	12	10	12	40	
Campbell, Neve		Entertainment	15			49	Actress. 'Scream', 'Party of Five' SP 65
Campbell, Nicky		Celebrity	10			15	television presenter
Campbell, Patrick, Mrs.	1865-1940	Entertainment	35	60		80	Vintage Stage Actress (Beatrice)
Campbell, Philip P.	1862-1944	Congress	12				Kansas
Campbell, William (Bill)		Entertainment	5	5	10	12	SP As Rocketeer 35. Star Trek SP 20
Campbell, William Bowen	1807-1867	Civil War	44	55	103		Union Gen., Congress TN
Campbell-Bannerman, Henry	1836-1908	Head of State	33	72	108		Br. Prime Minister
Campell of Airds, Brig. Lorne M.	1901-1992	Military	25				World War II British general
Campell, Maj. Gen. James	1886-1964	Military	25				World War II British general
Campell, Maj. Gen. John	1894-1942	Military	25				World War II British general
Campion, Jane		Celebrity	10			15	film industry
Campolo, Tony Dr.		Celebrity	10			15	motivational speaker
Campora, Giuseppe		Entertainment	10			40	It. Tenor, Opera
Campos, Ant=nio		Political	10			15	Member European Parliament
Campos, Pedro Marset		Political	10			15	Member European Parliament
Camre, Mogens N.j.		Political	10			15	Member European Parliament
Camus, Albert	1913-1960	Author	75	308	737		Nobel. Poet, Philosopher. AMsS (Poem) 595

NAME	DATE	CATEGORY	SIG	LS/DS	ALS	SP	COMMENTS
Canary, David		Entertainment	8			15	Actor
Canby, Edward Richard Sprigg	1817-1873	Civil War	81	260	598		Union Gen. ALS '64 330
Candal, Carlos		Political	10			15	Member European Parliament
Cander, John		Composer		40			Pop Music
Candler, Asa Griggs		Business	475	1275		595	Founder of Coca Cola
Candler, Warren Akin		Clergy	25	35	50		
Candlish, Robert Smith		Clergy	10	15	25	35	
Candy, John	1950-1994	Entertainment	41	74	75	90	Comedian. Died Prematurely
Canetti, Elia		Author	65	225	350		Bulg.-Br.Nobel Literature
Canfield, Jack		Celebrity	10			15	medical expert
Canham, Erwin		Journalist	10	20			Christian Science Monitor
Canham, Maj. Gen. Charles D.W.	1901-1963	Military	30				World War II U.S. general
Caniff, Milton*	1907-1988	Cartoonists	25	54	138	215	'Terry & the Pirates' & 'Steve Canyon'
Caniglia, Maria		Entertainment	15			88	Opera. Dramatic Sopr.
Canine, Lt. Gen. Ralph J.	1895-1969	Military	30				World War II U.S. general
Cannan, Maj. Gen. James H.	1882-1976	Military	30				World War II Australian general
Cannell, Stephen J.		Entertainment	6	10		10	TV Producer
Canning, Charles John	1812-1862	Head of State	35		65	50	Governor-General & 1st Viceroy of India
Canning, Effie I.		Author	45		300		AMsS 5000
Canning, George	1770-1827	Head of State	48	90	145		Prime Minister. Served only 3 Months .
Cannon, Annie Jump	1863-1941	Science			100		Great Woman Astronomer
Cannon, Chris C		Congress	10			15	Member U.S. Congress
Cannon, Dyan		Entertainment	5	7	12	18	Pin-Up 35-45
Cannon, Frank J.		Senate	5			10	Senator UT
Cannon, George Q.		Senate/Congress	50	140	200		Utah's 1st Congressman
Cannon, Howard W.		Senator	5	10	25	15	Senator NV
Cannon, Jos. G. 'Uncle Joe'		Congress	20	40	95	40	Speaker of the House
Cannon, Lt. Gen. Robert M.	1901-1976	Military	30				World War II U.S. general
Cannon, Martha H., Dr.		Science	25	30	60	30	
Canova, Antonio	1757-1822	Artist	85	250	612		It. Sculptor. Classical Revival
Canova, Diana		Entertainment	3	3	6	10	Pin-Up 22
Canova, Judy		Entertainment	12	15	22	30	Singer-Comedienne. Deceased
Cantey, James	1818-1874	Civil War	76		196		Confederate general
Cantinflas	1911-1995	Entertainment	33			87	
Cantlie, Lt. Gen. Sir Neil	1892-1975	Military	25				World War II British general
Canton, Frank (Joe Horner)	1849-1927	History		776			Western lawman
Cantor, Eddie	1892-1964	Entertainment	66	92		182	Early Comedian,Singer.Vaudeville,Films,Radio
Cantor, Eric C		Congress	10			15	Member U.S. Congress
Cantrell, Jerry		Entertainment	6			25	Music. Guitar, Vocals 'Alice in Chains'
Cantrell, Lana		Entertainment	3	3	6	10	
Cantwell, Maria		Senate	10			15	United States Senate (D - WA)
Canutt, Yakima		Entertainment	12	18	25	42	AA. Legendary Stuntman & Dir.
Canyon, Christy		Entertainment				35	Porn Queen
Capers, Ellison (WD)	1837-1903	Civil War	130		630		CSA General
Capers, Ellison	1837-1903	Civil War	82	166	267		CSA General

NAME	DATE	CATEGORY	SIG	LS/DS	ALS	SP	COMMENTS
Capers, Virginia		Entertainment	3	3	6	6	
Caperton, William		Military	25			50	Adm. WW I
Capito, Shelley Moore C.		Congress	10			15	Member U.S. Congress
Capka, Carol		Entertainment	3	3	6	6	
Caplin, Mortimer		Celebrity	5	5	10	10	
Capon, Robert F.		Clergy	10	15	20	15	
Capone, Al		Criminal	3840	10750		9400	Gangster. Special DS 15,000
Capote, Truman	1924-1984	Author	112	234	480	294	Novelist, Short Story Writer
Capp, Al*		Cartoonist	85	160		250	Li'l Abner, signed drawing 414
Cappato, Marco		Political	10			15	Member European Parliament
Capper, Arthur		Senate	12	25		30	Senator KS
Cappiello, Frank		Celebrity	10			15	financial expert
Capps, Lois C		Congress	10			15	Member U.S. Congress
Capra, Frank	1897-1991	Entertainment	25	155		98	AA Film Director. TLS Ltr/Poem 450
Caprice		Celebrity	10			15	celebrity model
Capshaw, Kate		Entertainment	6	10	35	43	Actress
Captain & Tennile		Entertainment	7	15	15	15	
Capuano, Michael E. C		Congress	10			15	Member U.S. Congress
Capucine		Entertainment	25	30	70	65	
Caraway, Hattie	1878-1950	Congress	25	30	35	40	1st Woman US Senator, AR
Caraway, Lt. Gen. Paul W.	1905-1985	Military	30				World War II U.S. general
Carberry, John J., Cardinal		Clergy	50	65	80	50	
Carden Roe, Brigadier William	1894-1977	Military	25				World War II British general
Cardigan, 7th Earl Brudenell		Military	75	175	250	130	Br.Gen. Charge of Light Brigade
Cardin, Benjamin L. C		Congress	10			15	Member U.S. Congress
Cardinale, Claudia		Entertainment	20			35	It. International Star. Pin-Up 45
Cardoza, Dennis A. C		Congress	10			15	Member U.S. Congress
Cardozo, Benjamin N.	1870-1938	Supreme Court	138	272	549	546	
Carere, Christine		Entertainment	5			20	Actress
Carey, Drew	1958-	Entertainment	12			45	Comedian-Actor
Carey, Harry Jr.		Entertainment	6	9	15	22	
Carey, Harry Sr.		Entertainment	100	110	175	250	
Carey, Hugh L.		Governor	10	15		15	Governor NY
Carey, MacDonald		Entertainment	7	7	9	18	'Days of Our Lives' Star. 50's-70's Movies
Carey, Mariah		Entertainment	10	65		62	Singer
Carey, Michele		Entertainment	5	6	15	25	
Carey, Ron		Entertainment	5	6	10	10	
Cargill, Henson		Country Music	4			18	Skip a Rope #1
Carias Andino, Tiburcio		Head of State	40	125		45	Pres. Honduras
Carl XIV Johan	1763-1844	Royalty	150	580			King Sweden
Carl XV	1826-1872	Royalty	125	425			King of Sweden & Nor. from 1859
Carl XVI Gustaf	1946-	Royalty	55	150			King Sweden
Carl, Marion		Aviation	15	25	48	75	ACE, WW II, 1st Marine Ace. Murdered
Carle, Frankie		Entertainment	12			42	Big Band Leader
Carleton, Brig. Gen. Don Emerson	1899-1977	Military	30				World War II U.S. general

NAME	DATE	CATEGORY	SIG	LS/DS	ALS	SP	COMMENTS
Carleton, Guy, Sir (Baron)	1724-1808	Military-Rev. War	250	583	800		Br. Commander-in-Chief
Carleton, James H.	1814-1873	Civil War	36	86	110		Union Gen. LS '63 825
Carleton, Will	1845-1912	Author	35	50	75	75	Ir. Novelist
Carlès, Lt Gen Emile-Jean-Gab.	1881-1943	Military	20				World War II French general
Carlin, George		Entertainment	6	10	12	18	Standup Comedian
Carlin, Lynn		Entertainment	3	3	6	6	
Carlin, William Passmore	1829-1903	Civil War	66		192		Conf. general
Carlisle, 7th Earl	1802-1864	Author-Politician	20	45	115		George W.F. Howard. Poet, Orator, Viceroy of Ireland
Carlisle, Belinda		Entertainment	8	12	18	40	'Go-Gos Lead Singer
Carlisle, John Griffin		Senate-Cabinet	15	25	35	30	Speaker. Sen. KY, Sec'y Treas.
Carlisle, Kitty		Entertainment	5	7	12	19	'What's My Line' Regular. Vintage SP 30
Carlisle, Mary	1912-	Entertainment	10	15	25	30	Actress
Carlo Alberto	1798-1849	Royalty	45	150	375		King of Sardinia
Carlotta (Marie-Charlotte-Amalie)		Royalty	340	770	1700		Empress of Mex. Became Insane
Carlotti, Marie-arlette		Political	10			15	Member European Parliament
Carlsen, Capt. Kurt		Celebrity	20	55	125	45	
Carlson, Frank		Governor-Senate	10	18	25	15	Governor, Senator KS
Carlson, Fred		Collectibles	3			10	'Lunch Box King'
Carlson, Richard		Entertainment	15			30	Film Leading Man. 40's-50's
Carlucci, Frank		Celebrity	10			15	political celebrity
Carlyle, Robert		Entertainment	10			20	Actor
Carlyle, Russ		Entertainment	5			15	Bandleader
Carlyle, Thomas	1795-1881	Author	70	175	337	235	Br. Philosopher, Social Critic, Essayist. AQS 150-300
Carman, Tex J.		Country Music	10			20	
Carmen, Jean		Entertainment	4	4	9	10	
Carmer, Carl		Author	20	45	175		
Carmichael, Hoagy	1899-1981	Composer	50	127		200	'Stardust'. AMusQS 250, 320, 375
Carmichael, Oliver C.		Educator	20	35		25	Pres. Univ. Alabama
Carnarvon, Henry 4th Earl		Statesman	15	35	80		Created Fed. Dominion Canada
Carne, Judy		Entertainment	6	8	15	22	Br. Comedienne. Pin-Up 35
Carnegie, Andrew	1835-1919	Industrialist	222	766	896	895	TLS/Cont.9800, Signed Stock Cert. 24000-125000
Carnegie, Dale	1888-1955	Author	37	35		50	Teacher.'How To Win Friends & Influence People'
Carnero González, Carlos		Political	10			15	Member European Parliament
Carnes, Kim		Entertainment	4			20	Singer
Carney, Art	1918-	Entertainment	12	15	20	34	'Norton' on The Honeymooners. Oscar Winner
Carney, Robert B.		Military	12	20	35	48	Eisenhower CNO
Carnot, Lazare N.M.		Fr. Revolution	90	250	325		Min. of War. Exiled
Carnot, Marie Francois Sadi	1837-1894	Head of State			110	190	Pres. France 1887-1894. Assassinated
Carnovsky, Morris		Entertainment	15		40	45	Character Actor
Carol I	1839-1914	Royalty					King Roumania & Queen Elizabeth. 2 SP's 1250
Carol, Cindy	1945-	Entertainment	5			25	Actress. Played 'Gidget'
Carol, Sue (Ladd)		Entertainment	10	14	18	28	Silent Screen. Wife & Agent of Alan Ladd
Carolan, Shirley		Celebrity	10			15	motivational speaker
Caroline (Monaco)		Royalty	25			80	Princess. Daughter of Grace
Caroline of Anspach		Royalty	335	450	1000		Queen of George II (Eng.)

NAME	DATE	CATEGORY	SIG	LS/DS	ALS	SP	COMMENTS
Caroline	1768-1821	Royalty	95	150	342		Estranged Queen George IV England
Caroline	1776-1841	Royalty		90	175		2nd Queen of Maximilian I (Bavaria)
Caron, George R.	1919-1995	Aviation/Military	28	40	118	80	Enola Gay Tail gunner WW II.
Caron, Leslie	1931-	Entertainment	12	30		36	Fr. Dancer-Actress
Carosio, Margherita		Entertainment	15			85	Opera
Carpenter, Edward	1844-1929	Author	5		60		
Carpenter, Francis Bicknell	1830-1890	Artist	50				Emancipation Proclamation Engraving DS 3500
Carpenter, John		Entertainment	10			25	Film Director-Writer
Carpenter, Joseph Estlin		Clergy	40	50	60	75	
Carpenter, Karen		Entertainment	75	250		150	Singer. Tragic Young Death
Carpenter, Maj. Gen. John Owen	1894-1967	Military	25				World War II British general
Carpenter, Mary-Chapin		Entertainment	5			35	Award Winning Country Singer-Composer
Carpenter, Matthew H.		Senate/Congress	10	15	30	35	Senator WI
Carpenter, Richard		Entertainment	5	4	9	15	Performer-Songwriter
Carpenter, Scott	1925-	Astronaut	50	52	125	78	Mercury 7 Astro
Carpenter, Sue		Celebrity	10			15	television presenter
Carpenter, W. Boyd, Bishop		Clergy	10	20	30		
Carpenter, William B.		Explorer	10	35	60		Br. Physiologist
Carpenter, William S.		Military	12	15	40	28	Viet Nam Hero
Carpenters, The		Entertainment	150	485		388	Richard and Karen
Carpentier, Gen. Marcel-Maurice	1895-1977	Military	20				World War II French general
Carper, Thomas		Senate	10			15	United States Senate (D - DE)
Carr, Brigadier Wm. Greenwood	1901-1982	Military	25				World War II British general
Carr, Eugene Asa	1830-1910	Civil War	46	162	200	220	Union Gen. CMH, ALS '63 2200.Indian Fighter
Carr, Gerald P.		Astronaut	5			15	
Carr, Jane		Entertainment	5			15	Actress
Carr, Jerry		Astronaut	6			22	
Carr, Joseph Bradford	1828-1895	Civil War	46	116	150		Union general
Carr, Lt. Gen. Laurence	1886-1954	Military	25				World War II British general
Carr, Tommy		Entertainment	20			35	
Carr, Vicki		Entertainment	3	3	6	10	Singer, Recording Artist. Award Winner
Carradine, David		Entertainment	7	20		27	Actor. 'Kung Fu' SP 28
Carradine, John		Entertainment	65	125	150	150	Versatile Actor. Many Characters. Many Films
Carradine, Keith		Entertainment	5			18	Stage, Screen, TV Star
Carradine, Robert		Entertainment	6			18	14 Page DS 150. 'Revenge Of Nerds' SP 22
Carranza, Venustiano		Head of State	52	205	400		Revolutionary Pres.Mex.Murdered
Carraro, Massimo		Political	10			15	Member European Parliament
Carrel, Dr. Alexis		Science	75	220	300	210	Nobel Medicine
Carreno, Terresa		Composer	25		118	90	Venez. Conductor- Pianist-Singer. Gottschalk Pupil
Carrera, Barbara		Entertainment	6	8	15	36	Actress
Carreras, Jose		Entertainment	25	40		65	Operatic Tenor
Carrere, Christine		Entertainment	5			15	Fr. Actress
Carrere, Tia		Entertainment				30	
Carrey, Jim		Entertainment	32			68	Comedian-Actor
Carrigain, Philip		Law	20	50			Surveyed NH, Named Granite St.

NAME	DATE	CATEGORY	SIG	LS/DS	ALS	SP	COMMENTS
Carrilho, Maria		Political	10			15	Member European Parliament
Carrillo, Leo	1880-1961	Entertainment	42	50	60	94	TLS/Content 150. 'Pancho'
Carrington, Brig Gen G. De L.	1894-1944	Military	30				World War II U.S. general
Carrington, Henry Beebee	1824-1912	Civil War	45	125	140		Union general
Carrington, Lt Gen Sir Robert H.	1882-1964	Military	25				World War II British general
Carrol, Eddie		Entertainment				40	Voice of Jimney Cricket
Carroll, Brig. Gen. Percy J.	1891-1987	Military	30				World War II U.S. general
Carroll, Charles	1737-1832	Revolutionary War	275	410	676		Signer. Important Rev. War ALS 8500
Carroll, Daniel		Revolutionary War	175	370	710		Continental Congress
Carroll, Diahann	1935-	Entertainment	6	9	14	30	Singer-Actress
Carroll, Earl		Entertainment	85	105	210	190	
Carroll, Georgia		Entertainment	5			15	Pin-Up SP 28
Carroll, Gladys Hasty	1904-	Author	15				US Novelist
Carroll, John Lee		Governor	10		30		Governor MD
Carroll, John		Entertainment	8	15	20	20	Singing-Strutting Leading Man.
Carroll, Julian M.		Governor	10		35		Governor KY
Carroll, Lee		Celebrity	10			15	comedian
Carroll, Leo G.		Entertainment	30			70	Br. Actor. 'Topper', 'U.N.C.L.E.'
Carroll, Lewis							(SEE DODGSON,C)
Carroll, Lisa Hart		Entertainment	6	8	15	19	
Carroll, Madeleine		Entertainment	49	150		84	Beautiful Brit. Star of 30's-40's
Carroll, Mickey		Entertainment	10			30	Wizard of Oz Munchkin
Carroll, Nancy		Entertainment	10	15	20	35	
Carroll, Samuel Sprigg	1832-1893	Civil War	62	92	140		Union general
Carroll, William H.	1810-1868	Civil War	75	176	302		CSA Gen.
Carroll, William		Military	25		90		Gen. TN Militia, Gov. TN 1821
Carrott, Jasper		Celebrity	10			15	comedian
Carryl, Guy Wetmore		Author	4	15	25		
Cars, The		Entertainment	50			85	
Carson, Benjamin Dr.		Celebrity	10			15	motivational speaker
Carson, Brad C.		Congress	10			15	Member U.S. Congress
Carson, Christopher Kit	1809-1868	Frontiersman	3650			4667	Union Gen'l, Scout, Indian Agt., Trapper, Explorer
Carson, Frank		Celebrity	10			15	comedian
Carson, Jack		Entertainment	15			50	
Carson, John		Military	10			35	General WW I
Carson, Johnny		Entertainment	8	20	35	42	Comedian. Tonight Show Host
Carson, Julia C		Congress	10			15	Member U.S. Congress
Carson, Leonard 'Kit'		Aviation	12	25	42	35	ACE, WW II
Carson, Rachel	1907-1964	Author-Science	75	205	318	275	ALS/Cont. 1,650. 1st Ed. 'Silent Spring' S 1,000
Carson, Sunset		Entertainment	20	25		45	
Carstares, William	1649-1715	Clery			120		Chaplin to William the Third
Carstens, Maj. Gen. Nicholas T.	1886-1945	Military	20				World War II Dutch general
Carter, Ann S.		Aviation	25	40		45	1st Woman Helicopter Pilot
Carter, Ben		Entertainment	100			250	
Carter, Benny	1907-	Entertainment	40	60	100	90	Jazz. Alto Sax, Trumpet. Arranger

NAME	DATE	CATEGORY	SIG	LS/DS	ALS	SP	COMMENTS
Carter, Betty		Entertainment	15			35	Lionel Hampton Vocalist
Carter, Billy		Celebrity	4	10	15	10	Pres. Carter's Brother
Carter, Boake		Radio	5	20	35	15	Radio Commentator-Vintage
Carter, Brig. Gen. Ellerbe W.	1884-1972	Military	30				World War II U.S. general
Carter, Brig. Gen. William V.	1883-1973	Military	30				World War II U.S. general
Carter, Carlene		Country Music	5			35	Grammy Nominee
Carter, Chris		Entertainment	5	15	25	30	Creator 'X Files'
Carter, Dixie		Entertainment	5		20	15	Actress. TV Star. 'Designing Women'
Carter, Elliott		Composer	32	175	202		Pulitzer Prize. 'The Minotaur'
Carter, Gen. Sir Charles Bonham	1876-1955	Military	25				World War II British general
Carter, Helen		Country Music	10			20	
Carter, Helena Bonham		Entertainment	13	30		44	Br. Actress. Frequent Oscar Nominee
Carter, Hodding		Consultant	4	8	12	10	White House Aide
Carter, Howard	1874-1939	Archaeologist	1295		1600		Egyptologist, King Tut's Tomb Discoverer RARE!!
Carter, Janis		Entertainment	4	4	9	9	
Carter, Jimmy & Rosalyn		Pres. & 1st Lady	100			295	
Carter, Jimmy (As President)		President		853	6674	185	TLS(content) 3000
Carter, Jimmy	1924-	President	50	234	880	90	Books S.75-200. War-dated ALS 3000
Carter, John Carpenter	1837-1864	Civil War	267				Confederate general, KIA Franklin, TN
Carter, John R. C		Congress	10			15	Member U.S. Congress
Carter, Leslie, Mrs.		Entertainment	20	75	90	70	Vintage Stage & Early Films
Carter, Lillian		Celebrity	12	25		15	Pres. Carter's Mother
Carter, Lynda		Entertainment	8	8	15	35	Actress. 'Wonder Woman'. Pin-Up SP 25
Carter, Maj. Gen. Arthur H.	1884-1965	Military	30				World War II U.S. general
Carter, Manly L.'Sonny'	1947-1991	Astronaut	25	75		150	Space Shuttle Discovery.Killed '91 in air crash.
Carter, Mother Maybelle		Country Music	40			80	
Carter, Nell (d.2002)		Entertainment	5			40	
Carter, Nick		Entertainment				30	
Carter, Robert	1633-1732	American Colonial		1400			VA official and Landholder
Carter, Rosalynn		First Lady	40	90	130	75	
Carter, Rubin		Celebrity	10			15	political celebrity
Carter, Samuel Powhatan	1819-1891	Civil War	43	142	210		Union general
Carter, Stephen L.		Celebrity	10			15	motivational speaker
Carter, Thomas H.		Senate	10		35	25	Senator MT. 1st Repr.from State
Carter, Tony		Entertainment	4	4	9	10	
Carter, Wilf		Country Music	10			20	
Carteret, George	1610-1680	Military		1600			Br. Naval Officer. Named New Jersey
Carteri, Rosanna		Entertainment	10			30	
Carter-Scott, Cheri		Celebrity	10			15	motivational speaker
Cartland, Barbara, Dame		Author	10	28	70	75	Br. Novelist. Over 500 Romantic Novels
Carton de Wiart, Lt Gen Sir Adr.	1880-1963	Military	25				World War II British general
Cartright, Joy		Entertainment	3			15	
Cartwright, Angela		Entertainment	5	6	15	20	'Lost in Space' TV Script S 40
Cartwright, Lionel		Country Music	4			18	Leap of Faith #1
Cartwright, Nancy		Entertainment	5			15	Voice of Bart Simpson. Signs as 'Bart'

NAME	DATE	CATEGORY	SIG	LS/DS	ALS	SP	COMMENTS
Cartwright, Veronica		Entertainment	8			22	Child Actress Now Grown. Older Sister of Angela
Carty, John J.		Science-Business	60	150	275	150	Telephone Pioneer. AT&T
Caruso, Anthony		Entertainment	25	29	70	52	
Caruso, David	1958-	Entertainment	10	35		35	Actor
Caruso, Enrico	1873-1921	Entertainment	244	356	763	597	Caricature Self-Portr. S 625-1450-2550
Caruso, Enrico, Jr.		Entertainment				25	Actor Son Of Caruso Sr.
Caruthers, Robert L.	1800-1882	Congress	12				Repr. TN, CW Gov. TN
Carvel, Elbert M.		Governor	10	15			Governor DE
Carver, Bill		Author	8			12	mountain humorist
Carver, Geo. Washington	1864-1943	Science	167	450	636	3495	Hall of Fame, Botanist, Educator. Internat'l Fame
Carvey, Dana		Entertainment	8			28	Comedian-Actor. 'Sat. Night Live'
Carville, Edward P.		Gov-Senate	12	15	40	20	Senator, Governor NV
Carville, James		Celebrity	10			20	political celebrity,commentator
Cary, Annie Louise		Entertainment	35	40		150	Opera. 1st Famous American Mezzo.
Cary, Jeremiah E.	1803-1888	Congress	10				Repr. NY
Cary, Phoebe		Author	10	15			Am. Poet/Sister Alice
Cary, Samuel Fenton		Senate/Congress	10		30	25	MOC OH
Casaca, Paulo		Political	10			15	Member European Parliament
Casadesus, Robert, Dr.		Composer	45		100	100	Fr. Concert Pianist-Composer
Casals, Pablo	1876-1973	Entertainment	101	98	253	338	Spanish Cellist,Conductor, Composer. AMusQS 350
Casanovo, Giacomo		Author	150	580	915		Adventurer, Gambler, Spy
Case, A. Ludlow	1813-1888	Civil War	50	95			Adm. North Atlantic Fleet
Case, Brig. Gen. Rolland W.	1882-1957	Military	30				World War II U.S. general
Case, Clifford P.		Senate/Congress	5	15		10	Senator, MOC NJ
Case, Ed C		Congress	10			15	Member U.S. Congress
Case, Francis H.		Senate/Congress	10	25		15	Senator, MOC IA
Case, Jerome I.		Business	30	60	155		Case Tractors & Farm Implements
Case, Kenny		Entertainment			35		Tenor of 4 Ink Spots
Case, Norman S.		Governor	10	25			Governor RI
Casella, Alfredo		Composer	35	130	250		Pianist, Conductor
Casella, Max		Entertainment	10			20	actor
Casellato, Renzo		Entertainment	20			50	Opera. Tenor
Caselotti, Adriana		Entertainment	5	15	35	39	Voice of Snow White
Casement, John S.	1829-1909	Civil War	30	75			Union Gen., 103rd Ohio
Casey, Bernie		Entertainment	5			18	Movie-TV-Artist
Casey, James S.		Civil War	30	125			1st Lt. Won CMH in Battle vs 'Crazy Horse'
Casey, Maj. Gen. Hugh J.	1898-1981	Military	30				World War II U.S. general
Casey, Silas	1807-1882	Civil War	24	70	110		Union Gen.ALS '63 550
Cash, Johnny & June Carter		Country Music	15			80	Husband/Wife Legends
Cash, Johnny		Country Music	18	25	40	88	CW singer
Cash, June Carter	d. 2003	Country Music	6			15	Singer. Carter Family
Cash, Kellye		Celebrity	8		12	12	
Cash, Rosanne		Entertainment	5	6	15	20	Pin-Up SP 25
Cash, Tommy		Country Music 5			10		
Cashman, Michael		Political	10			15	Member European Parliament

NAME	DATE	CATEGORY	SIG	LS/DS	ALS	SP	COMMENTS
Casimir-Perier, Jean Paul P.	1847-1907	Head of State			150		Pres. France 1894-95
Casper (Cast of)		Entertainment				100	Four Cast Members
Casper, John H.		Astronaut	8		95	20	
Cass, Brig. Edw. Earnshaw Eden	1898-1968	Military	25				World War II British general
Cass, Lewis	1782-1866	Cabinet	50	110	152		Jackson Sec'y War, Senator MI
Cass, Peggy		Entertainment	5			10	
Cassatt, Mary		Artist	225	475	1064		ALS/Content 4,500, 5,000
Cassavetes, John		Entertainment	20	15	25	50	Actor, Film Director
Cassels, Fld Msl Sir Archibald J H	1907-1997	Military	25				World War II British general
Cassels, General Sir Robert A.	1876-1959	Military	25				World War II British general
Cassidy, Bryan		Celebrity	10			15	political celebrity
Cassidy, David		Entertainment	5			28	
Cassidy, Jack		Entertainment	25			55	
Cassidy, Joanna		Entertainment	5	6	15	18	Actress. Pin-Up 35
Cassidy, Shaun		Entertainment	10			25	
Cassidy, Ted		Entertainment	175	225	325	775	
Cassin, Jimmy		Composer	10	40			Songwriter
Cassin, Rene		Statesman	30	75	175	45	Founder UNESCO, Nobel Peace
Cassini, Oleg		Business	12	25	40	45	Fashion Designer
Cassizzi, Vic		Author	8			12	religious historical novelist
Casson, Mel*		Cartoonist	10			20	Redeye
Castagna, Bruna		Entertainment	20			100	Opera. SP 4x5 40
Castanzo, Jack		Entertainment	10			30	Jazz Musician
Castelluccio, Federico		Entertainment				35	Furio Giunta, Soprano's
Castelnuovo-Tedesco, M.		Composer	65		300	125	Versatile Comp.All Fields.AMuQs 125-325
Casteneda, Jorge Ubico		Head of State	25	75			
Castle, Irene & Vernon		Entertainment	100			425	Dance Couple
Castle, Irene		Entertainment	50		75	75	
Castle, Lee		Entertainment	5	6	15	15	
Castle, Michael N. C		Congress	10			15	Member U.S. Congress
Castle, Peggy		Entertainment	10			25	
Castle, Vernon		Entertainment	50			150	
Castle, William		Entertainment	40			100	
Castlereagh, R. Stewart, Viscount	1769-1822	Statesman	25	142	250		Minister War vs Napol. Suicide
Castro, Emilio		Clergy	25	30	35	35	
Castro, Fidel	1927-	Head of State	518	1892	2987	1335	Communist Premier of Cuba
Castro, Raul H.		Governor	5			12	Governor AZ
Castro, Raul		Military				125	Younger Brother of Fidel
Cates, Clifton B.		Military	10	25	55	20	
Cates, Phoebe		Entertainment	10	8	15	48	Actress
Catesby, Robert	1573-1605	Fugitive		1065			Involved in Guy Fawkes Gunpowder Conspiracy
Cathcart, Wm. Schaw Sir		Revolutionary War	65	125			Cmdr.British Legionin America
Cather, Willa	1873-1947	Author	280	432	1425	550	Novelist.ALS/Cont 2,250
Catherine I (Rus)	1684-1727	Royalty	440	1733	3567		
Catherine II ('The Great')	1729-1796	Royalty	438	1367	2675		Empress Russia from 1762-96.

NAME	DATE	CATEGORY	SIG	LS/DS	ALS	SP	COMMENTS
Catherine, Marshall		Clergy	25	30	50	30	
Catherwood, Mary		Author	10	15	20		
Catlett, Mary Jo		Entertainment	4			18	Actress. Pin-Up 35
Catlett, Walter		Entertainment	10	15	25	25	
Catlin, George	1796-1872	Artist-Author	100	310	1000		Travel Books.Indian Scenes
Catlin, Isaac		Civil War	50	95	330		Union Gen., CMH
Catron, Brig. Gen. Thomas B.	1888-1973	Military	30				World War II U.S. general
Catron, John	1779-1865	Jurist	155				Supreme Ct. Justice
Catroux, General Georges	1877-1969	Military	20				World War II French general
Catt, Carrie Chapman	1859-1947	Women's Rights	66	190	259		Suffragette Leader. Feminist.
Catterson, Robert Francis	1835-1914	Civil War	42	102	190		Union general
Catton, Bruce		Author	30	70	125	75	Historian, Editor. Pulitzer
Cattrall, Kim		Entertainment				45	Samantha Jones, Sex in the City
Caudron, GTrard		Political	10			15	Member European Parliament
Caulfield, Jo		Celebrity	10			15	comedienne
Caulfield, Joan	1922-1991	Entertainment	15			40	Actress. Pretty 40's Ingenue. Pin-Up SP 35
Caullery, Isabelle		Political	10			15	Member European Parliament
Caunter, Brig. John Alan Lyde	1889-1981	Military	25				World War II British general
Cauquil, Chantal		Political	10			15	Member European Parliament
Cavalieri Muratore, Lina		Entertainment	50			220	Opera
Cavallaro, Carmen		Entertainment	15			35	Big Band Leader-Pianist
Cavanagh, Paul		Entertainment	7			20	
Cavanaugh, Hobart		Entertainment	15	18	20	35	
Cave-Brown, Maj. Gen. William	1884-1967	Military	25				World War II British general
Cavell, Edith	1865-1915	Science	225	375	1600		Br. Nurse. Allied Heroine. Court Martialed. Shot
Cavendish, William 1720-1764		Head of State	100	210	355		English Prime Minister. Duke of Devonshire.
Cavendish-Bentinck, William H.	1738-1809	Head of State	45	95	180		
Caveri, Luciano		Political	10			15	Member European Parliament
Cavett, Dick		Entertainment	4	8	12	14	Late Nite TV Host. Writer4
Cavour, Camillo, Count	1810-1818	Head of State		290			Architect of Italy's Unification. P.M.
Cawthorn, Maj. Gen. Walter Jos.	1896-1970	Military	25				World War II British general
Cayce, Edgar		Author	70	193			Am. Rural Healer, Seer
Cayvan, Georgia		Entertainment	6	8	15	15	
Ceausecu, Nicolae		Head of State	40	335		120	Pres. Romania. Assassinated
Cech, Thomas R., Dr.		Science	20	35		25	Nobel Chemistry
Cecil, Edg. Algernon, Lord	1864-1958	Diplomat	35	45	185		Statesman. Pres. League of Nations. Nobel Peace
Cecil, Robert A. 1830-1903		Head of State	40	45	72		British Prime Minister
Cederschiöld, Charlotte		Political	10			15	Member European Parliament
Cedric, the Magician		Entertainment	15			30	
Celeste		Entertainment				34	Porn Queen
Celine, Louis Ferd. (Destouches)		Author	175		912		1894-1961. Fr. Physician, Novelist
Celler, Emanuel		Senate/Congress	5	20		10	MOC NY
Celli, Giorgio		Political	10			15	Member European Parliament
Cellini, Benvenuto		Artist	1000	4800	13500		Florentine Goldsmith, Sculptor
Cello, Aldo		Business	3	9	10	10	TV Advertising

NAME	DATE	CATEGORY	SIG	LS/DS	ALS	SP	COMMENTS
Cenker, Robert		Astronaut	5			15	
Cercas, Alejandro		Political	10			15	Member European Parliament
Cerdeira Morterero, Carmen		Political	10			15	Member European Parliament
Cerf, Bennett	1898-1971	Author	15	20	30	15	Random House Editor, Author, Game Show Guest
Cermak, Anton J.		Politician	15	40	95	125	Assassinated Mayor of Chicago
Cernan, Eugene A.		Astronaut	48	40	75	87	Moonwalker Astro.
Cervantes, Miguel de		Author	10000	15000			Sp. Novelist. Poet. Don Quixote
Cesaro, Luigi		Political	10			15	Member European Parliament
Cesky, Charles J.		Aviation	10	22	38	28	ACE, WW II
Cetron, Marvin		Celebrity	10			15	financial expert
Cetywago, King of Zulu		Afr. Leader	375				
Ceyhun, Ozan		Political	10			15	Member European Parliament
Cezanne, Paul	1839-1906	Artist	1150	2300	7833		Fr. Impressionist to Cubism
Chabas, Paul Emile		Artist	35	60	135		
Chabert, Lacey		Entertainment	5			45	Child Actress
Chabot, Phillipe de Brion, Comte		Military	1750				1480-1543. Fr. Cmdr. In Chief
Chabot, Steve C		Congress	10			15	Member U.S. Congress
Chabrier, Alexis Emmanuel		Composer	70	255	408		Fr. Opera, Orchestral, Piano
Chadwick, Brig. Cecil Arthur H.	1901-1970	Military	25				World War II British general
Chadwick, James, Sir		Science	80	215	450		Nobel Phys. Discovered Neutron,. ALS content 1000
Chadwick, June		Entertainment	5			20	Brit. Actress. 'Riptide' etc.
Chafee, Lincoln		Senate	10			15	United States Senate (R - RI)
Chaffee, Adna R.	1842-1914	History	25	50	80		General Boxer Rebellion
Chaffee, Roger		Astronaut	225	265	484	679	Died Aboard Apollol I, 1-27-67
Chagall, Marc	1887-1985	Artist	208	286	734	753	Color Repro S 225-295-395-650-1095
Chaka Kahn		Entertainment	8			32	Singer
Chakiris, George		Entertainment	10	15	25	25	
Chalia, Rosalia		Entertainment	25	40	65		
Chaliapin, Feodor	1873-1938	Entertainment	120	278	500	306	Opera. Rus. Basso. SPc 450
Chalker, Jack		Author	10	20	40	30	
Chalmers, James R. (WD)	1831-1898	Civil War	250				CSA General
Chalmers, James R.	1831-1898	Civil War	135	452			CSA General
Chalmers, Judith		Celebrity	10			15	television presenter
Chalmers, Thomas	1780-1847	Clergy	55	69	90	75	Theologian, Philanthropist
Chalon, Alfred E.	1780-1860	Artist	200		375		Portr. Of Q. Victoria Appearing on 1st Postage Stmp
Chamberlain, Austen, Sir	1863-1937	Statesman	30	85	100	100	Br. Politician. Nobel Peace Prize 1925
Chamberlain, Brig. Gen. Edwin W.	1903-1966	Military	30				World War II U.S. general
Chamberlain, Daniel		Governor	50	125			Carpetbag Gov. SC
Chamberlain, Helen		Celebrity	10			15	television presenter
Chamberlain, Joseph A.	1836-1914	Br. Politician	60	85	85	90	Statesman, Nobel Peace Prize. Colonial Sec'y
Chamberlain, Joshua L.	1828-1914	Civil War	608	892	1094		ALS Re Gettysburg 3500. Union Officer. Gov. ME
Chamberlain, Neville	1869-1940	Head of State	90	223	293	165	Prime Minister Eng.
Chamberlain, Owen, Dr		Science	25	35	75	30	Nobel Physics
Chamberlain, Richard		Entertainment	12	15	30	27	Handsome Actor. 'Dr. Kildare' & Many Mini-series
Chamberlain, S.J.		Military	10	30	50		

NAME	DATE	CATEGORY	SIG	LS/DS	ALS	SP	COMMENTS
Chamberlain, Thomas		Civil War		875	1093		Brother to Joshua, 20th Maine
Chamberlaine, William		Military	10		35	20	General WW I
Chamberlin, Brig. Gen. Harry D.	1887-1944	Military	30				World War II U.S. general
Chamberlin, Clarence		Aviation	50	250	385	275	Record Non-Stop Flight NY-Ger.
Chamberlin, Jimmy		Entertainment	6			25	Music. Drummer 'Smashing Pumpkins'
Chamberlin, Lt. Gen. Stephen J.	1889-1971	Military	30				World War II U.S. general
Chambers Brothers (All)		Entertainment	50			200	Rock Group
Chambers, Alexander	1832-1888	Civil War	43	105	180		Union general
Chambers, Brig. Gen. William E.	1892-1952	Military	30				World War II U.S. general
Chambers, Henry Cousins	1823-1871	Civil War		130			Member of Confederate Congress
Chambers, Marilyn		Entertainment	7	15	22	28	Adult Film Star of 70's. Pin-Up SP 50
Chambers, Robert Wm.		Author-Artist	10	15	102		Novelist.Life Mag Illustrator
Chambers, Whittaker		Journalist	15	50	150	25	Charged Alger Hiss as Communist
Chambliss, John Randolph Jr.	1833-1864	Civil War	326				Confederate general
Chambliss, Saxby		Senate	10			15	United States Senate (R - GA)
Chaminade, Cecile	1857-1944	Composer	85	195	300	232	AMusQS 125
Champion, Gower & Marge		Entertainment	30			85	Dance Partner Legends
Champion, Gower		Entertainment	20	30	60	45	Successful Film-Stage Choreographer-Dancer
Champion, Marge		Entertainment	5	9	12	15	Dancer-Actress.
Champlin, Stephen Gardner	1827-1864	Civil War	102	162		184	Union general
Champollion, Jean-Francois	1790-1832	Archaeologist			2695		Fr. Translator of Egyptian Hieroglyphics 1st Time.
Chan, Genie*		Cartoonist	10			35	Conan
Chan, Jackie		Entertainment				75	Karate-Judo Films
Chancellor, John	1927-1996	Journalist	15			30	Radio-TV News & Commentator
Chandler, A.B. 'Happy'		Senate-Gov.	15	35		50	Sen., Gov. KY.Baseball Comm.
Chandler, Brig. Gen. Rex E.	1901-1964	Military	30				World War II U.S. general
Chandler, Christopher		Celebrity	6		40		
Chandler, Dorothy 'Buff'		Business	8	20	45	25	Buffums Dept. Stores
Chandler, George		Entertainment	5			25	Character Actor
Chandler, Helen		Entertainment	30			75	
Chandler, Jeff	1918-1961	Entertainment	54	75	150	137	Major Radio-Film Star. Early Death
Chandler, Joseph Ripley		Congress	15		35		Repr. PA 1843. Editor US Gazette
Chandler, Lane		Entertainment	20			40	
Chandler, Norman		Business	15	35	75	30	L.A. Times
Chandler, Otis		Business	20	45	95	40	Founder L.A. Times
Chandler, Raymond		Author	190	558	975		Novelist. Detective Fiction LS content 2950
Chandler, William E.		Cabinet-Senate	20	38	65		Senator NH, Sec'y Navy
Chandler, Zachariah		Cabinet-Senate	25	35	50		Senator NH, Sec'y Int.,Att'y Gen'l
Chandrasekhar, Subrahmanyan		Science	30	110	225		Nobel, Astrophysicist
Chandu the Magician		Entertainment	5	7	25	20	
Chanel, Coco		Business	50	110	235	85	Fashion Designer, Perfumer
Chaney, Lon, Jr.	1906-1973	Entertainment	331	410	500	707	
Chaney, Lon, Sr.	1881-1930	Entertainment	1150			1688	Man of a 1000 Faces. SP in Character 2000 & up
Chang		Entertainment	15			45	Chinese Giant
Chang, Franklin R.		Astronaut	5			15	

NAME	DATE	CATEGORY	SIG	LS/DS	ALS	SP	COMMENTS
Chang, Min-Chu	1909-1991	Science	50		145		Discoverer of 'In Vitro' Fertilization
Channing, Carol		Entertainment	4	24		18	Unique Broadway Musical Star. 'Hello Dolly'
Channing, Stockard		Entertainment	5	4	10	30	Actress
Channing, William Ellery	1780-1842	Clergy-Author	40	70	120		'Apostle of Unitarianism'
Channing, William Henry		Clergy	35	45	65	50	
Chanoine, Brig Gen Marie-J-H	1882-1944	Military	20				World War II French general
Chantrey, Francis Sir	1781-1841	Artist			185		Sculptor
Chaparral, John and Paul		Country Music	20			40	
Chapin, Brig. Gen. Willis McD.	1893-1960	Military	30				World War II U.S. general
Chapin, Edward Payson	1831-1863	Civil War	138	567			Union general
Chapin, Harry		Composer	100	107		295	Singer-Songwriter
Chapin, Lauren		Entertainment	10			25	Child actress
Chaplin, Ben		Entertainment	10			20	actor
Chaplin, Charles, Sir	1889-1977	Entertainment	342	620	750	891	Legendary Film Comedian. BS (Auto-Bio)550
Chaplin, Geraldine		Entertainment	9	12	28	25	Actress-Daughter of Charlie. Pin-Up 35
Chaplin, Lita Grey	1908-1995	Entertainment	20	25	45	25	
Chaplin, Sydney		Entertainment	15	15	35	30	
Chapman, Ben, Jr.		Entertainment	15			25	Actor. 'Creature From Black Lagoon' SP 75
Chapman, George Henry	1832-1882	Civil War	43	110	180		Union general
Chapman, Graham		Entertainment	15	20	25	30	
Chapman, Leonard, Jr.		Military	15	30		55	USMC General, WW II
Chapman, Maj. Gen. E. G. Jr.	1895-1954	Military	30				World War II U.S. general
Chapman, Marguerite		Entertainment	10			20	Pin-Up SP 25
Chapman, Mark David		Criminal	75	155			Murdered John Lennon
Chapman, Oscar L.		Cabinet	15	20	30	35	Sec'y Interior 1849
Chapman, Pat		Celebrity	10			15	Curry Chef
Chapman, Philip K.		Astronaut	6			20	
Chappell, Clovis G.		Clergy	20	25	30	30	
Chappell, William	1809-1888	Business	20	45	110	35	Music Publisher
Chappelle, Dave		Celebrity	10			20	
Chaptal, Jean Antoine, Count		Napoleonic	135	200			Chemist.Min.Agri., Interior
Charbonneau, Patricia		Entertainment	4			15	Actress. Pin-Up 28
Charcot, Jean Martin	1825-1893	Science	95	225	800		Fr. Neurologist & Prof. Of Pathological Anatomy
Charcot, Jean-Baptiste	1867-1936	Explorer		100	135		Headed 2 Arctic Exp. Drowned w/38 of his men
Charisse, Cyd		Entertainment	5	6	15	32	Dancing Star of Films. Pin-Up SP 40
Charles & Diana		Royalty		1886		3450	Prince & Princess of Windsor
Charles Albert (Sardinia)		Royalty			225		Count of Savoy
Charles Edw. Stuart	1720-1788	Royalty	110	362	1440		'The Young Pretender'; Jacobite Claiment
Charles Emmanuel I	1562-1630	Royalty	595	900			The Great
Charles I (Eng)	1600-1649	Royalty	558	2042	4000		Important DS (1642) 4500
Charles II (Eng)	1630-1685	Royalty	505	1454	3512		King Eng & Ireland. 'Merry Monarch'
Charles II (Sp)		Royalty	275	395			
Charles IV (Sp)	1748-1819	Royalty	185	518	762		Don Carlos. King of Sp. Forced to Abdicate
Charles IX (Fr)	1550-1574	Royalty	295	1428	1700		King of France 1560-1574
Charles V (Charles I {Sp})		Royalty	550	2100	5000		(Charles I & Juana DS 1500)

NAME	DATE	CATEGORY	SIG	LS/DS	ALS	SP	COMMENTS
Charles VI (Charles III {Sp})		Royalty	375	1562			Holy Roman Emperor 1711-1740
Charles VIII	1470-1498	Royalty		863			King of France
Charles X (Fr)	1757-1836	Royalty	150	407	725		King of France.
Charles XIV John (Swe)		Royalty	120	296	650		See also Bernadotte
Charles XV (Swe-Nor)		Royalty	45	140	320		
Charles, Craig		Entertainment	10			20	Actor
Charles, Ernest		Composer	20	80		45	
Charles, Josh		Entertainment	5			20	Actor 'Sports Night'
Charles, Prince of Wales	1948-	Royalty	775	842	1500	862	Philip Arthur George
Charles, Ray		Entertainment		200			Blind Afro-Am. Singer-Musician
Charles, Suzette		Entertainment	5	6	15	20	Miss American 1984
Charlie's Angels		Celebrity				125	Cast signed photo
Charlotte Sophia	1741-1818	Royalty	145	275	452		Queen of George III (Eng)
Charlotte, Grand Duchess		Royalty	25	75	180	55	Luxembourg
Charlton, Suzanne		Celebrity	10			15	weather presenter
Charmed (cast)		Entertainment				95	cast of 3
Charo		Entertainment	3	3	6	10	
Charpentier, Gustave	1860-1956	Composer	100	250	300	305	AMusQS 150-450-625-750
Charriere, Henri		Author		863			Papillon
Charrington, Brig. Harold V.S.	1886-1965	Military	25				World War II British general
Charteris, Leslie		Author	20	55	135	85	The Saint. FDC S 75
Charvet, David		Entertainment	12			45	Actor 'Baywatch'
Chase, Charley		Entertainment	20			150	Vintage Film Comedian
Chase, Chevy		Entertainment	6	7	15	35	Actor-Comedian. SP 'Xmas Vacation' 38
Chase, Ilka		Entertainment	12	15	20	25	Author
Chase, Maj. Gen. William C.	1895-1986	Military	30				World War II U.S. general
Chase, Mary Ellen	1887-1973	Author	25	70	150	80	Educator, Essayist, Pulitzer Prize ^"Harvey"^
Chase, Salmon P.	1808-1873	Supreme Court	87	403	481	300	Chief Justice Supr. Ct.,Lincoln's Sec'y Treas.
Chase, Samuel	1741-1811	Revolutionary War	275	815	1882		Signer Decl. of Indepen.
Chase, William C.		Military	6	20	35		
Chase, William Merritt	1849-1916	Artist	95				US Painter of Western Scenes
Chateaubriand, Francois R. de	1768-1848	Author	120	228	408		Fr. Novelist, Diplomat. Fndr. Fr.Romantic Movement
Chater, Maj Gen Arthur Reginald	1896-1979	Military	25				World War II British general
Chatterton, Ruth		Entertainment	15			55	
Chauncey, Isaac	1772-1840	Military	25	95	105		Am. Naval Off. Tripoli, War 1812
Chausson, Ernest		Composer	50	145	345		Fr. Opera, Symphonies
Chauvel, Henry, Sir		Military	25	75			Aussie General WW I
Chavez, Anna		Celebrity	10			15	media/TV personality
Chavez, Carlos		Composer	15	35	70	40	Mexican Conductor-Composer
Chavez, Cesar E.	1927-1993	Labor	40	155		182	Migrant Labor Organizer. Social Activist
Chavez, Dennis		Senate	10	25		25	Sen NM. 1st Hispanic MOC & Senator
Chavez, George A.		Aviation	45	60	175	65	
Chavez, Linda		Celebrity	10			15	motivational speaker
Chavin, Brig. Gen. Raphael S.	1894-1974	Military	30				World War II U.S. general
Chawla, Kalpana		Astronaut	100			250	Columbia Tragedy

NAME	DATE	CATEGORY	SIG	LS/DS	ALS	SP	COMMENTS
Chayefsky, Paddy (Sidney)		Author	52	155	188	125	Plays, TV Dramas, Screenplays
Cheadle, Brig. Gen. Henry B.	1891-1959	Military	30				World War II U.S. general
Cheadle, Don		Celebrity				35	
Cheap Trick		Entertainment	35			40	DS by Rick Nielsen Repr. For Band 50
Cheatham, Benj. Franklin	1820-1886	Civil War	253	481			CSA General
Cheatham, Benjamin F. (WD)	1820-1886	Civil War	390		652		CSA General
Checker, Chubby		Entertainment	10	20	25	34	Rock
Cheech & Chong		Entertainment	28			65	Raunchy Comic Duo
Cheek, John		Entertainment	10			25	Opera
Cheers (Cast) (6)		Entertainment				335	
Cheetham, Maj. Gen. Geoffrey	1891-1962	Military	25				World War II British general
Cheever, Charles A., Dr.		Science	40	100		75	
Cheever, George B.	1814-1890	Clergy	10		30		Author
Cheever, John	1912-1981	Author	45	125	220	88	Subtle, Ironic Novels. Pulitzer 1979
Chegwin, Keith		Celebrity	10			15	television presenter
Chekhov, Anton	1860-1904	Author	560	1815	4156		Rus.Dramatist. Novelist, Physician
Chen, Joan		Entertainment	15			60	Model-Actress
Chen, Tina		Composer	10	10		15	
Cheney, Dick		Celebrity	10			15	political celebrity
Cheney, Richard		Cabinet	10			50	Sec'y Defense. Vice President under George W. Bush
Cheney, Sherwood		Military	5		25		General WW I
Cheng, Nien		Celebrity	10			15	motivational speaker
Chennault, Anna	1925-	Celebrity	15	25	50	30	Aviation Exec.,Writer,Lecturer.Wife of the Gen'l.
Chennault, Claire L.	1890-1958	Aviation	250	250	675	638	Flying Tigers. USAAF Gen.
Cher		Entertainment	13	20	25	50	AA Winning Actress. Pin-Up SP 80
Cherkassky, Shura		Entertainment	20			60	Opera
Chernenko, Konstantin	1911-1985	Political		407			Soviet leader
Chernov, Vladimir		Entertainment	10			30	Opera, Rus. Baritone
Cherry, Don	1924-1996	Entertainment	5			30	Singer. Popular Decca Recording Artist
Cherry, R. Gregg		Governor	5	15		10	Governor NC
Cherubini, Luigi	1760-1842	Composer	175	352	540		It. 29 Operas, 15 Masses
Chesebrough, Amos	1709-1760	Colonial Am.		275			Lt.Col. 8th Reg. French-Ind. War
Chesebrough, George M.		Science		750			
Chesebrough, Robert		Business	15	30	50		Vaseline Products. Chesebrough Mfg. Co.
Cheshire, Leonard		Military	15	50	65	40	Br. RAF
Chesney, Kenny		Music	15			45	CW singer
Chesnutt, Mark		Country Music	4			22	Consistent Top 10 Artist
Chester, Bob		Entertainment	20			40	Big Band Leader
Chester, Colby M.		Business	10			55	CEO General Foods
Chester, John		Revolutionary War	35	80			Continental Army. Judge
Chesterfield, Fourth Earl of		Statesman		375			SEE STANHOPE, P.D.
Chesterton, Gilbert Keith		Author	44	305	325	190	'Father Brown, Detective'
Chestnut, James	1815-1885	Civil War	125				CSA Gen.
Chetlain, Augustus Louis	1824-1914	Civil War	40	95	145		Union general, Recruited a Black Regiment
Chevaerie, Kurt von der		Military	10			40	

NAME	DATE	CATEGORY	SIG	LS/DS	ALS	SP	COMMENTS
Chevalier, Albert	1861-1923	Composer	6	25	40	25	Br. Actor, Singer, Humorist
Chevalier, Maurice	1888-1972	Entertainment	52		150	102	Fr. Film & Vaudeville Actor-Singer. 'Gigi'
Chevallerie, Gen. of Inf. Kurt v der	1891-1945	Military	25				World War II German general
Cheves, Maj. Gen. Gilbert X.	1895-1985	Military	30				World War II U.S. general
Chevillon, Lt. Gen. André-Claude	1895-1953	Military	20				World War II French general
Chevrolet, Louis	1879-1941	Business	850	4858			Chevrolet Auto Mfg. & Glen Martin Aircraft
Chew, Virginia	1905-1987	Entertainment	5		25		Char. Actress. Longtime Broadway. Sometime Films
Chianese, Dominic		Entertainment				50	Uncle Jr. Soprano's
Chiao, Leroy		Astronaut	7			20	
Chiari, Walter	1924-1992	Entertainment	20			45	Comic Italian Actor. Internationally recognized.
Chicago (cast)		Entertainment				145	Gere, Zellweger, Zeta-Jones
Chicago		Entertainment	35			95	Rock Group
Chichester, Francis, Sir		Celebrity	35	100	165	40	Adventurer, Aviator, Sailed Gypsy Moth IV
Chichester, Giles Bryan		Political	10			15	Member European Parliament
Chickering, Brig. Gen. William E.	1895-1959	Military	30				World War II U.S. general
Chickering, Thos. E.	1824-1871	Civil War-Business	35	77	142		Union Gen. Chickering Piano
Chierel, Micheline		Entertainment	10			30	Actress
Chiklis, Michael		Entertainment	10			45	Emmy Award winner
Child, Julia		Celebrity Chef	5	12	22	15	TV Chef. Cookbook Author
Child, Lydia Maria		Author	30	90	155		Abolitionist, Reformer, Editor
Childress, Alvin		Entertainment	50			125	
Childs, George Wm.	1829-1894	Publisher	55	145	167		ALS content 925
Chiles, Lawton Mainor, Jr.		Senate	10	15	20	15	Senator FL
Chiles, Lois		Entertainment	5	6	15	22	Actress
Chilton, Kevin P.		Astronaut	4			15	
Chilton, Lt. Gen. Sir Maurice S.	1898-1956	Military	28				World War II British general
Chilton, Robert Hall (WD)	1815-1879	Civil War	395	3125			CSA General
Chilton, Robert Hall	1815-1879	Civil War	185		506		CSA General
Chilton, Samuel	1804-1867	Congress	50	145			MOC VA. John Brown's Att'y
Chirac, Jacques		Head of State	25	75	185	35	Fr. Prime Minister, Mayor Paris
Chirico, Giorgio de	1888-1978	Artist			765		Major Italian Surrealist
Chisholm, Maj. Gen. Brock	1896-1971	Military	20				World War II Canadian general
Chisholm, Shirley A.	1924-	Senate/Congress	25			100	1st Afro-Am. Congresswoman
Chittenden, Thos. C.	1788-1866	Congress	10				MOC NY
Chittenden, Uncle Russ		Author	8			12	cookbooks
Chlumsky, Anna		Entertainment	6			35	Young Actress
Cho, Lt. Gen. Isamu	1895-1945	Military	25				World War II Japanese general
Choate, Joseph H.	1832-1917	Diplomat	15	60	125	45	Prosecuted Tweed Ring
Choate, Pat		Celebrity	10			15	financial expert
Choate, Rufus	1799-1859	Senate	20	35	60		Boston Statesman, Orator, NY Sen
Chocola, Chris C		Congress	10			15	Member U.S. Congress
Choiseul, Leopold C. de, Card.		Clergy	100	165			
Chokachi, David		Entertainment	6			35	Actor. 'Baywatch'
Choltitz, Gen. of Inf. Dietrich von	1894-1966	Military	25				World War II German general
Chomsky, Noam		Celebrity	10			15	political celebrity

NAME	DATE	CATEGORY	SIG	LS/DS	ALS	SP	COMMENTS
Chong, Rae Dawn		Entertainment	5	8	15	35	Actress. Pin-Up 65
Chong, Tommy		Entertainment	8			15	Cheech & Chong
Chopin, Frederic		Composer	1200	4167	10000		ALS/Cont. 16,500, ALS/Cont.22,000
Chou En-Lai		Head of State	1155	4000	10000	5000	Chinese Communist Premier
Chouteau, Rene Auguste	1749-1829	Revolutionary War	350	1000	1515		American Pioneer. Fur Trader. Fndr. St. Louis
Chretien, Jean-Loup		Astronaut	10			20	France
Chris Steele, Dr		Celebrity	10			15	health and fitness expert
Christensen, Donna M. C		Congress	10			15	Member U.S. Congress
Christian IX (Den)	1818-1906	Royalty	90	250			King of Denmark 1863-1906
Christian VII (Den & Nor)	1749-1808	Royalty	125	325	625		King of Denmark
Christian, Brig. Gen. Thomas J.J.	1888-1952	Military	30				World War II U.S. general
Christian, Claudia		Entertainment	8			45	Actress. Pin-Up 65
Christian, George B.		Senate	5	20		10	Senator OH
Christian, Prince	1831-1917	Royalty	45		150		Prince Schleswig-HolsteinaVictoria's Son-in-Law
Christian, Spencer		Celebrity	10			15	media/TV personality
Christians, Mady		Entertainment	25	30	65	52	Star from Golden Years of American Theatre
Christiansen, Maj. Gen. James G.	1897-1982	Military	30				World War II U.S. general
Christianson, Helena		Celebrity	10			15	celebrity model
Christie, Agatha	1891-1976	Author	238	310	407	925	Classic Detective Novels, AMS 2300
Christie, Julie	1940-	Entertainment	28	15	28	49	Brit. Actress Oscar Winner.Pin-Up SP 45
Christie, Maj. Gen. Campbell M.	1893-1963	Military	25				World War II British general
Christina, Queen (Swe)		Royalty	250	2088	2400		
Christine, Virginia		Entertainment	6	4	15	25	
Christison, Gen. Sir Alex. F. P.	1893-1993	Military	25				World War II British general
Christmas, Maj. Gen. John K.	1895-1962	Military	30				World War II U.S. general
Christo*		Artist	5	15	20	85	Sculptor in Fabric
Christophe Novelli, Jean		Celebrity	10			15	Chef
Christophe, Henry	1767-1820	Head of State	1325	1500			Haitian Revolutionary, Sovereign.
Christopher, Dennis		Entertainment	3	4	6	6	
Christopher, Roy		Celebrity	10			15	film industry
Christopher, Warren		Cabinet	15	35		25	Sec'y State
Christopher, William		Entertainment	5	6	15	15	
Christy, Brig. Gen. William C.	1885-1957	Military	30				World War II U.S. general
Christy, Eileen		Entertainment	5			25	Vintage Actress
Christy, Howard Chandler	1873-1952	Artist	60	82	256	490	Illustrator, Portraitist. Books
Christy, June		Entertainment	10			20	Stan Kenton Vocalist. Recording Star
Chrobog, Jurgen		Celebrity	10			15	political celebrity
Chrysler, Morgan Henry	1822-1890	Civil War	42	110	161		Union general
Chrysler, Walter P. Jr.		Business	75	275	350	150	Walter's Son & Financier
Chrysler, Walter P.	1875-1940	Business	317	900	1175	1077	Founder Chrysler Motors.TLS 3500
Chrystall, Maj. Gen. John Inglis	1887-1960	Military	25				World War II British general
Chuikov, Vasily		Military		200			Soviet General
Chun Doo-Hwan		Head of State	25		50		
Chung, Connie		TV News	5	10	20	20	TV News Anchor
Chung, Kyung-Wha		Entertainment	10			65	Contemporary Violin Sensation

NAME	DATE	CATEGORY	SIG	LS/DS	ALS	SP	COMMENTS
Chung, Myung Whun		Conductor				75	Controversial Korean Maestro
Church, Benjamin		Rev War	205	530	1010		Am. Physician & Spy
Church, Brig. Gen. John H.	1892-1953	Military	30				World War II U.S. general
Church, Charlotte		Entertainment				30	Welsh soprano
Church, Frank		Congress	5	15		25	Senator ID
Church, Frederick E.	1826-1900	Artist	112	425	1020		Am. Dramatic Landscapes
Church, Frederick S.		Artist	40	65	122		ALS/Sketch 500, ANS/Sketch 225
Church, R.W.		Clergy	20	35	50		
Church, Thomas Haydon		Entertainment	10			20	actor
Churchill, Brig. John Atherton	1887-1965	Military	25				World War II British general
Churchill, Clementine S.	1885-1977	First Lady, Br.	74	200	265	160	Wife of Winston S.
Churchill, Jennie(Jerome)	1854-1921	Celebrity	15	100	305	95	W.S. Churchill's American Born Mother
Churchill, John	1650-1722	Military	360	785			1st Duke of Marlborough
Churchill, Mary		Celebrity	5		25		
Churchill, Randolph, Lord	1849-1895	Br. Statesman	45	90	225		Father of Winston S.
Churchill, Sarah		Entertainment	20	25	30	35	Actress-Daughter of Winston S.
Churchill, Sarah	1660-1744	Royalty	117	275			Powerful Confidante of Queen Anne. Duchess of
Churchill, Thomas James (WD)	1824-1905	Civil War	195	460			CSA General
Churchill, Thomas James	1824-1905	Civil War	75	107	223		CSA Gen., Gov. AR
Churchill, Winston S.	1874-1965	Head of State	841	1992	4017	3738	WW II P.M., Author, Artist. 3x5 SP 1500. Chk.S 3200
Churchill, Winston	1871-1947	Author	15	35	60	35	Historical Novelist
Chynoweth, Brig Gen Bradford G.	1890-1985	Military	30				World War II U.S. general
Cialini, Julie		Celebrity	10			15	model
Ciannelli, Eduardo		Entertainment	20			45	Actor
Ciano, Galeazzo, Conte		Royalty	65	295			Son-in-Law of Mussolini
Cibrian, Eddie		Entertainment	10			20	actor
Cicognani, A.G., Cardinal		Clergy	35	50	75	60	
Cigna, Gina		Entertainment	50	70		65	Opera
Cilea, Francesco		Composer	100			500	It. Composer of 'Adriana Lecouvreur'
Cimaro, Pietro		Entertainment	10	25	50		It. Conductor
Cimino, Michael		Entertainment	8	15	22	32	Film Director
Ciny, Alain	1908-	Entertainment	20			45	Fr. Character Actor 'La Dolce Vita' etc.
Cisneros, Henry	1947-	Cabinet	10			20	Sec'y HUD. Major Problems with FBI
Citroen, Andre-Gustaveé	1878-1935	Business	85	395		700	Engineer-Industrialist. Citroen Auto Mfg.
Civiletti, Benjamin		Cabinet	5	10	20	10	
Clack, Mrs. Louise		Author	8			12	'General Lee and Santa Claus
Clair, Ren	1898-1981	Entertainment	115	145	320		Fr. Film Maker, Actor, Writer
Clairborne, Liz		Business	10			20	Clothing Designer
Claire, Ina		Entertainment	15	15	35	35	Vintage Leading Lady. Stage-Films
Claire, Marion		Entertainment	10			25	Am. Soprano
Clamorgan, Jacques		Explorer-Trader		750			Missouri Co. 1795. Precursor of Louis & Clark
Clancey, Tom		Author	15	25		20	Am. Novelist
Clanton, James Holt	1827-1871	Civil War	135	567			Confederate general
Clanton, Jimmy		Entertainment	20			25	Rock
Clanton, N.H.		Celebrity	1100				Father of Billy, OK Corral

NAME	DATE	CATEGORY	SIG	LS/DS	ALS	SP	COMMENTS
Clapp, Gordon		Entertainment	10			20	actor
Clapton, Eric		Entertainment	30			89	Rock. 'August' Alb. S 110. Grammy Winner
Clark, Abraham	1726-1794	Revolutionary War	454	800	4500		Signer Decl. of Indepen.
Clark, Barzilla W.		Governor	5	12	20		Governor ID
Clark, Brig. Gen. Frank S.	1885-1975	Military	30				World War II U.S. general
Clark, Brigadier George Philip	1901-1977	Military	25				World War II British general
Clark, Buddy		Entertainment	10			25	40's Singer
Clark, Candy		Entertainment	4	3	7	15	Pin-Up 35
Clark, Carol Higgins		Author	5	15		20	All Around the Town
Clark, Champ	1850-1921	Political		20			Speaker of the house
Clark, Charles	1811-1877	Civil War	152	331	434		CSA General, CW Gov. of Miss.
Clark, Clarence D.		Senate	10		35	15	Senator WY
Clark, Cottonseed		Country Music	15			30	Singer
Clark, Dan		Celebrity	10			15	motivational speaker
Clark, Dane	1913-1998	Entertainment	18	20	25	35	Actor noted for 'Tough Guy' roles From 1942
Clark, Dick		Entertainment	6	14	15	22	American Bandstand Host
Clark, Edward	1815-1880	Civil War		150			Governor of TX
Clark, Francis E.		Clergy	10	15	25	20	
Clark, Frank		Senate/Congress	5	15		10	Congressman FL
Clark, Fred	1914-1968	Entertainment	25			50	Am. Character-Comedian Actor 1947-68
Clark, Gene		Entertainment	40			195	Deceased 'Byrds' Original
Clark, George Rogers	1752-1818	Revolutionary War	675	2450	4250		General, Frontier Leader
Clark, James B. (Champ)	1850-1921	Congress	60	40	145	95	Speaker of the House. MO
Clark, James, Sir		Medical	15	35	85		Phys.to Queen Victoria & Albert
Clark, Joe		Celebrity	10			15	motivational speaker
Clark, John Bullock, Jr. (WD)	1831-1903	Civil War	180				CSA Gen. ALS/Content 8250
Clark, John Bullock, Jr.		Civil War	82				Confederate gen.
Clark, Kenneth B.	1914-	Activist	20			55	Psychologist-Writer. Brown vs Board of Education
Clark, Laurel Blair		Astronaut	8			25	
Clark, Louis Gaylord		Author	20	35	122		Editor Knickerbocker Magazine
Clark, Lt Gen John Geo. Walters	1892-1948	Military	25				World War II British general
Clark, Marguerite	1883-1940	Entertainment	25			70	Stage.Film Rival Mary Pickford
Clark, Mark W.	1896-1984	Military	35	118	178	83	Gen. WW II 5th Army. FDC S 50
Clark, Mary Higgens		Author		38		20	Suspense Novels
Clark, Mary		Military	5	8	15	15	
Clark, Myron H.		Governor	10	20	35	15	Governor NY
Clark, Petula		Entertainment	8			31	Br. Singer-Actress
Clark, Ramsay		Cabinet	15	35	60	20	Att'y Gen.
Clark, Roy		Country Music	5	30		20	Singer-Guitarist-Comedian. 'Hee Haw'
Clark, Susan		Entertainment	5	9	12	18	Actress. Pin-Up SP 25
Clark, Terri		Entertainment	5			20	Singer-Country
Clark, Tim		Celebrity	10			15	comedian
Clark, Tom C.	1889-1977	Supreme Court	40	110	145	410	U.S. Attorney General
Clark, Walter J.		Aviation	10	22	38	28	ACE, WW II
Clark, Wesley General		Military	15	20	25	52	NATO Supreme Commander

NAME	DATE	CATEGORY	SIG	LS/DS	ALS	SP	COMMENTS
Clark, William A.		Senate	35	135	195		Railroad & Mining Magnate
Clark, William Thomas	1831-1905	Civil War	40	64	110		Union general
Clark, William	1770-1838	Explorer	375	1650	1988		Lewis & Clark Expedition.Gov. MO Territory
Clarke, Bruce C.	1901-1988	Military	30				World War II U.S. general
Clarke, Adam		Clergy	75	145	350		
Clarke, Annie		Entertainment	15	15	25	25	
Clarke, Arthur C.		Author	15	35	75	55	2001
Clarke, Brig. Gen. Carter W.	1896-1987	Military	30				World War II U.S. general
Clarke, Brig Frederick Arthur S.	1892-1972	Military	25				World War II British general
Clarke, Brigadier Terence Hugh	1904-1992	Military	25				World War II British general
Clarke, Brig. William Stanhope	1899-1973	Military	25				World War II British general
Clarke, Charles G.		Entertainment	6			15	Film Director
Clarke, Charles Mansfield		Medical	20	65	140		Br. Obstetrician
Clarke, George		Colonial Gov. N.Y	85	350			
Clarke, Henri J.G. Duc de		Napoleonic Wars	50	287	345		Marshal of Napoleon
Clarke, James Freeman		Clergy	40	50	89	60	
Clarke, James McClure		Senate/Congress	5			10	MOC NC
Clarke, Mae		Entertainment	28			65	Vintage Actress. Scene/James Cagney & Grapefruit
Clarke, Margi		Celebrity	10			15	television presenter
Clarke, Paul		Celebrity	10			15	Big Brother 2ª
Clarke, Robert		Entertainment	20			50	
Clarke, Roberta N.		Celebrity	10			15	medical expert
Clarke, Thomas		Revolutionary War	165	550			
Clarke, Warren		Entertainment	10			20	Actor
Clarkson, Jeremy		Celebrity	10			15	television presenter
Clarkson, Maj. Gen. Percy W.	1893-1962	Military	30				World War II U.S. general
Clarkson, Mathew	1758-1825	Military-Rev. War	45	95	175		Rev. Soldier, Philanthropist
Clarkson, Thomas	1760-1846	Reformer	35		100		Br. Devoted Entire Life to Abolition of Slavery
Clary, Alice		Author	15	25		15	
Clary, Julian		Celebrity	10			15	comedian
Clary, Robert		Entertainment	4	5	9	13	Diminuative Fr.Actor. 'Hogan's Heroes'
Clason, George S.		Celebrity	10			15	financial expert
Clavell, James		Author	10	25	55	15	Novelist
Clay, Cassius Marcellus	1810-1903	Civil War	91	283	500		Union Gen., Senate, Abolition.
Clay, Henry	1777-1852	Cabinet	122	561	654	350	Sec'y State, ALS Auct. 9,300, LS/Cont. 1500
Clay, Lucius D.	1897-1978	Military	35	110	150	118	Gen. WW II. US Military Gov. Berlin Blockade
Clay, William L., Sr.	1931-	Senate/Congress	10			27	Afro-Am. Congressman MO. Civil Rights Activist
Clay, Wm. Lacy C		Congress	10			15	Member U.S. Congress
Clayburgh, Jill	1945-	Entertainment	6	15	15	30	Actress. Twice Nominated for Oscar.
Clayton, Ethel	1882-1966	Celebrity				40	
Clayton, Henry D.		Senate/Congress	5	10			MOC AL
Clayton, Henry Delamar	1827-1889	Civil War	125				Confederate general
Clayton, Jan		Entertainment	12	6	15	30	Actress-Singer. Mother on 'Lassie'
Clayton, John M.		Cabinet	20	65	140		Taylor Sec'y State
Clayton, Joshua	1744-1798	Revolutionary War	220	425			1st Gov. DE. Senator DE

NAME	DATE	CATEGORY	SIG	LS/DS	ALS	SP	COMMENTS
Clayton, Maj. Gen. Edward Hadrill	1899-1962	Military	28				World War II British general
Clayton, Powell	1833-1914	Civil War	46	84	122		Union general
Clayton, S. J.		Senate/Congress	5	10			
Clear Sky, Chief		Native American	20			50	Iroquois Chief
Cleave, Mary		Astronaut	10			25	
Cleaveland, Moses		Revolutionary War	170	850			Cleveland, Ohio Namesake
Cleburne, Patrick R.	1828-1864	Civil War	2300	3600			CSA General, KIA Franklin, TN
Cleese, John		Entertainment	10			20	actor
Clegg, Nicholas		Political	10			15	Member European Parliament
Cleland, Brig. Gen. Joseph P.	1902-1975	Military	30				World War II U.S. general
Cleland, Brig. Donald Mackinnon	1901-1975	Military	20				World War II Australian general
Clem, John L. (Johnny)	1851-1937	Civil War	250	280	323	633	Union Drummer Boy, Chicamauga
Clemenceau, Georges	1841-1929	Head of State	100	140	185		Physician, Statesman, Journalist. AMsS 835
Clemens, Brig. Gen. Paul B.	1882-1960	Military	30				World War II U.S. general
Clemens, Clarence		Entertainment					
Clemens, Orion		Old West	125		160		Sec'y of Nevada Territory 1861 Brother of Samuel
Clemens, S.L., as Mark Twain	1835-1910	Author	756	1268	3170	4250	ALS/Content 19,500. P/C SP 2475. AQS 2530- 7500
Clemens, Samuel L.	1835-1910	Author	728	1506	2590	4732	ALS Content 19,000
Clement IX, Pope	1600-1669	Clergy		1310			Guilio Rospigliosi
Clement VIII, Pope		Clergy	550	1398			
Clement, Martin Withington		Business	3	8	16	6	Pres. CEO Pennsylvania RR
Clementi, Muzio	1752-1832	Composer			2000		Pianist. Remembered for Musical Combat/Mozart
Clements, Stanley Stash		Entertainment	10			20	
Clervoy, Jean-Francois		Astronaut	5			25	France
Cleveland, Carleton A.		Business	10	35	45	20	
Cleveland, Charles		Clergy	20	25	45		
Cleveland, Frances F.	1864-1927	First Lady	60	90	100	205	ALS As 1st Lady 300
Cleveland, Grover & Francis F.		President/1st Lady	418				
Cleveland, Grover (As Pres.)		President	250	537	668	1317	WH Card S 350, SP/1st Cabinet 1200
Cleveland, Grover	1837-1908	President	202	408	617	612	ALS/Content 1,250-3,500
Clewell, Brig. Gen. Edgar L.	1896-1973	Military	30				World War II U.S. general
Clewes, Henry		Business	25	45			Banker
Cliburn, Van		Entertainment	25	40	55	154	Am. Pianist
Clifford, Clark M.	1906-1998	Cabinet	20	25	42	35	Sec'y Defense. Advisor to Truman Thru Carter
Clifford, John Henry		Governor	10	55	95		
Clifford, Nathan	1803-1881	Supreme Court	75	175	240	150	Att'y Gen., Ambassador
Clifford, Rich		Astronaut	7			22	
Clift, Eleanor		Celebrity	10			15	media/TV personality
Clift, Montgomery	1920-1966	Entertainment	242	355	600	700	4 Oscar Nominations. Reclusive Non-Conformist
Clifton, Joseph C.		Aviation	15	35	60	40	
Cline, Patsy		Country Music	475			1450	Early Death
Clingan, William	d. 1790	Revolutionary War	50	185			Delegate Cont.Congress.Early Signer Articles Conf.
Clinger, Debora		Entertainment	3	5	7	8	Pin-Up 25
Clingman, Thomas Lanier	1812-1897	Civil War	108	295	410		CSA General
Clinton, Chelsea		Celebrity	10			15	political celebrity

NAME	DATE	CATEGORY	SIG	LS/DS	ALS	SP	COMMENTS
Clinton, De Witt	1769-1828	Statesman	63	205	299		Promoted Erie Canal. Mayor NYC. Pres. Candidate
Clinton, George	1739-1812	V.P.-Military	135	346	1098		Cont'l Congr.,Gen'l, Gov. NY. ALS/Cont. 7,000
Clinton, Henry, Sir	1730-1795	Military-Rev. War	425	1125	2200		Br. Commander Am. Rev. Blamed for Loss
Clinton, Hillary Rodham		Political	20	30	40	70	Fmr First Lady., Senator NY
Clinton, James G.	1804-1849	Congress	15		35		Repr. NY
Clinton, James		Military-Rev. War	200	490			General Revolutionary War
Clinton, Roger		Entertainment	25				Singer-Brother of President Clinton
Clinton, William 'Bill'		President	253	576	1959	282	42nd President. TLS/AN 1500. Pres. SP 895
Clinton, William J. (Bill) (As Pres.)		President	150	1266	2896	375	42nd U.S. President.
Clive, Colin		Entertainment	270			555	
Clive, E.E.		Entertainment	20			50	
Clive, Edward, Baron		Royalty			100		First Earl of Powys., Eldest son of Rbt. Clive
Clive, Robert		Military	250	600	1200		Baron Clive of Plassey
Clößner, Gen. of Infantry Heinrich	1888-1976	Military	25				World War II German general
Clokey, Art*		Cartoonist	20			150	Gumby. SP 35-45
Cloney, Thomas	1774-1850	History			2500		Irish rebellion
Clontz, Marie		Author	8			12	English grammar
Clooney, George		Entertainment	18	125		58	Actor-Director. Movies/TV. Check S 125
Clooney, Rosemary	d. 2002	Entertainment	5	6	15	55	Singer
Close, Glenn		Entertainment	13	17	25	40	Actress. Oscar Winner. Pin-Up 45
Clostermann, Pierre		Military	55	85	125	75	
Clover, Richardson		Military	35	125			USN Admiral
Clovio, Giorgio Guilio	1498-1578	Artist	650	1400	2000		It. Miniaturist
Clowe, John Lee		Celebrity	10			15	president of AMA
Clowes, Lt. Gen. Cyril A.	1892-1968	Military	20				World War II Australian general
Clowes, Maj. Gen. Norman	1893-1980	Military	25				World War II British general
Clune, Jackie		Celebrity	10			15	comedienne
Clunes, Alec	1912-1970	Entertainment	5	20		30	Brit. Stage, Film Actor. Director-Producer
Clunes, Martin		Entertainment	10			20	Actor
Cluseret, Gustave Paul	1823-1900	Civil War	40	91	160		Union general
Clutterbuck, Maj. Gen. Walter E.	1894-1987	Military	25				World War II British general
Clyburn, James E. C		Congress	10			15	Member U.S. Congress
Clyde, Andy		Entertainment	50			150	Vintage Comedian
Clyde, June		Entertainment	8	9	15	20	
Clymer, George	1739-1813	Revolutionary War	159	511	1071		Statesman. Signer Decl. of Indepen. FF 900
Coase, Ronald		Economist	20	35		25	Nobel Economics
Coates, Eric		Composer	25	55	85	130	
Coates, Phyllis		Entertainment	10			20	
Coats, Bob		Aviation	10	22	38	30	ACE, WW II
Coats, Michael L.		Astronaut	5			15	
Cobain, Kurt		Entertainment	45			168	Rock
Cobb, Calvin H.		Military	15	40	75		
Cobb, Howell (WD)		Civil War	225		575	950	CSA General
Cobb, Howell	1815-1868	Civil War	86	156	490		Speaker, Sec'y Treas.,CSA Gen., Gov. GA
Cobb, Irvin S.	1876-1944	Author	22	47	87	95	Journalist-Humorist-Playwright

NAME	DATE	CATEGORY	SIG	LS/DS	ALS	SP	COMMENTS
Cobb, Jerrie		Aviation	5	10	19	21	
Cobb, Lee J.		Entertainment	35	50	75	130	Fine Character Actor of Films & Stage
Cobb, Sylvanus	1823-1887	Author	12			40	
Cobb, Thos. Reade R. (WD)		Civil War	1250		2098		CSA Gen. KIA '62
Cobb, Thos. Reade R.	1823-1862	Civil War	628	1950	2495		CSA Gen. KIA '62
Cobbs, Brig. Gen. Nicholas H.	1896-1968	Military	30				World War II U.S. general
Cobham, Alan J., Sir	1894-1973	Aviation	40	110	220	62	Br. Aviation Pioneer. Pioneered Aerial Photography
Cobham, Gov. Gen. NZ		Head of State	5	8	15	10	New Zealand
Coble, Howard C		Congress	10			15	Member U.S. Congress
Cobo, Albert E.		Celebrity	10	15	45	15	Detroit's Cobo Hall
Coburn, Brig. Gen. Henry C. Jr.	1879-1958	Military	30				World War II U.S. general
Coburn, Charles	1877-1961	Entertainment	45	65	155	138	AA Winner. Monacle-wearing Character Actor
Coburn, James		Entertainment	10	12	22	35	Actor. 'Our Man Flint'. Academy Award '99
Coca, Imogene		Entertainment	9			35	Comedienne & TV Pioneer
Cochran, Eddie	1938-1960	Entertainment	220			595	Star of Early Rock. Died at 22
Cochran, Jacqueline		Aviation	45	175		145	Speed record holder
Cochran, John L (Johnny)		Legal	15			20	O.J. Simpson Trial Lawyer
Cochran, Robert L.		Governor	12	20	30	15	Governor NE
Cochran, Steve		Entertainment	15	15	30	28	
Cochran, Thad		Senate	10			15	United States Senate (R - MS)
Cochrane, Basil, Sir		Military	15	25	30		
Cochrane, John	1813-1898	Civil War	44	75	114		Union Gen. ALS '62 345
Cochrane, Ralph		Military	5	15	25	20	
Cocilovo, Luigi		Political	10			15	Member European Parliament
Cockburn, George, Sir		Military	40	100	140		Br. Admiral War 1812
Cockburn, Henry Thomas Lord	1779-1854	Jurist			110		Scottish Judge
Cockcroft, John Douglas, Sir		Science	60	110	245	75	Nobel Physics
Cocke, Philip St. George (WD)		Civil War			5500		CSA Gen. Suicide '61
Cocke, Philip St. George	1809-1861	Civil War	475	650			CSA Gen.
Cocker, Joe		Entertainment	12	40		40	Rock Star
Cockerell, Christopher, Sir	1910-	Inventor	35		90		Inventor of Hovercraft
Cockrell, Francis Marion	1834-1915	Civil War	78	160	227		CSA General, US Sen. MO
Cockrell, Ken		Astronaut	6			20	
Coco, James	1928-1887	Entertainment	15	20	40	35	Nomination Letter For Oscar From Academy 225
Cocteau, Jean	1889-1963	Author-Artist	200	225	592	650	Novelist, Playwright. Orig.Sketch S 500, 795, 900
Coda, Eraldo		Entertainment	5			25	Opera
Code, Maj. Gen. James A. Jr.	1893-1971	Military	30				World War II U.S. general
Cody, Buck		Entertainment	3	3	6	6	
Cody, Iron Eyes	1907-	Entertainment	30	45	50	60	Long Time Native American Star. Film & TV
Cody, John P., Cardinal		Clergy	25	35	50	45	
Cody, Lew		Entertainment	15	20	25	35	
Cody, Louisa		Celebrity		425			Wife of Wm. F. (Buffalo Bill) Cody
Cody, William F. & Buffalo Bill		Celebrity	1012	1483	2375	3221	Signed both Ways. ALS/Content 9300
Cody, William F.	1846-1917	Celebrity	593	1100	1436	1857	CW Scout, Pony Expr.,Showman, CMH
Coelho, Carlos		Political	10			15	Member European Parliament

NAME	DATE	CATEGORY	SIG	LS/DS	ALS	SP	COMMENTS
Coffee, Gerald		Celebrity	10			15	motivational speaker
Coffey, Brig. Gen. John W.	1897-1951	Military	30				World War II U.S. general
Coffin, Charles Carleton	1823-1896	Civil War-Author	92				Only Journalist to Cover Entire War
Coffin, Henry Sloane		Clergy	25	35	40	50	
Coffin, Howard C.		Manufacturer	30				Pioneer Auto Manufacturer
Coffin, Isaac, Sir	1759-1839	Military	20		75		Boston Born Br. Naval Officer
Coffin, John	1756-1838	Revolutionary War	175	500			Loyalist General
Coffin, Tris		Entertainment	20			35	
Coffin, William Sloane	1924-	Clergy	10	18	35	25	Political Activist. Tried with Dr. Spock
Coffyn, Frank		Aviation	40	65		95	
Coggan, Donald, Archbishop		Clergy	35	45	50	50	
Coghlan, Frank, Jr.		Entertainment	7			18	GWTW
Coghlan, Joseph B.		Military	25			60	Adm USN-Spanish American War
Cogswell, William	1838-1895	Civil War	15	35	75		Repr. MA
Cohan, Alexander		Entertainment					
Cohan, George M.	1878-1942	Composer	102	146	301	319	Actor,Playwright,Director,Singer SP-Fam.Portr.895
Cohen, Octavus Roy		Author	15	30	45	25	Novels, Screenplays, Radio
Cohen, Ronald M.		Celebrity	10			15	Film industry
Cohen, Stanley, Dr.		Science	20	35		25	Nobel Medicine
Cohen, Wilbur J.		Cabinet	5	14	22	10	Sec'y HEW
Cohen, William S.		Cabinet	10		25	40	Senator ME, MOC ME, Sec. Defense
Cohn, Harry		Business	35	85	165	65	Co-Founder Columbia Pictures
Cohn, Jack		Business	25	70	140	55	Co-Founder Columbia Pictures
Cohn, Roy		Lawyer	15	25	40	20	Legal Aide Sen. McCarthy
Cohn-bendit, Daniel Marc		Political	10			15	Member European Parliament
Coit, James Brolles		Civil War	25		125		Union General
Coke, Edward, Sir	1552-1634	Law		2162	3500		Eminent Eng. Jurist. Lord Chief Justice
Coke, Richard	1829-1897	Civil War	25		60		CSA Officer. Gov. TX, Senator
Coke, Thomas, Bishop		Clergy	250	350	750		
Coker, Jack		Entertainment	6	8	15	20	
Colbern, Maj. Gen. William H.	1895-1959	Military	30				World War II U.S. general
Colbert, Claudette	1903-1994	Entertainment	32	112		81	Chic Fr.-Am. Leading lady from 30's on
Colbert, Jean-Baptiste	1619-1683	History			328		Minister of finance under Louis XIV of France
Colby, Bainbridge	1869-1950	Cabinet	10	30	55		Sec'y State Under Wilson
Colby, Leonard		Military	40	90			General. Indian Fighter
Colden, Cadwallader		Revolutionary War	100	240			Am. Colonialist
Cole, Cornelius		Senate/Congress	15	25	40		MOC CA 1863, Senator CA
Cole, Edward N.		Business	5	12	30	10	Pres. General Motors
Cole, Graham		Entertainment	10			20	Actor
Cole, Maj. Gen. William E.	1874-1953	Military	30				World War II U.S. general
Cole, Maj. Gen. William Scott	1901-1992	Military	25				World War II British general
Cole, Michael	1945-	Entertainment	4	6	10	18	Actor 'Mod Squad'
Cole, Nat King	1919-1965	Entertainment	109	229		364	Am. Jazz Pianist, Singer
Cole, Natalie		Entertainment	9			37	Singer
Cole, Stephanie		Entertainment	10			20	Actress

NAME	DATE	CATEGORY	SIG	LS/DS	ALS	SP	COMMENTS
Cole, Sterling		Congress/Senate	5	10			Congressman NY
Cole, Timothy		Artist	35		135		Wood Engraver.
Cole, Tom C		Congress	10			15	Member U.S. Congress
Coleman, Booth		Entertainment	10			40	Planet of the Apes
Coleman, Cy		Composer	25			30	Arranger
Coleman, Dabney		Entertainment	5	6	15	15	Actor
Coleman, David		Celebrity	10			15	television presenter
Coleman, Gary		Entertainment	5	7	12	25	
Coleman, George		Entertainment	7			40	Jazz Sax
Coleman, Jonathon		Celebrity	10			15	television presenter
Coleman, Nancy		Entertainment	6	8	15	10	
Coleman, Norm		Senate	10			15	United States Senate (R - MN)
Colenso, John W., Bishop		Clergy	20	25	35		
Coleridge, Gen. Sir John F. S.	1878-1951	Military	25				World War II British general
Coleridge, John Duke		Celebrity	6	12	25		
Coleridge, Samuel Taylor	1772-1834	Author	325	575	1250		Br. Lyrical Poet, Literary Critic. AMsS 7,500
Coleridge-Taylor, Samuel	1875-1912	Composer	35	70	160	45	Choral, Musical Theatre, Songs. AMusQS 200
Coles, Charles 'Honi'	1911-1992	Entertainment	60			95	Legendary Tap Dancer-Choreographer. Tony Award
Colette, Sidonie-Gabrielle	1873-1954	Author	65	315	335	805	Fr. Novelist , Journalist, Critic. 15 Pg. DS 750
Colfax, Schuyler	1823-1885	Vice President	65	100	234	286	Speaker of House, Grant VP
Colgate. James C.		Business	10	25	50	40	Colgate University. Donor
Colgrass, Michael		Composer	20	35	85		Pulitzer, AMusQS 100
Colladay, Brig. Gen. Edgar B.	1885-1971	Military	30				World War II U.S. general
Collamer, Jacob		Cabinet	20	55	80		Taylor P.M. General
Collet, Maj. Gen. Philibert	1896-1945	Military	20				World War II French general
Collette, Toni		Entertainment	10			20	actress
Collier, Bo		Author	8			12	novelist
Collier, Constance	1878-1955	Entertainment	25		30	75	Vintage Br. Actress
Collier, James W.		Senate/Congress	5	15		10	MOC MS
Collier, Lt. Gen. John H.	1898-1980	Military	30				World War II U.S. general
Collier, Maj. Gen. Angus Lyell	1893-1971	Military	25				World War II British general
Collier, Peter F.		Business	14	35	70		
Collinge, Patricia		Entertainment	6	8	15	19	
Collingwood, Brigadier Sydney	1892-1986	Military	28				World War II British general
Collingwood, Charles		Journalist	5	35	62	15	News Analyst, War Correspondent,TV Moderator
Collins, Brig. Gen. Leroy P.	1883-1981	Military	30				World War II U.S. general
Collins, Brig. Arthur F. St Clair	1892-1980	Military	25				World War II British general
Collins, Cardiss	1932-	Congress	10	15		12	Longtime Dem. MOC MO
Collins, Eileen		Astronaut	7			25	1st Female commander of the Space Shuttle
Collins, General James F.	1905-1989	Military	30				World War II U.S. general
Collins, Gerard		Political	10			15	Member European Parliament
Collins, J. Lawton		Military	30	50	80	50	General WW II
Collins, Jackie		Author	10	15	28	28	Novelist. Her Novel Signed/Dust Jacket 25
Collins, Joan		Entertainment	15	23	30	34	Actress
Collins, Judy		Entertainment	5	10	15	31	Singer

NAME	DATE	CATEGORY	SIG	LS/DS	ALS	SP	COMMENTS
Collins, LeRoy		Governor	5	10		14	Governor FL
Collins, Lottie		Entertainment	15	15	25	25	
Collins, Lt. Gen. Joseph L.	1896-1963	Military	30				World War II U.S. general
Collins, Lt. Gen. Sir Dudley Stuart	1881-1959	Military	25				World War II British general
Collins, Mac C		Congress	10			15	Member U.S. Congress
Collins, Maj. Gen. Harry J.	1895-1963	Military	30				World War II U.S. general
Collins, Maj. Gen. James L.	1882-1963	Military	30				World War II U.S. general
Collins, Maj. Gen. Robert John	1880-1950	Military	25				World War II British general
Collins, Maj. Gen. Vivian B.	1883-1955	Military	30				World War II U.S. general
Collins, Michael		Astronaut	104	242	1381	338	Piloted Comm. Module 1st Moon Landing. Apollo XI
Collins, Michelle		Entertainment	10			20	Actress
Collins, Phil		Entertainment	8			45	Singer
Collins, Ray		Entertainment	50	60	150	175	
Collins, Reid		Celebrity	10			15	media/TV personality
Collins, Susan		Senate	10			15	United States Senate (R - ME)
Collins, Wilkie	1824-1889	Author	100	310	560	1380	Br. Novelist. Regarded as 1st Br.Det. Story Writer
Collis, Charles		Civil War	25		60		Union Gen., CMH
Collishaw, Raymond		Aviation	75	175	375	225	Brit. ACE, WW I
Collyer, Clayton 'Bud'	1908-1969	Entertainment	20			45	Actor. Radio, Early TV. Popular Game Show Host
Collyer, Robert, Dr.	1823-1912	Clergy	35	60	112		Unitarian. Lecturer. Author
Colman, Booth		Entertainment	4			15	Actor
Colman, Ronald	1891-1958	Entertainment	55	60	142	146	Suave, Sophisticated, Br. Leading Man Oscar Winner
Colman, Samuel	1832-1920	Artist	20		95		Landscapes. Fndr, 1st Pres. Am. Watercolor Soc.
Colom I Naval, Joan		Political	10			15	Member European Parliament
Colombo, Scipio		Entertainment	10			30	Opera
Colonna, Jerry	1903-1986	Entertainment	15	9	22	37	Buggy-Eyed Comedian Radio/Stage/Screen
Color Me Badd		Entertainment	25			55	Rock (Entire Group)
Colquitt, Alfred H.	1824-1894	Civil War	127	245	507	275	CSA Gen., US Sen. & Gov. GA. Sig/Rank 295
Colson, Brig. Gen. Charles F.	1896-1970	Military	30				World War II U.S. general
Colson, Charles W. 'Chuck'		Clergy	20	50	75	35	Convicted Watergate Figure
Colson, General Louis-Antoine	1875-1951	Military	20				World War II French general
Colston, Raleigh E.	1825-1896	Civil War	179	400			CSA Gen.
Colt, Samuel	1814-1862	Business-Inventor	538	2190	4325		Founder Colt Firearms
Colter, Jessie		Country Music	4			22	Wife of Waylon Jennings
Colton, Maj. Gen. Roger B.	1887-1978	Military	30				World War II U.S. general
Coltrane, John		Entertainment	20			40	Great Jazz Saxophonist.
Coltrane, Robbie		Entertainment	7			44	Br. Character Actor Mystery Series Star
Colum, Padraic		Author	38	68	110	120	Irish Poet & Playwright
Columbo, Franco		Entertainment	5			25	Actor-Body Builder
Columbo, Russ	1908-1934	Entertainment	50	90	200	165	Talented Crooner. Rival of Crosby.Shotgun Accident
Columbus, Christopher		Celebrity	10			20	film industry
Combe, Maj. Gen. John Fred. B.	1895-1967	Military	28				World War II British general
Combest, Larry C		Congress	10			15	Member U.S. Congress
Combs, Holly Marie		Entertainment	8			42	Actress. Pin-Up 55
Comden, Betty & Green, A.		Composers	20	45		50	Collaborators. Broadway Musicals

NAME	DATE	CATEGORY	SIG	LS/DS	ALS	SP	COMMENTS
Comden, Betty		Celebrity	10			15	media/TV personality
Comer, Jackie		Entertainment	10			20	actress
Comiskey, Charles A.	1859-1931	Business	400				Fndr.,Owner Pres. Chicago White Sox
Commager, Henry Steele		Civil War	25	60	125		Union General
Command Performance (5)		Entertainment	20			50	
Commodores		Entertainment	25			92	
Como, Perry	1912-2002	Entertainment	8	12	18	47	Singer. Radio,Recording,TV 1948-1963
Compere, Brig. Gen. Ebenezer L.	1880-1963	Military	30				World War II U.S. general
Compson, Betty	1897-1974	Entertainment	15	30	60	70	Actress. Films-1915-1948
Compton, Ann		Celebrity	10			15	media/TV personality
Compton, Arthur H.	1892-1962	Science	90	205	275	100	Nobel Physics. Atomic Bomb
Compton, Fay	1894-1978	Entertainment	30			45	Br. Actress. Starred in Barrie Plays..'Peter Pan'
Compton, Joyce		Entertainment	8	9	19	15	
Compton, Karl T.	1887-1954	Science	90	200		110	Physicist, Pres. M.I.T.
Compton-Burnett, Ivy		Author	40	85	175		Wrote Brilliant Original Comic Novels Family Life
Comstock, Cyrus B.	1830-1910	Military			195		US Commander
Comyn, Alison		Celebrity	10			15	newsreader
Conable, Barber		Celebrity	10			15	financial expert
Conant, A. Roger		Aviation	12	25	40	32	ACE, WW II, Marine Ace
Conant, James Bryant		Diplomat	10	15	30	20	Educator, US Ambassador
Conati, Lorenzo		Entertainment	20			65	Opera
Conchita, Maria		Entertainment	4			10	
Condé, General Charles-Marie	1876-1945	Military	20				World War II French general
Condé, Louis II	1621-1686	Military		750			One of France's Most Celebrated Generals
Condon, Eddie		Composer	40			60	Guitarist
Condon, Richard		Author	5	15	35	10	
Cone, Fairfax M.		Business	10	35	45	20	Foote,Cone & Belding, Adv.
Cone, Hutchinson		Military	25	35			Admiral WW I
Confalonieri, Carlo, Cardinal		Clergy	50	75	90	65	
Conforti, Gino		Entertainment	3	3	6	6	
Conger, Darva		Celebrity				22	
Congreve, William	1670-1729	Author	190	575	1050		Br. Drama. Restoration Comedy
Congreve, William, Sir		Science	45	125	235		Artillerist, Invented Rocket, 2nd Baronet
Coningham, Sir Arthur		Aviation	35	60			Cmdr. RAF 1st Tactical
Conkley, Brig. Gen. John F.	1891-1973	Military	30				World War II U.S. general
Conklin, Chester	1888-1971	Entertainment	112	125	220	110	Silent Film Comedian with Chaplin & W.C. Fields
Conkling, Roscoe		Senate	20	25		42	MOC, Senate NY Political Boss
Conlee, John		Entertainment	4			10	
Conley, Brian		Celebrity	10			15	comedian
Conley, Eugene		Entertainment	20	30		50	Opera
Conley, Joe		Entertainment	3	3	6	8	
Conn, Donny		Celebrity	10			15	motivational speaker
Connally, John B.		Cabinet	25	83	95	45	Gov. TX, Sec'y Treasury
Connally, Tom	1877-1963	Senate	20	25		70	Senator TX. Gov. TX
Connellan, Thomas		Celebrity	10			15	motivational speaker

NAME	DATE	CATEGORY	SIG	LS/DS	ALS	SP	COMMENTS
Connelly, Billy		Celebrity	10			15	comedian
Connelly, Jennifer		Entertainment	10			36	Winner Acadamy Award
Connelly, Marc	1890-1980	Author	20	75	75	35	Am. Dramatist. Pulitzer
Connelly, Matthew J.		White House Staff	10	25	35	15	Pres. Truman Aide
Conner, James	1829-1883	Civil War	112	274	329		CSA General. 1st Bull Run, Seven Pines
Conner, Nadine		Entertainment	10			33	Am. Opera, Radio, Records
Conner, Patrick E.		History	25				Father of Utah mining
Connery, Sean		Entertainment	53	69	75	132	Best Known for James Bond etc.Bond SP 200
Conness, John	1821-1909	Senate	45	85			Civil War Senator CA
Connick, Harry, Jr.		Entertainment	13	30		40	Big Band Leader-Singer-Pianist-Actor
Conniff, Ray	1916-	Entertainment	18	35	68	38	Composer, Conductor
Connolly, Maj. Gen. Donald H.	1886-1969	Military	30				World War II U.S. general
Connolly, Walter		Entertainment	81		90	85	
Connor, Harry P.		Aviation	15	30	45	50	
Connor, John T.		Cabinet	7	20	35	20	Sec'y Commerce
Connor, Maj. Gen. William D.	1874-1960	Military	30				World War II U.S. general
Connor, Patrick Edward	1820-1891	Civil War	48	95	130		Union General
Connor, Selden	1877-1947	Artist			92		American Artist
Connors, Chuck	1921-1992	Entertainment	20	35	30	56	Former Pro Baseball. 'The Rifleman' TV Series
Connors, Mike		Entertainment	6			22	Actor. 'Mannix'
Connors, Norman		Entertainment	4			10	
Connors, Patti		Entertainment	3	3	6	6	
Conolly, Brig. John James Pollock	1896-1950	Military	28				World War II British general
Conover, Harry		Business	10	17	25	15	Top Modeling Agency
Conquest, Ida		Entertainment	15	15	25	30	
Conrad, Brig. Gen. George B.	1898-1976	Military	30				World War II U.S. general
Conrad, Charles Magill	1804-1878	Cabinet	45	55	190		Sec'y War
Conrad, Charles, Jr.	1930-1999	Astronaut	50	230		104	3rd Moonwalker, DS cont 805
Conrad, Gerhard		Aviation	10	25	45	25	
Conrad, Joseph	1857-1924	Author	322	1125	1325	1250	Br. Novelist. 'Lord Jim' etc.
Conrad, Kent		Senate	10			15	United States Senate (D - ND)
Conrad, Michael		Entertainment	14	18	20	22	Actor. 'Hill St. Blues' SP 35
Conrad, Robert		Entertainment	7	10		30	Actor. 'Wild Wild West' SP 40
Conrad, William	1920-1994	Entertainment	20	25		45	Actor
Conried, Hans		Entertainment	15	20	40	40	
Conroy, Frances		Entertainment				40	Ruth Fisher, Six Feet Under
Conroy, Kevin		Entertainment	3	3	6	6	
Conroy, Pat		Author					Signed 1st Ed. 125-200
Consigny, Eugene F.		Banker		20			
Consort, Paul Winter		Entertainment	50			125	Enviromental Music, Grammy
Constable, Archibald	1774-1827	Publisher	30				Encyclopaedia Britannica
Constable, John	1776-1837	Artist	260	905	2400		Br. Landscapes, Rural Life
Constantine I	1868-1923	Royalty	95			425	King of Greece. Twice Abdicated.Plebicite Restored
Constantino, Florencio		Entertainment	75			365	Opera
Conte, John		Entertainment	4	5	9	12	

NAME	DATE	CATEGORY	SIG	LS/DS	ALS	SP	COMMENTS
Conte, Richard		Entertainment	7	10	15	15	
Conti, Bill		Composer	10	85	100	32	
Conti, Joseph		Entertainment	4			10	
Conti, Leorardo	d. 1945	Military	125				Nazi Doctor
Conti, Tom		Entertainment	10			20	Actor
Contino, Dick		Entertainment	3			8	Accordianist
Convy, Bert		Entertainment	10			20	Broadway, TV Star
Conway, Brigadier Albert Edward	1891-1974	Military	20				World War II New Zealand general
Conway, Henry Seymour	1721-1795	Military	25	60	135		Br. Fld. Marshal. MsDs 250
Conway, Martin F.	1827-1882	Congress	10				Repr. KS, U.S. Consul France
Conway, Rose A.		Cabinet	3	5	10	5	
Conway, Thomas		Revolutionary War	65	105	250		Maj. Gen. Rev. War
Conway, Tim		Entertainment	5	15	15	18	Comedian-Actor 'McHale's Navy' SP 25
Conway, Tom		Entertainment	50			128	The Saint
Conwell, Russell H.	1843-1925	Clergy	35	45	50		Baptist Fndr. & 1st Pres. Temple Univ.
Cony, Samuel		Governor	30	45	60		Civil War Gov. ME
Conyers, John	1929-	Senate/Congress	10	15		25	Afro-Am. Congressman MI
Coogan, Jackie	1914-1984	Entertainment	20	25	35	88	Actor. Major Child Star. 'Uncle Fester' Addams Fam
Coogan, Richard		Entertainment	5	6	15	15	
Coogan, Steve		Celebrity	10			15	comedian
Cook, Ann Turner		Model	10			25	Original Model For Gerber Baby Products
Cook, Elisha Jr.	1902-1995	Entertainment	15	25	35	82	
Cook, Eliza		Author			75		Poet
Cook, Everett R.		Aviation	10	30		50	ACE WW I
Cook, Francis Augustus		Military	75		55	30	Spanish American War
Cook, James, Capt.		Br. Naval Explorer	5267	9300	27000		Captain Cook
Cook, John	1825-1910	Civil War	42	92	140		Union general
Cook, Joseph, Sir		Politician	10	20	40		Australian Statesman
Cook, Kyle		Entertainment	6			25	Music. Lead Guitar 'Matchbox 20'
Cook, Maj. Gen. Gilbert R.	1889-1963	Military	30				World War II U.S. general
Cook, Philip	1817-1894	Civil War	198	354	395		CSA Gen.
Cook, Rachel Leigh		Entertainment	8			48	Actress. Young Star
Cook, Robin		Author	5			10	Novelist
Cook, Roger		Celebrity	10			15	television presenter
Cook, Sue		Celebrity	10			15	television presenter
Cook, Thomas		Business	35	110	545		Founder British Tourist Company
Cook, Tommy		Entertainment	15			30	Child Actor
Cook, Walter V.		Aviation	8	20	38	28	ACE, WW II
Cooke, Alistair		Celebrity	10			15	political celebrity
Cooke, Alistair, Sir		Author	20	95	140	75	TV Host. Masterpiece Theatre
Cooke, Brig. Gen. Elliot D.	1891-1961	Military	30				World War II U.S. general
Cooke, Brigadier Robert Thomas	1897-1984	Military	25				World War II British general
Cooke, Jack Kent		Business	10	22		15	
Cooke, Jay	1821-1905	Business	375	1494	1732	225	Banker, Financier of Union in Civil War
Cooke, John Rogers	1833-1891	Civil War	164	315			Confederate general

NAME	DATE	CATEGORY	SIG	LS/DS	ALS	SP	COMMENTS
Cooke, Nicholas		Revolutionary War		1100			Rev. War Gov. Rhode Island
Cooke, Philip St. George	1809-1895	Civil War	57	170			Union Gen. ALS/Cont.935
Cooke, Sam		Entertainment	232	675		500	Rock
Cooke, Terence J., Cardinal		Clergy	60	75	100	95	
Cool, Harry		Entertainment	4	4		6	
Cool, Phil		Celebrity	10			15	comedian
Cooley, Denton A., Dr.	1920-	Science	15	35	90	32	Heart Transplant Surgeon
Cooley, Lyman E.		Science	10		35		Civil Engineer
Cooley, Spade		Country Music	15			35	King of Western Swing
Coolidge, Calvin & Entire Cabinet		President	295			3500	
Coolidge, Calvin (As President)		President	195	473	3731	570	WH Card S 180-345. ALS/Content 6450
Coolidge, Calvin	1872-1933	President	152	297	643	402	Autogr. Speech Signed 6000
Coolidge, Grace	1879-1957	First Lady	68	136	142	146	FF 55-80
Coolidge, John		Celebrity	40	65			Father Of Pres. Coolidge
Coolidge, Martha		Celebrity	10			15	film industry
Coolidge, Rita		Entertainment	12	20		25	
Coolidge, T. Jefferson		Statesman	4	10	20		
Coolidge, William David, Dr.		Science	45	85	165	125	Dir. Research G.E., Inventor
Coolio		Entertainment				55	Rap singer
Coombs, Patricia		Artist	10	20	35	15	
Cooper, Alfred Duff		Statesman	10	25	60	15	1st Viscount Norwich. Author
Cooper, Alice		Entertainment	25		35	78	Rock. 'School's Out' Alb. S 50
Cooper, Douglas Hancock (WD)		Civil War			1125		Confederate gen.
Cooper, Douglas Hancock	1815-1879	Civil War	119	270	682		Confederate general
Cooper, Emil		Composer	30	50	80	70	Rus.Internat'l Conductor-Violinist
Cooper, Gary	1901-1961	Entertainment	212	301	338	489	Oscar winner., DS cont. 1552
Cooper, Gladys, Dame		Entertainment	40	35	65	55	Br. Stage & Film Actress
Cooper, Gordon		Astronaut	30	60		65	Mercury 7 Astro.
Cooper, Jackie	1921-	Entertainment	20	21	35	32	Child-Mature Actor, Director.'Little Rascal' SP40
Cooper, James Fennimore	1789-1851	Author	90	237	739		Am. Novelist. ALS/Cont.1,750
Cooper, James	1810-1863	Civil War	75	168			Union general
Cooper, Jeanne		Entertainment	8			15	Actress. Soap Star
Cooper, Jim C		Congress	10			15	Member U.S. Congress
Cooper, John Sherman		Senate/Congress	10	25			Senator KY, Statesman, Diplomat
Cooper, Joseph Alexander	1823-1910	Civil War	45	95	102		Union general
Cooper, Kenneth		Celebrity	10			15	medical expert
Cooper, Leon N., Dr.		Science	20	35	60	30	Nobel Physics
Cooper, Leroy, Jr.		Astronaut	40				Apollo VII (Early Sig.)
Cooper, Merian C.		Entertainment	100			250	King Kong, Four Feathers
Cooper, Michael 'Ibo'		Entertainment	6			25	Music. Calvinet, Organ 'Lenny Kravitz'
Cooper, Miriam		Entertainment	35			75	
Cooper, Peter	1791-1883	Industrialist	71	156	395	262	Am. Inventor, 1st Steam Locomotive. ALS cont. 2850
Cooper, Prentice		Governor	10	16			Governor TN
Cooper, Rick		Entertainment	5			10	Actor
Cooper, Samuel (WD)	1798-1876	Civil War	415	350	1860		CSA Gen.Special Content ALS 6325

NAME	DATE	CATEGORY	SIG	LS/DS	ALS	SP	COMMENTS
Cooper, Samuel	1798-1876	Civil War	111	220	322		CSA Ranking Gen.
Cooper, Thos. Sidney		Artist	10	20	35		
Coors, W. K.		Business	20	60	95	50	Coors Brewery
Coots, J. Fred		Composer	35	55	160	50	'Santa Claus isa.'AMusQS 150-195-1200
Coots, J.Fred & H. Gillespie		Composer					'Santa Claus Is Coming to Town' Sht.Mus. S 495
Copas, Cowboy		Country Music	100			225	
Copée, Frantois E.	1842-1908	Author	15	45	45		Fr. Poet, Novelist, Dramatist
Copeland, Brig. Gen. John E.	1891-1978	Military	30				World War II U.S. general
Copeland, C.C.		Clergy	30	80	225		
Copeland, Joseph Tarr	1813-1893	Civil War	45	85	131		Union general
Copeland, L. du Pont		Business	20		50		
Copeland, Royal S., Dr.		Senate	15	70			Senator NY. Author
Copeland, William John		Clergy	20	25	35		
Copland, Aaron	1900-1990	Composer	75	248	300	244	Major 20th Cent. Am. Composer.AMusQS 300-800
Copley, John Singleton	1738-1815	Artist	350	2612	6688		Outstanding Am. Portraitist
Copley, Teri		Entertainment	6			20	Pin-Up SP 40
Copmpanari, Giuseppe		Entertainment	35			125	Opera
Coppens, Willy (Baron de H)		Aviation	20	40	125	50	
Copperfield, David		Entertainment	8	15		38	Illusionist
Coppola, Francis Ford	b. 1939	Entertainment	20	58		43	Oscar Winning Film Director.Screenwriter
Coquelin, Benoit-Constant	1841-1909	Entertainment	25	40	55	155	Fr. Actor-Manager, 'Cyrano'
Coquelin, Ernest-Alex.-H.(Cadet)		Entertainment	15	30	50		Comedie-Francaise. Author
Coradin, Brig. Gen. Louis-Gus.-A.	1881-1949	Military	20				World War II French general
Corap, General André-Georges	1878-1953	Military	20				World War II French general
Corbe, Maj. Gen. René-Jean-Divy	1883-1942	Military	20				World War II French general
Corbett, Boston		Civil War	1591		1800		Shot John Wilkes Booth
Corbett, Henry Winslow		Senate/Congress	10	15	25	20	Senator OR
Corbett, John		Entertainment				35	Aidan Shaw, Sex in the City. Big Fat Greek Wedding
Corbett, Lt. Gen. Thomas William	1888-1981	Military	25				World War II British general
Corbett, Michael		Entertainment	4			10	Actor Young and the Restless
Corbett, Richard		Political	10			15	Member European Parliament
Corbey, Dorette		Political	10			15	Member European Parliament
Corbin, Henry Clarke		Civil War	30		115		Union General
Corbin, Maj. Gen. Clifford L.	1883-1966	Military	30				World War II U.S. general
Corbucci, Sergio	1927-1990	Entertainment	45			275	Known as Director of Spaghetti-Westerns
Corbusier, Le	1887-1965	Architect	115	575	1048	575	Jeanneret, Charles Edouard. Also Painter, Writer89
Corby, Ellen		Entertainment	12			30	Character Actress. Grandma Walton
Corcoran, Kevin		Entertainment	5			20	Actor. 60's Disney Star
Corcoran, Michael (WD)	1827-1863	Civil War		787	1264		Union Gen. RARE
Corcoran, Noreen		Entertainment	5			20	Actress. 'Batchelor Father'
Corcoran, William W.		Business	20	50			Banker, Philanthropist
Cord, Alex		Entereteaintment	8			12	
Corden, Henry		Entertainment	25	55		40	Fred Flintstone (Voice)
Cordtz, Dan		Celebrity	10			15	financial expert
Corea, Chick		Entertainment	15			35	

NAME	DATE	CATEGORY	SIG	LS/DS	ALS	SP	COMMENTS
Corelli, Franco		Entertainment	25	35	100	110	Opera
Corelli, Marie	1855-1924	Author	38	55	115	70	Eng. Romantic Novelist. (Mary Mackay)
Corena, Fernando		Entertainment	20			45	Opera
Corey, Elias		Science	20	35		30	Nobel Chemistry
Corey, Jeff		Entertainment	5			15	
Corey, Wendell		Entertainment	35	45	80	75	
Corgan, Billy		Entertainment	20			65	Music. Lead Singer 'Smashing Pumpkins'
Cori, Carl F.		Science	20	35	50	25	Nobel Medicine. (Insulin)Phil. Cover S. 150
Corio, Ann		Entertainment	15	15	20	35	Noted Exotic Dancer, Stripper. Films From '40's
Corlett, Irene		Entertainment	3	3	6	6	
Corlett, Lt. Gen. Charles H.	1889-1971	Military	30				World War II U.S. general
Corlin, Richard		Celebrity	10			15	medical expert
Cormack, Allan M.		Science	20	35	50	25	Nobel Medicine
Cormack, John, Dr.		Celebrity	10			15	health and fitness expert
Corman, Roger		Entertainment	5			20	
Cornbury, Edward Hyde, Lord		Colonial Gov.	135	450			1st Colonial Gov. NJ, Gov. NY
Corneliano, Mario N. di		Clergy	35	45	60	50	
Cornelius, Peter (Carl August)		Composer	55		325		Opera, Choral Works, Song Cycle
Cornell, Chris		Entertainment	12			40	Music. Lead Singer 'Soundgarden'
Cornell, Ezekiel		Military	60	200			Brig. Gen. American Rev.
Cornell, Ezra		Business	30	80	165	75	Financed Western Union Telegr.
Cornell, Joseph	1903-1972	Artist	135	400	700		Am. Surrealist Sculptor
Cornell, Katharine	1898-1974	Entertainment	20	35	75	77	Superb Am. Leading Stage Actress
Cornell, Lydia		Entertainment	5	3	10	20	Pin-Up SP 38
Corner, George W.		Science	75	150		100	
Cornfeld, Bernard		Business	10	20	55	35	
Cornforth, John W., Sir		Science	15	35	45	20	Br. Nobel Laureate in Chemistry
Cornillet, Thierry		Political	10			15	Member European Parliament
Corning, Erastus	1794-1872	Business	30	110	173		1st Pres. NY Central Railroad
Cornwallis, Charles E.	1738-1805	Revolutionary War	200	400	1241		Br. General Am. Revolution
Cornwell, Patricia		Author	4	7	9	15	'Southern Cross'
Cornyn, John		Senate	10			15	United States Senate (R - TX)
Corot, J.B. Camille	1796-1875	Artist	225	490	832	3000	Barbizon School. Impressionist, Landscape Painter
Corral, Elaine		Celebrity	10			15	media/TV personality
Corrie, John Alexander		Political	10			15	Member European Parliament
Corrigan, Douglas	1907-1995	Aviation	38	70	120	145	'Wrong Way' Corrigan
Corrigan, Mairead/B. William		Irish Activists	35	70	100	50	Nobel Peace Prize 1976
Corrigan, Michael A.		Clergy	10		30	20	Bishop
Corrigan, Ray Crash		Entertainment	40			150	
Corsan, Brig. Reginald Arthur	1893-1942	Military	25				World War II British general
Corsaut, Aneta	1933-1995	Entertainment	25			90	Actress Andy Griffith Show
Corse, John Murray	1835-1893	Civil War	58	94	118		Union General
Corse, Montgomery D.	1816-1895	Civil War	120	166	325		CSA General
Corso, Gregory		Author					AMSS 175
Corson, Fred P., Bishop		Clergy	20	30	50	45	

NAME	DATE	CATEGORY	SIG	LS/DS	ALS	SP	COMMENTS
Cortelyou, George B.	1862-1940	Cabinet	37	100	130		Served two Presidents.
Cortes, Hernando (Cortez)	1485-1574	Explorer		32500			Sp. Conqueror of Mex.
Cortez, Ricardo		Entertainment	25			40	
Corth, Brig. Gen. Hugh	1897-1974	Military	30				World War II U.S. general
Cortina, Juan N.		Military		1500			Mexican Gen'l. Rio Grande Bandit During Civil War
Cortot, Alfred	1877-1962	Entertainment	78			225	Pianist
Corwin, Thomas		Cabinet	30	55	125		Fillmore Sec'y Treasury
Cory, Lt. Gen. Sir George Norton	1874-1968	Military	25				World War II British general
Corzine, Jon		Senate	10			15	United States Senate (D - NJ)
Cosby, Bill	1937-	Entertainment	16	10	30	43	Comedian-Actor-Producer. Authentic Sigs. RARE
Cosby, Brig. Noel Robert Charles	1890-1981	Military	28				World War II British general
Cosby, George B.	1830-1909	Civil War	80	178	359		CSA General
Cosby, N. Gordon		Clergy	20	30	45		
Cosell, Howard		Entertainment	15			65	Radio-TV Sports News
Cosgrave, William T.	1880-1965	Head of State	70	150	275	225	Sinn Fe'in Easter Uprising.
Coslow, Sam		Composer-Author	50	200	300	350	Academy Award 1943
Cosmonauts (Russian)		Cosmonauts				5000	Titov,Gagarin,Tereshkova,Belyayev,Nikolayev,Popvch
Cosmovici, C. B.		Astronaut	12			25	
Cossotto, Fioranza		Entertainment	10			30	Opera
Cossutta, Armando		Political	10			15	Member European Parliament
Cossutta, Carlos		Entertainment	5			35	Opera
Costa Lo Giudice, Silvio		Entertainment	40			100	Opera
Costa, Mary		Entertainment	6			25	Singer. Opera-Light Opera
Costa, Michael, Sir		Composer	15	40	95	25	Br. Conductor.Opera, Ballet
Costa, Paolo		Political	10			15	Member European Parliament
Costa, Raffaele		Political	10			15	Member European Parliament
Costa-Gavras, Constantin		Entertainment	20			40	Film Director
Costas, Bob		TV Host	5			10	TV Host & Sports Commentator
Coste, Dieudonne & Bellonte, M.		Aviation	210			365	
Coste, Dieudonne	1898-1973	Aviation	125	255	385	235	Fr. Aviator. 1st Non-Stop Flight Paris-NY 1930
Costello, Delores (Barrymore)		Entertainment	28	35	65	60	
Costello, Elvis		Entertainment	12			56	Rock Entertainer
Costello, Jerry F. C		Congress	10			15	Member U.S. Congress
Costello, Lou	1906-1959	Entertainment	217	279		412	Radio, Film, TV Comedian
Costin, Maj. Gen. Eric Boyd	1889-1971	Military	28				World War II British general
Costner, Kevin		Entertainment	33			48	AA Actor-Director-Producer
Coswell, Henry T.		Aviation	55	105	150		1st Balloon ascent 1844
Cota, Maj. Gen. Norman D.	1893-1971	Military	30				World War II U.S. general
Cotrubas, Ileana		Entertainment	5			30	Opera
Cotsworth, Staats		Entertainment	8			15	
Cottam, Maj Gen Algeron Edward	1893-1964	Military	25				World War II British general
Cotten, Joseph	1905-1994	Entertainment	18	22	30	37	Actor. Orson Welles' Group. 'Citizen Kane' SP 40
Cotton, Carolina		Country Music	15			30	
Cottrell, Brig. Arthur Foulkes B.	1891-1962	Military	25				World War II British general
Cottrell-Hill, Maj Gen. Robt. Chas.	1903-1965	Military	25				World War II British general

NAME	DATE	CATEGORY	SIG	LS/DS	ALS	SP	COMMENTS
Coty, Francois		Business	100	325	475		Fr.Industrialist. Mfg. of Coty Perfume & Cosmetics
Couch, Darius Nash		Civil War	52	98	120		Union General
Couch, Orville		Country Western	10			35	Music. 50's Recording Artist
Couch, Virgil		Urban Designer	10	12	15		Dir. National Civil Defense
Coué, Emile	1857-1926	Science	175		500		Fr. Psychotherapist, Hypnotism
Cougar, John		Entertainment	10			35	
Coughlan, Marisa		Celebrity				40	
Coughlin, Albert L., Sr.		Business	10	20			Real Estate and Business Developer
Coughlin, Charles E.	1891-1979	Clergy	40	50	70		Activist Catholic Priest & Radio Evangelist
Coulouris, George		Entertainment	10			25	Character Actor
Coulter, Jessie		Country Music	6			15	
Coulter, Lt. Gen. John B.	1891-1983	Military	30				World War II U.S. general
Coulter, Richard		Civil War	37	84	106		Union Bvt. General
Courbet, Jean D. Gustave	1819-1877	Artist	225	600	1090		Leader of Realist School
Couric, Katie		TV Host	5			16	Host Today
Court, Hazel		Entertainment	6			30	Pin-Up 28
Courtney, Inez		Entertainment	15			35	
Courts, Ray		Entertainment	3			8	Show Promoter
Cousins, Norman		Author	10	25	40	22	Saturday Review Editor, Author
Cousins, Ralph P.	1891-1964	Aviation		165		95	Army Gen'l.Developed Radio Beam. Aviation Pioneer
Cousins, William E., Archbishop		Clergy	20	35	45	35	
Cousteau, Jacques		Science-Author	48	207	275	128	Underwater Explorer, Films
Cousteau, Jim (Son of Jacques)		Science	25			60	Underwater Explorer (Deceased)
Couteaux, Paul		Political	10			15	Member European Parliament
Couter, John B.		Military	15	47			
Couve de Murville, Maurice		Statesman	5	15	25	25	Fr. Premier, Foreign Minister DeGaulle Cabinet.
Couzens, James	1872-1936	Business	10	30		15	Ford Motor Co., US Senate
Covarrubias, Miguel		Artist	150	325			Mex. Book & Magazine Illustr.
Covell, Maj. Gen. William E.R.	1892-1975	Military	30				World War II U.S. general
Coventry, William Sir	1628-1686	Political			225		
Covey, Richard O.		Astronaut	6			22	
Covey, Steven Dr.		Celebrity	10			15	motivational speaker
Cowan, Edgar		Senate	15	25	35		Civil War Senator PA
Cowan, Jerome		Entertainment	10			35	
Cowan, Maj. Gen. David Tennant	1896-1983	Military	25				World War II British general
Coward, Noel, Sir	1899-1973	Author-Composer	122	179	260	252	Playwright, Actor, Producer. AMusQS 275
Cowdin, Robert	1805-1874	Civil War	45	106	130		Union general
Cowl, Jane		Entertainment	22		35	45	
Cowles, Brig. Gen. Miles A.	1894-1974	Military	30				World War II U.S. general
Cowles, Gardner		Business	12		25	15	Publisher Des Moines Register
Cowley, Maj. Gen. Sir John Guise	1905-1993	Military	25				World War II British general
Cox Family, The		Entertainment	25			45	Bluegrass
Cox, Archibald		Cabinet	15	40	55	25	Att'y Gen.,1st Watergate Spec. Prosecutor
Cox, Brig. Gen. Albert L.	1883-1965	Military	30				World War II U.S. general
Cox, Brig. Gen. Richard F.	1886-1964	Military	30				World War II U.S. general

NAME	DATE	CATEGORY	SIG	LS/DS	ALS	SP	COMMENTS
Cox, Brigadier Sir Matthew Henry	1892-1966	Military	25				World War II British general
Cox, Christopher C		Congress	10			15	Member U.S. Congress
Cox, Courtney	1964-	Entertainment	20			54	Actress 'Friends'
Cox, George H.		Author	5	15	30		Br. Historical Writer
Cox, Jacob D.	1828-1900	Civil War	40	85	112		Union Gen., Sec'y Interior, Gov. OH
Cox, James M.		Governor	15	60	75	25	Pres. Candidate,MOC,Gov. OH
Cox, Kenyon	1856-1919	Artist	30	55			Am. Mural Painter & Figural Compositions
Cox, Maj. Gen. Lionel Howard	1893-1949	Military	25				World War II British general
Cox, Nikki		Entertainment	15			45	Actress.
Cox, Palmer*	1840-1924	Artist	103	140	300	225	Author Children's Books, Illustrator 'Brownies'
Cox, Pat		Political	10			15	Member European Parliament
Cox, Ronny		Entertainment	10			20	actor
Cox, Samuel S.	1824-1889	Congress	20	45	103		Civil War Repr. OH
Cox, Sara		Celebrity	10			15	celebrity model
Cox, Wally		Entertainment	25		70	75	Actor-Comedian 'Mr. Peepers'
Cox, William R.	1832-1919	Civil War	84	133	295		CSA Gen. Sig/Rank 295, War Dte. DS 350
Coxe, Tenche		Revolutionary War	45	100	170		Continental Congress
Coxey, Jacob S.		Reformer	20	55	140	110	Led Coxey's Army to Wash. D.C
Coyote, Peter		Entertainment	10			35	
Coyte, Paul		Music	10			15	DJ
Crabbe, Buster	1909-1983	Entertainment	21	15	40	105	Actor.'Flash Gordon' or 'Tarzan' SP 85-125
Crabtree, John		Celebrity	10	20			Antique Expert
Crabtree, Lotta (Charlotte)		Entertainment	25	70	125	130	Am. Musical Comedy Actress
Craddock, Crash		Country Music	5	8	20	18	
Craig, Brig. Gen. Charles F.	1895-1982	Military	30				World War II U.S. general
Craig, Edward Gordon	1872-1966	Entertainment	15	40	155	190	Br. Stage Designer, Actor. AMS 650
Craig, James Henry, Sir	1748-1812	Military	75	185	200		Br. Gen. Wounded at Bunker Hill. Gov. Gen. Canada
Craig, James		Entertainment	15			35	Actor
Craig, James	1817-1888	Civil War	45	86	113		Union General. ALS War Dte.175, DS 134
Craig, Jenny		TV Personality	4			10	Talk Show Host. Diet Expert.
Craig, Larry		Senate	10			15	United States Senate (R - ID)
Craig, Maj. Gen. Archibald M.	1895-1953	Military	25				World War II British general
Craig, Maj. Gen. Louis A.	1891-1984	Military	30				World War II U.S. general
Craig, Malin General	1875-1945	Military	45	75	125		Cuba, Boxer Rebellion, France WW I, WWII
Craig, Yvonne		Entertainment	6	20		27	Pin-Up SP 30, 'Batgirl' 30
Craigavon, James C.	1871-1940	Head of State	20		35		1st P.M. Northern Ireland
Crain, Brig. Gen. James K.	1879-1972	Military	30				World War II U.S. general
Crain, Jeanne		Entertainment	15	20	40	45	Actress. Oscar Nominee 'Pinky'. Pin-Up SP 50
Cram, Donald J., Dr.		Science	20	35		30	Nobel Chemistry
Cramer Jr., Robert E. (Bud) C		Congress	10			15	Member U.S. Congress
Cramer, Floyd		Country Music	20			33	Pianist
Cramer, Grant		Entertainment	6	8	15	15	
Cramer, Maj. Gen. Kenneth F.	1894-1954	Military	30				World War II U.S. general
Cramer, Maj. Gen. Myron C.	1881-1966	Military	30				World War II U.S. general
Cranch, Christopher P.	1813-1892	Artist	5		25	35	

NAME	DATE	CATEGORY	SIG	LS/DS	ALS	SP	COMMENTS
Crane Frank		Clergy	15	20	35		
Crane, Andy		Celebrity	10			15	television presenter
Crane, Bob		Entertainment	150			225	Murdered TV Star Hogans Heroes
Crane, Brig. Gen. William C.	1891-1978	Military	30				World War II U.S. general
Crane, Charles Henry		Civil War	25	95	120		Union General.Surgeon
Crane, Cheryl		Celebrity	30			40	Killed Mother's Friend
Crane, Daniel (Scandal)		Congress	5		25	20	MOC IL
Crane, Frank		Clergy	15	25	45		
Crane, Fred		Entertainment	15			35	
Crane, Hart		Author	130	600	1500	350	Am. Poet, The Bridge
Crane, Henry Hitt		Clergy	25	30	50	35	
Crane, John		Military	100	250			Gen. Revolutionary War
Crane, Maj. Gen. John A.	1885-1951	Military	30				World War II U.S. general
Crane, Philip M. C		Congress	10			15	Member U.S. Congress
Crane, Richard		Entertainment	20			45	
Crane, Roy*		Cartoonists	30			200	Wash Tubbs, B. Sawyer
Crane, Stephen		Author	370	1100	4350		Died at 28. Red Badge of Courage
Crane, Walter	1845-1915	Artist - Poet	50	140	275		Br. Painter-Illustrator -Designer. ALS/Cont. 600
Crane, William H.	1845-1928	Entertainment	30	45	90	55	Vintage Actor
Crane, William M.	1784-1846	Military	15				War 1812 Navy
Crane, Winthrop M.		Senate-Business	10	25		35	Crane Stationery, Gov., Sen. MA
Cranston, Alan		Senate	15	20		22	Senator CA
Cranston, Brig. Gen. Joseph A.	1898-1973	Military	30				World War II U.S. general
Cranston, Henry Young	1789-1864	Congress	10				Repr. RI
Crapo, Michael		Senate	10			15	United States Senate (R - ID)
Crass, Franz		Entertainment	5			25	Opera
Craven, Frank		Entertainment	20			55	Vintage Film & Stage Actor
Craven, John		Celebrity	10			15	naturalist
Craven, Wes		Entertainment	10			25	Director
Cravens, Jordan E.		Civil War	45		80		CSA Officer, MOC AR
Crawford, Brig. Gen. David M.	1889-1963	Military	30				World War II U.S. general
Crawford, Brig. Gen. James B.	1888-1974	Military	30				World War II U.S. general
Crawford, Brig. Alastair W. E.	1896-1978	Military	25				World War II British general
Crawford, Broderick	1911-1986	Entertainment	30	35	40	89	Character Actor. Bad Guy Image
Crawford, Christina		Author	6	10	20	15	Daughter of Joan Crawford
Crawford, Cindy		Model	8			57	Model-Actress.Pin-Up SP 75
Crawford, Francis M.	1854-1909	Author	12	15	25		Am. Novelist
Crawford, Gen. Sir Kenneth Noel	1895-1961	Military	25				World War II British general
Crawford, Geo. W.	1798-1872	Cabinet		40	95		Sec'y War.Gov. GA Secessionist
Crawford, J. W.'Capt. Jack'	1847-1917	Military-Author	35		250		Indian Wars Scout.The Poet Scout
Crawford, Joan	1908-1977	Entertainment	42	94	214	169	AA Major Star. Pin-Up SP 200
Crawford, John W.		Author	60			405	
Crawford, Johnny		Entertainment	7			20	Actor. Remembered for 'The Rifleman' SP 25
Crawford, Maj. Gen. Geo. Oswald	1902-1994	Military	25				World War II British general
Crawford, Maj. Gen. John Scott	1889-1978	Military	25				World War II British general

NAME	DATE	CATEGORY	SIG	LS/DS	ALS	SP	COMMENTS
Crawford, Maj. Gen. Robert W.	1891-1981	Military	25				World War II U.S. general
Crawford, Maj. Gen. Roscoe C.	1887-1980	Military	30				World War II U.S. general
Crawford, Michael		Entertainment	20		35	70	
Crawford, Miles		Celebrity	10			15	comedian
Crawford, Robert		Composer	25				Air Force Song AMusQS 275
Crawford, Samuel Wylie	1829-1892	Civil War	55	85	180		Union Gen.
Crawford, William H.	1772-1834	Cabinet	40	90	150		Madison Sec'y War. ALS/Cont. 1500
Crawford-Frost, Wm. A.		Business	15	25	70	20	
Cream		Entertainment	50			190	Rock Band
Creatore, Giuseppe		Entertainment	30			120	Bandleader
Creed		Entertainment	32			75	Music. 4 Member Rock Group
Creedence Clearwater Revival		Entertainment	75			225	Rock
Creegor, Vivien		Celebrity	10			15	newsreader
Creeley, Robert	1926-	Contemp. Poet	5	12		10	Am. Poet. The Charm-1st Ed. S 150
Cregar, Laird	1916-1944	Entertainment	115	120	250	318	300 lb. Character Actor. Died at 28
Creighton, John O.		Astronaut	5			15	
Creighton, Johnston B.(WD)		Civil War	65	350			Union Adm.
Creighton, Mandell		Clergy	10	15	20		
Cremer, Peter Erich		Military	75		120		
Crenna, Richard	d. 2003	Entertainment	4	6	15	35	Versatile Film-TV Actor
Crenshaw, Ander C		Congress	10			15	Member U.S. Congress
Crerar, Gen Henry Duncan G.	1888-1965	Military	24				World War II Canadian general
Cresap, Mark		Business	4	6	15	7	
Crespin, Régine		Entertainment	10			60	Opera
Crestani, Lucia		Entertainment	30			120	Opera
Creston, Paul		Composer	10			125	
Creswell, John A. J.		Cabinet	20	25	40		Senator MD,CW MOC. P.M. Gen.
Crews, John R.		Military	10			20	Award CMH, WWII
Crews, Laura Hope	1880-1942	Entertainment	195			350	Aunt Pittypat-'Gone With the Wind'
Crewson, Wendy		Entertainment	4			15	Actress. Films
Crichlow, Maj. Gen. Robert W. Jr.	1897-1972	Military	30				World War II U.S. general
Crichton, Michael		Author	14	73		55	'Jurassic Park', etc.
Crick, Francis, Dr.		Science	50	112			Nobel in Medicine, Structure of DNA. FDC 75
Crier, Katherine		TV News	5			10	TV Commentary, Special Analysis
Crimi, Giulio	1885-1939	Entertainment	40			125	Opera. Puccini Tenor Role Creator
Crimson Tide (Cast Of)		Entertainment				130	Gene Hackman
Cringely, Robert X.		Celebrity	10			15	computer expert
Crippen, Hawley Harvey		Criminal		415	500		Murdered Wife. Executed in Eng.
Crippen, Robert L.		Astronaut	7			115	Shuttle Orbiter 102 Crew
Cripps, R. Stafford, Sir	1889-1952	Statesman	30	90	210		Br.Economist, King's Counsel
Crisp, Charles Frederick		Senate/Congress	20		35		CSA Officer,' Speaker of House
Crisp, Charles Robert		Senate/Congress	12	20		15	MOC GA
Crisp, Donald		Entertainment	50	60	90	150	
Crist, Brig. Gen. William E.	1898-1985	Military	30				World War II U.S. general
Cristal, Linda		Entertainment	8	12	22	22	Pin-Up SP 32

NAME	DATE	CATEGORY	SIG	LS/DS	ALS	SP	COMMENTS
Cristalli, Italo		Entertainment	60				Opera. Great Tenor. SP Pc as Faust 150 Rare
Crittenberger, Lt. Gen. Willis D.	1890-1980	Military	30				World War II U.S. general
Crittenden, George Bibb	1812-1880	Civil War	85	154	260		Confederate general
Crittenden, John J.	1787-1863	Cabinet	25	60	125		Sen.,MOC KY, Att'y General
Crittenden, Thomas L. (WD)	1819-1893	Civil War	85		1208	2500	Union Gen.
Crittenden, Thomas Leonidas	1819-1893	Civil War	50	135	220	250	Union Gen. Served also in Mex. War
Crittenden, Thomas Turpin	1825-1905	Civil War	45	90	142		Union general
Croce, Benedetto		Author-Philos.	25	35	80		It.Statesman, Critic, Historian
Croce, Jim	1943-1973	Entertainment	287			315	Rock, signed album 500-800
Crockatt, Brig. Norman Richard	1894-1956	Military	28				World War II British general
Crocker, Charles		Business	475	2800	3850		Am.Financier. Pres. S.P. RR
Crocker, Gen. Sir John Tredinnick	1896-1963	Military	25				World War II British general
Crocker, Marcellus Monroe	1830-1865	Civil War	65	110	175		Union general
Crockett, Brig. Gen. James C.	1888-1962	Military	30				World War II U.S. general
Crockett, David 'Davy'	1786-1836	Military	5731	11750	34250		Am. Frontiersman.Died at Alamo
Crockett, Samuel R.		Author	7	15	35		Scot.Abandoned Ministry
Croft, Dwayne		Entertainment	5			25	Opera
Croghan, George		Colonial America	195	420	850		Trader,Indian Agt,Treaty Maker
Croker, Richard Boss		Politician	20	45	80		Tammany Hall Leader
Croly, George		Clergy	15	25	40		
Crompton, Richmal	1890-1969	Author	48	62	155	85	(Lamburn) Novelist 'Just William' Series
Cromwell, James		Entertainment	10			40	SP Col./Babe 70
Cromwell, Oliver	1599-1658	Head of State	1200	6194	10225		Named Lord Protector Eng.
Cromwell, Richard		Entertainment	7	9	20	15	
Cronenberg, David		Entertainment	10			25	Film Director
Cronin, Archibald J.	1896-1981	Author	15	58	117	52	Br. Physician-Novelist. 'The Citadel'
Cronin, James W.		Science	15	25	35	20	Nobel Physics
Cronin, John		Celebrity	10			15	political celebrity
Cronkite, Walter		TV News	10	20	32	25	TV News Anchor, Commentator
Cronyn, Hume		Entertainment	10	18	25	28	Cronyn & Jessica Tandy SP 100-145
Crook and Chase		Entertainment	5			10	Lorianne & Charlie
Crook, George	1818-1890	Civil War	219	343	391	650	Union Gen. Sig/Rank 385
Crookes, William, Sir	1832-1919	Science	98	125	240		Br.Phys., Chem., Nobel. Thallium
Crooks, Richard		Entertainment	20	35	45	50	Opera. American Tenor
Crosbie, Annette		Entertainment	10			20	Actress
Crosby, Bing	1901-1977	Entertainment	58	110	238	152	Am. Singer-Actor. Academy Award. AMusQS 75
Crosby, Bob		Entertainment	20			35	Big Band Leader-Singer
Crosby, Cathy Lee		Entertainment	8	10	20	28	Pin-Up SP 30
Crosby, David		Entertainment	12			55	Rock & Roll HOF
Crosby, Gary		Entertainment	5	6	6	8	Actor Son of Bing
Crosby, Howard		Clergy	15	20	25		
Crosby, J.T.		Aviation	15	25	40	30	ACE, WW II, Navy Ace
Crosby, Kathryn		Entertainment	10	15	25	25	
Crosby, Mary		Entertainment	5	5	10	15	Actress wife of Bing
Crosby, Norm		Entertainment	5	10	15	22	Actor-Comedian

NAME	DATE	CATEGORY	SIG	LS/DS	ALS	SP	COMMENTS
Crosby, Percy*		Cartoonist	40	90		75	'Skippy' Sign Orig. Sketch 200
Crosby, Stills, Nash & Young		Entertainment	185	368		350	Super Star Rock Group (All Four)
Crosland, Brig. Harold Powell	1893-1973	Military	25				World War II British general
Crosland, Brigadier Walter Hugh	1894-1960	Military	25				World War II British general
Crosley, Powel Jr.		Business	20	75	95	35	Crosley Radio Corp.
Crosman, Henrietta		Entertainment	15			35	40 Years on Stage. Silent Films & Talkies
Cross, Christopher		Entertainment	10			23	Composer, Singer
Cross, Marcia		Entertainment	10			35	Actress, Melrose Place
Cross, Wilbur L.		Governor	5	10			Gov. CT
Crosse, Andrew	1784-1855	Science	45		165		Br. Electrical Pioneer/Copper-Zinc Battery
Crossfield, A. Scott		Aviation	15	30	45	55	1st U.S. Test Pilot of X-15
Crossman, George H.		Civil War	20		90	60	General
Crothers, Rachel		Author	10	30	40	20	Am. Playwright. 'Susan & God'
Crothers, Scatman	1910-1986	Entertainment	25	30	45	65	Black Character Actor. Disney Voice
Crouse, Lindsay		Entertainment	15	15	30	30	
Crouse, Russell		Author	10	15	45	50	Playwright. 'Life With Father'
Croves, H. (B.Traven) Torsvan	1890-1969	Author	250	800			Ger. Novelist, Actor, Pacifist
Crow, Sheryl		Entertainment	12			53	Rocker, Grammy winner
Crowe, Eyre		Statesman	5		20		British Circa 1923
Crowe, Sara		Entertainment	10			20	Actress
Crowe, William		Military	15	45		30	Admiral U.S. Navy
Crowell, Brig. Gen. Evans R.	1895-1982	Military	30				World War II U.S. general
Crowley, Brian		Political	10			15	Member European Parliament
Crowley, Joseph C		Congress	10			15	Member U.S. Congress
Crowley, Leo		Cabinet	5	5	12	10	Chm. FDIC. 9 Gov't Posts
Crowley, Pat		Entertainment	5	6	15	15	Promising Actress of 50's Films
Crowninshield, Benj. W.		Cabinet	30	85	185		Sec'y Navy 1814
Croxton, John Thomas	1836-1874	Civil War	43	96			Union general
Croy, Homer	1883-	Author	15	40			Novelist, Writer, Humorist
Crozier, William		Military	35			60	General WW I, Inventor
Crudup, Billy		Entertainment	10			20	actor
Cruft, Charles	1826-1883	Civil War	41	94	147		Union general
Cruikshank, Eliza		Celebrity			60		Mrs. George Cruicshank
Cruikshank, George*	1792-1878	Artist	92	86	365	375	Illustrator, Caricaturist, Etcher.,signed draw 213-242
Cruise, Tom		Entertainment	40	25	65	88	Leading Man. DS'Born on the 4thaa.' 495
Crumb, George		Composer	25		375		Pulitzer, AMusQS 200, 320
Crumb, Robert*		Cartoonist	25			265	Underground, Psychedelic Cartoons. Sp. Ed. S 805
Crume, Dillard		Entertainment	5			20	Blues Bassist/Koko Taylor
Crummit, Frank		Entertainment	5			15	Vintage Radio/Julia Sanderson
Cruzen, Richard H.		Explorer	20		50	75	Adm. Arctic-Antarctic/Byrd
Cruz-Romo, Gilda		Entertainment	5			30	Opera
Cryer, Barry		Celebrity	10			15	comedian
Crystal, Billy		Entertainment	20	25		45	Stand-up Comedian-Actor
Cubbison, Maj. Gen. Donald C.	1882-1968	Military	30				World War II U.S. general
Cuberli, Lella		Entertainment	10			35	

NAME	DATE	CATEGORY	SIG	LS/DS	ALS	SP	COMMENTS
Cubin, Barbara C		Congress	10			15	Member U.S. Congress
Cudahy, Michael F.		Business	25	65	135	50	Meat Packer. Refrigeration
Cuellar, Javier P.		Diplomat	5			15	Sec'y Gen. UN
Cuff, Maj. Gen. Brian	1889-1970	Military	25				World War II British general
Cugat, Xavier	1900-1990	Entertainment	20	30	35	72	Big Band Rhumba King. Performed in Films
Cui, Cesar	1835-1918	Composer	95	200	450		And Russian Military Engineer
Cukor, George		Entertainment	25	95		150	Stage and Screen Director
Culberson, John Abney C		Congress	10			15	Member U.S. Congress
Culbertson, Brig. Gen. Albert L.	1884-1956	Military	30				World War II U.S. general
Culbertson, Ely	1891-1955	Author	25	80		150	Invented Culbertson Contract Bridge
Culbertson, Frank L. Jr.		Astronaut	6			20	
Culbreth, Kennith		Author	8			12	War World II, postal rail
Culin, Maj. Gen. Frank L. Jr.	1892-1967	Military	30				World War II U.S. general
Culkin, Kieran		Entertainment	4			18	Actor. Mac's Younger Brother
Culkin, Macaulay		Entertainment	20			44	Child Actor, Now Married
Cullen, Countee		Author	200	343	400		Am. Black Poet. 1st Ed. S 230-450
Cullinan, Brigadier Edward Revill	1901-1965	Military	25				World War II British general
Cullom, Shelby M.	1829-1914	Congress	35	60			MOC 1865, Senator, Gov. IL
Cullum, George W.	1809-1892	Civil War	36	70	80		Union Gen
Culp, Julia		Entertainment	35			150	Opera
Culp, Robert		Entertainment	9	10	25	30	
Culshaw, Jon		Celebrity	10			15	impressionist
Culver, Roland		Entertainment	10	15	25	25	
Culverhouse, Hugh		Business	10		15		
Cumberland, Wm. Aug., Duke	1721-1765	Royalty	55	205			Third Son of George II. Army Cmdr.'Butcher Cumb..'
Cumming, Alfred	1829-1910	Civil War	100	295	330		CSA General
Cumming, Brig. Arthur Edward	1896-1971	Military	25				World War II British general
Cumming, Maj. Gen. Sir Duncan	1903-1979	Military	25				World War II British general
Cummings, e.e.(Edw. Estlin)		Author	200	240	314	695	Am. Poet, Painter
Cummings, Elijah E. C		Congress	10			15	Member U.S. Congress
Cummings, Homer	1870-1956	Cabinet	25	40	75	125	FDR Att'y Gen.
Cummings, Robert		Entertainment	15			40	Veteran Leading Man & Light Comedian from 1935
Cummins, Maj. Gen. Joseph M.	1881-1959	Military	30				World War II U.S. general
Cunard, Samuel, Sir		Business	90	130	210		Br. Shipowner.Cunard Line
Cunha, Arlindo		Political	10			15	Member European Parliament
Cunningham, Andrew B.	1883-1963	Military	35	100	200		Br. Adm. S. Afr. & WW I
Cunningham, Brig. Gen. James H.	1886-1963	Military	30				World War II U.S. general
Cunningham, E.V. (Howard Fast)		Author	20			35	Suspense Novels & Sci-Fi
Cunningham, John W.		Clergy	10	15	20	35	
Cunningham, Maj. Gen. Julian W.	1893-1972	Military	30				World War II U.S. general
Cunningham, Maj Gen Sir Wm. H.	1883-1959	Military	20				World War II New Zealand general
Cunningham, Merce	1922-	Entertainment	40		50	60	Dancer/Choreogr. Kennedy Award
Cunningham, R. Walter	1932-	Astronaut	10	20	30	42	
Cunningham, Randy 'Duke' C		Congress	10			15	Member U.S. Congress
Cunningham, Randy Duke		Aviation	12	25	45	38	ACE, Nam, Only Navy Ace

NAME	DATE	CATEGORY	SIG	LS/DS	ALS	SP	COMMENTS
Cunningham, Gen. Sir Alan G.	1887-1984	Military	25				World War II British general
Cuomo, Mario		Governor	15	35		65	Governor NY
Curb, Mike		Entertainment	4			15	Songwriter
Curie, Marie	1867-1934	Science	1139	2544	2932	4558	Fr Physicist-Nobel Prize. Curie Inst. DS 9,500
Curie, Pierre	1859-1906	Science	440	895	2650		Content ALS 9,000
Curless, Dick		Country Music	10			20	
Curley, Michael J., Archbishop		Clergy	45	55	65		
Curley, Pauline		Entertainment	4			20	Vintage Actress
Currie, Brig. Douglas Hendrie	1892-1966	Military	25				World War II British general
Currie, Donald, Sir		Business	10	20	40		Scot. Shipowner. Castle Line
Currier, Moody		Governor	4			10	Gov. NY
Currier, Nathaniel		Artist	225	800			Currier & Ives, Lithographers
Curry, Adam		Entertainment	10			20	actor
Curry, Ann		Celebrity	10			15	media/TV personality
Curry, B.		Civil War	45	70			CSA Officer
Curry, Bill		Celebrity	10			15	motivational speaker
Curry, Charles Forrest		Senate/Congress	10	15	35		MOC CA
Curry, George		Military	30	105			1st Territorial Gov. NM
Curry, Jabez L.M.	1825-1903	Civil War	35		40		CSA Congr. Lt. Col. Cavalry
Curry, John Steuart		Artist	65		370		Orig. Ink Sketch S 750, Murals
Curry, Mark		Celebrity	10			15	television presenter
Curry, Tim		Entertainment	15			48	Rocky Horror Picture Show
Curt Weldon		Senate	10			15	Member U.S. Congress
Curtin, Andrew G.		Governor	46	45			Civil War Gov. PA.
Curtin, Jane		Entertainment	10	15	20	30	
Curtin, John (Joseph A.)	1885-1945	Head of State	35				WW II Prime Minister New Zealand
Curtis, Alan		Entertainment	12	15	35	40	
Curtis, Benjamin R.	1809-1874	Supreme Court	35	140	235		Resigned. Protest of Dred Scott. Johnson Def. Att'y
Curtis, Charles	1860-1936	Vice President	55	110	180	95	Native Am. Descent. Hoover VP
Curtis, Cyrus H. K.		Business	35	55	140	95	Curtis Publishing Co.
Curtis, Edward Sheriff	1868-1952	Artist		500		1300	Photographer, Native Americans
Curtis, George Wm.	1824-1892	Author	33	40	55		Editor Harper's Weekly. Civil War
Curtis, Jamie Lee		Entertainment	15	20	25	40	Actress
Curtis, Ken	1916-1691	Entertainment	25			65	'Festus'. Country Music. 'Son of the Pioneers'
Curtis, Maj. Gen. Alfred Cyril	1894-1971	Military	25				World War II British general
Curtis, Maj. Gen. Charles C.	1893-1960	Military	30				World War II U.S. general
Curtis, Maj. Gen. Henry Osborne	1888-1964	Military	25				World War II British general
Curtis, Newton M.	1835-1910	Civil War	35	112			Union Gen. ALS '62 155
Curtis, Robin		Entertainment	10	12	20	20	'Star Trek'
Curtis, Samuel Ryan	1817-1866	Civil War	36	80	222		Union Gen'l. Hero of Pea Ridge
Curtis, Tony		Entertainment	18	22	25	40	Early Vintage SP 125
Curtis, Verna Maria		Entertainment	10			30	Am. Soprano
Curtis, Wilfred A.		Aviation	10	25	40	25	
Curtiss, Glenn		Aviation	285	400	650	850	Am. Inventor. Pioneer Aircraft Builder
Curtiz, Michael		Entertainment	30	75		100	Film Director

NAME	DATE	CATEGORY	SIG	LS/DS	ALS	SP	COMMENTS
Curzon, George Nathaniel	1859-1925	Head of State	25		65		1st Marquis, Viceroy & Gov. India 1898-1925
Curzon, Robert (Zouche)		Br. Explorer	10		25		
Cusack, Joan		Entertainment	4			25	Talented Actress-Sister of John Cusack
Cusack, John		Entertainment	15			40	Actor
Cusack, Niamh		Entertainment	10			20	Actress
Cushing, Caleb	1800-1879	Cabinet	34	65	75		Pierce Att'y Gen., Diplomat
Cushing, Harvey, Dr.		Science	165	475	1588		Specialist in Neurosurgery
Cushing, Peter	1913-1994	Entertainment	35	40	45	70	Brit. Actor., SP Star Wars 250
Cushing, Richard	1895-1970	Clergy	40	75	85	55	Rom. Cath. Cardinal
Cushing, Thomas	1725-1788	Colonial Am.	565	642			Patriot. Prominent in Col. Congr.
Cushman, Charlotte S.	1816-1876	Entertainment	20	35	60	90	19th Century Stage Actress. AM. HOF
Cushman, Robert E., Jr.	1914-	Military	25			40	Gen. U.S. Marines. Vietnam War
Cushman, Samuel		Senate/Congress	10	20	35		MOC NH 1835
Cushnahan, John Walls		Political	10			15	Member European Parliament
Custer, Elizabeth	1842-1933	Author-Civil War	85	220	551	360	Wife of George A. Custer
Custer, George A. (WD)	1839-1876	Civil War	4825	7883	11275	22500	Union Gen., Indian Fighter
Custer, George A.	1839-1876	Civil War	3312	6612	8500		Union Gen. LS/Cont. 15000. Killed Little Big Horn
Custine, Adam Philippe, Count de		Revolutionary War	100	350			Fr.Gen.Fought in Am. Revolution
Cutcheon, Byron M.	1836-1908	Civil War	30	55	90	122	Union Gen., U.S.V.-27th Mich. MOH.
Cutler, Brig. Gen. Elliott Carr	1888-1947	Military	30				World War II U.S. general
Cutler, Brig. Gen. Stuart	1896-1986	Military	30				World War II U.S. general
Cutler, Lysander	1807-1866	Civil War	67	142	215		Union General
Cutler, Manasseh	1742-1823	Revolutionary War	425	550			Am.Clergyman, Botanist, Pioneer
Cuvier, Georges, Baron	1769-1832	Science	98	270	365		Fr. Father of Comparative Anatomy. Naturalist
Cuyler, Theodore L.		Author	10	15	35		
Cyrus, Billy Ray		Country Music	25	70		48	Singer
Czerny, Carl		Composer	75	255	460		Master of Liszt. Etudes. Teacher
Czerny, Vincenz		Science	110		900		Ger. Leader Abdominal Surgery
Czerwenka, Oskar		Entertainment	5			25	Opera

D

NAME	DATE	CATEGORY	SIG	LS/DS	ALS	SP	COMMENTS
Da Ponte, Lorenzo		Librettist		1500			Don Giovanni, Cosi fan tutte, Marriage of Figaro
D'Abo, Maryan		Entertainment	8			32	Actress. Pin-Up SP 25-55
D'Abo, Olivia		Entertainment	10			30	Actress. Pin-Up 50
Dache, Lilly		Business-Designer	55	75	130	150	Coutourier. Specialty-Hats
Daddi, Francesco		Entertainment	5	8	15		
Dafoe, Allan Roy, Dr.	1883-1943	Science	52	60	135	225	Delivered Dionne Quintuplets
Dafoe, Willem		Entertainment	6	10	40	35	Actor
Dager, Maj. Gen. Holmes E.	1893-1973	Military	30				World War II U.S. general
Dagmar		Entertainment	20			35	
Dagover, Lil	b. 1897	Entertainment				195	Vintage Ger. Actress
Daguerre, Louis		Science	150	490	1250		Fr. Inventor Daguerreotype. Photography Pioneer

NAME	DATE	CATEGORY	SIG	LS/DS	ALS	SP	COMMENTS
Dahl, Arlene	1924-	Entertainment	8		15	20	Actress. Pin-Up SP 40
Dahl, Perry		Aviation	10	25	38	28	ACE, WW II
Dahl, Roald		Author	15	30	35	106	Br. Short Stories, Children's
Dahlberg, Edward		Author	20	30	35	45	Am. Writer & Critic
Dahlberg, Ken		Aviation	15	30	50	40	ACE, WW II
Dahlgren, John A.	1809-1870	Civil War	84	312	606		Adm. Union Navy. Dahlgren Gun. Sig./Rank 220
Dahlgren, Ulric	1824-1864	Civil War	275	325	964	2415	Union Col. Planned Capture Jeff. Davis. Killed
Dahlquist, General John E.	1896-1975	Military	30				World War II U.S. general
Dahmer, Jeffrey	1960-1994	Criminal	345				Serial killer
Dailey, Dan	1914-1978	Entertainment	20	25	45	40	Actor-Song & Dance Man. Many 20th Cent. Musicals
Dailey, Janet		Author	5	10		10	
Dailey, Peter F.		Entertainment	5	8	15	15	
Daille, Lt. Gen. Marius	1878-1978	Military	20				World War II French general
Daines, Claire		Entertainment				35	
Dal Monte, Toti		Entertainment	25			95	Opera. SP Pc 75
Daladier, Edouard		Head of State	30	85	150	50	Premier Fr. Arrested-Liberated
Dalai Lama XIV	1935-	Head of State	75	160	225	199	Exiled Tibetan Religious Leader
D'Albert, Eugen F.C.	1864-1932	Composer	55	75	130		Ger. Opera, Piano Concertos
Dalbey, Brig. Gen. Josiah T.	1898-1964	Military	30				World War II U.S. general
Dalby, Maj. Gen. Thomas Gerald	1880-1963	Military	25				World War II British general
Daley, Cass		Entertainment	5	9	20	15	Comedienne. Films
Daley, Maj. Gen. Edmond L.	1883-1968	Military	30				World War II U.S. general
Daley, Richard J.		Political	20	40	85	35	Mayor Chicago. Last of Big City Bosses
Daley, Richard M.		Political	5			18	Mayor Chicago & Son of Richard J.
Dali, Salvador	1904-1989	Artist	150	402	640	630	Sp. Surrealist Painter. AMsS/Sketches 5900-7500
Dali, Tracey		Entertainment	10			45	Model/actress
Dalison, Maj. Gen. John Bernard	1888-1954	Military	25				World War II British general
Dallapozza, Adolf		Entertainment	5			25	Vienna Operettas
Dallas, Alexander J.	1759-1817	Cabinet	52	175	261		Madison Sec'y Treasury
Dallas, George M.		Vice President	65	200	204		Dallas, Texas Named for Him. Polk VP
Dalmores, Charles		Entertainment	25			85	Opera
Dalton, Abby		Entertainment	4	6	15	18	Actress. Pin-Up 32
Dalton, Brig. Gen. James L.	1910-1945	Military	30				World War II U.S. general
Dalton, Charles		Entertainment	5	6	10	10	
Dalton, Dorothy		Entertainment	20	25	65	60	
Dalton, Emmett	1871-1937	Outlaw	650	1923	3150	2500	Western Train Robber
Dalton, Frank		Lawman	890	3000			U.S. Marshal-Old West
Dalton, John		Science	135	400	750		Br. Chemist & Philosopher
Dalton, Lacy J.		Entertainment	5			25	Singer
Dalton, Maj. Gen. Joseph N.	1892-1961	Military	30				World War II U.S. general
Dalton, Maj. Gen. Sir Charles J. G.	1902-1989	Military	25				World War II British general
Dalton, Timothy		Entertainment	18			50	One time OO7. 'James Bond' SP 45
Dalton, Tristram	1738-1817	Political			506		US Sen Mass
Daltry, Roger		Entertainment	15			65	Rock. 'Who' Lead Singer
Daluege, Kurt	1897-1946	Military	75				Chief police Prussian Ministry

NAME	DATE	CATEGORY	SIG	LS/DS	ALS	SP	COMMENTS
Daly, Brig. Gen. Cornelius M.	1891-1974	Military	30				World War II U.S. general
Daly, James		Entertainment	7	6	15	25	Actor. Movie-TV. Father of Tyne Daly. Deceased
Daly, John Charles		Entertainment	7			20	News Commentator.Game Show Host. TV Pioneer
Daly, Tim		Entertainment	15			30	Actor
Daly, Tyne	1947-	Entertainment	7	12	18	22	Actress
Dam, Henrik		Science	70			105	Danish Biochemist. Nobel. Phil. Cover S 125
D'Amato, Alfonse		Senate/Congress	10			45	Senator NY
Dame, Brig. Gen. Pierre	1887-1940	Military	20				World War II French general
Damião, Elisa Maria		Political	10			15	Member European Parliament
Damion, Michael		Entertainment	10			20	actor
Damita, Lili		Entertainment	32	80	85	75	Fr. Film Star. Mrs. Errol Flynn
Damon, Cathryn		Entertainment	5	6	15	20	Actress. Character
Damon, Les		Entertainment	5			20	Radio Actor. 'Nick Charles' in 'Thin Man'
Damon, Matt		Entertainment	20			61	Actor. AA 'Good Will Hunting'
Damone, Vic		Entertainment	5			24	Singer
Damrosch, Walter	1862-1950	Composer-Cond.	50	101	115	350	Pioneer of Symphonic Broadcasts. AMusQS 125
Dana, Bill		Entertainment	25			40	'Jose Jiminez'. Early 60's Comedian-TV Writer
Dana, Charles A.	1819-1897	Publisher-Editor	30	30	75	45	Owner & Editor NY Sun. Civil War Member War Dept.
Dana, James D.		Science	25	45	65		Scientific Observer Antarctic
Dana, Napoleon J.T.	1822-1905	Civil War	45	78	111	130	Union Gen. ADS '64 300
Dana, Richard Henry	1787-1879	Civil War	48	200	225		Prosecutor of Jefferson Davis
Dana, Richard Henry	1815-1882	Author	30	55	80		Sailor, author of ^"2 Years Before the Mast^"
Danaher, John A.		Senate/Congress	5	15		10	Senator CT
Dance, Bill		Author	8			12	fishing
Dandridge, Dorothy	1923-1965	Entertainment	45	55	82	400	Afro-Am. Singer, Actress, Dancer
Dandridge, Ruby		Entertainment	35			90	
Dandy, George B.	1830-1911	Civil War	40	95			Twice Brevetted Union Gen. Georgian
Dane, Karl		Entertainment	10			15	Actor
Dane, Nathan		Revolutionary War	25	65	130		Continental Congress
Danei, Paul Francis	1694-1775	Clergy		7500			Saint Paul of the Cross 1867
Danenhower, John Wilson		Explorer	20	45	115		De Long Arctic Expedition 1879
Danes, Claire		Entertainment	15			50	Actress
Danford, Maj. Gen. Robert M.	1879-1974	Military	30				World War II U.S. general
Danforth, Brig. Gen. Edward C.B.	1894-1974	Military	30				World War II U.S. general
Danforth, John C.		Senate	5			10	Senator MO
Danforth, Thomas	1622-1699	Colonial America	390	470			Deputy Governor MA
D'Angelo, Beverly		Entertainment	8			35	Actress. Pin-Up 60
Dangerfield, George		Author	5	10	25		
Dangerfield, Rodney		Entertainment	6	12	20	46	Comedian.,'No Respect'
Danges, Henry	1870-1948	Entertainment	35			70	Opera. Baritone. Sang in World Prem. Louise
Daniel, Brig. Gen. Maurice W.	1896-1986	Military	30				World War II U.S. general
Daniel, John W.		Senate	10	25			Senator VA, Disabled in CW
Daniel, Junius	1828-1864	Civil War	450				Confederate general, KIA Spotsylvania, VA
Daniel, Peter Vivian	1784-1860	Supreme Court	45	125	475		
Daniel, Price		Senate/Congress	15	40		25	Senator, Gov. TX

NAME	DATE	CATEGORY	SIG	LS/DS	ALS	SP	COMMENTS
Daniell, Henry		Entertainment	50			150	Vintage Villainous Character Actor
Daniels, Bebe		Entertainment	20	25	65	75	Vintage Actress. Major Star 30's
Daniels, Billy		Entertainment	10			20	Afr-Am. Vocalist. Supper Clubs & Early TV
Daniels, Charlie		Country Music	6			30	
Daniels, Faith		Celebrity	10			15	media/TV personality
Daniels, Jeff		Entertainment	10			38	Actor
Daniels, Josephus	1862-1948	Cabinet	25	50	160	125	Sec'y Navy WW I. Diplomat, Journalist, Editor
Daniels, Squire, Elizabeth		Author	8			12	mystery novels, forgetful detective
Daniels, William		Entertainment	5			20	
Danielson, Brig. Gen. Wilmot A.	1884-1966	Military	30				World War II U.S. general
Danielson, Maj. Gen. Clarence H.	1889-1952	Military	30				World War II U.S. general
Daniloff, Nicholas		Celebrity	10			15	political celebrity
Daniloff, Nick		Celebrity	20		25	20	
Danilova, Alexandra		Entertainment	20	35	65	80	Rus-Am Ballerina, Teacher
Dankworth, Johnny		Bandleader	5			20	Jazz Musician
Dannay, Frederick	1905-1982	Author	50	160	325		ELLERY QUEEN
Dannenberg, Konrad		Science	20			55	Rocket Pioneer/von Braun
Danner, Blythe		Entertainment	5	6	15	20	Actress. & Mother of Gwineth Paltrow
Danning, Sybil		Entertainment	8	10	20	25	Actress. Pin-Up 45
D'Annunzio, Gabriele	1863-1938	Author	75	120	150	450	It. Writer, Pro-Fascist Soldier
Dano, Royal		Entertainment	10	10	20	25	Vintage Character Actor
Danova, Cesare		Entertainment	5	8	15	20	
d'Anselme, Gen. André-Marie-M.	1891-1957	Military	20				World War II French general
Danson, Ted		Entertainment	20			45	Actor, 'Cheers' SP 45
Dantine, Helmut		Entertainment	15	15		35	Autrian Actor of 40's-50's. Frequent Nazi Officer
Danton, Georges-Jacques		Fr. Revolution	1080	2538			Guillotined Leader of Revolution
Danton, Ray		Entertainment	8			20	Actor
Danza, Tony		Entertainment	10	15	25	30	Actor. Ex-Boxer
Darby, Brig. Gen. William O.	1911-1945	Military	30				World War II U.S. general
Darby, Kim		Entertainment	15			35	Actress. Difficult Autograph. 'True Grit' SP 38
D'Arcleé, Haricleé		Entertainment	100				Fr. Soprano
Darcy		Entertainment	6			25	Music. Bass, Vocals 'Smashing Pumkins'
Darcy, Emery		Entertainment	15			40	Met. Heidentenor
D'Arcy, Lt. Gen. John Conyers	1894-1966	Military	25				World War II British general
Darden, Christopher		Law	18	125		20	O.J.Simpson Prosecuting Att'y
Darin, Bobby	1936-1973	Entertainment	148		250	255	Singer-Actor. 'Mack the Knife' Topped Charts d. 37
Darion, Joe		Composer	10			30	Jazz. AMusQS 50
Darlan, Francois	1881-1942	Military			448		Fr. Adm. Vichy. Assassinated
Darling, Charles John Lord	1849-1936	Jurist			90		
Darling, J.N. 'ding'*		Cartoonist	25			150	Political Cartoonist
Darlington, William	1782-1863	Naturalist-Author	25		155		Many Swiss & US plants named for him
Darman, Richard		Celebrity	10			15	political celebrity
Darnell, Linda	1923-1965	Entertainment	45	145		136	Died Tragically in Fire
Darrah, Thomas		Military	35	50		45	General WW I
Darrall, Chester B.		Senate/Congress	20	30	55		MOC LA. Union Surgeon CW

NAME	DATE	CATEGORY	SIG	LS/DS	ALS	SP	COMMENTS
Darras, Danielle		Political	10			15	Member European Parliament
Darre, Richard-Walther	1895-1953	Military	52				SS., German cabinet Minister
Darrell, Johnny		Country Music	10			20	
Darren, James		Entertainment	8			19	Actor-Singer
Darrieux, Danielle		Entertainment	8			25	Fr. Actress. Film & Stage
Darro, Frankie		Entertainment	50			150	Child Actor. Disney Voice
Darrow, Charles B.	1889-1967	Designer	395	995			Developed Best Seller 'Monopoly'
Darrow, Clarence	1857-1938	Law	337	1638	2250	1648	Scopes Trial('Monkey Trial'), Loeb & Leopold etc.
Dart, Justin		Business	50	100	250	75	Drugstore Chain. Art Museum
D'Artagnan, Comte de		Military			6500		Capt.Louis XIV Musketeers
Dartiguenave, Philippe Sudre		Head of State	40	100			President of Haiti 1915
Daru, Pierre Bruno	1767-1829	Political			65		Minister of France
D'Arville, Camille		Entertainment	15			45	Actress-Vintage
Darwell, Jane	1880-1967	Entertainment	122	110	200	200	Vintage Actress. 'GWT", 'Grapes of Wrath' Oscar
Darwin, Charles	1809-1882	Science	620	2372	3716	5462	Br. Naturalist.Theory of Evolution
Dary, Michel J.M.		Political	10			15	Member European Parliament
Daschle, Thomas		Senate	10			15	United States Senate (D - SD)
Dash, Stacey		Entertainment	10			35	actress
Dasher, Maj. Gen. Charles L.	1900-1968	Military	30				World War II U.S. general
Dassin, Jules		Entertainment	20			45	Film Director
Daubigny, Charles Francois		Artist	95	280	425		Fr. Landscape Painter
Daudet, Alphonse	1840-1897	Author	35	80	175	63	Fr. Stories, Novels, Plays
Daugherty, Harry M.	1860-1941	Cabinet	25	55	125	50	Att'y Gen.Tried for Fraud-Acquitted. (Harding Adm)
Daul, Joseph		Political	10			15	Member European Parliament
Daumier, Honore		Artist	240	630	1470		Fr. Caricaturist & Serious Art
Dauphin, Claude		Entertainment	35			75	Fr. Leading Man
Dausset, Jean, Prof.		Science	20	45		35	Nobel Medicine
Dauvray, Helen		Entertainment	4	3	6	8	
Daval, Danny		Entertainment	5	6	15	15	
Dave Weldon		Senate	10			15	Member U.S. Congress
Dave, Red River		Country Music	10			20	Country Singer
Davenport, Addington	1670-1736	Revolutionary War	140	265	500		Am. Colonial Jurist
Davenport, Fanny		Entertainment	20			50	Vintage Actress. 1889
Davenport, Harry		Entertainment	100			250	Veteran Char. Actor. 'GWTW' SP 595
Davenport, Homer C.		Cartoonist	30	60	135		Political Cartoons, Uncle Sam, signed draw. 391
David		Entertainment	5			25	Music. Drummer 'Korn'
David, Felicien-Cesar	1810-1876	Composer	100	500			AMusMsS 650-750
David, Ferdinand		Composer	45		225		Ger. Violinist
David, Hal		Composer	20	30	65	35	
David, Jacques Louis		Artist	175	400	610		Fr. Classical Painter
David, Larry		Entertainment	10	15	20	40	
David, Mack		Composer	20			40	Lyricist
Davidovich, Lolita		Entertainment	10			20	actress
Davidson, Allen Turner		Civil War	25	80	125		CSA Congress. Lawyer, Banker
Davidson, Arthur		Business	1100	5300			Harley-Davidson Motorcycle Founder. DS Stock Cert.

NAME	DATE	CATEGORY	SIG	LS/DS	ALS	SP	COMMENTS
Davidson, Gordon		Business	1500	4500			A Founder of Harley-Davidson. DS Stock Cert.
Davidson, Henry Brevard	1831-1899	Civil War	110	248	357		Confederate general
Davidson, Jim		Entertainment	4			18	Actor. 'Pacific Blue'
Davidson, Jo		Artist	35	75	126	105	Am. Sculptor
Davidson, Jo		Celebrity			58		songwriter
Davidson, John W.	1824-1881	Civil War	45	84	126		Union Gen. ALS '62 630
Davidson, John		Entertainment	4	6	6	14	Singer-Actor-Host
Davidson, Loyal		Military	35	60			
Davidson, Lt. Gen. Garrison H.	1904-1992	Military	30				World War II U.S. general
Davidson, Maj. Gen. Alexander E.	1880-1962	Military	25				World War II British general
Davidson, Maj. Gen. Francis H. N.	1892-1973	Military	25				World War II British general
Davidson, Peter		Entertainment	10			20	Actor
Davidson, Randall T., Archbishop		Clergy	25	35	45		
Davidson, Walter		Business	1200	5500			Harley-Davidson Motorcycle Founder. DS Stock Cert
Davidson, William B.		Entertainment	10			30	Character Actor
Davidson, William H.		Business	1000	3500	4300		Son of Wm. A.& Pres.Harley-Davidson 30's-40's
Davies, Chris		Political	10			15	Member European Parliament
Davies, Gail		Entertainment	4			10	Singer
Davies, Gilli		Celebrity	10			15	Welsh Chef
Davies, Henry E.	1836-1894	Civil War	58	80			Union General
Davies, Jeremy		Entertainment	3			6	
Davies, Maj. Gen. Henry L.	1898-1975	Military	25				World War II British general
Davies, Marion		Entertainment	49	65	105	154	C. Bull Original SP 275
Davies, Peter Maxwell		Composer	40			110	'Songs of a Mad King'. Opera
Davies, Ray (The Kinks)		Entertainment	18			45	Rock ' Give the Peopleaa' S Alb. 55
Davies, Rhys		Author	5	20	35	10	Welch. Novels, Stories
Davies, Ronald N.		Law	25		60	30	Nazi War Trials Jurist
Davies, Thomas F., Bishop		Clergy	30	35	45		
Davies, William		Revolutionary War	145	150	170		Sec'y War of VA
Davis, Angela	1944-	Activist	12	18	32	35	Afro-Am. Activist. Wanted Poster/Sig. 250
Davis, Ann B.		Entertainment	8			18	Character Actress. 'Brady Bunch'
Davis, Artur D		Congress	10			15	Member U.S. Congress
Davis, Benjamin F.		Civil War			161		Union Cavalry Commander
Davis, Benjamin O. Jr.		Aviation	15	15	38	45	ACE, WW II, 1st Afro-Am. Military Fighter Pilot
Davis, Bette	1908-1989	Entertainment	61	190	238	184	Actress Extraordinaire! Multi Oscar Winner
Davis, Brad		Entertainment	35			85	Actor. 'Midnight Express'
Davis, Brig. Gen. Addison D.	1883-1965	Military	30				World War II U.S. general
Davis, Brig. Gen. Benjamin O.	1877-1970	Military	30				World War II U.S. general
Davis, Brig. Gen. George A.	1892-1969	Military	30				World War II U.S. general
Davis, Brig. Gen. John F.	1892-1978	Military	30				World War II U.S. general
Davis, Brig. Gen. Leonard L.	1894-1975	Military	30				World War II U.S. general
Davis, Charles Henry	1807-1877	Civil War	33	89	128		Union Adm. ALS '63 275
Davis, Clifton		Entertainment	5			18	Actor TV
Davis, Cushman K.		Senate	12	25		30	Senator MN
Davis, Danny K. D		Congress	10			15	Member U.S. Congress

NAME	DATE	CATEGORY	SIG	LS/DS	ALS	SP	COMMENTS
Davis, David	1815-1886	Supreme Court	64	157	252		Sen. IL. Pres Pro Tem. Executor Lincoln Estate
Davis, Don		Celebrity	8			12	potter
Davis, Dwight F.	1879-1945	Cabinet	30	68	130	65	Sec'y War.Donor of Davis Cup.Gov.-Gen. Philippines
Davis, Ellabelle		Entertainment	10			40	Great Afro-Am Singer
Davis, Evelyn Redmon		Author	8			12	genealogy
Davis, Ewin L.		Senate/Congress	4	10			MOC TN
Davis, Fay	1872-1945	Entertainment	15	4	65	50	Actress. 1895 London Hit in 'Prisoner of Zenda'
Davis, Gail		Entertainment	14	18	22	35	Actress. 'Annie Oakley' SP 50
Davis, Geena		Entertainment	14	25	35	48	Oscar Winner
Davis, George	1820-1896	Civil War	68				Member of Confederate Congress, Atty. Gen
Davis, Henry Greene		Civil War	38	85			Union General
Davis, Henry Minton	1817-1865	Congress	15		50		Prevented MD from Joining CSA
Davis, James J.		Cabinet	20	50	95	75	Sec'y Labor, Founder of Moose
Davis, Jan		Astronaut	5			20	
Davis, Jefferson (WD)	1808-1889	Civil War	750	2859	4710	5500	President CSA. ALS/Cont. 15,900, LS/cont 13,500
Davis, Jefferson C.	1828-1879	Civil War	53	118	159		Union Gen. ANS '62 330, Sig/Rank 75
Davis, Jefferson	1808-1889	Civil War	620	1360	2180	4000	CSA Pres. ALS/Content 15,000, LS 55000
Davis, Jim D		Congress	10			15	Member U.S. Congress
Davis, Jim		Entertainment	40	40	70	70	Actor. 'Dallas'
Davis, Jim*		Cartoonist	35	68	225	175	'Garfield'. Repro Sketch S 75
Davis, Jimmie		Governor	30	45		60	Singing Gov. of LA, 'You Are My Sunshine'
Davis, Jo Ann		Congress	10			15	Member U.S. Congress
Davis, Jo		Entertainment	4	3	6	10	
Davis, Joan		Entertainment	25			88	
Davis, John Wm.	1873-1955	Congr.-Diplomat	20	45	75	40	Dem. Pres. Candidate. Defended R. Oppenheimer
Davis, John	1761-1847	Author	30	175	290		Historian, Comptroller US Treas
Davis, John	1787-1854	Governor	25	50	70		Gov. MA
Davis, Johnny 'Scat'		Entertainment	10	10	12	15	
Davis, Jonathan		Entertainment	12			48	Music. Lead Singer 'Korn'
Davis, Joseph Robert	1825-1896	Civil War	149	210	350		Confederate general
Davis, Kristin		Entertainment				48	Charlotte York, Sex in the City
Davis, Lincoln D		Congress	10			15	Member U.S. Congress
Davis, Mack		Country Music	7			15	Singer-Songwriter
Davis, Meyer		Entertainment	15			35	Big Society Band
Davis, Miles	1926-1991	Entertainment	183	210		588	Immortal Jazz Trumpet Player-Composer
Davis, Nancy (Reagan)		First Lady	80			170	
Davis, Nancy		Entertainment	50			150	
Davis, Nelson H.	1821-1890	Civil War	42	68	96		Union Gen. Chancellorsville
Davis, Noah		Senate/Congress	10	25	60		MOC NY 1869, Jurist
Davis, Ossie	1917-	Entertainment	9			16	Actor. Stage-Screen. Playwright, Political Activis
Davis, Patti (Reagan)		Entertainment	5	7	15	20	Model-Actress-Writer. Pin-Up 50
Davis, Patti		Celebrity	10			15	motivational speaker
Davis, Phil*		Cartoonist	30			250	Mandrake the Magician
Davis, Phyllis		Entertainment	6	12	18	20	Pin-Up 45
Davis, Reuben	1813-1890	Civil War	63	138	270		CSA General

NAME	DATE	CATEGORY	SIG	LS/DS	ALS	SP	COMMENTS
Davis, Richard Harding		Author	10	25	40	20	Correspondent 6 Wars, Novelist
Davis, Robert		Military	5		25		General WW I
Davis, Rufe		Entertainment	25			55	
Davis, Sammi		Entertainment	10			20	actress
Davis, Sammy, Jr.	1925-1990	Entertainment	40	50	80	137	Charter Member of Sinatra's Rat Pack. Most Talent
Davis, Susan A. D		Congress	10			15	Member U.S. Congress
Davis, Tom D		Congress	10			15	Member U.S. Congress
Davis, Varina		CSA First Lady	220	333	447	524	Mrs. Jeff. Davis.ALS/Cont 1600-6000
Davis, William George Mackey	1812-1898	Civil War	90	190	340		Confederate general
Davis, William W.H.	1820-1910	Civil War	42	71	120		Led 104th PA
Davision, Brig. Gen. Donald A.	1893-1944	Military	30				World War II U.S. general
Davison, Bruce		Entertainment	5			10	
Davison, Wild Bill		Entertainment	30			75	Jazz Cornet-Bandleader
Davisson, Clinton Joseph		Science	25	75			Nobel Physics.Bell Laboratories
Davout, Louis Nicolas, Duke		Fr. Revolution	45	210	248		Marshal of Napoleon
Davro, Bobby		Celebrity	10			15	comedian
Davy, Brig. George Mark Oswald	1898-1983	Military	25				World War II British general
Davy, Humphry, Sir	1778-1829	Science	118	322	643		Br.Chemist. ALS/Cont 3750,8,500,AMsS 2500
Dawber, Pam		Entertainment	8	10	20	20	Actress. Pin-Up 40
Dawes, Brigadier Hugh Frank	1884-1965	Military	25				World War II British general
Dawes, Charles G.		Vice President	30	110	175	275	Nobel Peace Prize
Dawes, William	1745-1799	Revolutionary War	3500				Patriot. Rode with Paul Revere
Dawley, Maj. Gen. Ernst J.	1886-1973	Military	30				World War II U.S. general
Dawm Chong, Rae		Entertainment	10			20	actress
Dawnay, Maj. Gen. Sir David	1903-1971	Military	25				World War II British general
Dawson, George		Clergy	20	35	60		
Dawson, John B.	1798-1845	Congress	10				Repr. LA, Maj. General of Militia
Dawson, John L.		Congress	20		70		Governor Kansas Terr. ,MOC PA
Dawson, Maj. Gen. Arthur Peel	1888-1958	Military	25				World War II British general
Dawson, Richard		Entertainment	5	20		23	Hogan's Heroes Co-Star
Dawson, Roger		Celebrity	10			15	motivational speaker
Dawson-Briggs, Roxanne		Entertainment				40	Actress. Star Trek
Dawson's Creek (cast)		Entertainment				150	Cast signed photo of 4
Day, Chon*		Cartoonist	10	35		50	Brother Sebastian
Day, Darren		Celebrity	10			15	television presenter
Day, Dennis		Entertainment	10	14	20	28	Vocalist-Comedian. Jack Benny Radio & TV Shows
Day, Doris		Entertainment	14	32		42	24 Page DS 'Do Not Disturb' 425.
Day, Frank		Celebrity	10		25		
Day, J. Edward		Cabinet	4	5	15	10	P.M. General
Day, Jeremiah		Clergy	15	20	35		
Day, Laraine		Entertainment	7			22	Actress. Pin-Up 28
Day, Linda (George)		Entertainment	5	8	15	17	Actress Turned Director
Day, Simon		Celebrity	10			15	comedian
Day, William R.	1849-1923	Supreme Court	40	90	135	65	Sec'y State
Dayan, Moshe	1915-1981	Military	188	171	220	306	Israeli General, Politician. Masterminded 3 Wars

NAME	DATE	CATEGORY	SIG	LS/DS	ALS	SP	COMMENTS
Dayan, Yael		Author	5			25	And Daughter of Moshe
Day-Lewis, Cecil	1904-1972	Author	15	50			Br. Poet-Laureate
Day-Lewis, Daniel		Entertainment	22			60	
Daymond, Gus		Aviation	12	25	55	40	ACE, WW II, Eagle Squadron
Dayne, Taylor		Entertainment	5			35	Rock
Dayton, Elias		Revolutionary War	90	210	395		General. Continental Congress
Dayton, Jonathan		Revolutionary War	175	165	243		Continental Congress
Dayton, Mark		Senate	10			15	United States Senate (D - MN)
Dayton, William L.	1807-1867	Senator NJ	25	40	110		John C. Fremont Running Mate
D'Azeglio, Massimo T., Marchese		Statesman/Author			120		
De Acosta, Mercedes		Author	10	25	45		Intimate of Greta Garbo
de Almeida, Antonio		Conductor	10			45	Specialist in Fr. Music
De Beauvoir, Simone		Author	35	95	200		Fr. Writer,Philosopher,Feminist
De Bono, Emilio		Military	75	225		375	It. Fascist Politician & Gen.
De Bray, Xavier B.	1818-1895	Civil War	125	174			CSA Gen. ALS/Cont.2500
De Broglie, Louis Victor	1892-1984	Scientist				184	Nobel prize 1929. Wave theory of electronics
de Burgh, General Sir Eric	1881-1973	Military	28				World War II British general
De Carlo, Yvonne		Entertainment				45	Munsters
De Clercq, Willy C.E.H.		Political	10			15	Member European Parliament
De Corsia, Ted		Entertainment	20	25		40	
De Courcey, Roger		Celebrity	10			15	comedian
de Duve, Christian R.		Science	10			40	Nobel
De Falla, Manuel	1876-1946	Composer	425	883	1200		Sp. AMusQS 2000
de Fonblanque, Maj. Gen. Edw. B.	1895-1981	Military	25				World War II British general
de Fonblanque, Maj. Gen. Philip	1885-1940	Military	25				World War II British general
De Forest, Lee, Dr.	1873-1961	Science	192	456	838	900	Invented Vacuum Tube. ALS Scientific Cont. 12,500
De Gaulle, Charles		Political	10			15	Member European Parliament
De Gaulle, Charles	1890-1969	Head of State	533	1034	3325	1382	Fr. WW II Gen., Wardate TLS/content 1000-2500
De Greiff, Monica		Celebrity	10			15	political celebrity
De Havilland, Geoffrey		Aviation	70	140	205	125	De Havilland Aircraft Co.
De Hidalgo, Elvira		Entertainment	45			150	Coloratura Soprano Teacher of Callas
De Keyser, VTronique		Political	10			15	Member European Parliament
De Kooning, Elaine*		Artist	50			242	Willem's Wife. Artist in her own right.
De Kooning, Willem	1904-1997	Artist	150	225	450	375	Dutch Abstract Impressionist. Repro S 285-550
de la Barra, Francisco Leon		Statesman	132	1225			Mex. Diplomat, Politician, Ambass. US, Prov. Pres.
De La Beckwith, Bryan		Activist	15		95	95	Convicted Murderer of Medgar Evers
De La Cierva, Juan		Aviation	90		295	350	Inventor Autogyro
De La Grange, Anna		Entertainment			80		Opera
De La Mare, Walter	1873-1956	Author	38	67	90	45	Br. Poet.Songs of Childhood. Novelist
De La Pena, George		Entertainment	3	3	6	6	
De La Perriere, Thierry		Political	10			15	Member European Parliament
De La Renta, Oscar		Business	10	15	35	20	Fashion Designer.Elegant Gowns
De la Rocha, Zack		Entertainment	8			42	Music. Lead Singer 'Rage Against the Machine'
De La Rue, Warren	1815-1889	Science			200		Br. Astron., Inventor Silver-Chlor. Battery
De Lagnel, Julius Adolph	1827-1912	Civil War	25	55			Confederate Lt. Col, Ordnance Dept.

NAME	DATE	CATEGORY	SIG	LS/DS	ALS	SP	COMMENTS
De Lancey, Stephen		Revolutionary War	75	180	225		Loyalist. Lawyer. Imprisoned
De Leo, Sarafina		Entertainment				40	Opera
De Link, Derek		Entertainment	3			8	
De Luca, Giuseppe		Entertainment	25	35	95	162	Opera
De Matteo, Drea		Entertainment	10			35	Adrianna La Cerva, Soprano's
De Mita, Luigi Ciriaco		Political	10			15	Member European Parliament
De Mornay, Rebecca		Entertainment	6	15		28	Pin-up Color 60
De Palma, Brian		Entertainment	10		20	22	Film Director
De Paul, Saint Vincent		Clergy	1100	1600	4500		
De Peyster, John W. Jr.		Civil War	10	20	55		Aide to Gen.Kearny
De Quincey, Thomas		Author	110	170	250		AMs 650-2,250
de Ravin, Emilie		Celebrity				40	
De Reszke, Edouard	1853-1917	Entertainment	68			150	Opera-Vintage. AMusQS 75
De Reszke, Jean	1850-1925	Entertainment	100	120	160	345	Opera-Vintage. SP/Brother Edouard 425
De Reszke, Marie		Entertainment			125		Opera
De Ridder. Anton		Entertainment	10		45	35	Opera
De Rita, Joe		Entertainment	32		65	66	Three Stooges SP 55, S Check 125
de Robeck of Sweden, Brig. J. H.	1895-1965	Military	28				World War II British general
De Roo, Alexander		Political	10			15	Member European Parliament
De Rossa, Proinsias		Political	10			15	Member European Parliament
De Rossetti, Curt		Business	10	20			Restaurateur
De Russy, Gustavus A.(WD)		Civil War	50	250	233		Union Gen.
De Sade, Marquis	1740-1814	Author	325	748	2212		Fr. Social Deviant. Abnormal Behavior. 'Sadism'
De Sarnez, Marielle		Political	10			15	Member European Parliament
De Seversky, Alex.	1894-1973	Aviation	90	140	205	238	TLS/Historical Cont. 1,200
De Smet, Pierre	1801-1873	Jesuit Missionary	225		800		Missionary to Western Indians
De Toth, André		Entertainment	10			20	Film Director
De Trobriand, Philippe R. (WD)		Civil War	50	109	395		Union Gen.
De Valera, Eamon (Ire)	1882-1975	Head of State	102	125	325	110	Pres. P.M. Cont.TLS 550
De Vere, Aubrey T.		Author	20	60	140		Ir. Poet,Critic,Hymns
De Veyrac, Christine		Political	10			15	Member European Parliament
De Veyrinas, Frantoise		Political	10			15	Member European Parliament
De Wilde, Brandon		Entertainment	100			300	
De Windt, Harry	1856-1933	Explorer	30	45	75	50	Br. Explorer
De Witt, Alexander		Senate/Congress	5		20		MOC MA
Deacon, Richard		Entertainment	25			50	
Deal, Nathan D		Congress	10			15	Member U.S. Congress
Dean, Billy		Country Music	5			20	
Dean, Donald J.		Military	15	45			WW I Victoria Cross
Dean, Eddie		Country Music	10	10	20	25	
Dean, Gilbert	1819-1870	Congress	9				Repr. NY
Dean, James	1931-1955	Entertainment	1862	2746	3250	5184	Short Lived Spectacular Career in Films
Dean, Jimmy		Country Music	5			21	Sausages & CW Singer
Dean, John W.		Law	5	15	25	95	Special Counsel to Nixon. Watergate
Dean, Julia		Entertainment	6	8	15	15	

NAME	DATE	CATEGORY	SIG	LS/DS	ALS	SP	COMMENTS
Dean, Letitia		Entertainment	10			20	Actress
Dean, Maj. Gen. Herbert R.	1882-1970	Military	30				World War II U.S. general
Dean, Maj. Gen. William F.	1899-1981	Military	30				World War II U.S. general
Dean, Maureen		Author	10	35			(Mrs. John Dean)
Dean, Millvina		Titanic Survivor	50	55	60	50	Titanic survivor Fatal Shipwreck Lithograph S 250
Dean, Pricilla	1896-1987	Entertainment	20			70	Silent Film Star of early 20's
Dean, William F.	1899-1981	Military	20	35	55	195	Gen. WW II. Hero of Korean War
Deane, Brig. Gen. John R.	1896-1982	Military	30				World War II U.S. general
Deane, Silas	1737-1789	Rev War	230	550	975		Diplomat. Negotiated Treaties. Cont'l Congress
DeAngelis, Jefferson		Entertainment	10				Actor
Dear, Brig. Gen. William R.	1883-1956	Military	30				World War II U.S. general
Dearborn, Henry A.S.	1783-1851	Senate/Congress	55	175	250		Collector Port Boston 1812-29
Dearborn, Henry	1751-1829	Cabinet	135	329	893		Rev. War Gen'l. Jefferson's Sec'y War.Statesman
Dearden, John, Cardinal		Clergy	30	35	45	40	
Dearing, James	1840-1865	Civil War	240				Confederate general
Deas, Zachariah Cantey	1819-1882	Civil War	138	294			Confederate general
Death on the Nile (Cast)		Entertainment				75	Signed by 6
Deayton, Angus		Celebrity	10			15	comedian
DeBakey, Michael, Dr.	1908-	Science	15	38		33	1st Coronary Artery Bypass Op.
Debar, William J.		Senate	10	15			Senator KY
DeBeaune, Charlotte		Celebrity		525			Mistress of Henry IV
DeBeck, Billy*		Cartoonist	30			260	Barney Google, Snuffy Smith
Debeney, General Marie-Eugène	1864-1943	Military	20				World War II French general
Debeney, Maj. Gen. Marie-C-V	1891-1956	Military	20				World War II French general
Debenham, Frank	1883-1965	Explorer		100			Antarctic explorer
Debizka, Hedwig von		Entertainment	40			150	Opera
DeBlanc, Jeff		Aviation	12	28	52	38	ACE, WW II, CMH
Debolt, Bob & Dorothy		Celebrity	10			15	motivational speaker
DeBray, Xavier B.	1818-1895	Civil War	95		690		CSA General
Debre, Michael		Head of State	5	20	50		
DeBroglie, Louis-C-V- Maurice		Science	35	90			Physicist. Pioneer in X-Rays
DeBruhl, Harold		Author	8			12	regional history
Debs, Eugene		Labor	96	276	388	450	U.S. Socialist Leader.Organizer
Debussy, Claude	1862-1918	Composer	256	525	949		Fr. Composer. AMusQS 7,500
DeButts, John D.		Business	10	35	45	20	
Debye, Peter J.W.		Science	55	110	175		NobelChemistry-Discovered Rayon
Decadenet, Amanda		Entertainment	10			20	actress
Decamp, Rosemary		Entertainment	5			40	Am.Radio & Film Star
DeCarlo, Yvonne	1922-	Entertainment	8	12	22	33	Actress Pin-Up 38
DeCasseres. Benjamin		Author	5	15	25		Columnist, Editorials NY Mirror
Decatur, Stephen	1779-1820	Military	368	3100	5000		American Naval Hero, War 1812
Dechaux, Brig. Gen. Louis-Léon	1883-1954	Military	20				World War II French general
DeCisneros, Eleanora		Entertainment	40			185	Opera
Decker, General George H.	1902-1980	Military	30				World War II U.S. general
Decker, Gen. of Panz. Troops Karl	1897-1945	Military	27				World War II German general

NAME	DATE	CATEGORY	SIG	LS/DS	ALS	SP	COMMENTS
DeCordova, Fred		Entertainment	5	8	15	15	
Decourriere, Francis		Political	10			15	Member European Parliament
Dee, Francis		Entertainment	8	6	18	32	Actress & Wife of Favorite Joel McCrea. Pin-Up 38
Dee, Jack		Celebrity	10			15	comedian
Dee, Ruby	1923-	Entertainment	10	12	15	20	1st Afr.-Am./Major Shakespearean Role Am. Festival
Dee, Sandra		Entertainment	8	10	15	38	Actress
Deedes, Lt. Gen. Sir Ralph Bouv.	1890-1954	Military	25				World War II British general
Deeley, Cat		Celebrity	10			15	celebrity model
Deems, Charles Force		Celebrity	5	10	20		
Deems, 'Cousin'		Country Music	4			15	And His 'Goat Herders'
Deere, Allan Christopher		Aviation-Ace	15	40	50		N.Z. Ace WWII, 22 confirmed
Deere, John	1804-1886	Business	300	3500	4100		Steel Plow. Deere Check 4750
Deering, James		Business	10	25	45	25	
Deering, Olive		Entertainment	15			35	
Dees, Morris		Legal	10			25	Lawyer, Political Activist. Tracks Hate Crimes
Dees, Rick		Country Western	2	5	15	5	Singer Radio-TV Host
DeFazio, Peter A. D		Congress	10			15	Member U.S. Congress
Defoe, Daniel	1660-1731	Author	1500	7500			Br. Journalist, Novelist
DeFord, Bailey		Country Music	20			75	Early Black Opry Star
DeFore, Don		Entertainment	9			20	Actor. Vintage SP 30
DeFranco, Buddy		Entertainment	12			25	Bandleader, Clarinetist
Defrank, Tom		Celebrity	10			15	media/TV personality
Degas, Edgar	1834-1917	Artist	250	760	1625		Fr. Impressionist. Ballet Scenes
DeGeneres, Ellen		Entertainment	18			53	Comedienne
DeGette, Diana D		Congress	10			15	Member U.S. Congress
DeHart, John		Revolutionary War	30	65	140		
DeHaven, Gloria		Entertainment	6	8	5	28	Glamor Actress-Singer-Dancer of MGM Musicals
DeHaven, Robert		Aviation	10	20	40	30	ACE, WW II
DeHavilland, Olivia		Entertainment	40	75	195	57	As 'Melanie' in GWTW. SP 90-150-225. AA
Dehmelt, Hans G., Dr.		Science	20	35		30	Nobel Physics
Dehner, John		Entertainment	10		10	15	
Dehousse, Jean-Maurice		Political	10			15	Member European Parliament
Deisenhofer, Johann		Science	27	36		35	Nobel
DeKalb, Johann	1721-1780	Revolutionary War			7500		Arrived w/Lafayette. Ordered to Capture Charleston
Dekker, Albert		Entertainment	6			10	
Dekker, Hank		Celebrity	10			15	motivational speaker
DeKlerk, F.W.		Head of State	75	150		90	Nobel Peace, Pr. Minister S.A.
DeKoven, Reginald	1859-1920	Composer	25	45	150	100	Versatile American Composer
Del Fuegos, The		Entertainment	20			50	
Del Monaco, Mario	1915-1982	Entertainment	50	65	150	208	Opera
Del Rio, Delores	1905-1983	Entertainment	30	35	55	75	Actress. Serenely Beautiful Mexican Performer
Del Toro, Benicio		Entertainment	10			52	Actor, AA
Del Tredici, David		Composer	15	35	80		Pulitzer, AMusQS 100
Delacroix, F.V. Eugene	1798-1863	Artist	175	385	643		Brilliant Colorist. Great Murals
DeLaCroix, Raven		Entertainment	3	3	6	8	

NAME	DATE	CATEGORY	SIG	LS/DS	ALS	SP	COMMENTS
Delafield, John R.		Military	8				General
Delafield, Richard		Civil War	56	92	483		Union General. Engineer
DeLagnel, Juius A.	1827-1912	Civil War	85	126	200		CSA General
Delahunt, William D. D		Congress	10			15	Member U.S. Congress
DeLancie, John		Entertainment				45	Actor. Star Trek
DeLand, Margaret		Author	12	25	75	25	Am. Novelist.Old Chester Tales
Delaney, Kim		Entertainment	8	35	70	46	Actress
Delano, Columbus		Cabinet	20				Sec'y Interior, Grant
Delany, Bessie		Author	5			20	Co-Author of Best Selling Memoirs
Delany, Dana		Entertainment	8	22	25	38	Actress
Delany, Sarah 'Sadie'		Author	5			20	Co-Wrote Best-Selling Memoirs
DeLauro, Rosa L. D		Congress	10			15	Member U.S. Congress
DeLay, Tom		Congress	10			15	Member U.S. Congress
Delbridge, Del		Entertainment	10			15	Radio Announcer
Delbruck, Max		Science	70		200		Nobel in Medicine
Deledda, Grazia		Author	45	105	320		Nobel Literature 1926
Deleon, Idalis		Celebrity	10			15	media/TV personality
DeLiagre, Alfred		Entertainment	5	7	12	10	
Delibes, Leo		Composer	85	220	270		Light Opera, Ballet
Deligne, Lt Gen Agathon-J-Jos.	1890-1961	Military	20				World War II French general
Delius, Frederick	1862-1934	Composer	300	400	770		Br.Orchestral, Concerti, Songs.AMusQS 4000
Dell, Gabriel		Entertainment	15	20	25	35	
Dell, Myrna		Entertainment	5	6	10	10	Pin-Up SP 15
Della Casa, Lisa		Entertainment	10			25	Swiss Soprano. Opera
Della Chiesa, Vivian		Entertainment	5	6	15	15	Soprano
Della Joio, Norman		Composer	35	115	240	55	Pulitzer, AMusQS 50-175
Della Vedova, Benedetto		Political	10			15	Member European Parliament
Dell'alba, Gianfranco		Political	10			15	Member European Parliament
Dellums, Ronald B.	1935-	Senate/Congress	10	15		20	Afro-Am. Congressman CA
Dell'utri, Marcello		Political	10			15	Member European Parliament
Delna, Marie		Entertainment	25			90	Fr. Contralto. Opera
Delon, Alain	1935-	Entertainment	15			35	Fr. Actor, Prod.,Dir.Leading Man Internat'l Films
DeLong, Phillip C.		Aviation	12	25	40	30	ACE, WW II
Delpy, Julie	1969-	Entertainment	20			55	Fr. Actress. 'Unbearable Likeness of Being'
DeLuca, Phil Dr.		Author	8			12	marriage and relationships
DeLuise, Dom	1933-	Entertainment	5	6	15	27	Comedian
DeMarco, Antonio		Entertainment	10	25			Producer
DeMarco, Tony		Entertainment		25			Dancer
Demarest, William	1892-1983	Entertainment	14		25	52	Vaudeville Star Turned Character Actor
DeMille, Agnes		Entertainment	55	200		170	Dancer,Innovative Choreographer
DeMille, Cecil B.	1881-1959	Entertainment	60	158	215	182	Director, Producer, Film Giant,TLS cont. 500-2500
DeMille, Katherine		Entertainment	10	12	15	25	
DeMille, William C.		Entertainment	15	45		50	Early Dir.,Playwright,Producer
Deming, W. Edwards		Business				75	Consultant
DeMint, Jim D		Congress	10			15	Member U.S. Congress

NAME	DATE	CATEGORY	SIG	LS/DS	ALS	SP	COMMENTS
Demme, Ted	d. 2002	Director				45	
DeMonvel, Boutes		Artist	25	70	125		
Dempsey, Gen. Sir Miles C.	1896-1969	Military	25				World War II British general
Dempsey, John		Governor	12				Gov. CT
Dempsey, Patrick		Entertainment	10			15	
Dempsey, Stephen W.		Congress	4	25			Repr. NY
Demslow, W.W.*		Cartoonist	50			175	Illustrator Of Wizard Of Oz
Demzn, Lev		Cosmonaut	20	30			
Denby, Edwin	1870-1929	Cabinet	20	50	75	50	Harding Sec'y Navy. 'Teapot Dome Scadal'
Dench, Judi		Entertainment	14			67	Actress, AA
Deneuve, Catherine	1943-	Entertainment	22	30	35	56	Actress, model
Denfeld, Louis E.		Military	10	25	40	25	Adm.Chief Naval Operations WWII
Dening, Maj. Gen. Roland	1888-1978	Military	25				World War II British general
DeNiro, Robert		Entertainment	11	30	45	89	Actor, AA Winner
Denis, Maurice	1870-1943	Artist	95		325		Fr. Religious Painter. Art Theoretician
Denison, Charles S.		Senate	5	10	15		Senator IL
Denison, John H.		Clergy	10	15	25		
Denit, Brig. Gen. Guy B.	1891-1976	Military	30				World War II U.S. general
Denman, G. Tony		Aviation	15	22	25	30	ACE, WW II, Navy Ace
Denman, Thomas, 3rd Baron		Head of State	10	15	35		Gov. General Australia
Dennehy, Brian		Entertainment	10	28		25	Mature Leading Man-Character Actor Movies/TV
Denning, Richard		Entertainment	5	8	15	15	Handsome Film Leading Man. 40's early 50's
Dennis, Cathy		Music	10			15	performing musical artist
Dennis, Les		Celebrity	10			15	comedian
Dennis, Maj. Gen. Meade Edward	1893-1965	Military	25				World War II British general
Dennis, Sandy	1937-1992	Entertainment	45	45		115	Oscar Winning Actress
Dennison, Jo Carroll		Entertainment	5	6	10	10	Actress
Dennison, William	1815-1882	Cabinet	40	95	210		Lincoln P.M. Gen. CW Gov. OH
Denny, Roz		Celebrity	10			15	TV Chef
Denos, John		Entertainment	7	10	30	15	TV actor 'The Young and the Restless'
Denson, Brig. Gen. Eley P.	1884-1970	Military	30				World War II U.S. general
Dent, Elliott		Aviation	12	25	35	30	ACE, WW II
Dent, Frederick T.	1820-1892	Civil War	35	71	179		Union Gen.
Dent, S. Hubert		Senate/Congress	5	15		15	MOC AL
Denton, Jeremiah A., Jr.		Military-Congress	15	25	30	25	Admiral WW II, MOC AL
Dentz, General Henri-Fernand	1881-1945	Military	20				World War II French general
Denver, Bob		Entertainment	10	12	15	28	Actor. 'Gilligan's Island'
Denver, James W.	1817-1892	Civil War	80	168	357		Denver, Colo... Union Gen.,Lawyer, Gov. KS Terr.
Denver, John	1943-1997	Music	44	15	15	118	Singer-Composer. Died in Air Crash 1997
Denza, Luigi	1846-1922	Composer					AMusQS 50-110
D'Eon, Charles de Beaumont		Adventurer	100		400		Louis XV's secret agent to Russ
Depardieu, Gerard		Entertainment	10			35	
Depew, Chauncey M.	1834-1928	Financier	50	140	285	475	Orator,NY Centr. RR, U.S. Sen.NY.
Depp, Johnny		Entertainment	11		40	46	Actor
Deprez, Gérard M.J.		Political	10			15	Member European Parliament

NAME	DATE	CATEGORY	SIG	LS/DS	ALS	SP	COMMENTS
Deprume, Cathryn		Entertainment	10			20	actress
Derain, André	1880-1954	Artist	125	210	342		Postimpression Fauvist.Repro Femme Nu Assise S285
Derby, Edw. Henry Stanley	1826-1893	Statesman	20		59		15th Earl of Derby. Sec'y of the Colonies
Derby, Edward Stanley	1799-1869	Head of State	50	60	102		14th Earl. Br. Prime Minister
Derek & Dominoes (all)		Entertainment	50			150	
Derek, Bo		Entertainment	16	20	25	50	Actress
Derek, John & Bo		Entertainment	20			75	Husband & Wife
Derek, John	1926-1998	Entertainment	15	28	35	48	Actor-Photographer
Deringer, Henry	1786-1868	Arms Mfg.	700		6500		Invented Derringer Pistol
Derleth, August		Author	20	75			
Dern, Bruce		Entertainment	6	8	15	32	Actor
Dern, George H.		Cabinet	10	20	35		Sec'y War, Mining Exec.,Gov. UT
Dern, Laura		Entertainment	8	10	25	35	Actress, Daughter of Bruce Dern
Derr, Richard		Entertainment	10			25	Actor
D'Errico, Donna		Entertainment	7			39	Actress
Dershowitz, Alan M.		Law	15	20		30	Trial Attorney, Author
Desai, M.R.		Head of State	5	15	25		Prime Minister India
Desanto, Sugar Pie		Entertainment	15			35	James Brown Vocalist
Descamps, Marie-Hélène		Political	10			15	Member European Parliament
Descartes, Rene		Philosopher	950	4035	10000		Mathematician.Analytic Geometry
Deschanel, Paul Eugène L.	1856-1922	Head of State			100		Pres. France 1920. Resigned
Descher, Sandy		Entertainment				30	Child Actress
Deshler, James	1833-1863	Civil War	372				Confederate general, KIA Chickamauga, GA
DeSilva, Howard		Entertainment	10	12	20	25	
Desmond, Johnny		Entertainment	3	5		8	Singer
Desmond, Shaw	1877-1960	Author	25	75			Irish Playwright. Pioneered Paranormal
Desmond, William		Entertainment	40				Vintage Film Actor
Desperado (cast)		Entertainment				85	Banderas / Hayek
Despretz, César		Science	5		30		Fr. Physician. Inventor Electric Arc Furnace
Dessalines, Jean-Jacques	1750-1806	Revolutionary		2500			Haitian Ruler
D'Estaing, V. Gistard		Head of State	15	40	100	60	Pres. France
Destinn, Emmy	1878-1930	Entertainment	110		225	325	Czech Dramatic Soprano
Detaille, Edwouard	1848-1912	Artist	110		325		Fr. Military & Portr. Painter
DeTreville, Yvonne		Entertainment	20			85	Opera, Light Opera
Deutekom, Cristina		Entertainment	10			35	Dutch Coloratura Soprano. Opera
Deutsch, Emery		Bandleader	5				
Deutsch, Patti		Entertainment	3	3	6	8	
Deutsch, Peter D		Congress	10			15	Member U.S. Congress
Deva, Nirj		Political	10			15	Member European Parliament
DeVane, William		Entertainment	8	10	12	23	Actor
Devens, Charles,	1820-1891	Military -Cabinet	69	88	108	250	Union Gen.-Att'y Gen.
Devereux, James P.S.		Military	35	70	90	150	Gen. WW II, Congress MD
Devers, Jacob L.	1887-1979	Military	30	45	60	60	General WW II
Devine, Andy	1905-1977	Entertainment	40	45	50	141	Comic Sidekick of Roy Rogers
Devine, Brig. Gen. James G.	1895-1972	Military	30				World War II U.S. general

NAME	DATE	CATEGORY	SIG	LS/DS	ALS	SP	COMMENTS
Devine, Magenta		Celebrity	10			15	television presenter
Devine, Maj. Gen. John M.	1895-1971	Military	30				World War II U.S. general
DeVito, Danny		Entertainment	7	15	20	32	As The Penguin 75. 'Get Shorty' Script S 50
Devlin, J. Greg		Author	8			12	
Devo		Entertainment	30			85	Rock Band
DeVoe, Brig. Gen. Ralph G.	1883-1966	Military	30				World War II U.S. general
DeVos, Rich		Business	18			25	Founder Amway
DeVries, William, Dr.		Science	15	25	40	20	
Dew, William, Bishop		Clergy	20	30	45		
Dewar, James		Science	85		375		Prof. Chemistry R.I., London. Liquified Air
DeWeese, Linda		Author	8			12	author and lecturer on abuse of women
Dewey, George	1837-1917	Military	78	157	190	300	Captured Manila. Span.-Am. War. Admiral
Dewey, John	1859-1952	Author	60	155	250	200	Philosopher, Educator, Psychol.
Dewey, Orville		Clergy	15	20	25		
Dewey, Thomas E.	1902-1971	Governor	40	79	165	95	Twice Presidential Candidate, Gov. NY
Dewhurst, Colleen		Entertainment	10		35	40	
DeWine, Mike		Senate	10			15	United States Senate (R - OH)
Dewing, Maj Gen Maurice Nelson	1896-1976	Military	25				World War II British general
Dewing, Maj. Gen. Richard Henry	1891-1981	Military	25				World War II British general
DeWitt, Brig. Gen. Calvin Jr.	1894-1989	Military	30				World War II U.S. general
DeWitt, Brig. Gen. Wallace	1878-1949	Military	30				World War II U.S. general
DeWitt, General John L.	1880-1962	Military	30				World War II U.S. general
DeWitt, Joyce		Entertainment	5	8	15	20	
DeWolf, H.G.		Military	5	15		20	Canadian Adm. WW II
DeWolfe, Billy	1907-1974	Entertainment	25	40	45	45	Actor. 'Prissy' Stage-Film Comic
Dexter, Al		Country Western	12			45	Western Singing Star of 40's.'Piston Packin' Mama'
Dexter, J.M.		Clergy	10	15	20		
Dexter, Timothy	1747-1806	Colonial-Rev.		175	275		Merchant, Speculator
Dey, Susan		Entertainment	7	10	20	26	Actress
DeYoung, Russell		Business	5			10	CEO Goodyear Tire & Rubber Co.
Díez González, Rosa M.		Political	10			15	Member European Parliament
Dhaene, Jan		Political	10			15	Member European Parliament
Dharma & Greg		Entertainment				200	Cast signed photo
Di Lello Finuoli, Giuseppe		Political	10			15	Member European Parliament
Di Pietro, Antonio		Political	10			15	Member European Parliament
Di Stefano, Giuseppe	1921-	Entertainment	30		65	75	It. TenorOpera
Diaghilev, Sergei	1872-1929	Entertainment	435	975	2250		Russian Ballet Impresario. Developed Ballet Russes
Diamond, Ann		Celebrity	10			15	television presenter
Diamond, David		Composer	25		35		AMusQS 200
Diamond, Domonik		Celebrity	10			15	television presenter
Diamond, Jack "Legs"	1897-1931	Criminal			1955		Bootlegger
Diamond, Neil		Entertainment	12	25	40	65	Composer-Singer. Difficult to Obtain
Diamond, Selma		Entertainment	20	25	30	50	
Diana, Princess (Eng)	1961-1997	Royalty	828	1517	2700	3264	Princess of Wales, signed Christmas cards 1500-3000
Diane E. Watson		Senate	10			15	Member U.S. Congress

NAME	DATE	CATEGORY	SIG	LS/DS	ALS	SP	COMMENTS
Diaz, Armando Vittorio		Military	35	100	175	120	It. General WW I
Diaz, Cameron	1973-	Entertainment	20			68	Actress
Diaz, Porfirio	1830-1915	Head of State	100	259	425	225	Dictatorial Pres.Mex. Fought Against Fr.Occupation
Diaz-Balart, Lincoln D		Congress	10			15	Member U.S. Congress
Diaz-Balart, Mario D		Congress	10			15	Member U.S. Congress
Dibdin, Thomas John	1771-1841	Actor			85		
Dibrell, George Gibbs (WD)		Civil War	290	546			CSA General
Dibrell, George Gibbs	1822-1888	Civil War	175	320	448		CSA General, MOC TN
DiCaprio, Leonardo		Entertainment	12			73	Actor
Dice Clay, Andrew		Entertainment	10			20	Comedian
Dicillo, Tom		Celebrity	10			15	film industry
Dick, Andy		Celebrity	10			20	Comedian
Dick, Fred		Aviation	10	22	40	30	ACE, WW II
Dick, Samuel	1740-1812	Revolutionary War	50	175	225		Continental Congress NJ. Col. 1st Battalion
Dickens, Charles	1812-1870	Author	529	948	1832	6280	Br. Novelist.'Christmas Carol', ALS cont 5000
Dickens, Charles	1837-1896	Celebrity			110		Eldest son of Charles Dickens
Dickens, Jimmy		Country Music	5			10	
Dickerson, Mahlon	1770-1853	Cabinet-U.S. Sen.	25	85	150		Jackson Sec'y Navy. Gov. NJ
Dickerson, Nancy		Journalist	3			12	Broadcast News Pioneer
Dickey, James	1923-	Author	15	75	135	55	Am. Poet, Novelist 'Deliverance'. Deceased
Dickey, Nancy Wilson		Physician	10			15	medical expert
Dickinson, Angie		Entertainment	6	14	18	35	Actress
Dickinson, Anna Eliz.	1842-1932	Author	25	70	142		Abolitionist-Lecturer
Dickinson, Clarence		Entertainment	15			95	Legendary Organist
Dickinson, Clement C.		Senate/Congress	5			15	MOC MO
Dickinson, Daniel S.		Senate/Congress	15	25			Senator from NY
Dickinson, Don M.		Cabinet	10	20			P.M. Gen. 1888
Dickinson, Emily		Author	750	2560	7250		Autographed Poem signed 20,000
Dickinson, Jacob M.	1851-1928	Cabinet	25	45	125		Taft Sec'y of War
Dickinson, James S.		Civil War	56	78	75		CSA Congressman
Dickinson, John P.		Revolutionary War	200	382			Continental Congress. Statesman, Administrator
Dickinson, Maj. Gen. Douglas P.	1886-1949	Military	28				World War II British general
Dickison, J. J.		Civil War	75	155	195		CSA Cav'ry Off.,Florida's Mosby
Dickman, Joseph		Military	50				General WW I
Dicks, Jacob		Governor	15	25	40		Governor NY
Dicks, Norman D. D		Congress	10			15	Member U.S. Congress
Diddley, Bo	1928-	Entertainment	20			85	R & B Singer-Composer-Guitarist. Rock HOF
Didelet, Maj. Gen. Henri-Antoine	1886-1945	Military	20				World War II French general
Didier-Pouget, W.		Artist	30	65	95		
Diefenbaker, John	1895-1979	Head of State	35	45	110	75	Prime Minister Canada
Diem, Ngo Dinh		Head of State	50				Pres. So. Viet Nam
Diemer, Louis		Composer	25			45	Fr. Pianist. AMusQS 100
Diemer, Walter E.		Business	20		75	90	Inventor Dubble Bubble Gum
Dies, Martin		Senate/Congress	15	50		25	MOC TX. Un-American Activities
Diesel, Rudolf		Science	900		3250		Ger. Mech. Engineer. Diesel Eng

NAME	DATE	CATEGORY	SIG	LS/DS	ALS	SP	COMMENTS
Diesel, Vin		Entertainment	10			45	Actor
Diesenhofer, Johann, Dr.		Science	20	25		40	Nobel Chemistry
Dieterle, William		Entertainment	30			75	Film Dirctor
Dietl, Colonel-General Eduard	1890-1944	Military	25			242	World War II German general
Dietrich, Dena		Entertainment	5			10	Mother Nature (Commercial)
Dietrich, Josef 'Sepp'	1892-1966	Military	195	690			SS Commander
Dietrich, Marlene	1901-1992	Entertainment	38	76	125	148	Actress
Digence, Richard		Celebrity	10			15	comedian
Dilke, Charles W. 2d Baronet		Author	10	25	45		Br. Travel Books, Politician
Dill, Field Marshal Sir John Greer	1881-1944	Military	25				World War II British general
Dillards		Entertainment	25			65	Herb, Dean, Rodney, Merle
Dillen, Karel C.C.		Political	10			15	Member European Parliament
Diller, Brig. Gen. LeGrande A.	1901-1987	Military	30				World War II U.S. general
Diller, Phyllis		Entertainment	6	9	15	20	Comedienne. Housewife Turned Funny-Girl
Dillinger, John		Criminal					DS - Typed Confession Signed 14,000. RARE
Dillingham, T.J.		Author	8			12	religion
Dillman, Bradford		Entertainment	8	9	15	15	
Dillon, Brig. Gen. Theodore H.	1884-1961	Military	30				World War II U.S. general
Dillon, C. Douglas		Cabinet	10	25	30	25	Ambassador, Diplomat
Dillon, Kevin		Entertainment	4			20	
Dillon, Matt		Entertainment	10	15	20	39	Actor
Dillon, R. Crawford		Clergy	15	45	60		
Dillon, Sidney		Business	283	590	723		RR Baron-Union Pacific RR. Jay Gould Aide
Dimbleby, David		Celebrity	10			15	television presenter
Dimbleby, Jonathan		Celebrity	10			15	television presenter
Dimbleby, Josceline		Celebrity	10			15	TV Chef
Dimitrakopoulos, Giorgos		Political	10			15	Member European Parliament
Dimitrova, Ghena		Entertainment	10			35	Opera
Dimmock, Charlie		Celebrity	10			15	home/gardening expert
Dimoline, Maj Gen William Alfred	1897-1965	Military	25				World War II British general
D'Indy, Vincent	1851-1931	Composer	40	125	362	375	Fr.Opera,Orchestral,Vocal Music AMusQS 300
Dinesen, Isak (Karen Blixen)	1885-1962	Author	100	500		500	Danish. Out of Africa
Dingell, John D. D		Congress	10			15	Member U.S. Congress
Dingley, Nelson, Jr.		Congress	10	20	35		Governor, Repr. ME
Dinkins, David	1927-	Political	15	35		17	1st Afr.Am. Mayor NYC
Dinning Sisters (3)		Entertainment	10			15	Jean, Jayne, Ginger
Dion, Celine		Entertainment	10			65	Singer. Grammy Winner
Dior, Christian		Fashion	85	170		175	Fashion Designer
Dippel, Andreas		Entertainment	35			125	Ger. Tenor. Impresario. Opera
Dire Straits		Entertainment	30			110	
Dirks, Rudolph*	1877-1968	Cartoonist	70		175	400	Katzenjammer Kids
Dirksen, Everett M.	1896-1967	Senate	20	58		40	Senator, MOC IL. Powerful Political Figure
Disney, Roy E.		Business	20	55		30	Brother of Walt. Disney Exec.
Disney, Walter E. (Walt)	1901-1966	Business	931	2675	3467	2681	Animated Film Producer, check signed 1500-2000
Disque, Brig. Gen. Brice P.	1879-1960	Military	30				World War II U.S. general

NAME	DATE	CATEGORY	SIG	LS/DS	ALS	SP	COMMENTS
Disraeli, Benjamin,	1804-1881	Head of State	147	154	679		Prime Minister, Novelist, Lord Beaconsfield
Disraeli, Isaac	1766-1848	Author	30	140	165		Br. Man of Letters. Novels
Ditka, Mike		Celebrity	10			25	motivational speaker
Ditmars, Raymond L.	1876-1942	Science	72				Herpetologist, Zoo Curator, Author
Ditto, Brig. Gen. Rollo C.	1886-1947	Military	30				World War II U.S. general
Divine		Entertainment	52			75	Rock. Short-lived Popularity
Divine, M.J., 'Father' (Geo. Baker)		Clergy	150	483	700	225	Communal Religious Soc., Rejected Matrimonya..
Dix, Dorothea L.	1794-1887	Civil War	98	188	472		Union Superintendent of Nurses. Social Reformer
Dix, Dorothy (Eliz. Gilmer)		Author	15	30	45	25	Am. Journalist, Editor, Advice
Dix, John Adams (WD)		Civil War	75	160	297		Union Gen.
Dix, John Adams	1798-1879	Civil War-Cabinet	40	98	114	300	Union Gen., Sec'y Treasury
Dix, Morgan		Clergy	25	35	50		Abolitionist
Dix, Richard		Entertainment	25	40	65	68	Vintage Movie Star
Dix, Robert		Entertainment				25	
Dixey, Henry E.	1859-1943	Entertainment	10	20	30	25	1st Success as Adonis
Dixie Chicks		Entertainment	20			116	Country Western trio
Dixon, Dean		Entertainment	35			175	Conductor. 1st Afro-Am. To Conduct NY Philharmonic
Dixon, Donna		Entertainment	8	10	15	20	Actress. Pin-Up 40
Dixon, Jeane		Celebrity	10			15	Forecasts the Future
Dixon, Julian C.		Senate/Congress	10	15		15	Afro-Am Dem. MOC CA
Dixon, Maj. Gen. Bernard Edw. C.	1896-1973	Military	25				World War II British general
Dixon, Thomas	1864-1946	Author-Clergy	15	30	75		The Clansman. Social Critic
Dixon, Willie		Entertainment	50			100	Rock HOF. Late Blues Man
Dizengoff, Meir	1861-1936	Celebrity	50	162	350		Early Jewish Settler in Palestine. Founder Tel Aviv
Djerassi, Carl		Celebrity	10			15	medical expert
Dmytryk, Edward	1908-	Entertainment	20			40	Film Director. Member Hollywood Ten
Dnhrkop Dnhrkop, Bárbara		Political	10			15	Member European Parliament
Doane, G.W.		Clergy		20	25	35	
Dobbie, Lt. Gen. Sir Wm. Geo. S.	1879-1964	Military	25				World War II British general
Dobbin, James C.	1814-1857	Cabinet	30	75	150		Pierce Sec'y Navy
Dobbin, John F.		Aviation	20	40	65	45	ACE, WW II, Marine Ace
Dobbs, Lou		Celebrity	10			15	financial expert
Dobehoff, F.L.		Aviation	15	50		75	
Dobie, Charles Cald.		Author	5	10	15	15	
Dobie, J. Frank		Author	20	50	130	75	Folklorist & Western Author
Dobrinyin, Anatole		Head of State	29	130	375	75	U.S.S.R. Political Power
Dobson, Kevin		Entertainment	5	6	15	15	
Docherty, Jack		Celebrity	10			15	television presenter
Dockery, Thomas P. (WD)	1833-1898	Civil War	275	490			CSA Gen.
Dockery, Thomas P.	1833-1898	Civil War	95	368	395		CSA General
Docking, Robert		Governor	5	15	22		Governor KS
Dockstader, Lew		Entertainment	75				
Doctorow, E. L.		Author	15	35	90	30	Am. Novelist. Ragtime
Doda, Carol		Entertainment	6			25	Actress. Pin-Up 40
Dodd, Christopher J.		Senate/Congress	5	15		10	Senator, MOC CT

NAME	DATE	CATEGORY	SIG	LS/DS	ALS	SP	COMMENTS
Dodd, Thomas J.		Senate & Congress	20	40	65	30	Chief of Counsel at Nuremberg
Dodd, William E.		Historian	15	60	75	25	Ambassador to Nazi Germany
Dodderidge, Philip		Clergy	25	35	45		
Dodge, Charles C.	1841-1910	Civil War	36	48	83		Union Gen.
Dodge, Grenville M. (WD)	1831-1916	Civil War	110	275	410		Union Gen.,Repr. IA.LS/Cont. 1950
Dodge, Grenville M.	1831-1916	Civil War	88	195	304	375	Post-War RR Tycoon. Stk.Cert.S 1750-2850
Dodge, Henry	1782-1867	Congress			45		Gov. Wisc.Terr.,1st Sen.,Indian Fighter
Dodge, Jerry		Entertainment	3	3	6	6	
Dodge, Joseph M.		Business	10	25	50		Banker, Built Jap. Economy
Dodge, Mary Abigail	1833-1896	Author	12	20	25		Am. Novelist
Dodge, Mary Mapes	1831-1905	Author	25	40	90	100	Children's Books.'Hans Brinker & the Silver Skates
Dodge, Theodore A.		Author	35				
Dodge, William Earl	1805-1883	Business	95	482	675		Phelps, Dodge & Co. YMCA Fndr.
Dodge, William G.		Civil War	25	55	85		
Dodgson, Charles L.	1832-1898	Author	275	1006	1884		Lewis Carroll 'Alice in Wonderland'
Dods, Marcus		Clergy	40	45	60		
Dodson, Jack		Entertainment	15	15	18	25	Actor. 'Andy Griffith Show' SP 45
Doe, Maj. Gen. Jens A.	1891-1971	Military	30				World War II U.S. general
Doenitz, Karl	1891-1980	Military	80	166	309	171	Ger. Adm., WW II.TLS/Cont. 7500, FDC S 90
Doerflinger, Joseph		Aviation	10		75	45	
Doering, Arnold		Aviation	10	20	35	25	
Doggett, Lloyd D		Congress	10			15	Member U.S. Congress
Dohanos, Stevan		Illustrator	5	15			
Doherty, Shannon		Entertainment	14			42	Actress.Pinup, SP 50
Dohihara, General Kenji	1883-1948	Military	25				World War II Japanese general
Dohnanyi, Erno von	1877-1960	Composer	55	135	165		Hung. Conductor. AMQS 350
Dohrn, Bernardine		Criminal					Terrorist. FBI Fingerprint Card S 150
Doi, Takao		Astronaut	15	25		25	
Doig, Andrew Wheeler		Senate/Congress	10	20			MOC NY 1839, Banker, Mining
Doisy, Edward A.		Science	20	45	78	50	Nobel Medicine. Vitamin K
Dolby, Ray		Science	20	35			Inventor Dolby Sound
Dolby, Thomas		Entertainment	20			40	
Dole, Charles F		Clergy	10	15	20		
Dole, Elizabeth		Senate	10			25	United States Senate (R - NC)
Dole, James D.		Business	55	145	235	175	Fdr.Hawaiian Pineapple Industry
Dole, Robert		Senate	20	20		75	Senator KS. Majority Ldr. Presidential Candidate
Dole, Sanford B.	1844-1926	Business	50	186	245	175	Pres. Repub.HI.1st Pres.Dole Pineapple.Chk.S 325
Dolenz, Ami		Entertainment	6			30	Pin-Up 45
Dolenz, Mickey		Entertainment	10		25	40	'The Monkees'
Doles, George Pierce	1830-1864	Civil War	350				Confederate general
Dolin, Anton		Entertainment	25	40	95	75	Ballet
Dollar, Robert	1844-1932	Business	20	55	130	50	Founder & Pres. Dollar Steamship Line.
Dolliver, Jonathan P.		Senate & Congress	20	35		25	Senator, MOC IA 1889
Dollmann, Col. General Friedrich	1882-1944	Military	25				World War II German general
Dolukanova, Zara		Entertainment	75				Rare SPc of Great Contralto 250

NAME	DATE	CATEGORY	SIG	LS/DS	ALS	SP	COMMENTS
Domenici, Pete		Senate	10			15	United States Senate (R - NM)
Domerque, Faith		Entertainment	12			40	Actress
Domingo, Placido		Entertainment	20		45	60	Opera, Concert
Dominguez, Oscar	1906-1957	Artist	70		250		Sp. Surrealist Artist
Dominick, Fred H.		Senate & Congress	5	15		10	MOC SC 1917-33
Domino, Fats	1928-	Entertainment	17	25	35	61	R&B Singer-Pianist-Composer.Rock HOF. AMusQS 376
Don, Monty		Celebrity	10			15	home/gardening expert
Donahue, Al		Entertainment	15			75	Big Band Leader
Donahue, Archie		Aviation	12	25	50	45	ACE, WW II, Ace in one day
Donahue, Elinor		Entertainment	5	6	15	24	'Father Knows Best' Actress.
Donahue, Phil		Entertainment	5			25	Tv host
Donahue, Troy	d. 2001	Entertainment	6	7	15	52	Actor. 60's Warner Bros. Star
Donaldson, Brig. Gen. Wm. H. Jr.	1894-1948	Military	30				World War II U.S. general
Donaldson, Jesse M.		Cabinet	10	20	35	25	1st Postman Becomes P.M. Gen.
Donaldson, Sam		Journalist	10			20	TV News Anchor, Commentator
Donan, Stanley		Celebrity	10			15	film industry
Donat, Peter	1928-	Entertainment	5	6	15	15	Canadian Character Actor
Donat, Robert	1905-1958	Entertainment	60	75	100	222	Br. From Shakespeare (30's)to AA 'Goodby Mr Chips'
Donat, Zdislawa		Entertainment	5			25	Opera
Donath, Ludwig	1900-1967	Entertainment	5			25	Played Al Jolson's Father. WW II Anti Nazi Films
Donavan, Elisa		Celebrity				35	
Donavon		Music				60	
Donelson, Daniel Smith	1801-1863	Civil War	325				Confederate general
Doniphan, Alexander William		Military	120	250	475		Fought Mex., Indians, Mormans
Donizetti, Gaetano	1797-1848	Composer	500	800	1442		AMusQS 2,750,AMusMs 3,000. ALS/Cont. 4750
Donlan, Roger		Military	10	25	40	30	
Donleavy, James Patrick	1926-	Writer		80			
Donlevy, Brian	1899-1972	Entertainment	20			100	Ir.With Pershing vs Pancho Villa.Pilot WW I.ACTOR
Donnell, Jeff	1921-	Entertainment	5	6	10	10	Columbia Pictures Teen-age Starlet. 2nd Leads
Donnelly, Ruth		Entertainment	10	15	25	25	Chorine-Stage-Films 1927 & Next 30 Years
Donner, Clive		Entertainment	5			25	Film Director
Donner, Richard		Entertainment	10			20	
Donner, Vyvyan		Editor	5			15	Fashion
Donohoe, Amanda		Entertainment	10			20	Actress
Donovan, Hedley		Editor	5	6	15	10	Time-Life Editor
Donovan, Jason		Entertainment	10			20	Actor
Donovan, King	1919-1987	Entertainment	15			25	Actor. Character- Supporting Roles
Donovan, Maj. Gen. Leo	1895-1950	Military	30				World War II U.S. general
Donovan, Maj. Gen. Richard	1885-1949	Military	30				World War II U.S. general
Donovan, Raymond J.		Cabinet	8	15	30	15	Sec'y Labor
Donovan, Wm. J. 'Wild Bill'	1883-1959	Military	80	217	325	100	Fighting 69th, OSS-CIA
Doobie Brothers		Entertainment	40			80	Signed by all
Doohan, James 'Scotty'		Entertainment	10	12	25	40	Star Trek Actor
Dooley, Calvin M. D.		Congress	10			15	Member U.S. Congress
Dooley, Paul		Entertainment	5	6	15	15	

NAME	DATE	CATEGORY	SIG	LS/DS	ALS	SP	COMMENTS
Dooley, Thomas A., Dr.	1927-1961	Science	125	185	400	250	Jungle Physician, SE Asia. Medical Mission
Dooling, Brig. Gen. Henry C.	1887-1972	Military	30				World War II U.S. general
Doolittle, Hilda	1886-1961	Author	75	205	475		Imagist Poet. Ed. 'The Egoist' Rare
Doolittle, James H.	1896-1993	Aviation	68	143	275	90	Gen. WW II, Test Pilot. Bombed Tokyo. Hero/MOH
Doolittle, James Rood		Senate	15	25	40		Civil War Senator WI
Doolittle, John T. D.		Congress	10			15	Member U.S. Congress
Doorn, Bert		Political	10			15	Member European Parliament
Doors & Jim Morrison (4)		Entertainment	1322	1531		1870	Rock, signed album 2527
Doors, The (3)		Entertainment	100	165		150	Rock 'Doors' Alb. 125
Doran, Ann	1914-	Entertainment	15	15	25	20	Am. Character Actress. Supporting Roles
Doran, Brig. Gen. Charles R.	1892-1984	Military	30				World War II U.S. general
Dorati, Antal		Conductor	15	25		85	Hung.-born
Dore, Gustave	1832-1883	Artist					French book illustrator 19th century., signed drw6650
Doré, Paul Gustave	1833-1883	Artist	60	235	508		Fantastic Imagination. Illustrated over 90 Books
Dorff, Stephen		Entertainment	10			20	actor
Dorfman, Dan		Celebrity	10			15	financial expert
Dorgan, Byron		Senate	10			15	United States Senate (D - ND)
Dorman-Smith, Maj. Gen. Eric	1895-1969	Military	25				World War II British general
Dorn, Brig. Gen. Frank	1901-1981	Military	30				World War II U.S. general
Dorn, Michael		Entertainment	10			20	actor
Dornan, Robert K.		Congress	4			20	MOC CA.
Dornberger, Walter R.	1895-1980	Science	40	100	120	75	Ger. Rocket Engineer. Bell Aircraft. FDC 225
Dorr, Julia C. R.	1825-1913	Author	4	5	15		Best Known for 10 Volumes of Poetry
Dorr, Thomas	1805-1854	Reformer		750	1250		Politician. Formed Own Party. Led 'Dorr Rebellion'
Dors, Diana	1931-1984	Entertainment	20			151	British 'Blonde Bombshell' of 40s.
D'Orsay, Alfred, Count	1801-1852	Artist	25	65	170		Fr.Wit, Fashion Arbiter, Society Leader
D'Orsay, Fifi		Entertainment	15	20	35	28	Fr. Canadian Actress. Vaudeville & 30's Films
Dorsey, Jimmy	1905-1956	Entertainment	50	150		157	Big Band Leader-Saxophone
Dorsey, Stephen	1842-1916	Business	35		125		RR Promoter. Rep. Sen. AR. Fraudulent RR Scandal
Dorsey, Tommy	1905-1956	Entertainment	75	150		135	Big Band Leader-Trombone
Dortch, William T.		Civil War	25	40	75		CSA Senator NC
Dos Passos, John	1896-1970	Author	20	50	75	60	Am. Novelist. Prolific Writer
Dos Santos, Manuel António		Political	10			15	Member European Parliament
Dostler, Gen. of Infantry Anton	1891-1945	Military	25				World War II German general
Dostoevsky, Fyodor	1821-1881	Author	1500	5700	13800		Rus. Novelist. 'Crime & Punishment'
Doty, James	1799-1865	Explorer	50		185		Politician, Land Speculator. C.W.Territorial Gov.
Doubleday, Abner	1819-1893	Civil War	391	700	900		Union Gen.-Credit for Inventing Baseball
Doubleday, Frank Nelson	1862-1934	Business	65	185	375		Book Publisher
Douce, Francis	1757-1834	Antiquary			120		
Doucette, John		Entertainment	6	8	15	20	Familiar Face & Voice. Excellent Supporting Actor
Doucette, Paul		Entertainment	6			25	Music. Drummer 'Matchbox 20'
Doug, Doug E.		Entertainment	10			20	actor
Dougherty, Dennis, Cardinal		Clergy	35	50	65	40	Card'l & Archbishop of Philadelphia
Douglas, Beverly B.		Civil War	35	50	65		CSA Officer, MOC VA
Douglas, Chas. W.H.	1850-1914	Military	25	70	195		Br. Gen.

NAME	DATE	CATEGORY	SIG	LS/DS	ALS	SP	COMMENTS
Douglas, Christopher		Entertainment	10			20	actor
Douglas, Donald W. Jr.		Business	25	60		45	Douglas Aircraft
Douglas, Donald W. Sr.	1892-1981	Aviation	150	257	450	360	Pioneer Aircraft Mfg. FDC S by Sr. & Jr. 250
Douglas, Donna	1933-	Entertainment	7	8	10	25	Actress. 'Ellie Mae' in TVs 'Beverly Hillbillies'
Douglas, Eric		Entertainment	9			18	Son of Kirk Douglas
Douglas, Helen Gahagan	1900-1980	Cong-Entertainment	30	55	98	55	MOC CA, Opera, Actress
Douglas, Jerry		Entertainment	10			20	actor
Douglas, Kirk	1916-	Entertainment	18	38	20	49	Versatile Actor. Lifetime Achiement Award
Douglas, Leon		Country Music	10			20	
Douglas, Lloyd C.	1877-1951	Author	25	45	75	30	Retired Minister.'The Robe','Magnificent Obsession
Douglas, Melvyn	1901-1981	Entertainment	20	23	30	52	Oscar Winning Film Actor. Tony Award for Stage
Douglas, Michael		Entertainment	20		25	51	Actor, AA
Douglas, Mike		Entertainment	5	6	10	16	Singer. Early TV Host
Douglas, Paul H.		Senate	10	20		15	Senator IL
Douglas, Paul P.		Aviation	15	25	45	35	ACE, WW II
Douglas, Paul	1907-1959	Entertainment	10	15		35	Pro-Football,Sportscaster,News.'48 'Born Yesterday
Douglas, Robert	1909-	Entertainment	10			25	Br.Actor. Leads & Supporting Parts
Douglas, Stephen A.	1813-1861	Senate	122	252	467	650	Statesman, Pres. Candidate. Debated vs Lincoln
Douglas, W. Sholto	1893-1969	Military	45			75	Br. Air Marshall. D-Day Coastal Operations
Douglas, William O.	1898-1980	Supreme Court	65	195	230	365	SC Judge
Douglas, William Taylor		Clergy	15	20	25		
Douglas-Home, Alec		Head of State	45	70	150	135	Br. Prime Minister
Douglass, Frederick	1817-1895	Abolitionist	262	570	4589	6325	Afro-Am. Author, Lecturer, Editor, Abolitionist
Douglass, Robyn		Entertainment	5	4	9	12	Pin-Up 32
Doulton, Henry, Sir	1820-1897	Potter-Inventor	25	35	145		Royal Doulton China & Appliances. Art Pottery
Doumer, Paul	1857-1932	Head of State	60		100		Pres. France 1931-32. Assassinated
Doumergue, Gaston	1863-1937	Head of State			195		Pres. France., P.M. France
Dove, Billie		Entertainment	10	15	30	40	30's Movie Star. Vintage SP 55
Dover, Den		Political	10			15	Member European Parliament
Dow, Charles H.	1851-1902	Business		1295			Dow-Jones
Dow, Neal	1804-1897	Civil War	40	75	175		Union Gen., Temperance Reformer
Dow, Tony		Entertainment	5	6	10	23	Actor., Wally Cleaver
Dowden, Edward	1843-1913	Author	10	15	25		Ir. Critic, Editor, Professor, Author
Dowding, Hugh C., Lord	1882-1970	Military	95		535		Br. Air Chief Marshal, Architect 'Battle of Brit'.
Dowler, Lt. Gen. Sir Arthur	1895-1963	Military	25				World War II British general
Dowling, Eddie	1895-1975	Entertainment	20	25	55	45	Major Broadway Star. 'Harvey'. Tony Winner
Down, Lesley-Anne	1954-	Entertainment	9	6	15	22	Actress. Leading Lady of Br.-Am. Films. Pin-Up 45
Down, Lt. Gen. Sir Ernest Edward	1902-1980	Military	25				World War II British general
Downes, Maj. Gen. Rupert M.	1885-1945	Military	20				World War II Australian general
Downey Jr., Robert		Entertainment	10			42	actor
Downey, Morton	1901-1985	Entertainment	20	20	20	32	Irish Tenor-Bandleader
Downey, Robert, Jr.	1965-	Entertainment	25			53	Contemporary Actor Plagued by Drug Problems
Downey, Roma		Entertainment	16			50	Actress. 'Touched By An Angel'
Downey, Sheridan	1884-1951	Senate	10	35		20	Dem. Senator CA 1938-50
Downing, Big Al		Entertainment	4	3	6	12	

NAME	DATE	CATEGORY	SIG	LS/DS	ALS	SP	COMMENTS
Downing, George, Sir	1623-1684	Statesman-Dipl	317	535			2nd Harvard Grad. Developed Downing St., So Named
Downliners Sect		Entertainment				75	Br. Rock Group (All 5)
Downs, Brig. Gen. Sylvester D. Jr.	1889-1957	Military	30				World War II U.S. general
Downs, Hugh	1921-	Entertainment	10	20	25	22	TV Co-Host 20/20. Perennial Host
Downs, Johnny	1913-1995	Entertainment	35			75	Actor 'Our Gang'.Broadway, Vaudeville, Films
Doyen, Lt. Gen. Paul-André	1881-1974	Military	20				World War II French general
Doyle, Arthur Conan, Sir	1859-1930	Author-Physician	583	870	1379	1750	Br. Novelist. Created 'Sherlock Holmes'
Doyle, Avril		Political	10			15	Member European Parliament
Doyle, Dinty		Journalist	5	20			Columnist
Doyle, Michael F. D		Congress	10			15	Member U.S. Congress
Doyle, Wendy		Celebrity	10			15	Research Dietician
D'Oyly Carte, Rupert		Entertainment	25	70	125	135	Producer of Original Gilbert & Sullivan Operettas
D'Oyly, George		Clergy	15	20	35		
Dozier, James		Military	12	30	45	20	
Dozier, Lamont		Entertainment	6			25	Singer/Songwriter
Dr. Dre		Entertainment	15			35	
Drabble, Margaret		Author	10	20	50		Br. Novelist, Editor
Dragonette, Jessica	1910-1980	Entertainment	15	20	25	50	Soprano. Radio, Stage Star 30s-40s
Dragoni, Maria		Entertainment	10			30	Opera
Drain, Brig. Gen. Jesse C.	1883-1974	Military	30				World War II U.S. general
Drake, Alfred	1914-1992	Entertainment	17			32	Singer-Actor. Musical Theatre, Concert
Drake, Betsy	1923-	Entertainment	5			15	Actress & Mrs. Cary Grant (Once upon a Time)
Drake, Brig. Gen. Charles C.	1887-1984	Military	30				World War II U.S. general
Drake, David		Author	25			50	military science fiction/fantasy
Drake, Frances	1906-1997	Entertainment	9	10	15	30	Am. Leading Lady of the 30s
Drake, Francis M.		Governor	10	25			Gov. IA. RR Builder. Fndr. Drake Univ.
Drake, Michele		Entertainment	4			15	Pin-Up SP 20
Drake, Samuel Adams	1833-1905	Civil War	28		55		Author
Drake, Stan*		Cartoonist	20			100	'Blondie'
Drake, Tom	1918-1992	Entertainment	5	6	8	20	Actor. The Boy Next Door in Many 40's Films
Drake-Brockman, Brig. Geoffrey	1886-1977	Military	30				World War II Australian general
Draper, Eben S.		Governor	5	12			Governor MA
Draper, Maj. Gen. William H. Jr.	1894-1974	Military	30				World War II U.S. general
Draper, Rusty		Country Music	5			15	Singer
Draper, Ruth	1884-1956	Entertainment	10	45	75	50	Am. Monologuist
Draper, William F.	1842-1910	Civil War	25	50			Union Brevet Brig. General
Draper, William H.		Clergy	20	35	40		
Drayton, Thomas F.	1808-1891	Civil War	95	250	290		CSA Gen..Sig./Rank 175. RR Stock S 295
Drayton, Gracie*		Cartoonist	20			188	Created Campbell Soup Kids
Drayton, William H.	1741-1779	Political		506			Congressman SC
Drees, Willem		Head of State	20	35	100		Survivor Buchenwald
Dreier, David D		Congress	10			15	Member U.S. Congress
Dreiser, Theodore	1871-1945	Author	70	200	300	300	'American Tragedy', 'Sister Carrie'.Magazine Editor
Drescher, Fran		Entertainment	15			38	Actress
Dresser, Louise	1878-1965	Entertainment	30			55	Broadway Musicals. Major Silent & Sound Film Star.

NAME	DATE	CATEGORY	SIG	LS/DS	ALS	SP	COMMENTS
Dressler, Marie	1869-1934	Entertainment	130			305	Vintage Actress. 1930 Academy Award 'Min & Bill'.
Drew, Daniel	1797-1879	Business	950	6800			'Great Bear of Wall Street' Fisk-Jay Gould
Drew, Ellen		Entertainment	6	8	13	15	Actress. 40's—. Pin-Up 32
Drew, John	1853-1927	Entertainment	60	75	185	100	Turn of the Century Stage Star
Drew, Maj. Gen. Sir James Syme	1883-1955	Military	25				World War II British general
Drewry, Brig. Gen. Guy H.	1894-1973	Military	30				World War II U.S. general
Drexel, Anthony J.	1826-1893	Banker		110			Fndr. Drexel, Morgan & Co. Stock Cert. S 975
Drexel, J. A.		Aviation	40	60	100	65	
Drexel, Joseph W.		Business					Drexel & Co. Phil., Established 1838. Stock S 1750
Dreyfus, Alfred	1859-1935	Military	145	300	802	1378	Framed for Treason, Sent to Devil's Isle.
Dreyfus, Julia Louis		Entertainment	17	45		49	Actress, 'Seinfeld'. Emmy Awards
Dreyfus, Lee Sherman		Celebrity	10			15	motivational speaker
Dreyfuss, Henry		Business		14	20		Self Sketch Henry 25
Dreyfuss, Richard		Entertainment	16	15	25	50	Talented, Versatile Actor. AA Winner
Dribrell, George Gibbs		Civil War	95	250	300		
Drinan, Robert, Father		Senate/Congress	5			15	Catholic Activist Priest
Drinkwater, John	1882-1937	Author	20	50	125	75	Poet, Playwright. Fndr., Mgr.'Pilgrim Players' '07
Driscoll, Bobby	1937-1968	Entertainment	145	155	190	373	AA '49. Best Child Actor. Died. Poverty-Drug Addict
Driver, Minnie		Entertainment	20			44	Actress
Driver, Samuel Rolles		Clergy	85	100	125		
Drouet, Robert		Entertainment	25	30	60	68	
Dru, Joanne	1923-	Entertainment	8			30	Actress. Screen, TV, Stage. Deceased
Druckman, Jacob		Composer	20	50	95		Pulitzer, AMusQS 250
Drudge, Matt		Celebrity	10			30	Internet journalist, http://drudgereport.com
Drum, Hugh A. Lt.Gen.		Military	25	55	125	50	General WW I, WW II
Drum, Richard C.	1825-1909	Civil War	30	58	93		Union General Sig/Rank 55, War Dte. DS 100
Drummond, Henry	1851-1897	Clergy	50	60	80		Scottish Evangelical Writer-Lecturer.
Drummond, James		Clergy	25	35	50		
Drury, Allen	1919-1998	Author	10	30	65	35	Novelist. Best Seller 'Advise & Consent' S 50
Drury, Frank		Aviation	10	25	40	30	ACE, WW II, Marine Ace
Drury, James		Entertainment	10			26	Actor. 'The Virginian' SP 25
Dryer, Fred		Entertainment	10		25	25	Actor TV Series 'Hunter'. Pro Football
Désir, Harlem		Political	10			15	Member European Parliament
Du Barry, Jeanne, Comtesse	1743-1793	Royal Mistress	285	960	1200		Louis XV Mistress. Banished, Arrested, Guillotined
Du Chaillu, Paul B.	1831-1903	Explorer	35	80	110	75	Brought 1st Gorillas out of Afr.
Du Maurier, Daphne, Dame		Author	45	140	150	65	Br. Novelist. 'Rebecca'
Du Maurier, George	1834-1896	Author	15	45	197		Artist, Novelist. Illustrator of 'Punch'
Du Maurier, Gerald, Sir	1873-1934	Entertainment	20	50		35	Actor-Manager
Du Pont, Alfred I.		Business	20				Banking
Du Pont, Elizabeth H		Business	20	75	110	35	
Du Pont, Henry A.	1838-1926	Civ. War-Business	98	357	750		CW, MOH. RR Pres.
Du Pont, Lammot		Business	20			50	CEO Du Pont Chemical
Du Pont, Pete		Celebrity	10			15	political celebrity
Du Pont, Pierre S.		Governor	15	35		50	Governor DE, Du Pont Chemical
Du Pont, Pierre-Samuel	1739-1817	Economist	500	1500	2700		Progenitor of Du Pont Lineage

NAME	DATE	CATEGORY	SIG	LS/DS	ALS	SP	COMMENTS
Du Pont, R.		Aviation	40	110			Am Aviation Exec.
Du Pont, Samuel Francis (WD)		Civil War	106	310	446		1803-1865, Union Adm.
Du Vigneaud, Vincent	1901-1978	Science	25	55	150	100	Nobel 1955. Synthesized Penicillin
Duala, Kevin		Celebrity	10			15	children's presenter
Duane, James	1733-1797	Revolutionary War	77	180	250		1st Continental Congress. NY Att'y Gen.
Dubcek, Alexander		Head of State	80	130			Czech. Reformer
Duberstein, Ken		Celebrity	10			15	political celebrity
DuBois, W. E. B.	1868-1963	Author	300	675		450	Black Rights, Educator-Writer
Dubose, Dudley McIver (WD)	1843-1883	Civil War	172	360			CSA Gen., MOC GA. Sig/Rank 325
Dubose, Dudley McIver	1834-1883	Civil War	114	267	350		Confederate general
DuBridge, Lee, Dr.		Science	30	100	145	50	Pres. Cal-Tech
Dubuffet, Jean	1931-1985	Artist	150	400	831		Swiss proponent of raw art
Dubuque, Julien	1762-1810	Am. Pioneer	600	2500			Am. Pioneer. 1st White Settler Near Dubuque
Ducarme, Daniel		Political	10			15	Member European Parliament
Duchamp, Marcel	1887-1968	Artist	125	350	775	1365	Fr. Avante Garde Artist
Duchin, Eddie		Entertainment	25	40		100	Big Band Leader, Pianist Father of Peter
Duchin, Peter		Entertainment	8	12	15	20	Pianist, Band Leader
Duchovny, David		Entertainment	24			45	Actor, 'X Files'
Duckworth, John T., Sir	1748-1817	Military	55	180			Br. Admiral, Gov. Newfoundland
Ducos, Jean Francois		Fr. Revolution	35	100	205		
Dudayev, Dzhokhar		Head of State	15			45	Pres. Chechen Republic
Dudenhoeffer, Matt		Entertainment	6			25	Music. Guitars 'Gravity Kills'
Dudicoff, Michael J.		Entertainment	8	15		20	Actor. Martial Arts SP 25
Dudley, Dave	1928-	Country Music	6			15	Singer
Dudley, Joseph	1647-1720	Colonial America	354	715	1200		Col.Gov.MA. Philosopher,Scholar, Divine
Dudley, Paul	1675-1751	Colonial America	115	310			Jurist. Religious Activist
Dudley, Thomas V., Bishop		Clergy	35	45	50	50	
Duer, William	1747-1799	Revolutionary War					War Dte/Cont. 1500
Duesenberg, Frederick S.	1877-1932	Business	550	1350			Champ. Bicyclist. Patented Duesenberg Motor etc.
Duff, Andrew Nicholas		Political	10			15	Member European Parliament
Duff, Arthur, Sir		Military	15	45	70		Br. Admiral
Duff, Brig. Gen. Robinson E.	1895-1979	Military	30				World War II U.S. general
Duff, Howard	1917-1990	Entertainment	14		25	35	Actor. Film & Radio Star.
Duff, James H.		Senate	5	15		10	Governor, Senator PA
Duff, Maj. Gen. Alan Colquhoun	1895-1973	Military	25				World War II British general
Duffer, Candy		Entertainment	20			45	Rock
Duffie, Alfred Napoleon	1835-1880	Civil War	35	75	90		Union Gen. War Dte. DS 235
Duffy, Brian		Astronaut	5			18	
Duffy, Francis P.		Clergy	15	20	25		
Duffy, Julia		Entertainment	7	10	20	20	Actress. 'Bob Newhart Show' Co-Star
Duffy, Patrick		Entertainment	6			28	Actor. 'Bobby Ewing' on 'Dallas' SP 30
Dufranne, Hector		Entertainment	20				Opera. Fr. Baritone
Dufy, Raoul	1877-1953	Artist	275	306	776	500	Fr. Impressionist, Fauvism
Duggan, Andrew	1923-1988	Entertainment	15			25	Character Actor. Tall, Stalwart Types
Duguid, Maj. Gen. David R.	1888-1973	Military	25				World War II British general

NAME	DATE	CATEGORY	SIG	LS/DS	ALS	SP	COMMENTS
Duhamel, George	1884-1966	Author		100			
Duhamel, Olivier		Political	10			15	Member European Parliament
Duigan, Maj. Gen. John E.	1882-1950	Military	20				World War II New Zealand general
Duin, Garrelt		Political	10			15	Member European Parliament
Dukakis, Kitty		Author	4			15	
Dukakis, Michael S.		Governor	10			20	Governor MA. Presidential Cand.
Dukakis, Olympia	1931-	Entertainment	15	25	35	30	Actress. Stage-Films. Character Leads
Dukas, Paul	1865-1935	Composer	55	160	355		French
Duke, Basil Wilson	1838-1916	Civil War	95	175	575		CSA Gen. War Dte ALS/Cont. 3900
Duke, Brig. Gen. James T.	1893-1970	Military	30				World War II U.S. general
Duke, Brig. Cecil Leonard Basil	1896-1963	Military	25				World War II British general
Duke, Charles M.		Astronaut	20	113	310	56	Moonwalker. SP of Earth 50
Duke, Clarence		Celebrity	4	10	25	10	Sports Announcer
Duke, David		Activist	40			95	Ex KKK Grand Wizard. Politically Active
Duke, Patty	1946-	Entertainment	14	20	30	34	Actress, AA
Duke, Paul		Celebrity	10			15	media/TV personality
Duke, Vernon	1903-1969	Composer	20	50	145		AMusQS 175-400
Dulac, Edmund	1882-1953	Artist			865		Illustrator, Sinbad.
Dulaney, Maj. Gen. Robert L.	1902-1984	Military	30				World War II U.S. general
Dulbecco, Renato		Science	20	35	60		Nobel Physiology-Medicine
Dullea, Keir		Entertainment	8	12	15	20	Actor. Films-Stage. '2001' SP 40
Dulles, Allen W.	1893-1969	Diplomat	30	95	165	100	State Dept., OSS, CIA. Author
Dulles, John Foster	1888-1959	Cabinet	35	128	155	100	Sec'y State, Diplomat, UN
Dumas, Alexandre (Fils)	1824-1895	Author	55	110	152	425	Fr. Dramatist, Novelist
Dumas, Alexandre (Pere)	1802-1870	Author	110	225	499	825	Fr. Novelist-Playwright. 'Count of Monte Cristo'
Dumas, Brig. Gen. Walter A.	1893-1952	Military	30				World War II U.S. general
Dumbrille, Douglass	1890-1974	Entertainment	40			75	Character Actor. Smooth, Suave Villain
Dummar, Melvin E.		Celebrity	20	30	45		Fraudulent H. Hughes Heir
Duna, Steffi	1913-	Entertainment	10		15	25	Dancer-Actress. Few Dramatic Roles in 30s
Dunagin, Ralph		Cartoonist	5			20	'The Middletons'
Dunaway, Faye	1941-	Entertainment	8	12	20	28	Actress
Dunbar, Bonnie J.		Astronaut	6			25	
Dunbar, Charles E., Sr.	1888-1959	Law	10	25			Chm. US War Trade Board 1914-18 WW I
Dunbar, Dixie	1915-1991	Entertainment	12	15	20	40	Actress-Dancer.Vaudev'l & Star of 30's Musicals
Dunbar, Paul Lawrence	1872-1906	Author	750	1725			Afro-Am. Poet, Novelist etc. Rare, signed book 1225
Duncan Jr., John J. D		Congress	10			15	Member U.S. Congress
Duncan, Charles T.		Celebrity	4	10	25	10	
Duncan, Isadora	1878-1927	Entertainment	350	649	950	1262	Am. Interpretive Dancer. Eccentric Personality
Duncan, James	1811-1849	Military	75				Mexican War Hero
Duncan, Johnny	1938-	Country Music	10			20	Guitar-Singer. 3 Years With Buddy Holly
Duncan, Johnson Kelly	1827-1862	Civil War	330				Confederate general, KIA Knoxville, TN
Duncan, Lee (Rin Tin Tin)		Entertainment	100				Dog Trainer & Actor
Duncan, Peter		Celebrity	10			15	television presenter
Duncan, Robert		Entertainment	10			20	Actor
Duncan, Sandy	1946-	Entertainment	5			23	Actress. TV-Stage-'Peter Pan'. Disney Voice SP 25

NAME	DATE	CATEGORY	SIG	LS/DS	ALS	SP	COMMENTS
Duncan, Thomas	1818-1887	Civil War	40	75	120		Union General
Duncan, Todd		Entertainment	45	125		112	First 'Porgy'. Rare
Dunckel, Maj. Gen. William C.	1893-1977	Military	30				World War II U.S. general
Dundas, Henry	1742-1811	Statesman	25	40	90		Br. Sec'y War. Pro War with Am. 1st Viscount
Dundas, Robert S.	1771-1851	Royalty	40	125			British Statesman Melville Sound
Dunham, Maj. Gen. George C.	1887-1954	Military	30				World War II U.S. general
Dunham, Sonny		Entertainment	15			25	Bandleader, Trumpet
Dunkel, Arthur		Celebrity	10			15	political celebrity
Dunkelberg, Maj. Gen. Wilbur E.	1898-1987	Military	30				World War II U.S. general
Dunlap, John	1747-1812	Am. Printer	450	2100			1st To Print Decl. of Independence & Daily News.
Dunlap, Robert P.	1794-1859	Congress	15				MOC ME, Gov. ME
Dunlop, Brig. Gen. Robert H.	1886-1970	Military	30				World War II U.S. general
Dunlop, John T.		Cabinet	5	10	15	15	Sec'y Labor
Dunn, Artie		Entertainment	10			20	Music. The Three Sons
Dunn, Bill Newton		Political	10			15	Member European Parliament
Dunn, Brig. Gen. Beverly C.	1888-1970	Military	30				World War II U.S. general
Dunn, Emma	1875-1966	Entertainment	10			35	Br. Character Actress. Longtime Film 'Housekeeper'
Dunn, Holly		Country Music	10			25	Singer
Dunn, James	1905-1967	Entertainment	60		100	125	Leading Man. AA For One Good Roll 'Tree Grows in..'
Dunn, Jennifer D		Congress	10			15	Member U.S. Congress
Dunn, William McKee		Civil War	25	40	70		Union Gen. (Judge, Adv. Gen.'75)
Dunnagan, Macon		Author	8			12	adventure, Kilimanjaro
Dunne, Dominick		Author		30		35	Columnist
Dunne, Irene	1901-1990	Entertainment	18	25	30	44	Actress-Singer. Major Star. Vintage SP 70
Dunne, Phillip	1908-1992	Author	15	20	35	35	Novelist, Director. Fndr. Screenwriters Guild
Dunne, Stephen		Entertainment				25	
Dunning, Debbie		Entertainment	5			15	Actress. Pin-up 67
Dunnock, Mildred	1904-1991	Entertainment	10		35	35	Actress. Broadway & Films. AA Nom. 'Death of a ..'
Dunovant, John	1825-1864	Civil War	220				Confederate general, KIA Vaughn Road, VA
Dunsany, Edw. J. Plunkett, Lord	1878-1957	Author	50		225	120	Traveller, Hunter, Playwright
Dunst, Kirsten		Entertainment	15			50	Actress
DuPonceau, Pierre		Military	25	60	140		
Duportail, Louis le Begue		Revolutionary War		496			Fr. Gen. in Continental Army
Dupré, Marcel		Composer	45			188	Celebrated Organist
Dupuis, Olivier		Political	10			15	Member European Parliament
Durais, C.		Artist	10	20	50		
Duran Duran		Entertainment	50			118	Rock Band (Entire Band)
Durand, Asher Brown	1796-1868	Artist	85	175	385		Hudson River School. Engraver, Painter
Durant, Ariel (Ida)	1898-1981	Author	25	50	115	35	Historian with Husband Will
Durant, Thomas C.	1820-1885	Business	350	950	1350		Pioneer Builder & Financer of Railroads
Durant, William Crapo	1861-1947	Business	250	850	1075		Durant Motor Car. GM, Chevrolet
Durant, William 'Will'		Author	30	35	60	45	Historian with Wife Aerial (Ida). Pulitzer
Durante, Jimmy	1893-1980	Entertainment	40	71	74	112	Comedian. Burlesque, Radio, TV & Films. 'Schnozz'
Durbin, Deanna		Entertainment	20			45	Child Singing Star. Retired Early.
Durbin, Richard		Senate	10			15	United States Senate (D - IL)

NAME	DATE	CATEGORY	SIG	LS/DS	ALS	SP	COMMENTS
Durenberger, David		Senate	5			15	Senator MN
Durer, Albrecht	1471-1578	Artist	3000	8200	21000		Foremost Ger. Renaissance Artist.
Durham, Bobby		Country Music	10			20	Singer
Durkin, Martin P.		Cabinet	10	25			Sec'y Labor, Eisenhower
Durnford, Lt. Gen. Cyril Maton P.	1891-1965	Military	25				World War II British general
Durning, Charles		Entertainment	5	15	15	22	Character Actor
Duroc, Geraud C.M.	1772-1813	Military	25	65	150		Napol. Grand Marshal-Diplomat
Duron, Maj. Gen. Amédée	1881-1949	Military	20				World War II French general
Durrell, Lawrence		Author	25	70	190	40	Br-Ir Poet, Playwright, Traveller
Durst, Fred		Entertainment				40	Frontman for Limp Bizket
Dury, Ian		Celebrity					Blockheads, Signed album 104
Duryea, Charles E.	1861-1938	Science-Business	280	625		2300	Built 1st Am. Gasoline Motor Car
Duryea, Dan	1907-1968	Entertainment	15	15	30	45	Character Actor. Star in 40's-50's. Vintage SP 55
Duryea, Hiram B.	1834-1914	Civil War	40		65		5th NY Infantry, Manassas
Duryee, Abram (WD)		Civil War		150	410		Union Gen. ANS '61 310
Duryee, Abram	1815-1890	Civil War	52	120	195		Union Gen. Raised Volunteer Reg. 'Duryee's Zouaves'
Duse, Eleanora	1859-1924	Entertainment	150	312	660	760	Great Italian Stage Actress
Dussault, Nancy		Entertainment	5	6	6	10	Character Actress
Dussek, Jan L	1760-1812	Composer	35	90	145		Marie Antoinette Patron to This Pianist-Composer
Dustinn, Emmy	1878-1930	Entertainment	30			170	Opera. Czech Soprano. 'Salome', 'Butterfly'
Dutra, Enrico Gaspar	1855-1974	Head of State	10	20	50	35	Pres. Brazil. General. Outlawed Communist
Duval, General Raymond-Francis	1894-1955	Military	20				World War II French general
Duvalier, Francois	1907-1971	Head of State	75	160		150	Papa Doc. Haitian President
Duvall, Gabriel	1752-1844	Supreme Court	60	272	360		
Duvall, Robert		Entertainment	10	15	25	45	AA Actor. Writer-Producer
Duvall, Shelley		Entertainment	8	8	15	21	Actress
Duvé, Christian de, Dr.		Science	20	35		30	Nobel Medicine
Duyckinck, Evart A.		Editor	40		150		Literary World
Duzenbury, Wyatt		military	25			65	Enola Gay flight engineer
Dvorak, Ann		Entertainment	10		30	35	Actress. Vintage Leading Lady of 30s
Dvorak, Antonin	1841-1904	Composer	350	760	2462		Czech. Symphonies. AMusQS 4160-6500
Dwan, Allan	1885-1981	Entertainment	15			35	Veteran Am Director-Ex Writer
Dwight, Theodore	1764-1846	Journalist	35	50	150		Harvard Wits, Hartford Convention
Dwight, Timothy	1752-1817	Author-Clergy	20	55			Pres, Yale. Equal Education of Women. Harvard Wits
Dwight, William	1827-1894	Author			150		Sanskrit scholar
Dwyer, Terri		Entertainment	10			20	Actress
Dybkjaer, Lone		Political	10			15	Member European Parliament
Dychtwald, Ken		Celebrity	10			15	medical expert
Dyer, Alexander Brydie	1815-1874	Civil War	40	84	134		Union general
Dyer, Edward	1543-1607	Author		1000			Br. Poet and Courtier
Dyer, Eliphlet	1721-1807	Revolutionary War	50	155	425		Continental Congress. Jurist
Dyer, George C.		Military	15	40	60		Admiral USN
Dyer, Leonidas Carstarphen		Senate/Congress	5			10	MOC MO 1915-1933
Dyer, Maj. Gen. Godfrey Maxwell	1898-1979	Military	25				World War II British general
Dyer, Nehemiah	1839-1910	Military	25			75	Admiral

NAME	DATE	CATEGORY	SIG	LS/DS	ALS	SP	COMMENTS
Dykes, Brigadier Vivian	1898-1943	Military	25				World War II British general
Dylan, Bob		Entertainment	184	494	525	472	Songwriter,Poet, Folksinger, rare signed contract 9500
Dymally, Mervyn M.		Congress	5			15	Afr-Am. Congressman CA
Dysart, Richard		Entertainment	5	15	20	20	Actor
Dzerzhinsky, Felix E.	1877-1926	Military		635			Bolshevik Leader, Sectry Secret police

E

NAME	DATE	CATEGORY	SIG	LS/DS	ALS	SP	COMMENTS
Eadie, Betty J.		Author	5			10	Non-Fiction
Eadie, John		Clergy	10	15	25		Scot. Theologian & Scholar
Eads, James Buchanan	1820-1887	Civil War	108	301	583		Engineer, Shipbuilder for Union
Eager, Brig. Gen. John M.	1889-1956	Military	30				World War II U.S. general
Eagleburger, Lawrence	1930-	Cabinet	15	25		35	Bush Sec'y of State.Dept. Career Diplomat
Eagles		Entertainment	100			225	Rock Alb. S/Frey,Henley,Walsh 185
Eagles, Gil		Celebrity	10			15	motivational speaker
Eagles, Maj. Gen. William W.	1895-1988	Military	30				World War II U.S. general
Eagleston, Glenn		Aviation	20	42	70	45	ACE, WW II
Eagleton, Thomas F.		Senate	10	50		20	Senator MO
Eaker, Ira	1896-1987	Aviation	50	80	95	145	WW II Air Force Cmdr
Eakes, Bobbie		Entertainment	10			20	actress
Eakins, Thomas	1844-1916	Artist	375		3250		Am. Painter-Sculptor. Master Draftsmanship,Anatomy
Eames, Charles	1907-1978	Art	75			250	Am. Architect-Designer. Best Known for Furniture
Earhart, Amelia	1898-1937	Aviation	543	1467		2189	TLS/Content 2,495. Her Book S 900-1100
Earle, George H.		Governor	10	15			Governor PA
Earle, Henry	1789-1838	Science			180		Surgeon
Earle, Merie	1889-1984	Entertainment	15			35	Character Actress into her 90's. 'The Walton's'
Earle, Virginia		Entertainment	6	8	15	15	
Early, Jubal A. (WD)	1816-1894	Civil War	797		3234		CSA General
Early, Jubal	1816-1894	Civil War	454	762	1221	1610	CSA General
Earnest, Maj. Gen. Herbert L.	1895-1970	Military	30				World War II U.S. general
Earney, Katherine		Celebrity	10			15	motivational speaker
Earp, Josephine		Celebrity			4950	1292	Wife of Wyatt Earp, ALS/ Cont 4950
Earp, Virgil		Lawman	650	4500	7150		US Marshal. S Auction 8,250
Earp, Wyatt	1848-1929	Lawman	3769	14500	27500		Legendary Gambler, Gunfighter
Easley, Brig. Gen. Cladius M.	1891-1945	Military	30				World War II U.S. general
Easley, Brig. Gen. Roy W.	1891-1985	Military	30				World War II U.S. general
East, Clyde B.		Aviation	25	35		35	Am. Highest Ranking Reconnaisance Ace.
East, James		Lawman	250	749			Western Cowboy
East, John		Senate	10	20	40	35	Senator NC, Suicide
Eastlake, Charles L., Sir	1836-1906	Artist	50	150	575		Critic, Historical Painter. Sec'y Royal Inst. Br.
Eastland, James O.		Congress	10	20		35	1943-78. Powerful Miss. Senator. Pres. Pro Tem.
Eastman, George	1854-1932	Business	228	957	1750	1543	Fndr Eastman Kodak. Rare DS 4900
Eastman, John		Artist	40		185		Am. Artist. Portraits & Genre

NAME	DATE	CATEGORY	SIG	LS/DS	ALS	SP	COMMENTS
Eastman, Max	1883-1969	Author	35	85	115		Communust & Editor-Fdr. 'The Masses'
Easton, Florence	1882-1955	Entertainment	45			175	Opera. Br. Soprano.Repertory 100 Roles-4 Languages
Easton, Sheena		Entertainment	15	15	25	45	Singer
Eastwood, Allison		Entertainment	7			38	Actress. Pin-Up 55
Eastwood, Brig. Gen. Harold E.	1892-1973	Military	30				World War II U.S. general
Eastwood, Clint	1930-	Entertainment	31			84	Actor-Producer-Dir. AA. 2'x3' Poster S 100
Eastwood, Lt Gen Sir Thos. Ralph	1890-1959	Military	25				World War II British general
Eather, Maj. Gen. Kenneth W.	1901-1993	Military	20				World War II Australian general
Eaton, Amos Beebe	1806-1877	Civil War	29	55	102		Union General. Seminole & Mex. War.Sig/Rank 50
Eaton, Brig. Gen. Ralph P.	1898-1986	Military	30				World War II U.S. general
Eaton, Dorman	1823-1899	Reformer	10	25	55		Jurist, Nat'l Civil Service Act
Eaton, John Henry		Cabinet	25	55	110		Senator TN 1818, Sec'y War
Eaton, Joseph H.	1816-1896	Civil War	35	75	75		Union Gen. ALS '65 605
Eaton, Shirley	1936-	Entertainment	10			67	Curvy Blonde Brit. Actress. 'Goldfinger'
Eaton, William	1764-1811	Military-Diplomat	38		88		U.S.Consul Tunis,Tripoli Action
Eban, Abba		Diplomat	15	75	75	65	Israeli Diplomat, Ambass. UN
Ebb, Fred		Composer	15		45	25	AMusQS Ebb & Kander 350
Ebbels, Brigadier Wilfred Austin	1898-1976	Military	25				World War II British general
Ebbets, Charles H.		Business	150			190	Orig. Brooklyn Dodgers Field (Ebbets Field)
Eben Emael		Military	30	85	140	60	
Eberbach, Gen. of Panz. Heinrich	1895-1993	Military	25				World War II German general
Eberhart, Adolph O.		Governor	5	22			Governor MN
Eberhart, Richard		Author	10	20	45	15	Major Poet 20th Cent.,Pulitzer
Eberlein, Gustav	1847-1926	Artist	20			72	Ger. Sculp. Mythological Subj & Bismark etc.
Eberly, Bob		Entertainment	5	15	10	40	Band Singer, Records
Eberly, Ray		Entertainment	10			60	Singer. Band, Records
Ebert, Roger		Entertainment	13			30	TV Movie Critic
Ebner, Michl		Political	10			15	Member European Parliament
Ebsen, Buddy	1908-	Entertainment	10	20	30	40	Actor. 'Beverly Hillbillies', original Tin-Man WOZ
Eccles, John C.		Science	20	30	40	30	Nobel Medicine
Echerer, Raina A. Mercedes		Political	10			15	Member European Parliament
Echols, John (WD)		Civil War	195	722	875		CSA General
Echols, John	1823-1896	Civil War	126	225	350		CSA General
Echols, Joseph Hubbard	1816-1885	Civil War	39				Member of Confederate Congress
Echols, Leonard Sidney		Senate/Congress	5	15			MOC WV 1919
Eckels, James H.	1858-1907	Statesman	15	50	100		U.S. Comptroller of Currency
Eckener, Hugo von	1868-1954	Aviation	165	322	440	506	Ger. Aeronaut, Built Graf Zeppelin
Eckert, Thomas T. (WD)	1825-	Civil War	150				Union Gen.Telegraph Giant.
Eckstine, Billy		Entertainment	20			50	Vocalist-Trumpet-Bandleader
Eclair, Jenny		Celebrity	10			15	comedienne
Ector, Matthew Duncan	1822-1879	Civil War	207	434			Confederate general
Ed, Carl		Cartoonist	10			30	'Harold Teen'
Eddington, Arthur Stanley, Sir	1882-1944	Science	25	140	185		Br. Mathematician, Astrophysicist
Eddleman, Lt. Gen. Clyde D.	1902-1992	Military	30				World War II U.S. general
Eddy, Duane		Entertainment	30			45	Rock Guitarist. HOF

NAME	DATE	CATEGORY	SIG	LS/DS	ALS	SP	COMMENTS
Eddy, Lt. Gen. Manton S.	1892-1962	Military	30				World War II U.S. general
Eddy, Mary Baker	1821-1910	Clergy	1138	1938	4572		Am. Fndr. Christian Science Church
Eddy, Nelson	1901-1967	Entertainment	40	132		100	30's-40's Baritone Favorite/Jeanette MacDonald
Edelsheim, Macmilian von		Military	40			65	German Panzer General
Eden, Anthony, Sir	1897-1977	Head of State	66	103	137	158	Prime Minister. 1st Earl Avon
Eden, Barbara		Entertainment	15	22	25	40	Actress, 'Jeannie'
Ederle, Gertrude 'Trudy'		Celebrity	25			60	1st woman to have swam the English Channel
Edeson, Robert		Entertainment	20			45	Silent Star. 'Ten Commandments'
Edge, Walter E.		Senate/Congress	15	25		20	Gov.NJ 1917, Senator PA, Ambassador
Edgecombe, Maj. Gen. Oliver	1892-1952	Military	25				World War II British general
Edgerton, H.K.		Celebrity	11			25	'March Across Dixie'
Edgerton, Maj. Gen. Glen E.	1887-1976	Military	30				World War II U.S. general
Edison, Charles	1890-1969	Cabinet	40	72	100	70	Sec'y Navy. Son of Thos. A.
Edison, Thomas Alva	1847-1931	Science	559	1306	2755	2500	Prolific Inventor.Rare DS re Electric Lights 4500
Edmonds, Maj. Gen. James E.	1879-1969	Military	30				World War II U.S. general
Edmonds, Noel		Celebrity	10			15	television presenter
Edmonds, Walter Dumanx	1903-1998	Author	5	. 30	40	25	'Drums Along the Mohawk'
Edmondson, Adrian		Entertainment	10			20	Actor
Edmunds, Geo.Franklin	1828-1919	Congress	10	15	30		Senator VT 1866-91
Edmundson, Henry A.		Civil War	40	55	80		CSA Officer, MOC VA
Edney, Kermit		Author	8			12	regional history, broadcasting
Edson, Merritt A.	1897-1955	Military	45	125		75	MOH Winner.Marine Cmdr. at Guadalcanal. WW II
Edward & Wallis (See Windsor)		Royalty					Duke and Duchess of Windsor
Edward III	1312-1377	Royalty					Doc. Written 1340 450. Doc.in Name of 1400
Edward IV (England)	1442-1483	Royalty	25000				
Edward VI (Reign of...)		Royalty					Land Grant 1551. 1750
Edward VII (Eng) (As King)	1841-1910	Royalty		588		1495	King From 1901-10
Edward VII (Eng.)	1841-1910	Royalty	110	282	347	600	As Albert Edw., Q.Vict. Eldest Son
Edward VIII (As King)	1894-1972	Royalty	328	852	2400	1232	
Edward VIII, as Prince of Wales	1894-1972	Royalty	129	316	868	525	Content TLS 1250. SP in Investiture Robes 2050
Edward, Brig. Gen. Harvey	1893-1947	Military	30				World War II U.S. general
Edward, Duke of Kent	1767-1820	Royalty	50	120	350		Father of Queen Victoria
Edwards, Anthony		Entertainment	20	50	70	50	Actor. 'ER' See Clooney, G
Edwards, Blake		Entertainment	10	24		22	Film Producer-Director. 'Pink Panther' etc.
Edwards, Chet E.		Congress	10			15	Member U.S. Congress
Edwards, Clarence		Military	35				General WW I
Edwards, Cliff	1895-1971	Entertainment	45	60	100	125	Singer-Actor Known as 'Ukelele Ike'. 'GWTW'
Edwards, Douglas		Journalist	5	10	15	15	Radio-TV News
Edwards, Edward Irving		Senate	10	15			Senator, Governor NJ
Edwards, Elaine S.		Senate	7	20		10	Senator LA, 8/1/72-11/13/72
Edwards, Gail J.		Entertainment	5	6	15	15	
Edwards, George		Congress	10				
Edwards, Gordon		Business	4			10	Business Exec., U.S. Steel
Edwards, James B.		Cabinet	10	15	35	10	Governor SC, Sec'y Energy
Edwards, Joan		Entertainment	5			10	Actress

NAME	DATE	CATEGORY	SIG	LS/DS	ALS	SP	COMMENTS
Edwards, Joe, Jr.		Astronaut	6			20	
Edwards, John		Senate	10			15	United States Senate (D - NC)
Edwards, John	1815-1894	Civil War	40	90	130		Union general
Edwards, Jonathan	1703-1758	Clergy-Author	110	350	380		Considered Greatest Theologian of Am. Puritanism
Edwards, Maj. Gen. Heber L.	1897-1962	Military	30				World War II U.S. general
Edwards, Maj. Gen. J.K.		Military	25				World War II British general
Edwards, Oliver	1835-1904	Civil War	35	105	125		Union General Sig/Rank 65
Edwards, Penny	1919-	Entertainment	5			20	Westerns Leading Lady of 40s
Edwards, Ralph		Entertainment	4	4	15	15	Radio-TV M.C. 'This Is Your Life' Host-Producer
Edwards, Vince		Entertainment	10			25	Actor, 'Dr. Ben Casey'
Edwin, John, the Younger	1768-1805	Actor			180		
Egan, Michael Richard		Clergy				25	Archbishop of NY
Egan, Richard	1921-1987	Entertainment	5	6	15	15	Actor.Leading Man. Mainly Action Drama & Westerns
Egan, Thomas Wilberforce	1834-1887	Civil War	48	112	160		Union general
Egan, Will		Entertainment	3			8	
Egan, William A.		Governor	5	12		10	Governor AK
Egbert, H.C.		Military	45			65	Gen. Spanish-Am. War
Egbert, Sherwood		Business	4	15	35	15	
Eggar, Samantha	1939-	Entertainment	10	12	15	22	Br. Leading Lady. Internat'l Films
Eggert, Nicole		Entertainment	5			30	Actress. 'Baywatch'
Eggerth, Marta	1912-	Entertainment	10			45	Opera. Reigning Star of Filmed Operettas in 40's
Eggleston, Benjamin	1816-1888	Congress	12	20	25		MOC OH
Eggleston, Edward	1837-1902	Author	5		30		Am. Regional Classic Novels
Eggleston, Geo. C.	1839-1911	Author	10	25			Editor, Novelist, Civil War & Boy's Books
Egleston, Brig. Gen. Nathaniel H.	1884-1981	Military	30				World War II U.S. general
Eglevsky, André	1917-1977	Entertainment	35	55	110	75	Rus-Am Ballet Teacher-Dancer
Eglseer, Gen. of Mtn. Troops Karl	1890-1944	Military	25				World War II German general
Ehlers, Vernon J. E		Congress	10			15	Member U.S. Congress
Ehrlich, Paul, Dr.	1854-1915	Science	150	1250	1850	1380	Nobel. Diphtheria, Syphillis
Ehrlichman, John	1925-1999	Political	20			29	Adv. To Nixon. Key in Watergate Scandal
Eibl, Gen. of Infantry Karl	1891-1943	Military	25				World War II German general
Eichelberger. Robert L.	1886-1961	Military	40	66	75	75	Gen. WW II. Cmdr I Corps
Eichelbrenner, E. A.		Science	45	95	225		
Eichmann, Karl Adolf	1906-1962	Military	275	800	1250	750	Nazi Leader. ALS/Cont.Offered 50,000-60,000
Eick, Alfred		Military	26	50			
Eiffel, Alexandre-Gustave	1832-1923	Arch.-Engineer	250	700	1025	1450	ALS/Content 1,750
Eigen, Manfred		Science	20	35	80	40	Nobel Chemistry
Eigenberg, David		Entertainment				30	Steve Brady, Sex in the City
Eikenberry, Jill		Entertainment	10			22	actress
Eilers, Sally	1908-1978	Entertainment	15	15	30	42	Actress. Low Key Leading Lady 30s
Eilshemius, Louis Michel	1864-1941	Artist	35	65	290		Am. Landscape Expressionist
Einem, Gottfried von		Composer					AMuQ 125
Einstein, Albert	1879-1955	Science	1058	2750	5166	3077	Nobel-Physics. ALS/Sci. Content 25,000
Eisele, Donn F.		Astronaut	50			128	
Eisenberg, Maurice		Entertainment	5	15		20	Cellist

NAME	DATE	CATEGORY	SIG	LS/DS	ALS	SP	COMMENTS
Eisenhower, Arthur B.		Business	5	15		10	Brother to Ike. Banker
Eisenhower, Barbara		Celebrity	5	15		10	Daughter-in Law to Ike
Eisenhower, David	1948-	Author	15	25		25	Historian & Writer
Eisenhower, Dwight D. (WWII dte)		Military	275	650	4750	650	Supreme Commander Allied Forces, ALS/Cont
Eisenhower, Dwight D.	1890-1969	President	271	590	2784	440	ALS/Content 3,750-17,500.
Eisenhower, Dwight D. (As Pres)		President	366	982	21510	715	Pres.chk 9500
Eisenhower, Edgar N.		Law	5	20		15	Brother & Lawyer to Ike
Eisenhower, John S. D.		Military	10	20	35	15	General & Only Son of Ike
Eisenhower, Julie Nixon		Celebrity	5	10	25	20	Daughter & Inlaw. Two Presidents
Eisenhower, Mamie Doud	1896-1979	First Lady	46	99	154	75	White House Card S 65, LS 85. FDC S 65
Eisenhower, Milton		Educator	10	30		20	Brother to D.D.E. Pres. Penn. State U.
Eisenhower, Susan		Celebrity	10			15	political celebrity
Eisenman, Robin G.		Entertainment	5	4	9	10	
Eisenstaedt, Alfred		Photographer	15	40		150	Celebrity Photographer, signed book 150
Eisenstein, Sergey	1898-1948	Entertainment		690	1350		Russ.Stage-Film Dir. Innovative Masterpieces
Eisley, Anthony	1925-	Entertainment	7			12	General Purpose Actor
Eisner, Michael O.		Business	32	66		45	CEO Walt Disney Co.
Eisner, William J.		Business	10	35	45	20	
Eizenstat, Stuart E.		Government	5	10	15	10	White House Staff
Ekberg, Anita	1931-	Entertainment	10			20	Voluptuous Swedish Blonde Actress. 50s-70s
Ekland, Britt		Entertainment	8	12	25	32	Actress.Am. & Internat'l Films. Pin-Up SP 40
Ekwall, William A.		Senate/Congress	5	10		10	MOC OR
El Fadil, Siddig		Entertainment	20			50	Actor. 'Star Trek Deep Space Nine'
Elam, Jack	1916-	Entertainment	8	10	15	28	Actor. Wall-eyed Western Character
El-Baz, Osama		Celebrity	10			15	political celebrity
Elbert, Samuel	1743-1788	Revolutionary War		110	170		Distinguished Officer. Gov. GA
Elder, Ruth (Camp)		Aviation	100	190	310	350	Pioneer Aviatrix
Elder, Will*		Cartoonist	30			100	Best Known for 'Little Annie Fanny' in Playboy Mag.
Elders, Joycelyn Dr		Celebrity	10			15	medical expert
Elders, M. Joycelyn		Cabinet	15	30		20	Clinton Surgeon General
Eldridge, Florence	1901-1988	Entertainment	10			30	Vintage Stage & Film Leading Lady.Mrs Fred. March
Eldridge, Louise		Reformer	10	15	30		Aunt Louisa AQS 25
Eldridge, Lt Gen Sir William John	1898-1985	Military	28				World War II British general
Eldridge, Roy		Entertainment	30			65	Jazz Trumpet
Electra, Carmen		Entertainment				42	Actress. Model.
Electric Light Orchestra		Entertainment	50			100	
Eleniak, Erika		Entertainment	10			35	Actress
Elfman, Jenna		Entertainment	10			48	Actress-Comedian. '99 Golden Globe
Elg, Taina		Entertainment	10			30	Fin. Ballet-Actress/Gene Kelly. Internat'l Films
Elgar, Edward, Sir	1857-1934	Composer	114	316	681	422	Br. Composer. AMusQS 1,500-2000
Elgart, Les		Bandleader	30			45	Arranger for Top Vocalists. Big Band
Elgin, 7th Earl (T.Bruce)		Diplomat					SEE Bruce, Thomas
Elgnozi, Brig. Gen. Jacob-Raoul	1883-1944	Military	20				World War II French general
Elion, Gertrude, Dr.		Science	20	65		35	Nobel Medicine. Biochemist-Leukemia-Herpes-AZT
Eliopulos, Marcus		Entertainment	6			25	Music. Guitar 'Stabbing Westward'

NAME	DATE	CATEGORY	SIG	LS/DS	ALS	SP	COMMENTS
Eliot, Charles W.	1834-1926	Educator	15	50	65		Pres. Harvard
Eliot, George (Pseud.)	1819-1880	Author	137	478	1530		Br. Novelist. (Mary Ann Lewes [Evans])
Eliot, T(homas) S(tearns)	1888-1965	Author	200	684	1322	860	Br. Poet, Critic, Editor, Nobel. Xmas Card S 375
Eliot, Thos. Dawes	1808-1870	Congress	5		15		CW MOC MA
Elisabeth, Queen	1876-1965	Royalty		208		350	Queen of Belgium. Wife of King Albert I
Elizabeth (Rus)	1709-1762	Royalty	267	760			Czarina of Russia. Daughter of Peter the Great
Elizabeth I (Eng.)	1533-1603	Royalty	4750	26140			
Elizabeth II & Philip		Royalty		862		1243	Queen of England and Consort
Elizabeth Mastantonio, Mary		Entertainment	10			20	actress
Elizabeth, II	1926-	Royalty	225	616	1188	875	Queen of Gr. Brit., ALS @Age 10 900
Elizabeth, Queen Mother	1900-2002	Royalty	120	300	538	750	Queen of George VI. Check Signed 950
Elizabeth, Shannon		Entertainment				50	
Elizondo, Hector		Entertainment	10			20	actor
Elkins, Maj. Gen. William Henry P.	1883-1964	Military	20				World War II Canadian general
Elkins, Stephen B.		Cabinet	15	25	60	25	Sec'y War, Senator WV
Ellen, Vera		Entertainment	20			45	Dancer, Films.
Ellender, Allen J.		Senate	4	5		10	Senator LA
Ellerbee, Linda		Journalist	10	35		15	TV News, Commentator
Ellers, Joseph C.		Author	8			12	Southern mountains mysteries
Ellery, William	1727-1820	Revolutionary War	175	398	657		Signer Decl. of Indepen.
Elles, James E.M.		Political	10			15	Member European Parliament
Ellet, Alfred Washington	1820-1895	Civil War	40	90	160		Union general
Ellicott, Andrew	1754-1820	Revolutionary War	60	185	320		Surveyor, Mathematician
Ellington, Buford		Governor	5	10	20		Governor TN
Ellington, Duke	1899-1974	Composer	172	472		465	Big Band Leader. AMusQS 300-1,200
Elliot, Maj. Gen. Gilbert Minto	1897-1969	Military	25				World War II British general
Elliot, Sam		Entertainment	10			20	actor
Elliott, Brig. Gen. Dabney O.	1890-1976	Military	30				World War II U.S. general
Elliott, Cass (Mama)		Entertainment	235	585		442	Rotund, Sweet-Voiced Singer. 'Mamas & Papas'
Elliott, David James		Entertainment	15			50	Actor
Elliott, Maj. Gen. James Gordon	1898-1990	Military	25				World War II British general
Elliott, Maxine		Entertainment	30	40	75	70	
Elliott, R.W.B., Bishop		Clergy	25	35	40	40	
Elliott, Robert B.		Senate/Congress	10	15		15	MOC SC
Elliott, Sam	1944-	Entertainment	20	10	35	45	Low Key Leading Man 70's to 90;s
Elliott, Stephen Jr.	1830-1866	Civil War	146	190	280		Confederate general
Elliott, Washington L.	1825-1888	Civil War	45	95	130		Union Gen. ALS '63 200
Elliott, Wild Bill	1904-1965	Entertainment	50			150	Vintage Cowboy Star from 20s-Late 50s
Ellis, Augustus Van Horne	1827-1863	Civil War		368			Died Gettysburg, Union Col.
Ellis, F. H.		Aviation	15	35		30	
Ellis, Havelock	1859-1939	Science	45	115	135	275	Br. Pioneer Advocate Sex Ed.
Ellis, Mary		Entertainment	20			50	Opera & Operetta Star. 1st 'Rose Marie'
Ellis, Robert H.		Military	10	25	45		
Ellison, James	1910-1993	Entertainment	15		20	30	Vintage Cowboy. Johnny in 'Hopalong Cassidy'
Ellison, Ralph W.	1914-1994	Author	55	175		125	Afr.-Am. Novelist. 'Invisible Man'

NAME	DATE	CATEGORY	SIG	LS/DS	ALS	SP	COMMENTS
Ellsberg, Daniel		Activist	20	35	50	30	Leaked Pentagon Papers
Ellsberg, Edward	1891-1983	Military	25	55	75	60	Naval Engineer, American WWII Admiral
Ellsworth, Ephraim E. (WD)		Civil War			6862	6325	Union Zouave Col. 1st CW Martyr
Ellsworth, Ephraim E.	1837-1861	Civil war	733	1875	2500		Union Zouave Col.
Ellsworth, Oliver	1745-1807	Supreme Court	90	269	431		3rd Chief Justice. Constitutional Conv.
Ellul, Jacques		Clergy	25	30	45		
Elman, Mischa	1891-1967	Entertainment	30	198		80	Rus.-Am. Violinist
Elman, Ziggy		Entertainment	25			75	Trumpet. Played With Major Bands 40's-50's.
Elmendorff, Karl		Entertainment	25			110	Ger. Conductor. 4x6 SP 85
Elmore, Brig. Gen. John A.	1902-1971	Military	30				World War II U.S. general
Elmore, E.C.		Civil War	55	105			Treas. CSA. ALS 3,500
Elphick, Michael		Entertainment	10			20	Actor
Elrod, Jack*		Cartoonist	10			35	'Mark Trail'
Elson, Edward L.R.		Clergy	15	20	25		
Elssler, Fanny	1810-1884	Entertainment	250				Austrian Ballerina
Elston, John A.		Congress	5	15			Congressman CA
Eltinge, Julian	1882-1941	Entertainment	25	20	35	40	Female Impersonator, Silent Films
Eluard, Paul	1895-1952	Author	110	225	375		Pseud: Eugene Grindel. Fr. Poet. Exponent Surrealism
Elvira		Entertainment	10	9	19	33	Pin-Up SP 35
Elwes, Cary		Entertainment	8			40	Actor. 'Robin Hood' SP 50
Ely, Joseph Buell		Governor	15	35	70		Gov. MA, Anti New Dealer
Ely, Paul General		Military	65		140	90	Fr. Cmdr. Indochina. Dienbienphu
Ely, Ron	1938-	Entertainment	15	20	25	45	Actor. One of Several 'Tarzans'. SP Tarzan 195
Ely, Smith		Congress	15				Mayor NYC, Repr. NY
Elzey, Arnold (Jones) (WD)	1816-1871	Civil War	257		1180		CSA General
Emanuel, David		Celebrity	10			15	Designer
Emanuel, Elizabeth		Celebrity	10			15	Designer
Emanuel, Rahm E		Congress	10			15	Member U.S. Congress
Emberg, Kelly		Model	10			25	Pin-Up SP 40
Embick, Lt. Gen. Stanley D.	1877-1957	Military	30				World War II U.S. general
Embry, Joan		Zoologist	10			25	San Diego Zoo TV Representative
Emerson, Faye	1917-1983	Entertainment	10			52	Film Actress-Early TV Panel Show Member
Emerson, George		Entertainment	8			30	
Emerson, Hope	1897-1960	Entertainment	15			35	6'2' Am. Character Actress. Early 30s-60s
Emerson, Jo Ann E		Congress	10			15	Member U.S. Congress
Emerson, Lake and Palmer		Entertainment	35	125		125	Rock. Alb. Signed (3) 125
Emerson, Ralph Waldo	1803-1882	Author-Clergy	250	410	891	2530	Essayist, Philosopher, Poet. ALS/Content 3,500
Emery, Brig. Gen. Ambrose R.	1883-1945	Military	30				World War II U.S. general
Emery, Ralph		Entertainment	4			8	TV Host
Eminem		Entertainment				63	Singer Marshall Mathers, Slim Shady
Emma B		Music	10			15	Rock
Emma, Queen (NT, Rooker)	1836-1885	Royalty	350				Wife of King Kamehameha IV
Emme		Celebrity	10			15	model
Emmerich, Roland		Celebrity	10			15	film industry
Emmett, Daniel D.		Composer	415	425	600		1st Minstral Show. Dixie

NAME	DATE	CATEGORY	SIG	LS/DS	ALS	SP	COMMENTS
Emmons, Conant H.		Author	8			12	novelist
Emmons, Ebenezer	1799-1863	Science	25	40	70		Early Prof. of Natural History
Emory, William Hemsley	1811-1887	Civil War	42	122	167		Union General. Sig/Rank 90, War Dte. ALS 355
Empey, James W., Lt. Col.		Aviation		25		35	Ace WW II
Enders, John Franklin, Dr.		Science	25	60	110	45	Nobel Medicine.
Endicott, William C.	1826-1900	Cabinet	25	30	55	150	Sec'y War
Enesco, Georges	1880-1955	Composer	125	275	550	550	AMusQS 475-850
Enevoldson, Einer		Astronaut	10			20	
Enfield, Harry		Celebrity	10			15	comedian
Engel, Eliot L. E		Congress	10			15	Member U.S. Congress
Engel, Georgia		Entertainment	10	12	15	25	Actress. 'Mary Tyler Moore' Show
Engel, Samuel G.	1904-1984	Entertainment	10			15	Producer
England, Anthony W.		Astronaut	7			28	
England, Sue		Entertainment	5			20	1940's Moppet
Engle, Frederick		Civil War	45				Union Commodore
Engle, Joe Henry		Astronaut	15			45	Engle & Truly SP 195
Englehart, Brig. Gen. Francis A.	1890-1969	Military	30				World War II U.S. general
Engler, Irvin		Author		25	30		Poet
English, Brig. Gen. Paul X.	1888-1964	Military	30				World War II U.S. general
English, Phil E		Congress	10			15	Member U.S. Congress
English, Thos. Dunn	1819-1902	Author-Congress	28	30	45		'Alice Ben Bolt'.Dr.,Lawyer, Poet, MOC NJ
Englund, Robert	1949-	Entertainment	10			28	Horror Movies. Character of 'Freddy Kruger'
Ennis, Maj. Gen. Riley F.	1897-1963	Military	30				World War II U.S. general
Ennis, Skinnay		Bandleader	25			65	Singer, Musician
Enola Gay		Aviation	150			350	Tibbets,Van Kirk,Ferebee
Enos, Roger	1729-1808	Military	55	175	295		General, Honored VT Citizen
Enright, Richard E.		Law	12	24			Police Commissioner
Enriques, Rene	1933-1990	Entertainment	35			60	'Hill Street Blues' 'Lt. Calletano'. AIDs Victiim
Ensign, John		Senate	10			15	United States Senate (R - NV)
Ensley, F. Gerald, Bishop		Clergy	20	35	50	25	
Ensor, James Sydney, Baron	1860-1949	Artist	75	172	385		Belg. Painter, Etcher. Bizarre Fantasies, Masks
Entwistle, John		Music				75	Bass guitar, Who
Enzi, Michael		Senate	10			15	United States Senate (R - WY)
Ephron, Henry	1912-1992	Entertainment	15			25	Screenwriter. Worked with wife, Nora.
Ephron, Nora	1941-	Author	15			25	Novelist-Screenwriter.Daughter of Phoebe & Henry.
Ephron, Phoebe	1914-1971	Entertainment	15			25	Screenwriter- Mother of Nora & Wife of Henry
Epp, Franz Xaver von	1868-1947	Military	50	175		175	WWII General, Nazi Storm Troops
Epstein, Brian		Entertainment	298	716	825		Beatles Manager & Promoter
Epstein, Jacob, Sir	1880-1959	Artist	150	210	375		Controversial Br.-Am. Sculptor
ER (cast)		Entertainment	98			275	All 6 Original. (5) 250 (4 males) 125
Erbsen, Wayne		Author	8			12	mountain music publisher/performer
Erdman, Paul		Celebrity	10			15	financial expert
Erdrich, Louise		Author	5			10	Novelist. 'The Bingo Palace'
Erhard, Ludwig	1897-1977	Head of State	25	70	170	60	Chancellor W. Germany
Erickson, Leif	1911-1986	Entertainment	15			40	Singer-Actor. Many 2nd Leads

NAME	DATE	CATEGORY	SIG	LS/DS	ALS	SP	COMMENTS
Ericsdotter, Siw		Entertainment	25			60	Opera
Ericson, B.A.		Aviation	10	25			Piloted XC-99
Ericson, Eric*		Cartoonist	15			75	Appeared 'New Yorker' Mag. 40's-50's
Ericsson, John	1803-1889	Civil War	95	195	624	1265	Designed & Built Monitor
Eriksson, Marianne		Political	10			15	Member European Parliament
Erlanger, Camille	1863-1967	Composer					AMQS 65
Ernest Augustus II	1771-1851	Royalty		225	360		1st King of Hanover(1837-51)
Erni, Hans		Artist	65		225		ALS-FDC/signed art
Ernouf, Manuel L.J., Baron		Fr. Revolution	35	85	160		
Ernst, Max	1891-1976	Artist	235	355	775		Surrealist-Dada Movement. Orig. Sketch S 825
Errant, James S.		Business	10			20	Restauranteur, Prima Inc.
Errol, Leon	1881-1951	Entertainment	45			93	Talented Character Actor in Comedy Roles
Erskine, Graves B.		Military	30	35	65	40	Led US Marines at Iwo Jima
Erskine, John	1879-1951	Author	35	83	125		Novelist, Pres. Juilliard, Musician
Erskine, Maj. Gen. Ian David	1898-1973	Military	28				World War II British general
Erté		Artist	102	187	400	195	
Ervine, St. John		Author	15	50			Br. Controversial Drama Critic
Erwin, Durward		Country Music	10			20	
Erwin, James		Military	45				General WW I
Erwin, Sam J.		Congress	20	45		25	Sen.NC. Watergate Investigator
Erwin, Stuart	1903-1967	Entertainment	20			42	Character Comedian. 20s-60s. Played Mr. Average
Esaki, Leo		Science	20	35	50	45	Nobel Physics
Escalante, Jaime		Celebrity	10			15	motivational speaker
Esclopé, Alain		Political	10			15	Member European Parliament
Escobar, Juan Andrés Naranjo		Political	10			15	Member European Parliament
Escobedo, Mariano	1827-1902	Military	50	225			Captured Maximillian
Eshkol, Levi	1895-1969	Head of State	94	189	400	225	Israeli P.M., Fndr. Histadrut
Eshoo, Anna G. E		Congress	10			15	Member U.S. Congress
Esnault-Pelterie, Robert	1881-1957	Aviation	75	250			Pioneer Aviator. Invented Aileron. Early Monoplane
Esperian, Kalen		Entertainment	10			30	Opera
Esposito, Jennifer		Entertainment	10			48	
Esquirol, Jean Etienne Dom.		Science		85			
Essame, Maj. Gen. Hubert	1896-1976	Military	25				World War II British general
Essex, David		Music	10			15	performing musical artist
Estaing, Charles Hector T. de	1729-1794	Revolutionary War	175	500	750		Fr.Gen-Adm. Pro American Hero
Este, George Peabody	1829-1881	Civil War	45	80	125		Union general
Este, Isabella d'	1474-1539	Royalty			10000		(Mantua) Art Patron, Diplomat. NPRA
Estefan, Gloria		Entertainment	12			45	Dancer-Singer.
Esterhasy, Gunt. A.		Head of State	20	70	175		Austria
Esterhazy, Prince Pal A.	1786-1866	Statesman	25		70		Austro-Hung. Diplomat. Ambassador to Eng.
Estes, Billy Sol		Celebrity	5	20	45	15	Grain Storage Scandal
Esteves, Maj. Gen. Luis R.	1893-1958	Military	30				World War II U.S. general
Estevez, Emilio	1962-	Entertainment	15	15	35	38	Actor-Son of Martin Sheen. Leading Man
Estil, Benjamin		Congress	15	25			Congressman VA 1825
Estrada, Erik	1948-	Entertainment	5	15	20	20	Leading Man. Puerto Rican Descent. 'Chips' TV

NAME	DATE	CATEGORY	SIG	LS/DS	ALS	SP	COMMENTS
Etheridge, Bob E		Congress	10			15	Member U.S. Congress
Etheridge, Melissa		Music	15			40	Rock
Etter, Philippe		Head of State	15	50			Switzerland
Etting, Ruth	1896-1978	Entertainment	25			60	Major Vint. Singing Star of 20s
Ettl, Harald		Political	10			15	Member European Parliament
Eubanks, Bob		Entertainment	5	8	10	18	Game Show Host
Eugene Griessman, B.		Celebrity	10			15	motivational speaker
Eugene-Francois De Savoie	1663-1736	Military	368				Austrian General
Eugenie, Empress (Nap. III)	1826-1920	Royalty	200	305	350		Influenced Nap. Fashion Leader
Euler-Chelpin, Ulf Svante von	1873-1964	Science	20	35	60	40	Nobel Medicine 1929
Eurythmics		Entertainment	40			90	
Eustis, Abraham		Military	65		350		War 1812. Promoted to Br. Gen.
Eustis, Henry Lawrence	1819-1885	Civil War	43	85	130		Union general
Eustis, William	1753-1825	Cabinet	35	118	185		Madison's Sec'y War, MOC MA 1801
Evan Galbraith, Amb.		Celebrity	10			15	financial expert
Evans, Alison		Celebrity	10			15	home/gardening expert
Evans, Brig. Gen. Henry C.	1895-1976	Military	30				World War II U.S. general
Evans, Chris		Music	10			15	DJ
Evans, Clement A. (WD)		Civil War	200	560	891		CSA General
Evans, Clement A.	1833-1911	Civil War	99	175	375		CSA General
Evans, Dale	1912-	Entertainment	20	30	60	53	Former Band Singer. Leading Lady to Roy Rogers
Evans, Daniel J.		Senate-Gov.	15	18		20	Gov., Senator, Washington
Evans, Edith Dame	1888-1976	Entertainment	20	30		40	Distinguished Br. Stage Actress. Few Films
Evans, Edw. R.G., Admiral	1880-1957	Explorer	35	90		75	Arctic Explorer. Lord Mountevans
Evans, Gene	1922-1998	Entertainment	15	20	30	45	Versatile Character Actor. 'My Friend Flicka' etc.
Evans, George De Lacy	1787-1870	Military	150	220			Br. Col. Who Burned White House
Evans, Geraint, Sir		Entertainment	10			35	Opera
Evans, Jillian		Political	10			15	Member European Parliament
Evans, Joan	1934-	Entertainment	5	10	15	10	Teenage Roles in Early 50s. Works now in Education
Evans, John V.		Governor	10	15			Governor ID
Evans, Jonathan		Political	10			15	Member European Parliament
Evans, Lane E		Congress	10			15	Member U.S. Congress
Evans, Lee		Entertainment	10			20	actor
Evans, Linda	1942-	Entertainment	8	12	20	30	Leading Lady. Successful TV Series 'Dynasty'
Evans, Lt. Col. D. M		Civil War	15	25	40		
Evans, Lt. Gen. Sir Geoffrey Chas.	1901-1987	Military	25				World War II British general
Evans, Madge	1909-1981	Entertainment	15	22	35	30	Film Debut at 5. Film Star Until 1943. Retiredt
Evans, Maj. Gen. David Sydney C.	1893-1955	Military	25				World War II British general
Evans, Maj. Gen. Roger	1886-1868	Military	25				World War II British general
Evans, Maj. Gen. Vernon	1893-1987	Military	30				World War II U.S. general
Evans, Marian		Author	137	478	1530		Br. Novelist. Mary Ann Lewes [Evans] See George Eliot
Evans, Mark		Celebrity	10			15	veterinarian expert
Evans, Maurice	1909-1989	Entertainment	42	73	85	78	Shakespearean Actor, Producer
Evans, Michael K.		Celebrity	10			15	financial expert
Evans, Michelle		Celebrity	10			15	Miss GB - celebrity model

NAME	DATE	CATEGORY	SIG	LS/DS	ALS	SP	COMMENTS
Evans, Nathan George 'Shanks'	1824-1868	Civil War	189	340	709		CSA Gen.
Evans, Nathan G. 'Shanks' (WD)		Civil War	265	800	1600		CSA General
Evans, Nicholas		Author		40			Novelist. 'The Horse Whisperer'
Evans, Oliver	1755-1819	Inventor		1500			Built Am. 1st Self-Propelled Land Vehicle 1787
Evans, Ray		Composer	15	35	45	40	Am. Songwriter. 'Buttons & Bows', 'Que Sera Sera'
Evans, Robert J.E.		Political	10			15	Member European Parliament
Evans, Robert		Celebrity	10			15	financial expert
Evans, Robley D.	1846-1912	Military	35	65	125	175	Admiral 'Fighing Bob Evans'
Evans, Ronald E.		Astronaut	40			100	
Evans, Walker	1903-1975	Photographer	75		270		Am. Photographer. Documented Everyday Life
Evanson, Maj. Gen. Arthur C. T.	1895-1957	Military	25				World War II British general
Evarts, William M.	1818-1901	Cabinet	40	65	95	150	Att'y Gen., Sec'y State, Sen NY
Evelegh, Maj. Gen. Vyvyan	1898-1958	Military	25				World War II British general
Everclear		Entertainment				95	Rock group
Everest, F.K. 'Pete'		Aviation	15	30	45	35	
Everett, Chad		Entertainment	5	10	15	30	Actor 'Medical Center' & More
Everett, Edward	1794-1865	Sen.-Cab.-Clergy	67	113	138	250	Fillmore Sec'y State, Sen. MA. Statesman, Scholar
Everett, Rupert		Entertainment				35	
Everett, Terry E		Congress	10			15	Member U.S. Congress
Everhart, Angie		Entertainment				30	Actress
Everly Brothers		Entertainment	35			95	Don & Phil. 1st R & R Duo. Influenced Later Artists
Everly, Phil		Entertainment	20			30	Singer-Songwriter-Guitarist. 'Everly Brothers'
Evers, Charles		Activist	5	20	40	53	Succeeded Brother Medgar as Sec'y NAACP '63
Evers, Medgar	1925-1963	Activist		2800			AM. Civil Rights Leader
Evetts, Lt. Gen. Sir John Fullerton	1891-1988	Military	25				World War II British general
Evigan, Greg		Entertainment	3	3	6	10	
Ewell, Richard Stoddert (WD)		Civil War	834	1294	1450		CSA General
Ewell, Richard Stoddert	1817-1872	Civil War	325	575	850		CSA General
Ewell, Tom		Entertainment	15	20	25	47	Actor. 'Seven Year Itch'
Ewing, Charles	1835-1883	Civil War	50	110	160		Union general
Ewing, Hugh Boyle	1826-1905	Civil War	40	85	110		Union general
Ewing, James	1736-1806	Rev. War	75	190	320		American Brig. General
Ewing, Thomas Jr	1829-1896	Civil War	40	75	120		Union general
Ewing, Thomas	1789-1871	Cabinet	30	65	95		Sen. OH,Sec'y Treas. & Interior
Exelmans, Remy J.I.	1775-1852	Fr. Revolution	65	140	230		Marshal of France
Exile (4)		Entertainment	20			50	Rock
Exon, J. James		Senator-Gov.	5	10		10	Senator, Governor NE
Eyre, Edward John	1815-1901	Explorer	55		150		Gov. Australia. Eyre Rock
Eyster, Brig. Gen. George S.	1895-1951	Military	30				World War II U.S. general
Eythe, William		Entertainment	10	15	20	20	
Eytinge, Rose	1838-1911	Entertainment	25		65	50	19th Cent.Actress/Laura Keene, Booth

NAME	DATE	CATEGORY	SIG	LS/DS	ALS	SP	COMMENTS
Fabares, Shelley	1942-	Entertainment	6	15	20	25	Actress. 'Coach'
Faber, John Eberhard	1822-1879	Business	140	500	725		Eberhard Faber Pencil Co.. 1st Pencil Mfg. In Am.
Fabian		Entertainment					See Forté, Fabian
Fabian, Ava		Entertainment	5			25	Actress. Pin-Up 45
Fabian, John M.		Astronaut	7			20	
Fabio		Model	15			38	Male Model
Fabius, Lt. Gen. Hendrik A.C.	1878-1957	Military	20				World War II Dutch general
Fabray, Nanette	1920-	Entertainment	5	6	15	30	Comedy Actress-Singer. 'Our Gang' as Child
Factor, Max Jr.		Business	10	30	55	45	Cosmetic Mfg.
Factor, Max		Business	25	125	175	60	Cosmetic Mfg.
Fagan, James Fleming	1828-1893	Civil War	110	274			CSA Gen.& U.S.Marshal For Indian Terr.
Fagerbakke, Bill		Entertainment	10			35	Actor 'Coach'
Fagoaga, Isidodo		Entertainment	15			50	Opera
Fahey, Jeff		Entertainment	8			35	Actor. Leading Man. 'The Marshal', 'Psycho III'
Fahnestock, Harris	1852-1914	Business			115		
Fair, James, G.	1831-1894	Capitalist	30	110	180		Mining, Financier, CA Developer
Fairbairn, Sir William	1789-1874	Engineer			180		
Fairbank, Brig. Gen. Leigh C.	1889-1966	Military	30				World War II U.S. general
Fairbank, Calvin		Abolitionist	40	85	150		Freed Fugitive Slaves
Fairbanks, Charles W.	1852-1918	Vice President	50	110	324	200	T. Roosevelt VP. US Sen.IN
Fairbanks, Douglas, Jr.	1909-2000	Entertainment	20	45	102	90	Actor-Son of the Famous Father
Fairbanks, Douglas, Sr.	1883-1939	Entertainment	90	135	210	285	Swashbuckling Silent Film Mega Star.United Artists
Fairbanks, Erastus	1792-1864	Governor	35		80		CW Gov. VT. Mfg. Platform Scales
Fairchild, Charles S.		Cabinet	20	35	55	40	Sec'y Treasury 1887
Fairchild, David G.	1869-1954	Science	5	10	20	15	Am. Botanist. Books on Plants
Fairchild, Lucius	1831-1896	Civil War	26	50	80		Union Gen., Gov. WI, Statesman. Sig/Rank 55
Fairchild, Morgan	1950-	Entertainment	10	15	20	33	Actress
Fairchild, Sherman		Business	25	60	115	40	Fairchild Camera & Equipment Co
Faircloth, Henry P.	1880-1956	Author	10	35			Noted US Social Scientist & Writer
Fairclough, Maj. Gen. Eric	1887-1944	Military	25				World War II British general
Fairfax, George Wm.	1787-	Rev. War	75	210	395		Companion of Geo. Washington
Fairfax, Thomas Lord	1691-1782	Colonial America	220	550			Historically Important Family.Settled in North-VA
Fairfield, Charles	1842-1924	Cabinet	25		40		Sec'y Treas. under Cleveland
Fairfield, John	1797-1847	Gov.-Senate	15	20	30		Senator, Gov. ME
Fairholt, Frederick	1814-1866	Artist	15		50		Engraver & Antiquarian
Fairless, Benjamin F.	1890-1962	Business	20	45	60	60	CEO US Steel
Fairley, Brigadier Neil H.	1891-1966	Military	20				World War II Australian general
Faisal, King	1906-1975	Royalty	25	50	95	125	Saudi Arabia. Many Benficial Reforms. Assassinated
Faith, Adam		Entertainment	10			20	Actor
Faith, Brig. Gen. Don C.	1896-1963	Military	30				World War II U.S. general
Faith, Percy		Composer	20			150	Conductor-Arranger For Top Artists

NAME	DATE	CATEGORY	SIG	LS/DS	ALS	SP	COMMENTS
Faithfull, Emily		Reformer	25	45	55		Br.Printer-Publisher Q.Victoria
Falck, Wolfgang		Aviation	20	45	60	40	
Falco, Edie		Entertainment				45	Carmela, Soprano's
Falconer, William	1732-1769	Author	60	350			Brit. Poet. Shipwrecked, Universal Marine Dict'y
Faleomavaega, Eni F. H. F		Congress	10			15	Member U.S. Congress
Fales, Maj. Gen. Eugene W.	1887-1963	Military	30				World War II U.S. general
Falk, Peter	1927-	Entertainment	8	10	15	28	SP As 'Columbo' 45
Falkenburg, Jinx	1919-	Entertainment	5	6	10	25	Model-Actress
Falkenhorst, Col Gen Nikolaus v.	1885-1968	Military	35		155		World War II German general
Fall, Albert B.	1861-1944	Cabinet	40	68	95	110	Sec'y Interior.Teapot Dome Scandal
Fall, Leo	1873-1925	Composer				105	Austrian Operetta Composer
Falla, Brigadier Norris S.	1883-1945	Military	30				World War II New Zealand general
Falla, Manuel de	1876-1946	Composer	162	360	600	900	Span. AMusQS 875, 1,000-1200
Fallieres, Clement Armand	1841-1931	Statesman		65			French statesman., 8th Pres. Of France
Fallon, Jimmy		Entertainment	15			40	Actor
Fallon, Walter A.		Business	4			10	CEO Eastman Kodak Co.
Falstaff, John, Sir		Military		8000			Model for Shakespeare's Play
Falvy, Lt. Gen. Maurice E.	1888-1970	Military	20				World War II French general
Falwell, Jerry		Clergy	15	20	25	18	
Fancourt, Darell		Entertainment	15			65	D'Oyly Carte Gilbert & Sullivan Baritone Star
Faneuil, Peter		Revolutionary War	125	225	555		Faneuil Hall, Boston
Fang, Wu Ting, Dr.		Statesman	10			20	Chinese Statesman
Fanshaw, Maj. Gen. Sir Evelyn D.	1895-1979	Military	25				World War II British general
Fantin-Latour, Henri	1836-1904	Artist	40	90	170		Fr. Illustrator, Lithographer
Far, Frances		Composer	5	15	30	10	
Faraday, Michael	1791-1867	Science	160	350	654	950	Br. Physicist, Chemist. ALS/Cont.1800
Farage, Nigel Paul		Political	10			15	Member European Parliament
Faranda, Tom Dr.		Celebrity	10			15	motivational speaker
Farentino, James	1938-	Entertainment	15			25	Actor. Leading Man. Mostly TV
Fargo, Donna		Country Music	8	15		20	Singer-Songwriter
Fargo, James C.		Business	210	633			Wells, Fargo & Co. Am. Express
Fargo, William G.	1818-1881	Business	368	950	1250		Wells-Fargo, Am. Express
Farias, Valentin Gomes	1781-1858	Head of State	205	490			President of Mexico until Defeated by Santa Ana
Farina, Dennis		Entertainment	10	35		27	Busy Mature Leading-Man-Character Actor
Farinelli, Patricia		Model	5			18	Pin-Up SP 20
Farjeon, Eleanor	1881-1965	Writer			325		
Farley, Chris	d. 1999	Entertainment	40			90	Comedian
Farley, James A.	1888-1976	Cabinet	15	50	63	30	FDR P.M. General. CEO Coca Cola. Politician
Farley, John Cardinal	1842-1918	Clergy	28			65	Religious Leader & Archbishop of New York
Farman, Henri	1874-1958	Aviation	60	110	175	165	Pioneer Aviator. Airplane Mfg.1st Flight over 1 Km
Farman, Maurice		Aviation	75		190		Pioneer Aviator. License #6. Brother of Henri
Farmer, Art		Entertainment	10			25	Jazz Fluegelhorn-Trumpet
Farmer, Brig. Gen. Archie A.	1892-1963	Military	30				World War II U.S. general
Farmer, Fannie Merritt	1857-1915	Author	190			250	Cookery Expert '...Boston Cooking School Cook Book'
Farmer, Frances	1914-1970	Entertainment	95	130	160	325	Tragic End for Beautiful Talented Actress

NAME	DATE	CATEGORY	SIG	LS/DS	ALS	SP	COMMENTS
Farmer, James	1920-1999	Activist	20			45	Founder CORE ('42).Led Freedom Riders 60's
Farnham, Ralph	1757-?	Military	150				Revolutionary War Soldier. Fought at Bunker Hill
Farnol, J. Jeffrey		Author	5	25			British
Farnsworth, Charles		Military	25			65	General WW I
Farnsworth, Daniel W.		Business		15	30		Founder Woolen Mills
Farnsworth, Elon John	1837-1863	Civil War	128				Union general, KIA Gettysburg
Farnsworth, John F.	1820-1897	Civil War	37	110	155	450	Union Gen. Sig/Rank 50
Farnsworth, Richard	1919-	Entertainment	12	12	15	34	Character Actor. AA winner
Farnum, Dustin	1874-1929	Entertainment	50	75	90	150	Silent Star. 'The Squaw Man', 'The Virginian'
Farnum, William	1876-1953	Entertainment	40			195	Vintage Leading Man. Silent Films. 'The Spoilers'
Farouk I	1920-1965	Royalty	298				King of Egypt. Inept Ruler. Overthrown By Nasser
F-Troop		Entertainment				65	Cast signed photo
Farquhar, John Hanson		Senate/Congress	10	20	30		MOC IN, Capt. Union Army
Farr, Hugh		Entertainment	12			35	Singer-Guitar Member of 'Sons of the Pioneers'
Farr, Jamie		Entertainment	5	8	10	15	MASH cast. 'Klinger'
Farr, Karl		Entertainment	12			35	Singer-Violin. Member 'Sons of the Pioneers'/Hugh
Farr, Sam F		Congress	10			15	Member U.S. Congress
Farragut, David G.	1801-70	Civil War	181	360	632	912	Union Adm. LS/Cont. 1,300. LS '64 2500
Farrakhan, Louis		Activist	70			150	Leads Nation of Islam
Farrar, Frederick W.		Clergy	25	35	50	50	
Farrar, Geraldine	1882-1967	Entertainment	50	80	100	105	Opera, Concert. Metropolitan. Legendary Star
Farrell, Charles	1901-1990	Entertainment	15	20	30	42	Top Star of Silents. Leading Man 30's-40's
Farrell, Eileen		Entertainment	10			95	Opera, Concert
Farrell, Glenda	1904-1971	Entertainment	25	30		75	Leading Lady-Wisecracking Comedienne 30s
Farrell, Lt. Gen. Francis W.	1900-1981	Military	30				World War II U.S. general
Farrell, Maj. Gen. Thomas F.	1891-1967	Military	30				World War II U.S. general
Farrell, Mike	1939-	Entertainment	5	6	20	22	Actor. 'Mash' and More. 'Providence'
Farrell, Terry		Entertainment				35	
Farrimond, Richard		Astronaut	10			25	
Farrow, Mia	1945-	Entertainment	12	30		32	Actress
Farwell, Chas. B.	1823-1903	Congress	15		20		Senator
Fassbaender, Brigitte		Entertainment	10			25	Ger. Mezzo Soprano,Opera
Fast, Howard	1914-	Author	15	70		25	Historical Novelist, Screenplays. 'Spartacus'
Faster Pussy Cat		Entertainment	25			55	Rock
Fat, Freddie M		Music	10			15	DJ
Father Knows Best		Celebrity				204	Cast signed photo
Fattah, Chaka F		Congress	10			15	Member U.S. Congress
Fatuzzo, Carlo		Political	10			15	Member European Parliament
Fauber, Bernard M.		Business	5	10		10	Pres. K Mart
Faubus, Orval E.		Governor	35		70	50	Gov. AR, Blocked Integration
Faucher, General Louis-Eugène	1874-1964	Military	20				World War II French general
Faulkner, Charles J., Jr.		Senate	15	25			Sen. WV. Battle of New Market
Faulkner, Chas. J.	1806-1884	Congress		40	150		Repr. WV. Authored Fugitive Slave Act
Faulkner, Lisa		Celebrity	10			15	celebrity model
Faulkner, William	1897-1962	Author	234	1103	2500	3600	Nobel Lit.1949, Pulitzer Fiction 1954, 1962,

NAME	DATE	CATEGORY	SIG	LS/DS	ALS	SP	COMMENTS
Fauquier, Francis		Colonial Gov. VA	200	575			Colonial Administrator
Fauré, Felix	1841-1899	Head of State	30		125		Pres. France 1895-99
Fauré, Gabriel	1845-1924	Composer	120	105	344	550	Fr. 100's Songs,Chamber Music. Organist
Faure, Jean-Baptiste	1830-1914	Entertainment	35	110			Opera. Bass-Baritone. 'Faust', 'Don Carlos'
Fausto, Cleva		Entertainment	30			65	Opera
Fava, Giovanni Claudio		Political	10			15	Member European Parliament
Faversham, William	1868-1940	Entertainment	30			55	Created Role 'Jim Carson' in 'Squaw Man'
Fawcett, Edgar	1847-1904	Author	45	110	225	150	Verse, Novels & Plays Satirizing NY High Society
Fawcett, Farrah	1947-	Entertainment	10	12	20	51	Actress
Fawcett, Millicent, Dame	1847-1929	Reformer	30	50	162		Br. Women's Suffrage Leader
Fay, Frank	1894-1961	Entertainment	15	25	45	45	Broadway Leads. Few Films. Barbara Stanwyck Husb.
Faye, Alice	1912-1998	Entertainment	10	15	30	30	20th Cent. Fox Musical Star. Films from Late 30s
Faye, Julia	1896-1966	Entertainment	4	6	10	14	Ex Max Sennett Bathing Beauty. Early DeMille Films
Faylen, Frank	1907-1985	Entertainment	30			55	Am. Character Actor from '36. Gangsters, Cops etc.
Faymonville, Brig. Gen. Philip R.	1888-1962	Military	30				World War II U.S. general
Fayon, James Fleming	1823-1893	Civil War	80				Confederate gen.
Fazenda, Louise	1895-1962	Entertainment	25			75	Mack Sennett Silent Film Star. Top Comedienne
Fearn, Thomas	1789-1863	Civil War	117	189			Member of Confederate Congress
Featherston, Winfield Scott	1820-1891	Civil War	102	255	305		CSA Gen. Sig/Rank 205
Feeney, Tom F		Congress	10			15	Member U.S. Congress
Fegelein, Hermann	1906-1945	Military	310	650			Nazi SS Leader
Fehr, Oded		Celebrity				40	
Feiffer, Jules		Cartoonist	10			50	Mag. Cartoonist
Feilden, Maj Gen Sir Randle Guy	1904-1981	Military	25				World War II British general
Feingold, Russell		Senate	10			15	United States Senate (D - WI)
Feinhals, Fritz		Entertainment	30			50	Ger. Baritone, Opera
Feinstein, Diane		Senate	10	12	25	20	Senator CA
Felber, Gen. of Inf. Hans-Gustav	1889-1962	Military	25				World War II German general
Feld, Fritz	1900-	Entertainment	8	9		20	Character-Comedian. Mad or Eccentric Characters
Feldany, Eric		Entertainment	4	5	6	10	
Felder, Rodney Dr.		Celebrity	5	8	15	15	
Feldman, Charles K.	1904-1968	Business	10	20	40	25	Fndr. Famous Artists Corp. Prod., Lawyer, Agent
Feldman, Corey		Entertainment	6			35	Actor. 'The Goonies'
Feldman, Maj. Gen. Herman	1889-1969	Military	30				World War II U.S. general
Feldman, Marty	1933-1983	Entertainment	35	67	95	105	Actor-Comedian. Pop-eyed Brit. Comedian
Feldon, Barbara	1939-	Entertainment	5	15	15	29	Actress. Leading Lady. 'Get Smart'
Feldshuh, Tovah	1952-	Entertainment	5	6	10	15	Actress. Leading Lady. 1st Noticed in 'Holocaust'-
Feliciano, Jose		Entertainment	5	6		20	Guitar-Vocalist. Blind
Felix, Maria	1915-	Entertainment	10			45	Major Star of Many Mex- Internat'l Films 40's-60's
Fellers, Brig. Gen. Bonner F.	1896-1973	Military	30				World War II U.S. general
Fellini, Frederico	1920-1993	Entertainment	37	98		86	AA Film Director-Producer
Fellows, Edith		Entertainment	10			23	Teen Singer-Actress of 30's
Fels, Joseph		Business	95	210	490		Fels Naptha Soap
Felt, Harry, Adm.		Military	10	30	50	25	
Felton, Cornelius C.	1807-1882	Educator	25	45	135		President Harvard 1860-62.

NAME	DATE	CATEGORY	SIG	LS/DS	ALS	SP	COMMENTS
Felton, Happy		Bandleader	15			35	Big Band
Felton, Rebecca L.	1835-1930	Senate	25	45	150		Sen. GA For 1 Day 11/21-11/22 1st Woman Sen.
Fenn, Brig. Gen. Clarence C.	1890-1971	Military	30				World War II U.S. general
Fenn, Sherilyn	1964-	Entertainment	10			34	Actress. Films From '85. 'Twin Peaks' '90. SP 45
Fenneman, George		Entertainment	12			25	Veteran Radio Personality. 'You Bet Your Life'-TV
Fenstermacher, Carol		Author	8			18	Glamour SP 42
Fenton, Brig. Gen. Chauncey L.	1880-1960	Military	30				World War II U.S. general
Fenton, Ruben E.		Governor	30	50	80		Civil War Gov. NY
Fenwick, B.J., Bishop		Clergy	20	25	30		
Fenwick, Maj. Gen. Charles Philip	1891-1954	Military	24				World War II Canadian general
Fenwick, Millicent	1910-1992	Senate/Congress	18	28		50	MOC NJ. Lampooned in 'Doonsbury'. Pipe Smoker
Feoktistov, Konstantin		Cosmonaut	25			75	Pioneer Russian Cosmonaut
Ferber, Edna	1887-1968	Author	85	169	287		Novelist,Screenplays,Pulitzer'24; 'So Big'; 'Giant
Ferber, Markus		Political	10			15	Member European Parliament
Ferdinand I	1503-1564	Royalty	425	1495			Holy Roman Emperor
Ferdinand I	1793-1875	Royalty	70	245			Emperor of Austria
Ferdinand I	1865-1927	Royalty	70			580	King of Roumania, Prince of Hohenzollern
Ferdinand II	1578-1637	Royalty	100	450			Holy Roman Emperor from 1619
Ferdinand II, and Isabella I		Royalty		4025			
Ferdinand V	1452-1516	Royalty		2850			King of Spain, Patron of Columbus, DS w/Isabella 6000
Ferdinand VII (Sp)	1784-1833	Royalty	125	475			His Reign Disastrous to Spain.
Ferebee, Thomas	1919-2000	Aviation	30	50	120	75	Major. Bombadier of Enola Gay, signed drwg 300
Ferenbaugh, Lt. Gen. Claude B.	1899-1975	Military	30				World War II U.S. general
Ferenczi, Sandor	1873-1933	Science	60	180	350		Hung. Psychoanalyst. Freud Friend
Ferguson, Clare		Celebrity	10			15	Food Stylist
Ferguson, Homer		Congress	5	15		10	Senator MI. Ambass. Philippines
Ferguson, Maynard		Entertainment	10			27	Fine Trumpet Player. Bandleader
Ferguson, Mike F		Congress	10			15	Member U.S. Congress
Ferguson, Miriam A. 'Ma'	1875-1961	Governor	60	150			Governor TX. Replaced Impeached Husband
Ferguson, Samuel W. (WD)	1834-1917	Civil War	238	631	839		CSA General
Ferguson, Samuel W.	1834-1917	Civil War	220	316	642		CSA Gen.
Ferguson, William J.		Entertainment	175	225	425		Actor 'Our American Cousin'
Ferkauf, Eugene		Business	8	10	15	15	
Ferlinghetti, Lawrence		Author	20	75	90	75	Am.Poet, Publisher. Beat Movement
Fermi, Enrico	1901-1954	Science	610	1850	3071		Nobel Phys. 1st Controlled Nuclear Chain Reaction
Fernandel	1903-1971	Entertainment	25			135	Actor-Comedian 'Around the World in 80 Days'
Fernández Martín, Fernando		Political	10			15	Member European Parliament
Ferrara, Franco		Entertainment	45			250	Conductor
Ferrare, Cristina		Entertainment	6	8	15	15	Model. TV Host
Ferrari, Enzo	1898-1988	Business	350	544	437	800	Luxury Sports Car Auto Mfg.& Race Car Driver
Ferraro, Geraldine		Congress	15	45	55	25	Congresswoman NY., V.P. Candidate
Ferreira, Anne		Political	10			15	Member European Parliament
Ferrer, Concepció		Political	10			15	Member European Parliament
Ferrer, Jose	1912-1992	Entertainment	20	25	40	57	AA Actor. 'Cyrano'
Ferrer, Mel	1917-	Entertainment	5			20	Actor. Former Radio Producer-Writer.

NAME	DATE	CATEGORY	SIG	LS/DS	ALS	SP	COMMENTS
Ferrer, Miguel	1955-	Entertainment	4			15	Actor son of Jose
Ferrero, Edward (WD)	1831-1899	Civil War	69	188		300	Union General. Commanded Colored Div. 1863
Ferrero, Edward	1831-1899	Civil War	52	108	150		Union General
Ferri, Enrico		Political	10			15	Member European Parliament
Ferrier, Kathleen	1912-1953	Entertainment	55			195	Opera. Br. Contralto. 'Carmen'
Ferrigno, Lou	1952-	Entertainment	5		10	23	Actor. 'The Hulk'. Muscular Former Mr. Universe
Ferrigno, Ursula		Celebrity	10			15	Vegetarian Chef
Ferrin, Brig. Gen. Charles S.	1892-1976	Military	30				World War II U.S. general
Ferris, Brig. Gen. Benjamin G.	1892-1982	Military	30				World War II U.S. general
Ferris, Scott		Senate/Congress	12	15		15	MOC OK
Ferry, Orris S. (WD)		Civil War	65	140	210	300	Union Gen., U.S. Sen. NY
Ferry, Orris Sanford	1823-1875	Civil War	40	80	125		Union general
Ferry, Thomas White	1827-1896	Senate	70	95			Sen. MI, Pres. Pro Tem Senate
Fersen, Hans-Axel, Count de	1755-1810	Revolutionary War		1250			With Rochambeau at Yorktown. Murdered
Fesch, Joseph, Cardinal	1763-1839	Clergy		220	305		Married Napoleon to Josephine.
Fess, Simeon Davison	1861-1936	Senate/Congress	10	27	45	40	MOC, Senator OH. Chmn. Nat. Rep. Committee
Fessenden, Francis (WD)		Civil War	73	152	210		Union Gen. Lost Leg at Monett's Bluff
Fessenden, Francis	1839-1906	Civil War	63	90	150		Union Gen.
Fessenden, James D.	1833-1882	Civil War	35	70	110		Union Gen.
Fessenden, William P.	1806-1869	Cabinet	45	75	142		Lincoln Sec'y Treasury
Festing, Fld. Mrshl. Sir Francis W.	1902-1976	Military	28				World War II British general
Fetchit, Stepin	1892-1985	Entertainment	35		55	150	Early Afro-Am. Actor-Comedian. Aka Lincoln Perry
Fetterman, William J.	1833-1866	Military		5900			Indian Fighter. With 80 Men..Ambushed & Killed
Feuillere, Edwige	1907-	Entertainment	15			38	Fr. Actress. Leading Member 'Comedie Francaise'
Few, William		Revolutionary War	200	714	750		Continental Congress. 1st GA Sen
Feynman, Richard P.		Science	25	40	85	30	Nobel Physics.
Fibich-Hanusova, Betty		Entertainment			250		Opera. Great Czech Alto
Fiderkiewicz, Alfred J., Dr.		Statesman	40	75			Polish Statesman
Fidler, Jimmy	1900-1988	Entertainment	20	25	30	45	Powerful Hollywood Gossip Columnist
Fiebiger, Christel		Political	10			15	Member European Parliament
Fiedler, Arthur	1894-1979	Entertainment	24	95		50	Conductor Boston Pops
Fiedler, John	1925-	Entertainment	5	6	8	10	Mild, Spectacled, Character Actor. '12 Angry Men'
Field, Charles E.		Clergy	20	35	45	25	
Field, Charles William	1828-1892	Civil War	125	210	340		Confederate general
Field, Cyrus W.	1819-1892	Business	75	210	260		Atl. Telegraph Cable, Financier. Signed stock cerf. 8800
Field, Davis Dudley	1805-1894	Legal	25		35		Counsel for J. Gould, J. Fiske. Law Codification.
Field, Eugene	1850-1895	Author	118	250	437	350	Children's Poet, Journalist. AMsS 900-1700
Field, Henry Martyn	1822-1907	Clergy	15		35		Presb. Younger Brother Cyrus, Davis, Stephen Field
Field, Kate		Author	10	15			
Field, Marshall, III	1893-1956	Business	55	95	160		Communications Empire. Major Publisher
Field, Marshall, IV.	1916-1965	Business	30	70	110	75	Pres., CEO Field Entertprises. Publisher, Editor
Field, Marshall, Sr.	1834-1906	Business	265	525	900	650	Marshall Field & Co.
Field, Mary French		Author	5	15	20	15	
Field, Rachel	1894-1942	Author	20	85			Am. Novels, 'All This & Heaven Too'. Children's Books
Field, Sally	1946-	Entertainment	10	15	25	33	AA Winning Actress

NAME	DATE	CATEGORY	SIG	LS/DS	ALS	SP	COMMENTS
Field, Stephen J.	1816-1899	Supreme Court	75	150	300	225	US Supreme Court Justice Under Lincoln
Field, Todd		Entertainment	3			8	
Field, Virginia	1917-1992	Entertainment	5	6	15	15	Br. Actress. Interesting 2nd Leads
Fielder, Brig. Gen. Kendall J.	1893-1981	Military	30				World War II U.S. general
Fielder, James F.		Governor	10	15	25	15	Governor NJ
Fielding, Copley		Artist	5		15		Brit. Watercolorist
Fielding, Yvette		Celebrity	10			15	children⁸s presenter
Fields, Benny	1894-1959	Entertainment				45	
Fields, Debbi		Entertainment	4			10	
Fields, Gracie, Dame	1898-1979	Entertainment	20	35	55	78	Br. Singer & Comedienne. Knighted for War Effort
Fields, James T.	1817-1881	Author	10	20	45		Publisher
Fields, Lew M.	1879-1946	Entertainment	50				SEE Weber & Fields
Fields, Shep		Entertainment	20			40	Big Band Leader-Songwriter-Singer 30's-40's
Fields, Stanley	1884-1941	Entertainment	15	15	30	35	Vintage Character Actor. Former Boxer, Vaudeville
Fields, W. C.	1879-1946	Entertainment	461	731	1240	1262	Comedian-Actor Stage & Screen. Check S 300-400
Fieldy		Entertainment	5			25	Music. Bass Guitar 'Korn'
Fiennes, Joseph (Finnes)		Entertainment	20			60	Br. Actor. 'Shakespeare In Love'
Fiennes, Ralph		Entertainment	15			52	Br. Actor. 'English Patient'
Fiennes, Ranulph		Explorer	10			30	
Fieseler, Gerhard		Aviation	25	55	85	85	
Fifteen (15)		Entertainment	30	40	50	60	Rock
Figgis, Mike		Celebrity	10			15	film industry
Figner, Medea							See Mei-Figner
Figueiredo, Ilda		Political	10			15	Member European Parliament
Figueres, Jose		Head of State	15	45	110	20	
Filacuridi, Nicola		Entertainment	15			45	Opera
Filippeschi, Mario		Entertainment	25			85	Opera
Fillmore, Caroline	?-1881	First Lady	400	625	800		2nd Wife
Fillmore, Millard (As President)		President	421	835	1865		FF 400-475. ALS/Cont. 27,500
Fillmore, Millard	1800-1874	President	260	627	793	10000	FF 375-400-475. Historic ALS 3750
Fillmore, Millard & Dan'l Webster		President		1917			President and Sectry of State
Filner, Bob F		Congress	10			15	Member U.S. Congress
Finch, Maj. Gen. Lionel Hugh K.	1888-1982	Military	25				World War II British general
Finch, Peter	1916-1977	Entertainment	80		110	165	Br. Actor.AA. Early Death. Protégé of L. Olivier
Findlay, William	1768-1846	Governor	45	60	115		Gov. PA 1817, Sen. 1821
Fine, Janine		Entertainment				40	Porn Queen
Fine, Larry	1911-1974	Entertainment	97	258	412	312	Member (1928) Of Three Stooges Comedy Team
Finegan, Bill (William J.)		Entertainment	20			40	Big Band Leader. (Arranger/Sauter)
Finegan, Joseph	1814-1885	Civil War	123				Confederate general
Finkel, Fyvush		Entertainment	5			20	Character Actor. 'Picket Fences' Emmy
Finlay, Frank	1926-	Entertainment	5	8	15	15	Br. Stage & Film Actor. Screen From '62. TV '84
Finletter, Thomas	1894-1980	Cabinet	7	15	30	20	Korean War Sec'y Air Force. Ambassador
Finley, Cameron		Entertainment	10			20	actor
Finley, Jesse J. (WD)	1812-1904	Civil War					CSA Gen., AMsS 6,600
Finley, Jesse J.	1812-1904	Civil War	96	152	297		CSA Gen. US Sen.

NAME	DATE	CATEGORY	SIG	LS/DS	ALS	SP	COMMENTS
Finley, John		Astronaut	5			15	
Finley, Maj. Gen. Thomas D.	1895-1984	Military	30				World War II U.S. general
Finney, Albert	1936-	Entertainment	10	15	20	25	Br. Actor. 'The Entertainer', 'Tom Jones'
Finney, Charles G.	1792-1875	Clergy	50	75	110		Presb. Revivalist-Evangelist.Withdrew-Pres.Oberlin
Finnie, Linda		Entertainment	10			30	Opera
Finnis, General Sir Henry	1890-1945	Military	25				World War II British general
Finston, Nat W.		Composer-Author	10			20	Conductor-Violinist
Fiorella, Pascal A.		Rev.War Era	20	55	125		
Fiorentino, Linda		Entertainment	18			63	Actress
Fiori, Francesco		Political	10			15	Member European Parliament
Fiorina, Carleton 'Carly'		Business		20	25	30	CEO of Hewlett-Packard
Fio-Rito, Ted		Entertainment	15			35	Big Band Leader
Firestone, Harvey S.	1868-1938	Business	360	825	1550	607	Fndr. Firestone Tire., Signed stock cert. 22000
Firestone, Jr., Harvey S.		Business	25	50	85	35	Pres. CEO Firestone Tire....
Firestone, Leonard K.		Business	15	40	70	30	
Firley, Douglas		Entertainment	6			25	Music. Keyboards 'Gravity Kills'
First Ladies (Four Repub.)		First Ladies	250			900	Nixon, Ford, Reagan, Bush
First Ladies (Kennedy thru Bush)		First Ladies	750				Six
Firth, Colin		Entertainment	10			20	Actor
Firth, Maj. Gen. Chas. Edw. Anson	1902-1991	Military	25				World War II British general
Fischer, Annie		Entertainment				250	
Fischer, Bobby	1943-	Celebrities	70	279	492	112	Champion Am. Chess Player.BS (Chess) 525
Fischer, Edmond H., Dr.		Science	20	45		30	Nobel Medicine
Fischer, Emil	1838-1914	Entertainment	40		75		Opera. Ger. Bass-Baritone. Excelled as 'Sachs'
Fischer, Harold E.		Aviation	10	25	45	35	ACE, Korea, Double Ace
Fischer, Siegfried		Aviation	10	15	25	15	
Fischer, Stanley		Celebrity	10			15	financial expert
Fischer-Dieskau, Dietrich		Entertainment	30			90	Opera
Fish, Hamilton	1808-1893	Cabinet	25	64	90	350	Gov., Senator,U.S.Grant & Hayes Sec'y State
Fish, Maj. Gen. Irwing A.	1881-1948	Military	30				World War II U.S. general
Fish, Michael		Celebrity	10			15	weather presenter
Fish, Nicholas		Revolutionary War	45	118	245		Aide-de-Camp Gen. Scott
Fish, Preserved		Colonial	45	165			Merchant Banker
Fish, Stuyvesant		Business	300	850			RR Baron, Financier
Fishburne, Laurence	1961-	Entertainment	12			50	Actor
Fishel, Danielle		Entertainment				30	
Fisher, Amy		Criminal	20		184		Shot alleged lover's wife.
Fisher, Anna L.		Astronaut	10			25	
Fisher, Bud* (Harry C.)	1885-1954	Cartoonist	75	95		425	'Mutt & Jeff'. 1st Regular Cartoon Strip, signed drw325
Fisher, Carrie		Entertainment	10	36	40	37	Actress, 'Star Wars' Authentic SP 60
Fisher, Cindy		Entertainment	4			10	
Fisher, Dorothy Canfield	1879-1958	Author	30	65	95		Am. Novelist, Essayist.
Fisher, Eddie	1928-	Entertainment	5	15	20	30	Singer
Fisher, Fred J.		Business	90				Mfg. Auto Body. Gen'l Motors.'Body By Fisher'
Fisher, Freddie		Entertainment	5			15	'Schnickelfritz'

NAME	DATE	CATEGORY	SIG	LS/DS	ALS	SP	COMMENTS
Fisher, Geoffrey F.	1887-1972	Clergy	35			50	Archbishop Canterbury
Fisher, Gregor		Entertainment	10			20	Actor
Fisher, Ham*		Cartoonist	100		225	250	'Joe Palooka', signed drwng 60
Fisher, Harrison		Artist	40				Orig. Art as Illustrator. S 700
Fisher, John S.		Governor	10	15	35		Governor PA
Fisher, John, Lord	1841-1920	Military	15	25			Brit. Adm. of the Fleet 1905.Prepared Navy For WW
Fisher, Lawrence P.		Business	90	150	410		Co-Founder Fisher Body (GM)
Fisher, Lt. Gen. Sir Bertie Drew	1878-1972	Military	25				World War II British general
Fisher, Maj. Gen. Arthur Francis	1899-1972	Military	25				World War II British general
Fisher, Maj. Gen. Donald R Dacre	1890-1962	Military	25				World War II British general
Fisher, William F.		Astronaut	5			20	
Fisk, Clinton B.	1828-1890	Civil War	42	85	110		Union Gen. Founded Fisk Univ.
Fisk, James, Jr.	1834-1872	Business	1000	1600	2250	2500	Rarest of Robber Barons.Stock Cert. S 25,000-42000
Fisk, Minnie Maddern	1866-1932	Entertainment	15			35	Am. Stage Actress. Made 2 Silent Films
Fiske, Bradley	1854-1942	Military	15		45		Admiral WW I. Holds 60 Patents for Navy
Fiske, John	1842-1901	Philosopher	20				American philosopher and historian
Fitch, Brig. Gen. Burdette M.	1896-1977	Military	30				World War II U.S. general
Fitch, Val L., Dr.		Science	20	35		30	Nobel Physics
Fitz, Reginald H.	1843-1913	Science	75		310		Physician. Identified Cause of Appendicitis
Fitzgerald, Barry	1888-1961	Entertainment	125	135	195	250	Character Actor.AA; Acquired Stardom'Going My Way'
FitzGerald, Edward	1809-1833	Author	90	250	760		Poet.Translator 'Rubaiyat.a'
Fitzgerald, Ella	1918-1998	Entertainment	97	126	128	301	Am. First Lady of Jazz DS (Conract) 350
Fitzgerald, F. Scott	1896-1940	Author	381	1545	3250	2500	Novelist, Screenwriter. ALS/Content 5,500
Fitzgerald, Garret		Statesman	10	30			Irish Statesman
Fitzgerald, Geraldine	1912-1992	Entertainment	12	22	15	40	Ir. Actress. 'Wuthering Heights'
Fitzgerald, John F.(Honey Fitz)		Political	40	55	95	260	Mayor Boston. JFK Grandfather
Fitzgerald, John		Revolutionary War	35	90	190		
Fitzgerald, Maj. Gen. Gerald M.	1889-1957	Military	25				World War II British general
Fitzgerald, Peter		Senate	10			15	United States Senate (R - IL)
Fitzgerald, Richard		Celebrity	10			15	photographer
Fitzgerald, Tara		Entertainment	10			20	Actress
Fitzherbert, Maj. Gen. Edward H.	1885-1979	Military	25				World War II British general
Fitzhugh, Gilbert		Business	4	5	12	10	
Fitzsimmons, Frank E.		Celebrity	3	8	25	10	
Fitzsimmons, Thomas	1741-1811	Revolutionary. War	244	278	575		Constitution Signer, Articles of Confed. ALS 6500
FitzSimons, Frank L.		Author	8			12	regional history
Fitzsimons, James (jim)		Political	10			15	Member European Parliament
Fitzwater, Marlin		Presidential Aide	5			12	
Fix	1901-1983	Entertainment	40			183	Actor. Good General Purpose Actor. Hundreds Roles
Fixx, Jim		Author-Runner	15	35			
Flack, Roberta		Entertainament	15			40	Rock
Fladgate, Maj Gen. Courtney Wm.	1890-1958	Military	25				World War II British general
Flagg, Fannie		Entertainment	5	10	20	20	Also Author, Playwright
Flagg, James Montgomery	1877-1960	Artist	59	200	330	375	Painter, Illustrator. Self Caricature S. 950
Flagler, D. W.		Military	15	20	25	20	

NAME	DATE	CATEGORY	SIG	LS/DS	ALS	SP	COMMENTS
Flagler, Henry M.	1830-1913	Business	750	2250	6500	1800	Stand. Oil Pioneer. Fndr. So. FL
Flagstad, Kirsten	1895-1962	Entertainment	102		150	260	Nor. Soprano
Flahaut, A.C.J., Count	1785-1870	Fr. Revolution	25		60		Exploits in Gallantry. General, Diplomat, Lover
Flahiff, George B., Cardinal		Clergy	35	40	60	40	
Flake, Floyd H.	1945-	Congress	4	10			Congressman NY
Flake, Jeff F		Congress	10			15	Member U.S. Congress
Flakus, Walter		Entertainment	6			25	Music. Keyboards 'Stabbing Westward'
Flammarion, Nicolas-Camille	1842-1925	Science	40	61	120		Fr. Astronomer
Flamsteed, John	1646-1719	Clergy-Science	750	2100			Br. 1st Astronomer Royal
Flanagan, Edward, Fr.	1886-1948	Clergy	45	110		195	Boy's Town Founder
Flanery, Sean Patrick		Entertainment	10			20	actor
Flannery, Sean Patrick		Entertainment	15			44	Actor. The Young 'Indiana Jones'
Flatt, Lester & Earl Scruggs		Country Music	50			125	Bluegrass Pioneers
Flaubert, Gustave	1821-1880	Author	175	635	1300		Fr. Novelist. Realist School
Flautre, Hélène		Political	10			15	Member European Parliament
Flavin, Dick		Celebrity	10			15	motivational speaker
Flavin, James	1906-1976	Entertainment	4	5	10	10	Ir.-Am. Supporting Actor. Usually Bewildered Cop
Flavin, Jennifer		Celebrity	10			15	model
Flaxman, John	1755-1826	Artist	55		200		Br.Sculptor & Illustrator. Designs for Wedgewood
Fleetwood Mac		Entertainment	186			306	Signed by All 6, signed album 275-500
Fleetwood, Mick		Entertainment	30			55	Member Fleetwood Mac
Fleischer, Charles		Entertainment	10			35	Voice of Roger Rabbitt
Fleischer, Leonore		Author	15		40	30	'Shadowlands'
Fleischer, Max*	1883-1972	Cartoonist	150	312		237	Animator. Creator of 'Betty Boop'
Fleischer, Richard	1916-	Entertainment	5			20	Film Director '46's-'87
Fleischmann, Charles L.		Business	110	450			Fleischmann's Yeast
Fleiss, Heidi		Business	10		30	45	Hollywood Madame
Fleming, Alexander, Sir	1881-1955	Science	235	281	1045	790	Scottish Bacteriologist. Nobel for Penicillin
Fleming, Ambrose	1849-1945	Science	175		467		Br. Electr. Engineer. Invented 1st Electron Tube
Fleming, Eric	1924-1966	Entertainment	225	250		350	Actor. Original 'Rawhide'-TV
Fleming, Francis		Aviation	10	22	40	30	ACE, WW II
Fleming, Ian	1888-1969	Author	475	900	1100	1400	'James Bond' Novels. 1st Ed. Signed 5,000-
Fleming, John Ambrose, Sir	1849-1945	Science	30	65	150		Br. Electrical Engineer. Many Contributions
Fleming, Maj. Gen. Philip B.	1887-1955	Military	30				World War II U.S. general
Fleming, Maj. Gen. Raymond H.	1889-1974	Military	30				World War II U.S. general
Fleming, Rhonda	1922-	Entertainment	9	18	25	41	Actress. Pin-Up SP 65
Fleming, Victor	1883-1949	Entertainment	255	325		600	Veteran AA Film Director.'Gone With The Wind'-'OZ'
Fleming-Sandes, Alfred		Military	18	50			WW I Victoria Cross
Flemming, Marialiese		Political	10			15	Member European Parliament
Flesch, Colette		Political	10			15	Member European Parliament
Fleta, Miguel	1897-1938	Entertainment	45			250	Opera. Span. Tenor
Fletcher, Bramwell	1904-1988	Entertainment	20			45	Br. Actor. Light Leading Man of 30s
Fletcher, Ernie F.		Congress	10			15	Member U.S. Congress
Fletcher, Frank Jack		Military	25	60	120	60	
Fletcher, Harvey	1884-1981	Science	225				Stereo Sound 1934

NAME	DATE	CATEGORY	SIG	LS/DS	ALS	SP	COMMENTS
Fletcher, James Cooley		Clergy	5		25		Missionary
Fletcher, James		NASA	10	20	35		Whistle Blower
Fletcher, John Gould	1886-1950	Author	18	35	100		Pulitzer Poet. Identified/Imagist Grp., Fugitives
Fletcher, Louise	1936-	Entertainment	6	10	15	35	Actress, AA
Flexner, Simon	1891-1946	Medicine					
Flindt, Flemming		Ballet	25			70	Royal Danish Ballet Star
Flint, Austin	1812-1886	Physician	70	215	400		Eminent Physician-Teacher
Flint, Keith		Entertainment	10			45	Music. Lead Singer 'Prodigy'
Flint, Lawrence		Aviation	10	16	35	25	
Flint, Sir William Russell	1880-1969	Artist			90		
Flippen, Jay C.	1898-1971	Entertainment	25			60	Actor. Vaudeville Background. Cops, Westerns
Flockhart, Calista		Entertainment	14			52	T.V.'s 'Ally McBeal'. Broad Stage Background
Floege, Ernest		Military		45		70	Commandant Paul.Fr.Resistance
Floren, Myron		Entertainment	4			10	Accordian. Lawrence Welk
Florence, William J., Mrs.		Entertainment	10		25	15	Actress-Malvina Pray. Stage. Appeared With Husband
Florence, William Jermyn	1831-1891	Entertainment	15	25	40	75	Actor, Songwriter, Playwright. Appeared With Wife
Florentino, Linda		Entertainment	10			20	actress
Florenz, Karl-heinz		Political	10			15	Member European Parliament
Flores, Juan Jose	1800-1864	Head of State		775			1st President of Equador
Florey, Howard Walter		Science	25	40	75	35	Nobel Medicine, Penicillin
Florey, Paul J., Dr.	1898-1968	Science	25	35	70	45	Nobel Medicine/Fleming. Penicillin
Florey, Robert		Entertainment	15			35	
Flörke, Lt. Gen. Hermann	1893-1979	Military	25				World War II German general
Flory, Brig. Gen. Lester D.L.	1899-1990	Military	30				World War II U.S. general
Flotow, Frederich von	1812-1883	Composer	75	220	450		Ger. Opera, Ballet, Concertos
Flotow, Maj. Gen. Erich von	1870-1940	Military	27				World War II German general
Flourens, Marie-Jean P.	1794-1867	Science		50	225		Fr. Physiologist
Flower, Jac		Celebrity	10			15	home/gardening expert
Flower, R.P.		Governor	10	15			Governor NY
Flowers, Bess	1900-1984	Entertainment	6	10	15	20	Over 1,000 films. 'Queen of Hollyw'd Extras'
Flowers, Jennifer		Celebrity	10			20	Alleged affair with Wm Clinton
Flowers, Wayland		Entertainment	15	15		36	Clever Marionette-Puppet Comedian
Floyd, John Buchanan (WD)		Civil War	242	450	1250		CSA Gen.(Buchanan's Sec'y War 1857-60)
Floyd, John Buchanan	1806-1863	Civil War	162	298	403		Gov. VA. Sec'y War, CSA General
Floyd, Kieth		Celebrity	10			15	TV Chef
Floyd, Maj. Gen. Henry Robert K.	1899-1968	Military	28				World War II British general
Floyd, William	1734-1821	Revolutionary War	350	1016	1370		Signer Decl. of Indepen. Maj.Gen. NY Militia
Floyer-Acland, Lt. Gen. Arthur N.	1885-1980	Military	25				World War II British general
Fluckey, Gene		Military	45		75	90	Top US Submarine Cmdr.
Flunger, Anna		Entertainment	6	8	15	15	
Fluster, Lafayette		Senate	40				Pres. Pro Tem of Senate
Flynn, Edward J.		Political	5	15	25	15	Democratic Boss NY. 'Boss Flynn'
Flynn, Errol	1909-1959	Entertainment	264	625	919	770	Actor, Chk275-400
Flynn, James		Entertainment	4	5	10	10	
Flynn, Joe	1925-1974	Entertainment	53	60	110	134	Am. Character-Comedian. TV 'McHale's Navy'

NAME	DATE	CATEGORY	SIG	LS/DS	ALS	SP	COMMENTS
Flynn, Steve		Entertainment	3			8	
Flynt, Larry		Publisher	15	30	35	31	'Hustler Magazine' Publisher
Foale, Mike		Astronaut	5			20	
Foch, Ferdinand	1851-1929	Military	50	125	285	220	Fr. General WW I, Marshal. Active in Major Battles
Foch, Nina	1924-	Entertainment	8	10	15	18	Dutch-Born Am. Leading Lady. Assoc. Dir.
Foer, Jonathan Safran		Author	20			30	Author, illustrator
Foertsch General Friedrich	1900-1976	Military	25				World War II German general
Foertsch, Gen. of Inf. Hermann	1885-1961	Military	25				World War II German general
Fogelberg, Dan		Entertainment	12			31	
Fogerty, John		Entertainment	15	50		47	Rock, CCR
Föhrenbach, General of Art. Max	1872-1942	Military	25				World War II German general
Fohstrom, Alma	1856-1936	Entertainment	125			600	Legendary Coloratura Soprano St. Petersburg
Fokker, Anthony H.	1890-1939	Aviation	200	295	525	500	Am. Aircraft Designer-Builder
Foley, David		Entertainment	6			30	
Foley, Mark F.		Congress	10			15	Member U.S. Congress
Foley, Red	1910-1968	Country Music	30			85	Top Country Star
Foley, Robert	1941-	Military	25	25		35	General & Vietnam Medal of Honor Recipient
Folger, Charles J.		Cabinet	10	15	35		Sec'y Treasury Under Arthur
Folger, William M.	1844-1928	Military	45	115			Adm. USN. Comm. Phillipine Squadron 189-1905
Folias, Christos		Political	10			15	Member European Parliament
Follett, Ken		Author	5	12		15	Br. Mystery Novelist
Fölsch, Surgeon-General Wilfried	1897-1967	Military	25				World War II German general
Folsom, Marion B.		Cabinet	15	25		20	Sec'y HEW. Drafter Soc.Sec.Adm.
Folsom, Nathaniel		Revolutionary War	125		450		Am. Gen., Continental Congress
Folttmann, Lt. Gen. Josef	1887-1958	Military	25				World War II German general
Foltz, Frederick		Military			45	100	General WW I
Fonck, Maj. Gen. Alfons	1872-1944	Military	25				World War II German general
Fonck, Paul-René	1894-1953	Aviation	1000	1900			ACE, Fr. WW I. Top Allied Ace
Fonda, Bridget		Entertainment	20			46	Actress
Fonda, Henry	1905-1982	Entertainment	50	96		108	AA Actor. Lifetime Achievement Award
Fonda, Jane	1937-	Entertainment	15	25	35	49	AA Winner
Fonda, Jelles		Revolutionary War	50	155	225		Colonial Leader,Rev.War Officer
Fonda, Peter	1939-	Entertainment	12	22	25	50	Actor., SP 'Easy Rider' 250-400
Fonda, Ten Eyck H.		Civil War	50		95		Military Telegrapher Hero
Fondren, Debra Jo		Entertainment	5			25	'Playboy' '78 Centerfold of the Year. Pin-Up 50.
Fong, Benson		Entertainment	25			40	
Fong, Hiram L.		Senate	5	10		15	Senator HI
Fonseca, Roberto A.		Head of State	5	16	40	20	
Fontaine, Joan	1917-	Entertainment	12	15	40	28	Oscar winning Actress. Pin-Up SP 45
Fontanne, Lynn	1887-1983	Entertainment	15			40	Stage Actress Wife of Partner Alfred Lunt
Fonteyn, Margot	1919-1991	Entertainment	40	55	135	195	Premier Ballerina. Fonteyn & Nureyev SP 250
Foot, Solomon		Congress	15	30	45		Repr. VT 1843, CSA Congress
Foote, Andrew Hull	1806-1863	Civil War	50	98	208		Union Adm ALS '63 3,500. Mortally Wounded 1863
Foote, Arthur Wm.	1853-1937	Composer	30	85	195		Organist. Church Music, Songs, Cantatas
Foote, H.R.B.		Military	10	20			Br. Maj. Gen. Victoria Cross WW II

NAME	DATE	CATEGORY	SIG	LS/DS	ALS	SP	COMMENTS
Foote, Henry S.		Civil War	25	40	70		US Senator, CSA Congress
Foote, Horton		Author	5		20	15	Playwright, Scriptwriter
Foote, Shelby		Author	15	35			
Foraker, Joseph B.	1846-1917	Senator-Gov.	10	32		20	Gov., Sen. OH. Secretly On Std.Oil Payroll as Sen.
Foran, Dick	1910-1979	Entertainment	15	20	35	45	Singer-Actor-Cowboy. 40 Year Career
Foray, June		Entertainment	10			25	Voices for Several 'Rocky & Bullwinkle' Characters
Forbes, Bertie Chas.	1880-1954	Business	45	80	120	90	Founder Forbes Magazine
Forbes, Emma		Celebrity	10			15	television presenter
Forbes, George Wm.	1869-1947	Head of State	25	65			NZ Prime Minister.
Forbes, J. Randy F		Congress	10			15	Member U.S. Congress
Forbes, M. Steve		Publisher	15			30	Twice Presidential Candidate
Forbes, Malcolm S.	1933-1991	Business	25	45	70	64	Publisher, Motorcyclist, Balloonist, Collector
Forbes, Ralph	1902-1951	Entertainment	15	20	30	25	Br. Stage as Child. Movies From 1921
Forbes-Robertson, John, Sir	1853-1937	Entertainment	25		98	58	Br.Vintage Stage, Films. SPc/Gertrude Elliott 125
Force, Manning Ferguson	1824-1899	Civil War	55	110	170		Union general, Medal of Honor
Ford , Anna		Celebrity	10			15	newsreader
Ford Coppola, Francis		Celebrity	10			35	film industry
Ford Jr., Harold E. F		Congress	10			15	Member U.S. Congress
Ford, Benson		Business	5	15	30	15	Ford Motor Car
Ford, Betty		First Lady	35	75		75	
Ford, Brig. Gen. William W.	1898-1986	Military	30				World War II U.S. general
Ford, Edsel B. II		Business	5	10	20	15	Ford Motor Co.
Ford, Edsel	1893-1943	Business	155	420		500	Pres. Ford Motor Co.
Ford, Eileen		Business	5	30		10	Ford Modelling Agency
Ford, Elaine		Business	20			30	
Ford, Faith		Entertainment	8			43	Actress. 'Murphy Brown'
Ford, Gerald & Betty		President-1st Lady				125	FDC S. 250
Ford, Gerald R. (As President)		President	114	344	1440	146	TLS/Cont. 1000-2500
Ford, Gerald R.		President	62	228	992	94	Signed Warren Attest. 200., Full Signed Pardon 1200
Ford, Glenn	1916-1995	Entertainment	37			65	Versatile Film Leading Man
Ford, Glyn		Political	10			15	Member European Parliament
Ford, Harold	1945-	Congress	5	20		15	Longtime Afr.-Am. Dem. MOC TN
Ford, Harrison		Entertainment	52			89	Actor, 'Star Wars' SP 144-309
Ford, Henry II	1917-1987	Business	10	45	55	55	Grandson, Pres.& CEO Ford Motor Co.
Ford, Henry	1863-1947	Business	825	2407	4667	2097	Pioneer Auto Mfg. Important DS 28,500
Ford, John Anson		Business	5	10	20	10	
Ford, John Thompson	1829-1894	Theatre Owner	342	500	650		Ford's Theater, Wash. D.C.
Ford, John	1895-1973	Entertainment	150			300	Classic Western Film Director
Ford, Lita		Entertainment	15			45	Singer
Ford, Maj. Gen. Elbert L.	1892-1990	Military	30				World War II U.S. general
Ford, Maj. Gen. John Randle M.	1881-1948	Military	25				World War II British general
Ford, Michael		Entertainment	5			15	Br. Actor
Ford, Paul	1901-1976	Entertainment	15			35	Am. Character Actor. Stage, TV, Films. 'OZ' Voices
Ford, Rosemarie		Celebrity	10			15	television presenter
Ford, Samuel Howard	1819-1905	Civil War	64	68	117		Member of Confederate Congress

NAME	DATE	CATEGORY	SIG	LS/DS	ALS	SP	COMMENTS
Ford, Sewell	1868-1946	Author		15	35		Short Story Writer
Ford, Tennessee Ernie	1919-	Country Music	18			36	'Sixteen Tons', 'Mule Train' etc.
Ford, Wallace	1898-1966	Entertainment	20			50	London Born. Played Strong Characters For 30 Years
Fordney, Joseph W.		Senate/Congress	15		30		MOC MI. Lumber, Banking
Forepaugh, Adam	1831-1890	Business-Circus	50		75		Early Circus Owner
Forester, Cecil Scott	1899-1966	Author	65	125	210	175	Known for 'Horatio Hornblower'
Forgy, Howell M.		Military Chaplain					'And Pass the Ammunition' S Book 395
Forman, Brig James Francis Robt.	1899-1969	Military	25				World War II British general
Forman, Milos	1932-	Entertainment	20			52	AA Director. 'One Flew Over the Cukoo's Nest'
Forman, Thomas M.		Revolutionary War	45	100			
Forman, Thomas March	1809-1875	Civil War	94				Member of Confederate Congress
Formentini, Marco		Political	10			15	Member European Parliament
Formes, Karl		Entertainment	5	6	15	15	
Formica, Fern		Entertainment	15	25		30	Munchkin,' Wizard of Oz'
Formica, Palma E.		Celebrity	10			15	medical expert
Fornay, John	1817-1881	Editor	20		48		Prominent Editor & Dem. Political Figure
Forney, John Horace	1829-1902	Civil War	125	126	234		CSA Gen. Sig/Rank 275, ALS '62 975
Forney, John W.	1817-1881	Journalist	5		25		Author
Forney, William H.	1823-1894	Civil War	96	180	388		CSA Gen., Wounded & Captured Twice. MOC AL
Forrest, Edwin	1806-1872	Entertainment	35	90	160	150	Early Great Am. Actor. ALS/Cont. 400
Forrest, Frederick	1936-	Entertainment	4			15	Actor. Leading Man of 70's-80's
Forrest, French (WD)		Civil War	175	660			CSA Naval Commander
Forrest, French	1796-1866	Civil War	136	145	195		CSA Naval Commander
Forrest, Hal*		Cartoonist	25			125	'Tailspin Tommy'
Forrest, Nathan Bedford (WD)		Civil War	1600		14500		CSA Gen., LS/Cont. 22,500
Forrest, Nathan Bedford	1821-1877	Civil War	1250	2750	6500		CSA General
Forrest, Sally	1928-	Entertainment	5			15	Ingenue-Dancer-Leading Lady in Early 50's
Forrest, Steve	1924-	Entertainment	7			15	Actor-Brother of Dana Andrews. Leads-2nd Leads
Forrestal, James	1892-1949	Cabinet	32	69		55	Sec'y Navy. 1st Sec'y Defense. Suicide
Forrester, Pat		Astronaut	6			20	
Forser, Brig. Gen. George J.	1891-1979	Military	30				World War II U.S. general
Forslund, Constance		Entertainment	5	6	15	15	
Forst, Lt. Gen. Werner	1892-1971	Military	25				World War II German general
Forster, Brig. Gen. George B. Jr.	1884-1949	Military	30				World War II U.S. general
Forster, Brig. Gen. Ivan L.	1896-1965	Military	30				World War II U.S. general
Forster, Edw. Morgan	1879-1970	Author	67	187	314		Br. Novelist. 'Howard's End', 'Passage to India'
Förster, Gen. of Inf. Sigismund	1887-1959	Military	25				World War II German general
Förster, Gen. Pioneers Otto-Wilh.	1885-1966	Military	25				World War II German general
Forster, John	1812-1876	Author	18	35	85		Br. Historian, Biographer of Dickens, Swift
Forster, Lt. Gen. Alfred Leonard	1886-1963	Military	25				World War II British general
Forster, Maj. Gen. Kurt	1891-1962	Military	25				World War II German general
Forster, Robert		Entertainment	5			35	Actor
Forster, Surgeon-General Edgar	1890-1975	Military	25				World War II German general
Forsyth, Bruce		Celebrity	10			15	comedian
Forsyth, Frederick		Author	10	25	40	20	Br., Master of Spy Novels

NAME	DATE	CATEGORY	SIG	LS/DS	ALS	SP	COMMENTS
Forsyth, James Wm.	1835-1906	Civil War	53	108	163		Union Gen.Fought at Wounded Knee ALS/Cont. 250.
Forsyth, James	1842-1915	Civil War	46	86	60		Admiral. Served w/Farragut. Also Span-Am. War
Forsyth, John	1780-1841	Cabinet	25	55	150		Sec'y of State (Jackson & Van Buren)Senator
Forsythe, John	1918-	Entertainment	10	10	20	30	Leading Man. Smoothe, Appealing. 'Dynasty'
Fort, Brig. Gen. Guy O.	1879-1942	Military	30				World War II U.S. general
Fort, George F.		Governor	15	35	50		Governor NJ 1850
Fort, John Franklin		Governor	5	15			New Jersey
Fort, Luigi		Entertainment	20			50	Opera
Fortas, Abe	1910-1982	Supreme Court	50	150	200		Resigned from Court
Forté, Fabian (Fabian)	1942-	Entertainment	5	8	25	20	Handsome Rock Singer. Teenage Idol
Forti, Carmen Fiorella		Entertainment	25			60	Opera
Fortier, Brig. Gen. Louis J.	1892-1974	Military	30				World War II U.S. general
Fortner, Lt. Gen. Johann	1884-1947	Military	25				World War II German general
Fortune, Maj. Gen. Sir Victor M.	1883-1949	Military	25				World War II British general
Forward, Walter	1786-1852	Cabinet	15	42	72		Sec'y Treasury 1841
Fosbury, Dick		Sportsman	25			45	Eponym for Fosbury Flop (High Jump)
Fosdick, Harry Emerson	1878-1969	Clergy	35	60	90	50	Baptist Minister, Author
Foss, Joe		Aviation	32	75	85	60	ACE, WW II, Medal of Honor
Foss, Sam Walter	1858-1911	Author	5	10	20	15	Editor, Humorist. 'House By The Side of The Road'
Fosse, Bob	1927-1987	Entertainment	35	60	90	80	AA. Choreographer-Film Director
Fossella, Vito F.		Congress	10			15	Member U.S. Congress
Fossett, Steve		Celebrity	10			30	Balloonist
Foster, Abiel	1735-1806	Clergy-Political	120	345			Cont. Congress. 1st MOC NH '89
Foster, Charles	1828-1904	Cabinet	35	55	100		Gov. OH, Sec'y Treas.
Foster, Dianne		Entertainment	5			20	Actress
Foster, Hal*	1892-1982	Cartoonist	100			550	'Tarzan', 'Prince Valiant'
Foster, Henry		Celebrity	10			15	medical expert
Foster, Jacqueline		Political	10			15	Member European Parliament
Foster, Jodie	1962-	Entertainment	30			139	Actress, Dir., AA Winner
Foster, John Gray (WD)	1823-1874	Civil War	55	105	275		Union General
Foster, John Gray	1823-1874	Civil War	50	65	106		Union Gen.
Foster, John W.	1836-1917	Cabinet	25		58	165	Sec'y State 1892, Diplomat, CW Union Officer
Foster, Lafayette S.	1806-1880	Senate	25	62	98		Civil War Senator CT. ALS As Acting VP 800
Foster, Lafayette Sabine	1806-1880	Law			32	35	Yale law professor
Foster, Lawrence		Entertainment	5	5	10	10	
Foster, Meg		Entertainment	10			20	actress
Foster, Myles B.		Artist	17	40	70		
Foster, Norman	1900-1976	Entertainment	15	20	35	45	Actor-Director. Stage & Films from 30's
Foster, Preston	1901-1970	Entertainment	28	85		52	Actor. Handsome Leading Man. Over 100 Films
Foster, Robert Sanford	1834-1903	Civil War	40				Union general
Foster, Stephen	1826-1864	Composers	1500	5500	10000		Pop Songs of Day. 'My Old Kentucky Home'
Foster, Susanna	1924-	Entertainment	15	30		25	Singer-Actress. One Major Prod. 'Phantom of Opera'
Foucauld, Charles E.	1858-1916	Explorer-Clergy	300		875		Fr. Priest & Explorer
Foucault, Leon	1819-1868	Science	150		715		Fr. Physicist. Speed of Light. Rotation of Earth
Fouché, Jos. Duc d'Otrante	1759-1820	Fr. Revolution	125	210	680		Politician, Advisor Nap.

NAME	DATE	CATEGORY	SIG	LS/DS	ALS	SP	COMMENTS
Foulkes, General Charles	1903-1969	Military	20				World War II Canadian general
Foulois, Benj. D.	1880-1967	Aviation	50			150	General. Pioneer Aviator
Fountain, Pete		Entertainment	10	10	25	43	Top Jazz-Dixieland Clarinetist
Fouquet, Maj Gen Hans-Joachim	1895-1944	Military	25				World War II German general
Four Seasons, The		Rock Group		125		125	60's Rock Group
Four Tops		Entertainment	40			95	Rock Singing Group
Fournet, Jean		Entertainment	25			70	Conductor
Fournier, G.		Military	55	85			
Fourtou, Janelly		Political	10			15	Member European Parliament
Fowkes, Maj. Gen. Charles C.	1894-1966	Military	28				World War II British general
Fowldes, Derek		Entertainment	10			20	Actor
Fowler, Brig. Gen. Raymond F.	1884-1949	Military	30				World War II U.S. general
Fowler, Gene	1890-1960	Author	20	60		30	Journalist, Biographer, Novelist
Fowler, Henry H.		Cabinet	5	20	35	15	Sec'y Treas.
Fowler, Jim		Entertainment	4			12	Animal Handler. Seen on 'Tonight Show'
Fowler, William, Dr.		Science	20	30	45	30	Nobel Physics
Fowles, John		Author	30	50	85	75	Br.Novelist.Fr. Lieut's Woman
Fowley, Douglas	1911-	Entertainment	10			30	Vet. Stage-Film Character Actor. Over 200 Films
Fox, Bernard		Entertainment	8			32	Actor. 'Hogan's Heroes', 'Bewitched', 'Titanic'
Fox, Brig. Gen. Leon A.	1890-1965	Military	30				World War II U.S. general
Fox, Charles	1749-1806	Statesman	40	65	134		Br.Reformer, Orator, Libel Bill
Fox, Edward	1937-	Entertainment	5			15	Br. Actor. Blonde-Brother of James. Similar Style
Fox, Fontaine T.*		Cartoonist	35	50		200	'Toonerville Trolley'
Fox, Fred S.		Entertainment	10		45		Actor 'Mayberry'
Fox, Gustavus V.	1821-83	Civil War	35		50		Asst Sec of Navy
Fox, James	1939-	Entertainment	5			15	Br. Actor. Leading Man. Similar in Style to Edward
Fox, Jamie		Entertainment	15			35	Actor
Fox, Kerry		Entertainment	10			20	actress
Fox, Lt. Gen. Alonzo P.	1895-1984	Military	30				World War II U.S. general
Fox, Maj. Gen. Wilhelm	1895-1985	Military	25				World War II German general
Fox, Matthew		Entertainment	10			45	Actor
Fox, Michael J.	1961-	Entertainment	20	37	40	45	'Back to the Future',actor
Fox, Samantha		Entertainment	12			49	Pin-Up 55
Fox, Samuel		Clergy	15	20	25	35	
Fox, William	1879-1952	Business	185	550		375	Founder Fox Film Corp.
Fox-Pitt, Maj. Gen. Wm. Aug. F. L.	1896-1988	Military	28				World War II British general
Foxworth, P. E.		Celebrity	5	15	35		
Foxworth, Robert	1941-	Entertainment	5	4	9	10	Actor. Good General Purpose . Mostly TV from '72
Foxworthy, Jeff		Entertainment	7			30	Comedian
Foxx, Redd	1922-1991	Entertainment	28	49		62	Comedian. Stand-up & Sit-Com. 'Sanford & Son'
Foy, Eddie, Jr.	1905-1983	Entertainment	20	25	40	45	Am. Vaudeville Entertainer. Few 50s-60s Films
Foy, Eddie, Sr.	1854-1928	Entertainment	25			60	Am. Vaudeville Comedian. Few Films
Foy, Maximilian S., Count	1775-1825	Fr. Revolution	75	140	225		Fr. Statesman, General. Waterloo
Fradona, Ramon*		Cartoonist	15			50	'Brenda Starr'
Frahm, Pernille		Political	10			15	Member European Parliament

NAME	DATE	CATEGORY	SIG	LS/DS	ALS	SP	COMMENTS
Fraisse, GeneviFve		Political	10			15	Member European Parliament
Fraizier, Brig. Gen. Thomas A.	1894-1969	Military	30				World War II U.S. general
Frakes, Jonathan		Entertainment	10	15	19	43	'Star Trek-Next Generation'
Frampton, George, Sir	1860-1928	Artist	20		48		Brit. Sculp. Edith Cavell Mem.' Peter Pan'
Frampton, Peter		Entertainment	10			30	Rock
France, Anatole (Thibault J.)	1844-1924	Author	50	75	119	225	Fr. Novels, Poetry, Critic. Nobel 1921
France, Hector		Author	30			60	adventurer, author
Francescatti, Zino		Entertainment	30			200	Violinist. 4x6 SP 150
Franchetti, Alberto, Baron	1860-1942	Composer	35		130	90	Wrote 9 Operas, Chamber Music, Symphony
Franchi, Sergio	1933-1990	Entertainment	10			30	Singer
Franciosa, Anthony	1928-	Entertainment	7	10	12	18	Broadway & Film 'Hatful of Rain'=AA Nomination
Francis Berry, Mary		Celebrity	10			15	political celebrity
Francis I Fr.	1494-1547	Royalty	410	750			France. Special DS 2,750
Francis I	1777-1830	Royalty	100	350			King Two Sicilies
Francis II	1768-1835	Royalty	125	400	650		Last Holy Roman Emperor(Aus)
Francis V	1819-1875	Royalty	110	275			Duke of Modena
Francis, Anne	1930-	Entertainment	7	10	15	25	Film Leading Lady. Radio Children. Soaps
Francis, Arlene	1912-	Entertainment	5	6	15	18	Gained Popularity as Radio-TV Hostess & Panelist
Francis, Connie	1938-	Entertainment	7	10	35	25	Singer. Top Vocalist late 50's-early 60's
Francis, David R.		Cabinet	15	30	50	75	Sec'y Interior 1896
Francis, Dick		Author	25	72	80	42	Br. Jockey Turned Mystery Writer
Francis, Genie		Entertainment	5	6	15	25	Actress. 'General Hospital'
Francis, Jan		Entertainment	10			20	Actress
Francis, Kay	1903-1968	Entertainment	25	30	70	95	One of Hollywood's Highly Paid Glamour Stars-30's
Franciscus, James	1934-1991	Entertainment	10	12	15	22	Actor
Franck, Cesar	1822-1920	Composer	300	460	658		AMusMsS 5,000
Francks, Cree		Entertainment	4			12	Actress/Voice Artist
Franco, Francisco	1892-1975	Head of State	75	260	1300	189	Sp. General & Dictator
Franco, James		Entertainment				40	
Francois, Maj Gen Henri-Nicholas	1882-1958	Military	20				World War II French general
Francois, Maj. Gen. Marie-J-V-L	1879-1962	Military	20				World War II French general
Franek, Lt. Gen. Friedrich	1891-1976	Military	27				World War II German general
Frank, August		Military	10	30	45		
Frank, Barney F		Congress	10			20	Member U.S. Congress
Frank, Brig. Gen. Selby H.	1891-1974	Military	30				World War II U.S. general
Frank, Diana		Entertainment	3			8	
Frank, Hans		Nazi Lawyer	225	500		368	Nazi Administrator of Poland
Frank, Marshall		Author	8			12	mystery novelist, political commentary
Frank, Otto	1889-1980	History	138	686			ANS on Hand Painted Card 2500. Ann Frank
Franke, Lt. Gen. Hermann	1878-1956	Military	25				World War II German general
Franke, Maj. Gen. Gustav H.	1888-1953	Military	30				World War II U.S. general
Franken, Rose		Author	10	25	40		Playwright
Frankenheimer, John	1930-2002	Entertainment	10		30	40	Film Director
Frankewitz, Lt. Gen. Bruno	1897-1982	Military	25				World War II German general
Frankfurter, Felix	1882-1965	Supreme Court	155	485	881	800	Founder Am. Civil Liberties Un. Special TLS 2900

NAME	DATE	CATEGORY	SIG	LS/DS	ALS	SP	COMMENTS
Franklin, Benjamin		Revolutionary War	4500	10228	26645		Rev. War Dte. DS 25,000
Franklin, Bonnie		Entertainment	5	10	15	22	Actress. 'One Day at a Time'
Franklin, Herbert H.	1867-1956	Business	35	125			Pioneer Auto Manufacturer
Franklin, Jane	1792-1875	Author	65		220		Wife of John Franklin, Traveller, Explorer
Franklin, John, Sir	1786-1847	Explorer	125	292	610		Proved NW Passage
Franklin, Maj. Gen. John M.	1895-1975	Military	30				World War II U.S. general
Franklin, William	1731-1813	Colonial & Revol.	150	375	722		Brit. Gov. NJ, Illegitimate Son of Benjamin
Franklin, Wm. Buell (WD)		Civil War	95	180	310	450	Union Gen. AES/3 Gen'ls 825
Franklin, Wm. Buell	1823-1903	Civil War	57	123	167	350	Union Gen.
Franklyn, Lt. Gen. Sir Harold E.	1885-1963	Military	25				World War II British general
Franks, Brig. Gen. John B.	1890-1946	Military	30				World War II U.S. general
Franks, Trent F.		Congress	10			15	Member U.S. Congress
Frann, Mary	1943-1998	Entertainment	10	15	15	35	Actress. 'Newhart'
Frantz, Charton C.		Business	10	35	45	20	
Frantzius, Maj. Gen. Botho von	1898-1942	Military	25				World War II German general
Franz Ferdinand	1863-1914	Royalty				1380	Archduke Austria. Assassinated
Franz Josef II, Crown Prince		Royalty	40	75	140	50	Liechtenstein
Franz Joseph I,	1830-1916	Royalty	155	672	875		Emperor of Austria
Franz, Arthur	1920-	Entertainment	10			20	Am. Leading Man & Character Actor; Radio, Stage, TV
Franz, Dennis		Entertainment	12			43	Actor. 'NYPD Blue' DS 95. Emmy
Franz, Maj. Gen. Gerhard Franz	1902-1975	Military	25				World War II German general
Fraser, Brendan		Entertainment	6			42	Actor
Fraser, Douglas A.		Labor	10	15		15	Union President
Fraser, James Earle	1876-1953	Artist	425	650			Am. Sculptor of Buffalo Nickel, Lincoln, St. Gaudens
Fraser, Maj. Gen. Alex. Donald	1884-1960	Military	25				World War II British general
Fraser, Maj Gen Wm. Archibald K.	1886-1969	Military	25				World War II British general
Fraser, Malcolm		Head of State	10			30	P.M. Australia
Fraser, Peter		Head of State	10	25		20	Prime Minister New Zealand
Frasier (Cast of)		Entertainment	102			250	All Five
Frasier		Entertainment				200	Cast signed photo
Frassoni, Monica		Political	10			15	Member European Parliament
Frawley, William	1887-1966	Entertainment	207	350		412	Dour Character Actor. 'Fred Mertz'
Frazer, James George	1854-1941	Science	120		650		Scottish Anthropologist-Classicist. 'Golden Bough'
Frazer, John Wesley	1827-1906	Civil War	198	255	805		CSA General. With no shot fired, surrendered!
Frazer, Joseph W.		Business	275	600			Kaiser-Frazer Auto Mfg.
Frazetta, Frank*		Cartoonist	50			375	'Johnny Comet'
Frazier, Brendon		Entertainment	5			30	Actor
Freddy & The Dreamers (All)		Entertainment	105				
Fredendall, Lt. Gen. Lloyd R.	1883-1963	Military	30				World War II U.S. general
Frederic, Harold		Author	10	35	70		Am. Novelist, Correspondent
Frederick Augustus I,	1750-1827	Royalty	55	275			The Just, Saxony
Frederick Augustus II	1797-1854	Royalty		250			King Saxony
Frederick I (Wurttemburg)	1754-1816	Royalty	100	230			Duke of Wurttemburg
Frederick II (The Great)	1712-1786	Royalty	350	700	2600		Prussia
Frederick III	1831-1888	Royalty	120	260	650	500	Queen Victoria's Son-in-Law. Ger. Emperor 99 Days

NAME	DATE	CATEGORY	SIG	LS/DS	ALS	SP	COMMENTS
Frederick IV	1671-1730	Royalty		320	700		Denmark
Frederick IX	1899-1972	Royalty	50	175	350		Denmark
Frederick Louis	1707-1751	Royalty		80	100		Prince of Wales
Frederick V	1723-1766	Royalty	90	270	500		Denmark
Frederick VI	1768-1839	Royalty	85	270			Denmark
Frederick VII	1808-1863	Royalty	90	220			Denmark
Frederick Wm. I	1688-1740	Royalty	145	388			Prussia
Frederick Wm. II	1744-1797	Royalty		168	490		Prussia. Succeeded by Uncle Frederick II, The Great
Frederick Wm. III	1770-1840	Royalty	80	207	475		Prussia
Frederick Wm. IV	1795-1861	Royalty	100	350	750		Prussia. Insane
Frederick, Maj. Gen. Robert T	1907-1970	Military	30				World War II U.S. general
Frederick, Pauline		Journalist	10		25	25	Pioneer TV Reporter. Debut 1949
Frederick, Pauline	1883-1938	Entertainment	20	35		80	Chorus Girl at 19. Silent Cinema Star from 1915
Frederick, Prince of Wales	1707-1751	Royalty		110			Son of Geo. II. Father of Geo. III
Fredericks, Fred*		Cartoonist	18		85	50	'Mandrake The Magician'
Fredericks, R.N.		Banker	12				
Freed, Bert	1919-	Entertainment	5	6	15	15	Am. Character Actor
Freedman, Larry		Celebrity	5	7	10	10	Lawyer, Die-hard Cub fan
Freeland, Maj. Gen. Rowan A.B.	1895-1970	Military	25				World War II British general
Freeland, Paul van		Head of State	8	16	40	20	Prime Minister
Freeling, Sir Francis	1764-1836	Celebrity			120		
Freeman, Alan		Music	10			15	DJ
Freeman, Kathleen	1919-	Entertainment	10	15		20	Long Time Character Actress. Films - TV
Freeman, Mona	1926-	Entertainment	5	8	15	18	Ingenue-Leading Lady.
Freeman, Morgan	1937-	Entertainment	15		50	50	Actor. Acadamy Award
Freeman, Orville		Cabinet	7	20	25	10	Sec'y Agriculture. Gov. MN
Freeman, Samuel		Revolutionary War	15	45	100		Rev. War Patriot
Freeman, Ted		Astronaut	10			48	
Freeman, Thomas W.	1824-1865	Civil War	100				Member of Confederate Congress
Freeman-Attwood, Maj. Gen. H. A.	1897-1963	Military	28				World War II British general
Fregeville, C.L.J.Marquis		Fr. Rev. War	20	35	75		
Frehley, Ace		Entertainment				45	Singer
Freleng, Friz*	1906-1995	Cartoonist	55	145		189	Animator Bugs Bunny, signed drawing 150-400
Frelinghuysen, Frederick T.	1817-1885	Cabinet	20	60	105	125	Sec'y State, Senator NJ
Frelinghuysen, Joseph S		Senate/Congress	5	15			Senator NJ
Frelinghuysen, Rodney P. F		Congress	10			15	Member U.S. Congress
Fremerey, Lt. Gen. Max	1889-1968	Military	25				World War II German general
Fremont, Jessie Benton	1824-1902	Author	35	80	270		Writer-'Far West Sketches'Wife of John C. Fremont
Fremont, John C. (WD)		Civil War	282	758	883		Union Gen. Explorer & Statesman
Fremont, John C.	1813-1890	Civil War	183	415	534	800	Union Gen.Content ALS 6,500., signed stock cert.1450
Fremstad, Olive	1871-1951	Entertainment	95			375	Swe-Am. Soprano. Opera. Europe & Met 1903-1917
French, Brig. Gen. Charles A.	1888-1982	Military	30				World War II U.S. general
French, Daniel Chester	1850-1931	Artist	70	140	200	175	Sculptor, Lincoln Memorial
French, Dawn		Celebrity	10			15	comedienne
French, John	1852-1925	Military	50		145		1st Earl Ypres. Field-marshal

NAME	DATE	CATEGORY	SIG	LS/DS	ALS	SP	COMMENTS
French, Michael		Entertainment	10			20	Actor
French, Samuel Gibbs	1818-1910	Civil War	120	292	527		CSA General
French, Victor		Entertainment	15			40	
French, William H.	1815-1881	Civil War	46	110	175		Union General
Freni, Mirella	1935-	Entertainment	10			45	It Soprano. Opera. 'Violetta', 'Mimi', 'Butterfly'
Frenking, Maj. Gen. Hermann	1894-1956	Military	25				World War II German general
Freron, Louis M.S.	1754-1802	Fr. Revolution	25	45	90		Revolutionary Politician. Conspiracy vs Robespierre
Fresnay, Pierre	1897-1975	Entertainment	10			45	Fr. Actor/Dir. Important Film Personality in 30s
Fretter-Pico, Lt. Gen. Otto	1893-1966	Military	25				World War II German general
Freud, Anna	1895-1982	Science		210	350		Daughter of Sigmund Freud
Freud, Emma		Music	10			15	DJ
Freud, Sigmund	1856-1939	Science	1433	2782	4363	9475	Psychoanalysis. ALS/Content 7,500-22,500
Freund, William		Celebrity	10			15	financial expert
Freutel, Maj. Gen. Lothar	1894-1944	Military	25				World War II German general
Frey, Richard		Aviation	25	50	100	65	
Freyberg, Lt. Gen. Bernard Cyril	1889-1963	Military	20				World War II New Zealand general
Freydenberg, Maj. Gen. Henry	1876-1975	Military	20				World War II French general
Freye, Maj. Gen. Johannes	1878-1952	Military	25				World War II German general
Freytag, Maj. Gen. Walter	1892-1982	Military	25				World War II German general
Frère, Gen. Aubert-Achille-Jules	1881-1944	Military	20				World War II French general
Friant, Louis, Count		Fr. Revolution	30	75	150		
Frick, Henry Clay	1849-1919	Business	250	410	650		Carnegie Steel. ,signed stock cert. 3800
Frick, Stephen		Astronaut	6			22	
Frick, Wilhelm	1877-1946	Military	185				Reich's Minister of the Interior
Fricke, Janie		Entertainment	5			10	Singer
Fricke, Richard I.		Business	10	35	45	20	
Fricker, Brenda	1944-	Entertainment	20	35	35	67	Ir. Character Actress. AA for 'My Left Foot'
Frid, Jonathan		Entertainment	10			50	
Frießner, Col-Gen Johannes	1892-1971	Military	25				World War II German general
Friedan, Bette		Feminist	15		25	20	
Friedgen, A.E.		Business	10	35	45	20	
Friedkin, William	1939-	Entertainment	10	20		25	Director. AA for 'The French Connection' 1971
Friedman, Herbert		Science	15	35	55	20	
Friedman, Jerome I.		Science	20	35		30	Nobel Physics
Friedman, Milton		Economist-Author	20	35		28	Nobel Economics
Friedman, Thomas		Celebrity	10			25	political celebrity
Friedrich, Ingo		Political	10			15	Member European Parliament
Friedrich, Klaus		Celebrity	10			15	financial expert
Friel, Anna		Entertainment	10			20	Actress
Friend, Maj. Gen. Arthur Leslie I.	1886-1961	Military	25				World War II British general
Friends (Cast Of)		Entertainment	90			212	Cast of 6 (Authentic)
Friganza, Trixie		Entertainment	5	7	9	10	Actress. Early Films
Friml, Rudolf	1879-1972	Composer	100	275	325	212	Operettas. Major Stage-Film Hits. AMusS 750
Frink, Maj. Gen. James L.	1885-1977	Military	30				World War II U.S. general
Frisch, Karl von		Science	15	30	40	25	Nobel Medicine

NAME	DATE	CATEGORY	SIG	LS/DS	ALS	SP	COMMENTS
Frist, Bill		Senate	10			15	United States Senate (R - TN)
Frist, William 'Bill' M.D.		Political		25	35	40	Sen. TN., Senate Majority leader
Fritchie, Barbara (Frietschie)		Civil War	12500				Patriotic Heroine of Civil War Incident
Frith, William P.	1819-1909	Artist	25	45	80		Crowded Scenes Contemporay Life. 'Derby Day' etc.
Fritsch, Werner von		Military	55	150	210	248	
Frizzell, Lefty	1928-	Country Music	25			65	Singer-Songwriter-Guitarist
Frobe, Gert	1913-1988	Entertainment	30			108	Ger. Character Actor
Frohman, Daniel	1851-1940	Entertainment	25		100	75	Dean of Am.Theatrical Producers
Frohnmeyer, John		Celebrity	10			15	motivational speaker
Froman, Jane	1907-1980	Entertainment	15	15	25	50	Major Singing Star. Suffered Air Crash. Crippled
Froment, Brig. Gen. Georges-Jos.		Military	20				World War II French general
Fromm, Col-General Friedrich	1888-1945	Military	25				World War II German general
Fromm, Erich	1900-1980	Science	42	130		75	Am. Ger. Born. Psychoanalist-Social Philosopher
Fromme, Lynette 'Squeaky'		Assassin	50	120	210	60	Charles Manson Follower. Attempted Assassination
Frondizi, Arturo		Head of State	15	35	75	55	President Argentina
Frontenac, Louis, Comte	1620-1698	Statesman			5400		Gov. La Nouvelle France(Canada)
Frontiersmen, The		Country Music	25			55	Populart Singing Group. Films-Records
Frost, Arthur B.	1851-1928	Artist	50	140		188	Illustrator, Uncle Remus Books
Frost, Daniel Marsh	1823-1900	Civil War	203	296	483		CSA Gen. Surrounded. Saw 1st Blood. Surrendered
Frost, David		Entertainment	5			15	Br. Interviewer of Major Personalities5
Frost, Edwin B.		Science	10	25	45		Am. Astronomer
Frost, Martin F		Congress	10			15	Member U.S. Congress
Frost, Robert	1874-1963	Author	129	380	1500	750	Poet. Pulitzer 1924,'31,'37,'43
Frost, Sadie		Entertainment	10			35	Br.Actress. 'Bram Stoker's Dracula' etc.
Frost, Stephen		Celebrity	10			15	comedian
Frost, Terry		Entertainment	10			40	Vintage cowboy actor
Frostrup, Mariella		Celebrity	10			15	television presenter
Frothingham, Octavius B.	1822-1895	Clergy	25	35	50		Am. Unitarian. Disciple of Theodore Parker
Frunze, Mikhail V	1885-1925	Military		460			Russian revolutionary general
Fruteau, Jean-Claude		Political	10			15	Member European Parliament
Fruyt van Hertog, Maj. Gen. J. H.	1879-1948	Military	20				World War II Dutch general
Fry, Birkett Davenport	1822-1891	Civil War	120	280			Confederate general, war date DS 2530
Fry, Brig. Gen. James C.	1897-1982	Military	30				World War II U.S. general
Fry, Christopher		Author	30	160	230		Br. Dramatist
Fry, Elizabeth	1780-1845	Clergy-Philanthro	40	125	185		Br. Quaker Philanthropist
Fry, Franklin C.	1900-1968	Clergy	20	25	35		Pres. Lutheran Church, World Relief, World Fed.
Fry, James Barnet	1827-1894	Civil War	37	96	135		Union Gen. Shiloh, 1st Bull Run....
Fry, Roger	1866-1934	Artist	35		200		Br. Art Critic & Artist. Lecturer
Fry, Speed Smith	1817-1892	Civil War	45		69		Union general
Fry, Stephen		Celebrity	10			15	comedian
Frye, Dwight	1899-1943	Entertainment	950		1750	2000	Cornered the Market in Crazed Hunchbacks
Frye, Wm. P. (Actg V.P.)		Acting V.P.	15				
FSrm, Göran		Political	10			15	Member European Parliament
Fuad I, King-Sultan	1868-1936	Royalty	95	300			King-Sultan of Egypt. Gen'l. Fndr. Egypt. Univ.
Fuchida, Mitsuo	1902-1976	Military-Aviation	256	606	627		Led Attack on Pearl Harbor 1941

NAME	DATE	CATEGORY	SIG	LS/DS	ALS	SP	COMMENTS
Fuchs, Rutger		Military	40	125	195	95	
Fuchs, Vivian E. Sir	1908-	Explorer	27	75	158		Br. Antarctic Explorer-Geologist
Fuentes, Daisy		Entertainment	12			43	
Fugard, Athol		Entertainment	10			20	actor
Fujii, Lt. Gen. Yoji	d. 1945	Military	25				World War II Japanese general
Fujimori, Alberto		Political				25	President of Peru
Fuka-Tu'itupou, Rev. Lynette		Author	8			12	Kingdom of Tonga religious history
Fukuda, Lt. Gen. Hikosuke	1875-1959	Military	25				World War II Japanese general
Fukuda, Takeo		Head of State	15		50	30	Prime Minister Japan
Fukui, Kenichi		Science	20	30	45	25	Nobel Chemistry
Fulbright, James W.	1905-1995	Congress	20	40	100	55	Senator AR, Fulbright Scholarship
Fulford, Millie Hughes		Astronaut	10			15	
Fulgham, Robert		Author	5			15	
Fulkerson, Abraham	1834-1902	Congress	20	35			CSA Colonel. MOC TN
Fuller, Alfred C.	1885-1973	Business	125		195	175	Fndr. Fuller Brush Co.Pioneered Door to Door Sales
Fuller, Alvan T.		Governor	15	25		20	Governor, MOC MA
Fuller, Brig. Gen. Howard E.	1892-1975	Military	30				World War II U.S. general
Fuller, Buckminster R.	1895-1983	Science	42	85	140	176	Br-Am. Architectural Engin'r, Geodetic Dome
Fuller, Charles		Entertainment	10			20	actor
Fuller, Delores		Entertainment	20			50	Actress/Ed Wood
Fuller, Eduard		Author	6	20	40		
Fuller, John G.		Celebrity	10	16			
Fuller, John Wallace	1827-1891	Civil War	53	106	157		Union general
Fuller, Loie	1862-1928	Entertainment	50	124	200	350	Am. Dancer
Fuller, Maj. Gen. Algernon C.	1885-1970	Military	25				World War II British general
Fuller, Maj. Gen. Horace H.	1886-1966	Military	30				World War II U.S. general
Fuller, Margaret	1810-1850	Reformer-Author	140	250	450		Feminist, ALS/Content 2,500
Fuller, Melville W.	1833-1910	Supreme Court	62	132	200	175	
Fuller, Robert	1934-	Entertainment	5	4	9	10	Am. Leading Man. Mostly TV. Many Westerns
Fuller, Sam	1912-	Entertainment	35			80	Film Writer-Director.
Fullerton, Chas. Gordon		Astronaut	10	30	35		
Fullerton, Fiona		Entertainment	10			20	Actress
Fullerton, Gordon		Astronaut	5			10	
Fulton, Brig. Gen. Walter S.	1879-1959	Military	30				World War II U.S. general
Fulton, Fitz		Astronaut	10		15	22	
Fulton, Robert	1765-1815	Inventor	404	1452	4600		Submarine, Steamboat. ALS/Content 6500
Fulton, William S.	1795-1844	Congress	16		45		Sen. AR, Gov. AR
Fulwood, Sam		Celebrity	10			15	motivational speaker
Funicello, Annette		Entertainment	31	15	32	47	Actress of 'Mickey Mouse Club'.
Funk, Brig. Gen. Arnold J.	1895-1980	Military	30				World War II U.S. general
Funk, Casimer		Science	25	65		30	Biochemist Discovered Thiamin
Funk, Isaac K.	1839-1912	Publisher	35	80	135		Funk & Wagnalls Dictionary
Funk, Larry		Bandleader	10			30	
Funk, Walther	1890-1960	Military	127	276			Hitler's personal advisor
Funsten, David	1819-1866	Civil War	117	254			Member of Confederate Congress

NAME	DATE	CATEGORY	SIG	LS/DS	ALS	SP	COMMENTS
Funston, Frederick	1865-1917	Military	75	195	300		Cuba, Span.-American War, MOH. Captured Aguinaldo
Funt, Alan		Celebrity	15			35	Candid Camera
Fuqua, James O.		Civil War			242		Louisiana capt.
Furcolo, Foster		Governor	10	25			Governor MA
Furnas, Robert W.		Governor	5	10			Governor NE
Furness, Betty	1916-1994	Entertainment	15	20	30	45	Actress. Early TV Hostess & Consumer Advocate
Furness, William H.		Clergy	10	15	20		
Furniss, Harry	1854-1925	Artist	40	120	250		Br. Illustrator-Caricaturist. Political & Social
Furrer, Reinhard		Astronaut	15			95	Germany
Furstenberg, Betsy von		Entertainment	5	10		20	Fashion Designer
Furtado, Nelly		Entertainment				40	Singer
Furtwangler, Wilhelm	1886-1954	Entertainment	200	360	525	825	Controversial Ger. Conductor WW II. SPpc 840
Fuseli, Henry	1741-1825	Artist	250	500			Br.-Swiss Romantic Painter, Author
Futch, Brig. Gen. Theodore L.	1895-1992	Military	30				World War II U.S. general
Futrell, J.M.		Governor	5	12		10	Governor AR
Fyfe, John		Military	15			30	WW II Hero. Submarine Ace

NAME	DATE	CATEGORY	SIG	LS/DS	ALS	SP	COMMENTS
Gabet, Sharon		Entertainment	5	6	15	15	
Gabin, Jean	1904-1976	Entertainment	35			255	Fr. Romantic Leading Actor
Gable, Clark	1901-1960	Entertainment	230	468	850	1289	Actor, signed check 450
Gable, Kay		Entertainment	8	9	15	20	Clark Gable's wife
Gabor, Eva	1920-1995	Entertainment	20	25	30	38	
Gabor, Zsa Zsa		Entertainment	5	6	15	30	
Gabreski, Frances J. 'Gabby'		Aviation	35	95	125	110	US ACE, WW II, 5th Leading Fighter Ace.
Gabriel, John Peter	1746-1807	Revolutionary War					General, Politician, Clergy.MsDS to Franklin 3500
Gabriel, Peter		Entertainment	15			50	Rock
Gabrielle, Monique		Entertainment	15			30	Pin-Up SP 35
Gabrilowitsch, Ossip	1878-1936	Entertainment	60	118	150	125	Rus.-Am. Pianist,Conductor. AMusQS 275
Gacy, John Wayne		Criminal	30	98	153	122	Convicted Serial Killer.Original Paintings 400-600
Gadsden, James		Diplomat-Business	110	250	350		Gadsden Purchase
Gadski-Tauscher, Johanna	1872-1932	Entertainment	40		85	125	Ger.-Born Wagnerian Soprano
Gaffey, Maj. Gen. Hugh J.	1895-1946	Military	30				World War II U.S. general
Gaffney, Drew		Astronaut	4			20	
Gagarin, Yuri	1934-1968	Astronaut	277	420		559	1st Man To Travel In Space, TLS/cont 1250
Gage, Brig. Gen. Philip S.	1885-1982	Military	30				World War II U.S. general
Gage, Lyman J.		Cabinet	15	25	50	45	Sec'y Treasury 1897
Gage, Nicholas		Author	10	25		15	
Gage, Thomas		Revolutionary War	225	602	817		Br. General. Commander-in-Chief
Gagnon, Ren, A.		Military	75	30		40	Iwo Jima Flag Raising FDC 225
Gahler, Michael		Political	10			15	Member European Parliament
Gahrton, Per		Political	10			15	Member European Parliament

NAME	DATE	CATEGORY	SIG	LS/DS	ALS	SP	COMMENTS
Gail, Max		Entertainment	10	12	15	20	
Gailey, Maj. Gen. Charles K. Jr.	1901-1966	Military	30				World War II U.S. general
Gailliard, Maj. Gen. Emile-Henri	1882-1961	Military	20				World War II French general
Gaines, John P.	1795-1857	Congress	20		35		MOC OR, Soldier, Gov. OR
Gaines, Rosie		Music	10			15	performing musical artist
Gaines, William		Celebrity	50	475			Founder Mad Magazine
Gainsborough, Thomas	1727-1788	Artist	275	603	1506		Br. Portraitist 'The Blue Boy'. Landscapes
Gairdner, Gen. Sir Charles Henry	1898-1983	Military	25				World War II British general
Gaither, Burgess Sidney	1807-1892	Civil War	64	117			Member of Confederate Congress
Gaither, Lt. Gen. Ridgely	1903-1992	Military	30				World War II U.S. general
Gajdusek, D. Carleton, Dr.		Science	20	35		35	Nobel Medicine
Galanos, James		Business	12	30	50	25	
Galard, Genevieve de		Celebrity	40			50	
Galbraith, John Ken.		Economist	15	35		25	Author Books Economics
Gale, General Sir Richard Nelson	1896-1982	Military	25				World War II British general
Gale, Lt. Gen. Sir Humfrey M.	1890-1971	Military	25				World War II British general
Gale, Robert		Celebrity	10			15	medical expert
Gale, Zona	1874-1938	Author	10	55	75	60	American Novelist Short Story Writer
Galella, Ron		Photographer	8	12		10	Celebrity Photographer
Galeote Quecedo, Gerardo		Political	10			15	Member European Parliament
Galer, Robert E., Jr.		Aviation				50	Gen'l WW II. MOH. Air Ace
Galileo	1564-1642	Science					Extremely rare
Gall, Bob		Business	4			10	Business Exec.
Gallagher, David		Entertainment				30	
Gallagher, Megan		Entertainment	8			35	Actress
Gallagher, Peter		Entertainment	4			28	Actor
Galland, Adolf	1912-1996	Aviation	48	68	188	120	ACE, Ger. WW II, Luftwaffe Head
Gallatin, Albert E.	1881-1952	Artist					Pencil Sketch 250
Gallatin, Albert	1761-1849	Cabinet	88	345	463		Jefferson's & Madison's-Sec'y Treas., ALS/cont 2415
Gallaudet, Thomas T.		History			130		founder of the first American school for the deaf
Galle, Emile	1846-1904	Artist	100	325	645		Fr. Artist in Glass & Furniture Mfg.
Gallegly, Elton G.		Congress	10			15	Member U.S. Congress
Gallian, Ketti		Entertainment	8	9	19	20	
Galliano, John		Celebrity	10			15	Designer
Gallico, Paul W.		Author	15	57		35	Am.Novelist. 'Poseidon Adventure'
Galli-Curci, Amelita	1889-1963	Entertainment	56	157	210	250	Opera
Galligan, Zach		Entertainment	4			12	Actor. 'Gremlins'
Gallinger, Jacob Harold	1837-1918	Congress	10	20	35	20	MOC.,Senator NH 1891-1919
Gallo, Ernest & Julio		Business	40	145		65	Award Winning Gallo Winery, Sonoma, CA
Gallo, Gustavo		Entertainment	20			50	Opera
Gallo, Joey	1929-1972	Criminal		550			gangster
Gallo, Robert, Dr.		Science	20	35		40	Research. Co-Discoverer HIV Virus
Galloway, Joseph	1731-1803	Revolutionary War		3250			Continental Congr.& Army. Tory Loyalist
Galloway, Lt. Gen. Sir Alexander	1895-1977	Military	25				World War II British general
Galloway, Marie S., 1st Lt. ANC		Medical	20		95		Nurse. Visited Hawaiian Leper Colony. 40's

NAME	DATE	CATEGORY	SIG	LS/DS	ALS	SP	COMMENTS
Gallup, Benadam		Military	40	150			Colonel French-Indian War. Groton, CT Selectman
Gallup, George, Jr.	1901-1984	Pollster	10	48		30	Gallup Poll. TLS/Original Poll re '76 Pres. 295
Galsworthy, John	1867-1933	Author	48	85	199	175	Br. Novelist, Playwright
Galvan, Elias G., Bishop		Clergy	20	25	35	35	
Galvin, Robert		Business	12	17	25	15	
Galway, James		Entertainment	10			40	Irish Flutist. AMusQS 50
Gam, Rita	1928	Entertainment	5	7	15	15	Actress
Gambee, Charles R.		Civil War	20	55			Col. 53rd Ohio Vol. KIA Resecca
Gambier, James, 1st Baron	1756-1833	Military	35	130			Br. Naval Cmdr. Admiral of the Fleet.
Gambino, Carlo	1902-1976	Criminal		274			Mafia boss
Gamble, Hamilton R.	1798-1864	Civil War	35		195		CW Gov. MO. Cmmdr.-in-Chief MO Militia
Gamble, William	1818-1866	Civil War	53	123	140		Union general
Gamelin, General Maurice	1872-1958	Military	20				World War II French general
Gammell, Lt. Gen. Sir James A. H.	1892-1975	Military	25				World War II British general
Gammon, James		Entertainment	10			20	actor
Gance, Abel	1889-1981	Entertainment		295	500		Fr. Actor, Dir., Writer. One of Greatest Directors.
Gandhi, Indira	1917-1984	Head of State	108	312	475	537	Assassinated P.M. India. TLS/Cont.600, FDC S 175
Gandhi, Mohandas K.	1869-1948	Political Leader	895	1600	4108	3825	Assassinated Spiritual Leader India
Gandhi, Rajiv		Head of State	40		85	150	Assassinated P.M. of India
Gandhi, Sonia		Political				30	India Politician
Gandier, D.M., Rev.		Clergy	10	20	35		Temperance Advocate
Gandolfini, James		Entertainment				112	Soprano's
Gann, Ernest K.		Author	10	20	35		
Gannett, Frank E.		Business	20	55	140	35	Newspaper, TV, Radio Empire
Gano, Richard Montgomery	1830-1913	Civil War	130				Confederate general, physician
Gantt, Harvey		Celebrity	10			15	political celebrity
Ganz, Rudolph		Conductor	25			60	Swiss/Am. Pianist/Conductor
Garat, Pierre (Fils)		Entertainment	45		120		Tenor Son
Garat, Pierre (Pere)	1762-1823	Entertainment	125		300		1st Great French Tenor
Garaud, Marie-frantoise		Political	10			15	Member European Parliament
Garber, Jan		Entertainment	15			35	Big Band Leader
Garbo, Greta	1905-1991	Entertainment	1319	2655	6742	11500	Major Internat'l Film Star. ALS/Cont.16,500.
García-margallo y Marfil, José M.		Political	10			15	Member European Parliament
García-orcoyen Tormo, Cristina		Political	10			15	Member European Parliament
Garcelon, Alonzo		Governor	5	12			Governor ME
Garchery, Gen. Jeanny-Jules-M.	1876-1961	Military	20				World War II French general
Garcia Menocal, Mario	1866-1941	Head of State	75	160		300	Pres. Cuba 1913-21
Garcia, Andy		Entertainment	15	10		52	Actor
Garcia, Jerry		Entertainment	68	88	150	239	Rock. 'Run For The Roses' Alb. S 225
Garcia, Judie		Celebrity	10			15	media/TV personality
Garcia, Manuel	1805-1906	Entertainment	20		75		Musician & Inventor of the Laryngoscope
Garcia-Robles, Alfonso, Dr.		Diplomat	35		130	60	Nobel Peace Prize, Disarmament
Gard, Maj. Gen. Robert G.	1899-1983	Military	30				World War II U.S. general
Gardanne, Gaspard A.		Fr. Revolution	40	115	250		
Garde, Betty		Entertainment	5			12	Actress

NAME	DATE	CATEGORY	SIG	LS/DS	ALS	SP	COMMENTS
Garden, Mary	1874-1967	Entertainment	36	45	68	100	Opera. Scottish Born, Am. Soprano
Gardenia, Vincent	1922-1992	Entertainment	5			20	Actor
Gardiner, Reginald		Entertainment	10			35	
Gardner, Alexander		Civil War	190				Photographer, Signed photo 6900
Gardner, Ava	1922-1990	Entertainment	52	78	110	121	Actress. Pin-Up SP 150
Gardner, Brig. Gen. John H.	1893-1944	Military	30				World War II U.S. general
Gardner, Dale A.		Astronaut	10			25	
Gardner, Erle Stanley	1889-1970	Author	85	204	275	175	Lawyer & Detective Novelist
Gardner, Franklin (WD)	1823-1873	Civil War	375	500	1510		CSA Gen.
Gardner, Franklin	1823-1873	Civil War	225	414	788		CSA General
Gardner, Guy S.		Astronaut	6			20	
Gardner, John L.	1793-1869	Civil War	30		105		Union Brevet Brig. Gen.
Gardner, John W.		Cabinet	5	30	35	10	Sec'y HEW. Fndr. 'Common Cause'
Gardner, Maj. Gen. Fulton Q.C.	1882-1963	Military	30				World War II U.S. general
Gardner, O. Max		Governor	15	20	35	20	Gov. NC. Lawyer, Industrialist
Gardner, Tony, Dr.		Celebrity	10			15	health and fitness expert
Gardner, William Montgomery	1824-1901	Civil War	120	221	327		Confederate general
Garfield, Allen		Entertainment	10			20	actor
Garfield, James A. (As President)	1831-1881	President	4000	13242	52000		Assassinated July 1881
Garfield, James A. (WD)	1831-1881	Civil War	290	1238	2750		Union general, President of the US
Garfield, James A.	1831-1881	President	226	563	791	1553	Union Gen., DS/War Dte 2,500, FF395
Garfield, James R.	1865-1950	Cabinet	20	35	70	35	Sec'y Interior 1907
Garfield, John	1913-1952	Entertainment	75	95		352	Warner Bros. Star. Died at 39. Born Julius Garfinkle
Garfield, Lucretia R.	1832-1918	First Lady	95	140	180		
Garfunkel, Art		Entertainment	25			38	Singer-Songwriter Frequently w/Paul Simon
Gargan, William	1905-1979	Entertainment	15	15	30	40	Vintage Leading Man. Films-Broadway. 1929
Gargan, Jack		Political				15	Chrm of thr Reform Party
Gargani, Giuseppe		Political	10			15	Member European Parliament
Garibaldi, Giuseppe	1807-1882	Head of State	140	291	330	650	It. Nationalist Leader, Soldier, Patriot
Garland, Augustus H.	1832-1899	Cabinet & CW	40	85	120		Att'y Gen. & CSA Congress, Gov.
Garland, Beverly		Entertainment	5	10		20	Actress
Garland, Hamlin	1860-1940	Author	30	40	173	85	Pulitzer 1921. Novelist, Essayist
Garland, Judy	1922-1969	Entertainment	401	672		792	Actress-Singer. 'Oz' Special DS 950. Chk S 550
Garland, Samuel Jr.	1830-1862	Civil War	950				Confederate general, KIA South Mt., MD
Garlington, Brig. Gen. Creswell	1887-1945	Military	30				World War II U.S. general
Garn, Jake		Senate-Astronaut	15	40		35	Senator UT
Garneau, Marc		Astronaut	9			25	
Garner, Erroll		Entertainment	75			150	Jazz Pianist
Garner, Francoise		Entetainment	10			35	Opera
Garner, James	1928-	Entertainment	10	18	22	44	Actor
Garner, Jennifer		Entertainment	15			45	Actress, 'Alias'
Garner, John Nance	1867-1967	Vice President	50	138	182	150	VP & Speaker. FDR VP
Garner, Max Sr.		Author	8			12	books for children
Garner, Peggy Ann		Entertainment	30			75	
Garnett, Francis H.		Author	20	60	125		

NAME	DATE	CATEGORY	SIG	LS/DS	ALS	SP	COMMENTS
Garnett, Richard Brooke	1817-1863	Civil War	1600	3200	5000		CSA Gen., ALS 1861 6600, KIA Gettysburg
Garnett, Robert Seldon	1819-1861	Civil War	1735		3450		Confederate general
Garnett, Tay		Entertainment	10	25		30	Director-Producer
Garnier, Charles	1825-1898	Architect	30		225		Designer Paris Opera House
Garofalo, Janeane		Entertainment				40	
Garot, Georges		Political	10			15	Member European Parliament
Garr, Terri		Entertainment	8	15	25	27	Actress
Garrard, Kenner	1827-1879	Civil War	50	75	160		Union Gen. War Date ALS 575
Garrard, Theophilus Toulmin	1812-1902	Civil War	43	84	110		Union general
Garretson, Melissa J.		Celebrity	10			15	medical expert
Garrett, Betty		Entertainment	7			18	Film & Stage Comedienne
Garrett, Brad		Entertainment	10			39	Actor, Emmy award winner
Garrett, Brig. Gen. Robert C.	1886-1981	Military	30				World War II U.S. general
Garrett, Finis J.		Senate/Congress	10	15	25	20	MOC TN 1905
Garrett, John W.	1872-1942	Political			155		US foreign minister
Garrett, Laurie		Celebrity	10			15	medical expert
Garrett, Leif		Celebrity				50	
Garrett, Patrick R. 'Pat'	1850-1908	Western Lawman	1600	2694	3190		Killed Billy the Kid. Became Sheriff. Assassinated
Garrett, Scott G		Congress	10			15	Member U.S. Congress
Garrett, Thomas		Emancipation	100	250	395		Chief Engineer Underground RR
Garriga Polledo, Salvador		Political	10			15	Member European Parliament
Garriott, Owen I.		Astronaut	5			20	
Garrison, Jim		Legal	55			150	Deceased Distr. Atty. Investigated Kennedy Assass.
Garrison, Lindley M.	1864-1932	Cabinet	30	65	80	75	Sec'y War 1913
Garrison, Vermont		Aviation	12	25	45	35	ACE, WW II & Korea
Garrison, Wm. Lloyd	1805-1879	Abolitionist	72	169	331	350	Reformer. Abolitionist. ALS/Cont. 1200
Garros, Roland		Aviation	125			425	Fr. ACE. 1st To Fly Mediterranean
Garrott, Isham Warren	1816-1863	Civil War	407	567			Confederate general, KIA Vicksburg, Miss.
Garroway, Dave		Entertainment	10			25	
Garson, Greer	1908-1996	Entertainment	25	95	45	70	Actress. Oscar Winner. DS 650 for 'Mrs. Miniver'
Garson, Willie		Entertainment				30	Stanford Blatch, Sex in the City
Garth, Jennie		Entertainment	10			42	Actress. Beverly Hills 90210
Gartland, Maj. Gen. Gerald I.	1889-1975	Military	28				World War II British general
Gartrell, Lucius J.	1821-1891	Civil War	95	285	317		CSA Gen.
Garvey, Marcus	1887-1940	Black Nationalist		1296		1250	Back to Africa Movement. Black Nationalism
Garvin, Maj. Gen. Crump	1898-1980	Military	30				World War II U.S. general
Gary, Elbert Henry	1846-1927	Business	142	423	575	525	CEO U.S. Steel, Gary, Ind., TLS/ALS cont 1500-2000
Gary, James Albert		Cabinet	15	25	40		P.M. Gen. Owned Cotton Mills 1897
Gary, John		Entertainment	20			35	Actor-Singer. Juvenile-Films. TV Personality
Gary, Martin Witherspoon	1831-1881	Civil War	125	267			Confederate general
Gascoigne, Jill		Entertainment	10			20	Actress
Gascoigne, Maj. Gen. Sir Julian A.	1903-1990	Military	28				World War II British general
Gasdia, Cecilie		Entertainment	10	15	35		35
Gasoliba I Böhm, Carles-alfred		Political	10			15	Member European Parliament
Gasser, Heber S.		Science	20	35	60	50	Nobel Medicine

NAME	DATE	CATEGORY	SIG	LS/DS	ALS	SP	COMMENTS
Gasser, Maj. Gen. Lorenzo D.	1876-1955	Military	30				World War II U.S. general
Gassman, Vittorio		Entertainment	25			85	
Gatehouse, Maj. Gen. Alex. Hugh	1895-1964	Military	25				World War II British general
Gately, George		Cartoonist	5			20	Heathcliff
Gates, Bill		Business	20	75		40	Microsoft Genius.
Gates, Daryl		Law Enforcement	15			30	Chief Police of L.A.
Gates, Horatio	1728-1806	Revolutionary War	217	588	909		General, Continental Army TLS/ALS cont 2000-4000
Gates, John W.	1855-1911	Business	500	1750			'Bet a Million Gates'. Steel Wire Baron
Gates, Robert		Celebrity	10			15	political celebrity
Gates, Seth	1800-1877	Congress	25	40	80		Anti-Slavery Repr. from NY
Gates, Thomas	1906-1983	Cabinet	10	35		35	Sec'y Defense under Eisenhower & Sec'y Navy
Gatlin, Larry & Brothers		Entertainment	10			20	C & W
Gatlin, Richard Caswell	1809-1896	Civil War	150	248			CSA Gen.
Gatling, Richard J.	1818-1903	Inventor-Business	400	975	1754		Gatling Gun, ALS on Ltrhd 9500, signed stk cert.33000
Gatti-Casazza, Giulio		Entertainment	50	150	250		It. Impresario. Opera Director
Gattie, Maj. Gen. Kenneth F. D.	1890-1982	Military	25				World War II British general
Gatty, Harold		Aviation	90	240	350	350	Australian. Wiley Post Navigator
Gauguin, Paul	1848-1903	Artist	750	2600	8825		Fr. Post-Impressionist. Important ALS 17,500
Gault, Willie		Entertainment	10			15	actor
Gaultier, Jean-Paul		Celebrity	10			15	Designer
Gaumont, Leon	1864-1946	Entertainment	55	330			Fr. Film Pioneer, Exec., Inventor Sound System
Gautier, Dick		Entertainment	5			12	
Gavarni, Paul		Artist	85		300		
Gavassi, Allesandro, Father		Clergy	75	100	150		
Gavaudan, Pierre	1772-1840	Entertainment			135		Opera. Tenor
Gavin, James M.	1907-1993	Military	40	83	185	112	Gen. WW II, 82nd Airborne, TLS/Cont.495
Gavin, John		Entertainment	5			20	Ambassador to Mexico
Gavin, Leon		Senate/Congress	5	10		10	MOC PA 1943
Gawronski, Jas		Political	10			15	Member European Parliament
Gaxton, William		Entertainment	10	15	25	25	
Gay, George A.		Civil War	15	25	45		Nat'l Commander GAR 1934
Gay, George H. Jr.	1917-1994	Military	35	50		75	Sole survivor of the Battle of Midway
Gay, Sydney Howard		Author	3	10	20		
Gaye, Marvin		Entertainment	75			150	
Gayheart, Rebecca		Entertainment	13			52	Actress. Pin-Up 75
Gayle, Crystal		Country Music	5			25	Singer
Gayle, John		Governor	10	35			Statesman, Jurist
Gayle, Michelle		Music	10			15	performing musical artist
Gayler, Paul		Celebrity	10			15	Chef
Gaylord, Mitch		Celebrity	10			15	motivational speaker, gymnast
Gaynor, Adam		Entertainment	5			22	Music. Rhythm Guitar 'Matchbox 20'
Gaynor, Gloria		Music	10			15	performing musical artist
Gaynor, Janet	1906-1984	Entertainment	22	35	50	78	Actress. First Oscar Winner. Vintage SP 140
Gaynor, Mitzi		Entertainment	10			25	Actress
Gaynor, William J.		Celebrity	20	55	115	30	

NAME	DATE	CATEGORY	SIG	LS/DS	ALS	SP	COMMENTS
Gazen, Waldemar von		Military	40			125	German Panzer General
Gazzara, Ben		Entertainment	5			25	
Geake, Maj. Gen. Clifford Henry	1894-1982	Military	25				World War II British general
Gear, John Henry	1825-1900	Congress	10	20	25		Senator IA 1887
Geary, Anthony 'Tony'		Entertainment	6	8	15	15	
Geary, John W.	1819-1873	Civil War	50	110	207	300	Un.Gen.,1st Mayor San Francisco
Gebel-Williams, Gunther		Entertainment	12			44	Circus animal trainer. Showman/Circus Performer
Gebhardt, Evelyne		Political	10			15	Member European Parliament
Gebhardt, Karl Dr.	d. 1948	Military	138				Nazi ^"doctor^"
Gedda, Nicolai		Entertainment	15		35	35	Swe. Tenor, Opera
Geddes, James	1763-1838	Engineer		567	850		Erie Canal Advocate, Chief Engineer & Surveyor
Gedrick, Jason		Celebrity				40	
Gee, Edwin A., Dr,		Business	5	10		10	CEO International Paper Co.
Geep, Maj. Gen. Cyril	1879-1964	Military	25				World War II British general
Geer, Ellen		Entertainment	4			12	Actress
Geer, Will	1902-1978	Entertainment	25			55	Actor, Folk Singer. On Stage & Films from 1930-
Geezinslaw, Sam & Dewayne		Country Music	15			30	
Geffrard, Nicholas Fabre		Head of State	35	125			Pres. Haiti
Gehlen, Reinhard	1902-1979	Military	40	95	140		German WWII General
Geiger, Johannes H.	1882-1945	Science	125	350	750		Ger. Physicist. Geiger Counter
Geisel, Ernesto		Head of State	12	20	25	15	
Geisel, Theodore		Author					SEE Dr. Seuss
Gell, William, Dr.		Science	25	40			Br. Archaeologist
Gellar, Sarah Michelle		Entertainment	12			77	Actress. 'Buffya..'. Pin-Up 80
Gelston, David		Revolutionary War	85	170			
Gemar, Charles 'Sam'		Astronaut	5			20	
Gemelli, Vitaliano		Political	10			15	Member European Parliament
Gemini 5 (3 Sigs)		Astronauts					US 1 Bill.Aboard Gem.5 Signed 2595
Gené, Jean	1910-1986	Author	175	295	450		Fr. LS/Content 1,275
Geneen, Harold S.		Business	5	10	25	10	
Genesis		Entertainment	40			85	
Genet, Edmond Citizen	1763-1834	Fr. Revolution	55	150	525		1st Fr. Minister to U.S.
Genet, Jean	1910-1986	Author		950	1575		French Black Prince of Letters
Genn, Leo		Entertainment	10	15	25	25	
Genscher, Hans-Dietrich		Celebrity	10			15	political celebrity
Gentilini, Amerigo		Entertainment	15			45	Opera
Gentry, Bobbie		Country Music	5			20	Composer 'Ode to Billy Joe' Sheet Mus. S 95
Gentry, Jerauld R.		Astronaut	5	25		15	
Gentry, Maj. Gen. Wiliam G.	1899-1991	Military	20				World War II New Zealand general
George (Prince Denmark)	1653-1708	Royalty		157			Consort of Queen Anne
George I (Eng)	1660-1727	Royalty	250	793	2300		Created Cabinet System of Gov.
George I (Gr)	1845-1913	Royalty	45	85	130		Assassinated Greek King
George II (Eng)	1683-1760	Royalty	250	597	1755		Last English Monarch to Lead His Troops in Battle
George II (Greece)		Royalty	70	80	185	400	Succeeded his Brother, Constantine to Throne
George III (Eng)	1738-1820	Royalty	230	572	1541		Last King of U.S. Colonies

NAME	DATE	CATEGORY	SIG	LS/DS	ALS	SP	COMMENTS
George IV (Eng)	1762-1830	Royalty	122	372	538		13 pp. Warrant 1815 3,500
George V (Eng)	1865-1936	Royalty	110	353	604	750	King of England
George V and Queen Mary (Teck)		Royalty	250			855	
George VI (Eng)	1895-1952	Royalty	100	304	376	500	WW II King of England. ALS as Duke York 275
George VI and Queen Elizabeth		Royalty	258	690		1750	
George, Boy		Music	10			15	DJ
George, Brig. Gen. Charles P.	1886-1946	Military	30				World War II U.S. general
George, Chief Dan		Entertainment	20			45	
George, Christopher		Entertainment	20	25	65	75	
George, David		Author	8			12	regional history, senior citizens
George, Duke of Cambridge	1819-1904	Military	40				Br. Cmdr. Crimean War
George, Duke of Kent	1902-1942	Royalty		110			Son of George V.
George, Gladys		Entertainment	20	25	40	40	
George, Grace		Entertainment	25			60	
George, Harold L.		Military	35	90	170	75	
George, Henry		Economist	30	105	200	35	Author, Reformer, Editor
George, Michael		Entertainment	3			8	
George, Phyllis		Entertainment	5	6	12	15	Miss America
George, Susan		Entertainment	6	8	15	15	
George, Walter F.	1878-1957	Congress	10	30		30	Senator GA 1922-57
Georges, Gen. Alphonse-Joseph	1875-1951	Military	20				World War II French general
Gephardt, Richard A. G		Congress	10			15	Member U.S. Congress
Gerard, James W.		Diplomat	12				Ambassador
Gerard, Francis R.		Aviation	10	22	38	28	ACE, WW II
Gerard, Gil		Entertainment	9	10	20	20	
Gerard, Richard		Composer	50	95	165		AMusQS 235
Gerardy, Jean		Entertainment	125			190	Belg. Violin-Cellist
Gere, Ashlyn		Entertainment					Actress-Model. Nude Pin-up 45
Gere, Richard		Entertainment	30	45	55	61	Actor. (Sometimes Uses paint pen)
Gerhardt, Elena		Entertainment	30			100	Opera, Remembered as Great Lieder Singer
Gerhardt, Maj. Gen. Charles H.	1895-1976	Military	30				World War II U.S. general
Gerhardt, Mike		Astronaut	5			18	
Gerlach, Jim G		Congress	10			15	Member U.S. Congress
Gerlache de Gomery, Adrien V.J.		Explorer	85	180	300		Belg. Naval Off'r., Antarctic
Gerland, Alfred		Aviation	15	35	55	40	
Germain, Lt. Gen. Georges-Louis	1877-1954	Military	20				World War II French general
German, Edward, Sir	1862-1936	Composer	35	60	64	85	Operettas. AMusQS 200
Germond, Jack		Celebrity	10			15	media/TV personality
Gernreich, Rudi		Business	10	15	40	25	Fashion Designer
Geronimo		Native American	6458			8500	
Gerow, Brig. Gen. Lee S.	1891-1982	Military	30				World War II U.S. general
Gerow, General Leonard T.	1888-1972	Military	30				World War II U.S. general
Gerri, Toni		Entertainment	4	4	9	9	
Gerry, Elbridge (VP)	1744-1814	Revolutionary War	275	625	1454		Signer Decl. of Ind. V.P., Gov. MA. FF 600-750
Gerry, James	1796-1873	Congress	10				Repr. PA, Physician

NAME	DATE	CATEGORY	SIG	LS/DS	ALS	SP	COMMENTS
Gerry, Peter G.	1879-1957	Congress	10	15		20	MOC, Senator RI 1913
Gersel Cemal		Head of State	20	65	90	75	Turkey
Gershon, Gina		Entertainment	10			20	actress
Gershwin, George & Ira		Composer	1125	3625			
Gershwin, George	1898-1937	Composer	803	2075	4250	3923	'Rhapsody in Blue', 'Porgy & Bess', signed check 1300
Gershwin, Ira	1896-1983	Composer	80	150	283	200	Lyricist. FDC S 95, AQS 880, Contract 2950
Gerson, Betty Lou		Entertainment	3			20	Major Radio Actress. Voice of Cruella de Vil
Gertz, Jami		Entertainment	7			42	
Gervais, John L.	1753-1798	Revolutionary War			100		Continental Congress
Gerville-Reache, Jeanne		Entertainment				275	Opera. Tragic French Mezzo
Gessendorf, Mechthild		Entertainment	10			25	Opera
Getaneh, Anna		Celebrity	10			15	model
Getty, Estelle		Entertainment	5	9	20	15	
Getty, George F.		Business		50			Founder Getty Oil Company
Getty, George Washington	1819-1901	Civil War	44	95	140		Union Gen. ALS/Cont. 740
Getty, George Washington (WD)	1819-1901	Civil War	70	210			Union Gen. Div. Cmdr.
Getty, J. Paul	1892-1976	Business	102	280	1255	400	Billionaire Oil Mogul Stk.Cert. S2400, ALS 2900
Getz, J. Laurence		Senate/Congress	10	15	20		MOC PA 1867. Publisher
Getz, Stan		Entertainment	85			225	Am. Jazz Saxophonist
Ghali, Boutros Boutros		Head of State	10			30	Pres. U.N.
Ghiaurov, Nicolai		Entertainment	10			25	Opera
Ghilardotti, Fiorella		Political	10			15	Member European Parliament
Gholson, Samuel J.	1808-1883	Civil War	106	292	575		CSA Gen.
Ghostley, Alice		Entertainment	5		15	15	Comedienne
Giancana, Antoinette		Celebrity	15			50	'Mafi Princess'
Giannini, A. P.		Business	150	290	500		Bank of America Founder
Gibb, Andy		Music	58	350			
Gibb, Cynthia		Entertainment	5	6	15	35	Pin-Up SP 20
Gibbon, Edward	1737-1794	Author	300	885	1800		Br. Decline & Fall Roman Empire
Gibbon, John (WD)		Civil War	215		870		Union Gen.
Gibbon, John	1827-1896	Military	60	263	378		Union Gen.ALS/Cont. 1760
Gibbons, Barry		Business	5			20	Founder Burger King
Gibbons, Brig. Gen. Lloyd H.	1895-1945	Military	30				World War II U.S. general
Gibbons, Cedric		Art	95	225	450		Hollywood Art Dir. 11 Awards
Gibbons, Floyd	1887-1939	Aviation-Journalist	56	132	205	200	Pioneer Aviator, Adventurer. Early Radio News
Gibbons, Herbert Adams		Celebrity	10	20	45		
Gibbons, James, Cardinal	1834-1921	Clergy	40	98	130	150	Established Washington Univ.,DC. Religious Leader
Gibbons, Jim G		Congress	10			15	Member U.S. Congress
Gibbons, Leeza		Entertainment	5			22	TV host
Gibbs, Addison C.		Governor	10	40			Governor OR
Gibbs, Alfred	1823-1868	Civil War	50	110	160		Union Gen. ALS '64 655
Gibbs, George C.		Civil War	250				CSA prison commander
Gibbs, Georgia		Entertainment	15			35	Big Band Vocalist
Gibbs, Marla		Entertainment	6	8	15	10	
Gibran, Kahlil	1883-1931	Author-Artist	150	571	1200	650	Syrian Poet, Novelist, Essayist

NAME	DATE	CATEGORY	SIG	LS/DS	ALS	SP	COMMENTS
Gibson, Brig. Gen. Herbert D.	1891-1980	Military	30				World War II U.S. general
Gibson, Charles Dana	1867-1944	Artist	60	250	285	240	Illustrator-Gibson Girl, Signed archive 1265
Gibson, Charles H.		Congress	5		15		Repr., Senator MD 1885
Gibson, Charles		Entertainment	4			18	TV News, '20/20' Co-Anchor
Gibson, Debbie		Entertainment	10			25	
Gibson, Edmund	1669-1748	Clergy		110			Bishop of London
Gibson, Edward G.		Astronaut	10			24	
Gibson, Henry		Entertainment	5			12	
Gibson, Hoot	1892-1962	Entertainment	170	195		368	Vintage Film Cowboy Star
Gibson, Horatio G.	1828-1924	Civil War	42				Union Brevet Brig. General
Gibson, James		Military	75	230	425		Officer War 1812. Wounded, Died
Gibson, Jim		Music	8			12	performer/publisher
Gibson, Maj. Gen. Ralph Burgess	1894-1962	Military	20				World War II Canadian general
Gibson, Mel		Entertainment	30			111	Actor
Gibson, Randall Lee (WD)		Civil War	190	4500	5250		CSA Gen.
Gibson, Randall Lee	1832-1892	Civil War	134	210	322		CSA General, US Sen. LA
Gibson, Robert L.		Astronaut	7			25	'Hoot'
Gibson, Thomas		Entertainment				30	
Gibson, William		Author	20		170		Playwright. The Miracle Worker
Giddings, De Witt C.		Senate/Congress	15	25	40		MOC TX. Served in CSA Army
Giddings, Joshua R.	1795-1864	Congress	12				Repr. OH
Gide, André	1869-1951	Author	150	270	329	350	Fr. Nobel Laureate Lit., Moralist, Philosopher
Gielgud, John, Sir	1904-	Entertainment	20	52		50	Noted British Actor
Gies, Jan		History	75				Helped shelter the Frank family during WWII
Gies, Miep		History	45	112	250		Befriended & hid Anne Frank's family
Gieseking, Walter	1895-1956	Entertainment	44			118	Fr.-born Concert Pianist
Giesler, Jerry		Law	10	20	40	15	Brilliant Trial Lawyer
Giffard, Gen. Sir George James	1886-1964	Military	25				World War II British general
Gifford, Francis		Entertainment	5	7	12	10	
Gifford, Kathie Lee		Entertainment	8			20	TV Personality-Singer.
Gifford, Walter S.		Business-Diplomat	5	15	25	10	Pres. AT&T 1925-48, Chm.-'50
Gigli, Beniamino	1890-1957	Entertainment	110	160	250	300	Opera, Concert. SPc 225-295
Gil, Brendan		Author	16			20	Writer New Yorker Mag.
Gilbert, Alfred C.	1884-1961	Business	60	95	175		Inventor Erector Set.
Gilbert, Billy		Entertainment	20	25	45	60	
Gilbert, Cass		Architect	20	60		35	Woolworth Bldg., Supr. Court...
Gilbert, Charles Champion	1822-1903	Civil War	41	92	140		Union general
Gilbert, H. E.		Celebrity	5	11	28	8	
Gilbert, James Isham	1823-1884	Civil War	45	110	160		Union general
Gilbert, John Sir	1817-1897	Artist			45		
Gilbert, John		Entertainment	125	175	325	300	Mega Star of Silent Movies. Romantic Hero
Gilbert, L. Wolfe		Composer	20	50	95	60	
Gilbert, Lynn		Entertainment	3	3	6	10	
Gilbert, Melissa		Entertainment	10	18		35	Actress
Gilbert, Sara		Entertainment	16			25	Actress Rosanne

NAME	DATE	CATEGORY	SIG	LS/DS	ALS	SP	COMMENTS
Gilbert, William. S., Sir	1836-1911	Composer	165	365	565	675	Gilbert & Sullivan Operettas. Pen Drawing S 3500
Gilbreath, Maj. Gen. Frederick	1888-1969	Military	30				World War II U.S. general
Gilbreth, Lillian		Engineer	30		100		1st Woman Engineer
Gilchrest, Wayne T. G		Congress	10			15	Member U.S. Congress
Gilder, Richard Watson	1844-1909	Author	25		70		Editor Century Magazine
Giles, Bill		Celebrity	10			15	weather presenter
Giles, Sandra		Entertainment	5			10	Pinup 30
Giles, William Branch		Senate	30	80	115		Early, influential VA Sen. 1801
Gilford, Jack	1907-1990	Entertainment	15		30	35	Character Actor.Film,Stage,TV. Blacklisted 1950's
Gill, Eric		Artist	20	66	150		Br. Sculptor, Engraver
Gill, Maj. Gen. John Galbraith	1889-1981	Military	25				World War II British general
Gill, Maj. Gen. William H.	1886-1976	Military	30				World War II U.S. general
Gill, Neena		Political	10			15	Member European Parliament
Gill, Vince		Country Music	10			40	
Gilland, Brig. Gen. Morris .	1898-1985	Military	30				World War II U.S. general
Gillem, Alvan Cullem	1830-1875	Civil War	48	94	140		Union general
Gillem, Lt. Gen. Alvan C. Jr.	1888-1973	Military	30				World War II U.S. general
Gillespie, Brig. Gen. Alexander G.	1881-1956	Military	30				World War II U.S. general
Gillespie, Dizzy	1917-1993	Entertainment	50			92	Jazz. Trumpet
Gillett, Frederick H.	1851-1935	Speaker of House	15	35	95		MOC, Senator MA
Gillette, Anita	1936-	Entertainment	5	15	35	20	Actress. Broadway Leads. TV Series. Films
Gillette, Francis		Senate	20	60			Free-Soiler Senator CT
Gillette, King Camp	1855-1932	Business-Inventor	375	950	3500	1250	Gillette Co. Invented Safety Razor
Gillette, William	1855-1937	Entertainment	58	110	215	165	Portrayed Sherlock Holmes.Actor, Playwright
Gilley, Mickey		Entertainment	8			20	C/W Singer
Gilliam, Terry*		Art-Entertainment	15			250	Clever 'Monty Python' Animator and Director
Gillig, Marie-hélène		Political	10			15	Member European Parliament
Gilligan's Island		Entertainment	511			558	Signd group photo, all 7
Gillis, J. H.		Military	5	15	25		
Gillmor, Paul E. G		Congress	10			15	Member U.S. Congress
Gillmore, Joseph A.		Governor	35	90			Civil War Gov. NY
Gillmore, Maj. Gen. William N.	1903-1990	Military	30				World War II U.S. general
Gillmore, Quincy A. (WD)		Civil War	60	145	235		Union Gen. LS '63 7975
Gillmore, Quincy A.	1825-1888	Civil War	38	121	157		Union Gen.
Gilman, John T.	1753-1828	Revolutionary War		100	140		Cont. Congr.Gov. NH
Gilman, Nicholas		Revolutionary War	110	285	575		Continental Congress
Gilmer, Jeremy F.	1818-1883	Civil War	130	100	412		CSA Gen.
Gilmer, John H.		Civil War	25		100		CSA Congress from NC
Gilmer, Thomas W.		Cabinet		95	145		Tyler Sec'y Navy
Gilmore, Gary		Celebrity	15	25	35		
Gilmore, James R.	1822-1903	Author	20	60	195		Merchant, Abolitionist, Novelist, Songwriter
Gilmore, Joseph A.	1811-1867	Civil War Gov.	35	135			Gov. NH
Gilmore, Laura E.	1832-	Celebrity	5		50		Wife of James R. Noted Medium
Gilmore, Patrick Sarfield	1829-1892.	Composer-CW	35	80	180		'When Johnny Comes Marching Home'. AMQS 275
Gilmore, Virginia		Entertainment	10	15	30	25	Actress. Pretty Wife of Yul Brynner

NAME	DATE	CATEGORY	SIG	LS/DS	ALS	SP	COMMENTS
Gilmour, Patrick S.	1829-1892	Bandleader	5				Bandmaster. Sig/Music 30
Gilpin, Henry D.	1801-1860	Cabinet	25	50	75		Van Buren Att'y Gen. 1840, Historian, Author
Gil-robles Gil-delgado, José M.		Political	10			15	Member European Parliament
Gilruth, Robert R.		Astronaut	10			20	
Gimbel Brothers (6)		Business	475				Gimbel Department Stores
Gimbel, Bernard F.	1885-1966	Business	75	175	375	175	Gimbel Bros. Dept. Stores
Gimbel, Ellis A.	1865-1950	Business	90	180			Last of Original Gimbel Bros.
Gimbel, Isaac		Business				242	Founder of Gimbel's
Giminez, Eduardo		Entertainment	10			30	Opera
Ginastera, Alberto		Composer		95	175	100	Opera, Ballet
Gingold, Hermione	1897-1987	Entertainment	10			25	Br. Comedienne. 'Gigi'
Gingrey, Phil G		Congress	10			15	Member U.S. Congress
Gingrich, Candace		Entertainment	10			20	actress
Gingrich, Newt		Senate/Congress	10	25	25	25	MOC GA Since 1973. Speaker of House. Resigned
Ginsberg, Ruth Bader		Supreme Court	40	70		75	Clinton Appointment to S.C.
Ginsburg, Allen	1926-1998	Author	42	191	272	115	Beat Poet. Social Activist. TMsS 575, FDC S 50
Giordano, Umberto	1867-1948	Composer	225	400	525	725	Opera Composer. AMusQS 450-750
Girard, Stephen	1750-1831	Revolutionary War	125	275	325		Philanthropist, Merchant, Banker
Girardey, Victor Jean Baptiste	1837-1864	Civil War	450	576			Confederate general
Giraud, General Henri-Honeré	1879-1949	Military	20				World War II French general
Gisborne, Thomas		Author	30				
Gish, Dorothy		Entertainment	75			132	Actress. Silent Film Star
Gish, Lillian	1896-1993	Entertainment	20	65	75	68	Silent Star. 'Birth of a Nation'
Gissing, George Robert	1857-1903	Author	50	175	345		Br. Novelist.
Gist, Mordecai	1742-1792	Rev. War			631		Led Maryland regiment against the British forces
Gist, States Rights	1831-1864	Civil War	975	1700	4200		Confederate Gen., RARE
Giuliani, Rudolph 'Rudy'		Political	25	50	35	75	Mayor of NYC
Giulmant, Felix-Alexandre	1787-1874	Musician				140	French organist
Given, Robin		Entertainment	10			30	Actress. 'Head of the Class'
Givenchy, Hubert de		Business	35	70	95	200	Fr. Fashion Designer
Givens, Charles		Celebrity	10			15	financial expert
Givens, Edward G. Jr.		Astronaut	10			25	
Givot, George		Entertainment	10			20	Comic. 'Greek Ambassador Good Will'
Gjelsteen, Maj. Gen. Einar B.	1900-1985	Military	30				World War II U.S. general
Glad, Gladys		Entertainment	10	12		20	Actress. Vintage
Gladden, Adley H.	1810-1862	Civil War	534	1178			CSA Gen. ALS '61 6325. Wounded & Died 1862
Gladden, Washington		Clergy	30	40	55		
Gladstone, William E.	1809-1898	Head of State	75	120	178	300	Br. Prime Minister
Glancy, Brig. Gen. Alfred R.	1881-1959	Military	30				World War II U.S. general
Glante, Norbert		Political	10			15	Member European Parliament
Glase, Anne-karin		Political	10			15	Member European Parliament
Glaser, Donald A.		Science	20	35	75	35	Nobel Phys. Invented Bubble Chamber
Glaser, Lillian		Entertainment	10			15	Mrs. DeWolf Hopper
Glaser, Lulu		Entertainment	10	12	20	20	
Glaser, Paul Michael		Entertainment	5			20	Actor

NAME	DATE	CATEGORY	SIG	LS/DS	ALS	SP	COMMENTS
Glaser, Tompall		Country Music	15			30	'Glaser Bros.& His Outlaw Band'. Harmony Group
Glasgow, Ellen		Author	40	115			Novelist. Pulitzer. VA Life
Glashow, Sheldon Lee, Dr.		Science	20	35		30	Nobel Physics
Glaspell, Susan		Author	25	65	110		Am. Playwright. Pulitzer
Glass, Carter	1858-1946	Cabinet	15	45	60	30	Sec'y Treas., Sen. VA 1902
Glass, Philip	1937-	Composer	30	50		190	Am.Orchestral, Opera, Film,Stage
Glass, Ron		Entertainment	5		25	20	Actor. 'Barney Miller'
Glassman, Alan		Entertainment	5			25	Opera
Glazunov, Alexander	1865-1936	Composer	150	225	450	350	Rus. AMusQS 1,000-2,750
Gleason, Jackie	1916-1987	Entertainment	50	100	130	157	Am. Comedian-Actor TV-Movies. 'Honeymooners'
Gleason, James		Entertainment	40			75	Grumpy Character Actor of 30's to 50's
Gledhill, Arthur		Business	4			10	Stanley Works
Glenn, John (As Astronaut)		Astronaut	40	153	223	107	1st To Orbit Earth. FDC 2/20/62 Canaveral 125
Glenn, John	1921-	Senator	20	30	40	50	Ohio Senator-Astronaut
Glenn, Scott	1942-	Entertainment	10	15	32	30	Actor. 'Silence of the Lambs', 'Nashville'
Glennon, John, Cardinal		Clergy	40	50	65	45	
Gless, Sharon		Entertainment	8	12	19	21	Actress.Long Running TV Series 'Cagney & Lacey'
Gliere, Reinhold	1875-1956	Composer	55		350		Rus. Symphony & Ballet
Globus, Yoram		Entertainment	5			16	Producer
Glossop, Peter		Entertainment	10			30	Opera
Gloucester, Henry Wm. F., Duke		Royalty	10	20	50	35	Son of Geo. V., Gov-Gen. Australia
Glover, Danny	1947-	Entertainment	10	12	15	39	Actor
Glover, John	1732-1797	Revolutionary War	250	610	1125		Gen. Continental Army. 27th Reg. (14th)
Glover, Julian		Entertainment	10			20	Actor
Glover, Maj. Gen. Malcom	1897-1970	Military	25				World War II British general
Glover, Maj. Gen. Sir Guy de C.	1887-1967	Military	25				World War II British general
Glubb, John, Sir Pasha	1897-1986	Military	22	45	60	125	Br. General. Formed & Commanded Arab Legion
Gluck, Alma		Entertainment	20	35	45	115	Opera, Concert, Recording
Glueck, Nelson		Archaeologist	10	25	50	20	Uncovered 1500 Ancient Artifact
Glunicke, Maj. Gen. Robert C.A.	1886-1963	Military	25				World War II British general
Glyn, Elinor 1864-1948		Author	20	70	165	125	Br. Novelist, Film Scenarios
Gnys, Wladek		Aviation	40			150	Shot Down 1st Plane in WW II
Goard, Nona		Aviation	10	15	25	15	
Gobbi, Tito	1913-1984	Entertainment	20			80	It. Baritone, Opera
Gobbo, Gian Paolo		Political	10			15	Member European Parliament
Gobel, George	1918-1991	Entertainment	10			35	Early TV
Godard, Benjamin Louis	1849-1895	Composer	75	125	238	150	Fr. Opera 'Jocelyn'. Familiar 'Berceuse'
Godard, Jean Luc	1930	Entertainment	200				Fr. Film Director, Writer. Scarce
Godard, Louis	1829-1885	Aviation-Balloon	300	1200			Balloonist, ALS/Content 6,500
Godard, Magdalena		Entertainment	15			75	Violinist
Goddard, Calvin	1768-1842	Political	15		55		Federalist Congress 1801-05
Goddard, Lt. Gen. Eric Norman	1897-1992	Military	25				World War II British general
Goddard, Paulette	1911-1990	Entertainment	28	45	80	85	Actress
Goddard, Robert H.	1882-1945	Science	426	950	1831	2495	Am. Physicist. Rocket Pioneer. TLS/Cont. 3500
Godden, Rumer	1907-	Author	15		65		Brit. Novelist. 'Black Narcissus', 'The River'

NAME	DATE	CATEGORY	SIG	LS/DS	ALS	SP	COMMENTS
Goderich, Fred. John Robinson		Head of State	15	40	95		Viscount Goderich. Br. P.M.
Godey, Louis A.	1804-1878	Publisher	40	95	175		Godey's Ladies Book
Godfrey, A. Earl		Aviation	30	60	110	75	
Godfrey, Arthur		Entertainment	15	50	55	25	Radio & Early TV Ukelele Playing-Singing Host
Godfrey, Brig. Gen. Stuart C.	1886-1945	Military	30				World War II U.S. general
Godfrey, Brigadier Arthur H.L.	1896-1942	Military	20				World War II Australian general
Godfrey, Capt. Johnny		Aviation	50				Ace/29 Victories
Godfrey, Gen. Sir Wm. Wellington	1880-1952	Military	25				World War II British general
Godin, Nesse		Celebrity	10			15	motivational speaker
Godolphin, Sidney, 1st Earl	1644-1712	Head of State	96	240			P.M. Eng. Lord High Treasurer to Queen Anne
Godoy, Manuel de	1767-1851	Head of State	295				Sp. Politician, Prime Minister
Godt, Eberhard		Military	15		70		
Godunov, Alexander	1949-1995	Entertainment	33			60	Ballet. Russian Star Defected
Godwin, Archibald Campbell	1831-1864	Civil War	500	1811	3479		Confederate general
Godwin, Linda		Astronaut	5			20	
Godwin-Austin, Gen. Sir Alfred R.	1889-1963	Military	25				World War II British general
Goebbels, Joseph	1897-1945	Nazi Leader WWII	250	900	1500	1100	Nazi Minister of Propaganda
Goebbels, Robert		Political	10			15	Member European Parliament
Goebel, Arthur		Aviation	40			110	Pioneer Aviator
Goepel, Lutz		Political	10			15	Member European Parliament
Goering, Hermann W.	1893-1946	Military	300	950	1578	1138	Nazi Leader. Marshal of the Reich. Suicide
Goethals, George W.	1858-1928	Military-Science	175	280	356	350	Panama Canal.TLS/Cont. 1,750
Goethe, Johann W. von	1749-1832	Author	1250	2400	5750		Ger. Poet, Dramatist, Novelist
Goettheim, F.		Business	10	20	45		
Goff Jr., Nathan	1834-1903	Civil War	35	60	85	150	Union Brevet Brig. General
Goggin, James Monroe	1820-1889	Civil War	144				Confederate general
Gogh, Vincent Van	1853-1890	Artist	3500	5500	16000		Dutch Painter. Individual Style
Gogol, Nicholai	1809-1852	Author	625	3350	6500		Father of Rus. Realistic Lit.
Going, Joanna		Entertainment	6			40	Actress Pin-Up 55
Golan, Menaham		Entertainment	5	6	15	15	Film Producer
Gold, Missy		Entertainment	8			20	'Benson'. Has Matured from Child Actress to Leads
Gold, Tracy		Entertainment	10			25	Actress
Goldberg, Arthur J.	1908-1990	Supreme Court	50	168		108	Resigned From Suprme Ct. To Become Ambass. UN
Goldberg, Lucianne		Celebrity	10			30	Internet journalist/opinion http://lucianne.com
Goldberg, Reiner		Entertainment	10			30	Opera
Goldberg, Rube*	1883-1970	Cartoonist	50	100		250	'Ike & Mike', 'Boob McNutt'. Pulitzer Prize '48
Goldberg, Stan*		Cartoonist	22			80	'Archie'. Repro Drawing S. 65 (4x6)
Goldberg, Whoopi	1935-	Entertainment	12	15	30	38	Oscar Winning Actress & Comedian
Goldblum, Jeff		Entertainment	10	12	15	37	Actor
Golden Eye (Cast Of)		Entertainment	80			150	Brosnan,Scorupco, Janssen
Golden Girls, The (Cast Of)		Entertainment	52			195	All Four
Golden, Charles, Bishop		Clergy	15	25	30	30	
Golden, Diana		Celebrity	10			15	motivational speaker
Goldenson, Leonard H.		Business	10	20	30	20	TV Broadcasting Exec.
Goldenthal, Elliot		Celebrity	10			15	film industry

NAME	DATE	CATEGORY	SIG	LS/DS	ALS	SP	COMMENTS
Golding, Louis		Author	50	85	125	60	Br. Verse, Stories, Novels
Golding, William	1911-1994	Author	65	125	260	150	Nobel Lit., 'Lord of the Flies'
Goldman, Edwin Franco		Composer	25	50	75		Bandmaster
Goldman, Emma		Anarchist	75	247	435	250	Deported. Author-Editor TLS /cont 1800
Goldman, Michael		Author	5	10	15	10	
Goldman, Nahum		Zionist	15		50		Pres. World Zionist Org.
Goldman, William		Author			125		'Soldier in the Rain', 'Princess Bride'
Goldmark, Peter C.		Science	25		40		Inventor. LP Records
Goldney, Maj. Gen. Claude le Bas	1887-1978	Military	25				World War II British general
Goldney, Maj. Gen. Henry W.	1885-1972	Military	25				World War II British general
Goldowsky, Boris		Conductor	8			35	Opera Coach. Dir. of own Opera Theatre
Goldsboro, Bobby		Country Western	10			18	Singer
Goldsborough, Louis M.	1805-1907	Civil War	65	135	200		Rear Admiral USN Sig/Rank 95
Goldschmidt, Berthold	1903-	Composer				175	Ger. Works Banned by Nazis WW II
Goldschmidt, Neil E.		Cabinet	4	10	25	15	Sec'y Transportation
Goldschmidt, Richard, Dr.	1890-1958	Science		20	40		World Famous Geneticist
Goldsmith, Jerry		Entertainment	4			10	
Goldthwaite, Brig. Gen. Ralph H.	1882-1969	Military	30				World War II U.S. general
Goldwater, Barry	1909-1998	Congress	18	73		38	Sen. AZ. Presidential Candidate
Goldwin, Tony		Entertainment	3			20	
Goldwyn, Sam		Business	100	124	255	195	Goldwyn Studios
Goldwyn, Sam, Jr.		Entertainment	4			12	Producer
Golino, Valerie		Entertainment	10			38	Actress
Gollnisch, Bruno		Political	10			15	Member European Parliament
Gollob, Gordon		Aviation		165		200	WWII Ger. Air Ace. RK
Golonka, Arlene		Entertainment	4	4	9	15	
Gombell, Minna		Entertainment	25	30	55	55	
Gomes, Carlos	1836-1896	Composer	25		175		Brazilian. Opera
Gomes, Francisco		Head of State	15	55	135	75	
Gomez, Aurea		Entertainment	5			20	Opera, Brazilian Soprano
Gomez, Thomas		Entertainment	20			50	
Gomme, George Laurence Sir		Science			60		
Gomolka, Alfred		Political	10			15	Member European Parliament
Gompers, Samuel	1850-1924	Labor Leader	100	195	290	300	Founder & 1st Pres. A.F.of L.
Gonclaves, Paul		Entertainment	10			20	actor
González álvarez, Laura		Political	10			15	Member European Parliament
Gonzalez, Charles A. G		Congress	10			15	Member U.S. Congress
Good Will Hunting (cast)		Entertainment				65	Damon / Affleck
Good, James W.		Cabinet	25	50		30	Hoover Sec'y of War
Goodall, Caroline		Entertainment	10			20	actress
Goode Jr., Virgil H. G		Congress	10			15	Member U.S. Congress
Goodfellas (cast)		Entertainment				150	Cast of 4
Goodier, Mark		Music	10			15	DJ
Gooding, Cuba		Entertainment	12			42	Actor. 'Jerry McGuire' SP 60
Goodlatte, Bob G		Congress	10			15	Member U.S. Congress

NAME	DATE	CATEGORY	SIG	LS/DS	ALS	SP	COMMENTS
Goodman, Al		Bandleader				45	
Goodman, Benny	1909-1986	Entertainment	52	162		177	Big Band Leader-Clarinetist
Goodman, Brig. Gen. John F.	1891-1947	Military	30				World War II U.S. general
Goodman, Dody		Entertainment	4	4	9	10	
Goodman, Ellen		Celebrity	10			15	media/TV personality
Goodman, Jerry		Celebrity	10			15	financial expert
Goodman, John		Entertainment	15			35	Actor
Goodman, Maj. Gen. William M.	1892-1958	Military	30				World War II U.S. general
Goodpaster, Andrew	1915-	Military	30	55	55	50	Gen. WW II. Highly Decorated Combat Officer etc.
Goodridge, Robin		Entertainment	6			25	Music. Drummer 'Bush'
Goodson, Mark		Entertainment	10			30	Producer TV
Goodway, Beverly		Celebrity	10			15	photographer
Goodwill, Robert		Political	10			15	Member European Parliament
Goodwin, E. S.		Aviation	3	5	10		
Goodwin, Hugh H.		Military	25	65	126	50	
Goodwin, Nat C.		Entertainment	20			30	Vintage Actor
Goody, Jade		Celebrity	10			15	¦Big Brother[a]
Goodyear, Charles Jr.		Business	20	60	150	30	Goodyear Tire & Rubber Co.
Goodyear, Charles	1800-1860	Inventor	350	1112	4400		Developed Rubber Vulcanization
Goodyear, Julie		Entertainment	10			20	Actress
Gookin, Dan		Author	10		35	20	Dos For Dummiesetc.
Goosens, Eugene, Sir		Composer	20	45	90	85	Br.Conductor. Opera/Orchestral Works
Goossens, Eugene		Entertainment	15			45	
Gorbachev, Mikhail (USSR)		Head of State	100	250	750	250	Instituted Perestroika,Glasnost.Nobel '90 FDC 175
Gorbachev, Raisa		Rus. 1st Lady	50			125	
Gorbato, Victor	b. 1934	Astronaut		45			Russian cosmonaut
Gorcey, Leo	1915-1969	Entertainment	90	100		161	The Bowery Boys
Gorder, Brig. Gen. Alexander O.	1893-1973	Military	30				World War II U.S. general
Gordon, Alex., 4th Duke of		Revolutionary War	20		35		
Gordon, B. Frank		Civil War		280			CSA gen.
Gordon, Bart G		Congress	10			15	Member U.S. Congress
Gordon, C. Henry		Entertainment	20				Actor
Gordon, Charles G.	1823-1886	Military	133	550	750	950	'Chinese Gordon',Gordon Pasha. Killed at Khartoum
Gordon, Charles W.		Clergy	20	25	30		
Gordon, Gale	1905-1995	Entertainment	25	20		71	Versatile Radio, TV/LUCY, Film Actor
Gordon, Gavin	1901-1983	Entertainment	40				Vintage
Gordon, George H.		Civil War	40	85	135		Union General
Gordon, George W.	1836-1911	Civil War	215	422	480		CSA General
Gordon, Gray		Entertainment	20			50	Big band leader
Gordon, Huntley	1897-1956	Entertainment	20	25		45	Silent Film Star. In over 50 films 1918-40
Gordon, James Byron	1822-1864	Civil War	338				Confederate general, KIA Yellow Tavern, VA
Gordon, John Brown (WD)		Civil War	350	900	2250		CSA Gen.
Gordon, John Brown	1832-1904	Civil War	187	287	429		CSA Gen., Gov. & US Sen. GA
Gordon, John F.		Business	4	6	15	10	
Gordon, Judah Leib	1830-1892	Journalist	175		1150		Russ. Born Writer For Jewish Haskalah

NAME	DATE	CATEGORY	SIG	LS/DS	ALS	SP	COMMENTS
Gordon, Mack		Composer	30	60	130	40	Lyricist
Gordon, Richard F. Jr.		Astronaut	22	75		46	
Gordon, Ruth		Entertainment	15	25	40	38	AA ' Harold and Maud ', Actress, Writer,Director
Gordone, Charles	1927-1995	Author	25			40	Afr-Am Pulitzer Prize Winning Playwright
Gordon-Finlayson, Gen. Sir Robt.	1881-1956	Military	25				World War II British general
Gore, Albert A., Jr.	1948-	Vice President	40	60		80	Vice President
Gore, Albert A., Sr.	1907-1998	Congress	15	60			Repr- Senator TN 1939-44, 53-71. Father of Gore Jr
Gore, Christopher		Senate	85	205	350		Gov. MA, Senator MA 1813
Gore, Howard W.		Cabinet	4	30			Sec'y Agriculture
Gore, Tipper		2nd Lady	5	12		10	
Gorgas, Josiah (WD)		Civil War	225	700	1025		CSA Gen.
Gorgas, Josiah	1813-1883	Civil War	206	314	475		CSA Gen.
Gorgas, William C., Dr.		Science	125	412	450		Eradicated Yellow Fever
Gorham, George H.		Senate/Congress	10	20	35		
Gorham, Nathaniel	1738-1796	Revolutionary War	375	396	1507		Pres. Continental Congress
Gorie, Dominic		Astronaut	5			19	
Goritz, Otto	1873-1929	Entertainment	30			65	Operatic Baritone
Gorki, Maxim	1868-1936	Author	350	1250	2190	1500	Rus.Writer emerged from lower classes. Novels
Görlach, Willi		Political	10			15	Member European Parliament
Gorman, Arthur P.	1839-1906	Senate	10	15	22		Senator MD 1881-99
Gorman, Brigadier Eugene		Military	20				World War II Australian general
Gorman, Margaret		Entertainment	40			75	1st Miss America 1921
Gorman, R. C.		Artist	25	222			American Indian Artist, signed repro 75-200
Gorman, Willis Arnold	1816-1876	Civil War	40	90	162		Union general
Gorney, Karen Lynn		Entertainment	5	3	6	15	
Gorostiaga Atxalandabaso, Koldo		Political	10			15	Member European Parliament
Gorshin, Frank	1933-	Entertainment	10	15	20	28	Actor, Impressionist. As 'The Riddler' 40 SP
Goschen, Maj. Gen. Arthur Alec	1880-1975	Military	25				World War II British general
Goss, Porter J. G		Congress	10			15	Member U.S. Congress
Gossard, Stone		Entertainment	6			25	Music. Vocalist 'Pearl Jam'
Gosse, Aristid V.		Science	30		80		
Gosse, Edmund, Sir	1849-1928	Author	20	35	50	35	Br. Poet, Man of Letters
Gosselaar, Mark Paul		Entertainment	10			30	actor
Gosselaar, Mark Paul		Entertainment	6			45	Actor
Gossett, Louis, Jr.		Entertainment	15	35		55	Actor
Gott, Lt. Gen. William Henry Ewart	1897-1942	Military	25				World War II British general
Gottfrederson, Floyd*		Cartoonist	100			500	Mickey Mouse Strip Art
Gotti, John		Crime	200		2013	500	Mafia Boss, signed check 878-1995
Gotto, Brig. Christopher Hugh	1888-1959	Military	25				World War II British general
Gottschalk, Louis Moreau	1829-1869	Composer	350	750	1250	2250	Pianist , AMusQS 1800-3250-4500
Goudal, Jetta		Entertainment	10	10	20	40	
Goudot, Maj. Gen. Victor-Nicolas	1876-1964	Military	20				World War II French general
Goudsmit, Samuel A.		Science	15	25	40	20	Dutch Born Atomic Physicist
Gough, John B.	1817-1886	Clergy	25	40	55	125	Temperance Advocate, Reformer
Gould, Charles L.		Business	10	35	45	20	

NAME	DATE	CATEGORY	SIG	LS/DS	ALS	SP	COMMENTS
Gould, Chester*	1900-1985	Cartoonist	50	80		179	Dick Tracy. Large Tracy Sketch S 500
Gould, Edwin	1866-1956	Business	50	250	350	150	son of Jay
Gould, Elliott		Entertainment	5	6	15	25	Actor
Gould, George	1864-1923	Business	95	225	350	175	Son of Jay.Lost Inheritance.TLS on RR Lttrhd 1900
Gould, Glenn	1932-1982	Entertainment		1165	1925	2948	Eccentric, Legendary Pianist. RARE
Gould, Gordon		Inventor	15	40			Commercial Laser Inventor
Gould, Harold		Entertainment	5	6	15	25	Actor
Gould, Jay	1836-1892	Business	275	716	1531	1500	Financier, ALS/cont 4500, Stk. Cert S 21,000
Gould, John	1804-1881	Science	110		700		Br. Ornithologist
Gould, Morton		Composer	20	45	70	40	AMusQS 200
Gould, Robert Simonton		Civil War	25	65	90		CSA Cmdr. Gould's Battalion
Gould, Samuel B.		Celebrity	4	8	20	10	
Gould, Sandra		Entertainment	4			15	Actress, Mrs. Kravitz 'Bewitched'
Goulding, Ray		Entertainment	3	3	6	10	
Goulet, Robert		Entertainment	10			20	Singer
Gounod, Charles	1818-1893	Composer	93	231	275	362	AMusQS 650-2,500. Score 'Sapho' S 985
Gouraud, Henri-Joseph E.	1897-1946	Military	40	70		100	Fr. Gen. WW I
Govan, Daniel C.	1829-1911	Civil War	90		540		CSA Gen.
Gowdy, John		Clergy	15	15	25		
Goya, Francisco		Artist	2200	7900	18750		Sp.Painter,Etcher,Lithographer
Goz, Harry		Entertainment	6	8	15	18	
Graªa Moura, Vasco		Political	10			15	Member European Parliament
Grabe, Ronald J.		Astronaut	8			25	
Grable, Betty	1916-1973	Entertainment	53	80	150	192	GI's WW II #1 Pin-up girl
Grace and Prince Rainier		Royalty	162	273	350	327	
Grace de Monaco (Grace Kelly)	1928-1982	Royalty	133	249	406	290	As Princess
Grace, Eugene G.		Industrialist	25	65	140	40	Pres.,Chmn. Bethlehem Steel
Grace, J. Peter		Celebrity	10			15	financial expert
Grace, William R.		Business	15	30	45	30	Mayor NYC. W.R. Grace & Co.
Gracen, Elizabeth Ward		Entertainment	5			25	Miss America '82, Pin-Up SP 55
Gracey, Gen. Sir Douglas David	1894-1964	Military	28				World War II British general
Gracie, Archibald Jr.	1832-1864	Civil War	450	1500			Confederate general, KIA Petersburg, VA
Grade, Lew, Lord	1906-1998	Entertainment	22			35	Br. Impresario of Entertainment. TV-Film Producer
Grady, Don		Entertainment	5			12	
Graefe Zu Baringdorf, Friedrich		Political	10			15	Member European Parliament
Graf, David		Entertainment	10			20	actor
Graf, Herman		Aviation	35			85	Ger. ACE. #9 Worldwide
Graham, Billy		Clergy	35	45	60	214	World-Wide Evangelist
Graham, Bob		Senate	10			15	United States Senate (D - FL)
Graham, Brig. Gen. Roy C.L.	1892-1980	Military	30				World War II U.S. general
Graham, Brig. Douglas M., Lord	1883-1974	Military	25				World War II British general
Graham, C.J.		Entertainment	4			10	Horror
Graham, Charles Kinnaird	1824-1889	Civil War	40	90	150		Union general
Graham, Donald		Business	10	25	40	15	
Graham, Elizabeth Candler		Author	5	7	10	15	Books about Coca-Cola

NAME	DATE	CATEGORY	SIG	LS/DS	ALS	SP	COMMENTS
Graham, George	1772-1830	Military-Cabinet	20	50	75		Monroe Sec. War (ad int) Soldier, Statesman
Graham, Heather		Entertainment	10			42	Actress. 'Shout' SP 65
Graham, Jim 'the Commish'		Author	8			12	NC Sec of Agriculture, cookbook
Graham, John	1774-1820	Diplomatist	65	215	430		Aided Jefferson, Madison, Monroe
Graham, Katherine	1917-	Publisher	15	25	60	25	Chm. CEO Washington Post
Graham, Lawrence Pike	1815-1905	Civil War	45	85	140		Union general
Graham, Lindsey		Senate	10			15	United States Senate (R - SC)
Graham, M. Gordon		Aviaton	25			50	ACE WW II
Graham, Maj. Gen. Douglas A. H.	1893-1971	Military	25				World War II British general
Graham, Maj. Gen. Sir Miles	1895-1976	Military	25				World War II British general
Graham, Martha	1895-1986	Entertainment	67	194	260	325	Dancer, Teacher, Choreographer
Graham, Robert		Artist	3			10	Sculptor
Graham, Sheila		Author	25		40	35	Journalist, Gossip Columnist
Graham, Sylvester		Inventor			100		The Graham Cracker
Graham, Thomas	1805-1869	Science			105		Scottish Chemist
Graham, Virginia	1912-1998	Entertainment	20			35	TV Hostess, Commentator, Panelist. Radio Actress
Graham, William A.	1804-1875	Cabinet	20	40	65		Fillmore Sec. Navy 1850
Grahame, Gloria	1924-1981	Entertainment	48	100		175	Academy Award
Grahame, Kenneth	1859-1932	Author	75	110	195		Br. Writer Wind in the Willows
Grahame-White, Claude	1879-1959	Aviation	60	100	250	125	1st Br. School of Aviation. Pioneer Aviator-Mfg.
Grahl, Briag. Gen. Charles H.	1894-1981	Military	30				World War II U.S. general
Grainger, Percy	1882-1961	Composer	40	95	165	250	Australian Pianist-Composer. SPc 150
Grainger-Stewart, Brig. Thomas	1896-1979	Military	25				World War II British general
Gramegna, Anna		Entertainment	45			95	Opera
Gramm, Phil		Senate	7			15	Senator TX
Grammer, Kelsey		Entertainment	10			40	TV Series-Frasier
Gran, Tryggve		Celebrity	12	30			
Granados, Enrique	1867-1916	Composer			975		Sp. Pianist. Piano Works, Opera AMusQS 1250
Granbury, Hiram Bronson	1831-1864	Civil War	450	6900			Confederate general
Grandi, Dino, Count	1895-1988	Diplomat	25	45	90	40	Mussolini Cabinet
Grandsard, Lt. Gen. Pierre-P-J	1881-1966	Military	20				World War II French general
Grandval, Marie F.C.		Composer	10		95		Fr. Woman Composer
Grandy, Fred		Entertainment	5	10		10	Congressman IA- Love Boat
Grange, E. R.		Aviation	10	25	45	35	
Granger, Farley		Entertainment	5	7	12	20	
Granger, Francis	1792-1868	Cabinet	30	60	100		Wm. H. Harrison P.M. General
Granger, Gideon	1767-1822	Cabinet	85	200	325		P.M. General 1801
Granger, Gordon	1822-1876	Civil War	49	110	163		Union General
Granger, Kay G		Congress	10			15	Member U.S. Congress
Granger, Robert S.	1816-1894	Civil War	52	100	140		Union Gen. Captured 1861
Granger, Stewart		Entertainment	20			51	Handsome, Swashbuckling Brit. Film Star
Granit, Ragnar		Science	25	50	120	100	Nobel Medicine
Granlund, Nils T. (NTG)		Entertainment	20			40	Producer Radio, TV, Night Club
Grant III, Ulysses	1881-1968	Military	30	55	75	75	
Grant, Amy		Entertainment	5	6	15	35	

NAME	DATE	CATEGORY	SIG	LS/DS	ALS	SP	COMMENTS
Grant, Cary	1904-1986	Entertainment	207	350		546	Actor, Oscar Winner
Grant, Duncan	1885-1978	Artist	100		300		Scot. Impressionist.Bloomsbury Grp.
Grant, Frederick Dent	1850-1912	Military	30	55	80		Son Of U.S. Grant
Grant, Gen Sir Charles John Cecil	1877-1960	Military	28				World War II British general
Grant, Gogi		Entertainment	3	5	10	10	
Grant, Hugh		Entertainment	20			55	Br. Actor
Grant, Jesse R.		Political	44				US Grant's son, author
Grant, Julia Dent	1826-1902	First Lady	250	325	511		
Grant, Kathryn		Entertainment	8			30	Actress-Widow of Bing Crosby
Grant, Kirby		Entertainment	15		25	35	
Grant, Lee		Entertainment	10	30		30	Oscar winner
Grant, Lewis Addison	1828-1918	Civil War	58	85	219	200	Union general, Medal of Honor
Grant, Lt. Gen. Harold George	1884-1950	Military	25				World War II British general
Grant, Maj. Gen. Ian Cameron	1891-1955	Military	25				World War II British general
Grant, Maj. Gen. Walter S.	1878-1956	Military	30				World War II U.S. general
Grant, Richard E.		Entertainment	10			20	actor
Grant, Russell		Celebrity	10			15	Astrologer
Grant, Ulysses S. (as President)	1822-1885	Presidents	683	1420	2478		18th President of USA
Grant, Ulysses S. (WD)	1822-1885	President	750	2169	5109	4000	ALS/Spec.Cont. 15000-17500, signed cdv 2500-5000
Grant, Ulysses S.	1822-1885	President	562	1235	1900	2238	
Grant, William T.	1876-1972	Business	42	122	315	275	1,176 W.T. Grant Stores in 40 States
Grantham, Leslie		Entertainment	10			20	Actor
Granville, Bonita		Entertainment	12	20	20	35	
Grapelli, Stephane		Entertainment	20			85	Unique Jazz Violinist. SPc 60
Grapewin, Charles	1869-1956	Entertainment	212			350	Am. Character Actor. 'Uncle Henry' in 'a.of Oz'
Grasett, Lt. Gen. Sir Arthur Edw.	1888-1971	Military	25				World War II British general
Grass Roots, The		Rock Group				188	60's Group (5) DS by Three 40
Grass, Gunter		Author	40	135	260	140	Ger. Novelist. Nazi Era
Grasser, Hartmann		Aviation	14	25	50	30	
Grassi, Rinaldo		Entertainment	35	95		85	Opera
Grassle, Karen	1944-	Entertainment	5	6	10	15	Actress. 'Little House on the Prairie'
Grassley, Chuck		Senate	10			15	United States Senate (R - IA)
Grasso, Ella		Governor	10	35		20	1st Woman Governor CT
Grateful Dead (All)		Entertainment	100			550	Rock HOF
Gratiot, Charles	1788-1855	Military	150	205			War 1812. General 1828
Gratz, Barnard		Revolutionary War	75	212	400		
Gratz, Rebecca	1781-1869	Philanthropist			2750		Noted Am.Jewish Philanthropist. RARE
Graue, Dave*		Cartoonists	10			65	Alley Oop
Grauman, Sid		Entertainment	30	45	90	75	Owner of Opulent Theaters
Gravatt, Andrea M.D.		Author	8			12	child safety
Gravatte, Marianne		Entertainment	4	4	9	10	
Gravel, Maurice Mike		Senate	5			20	Senator Alaska
Graveline, Duane E.M.D.		Astronaut	5			20	
Graves, Peter	1925-	Entertainment	15	10	25	35	Actor. 'Mission Impossible', 'Airplane' etc.
Graves, Robert	1895-1985	Author	65	175	310	110	Br. Poet, Novelist, Critic

NAME	DATE	CATEGORY	SIG	LS/DS	ALS	SP	COMMENTS
Graves, Sam G		Congress	10			15	Member U.S. Congress
Graves, William		Military	50				General WW I
Gravity Kills		Entertainment	30			65	Music. 4 Member Rock Group
Gray, Alexander	1902-1975	Entertainment	15			35	Actor-Singer. Broadway Musical Star. Radio-Films
Gray, Asa	1810-1888	Science	35	60	106		Am. Botanist. Darwin Supporter
Gray, Billy		Entertainment	8			30	
Gray, Bowman		Business	7	15	35	15	
Gray, Colin		Aviation	35		90		Top New Zealand ACE
Gray, Colleen		Entertainment	15	25	45	30	
Gray, Delores		Entertainment	40			85	Am. Singer, Dancer
Gray, Elisha	1835-1901	Inventor-Business	250	1800	2400		Founder Western Electric Mfg. Telephone Pioneer
Gray, Erin	1952-	Entertainment	9	10	20	25	Actress-Model
Gray, George	1840-1925	Congress	10		35	30	Senator DE. Jurist. Diplomat
Gray, Gilda	1901-1959	Entertainment	40			155	Popularized the Shimmy
Gray, Glen		Entertainment	15			35	Big Band Leader
Gray, Harold*	1894-1968	Cartoonists	100			450	Little Orphan Annie
Gray, Harry Jack		Business	5	10	20	10	CEO United Technologies
Gray, Henry	1816-1892	Civil War	130	166			Confederate general
Gray, Horace	1828-1902	Supreme Court	60	120	180	250	1882
Gray, Isaac P.		Governor	10	15			Governor IN
Gray, Jack Stearns		Aviation	150				TLS/Content 950. AVIATRIX
Gray, Linda		Entertainment	6	12	15	20	Dallas. Pin-Up SP 20
Gray, Maj. Gen. Carl R. Jr.	1889-1955	Military	30				World War II U.S. general
Gray, Oscar L.		Senate/Congress	5	15		10	MOC AL 1915
Gray, Peter W.	1819-1874	Civil War	38	122			Member of Confederate Congress
Gray, Sally		Celebrity	10			15	television presenter
Gray, Spalding		Entertainment	10			20	actor
Gray, Thomas	1716-1771	Author	950	1888	5100		Br. Poet.'Elegy Written in a Country Churchyard'
Gray, William H., III	1941-	Congress	10			20	Afr-Am MOC PA. Pres. United Negro College Fund
Gray, William	1750-1825	Revolutionary War	40		100		Merchant, Patriot, Privateer
Grayco, Helen		Entertainment	3	3	6	12	Vocalist & Wife Spike Jones
Grayson, Brig. Gen. Thomas J.	1896-1962	Military	30				World War II U.S. general
Grayson, Cary T.	1878-1938	Medical	95				White House Physician to 3 Presidents
Grayson, John Breckinridge	1806-1861	Civil War	152	436			Confederate general
Grayson, Kathryn	1922-	Entertainment	10	22	25	45	Singer-Actress. Starred in Many Lavish MGM Musicals
Great Expectations (cast)		Entertainment				85	DeNiro / Hawke
Grechaninov, Aleksandr	1864-1956	Composer			45		Russian born, American composer
Greco, Jose		Entertainment	18	15		60	Dance
Greeley, Andrew, Rev.		Clergy	6	15		10	
Greeley, Horace	1811-1872	Journalist	75	140	261	825	'Go West, Young Man',signed gun club stock cert.9500
Greely, Adolphus W.	1844-1935	Explorer	62	121	177	250	Arctic Explorer, General
Greely, Maj. Gen. John N.	1885-1965	Military	30				World War II U.S. general
Green, Adolph		Composer	10	15		20	Collaborated/Betty Comden
Green, Al		Entertainment	10			20	
Green, Anna Katherine	1846-1935	Author	50	85	125		Pioneer Am. Detective Fiction

NAME	DATE	CATEGORY	SIG	LS/DS	ALS	SP	COMMENTS
Green, Brian Austin		Entertainment	5			22	Beverly Hills 90210
Green, Charles	1785-1870	Aeronaut	40	100	250		Br. Balloonist
Green, Dorothy		Entertainment	5	6	15	15	
Green, Dwight H.		Governor	10	15			Governor IL
Green, Fitzhugh	1888-1947	Military	50	225			USN Cmdr.,Polar Explorer, Co-Author 'We'/Lindbergh
Green, Gene G.		Congress	10			15	Member U.S. Congress
Green, Henrietta (Hetty) H.	1834-1916	Financier	2000	9500			Wall St. Speculator. LS re Stocks 18,800
Green, Herschel		Aviation	12	28	48	35	ACE, WW II, Triple Ace
Green, Jeff		Celebrity	10			15	comedian
Green, Johnny	1908-1989	Composer	40	80	120	125	AMsS 250, 150, 350
Green, Kerri		Entertainment	8			38	Actree. Pin-Up 65
Green, Lt. Gen. Sir Wm Wyndham	1887-1979	Military	25				World War II British general
Green, Maj. Gen. Joseph A.	1881-1963	Military	30				World War II U.S. general
Green, Maj. Gen. Thomas H.	1889-1971	Military	30				World War II U.S. general
Green, Maj. Gen. William	1882-1947	Military	25				World War II British general
Green, Mark G		Congress	10			15	Member U.S. Congress
Green, Martin Edwin	1815-1863	Civil War	400		1455		Confederate general, KIA Vicksburg
Green, Mitzi	1920-1969	Entertainment	8	15	25	20	Actress.Musicals-Stage & Film
Green, Paul		Author		45			Playwright, Lost Colony. Pulitzer
Green, Richard		Entertainment	30			75	
Green, Seth		Entertainment	6			42	Actor. 'Buffy' Co-Star
Green, Theodore	1867-1966	Senate	10		20	15	Gov., Senator RI
Green, Thomas (WD)		Civil War	175	725	3250		CSA Gen. KIA. DS/Rare NM CSA '62 6500
Green, Thomas	1814-1864	Civil War	147	295	450		CSA Gen. KIA Mansfield, LA
Green, Tom		Celebrity	10			30	Comedian
Green, William F.	1873-1952	Labor Leader	30	72	85	100	Pres. A.F.of L.
Greenaway, Kate	1846-1901	Artist	543	650			Creator Children's Books. Sketch S 450-1,200+
Greenbaum, Brig. Gen. Edward S.	1890-1970	Military	30				World War II U.S. general
Greenbaum, Everett	1919-	Entertainment	15			25	TV & Film Writer. 'Andy Griffith', 'M A S H' etc.
Greene, Carl Franklin	1887-	Aviation	65	150			USAAC Col. Collier Award. 1st Pressure-Cabin Plane
Greene, Frank L.		Senate/Congress	10		20	15	MOC, Senator VT
Greene, George S.	1801-1899	Civil War	40	85			Union Gen.
Greene, Graham	1904-1991	Author	75	160	320	300	Br. Novelist, Dramatist, Critic
Greene, Lorne	1915-1987	Entertainment	32	100		106	Actor 'Bonanza'
Greene, Maj. Gen. Douglass T.	1891-1964	Military	30				World War II U.S. general
Greene, Michele		Entertainment	5	8	25	22	
Greene, Nathaniel	1742-1786	Military-Rev. War	750	2162	2730		Am.Rev. War Gen.ALS/Cont. 4800
Greene, Richard		Entertainment	10			40	Vint.Brit. Actor. Robinhood
Greene, Sarah Pratt Mc.	1856-1935	Author	20				
Greene, Shecky		Entertainment	5	6	15	25	Comedian
Greene, William		Author		142			
Greenfield, Terry D.		Author	8			12	cookbooks
Greenhouse, Kate		Entertainment	3			8	
Greenleaf, John		Clergy	30	50	85		
Greenslade, Brigadier Cyrus	1892-1985	Military	25				World War II British general

NAME	DATE	CATEGORY	SIG	LS/DS	ALS	SP	COMMENTS
Greenspan, Alan		Economist	15	30		35	Chairman Fed. Reserve Bd.
Greenstreet, Sidney	1879-1954	Entertainment	227		450	533	Casablanca, Maltese Falcon
Greenwood, Charlotte	1893-1978	Entertainment	25			82	Long-legged Comedienne-Dancer
Greenwood, Edward D.		Science	10	15	35		
Greenwood, Grace	1823-1904	Author	30	45	75	75	
Greenwood, James C. G		Congress	10			15	Member U.S. Congress
Greenwood, Lee		Country Music	5			10	
Greenwood, Pippa		Celebrity	10			15	home/gardening expert
Greer, Brig. Gen. Frank U.	1895-1949	Military	30				World War II U.S. general
Greer, Dabbs (Bill)		Entertainment	10			20	
Greer, Elkanah Brackin	1825-1877	Civil War	140				Confederate general
Greer, Jane		Entertainment	5	6	15	15	
Greer, Pam	1950-	Entertainment	10			30	Actress.'Jackie Brown'
Greeves, Maj. Gen. Sir Stuart	1897-1987	Military	25				World War II British general
Greg & Max		Celebrity	10			15	TV Chefs
Greg K		Entertainment	6			25	Music. Bass Guitar 'Offspring'
Gregg, Andrew	1755-1835	Congress	30	60			Sen., MOC PA ALS/Content 475
Gregg, David M. (WD)	1833-1916	Civil War	105	188	428		Union Gen.
Gregg, David M.	1833-1916	Civil War	40	75	182	175	Union Gen. Distinguished at Gettysburg
Gregg, John R.		Business	65	85	150	90	Inventor Gregg Shorthand System
Gregg, John	1828-1864	Civil War	350				Confederate general
Gregg, Judd		Senate	10			15	United States Senate (R - NH)
Gregg, Maxey (WD)		Civil War	565	4000			CSA Gen. KIA
Gregg, Maxey	1814-1862	Civil War	410	600			CSA Gen. KIA Fredericksburg, VA
Gregg, Virginia		Entertainment	10	12	20	25	
Gregg-Thomas, Delores J.		Author	8			12	African-American poetry
Gregory, Bettina		Celebrity	10			15	media/TV personality
Gregory, Bill		Astronaut	7			18	
Gregory, Dick	1932-	Entertainment	10	20	45	30	Comedian-Writer-Social Activist
Gregory, F. H. (WD)		Civil War	60	95	115		Union Naval Captain
Gregory, F.H.		Civil War	64	100	102		Union Naval Capt.
Gregory, Frederick D.		Astronaut	6	15		22	
Gregory, James		Entertainment	5	6	15	15	
Gregory, Lt. Gen. Edmund B.	1882-1961	Military	30				World War II U.S. general
Gregory, Thomas W.	1861-1933	Cabinet	20			45	US Att'y Gen. Woodrow Wilson
Gregson-Ellis, Maj. Gen. Philip	1898-1956	Military	25				World War II British general
Greico, Richard		Entertainment	10			45	
Grell, Mike*		Cartoonist	10			75	Tarzan
Grenfell, Wilfred T.	1865-1940	Physician-Clergy	35	55	75	125	Medical Missionary, Author
Grenville, George	1712-1770	Head of State	250	750			Br. P.M., Author of Stamp Act Vs Am. Colonies
Grenville, Peter	1913-	Entertainment	10		30	20	British Director. Stage & sometime Films.
Grenville, Wm. W., 1st Baron.	1759-1834	Head of State	100	285	650		Br. Prime Min. Pro Rom.Cath. Emancipation
Gresham, Walter Quintin	1832-1895	Civil War	45	75	100		Union general
Gretchaninoff, Alexander T.		Composer	65	180	395		AMsS 350
Grévy, Jules	1807-1891	Head of State	40				Pres. France 1879-87

NAME	DATE	CATEGORY	SIG	LS/DS	ALS	SP	COMMENTS
Grew, Joseph C.		Diplomat	10	25		35	Ambassador Japan 1931-41
Grey, Chas. 2nd Earl of	1764-1845	Head of State	85	98	160		Prime Minister
Grey, George Sir	1799-1882	Diplomat	5	25	55		Br. Statesman
Grey, Jennifer		Entertainment	8			38	Actress
Grey, Joel		Entertainment	6	8	15	35	
Grey, Nan		Entertainment	4	8	12	15	
Grey, Virginia	1917-	Entertainment	10	15	18	30	Actress 30's to early 40's
Grey, Zane	1875-1939	Author	78	128	415	400	Dentist Turned Western Writer
Gridley, Chas. Vernon	1844-1898	Military	250	410	895		Cmdr. of Adm. Dewey Flagship
Gridley, Richard	1711-1796	Revolutionary War	170	450	790		Gen. Continental Army, Artillery
Grieg, Edvard	1843-1907	Composer	236	600	1304	1449	19th Cent. Norge. AMusQS 1,800-2,800-3,250
Grier, David Alan		Entertainment	10			20	actor
Grier, Pam		Entertainment	5	6	15	25	Actress
Grier, Robert C.	1794-1870	Supreme Court	80	235	420		
Grierson, Benjamin H. (WD)		Civil War	165	235	545		Union General
Grierson, Benjamin H.	1826-1911	Civil War	80		235		Union Gen.
Griesbach, Franz	1826-1911	Military	25			50	Ger. Infantry General
Griesbach, Maj. Gen. William A.	1878-1945	Military	20				World War II Canadian general
Griessman, Eugene		Celebrity	10			15	motivational speaker
Griffes, Charles T.	1884-1920	Composer	175	515			Outstanding Am. Composer. ALS/Content 3,000
Griffeth, Bill		Celebrity	10			15	media/TV personality
Griffin, Angela		Entertainment	10			20	Actress
Griffin, Charles	1826-1867	Civil War	60	150			Union Gen., Indian Fighter
Griffin, Chris		Entertainment	10			25	Jazz Trumpet
Griffin, Cyrus	1749-1810	Revolutionary War	360	765			Continental Congress
Griffin, Maj. Gen. John Arnold A.	1891-1972	Military	25				World War II British general
Griffin, Merv		Entertainment	10			25	
Griffin, S. Marvin		Governor	10		30		Governor GA
Griffin, Simon Goodell	1824-1902	Civil War	40	80	120		Union general
Griffin, W.E.B.		Author	5			10	Fiction
Griffith, Andy		Entertainment	15	25	30	50	Actor
Griffith, Corinne		Entertainment	35	45	90	100	
Griffith, D(avid) W(ark)	1874-1948	Entertainment	350	612	875	1018	Pioneer Film Producer-Dir.
Griffith, Hugh	1912-1980	Entertainment	190	275		450	SP PC 200
Griffith, Joe		Celebrity	10			15	motivational speaker
Griffith, Leslie		Celebrity	10			15	media/TV personality
Griffith, Melanie		Entertainment	28	30	55	48	Actress
Griffith, Richard	1814-1862	Civil War	325				Confederate general
Griffiths, Rachel		Entertainment				40	Brenda Chenowith, Six Feet Under, Emmy winner
Griggs, John W.		Cabinet	12	45	110		Politician-Jurist, Gov. NJ
Griggs, S. David	1939-1989	Astronaut	60	150		140	
Grigson, Sophie		Celebrity	10			15	TV Chef
Grijalva, Raúl M. G		Congress	10			15	Member U.S. Congress
Grillo, Joann		Entertainment	4			10	
Grimaldi, Joesph	1779-1837	Actor			775		

NAME	DATE	CATEGORY	SIG	LS/DS	ALS	SP	COMMENTS
Grimblat, Pierre		Celebrity	10			15	film industry
Grimes, Bryan	1828-1880	Civil War	245	417	2013		Confederate general
Grimes, Maj. Gen. William M.	1889-1951	Military	30				World War II U.S. general
Grimes, Tammy		Entertainment	4	5	9	15	
Grimm, Jacob		Author	565	1840	3760		Grimm's Fairy Tales
Grimm, Wilhelm		Author	500	1425	3150		Grimm's Fairy Tales
Griner, Maj. Gen. George W. Jr.	1895-1975	Military	30				World War II U.S. general
Grinnell, Henry	1799-1874	Financier	45	160			Financed Arctic Expeditions
Grinnell, Josiah	1821-1891	Congress	25				Repr. IA, Founder Grinnell, IA & University
Grinnell, Moses H.		Business	25	60	120		MOC NY. Merchant Prince NY
Gris, Juan	1887-1927	Artist	175		1500		Sp Cubist Painter
Grisham, John		Author	20	70		45	The Firm, The Pelican Brief
Grisi, Giulia	1811-1869	Entertainment	100		215	190	It. Soprano. Great Diva of her time.
Grismer, Joseph R. 1849-1922	1849-1922	Entertainment	4	15			Actor-Manager
Grissom, Virgil I.'Gus'	1926-1967	Astronaut	322	787		983	Merc. 7. FDC S 750 (Deceased)
Griswald, O.W.		Military	15	35			
Griswold, John A.		Senate/Congress	10		25		MOC NY 1869
Griswold, Lawrence		Author	8			12	Real life 'Indiana Jones'!
Griswold, Lt. Gen. Oscar W.	1886-1954	Military	30				World War II U.S. general
Griswold, Matthew		Senate/Congress	12	115	160		MOC PA 1891
Griswold, Putnam		Entertainment	20			50	Opera
Grizzard, George		Entertainment	5	6	15	15	
Grizzard, Lewis		Author	20				Southern humorist
Groban, Josh		Music	15			40	
Grodin, Charles	1935-	Entertainment	8	8	15	28	Actor
Groener, Harry		Entertainment	4			20	Dear John
Groening, Matt*		Cartoonist	45			262	'The Simpsons'., signed orig art 250-500
Grofé, Ferde		Composer	100	200	245	130	AMusMsS 1,850, AMusQS 360
Grohl, Dave		Entertainment	15			48	Music. Drums, Vocals 'Nirvana' & 'Foo Fighters'
Gromyko, Andrei A.		Statesman	125	160	295	150	Rus.Diplomat. Ambass. to US
Gronau, Wolfgang von		Aviation	75	135	235	195	
Gröner, Lissy		Political	10			15	Member European Parliament
Grönfeldt Bergman, Lisbeth		Political	10			15	Member European Parliament
Groninger, Maj. Gen. Homer M.	1884-1963	Military	30				World War II U.S. general
Groom, Victor		Aviation	20	45	75	55	
Groom, Winston		Author	20				Forrest Gump
Gropius, Walter	1883-1969	Architect	125	200	600	425	Co-Founder of the Bauhaus Movement
Gropper, William*	1897-1977	Artist	30	85	200	350	Am. Social Protest Artist. Radical Cartoonist
Grosch, Mathieu J.H.		Political	10			15	Member European Parliament
Grose, William	1812-1900	Civil War	45	90	130		Union general
Gross, Calvin		Celebrity	8	20		15	
Gross, Chaim		Artist	35	75	165		4x6 Repro. Peace S 75
Gross, Clayton K.		Aviation	8	16	28	22	ACE, WW II
Gross, Courtlandt		Business	5	10	15	10	
Gross, Maj. Gen. Charles P.	1889-1975	Military	30				World War II U.S. general

NAME	DATE	CATEGORY	SIG	LS/DS	ALS	SP	COMMENTS
Gross, Mary		Entertainment	10			20	actress
Gross, Milt*		Cartoonist	20			100	Nize Baby
Gross, Samuel D.	1805-1884	Medical			1100		Leading Am. Surgeon Of His Time (Rare)
Grosser, Heinz		Science	15			45	Rocket Pioneer/von Braun
Grosset-te, Frantoise		Political	10			15	Member European Parliament
Grossinger, Jennie		Business	23	60	135	35	Grossinger's Hotel,Catskill Mts
Grossman, Loyd		Celebrity	10			15	Cuisine Expert
Grossmith, George	1874-1935	Entertainment	10			25	Br Musical Comedy,Films, Revues
Grosvenor, Charles H.		Civil War	40	75	110		Union Gen., MOC OH
Grosvenor, Gilbert H.	1875-1966	Business	60	100	195	95	Pres.National Geographic.Editor
Grosz, George	1893-1959	Artist	65	190	275		Expressionist Who Expressed Hatred of Bourgeoisie
Grotius, Hugo	1583-1645	Science		130			
Grouchy, Marquis E. de		Napoleonic Wars	100	250			Marshal of Napoleon. Exiled
Grover, Cuvier		Civil War	35	67	90		Union General
Grover, Maj. Gen. John Malcolm L	1897-1979	Military	25				World War II British general
Grover, Maj. Gen. Malcom	1897-1970	Military	25				World War II British general
Groves, Leslie R.		Military	65	145	220	150	Gen.WW II. Manhattan Project
Grove-White, Lt. Gen. Sir Maur. F.	1887-1965	Military	25				World War II British general
Grow, Galusha A.	1822-1907	Congress	25	55	75	125	Repr. PA, Speaker of the House
Grow, Maj. Gen. Robert W.	1895-1985	Military	30				World War II U.S. general
Grower,Brig. Gen. Roy W.	1890-1957	Military	30				World War II U.S. general
Grubbs, Gary		Entertainment	10			25	Will and Grace
Gruber, Brig. Gen. Wiliam R.	1890-1979	Military	30				World War II U.S. general
Gruberova, Edita		Entertainment	15			40	Opera. SP 4x6 25
Gruelle, Johnny		Cartoonist	35			250	Raggedy Ann & Andy
Gruen, George John		Business	30	80	150	55	Chm. Gruen Watch Co.
Gruenther, Alfred M.		Military	45		55	60	Gen. WW II, Pres. Am. Red Cr. Cmdr. NATO
Grumman, Leroy R.		Business	50	145		70	Grumman Aircraft
Grunert, Lt. Gen. George	1881-1971	Military	30				World War II U.S. general
Grunsfeld, John		Astronaut	5			20	
GTricault, Theodore	1791-1824	Artist			3000		Broke Classical Tradition.
GTrodias, Lt. Gen. Paul-Henry	1882-1956	Military	20				World War II French general
Guardia, R.A.C.		Head of State	15	50		25	Costa Rica
Guardino, Harry		Entertainment	6	15		20	Actor
Gubbins, Maj. Gen. Sir Colin McV.	1896-1976	Military	25				World War II British general
Guden, HIlde		Entertainment	25		75	50	Opera
Guderian, Heinz	1888-1954	Military	100	220	350	550	Ger. Panzer Gen. WW II
Gudger, V. Lamar		Senate/Congress	10	30		15	MOC NC
Gudin de la Sablonniere		Fr. Revolution	120	235			
Gudin, Theodore	1802-1880	Arist			130		
Gudunov, Alexander		Entertainment	15		40	35	Rus. Ballet
Guelfi, Piero		Entertainment	10			25	Opera
Guerard, Benjamin		Political		85			Govenor of SC
Guerin, Jules	b. 1866	Artist	10		35		Muralls at Lincoln Mem'l, Penn.RR Station
Guerre, Brig. Gen. Louis F.	1884-1966	Military	30				World War II U.S. general

NAME	DATE	CATEGORY	SIG	LS/DS	ALS	SP	COMMENTS
Guest, Christopher		Entertainment	10			25	actor
Guest, Edgar A.	1881-1959	Author	25	35	70	50	Am.Journalist-Poet of the People. Syndicated
Guest, Joanne		Celebrity	10			15	celebrity model
Guest, Lance		Entertainment	6	8	15	19	
Guest, Val		Celebrity	10			15	film industry
Guest, Winston Mrs.		Business	5	10	15	10	
Guevaro, Ernesto Che		Revolutionary	300	2179	9500		Aide to Fidel Castro in Cuba
Guffey, Joseph F.		Senate/Congress	5	10		10	Senator PA
Guggenheim, Daniel	1856-1930	Business	20	50	85	60	Guggenheim Foundation
Guggenheim, Harry F.		Aviation		75			Pres. Guggenheim Fund (Aeronautics)
Guggenheim, Peggy		Business	25	25	70	45	Patron of Arts. Collector
Guggenheim, William		Business	55	125		75	Industrialist, Philanthropist
Guidry, Thomas		Entertainment	3			8	
Guilbert, Yvette		Entertainment	40	65	130	150	
Guild, Curtis Jr.		Governor	12	15			Governor MA
Guild, Nancy		Entertainment	6	8	15	15	
Guildford, Henry, Sir	1489-1532	Royal Household	110	430			Henry VIII. Master of Horse & Comptroller of House
Guilfoyle, Paul		Entertainment	10	15	35	30	
Guillaumat, Gen. Marie-Louis-A.	1873-1940	Military	20				World War II French general
Guillaume, Gen. Augustin-Léon	1895-1983	Military	20				World War II French general
Guillaume, Robert		Entertainment	5	10	18	28	
Guillemin, Roger C.L.		Science	20	35	50	60	Nobel Medicine
Guillemont, Maj. Gen. Jean	1878-1939	Military	20				World War II French general
Guillotin, Joseph-Ignace		Science	275	1575			Fr. Doctor Supported Guillotin
Guinan, Texas (Mary Louise)		Entertainment	25	70	90	40	Actress, Hostess of Speakeasies
Guiney, Louise Imogen		Author	50		300		Poet-Essayist
Guingand, Francis		Military	15	35	50		Fr. General
Guinier, Lani		Law	10	20		15	Afr-Am Law Professer-Writer
Guinness, Alec, Sir		Entertainment	21	25	30	71	Br. Screen Actor. AA. 'Star Wars' SP85-100
Guinness, Benjamin L.	1798-1868	Business	30	50	110		Guinness Brewing Co.
Guinness, Edward C.	1847-1927	Business	15	25	45	20	Guinness Brewing Co.
Guion, David W.	1892-1981	Composer	100				'Home On The Range'. ANS 295
Guisewite, Cathy*		Cartoonists	25			85	Cathy
Guiteau, Charles	1842-1882	Assassin	350	675	3625	1750	Shot Pres. Garfield
Guitry, Maj. Gen. Jean-Marcel-R.	1874-1941	Military	20				World War II French general
Guizot, Francois	1787-1874	Politician			55		French statesman
Gulager, Clu		Entertainment	6		15	20	
Gullette, J. Carl		Author	8			12	Fort Sumter
Gullion, Maj. Gen. Allen W.	1880-1946	Military	30				World War II U.S. general
Gumbel, Bryant		Entertainment	5			20	
Gumbel, Greg		Celebrity	10			20	media/TV personality
Gummow, Bradley L.		Author	8			12	author financial
Gunner, Brig. Gen. Matthew J.	1886-1985	Military	30				World War II U.S. general
Guns 'N Roses (all)		Entertainment	80			135	
Gunsche, Otto		Military	50		85	55	

NAME	DATE	CATEGORY	SIG	LS/DS	ALS	SP	COMMENTS
Gunther, John	1901-1970	Author	20		75		Best Seller 'Inside Europe' etc.
Gur, Mordechai	1900-1979	Military	20	75			Israeli Gen. 6 Day War. Spec.AirMail Cov. 69.
Gurdon, Maj. Gen. Edw. Temple L	1896-1959	Military	25				World War II British general
Gurie, Sigrid		Entertainment	20	25	60	45	
Gurnett, Jane		Entertainment	10			20	Actress
Gurney, Brig. Gen. Augustus M.	1895-1967	Military	30				World War II U.S. general
Gurney, Maj. Gen. Russell	1890-1947	Military	25				World War II British general
Gurrag-gchaa,Jugderdemidij		Astronaut	15	50		35	Mongolian Astro.
Gusmeroli, Giovanni		Entertainment	5			15	Opera
Gustavus II Adolph (Swe)	1594-1632	Royalty-Military	350	1378	2355		Saved Protestantism in Germ. Great General
Gustavus III (Swe)	1746-1792	Royalty	175	403	985		King of Sweden from 1771
Gustavus IV Adolph (Swe)	1778-1837	Royalty	150				
Gustavus V (Swe)	1858-1950	Royalty	75	150		275	
Guston, Philip	1913-1980	Artist			175		Canadian-born Am. Painter
Guthner, Brig. Gen. William E.	1884-1951	Military	30				World War II U.S. general
Guthrie, Arlo		Country Music	15	35	45	72	Folk Singer in Tradition of His Father Woody
Guthrie, James	1792-1869	Cabinet-Senate	22	45	80		Pierce Sec'y Treas. Sen. KY
Guthrie, Thomas		Clergy	15	20	25		
Guthrie, Woody		Entertainer	300				Folksinger, Poet, Songwriter
Gutierrez, Luis V. G		Congress	10			15	Member U.S. Congress
Gutierrez, Sid		Astronaut	6			22	
Gutiérrez-cortines, Cristina		Political	10			15	Member European Parliament
Gutknecht, Gil G		Congress	10			15	Member U.S. Congress
Guttenberg, Steve		Entertainment	5		30	32	Actor
Guy, Jasmine		Entertainment	10			20	actress
Guy, Thomas		Celebrity	15	40	105		
Guynemer, Georges	1894-1917	Aviation	225	400	650	911	ACE, WW I. A French Legend
Guyot, Arnold	1807-1884	Science	25	45	195		Geographer, Mapmaker, Educator
Guyot, Pierre		Fr. Revolution	25	55	125		
Guy-quint, Catherine		Political	10			15	Member European Parliament
Guyton-Morveau, L.B.Baron	1737-?	Science	20	50	95		Fr. Chemist
Gwatkin, Maj. Gen. Sir Frederick	1885-1969	Military	25				World War II British general
Gwenn, Edmund	1875-1959	Entertainment	75	105	145	175	SP 'Miracle 34th St.' 1,650.,Sp. SP 2500
Gwin, William M.	1805-1885	Senate/Congress	20	45	60		MOC MS, Senator CA
Gwinnett, Button	1735-1777	Rev. War	150000	320000			Rare Signer Decl. Independence
Gwynne, Anne		Entertainment	6	8	15	15	
Gwynne, Fred		Entertainment	20			85	Actor, As 'Herman Munster' 150-175
Gye, Albani		Entertainment	10			25	
Gyllenhaal, Jake		Entertainment				45	Actor

NAME	DATE	CATEGORY	SIG	LS/DS	ALS	SP	COMMENTS
Haab, Robert		Head of State	25	70			Switzerland

NAME	DATE	CATEGORY	SIG	LS/DS	ALS	SP	COMMENTS
Haack, Maj. Gen. Werber	1894-1944	Military	25				World War II German general
Haag, Carl	1820-1915	Artist		30	80		Ger.-Born Br. Court Painter to Victoria
Haakon VII (Nor)	1872-1957	Royalty	120	205			1st King Independent of Sweden
Haakon VII and Maud		Royalty	200			450	King & Queen of Norway
Haarde, Lt. Gen. Johannes	1889-1945	Military	27				World War II German general
Haas, Lukas		Entertainment	10			20	actor
Haas, Maj. Gen. Franz	1898-1961	Military	25				World War II German general
Haase, Colonel-General Curt	1881-1943	Military	25				World War II German general
Haase, Lt. Gen. Konrad	1888-1963	Military	25				World War II German general
Haass, Richard		Celebrity	10			15	political celebrity
Habberton, John		Author	10	15	25		
Habenicht, Lt. Gen. Rudolf	1889-1980	Military	25				World War II German general
Habersham, John	1754-1799	Revolutionary War	40	115			Cont. Congr. Maj. 1st GA Cont. Reg. A Fndr. UofG
Habersham, Joseph	1751-1815	Revolutionary War	95	260	540		Continental Army,Cont.Congress
Habicht, Maj. Gen. Franz	1891-1972	Military	25				World War II German general
Haccius, Lt. Gen. Ernst	1893-1943	Military	25				World War II German general
Hachtel, Maj. Gen. Georg	1894-1943	Military	25				World War II German general
Hack, Shelley		Entertainment	4	7	12	15	Pin-Up SP 20
Hackett, Bobby		Entertainment	20			45	Cornet/Benny Goodman
Hackett, Buddy		Entertainment	5	10	20	32	Comedian
Hackett, Gen. Sir John Winthrop	1910-1997	Military	25				World War II British general
Hackett, James K.		Entertainment	12	15		30	Vintage Actor
Hackett, Joan		Entertainment	10	15	25	35	Talented Actress. Untimely Death
Hackleman, Pleasant Adam	1814-1862	Civil War	140	195			Union general
Hackman, Gene		Entertainment	20		35	48	SP/Denzel Washington 130
Hackstroh, Maj. Gen. Willem F.A.	1881-1951	Military	20				World War II Dutch general
Hadary, Jonathan		Entertainment	10			20	actor
Hadeln, Lt. Gen. Heinrich Baron v	1871-1940	Military	25				World War II German general
Haden, Pat		Celebrity	10			15	motivational speaker
Hadfield, Chris		Astronaut	7			25	
Hadley, Jerry		Entertainment	10			24	Concert, Opera
Hadley, Reed		Entertainment	15			30	
Hadley, Tony		Music	10			15	performing musical artist
Haeckel, Lt. Gen. Ernst	1890-1967	Military	25				World War II German general
Haehling, Maj. Gen. Kurt	1897-1983	Military	25				World War II German general
Haehnle, Lt. Gen. Hermann	1896-1966	Military	25				World War II German general
Haenicke, Gen. of Inf. Siegfried	1878-1946	Military	25				World War II German general
Haenschen, Gus		Entertainment	15		25	30	Big Band
Hagar, Sammy		Entertainment	10			25	Rock Singer-Guitarist
Hagegard, Hakan		Entertainment				30	Opera
Hagel, Chuck		Senate	10			15	United States Senate (R - NE)
Hagemann, Lt. Gen. Wolf	1898-1983	Military	25				World War II German general
Hagen, Jean		Entertainment	5			10	
Hagen, Johannes	1847-1930	Science	15	40	100		Austr. Astron.Hagen's Clouds
Hagen, Lt. Gen. Heinrich von dem	1873-1945	Military	25				World War II German general

NAME	DATE	CATEGORY	SIG	LS/DS	ALS	SP	COMMENTS
Hagen, Maj. Gen. Oskar von dem	1883-1940	Military	25				World War II German general
Hagen, Uta		Entertainment	7	12	20	20	
Hager, Gerhard		Political	10			15	Member European Parliament
Haggard, Henry Rider	1856-1925	Author	82	130	275	270	'King Solomon's Mines'
Haggard, Merle		Country Music	10			43	Singer
Haggerty, Dan		Entertainment	5	6	15	15	
Haggin, James Ben Ali		Business	75	275			Am Financier, Anaconda Copper. Hearst Partner
Hagl, Maj. Gen. August	1888-1972	Military	25				World War II German general
Hagman, Larry	1931-	Entertainment	8	10	15	31	Actor. 'I Dream of Jeannie', 'Dallas'
Hagood, Johnson	1829-1898	Civil War	159	326	408		CSA Gen, War Date S 200
Hague, Frank		Politician	10	25	40	15	Headed Major Dem. Machine
Hahm, Gen. of Infantry Walther	1894-1951	Military	25				World War II German general
Hahn, Jessica		Playboy Cover	4			15	Pin-Up SP 20
Hahn, Maj. Gen. Johannes	1889-1970	Military	25				World War II German general
Hahn, Otto	1879-1968	Science	98	160	275	350	Ger.Nobel Chem. Nuclear Fission. ALS/Cont 2000
Hahn, Reynaldo	1874-1947	Composer	70	160			Venezuelan. Critic, Dir. Paris Opera.AMusQS 285
Hahne, Maj. Gen. Hans	1894-1944	Military	25				World War II German general
Haider, Michael		Business	15			40	Pres. Standard Oil NJ
Haig, Alexander M.		Military	20	40	50	37	Gen. WW II, Sec'y State
Haig, Dorothy, Lady		Celebrity	4		25		Wife of Sir Douglas Haig
Haig, Douglas, 1st Earl	1861-1928	Military	35	112	130	65	Br.Gen., Boer War, India, WW I
Haig, General Sir Arthur Brodie	1886-1957	Military	25				World War II British general
Haight, Edward	1817-1885	Congress	10				Repr. NY, Founder NY Bank
Haight, Henry H.		Governor	15				San Francisco's Haight-Asbury Distr.
Haile, William	1797-1837	Congress	15				Repr. MS
Hailes, Brigadier William A.	1891-1949	Military	20				World War II Australian general
Hailey, Arthur		Author	25	40	65	40	Am. Novelist.Hotel,Airport
Haim, Corey		Entertainment	7			40	Actor
Haines, Brig. Gen. Oliver L.	1891-1981	Military	30				World War II U.S. general
Haines, Brig. Gen. Ralph E.	1883-1976	Military	30				World War II U.S. general
Haines, Connie		Entertainment	20			50	Big Band Vocalist
Haines, Daniel	1801-1877	Governor	30	45	90		Governor NJ
Haines, William	1900-1973	Entertainment	15	15	35	40	
Haining, Gen. Sir Robert Hadden	1882-1959	Military	25				World War II British general
Hairston, Jester		Entertainment	10			30	
Haise, Fred W. Jr.	1933-	Astronaut	15			55	Apollo 13
Haislip, General Wade H.	1889-1971	Military	30				World War II U.S. general
Hakewill Smith, Maj Gen Sir Edm.	1896-1986	Military	25				World War II British general
Halaby, Najeeb		Celebrity	10	30		15	
Halban, H.H., Dr.		Science	30	65			Fr. Pioneer Of Uranium Fission
Haldane, John B.S.	1892-1964	Science		125	195		Br. Geneticist & Author
Haldeman, George W.		Aviation	30	55	105	75	
Haldeman, H. R.		Political	10	20	62	20	Nixon-Watergate
Halder, Franz		Military	55	95	160	115	Ger.Gen.Opposed Hitler.Prison!
Hale, Alan Jr.	1918-1990	Entertainment	52	60	75	283	Actor. 'Gilligan's Island'

NAME	DATE	CATEGORY	SIG	LS/DS	ALS	SP	COMMENTS
Hale, Alan Sr.		Entertainment	52	55	95	100	
Hale, Barbara	1921-	Entertainment	10	15	22	25	Actress. Della Street On 'Perry Mason'
Hale, Edward Everett	1822-1909	Clergy	33	102	184	240	Author 'Man Without a Country'
Hale, Eugene	1836-1918	Senate	10	15	30		MOC 1869-75, Senator ME
Hale, George E.		Science	20	100			Invented Spectroheliograph
Hale, John Parker	1806-1873	Congress	15	45	100		Abolitionist., Senator NH
Hale, Lucretia Peabody	1820-1900	Author	25				
Hale, Monte	1921-	Entertainment	10	10	25	32	Big Time Cowboy Star
Hale, Nathan		Revolutionary War		15000			RARE 'I have but one life to give for my country'
Hale, Richard		Entertainment	6	8	15	15	
Hale, Robert		Entertainment	10			30	Opera
Hale, Sarah Josepha B.	1788-1879	Author	65	170	295		Editor. 'Mary Had A Little Lamb'
Halevy, Fromental		Composer	30		125		La Juive
Halevy, Jacques	1799-1862	Composer	45	80	135		Opera. Taught Gounod, Bizet
Halevy, Ludovic		Author	25	70	120		Novels, Libretti For Operas
Haley, Alex	1921-1992	Author	45	98	160	125	'Roots', 'Malcom X'.ALS/Cont. 2900
Haley, Bill	1925-1981	Entertainment	225	500		550	AND The Comets.S Alb. Pg/5 Orig. Members 375
Haley, Jack	1899-1979	Entertainment	56	107	120	162	Song & Dance Comedian, SP as 'Tin Man' SP 275-350
Haley, William J., Sir	1901-1987	Business	15		35	40	Dir. Gen'l BBC & Editor of the 'Times'
Halifax, Edw. Frederick L.	1881-1958	Statesman	20	60			1st Earl of...Viceroy of India, U.S. Ambassador
Halke, Maj. Gen. Hans	1881-1965	Military	25				World War II German general
Hall and Oates		Entertainment	20			45	
Hall, Abraham Oakey	1826-1898	Politician	15	35	84	125	NY Mayor, Tweed Ring, Tammany Hall
Hall, Alvin W.		Celebrity	5	10		35	
Hall, Arsenio		Entertainment	10			30	TV Talk Show Host, actor
Hall, Bridget		Celebrity	10			15	model
Hall, Brig. Gen. Gene W.	1891-1951	Military	30				World War II U.S. general
Hall, Charles M.		Clergy	10	15	20		
Hall, Christopher		Entertainment	8			32	Music. Lead Singer 'Stabbing Westward'
Hall, David		Governor	10			15	Governor OK
Hall, Deidre		Entertainment	10			35	Soaps
Hall, Edward Marshall, Sir	1858-1927	Law			60		British Lawyer
Hall, Ella	1976-1981	Entertainment	20			55	Actress. Universal Silent Star 1910-1920's
Hall, Fawn		Entertainment	10	15	40	20	Pin-Up SP 30
Hall, Gus		Communist	30	60	75	50	US Communist Party Leader
Hall, Harry		Entertainment	4	5	6	10	
Hall, Huntz		Entertainment	22	28	45	66	Actor. Early 'Dead End' Gang Type Films
Hall, Irma P.		Entertainment	10			20	actress
Hall, Jerry		Entertainment	10			32	
Hall, Jon	1913-1979	Entertainment	32	45	85	45	Bare-chested Hero of Many 40's Films
Hall, Josephine		Entertainment	5	8	15	15	
Hall, Joyce C.		Business	80	173		155	Hallmark Greeting Cards
Hall, Juanita	1901-1968	Entertainment	65			90	'Bloody Mary' in 'South Pacific'
Hall, Lt. Gen. Charles P.	1886-1953	Military	30				World War II U.S. general
Hall, Lyman	1724-1790	Revolutionary War	1567	2650	4875		Signer Decl. of Indepen.

NAME	DATE	CATEGORY	SIG	LS/DS	ALS	SP	COMMENTS
Hall, Michael C.		Entertainment				40	David Fisher, Six Feet Under
Hall, Monty		Entertainment	8	9	10	20	Game Show Host-TV
Hall, Nathan		Cabinet	25	40	115		Fillmore P.M. General
Hall, Pauline		Entertainment	10			30	Vintage Actress
Hall, Radclyffe		Author		45	135		'Well of Loneliness'
Hall, Ralph M. H		Congress	10			15	Member U.S. Congress
Hall, Rich		Celebrity	10			15	comedian
Hall, Robert, Sir	1761-1831	Clergy	30	80	125	35	Br. Baptist Minister. Great Pulpit Orator
Hall, Tom T.		Country Music	5			12	Singer
Hall, William	1775-1856	Military	40		100		General, War of 1812
Hallam, Henry	1777-1859	Author	35	115	180		Br. Historian
Halle, Wilhelmine		Entertainment	6	8	15	15	
Halleck, Fitz-Greene	1790-1867	Poet	30	80	105		Member of Knickerbocker Group
Halleck, Henry Wager (WD)	1815-1872	Civil War	182	475	925	375	Union Gen.ALS/Cont. 4,500
Halleck, Henry Wager	1815-1872	Civil War	98	213	584	700	Union general
Hallett, Mal		Entertainment	20			35	Big Band Leader
Halliburton, Lloyd		Author	8			12	Civil War
Halliburton, Richard	1900-1939	Explorer-Author	30	60		75	World Traveller, Lecturer
Halliwell, Geri		Music	15			35	performing musical artist
Halloran, Brig. Gen. George M.	1889-1965	Military	30				World War II U.S. general
Halm, Gen. of Infantry Hans	1879-1957	Military	25				World War II German general
Halmi Sr., Robert		Celebrity	10			15	film industry
Halop, Billy	1920-1976	Entertainment	75	75	120	150	One of Orig. Dead End Kids
Halpern, Seymour		Congress	5			15	MOC NY
Halpine, Charles G.	1829-1868	Civil War	40	65	90		Irish-Born Writer and General
Halsell, James, Jr.		Astronaut	10			25	
Halsey, Jeremiah		Colonial Am.		75	175		New London, CT Shipbuilder, Owner. Just. Of Peace
Halsey, Maj. Gen. Milton B.	1894-1990	Military	30				World War II U.S. general
Halsey, Wm. F. 'Bull'	1882-1959	Military	117	257	372	373	Adm. WW II. Top Adm. After Nimitz. SP/Nimitz 995
Halstead, Murat		Editor	5	20	35		Journalist
Halsted, Maj. Gen. John Gregson	1890-1980	Military	25				World War II British general
Halston		Business	15	20	40	30	Designer
Halstrom, Holly		TV Model	5			10	'Price is Right' Model
Hamann, Lt. Gen. Adolf	1885-1945	Military	25				World War II German general
Hamblen, Brig. Gen. Archelaus L.	1894-1971	Military	30				World War II U.S. general
Hamblen, Stewart		Country Music	15			30	Singer-Songwriter
Hamblin, Joseph Eldridge	1828-1870	Civil War	48	86	130		Union general
Hamel, Veronica		Entertainment	5	18	20	22	Actress
Hamer, Frank		Military	110	465			
Hamer, Rusty		Entertainment	63		55	75	Child Actor on 'Danny Thomas Show'
Hamill, Mark		Entertainment	10	20	25	49	Actor 'Star Wars'. DS (Gen'l Hosp.) 95
Hamilton, Alex. Jr.	1786-1875	Military	20	40	135		Officer War 1812, Lawyer
Hamilton, Alexander	1757-1804	Cabinet	1044	3091	3567		1st Sec'y Treas. FF 1200-1600. ALS/Cont. 7500
Hamilton, Andrew Jackson	1815-1875	Civil War	45	80	130		Union general
Hamilton, Charles Smith	1822-1891	Civil War	35	80	147		Union Gen.ALS/Content 575

NAME	DATE	CATEGORY	SIG	LS/DS	ALS	SP	COMMENTS
Hamilton, Donald		Author	7	15	25	10	
Hamilton, Emma, Lady	1765-1815	Celebrity	225	528	1062		Mistress of Lord Nelson Wife of Sir Wm. Hamilton
Hamilton, Gail		Author					See Dodge, Mary A.
Hamilton, George Alexander, Sir		Diplomatist	75	540			Archaeologist, Husband Emma H.
Hamilton, George		Entertainment	5			22	
Hamilton, Ian, Sir	1853-1947	Military	15				Brit. General. Led Gallipoli Exp.
Hamilton, James Alex.	1788-1878	Military	45	140			Officer War 1812
Hamilton, James		Colonial Am.	65	160			Colonial Gov. PA
Hamilton, John		Entertainment	15				Character Actor
Hamilton, Lee		Congress	5	20		10	Congressman IN
Hamilton, Linda		Entertainment	15			42	Actress
Hamilton, Margaret	1902-1985	Entertainment	112	160	210	267	SP 'Wicked Witch of West' 300
Hamilton, Neil		Entertainment	25	40	65	100	'Commissioner Gordon' in Batman
Hamilton, Schuyler	1822-1903	Civil War	40	80	128		Union general
Hamlin, Cyrus	1839-1867	Civil War	50	85	130		Union general, Hannibal Hamlin's son
Hamlin, Hannibal	1809-1891	Vice President	89	163	218		Lincoln VP, US Sen., Gov.ME., MOC. FF150- 350
Hamlin, Harry		Entertainment	8	15	28	22	Actor
Hamlin, V.T.*		Cartoonist	50			325	Alley Oop
Hamlisch, Marvin		Composer	15		45	50	Conductor. AMusQS 35, 85
Hammarskjold, Dag	1905-1961	Head of State	120	565	725		Swedish Sec'y General United Nations. Nobel 1961
Hammer		Entertainment	25			45	Rap
Hammer, Armand		Business	55	180	305	185	Occidental Petroleum. Physician in Soviet Union
Hammer, Lt. Gen. Ernst	1884-1957	Military	25				World War II German general
Hammer, Maj. Gen. Hans	1895-1944	Military	25				World War II German general
Hammerstein II, Oscar	1895-1960	Composer	183	249		375	Lyricist-Librettist. 'Oklahoma', 'Show Boat' etc.
Hammerstein, II & Kern		Composer		1200			
Hammett, Dashiell	1894-1961	Author	450	1348	1650	1500	Hard-Boiled Detective Fiction. 'Maltese Falcon'
Hammond, James B.		Inventor	20	100			Typewriter
Hammond, James H.	1807-1864	Congress		45	115		US Sen., Gov.SC.Cotton is King
Hammond, Jay S.		Governor	10	15			Governor AK
Hammond, L. Blaine		Astronaut	5			20	
Hammond, Maj. Gen. Arthur V.	1892-1982	Military	28				World War II British general
Hammond, Phil Dr.		Celebrity	10			15	health and fitness expert
Hammond, William A.		Civil War	50	120	400		Union Gen. /Surgeon Gen.Author
Hamnett, Katharine		Celebrity	10			15	Designer
Hampden, Renn D.		Clergy	10	25	30		
Hampden, Walter		Entertainment	20		45	45	
Hampe, Maj. Gen. Erich	1889-1978	Military	27				World War II German general
Hampson, Thomas		Entertainment	10			32	Opera
Hampton, Hope		Entertainment	40			70	
Hampton, Lionel	1913-2002	Entertainment	28			75	Big Band Leader-Vibes. Jazz Legend
Hampton, Wade (WD)	1818-1902	Civil War	350	1250	1800		CSA Gen.
Hampton, Wade	1818-1902	Civil War	281	578	860		CSA General, Gov., US Sen. SC
Hamsun, Knut (Pedersen)	1859-1952	Author	40	85	135	187	Nor. Nobel Lit. Neo-Romantic Novels.AMsS 1850
Hanami, Kohei		Military	80	250			

NAME	DATE	CATEGORY	SIG	LS/DS	ALS	SP	COMMENTS
Hanaya, Lt. Gen. Tadashi	1894-1957	Military	25				World War II Japanese general
Hance, Lt. Gen. Sir Jas. Bennett	1887-1958	Military	25				World War II British general
Hancock, Clarence E.	1885-1948	Congress	5	25			Repr. NY
Hancock, Herbie		Composer	10	25	45	27	
Hancock, John	1737-1793	Revolutionary War	2262	4972	8503		First Signer. ALS/Cont. 12,500,15,000. FF2500-3000
Hancock, Nick		Celebrity	10			15	television presenter
Hancock, Winfield Scott (WD)	1824-1886	Civil War	320		1212	1228	Union General
Hancock, Winfield Scott	1824-1886	Civil War	174	396	546	738	Union Gen. ALS/Cont. 3300. Pres. Candidate
Hand, Edward	1744-1802	Revolutionary War	185	475	1000		Gen. Cont. Army. Repr. PA 1784
Hand, Learned	1872-1961	Jurist	88	375	483	850	'Tenth Justice'. Distinguished Among Am. Jurists
Handel, George Frederick		Composer	1000	5800	22000		
Handelman, Stanley M.		Entertainment	3	3	6	6	
Handler, Ruth	d. 2002	Business	40	75		40	Founder Mattel Toys
Handwerk, Brig. Gen. Morris C.	1891-1967	Military	30				World War II U.S. general
Handy, General Thomas T.	1892-1982	Military	30				World War II U.S. general
Handy, W. C.	1873-1958	Composer	275	414	575	464	AMusQS500- 2200, Sheet Music S 795
Haney, Brig. Gen. Harold	1894-1973	Military	30				World War II U.S. general
Hanks, Tom		Entertainment	22	30	45	84	Actor. 'Forrest Gump' SP 100, Oscar winner
Hanly, Thomas Burton	1812-1880	Civil War	39	100			Member of Confederate Congress
Hann, Judith		Celebrity	10			15	television presenter
Hanna & Barbera		Cartoonists	35	90		125	Animators. Signatures/Characters Surrounding 85
Hanna, Bill		Cartoonist	30			85	'Flintstones', signed drwg 125-350
Hanna, Jack		Celebrity	10			15	media/TV personality
Hanna, Marcus A.	1837-1904	Industrialist	25	55	75	100	Sen. OH. Political Power Broker
Hannah, Daryl		Entertainment	15	38	45	46	Actress
Hannah, John A.		Educator	7			10	Pres. Michigan State Univ.
Hannan, Daniel J.		Political	10			15	Member European Parliament
Hannay, James Owen	1865-1950	Author		100			Pseudonym George A. Birmingham
Hanneken, Gen. of Inf. Hermann v	1880-1981	Military	25				World War II German general
Hannigan, Alyson		Entertainment	10			41	Actress. 'Buffy' Co-Star
Hannum, Brig. Gen. Warren T.	1880-1956	Military	30				World War II U.S. general
Hanover, Donna		Celebrity				15	Actress, Former wife of NYC Mayor Rudy Giuliani
Hansbrough, Henry C.	1848-1933	Congress	10	15	30		MOC, Senator ND
Hansen, Gen. of Artillery Christian	1885-1972	Military	25				World War II German general
Hansen, General of Cavalry Erik	1889-1967	Military	25				World War II German general
Hansen, Lt. Gen. Karl	1876-1965	Military	25				World War II German general
Hansen, Maj. Gen. Ottomar	1904-1993	Military	25				World War II German general
Hansen, Mark Victor		Celebrity	10			15	motivational speaker
Hansen, William		Entertainment	6	8	15	15	
Hansenne, Michel		Political	10			15	Member European Parliament
Hanson, Beck		Entertainment	8			48	Music. Lead Singer 'Beck'
Hanson, Brigadier Frederick M.H.	1895-1979	Military	20				World War II New Zealand general
Hanson, Howard		Composer	15	35	80	120	Pulitzer. Dir. Eastman Sch. Music
Hanson, John		Rev. War	2250	7500			1st Pres. Continental Congress
Hanson, Roger Weightman	1827-1863	Civil War	375	518			Confederate general

NAME	DATE	CATEGORY	SIG	LS/DS	ALS	SP	COMMENTS
Hanstein, Maj. Gen. Hans von	1883-1975	Military	25				World War II German general
Haralson, Hugh A.	1805-1854	Congress	10				Repr. GA, Maj. Gen'l State Militia
Harbach, Otto	1873-1963	Entertainment	60	100		175	Playwright, Lyricist, Music Publ
Harbaugh, Gregory J.		Astronaut	5			20	
Harberts, Maj. Gen. Jakob	1883-1962	Military	20				World War II Dutch general
Harbison, John		Composer	20		75		Pulitzer, AMusQS 150
Harbord, James G.		Military	50	92	135	150	Chief of Staff AEF WW I, RCA
Harbour, Malcolm		Political	10			15	Member European Parliament
Harburg, E. Y. 'Yip'		Composer	100	175	375		Over the Rainbow
Harcourt, Edward Venables		Clergy	25	30	40		
Hardaway, Brig. Gen. Francis P.	1888-1981	Military	30				World War II U.S. general
Hardaway, Brig. Gen. Robert M. II	1887-1978	Military	30				World War II U.S. general
Hardee, William J.	1815-1873	Civil War	437	663	1097	1100	CSA General
Hardeman, William Polk 'Gotch'	1816-1898	Civil War	135				Confederate general
Hardenberg, K.A. von Furst		Statesman	15	60	125		Prussian Politician
Hardie, J. Keir	1856-1915	Politician	75			200	Scottish, Founder of the Labour Party
Hardie, James Allen (War Date)		Civil War	80	205	245		Union General
Hardie, James Allen	1823-1876	Civil War	58	177	222		Union Gen.
Hardie, Russell		Entertainment	10	15	25	25	
Hardigg, Maj. Gen. Carl A.	1890-1967	Military	30				World War II U.S. general
Hardin, Clifford M.		Cabinet	5	10	18	15	Sec'y Agriculture
Hardin, Gus		Entertainment	4			10	Female Singer
Hardin, John Wesley	1853-1895	Outlaw	2592	6500			Notorious Gunslinger. Bullet Shot Card S 11,750
Hardin, Martin Davis	1837-1923	Civil War	51	85	130		Union general
Hardin, Ty		Entertainment	6	8	15	19	
Harding, Aaron	1805-1867	Congress	35	50			MOC KY. Contacts & Recommendations to Lincoln
Harding, Abner Clark	1807-1874	Civil War	40	75	120		Union general
Harding, Ann		Entertainment	15	15	35	30	
Harding, Brigadier-Horace	1896-1991	Military	30				World War II U.S. general
Harding, Florence Kling		First Lady	80	123	210	250	White House Card S 125
Harding, Maj. Gen. Edwin F.	1886-1970	Military	30				World War II U.S. general
Harding, Mike		Celebrity	10			15	comedian
Harding, Tonya		Celebrity	20			20	Infamous Ice Skater
Harding, Warren G. (As Pres)		President	250	662	13145	620	ALS/Cont.15000. TLS/cont 2500. WH Cd S 400-500
Harding, Warren G.	1865-1923	President	150	402	922	520	Pre-Nomination Political TLS/Cont 3500
Hardinge, Chas., 1st Baron		Diplomat	10	25	35	25	Br. Viceroy India, Ambass. Russia
Hardinge, Henry, Sir	1785-1856	Military			585		Br. Field Marshal
Hardwicke, Cedric, Sir		Entertainment	35	65	90	95	
Hardy, Brig. Gen. David P.	1890-1957	Military	30				World War II U.S. general
Hardy, Brig. Gen. Rosswell E.	1893-1961	Military	30				World War II U.S. general
Hardy, Gen. Sir Campbell Richard	1906-1984	Military	25				World War II British general
Hardy, Jeremy		Celebrity	10			15	comedian
Hardy, Oliver	1892-1957	Entertainment	238	375	480	500	1/2 of Popular Comedy Team
Hardy, Robert		Entertainment	10			20	Actor
Hardy, Thomas Masterman, Sir	1769-1839	Military	75	160	215		Br. Adm. w/Nelson. MsLS re War 1812 $750

NAME	DATE	CATEGORY	SIG	LS/DS	ALS	SP	COMMENTS
Hardy, Thomas	1840-1928	Author	205	450	850	1000	Br. Novelist, Poet, Dramatist
Hare, John, Sir		Entertainment	20	30		50	
Hare, Maj. Gen. James Francis	1897-1950	Military	25				World War II British general
Hare, WIlllam Hobart		Clergy	35	50	65	50	
Harewood, Dorian		Entertainment	10			20	actor
Hargest, Brigadier James	1891-1944	Military	20				World War II New Zealand general
Hargis, Billy James		Evangelist	10				Right Wing leader of extremist Christian Crusade
Haring, Keith*	1958-1990	Artist	78	100	175	350	Pop Artist-Cartoonist. ,signed drwg 500
Harjo, Suzan Shown		Celebrity	10			15	motivational speaker
Harker, Charles Garrison	1835-1864	Civil War	125		338		Union general
Harkin, Tom		Senate	10			15	United States Senate (D - IA)
Harkness, Georgia		Clergy	35	50	95	65	
Harlan, James	1820-1899	Cabinet	22	51	125		Andrew Johnson Sec'y Interior 1865
Harlan, John Marshall	1833-1911	Supreme Court	75	112	190		
Harlan, John Marshall	1899-1971	Supreme Court	40	85	125	150	
Harland, Edward	1832-1915	Civil War	40	54			Union general
Harland, Marion		Author	7	15	20		
Harley, William S.		Business	1500	7500			Co-Fndr. Harley-Davidson Motorcycles
Harlfinger II, Frederick J.		Military	10			25	
Harlow, Jean (Mama)		Entertainment	25	30		45	
Harlow, Jean	1911-1937	Entertainment	1042	1400	3000	3771	30's Sex Symbol. Died at 28. Mother Signed Most SP
Harman, Fred*		Cartoonist	25			250	Red Ryder
Harman, Jane H		Congress	10			15	Member U.S. Congress
Harmon, Angie		Entertainment	15			48	Actress
Harmon, Judson		Cabinet	10	25	40	20	U.S. Att'y Gen., Gov. OH
Harmon, Maj. Gen. Ernst N.	1894-1974	Military	30				World War II U.S. general
Harmon, Mark		Entertainment	9	10	20	28	Actor
Harmonica Rascals		Entertainment	10			25	Borah Minovitch and the......
Harned, Virginia		Entertainment	15			35	Vintage Actress, Mrs. Sothern
Harney, William S. (WD)		Civil War	50		330		Union Gen.
Harney, William Selby	1800-1889	Civil War	40	84			Union general
Haro, Daniel		Celebrity	10			15	motivational speaker
Harold Wilson, Lord		Celebrity	10			15	political celebrity
Harpe, Colonel-General Josef	1887-1968	Military	25				World War II German general
Harper, Joseph W.		Celebrity	10	30	80		
Harper, Maj. Gen. Arthur M.	1893-1972	Military	30				World War II U.S. general
Harper, Robert G.		Revolutionary War	65		150		Gen. Rev. War, Statesman
Harper, Tess		Entertainment	9	10	20	25	
Harper, Valerie		Entertainment	5	6	15	20	Actress
Harper, William	1790-1847	Political	25		95		SC Nullification Leader & Slavery Advocate
Harrel, Scotty		Entertainment	8			15	C & W
Harrell, Costen J., Bishop		Clergy	20	25	40	35	
Harrelson, Woody		Entertainment	15			40	Cheers
Harrendorf, Maj. Gen. Hermann	1896-1966	Military	25				World War II German general
Harrer, Heinrich		Mountaineer-Auth.	250				'Seven Years In Tibet'. Tutor of Dalai Lama

NAME	DATE	CATEGORY	SIG	LS/DS	ALS	SP	COMMENTS
Harridge, Will	1883-1971	Business		125			Pres. Org. Known as American League
Harries, George		Military	20	35	80		General WW I
Harriman, Brig. Gen. Joseph E.	1900-1963	Military	30				World War II U.S. general
Harriman, Edw. Henry	1848-1909	Business	250	900			U.S. RR Magnate. S RR Bonds 575+
Harriman, Edward Roland		Business	20	55	120	35	CEO Union Pacific RR. Banker
Harriman, W. Averell	1891-1986	Governor	20	56	100	50	Gov. NY, Statesman, Diplomat, Ambassador etc.
Harrington, Pat		Entertainment	4	5	10	15	
Harriot, Ainsley		Celebrity	10			15	TV Chef
Harris		Cartoonist	5			18	The Better Half
Harris, Arthur T., Sir 'Bomber'	1892-1984	Military	99	125	165	150	Cmdr.-in-Chief RAF WW 99II. Head of Bomber Comm.
Harris, Barbara C.		Clergy	10			20	
Harris, Barbara		Entertainment	5			20	Actress. Stage-Films
Harris, Bernard A., Jr.		Astronaut	10			25	Afro-Am. Astronaut
Harris, Brig. Gen. Arthur R.	1890-1968	Military	30				World War II U.S. general
Harris, Brig. Gen. Charles S.	1894-1993	Military	30				World War II U.S. general
Harris, Brig. Gen. Frederick M.	1900-1969	Military	30				World War II U.S. general
Harris, Cecil		Aviation	20	25	50	40	ACE, WW II
Harris, Ed		Entertainment	8	6	15	46	Actor
Harris, Emmy Lou		Entertainment	10			35	Country Singer
Harris, Fred R.		Senate/Congress	4	10			Senator OK
Harris, George E.		Senate/Congress	10	15			CSA Officer. MOC NC
Harris, Isham	1818-1897	Civil War	50	68	82		Civil War Gov. TN. ALS '64 450. US Senator
Harris, Jared		Entertainment	10			20	actor
Harris, Jean		Criminal	35	70	375		Murdered Dr. Herman Tarnower. ALS/cont. 375
Harris, Jed		Entertainment	5	20			Producer. Theatre
Harris, Joel Chandler	1848-1908	Author	219	398	700		Popular Books on Black Folklore. 'Uncle Remus'
Harris, John A.		Senate/Congress	4		15		
Harris, John	1726-1791	Frontier Leader	125	265	775		Founder Harrisburg, PA
Harris, Jonathan		Entertainment	7			21	Actor. 'Lost in Space'
Harris, Julie	1925-	Entertainment	8	10	15	32	Actress. Broadway 'Tony' Winner. Films, TV
Harris, Katherine H		Congress	10			20	Member U.S. Congress
Harris, Louis		Pollster	20	35		25	
Harris, Maj. Gen. Charles T. Jr.	1884-1961	Military	30				World War II U.S. general
Harris, Mel		Entertainment	8			35	Actress. '30 Something'
Harris, Nathaniel Harrison	1834-1900	Civil War	120	198			Confederate general
Harris, Neil Patrick		Entertainment	10			35	Young Actor in 'Doogie Howser'
Harris, Patricia Roberts	1924-1985	Cabinet	15	15	40	75	1st Afr-Am Woman To Serve in Cabinet. Authen.RARE
Harris, Paul Percy		Business	25	45		30	Fndr. & Pres.- Emeritus. Rotary
Harris, Phil		Entertainment	22			45	Bandleader-Actor-Singer and Disney Voice-Over
Harris, Richard (d.2002)		Entertainment	15		35	61	Irish-Br. Actor, Harry Potter SP 100
Harris, Robert H.		Entertainment	6	8	10	10	
Harris, Robert		Author	10	50			'Enigma'
Harris, Rolf		Celebrity	10			15	naturalist
Harris, Russell		Celebrity	10			15	'The Diceman' television presenter
Harris, Sam H.		Entertainment	4	25			Producer-Manager

NAME	DATE	CATEGORY	SIG	LS/DS	ALS	SP	COMMENTS
Harris, Thomas Maley	1817-1906	Civil War	43	70			Union general
Harris, Thomas S.		Aviation	15	45		30	ACE WW II, Test Pilot
Harris, Thomas		Author	20	55			'Silence of the Lambs'
Harris, William A.	1841-1909	Congress-Civil War	30		45		Repr.& Sen. KS, CW Adj. Gen'l
Harris, William L., Bishop		Clergy	15	25	35		
Harrison, Albertis S. Jr.		Governor	10	20			Governor VA
Harrison, Anna Symmes	1775-1864	First Lady	650	1375	3050		Free Frank 975
Harrison, Benj. & Roosevelt, T.		Presidents					Civ.Serv.Commission S 2250
Harrison, Benj.& Caroline		Pres.-1st Lady	600				Together on One Piece
Harrison, Benjamin (As Pres)		President	329	856	1493		Exec. Mansion Card S. 450, ALS/cont 10,755
Harrison, Benjamin	1833-1901	President	196	366	657	1525	TLS/Cont. 1600-2500. DS-Pres. Warrant 1450
Harrison, Benjamin	1726-1791	Revolutionary War	525	956	1683		Signer Decl. of Indepen., Gov. Virginia
Harrison, Brig. Gen. Eugene L.	1898-1981	Military	30				World War II U.S. general
Harrison, Burton, Mrs.		Celebrity	10			35	1890's Socialite
Harrison, Byron Patton 'Pat'		Senate/Congress	5	15		10	MOC, Senator MS
Harrison, Caroline Scott	1832-1892	First Lady	184	250	647	750	1st Pres. DAR. Died in White House/Tuberculosis
Harrison, Carter H.		Mayor	10	35	40		Mayor Chicago 1897
Harrison, George P., Jr. (WD)		Civil War	150	225			CSA Gen..
Harrison, George P.,Jr.	1841-1922	Civil War	95	188	283		CSA Gen.
Harrison, George		Entertainment	356	785	1478	743	Beatle.Check S 785. DS (Settlement 237,500)
Harrison, Gregory		Entertainment	9	15	20	20	Busy Actor
Harrison, Helen		Aviation	40	125			Am Aviatrix
Harrison, Henry B.		Governor	12		20		Governor CT 1885
Harrison, James Edward	1815-1875	Civil War	125	212			Confederate general
Harrison, Jenilee		Entertainment	4	4	10	15	Actress 'Three's Company'
Harrison, Linda		Entertainment	10			27	Actress. 'Planet of the Apes'
Harrison, Maj. Gen. Jas Murray R.	1880-1957	Military	25				World War II British general
Harrison, Maj. Gen. William H.	1892-1956	Military	30				World War II U.S. general
Harrison, Maj. Gen. William K. Jr.	1895-1987	Military	30				World War II U.S. general
Harrison, Mary Lord	1858-1948	First Lady	70	107	150	175	Niece of 1st Lady Caroline Scott & Second Wife
Harrison, Noel		Entertainment	8			18	Br. Actor-Son of Rex Harrison
Harrison, Rex, Sir	1908-1990	Entertainment	36	50	63	80	Br.Actor.' My Fair Lady' SP 150. Oscar Winner
Harrison, Richard B.	1865-1935	Entrtainment	25	85		150	Am. Vintage Black Actor. 'The Green Pastures'
Harrison, Robert Hanson		Revolutionary War	210	400	2502		Sec'y to G. Washington
Harrison, Thomas	1823-1891	Civil War	130	190	246		Confederate general
Harrison, William Henry (as Pres)		President		140000	210000		One Month in Office as President
Harrison, William Henry	1773-1841	President	657	1428	3614		ADS 1790's 1400. ALS/Content 6500-15000
Harrold, Kathryn		Entertainment	10	12	14	27	Actress
Harrold, Lt. Gen. Thomas L.	1902-1973	Military	30				World War II U.S. general
Harrow, William	1822-1872	Civil War	45	98	208		Union general
Harry, Debbie		Entertainment	25			66	Rock Singer-Actress. 'Blondie'
Harry, Jackee		Entertainment	5			15	
Harryhausen, Ray		Entertainment	10			35	Film Director
Harshaw, Margaret		Entertainment	10	12	40	65	Opera. U.S. Soprano
Hart, Brig. Gen. William L.	1881-1957	Military	30				World War II U.S. general

NAME	DATE	CATEGORY	SIG	LS/DS	ALS	SP	COMMENTS
Hart, Corey		Entertainment	8	8	15	22	
Hart, Dolores	1938-	Entertainment	5	10	15	20	Actress
Hart, Dorothy		Entertainment	15		25	30	
Hart, Eva		Celebrity	60	70	75	80	Titanic survivor
Hart, Gary W.		Senator	8	18		20	Senator CO. One Time Presidential Hopeful
Hart, John		Entertainment	10			28	SP as the Lone Ranger 50
Hart, John	1711-1779	Revolutionary War	335	457	1300		Signer Decl. of Indepen. Important DS 3490
Hart, Johnny*		Cartoonist	20			175	'B.C.' & 'Wizard Of Id'
Hart, Lorenz	1895-1943	Composer	300	450			Talented Lyricist for Richard Rodgers. Died Young
Hart, Maj. Gen. Charles E.	1900-1991	Military	30				World War II U.S. general
Hart, Mary		Entertainment	5	8	15	15	Pleasing 'Entertainment Tonight' Host.Pin-Up SP25
Hart, Melissa A. H		Congress	10			15	Member U.S. Congress
Hart, Melissa Joan		Entertainment	12			50	Actress. 'Sabrina The Teenage Witch'
Hart, Moss	1904-1961	Author	30	55	120	40	Playwright & Musical Librettist
Hart, Paul		Entertainment	5	8	15	15	
Hart, Roxanne		Entertainment	10			20	Pinup 30
Hart, Terry J.		Astronaut	8	15		30	
Hart, Thomas C.		Military	40			65	Adm. WW II
Hart, Tony		Celebrity	10			15	children's presenter
Hart, Veronica		Entertainment	8	15	30	35	Pin-Up SP 45
Hart, William S.	1870-1946	Entertainment	123	194	272	446	1st Western Movie Star. Silent Films
Harte, Francis Brett	1836-1902	Author	82	185	237		Diplomat. Author of Frontier Life, AMsS 25,000
Harteneck, Gen of Cavalry Gustav	1892-1984	Military	27				World War II German general
Hartford, George L.		Business	40	170	280		Great Atlantic & Pacific Tea Co.Huge Grocery Chain
Hartford, Huntington		Business	20	30	50	25	Arts Patron. Playboy. Huntington Hartford Theatre
Hartford, John		Composer	10	45	70		AMusQS 95
Hartle, Maj. Gen. Russell P.	1889-1961	Military	30				World War II U.S. general
Hartle, Russell	1889-1961	Military	20			35	General. Cmdr. US Forces in Britain early WW II
Hartley, David	1729-1813	Colonial			950		Br. Minister.Anti War/Colonies.Signed Peace Treaty
Hartley, Fred A.		Congress	20		50		Congressman NJ
Hartley, General Sir Alan Fleming	1882-1954	Military	25				World War II British general
Hartley, Mariette		Entertainment	5	8	15	15	Actress. Films, TV
Hartley, Nina		Entertainment	15			40	
Hartley, Roland H.		Governor	5	12		10	Governor WA
Hartley, Thomas	1748-1800	Revolutionary War	105		350		Lt. Col. War Content ALS 6500
Hartline, Haldan K.		Science	25	80	140	75	Nobel Medicine
Hartman, Brig. Gen. Charles D.	1886-1962	Military	30				World War II U.S. general
Hartman, Brig. Gen. George E.	1895-1968	Military	30				World War II U.S. general
Hartman, David		Entertainment	10	12	15	15	Early TV Host 'Good Morning America'
Hartman, Don		Entertainment	10			30	Producer
Hartman, Lisa (Black)		Entertainment	8	15	25	27	
Hartman, Phil	1948-1998	Entertainment	55			101	Comedian-Actor
Hartmann, Erich	1922-1996	Aviation	45	105	208	275	Ger.Ace WW II. #1 Worldwide/Most Kills
Hartmann, Gen. of Inf. Alex. von	1890-1943	Military	25				World War II German general
Hartmann, Gen. of Artillery Otto	1894-1952	Military	25				World War II German general

NAME	DATE	CATEGORY	SIG	LS/DS	ALS	SP	COMMENTS
Hartmann, Gen. of Artillery Walter	1891-1977	Military	25				World War II German general
Hartmann, Lt. Gen. Wilhelm	1894-1963	Military	25				World War II German general
Hartmann, Maj. Gen. Martin	1892-1971	Military	25				World War II German general
Hartness, Maj. Gen. Harlan N.	1898-1986	Military	30				World War II U.S. general
Hartranft, John F.	1830-1889	Civil War	55	98	122		Union Gen. Statesman. Gov. PA. ALS/Cont. 1045
Harts, William	1867-1961	Military	10		45		Span.-Am.War.General WW I. Extensive Career
Hartsfield, Henry W. Jr		Astronaut	10	40		20	
Hartsuff, George L.	1830-1874	Civil War	43	75	132		Union Gen. S/Rank 75-95
Hartwell, Alfred S.	1836-1912	Civil War	38	73	92		Union General
Hartwell, Maj. Gen. John R.	1887-1970	Military	28				World War II British general
Harvey, Andrew		Celebrity	10			15	newsreader
Harvey, George B. M.		Journalist-Dipl.	20	70		80	Fostered Woodrow Wilson Nomination
Harvey, Jan		Entertainment	10			20	Actress
Harvey, Lawrence		Entertainment	90			150	Br. Actor. Early Death
Harvey, Lilian		Entertainment	5	6	15	22	
Harvey, Maj. Gen. Geo. Alfred D.	1882-1957	Military	25				World War II British general
Harvey, Maj. Gen. Sir Chas. Offley	1888-1969	Military	25				World War II British general
Harvey, Marilyn		Entertainment	10			35	Star of 'The Astounding She Monster'
Harvey, Paul		Journalist	10	25		20	Popular Syndicated Columnist-TV Commentator
Harvey, William	1578-1657	Science	750	3750	11000		1st Theory Blood Circulation. (RARE in any form)
Hasbrouck, Maj. Gen. Robert W.	1896-1985	Military	30				World War II U.S. general
Hasbrouck, Robert W.		Military	50	165		75	Am. Gen. WW II
Hascall, Milo Smith	1829-1904	Civil War	45	82	130		Union general
Hasen, Irwin		Cartoonist	5			20	'Dondi'
Hashimoto, Maj. Gen. Gun	1886-1963	Military	25				World War II Japanese general
Haskell, James K.		Entertainment	8	15	30	22	
Haskell, Lt. Gen. William N.	1878-1952	Military	30				World War II U.S. general
Haskell, Peter		Entertainment	5			10	Actor
Haskil, Clara		Entertainment	120				Legendary Classical Pianist. RARE
Haskin, Joseph Abel	1818-1874	Civil War	50	51	105		Union General. Sig./Rank 65
Hassam, Childe	1859-1935	Artist	150	350	536		Foremost in Am. Impressionism. Etcher
Hassam, Crown Prince		Royalty	20	45	80	75	Morocco
Hassan, al Bakr, Ahmad		Head of State	10	35	90	18	
Hassan, Crown Prince		Royalty	10	15	50	20	
Hasse, Gen. of Infantry Wilhelm	1894-1945	Military	25				World War II German general
Hasselhoff, David		Entertainment	15	20	25	43	'Baywatch'
Hasselman, Maj. Gen. H. D. S.	1880-1943	Military	20				World War II Dutch general
Hassler, Maj. Gen. Joseph-L-F	1881-1966	Military	20				World War II French general
Hasso, Signe		Entertainment	5			20	Actress
Hasted, Maj. Gen. William Freke	1897-1977	Military	25				World War II British general
Hastert, J. Dennis		Political		15	20	25	Speaker of the House
Hastings, Alcee	1936-	Congress	10			15	Member U.S. Congress
Hastings, Daniel H.		Governor	10	25			Governor PA
Hastings, Doc H		Congress	10			15	Member U.S. Congress
Hastings, Warren	1732-1818	Head of State	60	237	335		1st Gov- Gen. India. Colonial Adm.

NAME	DATE	CATEGORY	SIG	LS/DS	ALS	SP	COMMENTS
Haswell, Charles H.	1809-	Civil War	46	77	109		Union Naval Architect War Dte DS 155-200
Hata, Field Marshal Shunroku	1879-1962	Military	27				World War II Japanese general
Hatch, Edward	1832-1889	Civil War	45	85	125		Union general
Hatch, John Porter	1822-1901	Civil War	44	78	125	250	Union Gen. CMH. ADS(Gen.Orders '62)4180
Hatch, Orrin		Senate	10			15	United States Senate (R - UT)
Hatch, Richard		Celebrity				15	Survivor
Hatcher, Maj. Gen. Julian S.	1888-1963	Military	30				World War II U.S. general
Hatcher, Richard G.	1933-	Political	5	10		25	Afro-Am. Mayor, Gary IN
Hatcher, Teri		Entertainment	10			52	Actress. 'Lois & Clark'-'James Bond'
Hatfield, Hurd		Entertainment	15	22	30	35	Actor. 'Portrait of Dorian Grey'
Hatfield, Lansing		Entertainment	15			95	Opera, Concert, Recital Artist
Hatfield, Mark O.		Senate	10	22		20	Senator OR, Governor Oregon. Long Time 'Dove'
Hathaway, Henry		Entertainment	40			95	Film Director
Hatlo, Jimmy*	1898-1963	Cartoonist	10	45		80	'Little Iodine'
Hatton, Christopher, Sir	1540-1591	Statesman		1138			Elizabeth Ist, Lord Chancellor
Hatton, Frank		Cabinet	50	70			Chester A. Arthur PMG
Hatton, Raymond		Entertainment	50			125	Vintage Actor
Hatton, Robert	1826-1862	Civil War	350	473	720		Killed at Fair Oaks 6/1/1862
Hatton, Rondo		Entertainment	450			1200	
Hatzidakis, Konstantinos		Political	10			15	Member European Parliament
Hauck, Frederick H.		Astronaut	10			25	
Hauer, Rutger		Entertainment	11			40	Actor. 'Lady Hawke'
Haug, Jutta D.		Political	10			15	Member European Parliament
Haugh, Maj. Gen. James W.N.	1894-1969	Military	25				World War II British general
Haught, Helmut		Aviation	10	15	30	20	
Haugton, Maj. Gen. Henry L.	1883-1955	Military	25				World War II British general
Haupt, Herman	1817-1905	Civil War	40	57	84		Union Gen. ALS '62 440
Hauptman, Herbert A., Dr.		Science	20	35		30	Nobel Chemistry
Hauptmann, Bruno Richard		Kidnapper	1420	1840			Convicted Killer Lindbergh Baby
Hauptmann, Gerhart		Author	90	295	575	375	Nobel Prize Literature 1912
Hauseman, Brig. Gen. David N.	1895-1981	Military	30				World War II U.S. general
Hauser, Dr. Gayelord		Medical	20			35	Healthfood Advocate. Garbo Companion
Hausner, Jerry		Entertainment	5	7	9	10	
Hautala, Heidi Anneli		Political	10			15	Member European Parliament
Havel, Vaclav		Head of State	20			45	Czech. Poet. President
Havemeyer, William F.		Business	125		305		Am. Sugar Refining Dynasty. Mayor NYC
Haven, Annette		Entertainment	9	10	20	25	Pin-Up SP 40
Havens, Beckwith		Aviation	18	40	55	50	
Havens, Richie		Music	15			40	Woodstock
Haver, June		Entertainment	5	10	12	20	40's-50's Blonde 20th Cent. Fox Star.Pin-Up SP 25
Havers, Nigel		Entertainment	10			20	actor
Havoc, June		Entertainment	10	8	20	25	Actress. 'Baby June' Sister of Gypsy Rose Lee
Hawes, Elizabeth		Artist	10	20	35		
Hawes, James Morrison	1824-1889	Civil War	110				Confederate general
Hawes, Maj. Gen. Leonard Arthur	1892-1971	Military	25				World War II British general

NAME	DATE	CATEGORY	SIG	LS/DS	ALS	SP	COMMENTS
Hawke, Ethan		Entertainment	18			43	Actor
Hawke, Robert	1929-	Head of State	20	40	130	30	Prime Minister Australia
Hawker, Harry	1886-1921	Aviation	185				Pioneer Australian Pilot & Airplane Builder. Rare
Hawkins, Anthony Hope, Sir		Author	38	42	85	38	Br.Novelist. 'Prisoner of Zenda'
Hawkins, Brig. Gen. Hamilton S.	1872-1950	Military	30				World War II U.S. general
Hawkins, Coleman		Entertainment	140			250	Jazz Tenor Sax. Band Leader
Hawkins, Erskine	1914-1992	Music				78	Jazz trumpeter
Hawkins, Jack		Entertainment	45			92	Br. Leading Man & Character Actor. Cancer Victim
Hawkins, John Parker	1830-1914	Civil War	42		140		Union general
Hawkins, Maj. Gen. George L. S.	1898-1978	Military	28				World War II British general
Hawkins, Paula		Senate/Congress	5	10		15	Senator FL
Hawkins, Rush C. (WD)	1831-1920	Civil War		245			Union Gen.
Hawkins, Rush C.		Civil War	63	112			Union General
Hawkins, William	1770-1819	Governor	35	85			Governor NC. War 1812
Hawks, Frank Monroe	1897-1938	Aviation	85	135	325	272	Pioneer Am. Aviator
Hawks, Howard		Entertainment	98	375		200	Diector-Producer-Studio Head
Hawks, Tony		Celebrity	10			15	comedian
Hawley, Joseph R.	1826-1905	Civil War	36	88	120		Union Gen., Gov. CT, Sen CT.Hero. Anti Slavery
Hawley, Maj. Gen. Paul R.	1891-1965	Military	30				World War II U.S. general
Hawley, Steven A.		Astronaut	10			20	
Hawn, Goldie		Entertainment	15	48	30	56	Actress-Comedianne
Haworth, Jill		Entertainment	5	7	9	10	Actress
Hawthorn, Alex. Travis	1825-1899	Civil War	212	372	628		CSA General
Hawthorn, Maj. Gen. Douglas C.	1897-1974	Military	25				World War II British general
Hawthorne, Julian	1846-1934	Author	40		225		Son of Nathaniel Hawthorne
Hawthorne, Nathaniel	1804-1865	Author	350	1019	1661		Novelist, Short Stories, US Consul
Hawthorne, Nigel		Entertainment	10			20	actor
Hay, Bill		Entertainment	10	15	20	20	Radio Announcer
Hay, John H.		Military	5		15		
Hay, John Milton	1838-1905	Cabinet	59	132	228	250	Lincoln Private Sec'y. ALS/Content 950 War Dte
Hay, Louise		Celebrity	10			15	medical expert
Hay, Maj. Gen. Arthur Kenneth	1884-1949	Military	25				World War II British general
Hay, William Henry		Military	5	15	30		
Hayakawa, Sessue		Entertainment	125			372	Japanese. Major Star in Jap., US & Foreign Films
Hayashi, Lt. Gen. Senjuro	1876-1942	Military	25				World War II Japanese general
Haydee, Marcia		Entertainment	10			35	Prima Ballerina in 'The Turning Point'
Hayden, Brig. Gen. Frederic L.	1901-1969	Military	30				World War II U.S. general
Hayden, Carl		Senate/Congress	10	25		20	MOC, Senator AZ. 42 Years
Hayden, Charles	1870-1937	Banker	20	45		40	Philanthropist. Hayden Planetarium
Hayden, Mellisa		Entertainment	5	6	15	15	Actress
Hayden, Nora		Entertainment	5			20	Actress. 60's Star 'The Angry Red Planet'
Hayden, Russell		Entertainment	25			75	Actor. Cowboy Star
Hayden, Sterling	1916-1986	Entertainment	25			50	Reclusive Actor
Hayden, Tom		Congress	5	15		15	MOC CA. Ex-Husband of Jane Fonda
Haydn, Franz Joseph	1732-1809	Composer	2850	15500	24000		Working Draft 4 String Quartets 1.04 Mil.

NAME	DATE	CATEGORY	SIG	LS/DS	ALS	SP	COMMENTS
Haydon, Benj. R.	1786-1846	Artist		115	232		Br. Historical Painter, Author, Teacher
Haydon, Maj. Gen. Joseph Chas.	1899-1970	Military	25				World War II British general
Hayek, Salma		Entertainment	15			54	Actress-'Desperado','Frida', director
Hayes, George 'Gabby'	1889-1965	Entertainment	138	220		450	Western Star. Grizzly 'Sidekick'
Hayes, Helen	1900-1994	Entertainment	20	40	45	50	Was First Lady of American Theatre
Hayes, Ira H., Corporal		Military	400				Iwo Jima Flag Raising FDC 550
Hayes, Isaac Israel	1832-1881	Explorer	72	143	195		Arctic Expl. ALS/Cont.1,500. War Dte. DS 375
Hayes, Isaac		Entertainment	9	10	15	30	Composer-Singer-Musician Recording Artist
Hayes, Joseph	1835-1912	Civil War	60	157	170	195	Union General
Hayes, Lucy Webb	1831-1889	First Lady	152		400	752	Mrs. Rutherford B. Hayes
Hayes, Maj. Gen. Eric Charles	1896-1951	Military	25				World War II British general
Hayes, Maj. Gen. Philip	1887-1949	Military	30				World War II U.S. general
Hayes, Maj. Gen. Thomas J.	1888-1967	Military	30				World War II U.S. general
Hayes, Margaret		Entertainment	9	10		15	Actress
Hayes, Patrick, Cardinal	1867-1938	Clergy	35	45	75	50	Founded Catholic Charities
Hayes, Peter Lind	1915-1998	Entertainment	20			32	Comedian, Actor, Singer/Wife Mary Healy
Hayes, Robin H		Congress	10			15	Member U.S. Congress
Hayes, Roland	1887-1977	Entertainment	80	72	175	250	Am. Tenor, Spingarn Medal '25
Hayes, Rutherford B. (As Pres.)		President	300	629	1053	1950	ALS/Cont. 7,500. WH Cd. 350-475
Hayes, Rutherford B. (WD)	1822-1893	Civil War	250	775	1192		Union general, US President
Hayes, Rutherford B.	1822-1893	President	204	498	622	1686	Union Gen.Post Pres.-Pro Education ALS 3500
Hayes, Sean		Entertainment	10			45	Will and Grace
Hayford, Brig. Gen. Bertram F.	1899-1985	Military	30				World War II U.S. general
Hayman-Joyce, Maj. Gen. H. John	1897-1958	Military	25				World War II British general
Hayne, Paul Hamilton	1830-1886	Author	80		562		ALS/Literary Content 2,500.'Laureate of South'
Hayne, Robert Young	1791-1839	Congress	75		180		Sen. SC, Gov. SC
Haynes, Brig. Gen. Loyal M.	1895-1974	Military	30				World War II U.S. general
Haynes, Linda		Entertainment	5	4	9	10	Actress
Haynie, Isham Nicholas	1824-1868	Civil War	45		110		Union general
Haynie, Will		Author	8			12	political commentary, Citadel controversy
Hayridge, Hattie		Celebrity	10			15	comedienne
Hays, Alexander	1819-1864	Civil War	192		1380		Union general
Hays, Frank A.		Aviation	35	55	95	65	ACE, WW II
Hays, Harry Thompson (WD)	1820-1876	Civil War	312	1205			CSA Gen.
Hays, Harry Thompson	1820-1876	Civil War	198	450			CSA General
Hays, Lt. Gen. George P.	1892-1978	Military	30				World War II U.S. general
Hays, Robert		Entertainment	5	8	12	18	Singer-Actor
Hays, Wayne L.		Senate/Congress	5	20		15	MOC OH
Hays, Will H.	1879-1854	Cabinet	28	45		45	Film Czar. Hays Code. Pres.DS 300. PMG
Hays, William	1819-1875	Civil War	45	90	165		Union Gen. ALS '64 385, Sig/Rank 85
Hayton, Lennie	1908-1971	Entertainment	20			75	Pianist, Composer, Musical Dir. MGM 1940-53
Hayward, George		Science	10	20	35	15	
Hayward, Louis		Entertainment	10	15	25	50	Br. Leading Man. Many Historical Films.
Hayward, Susan	1917-1975	Entertainment	155	200	380	425	Oscar Winning Actress. Early Death
Haywood, Thomas		Military	5	10	15	15	

NAME	DATE	CATEGORY	SIG	LS/DS	ALS	SP	COMMENTS
Hayworth, J. D. H		Congress	10			15	Member U.S. Congress
Hayworth, Rita	1918-1987	Entertainment	137	277	343	550	Glamour Star of the 40's
Hazan, Adeline		Political	10			15	Member European Parliament
Hazelwood, John	1726-1800	Revolutionary War	75	190	370		Commodore Continental Navy
Hazelwood, Joseph		Navy Captain	20			45	Capt. Exxon Valdez-Oil Spill
Hazen, Wm. Babcock	1830-1887	Civil War	34	55	98		Union Gen. War Dte. DS 150
Hazlett, Maj. Gen. Harry F.	1884-1960	Military	30				World War II U.S. general
Head		Entertainment	5			25	Music. Guitars, Vocals 'Korn'
Head, Edith		Entertainment	25			125	8 Academy Awards. Costume Design.
Headle, Marshall		Aviation	25	70		85	Lockheed Chief Test Pilot
Headly, Glenne		Entertainment	10			20	actress
Healey, Robert C.		Author	10	15	25		
Healy, Bernadine		Celebrity	10			15	medical expert
Healy, George Peter	1813-1894	Artist	105	164	838		Eminent 19th Cent. Portraitist
Healy, Ted		Entertainment	75	507	650	750	Vaudeville Song & Dance Man. DS Three Stooges1868
Heard, Brig. Gen. Ralph T.	1895-1993	Military	30				World War II U.S. general
Heard, John		Entertainment	10			20	actor
Heard, Maj. Gen. Jack W.	1887-1976	Military	30				World War II U.S. general
Hearn, Lafcadio	1850-1904	Author	300		1200		Irish-Greek-Am. Writer on Japanese Culture
Hearn, Maj. Gen. Frank A. Jr.	1896-1983	Military	30				World War II U.S. general
Hearnes, Warren E.		Governor	4	10		15	Governor MO
Hearst, George	1820-1891	Business-Senate	285		1175		Newspaper Dynasty. Stk.Cert. S 18,000-32000
Hearst, Patricia		Celebrities	275				Kidnapped daughter of Hearst, Jr.
Hearst, Phoebe A.(Mrs. George..)		Business	20	40	90		Philanthropies
Hearst, Wm. Randolph	1863-1951	Business	225	432	785	951	MOC. NY. Powerful Publisher. Pres. Cand. DS 1450
Hearst, Wm. Randolph, Jr.		Business	10	30	45	20	Son of Hearst, Sr. Newspaper Publisher
Heart		Entertainment	38			100	Rock
Heath, Edward		Celebrity	10			15	political celebrity
Heath, Edward	1916-	Head of State	30	90	110	45	Br.Prime Minister
Heath, Lt. Gen. Sir Lewis M.	1885-1954	Military	25				World War II British general
Heath, Maj. Gen. Gerard Wm. E.	1897-1980	Military	25				World War II British general
Heath, William	1737-1814	Revolutionary War	200	432	1267		Gen.Cont'l Army. DS War Dte.1275,1400
Heatherton, Joey		Entertainment	9	10	18	31	Actress-Dancer-Singer
Heatherton, Ray		Entertainment	20			70	Big band leader
Heaton, Patricia		Entertainment	15			35	Everybody Loves Raymond
Heaton-harris, Christopher		Political	10			15	Member European Parliament
Heavey, Brig. Gen. William F.	1896-1974	Military	30				World War II U.S. general
Heber, Reginald	1783-1826	Clergy	85	100	200		Br. Prelate, Hymn Writer. 'Holy, Holy, Holy'
Hebert, Louis (WD)		Civil War	202	505			CSA Gen.
Hebert, Louis		Civil War		1725			CSA General
Hebert, Louis	1820-1901	Civil War	112	258	685		CSA Gen.
Hebert, Paul O.	1818-1880	Civil War	110	350	458		CSA General Sig/Rank 200
Hebert, Paul		Civil War	117	382	396		CSA General
Heche, Anne		Entertainment	8			38	Actress
Hecht, Ben	1894-1964	Author	25	85		50	AA.Playwright, Novelist, Newsman

NAME	DATE	CATEGORY	SIG	LS/DS	ALS	SP	COMMENTS
Heckart, Eileen	1919-	Entertainment	12	10	15	35	Noted Character Actress of Stage, Film, TV
Heckerling, Amy		Entertainment	5	6	15	14	
Heckler, Margaret		Celebrity	10			15	medical expert
Heckman, Charles A.	1822-1896	Civil War	38	105			Union Gen. ALS (Autobiog.)550, Sig/Rank 50+
Hedin, Sven	1865-1952	Explorer	102	170	203	125	Swe. Asian Explorer, Geographer
Hedison, David		Entertainment	5	7	9	12	Actor. 'Voyage to Bottom of the Sea'
Hedkvist Petersen, Ewa		Political	10			15	Member European Parliament
Hedl, Walter		Composer	15	55	90		AMusQS 175
Hedley, Maj. Gen. Robert Cecil O.	1900-1973	Military	25				World War II British general
Hedman, Robert Duke		Aviation	25	45	75	50	ACE, WW II, Flying Tigers
Hedouville, G.M.T.J,Count		Fr. Revolution	70	125			Fr. Gen. Marshal of Fr.?
Hedren, Tippi		Entertainment	7	10	22	35	Actress. 'The Birds'
Hedrick, Brig. Gen. Lawrence H.	1880-1958	Military	30				World War II U.S. general
Hedrick, Roger		Aviation	15	25	40	35	ACE, WW II
Heflebower, Brig. Gen. Roy C.	1884-1973	Military	30				World War II U.S. general
Hefley, Joel H		Congress	10			15	Member U.S. Congress
Heflin, Howell		Senate	5	15	15	10	Senator AL
Heflin, James Thomas		Senate/Congress	10	20		15	MOC, Senator AL
Heflin, Van	1910-1971	Entertainment	35	75	95	100	Actor-Oscar Winner. Versatile. Leads to Westerns
Hefner, Christie		Business	5	10	30	20	Publisher Playboy Magazine
Hefner, Hugh		Business	10			25	'Playboy'TLS/Cont.500
Heft, Bob		Designer	20		25		Designed US 50 Star Flag
Hefti, Neal		Composer	15	35	50	40	AMusQS 195. 'Odd Couple' Theme AMusQS 45
Hegel, Geo. Wilhelm F.	1770-1831	Philosopher	750	1400	2250		Ger. Idealist Philosopher/Kant
Heggie, Oliver P.	1879-1936	Entertainment	350			750	Character Actor
Heidegger, Martin	1889-1976	Philosopher			884		Ger. Existential Phenomonologist
Heidt, Horace 'Musical Knights'		Entertainment	20			40	Big Band Leader. Sigs 12 Members 45
Heifetz, Jascha	1901-1987	Entertainment	175	260		625	Violin Virtuoso., AMusQS 700
Heigle, Katherine		Entertainment				45	Actress
Heileman, Maj. Gen. Frank A.	1891-1961	Military	30				World War II U.S. general
Heimlich, Henry Jay, Dr.		Science	20		45	40	Created Heimlich Maneuver
Heine, Heinrich	1797-1856	Author	570	4000	6500		Ger. Poet, Critic, Essayist
Heinlein, Robert A.		Author	55	165	350		Sci-Fi Fiction
Heinrich, Albert H.		Aviation	35		120		
Heinrici, Col. General Gotthard	1886-1971	Military	25				World War II German general
Heintzelman, Samuel P.	1805-1880	Civil War	36	95	144		Union General
Heintzelman, Samuel P.(WD)		Civil War	45	145	220		Union Gen.
Heinz, Henry John II		Business	35				Food Manufacturer
Heinz, Henry John III	1938-1992	Congress	15	30		25	Sen. PA. Air Crash Victim. Heir to Heinz Fortune
Heinz, Henry John	1844-1919	Business	110		800	385	Fndr/Brother& Cousin H&J. Heinz Co. Pickles etc.
Heinze, F. Aug.		Business	500	2450			Montana Mining Mogul
Heinze, Karl		Astronaut	35		75		
Heir, Doug		Celebrity	10			15	motivational speaker
Heise, Karl G.		Astronaut	10		20		
Heisenberg, Werner, Dr.	1901-1976	Science	102	418	675		Nobel Physics,ALS/Cont. 950

NAME	DATE	CATEGORY	SIG	LS/DS	ALS	SP	COMMENTS
Heiskell, Joesph Brown	1823-1913	Civil War	42		100		Member of Confederate Congress
Heitz, Colonel-General Walter	1878-1944	Military	27				World War II German general
Helbig, Joachim		Aviation	10	20	35	25	
Held, Anna	1865-1918	Entertainment	65	80	135	85	Mrs. Florenz Ziegfield.Star Fr.,Am.,Yid'sh Musical
Held, John, Jr.*	1889-1958	Cartoonist	165			385	Illustrator Created The 'Flapper'
Heldmann, Aloys		Aviation		70			Ger. WW I Ace
Heldy, Fanny		Entertainment	40			110	Opera
Helena, Princess		Royalty	15	52	150	65	3rd Daughter Queen Victoria. Fndr. Nursing Home
Helgenberger, Marg		Entertainment	15			35	Pin-Up SP 50
Heller, John R., Dr.		Science	12	20		20	
Heller, Joseph		Author	15	72	45	40	'Catch 22'
Heller, Walter E.		Business	5	15		15	Fndr.,Chm. Walter E. Heller
Heller, Walter W.		Cabinet	5	15	30	15	
Helletsgruber, Luise		Entertainment	25			75	Opera
Hellinger, Mark		Author	35	105	225	40	Columnist, Playwright
Hellman, Lillian	1905-1984	Author	60	133		225	Am. Dramatist, 'Little Foxes'
Hellyer, Paul T.		Celebrity	15	30			
Helm, Ben Hardin	1830-1883	Civil War	235	363			CSA General. Killed 9/20/63 Battle of Chicamauga
Helm, Briditte	1906-1996	Entertainment	25			100	Ger. Actress. 1926 Cult Film 'Metropolis'
Helm, Fay		Entertainment	15			50	Actress
Helmer, Roger		Political	10			15	Member European Parliament
Helmholtz, Hermann L.von	1821-1894	Science	195		600		Ger Physicist Biologist.Many Science Contributions
Helmick, Maj. Gen. Charles G.	1892-1991	Military	30				World War II U.S. general
Helmick, Robert		Celebrity	10			15	motivational speaker
Helmond, Katherine		Entertainment	8	10	20	20	Actress. Comedy & Straight Leads. TV-Films
Helms, Jesse		Congress	5	15		20	U.S. Senator NC
Helms, Richard		Celebrity	5	15	45	20	
Helms, Susan		Astronaut	8			25	
Helmsley, Leona		Business	10			25	Hotel Magnate
Heloise		Author	5			10	Columnist. Household Tips
Helper, Hinton R.	1829-1909	Author			270	368	American Writer
Helps, Arthur, Sir	1817-1875	Author	10	15	40		Historian Re America
Helton, Percy		Entertainment	20			65	
Hely, Brigadier Alfred Francis	1902-1990	Military	25				World War II British general
Hemingway, Ernest	1899-1961	Author	940	2426	4452	2580	Nobel Lit. Pulitzer., ALS/TLS /cont 27,500
Hemingway, Margaux		Entertainment	40			80	Actress-Daughter E. Hemingway
Hemingway, Mariel		Entertainment	15			50	Actress-Daughter E. Hemingway
Hemingway, Mary		Author	20	45	85		Mrs. Ernest Hemingway
Hemingway, Wayne		Celebrity	10			15	Designer
Hempel, Frieda		Entertainment	20	35		70	Ger. Soprano, Opera
Hemphill, John	1803-1862	Civil War	117				Member of Confederate Congress
Hemsley, Sherman		Entertainment	6	8	15	22	Actor. 'The Jeffersons'. TV Sitcom
Hemstridge, Natasha		Entertainment	20			72	Br. Actress
Hench, Philip S.	1896-1965	Science	40	75	150	150	Nobel Medicine & Physiology. Cortisone, Hormones
Henderson, Archibald		Military	65	195			Marine General War 1812

NAME	DATE	CATEGORY	SIG	LS/DS	ALS	SP	COMMENTS
Henderson, Don		Entertainment	10			20	Actor
Henderson, Fletcher		Entertainment	15			35	Bandleader
Henderson, Florence		Entertainment	6	8	10	20	'Brady Bunch' Mom. Singer-Actress-TV Announcer
Henderson, J. Pinckney		Statesman	390	525			Gen. TX Army, Gov. Texas
Henderson, John Brooks	1826-1913	Civil War Senator	25	65			Sen. From MO 1862-69. Frequent Contact/Lincoln
Henderson, Marcia		Entertainment	5			20	
Henderson, Skitch		Composer	16			35	Conductor, Bandleader
Hendon, Bill		Senate/Congress	3	5		5	Congressman NC
Hendricks, Barbara		Entertainment	10			35	Opera
Hendricks, Thos.A.	1819-1885	Vice President	60	130	200	350	Cleveland VP, U.S. Sen. IN
Hendrix, Jimi	1942-1970	Entertainment	823	1611		1977	Leading 'Acid Rock' 60's Singer. Signed album 2415
Hendrix, Wanda		Entertainment	10	15		25	Actress.
Hendry, Gloria		Entertainment	5			10	Afr.-Am. Actress
Hendy, Alastair		Celebrity	10			15	Chef
Heney, Hugh		Explorer	325	750			Scout & Interpretor for Lewis & Clark
Henie, Sonja	1910-1969	Entertainment	55	82		170	Gold in Olympic Figure Skating
Henize, Karl G.	1926-1993	Astronaut	10	15		50	
Henley, Don		Entertainment	20			47	Composer, Singer.'The Eagles' Alb. S 125
Henley, Thos. Jeff.	1810-1865	Congress	10		30		MOC IN, San Francisco Postmaster
Henley, William Ernest	1849-1903	Poet			120		
Henn, Mark		Cartoonist	10			35	Disney Animator. Little Mermain, Beauty & Beast
Henner, Marilu		Entertainment	8	8	20	29	Actress. 'Taxi'
Henning, Brig. Gen. Frank A. Jr.	1896-1983	Military	30				World War II U.S. general
Henninger, Brig. Gen. Guy N.	1895-1977	Military	30				World War II U.S. general
Henreid, Paul		Entertainment	32			91	Film Leading Man/Dir. 'Casablanca'
Henri, Robert		Artist	80	175	215		Portr. Painter, Ashcan School
Henricks, Terence T.		Astronaut	5			20	
Henrietta Maria	1609-1669	Royalty		3375			Queen Mother of Charles I
Henriksen, Lance		Entertainment	10			20	actor
Henry II (Fr)	1519-1559	Royalty	325	854	2250		France
Henry III (Fr)	1551-1589	Royalty	250	618	1500		France
Henry IV (Fr)	1553-1610	Royalty	212	643	1750		And Navarre. Assassinated
Henry IV (Sp)	1425-1474	Royalty		1675			King of Castile 'The Impotent'
Henry V (Fr)		Royalty	40	65	150		Pretender to Throne
Henry VI (Eng)	1421-1471	Royalty	850	3500	7250		England
Henry VII (Eng)	1457-1509	Royalty	825	6250	9250		
Henry VIII (Eng)	1491-1547	Royalty	5500	18000	26000		England. Father of Queen Mary & Elizabeth I
Henry, Bill		Aviation	10	25	40	30	ACE, WW II, Navy Ace
Henry, Buck		Entertainment	10	12	15	28	Actor. Films., writer
Henry, Gloria		Entertainment	5	7	10	15	Actress
Henry, Gustavous Adolphus		Civil War	52	117			Member of Confederate Congress
Henry, John	1750-1798	Revolutionary War	35	135	220		Continental Congress. Sen. MD
Henry, Joseph	1797-1878	Science	75	160	295		1st Electric Motor. 1st Dir. Smithsonian
Henry, Lenny		Celebrity	10			15	comedian
Henry, Maj. Gen. Guy V.	1875-1967	Military	30				World War II U.S. general

NAME	DATE	CATEGORY	SIG	LS/DS	ALS	SP	COMMENTS
Henry, Maj. Gen. Stephen G.	1894-1973	Military	30				World War II U.S. general
Henry, Mike		Entertainment	10			35	
Henry, O. (Pseud.) W.S. Porter		Author					SEE William Porter
Henry, Patrick	1736-1799	Revolutionary War	1275	2329	6500		Rev. War Leader, Statesman, ALS/cont 18,400
Hensarling, Jeb H		Congress	10			15	Member U.S. Congress
Henschel, George, Sir	1850-1934	Composer	70			150	Br.-Ger. Conductor, Singer
Henshaw, David	1791-1852	Cabinet	25	55	112		Tyler Sec'y Navy. MA Leader Dem. Party 30 Yrs.
Hensley, Dean		Author	8			12	NASCAR, sportswriter
Henslow, John Stevens		Science					Botanist. AMS 180
Henson, Jim	1936-1990	Entertainment	80	150	175	250	Created the Muppets. DS re 'Muppets' 275
Henson, John		Entertainment	10			20	actor
Henson, Matthew A.		Explorer	193	350			Afro-Am. Arctic Expl. Historical Statement 5000
Henstridge, Natasha		Entertainment	12			45	Actress
Henze, Hans Werner		Composer	45			165	Ger. Opera, Theater Works
Henze, Karl		Aviation	16	35	70	45	
Hepburn, Audrey	1929-1993	Entertainment	100	250	530	404	AA Winner. Belg.Born Actress-Humanitarian
Hepburn, Katherine	1907-2003	Entertainment	152	250	448	754	AA. 4 Times Oscar Winner. 3x5 SP 650.
Hepworth, Barbara, Dame		Artist	70	190		125	Br. Sculptor.Reclining Figure
Herb, Ritts	d. 2002	Photographer	15			50	Famous Hollywood photographer
Herbeck, Ray		Entertainment	5			15	Big Band Leader-Sax
Herbert, Caleb Claiborne	1814-1867	Civil War	72	168			Member of Confederate Congress
Herbert, F. Hugh		Author	12	20	30	20	Am. Playwright, Producer
Herbert, Frank		Author	15	20	35	20	Am. Sci-Fi. 'Dune Trilogy'
Herbert, Geo.E. (Carnarvon)	1866-1923	Archaeology	32	45	148		With Carter, King Tut Tomb. 5th Earl
Herbert, Hillary	1834-1919	Cabinet	15	35		30	Sec'y Navy Cleveland. Civil War Confed. Colonel.
Herbert, Hugh	1887-1952	Entertainment	35	45	70	75	Actor. Vaudeville-Stage Star. Over 100 Films
Herbert, Maj. Gen. Wm Norman	1880-1949	Military	28				World War II British general
Herbert, Sidney		Entertainment	15	25	30	25	
Herbert, Victor	1859-1924	Composer	50	148	265	312	Operettas.'Babes in Toyland' AMQS475,Spec SP1840
Herford,Oliver		Cartoonist	10	25			
Herger, Wally H		Congress	10			15	Member U.S. Congress
Hergesheimer, Joseph		Author	25	65	145	30	Am. Psychological Novels
Herget, Wilhelm		Aviation	20		50		
Hering, Constantine		Science	15	25	50		1st Homeopathic School
Hering, General Pierre	1874-1963	Military	20				World War II French general
Herkimer, Nicholas		Revolutionary War		3700			General of Militia.
Herkomer, Hubert von, Sir		Artist	25	60	80		Br. Portrait Painter
Herman, Alexis	1947-	Cabinet	4	20		15	Afro-Am. Sec'y Labor Clinton
Herman, Jerry		Composer	15	40	65	30	AMusQS 85 'Hello Dolly'
Herman, Pee Wee		Entertainment	15	15		40	
Herman, Woody		Entertainment	20	35		78	Big Band Leader-Clarinetist
Hermange, Marie-thérèse		Political	10			15	Member European Parliament
Hermann, Bernard	1911-1975	Composer		700			Music for Movies,Radio.Conductor CBS
Hermann, Hajo		Aviation	25	50		60	
Herman's Hermits		Entertainment	195			275	Popular Brit. Rock Group (5)

NAME	DATE	CATEGORY	SIG	LS/DS	ALS	SP	COMMENTS
Hermine, Princess Schonaich-C.		Royalty		125		250	Married Emp.Wilhelm II (after 1918 abdication)
Hernández Mollar, Jorge Salv.		Political	10			15	Member European Parliament
Herndon, William H.	1818-1891	Legal	130	294	525		Law Partner of Abraham Lincoln
Herne, James A.		Entertainment	15	15	30	28	Actor-Manager
Heron, William	1742-1819	Revolutionary War		1250			Double Agent for Americans & British.
Herr, Gen. Panz. Troops Traugott	1890-1976	Military	25				World War II German general
Herr, Maj. Gen. John K.	1878-1955	Military	30				World War II U.S. general
Herranz García, María Esther		Political	10			15	Member European Parliament
Herren, Lt. Gen. Thomas W.	1895-1985	Military	30				World War II U.S. general
Herres, Bob		Astronaut	5			16	
Herrick, Myron T.	1854-1929	Diplomat	25	35		45	Ambassador, Gov. OH, Banker.Lindbergh Friend
Herriman, George*		Cartoonist	50			525	'Krazy Kat'
Herring, Clyde L.	1879-1945	Congress	7			10	Senator IA
Herring, John F.	1795-1865	Artist	60		275		Br.Race Horses & Sporting Events
Herring, Lt. Gen. Edmund F.	1892-1982	Military	20				World War II Australian general
Herring, Thomas	1693-1757	Clergy		125	140		Archbishop York & Canterbury
Herrington, John		Astronaut	6			20	
Herriot, Edouard	1872-1957	Head of State	25	80	175		Premier of Fr., Nazi Prisoner
Herriot, James (Wight)		Author-Vet.	20	40	75	30	'All Creatures Great & Small'
Herrmann, Adelaide & Alexander		Magic	50			75	Magicians
Herrmann, Bernard	1911-1975	Composer		875			Film Composer
Herron, Francis J.	1837-1902	Civil War	42	110	160		Union Gen. Wounded, Captured, Exchanged
Herron, Lt. Gen. Charles D.	1877-1977	Military	30				World War II U.S. general
Herschbach, Dudley, Dr.		Science	25	35		40	Nobel Chemistry
Herschel, John Fred. Wm., Sir		Science	81	170	238	1265	1792-1871. Br. Astronomer, Mathematician
Herschel, William, Sir	1738-1822	Science	150	475	857		Ger.-Born Br.Astronomer, Discovered Uranus
Hersey, John	1914-1993	Author	20	40	70	60	'Bell for Adano'. Pulitzer
Hershey, Alfred D., Dr.		Science	20	30	45	30	Nobel Medicine
Hershey, Barbara	b. 1948	Entertainment	20			32	Actress. 1-Sheet Movie Poster 'Dealing:a' S 65
Hershey, Lewis B.		Military	15			25	Gen., Selective Service Adm.
Hersholt, Jean	1886-1956	Entertainment	20		95	64	Character Actor. Major Star & Humanitarian
Herter, Christian	1895-1966	Cabinet	15	25		45	Sec'y State. Gov. MA. Congressman
Hertz, Alfred		Entertainment	25			120	Conductor
Hertz, Gustav	1857-1894	Science	350				Ger. Physicist. Nobel 1925. Rare
Hertz, Heinrich	1857-1894	Science			1610		
Hertzberg, Maj. Gen. Chas. S. L.	1886-1944	Military	20				World War II Canadian general
Hertzberg, Maj. Gen. Halfdan F H.	1884-1959	Military	20				World War II Canadian general
Hervey, Brig. Gen. Harcourt	1892-1970	Military	30				World War II U.S. general
Hervey, Irene	1910-1998	Entertainment	15			35	Vintage Leading Lady. Films.
Herzberg, Gerhard, Dr.		Science	25	65		35	Nobel Chemistry
Herzl, Theodor	1860-1904	Zionist	250	2157	3677	1500	Writer-Journalist. Important DS 6,500-8,000
Herzner, Hans-Albrecht	1907-1942	Military	700				1st Ger. Engaged in Combat WW II
Herzog, Chaim	1918-1897	Head of State	35	65	175	65	Pres. Israel. Fndr & Head Military Intell. U.N.
Herzog, Philippe A.R.		Political	10			15	Member European Parliament
Herzog, Roman	1934-	Head of State	20			60	Pres. Of Germany

NAME	DATE	CATEGORY	SIG	LS/DS	ALS	SP	COMMENTS
Hesburgh, Theodore M., Rev.		Clergy	20	30	75	25	Longtime Pres. Notre Dame
Hesdin, General René de	1890-1966	Military	20				World War II French general
Hesketh, Brig. Gen. William	1895-1986	Military	30				World War II U.S. general
Hess, Brig. Gen. Walter W. Jr.	1892-1972	Military	30				World War II U.S. general
Hess, Myra, Dame	1890-1965	Entertainment	60	95	130	350	Br. Pianist
Hess, Rudolf	1894-1987	Military-Politici	175	450	825	800	Nazi WW II. Second to Hitler. Suicide in Spandau
Hess, Victor F.		Science	20	30	55	25	Nobel Physics
Hess, Walter R.		Science	20	30	50	25	Nobel Medicine
Hesse, Hermann	1877-1962	Author	95	242	430	400	Ger. Author, Artist, Poet. Nobel Prize
Hesseman, Howard		Entertainment	5	6	15	20	Actor. 'WKRP-Cincinnati'
Hesse-Nassau, Adolph von		Royalty	100	300			1st Duke of Luxembourg
Hester, Brig. Gen. Hugh B.	1895-1983	Military	30				World War II U.S. general
Hester, Maj. Gen. John H.	1886-1976	Military	30				World War II U.S. general
Heston, Charlton		Entertainment	12			30	Major Star. AA. SP As 'Moses' 150
Heth, Henry (WD)		Civil War	300	1172	3820		CSA Gen. Battle of Gettysburg. LS 3000
Heth, Henry	1825-1899	Civil War	158	475	812		CSA General
Heuss, Theodor	1884-1963	Head of State	45			95	First Pres. Of German Fed. Republic. 1949-59
Hewer, Maj. Gen. Reginald K.	1892-1970	Military	28				World War II British general
Hewes, Joseph	1730-1780	Revolutionary War	2500	7250	8500		Signer Decl. of Indepen.
Hewes,Joseph & John Penn		Revolutionary War		25000			Signers Decl. of Indepen.
Hewett, Charlston		Entertainment	4			10	
Hewish, Anthony		Science	20	40	85	30	Nobel Physics. Pulsars
Hewitt, Abram S.	1822-1903	Business	30	60	82		Iron Manufacturer, 1st Open Hearth Furnace
Hewitt, Gerald		Author	8			12	church 'troubleshooter'
Hewitt, H.K.	1887-1972	Military	20	50	85		Am. Adm'l WW II. Landings at N. Afr., Sicily, S.Fr
Hewitt, Jennifer Love		Entertainment	20			44	Actress
Hewlett, William R.		Business	25	70	145	35	Hewlett-Packard
Hexum, Jon-Erik		Entertainment	60			125	Actor
Heyde, John Leslie von der	1896-1974	Military	35				World War II British general
Heydeman, Maj. Gen. Cecil A.	1887-1967	Military	25				World War II British general
Heydrich, Reinhard	1904-1942	Military	200	953	1550	1000	Specialist in Nazi Terror. Assassinated
Heydt, Louis Jean		Entertainment	35			80	
Heyerdahl, Thor		Explorer	30	50	95	35	Norw. Ethnologist, Adventurer. 'Kon Tiki'
Heyman, Edward 'Eddie'		Author	5	10	25	10	
Heyman, Edward		Entertainment	4	5	6	10	
Heyrovsky, Jaroslav	1890-1967	Science				300	Czech. Nobel Chemistry 1959
Heyse, Paul	1830-1914	Author	45	135	300		Ger. Poet, Novelist, Nobel Literature
Heyward, Dorothy		Author	55	325			Co-writer of 'Porgy'. Signed Porgy contract 4500
Heyward, DuBose	1885-1940	Author	120	400			'Porgy & Bess'....LS/Cont. 2,250
Heyward, Thomas Jr.	1746-1809	Revolutionary War	300	818	1200		Signer Decl. of Indepen.
Heywood, Anne		Entertainment	10			20	Br. Actress
Heywood, Eddie		Entertainment	35			100	Big Band Leader-Piano
Heywood, Maj. Gen. Thos Geo. G.	1886-1943	Military	25				World War II British general
Hiaasen, Carl		Author	10			15	also columnist & motivational speaker
Hibbert, Maj. Gen. Hugh B.	1893-1988	Military	25				World War II British general

NAME	DATE	CATEGORY	SIG	LS/DS	ALS	SP	COMMENTS
Hibbs, Maj. Gen. Louis E.	1893-1970	Military	30				World War II U.S. general
Hichens, Robert S.		Author	15	40	150		Br. Novelist.'Garden of Allah'
Hickel, Walter J.		Cabinet	10	15	30	15	Governor Alaska, Sec'y Interior
Hickenlooper, Andrew		Civil War	30	55	80		Union Gen., Military Engineer
Hickenlooper, Bourke B.	1896-1971	Senate	10	5		20	Governor, Senator IA
Hickes, Maj. Gen. Lancelot Daryl	1884-1965	Military	25				World War II British general
Hickey, Brig. Gen. Daniel W. Jr.	1895-1980	Military	30				World War II U.S. general
Hickey, Lt. Gen. Doyle O.	1891-1961	Military	30				World War II U.S. general
Hickey, Lt. Gen. Thomas F.	1898-1983	Military	30				World War II U.S. general
Hickman, Darryl		Entertainment	10			20	Actor. Child-Juvenile-Adult
Hickman, Dwayne		Entertainment	5			15	Actor. Juvenile-Adult
Hickman, Maj. Gen. Henry T. D.	1880-1960	Military	25				World War II British general
Hickman, Ron		Inventor	20	50			Black & Decker. Workmate
Hickok, James Butler 'Wild Bill'	1837-1876	History			150000		rare
Hickox, Anthony		Celebrity	10			15	film industry
Hicks, Brig. Philip Hugh Whitby	1895-1967	Military	25				World War II British general
Hicks, Catherine		Entertainment	8		20	20	Actress
Hicks, Frank		Author	8			12	World II naval history
Hicks, Frederick Cocks		Senate/Congress	10	15			MOC NY
Hidalgo, Miguel y Costilla		Clergy	1525				Mexican Revolutionary & Priest
Hieb, Richard		Astronaut	5			15	
Hieronymi, Ruth		Political	10			15	Member European Parliament
Higgins, Andrew Jackson		Business	25		50		Inventor & Bldr. WW II Higgins Landing Boat
Higgins, Charles		Science	15	35			
Higgins, Edward	1821-1875	Civil War	125	212	281		Confederate general
Higgins, John Michael		Entertainment	15			25	Actor
Higginson, Henry L.		Business	10	20	35		
Higginson, Thos. W.	1823-1911	Civil War-Clergy	52	71	120	150	Antislavery Writer, Military CW
High Eagle		Old West				1650	Sioux Indian. Survived Battle of Little Big Horn
Highwaymen		Entertainment				395	Nelson, Jennings, Jennings, Cash, Kristofferson
Higuchi, Lt. Gen. Kiichiro	1888-1970	Military	25				World War II Japanese general
Hilary Jones, Dr		Celebrity	10			15	health and fitness expert
Hildebrand, Samuel		Civil War		2750			Quantrill Raider-Murderer. The Missouri Bushwacker
Hildegarde		Entertainment	5	6	18	15	Singer, Pianist, Entertainer
Hill, Ambrose P. (WD)	1825-1865	Civil War	3500	8500	12488		CSA Gen. KIA 1865
Hill, Ambrose Powell	1825-1865	Civil War	2500	5945		0	CSA General KIA
Hill, Annie		Entertainment	5	8	15	10	
Hill, Archibald V.		Science	25	45		35	Nobel Medicine 1922
Hill, Arthur		Entertainment	5	6	15	15	Actor
Hill, Baron P. H		Congress	10			15	Member U.S. Congress
Hill, Benjamin H.	1823-1882	Civil War-Senate	48	90	140	250	Signed CSA Constitution & GA Secession
Hill, Benjamin J.	1825-1880	Civil War	115	260	400		CSA Gen. Sig/Rank 175
Hill, Benny		Entertainment	20			30	Br. Comedian
Hill, Brig. Gen. Francis	1909-1973	Military	30				World War II U.S. general
Hill, Brig. Gen. Milton A.	1892-1976	Military	30				World War II U.S. general

NAME	DATE	CATEGORY	SIG	LS/DS	ALS	SP	COMMENTS
Hill, Dana		Entertainment	5	8	15	15	
Hill, Daniel H. (WD)	1821-1889	Civil War	600		1996		CSA General
Hill, Daniel H.	1821-1889	Civil War	359	545	655		CSA General
Hill, David B.		Senate	10	15			Governor NY, Senator
Hill, David Lee 'Tex'		Aviation	15	30	45	35	ACE, WW II, Flying Tigers
Hill, Dule		Entertainment	10			30	The West Wing
Hill, Edwin C.		Commentator	5	15		15	Vintage Radio News-Commentator
Hill, Faith		Entertainment	10			54	C & W Singer
Hill, Frank*		Cartoonist	10			50	
Hill, George Roy		Entertainment	5			35	AA director
Hill, George Washington		Business	80	220			American Tobacco Co.,Pres.
Hill, Grace Livingston		Author	25	40	75		Am. Novelist
Hill, Harry		Celebrity	10			15	comedian
Hill, Isaac	1789-1851	Senate/Congress	20	35	65		Governor, Senator NY
Hill, James J.	1838-1916	Business	650	2500	3000	950	Railrd. Exec., Financier. Created Great Norther RR
Hill, John F.		Governor	5	15			Governor ME
Hill, Jonathan A.	1831-1905	Civil War	25	35			Union Gen.
Hill, Katy		Celebrity	10			15	children's presenter
Hill, Lauryn		Entertainment	4			22	Singer. Grammy Winner
Hill, Maj. Gen. Leslie Rowley	1884-1974	Military	25				World War II British general
Hill, Maj. Gen. Sir Basil Alexander	1880-1960	Military	25				World War II British general
Hill, Maj. Gen. Walter Pitts Hendy	1877-1942	Military	25				World War II British general
Hill, Mel		Celebrity	10			15	'Big Brother'
Hill, Napoleon		Author	75	300			'Think & Grow Rich'. How to Succeed Books
Hill, Octavia		Celebrity			100		Philantropist
Hill, Rowland	1744-1833	Clergy	50	75	175		Eng. Evangelist. Ordained. Denied Priestly Orders
Hill, Rowland, 1st Viscount	1772-1842	Military	35	80	129		Cmdr. in Chief. England. General
Hill, Rowland, Sir	1795-1879	Postal Reformer	145	340	785		Originator of Penny Postage Stamp. England
Hill, Sam		Merchant		175	250		Storekeeper. 1st Postmaster New Salem
Hill, Teresa		Entertainment	5			40	Actress. 'Models, Inc.'
Hill, Thomas	1818-1891	Clergy-Educator	15	20	50		Pres. Harvard, Antioch.
Hill, Tiny		Entertainment	5	8	15	15	
Hill, Walter		Entertainment	5			20	Film Director
Hill, William		Entertainment	4	6	8	10	
Hill, Wm. J. Billy		Composer	30				'Last Roundup',' Wagon Wheels'. AMusQS 175
Hillary, Edmund, Sir	1919-	Mountaineer	59	155	195	150	1st To Climb Mount Everest
Hilldring, Maj. Gen. John H.	1895-1974	Military	30				World War II U.S. general
Hillegas, Michael	1729-1804	Revolutionary War	225	645			1st U.S. Treasurer 1777. Sugar Refiner, Iron Mfg.
Hillegess, C.K. Cliff		Author	10			25	'Cliff's Notes' Study Helps
Hiller, Arthur		Entertainment	5			15	Film Director
Hiller, Ferdinand	1811-1885	Composer	40	85	125		Ger. Conductor, Pianist, Composer Operas etc.
Hiller, Frank, Jr.		Aviation	75	150	330	160	
Hiller, Wendy, Dame	1912-	Entertainment	20		35	30	Br. Actress. AA
Hillerman, John		Entertainment	9	15	20	25	Actor
Hilles, Charles D.		Political	8	25			Chairman G.O.P. 1924

NAME	DATE	CATEGORY	SIG	LS/DS	ALS	SP	COMMENTS
Hillhouse, William	1728-1816	Politician			92		
Hilliard, Harriet		Entertainment	20			35	Band Singer& Wife of Ozzie Nelson
Hilliard, Henry W.	1808-1892	Civil War	39	80	110		Confederate Commissioner to TN
Hilliard, Robert		Entertainment	20			40	
Hillig, Otto		Aviation	40	85	150	115	
Hillis, Marjorie		Author	5	10	15		
Hillman, Brig. Gen. Charles C.	1887-1979	Military	30				World War II U.S. general
Hillman, Chris		Entertainment	8			38	'Byrds' Co-Founder
Hills, Carla A.		Cabinet	7	20	35	20	Sec'y HUD
Hills, Carla		Celebrity	10			15	political celebrity
Hilmers, David C.		Astronaut	7			25	
Hilpert, Colonel-General Carl	1888-1948	Military	25				World War II German general
Hilton, Barron		Business	10	15	25	20	Hilton Hotel Chain
Hilton, Conrad	1887-1979	Business	60	132	190	168	Fndr. Hilton Hotel Dynasty
Hilton, James, Sir		Author	35	75	150	125	'Lost Horizon', signed book 150-450
Hilton, Maj. Gen. Richard	1894-1978	Military	25				World War II British general
Himmler, Heinrich	1900-1945	Military	275	921	1500	712	Nazi Head of the Gestapo
Hinchey, Maurice D. H		Congress	10			15	Member U.S. Congress
Hinchingbrooke, Alex		Celebrity	10	20	45	15	
Hinckley, John, Jr.		Assassin	35	150	200		Attempt on Pres. Reagan's Life
Hincks, Edward W.	1830-1894	Civil War	72	262			Union General
Hind, Maj. Gen. Neville Godfray	1892-1973	Military	25				World War II British general
Hinde, Maj. Gen. Sir Wm. Robt. N.	1900-1981	Military	25				World War II British general
Hindemith, Paul	1895-1963	Composer	110	295	388	475	Ger. Violinist,Teacher,Critic.SP 350. AMQS 1200
Hindenburg, Paul von	1847-1934	Head of State	152	380	400	575	2nd Pres. Weimar Rep. of Ger. Field Marshal
Hindman, Thomas C. (WD)	1828-1868	Civil War	325	1028	1200		CSA General
Hindman, Thomas C.	1828-1868	Civil War	338		548		CSA Gen.
Hinds, Brig. Gen. John H.	1898-1993	Military	30				World War II U.S. general
Hinds, Brig. Gen. Sidney R.	1900-1991	Military	30				World War II U.S. general
Hines, Brig. Gen. Charles	1888-1966	Military	30				World War II U.S. general
Hines, Cheryl		Entertainment	10	15	20	40	
Hines, Duncan	1880-1959	Business	65	200		160	Food Critic. Duncan Hines Cake-Cookie Mix etc.
Hines, Earl K. 'Fatha'		Entertainment	78	210		300	Pianist, Composer, Bandleader
Hines, Frazer		Entertainment	10			20	Actor
Hines, Gregory		Entertainment	10	10	25	43	Dancer-Actor. Stage, TV, Films
Hines, Herm		Entertainment	10			25	Jazz Sax
Hines, Jerome		Entertainment	18			30	Opera, Concert. Basso
Hines, John E.		Clergy	10	15	15		
Hines, Mimi		Entertainment	5			10	Singer, Comedienne
Hingle, Pat		Entertainment	5	6	15	15	Actor. Character
Hinks, Edward W.		Civil War	53		55		CSA General
Hinman, Brig. Gen. Dale D.	1891-1949	Military	30				World War II U.S. general
Hinojosa, Rubén H		Congress	10			15	Member U.S. Congress
Hinshelwood, Cyril Norman, Sir	1897-1967	Science	20	45		35	Nobel Chemistry 1956
Hinton, Walter		Aviation	35	65	103	80	Pilot of NC-4. MOH

NAME	DATE	CATEGORY	SIG	LS/DS	ALS	SP	COMMENTS
Hippel, Hans Joachim von		Aviation	10			35	WW I & II Fighter Pilot. Stunt Flyer
Hirohito		Head of State	1500	6900		8108	Japan
Hirsch, Judd		Entertainment	10	15	20	25	Versatile Actor-Comedian. 'Taxi'
Hirschfeld, Al*		Caricaturist	50		142	250	Artist
Hirshfield, Harry*		Cartoonist	15			125	Abie The Agent
Hirshhorn, Joseph H.	1899-1981	Financier		150	225		Art Collector. Donated 4000 works of art
Hirt, Al		Entertainment	10			25	Jazz Trumpet. Sextet signed 110
Hislop, Ian		Celebrity	10			15	comedian
Hiss, Alger	1904-	Diplomat	40	65	190		Figure in Sensational U.S. Spy Case
Hitchcock, Alfred	1899-1980	Entertainment	232	381	525	692	Self-Caricature S 750-875-1250, Chk. 795
Hitchcock, Ethan Allen (WD)	1798-1870	Civil War	68	150	200		Union Gen., Also Author
Hitchcock, Ethan Allen	1798-1870	Civil War	54	105	148		Union general
Hitchcock, Frank H.		Cabinet	15	30	35	30	Sec'y Interior 1898
Hitchcock, Gilbert M.	1859-1934	Congress	10	20		15	Governor NE
Hitchcock, Michael		Entertainment	10			20	
Hitchcock, Raymond		Entertainment	20			35	
Hitchcock, Thomas	1900-1944	Aviation	120			200	Lafayette Escadrille. Greatest US Polo Player
Hitchings, George, Dr.		Science	20	30	70	35	Nobel Medicine
Hite, June		Research	5	15	25		Hite Research
Hite, Les		Entertainment	75			275	Saxophone. 'Hold Tight'
Hitler, A. & Goering, H.		Head of State		3200			
Hitler, Adolf	1889-1945	Head of State	1155	2375	17000	3524	DS relieving Rommel 35,000
Hitler, Adolph and Hess, Rudolf					1495		
Hittorff, Jacques	1792-1867	Architect	10	25	40		Fr. St. Vincent de Paul Church
Hitz, John		Celebrity	10	35	90		
Hitzfeld, Gen. of Infantry Otto M.	1898-1980	Military	25				World War II German general
Hitzfeld, Otto Maximilian		Military	20			50	Ger. Infantry General
Hix, John*		Cartoonist	15	50		60	Author 'Strange As It Seems'
Ho Chi Minh		Head of State	600	1225	2000	2600	Vietnam
Ho"bach, Gen. of Inf. Friedrich	1894-1980	Military	25				World War II German general
Ho, Don		Entertainment	5	6	10	12	Singer
Hoadley, Walter E.		Celebrity	10			15	financial expert
Hoag, R. C., Major		Astronaut	5			18	
Hoagland, Everett		Entertainment	20			55	Jazz Clarinetist. Bandleader
Hoar, Ebenezer R.	1816-1895	Cabinet	25		35		U.S. Att'y Gen 1869, Grant
Hoar, George F.	1826-1904	Senate	18	20	30		MOC, Senator MA 1877
Hoare, Maj. Gen. Lionel Lennard	1871-1955	Military	25				World War II British general
Hoban, James	1762-	Rev War	255	675			Architect White House, Wash.D.C
Hobart, Brig. James Wilfred L. S.	1890-1970	Military	25				World War II British general
Hobart, Garret A.	1844-1899	Vice President	60	110	210	200	VP under McKinley. Banker, Lawyer. Died in Office
Hobart, John Sloss	1738-1805	Senate/Congress	25	40	70		Delegate & Senator NY
Hobart, Maj. Gen. Sir Percy C. S.	1885-1957	Military	28				World War II British general
Hobart, Rose		Entertainment	5			20	Actress
Hobbes, Halliwell	1877-1962	Entertainment	25			45	Vint. Brit. Character Actor
Hobbs, Maj. Gen. Leland S.	1892-1966	Military	40				World War II U.S. general

NAME	DATE	CATEGORY	SIG	LS/DS	ALS	SP	COMMENTS
Hobby, Oveta Culp		Cabinet	15	25	40	30	1st Sec'y HEW
Hobson, Brig. Gen. William H.	1888-1960	Military	30				World War II U.S. general
Hobson, David L. H		Congress	10			15	Member U.S. Congress
Hobson, Edward Henry	1825-1901	Civil War	43	100			Union general
Hobson, Richmond P.		Military	88	120	160	200	Adm.CMH. Blew up USS Merrimac
Hobson, Valerie		Entertainment	25			60	Br. Vintage Film Star
Hoch, Danny		Entertainment	10			20	actor
Hoche, Louis-Lazare	1768-1797	Fr. Revolution	205	515			Rose From Corporal to General
Hock, Robt C.		Astronaut	5			15	Skylab
Hockney, David		Artist	58	65	75	95	
Hodes, Art		Entertainment	10			25	Pianist-Bandleader
Hodes, General Henry I.	1899-1962	Military	30				World War II U.S. general
Hodge, Al		Entertainment	25			200	
Hodge, General John R.	1893-1963	Military	30				World War II U.S. general
Hodge, George Baird	1828-1892	Civil War	110	495			Confederate general
Hodge, Patricia		Entertainment	10			20	Actress
Hodgen, Maj. Gen. Gordon West	1894-1968	Military	25				World War II British general
Hodges, Courtney	1887-1966	Military	39	70		75	Gen. WW II. Cmmdr. 10th, 3rd, & 1st Armies
Hodges, George H.		Governor	12		15		Kansas 1913-15
Hodgkin, Dorothy C.		Science	25		35		Nobel Chemistry
Hodgson, John		Clergy	20	25	35		
Hodiak, John	1914-1955	Entertainment	20	25	45	45	Radio Actor until WW II. Leading Roles
Hoe, Richard M.	1812-1886	Industrialist	90	310	532		Invented Rotary Press
Hoe, Robert	1839-1909	Business	30	55	95		Improved Hoe Rotary & Art Press
Hoeffel, Joseph M. H		Congress	10			15	Member U.S. Congress
Hoegh, Leo A.		Governor	5			12	Governor IA
Hoekstra, Peter H		Congress	10			15	Member U.S. Congress
Hoepner, Colonel-General Erich	1886-1944	Military	25				World War II German general
Hoest, Bill*		Cartoonist	10		35	40	'The Lockhorns'
Hoey, Clyde R.		MOC-Sen.-Gov.	8	20		15	MOC, Senator, Governor NC
Hoey, Dennis	1893-1960	Entertainment	75			200	Br. Actor. Character Roles in Br. Films
Hofer, Andreas		Military		3000			Tyrolean Patriot,executed
Hoff, Magdalene		Political	10			15	Member European Parliament
Hoff, Philip H.		Governor	5	15			Governor VT
Hoffa, James R.		Labor Leader	216	350		350	Teamsters Union (disappeared)
Hoffa, Portland		Entertainment	20				Comedienne, Mrs. Fred Allen. Major Radio Star
Hoffer, Eric		Celebrity	5	10	25	15	Self Made Philosopher
Hoffgen, Marga		Entertainment	10			35	
Hoffman, Abbie	1942-1994	Activist	90	175		125	Shortlived Author of Psychedelic 60's
Hoffman, Dustin		Entertainment	20	25	35	59	Oscar winner.'The Graduate' Orig. Soundtrk S 95
Hoffman, Felicity		Entertainment	5			32	Actress. 'Sports Night'
Hoffman, Harold Giles		Governor	12	30			Governor NJ
Hoffman, Jeffrey A.		Astronaut	6			30	
Hoffman, John Thompson		Governor	10	20	35		Governor NY 1868
Hoffman, Julius		Judge	50			295	Controversial. Prisided over 'Chicago 7'

NAME	DATE	CATEGORY	SIG	LS/DS	ALS	SP	COMMENTS
Hoffman, Kurt-Caesar		Military	25			65	
Hoffman, Maud		Entertainment	3	5		10	
Hoffman, Paul G.	1891-1974	Business	10	20	35	20	Auto Mfg.-Studebaker Cars. WW II Dir. Marshal Plan
Hoffmann, Brig. Gen. Hugh F.T.	1896-1951	Military	30				World War II U.S. general
Hoffmann, Oswald C.J.		Clergy	10	20	25		
Hoffmann, Peter		Entertainment	15			55	Opera
Hoffmann, Roald, Dr.		Science	20	30	45	25	Nobel Chemistry
Hoffmeister, Maj. Gen. Bertram M.	1907-1999	Military	20				World War II Canadian general
Hofmann, Albert		Science	75			565	Swiss Chemist. Identified Psychedelic LSD Effects
Hofmann, Josef	1876-1957	Entertainment	48	125	155	160	Pianist, Composer. AmusQS 75-150-200
Hofstadter, Robert		Science	20	30	45	25	Nobel Physics
Hogan, Hulk		Entertainment	15			35	Wrestler
Hogan, Paul		Entertainment	10	15	25	30	Australian Actor. 'Dundee'
Hogan's Heroes		Entertainment				750	signed cast picture
Hogarth, Burne*		Cartoonist	25			175	Tarzan-2nd Artist
Hogarth, Wm.	1697-1764	Artist	995	1665	3500		Br. Painter-Engraver.'The Rakes Progress'
Hoge, General William M.	1894-1979	Military	30				World War II U.S. general
Hogeback, Hermann		Aviation	10			40	Ger. Bomber Pilot. RK
Hogendorp, Katharine Harris van		Author	8			12	Red Cross, India
Hogg, Joseph Lewis (1806-62)	1806-1862	Civil War	300	381			Confederate general
Hogg, Maj. Gen. Doug. McArthur	1888-1965	Military	25				World War II British general
Hogshaw, Brigadier John Harold	1896-1968	Military	25				World War II British general
Hoiris, Holger		Aviation	40	85	155	95	
Hoke, Robert Frederick	1837-1912	Civil War	105		350		CSA Gen. ALS '62 625, Sig/Rank 180
Hokinson, Helen*		Cartoonist	20			100	Mag. Cartoonist-'The Ladies'
Holbrook, Brig. Gen. Willard A. Jr.	1898-1988	Military	30				World War II U.S. general
Holbrook, Hal		Entertainment	10	15	20	33	Actor. Very Versatile Film-TV Roles. 'Mark Twain'
Holbrooke, Richard C.		Political				20	Diplomat. 1995 Dayton Agreement(Bosnia)
Holcombe, Brig. Gen. William H.	1891-1980	Military	30				World War II U.S. general
Holcombe, David		Author	8			12	regional and eductional
Holden, Fay		Entertainment	20			50	Actress. Many 'Mother' Roles. 'Andy Hardy' Series
Holden, Joyce		Entertainment	10			25	Singer-Dancer/Donald O'Connor
Holden, Maj. Gen. William Corson	1893-1955	Military	25				World War II British general
Holden, Tim H		Congress	10			15	Member U.S. Congress
Holden, William	1918-1981	Entertainment	70	110		247	Actor. Oscar Winner for 'Stalag 17'
Holdrigde, Brig. Gen. Herbert C.	1892-1974	Military	30				World War II U.S. general
Hole, Jonathan		Entertainment	4	5	6	8	
Holiday, Billie	1915-1959	Entertainment	318	730		1680	Legendary Jazz-Blues Singer
Holladay, Ben	1819-1887	Business	135	350	925		Indian Trade, Army Contracts,RR-Esprss.Financier
Holland, Brig. Gen. Thomas L.	1879-1944	Military	30				World War II U.S. general
Holland, Clive		Celebrity	10			15	television presenter
Holland, Dexter		Entertainment	7			30	Music. Lead Singer 'Offspring'
Holland, Edmund M.		Entertainment	15			45	Vintage Stage Actor
Holland, John Philip		Inventor	70	160	345		1st Sub/Internal Combustion Eng
Holland, Jools		Music	10			15	performing musical artist

NAME	DATE	CATEGORY	SIG	LS/DS	ALS	SP	COMMENTS
Holland, Josiah Gilbert	1819-1881	Author	15	30	40		AKA Timothy Titcomb.Co-founder Scribner's
Holland, Maj. Gen. John Chas. F.	1897-1965	Military	25				World War II British general
Holland, Spessard L.	1892-1971	Congress	10	20			Governor, Senator FL
Hollar, Brig. Gen. Gordon C.	1887-1963	Military	30				World War II U.S. general
Hollen, Andrea Lee		Military	10	20	35	15	
Hollen, Chris Van H		Congress	10			15	Member U.S. Congress
Holley, Marietta	1836-1926	Author	10	15	35		Am. Humorist
Holley, Robert, Dr.		Science	15	20	35	20	Nobel Chemistry
Holliday, Frederick W.M.	1828-1899	Civil War	45	50	70		CSA Officer, Congress, Gov. VA Sig/Rank 75
Holliday, Judy	1922-1965	Entertainment	125			250	Academy Award Winning Actress 'Born Yesterday'
Holliday, Polly		Entertainment	10	12	15	20	Actress. Wise-Cracking 'Flo' in 'Alice'
Hollidt, Colonel-General Karl A.	1891-1985	Military	25				World War II German general
Holliman, Earl		Entertainment	5	8	10	18	Actor. Supporting Player & Co-Star From 50's
Holliman, John		Journalist	5			15	TV News Commentator
Hollings, Ernest 'Fritz'		Senate	10			15	Senator SC
Hollins, Geo. Nichols	1799-1878	Civil War	275	465			Commodore CSA Navy.Sig/Rank 375.War Dte DS 600
Hollis, General Sir Leslie C.	1897-1963	Military	25				World War II British general
Holloway, Stanley	1890-1982	Entertainment	95			110	Br. Character Actor. Oscar Nominee 'My Fair Lady'
Holloway, Sterling	1905-	Entertainment	25			50	Played Country Bumkins, Dim Wits. Disney Voices.
Hollowell, George		Aviation	12	25	38	35	ACE, WW II, Marine Ace
Holly, Brig. Gen. Joseph A.	1896-1987	Military	30				World War II U.S. general
Holly, Buddy	1936-1959	Music	723	871	2625	2520	Rock Singer-Songwriter. Sigs Holly & Crickets 750
Holly, Lauren		Entertainment	12			42	Actress
Hollywood Wives (Cast of)		Entertainment				65	Signed by 6
Holm, Celeste		Entertainment	5	6	15	28	Broadway Singer-Dancer. Film Actress. AA Winner
Holm, Eleanor		Entertainment	10			30	
Holman, Bill		Cartoonist		45			'Smokey Stover'
Holman, Libby		Entertainment	10	35		82	Vintage Torch Singer.TLS/Cont.150
Holman, Maj. Gen. Jonathan L.	1897-1975	Military	30				World War II U.S. general
Holman, William Steele		Senate/Congress	12	20	30		MOC IN 1859
Holmes, Augusta	1847-1903	Composer	10		85		Ir./Fr. Conventional Fr. Romantic Music
Holmes, Brent		Author	8			12	'The Road Less Gravelled'
Holmes, Brig. Gen. Henry B. Jr.	1892-1976	Military	30				World War II U.S. general
Holmes, Brig. Gen. Julius C.	1899-1968	Military	30				World War II U.S. general
Holmes, Burton	1870-1958	Author	15	20	45	30	In 1894 Originated Travelogues
Holmes, Christopher		Astronaut	15	25		25	
Holmes, D. Brainerd		Celebrity	10			25	
Holmes, Herbie		Bandleader	12			20	
Holmes, John Haynes		Clergy	15	20	30		
Holmes, Katie		Entertainment	8			38	Actress. 'Dawson's Creek' SP 75
Holmes, Lt. Gen. Sir William Geo.	1892-1969	Military	25				World War II British general
Holmes, Maj. Gen. Sir Noel G.	1891-1982	Military	25				World War II British general
Holmes, Oliver W., Jr.	1841-1935	Supreme Court	173	408	975	882	Thirty Year Supreme Court Veteran
Holmes, Oliver W., Sr.	1809-1894	Author-Physician	87	155	375	483	Poet. HOF, ALS/Content 1,800. AQS 475
Holmes, Robert D.		Governor	5	15		10	Governor OR

NAME	DATE	CATEGORY	SIG	LS/DS	ALS	SP	COMMENTS
Holmes, Theophilus H.	1804-1880	Civil War	190	285			CSA Gen. ALS '62 1100, Sig/Rank 215
Holmquest, Donald L.		Astronaut	10	15		20	
Holshouser, James E.		Governor	5		20	15	Governor NC
Holst, Art		Celebrity	10			15	motivational speaker
Holst, Gustav	1874-1934	Composer	45	175	300		AMusQS 275-1035
Holstrom, E.W. 'Brick'		Military	15	35	70	25	
Holt, Jack		Entertainment	40	60	100	100	Actor. Tight-Lipped Hero of Many Silents & Talkies
Holt, Jennifer		Entertainment	5			10	Actress. Leading Lady To Several Western Heroes
Holt, Joseph (WD)		Civil War	85	265	405		Union Gen. Lincoln's Judge Advocate
Holt, Joseph	1807-1894	Cabinet-Civil War	53	180	194		Lincoln Judge Adv.
Holt, Rush D.		Congress	10			15	Member U.S. Congress
Holt, Tim	1918-1973	Entertainment	45			120	Child-Juvenile-Mature. 'Magnificent Ambersons'
Holt, Victoria		Author	5		15	12	
Holten, Samuel	1738-1816	Revolutionary War	85	195			Patriot, Statesman, Activist. Cont'l Congr.
Holton, Linwood		Governor	7			15	Governor VA
Holtzclaw, James Thadeus	1833-1893	Civil War	130	232			Confederate general
Holworthy, Maj. Gen. Alan W.W.	1897-1983	Military	25				World War II British general
Holyoake, Keith, Sir		Head of State	45	95	125	50	NZ Prime Minister, Gov. General NZ
Holzer, Helmut		Science	20			40	Ger. Rocket Pioneer/von Braun
Homer & Jethro		Country Music	35			130	Henry Haynes (Guitar), Ken Burns (Mandolin)
Homer, Louise		Entertainment	35			225	Opera. Am Mezzo. SPc 95
Homer, Maj. Gen. John L.	1888-1961	Military	30				World War II U.S. general
Homer, Winslow	1836-1910	Artist	330	480	1150		Remarkable Seascapes, Landscapes
Homesteaders, The		Country Music	25			50	
Homma, Masaharu		Military	75	205	340	180	Jap. Gen. Invasion of Philippines
Homolka, Oscar		Entertainment	25	30	50	55	Imposing Character Actor. Ideal Heavy; AA Nomination
Honda, Lt. Gen. Masaki	1889-1964	Military	25				World War II Japanese general
Honda, Michael M. H		Congress	10			15	Member U.S. Congress
Honda, Soichiro	1904-1994	Business					Founder Honda Motors. RARE. No Current Prices
Hone, Maj. Gen. Sir Herbert R.	1896-1992	Military	25				World War II British general
Honegger, Arthur	1892-1955	Composer	45	202	381	150	Eminent & Prolific. 'Les Six', AMusQS 575-675
Honeyball, Mary		Political	10			15	Member European Parliament
Honeycombe, Gordon		Celebrity	10			15	newsreader
Honeymooners, cast		Entertainment	338			602	Signed by all 4
Honeywood, Phillip		Military			368		18th Century British Ragoons
Honjo, General Shigeru Baron	1876-1945	Military	25				World War II Japanese general
Honma, Lt. Gen. Masaharu	1887-1946	Military	25				World War II Japanese general
Honnen, Brig. Gen. George	1897-1974	Military	30				World War II U.S. general
Hood, Alexander Sir	1758-1798	Military	55	135	245		Accompanied Capt. Cook
Hood, Arthur Wm.	1824-1901	Military	20		105		Admiral, 1st Baron Hood of Avalon
Hood, Catherine, Dr.		Celebrity	10			15	health and fitness expert
Hood, Darla	1931-1979	Entertainment	125	162		309	Child Actress'Our Gang' Series
Hood, John Bell	1831-1879	Civil War	1000	2250	3750	3000	CSA Gen. ALS '62 18,150, Sig/Rank 1575
Hood, Lt. Gen. Sir Alexander	1888-1980	Military	25				World War II British general
Hood, Samuel, Sir	1762-1814	Military	35	85	135		Br. Adm. with Lord Nelson

NAME	DATE	CATEGORY	SIG	LS/DS	ALS	SP	COMMENTS
Hood, Thomas (Elder)	1799-1845	Author	40	140	275		Br. Humorist, Poet
Hood, Thomas, 'Tom' (Younger)		Author	15	30	70		
Hooft, W.A. Vlsser't		Clergy	15	20	25	20	
Hook, James Clarke		Artist	25	40	85		Brit. Royal Academy
Hooker, John Lee		Entertainment	75			195	Jazz Musician. Blues Legend. Guitar S 2000
Hooker, Joseph (WD)		Civil War	270	615	1110		Union Gen. ALS 4500
Hooker, Joseph	1814-1879	Civil War	182	396	462		Union Gen. ALS/Content 4,500
Hooker, Richard		Author	35			60	creator of M*A*S*H
Hooks, Benjamin L.	1925-	NAACP	10	15	25	20	NAACP Exec. Director. Civil Rights Leader
Hooks, Kevin		Entertainment	10			20	Afr.-Am. Actor
Hooley, Darlene H		Congress	10			15	Member U.S. Congress
Hooper, William Henry		Congress	10	20	35	30	MOC UT 1859
Hooper, William	1742-1790	Revolutionary War	750	4508	8500		Signer Decl. of Indepen. ADS 3,000
Hoosier Hot Shots		Entertainment	40			65	G Ward,Hezzie,K Trietsle,F Kettering. C & W
Hooten, Ernest A.		Science	25	65	140		Am. Anthropologist.Harvard Prof
Hoover, Herbert & Entire Cabinet		President	250				
Hoover, Herbert (As Pres)		President	195	471	33095	502	Historic TLS/Content 7,500, Unique DS 4100
Hoover, Herbert	1874-1964	President	88	246	1623	379	Cont.TLS 1300-4950, 2,500. WH Card S 450
Hoover, J. Edgar	1895-1972	Criminologist	36	103	182	132	Director of FBI for 48 Years
Hoover, Lou Henry		First Lady	75	124	163	185	WH Card S 95-125-150
Hope, Bob		Entertainment	30	40	50	74	Comedian-Actor-Singer. Stage, Radio, TV, Films
Hopekirk, Helen		Author	15		25		
Hopf, Hans		Entertainment	25			65	Opera
Hopkins, Anthony		Entertainment	20			58	Br. Oscar Winner. 'Silence of the Lambs'
Hopkins, Antony		Entertainment	20		32	42	Composer & Broadcaster
Hopkins, Bo		Entertainment	8	9	10	20	Actor
Hopkins, Claude		Entertainment	30			60	Pianist-Bandleader-Composer
Hopkins, Esek	1718-1802	Military	180	1200			1st Cmdr-in-Chief Continental Navy
Hopkins, Frederick G., Sir		Science	45	120	200		Nobel Medicine 1929
Hopkins, Harry L.	1890-1946	Cabinet	26	88		40	Sec'y Commerce.Important Advisor-Aide to FDR
Hopkins, James H.	1832-1904	Congress	10		22		MOC. PA, Banker
Hopkins, Johns	1795-1873	Business	175	371	625		Financier, Philanthropist. ALS/Content 3575
Hopkins, Joseph A.	1915-1980	Military		125	200	750	Fabulous Career Re Mt. Suribachi Flag-ALS 1500
Hopkins, Juliet	1818-1890	Military		305			CSA nurse
Hopkins, Mark	1802-1887	Educator	50	195	275		Inspired Teacher, Lecturer
Hopkins, Mark	1813-1878	Business		18500			Rarest RR 'Big Four'. signed Stk. S 35000-65000
Hopkins, Miriam	1902-1972	Entertainment	32	40	70	90	Vintage Leading Lady. Ballet to Chorus Girl to Star
Hopkins, Samuel	1721-1803	Revolutionary War	90	280	375		Officer Cont'l Army. Theologian
Hopkins, Stephen	1707-1785	Revolutionary War	225	667	1350		Signer. Gov. RI. Important ALS 6500
Hopkinson, Francis	1737-1791	Revolutionary War	265	705	1348		Signer, Author, Composer. Designer Am. Flag
Hopkinson, Joseph	1770-1842	Judge-Author	90	200			MOC PA. 'Hail Columbia'
Hopper, Dennis	1936-	Entertainment	15			65	Actor
Hopper, DeWolfe	1858-1935	Entertainment	20	40	55	75	Actor. Recitations.ALS/Casey at the Bat quote 395
Hopper, Edward		Artist	275	1050	1610		American artist
Hopper, Hedda	1890-1966	Entertainment	15		35	35	Actress. Gossip Columnist. Famous for her Hats

NAME	DATE	CATEGORY	SIG	LS/DS	ALS	SP	COMMENTS
Hopping, Brig. Gen. Andrew D.	1894-1951	Military	30				World War II U.S. general
Hordern, Michael, Sir	1911-	Entertainment	10	20	20	30	Br. Character Actor
Horenstein, Jascha		Entertainment	60			375	Conductor
Horii, Lt. Gen. Tomitaro	1890-1942	Military	25				World War II Japanese general
Horina, Louise		Entertainment	15			45	Opera
Horkan, Maj. Gen. George A.	1894-1974	Military	30				World War II U.S. general
Hormel, Jay C.		Business	45	95		75	George A. Hormel & Co. Meat Packing. New Ambass.
Horn, Alfred A. 'Trader'		Explorer	70	200			Br. Expl. Ivory Coast. African Rubber Trader
Hornberger, H. Richard		Author	20	30	45	25	
Hornby, Maj. Gen. Alan Hugh	1894-1958	Military	25				World War II British general
Horne, L. Donald		Business	5			10	CEO Mennen Co.
Horne, Lena	1917-	Entertainment	12	25		38	Afro-Am Film Actress & Recording Star
Horne, Marilyn		Entertainment	15			35	Opera, Concert
Horner, H. Mansfield		Business	5			10	Aircraft Exec.
Horner, Henry		Governor	10			20	Governor IL
Hornung, Ernest Wm.	1866-1921	Author	50		175		Brother-in-law A.Conan Doyle. Created 'Raffles'
Horowitz, David		Celebrity	3	7	15	8	
Horowitz, Scott		Astronaut	5			19	
Horowitz, Vladimir	1903-1989	Entertainment	139	195		350	Rus-born Am. Piano Virtuoso
Horrocks, Gen. Sir Brian		Military	20	25	50	40	Cmdr. XIII Corps WW II
Horrocks, June		Entertainment	6			35	Actress
Horrocks, Lt. Gen. Sir Brian G.	1895-1985	Military	25				World War II British general
Horsford, Eben N.	1818-1874	Science	15	25	70		Am. Analytical Chemist
Horsley, John Calcott		Artist	40		65		Brit. Royal Academy
Horsley, Lee		Entertainment	10	8	15	25	Actor. 'Matt Houston'
Hortefeux, Brice		Political	10			15	Member European Parliament
Horthy, Miklos, Adm.	1868-1957	Head of State	76	190	485	250	Hungarian Admiral & Politician
Horton, Edw. Everett	1886-1970	Entertainment	30	25	45	55	Actor. Delightful Comedy & Character Leads
Horton, Edward A.		Clergy	15	20	25		
Horton, Peter		Entertainment	15	11	40	38	
Horton, Robert		Entertainment	5	6	8	15	Actor
Hoskins, Allen 'Farina'		Celebrity				368	'Our Gang'
Hoskins, Bob		Entertainment	10			25	Actor
Hosmer, Titus	1736-1780	Revolutionary War	40	95	192		Continental Congress. Judge
Hospital, Brig. Gen. Ralph	1891-1972	Military	30				World War II U.S. general
Hostettler, John N. H.		Congress	10			15	Member U.S. Congress
Hotblack, Maj. Gen. Frederick E.	1887-1979	Military	25				World War II British general
Hotchkiss, Benjamin J.		Inventor-CW			995		Union Arms Supplier
Hotchkiss, Charles T.	1832-1914	Civil War			85		Union Gen. Atlanta Campaign
Hoth, Colonel-General Hermann	1885-1971	Military	35			235	World War II German general
Hottelet, Richard C.		Celebrity	10			20	news correspondent
Houdini, Harry (E.Weiss)	1874-1926	Entertainment	958	1867	2250	3676	Am. Magician, Escape Artist
Hough, Lynn Harold		Clergy	15	20	35		
Houghton, Amo H		Congress	10			15	Member U.S. Congress
Houghton, Katharine		Entertainment	30			45	Actress. 'Guess Who's Coming to Dinner?'

NAME	DATE	CATEGORY	SIG	LS/DS	ALS	SP	COMMENTS
Houldsworth, Brig. Sir Henry W.	1896-1963	Military	25				World War II British general
Hounsfield, Godfrey		Science	20	30	45	25	Nobel Medicine
Hounsou, Djimon		Entertainment	10			20	actor
House, Edw. M. 'Colonel'		Diplomat	35	100	310	45	Confidant of Pres. Wilson
Houseman, John		Entertainment	20	30		40	Actor/Director. Stage & Film Writer.
Housman, Alfred Edward	1859-1936	Author	65	225	430		Br. Poet, Classical Scholar
Houssay, Bernando A., Dr.		Science	65	135	250	100	Nobel Medicine 1947. Activist
Houston, David	1938-	Country Music	5			10	Singer-Guitar. 50's, 60's, 70,s
Houston, George		Senate	35	85			Civil War Senator AL
Houston, Sam	1793-1863	Military	638	1415	2350		Pres. Rep. TX, ALS/Cont.6500-9700 FF 850
Houston, Temple		Lawyer-Outlaw	375		1667	750	Son of Sam Houston
Houston, V. S. K.		Senate/Congress	10	25	40		MOC HI 1927
Houston, Whitney	1963-	Entertainment	28			55	Singer-Actress
Houston, William C.	1746-1788	Revolutionary War	55		145		Continental Congress, etc.
Hovey, Alvin P.	1821-1891	Civil War	45	90	125		Union Gen., Gov. IN Sig/Rank 95. War Dte.DS 135
Hovey, Charles Edward	1827-1897	Civil War	45	85	120		Union general
Hovhaness, Alan		Composer	70		375		Noted for Orchestral Works
Hovis, Larry		Entertainment	15			35	Actor. 'Hogan's Heroes'
How, William Walsham, Bishop		Clergy	15	20	25		
Howard, Brig. Gen. Edwin B.	1901-1993	Military	30				World War II U.S. general
Howard, Curley (Jerome)	1906-1952	Entertainment	556	500	950	1000	Rarest of the 'Three Stooges'
Howard, Edward, Cardinal		Clergy	35	50	75		
Howard, Jacob Merritt	1805-1871	Congress	15	30			Civil War MOC & Sen. MI
Howard, James H.		Aviation	20	30	55	45	ACE, WW II, CMH; Flying Tiger
Howard, John	1913-	Entertainment	10	20	45	35	Actor. 'Bulldog Drummond'. Navy Hero WW II
Howard, Ken		Entertainment	5	8	15	15	Actor. Tall, Blonde Leading Man of 70's Films
Howard, Leslie	1890-1943	Entertainment	265	325		387	GWTW. Br. Secret Serv. WW II. SP Pc 200
Howard, Maj. Gen. Gordon Byron	1895-1976	Military	20				World War II Canadian general
Howard, Milford W.	1862-1937	Congress	5			10	MOC AL
Howard, Moe	1895-1975	Entertainment	200	290	625	450	Three Stooges Leader
Howard, Oliver Otis (WD)	1830-1909	Civil War	145	204	391	1102	Union Gen.
Howard, Oliver Otis	1830-1909	Civil War	61	153	232	600	Union Gen. MOH
Howard, Robert, Sir	1626-1698	Author	85	325	475		Br. Restoration Dramatist/Dryden
Howard, Ron		Entertainment	20	40	55	50	Child, Juvenile, Mature Actor and AA Director
Howard, Shemp	1891-1955	Entertainment	468	519	625	650	Three Stooges
Howard, Sidney	1891-1939	Author	50	175	338	75	Am. Playwright. Pulitzer. Screenwriter from 1929
Howard, Trevor		Entertainment	27			113	Brit. Actor. Stage, Films. AA Nominated
Howard, Wiley C.		Author	8			12	Civil War history
Howard, Willie		Entertainment	5	9	20	15	
Howe, Albion P. (WD)		Civil War	40	125	510		Union General
Howe, Elias	1819-1867	Science	200	400	3000		Invented Sewing Machine
Howe, James Wong	1988-1976	Entertainment	40			65	AA Winning Cinematographer. 'Hud', 'Rose Tattoo'
Howe, Julia Ward	1819-1910	Author	78	168	332	529	'Battle Hymn of the Republic' AMS(BHR)49,500
Howe, Louis McHenry		Political	5	20			Secretary to FDR
Howe, Richard, Earl	1726-1799	Revolutionary War	175	420	440		Br. Adm. Rev. War.LS/Cont.1500

NAME	DATE	CATEGORY	SIG	LS/DS	ALS	SP	COMMENTS
Howe, Robert		Revolutionary War			2415		Continental Commander
Howe, Samuel Gridley	1801-1876	Humanitarian-Mil.	15	35	95		Philanthropist, Doctor, Clergy, Reformer
Howe, Timothy O.	1816-1883	Cabinet	5		30		PMG(Arthur).US Sen. WI. Recommended to Lincoln
Howe, William, Sir	1729-1814	Revolutionary War	200	550	900		Cmdr-in-Chief Br. Forces in Am. Colonies
Howell, Brig. Gen. George P. Jr.	1901-1979	Military	30				World War II U.S. general
Howell, Brig. Gen. Reese M.	1889-1967	Military	30				World War II U.S. general
Howell, C. Thomas		Entertainment	5		25	20	
Howell, Joshua Blackwood	1806-1864	Civil War	60	250			Union general
Howell, Maj. Gen. Fred. Duke G.	1881-1967	Military	25				World War II British general
Howells, William Dean	1837-1920	Author	35	75	158	391	Novelist, Critic, Editor
Howes, Barbara		Author	5	10	20	10	
Howitt, Richard		Political	10			15	Member European Parliament
Howland, Beth		Entertainment	5	6	15	15	Actress. TV-'Beth on 'Alice'
Howley, William	1766-1848	Clergy	25	35	40		Archbishop Canterbury
Howlin, Olin		Entertainment	45			70	Actor. 'GWTW' Collectible
Hoxie, Al		Entertainment	45			60	Actor. Westerns. Silents & Few Talkies
Hoxie, Jack	1885-1965	Entertainment	150				Actor-Cowboy Star in Silents & Early Talkies
Hoyer, Steny H. H		Congress	10			15	Member U.S. Congress
Hoyle, Edmond	1671-1769	Author	145	675	785		Card Games. Established Rules
Hoyle, Maj. Gen. Rene E.D.	1883-1981	Military	30				World War II U.S. general
Hoyt, John W.		Governor	50	85			Gov. WY Terr.,1st Pres. U. WY
Hruska, Roman		Senate & Congress	5	15		10	MOC, Senator NE
HSnsch, Klaus		Political	10			15	Member European Parliament
Huban, Maj. Gen. John Patrick	1891-1957	Military	25				World War II British general
Hubbard, Chester D.	1814-1891	Congress	10	15	30		MOC WV
Hubbard, Elbert	1856-1915	Author	50	195	275	118	Roycrofters. 'Message to Garcia'
Hubbard, Gardiner G.	1822-1897	Celebrity	30	55	170		Fndr.& 1st Pres. Nat'l Geographic Society
Hubbard, L. Ron	1911-1986	Author	200	1067			Religious Activist, Scientology, Dianetics
Hubbard, Richard B.		Governor		150			Gov. TX 1876-79
Hubbard, Thomas H.	1838-1915	Civil War	25	40			Union Gen. 30th ME
Hubble, Edwin P.	1889-1953	Science	20	80		65	Am. Astronomer.'Hubble Telescope' Named For Him
Hube, Colonel-General Hans V.	1890-1944	Military	25				World War II German general
Hubel, David H., Dr.		Science	20	30	45	25	Nobel Medicine
Huber, Oscar, Fr.		Celebrity	20		30		
Hubert, Lt. Gen. Louis-Eugène	1880-1966	Military	20				World War II French general
Hubley, Adam		Revolutionary War	75	300			Officer Cont. Army. Politician
Hubner, Herbert		Entertainment	25			75	Vintage German opera star
Huddleston, George		Senate/Congress	10	15		15	MOC AL 1915-1937
Hudghton, Ian Stewart		Political	10			15	Member European Parliament
Hudleston, Maj. Gen. Sir Hubert J.	1880-1950	Military	25				World War II British general
Hudson, Charles	1795-1881	Congress	10				MOC MA, Author Religious Textbooks
Hudson, George	1800-1871	Financier	20	50	175		Controlled 1,000 Miles Railrd. 'Railway King'
Hudson, Kate		Entertainment				50	
Hudson, Maj. Gen. Charles Edw.	1892-1959	Military	25				World War II British general
Hudson, Rochelle	1914-1972	Entertainment	25	30	50	46	Actress.Versatile Leading Lady of 30's Films.

NAME	DATE	CATEGORY	SIG	LS/DS	ALS	SP	COMMENTS
Hudson, Rock	1925-1985	Entertainment	71	108	118	178	Actor
Hudson, W.H.	1841-1922	Naturalist-Author		135	495		'Green Mansions'
Hudson, William Henry		Celebrity		120			Educator
Huebner, Maj. Gen. Clarence R.	1888-1972	Military	30				World War II U.S. general
Huemer, Dick*		Cartoonist	15			100	Disney Artist
Hueper, Brig. Gen. Remi P.	1886-1964	Military	30				World War II U.S. general
Huerta, Victoriano	1854-1916	Revolutionary	75	250	625	250	Mex. General, Politician. Provincial Pres. Exiled
Huffington, Arianna		Celebrity	10			15	political celebrity
Hufstedler, Shirley		Cabinet	5	10	15	15	Sec'y Education
Huger, Benjamin (WD)		Civil War	190	750			CSA Gen.
Huger, Benjamin	1805-1877	Civil War	100	260	399		CSA General
Huger, Isaac	1743-1797	Revolutionary War	110	240	825		General Continental Army
Huggins, Charles, Dr.		Science	25			35	Nobel Medicine
Huggins, Roy	1914-1996	Entertainment	20			30	TV Producer-Writer. 'Fugitive'
Huggins, William, Sir	1824-1910	Science	35	100	225	150	Br. Astron. Stellar Spectroscope
Hughes, Carol		Entertainment	12				Actress
Hughes, Charles E.	1862-1948	Supreme Court	42	122		192	Chief Justice, Sec'y of State. TLS/Content 750
Hughes, Coe D.		Author	8			12	regional history
Hughes, Edwin H., Bishop		Clergy	20	25	40	35	
Hughes, Harold E.	1922-	Congress	5			20	Senator IA
Hughes, Holly		Entertainment	10			20	actress
Hughes, Howard	1905-1976	Business	1500	2706	6125	2625	Aircraft, Oil Tools. RKO Films. Flight Cov S.2900
Hughes, Hugh Price		Clergy	15	20	25	20	
Hughes, John	1797-1864	Clergy	25		248		1st Archbishop NY. Laid Cornerstone St. Pat's
Hughes, Langston	1902-1967	Author	178	339	895	575	Afro-Am. Poet, Short Story Writer
Hughes, Maj. Gen. Everett S.	1885-1957	Military	30				World War II U.S. general
Hughes, Maj. Gen. Henry B. W.	1887-1953	Military	25				World War II British general
Hughes, Maj. Gen. Ivor Thomas P.	1897-1962	Military	25				World War II British general
Hughes, Maj. Gen. John H.	1876-1953	Military	30				World War II U.S. general
Hughes, Mary Beth	1919-	Entertainment	5	10	15	15	Actress. Supporting Parts & Leads. 40's to 70's
Hughes, Nerys		Entertainment	10			20	Actress
Hughes, Richard J.		Governor	5	15			Governor NJ
Hughes, Richard		Military-Rev. War	35	70			Br. Adm. during Rev. War
Hughes, Rupert		Author	20	50	95		Poet, Author, Historian
Hughes, Sarah T.		Law	30	40	65	50	Fed. Judge Swore In L.B. Johnson 1963
Hughes, Stephen		Political	10			15	Member European Parliament
Hughes, Thomas	1822-1896	Author	42		164		'Tom Brown's School Days'. Social Reformer
Hug-Messner, Regula		Aviation	15	30	50	35	
Hugo, Victor	1802-1885	Author	232	372	648	1100	Novelist-Politician-Poet
Huhne, Christopher		Political	10			15	Member European Parliament
Huidekoper, Henry		Civil War	60				Union Col., 'Bucktails'
Hull, Cordell	1871-1955	Cabinet-Statesman	50	135		112	Nobel Peace, Sec'y State. Father Fed. Income Tax
Hull, Fld. Mshl. Sir Richard Amyatt	1907-1989	Military	25				World War II British general
Hull, Henry	1890-1977	Entertainment	42	55		95	Veteran Am. Actor
Hull, Isaac	1773-1843	Military	165	340	602		Cmdr. U.S.S. Constitution 1812. Naval Hero 1812

NAME	DATE	CATEGORY	SIG	LS/DS	ALS	SP	COMMENTS
Hull, J.E.		Military	25				General
Hull, Jenny		Celebrity	10			15	childrenªs presenter
Hull, Josphine	1884-1957	Entertainment	150		200	275	Celebrated Stage Character Actress. AA 'Harvey'
Hull, Lt. Gen. John E.	1895-1975	Military	30				World War II U.S. general
Hull, Warren	1903-1974	Entertainment	25			50	Singer-Actor. Comic-strip Heroes. Radio & TV MC
Hull, William		Military	145	370	770		Revolutionary War Gen.
Hulse, Tom		Entertainment	10	15	20	30	Actor. 'Amadeus'
Hulshof, Kenny C. H		Congress	10			15	Member U.S. Congress
Hulthén, Anneli		Political	10			15	Member European Parliament
Humbard, Rex		Clergy	10	15	15	15	
Humboldt, Alex., Baron von	1769-1859	Science	84	125	267		Ger. Naturalist and Traveller
Hume, Benita	1906-1967	Entertainment	15			30	Br. Actress. Stage & Films. Wife of Ronald Colman
Hume, Brig. Gen. Edgar E.	1889-1952	Military	30				World War II U.S. general
Hume, Brit		Celebrity	10			15	media/TV personality
Hume, John		Political	10			15	Member European Parliament
Hume, Joseph	1777-1855	Politician	20	32	80		Br.Physician. Radical Politician
Hume, Mary-Margaret		Entertainment	5			12	Pin-Up SP 20
Humes, William Young C.	1830-1882	Civil War	168	235	557		CSA General. Sig/Rank 165, War Dte. DS 415
Hummel, Johann Nepomuk	1778-1837	Composer	150	190	725		Hung.-Born Child Prodigy. Piano Virtuoso
Humperdinck, Engelbert		Entertainment	10	10	20	30	Contemporary Vocalist
Humperdinck, Engelbert	1854-1921	Composer	115	225	297	250	AMusQS 450-675-950
Humphrey, George M.		Cabinet	10	20			Sec'y Treasury
Humphrey, Hubert H.	1911-1978	Vice President	35	70	110	63	V.P. & '68 Presidential Cand., MN Senator
Humphrey, Muriel	1912-1998	Congress	10	20		20	Senator MN. Replaced Husband, Hubert as Sen.
Humphreys, Andrews Atkinson	1810-1883	Civil War	44	160	253		Union Gen'l Sig/Rank 100
Humphreys, Benjamin Grubb	1808-1882	Civil War	70				Confederate general
Humphreys, David		Revolutionary War	55	150	200		ADC Washington. Poet,Diplomat
Humphries, Suzie		Celebrity	10			15	motivational speaker
Hungerford, Cy		Cartoonist	10			30	
Hungerford, Orville	1790-1851	Congress	15	45			MOC NY, W & R Railroad Pres.
Hunnicutt, Arthur	1911-1979	Entertainment	15			35	Stage Actor. Film Character Parts From Early 40's
Hunniford, Gloria		Celebrity	10			15	television presenter
Hunt, Bonnie		Entertainment	10			28	actress
Hunt, E. Howard		Gov't Official	15	25	90	25	21 Yr. Vet./CIA. Watergate
Hunt, Earl, Bishop		Clergy	20	25	35	25	
Hunt, George W. P.		Governor	15	35			Governor AZ
Hunt, H. L.	1889-1974	Business	57	147	254	162	TX Oil King. Arch Conservative
Hunt, Helen		Entertainment	25			56	Actress, AA
Hunt, Henry Jackson (WD)	1819-1889	Civil War	90	350	1108		Union Gen.
Hunt, Henry Jackson	1819-1889	Civil War	60	80	140		Union Gen. Gettysburg.
Hunt, James B. Jr.		Governor	5	10			Governor NC
Hunt, James Bunker		Business	5	15	35	15	Son of Oil Magnate H.L.Hunt
Hunt, John, Lord	1910-	Political	25	40	75		Leader 1st Successful Everest Expedition 1953
Hunt, Leigh	1784-1859	Author	30		40		Br. Essayist, Poet
Hunt, Lewis Cass	1824-1886	Civil War	58	80	120		Union general

NAME	DATE	CATEGORY	SIG	LS/DS	ALS	SP	COMMENTS
Hunt, Linda	1945-	Entertainment	20			65	Tiny AA Winning Character Actress.
Hunt, Marsha	1917-	Entertainment	10	12	20	20	Powers Model. Actress Since mid-30's
Hunt, Nelson Bunker		Business	10	20	40	15	Son of Oil Magnate H.L.Hunt
Hunt, Pee Wee		Entertainment	15			45	Trombone-Vocalist
Hunt, Ward		Supreme Court	65	80	175		1872
Hunt, Washington		Governor	35		60		MOC 1842, Governor NY 1850
Hunt, William H.		Cabinet	15	30	60	25	Sec'y Navy 1881
Hunt, William Holman	1827-1910	Artist	55	165	247		Br. Pre-Raphaelite Painter
Hunt, WIlliam Morris	1824-1879	Artist	50	215	500		American Portraitist
Hunt, Willie P.		Governor	40			100	1st Governor of Arizona
Hunter, Brig. Gen. George B.	1879-1965	Military	30				World War II U.S. general
Hunter, C. Bruce		Author	8			12	Masonic history/ritual
Hunter, David (WD)	1802-1886	Civil War	85	460	550		Union Gen.
Hunter, David		Civil War	58	154	172	257	Union General
Hunter, Duncan H		Congress	10			15	Member U.S. Congress
Hunter, Holly		Entertainment	20			51	AA Actress. 'The Piano' SP 75
Hunter, Jeff	1925-1969	Entertainment	35	50	100	90	Actor. 'Star Trek' Capt. For Short Time
Hunter, Kim		Entertainment	10	12	15	25	AA. 'Stella' SP 35. 'Planet of the Apes'
Hunter, Maj. Gen. Alan John	1881-1942	Military	25				World War II British general
Hunter, Moray		Celebrity	10			15	comedian
Hunter, R. M. T.	1809-1887	Civil War	110	175	222		CSA Sec'y State. US Sen. ALS '63 360
Hunter, Rachel		Cover Girl	15			45	Super Model
Hunter, Robert		Revolutionary War	220	508	1035		Br. Gen. Colonial Gov. VA,NY
Hunter, Ross	1921-1995	Entertainment.	25			35	Actor turned Producer. 'Pillow Talk' etc
Hunter, Tab		Entertainment	10	9		40	Actor
Hunter, William	1774-1849	Diplomat	55	80	125		Statesman, Senator RI
Huntington, Agnes		Opera	25			150	Am. & Brit. Productions
Huntington, Benjamin	1736-1800	Revolutionary War	60	175	275		Continental Congress
Huntington, Collis P.	1821-1900	Business	120	706	950	950	Am. RR Builder.,S RR Pass 9500, ALS cont 4500
Huntington, Daniel		Artist		155	250		Portrait Painter
Huntington, Ebenezer		Revolutionary War	110	250	380		Statesman, Army General
Huntington, Henry E.		Business	75	125	200		Railroad Magnate. Huntington Library, San Marino,
Huntington, Jabez W.		Senate/Congress	20	30	45		MOC 1829, Senator CT 1840
Huntington, Jabez	1719-1786	Revolutionary War	150	326			Maj.Gen. Militia. Merchant. Yale Grad. Legislature
Huntington, Jedediah	1743-1818	Military	75	121	490		Gen. Am. Continental Army. Collector of Customs
Huntington, Samuel	1731-1796	Revolutionary War	258	682	898		Signer Decl. of Indepen. Pres.Cont.Congr AL cont 8625
Huntington, Theo. Hastings	1650-1701	Royalty	75		185		7th Earl. Lord Lt. Leicester & Derby. Treason
Huntley, Chet	1911-1974	Journalist	30			100	Longtime TV News Anchorman/David Brinkley
Hunton, Eppa	1822-1908	Civil War	116	270	298		CSA General. Sig/Rank 195
Huntziger, Gen. Charles-Léon-C.	1880-1941	Military	20				World War II French general
Huppert, Isabelle	1955-	Entertainment	10			31	Actress
Huq, Konnie		Celebrity	10			15	children's presenter
Hurault, Maj. Gen. Louis-A-A	1886-1973	Military	20				World War II French general
Hurd, Peter		Artist	85	225	362		Fine Painter. His LBJ Portrait Rejected by LBJ
Hurdis,. Maj. Gen. Charles E.	1893-1977	Military	30				World War II U.S. general

NAME	DATE	CATEGORY	SIG	LS/DS	ALS	SP	COMMENTS
Hurlbut, Stephen A. (WD)	1815-1882	Civil War	70	135	504		Union Gen., ALS/Cont.2200
Hurlbut, Stephen Augustus	1815-1882	Civil War	40	90	130		Union general
Hurley, Brig. Gen. Thomas D.	1890-1963	Military	30				World War II U.S. general
Hurley, Charles F.		Governor	12	25			Governor MA
Hurley, Elizabeth		Entertainment	9			42	Actress-Model. Pin-Up 75
Hurley, Patrick J.	1883-1963	Cabinet	15	45	60	25	Sec'y War, Hoover
Hurrell, George		Photographer	15	50			Hollywood Stars.Orig.16x20 Ltd. Ed. Dietrich 1200
Hurst, Fannie	1889-1968	Author	25	35	60	50	Popular, Sentimental Novels
Hurst, Lee		Celebrity	10			15	comedian
Hurston, Zora Neale	1901-1960	Author	145		750		Am. Writer, Folklorist. Black Culture
Hurt, John		Entertainment	14	20	25	32	Br. Actor. Offbeat Character Portrayals.
Hurt, Mary Beth		Entertainment	6	8	15	21	Actress
Hurt, William		Entertainment	20	25	50	60	Actor. AA 'Kiss of the Spider Woman'
Hurwitz, Hank, Dr.		Science	20			35	Atomic Scientist
Husa, Karel		Composer	15	30	65		Pulitzer, AMusQS 150
Husak, Gustav		Head of State	30			100	Pres. Czechoslovakia. Communist Hard Liner
Huskisson, William		Celebrity			75		Statesman
Husky, Ferlin		Country Music	10			20	Singer- Comedian. AKA Terry Preston, Simon Crum
Hussein I, King	1935-1999	Royalty	92	165	385	450	King of Jordan. Hussein I & Queen Noor SP 675
Hussey, Olivia		Entertainment	5	8	12	32	Actress. 'Romeo & Juliet. Br. & International Film
Hussey, Ruth		Entertainment	5	6	12	15	Actress. 'Philadelphia Story'. Leading Lady in 40'
Husson, Brig. Gen. Paul-Louis	1878-1963	Military	20				World War II French general
Huston, Anjelica		Entertainment	8			39	AA Winning Actress. Daughter of John Huston
Huston, John	1906-1987	Entertainment	40	50	50	78	AA Film Director-Actor
Huston, Walter	1884-1950	Entertainment	67	75	130	150	AA Winning Actor. '..Treasure of the Sierra Madre'
Hutchence, Michael		Entertainment	20			50	
Hutchings, Brig. Gen. Henry Jr.	1892-1963	Military	30				World War II U.S. general
Hutchins, Will		Entertainment	10	15		15	Actor. 'Sugarfoot'
Hutchinson, Frederick Sharpe		Civil War	35		130		Union General
Hutchinson, John W.		Composer	15		50		
Hutchinson, Josephine	1904-	Entertainment	10	15	25	25	Vintage Actress.Child/Mary Pickford.Films from '34
Hutchinson, Lt. Gen. Balfour O.	1889-1967	Military	25				World War II British general
Hutchinson, Thomas	1711-1780	Colonial	185	306			Am. Colonial Administrator. Royal Gov. MA. Exiled
Hutchison, Kay Bailey		Senate	10			15	United States Senate (R - TX)
Hutchison, Maj. Gen. Joseph C.	1894-1982	Military	30				World War II U.S. general
Hutson, Don		Celebrity	10			15	motivational speaker
Hutson, Maj. Gen. Henry Porter W	1893-1991	Military	25				World War II British general
Hutton, Betty		Entertainment	10	15		30	Peppy Blond Actress-Singer of 40's Genre
Hutton, Gunilla		Country Music	5			10	
Hutton, Ina Ray		Entertainment	20			45	All-Girl Big Band Leader
Hutton, Jim	1933-1979	Entertainment	40	70	110	100	Actor.Tall Likeable Leading Man.Timothy's Father
Hutton, Lauren		Entertainment	9	10	20	30	Model-Actress
Hutton, Lt. Gen. Sir Thomas J.	1890-1981	Military	25				World War II British general
Hutton, Maj. Gen. Reginald A.	1899-1983	Military	25				World War II British general
Hutton, Robert		Entertainment	20	40	110	90	Actor

NAME	DATE	CATEGORY	SIG	LS/DS	ALS	SP	COMMENTS
Hutton, Timothy		Entertainment	18	20		40	AA Winner
Huxley, Aldous	1894-1963	Author	75	400	574	350	Br. Novelist.'Brave New World'. TLS/Content 1,200
Huxley, Julian Sorell	1887-1975	Science-Author	30	70	142		Br. Biologist, Educator
Huxley, Leonard	1860-1933	Author	20		75		Biographer, Poet. Son of Julian Huxley
Huxley, Thomas Henry	1825-1895	Science	52	150	220		Br. Biologist
Hyacinthe, Pere (Charles Loyson)	1827-1912	Clergy	50	130	275	200	Controversial Catholic Priest
Hyakatuke, Lt. Gen. Seikichi	1888-1947	Military	25				World War II Japanese general
Hyams, Leila	1905-1977	Entertainment	20	25	50	40	Leading Lady of 20's-30's
Hyde, Arthur W.		Cabinet	7	15	30	15	Sec'y Agriculture 1929
Hyde, Brig. Gen. James F.C.	1894-1944	Military	30				World War II U.S. general
Hyde, Edgar R.		Clergy	10	10	15		
Hyde, Henry J. H		Congress	10			15	Member U.S. Congress
Hyde, Herbert L.		Author	8			12	N.C. State senator/author
Hyde, Jonathan		Entertainment	10			20	actor
Hyder, Scott		Author	8			12	mountain poetry
Hyde-White, Wilfrid	1903-1991	Entertainment	20	25	35	73	Brit. Character Actor
Hyer, Martha		Entertainment	10	12	15	25	Actress. Oscar Winner
Hyland, Liam		Political	10			15	Member European Parliament
Hyland, Maj. Gen. Frederick G.	1888-1962	Military	25				World War II British general
Hylton, Jack	1892-1965	Entertainment	20			70	Major Br. Bandleader
Hylton, Lord		Politician	7	15	25		Chief Whip Unionist Party
Hyman, Earle		Entertainment	5			10	Afr.-Am Actor
Hymes, Myriam		Entertainment				20	
Hynde, Chrissie		Entertainment	25			40	Rock. 'The Pretenders'
Hyndman, Henry Mayers	1842-1921	Socialist	75		350		Br Marxist-Socialist. Interesting Political Career
Hyssong, Maj. Gen. Clyde L.	1896-1975	Military	30				World War II U.S. general

NAME	DATE	CATEGORY	SIG	LS/DS	ALS	SP	COMMENTS
I Remember Mama (Cast of 5)		Entertainment	125			395	50's Popular TV Program
Iacocca, Lee A.		Business	15	50		35	CEO Ford, Chrysler Motors
Ian, Janis		Entertainment	10	40		25	Singer-Actress
I'Anson, Lisa		Music	10			15	DJ
Ibert, Jacques-Francois		Composer	75		325	160	AMusQS 450
Ibsen, Henrik	1828-1906	Author	250	562	1415	1942	Nor. Poet & Dramatist. 'Peer Gynt', 'Doll's House'
Icart, Louis	1888-1950	Artist	115		875		Fr. Art Deco Painter-Illusrator
Ice Cube		Entertainment	15			45	Rapper, actor, writer
Ice T		Entertainment	20			50	Rock. Rapper
Ickes, Harold L.		Cabinet	20	35	65	25	Roosevelt Sec'y Interior
Idle, Eric		Entertainment	10			25	Actor
Idol, Billy		Entertainment	10			35	Rock Star
Iglesias, Enrique		Music	10			35	
Iglesias, Julio		Entertainment	15			48	Singer

NAME	DATE	CATEGORY	SIG	LS/DS	ALS	SP	COMMENTS
Iha, James		Entertainment	6			25	Music. Guitar 'Smashing Pumpkins'
Ihlefedl, Herbert		Aviation	25	55		60	
Ihler, Maj. Gen. Marcel	1880-1975	Military	20				World War II French general
Iida, Lt. Gen. Shojiro		Military	25				World War II Japanese general
Iivari, Ulpu		Political	10			15	Member European Parliament
Ikeda, Hayato		Head of State	15		65		Japan
Ikegami, Maj. Gen. Kenkichi		Military	25				World War II Japanese general
Ikehama, Maj. Gen. Seiji		Military	25				World War II Japanese general
Ikuta, Maj. Gen. Torao		Military	25				World War II Japanese general
Iler, Robert		Entertainment				35	Anthony Soprano Jr.
Ilgenfritz, Wolfgang		Political	10			15	Member European Parliament
Imai, Maj. Gen. Takeo		Military	25				World War II Japanese general
Imamura, Lt. Gen. Hitoshi	1886-1968	Military	25				World War II Japanese general
Iman		Model	25			55	Model
Imbeni, Renzo		Political	10			15	Member European Parliament
Imboden, John Dan'l (WD)		Civil War	375	810	2415		CSA Gen. Spec'l ALS 4500
Imboden, John Dan'l	1823-1895	Civil War	175	288	435		CSA Gen.
Imbruglia, Natalie		Entertainment	18			48	Rock Star
Immelmann, Max		Aviation	200	425	700	500	ACE, WW II, 1st German Ace
Impellitteri, Vincent		Celebrity	4	12	25	10	
Imperioli, Michael		Entertainment				40	Christopher Moltisanti, Soprano's
Imus, Don		Entertainment	10			25	Obnoxious talk show host
Inada, Maj. Gen. Masazumi		Military	25				World War II Japanese general
Ince, Thomas H.		Entertainment	40			125	Film Dir. Civil War Epics
Indecent Proposal (cast)		Entertainment				110	Douglas / Moore
Indiana, Robert		Artist	45	95	170	150	Colorful Contemporary Artist. Sports Specialy
Ingalls, John James	1833-1900	Congress	30	60	85		Senator KS
Ingalls, Laura		Aviation		295			Pioneer. 1st Non-Stop Transcontinental Flight
Ingalls, Rufus (WD)	1818-1893	Civil War	60		525		Union Gen., Explorer
Ingalls, Rufus	1818-1893	Civil War	34	105	211		Union General, Explorer
Inge, William R.		Clergy	50	100	115		Br. Prelate. 'Gloomy' Dean St. Paul's Cath., Writer
Ingels, Marty		Entertainment	8			28	
Ingersoll, Charles J.	1782-1862	Senate/Congress	20	25	50		MOC PA 1813
Ingersoll, Charles R.		Governor	5	15	25		Governor CT
Ingersoll, Jared	1749-1822	Revolutionary War	75	154	450		Continental Congr., Constitution Signer
Ingersoll, Robert Green		Celebrity	30	60	58	53	Agnostic Lecturer, Orator
Ingersoll, Robert H.		Business	80	175	300	225	Ingersoll 1 Watch
Ingersoll, Royal E.		Military	80	135		175	Adm. & Cmdr. Of Atlantic Fleet WW II
Ingham, Samuel D.	1779-1860	Cabinet	35	120	145		Sec'y Treasury 1829
Ingle, Red		Entertainment	25			80	
Ingle, Robert P.		Business	5	15	25	10	Ingles Grocery Chain
Ingles, Maj. Gen. Harry C.	1888-1976	Military	30				World War II U.S. general
Inglewood,		Political	10			15	Member European Parliament
Inglis, James		Business	5	20			Mfg.
Inglis, Maj. Gen. George Henry	1902-1979	Military	25				World War II British general

NAME	DATE	CATEGORY	SIG	LS/DS	ALS	SP	COMMENTS
Inglis, Maj. Gen. Lindsay M.	1894-1966	Military	20				World War II New Zealand general
Inglis, Maj. Gen. Sir John D.	1895-1965	Military	25				World War II British general
Ingold, Maj. Gen. Francois-Jos.-J.	1894-1980	Military	20				World War II French general
Ingraham, Duncan N.		Civil War		127	215		CSA
Ingraham, Duncan N.(WD)		Civil War	172		1100		Capt.CSA Navy
Ingraham, Porter	1810-1893	Civil War	40				Member of Confederate Congress
Ingram, Rex	1895-1969	Entertainment	100			300	Vintage Afro-Am. Actor
Ingres, Jean-Auguste-Dominique		Artist	205		750		Fr. Leader Among Classicists
Ingrid, Victoria, Queen		Royalty	20	40			Queen of Frederick IX (Denmark)
Inhofe, James		Senate	10			15	United States Senate (R - OK)
Ink Spots, The (4)		Entertainment	225			280	Vintage Singing Group. (All Four Sigs.)
Inman, Henry	1801-1846	Artist	110	305	650		American Portraitist. ALS/Content 1250
Inman, Jerry		Country Music	10			20	
Innes, Roy	1934-	Activist	15	15		25	Afr.-Am. Activist. Civil Rights. Pres. CORE
Inness, George	1824-1894	Artist	75	225	690		Am. Landscape Painter. ALS/Cont. 950
Inouye, Daniel		Senate	10			15	United States Senate (D - HI)
Inskeep, Jonathan		Revolutionary War	80	175			
Inskip, Maj. Gen. Roland D.	1885-1971	Military	25				World War II British general
Inslee, Jay I		Congress	10			15	Member U.S. Congress
Insull, Samuel	1859-1938	Financier	132	975	1300		Pvt. Sec'y Edison. Utilities Baron.TLS/Cont.685
International, Dana		Music	10			15	performing musical artist
Ionesco, Eugene	1912-1994	Author	40	145	225	55	Romanian-Fr. Dramatist.Theatre of Absurd. AQS 700
Ireland, Jill		Entertainment	25			60	Actress
Ireland, John M.F		Governor	40	150			Gov. TX 1883-87
Ireland, John		Entertainment	10			42	Actor
Ireland, Kathy		Cover Girl	20			52	Super model
Irish, James M.		Military	10	30	50		
Irons, Jack		Entertainment	6			25	Music. Drummer 'Pearl Jam'
Irons, Jeremy		Entertainment	10		25	40	Br. Actor
Ironside, Michael		Entertainment	10			20	actor
Irvin, James	1800-1862	Congress	18		35		Repr. PA, Merchant, Miller, Miner
Irvinc, Maj. Gen. Willard W.	1892-1969	Military	30				World War II U.S. general
Irvine, James	1735-1819	Revolutionary War	55	130	250		Gen. Militia. Cmdr. Fort Pitt
Irvine, William	1741-1804	Revolutionary War	125	275	425		Gen., Continental Congress
Irving, Amy		Entertainment	9	10	20	25	Actress
Irving, Clifford		Author	13	30	50	40	
Irving, Edward	1792-1834	Clergy	100		375		Founder 'Catholic Apostolic Church'
Irving, Henry, Sir	1838-1905	Entertainment	48	82	148	158	Vintage Actor-Manager. LS by Bram Stoker 225
Irving, John		Author	13	15	30	68	Am.'The World According to Garp'
Irving, Washington	1783-1859	Author	162	322	496		Am. Essayist. 'Rip Van Winkle'
Irwin, Bill		Celebrity	10			15	media/TV personality
Irwin, Brig. Gen. Constant L.	1893-1977	Military	30				World War II U.S. general
Irwin, David		Celebrity	10	20	45	15	
Irwin, James B.'Jim'	1930-1991	Astronaut	54	111	196	154	
Irwin, Lt. Gen. Noel Mackintosh S.	1892-1972	Military	25				World War II British general

NAME	DATE	CATEGORY	SIG	LS/DS	ALS	SP	COMMENTS
Irwin, Maj. Gen. Stafford L.R.	1893-1955	Military	30				World War II U.S. general
Irwin, Maj. Gen. Stephen F.	1895-1964	Military	25				World War II British general
Irwin, May		Entertainment	25		35	45	Vintage Stage Actress. 1st Film Kiss
Irwin, Noble E.	1869-1937	Military	55	150			USN Adm.1st Dir. Naval Aviation, Trans-Atl. Flight
Irwin, Will	1873-1948	Journalist			40		War Correspondent, Author
Isabella I, Of Castile	1451-1504	Royalty	850	2544	6500		Queen Spain. Columbus' Patron
Isabella II	1830-1904	Royalty	175	420	730		Spain. Strife, Intrigue. Abdicated
Isabey, Jean-Baptiste	1767-1855	Artist		115	350		Court Painter to Napoleon & Bourbons
Isakson, Johnny I		Congress	10			15	Member U.S. Congress
Ish Kabibble (Merwyn Bogue)		Entertainment	15			25	Novelty Singer, Kay Kyser Band
Isherwood, Christopher	1904-1986	Author	40	70	95	125	Br.-Am. Novelist, Playwright
Ishiguro, Kazuo		Author	15			40	'Remains of the Day'
Ishihara, Lt. Gen. Kanji	1889-1949	Military	25				World War II Japanese general
Ishii, Maj. Gen. Shiro	1883-1959	Military	25				World War II Japanese general
Isken, Edward		Aviation	15			35	Ger. Air Ace with 56 Victories
Isler BTguin, Marie Anne		Political	10			15	Member European Parliament
Ismay, Hastings Lionel		Military	25	35	60	45	Churchill Chief-of-Staff WW II
Isogai, Lt. Gen. Rensuke	1886-1967	Military	25				World War II Japanese general
Israel, Steve I		Congress	10			15	Member U.S. Congress
Israels, Jozef	1824-1911	Artist	55	180	350	225	Dutch. Hague School Genre Art. Landscapes
Issa, Darrell E. I		Congress	10			15	Member U.S. Congress
Istomin, Eugene		Entertainment	35			125	Pianist-Classical
Istook Jr., Ernest J. I		Congress	10			15	Member U.S. Congress
Itagaki, General Seishiro	1885-1948	Military	25				World War II Japanese general
Ito, Hirobumi (Prince)	1841-1909	Statesman	55	140			Japan. Prime Minister 1886
Ito, Lance, Judge		Law	20			55	O.J. Simpson Trial Judge
Ito, Marquis		Statesman	25				Japanese Statesman
Ito, Robert		Entertainment	4			10	Actor
Iturbi, Jose		Entertainment	20	40		50	Classical Pianist.Jose & Amparo Iturbi S 30-95
Iturbide, Augustin de	1783-1824	Revolutionary		875			Self Proclaimed Emperor of Mex.
Ivan IV, The Terrible		Royalty	35000				
Iverson, Alfred, Jr.	1829-1911	Civil War	191	300	475		CSA Gen. Sig/Rank 240-290
Ives, Burl		Entertainment	15	35		42	Folk-Singer Turned Oscar Winning Actor
Ives, Charles E.	1874-1954	Composer	792	1250	2000	800	Tonal Experiments. Pulitzer. Mysterious & Elusive
Ivey, Judith		Entertainment	10			35	Actress
Ivins, Marsha S.		Astronaut	7			25	
Ivins, Molly		Celebrity	10			15	media/TV personality
Ivogun, Maria		Entertainment	45			175	Opera
Iwakuro, Maj. Gen. Hideo	1897-1970	Military	25				World War II Japanese general
Izak, Edouard		Military	20	45			WW II CMH
Izquierdo Collado, Juan De Dios		Political	10			15	Member European Parliament
Izquierdo Rojo, Marfa		Political	10			15	Member European Parliament
Izzard, Eddie		Celebrity	10			15	comedian

NAME	DATE	CATEGORY	SIG	LS/DS	ALS	SP	COMMENTS

J

NAME	DATE	CATEGORY	SIG	LS/DS	ALS	SP	COMMENTS
Ja Rule		Music	15			45	Rap
Jabotinsky, Vladimir		Zionist	45	120	845	150	Zionist Leader WW I
Jabs, Hans-Joachim		Aviation	60	150			Famed Nazi Pilot.
Jack, Alison		Celebrity	10			15	newsreader
Jack, Thomas M.	1831-1880	Civil War	60				CSA Col. A.D.C. to A.S. Johnston
Jacks, L.P.		Clergy	15	20	45		
Jackson, Aaron		Entertainment	10			20	actor
Jackson, Alan		Country Music	18			52	C & W
Jackson, Alfred E.	1807-1889	Civil War	140		950		CSA General. Sig/Rank 220, War Dte. ALS 1200
Jackson, Andrew (As President)	1767-1845	President	683	2237	4552		Exceptional ALS26,000
Jackson, Andrew	1767-1845	President	553	1844	2647		Free Frank 1400, Land Grants(1829-1832) 750-1250
Jackson, Andrew & Van Buren		Presidents		3375			
Jackson, Anne		Entertainment	6	8	15	15	Actress. Broadway, Radio, TV, Films
Jackson, Brig. Gen. Harold R.	1894-1987	Military	30				World War II U.S. general
Jackson, Caroline F.		Political	10			15	Member European Parliament
Jackson, Charles T.	1805-1880	Science	200				Co-Discoverer of Ether
Jackson, Clairborne F.	1807-1862	Civil War		175	220		Civil War Gov. MO
Jackson, Conrad Feger	1813-1862	Civil War	90				Union general
Jackson, Eugene 'Pineapple'		Entertainment	15			25	'Our Gang' Comedies
Jackson, Glenda	1937-	Entertainment	15	20	30	35	Br. Oscar winner, Member of Brit. Parliament
Jackson, Gordon	d. 1996	Entertainment	15		50	55	Scot. 'Hudson' in 'Upstairs, Downstairs'
Jackson, Helen Hunt		Author	15	35	50	35	Am.Novelist, Poet. 'Ramona'
Jackson, Henry M. 'Scoop'		Senate/Congress	5	15		20	MOC, Senator WA
Jackson, Henry Rootes	1820-1898	Civil War	95	195	350		CSA Gen.
Jackson, Howell E.		Supreme Court	88	200		300	U.S. Senator 1881, Supr.Ct.1893
Jackson, James S. (WD)		Civil War	235		1018		Union Gen. KIA 1862
Jackson, James S.	1823-1862	Civil War	170		650		Union Gen. KIA 1862. ALS/Cont. 1375
Jackson, James, Dr.	1777-1867	Science	110	220	500		1st Am. to Perform Vaccinations
Jackson, Janet		Entertainment	25			60	Rock
Jackson, Jesse	1941-	Clergy	20	65	80	32	Reverend Jesse Jackson. Most Material Secretarial
Jackson, Jesse, Jr.	1965-	Congress	5	15		20	Dem. MOC IL. Civil Rights, Operation PUSH
Jackson, Joe		Entertainment	20			40	Vintage Entertainer
Jackson, John King	1828-1866	Civil War	260		920		CSA Gen. RARE
Jackson, Joshua		Entertainment	6			45	Young Actor
Jackson, Kate		Entertainment	10	15	32	32	One of 'Charlie's Angels'
Jackson, LaToya		Entertainment	20		38	44	Singer
Jackson, Mahalia	1911-1972	Entertainment	120			442	Gospel Singer. Queen of Gospel Music. SP 8vo 375
Jackson, Maj. Gen. Stonewall	1891-1943	Military	30				World War II U.S. general
Jackson, Mary Anna	d. 1915	Civil War			788		Wife to Stonewall Jackson
Jackson, Maynard		Entertainment	5	10	20	15	Big Band Trumpet
Jackson, Michael		Entertainment	56	246		125	Legendary Pop Music Mega Star

NAME	DATE	CATEGORY	SIG	LS/DS	ALS	SP	COMMENTS
Jackson, Nathaniel James	1818-1892	Civil War	40	85	110		Union general
Jackson, Peter		Entertainment				55	actor
Jackson, Rachel		First Lady	575				Mrs. Andrew Jackson
Jackson, Richard Henry	1830-1892	Civil War	45	70	120		Union general
Jackson, Robert H.		Supreme Court	50	295		125	Chief Prosecutor at Nuremberg
Jackson, Samuel L.		Entertainment	18			68	Versatile Afr-Am Actor
Jackson, Samuel M.	1833-1907	Civil War	35	80	130		Union Gen. Wilderness. ALS/Cont. 600
Jackson, Steve		Music	10			15	DJ
Jackson, T.J. Stonewall (WD)		Civil War	4000	13000	18375		CSA Gen. ALS 47,375
Jackson, T.J. Stonewall	1824-1863	Civil War	3250	8439	14000		CSA General
Jackson, Thomas		Clergy	25		40		
Jackson, Victoria		Entertainment	6	15		17	Actress-Comedian
Jackson, Wanda		Country Music	10			20	C & W Singer
Jackson, William Henry	1843-1942	Photographer	40	110			Photographed Indians etc. on Union Pac. RR Route
Jackson, Wm. Lowther 'Mudwall'	1825-1890	Civil War	140	218	417		Confederate general
Jackson, William	1759-1828	Revolutionary War	120	350	750		Gen. Washington Aide. Diplomat
Jackson, Wm. Hicks 'Red'	1835-1903	Civil War	110	237	250		CSA General. War Dte. DS 600
Jackson-Lee, Sheila	1950-	Congress	5			20	Afr-Am MOC TX
Jacob, Francois		Science	20	30	55	30	Nobel Medicine 1965
Jacob, General of Pioneers Alfred	1883-1963	Military	27				World War II German general
Jacob, Irene		Entertainment	10			20	actress
Jacob, John C.		CORE	10	15		15	Afro-Am. Leader CORE
Jacob, John J.		Governor	12	20			Governor WV
Jacob, Lt. Gen. Sir Edw. Ian Claud	1899-1993	Military	25				World War II British general
Jacobi, Derek		Entertainment	5		12	15	
Jacobi, Lou		Entertainment	5			15	Actor
Jacobs, Andy		Congress	4	15			Indiana
Jacobs, Brig. Gen. Fenton S.	1892-1966	Military	30				World War II U.S. general
Jacobs, Josef		Aviation	30	45	80	55	
Jacobs, Lee		Author	8			12	Civil War history
Jacobs, Lou		Entertainment	50	100		100	Clown
Jacobs, William Wymark	1863-1943	Author	250				Br. Monkey's Paw
Jacobsen, David		Celebrity	10			15	motivational speaker
Jacobsen, Fritz		Aviation	10	20	35	45	Ace WW I
Jacott, William E.		Celebrity	10			15	medical expert
Jacquemart, Nelie		Artist			92		
Jacques, Brigadier Leslie Innes	1897-1959	Military	25				World War II British general
Jacquet, Illinois Jean		Entertainment	30			70	Jazz Sax, Bandleader
Jacquot, Benoit		Celebrity	10			15	film industry
Jacquot, Richard James, Jr.		Author	8			12	Southern mountains geology
Jadlowker, Hermann		Entertainment	95			245	Opera
Jaeckel, Richard		Entertainment	15			25	Familiar Character Actor. Westerns-Tough Guys
Jaeger, James A.		Aviation	10		30		
Jaehnert, Erhard		Aviation	10	10	25	25	
Jaenecke, Colonel-General Erwin	1890-1960	Military	25				World War II German general

NAME	DATE	CATEGORY	SIG	LS/DS	ALS	SP	COMMENTS
Jaffe, Sam	1893-1984	Entertainment	25			41	Actor. Stage 1915. Films 30's. 'Gunga Din'. TV 50's
Jaffri, Madha		Celebrity	10			15	Indian Chef (US Based)
Jagger, Bianca		Entertainment	10			25	
Jagger, Dean	1903-1991	Entertainment	15	25	30	35	AA Winner
Jagger, Jade		Celebrity	10			15	Designer
Jagger, Mick	1943-	Entertainment	52			138	Lead singer of The Rolling Stones
Jahn, Sigmund		Cosmonaut	15			35	
Jakes, John		Author	15	50	70	50	'Holiday for Havoc'
James I & VI (Eng)	1566-1625	Royalty	750	2034	5250		King of Scotland from 1567—Eng. From 1603
James II (Eng)	1633-1701	Royalty	530	1378	3167		King Eng. 1685-88
James, Brigadier Manley Angell	1896-1975	Military	25				World War II British general
James, Daniel, Jr.		Military	20	35	85	45	AF Gen. 1st Black 4 Star Gen.
James, Dennis	1917-1997	Entertainment	25			30	1938 TV Pioneer. 1st Game Show Host. Emcee etc.
James, Etta		Entertainment	20			40	Rock
James, Frank	1844-1915	Outlaw	1252	2100	4250		Quantrill Raider. Rode With Him Throughout War
James, Harry	1916-1983	Entertainment	20	20	40	55	Big Band Leader-Trumpet SP Pc 30
James, Henry	1811-1882	Author	50		120		Theological & Social Scholar
James, Henry	1843-1916	Author	104	360	533		Am. Novelist, Essayist. ALS/Content 2500- 5,500
James, Kevin		Celebrity				40	
James, Manley		Military	10		45		WW I Victoria Cross
James, Merlin		Celebrity	10			15	motivational speaker
James, P.D.		Author	20	65	105		Notable Br. Mystery Writer
James, Sonny		Country Music	10			30	Singer. The Country Gentleman. Hits from 50's on
James, Susan Saint	1946	Entertainment	10			25	Actress
James, Thomas L.		Cabinet	15	25	45		P.M. General 1881
James, Will	1842-1942	Author	75	250	410	750	Illustrated own Western Novels
James, William	1842-1910	Science	90	350	495	300	Psychologist, Pragmatist, Philosopher
Jameson, (Margaret) Storm		Author		40			
Jameson, Charles Davis	1827-1862	Civil War	80	128	175		Union general
Jameson, Maj. Gen. Thos. Henry	1895-1985	Military	25				World War II British general
Jamet, Lt. Gen. Louis-Marie	1878-1958	Military	20				World War II French general
Jan & Dean		Entertainment	20			45	Rock
Janacek, Leos	1854-1928	Composer	140				Czech Composer AMusQS 2000
Janeway, Eliot		Author-Economist	16				
Janis, Conrad		Entertainment	5			15	Actor. 'Mork & Mindy'
Janis, Elsie		Entertainment	25		50	55	Stage, Screen Comedienne. WW I Entertainer
Janklow, William J. J		Congress	10			15	Member U.S. Congress
Janney, Allison		Entertainment	10			45	Emmy Award winner
Janney, Leon		Entertainment	35			75	Member Original 'Our Gang' Comedies
Jannings, Emil		Entertainment	150			275	1st Academy Award Winner
Janowitz, Gundula		Entertainment	10			65	Opera
Jansen, Marie		Entertainment	15			40	Opera
Jansons, Mariss		Conductor	10			45	Newly Discovered Latvian Conductor
Janssen, David	1930-1980	Entertainment	68	120		156	Actor 'The Fugitive' Original TV Series
Janssen, Famke		Entertainment	10			35	actress

NAME	DATE	CATEGORY	SIG	LS/DS	ALS	SP	COMMENTS
Janssen, Werner		Conductor	25			45	Conductor of Many US Leading Orchestras
Jantz, Gregory		Celebrity	10			15	medical expert
January, Lois		Entertainment	5	5	10	15	
Janus, Samantha		Entertainment	10			20	Actress
Jaray, Hans		Entertainment	5			20	Classical-Semi Classical Singer. Concert-Films
Jardine, Maj. Gen. Colin A.	1892-1957	Military	25				World War II British general
Jardine, William		Cabinet	10	15	55	20	Sec'y Agriculture 1925
Jardine, William, Sir	1800-1874	Author	55		200		Writer, Editor, Naturalist
Jarman, Claude, Jr.		Entertainment	15			35	Oscar winner. 'The Yearling'
Jarman, Maj. Gen. Sanderford	1884-1954	Military	30				World War II U.S. general
Jarman, Maxie		Business	15			55	Jarman Shoes
Jarmusch, Jim		Celebrity	10			15	film industry
Jaroff, Serge		Entertainment	15	20	25	35	Jaroff Ballet & Don Cossack Chorus
Jarreau, Al		Entertainment	20			40	Music
Jarrett, Art		Bandleader	15			30	Big Band
Jarriel, Tom		Journalist	5	10	15	15	TV News
Jarvik, Robert, Dr.		Science	15	35	60	40	Inventor Artificial Heart
Jarvis, Anna M.		Promoter	65	175			Campaigned for Mother's Day
Jarvis, Gregory B.		Astronaut	135	350		400	Killed in Challanger Disaster
Jarvis, Howard		Reformer-Tax	5	12	30	15	Sponsor Proposition 13. CA Property Tax
Jarzembowski, Georg		Political	10			15	Member European Parliament
Jasiak, Charles 'Chuck'		Business	10	20			American Entrepreneur
Jasmer, Brent		Entertainment	10			20	actor
Jason, David		Entertainment	10			20	Actor
Jason, Rick		Entertainment	5			15	Actor
Jason, Sybil		Entertainment	5	6	15	15	
Jassin, Lloyd		Author	7	11	25	12	Copyright author/attorney, rights expert
Javits, Jacob J.		Congress	10	20		25	MOC 1947, Senator NY 1957
Jawlensky, Aleksey von	1864-1941	Artist			600		Russ. Painter
Jaworski, Leon		Law	15	20	45	20	Dir. Watergate Prosecution Force
Jay, Brig. Gen. Henry D.	1891-1979	Military	30				World War II U.S. general
Jay, James, Sir	1732-1815	Science	90	275	400		Phys. to G. Washington; Inventor
Jay, John (Grandson)	1817-1894	Diplomat	30	65	95		Active Opposition to Slavery
Jay, John	1745-1829	Supreme Court	353	1529	2782		Pres. Continental Congr. ALS/cont 6,600
Jaynes, Maj. Gen. Lawrence C.	1891-1977	Military	30				World War II U.S. general
Jean, Gloria		Entertainment	5		20	25	Child Singer-Actress 30's-40's5
Jean, Norma		Country Music	10			20	
Jean, Shirley		Entertainment				58	Little Rascals
Jeannel, Lt Gen. Jos.-Chas.-Robt.	1883-1954	Military	20				World War II French general
Jean-Pierre, Thierry B.		Political	10			15	Member European Parliament
Jeans, James, Sir		Science	12	30	56	20	Br. Physicist, Astron., Author
Jedlichka, Ernest		Entertainment	45			200	Rus-Pol Pianist
Jeffe, Brig. Gen. Ephraim F.	1897-1986	Military	30				World War II U.S. general
Jeffers, Robinson	1887-1962	Author	65	350	450	95	Prize Winning Poet, Dramatist
Jeffers, William M.		Business	25	70	135	50	Pres. Union Pacific RR

NAME	DATE	CATEGORY	SIG	LS/DS	ALS	SP	COMMENTS
Jefferson Airplane (All)		Entertainment	125			300	Rock-The San Francisco Sound
Jefferson, Charles E.		Clergy	20	25	40		
Jefferson, Joe	1829-1905	Entertainment	45	70	107	80	Important Am.19th Century Actor
Jefferson, Martha Wayles		First Lady					Rare. Only 2 Known. No Current Price
Jefferson, Thomas & Madison		President	3038	6766			Special Doc. S 30,000, MLS 25,000
Jefferson, Thomas (As President)		President	3750	7000	30720		Free Frank 5,000-5950
Jefferson, Thomas	1743-1826	President	2893	6187	14793		Content ALS's 29,500-200,000. FF2800-4000
Jefferson, Thomas	1859-1932	Entertainment	20			125	Actor. Stage & Silent Films/D.W. Griffith
Jefferson, William J. J		Congress	10			15	Member U.S. Congress
Jeffords, James		Senate	10			15	United States Senate (I - VT)
Jeffrey, Francis, Lord	1773-1850	Jurist			110		Scottish Judge and critic
Jeffreys, Anne	1923-	Entertainment	10	14	22	25	Actress. 'Topper' etc.
Jeffries, Mark		Celebrity	10			15	conference facilitator / television presenter
Jeggle, Elisabeth		Political	10			15	Member European Parliament
Jellicoe, John R.	1859-1935	Military	35	70	125	167	Br.Adm. WW I, P.M. New Zealand
Jenckes, Joseph	1656-1740	Colonial Am.	90	250	520		Colonial Governor RI
Jenkins, Albert Gallatin	1830-1864	Civil War	250	316			Confederate general
Jenkins, Allen		Entertainment	25			45	Cigar-Chewing Character Actor
Jenkins, Butch		Entertainment	10			30	Freckle-Faced Child Actor
Jenkins, Lt. Gen. Reuben E.	1896-1975	Military	30				World War II U.S. general
Jenkins, Maj. Gen. Fred. A.M.B.	1891-1986	Military	25				World War II British general
Jenkins, Micah	1835-1864	Civil War	360				Confederate general
Jenkins, Richard		Entertainment				40	Nathaniel Fisher, Six Feet Under
Jenkins, Thornton Alex.	1811-	Civil War	35	95	160		Chief-of Staff Adm. Farragut Squad. Sig/Rank 65
Jenkins, William L. J		Congress	10			15	Member U.S. Congress
Jenner, Bruce		Celebrity	10			20	Olympic champion, motivational speaker
Jenner, Edward, Dr.	1749-1823	Science	375	650	1550		1st to Use. Smallpox Vaccination
Jenner, William E.	1908-1985	Congress	10	20			Senator IN
Jenner, William, Sir	1815-1898	Science	35	110	212		Identified Typhus-Typhoid. Phys. to Queen Victoria
Jennings, Al	1863-1961	Celebrity	450		850		Outlaw turned Hollywood actor
Jennings, Peter		Journalist	5	15	35	15	Broadcast Journalist, Anchor
Jennings, Waylon	d. 2002	Country Music	22	55		61	Country Singer
Jennison, Ralph D.		Business	10	35	45	20	
Jenrette, John W. Jr.		Congress	5	20		15	MOC. SC
Jenrette, Rita		Entertainment	4	6	15	18	
Jensen, Anne Elisabet		Political	10			15	Member European Parliament
Jensen, Karen		Entertainment	4	4	9	10	Actress
Jensen, Mike		Celebrity	10			15	media/TV personality
Jenson, May		Celebrity	10			15	political celebrity
Jepson, Helen		Entertainment	15			45	Opera, Concert
Jergens, Adele	1917-	Entertainment	10	12	15	20	Actress-Model. Over 50 Mostly B-Films.
Jeritza, Maria	1887-1984	Entertainment	50			95	Opera, Operetta, Films. 1st Met. 'Turandot'
Jernigan, Tamara E.		Astronaut	8			25	
Jernstedt, Ken		Aviation	10	25	40	35	ACE, WW II, Flying Tigers
Jerome, Addison G		Financier	300	975			Stock Market Legend in 1850's

NAME	DATE	CATEGORY	SIG	LS/DS	ALS	SP	COMMENTS
Jerome, Jerome K.	1859-1927	Author	50	70	108		Humorist, Playwright. 'Three Men in a Boat'
Jerome, Wm. Travers, III		Education	20	40		35	Pres. Bowling Green Univ.
Jerrard, Brigadier Charles Ian	1900-1977	Military	25				World War II British general
Jerry Weller		Senate	10			15	Member U.S. Congress
Jerusalem, Siegfried		Entertainment	15			45	Opera. Current Leading Wagnerian Tenor.SP 4x6 25
Jess, Lt. Gen. Carl H.	1884-1948	Military	20				World War II Australian general
Jesse, Edward	1780-1868	Author			65		Natural history
Jessel, George	1888-1972	Entertainment	28	80		77	Noted Emcee, Comic, Toastmaster
Jessup, Thomas S.	1788-1860	Military	57	138	183		War 1812, Seminole. Gen. LS/Content 950-1750
Jesup, William H.		Military	5	15	25		
Jeter, Michael		Entertainment	10			25	'Evening Shade'
Jethro Tull		Entertainment	30			75	Band
Jett, Joan		Entertainment	20	45		50	Rock. (And the 'Blackhearts')
Jeune, Maj. Gen. Francis le	1899-1964	Military	25				World War II British general
Jewel		Music	15	150		60	Singer
Jewell, Isabel		Entertainment	50			95	Longtime Vintage Actress.'Emmy Slattery' 'GWTW'
Jewell, Marshall		Governor-Cabinet	40	75	195		ALS/Cont. 400
Jewett, Sarah Orne	1849-1909	Author	45	200	262		New England Life & Folklore
Jewison, Norman		Entertainment	5			20	Film Director
Jewsbury, Geraldine Endsor	1812-1880	Author			70		
Jillian, Ann		Entertainment	8	8	15	22	Actress. Pin-Up SP 25
Jimenez, Enrique A.		Head of State	8	15	25	15	Panama
Jimenez, Marcos P.		Head of State	10	25	50	20	Venezuela
Joachim, Joseph	1831-1907	Composer	95	150	258	245	Hung.Violinist.AMuQS 250-575
Joad, Cyril Edwin Mitchinson	1891-1953	Author		30	35		Writer and teacher
Jodl, Alfred	1892-1946	Military	167	438	550	550	Nazi Chief-of-Staff To Keitel WW II
Jodl, Gen Mtn Troops Ferdinand	1896-1956	Military	25				World War II German general
Joel, Billy		Composer	20			61	Singer, Songwriter
Joel, Manuel	1826-1890	Judaica	45	125			Rabbi, Scholar. Defended Moderation vs Radicalism
Joffe, Julian Marc M.D.		Science	5	7	10	15	Famous Orthopedic surgeon, Author
Joffre, Joseph Jacques Cesaire		Military	58	101	250	160	Marshal of France WW I
Johann, Zita		Entertainment	20			45	Actor. 'The Mummy'
Johannson, Paul		Entertainment	4			20	Actor. 'Beverly Hills 90210'
John II, (King Castile)	1405-1454	Royalty	4700	5133			Patron of Literature & Arts. Father of Q. Isabella
John III (Port.)	1502-1557	Royalty	200	1400			King Portugal 1521-1557. Introduced Inquisition
John Kerr, Sir		Celebrity	10			15	political celebrity
John of Austria (Don John)	1629-1679	Royalty	150				
John VI	1769-1826	Clergy		230			King of Portugal
John, Augustus E.	1878-1916	Artist	50	135	330		Welch. Portraits, Landscapes
John, Christopher J		Congress	10			15	Member U.S. Congress
John, Elton		Entertainment	45	178	225	87	Br. Singer-Songwriter
John, Lee		Music	10			15	performing musical artist
Johns, Brig. Gen. Dwight F.	1894-1977	Military	30				World War II U.S. general
Johns, Glynis		Entertainment	15	15	30	30	Br. Actress. Leading Lady. Later, Character Roles
Johns, Jasper		Artist	40	75		75	Am. Pop Artist. FDC/Leroy Neiman 150

NAME	DATE	CATEGORY	SIG	LS/DS	ALS	SP	COMMENTS
Johns, Patrick		Author	8			12	
Johns, William Earl	1893-1968	Author		100			Creator of 'Biggles'
Johnson Jr., Daniel H.		Celebrity	10			15	medical expert
Johnson, Adam Rankin	1834-1922	Civil War	352				Confederate general, rare DS 3335
Johnson, Amy (Mollison)	1903-1941	Aviation	60	90	135	288	Br. Aviation Pioneer
Johnson, Amy Jo		Entertainment	5			28	Actress. Pin-Up 48
Johnson, Andrew (As Pres.)		President	474	1459	5806	3500	Impeached,.FF 775-1500
Johnson, Andrew	1808-1875	Civil War	475	1200			Union general, Mil. Gov. TN, US President
Johnson, Andrew	1808-1875	President	401	1032	4451	3000	ALS/Content 19,500. FF 675-775-1,400
Johnson, Art		Aviation	10	25	40	30	ACE, WW II, USAAF Ace
Johnson, Ben	d. 1998	Entertainment	35	70		60	Oscar winner. Popular Western Star
Johnson, Betty		Entertainment	3	3	6	8	
Johnson, Bradley T. (WD)	1829-1903	Civil War	150	280	550		CSA Gen.
Johnson, Bradley T.	1829-1903	Civil War	103	160	202		CSA Gen.,ALS/Content 4,500
Johnson, Brian		Entertainment	8			35	Music. Lead Singer 'AC/DC'
Johnson, Brig. Gen. Bernard A.	1898-?	Military	30				World War II U.S. general
Johnson, Brig. Gen. James H.	1887-1964	Military	30				World War II U.S. general
Johnson, Brig. Gen. Neal C.	1892-1979	Military	30				World War II U.S. general
Johnson, Brig. Gen. Robert W.	1893-1968	Military	30				World War II U.S. general
Johnson, Bunk		Entertainment	200			550	Jazz Trumpet
Johnson, Bushrod Rust	1817-1880	Civil War	145	300	365		CSA General. Mexican War
Johnson, Cave	1793-1866	Cabinet	50	110	195		P.M.Gen. 1st US Postage Stamps
Johnson, Chic		Entertainment	30			55	1/2 of Zany Comedy Team (Olsen & Johnson)
Johnson, Crockett*		Cartoonist	50			500	'Barnaby'
Johnson, David Earle		Author	8			12	Islamic history/influences
Johnson, Don		Entertainment	15			37	Actor
Johnson, Eastman	1824-1906	Artist	40	60	185	300	Am. Portrait & Genre Artist
Johnson, Eddie Bernice	1955-	Congress	5			20	Afr-Am Dem MOC TX
Johnson, Edward 'Old Alleghany'	1816-1873	Civil War	118	310			Confederate general
Johnson, Edward		Entertainment	25			75	Distinguished Canadian Tenor
Johnson, Eliza M.		First Lady	750	1500			
Johnson, Frank*		Cartoonist	5			40	
Johnson, Fred*		Cartoonist	10			45	'Moon Mullins'
Johnson, Gerald		Aviation	15	30	55	40	ACE, WW II
Johnson, H. Hank		Business	4			15	Pres. Spiegel. Catalog
Johnson, Harold K.		Military	15	35	50	35	WW II. Prisoner. 4 Star Gen.
Johnson, Haynes		Celebrity	10			15	media/TV personality
Johnson, Henry A.		Business	5			15	CEO Spiegel Inc.
Johnson, Herschel	1812-1880	Civil War	40	115			Gov. GA, CSA Senator, Member of CSA Congress
Johnson, Hiram W.	1866-1945	Congress	22	60		70	Powerful Senator CA
Johnson, Howard B.		Business	80			95	Howard Johnson Inns
Johnson, Howard S.		Business	12	30		25	
Johnson, Hugh S.		Cabinet	15	90	125	35	Gen., Dir. NRA During Depression. FDR
Johnson, James "Johnnie"	1916-1997	Aviation	50	75	135	118	Ace, WWII, Br. RAF Top Ace
Johnson, James K.		Aviation	10	25	40	35	ACE, Korea, Double Ace

NAME	DATE	CATEGORY	SIG	LS/DS	ALS	SP	COMMENTS
Johnson, James Weldon		Author	35	100	225		NAACP,1st Ed.'Black Manhattan' S 695-795
Johnson, Jesse G.		Military	35	85	170	90	Adm. WW II
Johnson, John H.	1918-	Publisher		50		65	1st Afro-Am Periodicals. 'Ebony', 'Jet'
Johnson, Jonathan Eastman		Artist	35	150			Am. Portrait, Genre Painter
Johnson, Keen		Governor	5	15		10	Governor KY
Johnson, L.B. & Lady Bird		Pres.-1st Lady				600	
Johnson, Lady Bird		First Lady	37	85		101	Vintage FDC 'Beautification of America' S 80
Johnson, LeRoy		Congress	4			10	
Johnson, Louis A.	1891-1966	Cabinet	15	40	60	35	Sec'y Defense 1949 Truman
Johnson, Lyndon B.	1908-1973	President	176	323		348	ALS As VP 4500. Rare ANS 950
Johnson, Lyndon B.(As Pres.)		President	195	983	3282	450	TLS as Pres. 1,250-4,200/Content
Johnson, Lynn		Cartoonist	27			65	'For Better Or Worst'
Johnson, Lynn-Holly		Entertainment	8	10	12	20	Actress
Johnson, Maj. Gen. Dudley G.	1884-1975	Military	25				World War II British general
Johnson, Maj. Gen. Harry H.	1895-1986	Military	30				World War II U.S. general
Johnson, Martin	1884-1937	Explorer-Photogr.	15	40		55	With Osa, Wild Animal Films. African Explorers
Johnson, Nancy L. J.		Congress	10			15	Member U.S. Congress
Johnson, Nunnally	1897-1977	Author	20	65		40	Am. Playwright, Screenwriter
Johnson, Oliver		Celebrity	5	15	30		
Johnson, Osa		Explorer-Photogr.	15	20	35	45	With Martin, Wild Animal Films
Johnson, Philip		Architect	22			108	Early Skyscrapers
Johnson, Reverdy	1796-1876	Cabinet	25	95	105		Statesman, Att'y Gen.,US Sen. MD
Johnson, Richard L.		Aviation	15	20	35	25	
Johnson, Richard M.	1780-1850	Vice President	56	152	190	400	Van Buren Vice Pres.
Johnson, Richard W	1827-1897	Civil War	40	110	140		Union general
Johnson, Robert S.		Aviation	20	25	45	80	ACE, WW II, #5 US
Johnson, Robert W.		Business	55	190			Fndr. Johnson & Johnson. Important DS 7750
Johnson, Robert Ward	1814-1879	Civil War	42	64	117		Member of Confederate Congress
Johnson, Russell		Entertainment	9		6	60	Actor, Gilligan's Island
Johnson, Sam J		Congress	10			15	Member U.S. Congress
Johnson, Samuel C.		Business	5			10	Pres. Johnson's Wax
Johnson, Samuel, Dr.		Author	1740	4080			Lexicographer, Critic
Johnson, Thomas	1812-1906	Civil War		84			Member of Confederate Congress
Johnson, Tim		Senate	10			15	United States Senate (D - SD)
Johnson, Van		Entertainment	14			28	MGM Leading Man in Straight Leads & Musicals
Johnson, Waldo Porter	1817-1885	Civil War		117			Member of Confederate Congress
Johnson, William B.		Business	5			10	CEO Railway Express
Johnson, William Cost		Senate/Congress	10	20	35		MOC MD 1833
Johnson, William Sam'l	1727-1819	Revolutionary War	130	358	675		Signer U.S. Constitution. Continental Congress
Johnson, William		Military	30		125	35	Maj. Gen'l USA 91st Div. AEF. WW I
Johnson, William	1715-1774	Colonial Amer.		2250			Br. Fur Trader. Superintendent Indian Affairs
Johnson, Willis, Dr.	1869-1951	Educator	8			15	
Johnston, Albert Sidney	1803-1862	Civil War	410	2700	3990	3500	CSA Gen.,TX Sec.War., DS 9500-21127, Sig/Rank 650
Johnston, Brig. Gen. Paul W.	1892- ?	Military	30				World War II U.S. general
Johnston, Frances	1864-1952	Photographer	5	25			1st Famous Female Photographer

NAME	DATE	CATEGORY	SIG	LS/DS	ALS	SP	COMMENTS
Johnston, George D.	1832-1910	Civil War	95	360	382		CSA Gen.
Johnston, Harriet Lane		Acting First Lady	200		625		Buchanan's Niece
Johnston, J. Lawson		Business	15	35	60		
Johnston, Johnny		Aviation	28	45		62	
Johnston, Joseph E. (WD)		Civil War	325	750	1326	2642	CSA Gen. ALS 12/1861/Content 10,000
Johnston, Joseph E.	1807-1891	Civil War	251	432	774	2250	CSA ALS/Cont 3,500-12,000. FF 500
Johnston, Kristen		Entertainment	10			20	actress
Johnston, Lynn*		Cartoonist	20			75	'For Better or Worse'
Johnston, Mary		Astronauts	5			20	
Johnston, Olin D.		Senate/Congress	5	15			U.S. Senator SC 1945
Johnston, Richard M.		Author	5	10	20		
Johnston, Robert Daniel	1837-1919	Civil War	110	193			Confederate general
Johnston, Robert	1818-1885	Civil War	42				Member of Confederate Congress
Johnstone, Maj. Gen. Reginald F.	1904-1976	Military	25				World War II British general
Jolie, Angelina		Entertainment	10			54	Actress
Joliot-Curie, Frederic & Irene		Science	200				Scientific Nobel Winning Team
Joliot-Curie, Irene	1897-1956	Science	45		205		
Joliot-Curie, Jean Frederic	1900-1958	Science		350	500		Fr. Physicist. Nobel '35.Son-in-law Pierre/Marie
Jolley, I. Stanford		Entertainment	20			50	
Jolly, Lt. Gen. Sir Gordon Grey	1886-1962	Military	25				World War II British general
Jolson, Al	1886-1950	Entertainment	117	204		281	Starred in 1st Talking Picture. SP in Blackface 500
Jonckheer, Pierre		Political	10			15	Member European Parliament
Jones, Allan	1907-1982	Entertainment	15	20	35	26	Film & Concert Singer. Many Popular 40's Musicals
Jones, Anne		Country Music	10			20	Singer
Jones, Annisa		Entertainment	150			325	TV Sitcom 'Family Affair'
Jones, Anson	1798-1858	Am. Politician	350		1200		Physician, Pres. Texas Repub.
Jones, Anthony Armstrong		Country Music	10			20	Singer
Jones, B.J.		Author	8			12	books for children
Jones, Bob		Clergy	15	25	60	25	'Bob Jones University'
Jones, Brig. Gen. Edwin W.	1896-1956	Military	30				World War II U.S. general
Jones, Brig. Gen. Thomas H.	1885-1947	Military	30				World War II U.S. general
Jones, Buck	1889-1942	Entertainment	170	230	300	427	Vintage Film Cowboy. Major Star
Jones, Carolyn	1929-1983	Entertainment	75	98	120	150	Actress. 'Morticia' on TV's 'Addams Family'
Jones, Casey		Aviation	32	82	175	117	
Jones, Catherine Zeta		Entertainment	12			60	Actress. AA Winner
Jones, Cherry		Entertainment	10			20	actress
Jones, Chuck*		Cartoonist	25			175	Animator
Jones, Claude A.		Military	40	65			
Jones, Daniel	1912-1993	Composer					Welsh composer AMuQS 80
Jones, David (Davy)		Entertainment	15			38	'The Monkees'
Jones, David C., Gen.	1879-1958	Military	8			42	Chairman/Chiefs of Staff
Jones, David R. (WD)	1825-1863	Civil War	472	2895	5175		CSA Gen.Died Richmond, VA 1/15/63. Coronary
Jones, David Rumph	1825-1863	Civil War	305	800			CSA Gen. Served/Beauregard & Longstreet
Jones, Dean	1933-	Entertainment	10	15	25	30	Actor. Numerous Disney Films
Jones, Dick		Entertainment	8			30	

NAME	DATE	CATEGORY	SIG	LS/DS	ALS	SP	COMMENTS
Jones, E. Stanley		Clergy	35	50	75	50	
Jones, Edward F.	1828-1913	Civil War	30	55	80	150	Union Gen. War Dte. DS. 210. Sig/Rank 80
Jones, Ernest	1879-1958	Science	20		75		Br. Psychoanalyst, Biographer of Freud
Jones, George Washington		Civil War	57	162			Member of Confederate Congress
Jones, George		Entertainment	10			25	C & W
Jones, Grace		Entertainment	18	20	30	40	'007' SP 65
Jones, Gwyneth		Entertainment	15			40	Opera
Jones, Henry Cox	1821-1913	Civil War	57		162		Member of Confederate Congress
Jones, Henry		Entertainment	5			15	Actor. Character
Jones, Howard		Entertainment	10			20	
Jones, Isham		Entertainment	15			40	Vintage Big Bandleader-Composer
Jones, J. Carey		Military	28	45		35	Admiral WW II
Jones, Jack		Entertainment	10			18	Pop Singer Son of Alan Jones
Jones, James Earl	1931-	Entertainment	10			40	Broadway-Films-TV Actor. Darth Vader Voice
Jones, James		Author	50	190		60	'From Here To Eternity'
Jones, Janet		Entertainment	10	15	30	30	Singer. Pin-Up SP 30
Jones, Jeffrey		Entertainment	4			20	Comic Bad Guy
Jones, Jennifer		Entertainment	140	200		361	AA Actress. Reluctant Signer
Jones, Jenny		Entertainment	10			20	TV Talk Show Host
Jones, Jesse H.		Cabinet	10	15	15	15	Sec'y Commerce 1940
Jones, Jim		Clergy	250	375	650	850	
Jones, John Marshall	1820-1864	Civil War	238	704			CSA Gen. Sig/Rank 1050, War Dte DS 2850
Jones, John Paul		Entertainment	50			175	Music. Drummer 'Led Zeppelin'
Jones, John Paul	1747-1792	Military-Rev. War	5750				Naval Hero.'I have not yet begun to fight!'
Jones, John Percival		Senate/Congress	10		25		U.S. Senator NV 1873
Jones, John Robert	1827-1901	Civil War	120	191	587		Confederate general
Jones, L.Q.		Entertainment	5			15	
Jones, Le Roi (See Baraka)		Author					Afr-Am Playwright, Poet, Novelist, Essayist
Jones, Lisa		Celebrity	10			15	motivational speaker
Jones, Lois Mailou	1905-1998	Artist	20		35		Noted Afr-Am Artist
Jones, Louis 'Grandpa'	1913-1998	Entertainment	20			35	'Grandpa' Jones. Country Singer, Banjoist.'Hee Haw
Jones, Louis R.		Military	10	30			
Jones, Luther 'Casey'		Celebrity	100				Legendary railroad engineer
Jones, Maj. Gen. Alan W.	1894-1969	Military	30				World War II U.S. general
Jones, Maj. Gen. Albert M.	1890-1967	Military	30				World War II U.S. general
Jones, Maj. Gen. David M.		Astronaut	10			25	
Jones, Maj. Gen. Henry L.C.	1887-1969	Military	30				World War II U.S. general
Jones, Maj. Gen. Lloyd E.	1889-1958	Military	30				World War II U.S. general
Jones, Marcia Mae		Entertainment	5	11	15	20	Child & Juvenile Actress
Jones, Mary H. 'Mother'	1830-1930	Labor	60	195	430		Agitator, Speaker, Organizer NYC Garment Workers
Jones, Norah		Celebrity	10			35	Grammy award winner
Jones, Patrick Henry	1830-1900	Civil War	45	80	130		Union general
Jones, Paula		Celebrity	8			25	Newsmaker, Clinton Accuser
Jones, Quincy		Composer	15	31	35	30	AMusQS 50
Jones, Rickie Lee		Entertainment	20			40	

NAME	DATE	CATEGORY	SIG	LS/DS	ALS	SP	COMMENTS
Jones, Robert McDonald	1808-1872	Civil War	54				Member of Confederate Congress
Jones, Samuel (WD)		Civil War	202	615	700		CSA Gen.
Jones, Samuel	1819-1887	Civil War	110	400			CSA General
Jones, Samuel Porter		Clergy	15	25	110		
Jones, Shirley		Entertainment	10	33		28	Actress. AA Award Winner. 'Partridge Family'
Jones, Simon		Entertainment	6			25	Music. Bass Guitar 'The Verve'
Jones, Spike	1911-1965	Entertainment	35			75	Big Band Leader. Novelty added
Jones, Star		Celebrity	10			15	media/TV personality
Jones, Stephanie Tubbs J		Congress	10			15	Member U.S. Congress
Jones, Terry		Entertainment	10			20	actor
Jones, Thomas McKissick	1816-1892	Civil War		100			Member of Confederate Congress
Jones, Thomas V.		Business	15	30		25	
Jones, Thomas		Astronaut	11			20	
Jones, Tom		Astronaut	6			21	
Jones, Tom		Entertainment	12	15	25	40	'Top Pop Singer 60's. Comeback in 90's
Jones, Tommy Lee		Entertainment	20			55	Col. SP Batman 60. Film DS 650, 495
Jones, Vinnie		Entertainment	10			20	Actor
Jones, Walter B. J		Congress	10			15	Member U.S. Congress
Jones, William E. (WD)	1824-1864	Civil War	275	750	1250		CSA Brig. Gen. 'Grumble' KIA Piedmont, Virginia
Jones, William E.	1824-1864	Civil War	152	212	525		
Jong, Erica		Author	10	14	25	15	Best Selling Bawdy Autobiography
Jongkind, Johan	1819-1891	Artist	200	450	860		Dutch. Master of Rendering Light
Jonnson, Ulrika		Celebrity	10			15	celebrity model
Jöns, Karin		Political	10			15	Member European Parliament
Jonson, Ben	1572-1637	Author	2850				Br. Playwright, Poet. 'Volpone', 'The Alchemist'
Jope, Bernhard		Aviation	10	25	40	30	
Joplin, Janis	1943-1970	Entertainment	712	1256	3134	2483	Blues & Rock Singer. Died of Heroin Overdose at 27
Joplin, Scott		Composer	700	1090	2000		Rag Time Composer
Jordan, Barbara	1936-1996	Senate/Congress	15	60		30	Highly Respected Afr-Am.Congresswoman TX
Jordan, Diane-Louise		Celebrity	10			15	television presenter
Jordan, Dorothy		Entertainment	15	20	35	30	
Jordan, Gen. of Infantry Hans	1892-1975	Military	27				World War II German general
Jordan, Hamilton		Gov't Official	5	15	25	20	Chief of Staff Carter Admin.
Jordan, Jim (FibberMcGee)		Entertainment	15	20	35	25	Top Radio Comedy Team 'Fibber McGee & Molly'
Jordan, John Alfred		Author	15			30	African adventure
Jordan, June		Celebrity	10			15	motivational speaker
Jordan, Louis		Entertainment	25			65	Big Band Leader
Jordan, Neil		Celebrity	10			15	film industry
Jordan, Thomas (WD)		Civil War	140	335	663		CSA Gen. Mexican War. ALS/Cont. 1195
Jordan, Thomas	1819-1895	Civil War	73	252	349		CSA General. Mexican War
Jordan, Vernon	1935-	Political	20	16		90	Powerful D.C. Fixer. Clinton Friend & Advisor
Jordanaires, The (4)		Entertainment	35			95	Gospel Quartet
Jordon, Richard		Entertainment	10		25	25	
Jorgensen, Christine	1926-1989	Celebrity	28	40	65	75	1st To Undergo Sex Change
Jorn, Carl		Entertainment	30			85	Opera

NAME	DATE	CATEGORY	SIG	LS/DS	ALS	SP	COMMENTS
Jory, Victor	1902-1982	Entertainment	52	60		152	Longtime Popular Character Actor. GWTW Collectible
Jose, Richard J.		Entertainment	8			15	Singer
Joseph I	1678-1711	Royalty		562			Holy Roman Emp., King Hungary, King of Romans
Joseph II	1741-1790	Royalty	125	359	875		King Ger. & Holy Roman Empire
Joseph, Lesley		Entertainment	10			20	Actress
Josephine, Empress	1783-1814	Royalty	912	1600	2857		Fr. (First) Wife of Napoleon
Joslyn, Allyn		Entertainment	17			55	Actor. Comedic Character Roles
Jossefy, Raphael	1853-1915	Entertainment	25			125	Pianist, Pupil of Liszt, Teacher. AMusQS 100
Jostyn, Jennifer		Entertainment	10			20	actress
Joswig, Wilhelm		Aviation	10			30	
Jouett, James		Civil War	25	55	125		Union Naval Officer/Farragut
Jouhaux, Benjamin	1879-1954	Reformer	25	60	140	50	Nobel Peace Prize 1951
Jourdan, Jean B., Count		Napoleonic Wars	55	260	305		Marshal of Napoleon
Jourdan, Louis	1919-1993	Entertainment	18	25	30	35	Handsome Fr. Leading Man. 'Gigi'
Journey		Entertainment	48			70	Entire Band Signed
Jové Peres, Salvador		Political	10			15	Member European Parliament
Jovovich, Milla		Entertainment	15			38	
Jowett, Benjamin	1817-1893	Scholar	10	25	35		Br. Master of Balliol.Plato & Socrates Translator
Jowett, Charles		Clergy	15	20	25		
Joy, James F.	1810-1896	Business	75	450	750		RR Baron,signed stock cert.1275
Joy, Jimmie		Bandleader	10			20	
Joy, Leatrice	1899-1985	Entertainment	25			35	Silent Film Star. 'Ten Commandments'
Joyce, Alice	1890-1955	Entertainment	15	25		60	Silent Star
Joyce, Brenda	1917-	Entertainment	15			25	Actress. 'Jane' in 5 Tarzan Films.
Joyce, Elaine		Entertainment	4	4	9	12	
Joyce, James	1882-1941	Author	442	595	4077	6300	Ir. Novelist, Poet, Playwright
Joyce, Maj. Gen. Keyton A.	1879-1960	Military	30				World War II U.S. general
Joyce, Richard		Military	40	100	175		
Juan Carlos, de Borbon		Royalty	55	120	245	150	King of Spain. So Designated by Franco in 1975
Juarez, Benito	1806-1872	Head of State	425	1008	1606	1500	Twice Pres. Mexico. Revolutionary
Judah, Henry Moses	1821-1866	Civil War	50	80	120		Union general
Judah, Theodore D.		Business		18000			Started Central Pac. RR .Rare DS 18,000
Judd, Ashley		Entertainment	15			49	Actress. Almost Nude Pin-up 80
Judd, Naomi & Wynona		Country Music	25			55	Beautiful Mother-Daughter Team
Judd, Norman B.	1815-1878	Congress	50		85		MOC. IL, Nominated A. Lincoln. Minister to Berlin
Judd, Walter H.	1898-	Congress	10	15		20	Congressman MN
Judge, Arline		Entertainment	10	15	35	17	Much Married Actress. 30's-40's
Judge, Mike*		Cartoonist	15			35	Printed Repro. S 50
Juin, Alphonse-Pierre	1888-1967	Military	20				Marshal of France, World War II French general
Julia, Raul		Entertainment	28			74	Actor. Premature Death. 'Addams Family' 'Gomez'
Julian, George W.	1817-1899	Congress	15	30	75		Co-Founder Free Soil Party, MOC. IN
Juliana, Queen		Royalty	100	250	710	350	Netherlands
Jumangi (Cast Of)		Entertainment				200	Williams, Hunt, Durst, Pierce
Jump, Gordon		Entertainment	8	10	15	20	Actor
Jung, Carl Gustav	1875-1961	Science	450	1783	3175	2320	Swiss Psychiatrist-Psychologist

NAME	DATE	CATEGORY	SIG	LS/DS	ALS	SP	COMMENTS
Junker, Karin		Political	10			15	Member European Parliament
Junkers, Hugo		Science	50		355		Ger. Airplane Engineer-Designer
Junot, Andoche 17		Military	70	235			Fr. Gen., Sec'y to Napoleon. Duc d'Abrante's
Jupitus, Phil		Celebrity	10			15	comedian
Jurgens, Curt		Entertainment	15			45	Scandanavian Actor
Jurgens, Dick		Entertainment	20			45	Big Band Leader
Jusserand, Jean Jules	1855-1932	Author		22	48		Pulitzer Prize. Fr. Diplomat, Author, Scholar
Justice, Bill*		Cartoonist	25			58	'The Chipmunks'. Full Size Color S 250
Juttner, Arthur		Military	10			30	Ger. RK Winner
Juxon, William	1582-1663	Clergy	125	400			Archbshp.Canterbury.Attended Chas. I on Scaffold

K

NAME	DATE	CATEGORY	SIG	LS/DS	ALS	SP	COMMENTS
Kabrich, Brig. Gen. William C.	1895-1947	Military	30				World War II U.S. general
Kadar, Janos	1912-1989	Head of State	50	130			Hungarian Prime Minister
Kader, Omar		Celebrity	10			15	political celebrity
Kaelin, Kato		Entertainment	30	65		45	Actor. Houseguest O.J. Simpson Turned Celebrity
Kafka, Franz	1883-1924	Author	850		2250		Ger. Novelist. Visionary Tales. Special ALS 16500
Kaganovich, Lazar		Military		256			Stalin's mass murderer
Kagesa, Lt. Gen. Sadaaki	1893-1948	Military	225				World War II Japanese general
Kahn, Alfred		Celebrity	10			15	financial expert
Kahn, Julius	1861-1924	Congress	5	15			Repr. CA 1899
Kahn, Madeline		Entertainment	5	6	15	32	
Kahn, Otto H.	1867-1934	Business	50	75	135	125	Banker, Philanthropist, Arts Patron
Kahn, Yahya		Head of State	30			50	Pakistan
Kahoutek, Lubos		Science	5	15	30	15	Am. Astronomer
Kaine, Jeff		Celebrity	10			15	photographer
Kaiser, Henry J.	1882-1967	Industrialist	125	225		312	S.F.Bay Bridge.Grand Coulee Dam etc.
Kai-Shek, Chiang & Mme.		Head of State				375	
Kai-Shek, Chiang	1887-1975	Head of State	100	220	450	300	Republic of China
Kai-Shek, Mayling Soong Chiang		Author	50	275		120	Madame Chiang
Kajisuka, Lt. Gen. Ryuji		Military	25				World War II Japanese general
Kalakaua, David	1836-1891	Royalty	271	425	775	1600	King Hawaii. Opposition To His Reform = Revolution
Kallen, Kitty		Entertainment		20		25	Big Band Vocalist
Kalmanoff, Martin		Composer	10		25		Numerous Works for Musical Theatre, Opera, etc.
Kaltenborn, H. V.		Radio	5	15	30	15	Radio Commentator
Kaltenbrunner, Ernst		Military	125	537		400	Perpetrator of Nazi Atrocities
Kalugin, Oleg		Celebrity	10			15	political celebrity
Kamburg, Arthur, Dr		Science	10	20			Nobel
Kamehameha II, Liholiho	1797-1824	Royalty	960		3850		King Hawaii
Kamehameha III, Kauikeaouli		Royalty	750	1585			King Hawaii
Kamehameha IV	1824-1863	Royalty		2500			King of Hawaii
Kamel, Stanley		Entertainment	10			20	actor

NAME	DATE	CATEGORY	SIG	LS/DS	ALS	SP	COMMENTS
Kamenev, Lev	b. 1883	Military		347			Bolshevik leader
Kamin, Daniel		Entertainment	10			20	actor
Kaminsky, Max		Entertainment	10			30	Dixieland Jazz Bandleader
Kamio, Mitsuomi		Military	110		225		
Kamionsky, Oscar		Entertainment				350	Great Jewish Baritone
Kammhuber, Josef		Aviation	20	30	65	35	Ger. Air Defense Gen. WW II. RK
Kampelman, Max		Celebrity	10			15	political celebrity
Kanaly, Steve		Entertainment	6	8	15	20	
Kander, John		Composer	10	45	95	25	Composed with Fred Ebb. 'Cabaret' etc.
Kandinski, Vasili	1866-1944	Artist	200	795			Rus. Painter. Cont. TLS 1,500
Kandor, John		Composer					See EBB, Fred
Kane, Bob*	1916-1999	Cartoonist	72			395	'Batman' Illustr.Drawing 230-795, Comic Bk. S 100
Kane, Brig. Gen. Paul V.	1892-1959	Military	30				World War II U.S. general
Kane, Carol		Entertainment	10	15	15	25	
Kane, Elisha Kent	1820-1857	Explorer	95	215	450		Grinnell Arctic Expedition
Kane, Helen	1904-1966	Entertainment	25			60	Boop-Boop-a-Doop Girl. Singer of the 20's
Kane, Richard		Military	20			90	
Kane, Thomas L.	1822-1883	Civil War	48	105	160		Union Gen.ALS '63 990
Kangaroo, Captain		Entertainment	5	6	15	30	
Kanin, Fld. Mrshl. Kotohito Prince	1865-1945	Military	25				World War II Japanese general
Kanin, Garson		Author	10	20	50	45	Playwright, Director, Screen.
Kanjorski, Paul E. K		Congress	10			15	Member U.S. Congress
Kansas		Entertainment	30			60	
Kant, Immanuel	1724-1804	Author	1005	3950	7375		Ger. Philosopher, Professor
Kantner, China		Entertainment	10			20	actress
Kantor, MacKinlay	1904-1977	Author	15	45	75	30	Am. Novelist. 'Andersonville', Pulitzer 1956
Kantor, Mickey		Celebrity	10			15	political celebrity
Kantrowitz, Adrian, Dr.		Science	25	70	145	30	
Kaper, Bronislaw		Composer	10	30	55	15	
Kapitza, Peter	1894-1984	Science		375	550		Nobel Prize Physics '78
Kaplan, Gabe		Entertainment	5			28	
Kaplan, Gilbert		Conductor				50	Mahler Specialist
Kaplinsky, Natasha		Celebrity	10			15	newsreader
Kapliolani	1834-1899	Royalty	250			1500	Queen Hawaii
Kappel, Frederick R.		Business	3	6	15	8	
Kappel, Gertrude		Entertainment	20			95	Wagnerian Soprano
Kaptur, Marcy K		Congress	10			15	Member U.S. Congress
Kapture, Mitzi		Entertainment	8			35	Actress. Pin-Up 60
Karajan, Herbert von	1908-1989	Conductor	58		325	409	Austrian Classical Conductor
Karamanou, Anna		Political	10			15	Member European Parliament
Karas, Anton		Composer	25	40	85	100	Third Man Theme AMusQS 350
Karas, Othmar		Political	10			15	Member European Parliament
Karloff, Boris	1887-1969	Entertainment	396	291	500	673	'Frankenstein'. 3x4 SPI 295
Karlsson, Hans		Political	10			15	Member European Parliament
Karlstad, Brig. Gen. Charles H.	1894-1960	Military	30				World War II U.S. general

NAME	DATE	CATEGORY	SIG	LS/DS	ALS	SP	COMMENTS
Karmakar, Romuald		Celebrity	10			15	film industry
Karman, Theodore von		Industrial	30	60	110	65	Automobile Designer. Karman-Ghia VW
Karn, Richard		Entertainment	10			20	actor
Karns, Roscoe		Entertainment	30			75	
Karpis, Alvin Creepy	1908-1979	Criminal	75	225	300	300	30's Public Enemy #1
Karras, Alex		Entertainment	5	6	15	15	
Karsavina, Tamara		Entertainment	50			362	Rus.-Br. Dancer
Karsh, Yousuf		Photographer	35	95	110	95	Portraits, Royalty, World Famous
Karslake, Lt. Gen. Sir Henry	1879-1942	Military	225				World War II British general
Kasaniff, Larry		Celebrity	10			15	film industry
Kasavubu, Joseph		Head of State	20	75	185	40	1st Pres. Dem. Repub. of Congo
Kaschmann, Giuseppe		Entertainment	60			325	Internationally Important Baritone Star
Kasdan, Sara		Author	8			12	Jewish life, humor, cooking
Kasem, Casey		Entertainment	5	8		20	Disc Jockey
Kasem, Jean		Entertainment	5	8		15	
Kasha, Al		Composer	15			45	
Kashfi, Anna		Entertainment	10		30	35	
Kassebaum, Nancy Landon		Senate	5	15		15	Senator KS
Kassell, Art		Bandleader	10			65	
Kassovitz, Mathieu		Celebrity	10			15	film industry
Kast, Sheilah		Celebrity	10			15	media/TV personality
Kasten, Maj. Gen. William H.	1891-1963	Military	30				World War II U.S. general
Kastler, Alfred, Dr.	1902-1984	Science	35	60		75	Nobel Physics '66. Orig'l Holograph Ms 850-975
Katchinsky, Victorin		Aviation	20			45	
Katiforis, Giorgos		Political	10			15	Member European Parliament
Kato, Maj. Gen. Sadamu		Military	25				World War II Japanese general
Katt, Nicky		Entertainment				35	
Katz, Bernard, Sir		Science	15	30	45	35	Nobel Medicine 1970
Katzenbach, Nicholas		Cabinet	10	20		15	Att'y General 1965
Katzenberg, Jeffrey		Business	15	25		25	Disney CEO
Katzir, Ephraim		Head of State	10			45	Pres. Israel '70's
Kaufman, Andy		Entertainment	85	150	225	162	Comedian-Actor. 'Taxi'. Very Early Death
Kaufman, George S.	1889-1961	Author	30	85	175	75	Dramatist, Critic, Director. Pulitzer. TLS/Cont. 275
Kaufman, Jonathan		Celebrity	10			15	media/TV personality
Kaufmann, Christine	1945-	Entertainment	5			20	Germ. Actress. Pretty 2nd Wife of Tony Curtis
Kaufmann, Sylvia-yvonne		Political	10			15	Member European Parliament
Kaunda, Kenneth		Head of State	40	150	350	122	1st Pres. Zambia
Kaupisch, Gen. of Art. Leonhard	1878-1945	Military	27				World War II German general
Kauppi, Piia-noora		Political	10			15	Member European Parliament
Kautz, August Valentine	1828-1895	Civil War	40	80	135		Union general
Kavelin, Al		Entertainment	10			20	Big Band Leader
Kawabe, General Masakasu	1886-1965	Military	25				World War II Japanese general
Kawabe, Lt. Gen. Torashiro	1890-1960	Military	25				World War II Japanese general
Kawasaki, Guy		Celebrity	10			15	motivational speaker
Kawato, Masajiro Mike		Aviation	40	100		150	Ace WW II, Downed Boyington

NAME	DATE	CATEGORY	SIG	LS/DS	ALS	SP	COMMENTS
Kay, Beatrice	1910-1981	Entertainment	10	20		22	Talented-Raucous Singer-Actress. Occasional Film
Kay, Dianne		Entertainment	3	3	6	6	
Kay, Herbie		Bandleader	10				
Kay, Mary (Ash)		Business	5	15	30	10	Cosmetics Empire
Kay, Mary Ellen		Entertainment				25	
Kay, Peter		Celebrity	10			15	comedian
Kay, Phil		Celebrity	10			15	comedian
Kaya, Lt. Gen. Tsunenori Prince	1900- ?	Military	25				World War II Japanese general
Kaye, Celia		Entertainment	4	5	10	12	
Kaye, Danny		Entertainment	80			125	
Kaye, Paul		Celebrity	10			15	comedian
Kaye, Sammy		Entertainment	15			40	Big Band Leader
Kaye, Stubby		Entertainment	10			25	
Kazamia, Andrew		Entertainment	10			20	Actor
Kazan, Elia		Entertainment	10	12	20	35	Director, Producer, Author
Kazan, Lainie		Entertainment	10			22	actress
Keach, Stacy		Entertainment	10	10		22	Actor. 'Mike Hammer' etc.
Kean, Jane		Entertainment	5	6	15	12	
Kean, Lt. Gen. William B.	1897-1981	Military	30				World War II U.S. general
Kean, Thomas H. Gov.		Celebrity	10			15	political celebrity
Keane, Bil*		Cartoonists	20	40		60	'The Family Circus'. Orig. Art 800
Keane, Edward		Entertainment	10			25	
Kearny, Philip (WD)		Civil War	409	650	1041		Union General KIA
Kearny, Philip	1815-1862	Civil War	256	330	558		Union general
Kearny, Stephen		Military-Governor	85	195	380		War of 1812, 1st Gov. of CA
Keating, Caron		Celebrity	10			15	children's presenter
Keating, Kenneth B.		Senate/Congress	5	15		10	Gen. WW II, MOC Senator 1947-65
Keating, Maj. Gen. Frank A.	1895-1973	Military	30				World War II U.S. general
Keating, Ronan		Music	10			15	performing musical artist
Keaton, Buster	1895-1966	Entertainment	169	250		415	Great Film Comedian
Keaton, Diane		Entertainment	15	35		48	AA Winning Actress. DS re 'Godfather III' 175
Keaton, Michael		Entertainment	15			47	As Batman SP 75
Keble, John	1792-1866	Clergy	75	125	232	295	Founder of Oxford Movement
Kedrova, Lila		Entertainment	10		25	40	
Keeble, John		Author	10	30	75		
Keegan, Andrew		Entertainment	10			20	actor
Keel, Howard		Entertainment	5	6	25	20	He-Man Singer-Actor
Keeler, Ruby	1909-1993	Entertainment	25			55	Once Busby Berkley Dancer. Wife of Al Jolson
Keena, Monica		Celebrity				35	
Keene, Carolyn		Author	5	15	30	10	Publisher Pseud.(5 Authors)
Keene, Charles S.		Entertainment	10			25	
Keene, Tom		Entertainment	25			50	Actor
Keerans, Brig. Gen. Charles L. Jr.	1899-1943	Military	30				World War II U.S. general
Kefauver, Estes		Senate	15	40		35	Senator TN
Keifer, Joseph W.		Civil War	25	45	60		Union Gen.& Speaker

NAME	DATE	CATEGORY	SIG	LS/DS	ALS	SP	COMMENTS
Keiffer, J. Warren (WD)		Civil War			1898		Union General
Keightley, Gen. Sir Chas. Frederic	1901-1974	Military	25				World War II British general
Keillor, Garrison		Author	15	25	35	20	Humorist
Keim, Betty Lou		Entertainment	5			12	Actress
Keim, George May	1805-1861	Congress	10				Repr. PA, Mayor Reading, PA
Keim, William High	1813-1862	Civil War	167	487			Union general
Keirstead, Wilfred C.		Clergy	10	15	20	15	
Keisha		Model	5			15	Pin-Up SP 25
Keitel, Harvey		Entertainment	15			52	Elusive Signer
Keitel, Wilhelm	1882-1946	Military	262	515	850	763	Ger. Fld. Marshal WWII
Keith, Arthur, Sir		Author	10		35		Anthropologist, Origins of Man
Keith, Brian		Entertainment	5	8	15	20	
Keith, David		Entertainment	5	6	15	10	
Keith, George Keith E.	1746-1823	Military	50	110	175		Br. Admiral. 1746-1823. Viscount
Keith, Ian		Entertainment	15				Vintage Actor
Keith, Penelope		Entertainment	10			20	Actress
Keith, Rosalind		Entertainment	10			75	
Keith, William,	1680-1749	Revolutionary War	135	552	700		Colonial Lt. Governor PA & DE
Kekkonen, Urho		Head of State	15	45			Finland
Kelcey, Herbert		Entertainment	10			20	Vintage Stage Actor
Keliher, Brig. Gen. John	1891-1964	Military	30				World War II U.S. general
Kelland, Clarence Buddington		Author	20	55	150	30	Am. Novelist, Short Stories
Kellar, Harry		Entertainment	15			35	Vintage Stage Actor
Kellard, Ralph		Entertainment	10			25	
Kellaway, Cecil		Entertainment	25			75	
Kelleghan, Fiona		Author	8			12	bibliographies
Keller, Helen & A. Sullivan		Author-Teacher	535			2200	
Keller, Helen	1880-1968	Author	155	512	1242	812	Blind, Deaf, Mute Author. TLS/Cont. 1450
Keller, Maj. Gen. Francois-P-L	1884-1981	Military	20				World War II French general
Keller, Maj. Gen. Louis-Marie-J-F	1881-1944	Military	20				World War II French general
Keller, Maj. Gen. Rodney Fred. L.	1900-1954	Military	20				World War II Canadian general
Keller, Ric K.		Congress	10			15	Member U.S. Congress
Kellerman, Annette		Entertainment	45		165	175	Aussie Dancer & Swimming Star
Kellerman, F.C., Duke Valmy		Military	75	285	405		7 Years' War. Marshal of Nap.
kellerman, Jonathan		Author	4			15	Author of 'Billy Straight'
Kellerman, Sally		Entertainment	10			25	
Kelley, Benjamin Franklin	1807-1891	Civil War	43		110		Union general
Kelley, Clarence	1911-1997	Cabinet	20	35	35	45	Dir. FBI
Kelley, David E.		Celebrity	10			25	film industry
Kelley, Deforest		Entertainment	10	15	25	35	Star Trek
Kelley, Kitty		Author	12			20	Celebrity Biography
Kelley, Patrick Henry		Senate/Congress	5	10		10	MOC MI 1913
Kelley, Virginia Clinton		President Mother	15	65			Mother of Bill Clinton
Kellogg, Charlotte		Philanthropist	7	20			Mrs. Vernon Kellogg
Kellogg, Frank B.	1856-1937	Cabinet	32	70	95	75	Nobel Peace Prize 1929

NAME	DATE	CATEGORY	SIG	LS/DS	ALS	SP	COMMENTS
Kellogg, John Harvey, Dr.		Food Business	15	35	75		Am. Phys.Health Reformer.Breakfast Cereal
Kellogg, Ray		Entertainment	5			9	Actor
Kellogg, W. K.		Business	110	150	325	200	Fndr. W.K. Kellogg Co.
Kellogg, William P.	1831-1918	Congress	50	100			U.S. Senator 1868, Gov. LA 1873-77
Kells, Maj. Gen. Clarence H.	1892-1954	Military	40				World War II U.S. general
Kelly , Lorraine		Celebrity	10			15	television presenter
Kelly, Brig. Gen. Paul B.	1896-1971	Military	30				World War II U.S. general
Kelly, Daniel Hugh		Entertainment	10			20	actor
Kelly, Edward J.		Political	10			15	Mayor Chicago
Kelly, Emmett, Sr.	1898-1979	Entertainment	52	150		244	Circus Clown ' Weary Willie' Circus FDC S 125
Kelly, Gene	1912-1996	Entertainment	33			126	AA Dancer, Actor, Choreographer, Director
Kelly, Grace	1928-1982	Entertainment	175	246	1030	607	AA, AA
Kelly, Howard A., Dr.		Science	20	35	60	40	Orig. Faculty Johns Hopkins U.
Kelly, Jack		Entertainment	15			45	
Kelly, John H.	1840-1864	Civil War	462	975			CSA Gen., Youngest Killed
Kelly, Kate		Celebrity	10			15	media/TV personality
Kelly, Kevin		Celebrity	10			15	media/TV personality
Kelly, Matthew		Celebrity	10			15	television presenter
Kelly, Moira		Entertainment	20			40	
Kelly, Nancy		Entertainment	10	20		25	
Kelly, Patsy	1910-1981	Entertainment	26	30	65	60	Comedienne-Actress. Wisecracking Hal Roach Star
Kelly, Paul		Entertainment	25			55	
Kelly, Paula		Entertainment	5		12	15	Pin-Up SP 18
Kelly, Ross		Celebrity	10			15	television presenter
Kelly, Scott		Astronaut	5			18	
Kelly, Sue W. K		Congress	10			15	Member U.S. Congress
Kelly, Thomas W.		Military	10	20		15	Gen. Desert Storm
Kelly, Walt*		Cartoonists	50	200		425	Pogo
Kelser, Brig. Gen. Raymond A.	1892-1952	Military	30				World War II U.S. general
Kelsey, Fred		Entertainment	25				Character Actor
Kelsey, Linda		Entertainment	5	6	15	15	
Keltie, Sir John Scott	1840-1927	Science			100		Geographer
Kelton, Pert	1907-1968	Entertainment	25		45	48	Comedienne. Original 'Alice' in The Honeymooners
Kelvin, William T., Lord	1824-1907	Science	85	195	288	175	Kelvin Scale, Atlantic Cable
Kemble, Charles	1775-1854	Actor			70		
Kemble, Edward W.*	1861-1933	Artist-Cartoonist	25		42	375	Am. Illustrator Huck Finn, etc., ALS/sketch 175
Kemble, Frances A. 'Fanny'		Entertainment	35	75	110		Vintage Br. Actress-Diarist
Kemble, Priscilla	1775-1845	Actress			70		Wife of John Philip Kemble
Kemp, Hal		Entertainment	15			40	Big Band Leader
Kemp, Jack		Cabinet	15			25	Sec'y HUD, Presidential Candidate
Kemp, Maj. Gen. Geoffrey C.	1890-1976	Military	25				World War II British general
Kemp, Ross		Entertainment	10			20	Actor
Kempenfelt, Richard	1720-1782	Military	120		410		Br.Admiral. Introduced Fr. Tactics & Signal System
Kemper, Jackson, Dr.	1789-1870	Clergy	20		95		Educator
Kemper, James L. (WD)		Civil War	375				CSA Gen. AES 1150 '64. Wounded,Captured,Exchng.

NAME	DATE	CATEGORY	SIG	LS/DS	ALS	SP	COMMENTS
Kemper, James L.	1823-1895	Civil War	168	295	420		CSA Gen.
Kemper, John M.		Celebrity	3	7	15	10	
Kempf, Gen. Panz. Troop Werner	1886-1969	Military	25				World War II German general
Kenchington, Brig. Arthur George	1890-1966	Military	25				World War II British general
Kendal, Felicity		Entertainment	10			20	Actress
Kendal, Madge, Dame	1848-1935	Entertainment	12		20	35	Shakespearean Actress
Kendall, Amos	1789-1869	Cabinet	48	116	260		Jackson P.M. Gen'l, Journalist. Partner S.F.B.Morse
Kendall, Cy		Entertainment	25			50	Vintage Character Actor
Kendall, David		Legal	3			8	Clinton Attorney
Kendall, Edward C., Dr.		Science	30	55	100	75	Nobel Medicine 1950
Kendall, Henry W.		Science	20	35		30	Nobel Physics 1990
Kendall, Kay	1926-1959	Entertainment	50			100	Brit. Actress-Comedienne. Died Leukemia at 32
Kendall, Lt. Gen. Paul W.	1898-1983	Military	30				World War II U.S. general
Kendren, John C.		Science	15	20	30	20	
Keneally, Thomas		Author	10			20	'Schindler's List'
Kenellopoulos, Panayotis		Head of State	15	35	90		Greece
Kenly, John Reese	1818-1891	Civil War	40	80			Union general
Kennan, George F.		Author	15	55			Am.Diplomat, Historian.Pulitzer
Kennedy, Anthony M.		Supreme Court	30			50	
Kennedy, Arthur		Entertainment	30	40	95	75	
Kennedy, Brig. Gen. John T.	1885-1969	Military	30				World War II U.S. general
Kennedy, Caroline		Celebrity-Author	15	30	40	25	Daughter of JFK, signed book 115
Kennedy, Carolyn Bessette		Celebrity	127				Wife of John Kennedy Jr.
Kennedy, Douglas		Entertainment	4			30	AKA Keith Douglas
Kennedy, Edgar		Entertainment	125			250	
Kennedy, Edward M.'Ted'		Congress	15	52	75	28	Senator MA 1962
Kennedy, Ethel		Celebrity	15	50	75	35	Mrs. Robert Kennedy
Kennedy, G.A.Studdert		Clergy	20				Br. Poet, Author.Woodbine Willie
Kennedy, George C.		Aviation	45			250	
Kennedy, George		Entertainment	5	20		45	AA Actor
Kennedy, Gerald, Bishop		Clergy	25	40	50	40	
Kennedy, Gordon		Celebrity	10			15	comedian
Kennedy, Jackie (As 1st Lady)		First Lady	575	1181	2282	2500	
Kennedy, Jackie	1929-1994	First Lady	464	844	1353	1264	Special SP 3300
Kennedy, Jayne		Entertainment	6	8	15	15	
Kennedy, John Doby	1840-1896	Civil War	125				Confederate general
Kennedy, John F. (As Pres.)		President	1331	2286	14072	3242	TLS/Cont. As Pres. 19,500-74,750
Kennedy, John F.	1917-1963	President	1036	1573	4521	2423	Young ALS 5750 , ALS WW II (WD) 6500-8500
Kennedy, John F. & Jackie		Pres.&1st Lady		4200		3233	Engr. WH Vignette S 3500
Kennedy, John F., Jr.		Business	50	62	483	118	Magazine Publisher 'George'
Kennedy, John P.		Cabinet	35	50	95		Fillmore Sec'y Navy 1852
Kennedy, Joseph P.	1888-1969	Business	138	225	248	300	Boston Financier, Father of JFK
Kennedy, Joseph Patrick II		Congress	15	30		70	Repr. MA 1987
Kennedy, Madge		Entertainment	10			30	
Kennedy, Maj. Gen. Sir John N.	1893-1970	Military	25				World War II British general

NAME	DATE	CATEGORY	SIG	LS/DS	ALS	SP	COMMENTS
Kennedy, Mark R.K.		Congress	10			15	Member U.S. Congress
Kennedy, Martin John		Senate/Congress	5	15			MOC NY 1930-45
Kennedy, Nigel		Music	10			15	performing musical artist
Kennedy, Patrick J. K		Congress	10			15	Member U.S. Congress
Kennedy, Robert F.	1925-1968	Cabinet-Congress	327	451	1200	736	Att'y Gen. Brother of JFK. Assassinated.WH Cd.975
Kennedy, Robert F., Jr.		Author					Signed Book 112
Kennedy, Rose Fitzgerald	1890-1995	Celebrity	86	117	240	175	Kennedy Family Matriarch
Kennedy, Sarah		Celebrity	10			15	television presenter
Kennedy, Tom		Entertainment	50			125	
Kenner, Maj. Gen. Albert W.	1889-1959	Military	30				World War II U.S. general
Kenney, George		Military	25	60	110	40	USAAF Gen. WW II
Kenny G.		Entertainment	20			35	Saxophonist
Kenny, Bill		Entertainment	25			75	Leader of Ink Spots
Kenny, Elizabeth, Sister	1886-1952	Science	175			275	Pioneer Polio Treatment. Autralian Nurse
Kenny, Nick		Entertainment		20			Singer/Ink Spots
Kensit, Patsy		Entertainment	10			60	Actress
Kent, A. Atwater		Inventor	20	195	90	35	Radio Mfg., Philanthropist
Kent, Edw. Augustus, Duke	1767-1820	Royalty	45	150			Son of Geo. III. Father of Queen Victoria
Kent, J. Ford		Military	90	195			Gen., Took San Juan Hill
Kent, Jack		Cartoonist	10			35	King Aroo
Kent, James	1763-1847	Revolutionary War	85	200	250		Legal Reporting System
Kent, Rockwell	1882-1971	Artist	42	180	244	225	Am. Landscape, Figure Painting, Illustrator
Kent, Walter		Composer	40	105		75	AMusQS 125-950 (I'll Be Home for Xmas)
Kent, William	1684-1748	Artist	175	920			Sculptor, Architect, Landscape Gardener. RARE
Kent, William	1864-1928	Congress	5	12		10	Repr. CA 1911
Kent-Lemon, Brig. Arthur Leslie	1889-1970	Military	28				World War II British general
Kenton, Simon	1755-1836	Pioneer	420	1783			Hunter, Trader, Spy, General
Kenton, Stan	1912-1979	Entertainment	35			110	Big Band Leader-Pianist
Kenyatta, Jomo		Head of State	125	220	525	150	Prime Min. Kenya
Kenyon, Doris		Entertainment	15	25	45	45	
Kenyon, William S.		Senate/Congress	10	15	35		MOC NY 1859
Kenzle, Leila		Entertainment	10			20	actress
Kepford, Ira		Aviation	15	30	48	42	ACE, WW II
Kephart, Horace		Author	20			50	Southern mountain culture/history
Kepner, Wm. E.		Military	15	35	60	25	
Keppel, Augustus		Military-Rev. War		375	750		Br. Admiral Who Influenced Br. Naval Strategy
Keppel, Francis		Celebrity	5	15	20	15	
Keppelhoff-wiechert, Hedwig		Political	10			15	Member European Parliament
Keppler, Joseph	1838-1894	Publisher	15		45		Founder Puck Magazine
Kerbs, Edwin G., Dr.		Science	20	30	55	35	Nobel Medicine
Kercheval, Ken		Entertainment	5			25	
Kerensky, Alexander	1881-1970	Head of State	150	325	525	475	Rus. Leader 1917 Revolution. Prime Minister. Fled
Kern, Jerome	1885-1945	Composer	200	425	725	1100	AMusQS 685-5175
Kern, Paul B., Bishop		Clergy	20	25	35	25	
Kernan, Brig. Gen. Redmond F.	1895-1982	Military	30				World War II U.S. general

NAME	DATE	CATEGORY	SIG	LS/DS	ALS	SP	COMMENTS
Kernan, Francis		Senate/Congress	10		35		MOC 1863, Senator NY 1875
Kerns, Joanna		Entertainment	5		10	15	
Kerns, Kurt		Entertainment	6			25	Music. Bass & Drums 'Gravity Kills'
Kerouac, Jack	1922-1969	Author	500	2422	2690	5500	Beat Generation Rep. Clebr. pd. 5000 for DS
Kerr, Brig. Gen. Francis R.	1890-1975	Military	30				World War II U.S. general
Kerr, Clark		Celebrity	5	10	20	10	
Kerr, Deborah		Entertainment	15	45	30	25	Pin-Up SP 35. Nominated 6 Times for Oscar
Kerr, Graham		Celebrity	10			15	media/TV personality
Kerr, John		Entertainment	10		25	30	Actor 'Tea And Sympathy', 'South Pacific'
Kerr, Maj. Gen. Sir Harold R.	1894-1974	Military	25				World War II British general
Kerr, Robert S.		Senate/Congress	5	15		10	Senator, Gov. OK
Kerr, Ruth		Business	25	35	40	50	Owner of Kerr Glass Co.. Queen of Home Canning
Kerrigan, J. Warren		Entertainment	35			75	Vintage Char. Actor. 'Johnny Gallegher' GWTW
Kerrl, Hans		Military		65			WW II German Reich minister
Kerry, John		Senate	10			15	United States Senate (D - MA)
Kerry, Margaret		Entertainment				38	Voice of Tinkerbell
Kerry, Robert		Senate	10			20	Senator
Kersee, Jackie Joyner		Celebrity	10			30	motivational speaker, Olympic champion
Kershaw, Joseph B.	1822-1894	Civil War	180	900	1625		CSA Gen. LS '61 3500, War Dte. Sig 350
Kerwin, Joseph P.		Astronaut	7	35		25	
Kesey, Ken		Author	66	42	110	35	'One Flew Over the Cukoo's Nest'
Kesselring, Albrecht	1885-1960	Military	122	220	360	250	Ger. Field Marshal WW II
Kessler, Margot		Political	10			15	Member European Parliament
Kestnbaum, Meyer		Business	15	30		25	Pres. Hart, Schaffner & Marx
Ketcham, Hank*		Cartoonist	25	75		108	'Dennis the Menace'. FDC S 50. ,signed drwg 100-150
Ketcham, John H. (WD)		Civil War	75	160	260		Union Gen.
Ketcham, John H.	1832-1906	Civil War	40	75	180		Union Gen. War Dte. S 150, DS 275
Ketchum, William Scott	1813-1871	Civil War	40		100		Union general
Ketelby, Albert W.		Composer	15		75		'In a Persian Marketa.', 'In a.Monastery Garden'
Kettering, Charles F.		Inventor	100	160	325	125	Engineer. Sloan-Kettering Inst.Kettering Engine
Kettley, John		Celebrity	10			15	weather presenter
Kevorkian, Jack, Dr.		Science	56		70	75	Euthanasia 'Dr. Death'
Key, David M.	1824-1900	Cabinet	30	45	90		P.M. General. CSA Officer
Key, Francis Scott	1779-1843	Lawyer-Author	500	664	988		Special ADS 2,500
Key, Maj. Gen. Berthold Wells	1895-1986	Military	25				World War II British general
Key, Maj. Gen. William S.	1889-1959	Military	30				World War II U.S. general
Key, Philip Barton	1857-1815	Senate/Congress	10	30	40		MOC MD 1807
Key, Ted*		Cartoonist	10			75	'Hazel', signed drawing 85
Keyes, Erasmus D.	1818-1895	Civil War	45	90	140	748	Union General. ALS/Cont. 1500
Keyes, Erasmus, D. (WD)		Civil War	75	160	260	300	Union Gen.
Keyes, Evelyn		Entertainment	22		40	58	Actress. SP in GWTW Costume 40-100
Keyes, Irwin		Entertainment	4			10	Character Actor
Keyes, Lt. Gen. Geoffrey	1888-1967	Military	30				World War II U.S. general
Keyes, Roger J.B.1st Baron	1872-1945	Military	35	30	65	75	Br. Adm.Fleet. Boxer Rebellion
Keynes, John Maynard	1883-1946	Economist	75	310	585	250	Br. Econ. Member'Bloomsbury Group'. TLS/Cont.1600

NAME	DATE	CATEGORY	SIG	LS/DS	ALS	SP	COMMENTS
Keys, Alicia		Music	15			35	Rock
Keys, Ancel		Science	5	15	30	10	
Keys, Henry W.		Governor	10	20	35		Governor NH
Keyser, Brig. Gen. George V.	1895-1972	Military	30				World War II U.S. general
Keyser, Herbert		Celebrity	10			15	medical expert
Keyser, Ralph S.		Military	30	50			
Keyserling, Hermann Graf	1880-1946	Philosopher	15	35	65	50	Ger. Social Philosopher (Spiritual Regeneration)
Khalid, King	1913-1982	Royalty	25	65	175	75	Saudi Arabia
Khama, Seretse, Sir		Head of State	65			250	1st Prime Minister of Botswana
Khambatta, Persis		Entertainment	22		30	60	Star Trek
Khan, Chaka		Entertainment	20			45	
Khan, Mohammad Ayub		Head of State	30	95			
Khan, Yasmin, Princess		Royalty	10			25	Daughter of Rita Hayworth
Khanbhai, Bashir		Political	10			15	Member European Parliament
Khanh, Nguyen, Gen.		Head of State	20	60	175	45	
Khanieff, Nikhandr S.	1922-1954	Entertainment				650	Leading Heroic Tenor at Bolshoi
Khatami, Mohammed		Political				135	President of Iran
Khatchaturian, Aram	1903-1978	Composer	110	180	350	316	AMusQS 300, 575, 625, 1275 ALS/cont 3000
Khomeini, Ruhollah, Ayatollah		Religious Leader	575				Iranian Moslem Leader
Khorana, Har G., Dr.		Science	15	25	45	25	Nobel Medicine 1968
Khrennikov, Tykhon		Composer		46			Russian Composer
Khrunov, Yevgeni		Astronaut				30	Russian cosmonaut
Khruschchev, Nikita S.	1894-1971	Head of State	300	525	625	1250	Premier Soviet Union
Kiam, Victor		Business	5	25		15	Remington Electric Razor Co.
Kibbee, Guy		Entertainment	20			40	Rotund, Ruddy Faced Comedian Char.Actor 30's
Kibler, Maj. Gen. Abram F.	1891-1955	Military	30				World War II U.S. general
Kid Jensen, David		Music	10			15	DJ
Kidd, Jemma		Celebrity	10			15	celebrity model
Kidd, Kandy		Celebrity	10			15	motivational speaker
Kidder, Margot		Entertainment	10			28	Actress. Pin-Up SP 30
Kiddoo, Jos. Barr		Civil War	35		90		Union General
Kidman, Nicole		Entertainment	20			66	Actress, AA winner
Kidron, Beeban		Celebrity	10			15	film industry
Kiefer, Brig. Gen. Homer W.	1898-1976	Military	30				World War II U.S. general
Kiel, Richard		Entertainment	5			15	
Kielmansegg, Graf J.A.		Military	20			35	Gen. German Army
Kielty, Patrick		Celebrity	10			15	television presenter
Kienzl, Wilhelm	1857-1941	Composer	15		55		Opera
Kiepura, Jan	1902-1966	Entertainment	42			125	Opera, Concert. Vintage, Trimmed SPc 40-50
Kier, Udo		Entertainment	10			20	actor
Kiernan, James Lawlor	1837-1869	Civil War	45		120		Union general
Kiker, Douglas		Celebrity	10			15	media/TV personality
Kilban, B.*		Cartoonist	10	25		100	Cat Cartoons, The New Yorker
Kilbourne, Charles E.		Military	15			75	Am. WW I Soldier. 3d Brig. 2d Div.
Kilbride, Percy	1888-1964	Entertainment	138			350	Wimpy Character Actor. 'Ma & Pa Kettle' Films

NAME	DATE	CATEGORY	SIG	LS/DS	ALS	SP	COMMENTS
Kilburn, Brig. Gen. Charles S.	1895-1978	Military	30				World War II U.S. general
Kilby, J. S. Jack		Science	20	35	70	35	Inventor of Micro Chip
Kildee, Dale E. K		Congress	10			15	Member U.S. Congress
Kiley, Richard	d. 1999	Entertainment	15	8	25	30	Fine Stage & Film Actor
Kilgore, Harley, M.		Senate/Congress	5	15		15	Senator WV 1941
Kilgore, Merle		Country Music	10			20	
Kilham, Hannah		Clergy	50	75	100		
Kilian, Victor		Entertainment	10		20	25	Character Actor. Many Dark, Brooding Parts
Killinger, John W.		Senate/Congress	10	15	30		MOC PA 1859
Kilmer, Joyce	1886-1918	Author	225	562			Poet. 'Trees'. AMsS 3000
Kilmer, Val		Entertainment	28	35		48	Batman SP w/Chris O'Donnell 150
Kilpatrick, Brig. Gen. John R.	1889-1960	Military	30				World War II U.S. general
Kilpatrick, Carolyn C. K		Congress	10			15	Member U.S. Congress
Kilpatrick, Hugh J. (WD)		Civil War	95	408	500	550	Union Gen.
Kilpatrick, Hugh J.	1836-1881	Civil War	87	185	260	415	Union Gen. Cavalry. '63 LS 1295
Kilpatrick, James		Celebrity	10			15	political celebrity
Kilpatrick, Kurt		Celebrity	10			15	motivational speaker
Kilroy-Silk, Robert		Celebrity	10			15	television presenter
Kimball, Brig. Gen. Allen R.	1886-1951	Military	30				World War II U.S. general
Kimball, Dan		Cabinet	20	35	40	25	Sec'y Navy. Aerojet General
Kimball, J. Golden		Clergy	25	150			Pioneer Mormon Leader
Kimball, John W.		Civil War	30		80		Union Gen.
Kimball, Nathan	1822-1898	Civil War	40	75	120		Union general
Kimball, Spencer W.		Clergy	25	25	35	30	Morman Leader
Kimball, Ward		Cartoonist	25			75	Musician-Discny Cartoonist. 'Firehouse 5 Plus 2'
Kimberly, John W., 1st Earl		Statesman	20	30	110		Br.Colon'l Sec'y. Kimberly S.A.
Kimberly, R. Lewis	1836-1913	Civil War	30	45	75		Union General
Kimbrough, Charles		Entertainment	10			20	actor
Kimbrough, Emily		Author	10	20	42	15	'Our Hearts Were Young & Gay'
Kimmel, Husband E.		Military	312	400		550	US Adm. Cmdr.At Pearl Harbor
Kimmel, Jimmy		Entertainment	10			20	TV host
Kimura, General Heitaro	1888-1948	Military	25				World War II Japanese general
Kind, Richard		Entertainment				30	
Kind, Ron K		Congress	10			15	Member U.S. Congress
Kindelberger, James H. Dutch		Business	45			75	Pres. No. American Aviation. Test Pilot
Kindermann, Heinz		Political	10			15	Member European Parliament
Kindermann, K. B.		Aviation	5	10	15	15	
Kindler, Hans		Conductor	25			100	Conductor Wash.,DC Nat'l Symphony
King, Alan		Entertainment	10	6	15	22	Stage, Film, TV, Vegas Top Comedian
King, Andrea		Enntertainment	15			25	Actress. 2nd Leads, Other Woman 40's-50's
King, B.B.		Entertainment	20	40		58	Grammy Winning R & B Singer, Guitarist
King, Ben E.		Composer	12			25	Singer-The Drifters. 'Stand by Me' AMusQS 95
King, Brig. Gen. Edgar	1884-1970	Military	30				World War II U.S. general
King, Brig. Gen. Henry L.P.	1895-1952	Military	30				World War II U.S. general
King, Brig. Gen. Woods	1900-1947	Military	30				World War II U.S. general

NAME	DATE	CATEGORY	SIG	LS/DS	ALS	SP	COMMENTS
King, Cammie		Entertainment	15		35	35	GWTW Child Actress.
King, Carole		Entertainment	15			30	Rock, songwriter
King, Charles		Civil War	50		175		Soldier-Civil War Author
King, Charles		Entertainment	20			50	
King, Claire		Entertainment	10			20	Actress
King, Coretta Scott		Celebrity	32	89	95	75	Mrs. Martin Luther King, Jr. Civil Rights Activist
King, Edward J., Bishop		Clergy	25	35	50		
King, Ernest J.	1878-1956	Military	30	120		125	Fleet Adm. Cmmdr. Chief US Fleet WW II
King, Frank*		Cartoonist	35			165	'Gasoline Alley'
King, Henry		Entertainment	30			75	Film Director
King, Horatio	1811-1897	Cabinet	45	175	275		P.M. General 1861
King, Jack	1903-1943	Composer					Pop Songwriter AMusQS 35
King, James	1791-1853	Business	20		65		Financier, RR Pres. Son of VP Rufus King
King, John Alsop		Governor	10		35		Gov. NY, a Founder Repub. Party
King, John 'Dusty'		Entertainment	20	30	45	55	
King, John Haskell	1820-1888	Civil War	42	75	110		Union general
King, Larry		Entertainment	10	20	35	22	Talk Show Host
King, Lt Gen Sir Chas. John Stuart	1890-1967	Military	25				World War II British general
King, Maj. Gen. Edward P. Jr.	1884-1958	Military	30				World War II U.S. general
King, Martin Luther, III		Activist	5			30	Civil Rights
King, Martin Luther, Jr.	1929-1968	Clergy	1662	2840	3500	3324	Advocate Peaceful Nonviolence. Assassinated
King, Martin Luther. Sr.		Clergy	35	45	60	65	
King, Pee Wee		Entertainment	10			20	C & W. Bandleader-Composer
King, Perry		Entertainment	5	8	15	20	
King, Peter T. K		Congress	10			15	Member U.S. Congress
King, Preston	1806-1865	Congress	15	45	100		Repr. 1843, Senate NY. Suicide 1865
King, Rodney		Celebrity	10				Afro-Am. L.A. Police Vicitim
King, Rufus	1814-1876	Civil War	42	80	110		Union General
King, Rufus (WD)	1814-1876	Civil War	75	260	320		Union Gen. ALS/Cont.'62 3200
King, Rufus	1755-1827	Revolutionary War	250	350	425		Cont'l Congr. Historical ALS 2500
King, Stephen		Author	40	90	310	150	Master of Horror and Suspense
King, Steve K		Congress	10			15	Member U.S. Congress
King, Thomas Starr	1824-1864	Clergy	25	35	95	40	
King, Walter Woolf		Entertainment	15		25	50	Broadway Singing Star. 'Vagabond King' in 30's
King, Wayne		Entertainment	15			25	Big Band Leader.
King, William R.	1786-1853	Vice President	181	340			Pierce VP. Died after 45 days
King, Wm. L. Mackenzie	1874-1950	Head of State	40	262		55	3 Times P.M. Canada
King, Yolanda		Celebrity	10			15	motivational speaker
Kingman, Brig. Gen. Allen F.	1893-1988	Military	30				World War II U.S. general
Kingman, Brig. Gen. John J.	1882-1948	Military	30				World War II U.S. general
Kingman, Dong		Artist	25	50	100		
Kingon, Alfred		Celebrity	10			15	political celebrity
Kingsford-Smith, Charles		Aviation	75	125		250	FDC Trans-Tasman Fl. 225
Kingsley, Ben	1943-	Entertainment	10	12	20	37	AA Winning Actor 'Gandhi'
Kingsley, Charles	1819-1875	Author-Clergy	45	95	145		Br. Novelist, Clergyman

NAME	DATE	CATEGORY	SIG	LS/DS	ALS	SP	COMMENTS
Kingston Trio		Entertainment	30			70	Folk Group of 50's
Kingston, Evelyn Pierrepont		Royalty			190		2nd Duke of Kingston
Kingston, Jack K		Congress	10			15	Member U.S. Congress
Kingston, William H.		Author	25		100		Br. Boy's Adventure Books
Kinks (5 Current Members)		Entertainment	40			85	Rock. LP Cover S 95
Kinman, Seth	1815-1885	History				368	Famous mountain-man, trapper
Kinmont, Kathleen		Entertainment	10			20	actress
Kinnear, Greg		Entertainment	10			25	actor
Kinney, John	d. 1919	History				635	Leader of the John Kinney Gang (NM rustlers)
Kinney, Sean		Entertainment	6			25	Music. Drummer 'Alice in Chains'
Kinnock, Glenys		Political	10			15	Member European Parliament
Kinsey, Alfred, Dr.	1894-1956	Science	80	139	210	250	Am. Sexologist Researcher
Kinskey, Leonid	1903-1995	Entertainment	20			35	Russian-Born Character Actor. 'Casablanca'
Kinski, Klaus		Entertainment	35		40	175	Actor-Director
Kinski, Natassja		Entertainment	15	25	45	69	Actress, Nude Pin-Up 110
Kinsley, Michael		Celebrity	10			15	media/TV personality
Kinstler, E.R.*		Cartoonist	10			100	Illustrator
Kintner, Robert		Business	5	10	30	10	
Kip, William I., Bishop		Clergy	50	85	125		
Kipling, Rudyard	1865-1936	Author	192	435	620	900	Nobel Lit., Novelist, Poet
Kiplinger, Austin		Business	10	20	45	15	Kiplinger Washington Newsletter
Kipnis, Alexander		Entertainment	35	75		95	Opera. Russ. Bass
Kippenberger, Maj. Gen. H. K.	1897-1957	Military	20				World War II New Zealand general
Kira, Maj. Gen. Goichi		Military	27				World War II Japanese general
Kirby, Bruno		Entertainment	10			20	actor
Kirby, Edmund	1840-1863	Civil War	325				Union general
Kirby, Fred. M.		Business		2450			Founded Dime Store Chain. Woolworth Partner
Kirby, George		Entertainment	5			15	
Kirby, Jack*		Cartoonist	25			170	'Captain America'
Kirby, Maj. Gen. Stanley W.	1895-1968	Military	28				World War II British general
Kirby, Rollin*		Cartoonist	20			90	
Kirk, Andy		Bandleader	15			65	
Kirk, Claude Jr.		Governor	7	15			Governor FL
Kirk, Eddie		Country Music	10			20	Country Singer-Recording Artist
Kirk, Edward Needles	1828-1863	Civil War	225				Union general
Kirk, Florence		Entertainment	10			30	Opera
Kirk, George		Aviation	12	22	40	35	ACE, WW II
Kirk, Grayson	1903-1997	Educator	20			40	Columbia University President for Many Years
Kirk, Maj. Gen. James	1890-1972	Military	30				World War II U.S. general
Kirk, Mark Steven K		Congress	10			15	Member U.S. Congress
Kirk, Norman T.	1888-1960	Military	30	50		55	U.S. Gen. WW II
Kirk, Phyllis		Entertainment	20		95	45	Rising Star in 50's.Cover Life Mag. Illness Struck
Kirk, Tommy		Entertainment	10			20	Juvenile Star
Kirkby-Lunn, Louise		Entertainment	30			95	Opera
Kirkconnell, Clare		Entertainment	4	5	9	10	

NAME	DATE	CATEGORY	SIG	LS/DS	ALS	SP	COMMENTS
Kirke, Gen. Sir Walter M. St. Geo.	1877-1949	Military	25				World War II British general
Kirkham, Ralph W.	1821-1893	Civil War	27	55	80		Union General
Kirkhope, Timothy		Political	10			15	Member European Parliament
Kirkland, Lane		Labor	8	15	30	15	Labor Leader. AFL-CIO
Kirkland, Sally		Entertainment	10			25	
Kirkland, Samuel	1741-1808	Missionary		2025	2150		Oneida Indian Missionary. Active during Rev. War
Kirkland, William Whedbee	1833-1915	Civil War	110				Confederate general
Kirkman, Gen. Sir Sidney C.	1895-1982	Military	25				World War II British general
Kirkman, Maj. Gen. John Mather	1898-1964	Military	25				World War II British general
Kirkpatrick, Jean J.		Cabinet	20		35	25	Ambassador U.N. Signature on Special Piece 115
Kirkwood, Joe, Jr.		Entertainment	45	75	110	100	Radio, Movies And Golfer
Kirkwood, Samuel J.	1813-1894	Cabinet	15	25	55	45	Sec'y Intertior, Gov, Senator IA
Kirman Sr., Richard.		Governor	10		30		Governor NV
Kirov, Sergey Mironovich	1886-1934	Political			632		Communist leader
Kirschlager, Angelika		Entertainment	10			30	Opera. Vienna's New Rising Star
Kirsebom, Vendela		Entertainment	15			50	Model-Actress 'Batman & Robin'
Kirshner, Mia		Celebrity				35	
Kirst, Michael		Celebrity	10			15	financial expert
Kirsten, Dorothy	1919-1992	Entertainment	20			48	Am. Lyric Soprano, Opera. Record 30 Yrs. At Met.
Kirwen, Dervla		Entertainment	10			20	Actress
Kisch, Brig. Frederick Hermann	1888-1943	Military	25				World War II British general
Kiser, Terry		Entertainment	10			20	actor
Kishigawa, Maj. Gen. Kenichi		Military	27				World War II Japanese general
Kisling, Moise	1891-1953	Artist			340		Polish Painter
Kiss (Entire Group)		Entertainment	50			125	Rock. Alb. S 145-225
Kissinger, Henry A.		Cabinet	28	70		52	Sec'y State, Stateman, Diplomat, Prolific Author
Kistiakowsky, G.B., Dr.		Science	40	135		70	Nobel Chemistry
Kita, Lt. Gen. Seiichi	1886-1951	Military	25				World War II Japanese general
Kitchener, Horatio H.	1850-1916	Military	85	205	278	210	Ir.-born Br. Field Marshal. 1st Earl, Statesman
Kitching, Maj. Gen. George	1910-	Military	20				World War II Canadian general
Kitt, Eartha	1928-	Entertainment	10			30	Actress-Singer. Pin-Up SP 35
Kittinger, Joe		Aviation	25	45			
Kittredge, Walter		Composer	30		45		'Tenting Tonight'...AMQS 300-1,150
Kitzhaber, John		Governor	3			8	Oregon Gov.
Klamt, Ewa		Political	10			15	Member European Parliament
Klass, Alisha		Entertainment	6			40	New Adult Film Star
Klass, Christa		Political	10			15	Member European Parliament
Kleber, Jean-Baptiste		Fr. Revolution	145	410	855		One of France's Greatest Gen'ls
Kleczka, Gerald D. K		Congress	10			15	Member U.S. Congress
Klee, Paul	1879-1940	Artist	200	615	1850		Swiss Surrealist Painter
Kleemann, Gen. of Panzer Ulrich	1892-1963	Military	27				World War II German general
Kleffel, General of Cavalry Philipp	1887-	Military	27				World War II German general
Kleiman, Jon		Entertainment	6			25	Music. Drummer 'Monster Magnet'
Klein, Calvin		Business	10	15	35	22	Fashion-Accessory Designer
Klein, Felix	1849-1925	Science	85		450		Ger. Mathematician Non-Euclidean Geometry

NAME	DATE	CATEGORY	SIG	LS/DS	ALS	SP	COMMENTS
Klein, Robert		Entertainment	5			22	Actor, Comedian
Kleist, Field Marshal Ewald von	1881-1954	Military	50	150			World War II German general
Kleist, Paul von		Military	50	85		100	Ger. WW II Tank Commander
Klemperer, Otto		Entertainment	73	161	310	260	German Conductor
Klemperer, Werner	1920-	Entertainment	15	25		25	Actor. 'Col. Klink' on 'Hogan's Heroes'
Kleppe, Thomas S.		Cabinet	5	15	30	10	MOC ND, Sec'y Interior
Klimt, Gustav	1862-1918	Artist	170	575	1112		Austrian. Allegorical Murals
Kline, John K		Congress	10			15	Member U.S. Congress
Kline, Kevin		Entertainment	15	12	45	48	Wanda Cast 120. Oscar Winner
Klingenberg, Fritz	1912-1945	Military				150	SS officer
Klose, Margarete	1902-1968	Entertainment	15			65	Opera. Ger. Mezzo-Soprano
Kluge, Hans Gunther von	1882-1944	Military	75		250		Ger. Gen'l WW II, Suicide
Kluge, Lt. Gen. Wolfgang von	1892-1976	Military	25				World War II German general
Klugman, Jack		Entertainment	10			24	Actor. 1/2 of the 'Odd Couple'
Klutznick, Philip M.		Cabinet	5	12		8	Sec'y Commerce
Kmentt, Waldemar		Entertainment	10			65	Opera. Eminent Tenor 3x5 SP 40
Knbler, Gen. Mtn. Troops Ludwig	1889-1947	Military	5				World War II German general
Knchler, Field Marshal Georg von	1881-1969	Military	25				World War II German general
Knern, H.H.*		Cartoonist	25		95	180	Katzenjammer Kids
Knibb, William		Clergy	45	60	75		
Knievel, Evel		Celebrity	10	15	35	48	Daredevil Motorcycle Rider
Knight, Austin		Celebrity	10			15	comedian
Knight, Evelyn		Entertainment	10				With the Star Dusters
Knight, Fuzzy		Entertainment	50			150	
Knight, Gladys		Entertainment	15	20	35	42	Rock. DS by Knight & 6 Pips 85
Knight, Goodwin J.		Governor	10	15		15	Governor CA
Knight, John S.		Business	10	35	45	20	Publisher
Knight, John T.		Military	25	75		35	Am. WW I Gen.
Knight, Jordan		Entertainment	10			45	
Knight, June		Entertainment	8	9	20	25	
Knight, Laura, Dame	1877-1970	Artist	60	100	175		Ranked Alongside Britain's Greatest
Knight, Phil		Business	22	35	45	25	Nike Athletic Shoes Etc.
Knight, Shirley		Entertainment	9	10	20	25	
Knight, Ted	1923-1986	Entertainment	15	35	40	62	Actor. Best Remembered in 'Mary Tyler Moore Show'
Knight, Wayne		Entertainment	10			35	Actor, 'Newman'
Knipe, Joseph Farmer	1823-1901	Civil War	45		120		Union general
Knolle, Karsten		Political	10			15	Member European Parliament
Knollenberg, Joe K		Congress	10			15	Member U.S. Congress
Knopf, Alfred A.		Business	7	20	35		Knopf Publishing
Knote, Heinrich		Entertainment	20			50	Opera
Knott, Walter & Cordelia		Business	150			475	Co-Founders Knott's Berry Farm
Knott, Walter		Business	35	70		150	Co-Founder Knott's Berry Farm
Knotts, Don		Entertainment	10			28	Self Sketch S 35
Knowland, William F.		Senate	10	20		25	Senator CA, Publisher
Knowles, Beyonce		Music	20			45	Rock singer

NAME	DATE	CATEGORY	SIG	LS/DS	ALS	SP	COMMENTS
Knowles, James S.	1784-1862	Author	10	25	60		
Knowles, John		Author	35			100	Br. Author
Knowles, Patrick		Entertainment	10			25	
Knox, Alexander		Entertainment	10	15	30	30	
Knox, Brigadier Errol	1889-1949	Military	20				World War II Australian general
Knox, Elyse		Entertainment	10	20	35	40	Actress-Wife Tom Harmon
Knox, Frank	1874-1944	Cabinet	50	75	95	100	Sec'y Navy. TLS/Cont 275
Knox, Henry	1750-1806	Cabinet-Military	162	387	625		Maj. Gen'l. Rev. War Dte. ALS 4,500
Knox, James, Cardinal		Clergy	30	30	35	35	
Knox, Philander C.	1853-1921	Cabinet	12	25	107	30	Att'y Gen., Senator PA
Knudsen, Lt. Gen. William S.	1879-1948	Military	30				World War II U.S. general
Knudsen, William S.		Business	20	35	85	45	Pres. GM. WW II War Prod. Dir.
Knutson, Harold		Senate/Congress	5	10		10	MOC MN
Koba, Maj. Gen. Toba		Military	25				World War II Japanese general
Kobayashi, Maj. Gen. Shigekichi		Military	25				World War II Japanese general
Kobayashi, Maj. Gen. Takashi		Military	25				World War II Japanese general
Kobayashi, Takeji		Author	25		60	45	Proletarian Literary Movement
Koch, Dieter-Lebrecht		Political	10			15	Member European Parliament
Koch, Edward I.		Political	10	20	35	15	Mayor NYC
Koch, Edward W.		Entertainment	20			35	Prod-Dir. 'Manchurian Candidate', 'Odd Couple'
Koch, Heinrich H. Robert	1843-1910	Science		1500	1813	2300	Nobel Bacteriology-Medicine'05, Koch's Postulates
Koch, Howard W.	1916-	Entertainment	20			35	Producer-Dir. of Multiple Film & TV Hits
Koch, Marvin		Author	8			12	genealogy
Koch-Erpach, Gen. of Cav. Rudolf	1886-	Military	25				World War II German general
Kodaly, Zoltan	1882-1967	Composer	135	300	685	472	Hung. Composer.Content ALS 1750.AMusQS 1150
Koehl, Herman		Aviation	75			250	1st East-West Crossing Atlantic
Koehler, Armin		Aviation	10	20	35	25	
Koeltz, Lt. Gen. Marie-Louis	1884-1970	Military	20				World War II French general
Koenig, Brig. Gen. Egmont F.	1892-1972	Military	30				World War II U.S. general
Koenig, Walter		Entertainment	20		45	50	Actor. 'Checkov' on Star Trek
Koetz, Maj. Gen. Karl	1908-1977	Military	25				World War II German general
Koga, Maj. Gen. Ryutaro		Military	25				World War II Japanese general
Kogan, Claude	1919-1959	Celebrity			150		adventurer
Kohl, Hannelove		Celebrity	5			10	Mrs. Helmut Kohl
Kohl, Helmut		Heads of State	15	30	65	25	Chancellor Germany
Kohl, Herb		Senate	10			15	United States Senate (D - WI)
Kohler, Walter J.		Business	10	30			Founder Kohler Corp. Plumbing
Kohlsaat, Herman H.		Editor	3		15		
Kohner, Susan		Entertainment	5			25	Actress. 'Imitation of Life'
Koiso, General Kuniaki	1880-1950	Military	25				World War II Japanese general
Kokoschka, Oskar	1886-1980	Artist	95	120	450	275	Austrian. PC Repro Painting S 180
Kokubu, Lt. Gen. Shishichiro		Military	25				World War II Japanese general
Kolbe, Jim K		Congress	10			15	Member U.S. Congress
Kolff, Willem J., Dr.		Science	15	55		40	Created Artificial Kidney
Kolker, Henry	1874-1947	Entertainment	15		65	35	Actor-Dir-Writer, Noted Stage, Film Char. Actor

NAME	DATE	CATEGORY	SIG	LS/DS	ALS	SP	COMMENTS
Kolleck, Teddy		Political	15	38		35	Mayor of Jerusalem
Kollo, Rene		Entertainment	10		35	25	Opera
Kollontay, Alexandra	1872-1952	Political		328			Russian revolutionary
Kollwitz, Kathe	1867-1945	Artist			362		Ger. Sculptor, Graphic Artist
Koloff, Nikita		Author	8			12	wrestler, religious books
Komarov, Vladimir M.	1927-1967	Cosmonaut	125			301	Rus. Cosmonaut. 1st To Die During Space Flight
Komatsubara, Lt. Gen. Michitaro	1886-1940	Military	25				World War II Japanese general
Kondo, Maj. Gen. Shihachi		Military	25				World War II Japanese general
Kondracke, Morton		Celebrity	10			15	media/TV personality
Konetzni, Anny		Entertainment	25			65	Opera
Konrad, Christoph Werner		Political	10			15	Member European Parliament
Konrad, Gen. Mtn. Troops Rudolf	1891-1964	Military	25				World War II German general
Konya, Sandor		Entertainment				40	Opera. Hung. Tenor
Kook, Abraham Isaac		Clergy	45	145			Palestinian Rabbi
Koontz, Dean	1945-	Author	20	55		65	Novelist. Horror. Signed Books VG+ 25
Koop, C.Everett, Dr.		Military	7	20	50	28	Adm., US Surgeon General
Kopell, Bernie		Entertainment	5			15	Actor. 'Get Smart', 'Love Boat'
Koppel, Ted		TV News	10	15	30	20	
Korakas, Efstratios		Political	10			15	Member European Parliament
Korda, Alexander		Entertainment	40	45	90	85	
Koren, Edward*		Cartoonist	10			75	New Yorker Cartoonist
Korfes, Maj. Gen. Otto	1889-1964	Military	225				World War II German general
Korhola, Eija-riitta Anneli		Political	10			15	Member European Parliament
Korman, Harvey		Entertainment	5	6	15	15	
Korn		Entertainment	35			115	Music. 5 Member Rock Group
Kornberg, Arthur		Science	20	30	45	25	Nobel Medicine
Kornby, Arthur		Science	15		20		
Korngold, Erich Wolfgang	1897-1957	Composer	75	200	350	250	Opera, Orchestral, Films. Spec'l Score S 985
Korolev, Sergei	1906-1966	Military		242		494	Russian missle designer, Sputnik
Korvin, Charles		Entertainment	10	15	20	20	
Kosciusko, Thaddeus		Revolutionary War	300	750	3148		Polish Patriot.
Kosleck, Martin		Entertainment	15			35	
Koslovsky, Ivan		Music		46			Opera singer
Kossa, Frank R.		Military	7	9	12	10	
Kossuth, Lajos	1802-184	Head of State	120	230	375	300	Hungarian Patriot, Journalist
Kostabi, Mark	b. 1960	Artist					Painting 750
Kostal, Irwin		Composer	3	10	20	10	
Kostelanetz, Andre	1901-1980	Entertainment	15	25	45	23	Conductor
Koster, Henry		Entertainment	15	35		40	Film Director
Kostunica, Vojislav		Political				45	President of Serbia
Kosygin, Aleksei		Head of State	200	443	625	500	Premier of Soviet Union
Koukiadis, Ioannis		Political	10			15	Member European Parliament
Koulourianos, Dimitrios		Political	10			15	Member European Parliament
Koussevitzky, Serge	1874-1951	Entertainment	65		170		Russ. Conductor.Pioneered Introducing Russ. Opera
Kovack, Nancy (Mehta)		Entertainment	4	4	9	10	

NAME	DATE	CATEGORY	SIG	LS/DS	ALS	SP	COMMENTS
Kovacs, Ernie	1919-1962	Entertainment	200			364	First Outrageous TV Comedian
Kovalevskaya, Sophia	1850-1891	Science			850		Rus. Mathematician, Novelist
Kovansky, Anatol		Artist	15		40	25	
Kove, Martin		Entertainment	6	8	15	15	
Kovic, Ron		Activist	20	35	65		Anti Viet Nam Autobio.'Born on the 4th of July'
Kowarski, L.		Science	10	25	60		
Kozhedub, Ivan		Military	75				Russian Ace WWII
Kozky, Alex*		Cartoonist	10			20	Apt. 3-G
Kozlovsky, Ivan	1900-1993	Entertainment				1500	Ukrainian Tenor. RARE
Krabbe, Jeroen		Entertainment	10			20	actor
Kraft, Chris		Astronaut	15			25	
Kraft, James L.		Business	30	95	175	50	Founder Kraft Foods Co.
Kragen, Ken		Business	5	10	20	20	Entertainment Business Mgr.
Kraigher, Sergej		Head of State				45	President Yugoslavia
Krakowski, Jane		Entertainment	5			32	Actress. 'Ally McBeal' Co-Star
Kral, Roy		Celebrity	10	25		15	
Kramer, Brig. Gen. Hans	1894-1957	Military	30				World War II U.S. general
Kramer, Jonathon		Celebrity	10			15	motivational speaker
Kramer, Maj. Gen. Herman F.	1892-1964	Military	30				World War II U.S. general
Kramer, Stanley		Entertainment	15	35		40	Film Producer, Director
Kramer, Stephanie		Entertainment	5			20	
Krantz, Judith		Author	25		40	35	Novelist
Krarup, Ole		Political	10			15	Member European Parliament
Krasner, Milton		Entertainment	20			45	Film Director. AA
Kratsa-tsagaropoulou, Rodi		Political	10			15	Member European Parliament
Kraus, Alfredo		Entertainment	15			35	Opera. 5x7 Half-Tone Portr. 20
Kraus, Clemens		Entertainment	65			220	Austrian Conductor
Kraus, Robert		Artist	10	25	50	25	
Krause, Charles		Entertainment	5			25	Actor. 'Sports Night'
Krause, Lt. Gen. Walther	1890-1960	Military	25				World War II German general
Krause, Peter		Entertainment	5			42	Actor. 'Sports Night'. Nate Fisher, 6 Ft. Under
Krauss, Werner		Entertainment	250				
Kravitz, Lenny		Entertainment	10			46	Music. Lead Singer 'Lenny Kravitz'
Kreber, Maj. Gen. Leo M.	1896-1973	Military	30				World War II U.S. general
Krebs, Gen. of Infantry Hans	1898-1945	Military	25				World War II German general
Krebs, Hans Adolf, Sir	1900-1981	Science	45	45	60	70	Ger.-Born Br. Biochemist. Nobel Medicine, Kreb's Cycle
Krebs, Nita	1904-1992	Entertainment	12	20		25	Actress-Dancer 'Wizard of Oz'. Munchkin
Kregal, Kevin		Astronaut	5			18	
Krehl, Constanze Angela		Political	10			15	Member European Parliament
Kreisler, Fritz	1875-1962	Composer	62	110	220	230	Violinist, AMQS 275
Kreissl-dörfler, Wolfgang		Political	10			15	Member European Parliament
Kremer, Andrea		TV News	5			12	ESPN News
Krenek, Ernst	1900-1991	Composer	22	35	141	55	Austrian-Am. AMusQS 95-150-225
Krenn, Fritz		Entertainment	15			35	Opera
Kreps, Juanita M.		Cabinet	4	10	15	12	Sec'y Commerce

NAME	DATE	CATEGORY	SIG	LS/DS	ALS	SP	COMMENTS
Kresge, Sebastian S. (S.S.)	1867-1966	Business	100	210	260	225	Kresge Stores
Kretschmer, Otto		Military	55	140		140	Highest Scoring U Boat Cmdr.
Kreutzer, Conradin		Composer	125	300	650		Ger. Composer/Conductor
Kreysing, Gen. Mtn. Troops Hans	1890-1969	Military	25				World War II German general
Kriebel, Gen. of Infantry Karl	1888-1961	Military	25				World War II German general
Krige, Alice		Entertainment	4	4	9	10	
Kristel, Sylvia		Entertainment	20			45	
Kristofferson, Kris		Entertainment	10		35	32	
Kristol, Irving		Celebrity	10			15	financial expert
Kristyon, Eldgorn		Head of State	20	35			President of Iceland
Krivine, Alain		Political	10			15	Member European Parliament
Kroc, Mrs. Ray (Joan)		Business	5	15	35	15	McDonalds
Kroc, Ray A.		Business	30	90	150	100	McDonalds
Krock, Arthur		Author	7	20	40	15	Bureau Chief, Columnist NY Times
Kroesen, Fred J.		Military	4	15	20	10	
Krofft, Marty		Entertainment	40	125		50	Puppeteer
Kroft, Steve		TV Journalist	5			24	60 Minutes
Krol, John, Cardinal	1910-1996	Clergy	30	40	75	50	Archbishop of Philadelphia 1961-88 & Cardinal '67
Kroll, Gustov		Science	10			30	Rocket Pioneer/von Braun
Kronberger, Hans		Political	10			15	Member European Parliament
Kroner, Brig. Gen. Hayes A.	1890-1975	Military	30				World War II U.S. general
Kropotkin, Pyotr A.	1842-1921	Political	75	175	350		Russian anarchist
Krosigk, Gen. Inf. Ernst-Anton von	1898-1945	Military	25				World War II German general
Krueger, Walter	1881-1967	Military	45	100			Sp.-Am., WW I & Full Gen. WW II
Krug, J. A.		Cabinet	10	20	30	15	Sec'y Interior
Kruger, Kurt		Entertainment	8	9	15	35	
Kruger, Otto	1885-1974	Entertainment	30			75	Distinguished Leading & Character Actor
Kruger, Stephanus J.P.	1825-1904	Head of State	125	450		660	Krugerrand Named For Him
Kruger, Stephanus Johannes P.		political		146			president of Transvaal republic
Krüger, Gen. Panz. Troops Walter	1892-1973	Military	25				World War II German general
Krulwich, Robert		Celebrity	10			15	media/TV personality
Krupa, Gene	1909-1973	Entertainment	40	110	160	93	Big Band Leader-Drums
Krupinski, Walter		Aviation	20	30	55	68	Ger. Ace. WW II . RK
Krupp, Alfred	1812-1902	Business	180	320	500		Founder Krupp Works
Krupp, Friedrich Alfred	1854-1902	Business	125	260			Arms Manufacturer
Krylov, Ivan A.		Author	15	40	75	20	Russion Fabulist. Fables
Krzyanowski, Wladimir	1824-1887	Civil War	50	95	140		Union general
Kschessinska, Matilda M.	1872-1971	Ballet	110		580	535	Prima Ballerina Assoluta Imperial Theatre
Kschessinsky, Joseph	1868-1942	Entertainment	75		250		Actor-Brother of Prima Ballerina Matilda K.
Kuatosov, Mikhail	1745-1813	Military		1750			Rus. Military Leader against Turks
Kubelik, Jan	1880-1940	Composer	40	92	250	225	Czech Violinist, AMQS 200-575
Kubelik, Rafael		Conductor	15	50		50	
Kubiszewski, Andrew		Entertainment	6			25	Music. Drummer, Vocals 'Stabbing Westward'
Kubitschek, Juscelino		Head of State	10	35	50	40	Brazil
Kubrick, Sidney		Entertainment	5	5	10	15	

NAME	DATE	CATEGORY	SIG	LS/DS	ALS	SP	COMMENTS
Kubrick, Stanley		Entertainment	30	65		125	Film Director.
Kuchel, Thomas	1910-	Congress	5	25			Sen. CA
Kuchler, Georg Von		Military				306	german general
Kuchta, Gladys		Entertainment	10			30	Opera
Kucinich, Dennis J.K.		Congress	10			15	Member U.S. Congress
Kuckelkorn, Wilfried		Political	10			15	Member European Parliament
Kudrow, Lisa		Entertainment	20			54	Actress. 'Friends'
Kuhlman, Katherine		Clergy	35		50		Radio Evengelist
Kuhn, Joseph E.		Military	30		125		Am. WW I Gen.
Kuhn, Maggie	1905-1995	Political	20			35	Political & Social Activist. Fndr Of Grey Panthers
Kuhne, Helmut		Political	10			15	Member European Parliament
Kuldell, Brig. Gen. Rudolph C.	1889-1973	Military	30				World War II U.S. general
Kullman, Charles		Entertainment	20			50	Popular Operatic Tenor/Met. 20 Yrs. Some Films
Kulp, Nancy		Entertainment	10			25	Comedienne-Actress
Kumalo, Dumisani		Celebrity	10			15	motivational speaker
Kuncewiczowa, Maria		Author	145		345		Escaped Nazi Ger.
Kung, Hans		Clergy	35	50	75	60	
Kunis, Mila		Entertainment				30	
Kunstler, William	1919-1995	Law	25	35	75	40	Defense of Radicals. Attny for Martin Luther King
Kuntz, Florence		Political	10			15	Member European Parliament
Kuntze, Gen. of Engineers Walter	1883-1968	Military	25				World War II German general
Kuntzen, Gen. Panz. Troops Adolf	1889-1964	Military	25				World War II German general
Kunzig, Brig. Gen. Louis A.	1882-1956	Military	30				World War II U.S. general
Kupka, Frantisek	1871-1957	Artist	110	225	387		Czech.Abstract Art, Illustrator
Kuralt, Charles		TV News	8	20	35	60	Commentator
Kuribayashi, General Tadamichi	1891-1945	Military	25				World War II Japanese general
Kurtz, Brig. Gen. Guy O.	1894-1969	Military	30				World War II U.S. general
Kurtz, Perry		Celebrity	10			15	comedian
Kurtz, Swoosie		Entertainment	5			26	Actress. Sisters
Kusch, Polykarp, Dr.		Science	20	50		25	Nobel Physics
Kutcher, Ashton		Celebrity				35	Actor
Kutosov, Mikhail	1745-1813	Military		1550			Rus. Military Leader against Turks
Kutschko, Brig. Gen. Emerick	1892-1969	Military	30				World War II U.S. general
Kutuzov, Mikhail Illarionovich		Military		1840			Soviet Field Marshall
Kutz, Brig. Gen. Harry R.	1889-1976	Military	30				World War II U.S. general
Kuwaki, General Takaaki		Military	25				World War II Japanese general
Kuykendall, Andrew J.	1815-1891	Congress	10				Repr. IL, Union Officer
Kwan, Nancy		Entertainment	9	16		45	
Ky, Nguyen Cao		Head of State	30	100	250	75	
Kÿchling, Gen. of Inf. Friedrich	1893-1970	Military	25				World War II German general
Kyl, Jon		Senate	10			15	United States Senate (R - AZ)
Kyne, Peter B.		Author	5	15	30	10	Homsey Family Novels
Kyser, Kay		Entertainment	15			30	Big Band Leader
Kÿstring, Gen. of Cavalry Ernest A.	1876-1953	Military	25				World War II German general

NAME	DATE	CATEGORY	SIG	LS/DS	ALS	SP	COMMENTS

L

NAME	DATE	CATEGORY	SIG	LS/DS	ALS	SP	COMMENTS
L A Guns		Entertainment	15			40	Rock
L A Law (Cast of)		Entertainment				275	10 Sigs.
La Belle, Patti		Entertainment	15			35	Singer
La Cava, Gregory		Entertaiinment	20			45	Film Director
La Farge, John	1835-1910	Artist	38	95	279		Am. Landscape & Figure Painter. Author
La Forge, Frank		Composer	15			45	
La Marr, Barbara		Entertainment	300			800	
La Motta, Vikki		Entertainment	10		10	15	Model-Actress. Wife of Jake La Motta. SP Nude 45
La Paglia, Anthony		Entertainment	10			20	actor
La Plante, Lynda		Celebrity	10			15	film industry
La Revelliere-Lepaux,L.		Fr. Revolution	25	70	145		Politician
La Rocque, Rod		Entertainment	20		45	55	
La Rue, Jack	1903-1984	Entertainment	10			35	Actor. Gangster Roles and Heavies
La Salle, Eriq		Entertainment	10			38	actor
La Verne. Lucille		Entertainment	75			150	
LaBeauf, Sabrina		Entertainment				15	Actress. Bill Cosby Show
Labouisse, Eve Curie		Science	15	60	90	35	Celebrity Daughter of Marie & Pierre Curie
Lacepede, Bernhard de		Science	30	75	145		Fr. Naturalist & Politician
LaCerva, Victor M.D.		Author	8			12	motivation, world peace
Lacey, Ingrid		Entertainment	10			20	Actress
Lachaise, Gaston	1882-1935	Artist		125	188		Fr.-Am. Sculptor
Laciura, Anthony		Entertainment	5			25	Opera
Ladd, Alan	1913-1964	Entertainment	70	80		187	Actor. Popular Leading Man of 40's-50's
Ladd, Brig. Gen. Jesse A.	1887-1957	Military	30				World War II U.S. general
Ladd, Cheryl		Entertainment	8	22	20	22	TV Star. 'Charley's Angels'.
Ladd, David		Entertaiinment	10			25	Producer
Ladd, Diane		Entertainment	5	6	15	15	
Ladd, Kenneth	d. 1944	Military	50			500	WWII Ace (rare)
Ladd, Sue Carol		Entertainment	5	6	15	15	
LaDelle, Jack		Entertainment	3	3	6	6	
Ladue, Brig. Gen. Laurence K.	1903-1951	Military	30				World War II U.S. general
Laemmle, Carl	1867-1939	Entertainment	78	175	525	625	Film Pioneer, Founder Universal
Laennec, Reneé T.H.	1781-1826	Science	2250	3100	4284		Fr. Phys., Invented Stethoscope
Lafayette, Marquis de	1757-1834	Revolutionary War	400	851	1447		Gilbert Motier. Fr. Statesman.ALS/Cont 4,900-9600
Laffer, Arthur Dr.		Celebrity	10			15	financial expert
Laffitte, Maj. Gen. David	1894-	Military	20				World War II French general
LaFlèche, Maj. Gen. Léo-Richer	1888-1956	Military	20				World War II Canadian general
LaFollette, Philip	1897-1965	Governor	15	35		50	Governor WI
LaFollette, Robert Jr.	1895-1953	Senate/Congress	10	25		20	Senator WI
LaFollette, Robert M.	1855-1925	Senate/Congress	35	95		40	Senator WI
Lafontaine, Brig. Gen. Henri-Jean	1882-	Military	20				World War II French general

NAME	DATE	CATEGORY	SIG	LS/DS	ALS	SP	COMMENTS
LaFontaine, Henri Marie		International Law	10	20	30		Nobel Peace Prize
Laforgue, Jules	1860-1887	Author	150				Fr. Symbolist Poet. Died at 27. ALS/Cont. 5500
Lagasse, Emeril		Celebrity	10			22	famous chef
Lage, Carlos		Political	10			15	Member European Parliament
Lagendijk, Joost		Political	10			15	Member European Parliament
Lagerkvist, P.		Author	30	70	175	100	Nobel Literature 1951
Lagerlof, Selma	1858-1940	Author	95	175		250	Nobel Literature 1909
Lagge, James		Clergy	20	25	35		
LaGuardia, Fiorello	1882-1947	Congress	44	94	110	150	Great Reform Mayor NYC. MOC NY. Colorful Char.
Laguiller, Arlette		Political	10			15	Member European Parliament
Lahm, Frank		Aviation	35	75	140	90	
LaHood, Ray L		Congress	10			15	Member U.S. Congress
Lahr, Bert	1895-1967	Entertainment	275	340		466	''Cowardly Lion' of OZ,SP as Lion 8000-11000
Lahti, Christine		Entertainment	6	8	15	24	
Laidlie, D. A.		Clergy	15	20	25		
Laine, Frankie		Entertainment	7	25		12	Singer. Recording artist of Top Hits
Laine, J.L.J., Viscount		Fr. Revolution	30	85	175		
Laingen, Bruce		State Dept.	5			15	Iran Hostage
Laird, Melvin		Cabinet	7	20	25	15	Sec'y Defense
Laithwaite, Eric R.		Inventor	25	95			Electromagnetic Propulsion & Air Cushion Suspensio
Lake, Alexander		Author	8			12	African adventure
Lake, Arthur	1905-1986	Entertainment	40	60	100	125	Dagwood Bumstead of 'Blondie'
Lake, Ricki		Entertainment	10			20	TV Host
Lake, Simon	1866-1945	Science-Business	30	56	325	409	Inv. Even-Keel Type Sub. Scientific Drwg 3750,chk25
Lake, Veronica	1919-1973	Entertainment	175	260		350	Actress
Laker, Freddie, Sir		Business	5			20	Airline President
Lakes, Gary		Entertainment	10			30	Opera
LaLanne, Jack		Entertainment	10	15	30	20	TV Body Builder
Lalique, Rene	1860-1929	Artist	150		600		Fr. Jeweler & Decorative Glass Artisan
Lalumiere, Catherine		Political	10			15	Member European Parliament
Lamacq, Steve		Music	10			15	DJ
Lamar, Joseph R.		Supreme Court	35	95	225		
Lamar, Lucius Q.C.	1825-1893	Supreme Court	82		235		CSA Officer, US Sen.
Lamar, Mirabeau B.	1789-1859	Head of State	88	284			Pres., V.P. & Sec'y State Repub. of TX
LaMarck, Jean Baptiste de		Science	400	950	1000		Forerunner of Darwin
Lamarr, Hedy	1913-	Entertainment	38	70	100	103	40's Beautiful Glamour Girl & Inventor
Lamarr, Mark		Music	10			15	DJ
LaMartine, Alphonse de	1790-1869	Author	90	130	190		Fr. Romantic Poet-Statesman
Lamas, Fernando		Entertainment	20	25	45	45	
Lamas, Lorenzo		Entertainment	9	10	20	25	
Lamassoure, Alain		Political	10			15	Member European Parliament
Lamb, Caroline, Lady	1785-1828	Celebrity			1395		
Lamb, Charles	1775-1834	Author	155	350	1025		Br. Essayist, Critic. Popularly Known as 'Elia'
Lamb, Gil		Entertainment	8			20	Stage-Film Dancer, Comic
Lambert, Christopher		Entertainment	6			35	Actor. 'Highlander' SP 45

NAME	DATE	CATEGORY	SIG	LS/DS	ALS	SP	COMMENTS
Lambert, Jean		Political	10			15	Member European Parliament
Lambert, Maj. Gen. Harold Roger	1896-1980	Military	25				World War II British general
Lambert, Ray		Celebrity	5	14		10	
Lambert, William C.		Aviation	75	135	175	150	ACE, WW I, 2nd Leading Ace
Lamm, Richard D.		Governor	5	26			CO Gov.
Lammers, Hans		Military	95	350			Nazi Official. Hitler Legal Advisor
Lammie, Maj. Gen. George	1891-1946	Military	25				World War II British general
Lamond, Frederic		Composer	25		82	120	Scot. Pianist & Composer
Lamont, Corliss		Activist	10		25		Author. Indicted for Contempt of Congress
Lamont, Daniel S.		Cabinet	15	25	40		Sec'y War, Journalist, Politician
Lamont, Forrest		Entertainment	25			65	Opera
Lamont, Robert P.		Cabinet	25	60	95		Sec'y Commerce
Lamont, Thomas S.		Business	8	25	40	10	Banker. Morgan Guaranty
Lamont, Thomas		White House	15	30	45		Cleveland's Pvt. Sec'y
Lamour, Dorothy	1914-1996	Entertainment	10	25	25	55	Pin-Up SP 35, 55
L'Amour, Louis	1908-1988	Author	75	130	260	150	Novels Re The Old West
Lamplough, Maj. Gen. Stephen	1900-1973	Military	28				World War II British general
Lampson, Nick L		Congress	10			15	Member U.S. Congress
Lampton, Mike		Astronaut	7			15	
Lamson, C.M.		Clergy	10	10	20		
Lancashire, Sarah		Entertainment	10			20	Actress
Lancaster, Burt	1910-1994	Entertainment	40	85		126	Rugged Leading Film Leading Man. Oscar Winner
Lancaster-Ranking, Maj Gen R. P.	1896-1971	Military	28				World War II British general
Lance, Bert		Business	3	5	15	10	Banker
Lanchester, Elsa	1902-1986	Entertainment	25	30	40	56	Eccentric English Actres Wife Of Chas. Laughton
Land, Edwin H.	1909-1992	Science-Business	262	212	500	1000	Polaroid Camera Inventor, rare in SP's
Land, Emory Scott		Military	25	65		35	Adm. Maritime Comm. WW II
Landau, Lev	1908-1968	Science					Russ. Physicist . '62 Nobel. TMsS 650
Landau, Martin		Entertainment	10			40	AA. As Dracula 75
Lander, Frederick West(WD)	1821-1862	Civil War	180	225	1317		Union Gen.
Landers, Ann		Columnist	8	20	30	20	Advice Column
Landers, Audrey		Entertainment	6	8	15	15	
Landers, Judy		Entertainment	5	6	15	15	Pin-Up SP 25
Landesburg, Steve		Entertainment	10			20	actor
Landi, Bruno		Entertainment	15			60	Opera
Landi, Elissa	1904-1948	Entertainment	30	45	60	70	Vintage
Landis, Carole	1919-1948	Entertainment	70			225	Suicide at 29
Landis, Jessie Royce		Entertainment	25			75	
Landis, John		Entertainment	15			25	Film Director 'Blues Brothers', 'Am Werewolf
Landis, Kenesaw Mountain		Jurist	169	317		525	And 1st Baseball Commissioner. HOF
Landon, Alfred M.	1887-1987	Governor	27	45	75	75	Rep. Pres. Candidate vs FDR. Gov. KS
Landon, Melville D.		Journalist	20				(aka Eli Perkins) Columnist
Landon, Michael		Entertainment	80	188		245	Actor-Writer-Dir. 'Little House', 'Bonanza'
Landowska, Wanda	1879-1959	Entertainment	155	165	350	295	Pol-Fr Harpsichordist-Composer
Landrieu, Mary		Senate	10			15	United States Senate (D - LA)

NAME	DATE	CATEGORY	SIG	LS/DS	ALS	SP	COMMENTS
Landrieu, Moon		Cabinet	6		15	10	Sec'y HUD
Landrum, Maj. Gen. Eugene M.	1891-1967	Military	30				World War II U.S. general
Landry, Robert B.		Military	15			25	Gen'l. Air Aide to Pres. Truman
Landseer, Charles		Artist	30		75		R.A. & Keeper of Royal Academy
Landseer, Edwin H., Sir	1802-1873	Artist	35	65	260		Extraordinary Landscape-Animal Painter
Landseer, John		Artist	25		125		Father of Edwin H.
Landseer, Thomas		Artist-Engraver	25	40	75		Brother of E.H.
Landsteiner, Karl, Dr		Science	50	90	210		Nobel Medicine
Lane, Abbe		Entertainment	15			20	Vocalist. Mrs.Xavier Cugat. Pin-Up SP 15
Lane, Allan Rocky		Entertainment	65			250	Cowboy-Actor
Lane, Christy		Entertainment	5	6	15	15	Gospel Singer
Lane, Diane		Entertainment	10	15		20	Actress
Lane, Evelyn		Entertainment	10			25	Brit. Actress. Vintage
Lane, Franklin K.		Cabinet	25	40		25	Sec'y Interior
Lane, Harriet		First Lady, Actg.	125	250	688		Actg. 1st Lady, Buchanan. RARE
Lane, Henry S.	1811-1881	Political			52		
Lane, James H. (WD)		Civil War-Congress	70	290	525		Special DS 7,500
Lane, James H.	1814-1866	Civil War-Congress	50	95	140	2990	Sen. KS, Union Gen.,Suicide
Lane, James Henry	1833-1907	Civil War	95	145	335	1970	CSA General
Lane, Joseph		Governor	40	75	130		Gov. OR Terr.& 1st US Sen.
Lane, Lola		Entertainment	22	15	30	25	
Lane, Nathan		Entertainment	15			55	Stage, Screen Actor-Comedian. Tony Award
Lane, Priscilla		Entertainment	12	15	25	25	
Lane, Rosemary		Entertainment	15	20	35	35	
Lane, Walter Page	1817-1892	Civil War	120				Confederate general
Lang, Anton		Entertainment	25	30	45	40	Play Christ in the Passion Play.
Lang, Belinda		Entertainment	10			20	Actress
Lang, Carl		Political	10			15	Member European Parliament
Lang, Cosmo Gordon		Clergy	25	35	45	35	
Lang, Fritz	1890-1976	Entertainment	154	375		188	Ger. Innovative Film Director
Lang, Johnny		Entertainment				45	Singer
Lang, June		Entertainment	10				Actress
Lang, K D		Country Music	20	20		68	
Lang, Rosa		Entertainment	4	4	9	10	
Lang, Sebastian		Entertainment	19	25	45	45	
Lang, Walter		Entertainment	20			45	Film Director. 40 Year Vet.
Langan, Glenn		Entertainment	8	15	35	25	
Langdon, Harry		Entertainment	82			314	
Langdon, John		Revolutionary War	210	400	1575		Continental Congr.,Gov. NH, Signer Const'n
Langdon, Loomis		Civil War				345	Union officer
Lange, Bernd		Political	10			15	Member European Parliament
Lange, David		Head of State	5	15	30	15	New Zealand
Lange, Hope		Entertainment	10			25	Pin-Up SP 30
Lange, Jessica		Entertainment	14	38		35	AA Actress. King Kong SP 75
Lange, Ted		Entertainment	5			15	

NAME	DATE	CATEGORY	SIG	LS/DS	ALS	SP	COMMENTS
Langella, Frank		Entertainment	15	20		40	Actor. Films-Stage
Langen, Werner		Political	10			15	Member European Parliament
Langenhagen, Brigitte		Political	10			15	Member European Parliament
Langer, Will		Senate	10	35			Senator ND
Langevin, James R. L		Congress	10			15	Member U.S. Congress
Langford, Frances		Entertainment	8			20	Big Band Vocalist-Films
Langley, Samuel P.	1834-1906	Aviation	148	388	438	450	1890's Aeronautical Pioneer, Astronomer
Langlie, Arthur		Governor	12	20		15	Governor Washington
Langmuir, Irving		Science	30	75	145		Nobel Chemistry 1932
Langtry, Lillie	1852-1929	Entertainment	243	310	409		Actress & Mistress of Edw. VII. 'Jersey Lilly'
Lanier, Sidney	1842-1881	Author	300	590	1165		Most Important So. Poet of Time. ALS/Cont 2400
Lannes, Jean		Fr. Revolution	675	1750			Marshal of France
Lannoye, Paul A.		Political	10			15	Member European Parliament
Lanphier, Thomas G., Jr.		Aviation	142	70	182	212	ACE, WW II, Yamamoto Mission
Lansbury, Angela		Entertainment	5	10	15	30	Br. Star of Stage-Screen-TV
Lansing, Robert		Cabinet	40	125			Sec'y State
Lansky, Meyer	1902-1983	Gangster	200	1040			Mob Boss, check 750-1250
Lantieri, Rita		Entertainment 5	5			20	Opera
Lantos, Tom L		Congress	10			15	Member U.S. Congress
Lantz, Walter*	1900-1994	Cartoonist	60	85	125	101	AA, 'Woody Woodpecker' signed draw 50-175
Lanz, Gen. of Mtn. Troops Hubert	1896-1982	Military	27				World War II German general
Lanza, Mario	1921-1959	Entertainment	175			725	Tragic Teno-Cinema Star. Early Death
LaPlace, P.M.,Marquis de	1749-1827	Science	535				Fr. Astronomer, Mathematician
Lapoype, J.F.C., Baron		Fr. Revolution	20		125		
Larch, John		Entertainment	6	10	15	10	Actor
Larcom, Lucy		Author	15	25	45		
Lardner, Dionysius	1793-1859	Author	45	85	162		Irish writer on Sci. & Math.
Lardner, James L.	1802-1891	Civil War	40	95	145		Union Naval Commodore. Sig/Rank 60, DS 170
Lardner, Ring Jr.	1915-	Author	10	20	35	15	Screenwriter. 'M.A.S.H.' One of 'Hollywood Ten'
Lardner, Ring	1885-1933	Author	65	195	310	250	Am. Humorist, Social Satirist
Laredo, Ruth		Entertainment	15	20	30	35	
Largent, Steve		Congress	5			20	Oklahoma. Star Football Player. MOC OK
Larminat, Gen. René-Marie-E. de	1895-1962	Military	20				World War II French general
Larmouth, Kathy		Entertainment	4	4	9	9	
LaRocca, D.J. Nick		Musician-Composer	50			225	AMusQS 250
Laroche, Loretta		Celebrity	10			15	motivational speaker
LaRosa, Julias		Entertainment	5			10	Singer Arthur Godfey Show
LaRoushe, Lyndon, Jr.		Pres. Candidate	20		35	25	Tax Evader
Larrey, Dominick, Baron		Fr. Revolution	45	155	310		
Larroquette, John		Entertainment	10			32	
Larsen, Rick L		Congress	10			15	Member U.S. Congress
Larsen-Todsen, Nanny		Entertainmnt	20			65	Opera
Larson, Gary*		Cartoonist	20			100	Far Side
Larson, John B. L		Congress	10			15	Member U.S. Congress
Larson, Leonard, Dr.		Science	5	15	30	10	

NAME	DATE	CATEGORY	SIG	LS/DS	ALS	SP	COMMENTS
LaRue, Lash		Entertainment	5	6	15	30	Western actor
Lasch, Gen. of Infantry Otto	1893-1971	Military	27				World War II German general
Laschet, Armin		Political	10			15	Member European Parliament
Lasker, Mary		Business	5	10	15	10	
Lasky, Jesse L.		Business	40	75	150	75	Pioneer Film Producer
Lasser, Louise		Entertainment	5	20		22	Character Actress-Comedian
Lasseter, John		Celebrity	10			15	film industry
Lassiter, William		Military	20	45	75	75	General WW I Under Pershing. TLS/Cont. 250
Laswell, Fred*		Cartoonist	25			150	B. Google & Snuffy Smith
Latham, Hubert		Aviation	25	35	90	75	
Latham, Louise		Entertainment	4			20	Current Character Actress
Latham, Tom L		Congress	10			15	Member U.S. Congress
Lathbury, General Sir Gerald Wm.	1906-1978	Military	28				World War II British general
Lathrop, George P.	1851-1898	Author	20	30	40	65	Am. Journalist, Writer
Latourette, Kenneth Scott		Clergy	20	30	45	30	
LaTourette, Steven C. L		Congress	10			15	Member U.S. Congress
Latour-Maubourg, M.V.N.F.		Napoeonic Wars	20		75		Cavalry Gen.
Latrobe, Benjamin H.	1764-1820	Artist	85	462	798		Am. Arch. of the White House
Latrobe, Osman		Civil War			575		CSA officer
Latter, Maj. Gen. John Cecil	1896-1972	Military	28				World War II British general
Lattimore, Richard		Author	10	15	25	15	
Lattler, Herman		West	70		165		Pioneer & American Indian Photographer of Note
Laubach, Frank C.		Clergy	35	50	90	60	
Lauck, Chet		Entertainment	10				Radio. Lum & Abner
Lauder, Estee		Business	10			30	Cosmetics
Lauder, Harry, Sir	1870-1950	Entertainment	60	90	145	125	Vintage Scottish Comedian-Singer
Lauer, Maj. Gen. Walter E.	1893-1966	Military	30				World War II U.S. general
Lauer, Matt		Celebrity	10			15	media/TV personality
Laughton, Charles	1899-1962	Entertainment	60	120	140	175	Brit. Actor. Versatile & Fine. Oscar Winner
Lauman, Jacob Gartner	1813-1867	Civil War	40	90	130		Union general
Lauper, Cyndi		Entertainment	25	35	85	43	Rock
Laurants, Arthur		Author	5			20	Playwright
Laure, Gen. Auguste-Marie-Emile	1881-1957	Military	20				World War II French general
Laurel, Stan & Hardy, Oliver		Entertainment	700			1249	SP (PC) 650-1050, SP 5x7 850
Laurel, Stan	1890-1965	Entertainment	128	264	420	456	Br.-Am Stage-Screen Comic Actor
Lauren, Dyanna		Entertainment				36	Porn Queen
Lauren, Ralph		Business	10	15	40	25	Fashion Designer.
Laurencin, Marie	1885-1956	Artist	125		450		Fr. Painter & Printmaker
Laurens, Henry	1724-1792	Revolutionary War	867	1644	2138		Pres. Continental Congress. SC Merchant
Laurie, Hugh		Celebrity	10			15	comedian
Laurie, Maj. Gen. Rufus Henry	1892-1961	Military	25				World War II British general
Laurie, Maj. Gen. Sir John Emilius	1892-1983	Military	25				World War II British general
Laurie, Piper		Entertainment	6	8	15	20	Pin-Up SP 30
Lausche, Frank J.		Governor	12	20		15	Governor OH
Lautenberg, Frank		Senate	10			15	United States Senate (D - NJ)

NAME	DATE	CATEGORY	SIG	LS/DS	ALS	SP	COMMENTS
Lauter, Harry		Entertainment	5			15	
Lauterbach, Johann Christoph		Entertainment		95	195		Ger. Violinist
Laux, Gen. of Infantry Paul	1887-1944	Military	27				World War II German general
Lauzanne, Maj. Gen. André-J-M	1879-	Military	20				World War II French general
Lavarack, Lt. Gen. John D.	1885-1957	Military	30				World War II Australian general
Lavarra, Vincenzo		Political	10			15	Member European Parliament
Lavi, Daliah		Entertainment	4			10	Pin-Up SP 10
Lavigne, Avril		Music	20			42	Rock
Lavin, Linda		Entertainment	5	6	15	20	
Lavoisier, Antoine L. de	1743-1794	Science	400	3625			Fr. Founder Modern Chemistry
Law, Andrew Bonar		Head of State	30	80	135		Br. Prime Minister
Law, Evander McIvor	1836-1920	Civil War	100	250	568		CSA Gen.
Law, George H.		Clergy	10		15	20	
Law, John Phillip		Entertainment	5			15	
Law, John	1671-1729	Reformer	150				Scot. Economist. LS/Cont.5000
Law, Jude		Entertainment	10			35	Actor
Law, Ruth		Aviation	30			100	
Law, Tony		Celebrity	10			15	comedian
Lawden, Frank O.		Celebrity	4	12	30		
Lawes, Lewis E.		Law Enforcement	20	40	65	50	Prison Warden. Sing Sing
Lawford, Betty	1910-1960	Entertainment	15	25		30	Brit. Actress. '25 Film Debut. 'a.Sherlock Holmes'
Lawford, Peter	1923-1984	Entertainment	20			62	Collected as Member of Sinatra's 'Rat Pack'
Lawler, Michael K.	1814-1882	Civil War	40	95			Union Gen. ALS '61 360
Lawless, Lucy		Entertainment	11			49	Xena, Warrior Princess.
Lawley, Sue		Celebrity	10			15	newsreader
Lawrence, 1st Baron		Head of State	10	30	75		India
Lawrence, Abbott	1792-1855	Congress	25				MA. Financier. Lawrence MA
Lawrence, Barbara		Entertainment	5			20	
Lawrence, Carol		Entertainment	5	6	15	15	
Lawrence, D(avid) H(erbert)	1885-1930	Author	225	718	2991		Br. Novelist.'Lady Chatterley's Lover'
Lawrence, David L.		Governor	17	20			Governor PA
Lawrence, Elliot		Entertainment	20			40	Big Band Leader. Multiple Emmys
Lawrence, Ernest O.	1901-1958	Science	100	170	240	200	Nobel Physics 1939. Invented Cyclotron.
Lawrence, Gertrude	1902-1952	Entertainment	20	42		55	Major Br. Actress. 1st Star of 'King and I'(Stage)
Lawrence, Herbert A., Sir		Military	10	30	50	25	
Lawrence, Jacob	1917-	Artist	15	30		30	Afro-Am. Painter, Educator. Print S 100
Lawrence, Jerome		Entertainment	10			20	actor
Lawrence, Joey		Entertainment	10			20	actor
Lawrence, John		Colonial Am.	35	90	175		CT Statesman, Rev. War Leader
Lawrence, Josie		Celebrity	10			15	comedienne
Lawrence, Maj. Gen. Thompson	1889-1973	Military	30				World War II U.S. general
Lawrence, Marc	1910-	Entertainment	10	15	25	25	Stage Actor, Films'33. Swarthy Pock-Marked Villain
Lawrence, Marjorie		Entertainment	15			90	Australian Opera, Concert Soprano
Lawrence, Rosina	1914-1998	Entertainment	20			55	Late Silent & Early Sound Film Star. 'Our Gang'
Lawrence, Sharon		Entertainment	10			25	NYPD Blue

NAME	DATE	CATEGORY	SIG	LS/DS	ALS	SP	COMMENTS
Lawrence, Steve		Entertainment	6	8	10	15	
Lawrence, Thomas, Sir	1769-1830	Artist	100	160	225		Br. Portr. Painter. Pres. Royal Academy
Lawrence, Thos. E.	1888-1935.	Author-Soldier	650	1250	4402	2917	Lawrence of Arabia
Lawrence, Tracy		Country Music	5			25	Singer
Lawrence, Vicki		Entertainment	5	6	15	15	
Lawrence, Wendy		Astronaut	8			25	
Lawrence, William	1819-1899	Congress	8				Repr. OH, Union Colonel
Lawson, James M.		Clergy	20	25	35	25	
Lawson, Maj. Gen. Edward F.	1890-1963	Military	28				World War II British general
Lawson, Nigella		Celebrity	10			15	TV Chef
Lawson, Ted		Aviation	15	30		40	
Lawton, Alexander R. (WD)	1818-1896	Civil War	195	652	900		CSA Gen.
Lawton, Alexander R.	1818-1896	Civil War	110	250	360		CSA Gen.
Lawton, Lt. Gen. Samuel T.	1884-1961	Military	30				World War II U.S. general
Laxalt, Paul		Senate/Congress	4	10		15	Governor, Senator NV
Lay, Brigadier William Oswald	1892-1952	Military	25				World War II British general
Lay, Herman W.		Business	10	25	50	30	Lay's Potato Chips
Lay, Philidda		Entertainment	3			8	Actress
Layard, Austen Henry, Sir	1817-1894	Archaeologist	75	160	410		Br. Diplomat. Excavator of Niveveh
Laycock, Maj. Gen. Sir Robt. Edw.	1907-1968	Military	25				World War II British general
Lazarev, Alexander		Conductor				65	Former Bolshoi Maestro
Lazarus, Emma	1849-1887	Author		2300			The New Colossus
Lazarus, Mel*		Cartoonist	5			20	Miss Peach, Momma
Lazarus, S. Ralph		Business	4	7	10	5	Pres.Benrus Watch.Philanthropis
Lazenby, George		Entertainment	10	15	30	52	
Lazzari, Virgillo		Entertainment	15			45	
Le Corbusier		Artist		600			French Architect,painter,writer
Le Pen, Jean-marie		Political	10			15	Member European Parliament
Lea, Homer		Military	55	175			Predicted US-Jap. War/HI as Key
Leach, James A. L		Congress	10			15	Member U.S. Congress
Leach, Robin		Entertainment	10			15	actor
Leachman, Cloris		Entertainment	9	15	20	25	AA
Leadbetter, Danville	1811-1866	Civil War	150	475			CSA General
Leahy, Patrick		Senate	10			15	United States Senate (D - VT)
Leahy, William Daniel		Military	35	145	105	195	Chief of Staff-FDR & Truman
Leake, Joseph Bloomfield	1828-1913	Civil War	30	55	75		Union Brevet Brig. General
Leakey, Louis B.		Science	45	80	120	125	Anthropologist, Archaeologist
Leakey, Mary D.		Science	15	25	70	30	Anthropologist, Archaeologist
Leakey, Meave, Dr.		Science	20	60			
Leakey, Richard, Dr.		Science	125				Br. Anthropologist
Lean, David, Sir		Entertainment	45			70	Film Director
Leander, Zarah		Entertainment	35			150	Opera
Lear, Edward	1812-1888	Artist	140		907		Br. Painter & Nonsense Poet
Lear, General Ben	1879-1966	Military	30				World War II U.S. general
Lear, Norman		Business	10	15	45	25	TV Film Producer

NAME	DATE	CATEGORY	SIG	LS/DS	ALS	SP	COMMENTS
Lear, Tobias		Revolutionary War	75	240	325		Pvt. Secretary to G. Washington
L'Enfant, Pierre Charles		Aviation	400	850	1500		
Lear, William P. Sr.		Business	35	125	195	200	Lear Jet Aircraft Founder
Learned, Michael		Entertainment	9	10	20	25	
Leary, Timothy, Dr.	1920-1996	Activist-Educator	25	80		57	Drug Cult Leader, Psychologist. Acid Print S 225
Lease, Mary Elizabeth		Reformer	15	20	40		Orator, Writer Woman Suffrage
Leavelle, James R.		Legal	20			85	Detective Handcuffed to Oswald when Shot
Leavenworth, Henry		Military	250		750		Frontier Soldier, General
LeBlanc, Matt		Entertainment	20			51	Actor.Friends
Leboeuf, Michael		Celebrity	10			15	financial expert
LeBrock, Kelly		Entertainment	10	15		30	
Lebrun, Albert	1871-1950	Head of State	30	50	125	75	Last Pres. 3rd French Repub.
Lebrun, Chas. F. Duc de	1739-1824	Napoleonic Wars	35	100	150		3rd Consul/Bonaparte
LeCarre, John (David Cornwell)		Author	20	45	75	30	Br. Realistic Spy Novels
Lechner, Kurt		Political	10			15	Member European Parliament
Leclerc, Maj. Gen. Pierre Eouard	1893-1982	Military	24				World War II Canadian general
Lecuona, Ernesto	1896-1963	Composer	150			635	AMusQS 400-600
Led Zeppelin (all-org.)		Entertainment	250			700	Alb.Cover Signed 850
Ledbetter, Brig. Gen. Louis A.	1890-	Military	30				World War II U.S. general
Lederer, Francis		Entertainment	10			25	
Lederman, Leon M., Dr.		Science	15	25	50		Nobel Phyics
Ledlie, James Hewett	1832-1882	Civil War	45	90	120		Union general
Ledoux, Harold*		Cartoonist	5			25	Judge Parker
Ledyard, John	1770-1771	Colonial America		70			Merchant, Justice of Peace. Progenitor of Line
Ledyard, John	1751-1789	Explorer		475			Accompanied Capt. Cook. Wrote Adventures.
Lee, Agnes	1869-1939	Author			299		Poet
Lee, Albert Lindley	1834-1907	Civil War	45	90	120		Union general
Lee, Alfred		Clergy	10	15	35		
Lee, Ang		Celebrity	10			15	film industry
Lee, Anna		Entertainment	5			15	
Lee, Barbara L		Congress	10			15	Member U.S. Congress
Lee, Bernard		Entertainment	15			25	
Lee, Brandon	1964-1993	Entertainment	241	444		571	Son of Bruce Lee. Tragic Death
Lee, Brenda		Country Music	5			15	
Lee, Brig. Gen. Raymond E.	1886-1958	Military	30				World War II U.S. general
Lee, Bruce	1940-1973	Entertainment	600	925	1275	1500	Legendary Cult Celeb
Lee, Canada	1731-1982	Entertainment	60			188	Afro-Am Actor. McCarthy Era Victim
Lee, Charles	1731-1782	Rev. War			3318		Turncoat Gen. Rev. War
Lee, Charles	1758-1815	Cabinet	110	250	550		Washington's Att'y Gen.
Lee, Christopher		Entertainment	20			49	Best Known for Role in Dracula
Lee, Dixie (Mrs Bing Crosby)		Entertainment	10	15	25	25	
Lee, Dr. Tsung-Dao		Science	20	30	45	25	Nobel Physics
Lee, E. Hamilton		Aviation	10	25	50	35	
Lee, Edwin G.	1836-1870	Civil War	165	290	410		CSA Gen.
Lee, Fitzhugh (WD)		Civil War	240		1388		CSA Gen.

NAME	DATE	CATEGORY	SIG	LS/DS	ALS	SP	COMMENTS
Lee, Fitzhugh	1835-1905	Civil War	115	198	243	417	CSA General. AQS 595, TLS/Cont. 575
Lee, Francis Lightfoot		Revolutionary War	977	1050	4250		Signer Decl. of Indepen.
Lee, Geo. Wash. Custis	1832-1913	Civil War	183	338	386	750	CSA General
Lee, Geo. Wash. Custis (WD)	1832-1913	Civil War	270		1300		CSA Gen.
Lee, Gordon 'Porky'		Entertainment	25			43	'Little Rascals'
Lee, Gypsy Rose	1913-1970	Entertainment	100	167		565	Burlesque Queen & Sometimes Movie Star
Lee, Harper	1926-	Author	110	263		350	'To Kill a Mocking Bird' Pulitzer
Lee, Heather		Entertainment				35	Porn Queen
Lee, Henry	1756-1818	Revolutionary War	220	623	733		Light-Horse Harry. General Revolutionary War
Lee, Henry, Sir	1533-1611	Knight	125		500		Model Knight to Queen Elizabeth I
Lee, Jason Scott		Entertainment	5			30	Actor. 'Jungle Book' SP 35
Lee, John Wayne		Celebrity	10			15	financial expert
Lee, John		Celebrity	10			15	motivational speaker
Lee, Lila		Entertainment	5	6	15	15	
Lee, Lt. Gen. John C.H.	1887-1958	Military	30				World War II U.S. general
Lee, Maj. Gen. Alec Wilfred	1896-1973	Military	25				World War II British general
Lee, Maj. Gen. William C.	1895-1948	Military	30				World War II U.S. general
Lee, Mark C.		Astronaut	7			25	
Lee, Martin		Celebrity	10			15	political celebrity
Lee, Mary Custis		Civil War	112		587	640	Mrs. Robert E. Lee
Lee, Michele		Entertainment	5	6	15	15	
Lee, Mildres	1846-1905	History			155		Daughter of Robert E. Lee
Lee, Pamela		Entertainment	10			20	actress
Lee, Peggy		Entertainment	10	22		53	Singer-Composer
Lee, Pinkie	1916-1693	Entertainment	15			30	Vaudeville & Early TV Comedian, Kid Shows
Lee, Richard Henry	1732-1794	Revolutionary War	275	2350	4058		Signer Decl. of Indepen.
Lee, Robert E. (WD)		Civil War	3423	12513	21540	8618	As CSA Gen. Auction 23K-36,000
Lee, Robert E.	1807-1870	Military	2785	5514	8400	5960	CSA Cmmdg. Gen. Mex. City 1848 ALS/Cont 25000
Lee, Rusty		Celebrity	10			15	TV Chef
Lee, Ruta		Entertainment	4			10	Pin-Up SP 10
Lee, Samuel P.	1812-1897	Civil War	60	210	275	265	Union Adm.
Lee, Spike		Entertainment	10	25		25	Afro-Am Film Director
Lee, Stan		Artist	45			100	Spiderman, signed drawing 140-225
Lee, Stephen Dill (WD)		Civil War	190	848			CSA Gen.
Lee, Stephen Dill	1833-1908	Civil War	120	195	325		CSA Gen.
Lee, Tenghui		Head of State	25			55	President Republic of China (Taiwan)
Lee, Tommy		Entertainment	20			42	Rock
Lee, William H.F. 'Rooney'	1837-1891	Civil War	185		630		CSA Gen.,ALS War Date/Cont.. 6050
Lee, William Raymond	1804-1891	Civil War	15	45	70		Union General
Lee, Yuan T., Dr.		Science	20	35	45	30	Nobel Chemistry
Leeb, Fld. Mshl. Wilhelm Knight v	1876-1956	Military	27				World War II German general
Leeb, General of Artillery Emil	1881-1969	Military	27				World War II German general
Leeb, Wilhelm Joseph Franz Von		Military				306	Nazi general
Leeb, Wilhelm R. Von		Military	45		135	210	
Leech, John	1817-1864	Artist	70	125	138		Br. Caricaturist-Illustrator. Orig. Piece S 875

NAME	DATE	CATEGORY	SIG	LS/DS	ALS	SP	COMMENTS
Leech, Richard		Entertainment	15			30	Opera
Leeds, Andrea		Entertainment	10			25	
Leeds, Peter	1917-1996	Entertainment	5	20			Actor. Appeared in over 8,000 TV shows
Leeming, Jan		Celebrity	10			15	newsreader
Leese, Lt. Gen. Sir Oliver Wm. H.	1894-1978	Military	25				World War II British general
Leese, Oliver, Sir		Military	20	50		35	Br. Gen. WW II/Montgomery. 8th Army
Leestma, David C.		Astronaut	5			20	
Leeves, Jane		Entertainment	10			20	actress
Lefavi, Bruce A.		Celebrity	10			15	financial expert
Lefebvre, F.J., Duke		Fr. Revolution	160	675			Marshal of Napoleon
Lefevre, Edwin		Financial Writer	4	8	15		Panamanian Ambass. to Spain
Leftwich, John W.		Senate/Congress	10	15	30		MOC TN 1866
LeGallienne, Eva		Entertainment	5	25	50	35	
LeGallienne, Richard		Author	35	50	162		Brit. Man of Letters
LeGarde, Tom and Ted		Country Music	10			20	
Leger, Fernand		Artist	80	199	462		Fr. Abstract Painter.AMsS 2750
Leggett, Mortimer Dormer	1821-1896	Civil War	45	75	120		Union General
Legrand, Michel		Composer	5	15	25	20	
Leguizamo, John		Celebrity				35	
Leguizamo, John		Entertainment	6			35	Versatile Movie Performer
LeHand, M. A. (Missy)	1898-1944	Gov't Exec. Aide	20	80	130	40	FDR Personal Sec'y 20 Years
Lehar, Franz	1870-1948	Composer	100	165	304	325	The Merry Widow. AMusQS 225
Lehman, Herbert H.	1882-1963	Governor	10	25		25	Gov. NY, Senator NY
Lehman, Maj. Gen. Raymond E.	1895-1964	Military	30				World War II U.S. general
Lehmann, Ernst August	1886-1937	Aviation	85		365		Ger. Aeronautical Engineer
Lehmann, Lilli	1848-1929	Entertainment	75		100	150	Ger. Soprano. 170 Operatic Roles
Lehmann, Lotte	1888-1976	Entertainment	50	75	158	195	Ger. Opera. Magnificent Soprano. SPc 80-135
Lehmann, Marie		Entertainment	50			175	Ger. Prima Donna. Mother Lilli
Lehne, Klaus-heiner		Political	10			15	Member European Parliament
Lehr, Lew		Entertainment	15	15	35	30	
Lehrer, Jim		Celebrity	10			15	media/TV personality
Leibman, Ron		Entertainment	5	6	15	15	
Leider, Frida		Entertainment	35			140	Opera. Great Brunhilde
Leiferkus, Sergei		Entertainment	10			25	Opera
Leigh, Barbara		Entertainment				40	
Leigh, Janet		Entertainment	5	9	15	52	Pin-Up SP 25
Leigh, Jennifer Jason		Entertainment	15			85	
Leigh, Mandy		Entertainment	3			18	Actress Pin-Up 40
Leigh, Richard		Composer	5	18			
Leigh, Vivien	1913-1967	Entertainment	255	377	572	745	Brit. Actress. Oscar Winner.SP Pc 575
Leigh, Vivien (As Scarlett O'Hara)		Entertainment				3450	SP Pc 750-1750
Leigh, Vivien & Laurence Olivier		Entertainment	350	712		1200	
Leighton, Frederic, Baron	1830-1896	Artist	25	90	150		Pres. Br.Royal Academy. Painter, Sculptor
Leighton, Laura		Entertainment	12			65	Actress. Melrose Place
Leighton, Margaret		Entertainment	15			40	

NAME	DATE	CATEGORY	SIG	LS/DS	ALS	SP	COMMENTS
Leik, Hudson		Entertainment	8			40	Actor. 'Xena' Pin-Up 70
Leinen, Jo		Political	10			15	Member European Parliament
Leinsdorf, Erich		Conductor	15			120	Austro-Amer Conductor
Leisure, David		Entertainment	5			10	
Lejeune, John Archer		Military	35	75	150	75	Commandant US Marine Corps
Lejeune, Maj Gen Francis St. D.B.	1899-1984	Military	25				World War II British general
Leland, Henry M.	1843-1932	Business	875	1783			Contract Creating Lincoln Motor Co. S 14000
Leland, W. C.		Business	20	55	140	40	
Leloir, Luis Frederico		Science	20	40	45	25	Nobel Chemistry
Lelong, Lucien		Designer	25				Fashion, Cosmetics
Lelouch, Claude		Entertainment	9	10	20	25	
LeMaire, Charles		Entertainment	15			25	Director
Lemass, Sean		Head of State	10	25	60	30	Prime Minister Ireland
LeMay, Curtis E.	1906-1990	Military	30	110		112	AF Gen. WW II. 200th Air Force, SAC
Lembeck, Harvey		Entertainment	30			75	
Lembeck, Michael		Entertainment	3	3	6	10	
Lemelsen, Gen. of Panz. Joachim	1888-1954	Military	25				World War II German general
Lemeshev, Sergei		Entertainment				500	Opera. Russ. Tenor of Soviet Era. RARE
Lemmon, Chris		Entertainment	10			20	actor
Lemmon, Jack		Entertainment	10	14	50	54	Academy Award, DS 75-200
Lemnitz, Tiana		Entertainment	40			125	Opera
Lemnitzer, Lyman L.	1899-1988	Military	30	40	90	45	Supreme Allied Commd'r WW II. 7th Inf. Korea
Lemon, Mark	1809-1870	Author	15		35		Br. Playwright, Humorist, Co-Founder Punch
Lenin, Vladimir Ilyich (N. Lenin)		Head of State					ALS/Content 29,000
Lennon Sisters, The (4)		Entertainment	20			45	
Lennon, John	1940-1980	Entertainment	904	1568	13803	1663	Lead singer of the Beatles, author, artist
Lennon, Julian		Entertainment	20			40	
Lennox, Vera		Entertainment	12			20	Br. Actress
Lenny Kravitz		Entertainment	35			90	Music. Rock Group
Leno, Jay		Entertainment	10			25	Self Caricature S 75
Lenoir, William B.		Astronaut	7			20	
Lenormand, René	1846-1932	Composer	30			175	Songs, String & Piano Music
Lenox, Lucie		Entertainment	15			40	
Lenske, Rula		Entertainment	4	4	9	15	
Lentaigne, Maj. Gen. Walter D. A.	1899-1955	Military	28				World War II British general
Lenya, Lotte		Entertainment	20	60		150	Cabaret Singer, Character Actr.
Leo XIII, Pope	1810-1878	Clergy	218	264			
Leonard, Ada		Entertainment	20			70	Big band leader
Leonard, Elmore		Author	15			25	Author of 'Get Shorty,' many other novels
Leonard, George		Jurist	40	100			Colonial Am. Jurist
Leonard, Gloria		Entertainment	5	6	15	15	
Leonard, Jack E.		Entertainment	5			22	Comedian
Leonard, Jack		Entertainment				25	Singer/Tommy Dorsey Orch.
Leonard, Maj. Gen. John W.	1890-1974	Military	30				World War II U.S. general
Leonard, Rosemary, Dr.		Celebrity	10			15	health and fitness expert

NAME	DATE	CATEGORY	SIG	LS/DS	ALS	SP	COMMENTS
Leonard, Sheldon		Entertainment	5	6	15	20	
Leonard, Steve		Celebrity	10			15	veterinarian expert
Leonard, Tom		Celebrity	10			15	motivational speaker
Leoncavallo, Ruggiero	1858-1919	Composer	175	427	772	675	AMusQS 750, 850, 925, 1200
Leone, Sergio	1921-1989	Entertainment	55			347	Master of Spaghetti Western.'Fistful of Dollars'
Leoni, Tea		Entertainment	10			20	actress
Leonov, Aleksei	1934-	Cosmonaut	75	112		148	Rus. Cosmonaut, 1st Space Walker
Leontif, Wassily, Dr.		Economist	20	35		40	Nobel Economics
Leontovich, Eugenie		Entertainment	15		30	45	
Leopardi, Giacomo		Author	80	350	475		Physically Deformed Italian Poe
Leopold (Prince)		Royalty				512	Duke of Albany. Q.Victoria's 4th Son. Hemophiliac
Leopold I	1640-1705	Royalty		1900			King of Hungary & Bohemia, Holy Roman Emperor
Leopold II	1835-1909	Royalty	120	325	540	253	Belgium
Leopold III	1901-1983	Royalty	80		175		King Belgium. Queen Astrid Tragic Death
Leopold V	1586-1633	Royalty		250			Archduke of Austria 1619-33. Papal Bishopric 1625
Leopold, Nathan F.	1905-1971	Criminal	125	310	575	250	Am. Criminal Convicted of Murder. Loeb & Leopold
Lerher, Jim		Journalist	3			12	Broadcast News. Radio/Tv
Lermontov, Mikhail	1814-1841	Author	540	2300	4625		Novelist, Poet. Killed in Duel
Lerner, Alan Jay	1918-1996	Composer	45	95	175	175	Am. Lyricist, Librettist/Loewe
Lerner, Max		Author	5	30	40	10	
Lerner, Michael		Celebrity	10			15	political celebrity
LeRoy, Hal	1914-1985	Entertainment	12			20	Tap Dancer. Director
LeRoy, Mervyn		Entertainment	50	65		75	Top Hollywod Film Director-Prod. 'Wizard of Oz'
Leslie, Frank	1821-1880	Publisher	95				Founder Illustrated Newspaper
Leslie, Frank, Mrs.		Publisher	20		75	75	Leslie's Magazine
Leslie, Joan		Entertainment	6	8	15	19	
Leslie, John		Celebrity	10			15	television presenter
Leslie, Maj Gen Robert Walter D.	1883-1957	Military	25				World War II British general
Leslie, Preston H.		Governor	10	15			Governor KY
Leslie, Thomas J.	1796-1874	Civil War	20		35		Union Gen. Paymaster's Dept. 50 Years
Lesseps, Ferdinand de	1805-1894	Engineer	123	235	375	700	Engineer& Diplomat. Promoted Suez Canal
Lester, Buddy		Entertainment	3	4	10	15	
Lesters, The (5)		Entertainment	10			25	Gospel Singers
Letcher, John	1813-1884	Civil War	49	191	592		CW Gov. VA, ALS/Cont. 2,500
Lethbrigde, Maj. Gen. John S.	1897-1961	Military	25				World War II British general
Leto, Jared		Entertainment	10			20	actor
Letson, Maj. Gen. Harry F. G.	1896-1992	Military	20				World War II Canadian general
Letterman, David		Entertainment	20	65		30	Comedian. TV Late Show CBS
Letterman, Jonathan	1824-1872	Civil War	95	175			Med. Services for CW Union Army
Leutze, Emanuel		Artist	75		320		Washington Crossing Delaware
Levant, Oscar		Entertainment	75			95	Pianist, Caustic Humorist, Actor, Author
Levene, Sam		Entertainment	10			20	
Levenson, Sam		Entertainment	10	35		15	Radio, TV Comic
Leventhrope, Collett	1815-1889	Civil War	90	165	325		CSA Gen.
Lever, Asbury		Senate/Congress	5	10		5	MOC SC

NAME	DATE	CATEGORY	SIG	LS/DS	ALS	SP	COMMENTS
Lever, Lord (Wm. Hesketh)		Business	30	100	190	60	Br. Soap Mfg. Lever Brothers
Leverett, John	1662-1724	Colonial	50	130	275		President of Harvard, Judge
Levi, Edward H.		Cabinet	7	25	45	10	Att'y General
Levi-Civita, Tullio	1873-1941	Science	50		250		Italian. Math. Helped Found Differential Calculus
Levi-Montalcini, Rita, Dr.		Science	20	65			Nobel Medicine
Levin, Carl		Senate	10			15	United States Senate (D - MI)
Levin, Ira		Author	25	35		30	Rosemary's Baby
Levin, Sander M. L		Congress	10			15	Member U.S. Congress
Levine, David*		Cartoonist	15			100	Caricaturist
Levine, Irving R.		TV News	4	10		5	Commentator
Levine, Jack		Artist	10	15	35		Color Print Repro 100
Levine, James		Entertainment	7	10	35	25	Conductor
Levinson, Barry		Entertainment	5			25	Director
Levi-Strauss, Claude	1908-	Science	25				Belg.-Fr. Anthropologist. Legion d'Honneur 1991
Levy, David H.		Science	15			20	Discovered Metor Crater
Levy, Eugene		Celebrity	10			32	
Levy, Steven		Author	8			12	computer journalist, historian
Lewellyn, Anthony		Astronaut	5	16		15	
Lewinsky, Monica		Presidential Aide	31			40	'Monica's Story' BS Monica 75-150
Lewis, (Percy) Wyndham	1882-1957	Artist-Writer	60		356		Br. Painter & Writer
Lewis, Al		Entertainment	10			35	
Lewis, Brig. Gen. Joseph H.	1888-1968	Military	30				World War II U.S. general
Lewis, C(live) S(taples)	1898-1963	Author	450	825	1520		Br. Medievalist, Philosopher, Scholar
Lewis, David 'Duffy'		Aviation	15	30	55	40	
Lewis, Drew		Cabinet	10		20	15	Sec'y of Transportation
Lewis, Edwin		Clergy	15	20	30		
Lewis, Emmanuele		Entertainment	6	8	15	15	
Lewis, Francis	1713-1803	Revolutionary War	375	1600	2500		Signer Decl. of Indepen.
Lewis, Geoffrey		Entertainment	4			10	Actor
Lewis, Gwilym H.		Aviation	20	45	80	55	
Lewis, Hannah Joy		Celebrity	10			15	television presenter
Lewis, Huey (And the News)		Entertainment	12			30	Rock. 'Sports' Alb. S by Lewis 30
Lewis, J.C.		Entertainment	12			25	Blues Drummer
Lewis, James		Entertainment	15	20	30	25	
Lewis, Jarma		Entertainment	5			12	Actress
Lewis, Jenifer		Entertainment	10			20	actress
Lewis, Jerry L		Congress	10			15	Member U.S. Congress
Lewis, Jerry Lee		Country Music	30			70	And Rock. DS re 'Shindig' 225
Lewis, Jerry	1926-	Entertainment	17	15	20	50	Comedian-Actor
Lewis, Joe E.		Entertainment	20	30	45	42	Nightclub Comedian
Lewis, John L		Congress	10			15	Member U.S. Congress
Lewis, John L.	1880-1969	Labor	38	68	110	86	AFL-CIO Labor Leader. TLS/Cont.275
Lewis, John	1940-	Activist	5	15			Civil Rights Leader.Sit-Ins-Freedom Rider. Injured
Lewis, Joseph Horace	1824-1904	Civil War	95	114	172		Confederate general
Lewis, Juliette	1973-	Entertainment	20			46	Actress

NAME	DATE	CATEGORY	SIG	LS/DS	ALS	SP	COMMENTS
Lewis, Kerrie McCarver		Entertainment	4			8	Mrs. Jerry Lewis
Lewis, Maj. Gen. Harold Victor	1887-1945	Military	25				World War II British general
Lewis, Maj. Gen. Robert Stedman	1898-1987	Military	25				World War II British general
Lewis, Maj. Gen. Sir Richard Geo.	1895-1965	Military	25				World War II British general
Lewis, Meriwether	1774-1809	Explorer	3500	5500	9500		Lewis & Clark Expedition
Lewis, Monica		Entertainment	10			30	Singer-Actress. Big Band Singer. Records
Lewis, Morgan		Revolutionary War	50	70	110		Gen.Gates Chief of Staff. Gov.
Lewis, Ramsey		Entertainment	25			50	Pianist-Composer
Lewis, Richard		Entertainment	5			28	Stand-up Comic-Actor
Lewis, Robert A.		Military	25			50	Enola Gay pilot
Lewis, Robert Q.	1921-1992	Entertainment	10			45	Radio-TV Star. Game Show Host. Actor
Lewis, Ron L		Congress	10			15	Member U.S. Congress
Lewis, Shari		Entertainment	10	16	25	48	Comedian-Pupeteer. Deceased
Lewis, Sheldon	1868-1958	Entertainment	30			55	Actor. Title Role 'Dr. Jekyll & Mr. Hyde' 1916 Film
Lewis, Sinclair	1885-1951	Author	60	229	325	346	1st Am. Awarded Nobel for Lit.
Lewis, Ted		Entertainment	20	25		75	Bandleader-Entertainer.'Me & My Shadow'
Lewis, Thyme		Entertainment	10			20	actor
Lewis, Tony		Celebrity	10			15	television presenter
Lewis, Vera		Entertainment	50				Character Actress
Lewis, William Arthur, Sir		Science	20	25	40	25	Nobel Economics
Lewis, William Gaston	1835-1901	Civil War	110		118		Confederate general
Lewis, William H.		Aviation	10	22	40	28	ACE, WW II
Lewishon, Ludwig		Author	20		25		Ger.-Born Author of 31 Books
Lewisohn, Adolph		Business	20	45	65	50	Mining, Investment
Lewitt, Sal		Artist	25			100	
Lewitz, Charlie		Celebrity	10			20	Revenge of the Nerds IV
Ley, Bob		TV News	5			15	ESPN News
Ley, Robert Dr.		Military		184			Nazi leader of Labour Front
Ley, Willy		Science	25	55	85	75	Rocker Expert, Sci-Fi Writer
Leyer, Lt. Gen. Roger	1888-1981	Military	20				World War II French general
Leyser, Gen. of Infantry Ernst von	1889-1962	Military	25				World War II German general
Leyshon, Paul		Entertainment	10			20	Actor
Lhermitte, Thierry		Entertainment	10			20	actor
Liardet, Maj. Gen. Claude Francis	1881-1966	Military	25				World War II British general
Libaud, Maj. Gen. Emmanuel-Ur.	1878-1955	Military	20				World War II French general
Libby, Willard F.		Science	20	35	55	25	Nobel Chemistry
Liberace	1919-1987	Entertainment	30	75		125	Sig/Piano Sketch 75-95-125
Liberace, George		Entertainment	8	15		15	Violinist Brother of Lee Liberace
Liberman, Evsei, Prof.		Celebrity	15	35		20	
Lichel, Gen. of Infantry Walther	1885-1969	Military	25				World War II German general
Lichfield, Lord		Celebrity	10			15	photographer
Lichtenberg, Byron, Dr.		Astronaut	10			20	
Lichtenstein, Roy	1923-1998	Artist	45	65	145	73	Repro S 175, 225
Lichty, George	1905-1983	Cartoonist	10		25		'Grin and Bear It'
Liddell, General Sir Clive Gerard	1883-1956	Military	25				World War II British general

NAME	DATE	CATEGORY	SIG	LS/DS	ALS	SP	COMMENTS
Liddell, Henry George		Clergy	20	35	40	45	
Liddell, St John Richardson	1815-1870	Civil War	110	180			Confederate general
Liddy, G. Gordon		Gov't Official	5	20	50	30	Lawyer, Watergate, Convicted
Lie, Jonas		Author	15	40	60		Nor. Novelist, Dramatist
Lie, Trygve	1896-1968	Head of State	37	75	130	140	Norwegian 1st Sec'y Gen'l U.N. His Bible S 475
Liebenow, William F.		Military	50			295	PT Boat Cmdr. Who Rescued JFK
Liebenstein, Maj Gen Kurt Baron v	1899-1975	Military	25				World War II German general
Lieber, Fritz		Entertainment	35			100	
Lieberman, Joseph		Political	20	25		35	Senator from Conn., VP candidate 2000
Liebermann, Max	1847-1935	Artist	75		250		Ger. Impressionist Painter. Orig. Pen Sketch 650
Liebig, Justus von,	1803-1873	Science	185		925	506	Ger. Chem. Discovered Chloroform. ALS/Content 1,750
Liebmann, Gen. of Infantry Kurt	1881-1960	Military	25				World War II German general
Lienart, Archille, Cardinal		Clergy	30	40	50	40	
Liese, Peter		Political	10			15	Member European Parliament
Lifar, Serge		Entertainment	15			80	Opera
Liggett, Hunter		Military	75	125	60	35	Am. Gen. WW I
Liggett, Louis Kroh		Business	85	170	350		Liggett's Drug Store Chain
Light, Enoch		Entertainment					Big Bandleader-Violinist
Light, Judith		Entertainment	12	15	25	22	
Lightbody, Andy		Celebrity	10			15	political celebrity
Lightburn, Joseph Andr. Jackson	1824-1901	Civil War	40	78	110		Union general
Lightner, Candy		Celebrity	12	30		20	1st Pres. MADD
Lightner, Winnie		Entertainment	19	25	45	45	
Ligi, Josella		Entertainment	5			25	Opera
Ligonier, John	1678-1770	Military	25				Br. Field Marshall of Queen Anne
Liles, Brooks		Aviation	8	20	38	22	ACE, WW II, USAAF Ace
Lilienthal, David E.		Business	15	30		20	Co-Fndr. I.J. Fox, Furriers
Lilienthal, Otto	1848-1896	Inventor	150		525		Aeronautical Eng'r , Author
Lillard, Mathew		Celebrity				40	
Lilley, Robert Doak	1836-1886	Civil War	110	154	389		Confederate general
Lillie, Beatrice	1894-1989	Entertainment	25	75	70	65	Br. Comedienne. WW II Entertainer
Lillie, Gordon W. (Pawnee Bill)	1860-1942	Entertainment	110	375	525	525	Buffalo Bill Partner. DS/Cody 3500
Lilly, Eli		Pharmaceuticals			1500		Pioneer Am. Manufacturer. Founder Eli Lilly & Co.
Liluokalini	1838-1917	Royalty	250	450	800	1000	Queen Hawaii. Last Monarch of Hawaii. Deposed
Liman, Arthur		Celebrity	4	12		20	
Limasset, Maj. Gen. Jean-B.	1881-1940	Military	20				World War II French general
Limbaugh, Rush		Radio/TV	10			20	Radio/TV Commentator
Limp Bizket		Entertainment				125	Rock Group
Lin, Y.S. Maya		Artist	25	100			Designed Viet Nam Wall
Lincke, Paul		Composer	70	185	325		AMusQS 675, 'Glow Worm'
Lincoln, Abraham (As President)		President	3500	7570	17813	45000	ALS/cont 25,000-1,000,000
Lincoln, Abraham	1809-1865	President	3250	6562	9510		ALS/cont. 35,000-101,500, ADS/cont 25,875
Lincoln, Benjamin	1700- ?	Justice of Peace	45	160			Father of Gen. Lincoln
Lincoln, Benjamin	1733-1810	Revolutionary War	100	218	425		Gen. Rev. War. Sec'y War
Lincoln, Blanche		Senate	10			15	United States Senate (D - AR)

NAME	DATE	CATEGORY	SIG	LS/DS	ALS	SP	COMMENTS
Lincoln, Elmo		Entertainment	475			871	
Lincoln, Evelyn		Gov't Official	15	20		35	JFK Presidential Sec'y
Lincoln, Joseph		Author	13	20	30		Writer of Cape Cod Stories
Lincoln, Levi	1749-1820	Cabinet	35	85	120		Memb. Continental Congr. Early Att'y General
Lincoln, Mary Todd	1818-1882	First Lady	992	2160	6635	7500	FF on Mourning Env. 3700- 4600
Lincoln, Robert Todd	1843-1926	Cabinet	125	325	525		Capt. CW. Sec'y War.Minister to Eng. LS/Cont. 750
Lincoln, Rufus		Revolutionary War		1650			Present at Burgoyne Surrender
Lind, Brigadier Edmund F.	1889-1944	Military	30				World War II Australian general
Lind, Don L.		Astronaut	6			20	
Lind, Jenny (Goldschmidt)	1820-1887	Entertainment	100	210	382	750	Concert, Opera. Called 'Swedish Nightingale'
Lindberg, Charles W.		Military	25	40		50	One of 6 Iwo Jimo Flag Raiser
Lindbergh, Anne Morrow		Author	15	45	150	30	Am. Writer-Poet.
Lindbergh, Charles A.	1902-1974	Aviation	469	1322	3765	2788	1st Fl. Cover S 975-2750, signed bk 750-1500
Lindemann, Col-General Georg	1884-1963	Military	27				World War II German general
Linden, Eric		Entertainment	25			75	'GWTW' (Amputation Case)
Linden, Hal		Entertainment	4	20		15	
Linder, John L		Congress	10			15	Member U.S. Congress
Linderman, H. R.		Civil War	10		25		Civil War Dir. of U.S. Mint.
Lindfors, Viveca		Entertainment	12			40	
Lindholm, Berit		Entertainment	10			25	Opera
Lindley, Audra		Entertainment	4			10	
Lindo, Delroy		Entertainment	10			20	actor
Lindsay, E. Lin		Aviation	10	22	38	30	ACE, WW II, USAAF Ace
Lindsay, Howard		Entertainment	10	15	25	25	Theatrical Producer
Lindsay, John		Politician	4	8		10	Lawyer, Author, Mayor NYC
Lindsay, Maj. Gen. George M.	1880-1956	Military	25				World War II British general
Lindsay, Margaret		Entertainment	15	25	45	50	Leading Lady. 30's-40's
Lindsay, Vachel	1879-1931	Author	50	120	260	250	Poet, Artist, Prairie Troubado
Lindsell, Lt. Gen. Sir Wilfrid G.	1884-1974	Military	25				World War II British general
Lindsey, Ben B.		Law	15				Jurist
Lindsey, George		Entertainment	6	8	15	25	Goober on the Andy Griffith Show
Lindstrom, Pia		Entertainment	3			15	Actress. TV News. Daughter Ingrid Bergman
Line, Shirly		Celebrity	10			15	Fish Chef
Linenger, J.M.		Astronaut	8			25	
Liney, John*		Cartoonist				50	Henry
Ling, Bai		Entertainment				30	
Linkletter, Art		Entertainment	10	25		15	Radio-TV MC. Master of the Interview
Linkohr, Rolf		Political	10			15	Member European Parliament
Linn, Archibald L.	1802-1857	Congress	10				Repr. NY, County Judge
Linnaeus, Carolus von	1707-1778	Science	925	7500			Carl vonLinne. Swe. Botanist.
Linn-Baker, Mark		Entertainment	5			15	
Linnehan, Richard		Astronaut	5			20	
Linville, Larry		Entertainment	20			55	Mash
Liotta, Ray		Entertainment	20			48	
Lipchitz, Jacques		Artist	130	210	225		Pol.-Fr.-Am. Cubist Sculptor

NAME	DATE	CATEGORY	SIG	LS/DS	ALS	SP	COMMENTS
Lipfert, Helmut		Aviation	35			70	#15 World Highest ACE. Ger.
Lipietz, Alain		Political	10			15	Member European Parliament
Lipinski, William O. L.		Congress	10			15	Member U.S. Congress
Lipkovska, Lydia		Entertainment	75			325	Rus. Soprano
Lipman, Clara		Entertainment	12			20	Stage Actress
Lipman, Maureen		Entertainment	10			20	Actress
Lipmann, Fritz A.		Science	25	45	70	30	Nobel Medicine 1953
Lipnicki, Jonathan		Entertainment	10			20	actor
Lipovsek, Marjana		Entertainment	10			30	Opera
Lippman, Walter		Author	25	75		30	Journalist, Editor, Pulitzer
Lipps, Lisa		Entertainment	6			35	Adult Star
Lipscomb, William N., Dr.		Science	20	35		30	Nobel Chemistry
Lipsner, B.B.		Aviation	30	65		90	Pioneer Air Mail Pilot
Lipton, Peggy		Entertainment	4	6	9	20	Actress
Lipton, Thomas, Sir	1850-1940	Business	75	175	425	460	Br. Tea Merchant-Yachtsman
Lisa, Manuel	1772-1820	Celebrity	763				American Fur Trader
Lisi, Giorgio		Political	10			15	Member European Parliament
List, Emanuel		Entertainment	35			95	
List, Eugene		Entertainment	20			75	
List, Field Marshal Wilhelm	1880-1971	Military	27				World War II German general
Lister, Joseph, Lord	1827-1912	Science	181	380	625		Pioneer of Antiseptic Surgery. 1st Baron
Liston, Robert	1794-1847	Science	15	30	50		Skilled Scottish Surgeon
Listowell, Earl of		Philosopher	20				Viscount Wm. Francis Hare
Liszt, Franz	1811-1886	Composer	350	590	1544	2500	Hung.-Born. Pianist. AMuQS 3,800,AMMsS 16,750
Litchfield, Grace D.	1849-1944	Author	5		25		
Litel, John	1892-1964	Entertainment	15	15	35	35	
Lithgow, John		Entertainment	5	6	15	20	Third Rock From the Sun
Litjens, Stefan		Aviation	7	15	25	20	
Littauer, Stephen		Celebrity	10			15	financial expert
Little Richard (Penniman)		Entertainment	22	20	45	130	Rock. DS re Lease of Master Recordings 150
Little River Band		Entertainment	25			50	
Little, Cleavon		Entertainment	20			55	
Little, Lewis Henry	1817-1862	Civil War	280				Confederate general
Little, Little Jack		Entertainment	15			35	Big Band Leader
Little, Mark		Celebrity	10			15	comedian
Little, Rich		Entertainment	3			20	
Little, Royal		Business	22		55		
Littlefield, Warren		Celebrity	10			15	film industry
Littlejohn, Abram N.		Clergy	10	20	35		
Littlejohn, Dewitt C.	1818-1892	Civil War	30	65	95		Union General
Littlejohn, Richard		Celebrity	10			15	television presenter
Litvak, Anatole		Entertainment	20			45	Film Director
Litvinov, Maksim M.		Diplomat	50		125	125	Soviet Foreign Minister
Liu, Lucy		Entertainment	7			40	Actress
Liu-Li Pei		Entertainment	10			25	Chinese Opera Star

NAME	DATE	CATEGORY	SIG	LS/DS	ALS	SP	COMMENTS
Livermore, Dan'l P.		Clergy	15	20	45		
Livermore, Mary A.	1820-1905	Reformer	24	64	175		Woman Suffrage, Temperance
Liverpool, 2nd Earl	1770-1828	Head of State	72	178	200		Robert Banks Jenkinson, P.M.
Livesay, Maj. Gen. William G.	1895-1979	Military	30				World War II U.S. general
Livingston, Alan		Composer	15	55			
Livingston, Derek		Celebrity	10			15	motivational speaker
Livingston, Edward P.	1764-1836	Cabinet	25	69	175		Jackson's Sec'y of State 1831
Livingston, Henry B.	1757-1823	Supreme Court	100	310	525		
Livingston, Jay		Composer	15	45	60	60	AMusQS 35-100-300-375 ('Silver Bells')
Livingston, John H.		Aviation	105			145	Premier Racing Pilot entering 139. 79 1st, 43 2nd
Livingston, Margaret		Entertainment	10			25	
Livingston, Mary		Entertainment	15	25	45	40	
Livingston, Peter Van Brugh		Revolutionary War		275			Patriot, Merchant
Livingston, Philip	1716-1778	Revolutionary War	290	800	1500		Signer Decl. of Independ. Etc. NY Merchant
Livingston, Robert R.	1746-1813	Revolutionary War	195	440	1250		Cont.Congr. Administered Pres. Oath To Washington
Livingston, Robert R., Sr.	1718-1775	Law		500			Att'y, Judge. Opposed Stamp Act.
Livingston, Robert		Entertainment	20			85	Known for 30's-40's Western Roles
Livingston, Robert	1742-1794	Revolutionary War	170	350	400		Dir. Bank of the U.S. (1792)
Livingston, William	1723-1790	Revolutionary War	300	888	1750		Continental Congr. Gov. NJ
Livingstone, David	1813-1873	Explorer-Clergy	175	460	725		Missionary, Explorer of Africa. Author
Livingstone, Ken		Political				20	Mayor of London
LL Cool J		Entertainment	15			35	Actor, rapper
Llamas, Lorenzo		Entertainment	10			20	actor
Llewellyn, Anthony		Astronaut	10			30	
Llewellyn, Roddy		Celebrity	10			15	home/gardening expert
Llewelyn-Bowen, Lawrence		Celebrity	10			15	Designer
Lloyd, Brigadier John E.	1894- ?	Military	20				World War II Australian general
Lloyd, Christopher		Entertainment	10	15	28	30	
Lloyd, Emily		Entertainment	10			40	
Lloyd, Frank A		Entertainment	20	50			Film Director AA
Lloyd, Harold	1894-1971	Entertainment	156	225		269	Film Comedian-Actor. Silent Into 30's
Lloyd, James	1769-1831	Senate/Congress	30	65	90		Senator MA 1808
Lloyd, Kathleen		Entertainment	4	4	9	15	
Lloyd, Kevin		Entertainment	10			20	Actor
Lloyd, Maj. Gen. Herbert W.	1883-1957	Military	20				World War II Australian general
Lloyd, Maj. Gen. Wilfrid Lewis	1896-1944	Military	25				World War II British general
Lloyd, Norman		Entertainment	4	4	9	10	
Lloyd, Sian		Celebrity	10			15	weather presenter
Lloyd, Sue		Entertainment	10			20	actress
Lloyd, Wendy		Celebrity	10			15	television presenter
Lloyd-George, David	1863-1945	Head of State	64	372	425	139	Br. Prime Minister WW I, 1st Earl
Lüdke, Gen. of Infantry Erich	1882-1946	Military	25				World War II German general
Lützov, Lt Gen Kurt-Jürg. Baron v.	1892-1961	Military	25				World War II German general
Lo Giudici, Franco		Entertainment	40			150	Opera
Loan, Nguyen Ngoc		Military	150			375	Gen. Viet Nam

NAME	DATE	CATEGORY	SIG	LS/DS	ALS	SP	COMMENTS
Loasby, Arthur W.		Business	5	20			Wall Street Banker
LoBianco, Tony		Entertainment	6	8	15	15	
LoBiondo, Frank A. L		Congress	10			15	Member U.S. Congress
Locane, Amy		Entertainment	15			35	Actress. Melrose Place
Loch, General of Artillery Herbert	1886-1975	Military	25				World War II German general
Loch, Lt. Gen. Sir Kenneth Morley	1890-1961	Military	25				World War II British general
Lochner, Maj. Gen. Rupert	1891-1965	Military	25				World War II British general
Locke, D. R.		Journalist					SEE Nasby, Petroleum
Locke, John	1632-1704	Author	700	1950	5000		Br. Philosopher. LS/Cont.12,500
Locke, Samuel	1813-1890	Politics			81		
Locke, Sandra		Entertainment	10	10	20	25	
Locke, William John		Author	20	35	75	30	Br. Novelist
Lockhart, Gene		Entertainment	20			50	Film Character Actor. 30's, 40's
Lockhart, June		Entertainment	5	6	20	22	Child Actress to Present. 'Lassie', 'Lost in Space
Lockheed, Alan		Aviation	80	150	300	150	Pioneer Aviator, Plane Designer
Locklear, Heather		Entertainment	10	20	30	47	Actress.
Locklin, Hank		Country Music	10			55	Country Star
Lockwood, Belva A.	1830-1917	Women's Rights	186	330	733		1st Woman to Practice Before Supr. Ct. AQS 360
Lockwood, Chas.W, Capt		Civil War	100				1st MN to Enlist,Last Survivor
Lockwood, Gary		Entertainment	5			20	Actor '2001'
Lockwood, Henry Hayes	1814-1899	Civil War	40	75	120		Union general
Lockwood, Margaret	1916-1990	Entertainment	12	20	55	55	Br. Film Actress
Lockyer, Herbert		Clergy	25	35	45		
Lodge, Henry Cabot	1850-1924	Senate	30	65	100	125	MOC 1887, Senator MA 1893.TLS/cont 368
Lodge, Henry Cabot, Jr.	1902-1985	Senate	20	42	65	50	Ambassador UN, Diplomat, VP Candidate
Lodge, Oliver J., Sir	1851-1940	Science	50	80	125	175	Br. Physicist, Spiritualist
Loeb, William		Business	10	25	55	35	
Loeder, Curt		Entertainment	10			20	actor
Loesser, Frank	1910-1969	Composer	120		450		Composer of Top Broadway Hits. Movie Hits
Loew, Marcus		Business	30	40	65	35	
Loewe, Frederick	1901-1988	Composer	38	75	145	55	AMusQS 220-650-895. 'My Fair Lady', 'Camelot'
Loewen, Gen. Sir Chas. Falkland	1900-1986	Military	25				World War II British general
Loewy, Raymond		Business	35	90	140	75	Designer
Lofgren, Zoe L		Congress	10			15	Member U.S. Congress
Lofting, Hugh	1886-1947	Author	95				& Illustrator Dr. Dolittle Books. S Illustr. 195
Loftus, Cissie (Cecilia)	1876-1943	Entertainment	35	65		175	Br. Actress. Vaudeville, Stage,Musical & Film Star
Logan, Benjamin	1752-1802	Military	350	560	675		Pioneer Hero, Indian Fighter
Logan, Ella		Entertainment	10	15	20	25	Pop Singer. Band Vocalist. 'A Tiskit, A Tasket'
Logan, John A. (WD)		Civil War	65	210	525	750	Union Gen.
Logan, John A.	1826-1886	Civil War	52	118	177		Union Gen., Father Memorial Day. Founder G.A.R.
Logan, Josh(ua)	1908-1988	Entertainment	20	40		45	Film & Stage Producer, Writer, Director
Logan, Michael		Celebrity	10			15	media/TV personality
Logan, Olive		Author	25	35			
Logan, Thomas M.	1840-1914	Civil War	95	225	422		CSA Gen.
Loggia, Robert		Entertainment	6	8	15	20	

NAME	DATE	CATEGORY	SIG	LS/DS	ALS	SP	COMMENTS
Loggins and Messina		Entertainment	25		50	50	
Loggins, Kenny		Entertainment	10	40		35	
Loisy, Alfred		Clergy	20	25	35		
Lollobrigida, Gina		Entertainment	12	15	30	57	Pin-Up SP35
Lom, Herbert		Entertainment	22			43	Character Actor
Lomax, Lunsford Lindsey	1835-1913	Civil War	100	275	352		CSA General
Lomax, Maj. Gen. Cyril Ernest N.	1893-1973	Military	25				World War II British general
Lomb, Henry	1828-1908	Science-Business		2600			Ger.Born Am. Optician. Co-Founder Bausch & Lomb
Lombard, Carole	1908-1942	Entertainment	240	375	550	649	Died in Air Crash 1942
Lombard, Louise		Entertainment	10			20	Actress
Lombardo, Guy	1902-1977	Entertainment	20	40	65	75	Big Band Leader. Royal Canadians
Lombardo, Raffaele		Political	10			15	Member European Parliament
Loncaine, Richard		Celebrity	10			15	film industry
London, Charmian		Celebrity	40			155	2nd Wife of Jack London
London, George		Entertainment	35			70	Opera, Concert, Met.
London, Jack	1876-1916	Author	215	729	1250	900	Am. Novelist, Adventurer. Suicide at 40,s chk 250-400
London, Julie		Entertainment	10	12	15	20	Vocalist-Actress. Recording Artist
London, Tom		Entertainment	50			100	
Long, Armistead L.	1825-1891	Civil War	85	100	370		CSA Gen.
Long, Dr. Loretta		Entertainment	10			20	actress
Long, Earl K.		Governor	20	30		25	Governor LA,
Long, Eli	1837-1903	Civil War					Union general
Long, Huey P.		Senate	127	208		175	Sen., Gov. LA. Assassinated, TLS cont 2415
Long, John D.		Cabinet	12	30	40	20	Sec'y Navy, Governor MA
Long, Johnny		Bandleader	25			50	Big Bandleader. Violinist
Long, Lotus		Entertainment	5			30	Actress-Oriental Dancer
Long, Pierse	1739-1789	Revolutionary War	30	75	180		Continental Congress
Long, Richard		Entertainment	20			50	
Long, Russell	1918-	Senate/Congress	5	20		10	Senator LA. Son of Huey Long
Long, Shelley		Entertainment	12	20	25	30	Actress 'Cheers'
Longacre, James B.	1794-1869	Engraver	140	400	950		Chief Engraver of the U.S. Mint
Longden, Maj. Gen. Harry L.	1900-1981	Military	25				World War II British general
Longet, Claudine		Entertainment	8	15	35	25	
Longfellow, Henry W.	1807-1882	Author	169	282	515	921	Poet, Harvard Prof.AMsS 2295, AQS 500
Longfellow, Samuel		Clergy	40	50	75	55	
Longfellow, Stephen	1775-1849	Senate/Congress	20	50	145		MOC ME 1823
Longley, Charles T.	1794-1868	Clergy	25				Archbishop Canterbury
Longley, James B.		Governor	9	15			Governor ME
Longmore, Brig. John Alexander	1899-1973	Military	25				World War II British general
Longrigg, Brig. Stephen Hemsley	1893-1979	Military	25				World War II British general
Longstreet, James (WD)	1821-1904	Civil War	625		4587	2600	CSA Gen.
Longstreet, James	1821-1904	Civil War	453	900	1346	1500	CSA General., Important ALS/cont 7500
Longworth, Alice Roosevelt		Pres. Daughter	35	45	125	150	
Longworth, Nicholas		Congress	15	65	85		Speaker of the House, Son-in-law of T. Roosevelt
Loo, Richard		Entertainment	20			55	

NAME	DATE	CATEGORY	SIG	LS/DS	ALS	SP	COMMENTS
Loomis, Gustavus	1789-1872	Civil War	30	65	105		Union General
Loos, Anita		Author	17	55	75	30	Am. Novelist, Film Scripts
Loos, Walter		Aviation	10	20	35	25	
Loper, Don		Business	5	15	35	10	Fashion Designer
Lopes, Lisa 'Left Eye'	d. 2002	Music	25			100	
Lopez, Jennifer		Entertainment	12			49	Actress, singer
Lopez, Vincent		Entertainment	20			55	Big Band Leader-Pianist
Lopez-Alegria, Michael		Astronaut	5			20	
Loraine, Robert		Aviation	15		55		
Lorca, Frederico Garcia		Author	440	1240	3150		Sp. Poet, Dramatist
Lord, Daniel, Rev.		Clergy	10			35	
Lord, E.J.		Congress	10		30		Senator CA
Lord, Herbert M.		Military	10	25			
Lord, Jack		Entertainment	30	110	140	125	Actor, Hawaii 5-0
Lord, John Wesley, Bishop		Clergy	20	35	45	45	
Lord, Marjorie		Entertainment	20	25		35	Danny Thomas Show
Lord, Phillips H.		Entertainment	20		35		Writer-Producer. Radio
Lord, Walter		Author	4	5	10	10	
Lords, Traci		Entertainment	10	15	30	39	Pin-up
Loren, Sophia		Entertainment	15	30		41	Pin-Up SP 50. SP from 'Two Women' 315. AA
Lorengar, Pilar		Entertainment	25			40	Opera
Lorentz, Hendrik A.	1853-1928	Science			1500		Dutch physicist. Nobel Prize winner 1902
Lorenz, Konrad	1903-1989	Science	62	275			Austrian Biologist
Lorillard, Peter		Business	125	260	475		Tobacco Industry
Lorimar, George C.		Clergy	20				Author
Loring, Gloria		Entertainment	10	12	15	15	
Loring, Israel		Clergy	25	75	125		
Loring, Lisa		Entertainment	5			30	Actress
Loring, William Wing (WD)	1818-1886	Civil War	180		745		CSA Gen.
Loring, William Wing	1818-1886	Civil War	120	277	315	425	CSA General
Loring-Days, Gloria		Entertainment	10			20	actress
Lorne, Marion		Entertainment	100			225	Broadway Character Actress-Comedian. TV-Films
Lorre, Peter	1904-1964	Entertainment	155	225		480	Hungarian Character Actor 'Maltese Falcon'
Losch, Tilly		Entertainment	10			65	3x5 SP 35
Losey, Joseph		Entertainment	15			60	Film Director
Losigkeit, Fritz		Aviation	12	15	30	20	
Lossing, Benson		Author	15	41	50		Am.Historian, Engraver
Lott, Felicity		Entertainment	15			30	Opera
Lott, Trent		Congress	12			25	Republican Majority Leader. Sen. MS
Loubet, Emile Francois	1838-1929	Head of State			125		Pres. France 1899-1906
Louge, Mike		Astronaut	8			26	
Lough, Brig. John Robert Stuart	1887-1970	Military	20				World War II Canadian general
Lough, Lt. Gen. Reginald D. H.	1885-1958	Military	25				World War II British general
Loughborough, Maj. Gen. Arth. H.	1883-1967	Military	25				World War II British general
Loughlin, Lori		Entertainment	5			40	Actress

NAME	DATE	CATEGORY	SIG	LS/DS	ALS	SP	COMMENTS
Louis II (Bavaria)	1845-1886	Royalty		525			King from 1864
Louis II (Monaco)	1870-1949	Royalty	50	150	210	200	Prince of Monaco
Louis Philippe (Fr)	1773-1850	Royalty	75	215	260		Citizen King. Duc D'Orleans
Louis XI (Fr)	1423-1483	Royalty		3500			Earliest Collectible King of France 1461-1483
Louis XII (Fr)	1462-1515	Royalty	800	1750	4200		King of France
Louis XIII (Fr)	1601-1643	Royalty	750	760	4000		King of France
Louis XIV (Fr)	1638-1715	Royalty	450	1019	3750		The Sun King
Louis XV (Fr)	1710-1774	Royalty	750	932	5500		King of France
Louis XVI (Fr)	1754-1793	Royalty	375	1400			King of France. Guillotined
Louis XVIII (Fr)	1755-1824	Royalty	200	191	1680		Louis Stanislas Xavier
Louise Caroline Alberta, Princess		Royalty	25		65	175	4th Daughter of Queen Victoria
Louise Vict.(Alex. Dagmar)	1867-1931	Royalty	20		83	170	Princess Royal. Daughter Edw. VII
Louise, Anita		Entertainment	15			45	Frail Leading Lady. Films 40's-50's
Louise, Tina		Entertainment	9	18	20	52	'Gilligan's Island'
Lounge, John M.		Astronaut	10			20	
Loup, Maj. Gen. Louis A.	1897-1991	Military	25				World War II British general
Lousma, Jack F.		Astronaut	10	20		53	
Love, Bessie		Entertainment	35		55	70	Vintage Actress
Love, Courtney		Entertainment	6			34	Actress. Pin-Up 55
Love, John A.		Governor	5	12		10	Governor CO
Love, Montagu		Entertainment	20			50	Vintage Character Actor
Love, Mother		Entertainment	4			10	Comedienne
Lovecraft, H.P.		Author	220	300	738	550	Reclusive Horror Story Writer
Love-Hewitt, Jennifer		Entertainment	8			40	Actress. Pin-Up 75
Lovejoy, Frank		Entertainment	25			50	Successful Radio Actor to Leading Roles in Films
Lovejoy, Owen		Clergy-Congress	15	30	45		MOC IL 1857-64
Lovelace, Linda	d. 2002	Entertainment	25			68	Activist, X-rated movie star
Loveless, Patty		Entertainment	15			35	Singer
Lovell, Bernard Dr.		Science	15	25	40	20	
Lovell, James A. Jr.	1928-	Astronaut	35	234		181	Cmmdr. of Aborted Apollo 13.Cont. TLS 375
Lovell, James	1737-1814	Revolutionary War	50	195	500		Continental Congress, Politician, Patriot
Lovell, Mansfield (WD)		Civil War	185	560	850		CSA Gen.
Lovell, Mansfield	1822-1884	Civil War	142	338	386		CSA Gen.
Loverboy		Entertainment	25			50	Music
Lovett, John	1761-1818	Senate/Congress	40		135		War 1812. ALS/Content 300
Lovett, Lyle		Country Music	20			58	Popular Country Music Singer
Lovett, Richard		Celebrity	10			15	film industry
Lovett, Robert		Cabinet	5	10	25	10	Sec'y Defense
Lovitz, Jon		Entertainment	10			25	actor
Lovkay, John		Business	4			10	CEO Hamilton Standard
Lovrenich, Rodger T.		Business	4	9	15	10	Inventor of electronic ignition
Low, Abiel Abbot	1811-	Shiipbuilder		110	175		Packet & Clipper Ships. Merchant, Civil War
Low, David, Sir*		Cartoonist	15	45	110	140	NZ-Br Political.'Colonel Blimp'
Low, Frederick F.		Governor	45		175		Gov, MOC CA 1860, Diplomat
Low, G. David		Astronaut	8			20	

NAME	DATE	CATEGORY	SIG	LS/DS	ALS	SP	COMMENTS
Low, Nicholas		Revolutionary War	105	245	450		Prominent NY, Backed Revolution. Merchant
Low, Seth	1819-1916	Mayor NYC	10	35	45		Merchant, Pres. Columbia Univ.
Lowe, Ed		Inventor	20			45	Kitty Litter
Lowe, Edmund		Entertainment	25	30	60	45	Handsome Leading-Man 30's-40's Films
Lowe, Hudson, Sir	1769-1844	Military		310	500		Last custodian of Napoleon, Gov. St. Helena
Lowe, Rob		Entertainment	17	35		40	Actor, The West Wing
Lowe, Thaddeus S. C.		Civil War	210	412	700		Aeronaut, Inventor, CW Balloonist
Lowell, Amy	1874-1925	Author	35	125	250		Am. Poet,Critic., Imagist School
Lowell, Carey		Entertainment	5			20	
Lowell, Charles Russell	1835-1864	Civil War	100				Union general
Lowell, James Russell	1819-1891	Author	45	115	152	375	Poet, Hall of Fame, Educator, Editor, Diplomat
Lowell, John H.		Aviation	15	25	40	35	ACE, WW II
Lowell, Joshua A.	1801-1874	Congress	10		45		MOC ME, Dem. Presidenial Elector
Lowell, Percival	1855-1916	Science	15	40	65		Am. Astronomer, Author. Brother of A.L. & Amy
Lowell, Robert	1917-1977	Author	42	90	185		Am. Poet. (2) Pulitzers 'Lord Weary's Castle'
Lowenstein, Allard		Congress	75			175	Dump Johnson Movement. Assassinated
Lowery, John		Senate/Congress	10	15		15	
Lowery, Joseph, Rev.		Celebrity	10			15	motivational speaker
Lowery, Robert		Entertainment	75	125		125	Actor. 'Batman' Serial
Lowey, Nita M. L		Congress	10			15	Member U.S. Congress
Lowman, Seymour	1868-1940	Cabinet	5	10			Ass't Sec'y Treas., Lt. Gov. NY
Lown, Bert		Entertainment	10			20	Bandleader. Bye Bye Blues
Lowrey, Mark Perrin	1828-1885	Civil War	110	225			Confederate general
Lowry, Robert		Governor	10	25			Governor MS
Lowry, Robert	1830-1910	Civil War	90	200			Confederate general
Loy, Myrna	1905-1993	Entertainment	24	40	50	62	SP as Nora Charles (Thin Man) 100
Loyd, General Sir Henry Charles	1891-1973	Military	28				World War II British general
Lubbers, Bob*		Cartoonist	10			70	Tarzan
Lubbock, Francis R.	1815-1905	Civil War	150	195	295	273	CSA Governor TX. Aide-de-camp Jeff. Davis
Lubbock, Sir John	1834-1913	Statesman-Author	10	22	42		Br. Banker. Author Science-Fiction Books
Lubin, Arthur		Entertainment	25			65	Film Director
Lubin, Germaine		Entertainment				275	Opera. Legendary Fr. Soprano. RARE
Lubitsch, Ernst	1892-1947	Entertainment	55		275	185	Ger.-Am. Vintage Film Director
Lubke, Heinrich	1885-1972	Head of State	10		30	50	Pres. Ger. Fed. Repub.
Lucan, Earl of		Military			75		George Charles Bingham, Field Marshal
Lucas, Caroline		Political	10			15	Member European Parliament
Lucas, Clyde		Entertainment	15			25	Bandleader
Lucas, David		Author	8			12	property rights
Lucas, Edward Verrall		Author	3	5	8	8	
Lucas, Frank D. L		Congress	10			15	Member U.S. Congress
Lucas, George		Entertainment	33	100	122	98	Film Director. 'Star Wars'
Lucas, John P.		Military	70	150		350	General. Cmdr. 4th Army WW II
Lucas, Ken L		Congress	10			15	Member U.S. Congress
Lucas, Thomas John	1826-1908	Civil War	45	80	120		Union general
Lucca, Pauline		Entertainment	30	70	100		Opera

NAME	DATE	CATEGORY	SIG	LS/DS	ALS	SP	COMMENTS
Lucci, Susan		Entertainment	8	10	15	37	Soap Star
Luccock, Halford E.		Clergy	20	35	50	40	
Luce, Clare Boothe		Author	30	60	70	50	Ambassador, Playwright, Congresswoman
Luce, Cyrus G.		Governor	5	15	25		Governor MI
Luce, Henry R.	1898-1967	Publisher	30	50	75	55	Time, Life, Fortune, Sports Illustrated
Luce, Stephen Bleecker	1927-1917	Military	15	35	95	40	Admiral. 1st Pres. Naval War College
Lucht, General of Artillery Walther	1882-1949	Military	25				World War II German general
Lucid, Shannon W.		Astronaut	10			50	Set New Space Record
Luckinbill, Laurence		Entertainment	22		40	50	Actor. Active in Star Trek Films
Luckner, Felix, von	1881-1966	Military	68	80	125	100	'The Sea Devil' WW II. Sank 14 Allied Ships 195
Luckner, Nicholas		Fr. Revolution	225	675			Marshal of Fr. Guillotined
Lucon, L. J., Cardinal		Clergy	45	55	75	60	
Ludden, Allan		Celebrity	25			45	TV Game show Host
Ludde-Neurath, Walter		Military	15	45		45	Aide-de-camp to Donitz
Ludendorff, Erich von	1865-1937	Military	100	225	300	206	Ger. Gen. WW I, Politician
Ludford, Sarah		Political	10			15	Member European Parliament
Ludin, Hanns		Military	130	350			Ger. Gen.-Storm Trooper WW II
Ludington, Marshall I.	1839-1919	Civil War	30	55	80		Union General
Ludlum, Robert		Author	10	25	35	20	Super Spy novels
Ludwig I	1786-1868	Royalty	65	400	450		King of Bavaria
Ludwig II	1845-1886	Royalty	55	255	470		King of Bavaria
Ludwig, Emil		Author	40	125	200		
Lufbery, Raoul		Aviation	125	350	590	400	ACE, WW I, Lafayette Escadrille
Lufburrow, W.A.		Political	5	25			Southern Racist Leader.
Luft, Lorna		Entertainment	12		15	19	Singer Sister of Liza Minelli. Daughter of Judy
Lugar, Richard G.		Congress	5	25			Sen. IN
Lugosi, Bela	1882-1956	Entertainment	316	525	700	1350	Hungarian Born, 'Dracula'
Luhan, Mabel Dodge		Author			388		
Luhman, Baz		Celebrity	10			15	film industry
Lujan, Albert		Artist	20		45		
Lukas, Foss		Composer	20			75	Versatile Ger./Am./Composer/Conductor
Lukas, Paul	1895-1971	Entertainment	50			100	AA Winner. 'Watch on the Rhine'
Luke, Frank		Aviation	150	400	600	500	ACE, WW I, MOH, #3 U.S. Ace
Luke, Keye		Entertainment	20			50	'#1 Son' in Charlie Chan Films
Lukis, Maj. Gen. Wilfrid Boyd F.	1896-1969	Military	25				World War II British general
Luks, George Benjamin	1867-1933	Artist	20	55	200		Member Ashcan Shool., signed drw 270
Lulling, Astrid		Political	10			15	Member European Parliament
Lulu Belle (& Scotty)		Entertainment	10				C & W Music. Popular Duo. 40's-50's
Lum & Abner		Entertainment	40			95	Top Radio Comedy Pr-30's.Chester Lauk-Norris Goff
Lumet, Sidney		Entertainment	15			40	TV Director-Dramatist
Lumholtz, Carl		Celebrity	3	8	20		
Lumiere, Louis	1862-1954	Inventor	175		501	375	Cinematographe Projector
Lumley, Carl		Entertainment	3			8	
Lumley, Joanna		Entertainment	10	12	15	22	
Lumsden, Lt. Gen. Herbert	1897-1945	Military	25				World War II British general

NAME	DATE	CATEGORY	SIG	LS/DS	ALS	SP	COMMENTS
Luna, Barbara		Entertainment	5			10	Actress
Lunacharsky, Anatoly		Author		368			Marxist writer
Lunceford, Jimmie		Entertainment	35			140	Big Band Leader-Arranger
Lund, John		Entertainment	5	6	15	15	Warner Bros. 40's-50's Leading Man
Lund, Lt. Gen. Sir Otto Marling	1891-1956	Military	25				World War II British general
Lund, Torben		Political	10			15	Member European Parliament
Lundberg, George		Celebrity	10			15	medical expert
Lunden, Jason		Entertainment	5			30	Actor
Lunden, Joan		TV Host	10			22	TV Host & Special Assignments MC
Lundgren, Dolph		Entertainment	15			35	Actor. Super Hero & Villain
Lundigan, William		Entertainment	15			30	Handsome Leading Man 40's-50's
Lundy, Jessica		Entertainment	10			20	actress
Lunn, George R.	1873-1948	Congress	4	15			MOC. NY
Lunney, G.		Astronaut	10			20	
Lunt, Alfred & Lynne Fontanne		Entertainment	40			80	Popular Stage Couple 30's. DS 'Idiot's Delight' 650
Lupino, Ida	1918-1995	Entertainment	17	50	75	65	Br-Am Actress, Director
Lupino, Stanley	1893-1942	Entertainment	15			35	Br. Comedian. Father of Ida
Lupone, Patti		Entertainment	10			20	actress
Lupton, John		Entertainment	10			20	
Luria, Salvador F.		Science	20	35	55	25	Nobel Medicine
Lurie, Bob		Business	10	25	45	15	
Luse, Harley		Country Music	10			20	
Lutes, Lt. Gen. Leroy	1890-1980	Military	30				World War II U.S. general
Luther, Hans		Head of State	35	55	85	55	Chancellor Ger., Ambass. US
Luther, Martin		Clergy		49500			
Lutoslawski, Witold	1913-1994	Composer		110			
Lutyens, Edw. Landseer, Sir	1869-1944	Architect		70			Br. Designed Cenotaph in London. Br. Embassy U.S.
Lutzi, Gertrude		Entertainment	15			30	Opera
Lutzow, Gunther		Aviation	175		445	450	
Lvov, Alexis F.	1798-1870	Composer	100		200		Rus.Commissioned by Czar. Russ. Nat'l Anthem
Lyautey, Louis	1854-1934	Military	20	40	105	40	Marshal of Fr., Statesman
Lyell, Charles, Sir	1797-1875	Science	95		425		Br. Founder of Modern Geology
Lyle, The Great		Entertainment	25			50	Vintage British Magician
Lyman, Abe		Bandleader	15			45	Big Band
Lyman, Charles Edwin		Clergy	15	25	50	30	
Lynam, Des		Celebrity	10			15	television presenter
Lynch, David		Entertainment	20			50	Movie-TV Director.' Twin Peaks'
Lynch, Jane		Entertainment	15			25	actor
Lynch, John R.		Congress		250			Former Slave. MOC MS 1873-77, '82-'83
Lynch, Kelly		Entertainment	10			40	Actress
Lynch, Peter		Celebrity	10			15	financial expert
Lynch, Richard		Entertainment	10			20	actor
Lynch, Stephen F. L		Congress	10			15	Member U.S. Congress
Lynch, Thomas Jr.	1749-1779	Rev. War	17825				Rare Signer Declaration of Independence
Lynde, Paul		Entertainment	14	20	25	23	Comedian from Original TV 'Tic Tac Dough'

NAME	DATE	CATEGORY	SIG	LS/DS	ALS	SP	COMMENTS
Lyndhurst, Nicholas		Entertainment	10			20	Actor
Lyndon, Josias		Politcal			391		Rhode Island's last Colonial governor
Lyne, Maj. Gen. Lewis Owen	1899-1970	Military	28				World War II British general
Lynen, Feodor		Science	20	40		25	Nobel Medicine
Lynley, Carol		Entertainment	10	18	35	25	Actress.
Lynn, Porsche		Entertainment	5			20	Porn Queen
Lynn, Diana	1926-1971	Entertainment	20	25	35	60	Actress. Talented Pianist. 'Bedtime for Bonzo'
Lynn, Ginger		Entertainment	5			20	Adult Film Star of 80's
Lynn, Jeffrey		Entertainment	9	10	20	15	40's Warner Bros. Leading Man
Lynn, Loretta		Country Music	6			15	Country Music
Lynn, Vera, Dame		Entertainment	30			112	Br. WW II Singing Star
Lynne, Elizabeth		Political	10			15	Member European Parliament
Lyon, Ben	1901-1979	Entertainment	25			40	Actor. Star Silents-Early Talkies. With RAF WW II
Lyon, Brigadier Cyril Arthur	1880-1955	Military	28				World War II British general
Lyon, Hylan Benton	1836-1907	Civil War	110				Confederate general
Lyon, Lucius	1800-1851	Congress	15		35		Sen. & MOC. MI
Lyon, Mary Mason	1797-1849	Educator	55	165	340		Provided Women's Advanced Edu. Mt. Holyoke Coll.
Lyon, Nathaniel	1818-1861	Civil War	256		1500		Union Gen. KIA. RARE, War date/rare 3950
Lyon, Sue		Entertainment	10	15	22	25	
Lyonne, Natasha		Entertainment	5			38	Actress
Lyons, Edmund, Lord	1790-1858	Military-Diplomat	50		252		Br, Admiral
Lyons, Judson W.		Public Office	30	125			1st Afr-Am Register of Treasury 1898-1906
Lyons, Rich'd B.P.,1st Earl	1817-1887	Diplomat	35		114		Br. Minister to US in Civil War.
Lyons, William		Business	40	80	175		
Lytell, Bert		Entertainment	30	45	90	65	Vintage Actor. Stage. Migrated to Films
Lytle, William Haynes	1826-1863	Civil War	100				Union general
Lytton, E. George Bulwer	1803-1873	Author	25	95	208		Novelist, Poet, Colonial Sec'y. 1st Baron

NAME	DATE	CATEGORY	SIG	LS/DS	ALS	SP	COMMENTS
Ma, Yo Yo		Entertainment	35			78	Cellist Superstar
Maas, Melvin G.	1898-1964	Military-Congress	25			125	Marine Corps Gen WW II. Wounded, Blinded. MOC MN
Maat, Albert Jan		Political	10			15	Member European Parliament
Maaten, Jules		Political	10			15	Member European Parliament
Mabley, Jackie Moms		Entertainment	75			200	
Mac, Bernie		Entertainment	15			30	
Macalevey, Maj. Gen. Gerald E.	1894-1969	Military	25				World War II British general
MacArthur, Arthur	1845-1912	Military	45	110	155	150	CW Officer, Sp.-Am. War. General
MacArthur, Charles		Author	15	30	55	25	Playwright Husband Helen Hayes
MacArthur, Douglas II		Diplomat	15	20	25	30	Ambassador to Japan. Nephew of the General
MacArthur, Douglas	1880-1964	Military	184	586	875	657	5 Star Gen. WW II, TLS/cont 1000-5000
MacArthur, James		Entertainment	12	14	15	30	Actor Son of Helen Hayes. 'Hawaii 5-0'
MacArthur, Jean		Military	15	20	30	20	Mrs. Douglas MacArthur

NAME	DATE	CATEGORY	SIG	LS/DS	ALS	SP	COMMENTS
MacArthur, Lt. Gen. Sir Wm Porter	1884-1964	Military	25				World War II British general
MacArthur-Onslow, Brig. Denzil	1904- ?	Military	20				World War II Australian general
Macartney, Clarence E.		Clergy	15	20	25	20	
Macartney, George		Head of State	10	35	85		
Macaulay, (Emilie) Rose, Dame		Author	10	20	68		Br. Novelist, Critic, Verse
Macaulay, Thos. B., Lord	1800-1859	Author	45	65	102		Historian & Poet. Politician
Macbeth, Florence		Entertainment	20			50	Am. Soprano
MacChesney, Nathan Wm.		Celebrity	10	20	85		
Macchio, Ralph		Entertainment	15			28	Young Actor. 'Karate Kid'
MacCormick, John	1884-1945	Entertainment		180			Irish tenor
Maccormick, Neil		Political	10			15	Member European Parliament
MacCracken, Henry M.		Clergy	20	35	45	30	
Macdonald, Brigadier J.A.		Military	25				World War II British general
MacDonald, Brigadier N.B.		Military	20				World War II Canadian general
MacDonald, Charles H.		Aviation	15	30	52	40	ACE, WW II
MacDonald, Cordelia H.		Entertainment	40	75	120		1st Eva in Uncle Tom's Cabin
MacDonald, George		Clergy	20	30	45		
MacDonald, George	1875-1961	Business	35				Public Utilities
MacDonald, J. Farrell		Entertainment	25			50	Char. Actor.SP as Detective in Maltese Falcon 495
MacDonald, J. Ramsey	1866-1937	Head of State	50	130	175	255	Twice Br. Prime Minister
Macdonald, Jacques E.J.A	1765-1840.	Fr. Revolution	75	110	250		Marshal of Napoleon
MacDonald, Jeanette	1901-1965	Entertainment	40	65	90	125	Teamed With Nelson Eddy in Top Movie Hits
MacDonald, John Alexander		Head of State	35	90			Premier 1857, 1st P.M. Canada
Macdonald, Maj. Gen. D.J.		Military	20				World War II Canadian general
Macdonald, Maj. Gen. Harry	1886-1976	Military	28				World War II British general
Macdonald, Maj. Gen. James B.	1898-1959	Military	25				World War II British general
MacDonald, Ross		Author	45	145	250		Mystery Writer
MacDonald, Torbet		Congress	10				MA. JFK Roommate & Lifelong Friend
Macdonogh, P. M. W.		Military	6	17	22		
MacDonough, Thomas	1783-1825	Military	95	290	700		Am. Naval Off'r. Tripoli, 1812
MacDougall, Clinton	1839-1914	Civil War	30	55	80		Union General
Macdougall, Maj Gen. Alastair Ian	1888-1972	Military	28				World War II British general
MacDowell, Andie		Entertainment	15			40	Col. Pin-Up 65
MacDowell, Edward	1861-1908	Composer	140	290	600	400	Songs, Concertos, Piano Pieces
MacDowell, Melbourne		Entertainment	15			40	Vintage Actor
Maceo, Jose	1846-1896	Military			2500		Liberator of Cuba
Macfadden, Bernarr		Business	15	45	96	35	Physical Culturist, Publisher
Macfadyen, Dugald		Clergy	45	45	50	50	
MacFarlane, Lt Gen Sir Frank N M	1889-1953	Military	25				World War II British general
Macfayden, Angus		Entertainment	10			20	actor
MacGraw, Ali		Entertainment	6	12		25	Actress. Pin-Up SP 25
MacGregor, Ewan		Entertainment	10			30	Actor, Star Wars
MacGregor, John 'Rob Roy'	1825-1892	Philanthropist	12		50		And Traveller
Machado, Anesia Pinheiro		Aviation	35	55	80	65	
Machiavelli, Niccolo	1469-1527	Author	2500	9000	12500		

NAME	DATE	CATEGORY	SIG	LS/DS	ALS	SP	COMMENTS
Machijiri, Lt. Gen. Kazumoto V.	1889-1950	Military	25				World War II Japanese general
Machimura, General Kingo		Military	25				World War II Japanese general
Machino, Maj. Gen. Kazuo		Military	25				World War II Japanese general
MacInnes, Helen		Author	5	15	20		Am Best Selling Novelist
MacIntosh-Walker, Brig. John R.	1898-1944	Military	25				World War II British general
Mack, Connie III		Senate	7	10		15	Senator FL
Mack, Helen		Entertainment	10			30	
Mack, Lee		Celebrity	10			15	comedian
Mack, Marion		Entertainment	10			35	
Mack, Ted		Entertainment	8			15	
Mackaill, Dorothy		Entertainment	20	30	70	65	Vintage Film Actress
MacKall, William W. (WD)	1817-1891	Civil War	250		1250		CSA Gen.
MacKall, William W.	1917-1891	Civil War	110	305			CSA General
MacKay, Charles		Clergy	20	25	35		
Mackay, John William		Business	40	100	215		Founder Postal Telegraph Co.
Mackay, Lt. Gen. Iven G.	1882-1966	Military	20				World War II Australian general
MacKaye, Percy	1875-1956	Author	40	90	150		Am. Poet, Dramatist
MacKelvie, Brig. Gen. Jay W.	1890-1985	Military	30				World War II U.S. general
Mackensen, August von		Military	12	25	40	85	Ger. Gen. Fld. Marshal WWI. RK
Mackensen, Col-Gen Eberhard v.	1889-1969	Military	25				World War II German general
Mackenzie, Brig. David Alex. L.	1897-1976	Military	25				World War II British general
MacKenzie, Gisele		Entertainment	3	5	6	15	
Mackenzie, Maj. Gen. John P.	1884-1961	Military	20				World War II Canadian general
Mackenzie, Morell, Sir		Science	60	165	350		Larygologist. Misdiagnosed
Mackenzie, Ranald Slidell	1840-1889	Civil War	40	75	110		Union general
Mackeson, Brig. Sir Harry Ripley	1905-1964	Military	25				World War II British general
Mackesy, Maj. Gen. Pierse Jos.	1883-1953	Military	25				World War II British general
Mackie, Bob		Business	5	10	25	15	Fashion Designer
MacLachlan, Kyle		Entertainment	10			32	Picket Fences. Trey MacDougal, Sex in the City
MacLagan, William D., Bishop		Clergy	15	25	35		
MacLaine, Shirley		Entertainment	15	25	35	37	Pin-Up SP 45
Maclane, Barton		Entertainment	50			125	Vint. Tough Guy. Maltese Falcon etc.
MacLaren, Donald M.		Military	25	40	95	75	
MacLean, Steve		Astronaut	7	15		16	
MacLeay, Lachlan		Astronaut	7			15	
MacLeish, Archibald	1892-1982	Author	30	55	90	75	Am. Poet, Lawyer. 3 Pulitzers
MacLeod, Gavin		Entertainment	6	8	15	20	
Macleod, George F.		Clergy	20	25	30		
MacLeod, Maj. Gen. Charles Wm.	1881-1944	Military	25				World War II British general
Macleod, Maj. Gen. Malcom N.	1882-1969	Military	25				World War II British general
Macleod, Maj. Gen. Minden W-M.	1896-1981	Military	25				World War II British general
MacMahon, Aline		Entertainment	20			60	
MacMahon, Marie E.P.		Head of State	35	110	225		Fr.Soldier, Politician, Marshal
MacMillan of MacMillan	1897-1986	Military	25				W W II British, General Sir Gordon Holmes Alexander
MacMillan, Donald B.	1874-1970	Explorer	40	60	95	75	Am. with Peary at North Pole

NAME	DATE	CATEGORY	SIG	LS/DS	ALS	SP	COMMENTS
MacMillan, Harold	1894-1987	Head of State	30	108	262	300	Br. P.M.. Lord Stockton
MacMullen, Maj. Gen. Hugh T.	1892-1946	Military	25				World War II British general
MacMurray, Fred	1908-1991	Entertainment	18	30		52	Film-TV Star
Macnab, Brigadier John Francis	1906-1980	Military	25				World War II British general
MacNee, Patrick	1922-	Entertainment	15			32	Brit. Actor. John Steed in 'The Avengers'
Macneil, Robert		Celebrity	10			15	media/TV personality
MacNelly, Jeff*		Cartoonist	30			200	Shoe
MacNider, Hanford		Military	3	9	15		
Macomb, Alexander	1748-1832	Business		98	115		Fur & Shipping Merchant. Associated/John J. Aster
Macon, Maj. Gen. Robert C.	1890-1980	Military	30				World War II U.S. general
Macon, Nathaniel	1758-1837	Congress	50	125			Sen. NC, Speaker of House, Rev. War Soldier
Maconie, Stuart		Music	10			15	DJ
Macpherson, Elle		Cover Girl	10			35	Pin-Up SP 40
MacQueen, Maj. Gen. John Henry	1893-1980	Military	20				World War II Canadian general
MacRae, Gordon		Entertainment	15			30	
Macrae, Maj. Gen. Albert Edward	1886-1958	Military	25				World War II British general
Macrae, Maj Gen Ian Macpherson	1882-1956	Military	25				World War II British general
MacRae, Meredith		Entertainment	5			20	
MacRae, Sheila		Entertainment	3			12	
MacReady, George		Entertainment	20			40	
Macready, Lt. Gen. Sir Gordon N.	1891-1956	Military	25				World War II British general
Macready, William C.	1793-1873	Entertainment	30		168		Foremost Br. Shakespearean Actor
Macsharry, Ray		Celebrity	10			15	political celebrity
MacVeagh, Franklin		Cabinet	10	25	60	20	Sec'y Treasury
MacVeagh, Wayne	1833-1917	Cabinet	65		98		Att'y Gen., Diplomat, CW Soldier
Macy, Bill		Entertainment	4			32	
Macy, William J.		Entertainment	6			38	Actor. 'Pleasantville'
Madden, Charles Edw.	1919-	Military	45	120	215	100	Brit. Adm.
Madden, John		Entertainment	10			20	Motion Picture Director
Maddox, Lester	-2003	Governor	15	40		30	Georgia Anti-Civil Rights Gov.
Madeira, Jean		Entertainment	18			52	Am. Contralto
Madero, Francisco I.		Head of State		3000			Revolutionary Pres. Mex. 1911-13
Madigan, Amy		Entertainment	10			35	
Madison, Dolley Payne	1768-1849	First Lady	717	1065	2436		Free Frank 750-850-1,200
Madison, Guy		Entertainment	6			25	
Madison, James & James Monroe		Presidents	550	2189			Unusual DS 4500
Madison, James (as Pres)	1751-1836	President	400	1511	4000		FF 460-600, ALS/cont 15,000-80,500
Madison, James	1751-1836	President	361	1178	2781		FF 695-775-925, ALS/Content. 7500-9500
Madonna		Entertainment	50	110		150	Singer, actress, ALS/cont 1200 Louise Veronica Cicone
Madriguera, Enric		Entertainment	15			30	Big Band Leader
Madsen, Chris		Pioneer Lawman		1396			Outlaw & Indian Fighter
Madsen, Michael		Entertainment	5			35	Actor
Madsen, Virginia		Entertainment	10			28	Pin-Up SP 35
Mae, Vanessa		Music	10			15	performing musical artist
Maes, Nelly		Political	10			15	Member European Parliament

NAME	DATE	CATEGORY	SIG	LS/DS	ALS	SP	COMMENTS
Maeterlinck, Maurice, Count	1862-1949	Author	35	115	200	425	Nobel Literature. 'Pelleas and Melisand'
Maffett, Debbie Sue		Entertainment	4	5	9	9	
Magee, John A.		Senate/Congress	10		35		MOC NY 1827. Banker, RR
Magee, Patrick		Entertainment	10			35	
Magee, Walter W.	1861-1927	Congress	12	25			Repr. NY
Magg, Alois		Aviation	4	9	16	15	
Magilton, Jerry		Astronaut	4			12	
Magnani, Anna	1908-1973	Entertainment	300			650	
Magnus, Kurt		Science				50	Rocket Pioneer. Peenemuende Team/USSR
Magnus, Sandra		Astronaut	7			25	
Magnusson, Magnus		Celebrity	10			15	television presenter
Magrath, Andrew G.	1813-1893	Civil War	35	60	80		CSA Gov.SC. ALS '61 150
Magritte, René Francois	1898-1967	Artist	188	580	842		Belg. Surrealist Painter. AMsS 2000
Magruder, John B.	1807-1871	Civil War	285	391	535		CSA Gen. Sig/Rank 450
Magruder, Maj. Gen. Bruce	1882-1953	Military	30				World War II U.S. general
Magsaysay, Ramon	1907-1957	Head of State	30	65	120	75	Pres. Philippines
Maguire, Frank		Celebrity	10			15	motivational speaker
Maguire, Tobey		Entertainment	7			75	Actor.
Maguire, W.A. Cpt.		Military	25	50	75	60	
Mahan, Alfred Thayer		Military	50	75	100		US Navy Off'r-Historian. CW
Maharis, George		Entertainment	10	25	25	20	Star of TV's 'Route 66' and Films
Mahen, Robert A.		Business	15	30	70	40	
Mahendra Bir Bikram		Royalty	35	50	135	50	King, Leader Nepal
Mahin, Maj. Gen. Frank C.	1887-1942	Military	30				World War II U.S. general
Mahler, Alma		Author	20		120		Author & Wife Gustav Mahler
Mahler, Gustav	1860-1911	Composer	550	1260	3303	2430	Austrian Composer. Signed etching 9000
Mahone, William (WD)		Civil War			3680		CSA general
Mahone, William	1826-1895	Civil War	106	250	285		CSA General, US Senator VA
Mahoney, Jock		Entertainment	20	35	55	45	
Mahurin, Walker M. Bud		Aviation	15	35	55	40	ACE, WW II, Legendary Ace
Maij-weggen, Hanja		Political	10			15	Member European Parliament
Maikl, George		Entertainment	5			20	Opera
Mailer, Norman	1923-1980	Author	25	55	75	75	'Naked & the Dead' Reprint Ed. Signed 50
Maillol, Aristide	1861-1944	Artist	200	460	796		Fr. Sculptor, Painter. Large Graceful Statues
Main, Marjorie		Entertainment	105			250	
Maintenon, Francoise, Marquise		Royalty			975		2nd Wife Louis XIV
Maison, Nicholas J.	1771-1840	Fr. Revolution	35	150	175		General under Napoleon
Maison, René		Entertainment	25			52	Opera
Maitland, Lester J.		Aviation	20		40		
Majendie, Maj. Gen. Vivian H. B.	1886-1960	Military	25				World War II British general
Majette, Denise L. M		Congress	10			15	Member U.S. Congress
Major, James Patrick	1836-1877	Civil War	64	261			Confederate general
Major, John		Head of State	5			20	Br. Prime Minister
Majorana, Gaetano (Caffarelli)		Entertainment			3200		Legendary Male Soprano (castrato)
Majors, Lee		Entertainment	5	6	15	15	

NAME	DATE	CATEGORY	SIG	LS/DS	ALS	SP	COMMENTS
Makarios III, Mikhail	1913-1977	Clergy-Head State	50	65	140	125	Archbishop & Pres. Cyprus
Makarova, Natalia		Entertainment	10			15	Ballet
Makino, Lt. Gen. Shira	1893-1945	Military	25				World War II Japanese general
Mako		Entertainment	6			20	
Malamud, Bernard	1914-1986	Author	25	40	75	75	Am. Novelist, Pulitzer
Malandro, Loretta Dr.		Celebrity	10			15	motivational speaker
Malcolm X	1925-1965	Black Leader	704	3084	7500		TLS/Content 10,000-15,000
Malden, Karl		Entertainment	10	35		35	Actor. Important DS 250
Malenkov, Georgi M.	1902-1988	Head of State	160	408	800	250	Union Sov. Russia. Premier
Malet, C. Francois de		Fr. Revolution	120	240			Gen'l. Court-martialed, Shot
Malher, J.P.F.		Fr. Revolution	25	80			
Malibran, Maria	1808-1836	Entertainment			2000		French Mezzo-soprano
Malik, Charles		Head of State	7	15	35	10	
Malik, Terrence		Entertainment	12			40	Movie Director. 'Thin Red Line'
Malina, Joshua		Entertainment	10			35	The West Wing
Malipiero, Gian-Francesco		Composer					Important 20th Cent.Comp.AMuQs 225
Malis, David		Entertainment	10			25	Opera
Malko, Nicolai	1833-1961	Entertainment	75		45	197	Rus. Conductor
Malkovich, John		Entertainment	10			44	Actor
Mallaby, Maj. Gen. Aubertin W. S.	1899-1945	Military	25				World War II British general
Mallarmé, Stephane	1842-1898	Author	150	750	1100		Fr. Poet. Symbolist Movement
Malle, Louis	1932-1996	Entertainment	35		45	50	Fr. Film Director.'My Dinner With Andre' etc.
Mallick, Don		Astronaut	5			15	
Malliori, Minerva Melpomeni		Political	10			15	Member European Parliament
Mallory, Charles M.		Aviation	10	22	38	30	ACE, WW II
Mallory, Francis	1807-1860	Congress	10				Repr. VA, Physician, RR Pres.
Mallory, Stephen R.		Civil War	125	280	360		CSA Sec'y of Navy.
Malmesbury, 1st Earl	1746-1820	Br. Diplomat	15	30	45		James Harris. Minister, Ambass.
Malmström, Cecilia		Political	10			15	Member European Parliament
Malo, Gina		Entertainment	3	3	6	6	
Malodva, Milada		Entertainment	7	9	20	15	
Malone, Dorothy		Entertainment	40	75		65	
Malone, Dumas		Author	10	30	75	40	
Maloney, Carolyn B. M		Congress	10			15	Member U.S. Congress
Maloney, Francis T.	1894-1945	Senate/Congress	10	20	40		Senator, MOC CT 1933-45
Maloney, Michael		Entertainment	10			20	actor
Malony, Maj. Gen. Harry J.	1889-1971	Military	30				World War II U.S. general
Maltby, Jasper Adalmorn	1826-1867	Civil War	40	85	110		Union general
Maltby, Maj. Gen. Christopher M.	1891-1980	Military	28				World War II British general
Malten, Leonard	1950-	Entertainment	10	25		35	Film Critic, Writer, TV Personality
Malten, Therese		Entertainment	35			150	Opera
Maltese, Lili		Celebrity	10			15	celebrity model
Malthus, Thomas Robert	1766-1834	Br. Economist	310	1100	1915		Educator, Author
Mamas and the Papas		Entertainment	350	900		650	Popular 60's singing group
Mamas and the Papas (NEW)		Entertainment	10			20	(Four)

NAME	DATE	CATEGORY	SIG	LS/DS	ALS	SP	COMMENTS
Mamet, David		Entertainment	10			25	Film Director
Mamoulian, Rouben		Entertainment	15	45		175	Top Film & Stage Director
Man Ray		Artist					SEE Ray, Man
Mana-Zucca (Zuckerman, Aug.)		Entertainment	20			100	Singer, Composer, Pianist
Manchester, Melissa		Entertainment	10	15		30	Singer. Concert & Recording Artist
Manchester, William		Author	5	10	20	15	
Mancini, Henry	1924-1994	Composer	25	30		50	Conductor-Pianist.AMusQS 85-250
Mandel, Howie		Entertainment	6	8	15	15	
Mandel, John		Entertainment	5	6	15	10	
Mandel, Marvin		Governor	10	15		22	Governor MD
Mandela, Nelson	1918-	Head of State	68	170		360	Leader African Nat'l Congress
Manders, Toine		Political	10			15	Member European Parliament
Manderson, Charles	1837-1911	Civil War	30	55	70		Union Gen. , U.S. Sen. NE
Mandoki, Luis		Entertainment	5			22	Movie Director
Mandrell, Barbara		Country Music	6			20	
Mane, Taylor		Entertainment				30	Actress
Manesh, Marshall		Entertainment	10			25	Will and Grace
Manet, Edouard	1832-1883	Artist	350	800	1544		Impressionist School Creator
Maney, George E.	1826-1901	Civil War	145				CSA Gen. ALS '62 760
Manfrini, Luigi		Entertainment	40			125	Opera
Mangano, Silvana		Entertainment	25	35	60	50	
Mangione, Chuck		Entertainment	5	6	15	15	
Mangold, James		Celebrity	10			15	film industry
Manhattan Transfer		Entertainment	35			80	
Manifold, Maj. Gen. John Alex.	1884-1960	Military	25				World War II British general
Manigault, Arthur M.	1824-1886	Civil War	105	288			CSA Gen. ALS '61 1650
Manilow, Barry		Entertainment	15	45		42	Composer, Vocalist, Pianist
Manisco, Lucio		Political	10			15	Member European Parliament
Manke, John		Astronaut	5			15	
Mankiewicz, Joseph L.		Entertainment	20		55	55	AA Film Director
Mankiller, Wilma		Author	5			20	
Mankiller, Wilma, Chief		Celebrity	10			15	Former Principal Chief of the Cherokee Nation
Manley, N. W.		Head of State	12		25	20	Prime Minister Jamaica
Mann, Daniel		Entertainment	10			35	
Mann, Delbert		Entertainment	20			45	Film Director
Mann, Erika		Political	10			15	Member European Parliament
Mann, Hank		Entertainment	100				Keystone Kop. Caricature S 250
Mann, Heinrich		Author	35	145	275		Ger. Novelist. Exiled, Interned
Mann, Horace	1796-1859	Educator	35	135	250		Education Reformer, Abolitionist
Mann, Johnny		Bandleader	16				
Mann, Manfred (All)		Entertainment	125				
Mann, Michael		Celebrity	10			50	Film industry
Mann, Orrin L.	1833-1908	Civil War	20	35	60		Union General
Mann, Thomas Clifton		Celebrity	3			10	
Mann, Thomas		Political	10			15	Member European Parliament

NAME	DATE	CATEGORY	SIG	LS/DS	ALS	SP	COMMENTS
Mann, Thomas	1875-1955	Author	214	724	1000	1080	Ger. Novelist, Nobel Prize. 'Death in Venice'
Mann, Thomas	d. 1967	Aviation	12	25	48	35	ACE, WW II, Double Ace
Manne, Shelly		Bandleader				45	Drummer
Mannerheim, C. Gustave, Baron		Head of State		290	850	594	Pres. Finland. Soldier, Patriot
Mannering, Mary		Entertainment	15			25	Vintage Stage Actress
Manners, David		Entertainment	10			35	
Manners-Sutton, Charles		Clergy	25	35	40		
Manning, Anne	1807-1879	Author			80		
Manning, Bernard		Celebrity	10			15	comedian
Manning, Daniel		Cabinet	18	35	65		Sec'y Treasury
Manning, Henry E., Cardinal		Clergy	40	60	95	50	
Manning, Irene		Entertainment	6	8	15	10	
Manning, Stephen H.		Civil War	30	55	110		Union General
Manning, Timothy J., Cardinal		Clergy	35	40	50	45	
Manning, William T., Bishop	1856-1947	Clergy	20	32	60	30	Episcopal Bishop of New York. 1924-46
Manoff, Dinah		Entertainment	5			20	
Manone, Wingy		Entertainment	10			50	Jazz Trumpet-Vocalist
Mansergh, Gen. Sir E.C. Robert	1900-1970	Military	25				World War II British general
Mansfield, Jayne	1933-1967	Entertainment	130			328	Blonde Glamour Actress. 5x7 SP 375, SP Pc 375
Mansfield, Joseph K.F. (WD)		Civil War	225		850		Union Gen.KIA 1862, ALS/cont 3150
Mansfield, Joseph King Fenno	1803-1862	Civil War	164	452	650		Union General
Mansfield, Katherine		Author		290			
Mansfield, Mike		Senate/Congress	10	25	40	15	MOC, Senator MT
Mansfield, Richard		Entertainment	50		175		Vintage Stage Actor, Manager, Producer
Manship, Paul Howard	1885-1955	Artist	40	275	412		Am. Sculptor of Prometheus Fountain
Manson, Charles		Criminal	75	215	455	143	Murderer, Cult Figure
Manson, Mahlon Dickerson	1820-1895	Civil War	45	65	110		Union general
Manson, Marilyn		Entertainment				35	Singer
Manson, Shirley		Entertainment	10			75	Music. Lead Singer 'Garbage'
Manstein, Erich von, General	1887-1973	Military	45	85	140	225	Planned Assault vs France WW II
Mantegna, Joe		Entertainment	10			20	actor
Mantell, Gideon A	1790-1852.	Science	10	25	40		Paleontologist. 4 Dinosaurs
Mantell, Robert B.		Entertainment	12			25	Vintage Shakespearean Actor
Mantelli, Eugenia		Entertainment	25			60	Opera
Manteuffel, Edwin F. von	1809-1885	Military	75	240	420		Prussian Fld. Marshal WW I
Manteuffel, Hasso von	1897-1978	Military	45	113	190	388	WW II Ger. Tank Commander-Panzer Divisions
Mantle, Clive		Entertainment	10			20	Actor
Mantovani		Entertainment	8	12		20	Conductor-Arranger
Mantovani, Mario		Political	10			15	Member European Parliament
Manuel II	1889-1932	Royalty	58	350			King of Portugal at 18. Father Assassinated
Manville, Tommy		Business	20		35		Much Married Asbestos Heir
Manzano, Sonia		Entertainment	10			20	actress
Manzarek, Ray		Entertainment	15	25		25	The Doors, bassist
Manzullo, Donald A. M		Congress	10			15	Member U.S. Congress
Mao Tse Tung	1893-1976	Head of State	3000				Chinese Communist Leader

NAME	DATE	CATEGORY	SIG	LS/DS	ALS	SP	COMMENTS
Maphis, Joe and Rose Lee		Country Music	10			20	
Maples, Marla		Entertainment	10			20	actress
Mapleson, James H.		Entertainment	75				Opera
Mapplethorpe, Robert	1946-1989	Artist	75		296		Controversial Am. Photographer
Mara, Adele		Entertainment	5	8		10	Actress
Maragliano, Luisa		Entertainment	5			15	
Marais, Jean	1913-1998	Entertainment	10		30	45	Fr. Actor. Stage & Film
Marat, Jean-Paul	1743-1793	Fr. Revolution		1600	3100		Politician-Doctor-Author. Murdered
Marbot, J.B.A.M., Marquis	1782-1854	Fr. Revolution	25	70	125		Napoleonic General
Marceau, Marcel		Entertainment	20	70		92	World Renown Mime
Marceau, Sophie		Entertainment	12			42	Actress. Pin-Up 65
Marcellino, Muzzy		Entertainment	10	15	25	25	Big Band. Trumpet
March, Barbara		Entertainment	5			30	Star Trek
March, Fredric	1897-1975	Entertainment	43	80	95	85	Long Respected Stage-Film Actor. AA 'Jekyll-Hyde'
March, Hal	1920-1970	Entertainment	5			15	Actor-TV Game Show Host
March, Jane		Entertainment	10			38	Actress. Pin-Up 65
March, Peyton C.	1864-1955	Military	50	125			Am. WW I Four Star Gen.
Marchand, Nancy		Entertainment				60	Livia Soprano
Marchesi, Mathilde	1821-1913	Entertainment	50		160	175	Ger. Mezzo-Sopr. From Famous Family of Singers
Marchiani, Jean-charles		Political	10			15	Member European Parliament
Marcinkus, Paul C., Archbishop		Clergy	45	65	100	50	
Marcks, General of Artillery Erich	1891-1944	Military	25				World War II German general
Marcks, Gerhard	1889-1981	Artist	45		345		Ger. Sculptor and Designer
Marconi, Guglielmo	1874-1937	Science	250	480	1250	1287	It. Physicist-Inventor. Nobel. Father of Radio
Marcos, Ferdinand E.		Head of State	50	135		130	Pres. Philippines
Marcos, Imelda		Head of State	15	35		25	Phillipines
Marcoux, Vanni	1877-1962	Entertainment	20			75	Opera, Buenos Aires. Fr. Bass-Baritone
Marcovicci, Andrea		Entertainment	10			20	
Marcus, Jerry*		Cartoonist	5			35	'Fatkat'
Marcus, Rudolph A., Dr.		Science	20	35		30	Nobel Chemistry
Marcus, Stanley		Business	30	75	160	60	Merchant. Nieman-Marcus
Marcy, Randolph B. (WD)		Civil War	50	175	460		Union Gen. ALS/Cont. 750
Marcy, Randolph B.	1812-1887	Civil War	35		180		Union Gen.
Marcy, William L.	1786-1857	Cabinet	40	110	135		Sec'y War, State. Senator NY
Maren, Jerry		Entertainment	10			25	Actor. 'Wizard of Oz'. Lollipop Kid
Marescot, Armand S.		Fr. Revolution	30	80	170		
Maressyev, Alexei		Aviation	135				Rus. ACE & Soviet Hero
Maret, Hugues B., Duke	1763-1839	Fr. Revolution	82	131	375		Napoleon Confidential Advisor., LS/cont 2500
Marey, Etienne		Science	50		700		Fr. Physiologist. Sphygmograph
Marey, Jules	1830-1904	Science			575		pioneer of early cinema
Margaret of Austria	1522-1586	Royalty	110	285	775		Duchess of Parma. Regent Of Netherlands
Margaret, Princess (d.2002)		Royalty	30	75	125	100	
Margie*		Cartoonist	20			250	Little Lulu
Margo (Mrs Eddie Albert)	1917-1986	Entertainment	20	20	35	30	Mex.-Born Actress-Dancer 'Lost Horizon'
Margolis, Jeremy		Law	5	7	10	15	World renowned attorney

NAME	DATE	CATEGORY	SIG	LS/DS	ALS	SP	COMMENTS
Margret, Ann		Entertainment	10			20	actress
Marguerite De Valois	1553-1615	Royalty		1910			Queen of Fr., 1st Wife of Henry of Navarre
Margulies, Julianna		Entertainment				45	Actress
Maria (Castile)		Royalty		2500			Queen of Alfonso V of Aragon
Maria Federovna		Royalty		213	230		Empress of Russia
Maria Theresa	1717-1780	Royalty	185	680	980		Archduchess, Qn Hung.-Bohemia
Marie Amelie de Bourbon (Fr.)	1782-1866	Royalty	100	240	322		Queen of Louis Phillippe I
Marie Antoinette (Fr)	1755-1793	Royalty	1255	5425			Queen of Louis XVI France
Marie Louise	1791-1847	Royalty	200	762	984		Empress of Fr. 2nd Wife of Napoleon I
Marie of Naples		Royalty	60	110	250		Queen of King Louis-Phillipe I
Marie	1875-1938	Royalty	80	115	240	350	Queen of Romania. Wife of Ferdinand I of Roumania
Marie, Rose		Entertainment	10	20		30	'Dick VanDyke Show', Actress-Singer-Comedienne
Marin, Cheech		Entertainment	5			30	Actor-Comedian (Cheech & Chong)
Marin, John		Artist	60	225	550		Am. Watercolorist, Etching
Marinaro, Ed		Entertainment	6	8	15	15	
Marinho, Lufs		Political	10			15	Member European Parliament
Marini, Franco		Political	10			15	Member European Parliament
Marinos, Ioannis		Political	10			15	Member European Parliament
Marion, Francis	1732-1795	Rev. War		6500	8500		The Swamp Fox
Mariscal, Don Ignacio		Statesman	20	35	55		V.P. Mexico
Maritain, Jacques		Clergy	40	45	95	75	
Maritza, Sari		Entertainment	8	9		20	
Markevitch, Igor		Entertainment	30			145	Conductor
Markey, Edward J. M		Congress	10			15	Member U.S. Congress
Markham, Albert H., Sir		Celebrity	5	20	45		
Markham, Clements, Sir	1830-1916	Geographer	15	25	125		Historian, Pres. Royal Geographical. Soc.
Markham, Edwin	1852-1940	Author	30	70	90	75	The Man With The Hoe
Markham, William		Colonial America	135	450			Colonial Gov. PA
Markov, Helmuth		Political	10			15	Member European Parliament
Markova, Alicia		Entertainment	20			50	Ballet
Markowitz, Harry M., Dr.		Economics	20	35	45		Nobel Economics
Marks, Johnny	1906-1985	Composer	35	95	125	100	AMusQS 175, TsS 'Rudolph' 850.
Marks, William, Jr.	1778-1858	Senate	35	140			PA Senator, ALS/Content 400
Marlborough, Consuelo	1876-1964	Royalty	35	185		350	Vanderbilt Heiress. 9th Duchess
Marlborough, James L.,	1550-1629	Judge	85	325			1st Earl of
Marley, Bob	1945-1981	Entertainment	919	1380		2258	Rock HOF. Reggae King. Held World Popularity
Marley, Maj. Gen. James P.	1882-1952	Military	30				World War II U.S. general
Marlin, Mahlon F.		Business	40	115	225		Pres-Treas. Marlin Firearms Co.
Marlow, Lucy		Entertainment	5	6	15	15	
Marlowe, Hugh		Entertainment	25			50	
Marlowe, Julia		Entertainment	19	35	70	60	Major Stage Star/E.H. Sothern
Marly, Florence		Entertainment	4	4	9	9	
Marmaduke, John S. (WD)	1833-1887	Civil War	167		2400		CSA Gen.
Marmaduke, John S.	1833-1887	Civil War	95	300			CSA Gen.
Marmont, A.F.L.V., Duke		Fr. Revolution	45	90			Marshal of Fr., Napoleon A-D-C

NAME	DATE	CATEGORY	SIG	LS/DS	ALS	SP	COMMENTS
Marney, Carlyle		Clergy	20	25	35	35	
Marquand, John P.		Author	40	125	165	100	Am. Novelist. Pulitzer
Marques, Antonio		Entertainnment	35			85	Opera
Marques, Sérgio		Political	10			15	Member European Parliament
Marquez, Gabriel		Author	70			245	Nobel. One Hundred Years of Solitude
Marriott, J.		Business	20	35	70	30	Marriott Hotel Chain
Marryat, Frederick	1792-1848	Military-Author	30	100	175		Br. Naval Cmmdr. Novelist
Marsala, Joe		Entertainment	20			65	Clarinet, Sax, Composer
Marsalis, Branford		Entertainment	10			25	Conductor, Sax
Marsalis, Wynton		Entertainment	15			30	Trumpet Virtuoso. Classic-Jazz
Marsden, Jason		Entertainment	10			25	The Munsters
Marsh, Jean		Entertainment	7			20	
Marsh, Joan		Entertainment	15	20	40	35	
Marsh, Mae		Entertainment	30	40	75	40	
Marsh, Marion		Entertainment	15			40	
Marsh, Ngaio, Dame		Author	20	35	50	40	New Zealand Mystery Writer
Marshall, Amanda		Music	15			35	Singer
Marshall, Brian		Entertainment	6			25	Music. Bass Guitar 'Creed'
Marshall, Catherine		Author	65	75	150	125	'A Man Called Peter', 'Christy'
Marshall, Cathy		TV News	7	10		10	CNN News
Marshall, Christopher		Revolutionary War	100				Am. Patriot & Diarist
Marshall, E.G.		Entertainment	10			25	
Marshall, Frank J.		History	125				Early US pioneer
Marshall, Gary		Celebrity	10			15	film industry
Marshall, George C.	1880-1959	Military-Statesman	144	329	550	436	WW II Chief Staff. Nobel Peace Prize. Statesman
Marshall, George E.		Entertainment	35			75	Film Director. 400+ Films
Marshall, George		Celebrity	25	127		15	impressionist
Marshall, Herbert	1890-1966	Entertainment	10	75		65	Sophisticated Br. Actor
Marshall, Humphrey (WD)		Civil War	270	512			CSA Gen.ALS/Cont 1825
Marshall, Humphrey	1812-1872	Civil War	90	195			CSA General
Marshall, Jim M		Congress	10			15	Member U.S. Congress
Marshall, John	1755-1835	Supreme Court	775	2607	3778		Chief Justice
Marshall, John, Sir		Head of State	10	20	35	20	Prime Minister New Zealand
Marshall, Maj. Gen. John Stuart	1883-1944	Military	25				World War II British general
Marshall, Maj. Gen. Richard J.	1895-1973	Military	30				World War II U.S. general
Marshall, Margaret		Entertainment	10			25	Opera
Marshall, Penny		Entertainment	8	15		20	Actress And Film Director
Marshall, Peter		Clergy	75	95	100	125	Senate Chaplain
Marshall, Thomas R.	1854-1925	Vice President	50	140	275	200	Wilson VP
Marshall, Thurgood	1908-1993	Supreme Court	105	200	260	250	1st Afro-Am. Justice
Marshall, Tully		Entertainment	20			50	
Marshall, William		Entertainment	15			25	Film Director
Marshall, William		Entertainment	8			25	Werewolf
Marshall, William	1825-1896	Civil War	25	40	75		Union Gen., Gov. MN
Marshall, William, Sir	1865-1939	Military	35			85	Brit. WW I General. France, Gallipoli, Salonika

NAME	DATE	CATEGORY	SIG	LS/DS	ALS	SP	COMMENTS
Marston, Gilman	1811-1890	Civil War	38	45	55		Union Gen. Legislator. Sen.NH
Martel, Lt. Gen. Sir G. Le Quesne	1889-1958	Military	25				World War II British general
Martelli, Claudio		Political	10			15	Member European Parliament
Martens, Maria		Political	10			15	Member European Parliament
Marterie, Ralph		Entertainment	10			20	Big Band Leader
Martin, Benny		Country Western	5			18	Western Recording Artist
Martin, Brig. Gen. Thomas L.	1891-1984	Military	30				World War II U.S. general
Martin, Charles H.		Governor	10	25			Governor OR
Martin, Chris Pin		Entertainment	50			100	
Martin, Clarence D.		Governor	5	15		10	Governor WA
Martin, David W.		Political	10			15	Member European Parliament
Martin, Dean & Jerry Lewis		Entertainment	125			195	Comedy Team
Martin, Dean Vincent		Entertainment	5	6	15	15	
Martin, Dean	1917-1995	Entertainment	28	50	75	78	Actor-Singer-Comedian. Member Sinatra 'Rat Pack'
Martin, Dewey		Entertainment	9			25	Leading Man
Martin, Dick		Entertainment	6	10	15	22	Comedian-Actor. 1/2 Rowan & Martin Team
Martin, Donna Boone		Author	8			12	motivational author/speaker
Martin, Frank	1890-1974	Composer	38		90	110	Prolific Swiss Composer. AMusQS 125
Martin, Freddie		Entertainment	35			65	Big Band Leader-Pianist
Martin, Gen. Henry-Jules-Jean	1888-1984	Military	20				World War II French general
Martin, Glenn L.	1886-1955	Aviation	75	175	275	250	Aeronautical Pioneer.Fndr.Airplane Mfg.Co./Wrights
Martin, Hans-peter		Political	10			15	Member European Parliament
Martin, Hugh		Composer					AMusQS 45
Martin, Hugues		Political	10			15	Member European Parliament
Martin, James Green (WD)	1819-1878	Civil War	182	663			CSA Gen.
Martin, James Green	1819-1878	Civil War	95	120	186		CSA General
Martin, James		Celebrity	10			15	TV Chef
Martin, John A.		Governor	12		30		Governor KS
Martin, John C.		Senate/Congress	5	10			MOC IL
Martin, Joseph W. Jr.	1884-1968	Congress	25	35		25	Speaker of the House
Martin, Kellie		Entertainment	10			20	actress
Martin, Lori		Entertainment				25	Former Ingenue
Martin, Lt. Gen. Hugh Gray	1887-1969	Military	25				World War II British general
Martin, Lt. Gen. Maurice-Paul-A.	1878-1952	Military	20				World War II French general
Martin, Luther	1748-1826	Revolutionary War	70	162	360		Continental Congress
Martin, Maj. Gen. Clarence A.	1896-1986	Military	30				World War II U.S. general
Martin, Maj. Gen. Edward	1879-1967	Military	30				World War II U.S. general
Martin, Maj. Gen. John Simson S.	1888-1973	Military	25				World War II British general
Martin, Maj. Gen. Kevin John	1890-1958	Military	25				World War II British general
Martin, Mary		Entertainment	35	45		50	
Martin, Pamela Sue		Entertainment	7		15	22	Actress. Pin-Up SP 20
Martin, Ricardo		Entertainment	15			45	Opera
Martin, Ricky		Entertainment				45	Singer
Martin, Ross		Entertainment	10	20	40	28	
Martin, Steve		Entertainment	12			55	Comedian-Actor.

NAME	DATE	CATEGORY	SIG	LS/DS	ALS	SP	COMMENTS
Martin, Strother		Entertainment	35	50		80	Character Actor
Martin, Theodore, Sir		Author	5	15	25	10	
Martin, Thomas S.	1847-1919	Congress	12	25			Senator VA 1893. CSA Army
Martin, Tony	1912-	Entertainment	13	22		30	Singer-Actor. 35 Top Hits
Martin, Victoria Woodhull	1838-1927	History			368		First woman to run for US Presidency
Martin, William C., Bishop		Clergy	15	25	30	35	
Martin, William T. (WD)		Civil War	170	440	488		CSA Gen.
Martin, William T.	1823-1910	Civil War	112	295	400		CSA General
Martindale, John Henry	1815-1881	Civil War	40	80	125		Union general
Martindale, Wink		Celebrity	10			20	TV game show host
Martine, James E.		Congress	5	15		10	Senator NJ
Martineau, Harriet	1802-1870	Author	50		75		Brit. Miscellaneous Writer
Martinek, Gen. of Artillery Robert	1889-1944	Military	27				World War II German general
Martinelli, Giovanni	1885-1969	Entertainment	35	60		125	It.-Am. Great Operatic Dramatic Tenor
Martinez, Jean-Claude		Political	10			15	Member European Parliament
Martinez, Luis, Cardinal		Clergy	30	45	55	50	
Martínez Martínez, Miguel Angel		Political	10			15	Member European Parliament
Martini, Nino		Entertainment	15			45	Opera, Films. Handsome Tenor
Martini, Steve		Author	5	10		10	Novelist
Martino, Al		Entertainment	3	5		8	
Martino, Donald		Composer	20	35	90		Pulitzer, AMusQS 180
Martinson, Leslie		Entertainment	15			25	Director TV & Films 'Bat Man', 'PT 109' etc.
Martinu, Bronislaw	1890-1959	Composer					Czech. Composer AMusQS 900-1500
Martiny, Philip		Artist	25	40	80	30	
Marton, Eva		Entertainment	20			50	Opera
Maruyama, Lt. Gen. Masao	1889-1957	Military	27				World War II Japanese general
Marvel, Ik		Author	10		30		Pseud. Donald G. Mitchell
Marvin, Lee	1924-1987	Entertainment	142	175		253	Supporting Actor to Star to Academy Award
Marwood, William		Executioner	75		350		Br. Lord High Executioner
Marx Brothers (3)		Entertainment	941			2158	Three Full Names
Marx Brothers (4)		Entertainment	1575			2925	4 Full Names Rare
Marx, Arthur		Author	7	15		15	
Marx, Chico	1886-1961	Entertainment	145	142	325	310	
Marx, Groucho	1890-1977	Entertainment	177	539	675	400	Comedian. Marx Bros. Leader. S Chk. 425
Marx, Harpo	1888-1964	Entertainment	200			466	
Marx, Karl	1818-1883	Author	1500	8000	22500	12650	Ger. Political Philosopher
Marx, Richard		Entertainment	20			50	Singer
Marx, Zeppo	1901-1979	Entertainment	65	120		189	
Mary (of Modena)	1658-1718	Royalty	140		750		Queen of James II
Mary (of Teck)	1867-1953	Royalty	120	370	205	330	Queen of George V (Eng.) Mother of Two Kings
Mary Adalaide (Dchs. Teck)		Royalty	35	70	150		
Mary I (Eng)	1516-1558	Royalty	900	3000	7500		Queen England, Bloody Mary
Mary II (Eng)	1662-1694	Royalty	370	1240	3100		Queen William II
Mary, Queen of Scots	1542-1587	Royalty		15000	18000		Executed by Elizabeth I
Masaryk, Jan	1886-1948	Head of State	95	155	275	550	Pres. Czechoslavakia

NAME	DATE	CATEGORY	SIG	LS/DS	ALS	SP	COMMENTS
Masaryk, Thomas G.	1850-1937	Head of State	100	250	717	425	Czech.Philosopher,1st President
Mascagni, Pietro	1863-1945	Composer	158	375	623	431	'Cavalleria Rusticana'. AMusQS 650-1,250.SPc 225
Mascherini, Enzo		Entertainment	15			50	Opera
Masefield, John	1878-1967	Author	35	81	215	110	Br. Poet Laureate
Mash (Show-Cast of)		Entertainment				448	Eight Main Characters
Mashburn, J.L.		Author	8			12	postcard price guides
Masini, Angelo		Entertainment				500	Opera. 19th Cent. Intern'l Star. RARE
Maskelyne, Nevil	1732-1811	Science	85	250	390		Br. Astronomer Royal. Inventor
Maslen, Scott		Entertainment	10			20	Actor
Mason, Alfred Edw. W.	1865-1948	Author	10	30	45	20	Br. Novelist
Mason, George	1725-1792	Rev. War	1775	4500			Am. Planter & Rev. Statesman
Mason, Jackie		Entertainment	5			10	Comedian
Mason, James M.	1798-1871	Civil War	49	115	200		US Sen.VA, CSA Diplomat/Trent Affair.ALS 700
Mason, James	1909-1984	Entertainment	40	70	80	105	Br. Actor-Film Director
Mason, John Sanford	1824-1897	Civil War	40	75	110		Union general
Mason, Jonathan	1756-1831	Federalist Am.	40		75		Federalist US Sen. MA. Exec. Council. Investor
Mason, LeRoy		Entertainment	50			150	
Mason, Marsha	1942-	Entertainment	8	10		25	Actress. Stage-Films From '66. AA Nom.'Goodby Girl
Mason, Nick		Entertainment	10			20	Actor
Mason, Sully		Entertainment	5	6	15	10	
Mason, Walt		Author	5			20	Poet
Mason, William E.	1850-1921	Congress	12	20		15	MOC, Senator IL
Massen, Osa	1915-	Entertainment	5	6	10	10	Dan-Am Actress. Hollywood Films From Late 30's
Massena, Andre, Duke	1758-1817	Fr. Revolution	100	375	450		Fr.Marshal.Greatest of Napoleon's Gen'ls
Massenet, Jules	1842-1912	Composer	65	222	132	465	'Manon', 'Thais'. AMusQS 375-650-2750-3500
Massey, Daniel		Entertainment	10			20	Actor
Massey, Eyre	1719-1804	Revolutionary War	300	1250			Br. Gen'l Serving in N.Am. During Am. Rev.
Massey, Gerald	1828-1907	Author	25	70	95		Br. Poet, Journalist, Editor
Massey, Illona		Entertainment	25		30	40	
Massey, Louise & Curt		Entertainment	25			45	Country Western
Massey, Raymond		Entertainment	33	20	46	65	Fine Vintage Canadian Actor. Stage & Screen
Massie, Paul		Entertainment	5	6	15	10	
Massie, Robert		Author		65			The Romanovs
Massine, Leonide		Entertainment	20			105	Ballet Dancer,Choreographer...
Masson, Andre		Artist	40	55	95		
Massy, Lt. Gen. Hugh Royds S.	1884-1965	Military	25				World War II British general
Mast, Gen. Charles-Emmanuel	1889-1977	Military	20				World War II French general
Mastella, Mario Clemente		Political	10			15	Member European Parliament
Masters, W H & Virginia Johnson		Sex Researchers	20			40	
Masters, Edgar Lee	1869-1950	Author	30	45	65	65	Poet, Novelist, Biographer. AMsS 600
Masters, Frankie		Entertainment	5			25	Big Band Leader
Masterson, Mary Stuart		Entertainment	10			40	
Masterson, Wm. B. 'Bat'	1853-1921	Lawman	4800	11500	12500		Scout, Sheriff, Gambler
Mastorakis, Emmanouil		Political	10			15	Member European Parliament
Mastracchio, Richard		Astronaut	5			19	

NAME	DATE	CATEGORY	SIG	LS/DS	ALS	SP	COMMENTS
Mastroantonio, Mary Eliz.		Entertainment	10	15	25	35	
Mastroianni, Marcello		Entertainment	20			45	
Mata Hari (M.G. Zelle)	1876-1917	Spy	350	930	4500	5300	Executed Secret Agent WW I
Matalin, Mary		Celebrity	10			15	political celebrity
Matchbox 20		Entertainment	30			85	Music. 5 Member Rock Group
Maté, Rudy		Entertainment	15			55	Top Cinematographer
Materna, Amalie		Entertainment	30		120		'Greatest Wagnerian Soprano of them all'
Materna, Gen. of Inf. Friedrich	1885-1946	Military	27				World War II German general
Mather, Cotton	1663-1728	Rev. War-Clergy	850	1950	4200		Author, Published 382 Books
Mathers, Jerry		Entertainment	15			30	'Beaver'
Matheson, Jim M		Congress	10			15	Member U.S. Congress
Matheson, Tim		Entertainment	10			30	
Mathews, Brander	1852-1929	Author	10		35		Novelist, Essayist, Drama Critic for NY Times
Mathews, Catharine VanCortlandt		Author	12				history of surveying
Mathews, George	1739-1812	Revolutionary War	85	190			Statesman, General
Mathias, Bob		Congress	10	15		20	MOC CA, Olymp. Decathlon Champ.Brief Actor
Mathieu, Véronique		Political	10			15	Member European Parliament
Mathis, Johnny		Entertainment	9	10	20	25	Alb. Cover S 55
Mathis, Samantha		Entertainment				80	Actress Broken Arrow
Mathiuci, Franca		Entertainment	5			15	
Matikainen-kallström, Marjo		Political	10			15	Member European Parliament
Matisse, Henri	1869-1954	Artist	500	800	1922	2242	Fr. Painter, Sculptor, Fauvist. SP (Pc)1550
Matlack, Timothy	1730-1829	Revolutionary War	85	275	450		Continental Congress. Am. Patriot. Franklin Aide
Matlin, Marlee		Entertainment	10		45	38	AA
Matoni, Walter		Aviation	10			35	Ger. Ace WW II. RK
Matsui, General Iwane	1878-1948	Military	25				World War II Japanese general
Matsui, Maj. Gen. Setsu		Military	25				World War II Japanese general
Matsui, Robert T. M		Congress	10			15	Member U.S. Congress
Matsumoto, Maj. Gen. Kenji		Military	25				World War II Japanese general
Matsura, Lt. Gen. Atsuo	d. 1942	Military	25				World War II Japanese general
Matsushita, Konosuke		Business	25	65	145	40	Japanese Electronic Giant
Matsuyama, Lt. Gen. Yuzo		Military	25				World War II Japanese general
Mattea, Kathy		Country Music	5			15	
Mattenklott, Gen. of Infantry Franz	1884-1954	Military	25				World War II German general
Mattern, Jimmie		Aviation	15	25	60	35	
Matthau, Walter		Entertainment	5		15	25	AA
Matthews, Christopher		Celebrity	10			15	media/TV personality
Matthews, Dave		Music	20			60	Rock
Matthews, DeLane		Entertainment	10			36	Actress Dave's World
Matthews, Frank Arnold		Clergy	20	25	35	25	
Matthews, Jessie		Entertainment	15			30	Br.Vintage Film Actress
Matthews, Maj. Gen. A. Bruce	1909-1991	Military	20				World War II Canadian general
Matthews, Maj. Gen. Francis R. G.	1903-1976	Military	25				World War II British general
Matthews, Maj. Gen. Harold H.	1877-1940	Military	25				World War II Canadian general
Matthews, Stanley		Supreme Court	45	150	275		

NAME	DATE	CATEGORY	SIG	LS/DS	ALS	SP	COMMENTS
Matthies, Charles (Karl) Leopold	1824-1868	Civil War	450	80	120		Union general
Mattingly, Thos. Ken		Astronaut	75			177	
Mattson, Conrad		Aviation	8	15	28	22	ACE, WW II
Mature, Victor		Entertainment	9	10	20	40	
Matzenauer, Margaret		Entertainment	25			85	Wagnerian Soprano
Matzky, Gerhard	1894-1983	Military	40	85			Nazi WW II Gen.
Mauborgne, Joseph O.	1881-1971	Military	45	150			USA Gen.Air-to-Ground Transmission.Broke Codes
Maubourg, Lafayette		Celebrity	5	12	20		Nephew
Mauch, Billy		Entertainment	10	15	25	25	
Mauch, Bobby		Entertainment	30			65	
Maude, Brig. Christian George	1884-1971	Military	25				World War II British general
Maugham, W. Somerset	1874-1965	Author	63	239	274	375	Br. Novelist and Playwright
Mauldin, Bill*		Cartoonist	25			250	Willie & Joe
Maupassant, Guy de		Author	275	795	1185		Fr. Master of Short Story
Maura, Antonio		Head of State	110	165			Sp. P.M. Provoked Rif War
Maurey, Pierre		Clergy	10	15	30	25	Pres. Reform Church France
Mauro, Ermanno		Entertainment	15			40	Opera
Mauro, Mario		Political	10			15	Member European Parliament
Maurois, Andre (Emile Herzog)		Author	22	75	120		Fr. Biographer, Novelist
Maury, Dabney H. (WD)	1822-1900	Civil War	142	280	750	1022	CSA General
Maury, Dabney H.	1822-1900	Civil War	72	230	257		CSA Gen.
Maury, Matthew F.	1806-1873	Civil War	79	225	455	1550	CSA Naval Cmdr., Hydrographer
Mauser, Paul von	1838-1914	Military	285				Ger. Weapon Mfg./Brother Wilhelm. Mauser Rifle
Mawson, Douglas, Sir		Explorer	50	160	375		Australian Polar Explorer
Max Muller, Friedrich	1823-1900	celebrity			100		Orientalist and philologist
Max, Peter		Artist	90	232			Am. Contemporary Art., signed Drwg 550
Maxey, Samuel Bell (WD)		Civil War	245		775		CSA Gen.
Maxey, Samuel Bell	1825-1895	Civil War	128	225	360		CSA General, US Sen. TX
Maxey, Virginia		Entertainment	5			10	
Maxim, Hiram Percy	1896-1936	Science	40	125	210		Radio amateur pioneer, W1AW
Maxim, Hiram Stevens	1840-1916	Science	75	150	310	300	Inventor Maxim Machine Gun. Engineer
Maxim, Hudson	1853-1927	Science	45	95	140	175	Inventor Smokeless Powder & Other Explosives
Maximilian II	1811-1864	Royalty	110	415	770		^"King of Bravaria^"
Maximilian	1832-1867	Royalty	310	878	1250		Emperor of Mexico
Maxon, R.*		Cartoonist	20			100	Tarzan
Maxwell, Brig. Richard Hobson	1899-1965	Military	25				World War II British general
Maxwell, Elizabeth		Author	8			12	regional history
Maxwell, Elsa		Columnist	8	25	35	15	Hostess & Professional Party
Maxwell, Lois		Entertainment	10			25	
Maxwell, Maj. Gen. Russell L.	1890-1968	Military	30				World War II U.S. general
Maxwell, Maj. Gen. Sir Aymer	1891-1971	Military	25				World War II British general
Maxwell, Marilyn		Entertainment	8	10		35	
Maxwell, Robert		Aviation	12	25	28	22	ACE, WW II
Maxwell, Robert		Publisher	45			120	Died Mysteriously
Maxwell, Wm. (Ld. Beaverbrook)		Publisher	25	110	180		Newspaper Proprietor, Statesman

NAME	DATE	CATEGORY	SIG	LS/DS	ALS	SP	COMMENTS
May, Billy		Bandleader	10				Arranger
May, Edna		Entertainment	18		30	32	Vintage Stage & Film. Darling of Brit. Music Hall
May, Jodhi		Entertainment	10			20	actress
Mayakovski, Vladimir V.	1893-1930	Author	300	795	2200		Russian Poet and Dramatist
Mayall, John		Entertainment	10			35	Rock
Mayall, Rik		Entertainment	10			20	Actor
Maybank, Burnet R.		Governor	10	18		15	Governor, Senator SC
Maye, Carolyn		Entertainment	10			25	
Mayer, Hans-peter		Political	10			15	Member European Parliament
Mayer, John		Music	20			40	Raok
Mayer, Louis B.	1885-1957	Business	68	166	220	225	MGM Film Studio, DS/TLS cont 750-900
Mayer, Maria, Dr.		Science	30	85		50	Nobel Physics
Mayer, Xaver		Political	10			15	Member European Parliament
Mayfair, Mitzi		Entertainment	10			10	
Mayhew, Anna Jean		Author	8			12	South Carolina history/attractions
Maynard, Bill		Entertainment	10			20	Actor
Maynard, Ken	1895-1973	Entertainment	103		145	175	Western Film Hero
Maynor, Dorothy		Entertainment	25			275	30's-50's Concert & Recording Career. 5x6 SP 75
Mayo, 6th Earl (Rich.Bourke)		Head of State	10		30		Br. Politician. Viceroy of India
Mayo, Charles H., Dr.	1865-1939	Science	140	290	380	425	Co-Founder Mayo Foundation
Mayo, Charles W., Dr.	1898-1968	Science	65	140	235	362	Surgeon Mayo Clinic.Prof. Surg.
Mayo, Frank	1839-1896	Entertainment	12				Actor
Mayo, Henry Thomas		Military	30	45	125	45	Adm. Cmdr. Atlantic Fl. WW I
Mayo, Simon		Music	10			15	DJ
Mayo, Virginia		Entertainment	8			22	Longtime Warner Bros. Actress. Pin-Up SP 40
Mayo, William J., Dr.	1861-1939	Science	105	290	380	462	Co-Founder Mayo Foundation
Mayol I Raynal, Miquel		Political	10			15	Member European Parliament
Mayron, Anie		Entertainment	10			20	actress
Mayron, Melanie		Entertainment	4			15	Actress 30 Something
Maytag, Frederick L.		Business	95	210	375	250	Maytag Electric Appliances
Mazaki, General Jinsaburo	1876-1956	Military	27				World War II Japanese general
Mazaki, Maj. Gen. Kumao		Military	27				World War II Japanese general
Mazar, Debi		Celebrity				35	
Mazarin, Jules, Cardinal	1602-1661	Clergy-Statesman		835			Succeeded Richelieu as Chief Minister Louis XIII
Mazurki, Mike		Entertainment	5	6	15	15	
Mazurski, Paul		Entertainment	5			20	Film Director
Mazzini, Giuseppe	1805-1872	Revolutionary	75	155	350		Italian Patriot. Unpublished ALS 2325
Mazzoleni, Ester		Entertainment	50			195	Opera. Dalmatian-Ital. Diva
Mbeki,Thabo		Political				35	President of South Africa
McAdam, John		Inventor		850			McAdamized Roads
McAdoo, John D.		Civil War			425		CSA General
McAdoo, William G.	1863-1941	Cabinet	25	55	95	75	Wilson Sec'y Treasury & Son-In-Law. RR Czar
McAfee, John P.		Author	8			12	the 'Catch-22' of Vietnam
McAfee, Robert		Celebrity	10			15	medical expert
Mcaffee, Johnny		Entertainment	3	3	6	6	

NAME	DATE	CATEGORY	SIG	LS/DS	ALS	SP	COMMENTS
McAllister, Lon		Entertainment	15			30	
McAndrew, James W.		Military	35			50	Am. WW I Gen. Gen'l Staff, Chief of Staff A.E.F.
McAndrew, Nell		Celebrity	10			15	celebrity model
McArdle, Andrea		Entertainment	5	6	15	15	
McArthur, John	1826-1906	Civil War	30			310	Union Gen.
McArthur, Kim		Playboy Bunny	4			8	Pin-Up SP 10
McArthur, William		Astronaut	7			20	
McAuliffe, Anthony C.	1898-1975	Military	120	383	454	525	WW II Gen ALS cont 5750, DS 'Nuts' 850-1500
McAuliffe, Christa		Astronaut	509	1235	2500	1346	Died in Challenger Disaster
Mcavan, Linda		Political	10			15	Member European Parliament
McAvoy, May		Entertainment	10			25	Vintage Film Actress
McBain, Diane		Entertainment	5	6	15	10	
McBain, Ed		Author	10	20	30	30	Novelist
McBride, George W.	1854-1911	Congress	5	15			Senator OR
McBride, John	1800-	Military	30	75			Brit. Adm. 1793
McBride, Jon A.		Astronaut	5	15		30	
McBride, Lt. Gen. Horace L.	1894-1962	Military	30				World War II U.S. general
McBride, Mary Margaret	1899-1976	Entertainment	5		25	20	Radio Talk Show Host. 30's-40's. Household Name
McCabe, Nick		Entertainment	6			25	Music. Lead Guitar 'The Verve'
McCaffrey, Anne		Author	5			10	Novelist
McCain, John S. III		Congress	5	30	45	40	Senator AZ, Vietnam war POW
McCain, John S. Jr.	1911-1981	Military	15	35			Admiral
McCain, John Sr.	1884-1945	Military	25	80	125		Vice Admiral WW II
McCall, Davina		Celebrity	10			15	celebrity model
Mccall, George Archibald	1802-1868	Civil War	40	75	120		Union general
McCall, Robert		Artist	25				
McCall, Tom		Governor	5	10		15	Governor OR
McCalla, Irish		Entertainment	10		25	25	Pin-Up SP 35
McCallister, Lon		Entertainment	10			30	
McCallum, David		Entertainment	5	6	15	25	
McCambridge, Mercedes		Entertainment	40			75	
McCampbell, David S.		Aviation	15	25	45	75	ACE, WW II, Top Navy Ace, MOH
McCandless, Bruce II		Astronaut	10		90	24	
McCann, Chuck		Business	5	15	30	10	
McCarey, Leo		Entertainment	35			65	Academy Award Director, Prod.
McCarthy, Andrew		Entertainment	10			20	actor
McCarthy, Arlene		Political	10			15	Member European Parliament
McCarthy, Carolyn M		Congress	10			15	Member U.S. Congress
McCarthy, Eugene J.		Congress	20	35	50	30	Senator MN. Pres. Candidate. '68 'Peace' Candidate
McCarthy, Jenny		Entertainment	6			36	Actress. Pin-Up 65-75
McCarthy, Joseph	1908-1957	Congress	40	110		100	Senator WI. McCarthyism. Notorious Red-Baiter
McCarthy, Karen M		Congress	10			15	Member U.S. Congress
McCarthy, Kevin		Entertainment	10			35	Actor.
McCarthy, Mary		Author	45	135		50	Novelist
McCarthy, Michael W.		Business	3	5	10	5	

NAME	DATE	CATEGORY	SIG	LS/DS	ALS	SP	COMMENTS
McCartin, John Joseph		Political	10			15	Member European Parliament
McCartney, Paul		Entertainment	133	450		517	Beatle. SP Paul & Linda 695
McCaskill, Ian		Celebrity	10			15	weather presenter
McCaulay, Rose, Dame		Br. Author	20			45	
McCausland, John	1836-1927	Civil War	120				Confederate general
McCay, Lt. Gen. Sir Ross Cairns	1895-1969	Military	25				World War II British general
McCay, Peggy		Entertainment	10			35	Actress. Mayberry
McCay, Winsor*		Cartoonists	50			600	Little Nemo
McClain, Gerald		Business	10	20			Pioneer in Assisted Living Development
McClanahan, Rue		Entertainment	10	10		25	
McClaran, John W.	1887-1948	Military	35	125			USN Adm. Round-the-World Bases For 1st Flight
McClellan, George B.	1826-1885	Civil War	175	341	419	863	Union Gen. ALS/Cont.'66 2200. Pres. Candidate
McClellan, George B.(WD)	1826-1885	Civil War	340	436	2189	1682	Union Gen.
McClellan, John L.	1896-1977	Congress	10	20		25	Repr., Senator AR
McClernand, John A. (WD)		Civil War	70	192	217		Union Gen.
McClernand, John A.	1812-1900	Civil War	45	110	140	600	
McClintic, James V.		Senate/Congress	5	10		7	MOC OK
McClintock, Francis L.	1819-1907	Explorer	61	115	127		Br. Adm., Arctic Navigator. Search for Franklin
McClintock, John		Astronaut	5	15		20	
McClinton, Delbert		Country Music	10			25	Singer-Musician. TX Blues Man
McCloskey, John, Cardinal		Clergy	95	125	250	100	
McCloskey, Lee		Entertainment	5	6	15	15	
McClosky, Pete		Senate/Congress	5	10		10	
McClung, J.T.M.		Senate/Congress	5	15		10	
McClure, Doug		Entertainment	5			28	
McClure, Maj. Gen. Robert B.	1896-1973	Military	30				World War II U.S. general
McClure, Samuel S.	1887-1949	Editor	12				Publisher
McClurg, Alexander C.	1832-1901	Civil War	30	55			Union General
McCollum, Betty M		Congress	10			15	Member U.S. Congress
McColpin, Carroll W.		Military	25	45	75	50	ACE WW II, Maj. Gen.
McComb, Henry S., Col.		Business	250	875			A U.P. RR Founder. Esposed Oakes Ames
McComb, William	1828-1918	Civil War	95	235	350		CSA Gen.
McConaughey, Matthew		Entertainment	10			44	Actor.
McConnel, Maj. Gen. Douglas F.	1893-1961	Military	28				World War II British general
McConnell, Calvin D., Bishop		Clergy	20	25	30	30	
McConnell, Francis J., Bishop		Clergy	20	25	50	30	
McConnell, James, Bishop		Clergy	20	25	35	30	
McConnell, Joseph, Jr.		Aviation	75	140	175	150	ACE, Korea, Top Korea Ace
McConnell, Mitch		Senate	10			15	United States Senate (R - KY)
McCoo, Marilyn		Entertainment	5	6	15	15	
McCook, Alex. M	1831-1903	Civil War	38	70	115		Union Gen.
McCook, Alex. M. (WD)	1831-1903	Civil War	45		195		Union Gen.
McCook, Anson	1835-1917	Civil War	30	55			Union Gen., MOC
McCook, Daniel Jr	1834-1864	Civil War	95				Union general
McCook, Edward Moody	1833-1909	Civil War	45	75	120		Union general

NAME	DATE	CATEGORY	SIG	LS/DS	ALS	SP	COMMENTS
McCook, Henry C.		Clergy	10	10	15		
McCook, Robert Latimer	1827-1862	Civil War	110	190	270		Union general
McCool, William		Astronaut	5			20	
McCormack, Eric		Entertainment	10			45	Will and Grace
McCormack, John W.		Congress	10	38	40	30	Speaker of the House
McCormack, John	1884-1945	Entertainment	60	105	220	170	Famed Irish Tenor. Opera & Popular Ballads
McCormack, Patty		Entertainment	5	8	15	15	
McCormic, Mary		Entertainment	20				Opera
McCormick, Anne O'Hare		Author	30	45	60	50	1st Pulitzer Woman Journalist
McCormick, Catherine		Entertainment	10			20	actress
McCormick, Cyrus H.	1809-1884	Science-Business	275	694	1888		Invented & Mfg. the Reaper. ALS/Content 4200
McCormick, Eric		Entertainment				35	Actor
McCormick, Maureen		Entertainment	10			20	actress
McCormick, Myron		Entertainment	15	25	45	40	
McCormick, Nettie Fowler		Business	25		90		Mrs. Cyrus McCormick
McCormick, Robert R., Col.		Business	35	140	165	60	Editor Chicago Tribune
McCorvey, Norma		Celebrity		150			A.K.A. Jane Roe (Roe vs Wade)
McCotter, Thaddeus G. M		Congress	10			15	Member U.S. Congress
McCown, John Porter (WD)		Civil War	245	1095			CSA Gen.
McCown, John Porter	1815-1879	Civil War	110	362			CSA Gen.
McCoy, Charles B.		Business	25		85	40	Pres. DuPont Co.
McCoy, Clyde		Entertainment	6	8	15	15	
McCoy, Frank		Military		25	50		Am. WW I Gen.
McCoy, Sylvester		Entertainment	10			20	Actor
McCoy, Tim		Entertainment	50			202	'Col'. Am. Cowboy Star. Innumerable Westerns
McCoy, Wilson*		Cartoonist	15			75	Phantom
McCracken, Paul		Celebrity	10			15	financial expert
McCrea, Joel		Entertainment	15	30		40	
McCready, Jack		Author	8			12	hunting and game preparation
McCready, Mike		Entertainment	6			25	Music. Guitarist 'Pearl Jam'
McCree, Laura		Celebrity	10			15	home/gardening expert
McCreery, Lt. Gen. Sir Richard L.	1898-1967	Military	25				World War II British general
McCreery, Richard L., Sir		Military	30	75		40	Br. Gen. WW II/Montgomery. 8th Army
McCrery, Jim M		Congress	10			15	Member U.S. Congress
McCuaig, Maj. Gen. George Eric	1885-1958	Military	20				World War II Canadian general
McCudden, James T.B.		Aviation	135	225	350	300	ACE, WW I, RAF
McCullers, Carson	1917-1967	Author	60	110	180	125	Am. Novelist. 'Heart is a Lonely Hunter'
McCulley, Michael J.		Astronaut	5			15	
McCulloch, Ben	1811-1862	Civil War	155	470	1202		CSA Gen. Morman War LS 2300
McCulloch, Henry E.	1816-1895	Civil War	145	350			CSA General
McCulloch, Hugh	1808-1895	Cabinet	45	95	135		Lincoln, Johnson, Arthur Sec'y Treas.
McCulloch, Maj Gen Sir Andrew J.	1876-1960	Military	25				World War II British general
McCullough, Colleen		Author	35	45	60	60	Austr. Novelist. Thorn Birds
McCullough, David		Author	8			12	private school history
McCullough, John	1832-1885	Entertainment	10			35	Vintage Stage Actor

NAME	DATE	CATEGORY	SIG	LS/DS	ALS	SP	COMMENTS
McCullough, Julie		Entertainment	7			27	Playboy Playmate
Mccurry, Mike		Celebrity	10			15	political celebrity
McCutcheon, George Barr	1866-1928	Author	10				
McCutcheon, John T.*	1870-1949	Cartoonist				30	Pulitzer, Political Cartoonist, Chicago Tribune
McCutcheon, Martine		Entertainment	10			20	Actress
McDaniel, Hattie	1895-1952	Entertainment	591	1500	2100	2250	AA 'Gone With the Wind'.
McDermont, Galt		Composer	10			25	'Hair'. 'Good Morning Sunshine' AMusQS 95
McDermott, Dylan		Entertainment	20			40	Actor.
McDermott, Jim M		Congress	10			15	Member U.S. Congress
McDevitt, Ruth		Entertainment	10			20	
McDivitt, James A.		Astronaut	30	96		40	Gemini 4 & Apollo 9 Astro.
McDonal, Michael		Entertainment	5			32	Singer. Lead Singer for Doobie Bros.
McDonald, A. J. (Al)		Astronaut	20			30	NASA Whistleblower
McDonald, Christopher		Entertainment	10			20	actor
McDonald, M. Nick		Celebrity	20	88		120	Police officer who captured Lee Harvey Oswald
McDonald, Marie		Entertainment	35	45	90	85	
McDonald, Richard J.		Business	92	260	450	225	MacDonald's, TLS/cont 1000-1500
McDonald, Skeets		Country Music	10			20	
McDonnell, James S.		Business	20	45	95	35	Founder, McDonnell Aircraft
McDonnell, Mary		Entertainment	20			50	
McDonough, John		Entertainment	10			20	actor
McDormand, Frances		Entertainment	10			20	actress
McDougall, Alexander		Revolutionary War	90	200	415		Gen. Cont. Army,Cont. Congress
McDowell, Andre		Entertainment	5			30	
McDowell, Irvin (WD)		Civil War	120	235	525	1250	Union Gen.Special DS 400
McDowell, Irvin	1818-1885	Civil War	62	165	271	977	Union Gen. Mexican War
McDowell, Malcolm		Entertainment	10			38	Br. Actor. US & Eng. Remember 'Clockwork Orange'
McDowell, Roddy	1928-1998	Entertainment	22		40	38	Talented Child and Mid-Life Actor & Photographer
McDuffie, George	1790-1851	Congress	15				Sen. & Repr. SC
McElmurry, Thomas		Astronaut	5			20	
McElroy, Neil H.		Cabinet	15	35		25	Sec'y Defense. Pres. P & G
McEnery, S.D.	1837-1910	Congress	12	25			Governor LA and Senator
McEntire, Reba		Country Music	15			30	
McEntyre, Joe (New Kids)		Entertainment	10			45	
McEwen, Mark		Entertainment	10			20	actor
McFadden, Bernar	1868-1955	Publisher-Physician	20	50			Eccentric Pulisher 'Physical Culture'-'True Story'
McFadden, Gates		Entertainment	5			15	Star Trek
McFadden, Obadiah B.		Senate/Congress	15	30	40		MOC WA 1873
McFaddon, Steve		Entertainment	10			20	Actor
McFarland, Spanky		Entertainment	28	45		52	Little Rascals Lobby Card S 195
McFarlane, Seth		Entertainment	4			22	'Family Guy' Creator/Voice
McFerrin, Bobby	1950-	Entertainment	10			23	Singer 'Don't Worry, Be Happy'. 4 Grammys
McGann, Paul		Entertainment	10			20	Actor
McGarru. William D.		Aviation	15	30	45	40	ACE, WW II, Flying Tigers
McGavin, Darren		Entertainment	15			37	

NAME	DATE	CATEGORY	SIG	LS/DS	ALS	SP	COMMENTS
McGee, Don		Aviation	25				WWII Am. Ace
McGee, Gale		Senate/Congress	5	15		10	Senator WY
McGill, John		Clergy	90		450		CW Bishop of Richmond
McGillis, Kelly		Entertainment	10		20	30	
McGinley, Phyllis		Author	10	30	45	20	Am Poet. Pulitzer
McGinnis, George Francis	1826-1910	Civil War	40	75	125		Union general
McGoohan, Patrick		Entertainment	20			45	
McGovern, Elizabeth		Entertainment	5			20	
McGovern, George		Senate	10	45		25	Senator SD, Pres. Hopeful
McGovern, James P. M		Congress	10			15	Member U.S. Congress
McGovern, John		Author	25	40			
McGowan, Alistair		Celebrity	10			15	impressionist
McGowan, Rose		Entertainment	7			40	Actress. Films. Pin-Up 70
McGowan, Samuel	1819-1897	Civil War	110		225		Confederate general
McGranery, James P.		Cabinet	10	15	25		Att'y General
McGrath, J. Howard		Cabinet	5	20	35	15	Att'y General
McGrath, Kathleen Capt.		Military				25	First US woman to command a warship
McGrath, Rory		Celebrity	10			15	comedian
McGraw, Phil Dr.		Celebrity				20	'Dr. Phil'
McGraw, Tim		Country Music	19			60	Singer
McGregor, Ewan		Entertainment	8			55	Actor. Films
McGuffy, William H.		Educator	95	475			McGuffy's Reader
McGugin, Harold C.	1893-1946	Congress	10	25			Repr. KS
McGuigan, James, Cardinal		Clergy	5	10	15	12	
McGuinn, Roger		Entertainment	10			40	'Byrds' Co-Founder
McGuire Sisters		Entertainment	60				Singing Group
McGuire, Barry		Entertainment	5	6		25	New Christy Minstrels
McGuire, Dorothy		Entertainment	15			30	
McGuire, Phyllis		Entertainment	4	15		10	McGuire Sisters
McGuire, Sean		Entertainment	10			20	Actor
McGuire, Thomas B.		Aviation	150	300	650	450	ACE, WW II, #2 U.S. Ace
McHenry, James	1753-1816	Cabinet-Military	202	327	629		Signer Constitution, Sec'y War. Sr. Surgeon
McHugh, Frank		Entertainment	20	25	65	60	
McHugh, Jimmy	1894-1969	Composer	25	75			
McHugh, John M.		Congress	10			15	Member U.S. Congress
McHugh, Joseph		Artist	5			10	
McIlvaine, Abraham R.	1804-1863	Congress	10				Repr. PA, Whig Presidential Elector
McInnis, Scott M		Congress	10			15	Member U.S. Congress
McIntire, John		Entertainment	20			50	
McIntosh, James McQueen	1828-1862	Civil War	275				Confederate general
McIntosh, John Baillie	1829-1888	Civil War	40	75	110		Union general
McIntosh, Lachlan	1725-1806	Revolutionary War	550	887	1375		Killed Button Gwinnett in Duel
McIntyre, Frank		Military	75	140			Am. WW I Gen.
McIntyre, James F., Archbishop		Clergy	40	65	75	60	
McIntyre, Marvin H.		Cabinet	3	10	15		Sec'y to FDR

NAME	DATE	CATEGORY	SIG	LS/DS	ALS	SP	COMMENTS
McIntyre, Mike M		Congress	10			15	Member U.S. Congress
McIntyre, O.O.		Author	15	25	40	20	Journalist, Synd. Columnist
McKay, Douglas	1893-1959	Cabinet	15	25		20	Governor OR, Sec'y Interior
McKay, Gardner		Entertainment	6	8	15	20	
McKay, Harry		Celebrity	10			15	motivational speaker
McKay, Jim		Celebrity	10			15	media/TV personality
McKay, Kelli		Entertainment	15			30	Miss USA 1991
McKean, Micheal		Entertainment	15			25	actor
McKean, Thomas Jefferson	1810-1870	Civil War	40	70	120		Union general
McKean, Thomas	1734-1817	Revolutionary War	225	458	2150		Signer. ADS 1778 2250
McKee, Thomas H.		Senate/Congress	10	20			
McKeen, Charles 'Chuck'		Author	8			12	sports autographs
McKeever, Chauncey (WD)	1829-1901	Civil War	45		175		Union Gen.
McKeldin, Theodore R.		Governor	5	17		10	Governor MD
McKellar, Kenneth D.	1869-1957	Congress	10	30			Senator TN
McKellen, Ian		Entertainment	12			45	Actor
McKenna, Gail		Celebrity	10			15	television presenter
McKenna, Joseph		Supreme Court	35	50	80	40	Att'y General
McKenna, Patricia		Political	10			15	Member European Parliament
McKenna, Siobhan		Entertainment	15			35	
McKenzie, Fay		Entertainment	5		15	15	
McKenzie, Jacqueline		Entertainment	3			8	
McKeon, Howard P. "Buck" M.		Congress	10			15	Member U.S. Congress
McKeon, Nancy		Entertainment	4	6		30	
McKeon, Phillip		Entertainment	5			20	
McKern, Leo		Entertainment	15			40	Rumpole
McKevitt, Anne		Celebrity	10			15	Designer
McKinley, Ida S.		First Lady	325	625	975	850	
McKinley, Ray		Entertainment	20			65	Bandleader, Drummer
McKinley, William (As Pres.)		President	337	650	2360	868	White House Card S 425-750
McKinley, William		Civil War/President		2500			
McKinley, William	1843-1901	President	204	425	850	583	Assassinated by Anarchist
McKinly, John		Revolutionary War	65	180			First Gov. DE, Captured by Br.
McKinstry, Justus	1814-1897	Civil War	56	75	105		Union general
McKnight, Kauffer E.	1890-1954	Artist	60		425		Br. Known For Book Illustrations, Poster Designs
McKone, John R.		Military	10	20	40	30	
McKuen, Rod		Author	20	25	35	50	Poet
McLachlan, Sarah		Entertainment	12			45	Actress.
McLaglin, Andrew V.		Entertainment	10		25		
McLaglin, Victor	1886-1959	Entertainment	165			335	AA 'The Informer'
McLain, Raymond S.	1890-1954	Military	30			45	Gen. WW II
McLains, The		Country Music	20			45	
McLane, Louis	1786-1857	Business	40	85	120		Jackson Sec'y Treasury
McLane, Robert		Diplomat-Gov.	35	80	135		Gov. MD, U.S. Minister to Jap.
McLaughlin, E.A.		Business	10	35	45	20	

NAME	DATE	CATEGORY	SIG	LS/DS	ALS	SP	COMMENTS
McLaughlin, James C.		Senate/Congress	10	15		15	MOC MI
McLaughlin, Kyle		Entertainment	20			75	
McLaughlin, Linda Murray		Author	8			12	religion
McLaws, Lafayette	1821-1897	Civil War	165	347	637		CSA Gen. Sig/Rank 290
McLean, Andrea		Celebrity	10			15	television presenter
McLean, Don		Entertainment	20			50	Rock
McLean, George P.		Senate	10	15	25		Gov., Senator CT
McLean, John	1785-1861	Supreme Court	55	200	285		Dissented Dred Scott Opinion
McLean, Lt. Gen. Sir Kenneth G.	1896-1987	Military	25				World War II British general
McLean, Nathaniel C.	1815-1905	Civil War	45	70	120		Union General
McLeod, Archibald Norman		Fur Trader		2500			Hudson's Bay Co. vs NW Co.
McLeod, Catherine	1921-	Entertainment	8	15	20	20	Actress. Films from 40's
McLeod, John Angus		Author	8			12	religious historian
McLeod, Lt. Gen. Sir Donald K.	1885-1958	Military	25				World War II British general
McLintock, Francis Sir		Celebrities	10	30	75		
McLuhan, Marshall		Author		37			
McMahon, Brien	1903-1952	Congress	10	40		15	Senator CT
McMahon, Ed		Entertainment	5			15	
McMahon, Horace		Entertainment	20			50	
McMahon, Martin T.	1838-1906	Civil War			175		Union general
McManus, George*		Cartoonist	50			247	'Bringing Up Father', Panel 1,500
McMichael, Morton		Journalist	45	95			1st Editor Saturday Evening Post
McMicking, Maj. Gen. Neil	1894-1953	Military	28				World War II British general
McMillan, Edwin M.		Science	20	35	69	30	Nobel Chemistry 1952
McMillan, James Winning	1825-1903	Civil War	40	75	110		Union General
McMillan, James	1838-1902	Congress	12	20	35		Senator MI 1889
McMillan, Kenneth		Entertainment	5	6	15	15	
McMillan, Terry		Entertainment	3	4	10	8	
McMillan-Scott, Edward H.C.		Political	10			15	Member European Parliament
McMillen, William L.		Civil War			65		US Commander
McMonagle, Donald		Astronaut	4			20	
McMorris, Charles H. Adm.		Military	10			35	WWII Naval Commander
McMullen, Clements	1892-	Military	50	150			WWI Aviator, WW II General
McMullen, Maj. Gen. Donald Jay	1891-1967	Military	25				World War II British general
McMullen, Richard C.		Governor	5	10			Governor DE
McNabb, Brigadier Colin V.O.	d. 1943	Military	25				World War II British general
McNair, Brigadier John Kirkland	1893-1973	Military	25				World War II British general
McNair, Evander	1820-1902	Civil War	115				Confederate general
McNair, General Lesley J.	1883-1944	Military	30				World War II U.S. general
McNair, Leslie J.		Military	35	95	165	80	WWI, General, WW II KIA
McNair, Robert		Governor	5	15		10	Governor SC
McNair, Ronald E.	1950-1986	Astronaut	75	130		262	Died in Challenger Crash
McNally, Eryl Margaret		Political	10			15	Member European Parliament
McNally, Stephen		Entertainment	10			20	
McNally, W.		Entertainment	5	6	15	15	

NAME	DATE	CATEGORY	SIG	LS/DS	ALS	SP	COMMENTS
McNamara, Robert S.		Cabinet	15	35		40	Sec'y Defense, Pres. World Bank
McNamara, William		Entertainment	5	8	25	25	
McNamee, Graham		Entertainment	20				Legendary Sports Announcer
McNarney, Joseph T.		Military	20	50			General WW II
McNary, Charles L.	1874-1944	Congress	15	35			Senator OR. McNary Dam
McNaughton, Kenneth		Military	4	9	15	10	
McNaughton, Lt. Gen. Andr. G. L.	1887-1966	Military	20				World War II Canadian general
McNear, Howard	d. 1969	Entertainment	20			35	Actor, Floyd the Barber on Andy Griffith Show
McNee, Patrick		Entertainment	10			25	
McNeil, Claudia		Entertainment	3			8	Actress
McNeil, John	1813-1891	Civil War	35	70	110		Union general, TLS/cont 668
McNeil, Robert		Entertainment	5			30	Star Trek
McNeill, Don	1907-1996	Entertainment	15	15	25	25	Radio-TV. Hosted 'Don McNeill's Breakfast Club'
McNichol, Kristy		Entertainment	10			20	Pin-Up SP 35
McNulty, Michael R. M		Congress	10			15	Member U.S. Congress
McNutt, Paul V.		Governor	15	30			Governor IN
McPartland, Jimmy		Entertainment	30	55		85	Jazz Trumpet
McPate, Randolph R.		Military	30			95	Commandant of U.S. Marine Corps
McPhatter, Clyde		Entertainment	400		800		Classic Rocker
McPherson, Aimee Semple		Clergy	198	392	495	350	
McPherson, Craig		Artists					
McPherson, Elle		Entertainment	22			60	Model-Actress
McPherson, Isaac V.		Senate/Congress	5	15			MOC MO
McPherson, James B. (WD)		Civil War	425	1100	2810		Union General KIA 1864
McPherson, James Birdseye	1828-1864	Civil War	309	610		1955	Union general, KIA 1864
McPherson, John R.	1833-1897	Congress	12	20	30		Senator NJ
McPherson, William		Author	15		70		Critic & Author. Pulitzer 1977 for Journalism
McQuade, James (WD)		Civil War	45	85			Union Gen.
McQuade, James	1829-1885	Civil War	25	70	178		Union General
McQueen, Butterfly	1911-1995	Entertainment	55	88		67	SP as Prissy 'GWTW' 125, SP 2'x4' 75
McQueen, Steve	1930-1980	Entertainment	167	362	400	333	
McRae, Dandridge	1829-1899	Civil War	100	210			Confederate general
McRae, William	1834-1882	Civil War	120	188			Confederate general
McRaney, Gerald		Entertainment	5			25	
McReynolds, James C.	1862-1946	Supreme Court	35	125	145	100	Wilson Att'y Gen. Justice 1914-41
McShane, Ian		Entertainment	9	10	20	25	
McShane, Mike		Celebrity	10			15	comedian
McShann, Jay		Entertainment	50			125	Jazz Pianist, Vocalist, Bandlead
McSheehy, Maj. Gen. Oswald Wm	1884-1975	Military	25				World War II British general
McWade, John		Entertainment	10				Character Actor
McWethy, John		Entertainment	4			20	ABC News
McWhorter, Hamilton		Aviation	12	25	45	35	ACE, WW II
McWilliams, Caroline		Entertainment	4	6	9	9	
Mead, Margaret	1901-1978	Science	70	125	170	225	Anthropologist, Lecturer, Author
Meade, Carl J.		Astronaut	5			22	

NAME	DATE	CATEGORY	SIG	LS/DS	ALS	SP	COMMENTS
Meade, George G. (WD)	1815-1872	Civil War	415	750	1250	2500	Union Gen. DS 1750
Meade, George G.	1815-1872	Civil War	250	422	625	1207	Union Gen. Special ALS Re. Officer's Service 1900
Meadowlarks		Entertainment	3			6	
Meadows, Audrey		Entertainment	15			30	actress
Meadows, Jayne		Entertainment	5			15	
Meagher, Thomas F. (WD)		Civil War	240	500	685		Union Gen.
Meagher, Thomas F.	1823-1867	Civil War	65	180	325		Union Gen.
Meaney, Colm		Entertainment	15			30	Star Trek
Means, Abigail		First Lady	125		1250		'Aunt Abby'. Surrogate First Lady for Pierce
Means, Russell		Entertainment	10			20	actor
Meany, George		Labor Leader	25	68		90	Pres. AFL-CIO
Meara, Anne		Entertainment	4	4		15	
Mears, Otto		History		85			Pathfinder of the San Juan
Meat Loaf		Entertainment	5		25	45	Rock
Mecham, Edwin L.		Senate	5	15		12	Governor, Senator NM
Medawar, Peter B., Sir		Science	20	30	60	25	Nobel Medicine 1960
Meddick, Jim*		Cartoonist	5			35	Illustrator of 'Robotman'
Medeiros, Humberto, Cardinal		Clergy	35	50	60	50	
Medici, Cosimo I, de	1519-1574	Royalty	375	1320			The Great. Duke of Florence
Medici, Fernando de	1549-1609	Royalty	370	1250	3125		Son of Cosimo I. Gr. Duke
Medici, Giovanni Gastone de	1671-1737	Royalty		375	525		Grand Duke of Tuscany
Medici, Leopoldo de, Cardinal		Clergy	300	385	550		Cardinal. Son of Cosimo II
Medicis, Catherine de	1519-1589	Royalty	270	800	2500		Queen of Henry II of France
Medicis, Francesco de		Royalty	100	200	500		
Medicis, Marie de	1573-1642	Royalty	350	728	2500		Queen of Henry IV (Fr)
Medill, Joseph	1823-1899	Journalist	125		250		A founder Repub. Party
Medill, William	1802-1865	Congress	12				Repr. OH, Gov. OH
Medina, Harold R.		Jurist	10	25		15	
Medina, Patricia		Entertainment	5	5		25	Brit. Actress
Medjugorje (Jugo) Children of		Religious	300				2 Who Saw Vision Virgin Mary
Medley, Bill		Country Music	6			20	
Meehan, Martin T. M		Congress	10			15	Member U.S. Congress
Meek, Kendrick B. M		Congress	10			15	Member U.S. Congress
Meeker, Ralph		Entertainment	25			40	
Meeks, Frank		Celebrity	10			15	motivational speaker
Meeks, Gregory W. M		Congress	10			15	Member U.S. Congress
Meen, Sally		Celebrity	10			15	weather presenter
Meese, Edwin III	1931-	Cabinet	10	35	35	32	Att'y General Reagan. Resigned abruptly
Meg, Mystic		Celebrity	10			15	Astrologer
Meganck, Glenn		Author	8			12	juvenile adventures
Mehta, Zubin		Conductor	12			50	International Conductor
Meier, Waltraud		Entertainment	15			35	Opera
Mei-Figner, Medea	1859-1952	Entertainment				1200	Opera. It.-Russian Mezzo-Soprano
Meighan, James		Entertainment				20	Radio Actor. The Falcon
Meighan, Tom		Entertainment	35			85	

NAME	DATE	CATEGORY	SIG	LS/DS	ALS	SP	COMMENTS
Meigs, Montgomery C.	1816-1892	Civil War	47	85	142	350	Union Quartermaster General
Meigs, Montgomery C.(WD)	1816-1892	Civil War	60	175	328		Union Gen., ALS/cont 2500
Meigs, Return J., Jr.	1764-1824	Military-Cabinet	80	205	360		Monroe P.M. General
Meijer, Erik		Political	10			15	Member European Parliament
Meiklejohn, G.D.		Cabinet	15	40			Ass't Sec'y War
Meinl, Tanaka		Entertainment	30			75	Opera
Meir, Golda	1898-1979	Head of State	114	273	600	207	TLS/Content1500-2500. FDC S 125
Meissonier, Ernst	1815-1891	Celebrity			50		German film producer
Meitner, Lise	1878-1968	Science	95			160	Austrian Physicist Uranium Fission Fermi Award
Melachrino, George		Bandleader	14				Arranger
Melasky, Maj. Gen. Harris M.	1893-1972	Military	30				World War II U.S. general
Melba, Nellie, Dame	1859-1931	Entertainment	70	135	200	307	Australian Operatic Soprano
Melbourne, Wm. Lamb, Lord	1779-1848	Head of State	70	85	138		Q. Victoria's1st Prime Minister
Melchior, Lauritz	1890-1973	Entertainment	65	100		184	Opera Danish Tenor. Wagnerian Roles at Met.
Melis, Carmen		Entertainment	35			85	Opera, Teacher
Mellencamp, John		Entertainment	35			56	Rock. Album Cover S 60-80
Mellnik, Steve		Military	5	25	35		
Mellon, Andrew W.	1855-1937	Business	150	260	450	450	Pitts. Millionaire Tycoon. Sec'y Treas. Financier
Mellor, Will		Entertainment	10			20	Actor
Melman, Yossi		Celebrity	10			15	media/TV personality
Melnick, Bruce E.		Astronaut	5			16	
Melohn, Tom		Celebrity	10			15	financial expert
Melton, James		Entertainment	10			55	Am.C oncert, Radio & Opera Tenor
Melvey, Justin		Celebrity	10			15	model
Melvill, Thomas	1751-1832	Revolutionary War	88	262	550		Memb. Boston Tea Party
Melville, George W.	1814-1912	Military	40	105	170		Admiral, Arctic Explorer
Melville, Herman	1819-1891	Author	3450	5000	12000		ALS's/Content 20,000-95,000
Melvin L. Watt		Senate	10			15	Member U.S. Congress
Memminger, Chris.G. (WD)	1803-1888	Civil War	178	456	817		CSA Sec'y of Treasury
Mencken, Henry L.	1880-1956	Author	102	250	365	450	Satirist, Editor, Essayist, Critic, Journalist
Mendel, Gregor Johann	1822-1884	Science	400	850	2000		Laws of Biological Inheritance
Mendeleyev, Dmitry	1834-1907	Science			1650		Rus. Chem. Developed Periodic Table
Mendelssohn, Felix	1809-1847			690	1840		
Mendelssohn-Bartholdy, F.	1809-1847	Composer	600	1098	3134		ALS/Content 6,500
Mendes, Abraham Caulle		Author	15	35	100		Fr. Poet. Plays, Verses, Libretti
Mendez, Arnaldo Tamayo		Astronaut	6			15	
Mendiluce Pereiro, José María		Political	10			15	Member European Parliament
Menéndez Del Valle, Emilio		Political	10			15	Member European Parliament
Menendez, Lyle		Criminal	50	175			Convicted Murderer of Parents. S Chk. 150
Menendez, Robert M		Congress	10			15	Member U.S. Congress
Mengelberg, Willem	1871-1951	Entertainment	75			210	Dutch Conductor. AMusQS 250
Mengele, Josef	1911-?	Science	3695				Auschwitz Dr. Experimented on Inmates. WW II
Menjou, Adolphe	1890-1963	Entertainment	25	45		68	Dapper, Well-dressed Film Actor. 20's into 40's
Menk, Louis W.		Business	5			10	CEO International Harvester
Menken, Helen	1902-1966	Entertainment	22	25	30	30	Stage Star & Occasional Films. Bogart's 1st Wife

NAME	DATE	CATEGORY	SIG	LS/DS	ALS	SP	COMMENTS
Menkes, Sara		Entertainment	20			55	Opera
Mennea, Pietro-paolo		Political	10			15	Member European Parliament
Mennin, Peter		Composer	10		65		AMusQS 75
Menninger, Karl	1893-1980	Science	35	66	120	75	Menninger Clinic & Foundation
Menninger, Roy		Science	10	25	55	30	
Menninger, William C., Dr.		Science	15	45	82	35	Psychiatrist, Pres. Foundation
Mennitti, Domenico		Political	10			15	Member European Parliament
Menon, V. Krisna		Diplomat	20		25		Ambassador Gr. Britain
Menotti, Gian Carlo	1911-	Composer	80	160	210	250	It.-Am. Composer
Menrad, Winfried		Political	10			15	Member European Parliament
Menuhin, Yehudi	1916-1999	Entertainment	40	78		222	Concert Violinist, Conductor, Child Prodigy
Menzies, Maj. Gen. Sir Stewart G.	1890-1968	Military	25				World War II British general
Menzies, Robert, Sir	1894-1978	Head of State	25	55	80	50	Australian Prime Minister
Meo, Sean		Celebrity	10			15	comedian
Merbold, Ulf		Astronaut	10	25		25	
Mercadante, Saverio	1795-1870	Composer	138		282		Dir. Royal Conservatory, Naples
Mercer, Archibald		Revolutionary War					Patriot. Cont. ALS 750
Mercer, Frances		Entertainment	5	8		15	
Mercer, Hugh W.	1808-1877	Civil War	90	111			CSA General. War Date Sig. 195
Mercer, Ian		Entertainment	10			20	Actor
Mercer, John Francis	1759-1821	Revolutionary War	70		125		Aide-de-Camp Gen Lee
Mercer, Johnny	1909-1976	Composer	40	75		135	Vocalist, Pianist
Mercer, Mabel		Entertainer	25			50	Jazz Singer
Mercer, Marian		Entertainment	10			35	
Merchant, Natalie		Entertainment	8			58	Music
Mercier, D. Joseph, Cardinal		Clergy	35	45	75		
Mercouri, Melina		Entertainment	25	30	45	65	
Mercury (4 Astronauts)		Astronaut					Schirra, Glenn, Slayton, Shepard S Phil. Cover 1050
Mercury (6 Astronauts)		Astronaut		1300		948	No Virgil Grissom. FDC 900
Mercury (7 Astronauts)		Astronaut				3579	All 7 Sigs
Mercury, Freddie	1946-1991	Entertainment	115			184	Lead singer Queen
Meredith, Burgess		Entertainment	10	32	35	48	Stage Actor before Films
Meredith, Edwin T.		Cabinet	5	20	30	15	Sec'y Agriculture 1920
Meredith, James H.		Activist	35	90	185	60	Afro-Am. Activist
Meredith, Samuel	1740-1817	Cabinet	90	300	370		Rev. War Gen., 1st US Treasurer. Financier, Patriot
Meredith, Solomon	1810-1875	Civil War	161		450		Union Gen. Iron Brig. of West
Meredith, Sullivan Amory	1816-1874	Civil War	45	75	110		Union general
Meriam, Ebenezer		Science			225		Meteorologist
Merivale, Philip		Entertainment	7		25	25	Vintage Br. Actor
Meriwether, Lee		Entertainment	5	10	12	35	
Merkel, Una		Entertainment	10			30	
Merli, Francesco		Entertainment	25			75	Opera. Dramatic Tenor
Merli, Gino J.		Military	5	25		22	WWII Hero CMH
Merlin, Philippe-Antoine	1754-1838	Fr. Revolution	60	140	250		Revolutionary. Min. of Justice
Merman, Ethel	1909-1984	Entertainment	30			78	Broadway Musical Star Before Movies

NAME	DATE	CATEGORY	SIG	LS/DS	ALS	SP	COMMENTS
Merriam, Frank F.		Governor	5	15		10	Governor CA
Merrick, David		Entertainment	20	30	70	60	Theatrical Producer
Merrick, Samuel Vaughan		Business	40	175			Financier
Merrill, Aaron, Adm.		Military	10			38	WWII Solomon Islands
Merrill, Dina		Entertainment	6	8	15	15	
Merrill, Frank D.	1903-1955	Military	150	250	325		Gen. WWII. Merrill's Marauders
Merrill, Gary	1914-1990	Entertainment	15	20	45	35	
Merrill, Henry T.		Aviation	30	45	100	100	
Merrill, Lewis	1834-1896	Civil War	30	65			Union General
Merrill, Richard 'Dick'		Aviation	30	55	105	75	
Merrill, Robert		Entertainment	22			50	Metropolitan Opera Co. Baritone
Merrill, Stuart		Author	30		125		Am. Poet. Wrote in French
Merriman, Nan	1920-	Entertainment	20			75	Opera. U.S. Mezzo-Sop.
Merrimon, Augustus S.	1830-1892	Congress	22	35			Senator NC
Merritt, Chris		Entertainment	10			30	Opera
Merritt, Wesley	1834-1910	Civil War	60	110	160		Union Gen., Indian Fighter
Merton, Paul		Celebrity	10			15	comedian
Merton, Thomas	1915-1968	Clergy	250	550			Priest-Writer, Poet
Mesmer, Franz Anton, Dr.	1734-1815	Science	115	285	535		Ger. Dr., 'Mesmerise', DS/cont 3750
Messenger, Melinda		Celebrity	10			15	celebrity model
Messerschmitt, Wilhelm	1898-1978	Aviation	144	275		395	Ger. Aircraft Designer-Mfg. 'Messerschmitt'
Messervy, Gen. Sir Frank Walter	1893-1974	Military	28				World War II British general
Messiaen, Olivier	1908-1990	Composer	70	200			Fr. Organist. AMusQS 475-1350
Messick, Dale*		Cartoonist	25			105	Brenda Starr, signed drawing 30
Messick, Don	1921-1997	Entertainment	15		30	45	Cartoon Voice of 'Scoobie Doo', 'Boo Boo Bear' etc.
Messing, Debra		Entertainment				45	Actress, Will and Grace
Messmer, Otto*		Cartoonist	55			400	Felix The Cat
Messner, Reinhold		Political	10			15	Member European Parliament
Mesta, Perle		Business	25	30	70	35	Washington Hostess
Metallica (4)		Entertainment				120	Rock. 'Metallica' CD Jacket S 85
Metcalf, Laurie		Entertainment	15			32	Actress. Roseanne
Metcalf, Victor H.	1853-1936	Cabinet	20	55	95		Sec'y Navy, Commerce, Labor
Metcalfe, Ralph H.		Senate/Congress	5	15		22	MOC IL
Metchnikoff, Elie	1845-1916	Science	60	150		250	Nobel Physiology 1908
Metternich, Clemens von, Prince		Head of State	50	110	140		Austrian Statesman
Metzenbaum, Howard		Senate	10			20	Senator OH
Metzer, Joe		Artist	10				Illustrator. Origianal Sm. Sketch 45
Meusel, Lucille		Entertainment	10			25	Soprano
Mewman, Larry		Aviation	25			75	
Meyer, Albert G., Cardinal		Clergy	35	40	50	40	
Meyer, E. C.		Military	6	10	30	20	
Meyer, George von L.		Cabinet	15	20	35	20	P.M. General 1907
Meyer, John C.		Aviation	35			195	Fighter Ace of WW II
Meyer, Joseph	1894-	Composer	75		225		'Calif. Here I Come', 'If You Knew Susiea.'
Meyer, Steve		Author	8			12	Civil War history

NAME	DATE	CATEGORY	SIG	LS/DS	ALS	SP	COMMENTS
Meyerbeer, Giacomo	1791-1864	Composer	170	255	438	300	Ger. Composer of Fr. Operas, AMusQ 750
Meyerhold, Vsevolod	1874-1940	Celebrity		483			Communist stage director
Meynell, Alice Christiana	1847-1922	Author					Poet, essayist, journalist. Autogr. Poem 160
Mfume, Kweisi		Congress	10			40	Head of NAACP
Miano, Robert		Entertainment	10			20	actor
Miaskovsky, Nikolai	1881-1950	Composer	125				27 Symphonies
Mica, John L. M		Congress	10			15	Member U.S. Congress
Michael, George		Entertainment	20	30	95	100	
Michaelmore, Maj. Gen. Godwin	1894-1982	Military	25				World War II British general
Michaels, Barbara		Author	5		25	15	
Michaels, Bret		Entertainment	10	20	50	45	
Michaels, Dolores		Entertaiment	10				Actress
Michaels, Lorne		Celebrity	10			20	Saturday Night Live
Michaels, Lorraine		Playboy Model	4			8	Pin-Up SP 10
Michaels, Marilyn		Entertainment	5		25	20	
Michael-Vincent, Jan		Entertainment	10			20	actor
Michaud, Michael H. M		Congress	10			15	Member U.S. Congress
Michel, Frank Curtis		Astronaut	5			15	
Michele, Denise		Entertainment	3	3		8	
Michelet, Jules	1798-1874	Author	30		77		Great Historian of Romantic School
Michelson, Albert A.	1852-1931	Science	120		450		Nobel Physics 1907
Michelson, Charles		Political	12	15			Speech Writer New Deal
Michener, James A.	1907-1998	Author	60	110	160	175	Am. Novelist. Pulitzer
Middleton, Arthur	1742-1787	Revolutionary War	2000	6900	15000		Signer Decl. of Indepen.
Middleton, Charles		Entertainment	75			250	
Middleton, Charles, Sir	1726-1813	Military					Issued Orders for Victory at Trafalgar
Middleton, Henry	1717-1784	Revolutionary War	3000	4500			Pres. of Congress. Special DS 9500
Middleton, Robert		Entertainment	50			150	
Middleton, Thomas Fanshaw		Clergy	30	50	80		
Middleton, Troy H.	1889-1976	Military	40	125		75	American WWII General
Middleton, Velma		Entertainment	30			70	Jazz Vocalist
Middleton, Walter T.		Author	10			15	World War II / Cherokee history
Midler, Bette		Entertainment	18			48	Singer-Actress
Midnight Cowboy (cast)		Entertainment				75	Hoffman and Voight
Midori		Entertainment	15			50	
Mielziner, Jo		Entertainment	15		40	35	Film Director
Mifflin, Thomas	1744-1800	Revolutionary War	125	375	483		Rev. War Gen'l. Pres. Continental Congr.
Mifune, Toshiro		Entertainment	20	25	75	50	Popular Japanese Star
Migenes, Julia		Entertainment	15			35	Opera
Miguélez Ramos, Rosa		Political	10			15	Member European Parliament
Mihalovivi, Marcel		Composer	20			150	Rumanian
Miklas, Wilhelm	1872-1956	Head of State	25				Pres. Austria
Mikoyan, Anastasy I.	1895-1970	Head of State	85	284		125	Pres. Presidium Supreme Soviet USSR
Mikulski, Barbara		Senate	10			15	U.S. Senate (D - MD)
Milano, Alyssa		Entertainment	20			40	

NAME	DATE	CATEGORY	SIG	LS/DS	ALS	SP	COMMENTS
Milanov, Zinka		Entertainment	20			120	Metropolitan Opera
Milburn, William H.	1823-1903	Clergy	35				Blind Circuit Rider Minister
Milch, Erhard	1892-1972	Aviation	80	160	250	250	Nazi general, Aviator
Miles, Brigadier Reginald	1892-1943	Military	20				World War II New Zealand general
Miles, Josephine		Author	7	15	25	10	
Miles, Lt. Gen. Sherman	1882-1966	Military	30				World War II U.S. general
Miles, Maj. Gen. Eric Grant	1891-1977	Military	28				World War II British general
Miles, Nelson A.	1839-1925	Civil War	79	166	326		Union General, MOH
Miles, Sarah		Entertainment	9	10	25	25	Pin-Up SP 35
Miles, Stuart		Celebrity	10			15	television presenter
Miles, Sylvia		Entertainment	10	20	35	35	
Miles, Vera		Entertainment	6	8	15	20	actress
Milestone, Lewis		Entertainment	35			85	Film Director
Milford, Brigadier Ernest William	1898-1944	Military	25				World War II British general
Milford, Maj. Gen. Edward J.	1894-1972	Military	30				World War II Australian general
Milhaud, Darius	1892-1974	Composer	100	187	240	302	Fr. Composer. AMusQS 475-500
Mill, James	1773-1836	Author	65	250	515		Scot. Philosopher, Historian, Econ
Mill, John Stuart	1806-1873	Author-Editor	177	325	711		Br. Economist, Philosopher, Reformer
Mill, William Hodge		Clergy	20	25	30		
Millais, John Everett, Sir	1829-1896	Artist	45	90	218		Pre-Raphaelite Painter
Milland, Ray		Entertainment	30	50		70	
Millay, Edna St. Vincent	1892-1950	Author	100	225	550	950	Am. Poet, Dramatist. Pulitzer
Millburn, Maj. Gen. Frank W.	1892-1962	Military	30				World War II U.S. general
Millender-McDonald, Juanita M		Congress	10			15	Member U.S. Congress
Miller, Alice Duer		Author	15	25	45		Novelist, Poet
Miller, Ann		Entertainment	15			50	
Miller, Arjay R.		Business	3	10	25	5	
Miller, Arthur		Celebrity	10			15	financial expert
Miller, Arthur	b. 1915	Author	58	82	138	86	Playwright. Pulitzer. TMsS & AMsS 3,900
Miller, Bill		Political	10			15	Member European Parliament
Miller, Brad M		Congress	10			15	Member U.S. Congress
Miller, Candice S. M		Congress	10			15	Member U.S. Congress
Miller, Caroline		Author	10	20			Pulitzer
Miller, Charles Henry	1842-1922	Artist	25			100	Landscape Painter
Miller, Cheryl		Celebrity	10			15	media/TV personality
Miller, Dennis		Entertainment	8	30		29	Comedian-Actor-Writer. Saturday Nite Live. HBO
Miller, Denny	1935-	Entertainment	5			25	Character actor
Miller, Eddie		Entertainment	20			45	Big Band Tenor Saxophonist
Miller, Frederick C.		Business	12	32	64	25	Miller Beer
Miller, G. William		Cabinet	5	15	25	12	Sec'y Treasury
Miller, Gary G. M		Congress	10			15	Member U.S. Congress
Miller, George M		Congress	10			15	Member U.S. Congress
Miller, Glenn	1904-1944	Entertainment	150	278	400	529	Big Band Leader-Trombonist. WW II Casualty
Miller, H.G.		Business	10			15	
Miller, Henry John	1869-1926	Entertainment	35	88	75	70	Br.-Am. Leading Man. Henry Miller Theatre

NAME	DATE	CATEGORY	SIG	LS/DS	ALS	SP	COMMENTS
Miller, Henry V.	1891-1980	Author	85	160	441	150	Autobiographical Novels. Tropic of Cancer
Miller, Henry		Entertainment	35	112		55	Vintage Actor
Miller, Jacob W.	1800-1862	Congress	12				Sen. NJ
Miller, James B.		Celebrity	10			15	financial expert
Miller, Jeff M		Congress	10			15	Member U.S. Congress
Miller, Joaquin	1839-1913	Author	62		108		Am. Poet, Journalist.Spec. TLS 3500
Miller, John F.	1831-1886	Civil War	38	51	60		Union Gen., U.S. Sen. CA
Miller, John James		Author	8		12		Southern religious practices
Miller, Ken		Entertainment	3			20	Child Actor
Miller, Leslie A.		Governor	10	20			Governor WY
Miller, Maj. Gen. Austin T.	1888-1947	Military	25				World War II British general
Miller, Maj. Gen. Charles Harvey	1894-1974	Military	25				World War II British general
Miller, Maj. Gen. Fred W.	1891-1946	Military	30				World War II U.S. general
Miller, Marilyn		Entertainment	72		240	215	Ziegfield Follies Dancing Star
Miller, Marla		Celebrity	10			15	media/TV personality
Miller, Marvin		law	15			35	Baseball lawyer
Miller, Mitch		Entertainment	5			15	Conductor, Arranger
Miller, Nathan L.		Governor	15	25		20	Governor NY
Miller, Oskar von	1855-1934	Science	115		325		Ger. Co-Founder of German Edison Co.
Miller, Patsy Ruth		Entertainment	25	35	55	45	
Miller, Penelope Ann		Entertainment	20			50	
Miller, Rebecca		Celebrity	10			15	film industry
Miller, Roger		Country Music	25			45	Composer
Miller, Samuel F.	1816-1890	Supreme Court	95	160	290		Appointed by Lincoln
Miller, Stanley		Science	15	35	65	20	
Miller, Stephen	1816-1881	Civil War	40	80	125		Union General
Miller, Taylor		Entertainment	4	4	9	10	
Miller, Warner	1838-1918	Congress	10	20	35		Repr., Senator NY
Miller, William H. H.		Cabinet	10	30	50	20	Att'y General 1889
Miller, William	1820-1909	Civil War	95	178			Confederate general
Miller, Zell		Senate	10			15	United States Senate (D - GA)
Millerande, Alexandre	1859-1943	Head of State	40	45	60	75	Socialist Pres. France 1920-24
Milles, Carl		Artist	30	55	90		Am. Sculptor
Millet, Aimé	1819-1891	Artist		30	75		Fr. Sculptor-Painter Works Adorn Paris Public Bldgs
Millet, Francis Davis	1846-1912	Artist	25	45	340		Am. Medal Winning Art. Journalist
Millet, Jean Frantois	1814-1875	Artist	200	450	2500		Fr. Religious,Classical,Peasant
Milligan, Edward		Business	5	15			Insurance Exec.
Millikan, John		Military	9	30	50	20	
Millikan, Robert A., Dr.	1868-1953	Science	123	182	425	200	Nobel Physics, Educator, Author
Milliken, William G.		Governor	5	15		10	Governor MI
Millikin, Maj. Gen. John	1888-1970	Military	30				World War II U.S. general
Millinder, Lucky		Entertainment	40			125	Band leader
Millman, William	1927-	Military	14			25	Israeli Independence Hero. Am.Vol. Sailor on Exodus
Millo, Aprile		Entertainment	10			35	Opera
Mills Brothers (4)		Entertainment	100			200	

NAME	DATE	CATEGORY	SIG	LS/DS	ALS	SP	COMMENTS
Mills, Billy		Celebrity	10			15	motivational speaker
Mills, Bob		Celebrity	10			15	comedian
Mills, Darius Ogden	1825-1910	Business	238	875	2750		Merchant, Calif. Banking Giant. Philan. RR DS 1550
Mills, Donna		Entertainment	9	10		25	actress
Mills, Earle W.		Military	12	30			
Mills, Elijah Hunt	1776-1829	Congress	20		50		MOC & Sen. MA.
Mills, Hayley		Entertainment	10	15	25	38	
Mills, Heather		Celebrity	10			25	celebrity model
Mills, John, Sir	1908-	Entertainment	20			40	Brit. Oscar Winner.
Mills, Juliette		Entertainment	10			20	
Mills, Madison	1811-1896	Civil War	35				Union Gen. Med. Officer, War Dte. ALS 275
Mills, Maj. Gen. Percy Strickland	1883-1973	Military	28				World War II British general
Mills, Ogden L.	1884-1937	Cabinet	10	23	45	15	Sec'y Treasury 1932. MOC NY
Mills, Roger Q.	1832-1911	Civil War	25	35	50		CSA Colonel, MOC TX
Mills, Wilbur	1909-	Congress	25			35	Senator AR
Milne, A. A.	1882-1956	Author	200	450	1438	1800	'Winnie-the-Pooh' Playwright, Poet, AMS 5950
Milner, Martin		Entertainment	4	6		15	
Milnes, Rich. M.		Celebrity	5	10	25	10	Man of Letters. Oxford Movement
Milnes, Sherrill		Entertainment	10			25	Opera. Am. Basso
Milosevic, Slobodan		Political	50			150	Fmr. President of Yugoslavia
Milosz, Czeslaw, Dr.		Author	30	60		75	Nobel Literature
Milroy, Robert H.	1816-1890	Civil War	40	80	120		Union Gen. LS '61 220
Milsap, Ronnie		Country Music	5	6	15	20	Singer. DS re 'Grammy Awards' 75
Milstein, Nathan	1904-1992	Entertainment	45			150	Rus. Violinist
Miltonberger, Butler		Military	35	60			
Mimieux, Yvette		Entertainment	5	8		26	Pin-Up SP 25
Minakami, General Genzo	d. 1944	Military	25				World War II Japanese general
Minami, General Jiro	1874-1951	Military	25				World War II Japanese general
Mincus, Leon		Composer	55			375	Austro-Rus. Many Ballets
Mindil, George W.		Civil War	35		210		Union Gen. MOH
Mindszenty, Jozef, Cardinal		Clergy	50	75	135	95	
Minelli, Liza	1946-	Entertainment	15	25	50	45	Actress-Singer
Minelli, Vincente	1910-	Entertainment	30			82	AA Film Director Father of Liza Minelli
Mineo, Sal	1939-1976	Entertainment	132			358	Murdered at 37, 2 Oscar Nominations
Miner, Jan		Entertainment	5	6	15	10	
Mingus, Charlie		Entertainment				2875	Jazz Musician, signed album 865
Minh, Duong Van Gen.		Military	15	40	75	40	
Minich, Peter		Entertainment	5			20	Opera, Light Opera
Mink, Patsy T.		Senate/Congress	5	15		10	MOH HI
Minor, Michael		Author	8			12	autographs, western history
Minor, Ruediger, Bishop		Clergy	25	40	45	50	
Minow, Newton N.		Law	12			15	Chairman FCC
Minshull-Ford, Maj. Gen. John R.	1881-1948	Military	25				World War II British general
Minter, Mary Miles		Entertainment	90	115	230	200	
Minton, Sherman	1890-1965	Supreme Court	40	95	150	125	

NAME	DATE	CATEGORY	SIG	LS/DS	ALS	SP	COMMENTS
Minton, Yvonne		Entertainment	5			25	Opera
Mintz, Eli	1904-1988	Entertainment	10	15	25	15	Yiddish Theatre Veteran Character Actor
Minvielle, Gabriel		Fr. Revolution	850				
Miollis, S.A.F.	1759-1828	Fr. Revolution	100	215			General of Napoleon
Mirabeau, Honore G.	1749-1791.	Fr. Revolution	120	350	575		Statesman, Diplomat, Politician
Mirabehin (M. Slade)		Celebrity	25		45		Companion-Follower of Gandhi
Miramon, Miguel (Mex)		Military	20	85	134		Cmdr. Army vs Juarez.
Miranda, Carmen	1913-1955	Entertainment	92	137		296	Brazilian-Portuguese Singer-Movie Star. 40's
Miranda, Isa		Entertainment	35			85	Fr. Actress
Miranda, Joaquim		Political	10			15	Member European Parliament
Mirisch, Walter		Entertainment	6	8	15	20	Motion Picture Producer
Miro, Joan	1893-1983	Artist	126	350	650	375	Spanish Surrealist Painter
Miroslava		Entertainment	25	30	70	65	
Mirren, Helen		Entertainment	10	20		65	Br. Actress
Mirrless, Maj. Gen. Wm. Henry B.	1892-1964	Military	28				World War II British general
Mischakoff, Mischa		Entertainment	25		85		Legendary Violinist. 'Toscanini's Concertmaster'
Mishima, Maj. Gen. Giichiro		Military	25				World War II Japanese general
Mishima, Yukio	1925-1970	Author		575	2500		Dichotomy Between Mind & Body. Ritual Suicide 1970
Mission Impossible (Cast)		Entertainment				195	4 Leads incl. Tom Cruise
Mister, Mister		Entertainment	15			55	
Mistinguett, Madamoiselle		Entertainment	90			272	Moulon Rouge Dancer-Actress
Mistral, Frederic	1830-1914	Author	40	110	175	200	Nobel Literature 1904
Mistral, Gabriela		Author	20	35	60	25	Nobel Lit. '43 'Godoy Alcayaga'
Mitchel, Ormsby M. (WD)	1809-1862	Civil War	125		475		Union Gen., Astronomy Prof.
Mitchel, Ormsby M.		Civil War	40	127	156		Union General
Mitchell, Andrea		Celebrity	10			20	media/TV personality
Mitchell, Cameron	1918-1994	Entertainment	20			40	Actor. Leading Roles in Rugged Parts
Mitchell, Charles E.		Business	20	35	65	25	Chmn. National City Bank
Mitchell, Edgar D.		Astronaut	28	142	322	71	Moonwalker. Apollo 14
Mitchell, Grant		Entertainment	35			80	
Mitchell, James P.		Cabinet	15	25	30		Sec'y Labor
Mitchell, John Cameron		Entertainment	20			40	Actor, writer, director
Mitchell, John Grant	1838-1894	Civil War	45	80	140		Union General
Mitchell, John Inscho	1838-1907	Civil War	20	45			U.S. Senator PA
Mitchell, John N.	1913-1988	Cabinet	25			50	Att'y General, TLS/Cont 200
Mitchell, John W.		Aviation	12	25	42	32	ACE, WW II
Mitchell, Joni		Entertainment	4			15	Singer
Mitchell, Maggie	1832-1918	Entertainment	50			125	Entertained 1st CSA Gov't & Troops
Mitchell, Maj. Gen. Philip Euen	1890-1964	Military	25				World War II British general
Mitchell, Margaret	1900-1949	Author	508	1750	3000		Pulitzer. TLS/Content 15,000
Mitchell, Maria	1818-1889	Science	90	185	375		Considered 1st Woman Astronomer. Mathematician
Mitchell, Martha		Celebrity	25	30		45	Wife Att'y Gen. Watergate
Mitchell, Ormsby M. (WD)		Civil War			957		Union Gen. Died 1862 RARE
Mitchell, Robert Byington	1823-1882	Civil War	40	75	110		Union general
Mitchell, Silas Weir		Science-Civil War	25	95	155		Civil War Surgeon

NAME	DATE	CATEGORY	SIG	LS/DS	ALS	SP	COMMENTS
Mitchell, Stephen Mix	1743-1835	Revolutionary War	65	295			Cont'l Congr. Federalist Sen. PA
Mitchell, Thomas	1892-1962	Entertainment	197	196	139	466	'GWTW'
Mitchell, Thomas, Sir		Military	10				Lord Provost Aberdeen
Mitchell, Warren		Entertainment	10			20	Actor
Mitchell, William (Billy)	1879-1936	Aviation	217	350	460	750	Gen. WW I. Pioneer Aerial Bombing. Courtmartialed
Mitchell, William D.		Cabinet	5	25	30	10	Att'y General
Mitchelson, Marvin		Law	13	25		20	Trial Att'y. Specialty Divorce
Mitchum, Robert	1917-1997	Entertainment	20	35	50	62	Actor. Versatile Leading Man
Mitford, Jessica		Author	15	25	25	20	
Mitford, Mary Russell	1787-1855	Author			128		Novelist and Dramatist.
Mitropoulous, Dimitri	1896-1960	Composer	45	50	95	135	Greek Conductor
Mitscher, Marc A.		Military	288			412	Adm.WW II (RARE)
Mittelhauser, Lt Gen Eugène-D-A	1873-1949	Military	20				World War II French general
Mitterand, Francois		Head of State	15	25	40	20	Pres. France
Mittford, Mary Russell		Author	15	20	40		Br. Poet. Historical Drama
Miura, Lt. Gen. Saburo		Military	25				World War II Japanese general
Miwa, Lt. Gen. Tetsuji		Military	25				World War II Japanese general
Mix, Tom	1880-1940	Entertainment	75		250	450	Cowboy Star of Hollywood Silent & Early Talkies
Mix, Victoria		Entertainment	8	9	15	10	
Miyake, Maj. Gen. Sadahiro		Military	25				World War II Japanese general
Miyamoto, Maj. Gen. Kiyokazu		Military	25				World War II Japanese general
Miyashita, Maj. Gen. Fumio		Military	25				World War II Japanese general
Miyazaki, Maj. Gen. Takeshi		Military	25				World War II Japanese general
Mizell, Jason		Music				60	Rap pioneer
Mizell, Wilmer D.		Senate/Congress	5	15			MOC KS, Prof. Baseball Pitcher
Mizrahi, Isaac		Celebrity	10			15	film industry
Mnller, Emilia Franziska		Political	10			15	Member European Parliament
Mnller, Rosemarie		Political	10			15	Member European Parliament
Moberly, Lt. Gen. Sir Bertrand R.	1877-1963	Military	28				World War II British general
Mobley, Mary Ann		Entertainment	5	8	15	12	
Mockler-Ferryman, Brig. Eric Edw.	1896-1978	Military	28				World War II British general
Model, Walter	1891-1945	Military	125	220	310	350	WWII German General
Modesti, Giuseppe		Entertainment	15			35	Opera
Modigliani, Amedeo	1884-1920	Artist	1200		4500		Italian Painter and Sculptor, Content ALS 35,000
Modine, Matthew		Entertainment	6			33	Actor
Modjeske, Helena		Entertainment	15	25	35	30	
Modrow, Hans		Political	10			15	Member European Parliament
Moessbauer, Rudolf, Dr.		Science	20			55	Nobel
Moeur, Benjamin B.		Governor	12	15	25		Governor Arizona
Moffat, Robert		Clergy	50	90	100		
Moffett, William A., Admiral	1869-1933	Military	15		50	55	MOH. With Adm. Dewey. FDC 90
Moffo, Anna		Entertainment	15			35	Opera, Concert
Mohammed, Seti		Political				35	Ruler of Morocco
Mohler, A. L.		Business	8	20	40	15	
Mohnke, WIlhelm		Military	35			150	Ger. Gen. SS

NAME	DATE	CATEGORY	SIG	LS/DS	ALS	SP	COMMENTS
Moholy-Nagy, Laszlo	1895-1946	Artist	80	265			Painter, Designer, Photographer
Mohr, Gerald		Entertainment	35			75	
Mohri, Momoru		Astronaut	12	25		25	
Mojica, Jose		Entertainment	60			225	Opera
Mol, Gretchen		Entertainment	20			65	'Vanity Fair' Cover S 75
Molders, Werner		Aviation	175	275	400	325	ACE, WW II, 1st to 100 Kills
Molesworth, Lt. Gen. Geo. Noble	1890-1968	Military	25				World War II British general
Molina, Alfred		Entertainment	10			20	actor
Molinari, Susan		Celebrity	10			15	political celebrity
Molinie, Maj. Gen. Jean-B-E	1880-1971	Military	20				World War II French general
Molitor, Gabriel J.J.	1770-1849	Fr. Revolution	75	175	250		Napoleon Gen., Marshal of Fr.
Moll, Kurt		Entertainment	15			35	Opera
Moll, Richard		Entertainment	6	8	15	15	
Molle, Lt. Gen. Marie-Eugène-A.	1895-1978	Military	20				World War II French general
Mollet, Guy		Head of State	20	40	65		Socialist Premier France
Mollohan, Alan B. M		Congress	10			15	Member U.S. Congress
Molnar, Ferenc	1878-1952	Author	72	140	275		Playwright, Novelist, Journalist
Moloney, Janel		Entertainment	10			35	The West Wing
Molotov, Vyacheslav M.	1890-1986	History		170	242	175	Russian revolutionary, 'Molotov cocktail'
Moltke, Helmuth Von, Count		Military	106	133	400	295	Prussian Field Marshal
Moltke, Helmuth von, Count	1800-1891	Military	15	30	60	30	Nephew Helmuth.
Moltmann, Jurgen		Clergy	50	75	100	80	
Momaday, N. Scott		Author	10	15	25	15	
Mombaur, Peter Michael		Political	10			15	Member European Parliament
Momo, Giuseppe		Entertainment	10			35	Opera
Mompou, Frederico		Composer					Reclusive Spanish Composer. AMusQS 495
Monaghan, Dominic		Entertainment				45	actor
Monaghan, Tom		Business	10			20	Domino's Pizza
Moncada, Fernando Rivera y		Military		4500			Spanish Gov of California 1774-77
Moncey, Bon-Adrien J. de		Fr. Revolution	45	135	160		Marshal of France
Monck, George	1608-1670	Military	95	430			1st Duke Albermarle. Restored Monarchy
Mondale, Walter		Vice President	25	32		28	
Mondell, Franklin W.		Senate/Congress	10	15		15	MOC WY
Mondrian, Piet	1872-1944	Artist	312	675	1542		Dutch. Traditional-Cubism
Monet, Claude	1840-1926	Artist	300	950	2050	1500	Fr. Impressionist Painter
Money, Hernando De Soto		Senate/Congress	10	25	45		MOC, Senator MS. CSA Army
Money, Ken		Astronaut	5	15		15	
Money, Maj. Gen. Robert Cotton	1888-1985	Military	28				World War II British general
Monk, Thelonious		Entertainment		1093			Jazz Musician
Monkees, The (4)		Entertainment	75			120	Rock Group. Jones, Nesmith, Dolenz, Tork
Monkhouse, Bob		Celebrity	10			15	comedian
Monroe, Bill		Entertainment	45		150		Father of Blue Grass Music
Monroe, Elizabeth		First Lady					Rare 10-12 Known
Monroe, James & Adams, John Q.		President		2850			SEE Adams, John Quincy
Monroe, James (as Pres)		President	425	1313	3314		5th Pres. Of USA, ALS/cont 14,340

NAME	DATE	CATEGORY	SIG	LS/DS	ALS	SP	COMMENTS
Monroe, James	1758-1831	President	356	900	2375		Free Frank 525, ALS/cont 5000
Monroe, Marilyn (Norman Jean)		Entertainment			15000		Signed Norma Jean, Contract 9500
Monroe, Marilyn	1926-1962	Entertainment	1762	2575	7500	5674	ALS/Cont.15,000, signed check 1250-2000
Monroe, Vaughn		Entertainment	15	25		30	
Monster Magnet		Entertainment	32			80	Music. 5 Member Rock Group
Montagu, Charles	1661-1715	Politician		210			Lord Halifax. Wit, Author. Created Bank of England
Montagu, Edwin Samuel	1879-1924	Politician	15	50	80	35	Br. Statesman
Montagu, John (Earl of Sandwich)		Celebrity	65	205	450		Sandwich Named For Him
Montague, Andrew J.		Congress	5	15	35		Repr., Senator VA
Montague, Lt. Gen. Percival John	1882-1966	Military	20				World War II Canadian general
Montal, Lisa		Entertainment	5			20	Actress, Vintage
Montalban, Ricardo		Entertainment	10	15	25	22	SP/Herve Villechaize & Montalban 50
Montalivet, J.P.B. Count		Fr. Revolution	35	100	225		
Montana, Bob*		Cartoonist	40			175	Archie
Montana, Bull		Entertainment	25			50	
Montana, Monte		Entertainment	5			24	
Montana, Patsy		Country Music	15			35	
Montand, Yves		Entertainment	10			35	
Montbarey, Alex-Marie	1732-1796	history			633		French Stateman, minister of war 1777-80
Montcalm, Louis J. Marquis de		Military	575	1765	3077		Cmdr. Fr. Troops in North Am.
Montefiore, Moses, Sir	1784-1885	Philanthropist	75	160	275		Br.-Jewish Philan. Sheriff of London
Montell, Lisa		Entertainment				15	Retired Actress-Heiress
Montenegro, Conchita		Entertainment	8	9	19	19	
Montessori, Maria	1870-1952	Educator	275		1050		1st Italian Woman Doctor, Montessori schools
Monteux, Pierre	1875-1964	Entertainment	35	50		68	Conductor
Montevecchi, Liliane		Entertainment	10			20	actress
Monteverde, Alfred de		Aviation	25	50	85	55	
Monteverde, George de		Aviation	25	50	85	55	
Montez, Lola	1818-1861	Adventuress	200		725		Seductress of Louis I of Bavaria. RARE
Montez, Maria		Entertainment	50	55		100	
Montfort, Elizabeth		Political	10			15	Member European Parliament
Montgolfier, Jacques-Etienne	1745-1799	Aviation		750	1800		With Joseph, 1st hot air Balloon
Montgolfier, Joseph-Michel	1740-1810	Aviation		160			Special Content ALS 63,000
Montgomery, Bernard Law, Sir	1887-1976	Military	73	184	192	328	Of Alamein. War-date 500-2500
Montgomery, Douglass		Entertainment	10	15	25	25	
Montgomery, Elizabeth	1933-1995	Entertainment	35	65		85	Star of TV's 'Bewitched' Pin-Up SP 25
Montgomery, George		Entertainment	10	15	25	20	Western Actor & Talented Furniture Maker
Montgomery, James Shera		Clergy	50	65	75		Chaplain U.S. Congress
Montgomery, James	1771-1854	Composer	15		195		Scot. Poet-Hymnwriter
Montgomery, M., Lady		Celebrity	5	10	20		Mother of Bernard L. Montgomery
Montgomery, Melba		Country Music	10			20	
Montgomery, Robert	1904-1981	Entertainment	15	30	60	30	Actor. Young & Mature Leading Man. Films.
Montgomery, William Reading	1801-1871	Civil War	45	75	110		Union general
Monti, Carlotta		Entertainment	15		75	40	W. C. Fields Paramour
Monti, Nicola		Entertainment	35			85	Opera

NAME	DATE	CATEGORY	SIG	LS/DS	ALS	SP	COMMENTS
Montoya, Carlos		Entertainment	10	15	25	30	Classical Guitarist
Moody Blues (All 5)		Entertainment	145			275	60's Rock Group
Moody, Dwight L.	1837-1899	Clergy	100	287	391	300	Evangelist, LS/Content 500
Moody, William H.	1853-1917	Supreme Court	45	125	175	150	Sec'y Navy, Att'y Gen'l, MOC
Moody, William V.		Author	30	85	125		Poet, Playwright
Moody, Young Marshall	1822-1866	Civil War	120				Confederate general
Moog, Bob		Science	50	70	110	65	Inventor. Synthesizer
Moon, Keith		Entertainment	175	280		452	Rock. 'The Who' Deceased Member
Moon, Sun Myung		Clergy				65	Rev. Unification Church
Mooney, Art		Entertainment	10			20	Big Band Leader
Mooney, Edward, Cardinal		Clergy	30	40	55	40	
Mooney, Tom	1883-1942	Labor Activist	25	60	180	275	Bombed Parade. TLS/Cont.550
Moonlighting		Entertainment				100	Cast signed photo
Moonwalkers		Astronaut				2338	All 12
Moore, Alfred	1755-1810	Supreme Court	3000				Rev. War Soldier, NC Planter, Politician—RARE—
Moore, Andrew B.	1806-1873	Civil War	45	115	145		CSA Gov. AL. ALS '61 1485
Moore, Arch A. Jr.		Senate/Congress	5	15			Governor, MOC WV
Moore, Arthur J., Bishop		Clergy	20	25	40	40	
Moore, Barbara, Dr.		Celebrity	5		20		Br. Marathon Walker
Moore, Clayton		Entertainment	18			77	Longtime 'The Lone Ranger'
Moore, Clement C.	1779-1863	Author	230	340	1045		''Twas the Night Before...' Am. Educator & Poet
Moore, Colleen	1900-1988	Entertainment	10	20	52	38	Silent Screen Major Star/Travelling Doll House
Moore, Constance		Entertainment	8			20	Actress-Singer
Moore, Dan K.		Governor	5	15	30		Governor NC
Moore, Demi		Entertainment	40	140		84	Advanced from 'Soaps' to Highest Paid Actress
Moore, Dennis M		Congress	10			15	Member U.S. Congress
Moore, Dick		Entertainment	10			25	'Dickey Moore' Child Actor
Moore, Dudley	d. 2002	Entertainment	18			55	Actor-Pianist. Light Comedy Parts
Moore, Edward C.		Clergy	10	20	30		
Moore, Foster*		Cartoonist	15			50	'Napoleon'
Moore, Francis D., Dr.		Science	10	30	55	20	
Moore, Gary		Entertainment	15			28	TV Host-Comedian. Early TV
Moore, General James E.	1902-1986	Military	30				World War II U.S. general
Moore, George	1852-1933	Author	45	115	125		Irish Novelist
Moore, Grace	1901-1947	Entertainment	70	95		173	Met. Opera Star-Films.Died in Plane Crash. SPc 200
Moore, Henry	1898-1986	Artist	50	154	200	125	Br. Sculptor. 'The Thinker', signed print 529
Moore, Jeremy, Sir		Military	5	15	25	15	General
Moore, Joanna		Entertainment	8			20	Actress
Moore, John Bassett		Law-Jurist	65		250		Internat'l Law.Permanent Court Internat'l Justice.
Moore, John Creed	1824-1910	Civil War	100	188			Confederate general
Moore, John, Sir	1761-1809	Military	60	225	350		Br. General vs Am.'til 1783. KIA 1809
Moore, Julianne		Entertainment	10			40	Actress
Moore, Maj. Gen. Bryant E.	1894-1951	Military	30				World War II U.S. general
Moore, Maj. Gen. Francis Malcom	1897-1974	Military	25				World War II British general
Moore, Maj. Gen. George F.	1887-1949	Military	30				World War II U.S. general

NAME	DATE	CATEGORY	SIG	LS/DS	ALS	SP	COMMENTS
Moore, Mandy		Entertainment				40	Singer
Moore, Marianne C.	1887-1972	Author	60	111		75	Am. Poet. Pulitzer
Moore, Mary Tyler (Cast of Show)		Entertainment	135			388	Six Main Characters
Moore, Mary Tyler		Entertainment	10	32		37	
Moore, Michael		Celebrity	10			22	film industry,director ,AA winner
Moore, Patrick Theodore	1821-1883	Civil War	110				Confederate general
Moore, Ray*		Cartoonist	25			175	'Phantom'
Moore, Rich'd Channing		Clergy			160		Episcopal Bishop 1814-41
Moore, Roger		Entertainment	18			51	Followed Connery as 'James Bond'. SP as 007 65
Moore, Roy D.		Business	10	25		20	Fndr. Newspaper-Radio Chain
Moore, Samuel P.		Civil War	522	484	800		Surgeon General CSA
Moore, Sara Jane		Radical	30	80	200		Attempted Assassination Pres. Ford
Moore, Sydenham	1817-1862	Congress-CW	40	55	90		MOC AL. CSA Officer
Moore, Terry		Entertainment	15	20	25	35	
Moore, Thomas O.	1804-1876	Civil War	40	75	184		Civil War Gov. of Louisiana
Moore, Thomas		Celebrity	10			15	medical expert
Moore, Thomas	1779-1852	Author	50	105	475		Irish Poet. ''Tis The Last Rose of Summer''
Moore, Victor	1876-1962	Entertainment	25			55	Vaudeville Headliner. Film Wimpy Comedian
Moore, William		Colonial Am.	90	225			Colonial Am. Statseman-Jurist
Moorehead, Agnes		Entertainment	40			88	Fine Radio-Film Character Actress. 'Bewitched'
Moorer, Thomas		Military	20	45	70	40	Adm. Survivor-Twice
Moores, Dick*		Cartoonist	10			30	'Gasoline Alley'
Moorhead, Maj. Gen. Charles D.	1894-1965	Military	25				World War II British general
Moraes, Claude		Political	10			15	Member European Parliament
Morales, Ramon V.		Head of State	15	35			Ecuador
Moran, Diana		Celebrity	10			15	health and fitness expert
Moran, Dylan		Celebrity	10			15	comedian
Moran, Erin		Entertainment		25		35	Actress. 'Happy Days' Cast
Moran, James P. M		Congress	10			15	Member U.S. Congress
Moran, Jerry M		Congress	10			15	Member U.S. Congress
Moran, Lois		Entertainment	6	8	10	25	Actress
Moran, Thomas	1837-1926	Artist	80	225	350		Specialized in American West
Moranis, Rick		Entertainment	8			22	
Moranville, H. Blake		Aviation	15	25	40	35	ACE, WW II, Navy Ace
Mordacq, Maj. Gen. Jean-Jos.-L	1880- ?	Military	20				World War II French general
Mordant, Maj. Gen. Eugène	1885-1959	Military	20				World War II French general
Mordecai, Alfred		Military	15		95		West Point Instructor. General
More, Johnny		Celebrity	10			15	impressionist
More, Thomas, Sir	1478-1535	Author	19750				'Utopia'
Moreau, Gustave	1826-1898	Artist	35		192		Important Teacher of Matisse, Rouault
Moreau, Jeanne		Entertainment	10			20	actress
Moreau, Jean-Victor		Fr. Revolution	90	275	300		Fr. General under Napoleon
Morehead, James B.		Aviation	10	22	38	28	ACE, WW II, USAAF Ace
Morehead, John M.		Governor	10	25			Governor NC
Morehouse, A.P.		Governor	10	20		25	Governor MO

NAME	DATE	CATEGORY	SIG	LS/DS	ALS	SP	COMMENTS
Moreira Da Silva, Jorge		Political	10			15	Member European Parliament
Moreland, Mantan		Entertainment	100	125		200	
Morell, George W. (WD)		Civil War	45	95	300		Union Gen.
Morell, George W.	1815-1883	Civil War	30		80		Union Gen.
Morello, Tom		Entertainment	6			25	Music. Guitar 'Rage Against the Machine'
Moreno, Anthony		Entertainment	3	3	6	6	
Moreno, Bertha		Entertainment	20			95	Opera
Moreno, Buddy		Bandleader				45	
Moreno, Rita		Entertainment	9	10	25	28	Pin-Up SP 30. AA. 'West Side Story' Script S 50
Morgan, Barbara		Astronaut	5	35		15	
Morgan, Charles Hale	1834-1875	Civil War	40	70	110		Union general
Morgan, Charles L.	1894-1958	Author	25	70	80		Br. Novelist, Dramatist, Critic
Morgan, Dennis		Entertainment	8		15	15	Actor-Singer
Morgan, Edward J.		Entertainment	10	12		25	
Morgan, Edwin Barber	1806-1881	Business	40	75	160		NY, 1st Pres. Am. Express ALS 485-985
Morgan, Edwin Denison, Jr.	1811-1883	Civil War	40	72	98		Union Gen.,CW Gov.,NY. ALS '62 200, US Sen.
Morgan, Eluned		Political	10			15	Member European Parliament
Morgan, F. Crossley		Clergy	10	15	15	15	
Morgan, Frank	1890-1949	Entertainment	375	632		673	Collected as 'Wizard of OZ', SP as WOZ 9184
Morgan, G. Campbell		Clergy	20	30	45		
Morgan, General Sir Wm. Duthie	1891-1977	Military	25				World War II British general
Morgan, George W.	1820-1893	Civil War	40	80	120		Union Gen, War Date ALS/Cont. 1650
Morgan, George		Country Music	15			35	
Morgan, George	1743-1810	Revolutionary War	125	425	675		Indian Agent, Speculator
Morgan, Harry		Entertainment	5	10	20	15	
Morgan, Helen	1900-1941	Entertainment	43	175		200	1st Julie in 'Show Boat'. Noted Blues singer
Morgan, James Dada	1810-1896	Civil War	40	75	100		Union general
Morgan, Jaye P.		Entertainment	5			15	
Morgan, John Hunt	1825-1864	Civil War	1840	5462	8000		CSA Gen. War dte DS/cont 12,500
Morgan, John Pierpont, Jr.	1867-1943	Business	75	1978	280	250	Banker, Financier
Morgan, John Pierpont, Sr.	1837-1913	Business	318	1038	2500	1025	Banker, Financier, Philanthropist. Legal DS 2400
Morgan, John Tyler (WD)		Civil War	190	650	1600		CSA Gen.
Morgan, John Tyler	1825-1907	Civil War	54	198	293	240	CSA Gen., US Sen. AL.TLS/Cont. 1250
Morgan, Lt. Gen. Sir Fredrick E.	1894-1967	Military	25				World War II British general
Morgan, Maj. Gen. Harold de R.	1888-1964	Military	25				World War II British general
Morgan, Marion		Entertainment	6			14	Singer
Morgan, Michele		Entertainment	10			25	
Morgan, Ralph		Entertainment	35			65	
Morgan, Russ		Bandleader	20			65	Big Band leader. Arranger
Morgan, Sydney, Lady		Author	15	35	60		Ir. Author. TheWild Irish Girl
Morgan, Thomas H.		Science	95	200	425	125	Nobel Medicine 1933
Morgan, Thos. Jeff.	1839-1902	Civil War	30	55	75		Union General
Morgan, Wm. H.	1825-1878	Civil War	25	55	75		
Morganna		Entertainment	5	8	20	18	Pin-Up SP 30
Morgantini, Luisa		Political	10			15	Member European Parliament

NAME	DATE	CATEGORY	SIG	LS/DS	ALS	SP	COMMENTS
Morgenthau, Henry Jr.	1891-1967	Cabinet	35	65	145	60	FDR Sec'y Treasury
Mori, Lt. Gen. Takeshi	1894-1945	Military	25				World War II Japanese general
Mori, Yoshiro		Political				35	PM of Japan
Moriarty, Cathy		Entertainment	7			30	Actress
Moriarty, Michael		Entertainment	10			32	Actor
Morillon, Philippe		Political	10			15	Member European Parliament
Morimoto, Maj. Gen. Yukio		Military	25				World War II Japanese general
Morimura, Maj. Gen. Tsunetaro		Military	25				World War II Japanese general
Morin, Maj. Gen. Charles-Eugène		Military	20				World War II French general
Morini, Erica		Entertainment	20			50	Austrian-born Violinist
Morioka, Lt. Gen. Susumu		Military	25				World War II Japanese general
Morison, Patricia		Entertainment	15	15	30	25	
Morison, Samuel E.	1887-1976	Author	35	55	155		Am. Historian. Pulitzer Prize Twice
Morita, Pat		Entertainment	10		25	25	actor
Morland, Mantan		Entertainment	25			50	
Morley, Christopher	1890-1957	Author	25	45	75	60	Am. Writer, Editor, Novelist
Morley, Ken		Entertainment	10			20	Actor
Morley, Margaret W.		Author	10			25	education, Southern mountains
Morley, Robert	1908-1992	Entertainment	32	75		78	Noted Br. Actor
Morphis, Joseph L.	1831-1913	Congress	10				Repr. MS, U.S. Marshal
Morrill, Justin Smith	1810-1898	Congress	45	60	110		Repr., U.S. Senate VT 1855-98
Morrill, Lot M.		Cabinet	15	30	60		Sec'y Treas., Gov., Senator ME
Morris, Anita		Entertainment	6	8		20	
Morris, B. Wistar		Clergy	10		20		
Morris, Brig. Herbert Edwin A.	1894-1969	Military	25				World War II British general
Morris, Charles		Military	20	60			Commodore USN
Morris, Chester	1901-1970	Entertainment	25	40		70	Silent Child Star to Adult '29 Oscar Nominee
Morris, Clara	1846-1913	Entertainment	12				Vintage Actress
Morris, Edmund		Author				15	Pulitzer-prize winning author., Dutch
Morris, Edward Joy	1815-1881	Congress	10				Repr. PA, Minister Turkey
Morris, Eugene 'Mercury'		Celebrity	10			15	motivational speaker
Morris, Felix J.		Entertainment	15			40	Vintage Stage Actor
Morris, General Sir Edwin Logie	1889-1970	Military	28				World War II British general
Morris, Gouverneur	1752-1816	Revolutionary War	150	325	638		Continental Congr., Diplomat
Morris, Greg	1934-1996	Entertainment	15			35	Actor. 'Mission Impossible' Original TV Series
Morris, Harrison Smith		Publisher	30	55			Magazine Editor
Morris, Howard		Entertainment	3			15	Comedian-Actor
Morris, James		Entertainment	5			25	Opera
Morris, Juliet		Celebrity	10			15	news reader
Morris, Lewis	1726-1798	Revolutionary War	675	1109	1894		Signer Decl. of Indepen. DS/Fran. Lewis 3500
Morris, Lewis, Sir		Author	5	10	20		
Morris, Lt. Gen. Wm. Henry H. Jr.	1890-1971	Military	30				World War II U.S. general
Morris, Maj. Gen. Basil M.	1888- ?	Military	30				World War II Australian general
Morris, Robert & J. Nicholson		Revolutionary War		1475			Content DS 45,000, Content DS 29,500
Morris, Robert Page W.		Senate/Congress	5	10			MOC MN

NAME	DATE	CATEGORY	SIG	LS/DS	ALS	SP	COMMENTS
Morris, Robert	1734-1806	Revolutionary War	350	787	1168		Signer. Important DS 13500-22,000. Financier
Morris, Thomas A. (WD)	1811-1904	Civil War			3520		Union Gen.
Morris, Tom		Celebrity	10			15	financial expert
Morris, Wayne		Entertainment	25			60	
Morris, William Hopkins	1827-1900	Civil War	40	75	105		Union general
Morris, William Walton	1801-1865	Civil War	36	70	80		Union Gen. ALS '62 160
Morris, William	1834-1896	Artist	125	275	675		Br. Poet, Artist, Designer, Printer, Social Reform
Morrison, Harold		Country Music	10			20	
Morrison, Henry Clay		Clergy	25	35	50	40	
Morrison, Herb		Aviation	40	85	160	100	Announcer of Hindenburg Crash
Morrison, Jim	1943-1971	Entertainment	704	4698		1601	Lead Singer 'The Doors', chk sgn 900-2000
Morrison, Robert	1782-1834	Clergy		125	240		English Divine. 1st Missionary to China
Morrison, Samuel E.		Author	12	20			Historian
Morrison, Shelley		Entertainment	10			25	Will and Grace
Morrison, Toni		Author	35	45	70	50	Afro-Am. Nobel Literature
Morrison, Van		Entertainment	18			45	
Morrison, William Ralls		Civil War	25		80		Union Officer, MOC IL
Morrissey, John	1831-1878	Political	212	104			NY Congressman
Morrissey, Neil		Entertainment	10			20	Actor
Morrow, Buddy		Bandleader	20			45	
Morrow, Dwight W.		Diplomat	10	35			Lawyer, Banker, Amb. to Mex.
Morrow, Jeff		Entertainment	5	6	15	15	
Morrow, Rob		Entertainment	15			30	
Morrow, Vic	1932-1982	Entertainment	100	132		150	Died in Tragic Helicopter Accident
Morse, Carleton E.		Writer-Producer	20	25		30	One Man's Family Vint. Radio
Morse, David		Entertainment	10			30	actor
Morse, Jedediah	1761-1826	Science		75	125		Father of American Geography
Morse, Samuel F. B.	1791-1872	Science-Artist	400	1250	1612	3718	Telegraph, Pioneer Photographer. ALS/Cont. 7500
Morse, Wayne	1900-1974	Congress	10	25		55	Senator OR
Morshead, Lt. Gen. Leslie J.	1889-1959	Military	30				World War II Australian general
Mortell, Art		Celebrity	10			15	motivational speaker
Mortensen, Viggio		Entertainment				65	actor
Mortier, Edouard A.C.J.		Fr. Revolution	35	115	230		Marshal of Fr., Statesman
Mortimer, Charles		Business	5	15	25	10	CEO General Foods
Morton, J. Sterling		Cabinet	25	50	145	75	Father Arbor Day, Sec'y Agri.
Morton, James St Clair	1829-1864	Civil War	120	250			Union general, KIA Petersburg
Morton, John	1724-1777	Revolutionary War	400	850	1375		Signer Decl. of Indepen., Continental Congr.
Morton, Levi P.	1824-1920	Vice President	50	110	160	350	Gov. NY. VP. MOC, Minister to Fr.
Morton, Oliver P.		Senate	16	25	50		Governor, Senator IN
Morton, Peter A.		Business	40	195			Founder 'Hard Rock Café' Chain
Morton, Wm. Thos. Green		Science	170	450	825		1st To Use Ether as Anesthetic
Mosby, John S. (WD)		Civil War		8500	9600		'Gray Ghost', Mosby's Rangers
Mosby, John S.	1833-1916	Civil War	500	1617	2706	2500	CSAOfficer, Content ALS 12,500
Moscona, Nicola		Entertainment	25			45	Opera
Moscone, George R.		Celebrity	80		95		

NAME	DATE	CATEGORY	SIG	LS/DS	ALS	SP	COMMENTS
Mosel, Tad		Author	16	20	30	25	Am. Dramatist
Moseley, Corliss Champion	1894-	Aviation	65	150			1st Pulitzer Aviation Speed Prize Winner-1920. ETC
Moseley, George Van Horn		Military	30	110			MacArthur's Dep. Chief of Staff
Moseley-Braun, Carol		Celebrity	10			15	political celebrity
Moser, Edda		Entertainment	5			25	Opera
Moses, Anna Mary R. (Grandma)	1860-1961	Artist	223	378	860	548	ALS/Content1,500, signed repro 425
Moses, George H.		Senate/Congress	7	15	35		Senator NH. Diplomat
Moses, Robert	1888-1981	Public Official	15	40	65		Dominated NY Politics. Father of Interstate Hwy Sys
Mosher, Terry		Celebrity	5		10		
Mosimann, Anton		Celebrity	10			15	Chef
Mosley, Jack*		Cartoonists	25			105	Smilin' Jack
Mosley, Oswald, Sir	1896-1980	Political	30	75	210	140	Founder Br. Union of Fascists
Moss Kanter, Rosabeth		Celebrity	10			15	motivational speaker
Moss, Kate		Model	10			40	Model
Moss, Ralph W.		Senate/Congress	10	15	25		MOC IN 1909
Mossadegh, Muhammad		Head of State	40	75	165		Premier Iran. Nationalized Oil
Mossbauer, Rudolf L.		Science	25	55	90	45	Nobel Physics
Mossdorf, Martin		Aviation				25	Ger. RK Winner. Stuka Pilot
Mostel, Zero	1915-1977	Entertainment	30	80		248	Stage, Film Comedy Star
Mostue, Trude		Celebrity	10			15	veterinarian expert
Moszkowski, Moritz	1854-1924	Composer	50		200		Ger. Pianist. AMusQS
Moten, Brigadier Murray J.	1899- ?	Military	30				World War II Australian general
Motherwell, Robert	1915-1991	Artist	60	160	325		Am. Abstract Expressionist. Pc Repro S175
Motion, Andrew		Author			30	40	England's poet laureate
Motivator, Mr.		Celebrity	5			10	health and fitness expert
Motley Crue (4)		Entertainment	45			185	Rock group
Motley, John Lothrop	1814-1877	Author	30	50	118		Am. Historian, Diplomat, Hall of Fame
Motson, John		Celebrity	10			15	television presenter
Mott, Charles S.		Business	25				Pioneer Auto.Exec. A Founder Gen'l Motors
Mott, Frank L.		Journalist	10		35	20	Educator, Pulitzer
Mott, Gershom (WD)		Civil War	65	150			Union Gen.
Mott, Gershom	1822-1884	Civil War	40	80	95		Union Gen.
Mott, John R.		Clergy	30	45	75	100	Nobel Peace Prize
Mott, Lucretia	1793-1880	Women's Rights	78	150	225	309	Reformer, Abolitionist, Suffrage
Mott, Neville F. Dr.		Science	20	35	50	25	Nobel Physics
Moulton, Louise Chandler	1835-1908	Author	25	70	125		Bed Time Stories
Moulton, Samuel W.	1821-1905	Congress	10				Repr. IL
Moulton, William		Revolutionary War	20	145			
Moultrie, William	1730-1805	Governor-Military	206	481			Revolutionary War Gen. Fort Moultrie Namesake
Mount, James A.		Governor	30	100			Gov. IN
Mountbatten, Edwina, Lady		Celebrity	10	35			Wife of Louis Mountbatten
Mountbatten, Louis, Lord	1900-1979	Military	99	158	315	188	Of Burma. Adm. of Fleet WW II. 1st Earl
Mountevens,Baron (E Evans)		Military	20	45		335	Br. WW I Naval Hero
Moured, David		Celebrity	10	20			Computer Guru
Mouton, Alfred		Civil War		3220			CSA General

NAME	DATE	CATEGORY	SIG	LS/DS	ALS	SP	COMMENTS
Mouton, Jean Jacques Alfred A.	1829-1864	Civil War	140				Confederate general
Moutrie, Alexander		Revolutionary War	35		200		
Mowbray, Alan		Entertainment	45			75	
Mowbray, H. Siddons		Artist	25	40	70		Murals. J.P. Morgan Library etc
Mower, Joseph A.		Civil War	35	90	115		Union General
Mowry, Tamera		Entertainment	10			20	actress
Mowry, Tia		Entertainment	10			20	actress
Moyers, Bill		Author	5	15	45	15	TV Host
Moynihan, Daniel Patrick	d. 2003	Senate/Congress	10	20		30	Senator NY
Mozart, Wolfgang A.	1756-1791	Composer	35000	47500	80000		
Mroczyk, Peter		Celebrity	10			15	media/TV personality
Méndez De Vigo, -ligo		Political	10			15	Member European Parliament
Mubarak, M. Hosni		Head of State	75	110	275	125	President Egypt
Mucha, Alphonse	1860-1939	Artist	64		444		Czech-Born French Painter- Illustrator Art Nouveau
Muck, Karl, Dr.		Conductor	10			50	
Mudd, Roger		News	5	10	30	15	Radio-TV News
Mudge, Maj. Gen. Verne D.	1898-1957	Military	30				World War II U.S. general
Mueller, Frederick H.		Gov't Official	5	15	30		
Mueller, Maj. Gen. Paul J.	1892-1964	Military	30				World War II U.S. general
Mueller, Reuben H., Bishop		Clergy	20	25	35	25	
Mueller-Stahl, Armin		Entertainment	4			12	
Muench, Aloisius J., Cardinal		Clergy	35	50	65	50	
Mugabe, Robert G.		Head of State	20	60	145	40	
Muggeridge, Malcolm		Clergy	30	40	50	40	
Muhammed, Elijah	1897-1975	Muslim Leader	213	243		425	Leader, 'Nation of Islam'
Muhlenberg, Frederick A.	1750-1801	History		275			Member of Cont. Congress
Muhlenberg, John Peter Gabriel	1746-1807	Revolutionary War	125	260	375		Gen. Cont. Army, ALS/Cont. 2400
Muhlenberg, W. Augustus		Clergy	25	40	60		
Muir, Jean		Entertainment	8	9		20	
Muir, John	1838-1914	Science	350	725	1200	1000	Scot.-Am. Naturalist, Explorer
Muir, Maj. Gen. James I.	1888-1964	Military	30				World War II U.S. general
Mukai, Chiaki		Astronaut	10	25		27	
Muldaur, Diana		Entertainment	6	8	15	20	
Muldaur, Maria		Entertainment	5			15	
Mulder, Jan		Political	10			15	Member European Parliament
Muldoon, Robert		Head of State	10	20	30	20	Prime Minister New Zealand
Mulgrew, Kate		Entertainment	6	6	15	42	As 'Janeway' from Voyager 55
Mulhare, Edward		Entertainment	15			40	
Mulheen, R.J.		Business	3	5		8	CEO Boston & Maine RR Corp.
Mull, Martin		Entertainment	5	6		20	
Mullally, Megan		Entertainment	10			45	Will and Grace
Mullane, Richard M.		Astronaut	5			10	
Muller, Herman J.		Science	20	35	75	60	Nobel Medicine 1946
Muller, Hermann	1876-1931	Statesman	45		200		Ger. Foreign Minister. Chancellor
Mullican, Moon		Country Music	10			20	

NAME	DATE	CATEGORY	SIG	LS/DS	ALS	SP	COMMENTS
Mulligan, Gerry		Entertainment	12			25	Baritone Sax. Arranger-Composer
Mulligan, James A.	1830-1864	Civil War	227	500	690		Union Col. KIA; Irish Brig. War Dte.LS 550-850
Mulligan, Richard		Entertainment	5	5		15	
Mulligan, Robert		Entertainment	5			20	
Mullin, Willard		Cartoonist	10			30	Sports Cartoonist
Mullins, Maj. Gen. Charles L. Jr.	1892-1976	Military	30				World War II U.S. general
Mullowney, Deborah		Entertainment	4	6	10	15	
Mumpower, Carl		Author	8			12	Vietnam and self help books
Mumy, Bill		Entertainment	5	10	15	15	Child Actor
Munch, Charles		Entertainment	45		335	35	Ger. Conductor
Munch, Edvard	1863-1944	Artist	65	350	1118		Nor. Painter-Printmaker
Mundel, Ed		Entertainment	6			25	Music. Lead Guitar 'Monster Magnet'
Mundelein, Geo. Wm., Cardinal		Clergy	65	110	225	90	
Mundt, Karl E.		Senate	10	20		35	MOC, Senator SD, Educator
Munford, Thomas T.	1831-1918	Civil War	110		220		CSA Gen. Sig/Rank 310
Muni, Paul	1895-1965	Entertainment	7595	72	120	207	Academy Award 'Story of Louis Pasteur' 1936
Munky		Entertainment	5			25	Music. Guitar 'Korn'
Munnekrede, Lt. Gen. Petrus J. v.	1878-1948	Military	20				World War II Dutch general
Munro, Caroline		Entertainment	5	6	15	40	
Munro, Janet		Entertainment	12			30	Br. Actress. Disney Charmer
Munro, Leslie K., Sir		Diplomat	10	15		25	Pres. UN Assembly
Munro, Maj. Gen. Archibald C.	1886-1961	Military	225				World War II British general
Munro, Peter Jay	1767-1833	Jurist	30	65	155		Nephew of John Jay
Munsel, Patrice		Entertainment	10	20	50	50	Met. Debut at 18
Munsey, Frank A.		Editor	15		35		Muncey's Magazine
Munson, Ona		Entertainment	225			250	Became Classic as 'Belle Watling' in 'GWTW'
Munster, Earl of		Military	10	25	40		
Munsterberg, Hugo	1863-1916	Science		70		95	Ger-Born Am. Psychologist
Munsters		Entertainment				325	signed group
Munteanu, Petre		Entertainment	35	110	165		Opera
Muntz, Earl 'Madman'		Business	13	18	25	20	Pioneer TV Advertiser-Owner
Mura, Maj. Gen. Takaiki		Military	25				World War II Japanese general
Murai, Maj. Gen. Kenjiro	d. 1944	Military	25				World War II Japanese general
Muraji, Maj. Gen. Toshio		Military	25				World War II Japanese general
Murakami, Maj. Gen. Makoto		Military	25				World War II Japanese general
Murat, Joachim	1767-1815	Fr. Revolution	135	342	548		Napoleon Marshal, Gov. Paris, King Naples
Murata, Maj. Gen. Takaiki		Military	25				World War II Japanese general
Murchie, Lt. Gen. John Carl	1895-1966	Military	20				World War II Canadian general
Murchison, Clint		Business	10	15	25	20	TX Oil Entrepreneur Millionaire
Murchison, Clint, Jr.		Business	5	10	20	12	
Murdoch, Rupert		Business	10	35	55	30	International Newspaper Publ.
Murison, Maj. Gen. Charles A. P.	1894-1981	Military	25				World War II British general
Murkowski, Lisa		Senate	10			15	United States Senate (R - AK)
Muroya, Maj. Gen. Chuichi		Military	25				World War II Japanese general
Murphy Brown (Show-Cast of)		Entertainment				275	Seven Main Characters

NAME	DATE	CATEGORY	SIG	LS/DS	ALS	SP	COMMENTS
Murphy, Audie	1924-1971	Military	128	212	325	412	Western Film Star & WW II MOH Winner
Murphy, Ben		Entertainment	5	6	15	15	
Murphy, Brittany		Celebrity				40	
Murphy, Eddie		Entertainment	25			42	
Murphy, Edward, Jr.	1836-1911	Congress	6	12			Senator NY
Murphy, Erin		Entertainment	5			15	Actress. Tabitha
Murphy, Frank	1890-1949	Supreme Court	40	80	120	150	
Murphy, Franklin		Governor	5	10		10	Governor NJ
Murphy, George L.	1902-1992	Entertainment	20	25	35	45	U.S. Senator from CA., Film Song & Dance Man
Murphy, John Cullen*		Cartoonist	5			45	Big Ben Bolt & Prince Valiant
Murphy, Richard		Author	15		25		Screenwriter
Murphy, Simon Francis		Political	10			15	Member European Parliament
Murphy, Tim M		Congress	10			15	Member U.S. Congress
Murphy, Turk		Entertainment	20	40		50	Bandleader, Composer, Trombone
Murphy, William P., Dr.		Science	30	75	120	80	Nobel Medicine 1934
Murray, Al		Celebrity	10			15	comedian 'the Pub Landlord'
Murray Abraham, F.		Entertainment	10			35	actor
Murray, Anne		Entertainment	5	35		22	Singer
Murray, Arthur		Business	10	15	30	25	Ballroom Dance Studios
Murray, Bill		Entertainment	12			44	Comedian, actor
Murray, Bob		Aviation	12	24	42	30	ACE, WW II
Murray, Brig. Sir Geo. David Keith	1898-1965	Military	25				World War II British general
Murray, Brig. Terence Desmond	1891-1961	Military	25				World War II British general
Murray, Don		Entertainment	5			15	
Murray, Eli	1844-1896	Civil War	30	65			Union Gen., Gov. UT Territory
Murray, General Sir Horatius	1903-1989	Military	25				World War II British general
Murray, George, Bishop		Clergy	25	40	50		
Murray, James A.H..	1837-1915	Lexicographer			225		Oxford English Dictionary
Murray, Jan		Entertainment	4			20	
Murray, Jim		Journalist	5			20	Sports Writer, L.A. Times
Murray, John C., S.J.		Clergy	10	15	35	20	
Murray, Joseph E., Dr.		Science	20	30		25	Nobel Medicine
Murray, Ken	1903-1988	Entertainment	15	20	25	50	Wisecracking Comedian. Radio-TV-Film
Murray, Mae		Entertainment	22	35	50	60	Major Silent Star
Murray, Maj. Gen. Maxwell	1885-1945	Military	30				World War II U.S. general
Murray, Patty		Senate	10			15	United States Senate (D - WA)
Murray, Philip		Labor Leader	35	45	70	50	Pres. CIO, United Steel Workers
Murray, Stuart S.		Military	25	75		45	
Murray, William Vans		Revolutionary War	25	40	90		Diplomat, Lawyer, MOC MD
Murrow, Edward R.	1908-1965	Journalist	53	117		152	'...See It Now'. Live WW II Reports From London etc
Murtha, John P. M		Congress	10			15	Member U.S. Congress
Musante, Tony		Entertainment	4	4		15	
Muscardini, Cristiana		Political	10			15	Member European Parliament
Musgrave, Marilyn N. M		Congress	10			15	Member U.S. Congress
Musgrave, Story, Dr.		Astronaut	10			28	

NAME	DATE	CATEGORY	SIG	LS/DS	ALS	SP	COMMENTS
Musharraf, Pervez		Political	35			102	Prime Minister of Pakistan
Muskie, Edmund		Cabinet	10	25	40	35	Sec'y State. V.P. Candidate/H.H. Humphrey
Musotto, Francesco		Political	10			15	Member European Parliament
Muspratt, Gen. Sir Sydney Fred.	1878-1972	Military	25				World War II British general
Mussa, Antonio		Political	10			15	Member European Parliament
Mussolini, Benito	1883-1945	Head of State	143	226	2223	854	Fascist Italian Dictator. DS/Emanuelle III 150-200
Musumeci, Sebastiano (nello)		Political	10			15	Member European Parliament
Mutaguchi, Lt. Gen. Renya	1888-1966	Military	25				World War II Japanese general
Muto, Fld Mrshl. Nobuyoshi Baron	1866-1933	Military	25				World War II Japanese general
Muto, Lt. Gen. Akira	1892-1948	Military	25				World War II Japanese general
Muybridge, Eadweard		Photographer	150		400		Br.-Am Pioneer Motion Pictures
Muzio, Claudia		Entertainment	200			525	It. Soprano
Myers, Carmel		Entertainment	10				Silent Screen Vamp
Myers, Dee, Dee		Celebrity	10			15	political celebrity
Myers, Mike & Dana Carvey		Entertainment				75	Wayne's World
Myers, Mike		Entertainment	6			40	Actor. 'Austin Powers'
Myers, Russell*		Cartoonist	10		25	70	Broom Hilda
Myerson, Bess		Celebrities	10	20		20	Miss America. NYC Official
Myller, Riitta		Political	10			15	Member European Parliament
Myrick, Daniel		Entertainment				20	writer (with E. Sanchez) of The Blair Witch Project
Myrick, Sue Wilkins M		Congress	10			15	Member U.S. Congress
Myrt and Marge		Entertainment	20			60	Vintage Radio Series

N

NAME	DATE	CATEGORY	SIG	LS/DS	ALS	SP	COMMENTS
Nabokov, Vladimir	1899-1977	Author	250	550	1750	1250	Novelist, Critic, Researched Butterflies. 'Lolita'
Nabors, Jim		Entertainment	15	20	30	60	Actor-Comedian-Singer. 'Gomer Pyle'
Nache, Maria Luise		Entertainment	20			45	Opera
Nadar (F. Tournachon)	1820-1910	Artist-Author	85	175	510		Fr. Caricaturist, Photographer, Balloonist
Nader Khan, Muhammad	1880-1933	Royalty	65			140	King Afghanistan, Assassinated
Nader, George		Entertainment	15		45	40	Actor. Fine Performer. Victim of Studio Politics
Nader, Ralph		Political	10			22	Politician, activist
Nadler, Jerrold N		Congress	10			15	Member U.S. Congress
Nadler, Paul S. Dr.		Celebrity	10			15	financial expert
Nagaoka, Guishi, Gen.	1858-1933	Military	150			975	Father of Japanese Aviation
Nagel, Anne	1912-1966	Entertainment	25			50	Leading Lady 30's-40's
Nagel, Conrad		Entertainment	20	25	45	70	Stage-Film Leading Man to Character Actor
Nagel, Steven R.		Astronaut	5			18	
Nagino, Lt. Gen.		Military	27				World War II Japanese general
Nagle, James	1822-1866	Civil War	45	70	95		Union general
Naglee, Henry M.	1815-1886	Civil War	38	80			Union Gen. War Dte. DS 375
Nagy, Imre	1896-1958	Head of State	90	188			Communist Premier Hungary. Executed
Nail, Jimmy		Entertainment	10			20	Actor

NAME	DATE	CATEGORY	SIG	LS/DS	ALS	SP	COMMENTS
Nair, Sami		Political	10			15	Member European Parliament
Naisbitt, John		Celebrity	10			15	financial expert
Naish, J. Carrol		Entertainment	25			85	Familiar Character Actor
Nakasone, Y.		Head of State	25	35	85	35	Japan.FDC S 35
Nakayama, Maj. Gen. Masayasu		Military	27				World War II Japanese general
Nakazawa, Lt. Gen. Mitsuo		Military	27				World War II Japanese general
Nakoka, Lt. Gen. Yataka		Military	27				World War II Japanese general
Nalder, Maj. Gen. Reginald F. H.	1895-1978	Military	28				World War II British general
Naldi, Nita		Entertainment	20			35	Silent Movies Star
Nanbu, Maj. Gen. Johkichi		Military	27				World War II Japanese general
Nansen, Fridtjof	1861-1930	Explorer	125	230	375	450	Nor. Zoologist, Statesman, Arctic Explorer, Nobel
Napavilova, Zofie		Entertainment	25			65	Opera
Napier, Alan		Entertainment	30			55	Sometimes Menacing Character Actor
Napier, Charles		Entertainment	4	4	9	9	
Napier, Chas. James, Sir		Military	25	60	150		Br. Gen. vs U.S. War 1812
Napier, Maj. Gen. Charles Scott	1899-1946	Military	225				World War II British general
Napier, McVey	1776-1847	Law	10	15	30		Editor 4-7th Encyclopedia Britannica
Napier, Robert C., Sir	1810-1890	Military	45	80	125		Field Marshal, Gov. Gen. India
Napier, Sir Wm. F.P.		Military	20	40	70		Br. General
Napier-Clavering, Maj Gen. N. W.	1888-1964	Military	28				World War II British general
Napoleon I	1769-1821	Royalty	600	1826	15000		Import.LS 7360, DS 6500-10350, Short ANS1897-5500
Napoleon II (Duke Reichstadt)	1811-1832	Head of State	260	1400	1850		Francois-Charles-Jos. Bonaparte
Napoleon III	1808-1873	Royalty	100	260	525		Louis Napoleon, Nephew of Napoleon
Napoleon, Eugene L.J.J.	1856-1879	Military				575	Son of Nap. III. KIA at 23
Napoletano, Pasqualina		Political	10			15	Member European Parliament
Napolitano, Giorgio		Political	10			15	Member European Parliament
Napolitano, Grace F. N		Congress	10			15	Member U.S. Congress
Nares, Maj. Gen. Eric Paytherus	1892-1947	Military	28				World War II British general
Nasby, Petroleum (D. Locke)		Author	50	75	160		Outstanding Humorist
Nash, Charles W.		Industrialist		500			Am. Mfg. Nash Motors. Leading Independent Auto
Nash, Clarence		Entertainment	58			150	
Nash, Graham		Entertainment	10			50	Rock, CSN and Y
Nash, John		Celebrity	10			25	'ABeautiful Mind'
Nash, Ogden	1902-1971	Author	42	60	108	75	Poet-Humorous, Unorthodox
Nash, Walter		Head of State	15	40	85	20	Prime Minister New Zealand
Nashimoto, Fld. Mrshl. Morimasa	1874-1951	Military	27				World War II Japanese general, Prince
Nasir-edun, Shah Qajar		Royalty	750		3500		King (Shah) Persia
Nasmyth, James	1808-1890	Inventor	100		185		Machinist, Engineer. Inv. Steam Hammer
Nassauer, Hartmut		Political	10			15	Member European Parliament
Nasser, Gamal Abdel	1918-1970	Head of State	100	180	350	350	President Egypt
Nast, Conde	b. 1874	Business	10	60			traveler's guides, magazine owner
Nast, Thomas*	1840-1902	Cartoonist	87	250		1442	Political Cartoonist. Signed drwg 250-1000
Nat, Yves		Entertainment					Legendary Pianist. AMusQS 65
Nathan, George Jean		Author	10	15	35	15	Powerful Drama Critic, Editor
Nathans, Daniel, Dr.		Science	25	35	45	30	Nobel Medicine

NAME	DATE	CATEGORY	SIG	LS/DS	ALS	SP	COMMENTS
Nation, Carry	1846-1911	Reformer	175	252	328	2300	Temperance Agitator. Went wrecking in KS w/Hatchet
Natividad, Kitten		Entertainment				20	Model
Natta, Giulio		Science	25	35	80		Nobel Chemistry 1963
Natwick, Mildred		Entertainment	10			25	
Nava, Gregory		Celebrity	10			15	film industry
Navarro, Ramon		Actor	35		125	150	Latin Silent Star.
Navatril, Michel		Titanic	195				Survivor
Navon, Yitzhak		Head of State	20			50	Israel
Naylor, Maj Gen Robt. Francis B.	1889-1971	Military	25				World War II British general
Nazimova, Alla	1879-1945	Entertainment	70			100	Russian Stage & Screen Star
Neagle, Anna, Dame	1904-1986	Entertainment	10	34		35	Beautiful Br. Leading Lady. Stage-Films-Musicals
Neal, Bob		Aviation	20	35	50	40	ACE, WW II, Flying Tigers
Neal, Patricia		Entertainment	6	8		28	Academy Award
Neal, Richard E. N		Congress	10			15	Member U.S. Congress
Neal, Tom		Entertainment	10			20	
Neale, Bob		Aviation	22			70	Flying Tiger Ace. WW II
Neame, Lt. Gen. Sir Philip	1888-1978	Military	25				World War II British general
Nebel, Rudolf		Science	40	125			
Neblett, Carol		Entertainment	10			35	Opera. U.S. Soprano
Necker, Jacques	1732-1804	Fr. Revolution	125	268			Fr. Financier & Statesman
Needham, Hal		Entertainment	10			20	Film Director-Stuntman
Needham, Maj. Gen. Henry	1876-1965	Military	28				World War II British general
Neel, Louis Eugene Felix		Science	20	30	40	25	Nobel Physics
Neely, Thomas B., Bishop		Clergy	15	25	35		
Neeson, Liam		Entertainment	32			62	Actor. AA
Neff, Francine I.		Cabinet	5	10	25	10	
Neff, Hildegarde		Entertainment	20			35	Ger. 40's-50's Leading Lady & Author
Neff, Pat Morris		Governor	10	15		15	Governor TX, Pres. of Baylor U.
Negley, James S.	1826-1901	Civil War	60	65	95		Union Gen., MOC. War Dte. ALS 105
Negri, Pola	1894-1987	Entertainment	38	75		105	Ger. Import to Am. Silent Films
Neher, Fred*		Cartoonist	18			73	
Nehring, Walter	1892-1983	Miltary	40	75			Ger. Gen. WW II
Nehru, B.K.		Diplomat	10	15		20	Ambassador
Nehru, Jawaharlal	1889-1964	Head of State	100	325	600	367	Assassinated.1st Prime Minister India
Neidlinger, Gustav		Entertainment	15			40	Opera
Neil, Stephen, Bishop		Clergy	10	15	35	20	
Neil, Vince		Entertainment	20			50	Rock
Neill, James		Entertainment	15			35	Vintage Stage Actor
Neill, Noel		Entertainment	10			25	Actress 'Lois Lane' 'Superman'
Neill, Sam		Entertainment	15			45	Aussie Leading Man
Neill, Thomas Hewson	1826-1885	Civil War	40	70	110		Union general
Neilson, Adelaide		Entertainment	20				Vintage Actress
Neiman, LeRoy		Artist	45	110	160	125	Colorful Modern Artist
Nell, Stephen, Bishop		Clergy	10	15	35		
Nelligan, Kate		Entertainment	5	8	20	22	

NAME	DATE	CATEGORY	SIG	LS/DS	ALS	SP	COMMENTS
Nelly		Music	20			45	Rap
Nelson, Allison	1822-1862	Civil War	352				Confederate general
Nelson, Ben		Senate	10			15	United States Senate (D - NE)
Nelson, Bill		Senate	10			15	United States Senate (D - FL)
Nelson, Craig T.		Entertainment	10			20	actor
Nelson, David		Entertainment	15			45	Early Family Sitcom. 'Ozzie & Harriett'
Nelson, Ed		Entertainment	10			15	
Nelson, Gaylord		Senate	10	25	40		Gov., Senator WI
Nelson, Gene	1920-1996	Entertainment	15			60	Dancer-Actor. Films & Stage
Nelson, George D.		Astronaut	5			15	
Nelson, Harriet Hilliard		Entertainment	25			58	Band Singer-Actress. 'Ozzie & Harriet'
Nelson, Horatio, Lord	1758-1805	Military	813	2795	4570		Br. Adm. Trafalgar Hero. ALS/Right Hand 3600
Nelson, Jack		Celebrity	10			15	media/TV personality
Nelson, Jimmy		Entertainment	3	3	6	6	
Nelson, John C.		Author	8			12	World War II, naval
Nelson, John		Cabinet	20	50	95		Tyler Att'y General
Nelson, Judd		Entertainment				40	Actor
Nelson, Knute	1843-1923	Senate	5	15		10	Senator MN
Nelson, Lori		Entertainment	5	6	15	15	Pin-Up SP 15
Nelson, Ozzie & Nelson, Harriet		Entertainment		250		272	Contract Signed By Both
Nelson, Ozzie		Entertainment	35	50		85	Big Band Leader, Actor
Nelson, Paula		Celebrity	10			15	financial expert
Nelson, Richard H.		Military	25			50	Enola Gay radio operator
Nelson, Rick		Entertainment	112	240	410	426	Nelson Family, Teen Idol Star, singer
Nelson, Samuel	1792-1873	Supreme Court	50	175	225		Appointed by Tyler
Nelson, Thomas Jr.	1738-1789	Revolutionary War	600	2600	4500		Signer, Important ALS 17,500
Nelson, Tracy		Entertainment	10			22	Actress-Daughter of Ricky Nelson
Nelson, Trevor		Music	10			15	DJ
Nelson, William 'Bull'	1824-1862	Civil War	368		1380		Union general
Nelson, William L.		Senate/Congress	5	15			MOC MO
Nelson, Willie		Country Music	15			45	Singer-Composer. Alb. S 45
Nelson, Wm. Rockhill	1841-1915	Author	10				Journalist
Nemerov, Howard		Author	10		35	25	3rd Poet Laureate US, Teacher
Nero, Peter		Entertainment	6	8	15	15	Jazz Pianist
Neruda, Pablo	1904-1973	Author	450	2600			Latin American Poet-Nobel Prize Winner
Nesbit, Evelyn	1884-1967	Entertainment	50			525	Girl in the Red Velvet Swing
Nesbit, Wilbur		Author		20	30		
Nesbitt, Cathleen		Entertainment	15			30	
Nesmith, Michael		Entertainment	20			48	Rock, Monkees
Ness, Eliot		Law Enforcement	302	1094		600	
Nesselrode, Carl von		Head of State	75		462		Rus. Count, Foreign Minister, Chancellor
Netanyahu, Benjamin		Political	25			50	Israel PM
Nethercutt Jr., George R. N		Congress	10			15	Member U.S. Congress
Nethersole, Olga		Entertainment	15	40		45	Vintage Stage Actress
Nettles, John		Entertainment	10			20	Actor

NAME	DATE	CATEGORY	SIG	LS/DS	ALS	SP	COMMENTS
Nettleton, Lois		Entertainment	5	6	15	15	
Neubert, Frank		Aviation	25	75			Scored 1st Air Victory 9/1/39
Neuharth, Allen H.		Celebrity	10			15	financial expert
Neuling, Gen. of Inf. Ferdinand	1885-1960	Military	25				World War II German general
Neumann, Theresa	1898-1962	Religious	65	175	395	250	German Stigmatic
Neurath, Konstantin von	1873-1956	Diplomat	75	80	150	115	Ger. Imprisoned For War Crimes
Nevelson, Louise	1900-1988	Artist	50	85	155	200	Russ-Am. Sculptor. Large Abstract Wood Pieces
Neville, Aaron		Entertainment	4			15	Singer Neville Brothers
Neville, Henry		Entertainment	4	4	9	10	
Nevin, Ethelbert	1862-1901	Composer	75	140	320	250	Short Piano Pieces & Songs
Nevins, Allan		Author	12	30			Am. Historian, Editor, Professor
New Kids on the Block		Entertainment	50			175	
New, Harry S.	1858-1937	Cabinet	15	30	50	20	PMG 1923. US Senn, IN
Newberry, Truman H.		Cabinet	15	20	35		Sec'y Navy 1908
Newcomb, Simon	1835-1909	Science	65	195	228		Am. Astronomer, Mathematician
Newcome, Jack		Author	8			12	sports history
Newell, Frederick B., Bishop		Clergy	20	25	50	30	
Newell, Richard		Business	10	20			American Entrepreneur
Newgarden, Maj. Gen. Paul W.	1892-1944	Military	30				World War II U.S. general
Newhart, Bob		Entertainment	6	12	15	28	Comedian. 3 Successful TV Series
Newhouse, Samuel		Business	15	25	60	25	Newspaper-Radio-TV Empire
Newley, Anthony	1931-1999	Composer	40			58	Talented Composer-Actor-Singer
Newman, Barry		Entertainment	4	6		10	
Newman, Edwin		Celebrity	4	10	20	15	News Broadcaster
Newman, James		Astronaut	5			20	
Newman, John Henry, Card'	1801-1890	Clergy	112	275	608	395	Leader Oxford Movement. ALS/Cont. 1600-1800
Newman, Maj. Gen. Arthur	1896-1976	Military	25				World War II British general
Newman, Maj. Gen. Hubert Thos.	1895-1965	Military	25				World War II British general
Newman, Nanette		Entertainment	10			20	Actress
Newman, Paul		Entertainment	75	171		169	Major Motion Picture Star. Authentic Sigs. Rare
Newman, Phyllis		Entertainment	10			20	actress
Newman, Randy		Entertainment	10			38	AA songwriter
Newman, Rob		Celebrity	10			15	comedian
Newmar, Julie		Entertainment	8	10	20	30	
Newsom, Tommy		Entertainment				15	Band Leader
Newton, Helmut		Celebrity				40	Photographer
Newton, Huey P.		Activist	100			1150	Afro-Am. Activist
Newton, Isaac, Sir	1642-1727	Science	4750	10425	17500		LS/cont 16,500
Newton, John	1822-1895	Civil War	40	85	140		Union General, War Date ALS 325
Newton, Juice		Entertainment	10	12	15	25	Singer
Newton, Maj. Gen. Thomas C.	1885-1976	Military	25				World War II British general
Newton, Robert		Clergy	35	45	45	60	
Newton, Robert		Entertainment	50	65	95	128	Deceased British actor
Newton, Wayne		Entertainment	9	10		47	Singer
Newton-John, Olivia		Entertainment	15			248	Singer-Actress

NAME	DATE	CATEGORY	SIG	LS/DS	ALS	SP	COMMENTS
Ney, Michel, Duc d'	1769-1815	Fr. Napoleon	125	310	718		Marshal of France
Ney, Richard		Entertainment	15			35	
Ney, Robert W. N		Congress	10			15	Member U.S. Congress
Ngo Dinn Diem	1901-1963	Head of State	100				Pres. South Vietnam
Ngor, Haing S., Dr.	d. 1996	Entertainment	30		50	100	Murdered AA winner
Nianick, Jack		Military	5	10	15	20	WW II P-51 flight instructor
Niarchos, Stavro		Business	45	110	190	75	Gr. Millionaire Shipping Magnate
Niblack, Albert P.		Military	50		145		Am. WW I Adm.
Nichol, Phil		Celebrity	10			15	comedian
Nicholas I	1796-1855	Royalty	175	515			Emperor of Russia (Iron Czar)
Nicholas I	1841-1921	Royalty	50	110	225		King of Montenegro
Nicholas II	1868-1918	Royalty		1050	4600	4850	Last Czar of Russia. Executed
Nicholas, Denise		Entertainment	5	5		15	
Nicholas, Grand Duke of Russia	1856-1929	Royalty				1200	Grandson of Czar Nicholas I
Nicholas, Harold and Fayard		Entertainment	50			100	tap dancers, 'Brotherhood in Rhythm', 100+ movies
Nicholas, Thomas Ian		Entertainment	10			20	actor
Nicholls, Francis R. T.	1834-1912	Civil War	110	160	240		CSA General, Gov LA
Nicholls, Maj. Gen. John S.	1896-1954	Military	25				World War II British general
Nicholls, Maj. Gen. Sir Leslie B.	1895-1975	Military	25				World War II British general
Nichols, (John) Beverley	1893-1983	Author		125	175		
Nichols, Barbara		Entertainment	10			25	
Nichols, Ebenezer B.		Business	35	195			Major Early TX Entrepreneur. Banker
Nichols, John Anthony		Senate/Congress	5		15		MOC NC
Nichols, Mike		Entertainment	35	75		92	Film Director
Nichols, Nichelle		Entertainment	15			35	Actress. 'Star Trek'
Nichols, Red		Entertainment	35			60	Jazz Instrumentalist
Nichols, Ruth Roland	1901-1960	Aviation	125	180		250	Holder of Flying Records
Nichols, William A.	1818-1869	Civil War	25	80			General
Nicholson Of Winterbourne,		Political	10			15	Member European Parliament
Nicholson, Dana Wheeler		Entertainment	10			20	actress
Nicholson, Jack		Entertainment	22			64	SP as 'Joker' 65-80. Academy Award Winner
Nicholson, James		Political	10			15	Member European Parliament
Nicholson, John	1783-1846	Military	30	75	190		Commodore U.S. Navy
Nicholson, Maj. Gen. Francis L.	1884-1953	Military	25				World War II British general
Nicholson, Meredith	1866-1947	Author	20	80	125	60	
Nick, Nasty		Celebrity	10			15	reality TV
Nickerson, Francis Stillman	1826-1917	Civil War	40	75	115		Union General
Nickles, Don		Senate	10			15	United States Senate (R - OK)
Nicks, Stevie		Entertainment	18			48	Fleetwood Mac
Nicol, Alex		Entertainment	10			25	Actor
Nicola, Nassira		Entertainment	10			20	actress
Nicolai, Elena		Entertainment	30			85	Opera
Nicolay, John G.	1832-1901	Civil War	52	138	312		Lincoln Personal Sec'y. Author
Nicollet, Joseph N.		Explorer	105	225	345		1st Expedition Headwaters Mississippi River
Nicollier, Claude		Astronaut	10			30	

NAME	DATE	CATEGORY	SIG	LS/DS	ALS	SP	COMMENTS
Niebler, Angelika		Political	10			15	Member European Parliament
Niebuhr, H. Richard	1892-1971	Clergy	35	60	95	50	
Niebuhr, Reinhold		Clergy-Author	58	110	135	85	Am. Major Theologian
Niehoff, Gen. of Infantry Hermann	1897-1980	Military	25				World War II German general
Nielsen, Alice	1876-1943	Entertainment	35			150	Opera-Operetta
Nielsen, Asta		Entertainment	20			50	Opera
Nielsen, Brigitte		Entertainment	5			25	
Nielsen, Carl	1865-1931	Composer	180	450	1025		Danish Composer, Conductor
Nielsen, Gertrude		Entertainment	10			25	
Nielsen, Leslie		Entertainment	10			32	actor
Nielsen, Terry		Entertainment	8	9		15	
Niemack, Horst		Military	40		125	50	German WW II Major General
Niemoller, Martin	1892-1984	Clergy	72	270	410	200	In Concentration Camp WW II
Niesen, Gertrude		Entertainment	10			15	Singer
Nietzsche, Friedrich	1844-1900	Author	750	3500	7765		Ger. Poet, Philosopher, Philology
Nigh, William		Entertainment	10			30	Actor-Director
Nightingale, Florence	1820-1910	Science	425	728	1264		Br. Nurse, Hospital Reformer, Humanitarian
Nijinsky, Vaslav	1890-1950	Entertainment	440			3250	Ballet
Nikisch, Artur		Conductor	25	65	85	375	Hung. Conductor. AMusQS 100
Nikolayev, Andryan G.		Cosmonaut	48			65	Russian Cosmonaut
Nillson, Christine	1843-1921	Entertainment	60		125		Swedish Opera Singer
Nilssen, Anna Q.		Entertainment	15	20		45	
Nilsson, Birgit	1918-19??	Entertainment	15			35	Swe.Soprano, Opera
Nilsson, Harry		Entertainment	50			100	
Ni'matullah, Hajji		Author	4200		7200		Mystic Scholar. Clergy
Nimersheim, Jack		Author	5	8	20	20	Campbell Award nominee
Nimitz, Chester W.	1885-1966	Military	114	233	390	487	Fleet Adm. WW II., SP Surrender 1500,TLS/cont 1500
Nimoy, Leonard		Entertainment	35	65	75	68	'Star Trek'
Nin, Anais	1903-1977	Author	45	125	250	150	Fr. Born Am. Author. Content ALS 395
Nina		Model	4			15	
Nirenberg, Marshall W.		Science	15	25	45	20	Nobel Medicine 1968
Nirvana (3)		Entertainment				318	Rock
Nisbit, Eugenius Aristides		Senate/Congress	20	80	150		MOC GA 1839
Nissen, Greta		Entertainment	10			25	
Nissen, Hans Hermann		Entertainment	25			80	Opera
Nistico', Giuseppe		Political	10			15	Member European Parliament
Niven, David	1909-1983	Entertainment	50	92	130	85	AA.Sophisticated Versatile Br. Actor
Nivernais, Louis Mancini-. Duc de		Military			725		French Soldier-Diplomat
Nixon, Cynthia		Entertainment				42	Miranda Hobbes, Sex in the City
Nixon, John	1733-1808	Revolutionary War	125	320			Proclaimed Decl. Ind. 1st Time
Nixon, Marion		Entertainment	15			40	
Nixon, Marni		Entertainment	8			20	Sang for Audrey Hepburn, Susan Hayward
Nixon, Patricia	1912-1992	First Lady	47	79	325	127	SWH Card 75-130
Nixon, Richard & Pat Nixon		President-1st Lady	300			498	
Nixon, Richard M. (As Pres.)		President	200	590	28680	435	TLS/cont2000-7475. DS/cont 4900, Special SP 1035

NAME	DATE	CATEGORY	SIG	LS/DS	ALS	SP	COMMENTS
Nixon, Richard M.	1913-1994	President	178	314	4311	246	Signed resignation 1250-2000. TLS/cont 1500-2500
Nizer, Louis		Law	25	40	65	50	Noted Trial Attorney
Nkomo, Joshua		Head of State	55	125	275	85	African Nationalist, Zimbabwe
No Doubt		Entertainment				125	Rock group
Nobel, Alfred	1833-1896	Science	250	750	2415	1000	ALS/Content 3,500
Nobile, Umberto	1885-1978	Aviation	75	276	335	225	It. Aeronautical Arctic Pioneer Engineer
Nobilia, Mauro		Political	10			15	Member European Parliament
Noble, Edward J.	1881-	Business	95		395		Candy Mfg. Popularized 'Lifesavers'
Noble, Emma		Celebrity	10			15	celebrity model
Noble, James		Entertainment	5	6	15	15	
Noble, John W.	1831-1912	Civil War	35	50	75	150	Union Gen. CW. Sec'y Interior
Noble, Ray		Bandleader	25				British
Noble, Robert	1861-1939	Military	20		50	35	General.Campaigns from Geronimo to WW I
Noboa, Gustavo		Political				25	President of Ecuador
Nodl, Lt. Gen. Onésime-Paul	1880-1944	Military	20				World War II French general
Noe, Sydney P.		Numismatist	5	15			
Noel, Baptist W.	1798-1873	Clergy	20	35	38		Br. Evangelical Minister
Noel-Baker, Philip	1889-1982	Statesman	30	40	75	75	Nobel Peace Prize
Noguchi, Isamu		Artist	25		65		Am. Sculptor, Designer
Noguchi, Thomas T.		Celebrity	10	30		18	Coroner, Los Angeles
Nogueira Román, Camilo		Political	10			15	Member European Parliament
Noguès, Gen Chas.-Auguste-Paul	1876-1971	Military	20				World War II French general
Nolan, Jeanette		Entertainment	5	6	15	15	
Nolan, Kathleen		Entertainment	8			15	
Nolan, Lloyd	1902-1985	Entertainment	10	35		50	Fine Versatile Film Actor
Nolan, Mae E.		Congress	10	18			Repr. CA 1923
Nolin, Gene Lee		Entertainment	20			45	Actress. 'Baywatch'
Nolte, Nick		Entertainment	10	25		40	
Nomura, Kichisaburo		Diplomat	275				Japanese Ambassador 12/7/41
Nono, Luigi	1924-1990	Composer	115			175	Opera. Conductor
Nonweiler, Maj. Gen. Wilfrid Ivan	1900-1953	Military	28				World War II British general
Noodles		Entertainment	6			25	Music. Guitar 'Offspring'
Noonan, Fred J.	1893-1937	Aviation		368			Guam-San Francisco Flight Cover S 995
Noonan, Peggy		White House	5	20			Reagan Speech Writer
Noone, Peter		Entertainment	20			45	Herman's Hermits
Noor, Queen		Head of State	15	40	125	70	Queen of Hussein (Jordan)
Norblad, Albin W.		Congress	15	30		20	Repr. OR. Intelligence Officer WW II
Norblin, Emile		Entertainment	85			350	Celebrated Cellist
Nordau, Simon Max	1849-1923	Science	65	95	175	150	Hung. Phys.-Writer, AMsS 1750, ALS/cont 1208
Nordenskjold, Nils Adolf E.		Explorer	200			340	Navigated North-East Passage
Nordenskjold, Nils Otto		Explorer	215			300	Led Antarctic Expedition, Rescued
Nordhoff, Charles		Author	20	35	37		Collaborator 'Mutiny on the Bounty'
Nordhoff, Heinz, Dr.		Business	25			50	Auto Mfg.-VW
Nordica, Lillian	1859-1914	Entertainment	60			350	Am. Soprano
Nordmann, Jean-thomas		Political	10			15	Member European Parliament

NAME	DATE	CATEGORY	SIG	LS/DS	ALS	SP	COMMENTS
Nordsieck, Kenneth		Astronaut	6			16	
Norgay, Tenzing		Celebrity	40	110	255	150	Sherpa uide. Mt. Everest
Noriega, Carlos		Astronaut	6			20	
Noriega, Manuel A.		Head of State	50	75		75	Gen., Notorious Pres. Panama
Norman, Barry		Celebrity	10			15	television presenter
Norman, Brian		Music	10			15	DJ
Norman, Emma		Celebrity	10			15	television presenter
Norman, Jessye		Entertainment	20			35	Opera.US Soprano
Norman, Lucille	1926-	Entertainment	10			35	Film Actress from 1942
Norman, Maj. Gen. Charles Wake	1891-1974	Military	25				World War II British general
Norman, Sam		Celebrity	10			15	television presenter
Normand, Mabel		Entertainment	135			379	Silent Screen Comedienne. Talented-Popular
Norris, Chuck		Entertainment	8	10		35	
Norris, Frank	1870-1902	Author	125	275	525		Novelist, War Correspondent
Norris, George W.		Senate/Congress	15	30		40	MOC, Sen.NE. Fathered TVA
Norris, J. Frank Dr.		Clergy	5	15	25	10	Fundamentalist Baptist Pastor
Norris, Kathleen		Author	20	40	65	25	Prolific Am. Novelist
Norstad, Lauris	1907-1989	Military	40	60		75	Gen.WW II
North, Brownlow		Clergy	15	25	40		
North, Frederick, Lord	1732-1792	Head of State	102	420	595		Br. P.M. During Am. Revolution. 2nd Earl Guilford
North, Jay		Entertainment	10			28	Child actor, 'Dennis the Menace'
North, John Jr.		Author	8			12	gangland history
North, John Ringling		Business	40	82	135	85	Ringling Brothers Circus
North, Oliver L.		Military	20	40	75	55	Iran-Contra Affair
North, Sheree		Entertainment	5	6	15	15	Actress
North, William	1755-1836	Military	75	185	488		Gen. Cont. Army. US Senator NY
Northam, Jeremy		Entertainment	10			20	actor
Northcott, General John	1890-1966	Military	20				World War II Australian general
Northrop, John K.	1895-1981	Industrialist	45	125	275	110	Engineer-Designer. Founder Northrop Aircraft etc
Northrop, Lucius Bellinger	1811-1894	Civil War	175	278			Confederate general
Northrup, John H.	1893-1987	Science	45	150		100	Nobel Chemistry 1946
Northup, Anne M. N		Congress	10			15	Member U.S. Congress
Norton, Daniel Sheldon		Senate/Congress	7	10	25		Senator MN 1865
Norton, Edward		Entertainment	7			55	Actor.
Norton, Eleanor Holmes N		Congress	10			15	Member U.S. Congress
Norton, Gerald		Military	20			45	Brit. WW II Hero. Victoria Cross
Norton, Graham		Celebrity	10			15	television presenter
Norton, Lt. Gen. Edward Felix	1884-1954	Military	25				World War II British general
Norton, Mary Teresa		Senate/Congress	10	25		15	MOC NJ 1925-51
Norton-Taylor, Judy		Entertainment	10	15		20	Pin-Up SP 25
Norville, Deborah		Journalist	8			20	TV News Anchor
Norvo, Red		Entertainment	15			40	Band Leader, Vibes, Xylophone
Norwood, Charlie N		Congress	10			15	Member U.S. Congress
Norworth, Jack	1879-1956	Composer	130		372		'TakeMe Out to the Ball Game'
Noseworthy, Jack		Entertainment	10			20	actor

NAME	DATE	CATEGORY	SIG	LS/DS	ALS	SP	COMMENTS
Nosworthy, Lt. Gen. Sir Francis P.	1887-1971	Military	25				World War II British general
Noth, Chris		Entertainment				35	Mr. Big, Sex in the City
Notkin, Boris		Celebrity	10			15	political celebrity
Nott, Eliphalet	1773-1866	Clergy-Inventor	20	80			Pres. Union College 62 Years
Nouira, Hedi		Head of State	7		15		Tunisia
Nouri, Michael		Entertainment	7			20	Actor
Nourse, Amos, Dr.		Senate/Congress	35	50			Senator ME 1/16-3/3/1857
Nourse, Carl C.		Business	10	20			Noted Ohio Businessman
Nourse, Joseph	1754-1841	Military	100	260			DS/Content 2,000
Novaes, Guiomar		Entertainment	30			155	Great Classical Pianist of 20th Century.
Novak, Kim		Entertainment	20	30	40	57	Actress
Novak, Michael		Clergy	15	20	35		
Novak, Robert		Celebrity	10			15	political celebrity
Novak, Vitezslav		Composer	40			150	Czech. Composer
Novarro, Ramon	1899-1968	Entertainment	55		195	110	Mexican Silent Movie Star. Murdered 1968
Novatna, Jarmila		Entertainment	15	45		35	Czech. Soprano
Novello, Ivor		Entertainment	25		80	75	Br. Actor, Composer, Film Star
Novoselic, Krist		Entertainment	10			38	Music. Bass Guitar, Vocals. 'Nirvana'
Nowak, Max		Science	15			45	Rocket Pioneer w/von Braun
Noyce, Philip		Celebrity	10			15	film industry
Noyes, Alfred	1880-1958	Author	25	60	75	40	Br. Poet, Poetic Plays, Stories
Noyes, Edward F.		Governor	10	20		15	Governor OH
Noyes, General Sir Cyril Dupré	1885-1946	Military	25				World War II British general
N'Sync (5)		Entertainment	55			155	Rock Group (5)
NTmeth, Maria		Entertainment	20			60	Opera
Nucci, Danny		Entertainment	10			20	actor
Nugent, Elliott		Entertainment	6	10		15	Broadway & Film Actor
Nugent, Maj. Gen. John Fagan H.	1889-1975	Military	28				World War II British general
Nugent, Ted		Entertainment	12		35	60	Guitarist 'Amboy Dukes'
Nugent, Thomas	1700-1772	Author			120		
Nuland, Sherwin		Celebrity	10			15	medical expert
Numans, Maj. Gen. Anthoine	1880-1948	Military	20				World War II Dutch general
Numata, Lt. Gen. Takazo		Military	25				World War II Japanese general
Nunes, Devin N		Congress	10			15	Member U.S. Congress
Nungesser, Charles		Aviation	135	233	548	300	
Nunn, Sam		Senate	15			40	Senator GA
Nureyev, Rudolf	1938-1993	Entertainment	90	125	212	303	Kirov Ballet Dancer-Choreographer
Nurmella, Kari		Entertainment	15			35	Opera
Nurse, Brigadier Harry S.	1896- ?	Military	30				World War II Australian general
Nussle, Jim N		Congress	10			15	Member U.S. Congress
Nutkins, Terry		Celebrity	10			15	naturalist
Nutt, Clifford C.	1896-	Military	55	150			USA Gen.-Command Pilot. Decorated; Mackay Trophy
Nutter, Mayf		Country Music	10			20	
Nuyen, France		Entertainment	8	8	15	15	Actress. Interesting, Short-lived Career
Nye, Bill (Edgar Wilson)		Author	18		85		Humorist

NAME	DATE	CATEGORY	SIG	LS/DS	ALS	SP	COMMENTS
Nye, Gerald P.		Senate	8	15		15	Senator ND
Nye, James W.	1815-1876	Senate	75	140	175		Gov. Nevada Terr. 1861. Sen. NE '64
Nye, Lt Gen Sir Archibald Edward	1895-1967	Military	25				World War II British general
Nyerere, Julius		Head of State	30	50	85	150	Prime Minister, President Tanzania.
Nykvist, Sven		Celebrity	10			15	film industry

NAME	DATE	CATEGORY	SIG	LS/DS	ALS	SP	COMMENTS
Oak Ridge Boys, The (4)		Country Music	10			58	Country Western singing group
Oakes, Randi		Entertainment	5			15	
Oakie, Jack		Actor	25			127	
Oakie, Jack		Entertainment	20	95		89	
Oakley, Annie	1860-1926	Markswoman	1815		7964	4500	Am. Markswoman/Buffalo Bill, signed chk 3795-6158
Oakley, Violet		Artist	35	95			Her 'The Tragic Muse' Famous
Oates, Joyce Carol		Author	18	30	60	30	Am. Novelist, Critic, Poet, Teacher
Oates, Lawrence E. G.	1880-1912	Explorer	100		575		Antarctic Explorer
Oates, Warren		Entertainment	25			50	
Oates, William C.	1833-1910	Civil War		397			Col. CSA, Little Round Top
Obasanjo, Olusegun		Political				50	President of Nigeria
Obata, General Hideyoshi	1880-1944	Military	27				World War II Japanese general
Ober, W.O. 'Willy'		Aviation	25		55		
Oberhardt, William		Artist	30	65	135		Portraits. Eisenhower, Hoover....
Oberon, Merle		Entertainment	45			180	Major Star. Of Mysterious Heritage
Oberstar, James L. O.		Congress	10			15	Member U.S. Congress
Oberth, Hermann, Dr.	1894-1989	Science	68	225		180	Hung. Early Rocket Pioneer. TLS/Cont. 4250
Obey, David R. O.		Congress	10			15	Member U.S. Congress
Obiols I Germà, Raimon		Political	10			15	Member European Parliament
Oboler, Arch		Entertainment	12		35	25	Writer-Producer of Radio Dramas
Obratszova, Elena		Entertainment	10			40	Opera. Glamourous Rus. Mezzo
O'Brien, Conan		Entertainment	4			30	Late Night TV Host
O'Brien, Cubby		Entertainment	5			20	Mickey Mouse Club
O'Brien, Edmond		Entertainment	20	40		50	AA
O'Brien, Frederick		Author	8			12	South Seas true adventure
O'Brien, George		Entertainment	20			40	
O'Brien, Hugh		Entertainment	6			20	TV Wyatt Earp
O'Brien, James		Business	5	10	35		
O'Brien, Lawrence F.	1917-1990	Cabinet	10	20	40	70	JFK Adviser-Strategist.P.M.Gen.
O'Brien, Margaret		Entertainment	15			38	Sig. As Child 50
O'Brien, Pat	1899-1963	Entertainment	45	65		88	Actor. Knute Rockne
O'Brien, Virginia		Entertainment	5			10	Singer-Actress, Somber-faced Comedienne
Obstfelder, Gen. of Inf. Hans von	1886-1976	Military	27				World War II German general
Obukhova, Nadezhda	1886-1961	Entertainment	75		400		Opera.Greatest Russ. Contralto of Century
O'Callaghan, Mike		Governor	5	15		10	Governor NV

NAME	DATE	CATEGORY	SIG	LS/DS	ALS	SP	COMMENTS
Ocasek, Ric		Entertainment	25			50	Rock
O'Casey, Sean	1880-1964	Author	112	197	384	350	Irish Playwright. Abbey Theatre. 'Plough & the Stars'
Ochles, Wubbo		Astronaut	10	25		25	
Ochoa, Ellen		Astronaut	6			22	
Ochoa, Severo, Dr.		Science	22	35	85	30	Nobel Physiology & Medicine
Ochs, Adolph S.	1858-1935	Business	75	110		125	Publisher-Founder NY Times
Ochsner, Albert John	1858-1925	Science	15			31	American physician and surgeon
O'Connell, Arthur		Entertainment	30			65	
O'Connell, Charles		Business	10	15	30	15	
O'Connell, Daniel	1775-1847	Statesman-Patriot	75	250	633		Irish Nationalist Leader
O'Connell, Helen		Entertainment	15			30	
O'Connell, Jerry		Entertainment	5			30	Actor. 'Scream' SP 42
O'Connell, William H., Cardinal		Clergy	50	65	75	65	
O'Conner, Flannery		Author	300	925			Am. Author. Died At Age 39
O'Conner, Gen. Sir Richard N.	1889-1981	Military	28				World War II British general
O'Connor, Basil		Celebrity	15	25		35	1st Pres. March of Dimes Foundation
O'Connor, Bryan D.		Astronaut	5			20	
O'Connor, Carroll		Entertainment	15	45		50	'Archie Bunker', actor
O'Connor, Donald		Entertainment	12			25	Singer-Dancer-Actor. 'Singin' in the Rain' SP 45
O'Connor, Glynnis		Entertainment	5			15	
O'Connor, Sandra Day		Supreme Court	35	70	110	60	Bush Appointee
O'Connor, Una		Entertainment	40			148	Character Actress
O'Connor, Thos. P.	1848-1929	Author	65	120	170		Irish Journalist & Nationalist. (Tay Pay) AMsS 325
O'Conor, Charles	1804-1884	Law-Politician	60	75	175		1st Catholic Presidential Cand.
O'Conor, Herbert R.		Governor	5	10			Gov. MD
O'Daniel, Lt. Gen. John W.	1894-1975	Military	30				World War II U.S. general
O'Daniel, W. Lee 'Pappy'		Senate/Congress	15	50		45	Governor, Senator TX
O'Day, Anita		Entertainment	20				Big Band-Jazz Vocalist
Oddie, Bill		Celebrity	10			15	naturalist
Odell, Benjamin Baker, Jr.		Senate/Congress	10	30	40		MOC 1895, Governor NY 1900
O'Dell, Doye		Entertainment	5			15	C & W Singer-Actor
Odell, George C.D.		Author	5	15	30		Educator, Theatre Arts
Odell, Moses F.	1818-1866	Congress	10	20	30		Repr. NY 1861
Odets, Clifford	1906-1963	Author	40	80	120	140	Playwright. Golden Boy, etc.
O'Diear, James		Author	8			12	WW II novelist/historian
Odlum, Maj Gen Victor Wentworth	1880-1971	Military	24				World War II Canadian general
O'Donald, Emmett		Aviation	15	30	50	35	
O'Donnell, Chris & Val Kilmer		Entertainment					Batman SP 125
O'Donnell, Chris		Entertainment	10			42	'Robin' in Batman
O'Donnell, Maj. Gen. Eric Hugh	1893-1950	Military	25				World War II British general
O'Donnell, Rosie		Entertainment	10			35	Comedienne
O'Donovan, Brig Morgan John W.	1893-1969	Military	25				World War II British general
O'Driscoll, Martha	1922-1989	Entertainment	5			20	40's Film Leading Lady. 30's Pin-up 45
Oe, Kenzburo	1935-	Author	90				Japanese Writer. One of Rarest Living Nobel Winners
Oechmichen, Maj Gen Jean-Fréd.	1876- ?	Military	20				World War II French general

NAME	DATE	CATEGORY	SIG	LS/DS	ALS	SP	COMMENTS
Oersted, Hans Christian	1777-1851	Science	2500	4750			Discovered Electromagnetism
Oesau, Walter 'Gulle'		Aviation	130		415	275	
Offenbach, Jacques	1819-1880	Composer	125	210	493	500	Fr. Composer. Many Operettas. ALS/Content 1,400
Offenhauser, Fred		Engineer	130	395			Automobile, Racing Engine Mfg.
Offspring		Entertainment	28			75	Music. 4 Member Rock Group
O'Flaherty, Liam		Author	90	254			Ir. Novelist. The Informer
Ogden, Aaron		Senator	35	110	225		Am. Rev. War Soldier, Gov. NJ
Ogden, Francis B.	1783-1857	Military	15	68	95		Inventor. Steam Eng. Pioneer
Ogden, Thomas L.	1773-1844	Law	20		45		Law Partner Alexander Hamilton
Ogden, William B.		Political	150	525	925		1st Mayor of Chicago 1837.
Oger, Brig. Gen. J.V.P.G.	1889- ?	Military	20				World War II French general
Ogilvie, Maj. Gen. Sir William H.	1887-1971	Military	25				World War II British general
Ogle, Samuel	d. 1751	Colonial Am.	180	550			Colonial Gov. MD
Ogle, William		Celebrity	5	10	15	8	
Oglesby, Richard J.	1824-1899	Civil War	33	78	105	150	Union Gen., Gov. IL, US Sen. IL
Oglethorpe, James Edward	1696-1785	Colonial Am.		5500	6325		Oneof the Rarest of Colonial Autographs
O'Grady, Gail		Entertainment	10				Actress NYPD Blue Pin-Up 60
Oh, Soon-Teck		Entertainment	5			15	
O'Hair, Madalyn Murray	1919-1995	Celebrity	40	75	160		Atheist, Activist, Mysteriously Disappeared 1955
O'Hanlon, Ardal		Entertainment	10			20	Actor
O'Hanlon, George		Entertainmment	15				Actor-Comedian
O'Hara, Catherine		Entertainment	10			30	
O'Hara, Geoffrey		Composer	20	45		25	AMusQS 65
O'Hara, John F., Cardinal		Clergy	50	85	100	75	
O'Hara, John		Author	160	500	660		Am. Novelist, Short Stories
O'Hara, Mary (Alsop)		Author	20	50	75		Am. Novelist. 'My Friend Flicka'
O'Hara, Maureen		Entertainment	16			30	Irish-Am. Actress. Starred Frequently w/John Wayne
O'Hare, Edward 'Butch'		Military	225	1050			WW II Ace, shot down Nov. 1943
O'Herlihy, Dan		Entertainment	7			15	
O'Higgins, Bernardo	1778-1842	Head of State	450	1250			Chile. Soldier, Statesmn, Dictator
O'Higgins, Harvey		Author	10	20	75	15	Am. Journalist, Novelist
Ohms, Elizabeth		Entertainment	35			150	Opera
Ohrbach, Jerry		Entertainment	8			20	
Oi, Narimoto		Military	40	125	195		
Oistrakh, David	1908-1974	Music				150	Soviet Violinist, Conductor
Ojeda Sanz, Juan		Political	10			15	Member European Parliament
Okamura, General Yasutsugu	1884-1966	Military	27				World War II Japanese general
Oke, Femi		Celebrity	10			15	weather presenter
O'Keefe, Dennis		Entertainment	5	6	15	15	
O'Keefe, Georgia	1887-1986	Artist	306	360	1235	508	Scenes SW Desert. TLS/Cont.3500
O'Keefe, Jodi Lyn		Celebrity				35	
O'Keeffe, Adrian		Business	5	15		10	CEO First National Stores
Okking, Jens Dyhr		Political	10			15	Member European Parliament
Oland, Warner	1880-1938	Entertainment	150			252	Most Famous Charlie Chan
O'Laughlin, Gerald S.		Entertainment	10			20	

NAME	DATE	CATEGORY	SIG	LS/DS	ALS	SP	COMMENTS
Olav V	1903-1991	Royalty	45	125	.		King of Norway
Olbricht, Gen. of Infantry Friedrich	1888-1944	Military	27				World War II German general
Olcott, Chauncey	1860-1932	Composer	44	90	150	90	My Wild Irish Rose etc.Noted Tenor
Oldenburg, Claes Thure	1929-	Artist	20	35	95	40	Swe. Sculptor. Soft Scuptures. Pc Repro S 125
Older, Charles H.		Aviation	12	30	45	32	ACE, WW II, Flying Tigers
Older, Charles S.		Civil War-Gov.	25	40	55		CW Gov. NJ
Oldman, Gary		Entertainment	10			38	Talented, Versatile Actor. 'Dracula'
Olds, Ransom E.	1864-1950	Business	238	1235			REO & Oldsmobile Motor Cars. Stock Cert. S 975
Olds, Robin		Aviation	15	30	45	32	ACE, WW II, Korea, Nam
O'Leary, Brian		Astronaut	5			15	
Oleynik, Larisa		Entertainment	10			20	actress
Olin, John M.		Business	6	12	20	12	Olin Industries
Olin, Ken		Entertainment	5			15	Actor
Olin, Lena		Entertainment	20			50	
Oliphant, Laurence		Author	10	25	60		Br. Writer. Cape Town, S.A.
Oliphant, Pat		Cartoonist	5			30	
Olitzka, Rosa		Entertainment	35	.		125	Pol./Ger. Mezzo
Oliver, Andrew		Revolutionary War	65	185	240		Am.Colonial Politician
Oliver, Daniel		Celebrity	10			15	financial expert
Oliver, Edna May		Entertainment	45			120	
Oliver, George	1873-1961	Author		70			
Oliver, Henry W., Jr.	1840-1904	Business	45	60			Iron & Steel Tycoon
Oliver, Jamie		Celebrity	10			15	TV Chef
Oliver, Jane		Entertainment	6			15	
Oliver, John Morrison	1828-1872	Civil War	45	65	110		Union general
Oliver, Maj. Gen. Lunsford E.	1889-1978	Military	30				World War II U.S. general
Oliver, Paul A.	1830-1912	Civil War	25	50	75		Credit For Inventing Dynamite
Oliver, Sy		Entertainment	30			75	Trumpet, Composer, Arranger
Olivero, Magda		Entertainment	20			100	Opera
Olivetti, Adriano		Industrialist		200		150	Owner Olivetti Typewriter & Business Machines
Olivier, Laurence & Leigh, Vivien		Entertainment					SEE Leigh, Vivien
Olivier, Laurence, Sir	1907-1989	Entertainment	49	98		138	Special DS 2,000. AA. FDC S 95
Olmos, Edward James		Entertainment	8	20	15	20	Actor
Olmstead, Frederick Law	1822-1903	Architect	102	175	412		Landscape Arch, NY Central Park.US Capitol Grounds
Olney, Richard	1835-1917	Cabinet	15	25	45	75	Att'y General, Sec'y State
Olney, Thomas		Clergy	85	125	250		
Olry, General René-Henri	1880-1944	Military	20				World War II French general
Olsen & Johnson		Entertainment	35			75	'Hellzapoppin' 30's Comedy Team
Olsen, Ashley		Entertainment	8			25	Actress 'Full House'
Olsen, George		Entertainment	25			120	Bigband leader
Olsen, Mary Kate & Ashley		Entertainment	15			45	Twin Sister Stars of 'Full House'
Olsen, Mary Kate		Entertainment	8			25	Actress 'Full House'
Olsen, Merlin		Entertainment	9	10	20	25	
Olsen, Ole		Entertainment	25			50	.
Olson, Nancy		Entertainment	6	8	15	15	

NAME	DATE	CATEGORY	SIG	LS/DS	ALS	SP	COMMENTS
Olsson, Karl Erik		Political	10			15	Member European Parliament
Olver, John W.		Congress	10			15	Member U.S. Congress
O'Mahoney, Joseph	1884-1962	Congress	10	35			Senator WY
O'Malley, J. Pat		Entertainment	25			50	
Onassis, Aristotle		Business	175	475		400	Gr. Millionaire Shipping Magnate
Ondricek, Frantisek		Composer				950	Czech Violinist & Composer
O'neachtain, Seán		Political	10			15	Member European Parliament
O'Neal, Alexander		Music	10			15	performing musical artist
O'Neal, Edward Asbury	1818-1890	Civil War	95				Confederate general
O'Neal, Frederick		Entertainment	5			15	Afro-Am. Actor
O'Neal, Ralph A.		Military	22	40	85	70	
O'Neal, Ryan		Entertainment	10			35	
O'Neal, Tatum		Entertainment	15			50	AA
O'Neil, Barbara	1909-1980	Entertainment	250			595	Scarlett O'Hara's Mother in GWTW
O'Neill, Charles	1821-1893	Congress	10		40		Repr. PA 1863
O'Neill, Eugene	1888-1953	Author	138	403	692	1400	Playwright. Nobel & 3 Pulitzers
O'Neill, Henry	1891-1964	Entertainment	10			50	Major Vint.. Character Actor
O'Neill, James		Entertainment	20	25	45	45	Vintage Actor
O'Neill, Jennifer		Entertainment	5	6	15	15	
O'Neill, Peggy		Entertainment	5	6	15	15	
O'Neill, Thomas 'Tip'	1912-1994	Congress	20	35		48	Speaker of the House. MA MOC
Onesta, Gérard		Political	10			15	Member European Parliament
Onizuka, Ellison S.	1946-1986	Astronaut	125			208	Challanger
Ono, Yoko		Entertainment	40		100	75	Jap. Artist, Songwriter. Former John Lennon Wife.
Ontkean, Michael		Entertainment	5	6	15	15	
Oomen-ruijten, Ria G.h.c.		Political	10			15	Member European Parliament
Oostlander, Arie M.		Political	10			15	Member European Parliament
Opatoshu, David	1918-1996	Entertainment	20	35		30	Actor. Many Faceted Character Actor
Opdycke, Emerson	1830-1884	Civil War	45	70	100		Union general
Opdyke, George	1805-1880	Civil War	20	45			CW Mayor of NY.Chk.S '62 900
Opp, Julie		Entertainment	12			25	Opera
Oppenheimer, J. Robert, Dr.	1904-1967	Science	533	1236	4500	1200	Exec. Dir. Manhattan Project.Father of Atomic Bomb
Opper, Frederick Burr*	1857-1937	Cartoonist	25		100	275	Happy Hooligan, signed drwg 750
Orbach, Jerry		Entertainment	10			35	Versatile Stage, Film, TV Actor
Orbison, Roy	1936-1988	Country Music	115	200		244	Blind Singer-Pianist
Orczy, Emmuska, Baroness	1865-1947	Author	40	125	160	150	Br. Novelist, Playwright. 'Scarlet Pimpernel' etc.
Ord, Edward O.C.	1818-1883	Civil War	41	145	375	750	Union Gen-Indian Fighter
Ordzhonikidze, Grigory	1886-1937	Political		242			Russian Communist leader
Oreja Arburúa, Marcelino		Political	10			15	Member European Parliament
Orenstein, Leo		Composer				100	Russ.-US Pianist-Composer
Orff, Carl	1895-1982	Composer	25			172	Ger. Opera. 'Carmina Burana'
Orfila, Matthieu		Science			65		Founder of Toxicology
Orgonotzova, Ludmilla		Entertainment	5			25	Opera
Orient, John H., Bishop		Clergy	5	10	15		
Orita, Zenji		Military	50	160	255	100	

NAME	DATE	CATEGORY	SIG	LS/DS	ALS	SP	COMMENTS
Orlando, Vittorio E.	1860-1952	Head of State	65	135	275		It. Prime Minister, Pres. One of Big Four
Ormandy, Eugene		Conductor	40	40	100	85	Hung.-Am. Conductor Philadelphia Symph. Orch.
Orme, William Ward	1832-1866	Civil War	45	70	120		Union general
Ormond, Julia		Entertainment	25			75	Actress
Orne, Azor	1731-1796	Revolutionary War	100	450			Maj. Gen. Am. Forces
Ornish, Dean		Celebrity	10			18	medical expert, author
O'Rorke, Patrick Henry		Civil War			1236		Union, KIA Little Round Top 1863
Orpen, William, Sir	1878-1931	Artist	45	120	390	350	Portrait, Genre, War Painter
Orr, Marjorie		Celebrity	10			15	Astrologer
Orr, Robert L.		Civil War	45	110			MOH Major 61st Pennsylvania Inf.
Orr, William T.		Entertainment	25				Film Director-Producer
Ortega, Katherine D.		Gov't Official	3	8		10	
Ortega, Manuel Medina		Political	10			15	Member European Parliament
Orth, Godlove Stein	1817-1882	Conngress	20		45		MOC IN. CW Officer. Minister to Austr-Hung
Ortiz, Solomon P. O		Congress	10			15	Member U.S. Congress
Orton, Arthur	1834-1898	Celebrity			180		The Tichborne Claimant
Ortuondo Larrea, Josu		Political	10			15	Member European Parliament
Orvis, Charles F.		Business		322	633		Founder Orvis
Orwell, George	1903-1950	Author		1600			Pen-name of Eric Blair. Rare if Signed Pen-name
Ory, Edward Kid		Entertainment	100			200	Dixieland Band Leader
Osborn, Joan		Entertainment	10			70	Singer
Osborn, Super Dave		Entertainment	12			20	Comic Daredevil
Osborn, Thomas Ogden	1832-1904	Civil War	50	70	125		Union general
Osborne, Baby Marie		Entertainment	10			20	
Osborne, Henry Z.		Senate/Congress	10	20		15	MOC CA 1917
Osborne, John	1929-1994	Author	10	20	40	20	Br. Playwright, Screenwriter
Osborne, Lt. Gen. Edmund A.	1885-1969	Military	25				World War II British general
Osborne, Maj. Gen. Coles Alex.	1896-1964	Military	25				World War II British general
Osborne, Sidney P.		Governor	10	15		10	Governor AZ
Osborne, Thomas A.		Governor	10	15		10	Governor KS
Osborne, Tom O		Congress	10			15	Member U.S. Congress
Osborne, Will	1906-1981	Bandleader	20			35	1st Crooner. Band Leader 1924 to Late 50's
Osbourne, Jack		Celebrity	10			20	Osbourne's
Osbourne, Kelly		Celebrity	10			20	Osbourne's
Osbourne, Ozzy		Entertainment	20			50	
Osbourne, Sharon		Celebrity	10			25	Osbourne's
Oscar I	1799-1859	Royalty	100	280	550		King Sweden & Norway
Oscar II	1829-1907	Royalty	60	190	300		King Sweden & Norway
Ose, Doug O		Congress	10			15	Member U.S. Congress
Osgood, Charles		TV News	4			15	TV News, Host
Osgood, Samuel		Revolutionary War	125	385	535		Cont'l Congress, First P.M. Gen.
O'Shea, Michael	1906-1973	Entertainment	9	35		20	Actor- Films from 30's.Career Ended as Detective
Oshima, Lt. Gen. Hiroshi	1886-1975	Military	27				World War II Japanese general
Osler, William, Dr.	1849-1919	Science	238	410	750		Can. Phys., Important Medical Historian
Oslin, K.T.		Entertainment	5			20	

NAME	DATE	CATEGORY	SIG	LS/DS	ALS	SP	COMMENTS
Osman, Mike		Celebrity	10			15	impressionist
Osmena, Sergio		Head of State	65	200			Pres. Philippines 1944-46
Osment, Haley Joel		Celebrity				40	
Osmond Brothers (3)		Entertainment	10			30	
Osmond, Donny		Entertainment	5	8	15	15	
Osmond, Marie		Entertainment	5	15	20	22	
Osten, Hans Georg von der		Aviation				60	Ger. Ace WW I/Richthofen
Ostenso, Martha		Author	25	45	70		Am. Novelist, Poet
Osterhaus, Peter J.	1823-1917	Civil War	45	79	116		Union Gen.
Osterkamp, Theo		Aviation	35	60	130	70	
Osterman, Kathryn		Entertainment	20			50	Silent Films
O'Sullivan, Gilbert		Entertainment	25	75			
O'Sullivan, Maureen		Entertainment	15	25	35	59	Irish Actress. Jane to 'Tarzan'. Mia Farrow's Mother
Osvoth, Julia		Entertainment	20			45	Opera
Oswald, Lee Harvey	1939-1963	Assassin	1662	7000	9212		Assassin of John F. Kennedy
Oswald, Marguerite		Celebrity			690		Mother to Lee Harvey Oswald
Oswald, Marina (now Porter)		Celebrity	50	125	150	55	Mrs. Lee Harvey Oswald
Oswald, Mark		Entertainment	10			25	Opera
Oswald, Steve		Astronaut	5			20	
Otis, Carre		Model	4				Mrs. Mickey Rourke
Otis, Elita Proctor		Entertainment	10	15	25	25	
Otis, Elwell S.		Civil War	45	66	90		Union Gen.
Otis, Harrison Gray	1765-1848	Congress	25	68	75		Repr. 1797, Sen. MA 1817 MA
Otis, Harrison Gray	1837-1917	Business	75	125	250		General. Publisher. L.A. Times
Otis, James	1725-1783	Revolutionary War	180	436	750		Statesman, Eloquent Lawyer
Otis, Johnny		Entertainment	25			40	R & R Producer, Director. HOF
Otis, Samuel A.	1740-1814	Revolutionary War	242	340	650		Continental Congr.
O'Toole, Annette		Entertainment	10			30	
O'toole, Barbara		Political	10			15	Member European Parliament
O'Toole, Peter		Entertainment	15			73	Actor. AA winner
Otter, C. L. "Butch" O		Congress	10			15	Member U.S. Congress
Otto I (Otho I)	1815-1867	Royalty	105	248	375		King of Greece
Oudinot, Charles N. Duc de		Napoleonic Wars	70	162			Marshal of Napoleon
Ouida, Marie Louise de la Ramee	1839-1905	Author	25	60	118		Br.Novelist. 'A Dog of Flanders'
Ould, Robert	1820-1882	Civil War	60	142	168		CSA Col. POW Exch. ALS '65 690
Ouspenskaya, Maria	1876-1949	Entertainment	235			544	Wolf Man's mother
Outcault, Richard*		Cartoonist	75			450	Yellow Kid, Buster Brown
Outlaw, Edward C.		Aviation	12	25	40	32	ACE, WW II, Ace in a Day
Overakker, Maj. Gen. Roelof T.	1890-1945	Military	20				World War II Dutch general
Overall, Park		Entertainment	5			20	
Overman, Lynn		Entertainment	15			45	30's-40's Film Character Actor
Overmyer, Robert	1936-1996	Astronaut	5			95	2nd Space Shuttle Flight
Ovington, Earle	1879-1936	Aviation	45	80	140	180	Pilot 1st Air Mail Plane
Owanneco, Chief	1645-1710	Mohawk Chief		50000			Last of the Mohicans
Owen, David, Sir		Economist	10	25	40	15	Internat'l Planned Parenthood

NAME	DATE	CATEGORY	SIG	LS/DS	ALS	SP	COMMENTS
Owen, John		Clergy	10	10	15	20	
Owen, Joshua T. (WD)		Civil War	70		225		Union Gen.
Owen, Joshua T.	1821-1887	Civil War	32				Union Gen.
Owen, Nicholas		Celebrity	10			15	news reader
Owen, Reginald		Entertainment	25			35	
Owen, Rhodri		Celebrity	10			15	children's presenter
Owen, Richard, Sir	1804-1892	Science	75	130	175		Anatomist, Zoologist. Inventor of Name 'Dinosaur'
Owen, Robert Dale	1801-1877	Congress-Clergy	20		150		Scottish Born. Repr. IN. Reformer
Owen, Robert	1771-1858	Political		149	250		Br. Utopian Socialist
Owen, Ruth Bryan (Rohde)		Diplomat	20	30		30	1st US Woman Diplomat-MOC FL
Owens, Buck		Aviation	12	28	45	30	ACE, WW II, Marine
Owens, Buck		Country Music	5			20	
Owens, Charlie		Artist					LA Times. Art work signed 950
Owens, Major R. O		Congress	10			15	Member U.S. Congress
Owens, Tex		Country Music	10			20	Wrote 'Cattle Call'
Oxborrow, Brig. Claude Catton	1898-1972	Military	25				World War II British general
Oxenberg, Catherine		Entertainment	25			35	
Oxley, Maj. Gen. Walter Hayes	1891-1978	Military	25				World War II British general
Oxley, Michael G. O		Congress	10			15	Member U.S. Congress
Oxnam, G. Bromley, Bishop		Clergy	35	50	95	45	
Oxnam, Robert		Celebrity	10			15	political celebrity
Oy, Jenna von		Entertainment	5			15	Blossom
Oyen, Lt. Gen. Ludolph H. van	1889-1953	Military	20				World War II Dutch general
Oz, Frank		Entertainment	5	20		25	Self Caricature S 50
Ozanne, Maj. Gen. Wm. Maingay	1891-1966	Military	25				World War II British general

NAME	DATE	CATEGORY	SIG	LS/DS	ALS	SP	COMMENTS
Paar, Jack		Entertainment	6	8	25	25	
Paasilinna, Reino		Political	10			15	Member European Parliament
Pabst, Fred		Business	190	402		322	Pabst Brewing Co.
Paca, William	1740-1799	Revolutionary War	750	1248	2455		Signer. LS (War Date) 2750
Pacca, Bartolomeo, Cardinal		Clergy	45	300			Sec'y of State to Pope Pius VII
Pacetti, Iva		Entertainment	25			108	Opera
Pache, Jean Nicholas		Fr. Revolution	20	65	145		
Pacheco Pereira, José		Political	10			15	Member European Parliament
Pacino, Al		Entertainment	12			62	Actor
Paciotti, Elena Ornella		Political	10			15	Member European Parliament
Pack, Denis, Sir		Military	25	80	125		
Pack, Doris		Political	10			15	Member European Parliament
Packard, David		Business	20	45	90	60	Co-Founder Hewlett-Packard Co.
Packard, James Ward	1863-1928	Business		5800			Founder of Packard Automobile
Packard, Vance		Author	10	20	45	15	Am. Nonfiction Writer

NAME	DATE	CATEGORY	SIG	LS/DS	ALS	SP	COMMENTS
Packer, Mason R.		Celebrity			950		Gold Rush speculator
Packham, Chris		Celebrity	10			15	naturalist
Packwood, Bob		Senate/Congress	10	25		35	Senator OR
Pacula, Joanna		Entertainment	9	10		25	
Paderewski, Ignace J.	1860-1941	Composer	155	310	450	430	Pianist, AMusQS550, 750, 850. Pres. Poland
Padgett, Lemuel P.		Senate/Congress	5	15		10	MOC TN 1901-22
Paduca, Duke of		Country Music	20			40	
Paer, Ferdinando		Composer	40	110	200		Italian Opera Buffo
Paganini, Nicolo	1782-1840	Composer	400	1100	2250		Revolutionized Violin Technique. Violin Virtuoso
Page, Anita		Entertainment	8			15	
Page, Bettie		Celebrity				212	The 'Gibson Girl' Model. Vintage Sketch S
Page, Carroll S.		Senate/Congress	10	25		20	Governor 1890, Senator VT 1908
Page, Geraldine		Entertainment	30			60	AA
Page, Jimmy		Entertainment	15			75	Music. 'Led Zeppelin'
Page, Joanne		Entertainment	5			15	
Page, John	1743-1808	Revolutionary War		275			Patriot, Activist, Gov. VA
Page, Maj. Gen. Lionel Frank	1884-1944	Military	20				World War II Canadian general
Page, Maj. Gen. Sir Charles Max	1882-1963	Military	25				World War II British general
Page, Patti		Entetainment	4			12	
Page, Richard Lucian	1807-1901	Civil War	100	190	542		CSA Gen. Sig/Rank 150
Page, Thomas Nelson	1853-1922	Author	10	20	40		Am. Novelist, Diplomat, Lawyer
Page, William Tyler		Congress	20				
Page, William	1811-1885	Artist	150		410		Am. Portr. Painter. ALS/Cont. 1150
Paget, Charles, Sir	1778-1839	Military	25				Brit. Adm. Napoleonic Wars
Paget, Debra		Entertainment	10			45	Actress
Paget, Gen Sir Bernard Charles T	1887-1961	Military	28				World War II British general
Paget, James, Sir	1814-1899	Science	40	75	140		English Physician. Pathology. Paget's Disease
Pagliughi, Lina		Entertainment	35			140	Opera
Pahlavi, Mohammed Riza	1919-1980	Head of State	150	225	310	350	SP Shah of Iran & Farah Diba Pahlavi 475
Paige, Janis		Entertainment	10		15	28	Actress. Warner Bros. Musicals & Light Comedy
Paige, Mabel		Entertainment	10			25	Vintage Radio Comedienne-Actress
Paige, Maj. Gen. Douglas	1886-1958	Military	28				World War II British general
Paine, Charles Jackson	1833-1916	Civil War	60	95	130		Union general
Paine, Eleazar Arthur	1815-1882	Civil War	40	75	110		Union general
Paine, Halbert Eleazer	1826-1905	Civil War	35	75	120	400	Union general and lawyer
Paine, John Knowles		Composer	15	40	50		Paine Hall at Harvard
Paine, Robert Treat	1731-1814	Revolutionary War	212	447	850		Signer Decl. of Indepen., Cont. Congr.
Paine, Thomas	1737-1809	Revolutionary War	5500		22500		Am. Philosopher-Author
Paine, William A.		Business		875			Founder Paine-Webber Brokerage House
Painter, Brig. Gordon Whistler A.	1893-1960	Military	25				World War II British general
Painter, Joseph T.		Celebrity	10			15	medical expert
Paisley, Ian R.k.		Political	10			15	Member European Parliament
Pakenham-Walsh, L. Gen Ridley P	1888-1966	Military	25				World War II British general
Pakula, Alan J.		Entertainment	5	10		20	Producer-Director
Pal, George	1908-1980	Entertainment	50			125	Producer-Director. Special Effects Expert. Puppets

NAME	DATE	CATEGORY	SIG	LS/DS	ALS	SP	COMMENTS
Palacio, Ernesto		Entertainment	5			30	Opera
Palade, George E., Dr.		Science	20	35		25	Nobel Medicine 1974
Palance, Jack		Entertainment	20			63	AA Actor
Palet, Jose		Entertainment				220	Opera. Fonotipia Tenor
Paley, Petronia		Entrtainment	5			20	Pretty Afro-Am. Actress. 'Annie Hall' etc.
Paley, William S.		Business	20	30	70	30	Founded CBS in 1928
Palfrey, Francis Winthrop		Civil War	25		75		Union Gen.
Palfrey, John G.	1796-1881	Abolitionist	32	50	68		
Palin, Michael	1943-	Entertainment	15			35	Comedian. Mony Python.'Full Circle' Book S. 65
Pall, Gloria		Entertainment	15			35	DS re Voluptua 40
Pallette, Eugene		Entertainment	60			85	Rotund, Gravel Voiced Character actor
Pallone Jr., Frank P		Congress	10			15	Member U.S. Congress
Palma, Tomas Estrada	1835-1908	Head of State	75	160	250		1st President Cuba
Palme, Olaf	1927-1986	Head of State	45	70	145	150	Premier Sweden. Assassinated '86
Palmer, A. Mitchell		Cabinet	10	25	40	30	MOC PA. Att'y General
Palmer, Alice Freeman	1855-1902	Educator	20	35	50		Pres. Wellesley. Member HOF
Palmer, Betsy		Entertainment	5	7	9	12	Actress. Stage-Films. Active Early TV Panelist
Palmer, Chuck		Entertainment	3			8	Promoter
Palmer, Geoffrey		Entertainment	10			20	Actor
Palmer, Gregg		Entertainment	10			30	Actor. Supporting Roles, 2nd Leads Since Early 50's
Palmer, Innis N.	1824-1900	Civil War	55	65			Union Gen. Led Only Cavalry at Bull Run
Palmer, Jimmy		Entertainment	15			40	Band Leader
Palmer, John McCauley	1817-1900	Civil War	55	110	176		Union General & Political Figure. US Sen.-Gov. IL
Palmer, Joseph Benjamin	1825-1890	Civil War	110	977			Confederate general
Palmer, Lilli	1912-1986	Entertainment	20	35		70	Ger. Actress. Charming, Elegant Leading Lady
Palmer, Patsy		Entertainment	10			20	Actress
Palmer, Potter		Business	275	975	1650	475	Palmer House Hotel, Chicago. Stock S 1450
Palmer, Robert		Entertainment	20			45	
Palmerston, Henry J.T., Lord	1784-1865	Head of State	48	95	147		Prime Minister Eng. Ended Crimean War
Palminteri, Chaz		Entertainment	10			35	actor
Paltrow, Bruce	d. 2002	Entertainment	25			40	Producer
Paltrow, Gwyneth		Entertainment	20			65	Actress. 'Shakespeare in Love'. AA
Paluzzi, Luciana		Entertainment	5			15	Actress. Leads & 2nd Leads. Italian-Internat'l Pix
Pan, Hermes	1933-1973	Entertainment	30			65	Choreographer. Dance Director. AA
Pancake, James		Business	10	20			Ohio Businessman and Race Driver
Pancero, Jim		Celebrity	10			15	motivational speaker
Panerai, Rolando		Entertainment	5			25	Opera
Panetta, Leon		Congress	15			30	NY. White House Chief of Staff
Pangborn, Clyde		Aviation	75	140	250	250	Aviation Pioneer
Pangborn, Franklin	1894-1958	Entertainment	42			65	Comedic Character Actor
Pankhurst, E. Sylvia	1882-1960	Women's Rights	55	118	250	660	Br. Woman Suffrage Advocate. Newspaper Editor
Pankhurst, Emmeline	1858-1928	Women's Rights	40	125	240	500	Br. Leader of Women's Suffrage
Pankhurst, Christabel, Dame	1880-1958	Women's Rights	25	65	160		Br. Woman Suffrage Advocate
Pannella, Marco		Political	10			15	Member European Parliament
Pannenberg, Wolfhart A.		Clergy	35	85	100	75	

NAME	DATE	CATEGORY	SIG	LS/DS	ALS	SP	COMMENTS
Pannwitz, Lt. Gen. Helmuth	1898-1947	Military	25				World War II German general
Pantaleoni, Romilda		Entertainment			200		Opera.1st Desdemona
Pantas, Lee		Author	8			12	Southern mountains guide books
Pantoliano, Joe		Entertainment	5			38	Ralphie Cifaretto, Soprano's
Papanin, Ivan Dmitrijewicz	1894-1986	Celebrity	30	52	125		Russian Polar explorer
Papayannakis, Mihail		Political	10			15	Member European Parliament
Papen, Franz von	1879-1969	Head of State	88	175	350	350	Served under Adolph Hitler
Papp, Joseph		Entertainment	30	40		55	Major Theatrical Producer
Pappas, Ike		Celebrity	10			15	media/TV personality
Paquin, Anna		Entertainment	35			44	New Zealand Child Actress. 'The Piano', AA
Paradis, Vanessa		Entertainment	5			22	Singer-Actress
Parazynski, Scott		Astronaut	6			20	
Pargiter, Maj Gen Robert Beverly	1889-1984	Military	25				World War II British general
Parham, Maj. Gen. Hetman Jack	1895-1974	Military	25				World War II British general
Paris, Joel B., III		Aviation	15	25	40	35	ACE, WW II
Parish, Neil		Political	10			15	Member European Parliament
Parisot, Lt. Gen. Henri	1881-1963	Military	20				World War II French general
Park, Charles E.		Clergy	15	20	25		
Park, Chung Hee	1917-1979	Head of State	50			150	Pres. Korea. Assassinated
Park, Frank		Senate/Congress	5	15	25		MOC GA 1913
Park, Ray		Entertainment				40	Darth Maul, Star Wars I
Park, Roy H.		Business	10	25	55	20	Owner 'Duncan Hines' & Broadcast Stations
Parke, John Grubb	1827-1900	Civil War	39	95	150		Union General. Sig/Rank 55, DS 115
Parker, Alton B.	1852-1926	Jurist-Pres.Cand.	20	35	101	100	Judge, Pres. Candidate 1904
Parker, Amelia, Mrs.		Celebrity	5	15	25		Alton B. Parker Wife
Parker, Cecilia	1905-1993	Entertainment	5			15	Actress. 'Andy Hardy's' Sister
Parker, Charlie	1920-1955	Entertainment	689	900		3600	Alto Sax Jazz Musician. 'The Bird'.
Parker, David		Military	15	35	60		
Parker, Dorothy		Author	25	40	95	30	Critic, Poet, Humorist
Parker, Edward P.		Business	65	150			Parker Bros. Pen Co.
Parker, Eleanor		Entertainment	6	8	15	15	Pin-Up SP 20
Parker, Ely Samuel	1828-1895	Civil War	80	195			Seneca Indian Chief, Union Gen.
Parker, Fess	1925-	Entertainment	10	15	25	32	Actor. Remembered Lovingly as 'Davy Crockett'
Parker, Frank		Entertainment	10			35	Jack Benny's 1st Vocalist
Parker, Frank		Military	50	75			Am. WW I Gen.
Parker, Gilbert	1861-1921	Author	12		50		
Parker, Graham		Entertainment	20			35	
Parker, Isaac C.	1838-1896	Law	451	805	1725		'TheHanging Judge'
Parker, Isaac	1768-1830	Law	25		140		Founded Harvard Law School
Parker, James	1768-1837	Congress	12				Repr. MA
Parker, James	1776-1868	Congress	12				Repr. NJ
Parker, Jameson		Entertainment	5			20	
Parker, Jean		Entertainment	15		30	30	
Parker, Joel	1816-1888	Governor-CW	15	30	75		Civil War Gov. NJ
Parker, Maj. Gen. Edwin P. Jr.	1891-1983	Military	30				World War II U.S. general

NAME	DATE	CATEGORY	SIG	LS/DS	ALS	SP	COMMENTS
Parker, Maj. Gen. George M. Jr.	1889-1968	Military	30				World War II U.S. general
Parker, Mary Louise		Entertainment	12			36	Actress
Parker, Moses		Revolutionary War					POW ALS 625
Parker, Robert A.		Astronaut	6			20	
Parker, Roy, Jr.		Entertainment	5	6	15	10	
Parker, Sarah Jessica		Entertainment	20			55	Carrie Bradshaw, Sex in the City
Parker, Suzy		Entertainment	6	8	15	20	
Parker, Theodore	1810-1860	Clergy	50	70	175		Abolitionist, Social Reformer
Parker, Thomas		Revolutionary War	55	90	145		Officer Cont. Army. General
Parker, Tom, Colonel		Entertainment	10	70		42	Elvis Presley's Manager-Agent
Parker, Willard		Entertainment	10			25	Actor-Husband Virginia Field
Parker, William, Sir	1781-1866	Military	145		300		Br. Adm. Captured Ports thus Ending 'Opium War'
Parkhurst, Charles H.	1842-1933	Clergy	36	30	60	50	Reformer. Anti Tammany Hall
Parkins, Barbara		Entertainment	6	8	15	20	Pin-Up SP 25
Parkinson, Dian		Playboy Cover	5			20	pin-up
Parkinson, Maj. Gen. Graham B.	1896-1979	Military	20				World War II New Zealand general
Parkman, Francis	1823-1893	Author	25	70	150		Historian. The Oregon Trail
Parks, Bert		Entertainment	10			32	
Parks, Elizabeth		Entertainment				25	
Parks, Gordon	1912-	Author	20	50	75	40	Learning Tree. Photojournalist-Prod.-Director
Parks, Larry		Entertainment	20			50	
Parks, Rosa L.	1913-	Activist	90	145		196	Civil Rights Activist, Bus Boycott
Parkyakarkus	d. 1958	Celebrity				22	Comedian
Parnell, Charles Stewart	1846-1891	Statesman	55	145	356		Ir. Nationalist Leader. Fought for Home Rule.
Parr, Ralph		Aviation	12	28	42	32	ACE, Korea, Double Ace
Parran, Thomas		Senate/Congress	5	8	10		MOC MD
Parrish, Anne	1888-1957	Author	15	20	30		Am. Novelist
Parrish, Helen		Entertainment	8			43	
Parrish, Julie		Entertainment	4	4	9	10	
Parrish, Maxfield	1870-1966	Artist	200	384	742	750	Repro S 600. TLS/cont 950, ALS/cont 1840, S Chk 250
Parry, Charles Hubert H., Sir		Composer	10	25	50		Historian, Dir. Royal Coll. Music
Parry, William E., Sir	1790-1855	Explorer	75	95	225		Br. Adm. Arctic Explorer
Parseval, August von		Aviation	80				Ger. Aeronautical Engineer
Parsons, Albert Ross		Composer	5	10	15	10	
Parsons, Dave		Entertainment	6			25	Music. Bass Guitar 'Bush'
Parsons, Estelle		Entertainment	5	10		30	
Parsons, Lewis Baldwin	1818-1907	Civil War	40	70	100		Union general
Parsons, Louella O.		Entertainment	20	30	75	45	Very Powerful Hearst Entertainment Journalist
Parsons, Lynn		Music	10			15	DJ
Parsons, Mosby M.	1822-1865	Civil War	170				CSA Gen.ALS '65 1650, Sig/Rank 250
Parsons, Samuel Holden	1737-1789	Revolutionary War		400	475		Cont'l. Gen'l. MsLs/Content 1500
Parsons, Squire		Music	8			12	award-winning gospel songwriter/singer
Part of Five (cast)		Entertainment				175	Cast of 7
Parton, Dolly		Country Music	10			40	
Parton, James	1822-1891	Author	15				

NAME	DATE	CATEGORY	SIG	LS/DS	ALS	SP	COMMENTS
Parton, Stella		Country Music	4			10	
Partridge, Bernard, Sir		Artist			45		Brit. Punch Cartoonist
Partridge, Wm. Ordway		Artist	10	20	50	30	Am. Sculptor. Portrait Busts
Parvis, Taurino		Entertainment	40			110	Opera
Pasch, Moritz		Science	60		95		Ger. Mathemat'n. Pasch's Axiom
Pascrell Jr., Bill P		Congress	10			15	Member U.S. Congress
Pasero, Tancredi		Entertainment	30			75	Opera
Paskalis, Kostas		Entertainment	15			45	Opera
Pasqua, Charles		Political	10			15	Member European Parliament
Pasquarella, Gus		Photographer	55				Photo Hindenburg Burning 1500
Passman, Otto E.		Senate/Congress	5			10	MOC LA
Pasternak, Boris	1890-1960	Author	375	750	1562		Rus. Poet, Novelist. 'Dr.Zhivago'. Nobel Prize 1958
Pasternak, Joe		Entertainment	30	65	100	70	Film Director
Pasteur, Louis	1822-1895	Science	500	825	1553	2549	Fr. Biologist. Pasteurization, Vaccines. AMsS 15,000
Pastor, Ed P		Congress	10			15	Member U.S. Congress
Pastor, Tony		Entertainment	10			35	Big Band Leader
Pastore, John A.		Governor	5	10		15	Governor RI
Pastore, Vincent		Entertainment				40	Big Pussy Bompensiero, Soprano's
Pastorelli, Paolo		Political	10			15	Member European Parliament
Patakis, Ioannis		Political	10			15	Member European Parliament
Patat, Frederic		Astronaut	12	25		25	
Patch, Alexander M.	1889-1945	Military	60	175	260	250	Am. General WW II
Patch, Maj. Gen. Joseph D.	1885-1965	Military	30				World War II U.S. general
Pate, Michael		Entertainment	5			15	
Paterson, Caroline		Entertainment	10			20	Actress
Paterson, John	1744-1808	Revolutionary War	70	200	325		Berkshire Minute Men. General
Patey, Janet		Entertainment	25		80		
Patinkin, Mandy		Entertainment	20			38	Actor-Singer. Chicago Hope
Patman, J. Wm. Wright		Senate/Congress	5			10	MOC TX 1929
Paton, Alan	1902-1989	Author	40	120	260		S.Afr. Author, Political Activist
Paton, Maj. Gen. William Calder	1886-1979	Military	25				World War II British general
Patric, Jason		Entertainment	10			25	actor
Patrick, Butch		Entertainment	10		25	27	Eddie Munster
Patrick, Dennis		Entertainment	4			10	
Patrick, Gail		Entertainment	9	10	20	15	
Patrick, John		Author	4	15			
Patrick, Marsena R. (WD)	1811-1888	Civil War	45	85	118		Union General
Patrick, Marsena R.	1811-1888	Civil War	35	50	122		Union General
Patrie, Béatrice		Political	10			15	Member European Parliament
Patten, Gilbert (Burt Standish)		Author	30	70	160	50	Fictional Hero Frank Merriwell
Patten, Luana		Entertainment	15			25	
Patterson, Annie W.		Composer					S Bars of Music 50
Patterson, Basil	1926-	Political	10	20		30	Vice-Chm. Dem. National Committee
Patterson, Daniel Tod	1786-1839	Military	45	145	225		Navy Commandant vs Jean Lafitte
Patterson, Francis Engle	1821-1862	Civil War	110				Union general

NAME	DATE	CATEGORY	SIG	LS/DS	ALS	SP	COMMENTS
Patterson, John		Governor	12	25			Governor AL
Patterson, Melody		Entertainment	5			35	Actress. 'Wrangler Jane' on 'F Troop'
Patterson, Paul L.		Governor	5	10		10	Governor OR
Patterson, Richard North		Author	5			10	Fiction
Patterson, Robert P.		Cabinet	20	35	45	25	Sec'y War
Patterson, Robert	1792-1881.	Civil War	25	55	80		Oldest Commissioned CW Maj.Gen.
Patterson, William Allan		Business	3	7	12	5	
Patti, Adelina (Niccolini)	1843-1919	Entertainment	114	121	330	276	Great Operatic Coloratura. (Baroness Ledenbrun)
Patti, Amalia		Entertainment	40		135	150	Opera
Pattison, Robert T.		Governor	10	25		15	Governor PA
Patton, Francis L.		Clergy	15	20	25	20	
Patton, George S.	1833-1864	Civil War	280		3750		(Grandfather) KIA in Civil War. ALS 6/26/63 7500
Patton, George S., III		Military	10	20	45	15	Son Of WW II General
Patton, George S., Jr.	1885-1945	Military	955	1879	3518	4681	Cmmdr. 3rd Army WW II, TLS/ALS cont 5000-15000
Paul I & Frederica		Royalty	200			250	King & Queen of Greece
Paul I (Rus)	1754-1801	Royalty	180	550	1400		Czar Russ. Son of Cath. Great. Assassinated
Paul, Adrian		Entertainment	7			42	Actor. 'Highlander'
Paul, Alexandra		Entertainment	4			15	Pin-Up SP 20
Paul, Arthur		Celebrity	5	7	20	32	
Paul, Brig. Gen. Georges-Eugène	1883- ?	Military	20				World War II French general
Paul, Gabriel Rene	1813-1886	Civil War	70	160			Union general
Paul, Les		Entertainment	25	35		75	And Manufacturer of Guitars
Paul, Maj. Gen. Willard S.	1894-1966	Military	30				World War II U.S. general
Paul, Ron P		Congress	10			15	Member U.S. Congress
Paul, Ru		Music	10			15	performing musical artist
Paul, Wolfgang	1913-	Science		30		30	Nobel Physics 1989
Paulding, Hiram	1797-1878	Civil War	28	50	170		Adm. Commanded Navy Yard NY During Civil War
Paulding, James Kirke	1778-1860	Cabinet -Author	35	125	165		VanBuren Sec'y Navy, War
Pauley, Ed		Business	10	45		25	Powerful CA Oil Tycoon. Treas. Dem. Party
Pauley, Jane		Celebrity	4	10	15	20	TV news anchor
Paulham, Louis		Aviation	40	75	135	80	
Pauling, Linus	1901-1994	Science	68	280	410	138	Nobel in Chemistry, Nobel Peace. SP(Pc) 125
Paulsen, Marit		Political	10			15	Member European Parliament
Paulsen, Valademar		Science	40	120			
Paulsson, Pat		Entertainment	5	6	15	25	
Paulter, Thomas C.		Celebrity	12	20			
Paulton, Harry		Entertainment	3	3	6	8	
Paulucci, Jeno F.		Business	15	25	35	20	
Paulus, Friedrich von	1890-1957	Military	200	750			German Field Marshal. Stalingrad
Pauly, Rose		Entertainment	20			60	Opera. Unequaled as Elektra
Pavarotti, Luciano		Entertainment	25	55	85	75	Opera, Concert
Pavie, Auguste-Jean-Marie		Diplomat	40	145	230		Fr. Explorer. Laos, Mekong
Pavlov, Ivan	1849-1936	Science			3100	7675	Rus. Physiologist.
Pavlova, Anna	1885-1931	Entertainment	271		450	558	Russian Premiere Ballerina. SP Pc 450
Pavon, Jose Maria M. y	1765-1815	Clergy		3250			Revolutionary Mex. Priest. Leader of Rebel Forces

NAME	DATE	CATEGORY	SIG	LS/DS	ALS	SP	COMMENTS
Pawnee Bill		Entertainment					SEE Lillie, G.A.
Paxinou, Katina		Entertainment	150		300	275	
Paxton, Bill		Entertainment	10			40	Twister w/Helen Hunt SP 130
Paxton, Elisha F. (WD)		Civil War	638	2700			CSA Gen., Stonewall Brigade
Paxton, Elisha Franklin 'Bull'	1828-1863	Civil War	341	1064			Confederate general
Paycheck, Johnny	d. 2002	Country Music	8			35	
Payer, Julius von		Explorer-Artist	90	225		285	Austr-Hung. No. Polar Expedition
Payne, Cril		Celebrity	4	8	15	10	
Payne, Donald M. P		Congress	10			15	Member U.S. Congress
Payne, Eugene B.	1835-1910	Civil War	25	45	65		Union General
Payne, Freda		Entertainment	10			20	'Band of Gold' Singer
Payne, Frederick	1903-1978	Political	5		25		Mayor, Governor, US Senator from Maine
Payne, Henry C.		Cabinet	15	20	35		P.M. General 1902
Payne, John Barton		Cabinet	7		15		
Payne, John Howard	1791-1852	Composer	68	210	271		Actor,Author.Home Sweet Home
Payne, John	1912-1991	Entertainment	15	30	55	67	Film Actor
Payne, Michael		Celebrity	10			15	veterinarian expert
Payne, T.H.		Cabinet	5	25			
Payne, William H. (WD)	1830-1904	Civil War	170	390			CSA Gen.
Payne, William H.	1930-1904	Civil War	85		356		CSA Gen.
Payne, William W.	1807-1874	Congress	10				Repr. AL, Lawyer, Planter
Pays, Amanda	1959-	Entertainment	4			20	Brit. Actress 'Max Headroom', 'The Flash' etc
Payton, Gary		Astronaut	8	20		15	
Payton-Noble, Jo Marie		Entertainment	10			25	Will and Grace
Peabody, Andrew Preston	1781-1883	Clergy	15	20	35	30	Unitarian Theologian, Author
Peabody, Charles, Dr.		Science	10	20	25		
Peabody, Eddie		Entertainment	15	15	35	30	
Peabody, Endicott 'Chub'	1920-1997	Political	5	28	35		Gov. MA. Coll.Football Hall of Fame at Harvard
Peabody, Endicott		Clergy	35	45	60		Fnder. Of Groton School.
Peabody, Francis		Celebrity	10	25	85		
Peabody, George F.	1852-1938	Banker	35	90	385	150	Merchant, Financier, Philanthropy
Peabody, George	1795-1869	Business	54	140	406		Merchant, Financier
Peabody, Nathaniel	1741-1823	Rev. War	40	125	180		New Hampshire patriot
Peale, Chas. Wilson	1741-1827	Artist-Rev. War	268	525	920		Officer. Portrait Painter, Engr.
Peale, Norman Vincent	1898-1993	Clergy	23	58	112	75	And Bestselling Author. Marble Collegiate Church
Peale, Rembrandt	1778-1860	Artist	295	550	1300		Am. Portrait & Historical Artist AmsS 1800
Peale, Titian	1799-1885	Artist		225	562		ALS/Content 975
Pearce, Dave		Music	10			15	DJ
Pearce, Guy		Entertainment				40	
Pearce, James Alfred		Senate/Congress	10	30	35		MOC, Senator MD 1835
Pearce, Richard		Entertainment	10	15		20	Film Director
Pearce, Stevan P		Congress	10			15	Member U.S. Congress
Pearkes, Maj Gen Geo. Randolph	1888-1984	Military	20				World War II Canadian general
Pearl Jam (Entire Group)		Entertainment	35			115	Rock, Alb. S 125-150
Pearl, Minnie		Country Music	10			35	Grand Ole Opry Star

NAME	DATE	CATEGORY	SIG	LS/DS	ALS	SP	COMMENTS
Pearson, Lester B.	1897-1972	Head of State	35	60	90	75	P.M. Canada, Nobel Peace Prize
Pearson, Neil		Entertainment	10			20	Actor
Peary, Harold		Entertainment	20			45	
Peary, Robert E.	1856-1920	Military-Explorer	108	243	505	575	Am. Adm. Arctic Explorer. 1st To Reach North Pole
Pease, Charles E.		Civil War	25				Carried Surrender Letter. ALS 1862 225
Pease, Elisha M.		Governor		395			Comptroller Repub. TX. Gov. TX
Peck, Gregory	1916-2003	Entertainment	18	30	35	67	Oscar Winning Actor
Peck, John James	1821-1878	Civil War	40		110		Union general
Peck, Robert Newton		Author	10	15	25		Am. Novelist
Peck, William Raine	1818-1871	Civil War	100	162			Confederate general
Peckham, Rufus W.	1838-1909	Supreme Court	50	120	195	150	
Peckinpah, Sam		Entertainment	25			50	Director
Peddie, G.		Military	10	25			Gen. WW II
Pedersen, Laura		Celebrity	10			15	financial expert
Pederson, Monte		Entertainment	10			30	Opera
Pederzini, Gianna	1900-1988	Entertainment	25			103	Opera. Mezzo-Soprano. 5x7 SP 50
Pedro II	1825-1891	Royalty	85	242	305		Emperor Brazil 1831-89
Peek, Kim		Celebrity	10			15	motivational speaker
Peek, Maj. Gen. Ernest D.	1878-1950	Military	30				World War II U.S. general
Peel, John		Music	10			15	DJ
Peel, Robert, Sir	1788-1850	Head of State	45	75	110		Prime Minister Eng. 'Bobbies' Named for Him
Peeples, Nia		Entertainment	15			25	
Peerce, Jan	1904-1984	Entertainment	28	40		68	Great Operatic Tenor. Long Career With Met.
Pegler, Westbrook		Author	20	20	35	20	Am. Journalist, Columnist
Pegram, John (WD)		Civil War	895	1795	7062		CSA Gen.
Pegram, John	1832-1865	Civil War	650	838	1800		CSA Gen.
Pei, I.M.		Architect	35	75	140		Internationally Recognized
Peijs, Karla M.h.		Political	10			15	Member European Parliament
Peirce, Benjamin	1809-1880	Science	20	30	80		Mathematician, Astronomer
Pelham, Henry	1696-1754	Head of State	45	150	265		Prime Minister
Pelham-Holles, Thomas		Head of State	50	105	170		Brother of Henry. Prime Min.
Pell, John		Historian	10	25			Museum Director
Pell, Stephen H.P.		Historian	10	25			Curator
Pellegrini, Margaret		Entertainment	15	20		35	Munchkin, Wizard of Oz
Pellegrino, Francis		Aviation				112	Pilot 509th Bomb Gp. (Atomic Bomb)
Pelletier, St. Marie Euphraise	1796-1868	Clergy			2500		Saint Canonized 1940
Pelosi, Nancy P		Congress	10			15	Member U.S. Congress
Pelouze, Louis H.	1831-1878	Civil War	35	65	110		Union Gen. War Dte. DS 350
Pemberton, John C. (WD)		Civil War	210	714	812	1250	CSA Gen. Originator COCA COLA
Pemberton, John C.	1814-1881	Civil War	120	220	360	550	CSA Gen. Originated Coca-Cola
Pemberton-Pigott, Maj Gen A.J.K.	1892-1969	Military	25				World War II British general
Pemsel, Max		Military				40	Nazi General
Pena, Elizabeth		Entertainment	10			20	
Pence, Mike P		Congress	10			15	Member U.S. Congress
Pendarvis, Paul		Bandleader	10				

NAME	DATE	CATEGORY	SIG	LS/DS	ALS	SP	COMMENTS
Pender, William Dorsey	1834-1863	Civil War	475	1265			CSA Gen. War Dte. ALS 3,250
Penderecki, Krzysztof		Composer	20		90		Pol. Opera, Religious Music
Pendergast, Thomas J.		Political	17	50	105	35	KS Democratic Political Boss
Pendleton, Alex 'Sandie'	1840-1864	Civil War	175	350	475		CSA Staff Officer-T.J. Jackson
Pendleton, Edmund	1721-1803	Revolutionary War	350	680	975		Continental Congress
Pendleton, George Hunt	1825-1889	Congress	20	35	75		Presidential Candidate. Sen. OH
Pendleton, Nat		Entertainment	30	45	60	45	
Pendleton, Nathanael G.	1793-1861	Congress	10				Repr. OH, Father of G.H. Pendleton
Pendleton, William Nelson	1809-1883	Civil War	196		560	935	CSA Gen., Pre War Clergyman
Penn & Teller		Entertainment	10			25	
Penn, Arthur		Entertainment	10			20	
Penn, Chris		Entertainment	10			20	actor
Penn, John	1729-1795	Colonial Am.		244	375		Lt. Governor of Pennsylvania
Penn, John	1740-1788	Revolutionary War	1525	4500	7500		Signer Decl.of Indepen. Signed Book 7500
Penn, Sean	1962-	Entertainment	10	30	30	43	Actor-Director-Writer. 'ThinRed Line' SP 125
Penn, Thomas	1702-1775	Colonial		150			Son of William. Proprietor of PA
Penn, William	1644-1718	Religious Reform	1500	4641	7500		Eng. Quaker Founder PA. AMsS 9,000.
Pennell, Joseph	1857-1926	Artist	55	160	320		Am. Artist, Printmaker
Penner, Joe		Entertainment	20	25	45	45	
Penney, J.C.	1875-1971	Business	48	180	210	225	Founder of J.C. Penney. Informative TLS 1500
Penney, Joe		Entertainment	8		25	20	
Pennington, Ann		Entertainment	25	30	70	70	Ziegfield Star
Pennington, William	1796-1862	Congress	48	70			Gov. PA. Speaker of House
Pennoyer, Sylvester		Governor	10	15			Governor OR
Penny, Joe		Entertainment	10			20	actor
Penny, Little Joe		Country Western	5			15	Music. 50's Western Recording Artist
Pennypacker, Galusha	1844-1916	Civil War	140	260	375		Union. Boy General
Pennypacker, Samuel W.		Governor	15	25		30	Jurist, Author, Gov. PA
Penrose, Boies	1860-1921	Congress	12	15			Senator PA. Pres. Pro Tempore
Penrose, William Henry	1832-1903	Civil War	45	80	115		Union general
Penske, Thomas H.		Business	10	30		20	
Penzias, Arno, Dr.		Science	15	35	65	25	Nobel Physics
Pepin, Jacques		Celebrity	10			15	famous chef
Peppard, George		Entertainment	6	8	15	25	
Pepper, Art		Entertainment	30			75	Bandleader
Pepper, Brigadier Ernest Cecil	1899-1981	Military	25				World War II British general
Pepper, Claude	1900-1989	Congress	22	38		25	Champion of the Elderly Sen.FL. Sorely Missed
Pepper, Don		Celebrity	10			15	motivational speaker
Pepper, George Wharton		Congress	5	15			Senator PA 1922
Pepperell, William, Sir	1696-1759	Military	175	360	550		Merchant. Gen. in Fr-Indian War
Pepys, Samuel	1633-1703	Author-Diarist	570	1890			Br. Sec'y of the Navy. Revealing Diarist.
Pequet, Henri		Aviation	16		37		
Perceval, Maj Gen Chris. Peter W.	1890-1967	Military	25				World War II British general
Perceval, Spencer	1762-1812	Head of State	120	250			Only Br. P. M. Assassinated
Percival, John 'Mad Jack'		Military	30	95	145		Am. Navy. War 1812 Exploits

NAME	DATE	CATEGORY	SIG	LS/DS	ALS	SP	COMMENTS
Percival, Lt. Gen. Arthur Ernest	1887-1966	Military	25				World War II British general
Percy, Charles		Senate/Congress	10	15		25	Senator IL
Percy, Hugh	1742-1817	Military	50	145	250		British General
Percy, Walker	1916-1990	Author-Doctor	30	55	75	60	Am. Novelist
Pereira, William L.		Architect	10	35	75	20	Internationally Recognized Architect
Perelman, S.J.		Author	45		160		Humorist, Film Scripts
Peren, Brigadier Geoffrey S.	1892-1980	Military	20				World War II New Zealand general
Peres, Shimon		Head of State	35	110		145	Israeli Prime Minister. Nobel Peace Prize
Perez De Cuellar, Javier		Celebrity	10			15	political celebrity
Perez, Charles		Celebrity	10			15	media/TV personality
Perez, Mariano		Head of State	15	25	85	20	President Colombia
Perez, Rosie		Entertainment	10			45	Actress
Perez, Rosita		Celebrity	10			15	motivational speaker
Perez, Vincent		Entertainment	25			70	The Crow Star
Perham, Josiah		Business			75		1st President of Northern Pacific RR
Perier, Jean		Entertainment	25			75	Fr. Baritone. 45 Year Career
Perignon, D.C. Marquis de	1754-1818	Military	65	180	375		Marshal of Napoleon
Perkins, Anthony	1932-1992	Entertainment	20			52	'Psycho' SP Premium. AIDs Victim.
Perkins, Carl	1932-1998	Country Music	15		50	65	Singer-Songwriter. Rock 'n Roll HOF.
Perkins, Elizabeth		Entertainment	10			20	actress
Perkins, Frances		Cabinet	25	70	145	60	1st Woman Cabinet Member. Sec'y Labor
Perkins, George C.	1839-1923	Congress	14	20			Governor, Senator CA 1893
Perkins, Marlin		Zoo Director	12			20	Animal Expert
Perkins, Millie		Entertainment	10			30	
Perkins, Osgood		Entertainment	35			75	
Perkins, Thomas H.		Business	20	45	90		
Perlman, Itzhak		Entertainment	20			55	Am. Violinist
Perlman, Rhea		Entertainment	5	6	15	20	Cheers SP 45
Perlman, Ron		Entertainment	10			20	actor
Perlman, Ronuy		Entertainment	8	12	40	30	
Peron, Eva (Evita)	1919-1952	Head of State	250	458		718	Argentina. Statesman
Peron, Juan & Peron, Eva		Heads of State		750			
Peron, Juan Domingo	1895-1974	Head of State	125	280	338	456	President & Dictator of Argentina
Perot, H. Ross		Business	15	35		30	Presidential Candidate
Perpich, Rudolph G.		Governor	10	15		15	Governor MN
Perrault, Charles	1628-1703	Author		1250	2600		Fr. Poet. Fairy Tales.
Perret, Gene		Celebrity	10			15	motivational speaker
Perrin, Abner Monroe	1827-1864	Civil War	280				Confederate general, KIA Spottsylvannia 1864
Perrin, Claude	1784-1841	Military		160			Marshal of France
Perrin, Jean	1870-1942	Science	75	375			Nobel Prize '26 Physics.TMsS 1,000
Perrine, Valerie		Entertainment	5	6	15	10	Pin-Up SP 30
Perris, Adriana		Entertainment	5			30	Opera
Perry, Alexander J.	1829-1913	Civil War	25	45			Union Brvt. Gen., Nephew Commodore Perrry
Perry, Antoinette		Entertainment		200			Tony Award
Perry, Edward Aylesworth	1831-1889	Civil War	110	200			Confederate general

NAME	DATE	CATEGORY	SIG	LS/DS	ALS	SP	COMMENTS
Perry, J. Mitchell		Celebrity	10			10	motivational speaker
Perry, Jim		Celebrity	10			15	motivational speaker
Perry, Lila	1959-	Entertainment	5			25	Afro-Am Child Star. TV Shows of Mid 60's
Perry, Lucas		Entertainment	20			35	
Perry, Madison S.		Governor	15	45			Governor FL
Perry, Matthew C.	1794-1858	Military	260	625	1245		Father of the Steam Navy
Perry, Matthew		Entertainment	10			53	Friends Actor
Perry, Nora		Author	3	10	20		Novelist
Perry, Oliver H.	1785-1819	Military	550	850	1250		
Perry, Ralph Barton		Author	10	20	35		Philosopher, Pulitzer Prize
Perry, Roy		Political	10			15	Member European Parliament
Perry, Susan		Entertainment	20				Actress
Perry, William Flank	1823-1901	Civil War	110	168			Confederate general
Perryman, Lloyd		Country Music	10			20	
Persaud, Raj, Dr.		Celebrity	10			15	health and fitness expert
Pershing, John J.	1860-1948	Military	79	244	460	525	Comm.-in-Chief AEF WW I. Important ALS 895
Persichetti, Vincent		Composer	10	25	60	15	
Persoff, Nehemiah		Entertainment	5	6	15	15	
Persons, Lt. Gen. John C.	1888-1974	Military	30				World War II U.S. general
Persons, Wilton B.		Gov't Official	5	15	25	10	Gen. Chief Ass't to Pres. DDE
Pert, Maj. Gen. Claude Ernest	1898-1982	Military	28				World War II British general
Pertile, Aureliano	1855-1952	Entertainment	40			137	Opera. Favorite of Toscanini at La Scala
Perulli, Franco		Entertainment	20			50	Opera
Perutz, Max		Science	20	40	75	50	Nobel Chemistry 1962
Pesci, Joe		Entertainment	15			55	AA
PesSIS, Mikko		Political	10			15	Member European Parliament
Petain, Henri-Phillippe.	1856-1951	Head of State	60	125	225	200	Hero WW I. Treason WW II
Peter & Gordon (Both)		Entertainment	75			125	Singing Duo
Peter I	1844-1921	Royalty	90	225	400		King of Serbia
Peter I, The Great	1672-1725	Royalty	1250	4928	9200		Czar of Russia
Peter, Paul & Mary		Entertainment				35	SP All three/full name 35
Peters, Absalom		Clergy	15	20	35		
Peters, Andi		Celebrity	10			15	television presenter
Peters, Bernadette		Entertainment	5	6	20	32	Pin-Up SP 35
Peters, Brock		Entertainment	5	6	15	15	
Peters, Jean		Entertainment	30	45	50	85	
Peters, Mike*		Cartoonist	5			45	Mother Grimm
Peters, Richard Jr.	1744-1828	Revolutionary War	40	95	150		Soldier, Jurist, Continental Cong
Peters, Roberta		Entertainment	10			25	Opera, Concert
Peters, Susan		Entertainment	75	85	95	100	
Peters, Tom		Celebrity	10			15	motivational speaker
Petersen, Paul		Entertainment	5			15	
Peterson, Bruce A.		Astronaut	5			20	
Peterson, Chesley		Aviation	15	30	55	40	ACE, WW II, Eagle Squadron
Peterson, Collin C. P		Congress	10			15	Member U.S. Congress

NAME	DATE	CATEGORY	SIG	LS/DS	ALS	SP	COMMENTS
Peterson, Donald H.		Astronaut	6			20	
Peterson, Forrest (RADM)		Astronaut	5			15	
Peterson, John E. P		Congress	10			15	Member U.S. Congress
Peterson, Oscar		Entertainment	25			45	Jazz Pianist
Peterson, Roger Tory		Author	20	35		25	
Peterson, Rudolph A.		Business	4	6	15	10	
Petiet, Claude		Fr. Revolution	125	265			
Petion, Alexandre	1770-1818	Head of State	225	292			Haitian General, President Southern Haiti
Petre, Maj. Gen. Roderic Loraine	1887-1971	Military	25				World War II British general
Petrella, Clara		Entertainment	20			50	Opera
Petri, Thomas E. P		Congress	10			15	Member U.S. Congress
Petrie, Wm. Matthew Flinders, Sir		Archaeologist	125	166			Pyramids At Giza. Paved the Way For Carter et al
Petrillo, James C.		Labor	20	55			Czar of Musician's Union
Petrocelli, Daniel		Law	15			20	Prosecuted O.J. Simpson in Civil Suit for Goldman
Petroff, Paul		Entertainment	30			100	Am. Ballet Dancer-Teacher
Petrova, Olga		Entertainment	35			75	Silent Films
Pettet, Joanna		Entertainment	5	6	15	15	
Pettigrew, James J.	1828-1863	Civil War	222	608			CSA Gen.
Pettigrew, James, J. (WD)	1828-1863	Civil War	525	5750			CSA Gen. AES '61 13,200
Pettit, Charles		Revolutionary War	70	185	315		Continental Congress
Pettit, Don		Astronaut				20	
Pettus, Edmund W.	1821-1907	Civil War	123	213	559		CSA Gen. ALS War Dte 3500
Pettus, John J.	1813-1867	Civil War	30	55	70		Mississippi War Gov.
Petty, Tom		Entertainment	35			72	Rock, Heartbreakers
Peugeot, Eugene		Business	50	130	315		Fndr. Peugeot Automobile Co.
Pfeiffer, Michelle		Entertainment	15	20		74	Actress
Pflug, Jackie		Celebrity	10			15	motivational speaker
Pflug, Jo Ann		Entertainment	3	5	15	12	
Phelan, James D.	1864-1930	Congress	10	25	40		Senator CA 1915
Phelan, Maj. Gen. Frederick Ross	1885-1970	Military	24				World War II Canadian general
Phelps, Austin		Clergy	20	30	40		
Phelps, John Smith	1814-1886	Civil War	35	65	100		Union General, Gov. MO
Phelps, John Wolcott	1813-1885	Civil War	35	135	200		Raised 1st Negro Troops
Phelps, Noah	1740-1809	Military	100	275			Soldier, Patriot, Spy
Phelps, William Walter	1839-1894	Congress	10		25		Repr. NJ
Philbin, Mary	1903-1993	Entertainment	25			55	Silent Film Star & Beauty Queen
Philbin, Regis		Celebrity	5			28	TV Host
Philbrick, Herbert A.		Celebrity	15	30	60	25	I Led Three Lives Agent
Philip (Duke Edinburgh)		Royalty	110	175	325	350	Prince Consort Elizabeth II
Philip II (Sp)	1527-1598	Royalty	275	1252			King of Spain 1556-1598. Husband of Mary Tudor
Philip III (Sp)	1578-1621	Royalty	250	675			Ruled Portugal, as Philip II
Philip IV (Sp)	1605-1665	Royalty	150	361	1250		Ruled Portugal, as Philip III
Philip V (Sp)	1683-1746	Royalty	138	255			Founder Bourbon Dynasty
Philip, John		Entertainment	10			20	actor
Philipp, Isadore		Entertainment	20		65		Pianist

NAME	DATE	CATEGORY	SIG	LS/DS	ALS	SP	COMMENTS
Philippe II (Duc d'Orleans)		Royalty		500			Regent of Fr. for Louis XV
Philippi, Alfred		Military	5	15			Ger. Gen. WW II. RK
Philippon, Brig. Gen. Marie-Louis	1869-1943	Military	20				World War II French general
Philips, Maj. Gen. Charles G.	1889-1982	Military	28				World War II British general
Philips, Maj. Gen. Leslie G.	1892-1966	Military	25				World War II British general
Philipson, Maj. Gen. Irving J.	1882-1955	Military	30				World War II U.S. general
Phillip, Jack W.		Military	27	80			Captain USN
Phillippe, Ryan		Entertainment	10			55	Promising Young Movie Star
Phillips, Bill		Country Music	10			20	
Phillips, Chynna		Entertainment	30			75	Singer-Actress
Phillips, Craig		Celebrity	10			15	'Big Brother'
Phillips, Fiona		Celebrity	10			15	television presenter
Phillips, Irna		Entertainment	10			15	Actress. Today's Children
Phillips, J.B.		Clergy	35	50	95	50	
Phillips, John		Astronaut	6			20	
Phillips, John	d. 2002	Entertainment	25			100	Founder The Mamas & the Papas
Phillips, Julia		Celebrity	10			15	film industry
Phillips, Julianne		Entertainment	25			42	Pin-Up SP 72
Phillips, Lou Diamond		Entertainment	10	15	45	30	
Phillips, Mackenzie		Entertainment	10			35	
Phillips, Maj. Gen. Owen F.	1882-1966	Military	20				World War II Australian general
Phillips, Michelle		Entertainment	10			38	
Phillips, Phil		Composer	15			35	Singer-Songwriter
Phillips, Robert		Astronaut	6			16	
Phillips, Scott		Entertainment	6			25	Music. Drummer 'Creed'
Phillips, Wendell	1811-1884	Reformer	27	74	125	125	Abolitionist, Orator,Civ.Rights
Phillips, William		Revolutionary War	225	644	825		Br. Major General
Phillips, Wm.		Cabinet	4	15	20		
Phillpotts, Eden (Harrington Hext)		Author	10	35	55		Br. Novelist. Plays, Poems, Mystery
Phillpotts, Henry		Clergy	25	35	40		Under Sec'y
Phipps, Brig. Charles Constantine	1889-1958	Military	25				World War II British general
Phipps, Spencer	1685-1757	Colonial	125	375			Br. Colonial Gov. MA
Phoenix, Joaquin		Entertainment	10			20	actor
Phoenix, River	1971-1993	Entertainment	167			288	actor, died young
Physick, Philip Syng	1768-1837	Science		775			'Father of Am. Surgery'
Piaf, Edith	1915-1963	Entertainment	112	220	338	433	Legendary Internat'l Chanteuse
Piaget, Jean	1896-1980	Science		375			Swiss Psychologist
Pianchettini, Pio	1799-1851	Composer					Pianist. ANS Framed/Portrait 3500
Piatigorsky, Gregor	1903-1976	Entertainment	75	130	220	275	Rus./Am.Cellist. AMusQS 100
Piatt, Abram Sanders	1821-1908	Civil War	40		95		Union general
Piazza, Marguerite		Entertainment	10			30	Am. Met Sopr.
Picabia, Francis	1879-1953	Artist			225		Fr. Painter. A Leader of Dadaist Movement
Picard, Brig. Gen. Francois	1883-1961	Military	20				World War II French general
Picard, Brig. Gen. Jean-Jules-Ern.	1881- ?	Military	20				World War II French general
Picard, Charles-Emile	1856-1941	Science	70	240	430		Fr. Mathematician

NAME	DATE	CATEGORY	SIG	LS/DS	ALS	SP	COMMENTS
Picardo, Robert		Entertainment				40	Actor. Star Trek Voyager.
Picasso, Pablo	1881-1973	Artist	468	1213	2231	2149	Signed sketch 2,000-12500
Picasso, Paloma		Artist	25		95		Artist-Designer. Daughter
Piccaluga, Nino		Entertainment	30			80	Opera
Piccard, Auguste	1884-1963	Science	45	115	195	115	Sw. Physicist. Bathyscaphe
Piccard, Jacques		Science	15	40	75	20	
Piccard, Jean-Felix		Science	65	195		125	Chemist, Aeronautical Eng.
Piccaver, Alfred		Entertainment	75			225	Br. Tenor, Opera
Piccolomini, Marietta		Entertainment	100	275		275	It. Soprano
Pichegru, Charles		Fr. Revolution	35	115	195		Fr. Gen. Strangled In Prison
Pick, Lewis A.	1890-	Military	35	125		40	Gen. WW II
Pickens, Francis W.		Civil War	40	150	200		CSA Gov SC
Pickens, Jane		Entertainment	25			50	Pickens Sisters & Actress/Singer
Pickens, Slim		Entertainment	100			185	
Pickens, T. Boone		Business	20	55		45	Corporate Raider. Controversial
Pickering, Charles W. "Chip"		Congress	10			15	Member U.S. Congress
Pickering, John	1737-1805	Revolutionary War	175	250			Impeached & Convicted by Congr.
Pickering, Thomas		Diplomat	10			20	Ambassador to Russia
Pickering, Timothy	1745-1829	Cabinet-Military	200	583	1058		Sec'y War, Sec'y State,TLS/cont 2300,ALS/cont 2500
Pickering, William, Dr.		Science	15	35	60	25	Astronomer. Lowell Observatory
Pickett, Cindy		Entertainment	3	3	6	6	
Pickett, George Edward	1825-1875	Civil War	1652	3612	7919		Rare war-date ALS 15,000
Pickford, Jack		Entertainment	50			150	
Pickford, Mary & Buddy Rogers		Entertainment	95			275	
Pickford, Mary	1893-1979	Entertainment	55	125	150	151	Co-Founder United Artists. Major Silent Star. AA
Picon, Molly		Entertainment	35	30		45	Stage & Film Star of Yiddish & Am. Theatre
Picquart, Georges	1854-1914	Military		150			French General. Dreyfus affair
Pidgeon, Walter	1897-1984	Entertainment	20	40		75	Am. Film Actor
Piecyk, Wilhelm Ernst		Political	10			15	Member European Parliament
Pied Pipers, The (3)		Entertainment	20			45	Big Band Singing Group
Pierce, Benjamin	1757-1839	Revolutionary War	60	135	200		Father of Pres., Gov. NH
Pierce, Benjamin	1809-1880	Science	20		62		Am. Math.& Astronomy.Harvard Prof.
Pierce, Byron Root	1829-1924	Civil War	64	85	114		Union general
Pierce, David Hyde		Entertainment	5	15	20	42	'Niles' in Frasier
Pierce, Franklin (as Pres)		President	362	1110	1566		14th Pres. Of USA
Pierce, Franklin & Jefferson Davis		President		3469			President and Sectry of War
Pierce, Franklin	1804-1869	President	328	741	990		FF 300-595
Pierce, Guy		Entertainment	5			35	
Pierce, James		Entertainment	25			45	Vintage Tarzan
Pierce, Jane M.	1806-1863	First Lady	215	500	1212		Wife of Franklin Pierce. Tragic Life
Pierce, Maj. Gen. John L.	1895-1959	Military	30				World War II U.S. general
Pierce, Mark Robert		Business	5	7	10	20	Advertising, a '10', songwriter
Pierce, Samuel, Jr.	1922-	Cabinet	25		40	70	Afr-Am Sec'y HUD Under Reagan. Key in HUD Scandal
Pierce, Walter M.		Senate/Congress	3	5	10		MOC OR
Pierce, Web		Country Music	4			10	

NAME	DATE	CATEGORY	SIG	LS/DS	ALS	SP	COMMENTS
Pierné, H.C. Gabriel	1863-1937	Composer	15	50	135	225	Conductor. AMusQS 250
Pierre White, Marco		Celebrity	10			15	Chef
Pierrepont, Edwards	1817-1892	Cabinet	45	55	92		Grant Att'y General 1875. Prosecution of Surratt
Pierson, Roland		Aviation	10	25	35	30	
Piétrasanta, Yves		Political	10			15	Member European Parliament
Pigni, Renzo		Entertainment	15			35	Opera
Pigott, Maj. Gen. Alan John Keefe	1892-1969	Military	28				World War II British general
Pike, Albert	1809-1891	Civil War	148	210	360		CSA Gen. Sig/Rank 180
Pike, Christopher		Author	4		15	10	Novelist
Pike, James A., Bishop	1913-1969	Clergy	70	120	262	90	Episcopal Bishop.
Pike, Zebulon M.	1779-1813	Military	245	716	1250		General. Discovered Pike's Peak
Pike, Zebulon	1751-1834	Revolutionary War	40	75	135		Officer Revolutionary Army
Pilatre De Rozier, Jean Francois		Aeronaut	125		500		Pioneer Balloonist
Pile, General Sir Frederick Alfred	1884-1976	Military	25				World War II British general
Pile, William Anderson	1829-1889	Civil War	50		150		Union general
Pileggi, Mitch		Entertainment	10			20	actor
Pillau, Maj. Gen. Gerald Arthur	1896-1964	Military	28				World War II British general
Pillow, Gideon J. (WD)	1806-1878	Civil War	168	440	750		CSA General. ALS/Cont. 3,750
Pillow, Gideon J.	1806-1878	Civil War	135		473		CSA Gen.
Pillsbury, George A.		Business		1759	2400		Founder Pillsbury Flour. ALS on Lttrhd. 3850
Pillsbury, John S.		Business	85	675			Governor MN, Pillsbury Flour
Pillsbury, Parker		Reformer	15	25	60		
Pilsudski, Joseph Klemens		Military	115	320	550	275	Pol. Gen., Statesman, Dictator
Pinay, Antoine		Head of State	15	35	50		Fr.
Pinchback, Pinckney		Senate	125	350	495		Early Black Elected Official
Pinchot, Bronson		Entertainment	5			15	
Pinchot, Gifford	1865-1946	Governor	35	100	125		Governor PA, Forester
Pinckney, Charles C.	1746-1825	Revolutionary War	175	475	1231		General, Diplomat, XYZ Affair
Pinckney, Charles	1757-1824	Revolutionary War	375		1500		Continental Congress, MOC, Sen. SC
Pinckney, Pauline		Author	5	10	20		
Pinckney, Thomas	1750-1828	Revolutionary War	200	458			Continental Army, Gov. SC
Pincus, Harry		Artist	10	30	60		
Pine, Courtney		Music	10			15	performing musical artist
Pine, Phillip		Entertainment	3	3	6	8	
Pinero, Arthur Wing, Sir	1855-1934	Author	20	35	65	60	Br. Dramatist, Actor
Ping, Deng Xiao		Head of State	200		700		China
Pingel, Rolf		Aviation	10	15	30	25	
Pingree, Hazen S.		Governor	10	15			Governor MI
Pink Floyd		Entertainment	75			170	signed album 368
Pink		Entertainment				45	Singer
Pinkerton, Allan	1819-1884	Am. Detective	275	807	1365	1150	Dir. Union Secret Service Bureau During Civil War
Pinkerton, Robert A.		Business	35	105	220	75	CEO Pinkerton's Inc. Detectives
Pinkett, Jada		Entertainment	10			22	actress
Pinkney, William	1764-1822	Cabinet	90	225	275		MOC, Senator MD. Att'y Gen. 1811
Pinochet, Augusto		Head of State	30	115	245	125	Chilean Mil. Leader

NAME	DATE	CATEGORY	SIG	LS/DS	ALS	SP	COMMENTS
Pinter, Harold		Author	20			95	Br. Playwright. Small (4x5) SP 50
Pinza, Ezio	1892-1957	Entertainment	70	140		202	It.-Am. Basso, Opera, Films
Piper, William Thomas		Aviation	175	380	460		Founder Piper Aircraft Corp.
Pirandello, Luigi	1867-1936	Author	70	175	425	390	Nobel Lit. ALS/Content 2,400
Pirchoff, Nelly		Entertainment	10			30	Opera
Pire, Dominique George		Clergy	55		90	65	
Pirker, Hubert		Political	10			15	Member European Parliament
Piscarreta, Joaquim		Political	10			15	Member European Parliament
Piscopo, Joe		Entertainment	10			32	
Pisicchio, Giuseppe		Political	10			15	Member European Parliament
Pissarro, Camille	1830-1903	Artist	200	695	1108		Fr. Impressionist-Pointillist
Piston, Walter	1894-1976	Composer	60	95	125	150	Pulitzer Music 1947 & 1960
Pitcher, Thomas Gamble	1824-1895	Civil War	45	75			Union general
Pitkin, William	1694-1769	Colonial Am.	65	475			Soldier, Colonial Judge & Gov. CT
Pitkin, William	1729-1789	Colonial Am.	30	102			Jurist, Army Major., Mfg. Gunpowder. Chf.Just. CT
Pitney, Gene		Entertainment	5			25	
Pitney, Mahlon	1858-1924	Supreme Court	45	85	160	150	MOC NJ 1895
Pitt, Brad		Entertainment	18			59	actor
Pitt, Ingrid		Entertainment	3			10	Actress
Pitt, John, Sir	1756-1835	Military	45		80		Gen. Cmdr. Failed Walcheren Exp.
Pitt, William (Elder)	1708-1778	Head of State	110	225	360		The Great Commoner
Pitt, William (Younger)	1759-1815	Head of State	115	280	430		England'sYoungest Prime Min.
Pittella, Giovanni		Political	10			15	Member European Parliament
Pittenger, William	1840-	Clergy	15		25		Military (Civil War)
Pittner, William		Civil War-Clergy	15				
Pitts, Joseph R.		Congress	10			15	Member U.S. Congress
Pitts, Zazu		Entertainment	40			100	
Plainsmen, The		Country Music	25			50	
Planck, Max	1858-1947	Science	238	850	1650	2500	Nobel Physics 1918. ANS Pc 500
Plancon, Pol	1854-1914	Entertainment	125		210	400	Opera
Planer, Nigel		Entertainment	10			20	Actor
Plant & Page (Both)		Enertainment				175	Rock, Led Zeppelin
Plant, Maj. Gen. Eric C.P.	1890-1950	Military	20				World War II Australian general
Plant, Robert		Entertainment	35			65	
Plato, Dana		Entertainment	5			25	
Platt, Ed		Entertainment	75			160	
Platt, General Sir William	1885-1975	Military	25				World War II British general
Platt, Marc		Entertainment	5			35	Dancer-Choreographer
Platt, Orville H.	1827-1905	Congress	5	15			Senator CT
Platt, Thomas C	1833-1910	Congress	15		33	40	Senator NY
Platters, The (Group of 5)		Entertainment				250	Black Singing Group
Platts, Todd Russell P		Congress	10			15	Member U.S. Congress
Playfair, Lyon, 1st Baron		Science	10	25	40		Br. Chem. Modern Sanitation
Playfair, Maj Gen. Ian Stanley Ord	1894-1972	Military	25				World War II British general
Pleasant, Mary E. 'Mammy'	1813-1904	Celebrity	400				Former Slave who became wealthy

NAME	DATE	CATEGORY	SIG	LS/DS	ALS	SP	COMMENTS
Pleasence, Donald		Entertainment	15			40	
Pleasonton, Alfred (WD)		Civil War	90	185	425		Union Gen. Sherman's Chief Cavalry
Pleasonton, Alfred	1824-1897	Civil War	58	120	200		Union Gen.ALS War Dte 1,200
Pleshette, Suzanne		Entertainment	6	8	15	225	
Plimpton, George		Author	7	20	25	20	
Plishka, Paul		Entertainment	5			25	Opera
Plitsetskaya, Maya		Entertainment	15			40	Ballet
Plooij-van Gorsel, Elly		Political	10			15	Member European Parliament
Plow, Maj. Gen. Edward Chester	1904-1988	Military	20				World War II Canadian general
Plowright, Joan		Entertainment	10			25	
Plum, Rev. Angela		Author	8			12	interfaith manuals
Plumb, Charlie		Celebrity	10			15	motivational speaker
Plummer, Amanda		Entertainment	16			25	Actress
Plummer, Christopher		Entertainment	7	10		28	Actor
Plummer, Joseph Bennett	1816-1862	Civil War	120				Union general
Plunkett, Charles P.	1864-1930	Military	45	135			USN Adm. Transatlantic Flight Operations 1919
Pocahontas (Cast Of)		Entertainment				130	Mel Gibson & Two Others
Podestå, Guido		Political	10			15	Member European Parliament
Podesta, Rossana		Entertainment	10			35	International Films. Beautiful Italian Actress.
Podgorney, Nikolay V.	1903-1983	Political		140			Soviet Communist leader
Podmore, Thomas		Clergy	10	10	15	20	
Poe, Edgar Allan	1809-1849	Author	6810		19500		AMsS 35,000, ALS 39,000
Poe, Orlando Metcalfe	1832-1895	Civil War	40	70	105		Union general
Poett, Gen. Sir Jos. Howard Nigel	1907-1991	Military	25				World War II British general
Poettering, Hans-gert		Political	10			15	Member European Parliament
Pogany, Willy	1882-1955	Artist	70	190			Illustrator, Muralist, Designer
Poggi, Gianni		Entertainment	10			25	Opera
Pogue, William R.		Astronaut	6			30	
Pohjamo, Samuli		Political	10			15	Member European Parliament
Pohl, Karl Otto		Celebrity	10			15	political celebrity
Poignant, Bernard		Political	10			15	Member European Parliament
Poincaré, Raymond	1860-1934	Head of State	40	60	100	105	3 Times Prime Minister France
Poindexter, John		Military	20			40	US Adm. Iran-Contra
Poindexter, Joseph B.		Governor	10	15			Governor Hawaii, Federal Judge
Poindexter, Miles		Congress	5	15		10	Repr., Senator WA 1909
Poinsett, Joel R.	1779-1851	Cabinet	40	110	160		Sec'y War. Poinsettia Flower
Pointer Sisters		Entertainment	30			68	
Poiret, Paul	1879-1944	Designer	125	525			Fr. Dress Designer
Poitier, Sidney	1924-	Entertainment	13	65		58	1st Afr-Am AA Winning Actor
Poland, Luke P.		Senate/Congress	10	15	30		MOC, Senator VT 1865
Polando, John		Aviation	30	60	110	75	
Polanski, Roman		Entertainment	35			115	Fugitive Director, AA winner
Polansky, Mark		Astronaut	5			19	
Polaski, Deborah		Entertainment	5			25	Opera
Poli, Afro		Entertainment	10			45	Opera

NAME	DATE	CATEGORY	SIG	LS/DS	ALS	SP	COMMENTS
Police, The		Entertainment	70			275	
Polignac, Camille J.	1832-1913	Civil War	110				Confederate general
Poling, Daniel A.		Clergy	20	30	60	35	
Polizzi, Harry		Celebrity	10	20			Book Dealer
Polk, James K & James Buchanan		Presidents	1150	2675			
Polk, James K. (As Pres.)		President	575	1537	2371		FF 975-1200
Polk, James K.	1795-1849	President	518	1379	2147		Political ALS 5250
Polk, Leonidas (WD)	1806-1864	Civil War	500	1750	3295		CSA General
Polk, Leonidas	1806-1864	Civil War	382	958	2121		CSA Gen. KIA. Episcopal Bishp.Fndr.Univ. of South
Polk, Lucius Eugene	1833-1892	Civil War	100				Confederate general
Polk, Sarah Childress		First Lady	388	625	907	1250	Banned Dancing & Drinking in WH
Pollack, Sidney		Entertainment	12	30	30	25	AA Director-Actor
Pollack, Sir George	1786-1876	Military			260		
Pollan, Tracy		Entertainment	10			25	married to Michael J. Fox
Pollard, Michael J.	1939-	Entertainment	8			22	Character Actor. 'Bonnie & Clyde','Dobie Gillis'
Pollard, Snub		Entertainment	50			200	Keystone Cop
Pollard, Sue		Celebrity	10			15	comedienne
Pollard, Sue		Entertainment	10			20	Actress
Pollock, Channing	1880-1946	Author	30	55	80	75	Am. Playwright, Essayist
Pollock, Maj Gen Arthur Jocelyn C	1891-1968	Military	25				World War II British general
Pollok, Maj. Gen. Robt. Valentine	1884-1969	Military	25				World War II British general
Pombo, Richard W. P.		Congress	10			15	Member U.S. Congress
Pomeroy, Earl P		Congress	10			15	Member U.S. Congress
Pomeroy, Samuel Clarke	1816-1891	Congress	35	50	75		Civil War Senator KS 1861. Twice Cleared of Bribery
Pomés Ruiz, José Javier		Political	10			15	Member European Parliament
Pometti, Vincenzo		Entertainment	5			15	
Pompadour, Mme. J. A., Duchess	1721-1764	Royalty	250	525	1130		Louis XV Mistress
Pompidou, Georges		Head of State	10	25		20	Premier, President France
Ponchielli, Amilcare		Composer	175		1200		It. Opera. La Gioconda.Ballets
Pond, Enoch		Clergy	15	25	30		
Pond, Julian		Science	50		325		
Ponder, James		Governor	12	20			Governor DE
Poniatowski, Jozef A., Prince	1763-1813	Military	470	950	2150		Rarest Napoleon Marshal
Pons, Juan		Entertainment	5			25	Opera
Pons, Lily	1904-1976	Entertainment	40	75	125	150	Fr.-Born Am. Coloratura Soprano Met. Star.
Ponselle, Carmela		Entertainment	25				Mezzo Sister of Rosa
Ponselle, Rosa	1897-1981	Entertainment	62		150	225	Acclaimed for 'Norma'. SP in Opera Debut Role 475
Pontchartrain, Louis de	1643-1727	Diplomat	250		1250		French Statesman
Ponti, Carlo		Entertainment	15	20		30	It. Film Producer
Ponting, Herbert George		Celebrity	25	60	165		
Ponty, Jean-Luc		Entertainment	6	8	15	15	
Pool, Tilaman E.		Aviation	10	22	38	28	ACE, WW II, Navy Ace
Poole, Maj. Gen. Leopold Thos.	1888-1965	Military	25				World War II British general
Poor, Enoch		Revolutionary War	175	550	875		General. Patriot, Hero
Poore, Benjamin A.	1866-1940	Military		75		40	Am. WW I Gen.

NAME	DATE	CATEGORY	SIG	LS/DS	ALS	SP	COMMENTS
Poorten, General Hein Ter	1887-1968	Military	20				World War II Dutch general
Poos, Jacques F.		Political	10			15	Member European Parliament
Pope Gregory XVI	1765-1846	Clergy		1200			Roman Catholic Pope 1831-46
Pope John Paul I	1912-1978	Clergy		682			Pope From August-September 1978. 33 Days.
Pope John Paul II	1920-	Clergy	150	400		1065	Karol Wojtyla. Polish Roman Catholic Pope since 1978
Pope John XXIII	1881-1963	Clergy	645	1350		2254	Angelo Giuseppe Roncalli
Pope Paul III	1468-1549	Clergy		1850			
Pope Paul VI	1897-1978	Clergy		500		865	SP Pope Paul VI & Cardinal Jozef Mindszenty 925
Pope Pius IX	1792-1878	Clergy	337	650	400		Giovanni M. M. Ferretti
Pope Pius VII	1740-1823	Clergy	300	820		750	Barnaba Chiaramonti
Pope Pius X	1835-1914	Clergy		592	633	1750	Giuseppe Melchiorre Sarto
Pope Pius XI	1857-1939	Clergy	275	695	3200	1250	Achille Ambrogio Damiano Ratti
Pope Pius XII	1876-1958	Clergy		1127		940	Eugenio Pacelli
Pope, A.J.		Aviation	20	35			WW II Am. Ace
Pope, Alexander	1688-1744	Author	650	1200	2600		Br. Poet, Satirist, Critic
Pope, Alexander	1849-1924	Artist	150	370	600		Am. NY Auction Still Life Sold 475,000 '82
Pope, Generoso Jr.		Business	10	40	50	25	It.-Born Publ. Il Progresso
Pope, James Pinckney	1884-1966	Congress	10	15		20	Senator ID. Dir. TVA
Pope, John (WD)		Civil War	70	160	633		Union Gen.
Pope, John	1822-1892	Civil War	52	138	210	400	Union Genl. Cmdr. 2nd Bull Run
Pope, Lt. Gen. Maurice Arthur	1889-1978	Military	20				World War II Canadian general
Pope, Lt. Gen. Vyvyan Vavasour	1891-1941	Military	25				World War II British general
Popescu, Petru		Celebrity	10			15	film industry
Popham, William	1752-1847	Revolutionary War			375		Aide-de-Camp to Gen. Clinton
Popkin, John S.	1771-1850	Clergy		40	75		Greek Scholar & Harvard Prof. of Greek
Popovic, Cojetko		Celebrity	40		270		
Popovich, Pavel		Cosmonaut	35			58	Rus. Cosmonaut
Popp, Lucia		Entertainment	15			50	Opera
Porizkova, Paulina		Entertainment	25			58	Model-Actress. Pin-Up SP 80
Porritt, Brigadier Arthur E.	1900-1994	Military	30				World War II New Zealand general
Porsche, Ferdinand	1909-1998	Business	350	525		750	Creator of Sports car
Porsche, Ferdinand, Dr.	1875-1951	Business	350	475		650	Designed Volkswagon Beetle
Portal, Charles		Aviation	20	40	80	50	
Porter, Andrew	1820-1872	Civil War	40		75		Union general
Porter, Cole	1891-1964	Composer	225	410	546	1073	AMusQS 1250, S Chk 1050
Porter, David Dixon	1813-1891	Civil War	81	157	300	370	Union Adm., Mex. War, Civil War
Porter, David	1780-1843	Military	56	110	232		Am. Naval Off. Fought 3 Wars
Porter, Don		Entertainment	5	5	10	13	
Porter, Fitz-John	1822-1901	Civil War	34	110	208	997	Union Gen. Special ALS 825-900
Porter, Gail		Celebrity	10			15	celebrity model
Porter, Gene Stratton		Author	50	110	175	125	Am. Novelist. Freckles
Porter, George, Sir		Science	15	35	60	25	Nobel Chemistry 1967
Porter, Horace	1837-1921	Civil War	45	75	98		Union General MOH LS/Cont.1750
Porter, James D.		Governor	5	20	35		Governor TN
Porter, James M.	1793-1844	Cabinet	20	77	120		Sec'y War 1843, Jurist, RR Pres.

NAME	DATE	CATEGORY	SIG	LS/DS	ALS	SP	COMMENTS
Porter, Jane	1776-1850	Author	100		325		Br. Romance Novelist
Porter, Jon C. P		Congress	10			15	Member U.S. Congress
Porter, Katherine Anne	1890-1980	Author	40	95	160	150	Am. 'Ship of Fools', Pulitzer
Porter, Maj. Gen. Ray E.	1891-1963	Military	30				World War II U.S. general
Porter, Mark Dr.		Celebrity	10			15	health and fitness expert
Porter, Noah	1811-1892	Clergy	30	65	100		Editor. President of Yale
Porter, Peter		Cabinet	65	145	180		Sec'y War J.Q.Adams
Porter, Quincy		Composer	17	45			Dean & Dir.New Eng.Conservatory
Porter, William Sidney	1862-1910	Author	300	725	1548		as O. Henry, Am. Short-Story Writer
Portes-Gil, Emilio		Head of State	35		85		Pres. Mexico
Portman, Eric		Entertainment	35			95	
Portman, Natalie		Entertainment	10			58	Young Actress, Star Wars
Portman, Rob P		Congress	10			15	Member U.S. Congress
Portsmouth, Duchess (Chas II)	1649-1734	Royalty	65	465	625		Louise-Renee'de Keroualle.
Posey, Carnot	1818-1863	Civil War	275				Confederate general
Posey, Parker		Entertainment	20			47	
Poshetko, Joseph		Aviation	10	15	25	30	WW II Flying Tiger Ace
Possart, Ernst		Entertainment	15		55	50	Classical Musician
Posselt, Bernd		Political	10			15	Member European Parliament
Post, Augustus		Aviation	25	45	55	50	Pioneer Aviator, Balloonist
Post, Emily	1873-1960	Author	30	50	80	60	US Etiquette Authority of Her Time
Post, Marjorie Merriweather		Business	15	35	70	25	Philanthropist, Postum Cereal
Post, Markie		Entertainment	6	8		25	
Post, Wiley	1900-1935	Aviation	300	460	700	956	1st Solo Around the World Flight. FFC '31 595
Post, Wiley, & Gatty, Harold		Aviation	425			529	
Postlethwaite, Pete		Entertainment	10			20	actor
Poston, Tom		Entertainment	5			25	
Potter, (Helen) Beatrix	1866-1943	Author	250	600	1788	750	& Illustr. Children's Books. 'Peter Rabbit',sgn bk 1550
Potter, Alonzo	1800-1865	Clergy			40		Am. Episcopal Bishop
Potter, Cora		Entertainment	10	15	30	25	
Potter, Edward E.	1823-1889	Civil War	40	75	110		Union General 1st North Carolina
Potter, Joseph Haydn	1822-1892	Civil War	35		95		Union general
Potter, Robert Brown	1829-1887	Civil War	50	95			Union general
Potts, Annie		Entertainment	10			35	
Potts, Benjamin Franklin	1836-1887	Civil War	35	60	95		Union general
Potts, Brigadier Arnold W.	1896- ?	Military	20				World War II Australian general
Poulenc, Francis-Jean	1899-1963	Composer	135	337	484		Member Group of Six. Pianist
Poulson, Norris		Mayor	4	10		10	Mayor L.A.
Poulter, Thomas C.		Explorer	20	40			2nd Arctic Expedition
Pound, Ezra	1885-1972	Author	182	746	1206	1052	Poet, Editor, Critic, Translator
Poundstone, Paula		Entertainment	7			25	Standup Comedienne
Povey, Len		Aviation	10	15	25	20	
Povich, Maury		TV Host	10			22	TV Host
Pow, Rebecca		Celebrity	10			15	home/gardening expert
Powderly, Terence V.	1849-1924	Labor	45	95		50	Am. Labor Leader

NAME	DATE	CATEGORY	SIG	LS/DS	ALS	SP	COMMENTS
Powell, Adam Clayton	1908-1972	Congress	30	40	55	50	Contoversial Minister, MOC NY. Barred, Reelected
Powell, Colin L.	1937-	Military	35	75		88	General. Secretary of State
Powell, Dick	1904-1963	Entertainment	35	45	60	52	Actor, SP 11x14 Bachrach 145
Powell, Eleanor	1910-1982	Entertainment	10	25	35	55	Popular 40's Film Tap Dancer Musical Star
Powell, Jane		Entertainment	9	10	20	25	
Powell, Jenny		Celebrity	10			15	television presenter
Powell, Jeremiah		Revolutionary War	75		245		President of Mass. Bay Colony Rev. Times
Powell, John Wesley		Explorer	250	391			Geologist. Pioneer Expl. West US
Powell, Lewis F., Jr.	1907-1998	Supreme Court	40	95		125	Supreme Court Justice
Powell, Maud		Entertainment	20			90	Violinist
Powell, Max		Country Music	10			20	
Powell, Robert		Entertainment	4			10	Actor
Powell, Ross E.		Military	10	15	30		
Powell, Talmage		Author	10	20	45	15	Am. Novelist Mysteries
Powell, Teddy		Entertainment	20			70	Big Band Leader
Powell, William Henry	1825-1904	Civil War	45	75	138		Union general
Powell, William	1892-1985	Entertainment	30	50		90	Actor
Power, Paul		Entertainment				20	Character Actor
Power, Tyrone	1913-1958	Entertainment	80	123		250	Actor
Powers, Bert		Celebrity	4	10	15	10	White House Aide
Powers, Francis Gary		Aviation	110	148		125	U2 Pilot Downed Over USSR LS/Cont 795
Powers, Hiram	1805-1873	Artist	60	160	325	350	19th Cent. Major Sculptor
Powers, John Robert		Business	10	20	25	20	Fndr. One of 1st Modelling Agy.
Powers, John 'Shorty'	1923-1980	Celebrity	30	40		50	NASA Spokesman. A-OK
Powers, Mala		Entertainment	5	7		15	
Powers, Preston		Artist	25	65	165		
Powers, Richard							SEE Tom Keene
Powers, Ridgely C.		Governor	10	15	30		Governor MS
Powers, Stephanie		Entertainment	9	10	20	25	Pin-Up SP 25
Pownall, Lt Gen Sir Henry Royds	1887-1961	Military	25				World War II British general
Pownall, Thomas	1722-1805	Colonial Am.	150	311	630		Lt.Gov. NJ, Gov. MA Bay, SC
Powter, Susan		Author	5			10	Non-Fiction
Powys, John C.	1872-1963	Author	28	60			Novelist, Poet, Critic, Philosopher
Powys, Llewelyn		Author	30	45	50	60	Essayist, Novelist
Powys, Theodore Francis	1875-1953	Author	80		350		Br. Allegorical Novels. AMsS 1980
Poynter, Edward John, Sir		Artist	10	35	75		Pres. Royal Academy
Pozzo di Borgo, Carlo Andrea	1764-1842	Corsican Diplomat	100		260		Opponent of Napoleon
Prado, Perez		Bandleader	25			85	
Praed, Michael		Entertainment	10			20	Actor
Praed, Winthrop M.	1802-1839	Author	50		230		Poet
Pran, Dith		Celebrity	10	20	45	20	Cambodian photographer
Pratt, Brig. Gen. Don F.	1892-1944	Military	30				World War II U.S. general
Pratt, Calvin Edward	1828-1896	Civil War	40		105		Union general
Pratt, Elmer 'Geronimo'		Celebrity	10			15	political celebrity
Pratt, Francis & Whitney, Amos		Inventor		465			Pratt & Whitney Engine

NAME	DATE	CATEGORY	SIG	LS/DS	ALS	SP	COMMENTS
Pratt, Maj. Gen. Douglas Henry	1892-1958	Military	25				World War II British general
Pratt, Maj. Gen. Fendall Wm. H.	1892-1960	Military	25				World War II British general
Pratt, Ruth	1877-1965	Congress	10	30			Repr. NY 1929-33
Pratt, Thomas G.		Congress	5	20	25		Gov. 1845, Senator MD 1849
Praun, Gen Signals Troops Albert	1894-1975	Military	27				World War II German general
Preble, George H.		Civil War	20	60	85		Adm. USN. DS/Cont. 250
Precourt, Charlie		Astronaut	7			20	
Preddy. George E.		Aviation	10	30	45	30	
Preger, Kurt		Entertainment	5			20	Opera
Prelog, Vladimir		Science	20	30	45	25	Nobel Chemistry 1975
Premice, Josephine		Entertainment	20			35	Afr.-Am. Actress
Preminger, Otto	1906-1986	Entertainment	50			125	Important Film Director
Prentice, John*		Cartoonist	10			40	Rip Kirby
Prentiss, Benjamin M. (WD)		Civil War	75	160	275		Shiloh
Prentiss, Benjamin M.	1819-1901	Civil War	45	85	125		Union Major General
Prentiss, Paula		Entertainment	12			20	Pin-Up SP 25
Prepon, Laura		Entertainment				35	
Prescott, Oliver	1731-1804	Revolutionary War	125	276	525		Suppression of Shay's Rebellion
Prescott, Wm. Hickling		Author	30	60			
PRESIDENTIAL OATH		President		4417			FIVE PRES.(Printed Transcript), signed by 5
PRESIDENTS (4)		President	1250			1446	4 PRESIDENTS (Reagan-Ford-Carter-Nixon)
PRESIDENTS (5)		President	1412			3783	Ford, Nixon, Bush, Reagan, Carter WH Engr.S 3700
Presley, Elvis	1935-1977	Entertainment	597	1390	2912	1228	ALS/Content 10,000-13,000
Presley, Lisa Marie		Celebrity	20			35	Singer, Daughter to Elvis and Priscilla
Presley, Priscilla		Entertainment	20		40	30	Pin-Up SP 35. Legal DS 500., SP with Elvis 1500
Presley, Vernon		Celebrity	15			60	Father of Elvis Presley
Presnell, Lowell		Author	8			12	history of mining
Presser, Jackie		Celebrity	10	25		15	
Preston, J.A.		Entertainment	10			20	actor
Preston, John Smith	1809-1881	Civil War	95				Confederate general
Preston, Kelly		Entertainment	5			30	
Preston, Richard		Celebrity	10			15	medical expert
Preston, Robert	1918-1987	Entertainment	50			75	Actor-Singer 'Music Man'
Preston, William (WD)		Civil War	157	590	735		CSA Gen.
Preston, William Ballard	1805-1862	Cabinet	25	50	110		CSA Senator., War dte SP 3,000
Preston, William	1816-1887	Civil War	125	423	540		CSA Gen.
Preston, Wm. C.	1794-1860	Congress	15	35			Sen. SC
Pretelat, General André-Gaston	1874-1969	Military	20				World War II French general
Pretenders		Entertainment	12			65	
Pretorius, Major P.J.		Author	15			40	African adventure
Prets, Christa		Political	10			15	Member European Parliament
Pretty Things, The		Entertainment				80	Br. Rock Group (All 5)
Preuss, Georg		Military	20		40		
Previn, Andre		Conductor-Comp.	20	40	80	75	
Previn, Dorey		Composer	5	10	20	10	

NAME	DATE	CATEGORY	SIG	LS/DS	ALS	SP	COMMENTS
Prevost, Eugene-Marcel		Author	10	25	55		Fr. Moralist, Feminist Fiction
Prey, Hermann		Entertainment	10			30	Opera
Price, Brig. Thomas Reginald	1894-1978	Military	25				World War II British general
Price, Bruce D		Author	8			12	genealogy
Price, Channing	1843-1863	Civil War	75		1668		CSA Adjutant General
Price, David E. P		Congress	10			15	Member U.S. Congress
Price, James H.		Governor	5	15			Governor VA
Price, Leontyne		Entertainment	25		45	55	Am. Soprano, Opera
Price, Lindsay		Celebrity				20	
Price, Maj. Gen. Charles Bacil	1889-1975	Military	20				World War II Canadian general
Price, Margaret		Entertainment	15			45	Opera
Price, Ray		Entertainment	5			15	C & W
Price, Sterling (WD)		Civil War	380		4500		CSA Gen. AES 575
Price, Sterling	1809-1867	Civil War	218	271	374		CSA Gen. Gov. MO
Price, Vincent	1911-1993	Entertainment	45	65	80	80	Self Sketch S 90. 'Egghead' SP 125
Prichard, Maj. Gen. Vernon E.	1892-1949	Military	30				World War II U.S. general
Prickett, Maj. Gen. Fay B.	1893-1982	Military	30				World War II U.S. general
Pride, Charley	1938-	Country Music	10			20	1st Afr-Am Major Country Music Star
Prien, Guenther	1908-1941	Military	300			950	German WW II U-Boat Commander
Priest, Ivy Baker		Cabinet	10	15	30	20	U.S. Treasurer
Priest, Maj. Gen. Robert Cecil	1882-1966	Military	25				World War II British general
Priest, Pat		Entertainment	4			20	Actor. 'Munsters'. 'Marilyn Munster'
Priest, Royce W.		Aviation	10	22	35	30	ACE, WW II, USAAF Ace
Priestley, John Boynton	1894-1984	Author	20	35	60	50	Playwright, Novelist, Playwright
Priestley, William O., Sir		Medical	50	120	200		Obstetric Physician
Priestly, Jason		Entertainment	20			35	Actor
Priestly, Joseph	1783-1804	Science	350	1200	2200		Br. Clergyman, Chemist.
Priestman, Maj. Gen. John H. T.	1885-1964	Military	28				World War II British general
Prieur-Duvernois, Claude-A		Fr. Revolution	35	125			Fr. Revolutionary
Prigogine, Ilya		Science	20	30	45	25	Nobel Chemistry 1977
Prima, Louis		Entertainment	20			45	Big Band Leader-Trumpeter
Primrose, Archibald P.	1847-1929	Head of State	30	70	145		Br. Prime Minister
Primrose, William		Entertainment	75			250	Great Violinist
Prince		Entertainment	110			175	
Prince, Harold 'Hal'		Entertainment	15	20	30	30	
Prince, Henry	1811-1892	Civil War	30	65	85		Union Gen.Pre War ALS 650
Prince, John Dyneley		Educator	10	25		15	Dean Graduate School NYU
Principal, Victoria		Entertainment	10	10	25	30	
Pringle, Aileen		Entertainment	15	15	35	30	
Prinz, Dianne		Astronaut	4			12	
Prinz, Rosemary		Entertainment	3	4		10	
Prinze, Freddie		Entertainment	45	60		85	Comedian
Prinze, Freddie, Jr.		Entertainment	8			39	Actor
Pritchard, Brig. Charles Hilary V.	1905-1976	Military	25				World War II British general
Pritchard, Jeter C.	1857-1921	Congress	10	15			Senator NC 1895

NAME	DATE	CATEGORY	SIG	LS/DS	ALS	SP	COMMENTS
Pritchard, John, Sir		Conductor				45	Opera & Mozart Specialist
Procacci, Giovanni		Political	10			15	Member European Parliament
Procol Harum		Entertainment	35			125	
Proctor, Edna Dean	1838-	Author	35		80		Am. Poet, Magazine Writer
Proctor, Redfield	1831-1908	Cabinet	12	25	50	30	Gov, Senator VT, Sec'y War
Proctor, Richard Anthony		Science	5	15	35		Br. Astonomer, Science Writer
Profumo, John		Politician	40	65		100	Br. Traitor. Member of Parliament
Profumo, Valerie (Hobson)		Entertainment	10		25	25	Br. Film Star
Prokofieff, Serge	1891-1953	Composer	425	1250	1888	1500	Russ. AMusQS 2500-5,000
Pronk, Bartho		Political	10			15	Member European Parliament
Proops, Greg		Celebrity	10			15	comedian
Prosky, Robert		Entertainment	5	6	15	15	
Prosser, Maj. Gen. Walter E.	1882-1981	Military	30				World War II U.S. general
Protti, Aldo		Entertainment	5			20	Opera
Prouse, Juliet		Entertainment	10	12	15	35	Actress, dancer
Proust, Marcel	1871-1922	Author	500	875	1550	6000	ALS/Content 3,300, 3,500
Prout, William	1785-1850	Science		110	175		English Chemist and Physician
Prouty, Jed		Entertainment	30			45	
Proval, David		Entertainment				35	Richie Aprile, Soprano's
Provan, James L.C.		Political	10			15	Member European Parliament
Provine, Dorothy		Entertainment	5	6		10	
Provost, Jon		Entertainment	18			22	Young Actor. 'Timmy' from 'Lassie' TV Series
Prowse, Dave		Entertainment	10			35	Actor. Darth Vadar 35
Proxmire, William		Senate/Congress	5	10		15	Senator WI
Prudhomme, Paul		Celebrity	10			15	famous chef
Prudhomme, Rene Francois		Author			175		Fr. Poet and Philosopher
Prutzmann, Hans-Adolf	d. 1945	Military	125				Nazi SS leader. 'Werewolf' Bands
Pryce, Deborah P		Congress	10			15	Member U.S. Congress
Pryce, Jonathan		Entertainment	10			20	actor
Pryor, David		Governor	5	15			Governor AR
Pryor, Mark		Senate	10			15	United States Senate (D - AR)
Pryor, Richard		Entertainment	9	10	35	25	
Pryor, Roger A. (WD)		Civil War	175		650		CSA Gen.
Pryor, Roger A.	1828-1919	Civil War	127	210	244		CSA Gen. US MOC. 1859-61
Pryor, Roger		Entertainment	15	20		45	
Pérez álvarez, Manuel		Political	10			15	Member European Parliament
Pérez Royo, Fernando		Political	10			15	Member European Parliament
Pucci, Emilio		Business	10	25	40	15	It. Fashion Designer
Puccini, Giacomo	1858-1924	Composer	375	750	1203	1378	AMusQS 1,400-1950-4,000
Puck, Wolfgang		Business	5	10		20	Successful Chef & Owner of 'Spago'
Puckrik, Katie		Celebrity	10			15	television presenter
Pudovkin, Vsesolod	1893-1953	Celebrity	75		322	368	Russian film director
Puelo, Johnny		Entertainment	10			25	
Puente, Tito		Entertainment	10			45	Big Band Leader.
Puerta, Alonso José		Political	10			15	Member European Parliament

NAME	DATE	CATEGORY	SIG	LS/DS	ALS	SP	COMMENTS
Puett, Clay		Business	25	60		35	
Pulitzer, Joseph	1847-1911	Business	125	350	595		Pulitzer Prize. Editor-Publisher. Rare ALS 4500
Pulitzer, Joseph, Jr.		Business	20	25		30	Editor-Publisher
Pulitzer, Ralph	1879-1939	Business	54		250		Journalist, Pres. Press Publishing NY World
Pulitzer, Roxanne		Celebrity	5	15	35	20	Pin-Up SP 25
Pullenberg, Albert		Science	20			60	Rocket Pioneer w/von Braun
Pullman, Bill		Entertainment	12			35	Actor
Pullman, George M.	1831-1897	Business-Inventor	350	650	900	1000	Pullman RR Car. ALS on Lttrhd. 9600
Pullman, Hattie Sanger		Philantropist	15	25	30		Mrs. George M. Pullman
Pulp Fiction (cast)		Entertainment				75	Travolta/ Jackson
Pulsford, Nigel		Entertainment	6			25	Music. Guitar 'Bush'
Puma, Salvatore		Entertainment	5			20	Opera
Punshon, W. Morley		Clergy	25	40	50		
Pupin, Michael, Dr.	1858-1935	Science	64	150	210	250	Physicist-Inventor-Author
Purcell, Edward M., Dr.		Science	20	30	45	25	Nobel Physics 1952
Purcell, Lee		Entertainment	4	5	12	10	
Purcell, Sarah		Entertainment	5	6	15	20	
Purdy, James		Author	15	50			
Purl, Linda		Entertainment	6	8	15	20	
Purser, Maj. Gen. Arthur William	1884-1953	Military	28				World War II British general
Purvis, John		Political	10			15	Member European Parliament
Purvis, Melvin	1903-1960	Lawman	45	120	175	150	FBI. Noted Agent. Hunted Down 'Most Wanted'
Purvis, Robert		Anti-Slavery	15	40	85		Underground Railroad
Pusey, Edward B.	1800-1882	Clergy	45	55	110	150	Anglican High Church Leader of Oxford Movement
Pusey, Nathan M.	1907-	Educator	15	30	75	50	President Harvard
Pusey, Pennock		Political	10	15			Government Official
Pushkin, Alexander	1799-1837	Author	2200	5250	16200		Rus. Poet, Dramatist, Novelist
Pusser, Buford		Lawman	50	150			Walking Tall Tennessee Sheriff
Putin, Vladimir V.		Political	75	220		250	President of Russia
Putman, Frederick Ward	1839-1915	Science		30	55		Anthropologist-Naturalist. Curator of Top Museums
Putnam, Adam H. P		Congress	10			15	Member U.S. Congress
Putnam, George Haven	1844-1930	Business	30	80			Publishing House. Putnam & Sons
Putnam, George Palmer	1814-1872	Business	40	75	110		Book Publisher, Author
Putnam, Israel	1718-1790	Revolutionary War	200	725	1250		'Don't Fire Till...' War Dte. MsLS 3500
Putnam, Rufus		Revolutionary War	175	405	592		General. Ohio Pioneer
Putney, Mahlon		Celebrity	20	55			
Puttick, Lt. Gen. Edward	1890-1976	Military	30				World War II New Zealand general
Puzo, Mario	1921-1999	Author	20	40	65	50	Am. Novelist. The Godfather
Py, Gilbert		Entertainment	5			25	Opera
Pyle, Denver		Entertainment	4	6	10	20	
Pyle, Ernie	1900-1945	Author	212	376	485	350	Correspondent WWII, Pulitzer. KIA
Pyle, Howard	1853-1911	Artist	170	375	750		Am. Art Nouveau Illustrator-Auth
Pyman, Gen. Sir Harold English	1908-1971	Military	25				World War II British general
Pynchon, John	1626-1703	Colonial America			3750		Statesman, Soldier.

NAME	DATE	CATEGORY	SIG	LS/DS	ALS	SP	COMMENTS
Qaddafi, Muammar el-(Alg)		Head of State	85	225	500	350	Chairman Libyan-Arab Republic
Quackenbush, Stephen (WD)	1823-1890	Civil War	35		165		Union Naval Officer
Quaid, Dennis		Entertainment	20			42	Actor
Quaid, Randy		Entertainment	6	15		25	Actor
Quale, Anthony		Entertainment	20	25	55	42	
Qualen, John		Entertainment	10			20	
Quang, Thich Tri		Head of State	20	45	125	30	
Quant, Mary		Business	5	10	20	10	Br. Fashion Designer.
Quantrill, William C.	1837-1865	Civil War	2750	6500	12000		CSA Army Guerilla Leader
Quarles, William A.	1825-1893	Civil War	97	308			CSA General. Sig. War Dte. 150
Quarry, Robert		Entertainment	10			25	
Quasimodo, Salvatore		Author	25	40	55	30	Nobel Literature 1959
Quay, Matthew Stanley	1833-1904	Civil War	30	75	120		Union Colonel, MOH
Quayle, Dan	1947-	Vice President	58	78		56	Sen. IN. Bush VP. Signed White House Card 50
Quayle, Marilyn		2nd Lady	20			35	
Queen Latifa		Celebrity	20			45	Actress, singer
Queen		Music	472				Rock, Signed album 450-744
Queen, Ellery		Author					SEE DANNAY
Queensberry, Wm. Douglas		Celebrity	15	40	95		
Queiró, Luís		Political	10			15	Member European Parliament
Quentin, Caroline		Entertainment	10			20	Actress
Quesada, Elwood R.		Aviation	16	30	45	30	
Quesada, Vincente Fox		Political				30	President of Mexico
Questel, Mae		Entertainment	50				Original Voice of Betty Boop
Quie, Albert Harold		Senate/Congress	5			10	MOC MN
Quigg, Lemuel Ely		Senate/Congress	5	10			MOC NY 1894
Quillan, Eddie		Entertainment	20			45	
Quinan, Gen. Sir Edward Pellew	1884-1960	Military	28				World War II British general
Quinby, Isaac Ferdinand	1821-1891	Civil War	35	65	80		Union general
Quincy, Josiah	1772-1864	Congress	40	60	95		Repr. MA. Pres. Harvard
Quine, Richard		Entertainment	10			20	Actor turned Director
Quinlan, Kathleen		Entertainment	10			20	actress
Quinn, Aidan		Entertainment	10			20	actor
Quinn, Anthony		Entertainment	15	38		61	AA Winning Mex.-Irish Actor. 'Zorba'
Quinn, Carmel		Entertainment	5			15	
Quinn, Jack Q		Congress	10			15	Member U.S. Congress
Quinn, Jane Bryant		Celebrity	10			15	financial expert
Quinn, Martha		Entertainment	4			10	MTV
Quinn, Robert E.		Governor	10	15			Governor RI
Quinn, William F.		Governor	5	10		15	Governor HI
Quinones, John		Celebrity	10			15	TV personality

NAME	DATE	CATEGORY	SIG	LS/DS	ALS	SP	COMMENTS
Quintard, Charles Todd		Clergy	75	95	160		Served Confed. Army as Phys.
Quirk, Michael J.		Aviation	12	25	40	30	ACE, WW II
Quirke, Pauline		Entertainment	10			20	Actress
Quiros, Jean B.		Head of State	45	70			
Quisling, Vidkun	1877-1955	Military	115	220	475	450	Executed Nazi Collaborator
Quisthoudt-rowohl, Godelieve		Political	10			15	Member European Parliament
Quitman, John A.	1799-1858	Millitary-Congr.-Gov.	25				General. Gov. & Sen. MS
Quivers, Robin		Celebrity	10			15	media/TV personality

NAME	DATE	CATEGORY	SIG	LS/DS	ALS	SP	COMMENTS
R. Kelly		Music	20			45	Rap
Raab, Julius		Head of State	5	15	35	15	Chancellor Austria
Raabe, Meinhardt		Entertainment	25			35	Munchkin WOZ
Rabaud, Henri	1873-1949	Composer	35			200	Fr. Composer-Conductor. Opera. AMusQS 120
Rabi, Isador I.	1898-1988	Science	42	60	80	40	Nobel Physics 1944. Development of Radar, A Bomb
Rabin, Yitzhak	1922-1996	Head of State	116	278	525	384	PM Israel, Nobel. Assassinated '96
Rabinowitz, Solomon		Author					SEE Aleichem, S. (Pen Name)
Raboy, Mac*		Cartoonist	10			95	Flash Gordon
Rachin, Alan		Entertainment	5			15	
Rachmaninoff, Sergei	1873-1943	Composer	358	868	1383	1341	AMusQS 2,000- 4500
Racine, Jean	1639-1699	Author	4500				Fr. Dramatist
Rack, Reinhard		Political	10			15	Member European Parliament
Rackham, Arthur	1867-1939	Artist	60	175	325		Br. Illustrator Children's Books. Water Color
Radanovich, George R		Congress	10			15	Member U.S. Congress
Radford, Michael		Celebrity	10			15	film industry
Radford, William	1808-1890	Civil War	40	125	170		Union Commodore
Radford, William	1814-1870	Congress	10	15	30		Repr. NY
Radhakrishnan, Sarvepalli	1888-1975	Head of State	75	167	380	250	Pres. India, Philosopher, Educator, Author
Radner, Gilda	1946-1989	Entertainment	50	62		250	Am. Comedienne
Radwan, Alexander		Political	10			15	Member European Parliament
Radziwill, Lee		Celebrity	20	35		20	Sister to Jackie Kennedy
Rae, Cassidy		Entertainment	5			40	Actress Models, Inc.
Rae, Charlotte		Entertainment	5			15	
Raeder, Erick	1876-1960	Military	115	208	360	250	Ger. Navy Cmdr., Convicted of War Crimes WW II
Raff, Joseph Joachim		Composer	25		150		Ger. Wide Variety Of Music
Rafferty, Frances		Entertainment	4			10	
Raffin, Deborah		Entertainment	10	12	15	42	
Rafko, Kaye Lani		Entertainment	8			15	Miss America 1988
Raft, George	1895-1980	Entertainment	45	120		170	11x14 Vintage SPI 200
Rage Against the Machine		Entertainment	32			90	Music. Rock Group
Raglan, Fitzroy Somerset, Lord		Military	40	115	150		Crimean War. Raglan Sleeve
Ragsland, Rags		Entertainment	40			75	

NAME	DATE	CATEGORY	SIG	LS/DS	ALS	SP	COMMENTS
Rahall II, Nick J. R		Congress	10			15	Member U.S. Congress
Rahman, Abdul		Head of State	10	35	80	15	Malaysia.1st Ambass. U.S.
Raikes, Maj. Gen. Sir Geoffrey T.	1884-1975	Military	25				World War II British general
Raimondi, Ruggero		Entertainment	20			50	Opera
Rainer, Luise		Entertainment	15	35	40	50	Austrian Two Time Oscar Winner. Back to Back
Raines, Ella		Entertainment	7			18	
Rainey, Ford		Entertainment	3	5		10	
Rainey, Henry Thomas		Senate/Congress	5	15			MOC IL 1903-21, Speaker
Rainger, Ralph		Composer	20			40	AMusQS 55, 85
Rainier III, Prince		Royalty	70	95	205	125	Monaco
Rain-in-the-Face		Indian Chief	5750			8260	
Rains, Claude	1899-1967	Entertainment	113			241	Brit. Character Actor. 'Casablanca'
Rains, Gabriel James	1803-1881	Civil War	110	417			Confederate general
Rains, James E. (WD)	1833-1862	Civil War		4850			CSA Gen. KIA
Rainwater, Leo James		Science	20	30	45	25	Nobel Physics 1975
Rainwater, Marvin		Country Music	15			30	
Raisa, Rosa	1893-1963	Entertainment	30	45		60	Opera. Created Title Role in Turandot
Raitt, Bonnie		Entertainment	5			45	rock
Raitt, John		Entertainment	5	7	15	15	
Raksin, David		Composer					AMQS 75
Raleigh, Cecil		Entertainment	6	8		10	
Raleigh, Sara		Entertainment	6	8		10	
Raleigh, Walter, Sir	1552-1618	History	5750	23000			Renaissaince explorer, poet
Rall, Guenther		Military-Aviation	30	75	150	82	#3 ACE, WW II, Ger. 275 Kills.
Ralston, Esther		Entertainment	10	15	45	33	Am. Leading Lady 20's-30's
Ralston, Jobyna		Entertainment	25	35	65	50	
Ralston, Vera Hruba		Entertainment	7	15		25	
Ralston, William		Business	55	90	150		Founder Bank of California
Rama VI	1881-1925	Royalty	135				King Siam (Thailand)
Rambeau, Marjorie		Entertainment	20	25	45	45	
Rambo, Dirk		Entertainment	20			40	
Ramey, Samuel		Entertainment	10			35	Opera
Ramirez, Carlos		Entertainment	8			25	Baritone
Ramone, Johnny		Entertainment	16			76	Romones Rock Group
Ramos, Ramon		Entertainment	10			35	1930's Big Band Leader
Rampling, Charlotte		Entertainment	5			27	Brit. Actress-Model. Pin-up SP 35
Ramsay, George Douglas	1802-1882	Civil War	40	75	100		Union general
Ramsay, Maj. Gen. Alan H.	1895-1973	Military	20				World War II Australian general
Ramsay, William, Sir	1852-1916	Science	150	410	750		Nobel Chemistry 1904
Ramsden, Lt. Gen. Wm. Havelock	1888-1969	Military	25				World War II British general
Ramseur, Stephen D. (WD)	1837-1864	Civil War		13000			CSA Gen. RARE
Ramseur, Stephen Dodson	1837-1864	Civil War	354	775			Confederate general
Ramsey, Alexander		Cabinet	20	45	90		CW Gov. MN, Hayes Sec'y War
Ramsey, Gordon		Celebrity	10			15	TV Chef
Ramsey, Michael, Archbishop		Clergy	35	45	50	45	

NAME	DATE	CATEGORY	SIG	LS/DS	ALS	SP	COMMENTS
Ramsey, Norman F., Dr.		Science	15	25		20	Nobel Physics 1989
Ramstad, Jim R		Congress	10			15	Member U.S. Congress
Rance, Maj. Gen. Sir Hubert Elvin	1898-1974	Military	25				World War II British general
Rand, Ayn	1905-1982	Author	750	2962		1500	Objectivist Novels, AMS2128
Rand, Sally	1903-1979	Entertainment	25	60		70	Fan Dancer 20's-30's
Randall, James R.	1839-1908	Writer-Composer	100		350		'Maryland, My...' MsS 1,900, AMsS 9,500
Randall, Richard		Celebrity	10			15	home/gardening expert
Randall, Samuel J.		Senate/Congress	7	20			MOC PA 1863-90
Randall, Tony		Entertainment	5	5	15	30	
Randell, Mike		Business	3			5	TV Exec.
Randolph, A. Philip	1889-1979	Labor	65	75			US Black Labor Leader 1925. Train Porter's Strike
Randolph, Beverly	1755-1797	Revolutionary War	100	325			Early Gov. Virginia 1788
Randolph, Boots		Entertainment	5			15	Country Rockabilly Saxaphonist
Randolph, Charles D.		Showman	75	210	315		Buckskin Bill Assoc./Wm. Cody
Randolph, Edmund J.	1753-1813	Revolutionary War	188	491	625		Sec'y State, Washington Aide-de-camp ADS/Cont.1600
Randolph, Geo. Wythe	1818-1867	Civil War	268	410	565		CSA Gen. ALS '62 825
Randolph, John (of Roanoke)	1733-1883	Revolutionary War	85	265	485		MOC, Senator VA
Randolph, Joyce		Entertainment	5	10		25	Actress. 'Trixie' on 'The Honeymooners'
Randolph, Lillian		Entertainment	100			250	
Randolph, Peyton	1721-1775	Am. Revolution	400	2250			1st Pres. Continental Congress
Randolph, Thos. Mann, Jr.	1768-1828	Congress	75	275			Repr. & Gov. VA. Special ALS 2800
Randy & the Rainbows (3)		Entertainment	20			40	Rock
Randzio-Plath, Christa		Political	10			15	Member European Parliament
Rangel, Charles B.	1930-	Congress	10			15	Afr-Am MOC NY. Advocate for Disadvantaged
Rank, J. Arthur, 1st Baron		Entertainment	25		75	55	Br. Industrialist, Film Magnate
Rank, Otto	1884-1939	Science	200		425		Austrian Psychoanalyst
Rankin, Jeannette	1880-1973	Congress	80	200			Voted against both World Wars
Rankin, Nell		Entertainment	10	20		25	Am. Contralto-Mezzo
Rankin, Paul & Paul		Celebrity	10			15	TV Chefs
Rankin, Robert J.		Aviation	12	25	42	35	ACE, WW II, Ace in a Day
Ranking, Maj. Gen. Robt. Philip L.	1896-1971	Military	25				World War II British general
Ransier, Alonzo Jacob		Senate/Congress	75				MOC SC
Ransom, John Crowe		Author	35	85	200		Am. Poet, Critic, Professor
Ransom, Maj. Gen. Algernon Lee	1883-1969	Military	25				World War II British general
Ransom, Maj. Gen. Paul L.	1894-1985	Military	30				World War II U.S. general
Ransom, Matthew W.	1826-1904	Civil War	110	186	245		CSA Gen.
Ransom, Robert Jr	1828-1892	Civil War	100				Confederate general
Ransom, Robert, Jr. (WD)	1828-1892	Civil War	220	1250	2850		CSA Gen.
Ransom, Thomas E. G.	1834-1864	Civil War	120		288		Union general
Rantzen, Esther		Celebrity	10			15	television presenter
Rapaport, Lester		Artist	10	15	30	15	
Rapee, Erno		Conductor	15			45	Hung.-Am. Radio City Music Hall
Raphael, Sally Jessy		TV Host	5			23	TV Talk Show Hostess
Rapkay, Bernhard		Political	10			15	Member European Parliament
Rapper, Irving	1898-	Entertainment	15			35	40's Film Director. 'Now Voyager'

NAME	DATE	CATEGORY	SIG	LS/DS	ALS	SP	COMMENTS
Rappold, Marie		Entertainment	30			95	Opera, Concert
Raschhofer, Daniela		Political	10			15	Member European Parliament
Rash, Steve		Celebrity	10			15	film industry
Rashad, Phylicia		Entertainment	5			25	
Raskob, John J.		Business	10	20		15	CEO General Motors
Rasmussen, Knud J.V.	1879-1933	Explorer	200		325	350	Danish Arctic Explorer, Author
Rasp, Gen. of Infantry Siegfried	1886-1968	Military	25				World War II German general
Raspberry, William		Celebrity	10			15	motivational speaker
Rasputin, Gregori E.	1872-1916	Clergy	2000	3170	7250		Rus. Mystic. Influenced Royal Family. Assassinated
Rathbone, Basil	1892-1967	Entertainment	165	292	349	416	Menacing, Leading Man & Sophisticated 'Villain'
Rathbone, Henry Reed	1837-1911	History		1380	1500		Union Col., Accompanied Lincoln to Ford's theater
Rathbone, Monroe J.		Business	4	8	15	10	Exxon. Important Oil Innovations
Rather, Dan		Celebrity	10			25	media/TV personality
Ratner, Payne		Governor	5	15			Governor KS
Ratoff, Gregory		Entertainment	20	65		60	Film Director
Ratzenberger, John		Entertainment	5			25	Cheers SP 35
Rau, Johannes		Political				20	President of Germany
Raum, Green B.	1829-1909	Civil War	28	65		127	Union Gen., MOC IL
Raus, Colonel-General Erhard	1889-1956	Military	25				World War II German general
Rauschenberg, Bob		Artist	50				Color Pc Repro. S 165
Ravel, Maurice	1875-1937	Composer	358	877	1289	1500	AMusQS 1,675-3,800-4,800
Rawdon-Hastings, Francis, Lord	1754-1826	Revolutionary War	100	220	310		Br. Officer. Bunker Hill
Rawlings, Edward V.		Military	10	20			
Rawlings, Marjorie Kinnan		Author	45	150			Am. Pulitzer. The Yearling
Rawlins, John A.	1831-1869	Civil War	60	75	184		Union Gen., Sec'y War 1869
Rawlins, Maj. Gen. Stuart Blundel	1897-1955	Military	25				World War II British general
Rawlinson, Herbert	1886-1853	Entertainment	15	20	45	65	Br. Actor. Starred in dozens of B Westerns,
Rawls, Lou		Entertainment	15	25		40	Singer
Rawson, Edward	1615-1693	Colonial America	125	350	685		Colonial Sec'y. ADS 1500
Rawson, Maj. Gen. Geoffrey G.	1887-1979	Military	25				World War II British general
Rawstorne, Brig Geo. Streynsham	1895-1962	Military	25				World War II British general
Ray, Aldo		Entertainment	4	5		15	
Ray, Charles		Entertainment	25	35	65	60	
Ray, Dixie Lee		Governor	15			40	Governor WA
Ray, James Earl	1928-1976	Assassin	65	125	194		Shot Martin Luther King, Jr.
Ray, Johnny		Entertainment				40	Singer-Actor
Ray, Leah		Entertainment	10			15	
Ray, Man (Rudnitsky)	1890-1976	Artist	262	575			Surrealist Painter, Photographer. ANS 285
Ray, Robert D.		Governor	5			10	Governor IA
Ray, Susan		Country Music	5			10	
Rayburn, Gene		Celebrity	15			35	TV Gameshow host
Rayburn, Sam	1882-1961	Congress	35	94		75	Speaker of the House, TX. Was Speaker Longest
Raye, Cassidy		Entertainment				40	Models, Inc.
Raye, Collin		Country Music	10			30	
Raye, Martha	1916-1994	Entertainment	20	30		40	Comedienne

NAME	DATE	CATEGORY	SIG	LS/DS	ALS	SP	COMMENTS
Rayleigh, John W. S.	1842-1919	Science			402		Nobel Physics. 3rd Baron
Raymond, Alex*		Cartoonist	60		95	55	Flash Gordon. Spec. Ltrhd. TLS 225
Raymond, Gene		Entertainment	10	15	25	25	
Raymond, Henry J.		Business	30	75	150		Fndr. New York Times, MOC NY
Raymond, Jim*		Cartoonist	15			75	Blondie
Raymond, John T.	1836-1887	Entertainment	20				Vintage Actor
Raymond, Michel		Political	10			15	Member European Parliament
Raymond, Paula		Entertainment	5			15	
Razaf, Andy		Composer	45		225		Lyricist 'Ain't Misbehavin'
Rea, Stephen		Entertainment	10			20	actor
Read, Albert Cushing		Aviation	40	85	180	115	Adm. Record Flight, WW I & II
Read, Dolly		Entertainment	5	6	15	15	Pin-Up SP 15
Read, George	1733-1798	Revolutionary War	388	650	1695		Signer Decl. of Indepen.
Read, Imelda Mary		Political	10			15	Member European Parliament
Read, Jacob	1752-1816	Rev War	75	180	240		Rev War Colonel. Politician.
Read, James	b. 1953	Entertainment	10			20	Actor
Read, T. Buchanan	1822-1872	Artist	17	30	40		Poet. 'Sheridan's Ride'
Readdy, William F.		Astronaut	5			20	
Reade, Charles		Author	30	70	135		Br. Novelist, Dramatist
Reagan, John H.	1818-1905	Civil War	113	303	408		CSA Postmaster Gen., DS cont 1610
Reagan, Maureen		Celebrity	5	15	30	25	Political Daughter of President
Reagan, Nancy		1st Lady	65	82	172	103	
Reagan, Ron		Celebrity	10			15	media/TV personality
Reagan, Ron, Jr.		Entertainment	4			30	Dancer
Reagan, Ronald (As Pres.)		President	407	1022	5012	523	R. Reagan & Nancy SP 380-500.
Reagan, Ronald	1911-	President	252	600	1327	331	Personal Paternal ALS 18,000
Real, Pierre F., Count		Fr. Revolution	15	35	80		
Reale, Antenore		Entertainment	20			55	Opera
Ream, Vinnie		Artist			450		Am. Sculptor
Reardon, Thomas R.		Celebrity	10			15	medical expert
Reason, Rex		Entertainment	10			20	
Reasoner, Harry		TV News	15			40	60 Minutes
Reckell, Peter		Entertainment	10			20	actor
Reckord, Maj. Gen. Milton A.	1879-1975	Military	30				World War II U.S. general
Rector, George		Business	20			35	World Famous Chef-Rector's NY
Rector, Henry M.	1816-1901	CSA Governor	75	180			CSA Gov. AR. War Dte. DS 875
Red Hot Chili Peppers (4)		Entertainment	75				Funk Rock Band 'Under the Bridge'
Reddy, Helen		Entertainment	6	20	20	20	
Redenbacker, Orville	1907-1995	Business	10	30	35	35	Popcorn King. Agricultural Expert Popcorn
Redfield, Billy		Entertainment	4	7		15	
Redfield, William C.	1889-1932	Cabinet	10	30	45	15	Sec'y Commerce 1913
Redford, Robert		Entertainment	55	195		205	Actor-Producer, Director, Writer. MANY SECRETARIALS
Redgrave, Lynn	1943-	Entertainment	8			25	SB 'This is Living' 35. AA Nominations
Redgrave, Michael, Sir	1908-1985	Entertainment	24		55	45	Tall, Distinguished Actor. Stage-Films from 30's
Redgrave, Vanessa	1937-	Entertainment	20	35		55	Br. Leading Lady. Numerous AA Nominations

NAME	DATE	CATEGORY	SIG	LS/DS	ALS	SP	COMMENTS
Redman, Don		Entertainment	20			45	Jazz Musician
Redman, Lt. Gen. Sir Harold	1899-1986	Military	25				World War II British general
Redmond, John E.	1856-1918	Politician	5	15	40	50	Irish Leader of Home Rule
Redon, Odilon	1840-1916	Artist	70		435		Flowers-Phantoms. Also Lithographer & Engraver
Redondo Jiménez, Encarnación		Political	10			15	Member European Parliament
Redouté, Pierre Joseph	1759-1840	Artist	200	625	1392		Belg-Fr. Painter, Lithographer. Known for Flowers
Reed, Alan	1907-1977	Entertainment	25			50	Character Actor, Original 'Fred Flintstone' Voice
Reed, Barry		Celebrity	10			15	motivational speaker
Reed, Carol, Sir	1906-1976	Entertainment	45	100		150	Influential Br. Film Director
Reed, David H.C.		Clergy	20	25	35	30	
Reed, Donna	1921-1986	Entertainment	87	150		196	AA Winner. 'It's A Wonderful Life'. Pin-Up SP 180
Reed, Erik		Entertainment	5			10	
Reed, Frances		Entertainment	10	12		20	
Reed, Jack		Senate	10			15	United States Senate (D - RI)
Reed, James Alexander		Senate/Congress	5	15		10	Senator MO 1910
Reed, James F.		Celebrity	1250				
Reed, Jerry		Entertainment	5			15	Singer-Actor
Reed, John	1887-1920	Author	188	525	1050	1250	Radical Am.Journalist & Revolutionist
Reed, Joseph	1741-1785	Revolutionary War	84	125	275		PA Statesman, Continental Cong.
Reed, Lou		Entertainment	20			50	
Reed, Oliver	1938-	Entertainment	15			65	Br. Actor. Br., Am. & Internat'l Films. Leading Man
Reed, Phillip	1908-	Entertainment	10	20	35	30	Handsome Leading Man & 2nd Lead. From Early 30's
Reed, Rex	1938-	Entertainment	8	6	15	15	Showbiz Interviewer and Gossip Columnist
Reed, Robert		Entertainment	40	70		68	Actor. 'The Brady Bunch'
Reed, Roland		Entertainment	15			35	Vintage Actor
Reed, Stanley	1884-1980	Supreme Court	48	120	175	125	TDS 1500 (Opinion) F.D.R. Court
Reed, Thomas Brackett	1839-1902	Congress	15	35	45		Speaker of the House. ME
Reed, Walter		Entertainment	10			25	Actor
Reed, Walter	1851-1902	Science	400	925	2040	1250	Am. Army Surgeon. Proved Mosquito=Yellow Fever
Reedy, George		Cabinet	4			8	
Rees, Maj. Gen. Thomas Wynford	1898-1959	Military	25				World War II British general
Rees, Roger		Entertainment	4			10	
Rees, Thomas		Business	10	25	45	25	
Reese, Della		Entertainment	15	45		40	Actress-Singer'Touched By An Angel'
Reese, Jim		Celebrity	10			15	motivational speaker
Reeve, Christopher		Entertainment	58		150	117	Actor. 'Super Man'
Reeve, Maj. Gen. John Talbot W.	1891-1983	Military	25				World War II British general
Reeves, Chuck		Celebrity	10			15	motivational speaker
Reeves, George	1914-1959	Entertainment	681	1100	1350	2387	Orig. TV 'Superman'. 'GWTW', ALS/ DS/cont 6000
Reeves, Jim	1923-1964	Entertainment	675			1500	Country Singer. Signed album 155
Reeves, Keanu	1965-	Entertainment	20	70		47	Actor
Reeves, Martha		Composer	5			20	Composer-Entertainer
Reeves, Ronna		Entertainment	5			10	Singer
Reeves, Steve	1926-	Entertainment	18			43	Actor, Mr. America, World & Universe
Reeves-Smith, Olive		Entertainment	5	7	15	15	

NAME	DATE	CATEGORY	SIG	LS/DS	ALS	SP	COMMENTS
Refice, Licinio	1855-1954	Composer-Clergy	20			55	Mostly Church Music. 2 Operas. AMusQS 85
Regan, Donald		Cabinet	10	15		30	Sec'y Treasury
Regan, Phil		Entertainment	10			35	Handsome Actor-Singer. Films From 1930's
Reger, Max	1873-1916	Composer	75	250	550		Ger. Composer
Reginald, Lionel		Entertainment	10			20	
Regnault de Saint-Jean	1761-1819	Fr. Revolution	35		105		Fr. Politician. Aided Napoleon. Exiled
Regula, Ralph R		Congress	10			15	Member U.S. Congress
Rehan, Ada		Entertainment	20			40	FineVintage Shakespearean Actress
Rehberg, Dennis R. R		Congress	10			15	Member U.S. Congress
Rehm, Dan		Aviation	12	25	45	30	ACE, WW II
Rehnquist, William H.		Supreme Court	65	160	182	138	Chief Justice. Confirmation Ballot S 3900
Reich, Wilhelm	1897-1857	Science	120	325	650		Austr. Psychoanalyst. Author.
Reichenau, Fld Mrshl. Walter von	1884-1942	Military	40			108	World War II German general
Reichers, Lou		Aviation	30	45	60	65	
Reid, Albert T.*		Cartoonist	20			112	Political Cartoonist. FDR Genre
Reid, Christian		Author	8			12	19th cen. 'The Land of the Sky'
Reid, Harry		Senate	10			15	United States Senate (D - NV)
Reid, Hugh Thompson	1811-1874	Civil War	40	70	110		Union general
Reid, Maj. Gen. Denys Whitehorn	1897-1970	Military	28				World War II British general
Reid, Mike		Celebrity	10			15	comedian
Reid, Samuel C.	1783-1861	Military	70	195			Naval Cmdr. War 1812. Designed US Flag
Reid, Tim		Entertainment	5	6	15	15	Actor
Reid, Wallace	1891-1923	Entertainment	195			650	Actor-Dir-Screenwriter. Died Drug Addict
Reid, Whitelaw	1837-1912	Journalist	30	45		50	Correspondent, Ambassador
Reifel, Benjamin		Senate/Congress	5			10	MOC SD
Reightler, Ken		Astronaut	5			25	
Reik, Theodor	1888-1969	Science	90	218	360		Austrian Psychoanalyst
Reilly, Charles Nelson		Entertainment	5			12	Actor
Reilly, James William	1828-1905	Civil War	35	65	90		Union general
Reinburg, J. Hunter		Aviation	15	35	50	40	ACE. WW II, Marine Ace
Reinecke, Gen. of Inf. Hermann	1888-1973	Military	25				World War II German general
Reinecke, Karl		Composer	55	145	225	250	Ger. Pianist, Conductor, Teacher
Reiner, Carl	1922-	Entertainment	10	28	30	25	Movie-TV Actor-Writer-Director
Reiner, Fritz		Entertainment	50	150		225	Hung. Conductor
Reiner, Ira		Celebrity	10			15	media/TV personality
Reiner, Rob		Entertainment	10	25		25	Like Father, Carl, Writer-Director-Actor
Reinert, Ernst Wilhelm		Aviation	20			50	Ger. ACE. RK
Reinhardt, Col-Gen. Georg-Hans	1887-1963	Military	25				World War II German general
Reinhardt, Maj. Gen. Emil F.	1888-1969	Military	30				World War II U.S. general
Reinhardt, Max	1873-1943	Entertainment	105	175	410	358	Austrian Innovative Theatre Dir.
Reinhardt, Uwe E.		Celebrity	10			15	medical expert
Reinhart, Maj. Gen. Stanley E.	1893-1975	Military	30				World War II U.S. general
Reinhold, Judge		Entertainment	5			33	Actor. 'Beverly Hills Cop' SP 35
Reinking, Ann	1949-	Entertainment	10	10	20	20	Dancer-Choreographer. Tony. 'All That Jazz'
Reisch, Walter	1900-1983	Entertainment	10			20	Screenwriter. AA (Shared) for 'Titanic' Script 1953

NAME	DATE	CATEGORY	SIG	LS/DS	ALS	SP	COMMENTS
Reischauer, Edwin O.		Celebrity	4	5	10	10	
Reiser, Paul		Entertainment	20			48	Actor-Comedian. 'Mad About You'. Emmy
Reiserer, Russell		Aviation	15		40		ACE WW II
Reitsch, Hanna	1912-1979	Aviation	65	165	270	185	Flew 1st Practical Helicopter.
Reitz, Francis W.		Head of State	50	135			South Africa
Reizen, Mark		Entertainment				750	Opera
Rejane, Gabrielle-Charlotte		Entertainment	35		80	85	Vintage Fr. Tragedienne
Remarque, Erich Maria	1898-1970	Author	98	240	375	75	'All Quiet on the Western Front' etc
Remer, Otto		Military	40			125	SS Gen. WW II. RK
Remick, Lee	1935-1991	Entertainment	30			60	Perky-Talented-Attractive Actress
Remington, Eliphalet	1793-1861	Business	350	440			E. Remington & Sons, Guns. Bond S 6500
Remington, Frederic	1861-1909	Artist	499	805	1653	1850	Sculptor, Writer, War Correspond.
Remington, Samuel		Business			1450		Gun Manufacturer. ALS on Lttrhd. 1450
Renaldo, Duncan	1904-1980	Entertainment	25		100	175	Actor, 4th 'Cisco Kid'
Renaud, Maj. Gen. Ernest James	1890-1967	Military	20				World War II Canadian general
Renaud, Maurice		Entertainment	35			175	Opera. Important Fr. Baritone
Renaud, Paul		Head of State	50			100	Premier France
Renault, Louis	1877-1944	Jurist	35	95	125		Fndr. Renault Freres. Autos.Nobel Peace Prize 1907
Renay, Liz		Entertainment	20				Actress-Model.Mafia Connection/Mickey Cohen
Rendulic, Colonel-General Lothar	1887-1971	Military	25				World War II German general
Renner, Karl, Dr.	1870-1950	Head of State	25	50	105	80	Fndr., Pres. Austrian Republic
Rennie, George	1791-1866	Science			80		Civil engineer
Rennie, John	1761-1821	Engineer			625		Br. Civ. Eng. Built Waterloo Bridge
Rennie, Maj. Gen. Tom Gordon	1900-1945	Military	28				World War II British general
Rennie, Michael	1909-1971	Entertainment	95			205	Actor, 'The Day the Earth Stood Still'
Reno, Jean		Entertainment	10			30	actor
Reno, Jesse Lee	1823-1862	Civil War	776				Union general, KIA 1862 South Mountain
Reno, Kelly		Entertainment	5			20	Young Actor Star of 'Black Stallion' DS 35
Reno, Marcus A.	1835-1889	Military	892	2507	11500		Battle of Little Big Horn., ALS cont. 16,500
Renoir, Jean	1894-1979	Entertainment	120	312			Fr. Inovative Film Maker-Son of Impressionist
Renoir, Pierre-Auguste	1841-1909	Artist	275	788	2082	3245	Repro Artwork S 3,000-5,000
Rent (Cast of)		Entertainment	75			120	Tony Award Winning Broadway Musical. 20-25 Sigs.
Renton, Maj Gen Jas. Malcom L.	1898-1972	Military	25				World War II British general
Renwick, Edward Sabine	1823-1912	Inventor	25	55	195		Inventor Breech-Loader & Modern Poultry Indust
Renzi, Rick R		Congress	10			15	Member U.S. Congress
REO Speedwagon		Entertainment	35			65	Rock (Signed by All)
Repplier, Agnes	1855-1950	Author	5	15	35	50	Am. Dean of Essayists. Biographer
Requesens, Luis de Zuniga	1528-1576	Military	750				Sp. Soldier. Succeeded Duke of Alba as Gov.
Resnick, Laura		Author	8			12	novelist
Resnick, Mike		Author	12	20	40	15	Hugo & Nebula SF award winner
Resnick, Regina		Entertainment	15			60	Opera
Resnik, Judith A.	1946-1986	Astronaut	108	300		323	Postal Cover 125-175, Challenger
Respighi, Ottorino	1879-1936	Composer	75	200	550		It. Opera, Orchestral, Choral. AMusQS 550
Ressler, Robert		Celebrity	10			15	political celebrity
Reston, John 'Scotty'		Author	15	20	35	25	Journalist, Synd. Columnist

NAME	DATE	CATEGORY	SIG	LS/DS	ALS	SP	COMMENTS
Rethberg, Elisabeth	1894-1976	Entertainment	40			140	Ger-Am Sopr.Opera. Admired by Toscannini-Strauss
Rethers, Harry F.		Military	40				Am. WW I Quartermaster Gen.
Rethy, Ester		Entertainment	10	15	35	30	Opera, Operetta
Rettig, Tommy	1941-1996	Entertainment	10			25	Juvenile Actor. 'Jeff' on 'Lassie'
Reuter, Edzard		Business	40	60	250	150	
Reuther, Walter P.	1907-1970	Labor	25	40	65	50	Pres. UAW-CIO. Gained Many Benefits for Union
Revelle, Hamilton		Entertainment	5	5	10	10	
Revell-Smith, Maj Gen Wm Revell	1894-1956	Military	225				World War II British general
Revels, Hiram Rhoades	1822-1901	Clergy-Civil War	300				1st Elected Black U.S. Senator, MS
Revere, Anne	1903-1990	Entertainment	25		45	60	Stage-Screen Char. Actress. AA 'National Velvet'
Revere, Joseph Warren	1812-1880	Civil War	50	92	130		Union general
Revere, Paul	1735-1818	Rev. War	2263	8133	18200		ALS 26000, DS cont 75000,DS w/ J Hancock 95,000
Revers, Gen. Georges-Marie-Jos.	1891-1974	Military	20				World War II French general
Rexroth, Kenneth	1905-1982	Author	10	35	65	20	Am. Columnist, Poet, Avant-Garde
Rey, Alejandro	1930-1987	Entertainment	25		45		Actor. Handsome Argentine-Born
Rey, Alvino		Entertainment	20			75	Big Band Leader
Reybold, Lt. Gen. Eugene	1884-1961	Military	30	35	55		World War II U.S. general
Reyes, Silvestre R		Congress	10			15	Member U.S. Congress
Reymann, Hellmuth		Aviation	30		75		
Reynders, General Izaak H.	1879-1966	Military	20				World War II Dutch general
Reynolds, Albert		Head of State	20			30	P.M. Ireland
Reynolds, Alexander W.	1816-1876	Civil War	116	175	486		CSA General. Captured-Exchanged. Sig/Rank 195
Reynolds, Burt	1936-	Entertainment	16	37		28	Actor 'Smokey& The Bandits', 'Boogie Nights'
Reynolds, Craig		Entertainment	10			25	Actor
Reynolds, Daniel H.	1832-1902	Civil War	92		385		CSA Gen. Sig/Rank 125-160
Reynolds, Debbie	1932-	Entertainment	10		50	25	Still Cute & Charming. Pin-Up SP 25
Reynolds, Donn		Country Music	10			20	Aussie 50's Yodeling Cowboy
Reynolds, Frank		Journalist	9			20	Broadcasting News Pioneer
Reynolds, Gene	1925-	Entertainment	5	6	15	20	Juvenile Actor. Mature Director
Reynolds, John Fulton	1820-1863	Civil War	515	1428			Union Gen. KIA Gettysburg. Sig/Rank 1375
Reynolds, Joseph Jones	1822-1899	Civil War	30	110	132		Union General, Indian Fighter. Sig/Rank 75
Reynolds, Joshua, Sir	1723-1792	Artist	350	1300	1690		Br. Portraitist, 1st Pres. Royal Academy
Reynolds, Maj. Gen. Roger C.	1895-1983	Military	25				World War II British general
Reynolds, Marjorie		Entertainment	20	30	40	45	Actress. 'Holiday Inn', 'GWTW' Collectible
Reynolds, R.J.		Business	225	750			Founder Tobacco Empire
Reynolds, Richard Samuel		Business	45	110	240	125	Reynolds Metal Co., Aluminum
Reynolds, Thomas M. R		Congress	10			15	Member U.S. Congress
Reynolds, William H.	1910-	Entertainment	15			25	Film Editor. AA 'The Sting'. Three AA Nominations
Reynolds, William		Entertainment	5			15	Actor. TV 'FBI'
Rezner, Trent		Entertainment	10			45	Music. Lead Singer 'Nine Inch Nails'
Rhames, Ving		Entertainment	10			30	actor
Rhea, Caroline		Entertainment	10			25	actress
Rhee, Syngman	1875-1965	Head of State	125	180	280	250	1st Pres. So. Korea
Rhett, Alicia		Entertainment	300				SPN/A. 'GWTW' Collectible
Rhett, Robert Barnwell	1800-1876	Civil War	143	285	440		ALS/Content 2,500. The Father of Secession

NAME	DATE	CATEGORY	SIG	LS/DS	ALS	SP	COMMENTS
Rhett, Robert G., Mrs.		Celebrity	3		10		Blanche Rhett
Rhodes, Billie	1894-1988	Entertainment	15			35	Am. Star of Al Christie Comedies from 1911
Rhodes, Cecil John	1853-1902	Head of State	135	230	438	1175	S. Afr. Fndr. Rhodesia. Rhodes Scholarship Fund
Rhodes, Erik	1906-1990	Entertainment	20			45	Am. Comic Actor From Musical Comedy Stage. Films
Rhodes, Gary		Celebrity	10			15	TV Chef
Rhodes, John J.		Senate/Congress	5	15		10	MOC AZ 1953-83
Rhodes, Zandra		Celebrity	10			15	Designer
Rhys-Davies, John		Entertainment	15			38	Br. Actor. 'Indiana Jones' Films
Rhys-Jones, Griff		Celebrity	10			15	comedian
Ribbentrop, Joachim von	1893-1946	Military	165	388	645	325	Hitler Foreign Affairs Advisor. Convicted & Hung
Ribbentrop, Rudolf von		Military	65	95	150		
Ribeiro E Castro, José		Political	10			15	Member European Parliament
Ribicoff, Abraham	1910-	Cabinet	10	15	35	20	Gov., Senator CT. Sec'y HEW
Ricard, Brig. Gen. Emile-Pierre-E.	1888- ?	Military	20				World War II French general
Ricardo, David	1772-1823	Economist	425				Founder Classical School of Political Economy
Ricci, Christina		Entertainment	20			48	Actress.
Ricciarelli, Katia		Entertainment	5			25	Opera
Rice, Alexander H.	1818-1895	Congress-Gov.	10	15	20		Sen.& Gov. MA
Rice, Alice C.	1870-1942	Author	70		220		Children's Books. 'Mrs. Wiggs of Cabbage Patch'
Rice, Americus Vespucius	1835-1904	Civil War	40	75	110		Union general
Rice, Anne		Author	25			50	Novelist
Rice, Anneka		Celebrity	10			15	television presenter
Rice, Dan (Dan'l McLaren)	1823-1900	Business	38	100	341		Circus Clown & Owner
Rice, Don III		Celebrity	10			15	motivational speaker
Rice, Donna		Model	15			20	
Rice, Elliott Warren	1835-1887	Civil War	45		95		Union general
Rice, Elmer	1882-1967	Author	80	120		130	Pulitzer Prize. Playwright
Rice, Florence	1907-1974	Entertainment	5	10		15	Actress. Pleasing Leading Lady of Late 30's
Rice, Gillian, Dr.		Celebrity	10			15	health and fitness expert
Rice, Grantland	1881-1954	Journalist	25			75	Sportswriter-Sportscaster.One Reel Sports Films
Rice, Henry M.		Senate/Congress	5		15		Senator MN 1858-63
Rice, James Clay	1829-1864	Civil War	110	379	488		Union general
Rice, Merton S.		Clergy	20	30	40		
Rice, Samuel Allen	1828-1864	Civil War	110		468		Union general
Rice, Tim		Composer	10	30	65	30	Composer. Disney Films
Rice-Davies, Mandy		Celebrity	5	10	25	20	Involved In Br. Scandal
Rich, Adam		Entertainment	10			20	actor
Rich, Buddy	1917-1987	Entertainment	38			132	Big Band Leader-Drummer
Rich, Charlie	1932-1995	Entertainment	15			30	Rock/Rockabilly Singer 50'-60's. Country Superstar
Rich, Irene	1891-1988	Entertainment	25	38	55	150	Silent Film Star. Few Talkies. Radio Star
Rich, Maj. Gen. Henry Hampden	1891-1974	Military	25				World War II British general
Richard II (Anjou-Plantagenet)	1367-1400	Royalty					Writ of Privy Seal in Name of Richard II 2000
Richards, Adriana		Entertainment	10			30	Juvenile Actress in 'Jurassic Park'
Richards, Ann		Governor	7			20	Attractive, Outspoken, Admired Governor TX
Richards, Cliff		Entertainment	15			40	Rock

NAME	DATE	CATEGORY	SIG	LS/DS	ALS	SP	COMMENTS
Richards, Denise		Entertainment	10			48	
Richards, Dickinson W.	1895-1973	Science	25	35	70	50	Nobel Medicine 1956. Perfected Heart Cath.
Richards, Jeff	1922-1989	Entertainment	5			20	Was Young MGM Star
Richards, Keith		Entertainment	25			110	Rock. 'Rolling Stones' Guitarist
Richards, Kelly		Entertainment				60	Singer
Richards, Lloyd	1923-	Entertainment	10			20	Afr-Am Stage Director
Richards, Maj. Gen. Geo. Warren	1898-1978	Military	25				World War II British general
Richards, Maj. Gen. Wm. Watson	1892-1961	Military	25				World War II British general
Richards, Michael		Entertainment	20			60	'Kramer'on Seinfeld
Richards, Richard N.		Astronaut	10			35	
Richards, William		Senate/Congress	15		50		Rep. NY 1871
Richardson, Dorothy	1872-1857	Author	32	115	187		Br. Introduced Stream of Consciousness Technique
Richardson, Elliot		Cabinet	7	25	45	20	Att'y Gen. Watergate Period
Richardson, Friend W.		Governor	5		15		Gov. CA 1923-27
Richardson, Gen. Robert C. Jr.	1882-1954	Military	30				World War II U.S. general
Richardson, Ian	1934-	Entertainment	5	6		15	
Richardson, Israel Bush	1815-1862	Civil War	125	292			Union general, KIA Antietam
Richardson, Joely		Entertainment	10			20	actress
Richardson, John P.		Governor	15	25	86		Governor SC 1840
Richardson, John, Sir	1787-1865	Science-Explorer	20	60	118		Surgeon-Naturalist. Franklin Expedition
Richardson, Maj. Gen. David T.	1886-1957	Military	25				World War II British general
Richardson, Maj. Gen. Roland	1896-1973	Military	25				World War II British general
Richardson, Maj. Gen. Thos. Wm.	1895-1968	Military	25				World War II British general
Richardson, Miranda	1958-	Entertainment	22			50	Br. Actress. 'Enchanted April', 'The Crying Game'
Richardson, Natasha		Entertainment	15			60	Br. Actress-Daughter of Vanessa Redgrave
Richardson, Patricia		Entertainment	10			35	'Tool Time' Hostess
Richardson, Ralph, Sir	1902-1983	Entertainment	20	25	50	45	Distinguished Br. Stage-Film Actor. AA Nominations
Richardson, Robert Vinkler	1820-1870	Civil War	260	525			CSA General
Richardson, Tony	1828-1891	Entertainment	20			30	Br. Stage & Film Director. AA 'Tom Jones'. Aids
Richardson, William A.	1821-1896	Cabinet	18	48	95		Sec'y Treas.1873
Richardson, William Alex.	1811-1875	Congress	10		20		Sen. IL
Richelieu, Armand E. du	1766-1822	Head of State	105	240	350		French Statesman & Cardinal
Richelieu, Armand-Jean, Cardinal	1585-1642	Head of State	275	1177	2150		Statesman & Cardinal. Special DS 3,450
Richens, Gabrielle		Celebrity	10			15	celebrity model
Richey, Helen		Aviation	25	50		55	
Richey, Lawrence		Cabinet	4	10			
Richie, Lionel		Composer	10	52		38	Composer-Singer-Arranger
Richie, Shane		Celebrity	10			15	comedian
Richman, Charles		Entertainment	10	15	30	25	
Richman, Harry	1895-1972	Entertainment-Avia.	15	25	35	35	And Flew 'Lady Peace' 1st R/T Atlantic Crosssing
Richter, Burton, Dr.		Science	20	45	70	35	Nobel Physics 1976
Richter, Charles, Dr.	1900-1985	Science	25	175		65	Devised Richter Scale. Earthquake Measure
Richter, Hans (Janos)	1843-1916	Conductor	150		583		Ger. Conductor. AMusQS 350
Richter, Jason James		Entertainment	10			20	actor
Richters, Christine		Playboy Ctrfold	5			15	Pin-Up SP 25

NAME	DATE	CATEGORY	SIG	LS/DS	ALS	SP	COMMENTS
Richthofen, Manfred von	1892-1918	Aviation	1750	3200	5000	8000	ACE, WW I, 'The Red Baron'
Rickard, George L. Tex		Business	350	525		675	Boxing Promoter & Entreprenuer. DS 2,000
Rickards, Maj. Gen. Gerald Arthur	1886-1972	Military	25				World War II British general
Rickenbacker, Edw V.	1890-1973	Aviation	82	181	225	197	ACE, WW I, Auto Race, Exec. TLS/Cont. 1500
Ricketts, Charles	1866-1931	Artist	40	60	136		artist, designer
Ricketts, James Brewerton	1817-1887	Civil War	45	70	110		Union general
Ricketts, Maj. Gen. Abby Henry G.	1905-1993	Military	25				World War II British general
Rickles, Don	1926-	Entertainment	5	6	15	30	Comedian. Rare Authentic Sigs
Rickman, Alan		Entertainment	10			30	Actor
Rickover, Hyman G.	1900-1986	Military	75	191	442	350	Rus-Born Am. Admiral. Father of Atomic Sub.
Riddell, Maj. Gen. Ralph A.	1900-1979	Military	25				World War II British general
Riddle, George		Country Music	10			28	
Riddle, Georgie		Country Western	10			35	50's Western Recording Artist
Ride, Sally K.		Astronaut	15	36	63	52	1st US Woman in Space
Riders in the Sky (3)		Entertainment	5			20	
Ridgway, Matthew B.	1895-1993	Military	44	102	146	87	Supr. Allied Cdr. WW II & KW, TLs/ALS cont500-1500
Ridley, Maj. Gen. Clarence S.	1883-1969	Military	30				World War II U.S. general
Ridruejo, Mónica		Political	10			15	Member European Parliament
Riefenstahl, Leni	1902-	Celebrity	26	42	80	69	German-actress Hitler's Favorite
Rieger, Vince		Aviation	12	25	40	30	ACE, WW II, Navy Ace
Riegger, Wallingford	1885-1961	Composer	20	65	125	80	Am. Orchestral, Choral, 12 Tone
Ries, Frédérique		Political	10			15	Member European Parliament
Rifkin, Adam		Celebrity	10			15	film industry
Rigal, Delia		Entertainment	15			45	Opera
Rigg, Diana	1938-	Entertainment	20	35	45	95	Br. Leading Lady. Prominence in 'The Avengers'
Riggs, Clinton E.		Inventor	24			40	Created Highway Yield Sign
Riggs, Tommy		Entertainment	5	8	15	15	Ventriloquist? (And Betty Lou)
Righteous Brothers		Entertainment	45			118	Bill Medley & Bobby Hatfield
Riis, Jacob A.	1849-1914	Author-Reformer	18	50	85		Dan.-Am. Journalist. ALS/Cont. 350
Riis-Jorgensen, Karin		Political	10			15	Member European Parliament
Rilay, Maj. Gen. Sir Henry Guy	1884-1964	Military	25				World War II British general
Riley, James Whitcomb	1849-1916	Author	95	175	310	300	The Hoosier Poet. 'Little Orphant Annie' etc.
Riley, Jeannie C.	1945-	Country Music	5			15	Singer. Internat'l Star with 'Harper Valley PTA'
Riley, Larry		Entertainment	5			10	
Riley, Lisa		Entertainment	10			20	Actress
Riley, Mark		Music	10			15	DJ
Riley, Richard		Celebrity	10			15	political celebrity
Rilke, Rainer Maria	1875-1926	Author	138	345	1529		Czech. Lyric Poet-Translator. Highly Influential
Rimes, Leann		Entertainment	15	60		38	Singer. Country-Pop
Rinehart, Mary Roberts	1876-1958	Author	20	45	75	75	Am. Novelist, Playwright. Mysteries-Romances
Rinfret, Pierre		Celebrity	10			15	financial expert
Ring, Blanche		Entertainment	15			40	Vintage Silent Star
Ringel, Julius		Military	30			76	German general WWII
Ringgold, George H.	1814-1864	Civil War	20	40	55		Union Paymaster War Dte DS 80
Ringling, Albert C.	1852-1916	Business-Circus	132	425			Ringling Bros.& Barnum & Bailey

NAME	DATE	CATEGORY	SIG	LS/DS	ALS	SP	COMMENTS
Ringling, Charles	1863-1926	Business-Circus	120	453			Ringling Bros.& Barnum & Bailey
Ringling, Henry		Business-Circus	112	337		125	Special DS 1,250
Ringling, John	1866-1936	Business-Circus	145	565	620	700	Ringling Bros(Owner-Performer)& Barnum & Bailey
Ringling, Otto	1858-1911	Business-Circus	230	650			Ringling Bros.& Barnum & Bailey
Ringling, William		Business-Circus	70	130		150	2nd Generation Owner
Ringo, John		Outlaw	2000	6500			Early West. Cowboy Gunslinger
Ringwald, Molly		Entertainment	10	20	40	40	Actress
Rinna, Lisa		Entertainment	6			35	Actress
Rio Rita		Entertainment	15			40	And Her All-Girl NBC Orchestra. 1930's
Riorden, Shane		Author	8			12	reading for children
Ripley, Eleazar W.	1782-1839	Military	68		250		General War 1812
Ripley, George	1802-1880	Social Reformer	140	350	780		Critic, Editor, Unitarian Clergy
Ripley, J.R.		Author	8			12	mystery novelists
Ripley, James Wolfe	1794-1870	Civil War	35	65	95		Union General
Ripley, Robert*	1893-1949	Cartoonist	112	105	225	298	'Believe It Or Not'
Ripley, Roswell S. (WD)	1823-1887	Civil War	290	450	1025		CSA Gen.
Ripley, Roswell S.	1823-1887	Civil War	122	220	425		CSA Gen. Nephew of Union Gen.
Ripoll y Martínez de Bedoya, Car.		Political	10			15	Member European Parliament
Rippon, Angela		Celebrity	10			15	news reader
Risner, James R.		Military	10	25	35	20	
Ritchard, Cyril	1896-1977	Entertainment	20			60	Br. Dancer & Comedian.
Ritchie, Adele		Entertainment	20		50	45	Vintage Musical Theater Star
Ritchie, Albert C.		Governor	10		35		Gov. MD
Ritchie, General Sir Neil Methuen	1897-1985	Military	225				World War II British general
Ritchie, Neil, Sir		Military	15	35	60	30	General
Ritchie, Steve		Aviation	15	35	45	40	ACE, Nam, Only AF Ace
Ritt, Martin	1919-1990	Entertainment	30			65	Film-Stage-TV Director. Taught at Actor's Studio
Rittenberg, Sidney		Celebrity	10			15	political celebrity
Rittenhouse, David	1732-1796	Science	850	1150	4500		Am Astronomer, 1st US Telescope
Ritter, John	1948-	Entertainment	8	10	15	30	Light Romantic-Comedy Roles. Son of Tex Ritter
Ritter, Tex	1907-1974	Country Music	100			232	Major Singing Cowboy Star,signed album 92
Ritter, Thelma	1905-1969	Entertainment	45			150	Am Character Actress & Comedienne.
Ritterscheim, Karl		Entertainment	5			25	Opera
Ritz Brothers, The (3)		Entertainment	80			106	Jimmy, Al, Harry. Zany Nightclub Act. A Few Films
Ritz, Jimmy	1903-1985	Entertainment	15			40	The Middle Ritz Brother
Rivera, Chita		Entertainment	10			20	actress
Rivera, Diego	1886-1957	Artist	272	730	970	1375	Mex. Political-Social Muralist, signed repro 425-1265
Rivera, Geraldo		Entertainment	20	42		30	TV Host
Rivers, Joan	1933-	Entertainment	5	8	25	15	Comedienne. Cabaret, Standup, TV Hostess
Rivers, Larry	1923-2002	Artist	40	75	250		Forerunner Pop Art Movement
Rives, Amelie	1863-1945	Author	12	60	85		
Rivington, James	1724-1802	Revolutionary War	100	225			Journalist-Publisher-Spy
Rivron, Roland		Celebrity	10			15	comedian
Rizzo, Frank L.		Political	10	20		25	Mayor Phila. Fmr. Chief of Police
Rnbig, Paul		Political	10			15	Member European Parliament

NAME	DATE	CATEGORY	SIG	LS/DS	ALS	SP	COMMENTS
Rnhle, Heide		Political	10			15	Member European Parliament
Roach, Hal, Jr.		Entertainment	5			15	
Roach, Hal, Sr.	1892-1992	Entertainment	80	175		200	AA Film Pioneer. Our Gang Comedy. Silent-Sound
Ro'Al, Zhang	1713-1746	Artist		700			Chinese Painter
Roane, John Selden	1817-1867	Civil War	110				Confederate general
Roarke, Hayden		Entertainment	52			65	Actor. 'Jeannie' 'Dr. Bellows'
Roarke, John		Entertainment	10			20	actor
Robards, Jason, Jr.	1920-	Entertainment	15	22		30	Am. Stage-Film Actor. AA 'Julia'
Robb, Maj. Gen. W.		Military	25				World War II British general
Robb, Robert G.		Civil War		178			CSA Navy Commander
Robbins, Frederick C., Dr.		Science	20	30	45	25	Nobel Medicine 1954
Robbins, Gale	1922-1980	Entertainment	15	20	35	30	Singer-Leading Lady
Robbins, Harold	1916-	Author	20	40	75	60	Am. Novelist. The Carpetbaggers
Robbins, Jay T.		Aviation	10	25	40	35	ACE, WW II
Robbins, Jerome	1918-	Entertainment	40	75	110	79	Ballet Dancer, Choreographer. AA 'The King & I'
Robbins, John	1808-1880	Congress	12		25		Repr. PA, Steel Mfg.
Robbins, Marty	1925-	Country Music	25			60	Country & Pop Singer-Songwriter
Robbins, Reg. L.		Aviation	25			60	Pioneer Aviator
Robbins, Tim	1958-	Entertainment	23			46	Actor-Singer-Songwriter-Screenwriter-Director
Robert Wexler		Senate	10			15	Member U.S. Congress
Roberti, Margherita		Entertainment	15			30	Am. Soprano
Roberts, Barbara		Governor	7			20	Governor OR
Roberts, Benjamin Stone	1810-1875	Civil War	35	65	90		Union general
Roberts, Beverly		Actor	10			35	
Roberts, Cokie		Journalist	10			20	TV-Radio Journalist
Roberts, David	1896-1964	Artist	40	90	162		Scottish Painter
Roberts, Doris		Entertainment	10	15	15	37	Character-Comedienne. 'Everybody Loves Raymond'
Roberts, Eric	1956-	Entertainment	10			25	Leading Man, 70's. AA Nom. 'Runaway Train'
Roberts, Frederick Sleigh	1832-1914	Military	40	65	125	100	1st Earl. Field Marshal, Kandahar
Roberts, Gen. Sir Ouvry Lindfield	1898-1986	Military	25				World War II British general
Roberts, Jack		Country Music	10			20	
Roberts, Jonathan	1771-1854	Senate	30		75		Introduced Important Legislation
Roberts, Julia	1967-	Entertainment	40	60		85	Actress, AA Winner
Roberts, Kenneth	1885-1957	Author	25	80	150		Am. Historical Novels. 'Northwest Passage' etc
Roberts, Lee S.		Composer	30	65	150		AMusQS 285
Roberts, Maj Gen Frank Crowther	1891-1982	Military	25				World War II British general
Roberts, Maj. Gen. Geo. Philip B.	1906-1997	Military	25				World War II British general
Roberts, Maj. Gen. John Hamilton	1891-1962	Military	20				World War II Canadian general
Roberts, Oral		Clergy	18	35	50	45	Am. Evangelist. Oral Roberts Univ. 5x7 SP 25
Roberts, Oran M.		Governor	15		30		Gov. TX 1879-83
Roberts, Owen J.	1875-1955	Supreme Court	50	150	220	100	Justice 1930-45. Dean U. of Penn. Law School
Roberts, Pat		Author	5			10	Cookbook author, editor
Roberts, Pat		Senate	10			15	United States Senate (R - KS)
Roberts, Pernell	1930-	Entertainment	40	75		80	Actor. Original 'Bonanza' Brother. 'Trapper John'
Roberts, Ralph		Author	10	20	40	15	1st U.S. book on computer viruses, 100 other books

NAME	DATE	CATEGORY	SIG	LS/DS	ALS	SP	COMMENTS
Roberts, Robin		Journalist	5			10	ESPN News
Roberts, Roy		Entertainment	15			35	
Roberts, Tanya		Entertainment	10			25	Actress. Pin-Up SP 35
Roberts, Tony	1939-	Entertainment	5	6	15	20	Actor
Roberts, William Paul	1841-1910	Civil War	85	180	320		CSA Gen. Youngest In CSA Service. Sig/Rank 150
Roberts, Xavier		Business	15	20	35	25	Cabbage patch dolls
Robertson, Alice Mary		Senate/Congress	5		20	25	MOC OK, Self-Taught Creek Indian
Robertson, Beverly H.	1827-1910	Civil War	113	158	320		CSA General. Sig/Rank 185
Robertson, Cliff	1925-	Entertainment	20	25		35	Am. Leading Man. Stage-Films. AA 'Charley'
Robertson, Dale	1923-	Entertainment	10			35	Am. Actor. Western Star
Robertson, Felix H.	1839-1928	Civil War	85		262		CSA General Sig/Rank 150
Robertson, James	1720-1788	Revolutionary War			975		Br. Gen. Fought in Rev. War
Robertson, Jerome Bonaparte	1815-1891	Civil War	125	368			Confederate general
Robertson, Lt. Gen. Horace C.H.	1894-1960	Military	20				World War II Australian general
Robertson, Maj. Gen. Cecil Bruce	1897-1977	Military	25				World War II British general
Robertson, Maj. Gen. Walter M.	1888-1954	Military	30				World War II U.S. general
Robertson, Morgan		Author	15		60		Sea Stories
Robertson, Pat, Rev.		Clergy	20	25	50	30	Rt. Wing Evangelical, Presidential Hopeful
Robertson, Willard	1886-1948	Entertainment	15			25	Am. Character Actor. Lawyers & Wardens
Robeson, George M.	1834-1896	Cabinet	15	62	92		Sec'y Navy 1869-1877
Robeson, Paul	1898-1976	Entertainment	101	163	280	528	Am. Singer, Actor, Athlete, Activist
Robespierre, Maximilien	1758-1794	Fr. Revolution	1200	2650	12500		Revolutionist Leader. 'Reign of Terror'. DS 4,275
Robilio, Victor		Author	8			12	fine wines, wineries
Robin, Mado		Entertainment	40			225	Opera. Coloratura. Young, Tragic Death
Robinson, Anne		Celebrity	10			15	television presenter
Robinson, Bill 'Bojangles'	1878-1949	Entertainment	72	235	450	442	Afro-American Tap-Dancer, Entertainer. 30's Films
Robinson, C. Roosevelt		Celebrity	5	15	20	15	
Robinson, Dwight P.		Business	5	15	25	15	
Robinson, Edward A.	1869-1935	Author	55	125	215		Am. Poet, 3 Pulitzers
Robinson, Edward G.	1893-1973	Entertainment	55	100	150	153	Actor Famous for Gangster Roles & Art Collection
Robinson, Edward	1794-1863	Archaeologist		185	395		Biblical Scholar. Explored Palestine-Syria.
Robinson, Gary Edward		Business	5	7	10	20	World renowned investor
Robinson, George D.	1834-1896	Governor	10			35	Repr. & Gov. MA
Robinson, James Sidney	1827-1892	Civil War	40	75	110		Union general
Robinson, John C.	1817-1897	Civil War	52	185	220		Union Gen., MOH Gettysburg. Sig/Rank 100
Robinson, John	1761-1828	Revolutionary War	60	175	340		Soldier, Merchant
Robinson, Joseph T.	1872-1937	Congress	20		25		Sen. Arkansas
Robinson, Lucius		Governor	10	20	40		Governor NY 1876
Robinson, Maj. Gen. Alfred Eryk	1894-1978	Military	25				World War II British general
Robinson, Maj. Gen. Guy St. Geo.	1887-1973	Military	25				World War II British general
Robinson, Patrick		Entertainment	10			20	Actor
Robinson, Rachel		Celebrity	10			15	motivational speaker
Robinson, Smokey		Entertainment	25			48	Motown artist
Robinson, Tony		Entertainment	10			20	Actor
Robson, Flora, Dame	1902-1984	Entertainment	28	25	40	70	Distinguished Br. Stage & Film Actress. 30s-80s

NAME	DATE	CATEGORY	SIG	LS/DS	ALS	SP	COMMENTS
Robson, Linda		Entertainment	10			20	Actress
Robson, May	1858-1942	Entertainment	40			75	Australian-Am. Stage Actress. Films 1915-1942
Robson, Stuart		Entertainment	20	25	45	45	Vintage Actor
Rocard, Michel		Political	10			15	Member European Parliament
Rochambeau, Count de	1725-1807	Revolutionary War	350	750	826		Fr. Gen. in Am. Revolution, DS/cont 1725
Rochan, Debbie		Entertainment	4			25	Actress. Pin-Up Col.45
Roche, James M.	1906-	Business	10	15	30	20	Pres. Ford Motor Co.,CEO Gen. Motors
Rochefort, Henri, Marquis de	1830-1913	Author	18	30	50		Fr. Journalist.Anti Napoleon III
Rochester, Laurence Hyde		Politics		180			
Rochford, Leonard		Aviation	20	40			Br. Ace WW I
Rock, Blossom (Blake, Marie)	1896-1978	Entertainment	175			225	Sister-Jeanette MacDonald. 'Addams Family''Granny'
Rock, Chris		Entertainment				40	Comedian
Rock, John	1890-	Science	25	80			Developed 1st Birth Control Pill
Rockefeller, Abby A.		Business	15	30	52	25	Socialite-Wife of John D., Jr.
Rockefeller, David		Business	15	38	55	25	Banker
Rockefeller, Happy		Business	5	15	25	10	Wife of Nelson Rockefeller
Rockefeller, John D.	1839-1937	Business	369	1350	1983	1417	Standard Oil. Philanthropist. DS Oil Contract 9450
Rockefeller, John D., Jr.	1874-1960	Business	35	80	150	125	Rockefeller Ctr. Philanthropist. Son of John D.
Rockefeller, John		Senate	10			15	United States Senate (D - WV)
Rockefeller, Laurance		Business	5	15	25	10	Philanthropist
Rockefeller, Nelson A.	1908-1979	Vice President	28	56	75	58	Governor NY. Ford's VP. TLS as VP 325
Rockefeller, Winthrop		Governor	10	20		15	Governor AR
Rockerfeller, John (Jay) D., IV		Governor	5	15		10	Governor WV. Confidential Political ALS 450
Rockwell, George Lincoln		Activist	45	126	155	92	American Nazi Party
Rockwell, Norman*	1894-1978	Artist	108	207	535	394	Am. Illustrator-Artist. FDC S 125. Print S 295+
Rockwell, Robert		Entertainment	5	10		20	Actor. Leads & Supporting Actor. 'Our Miss Brooks'
Rocos, Cleo		Celebrity	10			15	television presenter
Rod, Didier		Political	10			15	Member European Parliament
Roddenberry, Gene	1931-1991	Entertainment	119	235		212	Creator of 'Star Trek'
Roddey, Philip D. (WD)	1826-1897	Civil War	200	878	2498		CSA Gen.
Roddey, Philip D.	1826-1897	Civil War	105	375	415		CSA Gen.
Rodenburg, Carl	1894-1992	Military	40			75	Ger. Gen. Stalingrad. WW II.
Roderick, Milton David		Business	5			10	CEO U.S. Steel
Rodes, Robert Emmett (WD)		Civil War	750		8425		CSA Gen. RARE
Rodes, Robert Emmett	1829-1864	Civil War	425		1675		CSA General KIA RARE
Rodgers, Anton		Entertainment	10			20	Actor
Rodgers, Geo. Washington	1822-1863	Civil War	75	130	260		Union Navy. KIA Fort Wagner
Rodgers, Jimmie	1897-1933	Entertainment	225			500	Legendary Country Music Singer-Composer
Rodgers, John		Aviation	65	125	240	135	
Rodgers, John	1771-1838	Military	50	75	100		Distinguished US Naval Officer
Rodgers, John	1812-1882	Civil War	60	160	275		U.S. Naval Commodore,-Explorer
Rodgers, Richard & Hammerstein		Composers	500				Oscar Hammerstein III
Rodgers, Richard & Hart, Lorenz		Composers	675	1350			Rodgers AND HART Very Rare. Hart Died 1943
Rodgers, Richard	1902-1979	Composer	88	345		164	Pulitzer. AMusQS 460. FDC S 110
Rodham, Brig. Cuthbert Harold B.	1900-1973	Military	25				World War II British general

NAME	DATE	CATEGORY	SIG	LS/DS	ALS	SP	COMMENTS
Rodin, Auguste	1840-1917	Artist	222	342	658	1056	Fr. SP of Sculpture 1250-1700
Rodll, Lt. Gen. Willem	1873-1958	Military	20				World War II Dutch general
Rodman, Hugh		Military	55				Adm. USN, Am. WW I
Rodman, Isaac Peace	1822-1862	Civil War	110				Union general
Rodman, Judy		Entertainment	5	6	15	15	
Rodney, Caesar	1728-1784	Rev. War-Cabinet	386	985	1688		Signer Decl. of Indepen.
Rodr-guez Ramos, Marfa		Political	10			15	Member European Parliament
Rodriguez, Ciro D. R		Congress	10			15	Member U.S. Congress
Rodriquez, Freddy		Entertainment				40	Fererico Diaz, Six Feet Under
Rodwell, Brig. Gen. James S.	1896-1962	Military	30				World War II U.S. general
Rodzinski, Artur	1892-1958	Conductor	30	75		75	Pol.-Am. Conductor. 4x5 SP 50
Roe, Edward Payson	1838-1888	Author	15	25	35		Novelist, Clergy
Roe, Tommy		Entertainment	25	40		32	Singer
Roebling, John A.	1806-1869	Engineer	85	175	325		Designed the Brooklyn Bridge
Roebling, Washington A.	1837-1926	Engineer	92	225	360		Built the Brooklyn Bridge
Roebuck, Alva Curtis		Business	175	215		375	Co-Fndr. Sears & Roebuck. Stock Cert. S 1900
Roederer, Pierre C., Count		Fr. Revolution	20	50	95		
Roeg, Nicolas		Celebrity	10			15	film industry
Roell, Werner		Aviation	5			20	Ger. RK Winning Stuka Pilot
Roentgen, Wilhelm	1845-1923	Science	604	1300	3158		1st Nobel in Physics. Discovered X Rays
Roethke, Theodore		Author	35	60	125	75	Am. Poet. Pulitzer
Roffman, Marvin		Celebrity	10			15	financial expert
Rogallo, Francis M.		Inventor	27		45		Invented Hang Glider.
Rogatchewsky, Joseph		Entertainment	20			85	Ukranian. Lyric/Dramatic Tenor
Roger, Gustav		Entertainment	40		160		Opera. Creator of Important Tenor Roles
Rogers, Charles 'Buddy'	1904-	Entertainment	15	20	35	23	Actor. Light Leads & Support. 20's-30's
Rogers, Andrew Jackson	1828-1900	Congress	10				MOC NJ, Teacher, Lawyer
Rogers, Bernard W.		Military	10	25	50	40	
Rogers, Carroll P.		Business	8	15	35	15	
Rogers, Fred		Entertainment	8	15		32	'Mr. Rogers'
Rogers, Ginger	1911-1995	Entertainment	40	135		125	Actress, Dancer. AA 'Kitty Foyle'. SP/Astaire 675
Rogers, Harold R		Congress	10			15	Member U.S. Congress
Rogers, Jean	1916-1991	Entertainment	25			58	40's Adventure Serial Queen. 'B' Movie Leads
Rogers, John	1829-1904	Artist	150	250	305		Sculptor of the Rogers Groups
Rogers, Joseph W.		Aviation	15	30	60	35	
Rogers, Kenny		Entertainment	20	40		40	Singer-Actor-Producer
Rogers, Marianne and Kenny		Country Music	10			35	
Rogers, Mike R		Congress	10			15	Member U.S. Congress
Rogers, Mimi	1956-	Entertainment	15			32	Actress. Leading Lady Film & TV
Rogers, Randolph	1825-1892	Artist	18		30		Sculptor
Rogers, Richard		Astronaut	6			20	
Rogers, Robert	1731-1795	Revolutionary War	335	1195	3300		Frontier Soldier. 'Rogers Rangers'. Fled to Eng.
Rogers, Roy	1912-1998	Entertainment	45	160		160	'King of the Cowboys' SP/Roy & Dale 135-195
Rogers, Samuel	1763-1855	Author	15	30	59		Br. Poet. Patron Of The Arts
Rogers, T.S.		Military	75				Am. WW I Rear Adm. U.S.N., U.S.S. Utah

NAME	DATE	CATEGORY	SIG	LS/DS	ALS	SP	COMMENTS
Rogers, Wayne		Entertainment	15			30	Actor. 'Mash'
Rogers, Will Jr.		Senate/Congress	10			25	Congressman CA, Actor
Rogers, Will	1879-1935	Entertainment	244	392	1030	734	America's Favorite Humorist. Plane Crash w/Wiley Post
Rogers, William F.	1820-1899	Civil War	22	40	55		Union General
Rogers, William Findlay		Senate/Congress	5		10		MOC NY, Soldier CW
Rogers, William P.		Cabinet	12	20	35	25	Sec'y State
Roget, Peter M., Dr.	1779-1869	Author	75	85	220		Br. Physician & Savant. Roget's Thesaurus
Rohan, Louis Prince de	1734-1803	Clergy		225			Cardinal and Grand Aumonier of France
Rohm, Ernst	d. 1934	Military	250	750	1265		Nazi commander of SA (storm troopers)
Rohmer, Eric	1920-	Entertainment	40	218			Fr. Director. Literate, Articulate Searching .60's
Rohmer, Sax (A.S.Ward)	1886-1959	Author	75	120	175	182	Br. Mystery Novels. 'Fu Manchu'
Rohrabacher, Dana R		Congress	10			15	Member U.S. Congress
Rohrer, Henreich	1933-	Science	20		45		Nobel Physics 1981
Röhricht, Gen. of Infantry Edgar	1892-1967	Military	25				World War II German general
Rojo, Gustavo		Entertainment	10			30	On Screen from 1948
Roker, Al		Entertainment	10	15		20	TV Weatherman
Rokossovsky, Konstantin K.		Military	125	391			Soviet WW II general
Rokuro, Umewaka		Entertainment	10			20	actor
Roland de La Platiere, Jean	1734-1793	Fr. Revolution	40	95	185		Fr. Statesman. Leader of Gerondists. Suicide
Roland, Gilbert	1905-1994	Entertainment	20	21		50	Latin Romantic Leading Man Silent & Sound Films
Roland, Ruth	1893-1937	Entertainment	22	35		42	Silent Serials & One Time Child Star.'Baby Ruth'
Roldan, Salv. C.		Head of State	10	20	50	15	Columbia
Rolfe, William James		Author	5	10	20	10	
Rolland, Romain	1866-1944	Author	35	85	130	105	Nobel Lit. 1915, AMsS 2,000
Rolle, Esther		Entertainment	10			35	Actress
Rolling Stones (5)		Entertainment	546	375		769	Rock Group (5) ., SP with Brian Jones 1200
Rollins, Ed		Celebrity	10			15	political celebrity
Rollins, Edward Henry		Senate	15	22	35		NHRR Tycoon & Bank Executive
Rollins, Edward		Celebrity	10			15	media/TV personality
Rollins, Sonny		Entertainment	30			55	Jazz Tenor Sax
Rolls, Charles S.	1877-1910	Business	300	375	588		Roll-Royce Motors. Aviator. Flying Record.
Rolph, James		Governor	10		35	20	Governor CA
Roman, Ruth	1924-	Entertainment	10			25	Leading Lady Films from 40's
Romano, Ray		Entertainment	15			40	Everybody Loves Raymond
Romanoff, Michael, 'Prince'	1890-1972	Business	30	65	145	55	Romanoff's Restaurant. Hollywood. (H. Gurgason)
Romanov, Stephanie		Entertainment	10			40	Actress. Models, Inc.
Rombauer, Irma S.		Author	5	15	30	10	'The Joy of Cooking'
Romberg, Sigmund	1887-1951	Composer	105	179	350	225	Hung.-Am. Composed 'Hit' Operettas. AMusQS 650
Rome, Harold		Composer	15	50	100	30	AMusQS 125. Many Pop Hits
Rome, Sydney		Entertainment	5	8	15	15	
Romero, Cesar	1907-1993	Entertainment	30	38		73	Actor. Handsome Film Star from '30's. 'Batman'
Romijn, Rebecca		Entertainment	7			37	Actress
Rominger, Kent		Astronaut	6			20	
Romjue, Milton Andrew		Senate/Congress	5	12		10	Rep. MO 1917
Rommel, Erwin	1891-1944	Military	461	762	3611	2069	Ger. Field Marshal WW II, D-Day cont LS 20,000

NAME	DATE	CATEGORY	SIG	LS/DS	ALS	SP	COMMENTS
Romnes, Haakon I.		Business	5	10		10	CEO AT&T
Romney, George W.		Business-Governor	20	30	55	22	Pres. American Motors. Gov. MI., Pres. Candidate
Romney, George	1734-1802	Artist	150	475	600		Signed Original Sketch 1,500
Romulo, Carlos P.	1901-1985	Head of State	48	80	95	75	Philippines. Pres. UN, Pulitzer. General WW II
Ronne, Edith M. (Mrs. Finn)		Explorer	20	30			Antarctic Land Named Edith Ronne Land
Ronne, Finn	1899-1980	Explorer	25		70		Proved Antarctic a Continent. 'Ronne Ice Shelf'
Ronstadt, Linda		Entertainment	20	38	40	42	Singer. Versatile Vocalist. Pop-Standards-Country
Rook, Susan		Celebrity	10			15	media/TV personality
Rooker, Michael		Entertainment	10			20	actor
Rooks, Maj. Gen. Lowell W.	1893-1973	Military	30				World War II U.S. general
Rool, Micheal		Entertainment	10			20	actor
Roome, Maj. Gen. Sir H.	1887-1964	Military	28				World War II British general
Rooney, Andy		Entertainment	10			20	actor
Rooney, Mickey	1920-	Entertainment	25	35		70	Talented Versatile Actor From Young Boy to Old Man
Roosa, Stuart R.		Astronaut	125			225	
Roosevelt, Edith Kermit	1861-1948	First Lady	60	110	130	375	FF 70
Roosevelt, Eleanor (As 1st Lady)		First Lady	138	251	1250	300	TLS/Content 1500-4025, ALS/cont 3950
Roosevelt, Eleanor	1884-1962	First Lady	81	183	270	175	Own Persona as UN Delegate & Social Worker
Roosevelt, Franklin & Eleanor		President		200		1466	
Roosevelt, Franklin D.	1882-1945	President	246	804	1500	753	TLS content 1500-5000, ALS/cont 9500
Roosevelt, Franklin D.(As Pres.)		President	301	1506	18571	846	WH Card 525.ALS/Cont 19,000,TLS/cont 5000-25000
Roosevelt, Franklin & W Churchill		President		20350			
Roosevelt, Franklin Jr.		Senate/Congress	10			20	MOC NY. Businessman-Farmer
Roosevelt, James		Senate/Congress	10	25	45	20	MOC CA. Marine Corps General
Roosevelt, John A.		1st Family	20	35			FDR Son
Roosevelt, Nicholas J.		Revolutionary War	25	60	135		Inventor
Roosevelt, Quentin	1897-1918	Military	50	120	200	200	Shot Down in France. WW I, TR's son
Roosevelt, Sarah D.	1854-1941	Presidential	75	110	140	125	FDR Mother
Roosevelt, Theodore (As Pres)		President	455	984	2800	1728	ALS/TLS/Cont.12,000,WH Cd. 500
Roosevelt, Theodore	1858-1919	President	231	718	1439	1162	TLS/Content 3000-9,000 ALS/TLS war-date 4950
Roosevelt, Theodore, Jr.	1887-1944	Military-Author	30	125	200	80	TR's son. KIA Normandy
Root, Elihu	1845-1937	Cabinet	50	80	120	140	Sec'y War, Sec'y State, Nobel Peace Prize
Root, George F. (G.Wurzel)	1820-1895	Composer	50	90	135		Many Popular & Civil War Songs.AMQS 895-1,195
Root, Jesse		Revolutionary War	25	75	125		Continental Congress
Rootes, Thomas Read		Civil War	215	360	475	1765	CSA Naval Commander, War Date LS 975
Roper, Daniel	1867-1943	Cabinet	10	30	50	50	Sec'y Commerce 1933
Röpke, Gen. of Infantry Kurt	1896-1966	Military	25				World War II German general
Rops, Felicien	1833-1898	Artist	65	165	477		Belg. Licentious Subjects. Graphic Artist
Rorem, Ned		Composer	20	45	332		Pulitzer 1976, AMusQS 175
Rorschach, Hermann	1884-1922	Science	200	3400			Swiss Psychiatrist Developed Ink Blot Test
Rosas, Juan M. de		Head of State	10	25	40		Argentina
Rose, Axl (Guns N' Roses)		Entertainment	25			82	Rock
Rose, Billy	1899-1966	Entertainment	25	75	100	80	Entrepreneur, Producer. Husband of Fanny Brice
Rose, Charlie		Celebrity	10			20	media/TV personality
Rose, David		Composer	10	20	35	20	Musical Dir. MGM. 'Holiday for Strings'.

NAME	DATE	CATEGORY	SIG	LS/DS	ALS	SP	COMMENTS
Rose, Fred	1897-1954	Country Music	30			60	Country Music HOF. Fndr. Acuff-Rose Publishing Co.
Rose, Juanita		Country Music	10			20	
Rose, Maj. Gen. Maurice	1899-1945	Military	30				World War II U.S. general
Rosecrans, William S.	1819-1902	Civil War	78	248	300		Union Gen.
Rosecrans, William S.(WD)	1819-1902	Civil War	144		1348		Union Gen.
Rosellini, Albert D.		Governor	5	15		10	Governor WA
Rosenbaum, Edward E.		Celebrity	10			15	medical expert
Rosenbaum, Michael		Celebrity				25	Actor
Rosenberg, Alfred	1893-1946	Military	175	345		450	Nazi Head of Foreign Policy. Hanged as War Criminal
Rosenbloom, 'Slapsie Maxi'		Entertainment	55			120	Heavyweight Boxer-Actor
Rosendahl, Charles E.		Aviation	75	170	225	200	Am. Adm. Premiere U.S. Dirigible Capt.
Rosenfeld, Isadora		Celebrity	10			15	medical expert
Rosenman, Samuel I.		Jurist	5	20	55	15	Confidant-Advisor to FDR
Rosenquist, James		Artist	20	55	150		Am. Pop Art. Huge Canvases. Pc Repro. S 85
Rosenthal, Jim		Celebrity	10			15	television presenter
Rosenthal, Joe		Artist-Photographer	70	258	290	390	Iwo Jima Special 1st Day Issue 450. FDC S 100
Rosenthal, Laurence		Composer	5	10	20	10	
Rosenthal, Moriz		Entertainment	75		105		Pol. Pianist
Rosenwald, Julius	1862-1932	Business	283	1325			Bought out Roebuck (of Sears) DS/Sears Sig. 12500
Rosing, Bodil		Entertainment	10			30	
Ros-Lehtinen, Ileana R		Congress	10			15	Member U.S. Congress
Roslin, Gaby		Celebrity	10			15	television presenter
Ross, Charles J.		Entertainment	5	8	15	15	
Ross, Charlotte		Entertainment	5	6		10	
Ross, Craig		Entertainment	6			25	Music. Guitar 'Lenny Kravitz'
Ross, David	1755-1800	Revolutionary War			385		Cont'l Army & MOC MD.
Ross, Dianna	1944-	Entertainment	35	70	150	72	Mega Star Singer-Actress. Of the 'Supremes'
Ross, George	1730-1779	Revolutionary War	300	801	1340		Signer Decl. of Indep. Cont. Congress, LS/cont1900
Ross, Herbert		Celebrity	10			15	film industry
Ross, Jerry L.		Astronaut	6			20	
Ross, Joe E.		Entertainment	100			250	Short, Fat American Comedian. Frazzled Character
Ross, John	1790-1866	Am. Indian Chief	312	1260	1842		Chief Cherokee Nation. Coowescoowe
Ross, John, Sir	1777-1856	Explorer	70	180	275		Arctic Expeditions. Author
Ross, Jonathon		Celebrity	10			15	television presenter
Ross, Katharine	1942-	Entertainment	15	30		40	Leading Lady. AA Nom. 'The Graduate'.
Ross, Lanny		Entertainment	15		25	25	Vintage Radio Tenor of 30's & 40's
Ross, Lawrence Sullivan	1838-1898	Civil War	165	310	475		CSA General, Texas Governor. In Over 100 Battles
Ross, Leonard Fulton	1823-1901	Civil War	40	75			Union general
Ross, Lewis W.		Senate/Congress	10	15	30		MOC NY 1863
Ross, Maj. Gen. Robert Knox	1893-1951	Military	25				World War II British general
Ross, Marion		Entertainment	15	25		35	Actress. 'Happy Days' & Many More
Ross, Mike R		Congress	10			15	Member U.S. Congress
Ross, Nellie Tayloe	1876-1977	Governor	35	75	145		1st Woman Governor in U.S., WY
Ross, Nick		Celebrity	10			15	news reader
Ross, Robert		Author	5	10	20	10	Mystery Writer. Poe Award

NAME	DATE	CATEGORY	SIG	LS/DS	ALS	SP	COMMENTS
Ross, Ronald, Sir	1857-1932	Science		125	275		Br. Phys. Nobel 1902 for Studies in Malaria
Ross, Samuel	1822-1880	Civil War	30	55	70		Union General. 20th Conn.
Ross, Sobieski		Senate/Congress	10	15	25		MOC PA 1873
Ross, Vernon 'Gene'		Author	8			12	agriculture
Rossdale, Gavin		Entertainment	12			55	Music. Lead Singer 'Bush'
Rosselini, Isabella	1952-	Entertainment	15			40	Leading Lady Daughter of Ingrid Bergman
Rosser, Thomas L.	1836-1910	Civil War	125	302	550	375	CSA Gen. Sig/Rank 175
Rossetti, Christina	1830-1894	Author	45	125	250		Br. Poet. Sister of Dante
Rossetti, Dante Gabriel	1828-1882	Artist	130	235	630		Br. Poet & Painter
Rossetti, Wm. M.	1829-1919	Author	75		408		Pre-Raphaelite Art Critic.AQS 300
Rossi, Dick		Aviation	10	25	45	30	ACE, WW II, Flying Tigers
Rossini, Gioacchino	1792-1868	Composer	500	1075	1720	3408	AMusMsS 3900. Spec, Engr.S 4500.AMusQS 3900
Rossman, Edmond		Aviation	10	30	45	25	
Rossmann, Edmund		Aviation	20			50	Ger. Ace WW II. RK
Rostand, Edmond	1868-1918	Author	70	200	450	860	Fr. Playwright. 'Cyrano de Bergerac'.
Rostenkowski, Dan		Congress	15	25		30	Powerful Rep. IL
Rostropovich, Mstislav		Entertainment	25	75	100	70	Cello Virtuoso, Conductor. 5x7 SP 45
Roth, David Lee		Entertainment	30	75		60	Ex Van Halen Group
Roth, Lillian	1910-1980	Entertainment	35	52	85	62	Tragic 20's-30's Vocal Star. Problems with Alchohol
Roth, Philip	1933-	Author	20	60	90	45	Novels. 'Portnoy's Complaint', 'Goodbye Columbus'
Roth, Tim	1961-	Entertainment	20			45	'Pulp Fiction'
Rothafell, S. L. 'Roxy'		Entertainment	15	25	40	45	NY Entrepreneur, Theatre Owner
Roth-behrendt, Dagmar		Political	10			15	Member European Parliament
Rothe, Mechtild		Political	10			15	Member European Parliament
Rothenstein, William, Sir	1872-1945	Artist-Writer	20	45	75		Off'l Artist WW I & II
Rothes, John Leslie, first Duke of	1630-1681	Royalty		180			
Rothley, Willi		Political	10			15	Member European Parliament
Rothman, Steven R. R		Congress	10			15	Member U.S. Congress
Rothrock, Cynthia		Entertainment	10			20	actress
Rothschild, Alfred	b. 1843	Banker	35	90	150		Grandson of Nathan Mayer
Rothschild, Alix de		Banker	70	190	375		
Rothschild, Amschel Mayer	1773-1855	Banker		1000			Eldest Son of Mayer Amschel
Rothschild, Guy de		Banker	15	40	80	85	
Rothschild, Jakob	1792-1868	Banker	125	588			Founded Paris Branch
Rothschild, Karl	1788-1855	Banker	200	575			Founder of Naples Branch
Rothschild, Leopold	b. 1845	Banker	35	75	150		Grandson of Nathan Mayer
Rothschild, Lionel Nathan	1808-	Banker	25	75	125		Son of Nathan Mayer
Rothschild, Mayer Amschel	1743-1812	Banker	145	400	550		Founder House of Rothschild
Rothschild, Nathan Meyer	1777-1836	Banker	260	650			Founder London Bank Branch. Banking Empire
Rothschild, Nathan	1840-	Banker	50	150			Eldest son of Lionel
Rotia, Rocky		Business	5	15	30	25	
Rotten, Johnny		Entertainment	18	40		48	
Röttiger, Gen. Panz. Troops Hans	1896-1960	Military	25				World War II German general
Rouault, Georges	1871-1958	Artist	200	475	783	1150	Landscapes, Religious, Clowns. aSP(Pc) 840
Roubertie, Brig Gen Jean-S-Louis	1887- ?	Military	20				World War II French general

NAME	DATE	CATEGORY	SIG	LS/DS	ALS	SP	COMMENTS
Roucaud, Brig Gen Guill.-Charles	1883-1944	Military	20				World War II French general
Rouget de Lisle,Claude-Joseph	1760-1836	Military,Composer	118	295	912		Composed 'La Marseillaise'. Fr. National Anthem
Rountree, Richard		Entertainment	10			30	Opera, Concert
Roure, Martine		Political	10			15	Member European Parliament
Rourke, Mickey	1950-	Entertainment	20			45	Actor
Rous, F. Peyton, Dr,	1879-1970	Science	20	30	45	25	Am. Pathologist. Nobel Medicine 1966. Tumor Viruses
Roush, Clara		Author	10	15		15	
Rousseau, Jean-Jacques	1712-1778	Author	398	1050	2950		Fr. Philosopher, Political
Rousseau, Lovell H.	1818-1869	Civil War	45	85			Union Gen. Congress
Rousseau, Theodore	1812-1867	Artist	75	175	475		Fr. Leader of Barbizon School
Roussel, Albert-Charles	1869-1937	Composer			610		Leading Fr. Composer after WW I
Routledge, Patricia		Entertainment	10			20	Actress
Roux, Albert		Celebrity	10			15	Chef
Roux, Pierre Paul Emile	1853-1933	Science	20	45	90	40	Fr. Bacteriologist with Pasteur. Dir. Pasteur Inst
Rovero, Ornella		Entertainment	15			45	Opera
Rovsing, Christian Foldberg		Political	10			15	Member European Parliament
Rowan, Andrew S.		Military	35	95	165	95	Delivered Message to Garcia
Rowan, Carl	1925-	Journalist	15	35		45	1st Afr-Am Ambass to Finland. Head U.S. Info. Agy.
Rowan, Dan	1922-1987	Entertainment	25	35		40	Comedian Partner of Dick Martin. 'Laugh-In'
Rowan, John	1773-1853	Senate/Congress	30	75			Rep.1807, Senator KY 1825
Rowan, Stephen C.	1808-1890	Civil War	40	75	155		Union Naval Commodore
Rowcroft, Maj. Gen. Sir Eric B.	1891-1963	Military	225				World War II British general
Rowe, Leo S.		Cabinet	5	20	35	10	Ass't Sec'y
Rowe, Misty		Entertainment	8			20	Pin-Up SP 25
Rowell, Lt. Gen. Sydney F.	1894-1975	Military	20				World War II Australian general
Rowland, Adele	1883-1971	Entertainment	10			20	Silent Film Actress
Rowland, David		Colonial America	45	150			Member Stamp Act Congress
Rowlands, Gena	1934-	Entertainment	10	20	25	36	Actress. Multi AA Nominations
Rowlandson, Thomas	1756-1827	Artist	250	625	900		Br. Portrait Painter-Caricaturist, Illustrator
Rowley, Thomas Algeo	1808-1892	Civil War	40		110		Union general
Rowling, J. K.		Author	30	50	102	85	Harry Potter
Rowling, William E.		Head of State	10	15	20	35	Prime Minister New Zealand
Roxas y Acuna, Manuel	1892-1948	Head of State	35	90	230	110	1st Pres. Philippines Republic
Roy and Siegfried		Entertainment				45	Animal Trainers
Roy, Maurice, Cardinal		Clergy	30	30	40	35	
Roybal-Allard, Lucille R		Congress	10			15	Member U.S. Congress
Royce, Edward R. R		Congress	10			15	Member U.S. Congress
Royce, F. Henry, Sir	1863-1933	Business	350	700	900		Co-Founder Rolls-Royce, Ltd.
Roylance, Pamela		Entertainment	4	5	6	10	
Roze, Marie		Entertainment	40			145	Opera
Rozema, David Lee		Clergy	10	15	25	15	
Rozsa, Miklos	1907-	Composer			500		Hung. Known Best for Film Music. AA(3). AAN (6)
RTjane, Gabrielle-Charlotte RTju		Entertainment	15	70	105		
Rubattel, Rudolph		Head of State	30	55			Switzerland
Rubens, Alma	1899-1931	Entertainment	65	85	165	175	Actress. Major Film Star Early 20th Cent.

NAME	DATE	CATEGORY	SIG	LS/DS	ALS	SP	COMMENTS
Rubens, Paul A.		Composer	15		60		Br. Musical Comedy. AMusQS 75
Rubens, Peter Paul	1577-1640	Artist		9250	21750		Flem. Baroque Landscapes, Portraits
Rubenstein, Bill		Celebrity	10			15	motivational speaker
Rubik, Erno		Science	35	65	85	45	Hung. Mathematician. Remember 'Rubik's Cube'?
Rubin, Jerry		Celebrity	15		35	30	activist, Chicago 7
Rubin, Robert		Political				15	Prior Sect'y of the Treasury
Rubini, Jan		Entertainment	20			65	
Rubinoff, David	1897-1986	Entertainment	18			45	Rubinoff & His Violin. Eddie Cantor Show Regular
Rubinstein, Anton	1829-1894	Composer	90	230	530	445	Pianist. AMusQS 625-1250 AMsS 4,750
Rubinstein, Artur	1887-1983	Entertainment	50	125	205	383	Pol.-Am. Pianist, AMusQS 425
Rubinstein, Helena	1870-1965	Business	72	150	225	312	Beautician Who Invented the Cosmetics Industry
Rubinstein, Ida		Entertainment	125			500	Rus. Ballerina/Nijinsky
Rubinstein, John	1946-	Entertainment	8	10	15	18	Actor-Director-Composer. Son of Artur
Rubio, P. Ortiz		Head of State	35			50	Pres. Mex. 1930-32
Ruby, Brig Gen Edmond-Auguste	1890- ?	Military	20				World War II French general
Ruby, Harry	1895-1974	Composer	30	90	162	110	AMusQS 265
Ruby, Jack	1911-1967	Assassin	150	350	1600		Killed Lee Harvey Oswald. AMsS 1300, Chk250
Rucker, Daniel H.	1812-1910	Civil War	30	65	90	150	Union Col., Bvt. General
Ruckman, John W.		Military	75				Am. Gen.
Rudel, Hans-Ulrich	1916-1982	Aviation	118	295	425	345	Most Highly Decorated Ger. Ace
Rudman, Warren B.		Senator	10			20	Senator NY
Rudner, Rita		Entertainment	5			20	Actress-Standup Comedienne
Rudnick, Paul		Entertainment	10			20	actor
Rudolf, Archduke (Aus)	1858-1889	Royalty			750	985	Dual Suicide at Mayerling/Baroness Marie Vetsera
Rudorffer, Erich		Aviation	40			75	Ger. World's 7th Highest Ace
Ruehl, Mercedes	1954-	Entertainment	25			60	Actress-Stage-Films. AA 'The Fisher King'
Ruff, Charles F.	1817-1885	Civil War	30	55	85		Union General
Ruffo, Titta	1887-1953	Entertainment	100		765	410	It. Operatic Bariton
Ruffolo, Giorgio		Political	10			15	Member European Parliament
Ruge, Friedrich		Military	68			175	Ger. Vice Adm.
Ruger, Thomas H.	1833-1907	Civil War	30	50	85		Union General
Ruggles, Charles 'Charlie'	1886-1970	Entertainment	40			75	Character Comedian. 100s Films 1928-66
Ruggles, Daniel (WD)		Civil War	162	637	962		CSA General, ALS/cont 2295, TLS/cont 1980
Ruggles, Daniel	1810-1897	Civil War	120	249	608		CSA Gen. ALS/Cont. 4900
Ruggles, Wesley	1889-1972	Entertainment	20	25	45	45	Film Dir. Original Keystone Cop. Director 1922-46
Ruick, Barbara	1932-1974	Entertainment	5	6	15	10	Actress-Daughter of Lorene Tuttle Radio Star
Rukeyser, Louis		Business	5	15	20	20	'Wall Street Week' Host
Rumpler, Edward		Aviation	20	40	75	50	
Rumsfeld, Donald		Cabinet	10	20	45	25	Sec'y Defense
Runcie, Robert A.K., Archbishop		Clergy	30	40	50	40	
Runco, Mario		Astronaut	8			16	
Rundstedt, Karl R. Gerd von	1875-1953	Military	150	240	310	350	Ger. Fld. Marshal. Cmdr. Armies in Pol., Fr., USSR
Runger, Gertrud		Entertainment	15			50	Opera
Runkel, Louis		Business	5	15		10	
Running Horse, Chief		Native American	5		30		

NAME	DATE	CATEGORY	SIG	LS/DS	ALS	SP	COMMENTS
Running Water, Chief		Native American	75		275		Model For US Indian Head Nickel
Runyon, Damon	1884-1946	Author	160	388	425	210	Short Stories & Sports Writer
Ruoff, Colonel-General Richard	1883-1967	Military	25				World War II German general
Ruppersberger, C. A. Dutch R		Congress	10			15	Member U.S. Congress
Ruppert, Jacob	1867-1939	Business	88	244	415	225	Founder Ruppert Brewing Co.
Rush, Barbara	1927-	Entertainment	8	10	15	20	Actress
Rush, Benjamin	1745-1813	Revolutionary War	650	967	2303		Signer Decl. of Indepen. Prominent Physician
Rush, Bobby L. R		Congress	10			15	Member U.S. Congress
Rush, Geoffrey		Entertainment	15			45	Autralian Oscar Winning Actor.
Rush, Isadore		Entertainment	10			30	Stage
Rush, Richard	1780-1859	Cabinet	76	175	260		Att'y General, Sec'y Treas, Sec'y State., TLS/cont 800
Rusher, William		Celebrity	10			15	media/TV personality
Rusk, Dean	1904-1994	Cabinet	20	58		40	Sec'y State Under JFK
Rusk, Jeremiah M.	1830-1893	Civil War-Cabinet	28	55	75		Union Brevet Brig. General
Rusk, Johnny		Country Music	5			15	
Rusk, Thos. Jefferson	1803-1857	Military	185	445	700		TX Provisional Gov. & Sec'y War. U.S. Sen. TX
Ruskin, John	1819-1900	Artist-Critic	60	208	364		Br. Painter, Art Critic, Author, Social Reformer
Rusling, James F.	1834-1918	Civil War	15	30	45		Union Gen. Bvt.
Russell, Annie		Entertainment	10		25	25	Vintage Stage
Russell, Bertrand	1872-1970	Author	72	158	528	292	Philosophy, Math., Nobel Prize Lit.
Russell, Brigadier Nelson	1897-1971	Military	25				World War II British general
Russell, Bruce*		Cartoonist	25			50	Political Cartoonist, Pulitzer
Russell, Charles M.	1864-1926	Artist	525	1400	4300		Known For Cowboy-West Art
Russell, Charles		Governor	5	15			Governor NV
Russell, David Abel		Congress	10	25	35		Repr. NY 1835
Russell, David Allen	1820-1864	Civil War	175	922			Union Gen., KIA Winchester
Russell, Donald J. M.		Business	5	10	20	10	
Russell, Harold		Entertainment	10	15	25	35	Military Hero, AA 'Best Years Of Our Lives'
Russell, Henry	1874-1936	Entertainment	10	20			Theatrical Mgr. & Singer
Russell, Jane	1921-	Entertainment	12	40	20	41	Actress Famous for 'The Outlaw'. Pin-Up SP 35
Russell, John	1921-1991	Entertainment	20			45	Actor. Western Star in 'The Lawman'
Russell, John, Lord	1792-1878	Head of State	38	80	125		Br. Prime Minister, 1st Earl
Russell, Johnny		Entertainment	5			15	Singer-Songwriter
Russell, Jonathan	1771-1832	Diplomat	390	800			Treaty of Ghent
Russell, Keri		Entertainment	18			45	TV 'Felicity'.
Russell, Kurt	1947-	Entertainment	25			45	Former Child Actor. Successful Leading Man
Russell, Leon		Entertainment	8			38	Legendary Rocker
Russell, Lillian	1861-1922	Entertainment	73	145	300	400	Vintage Musical, Operetta Star
Russell, Lt. Gen. Sir Dudley	1896-1978	Military	28				World War II British general
Russell, Maj. Gen. George Neville	1899-1971	Military	25				World War II British general
Russell, Maj. Gen. Henry D.	1889-1972	Military	30				World War II U.S. general
Russell, Mark		Entertainment	5			10	
Russell, Richard B., Jr.	1897-1971	Congress	20	35		35	Gov., Senator GA. Content TLS 300
Russell, Richard M.		Congress	5	10			Rep. MA
Russell, Rosalind	1911-1976	Entertainment	48	56		98	Actress. Sophisticated Comedy. AA Nom.(4)

NAME	DATE	CATEGORY	SIG	LS/DS	ALS	SP	COMMENTS
Russell, Sol Smith		Entertainment	20			40	Vintage Comedian
Russell, Theresa	1957-	Entertainment	8	15	30	25	Am. Leading Lady. US Films from 1977
Russell, William H.	1802-1873	History			167		Pvt sect'y to Henry Clay
Russell. George W.	1867-1935	Author	40	145		55	Leader Irish Literary Renaissance
Russell-McCloud, Patricia		Celebrity	10			15	motivational speaker
Russert, Tim		Celebrity	10			20	media/TV personality
Russo, René		Entertainment	10			40	Actress-Model. 'Ransom'
Rust, Albert	1818-1870	Civil War	90	200	256		CSA Gen. AES 155
Rustin, Bayard		Activist	15	35	70	25	Afro-Am Civil Rights Activist
Rutan, Dick & Jeana Yeager		Aviation		75		125	Non-Stop Trans-World w.o. Refueling
Rutan, Dick		Aviation	15	30		30	
Rutelli, Francesco		Political	10			15	Member European Parliament
Rutgers, Henry	1745-1830	Revolutionary War	95	210	298		Benfactor Rutgers University
Ruth, Babe	1895-1948	Entertainment	1024	2659	12675	3121	Baseball Immortal
Rutherford, Ann	1917-	Entertainment	18	15		50	Pin-Up SP 35. 'GWTW' Collectible. SP50-75
Rutherford, Brig. Thomas John	1893-1975	Military	20				World War II Canadian general
Rutherford, Ernest	1871-1937	Science	128	375	750	600	NZ Born Physicist. Nobel Chem. 1908
Rutherford, Kelly		Entertainment	15			40	Actress
Rutherford, Margaret, Dame	1892-1972	Entertainment	50	145	160	362	Brit. Actress. Oscar Winner. 'Miss Marple' SPc 330
Rutledge, Edward	1739-1800	Revolutionary War	225	554	2108		Signer
Rutledge, John	1739-1800	Supreme Court	195	600	2432		Continental Congress.Chief Just. Brother to Edward
Rutledge, Wiley B.	1894-1949	Supreme Court	46	115	265	50	
Ruttan, Susan		Entertainment	5			15	Actress
Ryan, Bill		Celebrity	10			15	film industry
Ryan, George		Political				15	Gov IL
Ryan, Irene	1903-1973	Entertainment	75			180	Comedienne/Partner Tim
Ryan, James W.	1858-1907	Congress	12				Repr. PA
Ryan, Jeri		Entertainment	14			48	Actress. 'Star Trek'
Ryan, Meg		Entertainment	30			65	Adorable 'Sleepless In Seattle' Star
Ryan, Mitchell		Entertainment	5				Actor
Ryan, Paul R		Congress	10			15	Member U.S. Congress
Ryan, Peggy		Entertainment	10	15	35	30	
Ryan, Robert		Entertainment	20	30		75	
Ryan, Sheila		Entertainment	5	6	15	15	
Ryan, T. Claude		Aviation	85	300		225	Ryan Aircraft Mfg.-Designer
Ryan, Timothy J. R		Congress	10			15	Member U.S. Congress
Rydell, Bobby		Entertainment	12			25	50's singer
Ryder, Albert P.	1847-1917	Artist	90	250	560		Am. Landscapes, Marine, Portraits
Ryder, Maj. Gen. Charles W.	1892-1960	Military	30				World War II U.S. general
Ryder, Winona		Entertainment	20			54	Actress
Ryder-Richardson, Anna		Celebrity	10			15	home/gardening expert
Ryle, Martin, Sir		Science	35	110	190	45	Nobel Physics 1974
Ryun, Jim R		Congress	10			15	Member U.S. Congress

NAME	DATE	CATEGORY	SIG	LS/DS	ALS	SP	COMMENTS

S

NAME	DATE	CATEGORY	SIG	LS/DS	ALS	SP	COMMENTS
Saarinen, G. Eliel		Architect	20	65	150	40	Am. Foremost Arch. Of His Day
Sabatier, Paul		Science	60		180		Fr. Chem. Nobel 1912
Sabatini, Rafael	1875-1950	Author	30	70	105		It. Historical Romance Novels, Dramatist.
Sabato, Antonio Jr.		Entertainment				40	Model
Sabin, Albert Bruce, Dr.	1906-1993	Science	60	108	150	163	Physician-Virologist. Oral Polio Vaccine
Sabin, Dwight May		Senate/Congress	5	10		10	Rep. MN 1883
Sabin, Florence R.,Dr.	1871-1953	Science	25		145		1st Woman Elected to Nat'l Acad.of Sciences
Sabine, Edward, Sir	1788-1883	Military	45		190		Br. Gen. With Ross & Parry on Arctic Exped.
Sablon, Jean		Entertainment	20	25	45	45	Vintage Fr. Romantic Singer
Sabo, Martin Olav S		Congress	10			15	Member U.S. Congress
Sabu (Dastagir)	1924-1963	Entertainment	50			126	Overnight Star in 'Elephant Boy'
Sacco, Nicola	1891-1927	Political Radical			3700		With Vanzetti Convicted of Murder
Sacconi, Guido		Political	10			15	Member European Parliament
Sacher-Masoch, Leopold von	1836-1895	Author	135	275	420		Word Masochism Attributed to Abnormality
Sackett, Frederic	1868-1941	Congress	5	25			Sen. KY. Business. Ambass. Germany
Sackler, Howard		Author	5	15	25	10	
Sacks, Oliver, Dr.		Science	15	45		30	'Awakenings'. Neurologist
Sackville-West, Lionel, Sir		Diplomat	10	25	40		2nd Baron
Sackville-West, Victoria Mary	1892-1962	Author	100	301	425		Br. Poet and Novelist
Sacrédeus, Lennart		Political	10			15	Member European Parliament
Sadat, Anwar	1918-1981	Head of State	50	145	325	567	Assassinated Pres.of Egypt
Sade		Entertainment	20			38	Vocalist
Sade, D.A.F., Marquis de	1740-1814	Author	402	725	2050		Sadist, Sadistic Attributed.Prison Confinement.
Safer, Morley		Journalist	5	10		15	'60 Minutes' Regular
Saffro, Yale L.		Artist	5	10	15	50	80th Fghter Sq. WWII., Artist., Signed Artwork
Safire, William		Author	5			15	Journalist. Newspaper Columnist. TV Guest
Sagan, Carl, Dr.		Science	25	40	55	75	Am. Astronomer, Author. Pulitzer
Sage, Russell	1816-1906	Business	100	425	1100	550	Financier, Speculator w/J.Gould. Invented 'Options'
Sagendorf, Bud*	1915-1994	Cartoonist	45			250	'Popeye'-after Segar
Sager, Carole Bayer		Composer	5	15	20	20	
Saget, Bob		TV Host	10			20	TV Host & Actor. 'Full House'
Sahl, Mort		Entertainment	5	10	15	18	Political Humorist
Said, Nuri		Head of State	5	15	35	10	Pr. Minister Iraq
Sailing, John	1847-1959	Civil War	100		395		Last Surviving Certifiable Confed. C.W. Soldier
Saint Hilaire, L.V. Jos.		Fr. Revolution	30	75	155		
Saint Laurent, Yves		Business	25	40	70	40	Fashion Designer
Saint Phalle, Niki de	1930-	Artist	80				Fr. Artist. Scarce Autograph
Saint, Eva Marie	1924-	Entertainment	10	15		30	Leading Lady. AA For 'On the Waterfront'
Saint-Cyr, Gouvion		Military	50	175	190		Fr. Marshal, Minister of War
Saint-Exupery, Antoine de	1900-1944	Aviation	192	145	225	135	Fr. Aviator. auth. Children's Books, signed bk 920
Saint-Gaudens, Augustus	1848-1907	Artist	225	335	825	1150	Known For Monumental Sculptured Projects

NAME	DATE	CATEGORY	SIG	LS/DS	ALS	SP	COMMENTS
Saint-josse, Jean		Political	10			15	Member European Parliament
Saint-Just, Louis A.L. de	1767-1794	Fr. Revolution	375	1368			Guillotined. Fr. Revolutionary
Saint-Saens, Camille	1835-1921	Composer	140	371	426	501	Organist, Opera, AMusQS 450-865
Saito, Hiroshi	d. 1939	Political	5	15	35	20	Japanese Ambassador to U.S.
Saito, Lt. Gen. Yoshitsugu	1890-1944	Military	25				World War II Japanese general
Saito, Makoto, Baron		Head of State	90	205	350		Prime Minister Japan
Sakai, Saburo		Aviation	40			90	3rd Highest Japanese Ace
Sakall, S.Z. 'Cuddles'	1884-1955	Entertainment	150			325	Also: Szakall. Hungarian Character Actor from 1916
Sakellariou, Jannis		Political	10			15	Member European Parliament
Sakharov, Andrei & Elena Bonner		Science	425				Nobel Phys., Political Activists
Sakharov, Vladmir		Celebrity	20			40	Communist agent
Salafranca Sánchez-neyra, José I		Political	10			15	Member European Parliament
Salalm, Abdus		Science	20	30	55	25	Nobel Physics 1979
Salan, Gen. Raoul-Albert-Louis	1899-1984	Military	20				World War II French general
Salan, Raoul		Military	20	45	95	50	
Salazar, Jose, Cardinal		Clergy	30	30	35		
Sale, Charles 'Chic'	1885-1937	Entertainment	28	40	65	95	Comedian-Actor
Salenger, Meredith		Entertainment	10			20	actress
Sales, Soupy		Entertainment	5	15	25	20	Comedian.Early Entry to Children's Programming
Saleza, Albert		Entertainment	40			70	Opera. Tenor
Salinger, J [erome] D [avid]		Author	1272	5352	6500		Novelist 'Catcher in the Rye'. RARE in any Form!
Salinger, Pierre		Journalist-Author	10	25	35	25	Press Sec'y Pres. JFK
Salisbury, Frank O.	1874-1962	Artist	25	75	125		presidential portrait painter
Salisbury, Harrison		Author	15			25	Pulitzer Journalist, Editor
Salisbury, Peter		Entertainment	6			25	Music. Drummer 'The Verve'
Salisbury-Jones, Maj Gen Sir A.G.	1896-1985	Military	25				World War II British general
Salk, Jonas, Dr.	1914-1995	Science	78	173	300	244	Polio Vaccine Booklet S 200
Salmi, Albert		Entertainment	25			40	
Salminen, Sally		Author	15	40	75		
Salmon, Maj. Gen. Harry L.N.	? -1943	Military	20				World War II Canadian general
Salmuth, Col-General Hans von	1888-1962	Military	25				World War II German general
Salomon, Friedrich (Frederick)	1826-1897	Civil War	44	75	110		Union general
Salt, Jennifer		Entertainment	3			10	
Salt, Titus, Sir	1803-1876	Business	5	20	40		Pioneer Wool Industry.Inventor
Salten, Felix	1870-1946	Author	75	100	235		Austrian Author of Bambi
Saltonstall, Leverett	1892-1979	Congress	12	20		15	Senator MA
Salvini, Tomaso		Entertainment	45			175	Tragedian with Booth
Salz, Jeff Dr.		Celebrity	10			15	motivational speaker
Salzedo, Carlos	1885-1961	Music	25			96	Classical harpist
Sam the Sham		Entertainment	10			20	Rock
Samaroff-Stokowski, Olga		Entertainment	20			88	Acclaimed Pianist,Teacher,Critic
Sambora, Richie		Entertainment	10			40	Rock
Samms, Emma		Entertainment	6	8		20	Pin-Up SP 35
Sammt, Albert		Aviation	30			65	
Samples, Candy		Entertainment	25			60	

NAME	DATE	CATEGORY	SIG	LS/DS	ALS	SP	COMMENTS
Sampson, Will		Entertainment	35	55	85	100	
Sampson, William T.	1840-1902	Military	40	70	110	150	Am. Adm. Cmdr-in-Chief, Sp.-Am. War
Samuel, Herbert		Statesmand	28		150		1st Jew to Govern Palestine Since Romans
Samuelson, Paul A., Dr.		Economics	25	40		35	Nobel Economics
San Giacomo, Laura		Entertainment	15			40	Actress. TV Series 'Don't Shoot Me'
San Juan, Olga		Entertainment	5			10	Singer-Dancer-Actress
San Martin, Jose de	1778-1850	Head of State	500	800	2650		Soldier Hero of Argentina
Sanborn, Franklin B.	1831-	Author-Reformer	5	15	15		Journalist, Editor, Biographer
Sanborn, John Benjamin	1826-1904	Civil War	35	65	90		Union general
Sanborn, Katherine A.		Author	5	20	35		
Sánchez García, Isidoro		Political	10			15	Member European Parliament
Sanchez, Eduardo		Entertainment				20	writer of The Blair Witch Project (with Myrick)
Sánchez, Linda T. S		Congress	10			15	Member U.S. Congress
Sanchez, Loretta S		Congress	10			15	Member U.S. Congress
Sanchez, Oscar		Celebrity	10			15	political celebrity
Sanchez, Sonia		Celebrity	10			15	motivational speaker
Sanchez-Gijon, Aitana		Entertainment	10			20	actress
Sand, George	1804-1876	Author	88	207	536		Fr. Non-Conformist. ALS/Cont.3500. (A.A.Dupin)
Sand, Shauna		Celebrity	10			15	model
Sandbæk, Ulla Margrethe		Political	10			15	Member European Parliament
Sandburg, Carl	1878-1967	Author-Poet	82	188	250	425	Biographer, Journalist. Orig. Pencil Portr. S 750
Sanders, Bernard S		Congress	10			15	Member U.S. Congress
Sanders, George R.	1926-1998	Author	5			10	'Autograph Price Guide' Author
Sanders, George	1906-1972	Entertainment	90		92	165	Laid Back Br. Actor. AA Award
Sanders, Gregg		Entertainment	10	12	25	20	Supporting Actor
Sanders, Harland 'Colonel'		Business	30	75	150	125	KFC Colonel Sanders
Sanders, Helen Doolittle		Author	5			10	Autograph Price Guide expert
Sanders, Horace T.	1820-1865	Civil War	32	75	180		Union Gen'l. Sig/Rank 50. Wounded-Bled to Death
Sanders, John Caldwell Calhoun	1840-1864	Civil War	650				Confederate general
Sanders, Sanders & Roberts		Author	25	35			first full autograph price guides
Sanders, William Price	1833-1863	Civil War	234				Union general
Sanderson, Julia		Entertainment	10	20	30	30	Vintage Radio Team With Frank Crummit
Sandie, Brigadier John Grey	1897-1975	Military	25				World War II British general
Sandler, Adam		Entertainment	9			40	Actor. Comedian
Sandlin, Max S		Congress	10			15	Member U.S. Congress
Sandoz, Mari	1896-1966	Author	25	50	95	75	Western Writer
Sands, Tommy		Entertainment	10			15	
Sandstrom, Beatrice		Celebrity	50	55	60	65	Titanic survivor
Sanford, Edw. Terry		Supreme Court	75	195			
Sanford, Isabel		Entertainment	5	7	15	18	
Sanger, Frederick		Science	20	35	60	45	Nobel Chemistry 1958
Sanger, Margaret	1883-1966	Reformer	82	210	350	200	Birth Control Advocate
Sangster, Margaret E.		Author	30	55	175		Journalist, Poet, Editor
Sangster, William E.		Clergy	25	40	55		Br. Meth. Minister-Author
Sankey, Ira D.		Clergy	120	127	259	100	Singing Evangelist. Associated w/Dwight Moody

NAME	DATE	CATEGORY	SIG	LS/DS	ALS	SP	COMMENTS
Sankford, Henry		Clergy	35	50	60		
Sano, Lt. Gen. Tadayoshi	1889-1945	Military	25				World War II Japanese general
Sano, Roy L., Bishop		Clergy	20	25	35	25	
Sansom, Art		Cartoonist	5			20	The Born Loser
Sansom, Lt. Gen. Ernest William	1890-1982	Military	20				World War II Canadian general
Santa Anna, Antonio L. de	1794-1876	Head of State	300	1222	2757	2500	General, Revolutionary, Pres.Mex.
Santa Cruz, Andres	1792-1865	Head of State	95	245			General. Pres.Bolivia. Exiled
Santa Rosa, Annibale S.,Count		Military	25	70	150		It. Piedmontese Insurgent
Santana		Entertainment	10			58	Singer-Musician
Santander, Francisco de Paula	1792-1837	Head of State			450		Pres. Columbia.
Santayana, George		Author	65	175	350		Poet, Philosopher, Critic
Santelmann, William H.		Entertainment		25			Marine Corps Bandmaster
Santer, Jacques		Political	10			15	Member European Parliament
Santerre, Antoine J.	1752-1809	Science		175			Proved theory of modern combustion
Santiago, Tessie		Celebrity				20	Actress
Santini, Giacomo		Political	10			15	Member European Parliament
Santley, Charles, Sir	1834-1922	Entertainment	40			175	Baritone. Debut 1857. Retired 1911
Santorum, Rick		Senate	10			15	United States Senate (R - PA)
Santos, Joe		Entertainment	5	6	15	15	
Santos-Dumont, Alberto	1873-1932	Aviation	217	345	580	610	Brazil. Aeronaut. Pioneer Airman
Santunione, Orianna		Entertainment	5			20	Opera
Saperstein, Abe M.		Business	50	120		150	Owner-Coach-Founder Harlem Globetrotters
Sara, Mia		Entertainment	15			45	Actress
Sarandon, Chris		Entertainment	4			15	Actor
Sarandon, Susan		Entertainment	12	22	40	45	AA, Actress.
Sarasate, Pablo de	1844-1908	Composer	113	172	250		Violin Virtuoso, AMusQS 275-460
Sarbanes, Paul		Senate	10			15	United States Senate (D - MD)
Sardi, Vincent		Business	4	15	25	10	Fndr. Sardi's Restaurant NYC
Sardou, Victorien	1831-1908	Playwright	20	45	125	150	Fr. Librettist, Bourgeois Drama
Sarett, Lew		Author	75	100			
Sarfatti, Margherita		Author	10	30	50		
Sarg, Tony*	1882-1942	Artist	15			75	Illustrator-Marionette Maker
Sargent, Dick	1930-1994	Entertainment	25			105	Darren, Bewitched
Sargent, John G.		Cabinet	15	30	60	25	Att'y General 1925
Sargent, John Osborne	1811-	Legal	10		65		Lawyer, Author. Political Activist
Sargent, John Singer	1856-1925	Artist	95	238	316		Am. World Famous Portraitist
Sargent, Kenny		Entertainment	20			45	Big Band Singer
Sargent, Sir Malcolm	1895-1967	Entertainment				100	Orchestral composer
Sargent, Winthrop		Revolutionary War	30	100	240		Cont'l Army, 1st Gov. MS Terr.
Sarnoff, David	1891-1971	Business	80	465	650	300	Broadcasting Pioneer. TLS on RCA Lttrhd. 1450
Sarocco, Suzanne		Entertainment	10			25	Opera
Saroyan, William	1908-1981	Author	60	158	210	150	Playwright. Pulitzer 'The Time of Your Life'
Sartain, John	1808-1897	Artist-Engraver	25	85	100		Sartain's Union Magazine
Sarton, May		Author	5	15	40		
Sartori, Amalia		Political	10			15	Member European Parliament

NAME	DATE	CATEGORY	SIG	LS/DS	ALS	SP	COMMENTS
Sartre, Jean-Paul	1905-1980	Author	110	383	698		Leader Existentialist Movement. ALS/Cont. 1350
Sassoon, Beverly		Entertainment	3	3	6	20	
Sassoon, Siegfried	1886-1967	Author	50	225	420		Br. Poet. Anti-War Verses
Sassoon, Vidal		Business	15	20	25	20	Hair Design & Products
Satie, Erik	1866-1925	Composer	185	825	1285		Eccentric, Avant Garde Music
Sato, Eisaku		Head of State	20	55	150	35	Premier Japan. Nobel Peace
Sato, Lt. Gen. Kotoku	1893-1959	Military	25				World War II Japanese general
Sauckel, Fritz	1894-1946	Military	50	302			Nazi War Criminal. Hanged
Sauer, Emil		Entertainment	15	15	75	30	
Sauguet, Henri		Composer	65		275		Fr. Opera, Ballet AMQS 250
Sauken, Dietrich von		Military	25			75	Panzer General
Saul, Sonya		Celebrity	10			15	television presenter
Saulsbury, Grove		Governor	5	15	30		Governor DE
Saumarez, James, Sir,	1757-1836	Military	90	265	600		Br. Adm., Battle of the Nile
Saunders, Alvin		Senate/Congress	15	35	80		Sen. KY, CW Gov. Nebr. Territory
Saunders, Edward Watts		Senate/Congress	10	20			Rep. VA 1906
Saunders, Hugh W.		Aviation	5	10	20	15	
Saunders, Jennifer		Entertainment	10			20	actress
Saunders, John Monk		Entertainment	10	25			ANS 35, writer/director
Saunders, Lori		Entertainment	4			15	
Saunders, Maj. Gen. Macan	1884-1956	Military	25				World War II British general
Saunders, Stuart J.		Business	3	7	15	10	
Saunders, Stuart T.	1909-	Business	5			10	CEO Penn-Central RR
Sautet, Claude		Celebrity	10			15	film industry
Savage, Ann		Entertainment	12	15		35	
Savage, Fred		Entertainment	7			18	
Savage, Jeannie		Celebrity	10			15	photographer
Savage, Lily		Celebrity	10			15	comedian
Savage, M. J.		Clergy	15	30	45		
Saval, Dany		Entertainment	5		25	20	Pin-Up SP 25. Fr. Actress
Savalas, George		Entertainment	15			40	
Savalas, Telly	1924-1994	Entertainment	15	43		40	Actor. TV's 'Kojak'. Oscar Nominee
Savary, Gilles		Political	10			15	Member European Parliament
Savige, Lt. Gen. Stanley G.	1890-1954	Military	20				World War II Australian general
Saving Private Ryan (cast)		Entertainment				110	Hanks/ Damon., Hanks and Sizemore 85
Savitch, Jessica		Journalist	35			125	TV-News. Died Young in Car Accident
Savitt, Jan		Bandleader	15			45	
Savles, Thomas F, Bishop		Clergy	30	40			
Savoia, Attilio		Artist	15	40	75		
Savory, Lt. Gen. Sir Reginald Arth.	1894-1980	Military	25				World War II British general
Sawhala, Julia		Entertainment	10			20	Actress
Sawyer, Charles		Cabinet	5	25	30	25	Sec'y Commerce 1948
Sawyer, Diane		Journalist	5	20		25	TV Broadcast Journalist
Sawyer, Forest		Celebrity	10			20	media/TV personality
Sawyer, Joe		Entertainment	75			200	

NAME	DATE	CATEGORY	SIG	LS/DS	ALS	SP	COMMENTS
Sax, Adolphe		Science	55	180	375		Invented Saxophone & Others
Saxbe, William B.		Cabinet	8	12	20	15	Att'y General 1974
Saxe, John G.		Author	10	30	55	30	
Saxon, John		Entertainment	5			20	
Saxton, Jim S		Congress	10			15	Member U.S. Congress
Saxton, Rufus	1824-1908	Civil War	45	68	113		Union General
Say, Jean-Baptiste	1767-1832	Economist			1200		French political economist.
Sayao, Bidu		Entertainment	15			75	Opera Soprano
Sayer, Leo		Music	10			15	performing musical artist
Sayers, Dorothy	1893-1957	Author	183	467	565	350	Br. Mystery Novelist. Created Lord Peter Wimsey
Sayle, Alexei		Celebrity	10			15	comedian
Sayles, John		Celebrity	10			20	film industry
Saylor, Anna, Mrs.		Socialite	5	10			
Sbarbati, Luciana		Political	10			15	Member European Parliament
Scacchi, Greta		Entertainment	10			35	Actress
Scaggs, Boz		Entertainment	15			40	rock
Scagliarini, Eleanora		Entertainment	10			40	Opera
Scalchi Lolly		Entertainment	35			75	
Scales, Alfred Moore (WD)		Civil War	165		342		CSA Gen.
Scales, Alfred Moore	1827-1892	Civil War	124				Confederate general
Scales, Prunella		Entertainment	10			20	Actress
Scalia, Antonin		Supreme Court	30	45		55	TLS/cont. 575
Scalia, Jack		Entertainment	10			25	
Scallon, Dana Rosemary		Political	10			15	Member European Parliament
Scammell, Alexander	1746-1781	Revolutionary War	350		1500		Officer. Wounded Died 1781
Scammon, Eliakim Parker	1816-1894	Civil War	45	70	110		Union general
Scancarelli, Jim*		Cartoonist	10			45	Gasoline Alley
Scapagnini, Umberto		Political	10			15	Member European Parliament
Scarbonchi, Michel-ange		Political	10			15	Member European Parliament
Scarborough, John		Clergy	10	15	20		
Scarlatti, Alessandro	1660-1725	Composer	725	4150	12000		115 Operas, Over 600 Cantatas
Scarlett, Maj. Gen. Gerald	1885-1957	Military	25				World War II British general
Scarwid, Diana		Entertainment	5		15	20	
Schaal, Gen. of Panz. Ferdinand	1889-1962	Military	27				World War II German general
Schaal, Richard		Entertainment	3	3	6	8	
Schaal, Wendy		Entertainment	3	3	6	6	
Schacht, Hjalmar	1877-1970	WW II	51	172	300		Nazi. President of Reichsbank
Schaech, Johnathon		Celebrity				35	Actor
Schafer, Natalie		Entertainment	20			58	Actress, Gilligan's Island, SP with Jim Backus 138
Schaff, Phillip		Clergy	40	55	75	50	
Schaffner, Anne-marie		Political	10			15	Member European Parliament
Schaffner, Franklin J.		Entertainment	30			75	
Schaffner, Hans		Head of State	10			20	Pres. Austria
Schakowsky, Janice D. S.		Congress	10			15	Member U.S. Congress
Schall, Thomas D.		Senate/Congress	5	15			Rep., Senator MN 1915

NAME	DATE	CATEGORY	SIG	LS/DS	ALS	SP	COMMENTS
Schallert, William		Entertainment	5	6	15	15	
Schally, Andrew V., Dr.		Science	22	30	45	30	Nobel Medicine 1977
Schanberg, Sydney, H.		Author	10	30	75	15	
Scharwenka, Franz Xavier		Composer	25		75	150	Pianist. Founder of Conservatory
Schary, Dore		Entertainment	15		25	30	Producer, Director, Writer
Schary, Emanuel		Artist	10	25	35		
Schaub, Julius	1898-1967	Military	86			175	SS General. Hitler's Adjutant
Schawlow, Arthur L., Dr.		Science	22	30	35	25	Nobel Physics 1981
Scheel, Jeff		Entertainment	8			40	Music. Lead Singer 'Gravity Kills'
Scheele, Karin		Political	10			15	Member European Parliament
Scheer, Reinhard	1863-1928	Military	35	45	100	55	Ger. Adm. Battle of Jutland.
Scheff, Fritzi	1882-1954	Entertainment	20	15	30	25	Austr-Am. Soprano. Musical Theatre & Silent Films
Scheidemann, Philippe		Head of State	10	20	50	40	1st Chancellor of Repub. 1919
Scheider, Roy		Entertainment	7	20		20	Actor
Schell, Augustus	1812-1884	Business	275	850			Financier & C. Vanderbilt Attorney
Schell, Maria	1926-	Entertainment	5	7	20	25	International Austrian Film Star 50's
Schell, Maximillian		Entertainment	10	15	35	45	AA
Schell, Richard	1810-1879	Business		975			Commodore Vanderbilt's Aide During 'Erie War'
Schenk, Robert C.		Civil War	33	60	61		Union Gen., Rep OH, Ambassador
Scherchen, Hermann		Conductor	20	242		125	
Scherer, Paul		Clergy	20	25	40	30	
Schick, Bela, Dr.		Science	60	135	225	125	Hung.-Am Pediatrician. Schick Test for TB
Schiele, Egon		Artist		1400			Austrian Expressionist Painter
Schierhuber, Agnes		Political	10			15	Member European Parliament
Schiff, Adam B. S		Congress	10			15	Member U.S. Congress
Schiff, Jacob H.	1847-1920	Business	75	140	265		Banker, Philanthropist. Wall Street Brokerage
Schiff, Richard		Entertainment	10			35	The West Wing
Schiffer, Claudia	1972-	Entertainment	18			49	German Model. Pin-Up SP 65
Schifrin, Lalo		Composer	10	20	25	30	Argentine Composer. Film Themes. AMusQS 40
Schildkraut, Joseph		Entertainment	75	150		220	Oscar winner
Schiller, Hans von		Aviation	20		45		
Schilling, David		Aviation	18	38	60	45	ACE, WW II
Schilling, Maj. Gen. Wijbrandus	1890-1958	Military	20				World War II Dutch general
Schimmelfennig, Alexander	1824-1865	Civil War	45	80			Union general
Schine, G. David		Business	20			40	Hotel Chain Owner
Schiotz, Fredrik A.		Clergy	20	25	35	30	
Schipa, Tito	1889-1965	Entertainment	65			140	Opera. Important Tenor
Schirach, Balder von	1907-1974	Ger. Politician	75	242	375		National Dir. Hitler Youth Movement
Schirra, Walter M.		Astronaut	40	85	158	59	Mercury 7 Astro.
Schirripa, Steven R.		Entertainment				35	Bobby 'Bacala' Baccalieri, Soprano's
Schlafly, Phyllis		Political	10	20	35	25	Activist, Feminist
Schleicher, Ursula		Political	10			15	Member European Parliament
Schlemmer, Gen Mtn Troops Hans	1893-1973	Military	25				World War II German general
Schlender, Brent		Celebrity	10			15	motivational speaker
Schlesinger, Arthur Jr.		Author	10	38	50	20	Historian. Special Ass't to JFK. Pulitzer 1946

NAME	DATE	CATEGORY	SIG	LS/DS	ALS	SP	COMMENTS
Schlesinger, James R.		Cabinet	5	10	25	15	Sec'y Defense 1973
Schlesinger, John		Entertainment	5			20	Film Director
Schlesser, Lt. Gen. Guy	1896-1970	Military	20				World War II French general
Schlessinger, Laura Dr.		Celebrity				20	
Schley, Winfield Scott	1839-1909	Military	87	128	183	150	Am.Naval Officer. Arctic rescue of Greely
Schlieben, Lt Gen. Karl-Wilhem v.	1894-1964	Military	25				World War II German general
Schliemann, Heinrich	1833-1890	Archaeologist	245	750	1665		Discovered Ancient Troy. ALS re Mycenae 5,000
Schlieper, Lt. Gen. Fritz	1892-1977	Military	25				World War II German general
Schlossstein, Steven		Celebrity	10			15	financial expert
Schmalz, Wilhelm		Military	15	40	75	30	
Schmid, Gerhard		Political	10			15	Member European Parliament
Schmid, Herman		Political	10			15	Member European Parliament
Schmidt, Colonel-General Rudolf	1886-1957	Military	25				World War II German general
Schmidt, Friedrich		Astronaut	30				
Schmidt, Gen. of Infantry Hans	1877-1948	Military	25				World War II German general
Schmidt, Helmut		Head of State	15	25	40	20	Ger. Political Leader, Chanc.
Schmidt, Maarten, Dr.		Science	10	25	30	20	
Schmidt, Maj. Gen. William R.	1889-1966	Military	30				World War II U.S. general
Schmidt, Olle		Political	10			15	Member European Parliament
Schmidtmer, Christiane		Entertainment	4			15	Ger. Actress. Pin-Up SP 25
Schmied, Francois-louis	1873-1941	Artist	90		375		Fr. Art Deco Painter - Illustrator
Schmitt, Harrison H.		Astronaut	48	76	130	126	Apollo 17 Moonwalker, TLS/cont 632
Schmitt, Ingo		Political	10			15	Member European Parliament
Schmitt-Walter, Karl		Entertainment	10			35	Opera. Baritone. Wide Repertoire
Schnabel, Artur	1881-1951	Entertainment	40	135	220	105	Austrian Pianist
Schnaut, Gabriella		Entertainment	5			25	Opera
Schneider, John		Entertainment	4	10		15	Singer-Actor
Schneider, Rob		Entertainment				30	Comedian
Schneider, Romy		Entertainment	75			130	
Schneider, Wm. C.(SKYLAB)		Astronaut	6			20	
Schnellhardt, Horst		Political	10			15	Member European Parliament
Schnittke, Alfred	b. 1934	Music	20		170		Composer
Schnitzer, George C. Jr.		Author	8			12	author/publisher
Schnitzler, Arthur	1862-1931	Author	40	125			Austrian playwrite
Schochet, Bob*		Cartoonist	5			35	
Schoenberg, Arnold	1874-1951	Composer	262	576	690	675	Austrian-Born. AMusQS 2,250, 2500
Schoenebeck, Karl August		Aviation	30	65		75	
Schoenert, Rudolf		Aviation	10	20	40	25	
Schoepf, Albin Francisco	1822-1886	Civil War	45		90		Union general
Schoepfel, Gerhard		Aviation	5	15	25	15	
Schofield, John McAllister (WD)	1831-1906	Civil War	125	155	340		Union General, Sec'y War 1868
Schofield, John McAllister	1831-1906	Civil War	42	80	150		Union Gen. MOH At Wilson's Creek
Schofield, Philip		Entertainment	10			20	Actor
Schopenhauer, Arthur	1788-1860	Author	700	2250	5000		Ger. Philosopher
Schörling, Inger		Political	10			15	Member European Parliament

NAME	DATE	CATEGORY	SIG	LS/DS	ALS	SP	COMMENTS
Schorner, Ferdinand		Military	40		120		
Schörner, Fld. Marshal Ferdinand	1892-1973	Military	25				World War II German general
Schorr, Daniel		Journalist	10			45	CBS Correspondent Till 1976. Nat'l Public Radio Now
Schrader, Paul		Entertainment	5	15		20	Film Director
Schram, Emil		Business	3	10	20	5	
Schramm, Margit		Entertainment	5			15	Opera, Operetta
Schreiber, Avery		Entertainment	3	5	8	12	
Schreiber, Lt Gen Sir Edm. Chas.	1890-1972	Military	25				World War II British general
Schricker, Henry F.		Governor	5	20		10	Governor IN
Schrieffer, John R.		Science	10	20	35	15	Nobel Physics 1972
Schriver, Edmund	1812-1899	Civil War	20	40			Union Gen.
Schriver, Edmund	1812-1899	Civil War	30	55	70		Union General
Schrock, Edward L. S.		Congress	10			15	Member U.S. Congress
Schröder, Ilka		Political	10			15	Member European Parliament
Schröder, Jürgen		Political	10			15	Member European Parliament
Schroeder, Barbet		Celebrity	10			15	film industry
Schroeder, Patricia		Senate/Congress	5	10		15	Rep. CO
Schroeder, Patrick A.		Author	8			12	Civil War
Schroeder, Rick		Entertainment	10			20	actor
Schroeder, Ricky		Entertainment	10			35	Actor
Schroeder-Feinen, Ursula		Entertainment	5			30	Opera
Schroedter, Elisabeth		Political	10			15	Member European Parliament
Schroer, Werner		Aviation				65	Ger. Ace WW II. RK
Schroeteler, Heinrich		Military				60	Ger. Capt. U-667, U1023. RK
Schubert, Franz	1797-1828	Composer	2200	4567	10000		
Schuk, Walter		Aviation	25	45		85	Ger. 12th Highest ACE
Schulberg, Budd		Author	30	55		50	Novelist, Screenwriter. 'On The Waterfront'
Schuller, Gunther		Music	35			55	Pulitzer '94 in Music. AMusQS 250
Schuller, Robert		Clergy	15	20		25	
Schulmann, Horst		Celebrity	10			15	financial expert
Schultz, Charles		Celebrity	10			15	financial expert
Schultz, Theodore William		Agri-Science	10	15	25		Nobel Economics
Schulz, Charles	1922-2000	Cartoonist	115	180	490	355	Snoopy Sktch S 750, Peanuts S Orig. Strip 1,500-3000
Schulz, Gen. of Infantry Friedrich	1897-1976	Military	27				World War II German general
Schulz, Martin		Political	10			15	Member European Parliament
Schulze, William		Science	15			45	Rocket Pioneer w/von Braun
Schumann, Clara	1819-1896	Composer	70	195	396	925	Ger. Pianist-Composer. ALS/Content 3,000, AMQS 635
Schumann, Elizabeth		Entertainment	45			140	Opera
Schumann, Robert	1810-1856	Composer	800	1100	4000		AMusQS 15,000 (3rd Symph).22,000(Die Nonne)
Schumann-Heink, Ernestine		Entertainment	45		100	150	Opera, Concert. Contralto
Schumer, Charles		Senate	10			15	United States Senate (D - NY)
Schurz, Carl	1829-1906	Civil War	30	60	112		Union Gen., U.S. Sen. MO. Advisor to 5 Presidents
Schuschnigg, Kurt von	1897-1977	Head of State	50	85	225	1125	Austrian Chancellor. Deposed & Imprisoned by Nazis
Schuyler, Philip J.	1733-1804	Revolutionary War	275	529	889		Soldier, Statesman. Rev. War General. Cont'l Congr
Schwab, Charles M.	1862-1939	Industrialist	138	390	1150	312	Pres. Carnegie, US & Bethlehem Steel/Mil. Salary

NAME	DATE	CATEGORY	SIG	LS/DS	ALS	SP	COMMENTS
Schwab, Frank X.		Political	5	20			Mayor Buffalo, NY
Schwaiger, Konrad K.		Political	10			15	Member European Parliament
Schwantner, Joseph		Composer	10		55	40	Pulitzer, AMusQS 95
Schwartz, Arthur		Composer					Dancing in the Dark AMQS on Ph. 410
Schwartz, Melvin, Dr	1932-	Science	24			30	Nobel Physics 1988
Schwartz, Scott		Entertainment	6			25	Actor. 'Xmas Story' SP 30
Schwartz, Stephen		Composer	55	200			'Godspell'
Schwartz, William B.		Celebrity	10			15	medical expert
Schwarzenegger, Arnold		Entertainment	38	35	55	67	Actor-Producer
Schwarzkopf, Brenda		Celebrity	10			15	political celebrity
Schwarzkopf, Elizabeth		Entertainment	15			50	Opera
Schwarzkopf, Norman		Military	25	92		70	Gen. Desert Storm
Schwatka, Frederick	1849-1892	Military	150	350	625		Indian Fighter
Schwedtman, Ferd. D.		Science	5	15		10	
Schweickart, Russell L.		Astronaut	25	125		75	
Schweiker, Richard S.		Senate/Congress	5	10		10	Rep., Senator PA 1961
Schweitzer, Albert, Dr.	1875-1965	Science-Music	180	353	641	885	Nobel. Clergy. 3x4 SP 350-650. AMusQS 650
Schwellenback, Lewis B.		Cabinet	10	35	70	45	Sec'y Labor 1945
Schwimmer, David		Entertainment	15			50	Actor. Friends
Schwinger, Julian, Dr.		Science	20	30	55	25	Nobel Physics 1965
Schwitters, Kurt	1887-1948	Artist	250	775			Ger. Best Know For His Collages
Sciorra, Annabella		Entertainment	10			30	Actress
Scitar, Ted		Music	10			20	Rhythm guitar, sax, vocals, 'The VooDoos'
Scobee, Dick	1939-1989	Astronaut	100	250		325	Challenger
Scobie, Lt. Gen. Sir Ronald MacK.	1893-1969	Military	25				World War II British general
Scofield, Glenni W.		Senate/Congress	10	15	25		Rep. PA 1863
Scofield, Paul	1922-1996	Entertainment	25		125	85	Brit. AA Winner. 'Man for All Seasons' etc
Scoggins, Tracy		Entertainment	5	8	25	20	Pin-Up SP 50
Scoones, Gen Sir Geoffry Allan P.	1893-1975	Military	25				World War II British general
Scoones, Maj Gen Sir Reginald L.	1900-1991	Military	25				World War II British general
Scopes, John T.	1900-1970	Educator	200	1200		1495	Defendant In Monkey Trial
Scorsese, Martin		Entertainment	15	55		49	Film Director
Scorupco, Izabella		Entertainment	5				Actress. Golden Eye Pin-Up 55
Scotchie, Joseph		Author	8			12	conservative politics, literary critism
Scott, Blanch Stuart	1891-1970	Aviation	50		225	250	1st Fem. Pilot to Solo
Scott, Charles Wm. A.		Aviation	25	50	80	50	Br. Won Harmon Trophy
Scott, Charles	1739-1813	Revolutionary War	125	275	525		General, Indian Fighter, Gov. KY
Scott, Chuck Col.		Celebrity	10			15	motivational speaker
Scott, Cyril Meir		Composer	15	30	55	60	Br. Orchestral, Piano, Chamber
Scott, David C.		Business	5	10		10	CEO Allis-Chalmers
Scott, David R.		Astronaut	58	175		230	
Scott, David S		Congress	10			15	Member U.S. Congress
Scott, E. Irwin		Business		965	1475		One of Founders of Scott Paper Co.
Scott, Earl		Country Western	10			35	Music. 50's Western Recording Artist
Scott, Eric		Entertainment	4	6		10	

NAME	DATE	CATEGORY	SIG	LS/DS	ALS	SP	COMMENTS
Scott, Fred		Entertainment	18			42	Vintage Cowboy Actor
Scott, George C.		Entertainment	20			90	AA Patton
Scott, Gordon		Entertainment	15			35	
Scott, Gustavus		Revolutionary War	35	90	140		Lawyer, Patriot (MD)
Scott, Hazel		Entertainment	35	45		130	Piano-Organ
Scott, Hugh L.		Military	30	95	250		Am. WW I Gen. 7 Chief of Staff
Scott, Hugh		Senate/Congress	5	15		25	Senator PA
Scott, Jack		Entertainment	10			25	Rock
Scott, Jerry*		Cartoonist	10			45	Nancy
Scott, John Morin		Revolutionary War	35	120	150		General, Patriot, Rep. NY
Scott, Lizabeth		Entertainment	8	10		20	Pin-Up SP 25
Scott, Maj. Gen. Anthony Gerald O	1899-1980	Military	25				World War II British general
Scott, Maj. Gen. James Bruce	1892-1974	Military	25				World War II British general
Scott, Maj Gen John Walter Lenox	1883-1960	Military	25				World War II British general
Scott, Maj. Gen. Thomas	1897-1968	Military	25				World War II British general
Scott, Martha		Entertainment	5			20	
Scott, Pippa		Entertainment	6			15	Actress
Scott, Randolph	1903-1987	Entertainment	40	55		104	Actor. Handsome Western Hero
Scott, Raymond		Composer	25	40	65	50	Big Band Leader, Arranger
Scott, Robert C. S		Congress	10			15	Member U.S. Congress
Scott, Robert Falcon	1868-1912	Explorer	90	160	240	300	Br. Arctic Expeditions
Scott, Robert Kingston	1826-1900	Civil War	45		90		Union Gen., Gov. SC
Scott, Robert Lee, Jr.		Aviation	25	35	60	40	ACE, WW II, 'God Is My Co-Pilot'
Scott, Selina		Celebrity	10			15	television presenter
Scott, Thomas A.	1824-1881	Business	238	762	1125		Pennsylvania RR Baron
Scott, Thomas Moore	1829-1876	Civil War	90				Confederate general
Scott, Thomas		Clergy	40	50	75		
Scott, Tony		Celebrity	10			15	film industry
Scott, W. Kerr		Senate	5			25	Gov. NC 1949, Senator NC 1954
Scott, Walter, Sir	1771-1832	Author	135	588	711		Poet, Novelist, Historian
Scott, Willard		Entertainment	4	4		10	
Scott, William R.		Business	5	15			RR Exec.
Scott, Winfield (WD)		Civil War	130	375	525		Union General
Scott, Winfield	1786-1866	Civil War	108	210	331	386	Union Gen.
Scott, Zachary		Entertainment	25			50	
Scotti, Antonio		Entertainment	40		100	185	It. Baritone, Opera
Scotto, Renata		Entertainment	15			50	Opera
Scowcroft, Brent		Military	10	30		20	Gen., Statesman, Pres. Advisor
Scranton, Bill		Governor	5	15		15	Gov. PA. Pres. Candidate
Scriabin, Alexander	1872-1915	Composer	650	3500	5000	3200	Rus. Symphonies, etc. AMusQS 3500-6000
Scribe, Eugene	1791-1861	Author	10	35	130		Fr. Librettist. Meyerbeer, Halevy
Scribner, Charles		Publishing	110	215			Publishing Giant. Stk. Cert. S 1750
Scrimm, Angus		Entertainment	6			20	Actor
Scripps, William E.		Aviation	15	90		40	
Scruggs, Jan		Celebrity	10			15	motivational speaker

NAME	DATE	CATEGORY	SIG	LS/DS	ALS	SP	COMMENTS
Scryabin, Alexander	1872-1915	Composer			3500		Russian composer and pianist
Scudder, Horace E.	1838-1902	Author	10	30	55		Ed. Atlantic Monthly, Biographer
Scuderi, Sara		Entertainment	35			85	Opera
Scullin, James H.	1876-1953	Head of State	40			70	P.M. Australia
Scully-Power, Paul		Astronaut	25			65	
Scura, Maggie		Celebrity	10			15	media/TV personality
Scurry, William Read	1821-1864	Civil War	488		4255		Confederate general
Seaborg, Glenn T.	1912-1999	Science	25	105	150	75	Chm. AEC. Nobel Chemistry 1951. Plutonium-A Bomb
Seaforth, Susan		Entertainment	5			20	Pin-Up SP 30
Seale, Bobby	1936-	Activist	25			55	Political Activist. Co-Fndr. Black Panthers, Chicago 8
Seals, Dan		Country Music	5			15	
Searle, Ronald		Cartoonist	20	45	80		Painter, Author. 'St. Trinians School Girls'
Sears, Barry		Celebrity	10			15	medical expert
Sears, Claudius Wistar	1817-1891	Civil War	105				Confederate general
Sears, Edmund		Clergy	20	25	35		
Sears, Richard Warren		Business		6500			Sear's Founder. DS Sears Contract 12,500
Seath, Maj. Gen. Gordon Hamilt'n	1886-1952	Military	25				World War II British general
Seaton, George		Entertainment	35			70	Film Director
Seawell, Molly Elliot		Author	5	15	35	10	
Seawell, William T.		Business	3	10	15	15	
Sebastian, John		Entertainment	15			40	Singer-Songwriter. The Lovin' Spoonful
Sebastini, H.F.B.	1772-1851	Fr. Military		80	150		Gen. under Napoleon, Marshal of Fr.
Seberg, Jean	1838-1879	Entertainment	75	110		165	Early Suicide
Sebold, Alice		Author	10			20	Bestselling Author
Sebree, Maj. Gen. Edmund B.	1898-1966	Military	30				World War II U.S. general
Sechelles, Marie-Jean Herault de		Fr. Revolution			895		Att'y to Louis XVI
Sedaka, Neil		Composer	10			25	Entertainer. AmusQS 35
Seddon, James A. (WD)		Civil War	210	905	2675		CSA Sec'y War Dte.
Seddon, James A.		Civil War	150	450	650		CSA Sec'y War
Seddon, Margaret R.		Astronaut	6			25	
Sedgewick, Kyra		Entertainment	10			20	actress
Sedgwick, Catherine M.	1789-1867	Author	10	20	45		Am. Early Novelist. Moral Tales
Sedgwick, John	1813-1864	Civil War	228	497	632		Union General (Uncle John). KIA Spotsylvania
Sedgwick, Kyra		Entertainment	15			75	Actress
See, Elliot M. Jr.		Astronaut	225			350	Died in Launching Tragedy
Seeburg, Justus Percival		Business	40	120	195		
Seeger, Pete		Composer	20	50	95	45	Folk Singer
Seeley, Blossom		Entertainment	5	6	15	15	
Seeley, Jeannie		Country Music	10			20	
Seelye, Julius Hawtry		Clergy	15	20	25		College Pres., Rep.MA
Segal, Erich		Author	20	30			Love Story
Segal, George		Artist	35		60	125	Sculptor
Segal, George		Entertainment	5	8	15	30	Actor
Segal, Steven		Entertainment	15			50	Actor. Major Action Films
Segar, Elzie C.*		Cartoonist	125			575	Popeye

NAME	DATE	CATEGORY	SIG	LS/DS	ALS	SP	COMMENTS
Segar, Joseph E.		Senate/Congress	10	20			Rep. VA 1862
Seger, Bob		Entertainment	20			45	rock
Seger, C.B.		Business	15	45	85	40	
Segni, Mariotto		Political	10			15	Member European Parliament
Segonzac, Andre Dunoyer de	1884-1974	Artist				130	Painter and engraver
Segovia, Andres	1894-1987	Entertainment	100	300	475	350	Classical Guitar Virtuoso
Segre, Emilio, Dr.		Science	20	35	50	30	Nobel Physics 1959
Segura, Wiltz P.		Aviation	15	25	40	30	ACE, WW II, USAAF Ace. Flew w/Chennault
Segurola, Andres de		Entertainment	45			150	Sp. Bass
Seidel, Toscha		Entertainment	20			75	Noted Rus.-Am. Violinist
Seidelman, Susan		Entertainment	5	10		10	Film Director
Seignolle, Claude		Author	120	175	220		
Seinfeld (Cast)		Entertainment	150			272	Four Main Characters
Seinfeld, Jerry		Entertainment	15			52	
Seipel, Ignas Dr.		Head of State	10	30	80	40	Austrian Prelate & Chancellor
Seka		Entertainment	9	10	20	25	Pin-Up SP 35
Selassie, Haile	1891-1975	Head of State	327	439	730	900	(Tafari Makonnen) Emperor of Ethiopia
Selby, Maj. Gen. Arthur Roland	1893-1966	Military	25				World War II British general
Seldes, Gilbert		Author	25	126			American playwrite, screenwriter
Selfridge, Harry G.	1858-1947	Business	15	65	110	75	Founder Selfridge's, London Dept. Store
Selfridge, Thos. O.	1836-1924	Civil War	40	85	120		Union Naval Commander
Sellecca, Connie		Entertainment	10			30	
Selleck, Tom		Entertainment	10	15	30	32	'Magnum P.I.' TV Star. SP 75
Sellers, David Foote		Military	20	55	95	50	
Sellers, Jim		Entertainment	6			25	Music. Bass Guitar 'Stabbing Westward'
Sellers, Peter	1925-1980	Entertainment	112	151	188	210	British comic actor
Sellers, Winfield S.		Military	15	40	75	40	
Selman, John Henry	1839-1896	Outlaw-Lawman	1200	1931			Killed John Wesley Hardin
Selous, Frederick Courteney		Author	20			40	African adventure
Selznick, David O.	1902-1965	Business	95	319		350	Film Producer 'GWTW'. S Chk 350
Selznick, Irene		Entertainment	10	15		20	Film Executive
Sembrich, Marcella	1858-1935	Entertainment	85		300	350	Opera, Concert. Polish Soprano
Semenov, Mikhail		Science	10	20			Russian/American Physicist
Semenov, Nikolai		Science		55		75	Rus. Chem., Physicist. Nobel 1956
Semmelweis, Ignaz	1818-1865	Science	500	1200	3200		Hung. Obstetrician. Antisepsis
Semmes, Paul J.	1815-1863	Civil War	831	1365	1875		CSA Gen. Sig/Rank 1450
Semmes, Raphael	1809-1877	Civil War	483	825	2640	1750	CSA Admiral Sig/Rank 475
Semple, James	1798-1866	Congress	15				Sen. IL, Elsa, IL Founder
Sendak, Maurice		Author	20	65			Writer & Illustrator of Many Children's Books
Senechal, Michel		Entertainment	5			25	Opera
Senior, Brigadier Ronald Henry	1904-1988	Military	25				World War II British general
Senn, Nicholas		Science	35		80		Physician. Spanish American War
Sennett, Mack	1880-1960	Entertainment	225	475		591	Historic DS 4,500
Sensenbrenner Jr., F. James S		Congress	10			15	Member U.S. Congress
SeppSnen, Esko Olavi		Political	10			15	Member European Parliament

NAME	DATE	CATEGORY	SIG	LS/DS	ALS	SP	COMMENTS
Sergeant, John		Celebrity	10	20	35		
Sergeant, John	1779-1852	Congress	65	85	135		Rep. PA. ALS/Cont 1600
Sergievsky, Boris		Aviation	75			150	
Sergison-Brooke, Lt. Gen. B. N.	1880-1967	Military	25				World War II British general
Serkin, Rudolf	1903-1991	Entertainment	40	130	155	162	Austr.-Born Piano Virtuoso, AMusQS 50-175
Serkis, Andy		Entertainment				50	Entertainment
Serling, Rod	1924-1975	Author-Entertain.	116	250	375	340	Creator 'Twilight Zone'. MGM DS 425
Serpico, Frank		Law	10	20	45	20	Undercover Detective-Hero
Serrano, José E. S.		Congress	10			15	Member U.S. Congress
Serurier, Jean M. P., Count		Fr. Revolution	50	145	215		Marshal of Napoleon
Service, Robert W.	1874-1958	Author	75		235	400	Canadian Poet, Author, Versifier
Sessions, Jeff		Senate	10			15	United States Senate (R - AL)
Sessions, John		Celebrity	10			15	comedian
Sessions, Pete S		Congress	10			15	Member U.S. Congress
Sessions, Roger		Composer	25	45	203		Pulitzer, AMusQS 250
Sessions, William L.		Government	25	75		30	Dir. FBI
Seton-Thompson, Ernest	1860-1946	Author	75	115	216	180	Co-Fnd. Boy Scouts of Am. Wild Life Stories. Illustr
Setzer, Brian		Entertainment				35	Singer. Brian Setzer Orchestra.
Seuss, Dr. (Theodore Geisel)*	1904-1992	Author	135	345	425	530	Orig. Sketch 500-3000., Print S 300, signed FDC 540
Severance, Joan	1904-1991	Entertainment	5			25	Nude Pin-Up S 85
Severeid, Eric	1912-1992	Journalist	15			40	TV-Radio Anchor & Sr. Commentator/Cronkite
Severeid, Susanne		Model	4			15	Pin-Up SP 20, Actress
Severinson, Doc		Entertainment	6	8	25	25	Trumpet, Big Band
Sevez, Lt. Gen. Francois-A-L	1891-1948	Military	20				World War II French general
Sevier, John	1745-1815	Revolutionary War	525	1350	2100		Hero of Battle of King's Mt. Historical DS 3,750
Sewall, David		Revolutionary War	20	50	110		Jurist, Patriot, Justice Peace
Sewall, Samuel	1652-1730	Colonial America	275	1068	1300		Salem Witchcraft Trials
Sewall, Samuel	1757-1814	Senate/Congress	25		60		Rep. MA 1796. MA Chief Justice
Seward, Frederick Wm.	1830-1915	Cabinet	30	48	80		Ass't Sec'y State
Seward, William H.	1801-1872	Cabinet	53	180	292	745	Lincoln's Sec'y State. LS/Re Assassination 1,750
Sewell, Stephen		Jurist	125	690			Am. Chief Justice 1752-1760
Sewell, William J.	1835-1901	Civil War	30	65	90		Union Gen., U.S. Sen. NJ
Sex Pistols		Music		435		250	Rock
Sexton, Anne	1928-1974	Author	65	420			Am. Poet. 1967 Pulitzer. Suicidal Breakdown '55
Sexton, Dr. Ralph Jr.		Clergy	8			12	television evangelist
Sexton, Dr. Ralph Sr.		Clergy	8			12	author, longtime evangelist
Sexton, Walton R.		Military	10	30	45	30	Adm. US Navy. WW II
Seyffradt, Lt. Gen. Hendrik A.	1872-1943	Military	20				World War II Dutch general
Seymour, Anne		Entertainment	10			20	
Seymour, George F., Bishop		Clergy	25	25	40		
Seymour, Horatio	1810-1886	Governor	30	60	80		Civil War Gov. NY. Pres. Candidate
Seymour, Jane		Entertainment	15			48	Br. Actress.
Seymour, Stephanie		Entertainment	20			62	Model-Actress
Seymour, Truman	1824-1891	Civil War	64	115	292		Union General. At Ft. Sumter When Surrendered
Seyss-Inquart, Artur von	1892-1946	Military	150				Nazi Brute. War Criminal

NAME	DATE	CATEGORY	SIG	LS/DS	ALS	SP	COMMENTS
Shabazz, Attallah		Celebrity	10			15	motivational speaker
Shackelford, James Murrell	1827-1909	Civil War	45	84			Union general
Shackelford, Ted		Entertainment	5			15	
Shackleton, Ernest H., Sir	1874-1922	Explorer	450	725	900	900	Br. Antarctic Explore., AQS 2415-4370
Shadegg, John B. S		Congress	10			15	Member U.S. Congress
Shaffer, Paul		Entertainment	5			15	
Shaffer, Peter L.		Author	10	20	35	15	
Shafter, William R.	1835-1906	Civil War	30	65	104	150	Union Gen. MOH. Indian Fighter
Shaftesbury, A.A.C. 7th Earl	1801-1885	Reformer	25	80	160		Politician, M.P., Statesman, Social Reformer
Shah, Zahir		Royalty	50				King Afghanistan
Shahn, Ben		Artist	55	150	240	145	Am. Painter-Graphic Artist
Shain, Edith		Celebrity				138	Nursein Famous VJ Day photo, w/ Muscarello 350
Shakira		Entertainment				55	singer
Shakur, Tupac	1971-1996	Entertainment	125			188	Assassinated rapper/actor
Shalamar		Entertainment	12	15	60	50	
Shaler, Alexander	1827-1911	Civil War	42	55	78		Union General. MOH
Shalikashvili, John		Military	10	25		20	Chm. Joint Chiefs of Staff
Shamir, Yitzhak		Head of State	25	95	105	125	7th Prime Minister Israel
Shamroy, Leon		Entertainment	20				Director, Cinematographer. AA
Shandling, Gary	1949-	Entertainment	15			42	Comedian. TV Emmy Winner
Shannon, Del		Entertainment	35			80	Country Music
Shannon, Wilson		Governor	25	65	100		Kansas Peacemaker 1870
Shapely, Harlow	1885-1972	Science	20	80			Noted for work on Photometry & Spectroscopy
Shapiro, Harry		Artist	10	25	45		
Shapiro, Karl		Author	10	30	70	20	
Shapiro, Robert		Law		15		20	O.J. Simpson Trial Attorney
Shapland, Maj. Gen. John Dee	1897-1971	Military	25				World War II British general
Shapley, Alan		Military	10	35	50		
Shapley, Harlow	1885-1972	Science	35	90	150		Astronomer. Dir. Harvard Observ.
Shapp, Milton J.		Governor	10	20			Governor PA
Sharan, Shri Chakradhar		Head of State	15	35		75	Pres. India
Sharett, Moshe (Shertok)	1894-1965	Head of State	50		325		Israeli Prime Minister
Sharif, Omar		Entertainment	15	25	60	52	Egyptian Actor-Champion Tournament Bridge
Sharkey, Ray		Entertainment	7	22		25	
Sharman, Helen		Astronaut		55		45	First British Astronaut in Space Aboard A Soyuz
Sharnova, Sonia		Entertainment	10			25	Am. Contralto
Sharon, Ariel		Military	25	65	125	80	Israeli General, PM
Sharon, William		Senate-Business	45	110	200		Senator NV, Banker & Financier
Sharp, Jacob Hunter	1833-1907	Civil War	110				Confederate general
Sharp, Maj. Gen. William F.	1885-1947	Military	30				World War II U.S. general
Sharp, U. S. Grant		Military	10	25	35	15	
Sharp, William		Artist	15	40	105		
Sharpe, George H.	1828-1900	Civil War	30	45			Union Gen., 120th New York
Sharpe, Karen		Entertainment	4	6		8	
Sharpe, William, Dr.		Economist	22	30		25	Nobel Enconomics 1990

NAME	DATE	CATEGORY	SIG	LS/DS	ALS	SP	COMMENTS
Sharpton, Al, Rev.		Clergy	20			35	
Shatner, William		Entertainment	12	15		55	Star Trek SP 75
Shaud, Grant		Entertainment	10			30	Murphy Brown
Shaunessy, Charles		Entertainment	5	6	15	15	
Shavelson, Melville		Entertainment	5	10		25	
Shaver, Helen		Entertainment	10			25	
Shaw, Andrew J.		Celebrity	10	20			Explorer and Musician
Shaw, Anna Howard	1847-1919	Women's Rights	35	80	175		Physician, Suffragist, Clergy
Shaw, Artie		Entertainment	25			60	Big Band Leader-Clarinetist
Shaw, Bernard		Journalist	10			25	TV Broadcast Journalist
Shaw, Brewster H.		Astronaut	6			15	
Shaw, Clay		History	45	437			acquitted in conspiracy to assassinate Pres. JFK
Shaw, Elizabeth		Entertainment	10	20			Noted Actress (Ohio)
Shaw, Eugene Clay, Jr.		Congress	10			15	Member U.S. Congress
Shaw, George Bernard	1856-1950	Author	245	725	894	1495	Ir. Playwright, Critic. Nobel Prize. FDC 500
Shaw, Irwin	1913-1984	Author	20	40	65	50	Am. Novelist, Short Story Writer
Shaw, Lemuel	1781-1861	Revolutionary War	30	75	140		Chf. Justice MA Supreme Court
Shaw, Leslie M.	1848-1932	Cabinet	30	35	50		Sec'y Treasury 1902
Shaw, Robert	1916-1999	Entertainment	32			122	Conductor Robert Shaw Chorale
Shaw, Suzanne		Celebrity	10			15	media/TV personality
Shawn, Dick		Entertainment	40			100	
Shawn, Ted		Entertainment	45			100	Am. Dancer-Choreographer
Shay, John		Entertainment	4	6		10	
Shayne, Robert		Entertainment	10			30	
Shays, Christopher S		Congress	10			15	Member U.S. Congress
Shays, Daniel	1747-1825	History		747			Led Shay's rebellion
Shazar, Zalman		Head of State	20			60	Israel
Shea, George Beverly		Clergy	15	20	25	30	Singing Evangelist
Shea, John		Entertainment	4			15	Actor
Shea, William A.		Business	5	20	40	10	
Shear, Rhonda		Entertainment	4			10	TV Personality
Shearer, Brigadier Eric James	1892-1980	Military	28				World War II British general
Shearer, Harry		Entertainment	15			25	actor
Shearer, Moira		Entertainment	50		70	85	Ballet. 'TheRed Shoes'
Shearer, Norma	1902-1983	Entertainment	84	202	293	255	AA. Bull Orig. SP 650
Shearing, George		Entertainment	20			45	Jazz Pianist
Shears, Maj. Gen. Philip James	1888-1972	Military	28				World War II British general
Sheedy, Ally		Entertainment	10	15		35	
Sheehan, John		Entertainment	10				Character Actor
Sheen, Charlie		Entertainment	10	15		48	
Sheen, Fulton J.	1895-1979	Clergy-TV Star	40	60	95	75	Archbishop Rochester, NY. Television Personality
Sheen, Martin		Entertainment	9	45		50	AA, The West Wing
Sheffer, Chris		Entertainment	6	8	15	15	
Sheffer, Craig		Entertainment	10			20	actor
Sheffield, Johnny		Entertainment	10			29	As Child Played Tarzan's Son

NAME	DATE	CATEGORY	SIG	LS/DS	ALS	SP	COMMENTS
Shehan, Lawrence J., Cardinal		Clergy	35	45	50	60	
Sheilds, Mark		Celebrity	10			15	political celebrity
Sheinberg, Sheila Dr.		Celebrity	10			15	motivational speaker
Shekoni, Judith		Entertainment	10			20	Actress
Shelby, Isaac	1750-1826	Revolutionary War	300	339	550		Officer VA Militia. 1st Gov. KY
Shelby, Joseph O. (WD)	1830-1897	Civil War	450				CSA Gen.
Shelby, Joseph O.	1830-1897	Civil War	385	828	1250	2200	CSA General
Shelby, Richard		Senate	10			15	United States Senate (R - AL)
Sheldon, Charles M.		Clergy	20	35	50	40	
Sheldon, Sidney		Author	5	15	25	15	Am. Novelist
Shelley, Charles Miller	1833-1907	Civil War	125	977			Confederate general
Shelley, Mary Wollstonecraft	1797-1851	Author	525	1050	1750		Frankenstein
Shelley, Percy Bysshe		Author	1060	2500	4375		ALS/Content 14,000
Shelton, Deborah		Entertainment	8	9		20	Pin-Up SP 30, Miss USA
Shenkenberg, Marcus		Celebrity	10			15	model
Shepard, Alan B.	1923-1998	Astronaut	56	246		215	1st Am. In Space. Mercury 7 Astro., Moonwalker
Shepard, Ernest Howard		Illustrator	45	184			Illustrator for 'Winnie the Pooh', signed drwg 1840
Shepard, Isaac Fitzgerald	1816-1889	Civil War	35	60	90		Union general
Shepherd, Ben		Entertainment	6			25	Music. Bass, Vocals 'Soundgarden'
Shepherd, Cybill		Entertainment	10	25		45	actress
Shepherd, William M.		Astronaut	5			15	
Shepis, Tiffany		Entertainment	5			15	Actress. Pin-Up 22
Shepley, George Foster	1819-1878	Civil War	52	70	110		Union general
Sheppard, Dick		Clergy	25	35	50	30	
Sheppard, Morris		Senator/Congress	10	20		15	Rep., Sen. TX. Author 18th Amend.
Sheppard, Sam		Celebrity					acquitted murder suspect AQS 1035
Shera, Mark		Entertainment	5			20	
Sheridan, Ann		Entertainment	35			88	40's Oomph Girl
Sheridan, Jim		Celebrity	10			15	film industry
Sheridan, Nicollette		Entertainment	15			40	Pin-Up SP 60
Sheridan, Philip H. (WD)	1831-1888	Civil War	261	1050	2675	1892	Union Gen.
Sheridan, Philip H.	1831-1888	Civil War	123	276	425		Cavalry
Sheridan, Richard Brinsley	1751-1816	Author	65	120	370		Ir. Dramatist, Politician. 1751-1816
Sherlock, Nancy		Astronaut	7			20	
Sherman, Brad S		Congress	10			15	Member U.S. Congress
Sherman, Forrest P.		Military	20	50	95	50	Adm. WWII.Ch. Naval Operationsl
Sherman, Francis Trowbridge	1825-1905	Civil War	45	75	100		Union general
Sherman, Frederick C.		Military	35	45	70	50	Adm. Cmdr Carrier Lexington
Sherman, George		Entertainment	10			25	
Sherman, James S.	1855-1912	Vice President	60	140	210	200	Taft VP. MOC
Sherman, John	1823-1900	Cabinet-Senate	62	140	213	150	Sherman Anti-Trust Act, TLS/cont 600,. RR ALS 1450
Sherman, Richard and Robert		Composer	40	60	100		AMusQS 150
Sherman, Roger	1721-1793	Revolutionary War	205	573	975		Signed All 4 Major Fed. Papers
Sherman, Thomas West		Civil War	30	55	85		Union General
Sherman, William T. (WD)	1820-1891	Civil War	350	1500	4500	2426	Content ALS's go up to & incl.50,000+

NAME	DATE	CATEGORY	SIG	LS/DS	ALS	SP	COMMENTS
Sherman, William T.	1820-1891	Civil War	294	525	702	2117	Union Gen.War. Content ALS 7500- 17,500
Sherriff, Robert C.	1896-1975	Author	45		140	80	Playwright, Novelist, Screenwriter
Sherrill, Carolyn		Author	8			12	children
Sherwood, (Mary) Martha	1775-1851	Author	10	15	35		Br. Author Juvenile Tales
Sherwood, Bobby		Entertainment	6	8	15	15	
Sherwood, Don S		Congress	10			15	Member U.S. Congress
Sherwood, Isaac R.		Senate/Congress	10	15		20	Rep.OH 1873
Sherwood, Percy		Composer	25			60	Ger. Pianist. AMusQS 75
Sherwood, Robert E.	1896-1955	Author-Cabinet	30	55	80	75	Am. Plays, Speeches FDR, Pulitzers
Sherwood, Samuel	1779-1862	Cogress	20	35	50		Rep.NY 1813
Sheur, Barry		Celebrity	10			15	medical expert
Shields, Arthur		Entertainment	10			25	Actor-Brother Barry Fitzgerald
Shields, Brooke	1965-	Entertainment	10	12	35	45	Actress. Films & TV
Shields, James	1806-1879	Civil War	42	65	80		Challenged Lincoln to a Duel
Shields, Mark		Celebrity	10			15	media/TV personality
Shigeta, James		Entertainment	6	8	15	20	
Shillaber, Benjamin P.	1814-1890	Author		50	110		Humorist-Editor
Shimkus, John S		Congress	10			15	Member U.S. Congress
Shimmerman, Armin		Entertainment	15			35	Star Trek
Shinn, Conrad S.		Aviation		35		25	Landed 1st Plane at South Pole
Shinokura, General	d. 1945	Military	27				World War II Japanese general
Shipman, Nina		Entertainment	4			15	Hawaiian Leading Lady
Shippen, Edward		Revolutionary War	45	95	165		Ch. Justice PA, Statesman
Shipstad, Henrik	1881-1960	Congress	5	20		25	Senator MN 1922
Shiras, George, Jr.		Supreme Court	90	250	375		
Shire, David		Composer	15			30	Oscar winner
Shire, Talia		Entertainment	15			30	
Shirer, William L.		Author	15	40		25	News Commentator. 'Berlin Diary' S 50
Shirley, Anne		Entertainment	15	15	35	30	
Shirley, William	1693-1771	Colon'l Gov. MA	165	350	885		Cmdr.-in-Chief, Explorer, Colonial Gov. MA
Shivers, Allan		Governor	12			30	Governor TX
Shockley, William, Dr.		Science	35	144	165	82	Nobel Physics 1956. Transistor, signed drwg 225
Shoemaker, Eugene M. & Carolyn		Science	45			75	Discovered Meteor Crater
Shoemaker, Lazarus D.		Senate/Congress	10	20		15	Rep. PA 1871
Shoemaker, Vaughn*		Cartoonist	10			75	Pulitzer Prize Editorial Cartoonist.John Q. Public
Shoemaker, William L.		Author	5	8	15		
Shoen, Sam		Business	5	15	35	25	
Shoma, William		Aviation	15	32	50	40	ACE, WW II, CMH
Shoop, Pamela Susan		Entertainment	5	6	15	15	
Shor, Bernard Toots		Business	30	45	75	35	NY Restaurateur. Celebrity Host
Shore, Dinah	1917-1994	Entertainment	15	31	40	52	Singer-Actress-TV Host. Golf Sponsor
Shore, Pauley		Entertainment	10			20	actor
Shore, Roberta		Entertainment	7			25	Actress. Movies-TV Disney Star. 'The Virginian'
Short, Bobby		Entertainment	5			32	Nightclub Pianist-Vocalist
Short, Lt. Gen. Walter C.	1880-1949	Military	30				World War II U.S. general

NAME	DATE	CATEGORY	SIG	LS/DS	ALS	SP	COMMENTS
Short, Martin		Entertainment	15			50	
Shortridge, Samuel	1861-1952	Congress	10	20			Senator CA 1920
Shostakovich, Dmitri	1906-1975	Composer	306	704	1599	1920	ALS/Content3,200, 4000, AMusQS 750-2500
Shoumatoff, Elizabeth		Artist	35	45	75		Painting FDR Portrait At Time Of Death.Repro S 295
Shoup, David M.	1904-1983	Military	25	40	80	95	MOH Winning Cmdr. 2nd Marines. Commandant
Shoup, Francis, A.	1834-1896	Civil War	115		506		CSA Gen.
Shoup, George L.	1836-1904	Congress	12	20	35		1st Gov. ID, Senator ID 1890
Show, Grant		Entertainment	6			32	Actor
Showalter, Max		Entertainment	6	10	15	15	
Shower, Kathy		Entertainment	5				Actress-Model.Nude SP 60
Shrimpton, Jean		Entertainment	5	6	15	10	
Shriner, Herb		Entertainment	4	5		15	
Shriner, Wil		Entertainment	10			20	actor
Shriver, Eunice Kennedy		Celebrity	15			35	Sister JFK, Wife Sargent Shriver
Shriver, Loren J.		Astronaut	7			28	
Shriver, Maria		Journalist	6			20	Broadcast Journalist
Shriver, Sargent		White House	4	10	25	20	Created Job Corps
Shroyer, Sonny		Entertainment	3			7	
Shrum, Cal		Entertainment	4			25	Cowboy Actor
Shubert, John		Entertainment	5	9		15	
Shubert, Lee	1873-1953	Business	20	70	85	40	Theatrical Mgr.-Producer
Shubrick, William B.		Military	25				Commander Frigate Constitution, War 1812
Shue, Andrew		Entertainment	8			52	Actor
Shue, Elizabeth	1963-	Entertainment	10			52	Actress
Shugart, Alan		Inventor	10	20		20	Computer Disk Drive
Shulman, Ellen L.		Astronaut	6			25	
Shulman, Max		Writer	10			20	Creator Dobie Gillis
Shultz, George P.		Cabinet	15	25	40	35	Sec'y State, Labor, Treasury
Shum, Mina		Celebrity	10			15	film industry
Shuman, Charles B.		Celebrity	3	7	15	5	
Shuman, Eleanor		Celebrity	50	60	70	75	Titanic survivor Deceased 3/98
Shumard, Bob		Military	25			50	Enola Gay asst flight engineer
Shuster, Bill S		Congress	10			15	Member U.S. Congress
Shuster, W. Morgan		Business	10	15	35	15	Chm. Appleton-Century-Crofts
Sibelius, Jan	1865-1957	Composer	313	680	1625	1142	Fin. Symph. AMusQS 1600-1850-3500, SPc 1115
Sibert, Maj. Gen. Franklin C.	1891-1980	Military	30				World War II U.S. general
Sibley, Henry Hastings	1811-1891	Civil War	45				Union General. Indian fighter. First Gov. of Minn.
Sibley, Henry Hopkins	1816-1886	Civil War	102	316	474		CSA Gen., Indian Fighter, Inventor of the Sibley tent
Sicé, Gen Marie-Eugène-Adolphe	1885-1957	Military	20				World War II French general
Sichrovsky, Peter		Political	10			15	Member European Parliament
Sickles, Daniel E.	1819-1914	Civil War	80	198	253	437	Union General, MOH winner
Sickles, Noel*		Cartoonist	20			175	Scorchy
Siddons, F. Scott, Mrs.		Entertainment	25			50	Vintage Actress
Siddons, Sarah Kemble	1755-1831	Entertainment	175		850		18th-19th Cent. Br. Tragedienne
Sidey, Hugh		Celebrity	10			15	media/TV personality

NAME	DATE	CATEGORY	SIG	LS/DS	ALS	SP	COMMENTS
Sidgwick, Henry	1838-1900	Philosopher			125		
Sidney, George		Entertainment	15			35	Film Director
Sidney, Robert, Sir	1563-1626	Miltary	150	920			Poet Brother of Sir Philip. Earl of Essex
Sidney, Sylvia		Entertainment	10	15	25	35	Vintage Actress from 30's. Still Active
Siegbahn, Kai Manne		Science	30	55	100	90	Nobel Physics 1981
Siegel & Shuster*		Cartoonist	150			900	Superman
Siegel, Bernie		Celebrity	10			15	medical expert
Siegel, Don		Entertainment	15	30		40	Film Director
Siegel, Jerry	1915-1996	Entertainment	10	25		15	One of Creators. Superman
Siegel, Joel		Journalist	4			15	TV Film Reviewer
Siegfried & Roy		Entertainment	10			50	Animal Trainers
Siegmeister, Elie		Composer	25	40	80	60	
Siems, Margarethe		Entertainment	45			110	Opera
Sienkiewicz, Henryk	1846-1916	Author			350		Polish Writer. Nobel. Quo Vadis
Siepi, Cesare		Entertainment	15			65	Opera. Self-Taught Bass
Sierra, Gregory		Entertainment	4	4	9	9	
Sierra, Margarita		Entertainment	3	3	6	6	
Sievers, Wolfram		Military	46				Asst. to Himmler
Sigall, Joseph		Artist	100	190	385		Pres. Portraits & Eur. Royalty
Sigel, Franz	1824-1902	Civil War	41	109	174		Union General
Sighele, Mietta		Entertainment	10			30	Opera
Sigler, Jamie Lynn		Entertainment				35	Meadow Soprano
Sigler, Kim		Governor	5	15		10	Governor MI
Signac, Paul	1863-1935	Artist	110	179	464		Fr. Watercolor Land & Seascapes. Neo-Impressionist
Signoret, Simone	1921-1985	Entertainment	52			168	Oscar winner
Sigourney, Lydia Howard H.	1791-1865	Author		76	175		Most Famous Lady Writer in Am 1830's. Professional
Sigsbee, Charles D.		Military	35	105	165	75	Capt. USN The Maine
Sihanouk, Norodom, Prince		Head of State	50	95	155	125	Cambodia
Sikes, Cynthia		Entertainment	5			15	Pin-up SP 25
Sikking, James B.		Entertainment	6	8	15	20	
Sikorsky, Igor I.	1889-1972	Aviation	75	135	180	251	Designed & Built 1st Helicopter. Aviation HOF
Silhouette, Etienne de	1709-1767	Cabinet		950			Fr. Controller Gen., Financier, Silhouette so Named
Silja, Anja		Entertainment	15			40	Opera
Sill, Joshua Woodrow	1831-1862	Civil War	125	440			Union general, KIA Stone River TN
Sill, Susan		Astronaut	7			25	
Silla, Felix		Entertainment	5			15	Actor. 'Addams Family'
Silliman, Benjamin	1816-1885	Science	30	52	125		Am. Chemist. Editor. Professor
Silliman, Gold Selleck	1732-1790	Revolutionary War	70	142			Colonel & Brig. General
Sills, Beverly		Entertainment	15		25	33	Am. Soprano
Sills, Milton	1882-1930	Entertainment	30	40	75	80	Leading Man of Silent Films
Siloti, Alexander		Composer	50		225	75	Pianist, Conductor
Silva, Henry		Entertainment	10			25	actor
Silva, Jose		Celebrity	10			15	financial expert
Silva-Herzog, Jesus		Celebrity	10			15	political celebrity
Silver, Abba Hillel		Zionist	15	50			Zionist Leader

NAME	DATE	CATEGORY	SIG	LS/DS	ALS	SP	COMMENTS
Silver, Joe	1921-1989	Entertainment	10			20	Actor
Silver, Ron		Entertainment	15			30	Actor-Director
Silverberg, D.M. 'Dave'		Science	8			15	Founder of Aestiva, creator of webcentric HTML/OS
Silverheels, Jay		Entertainment	175			425	Tonto
Silverman, Fred		Business	3	9	20	10	Broadcasting Executive
Silverman, Jonathan		Entertainment	5			35	Actor
Silverman, Robert		Entertainment	10	15		45	Contemporary Pianist
Silvers, Phil	1912-1985	Entertainment	32	60	125	88	Am. Comedian-Actor. 'Sgt Bilko'
Silverstone, Alicia	1976-	Entertainment	10	35		58	Actress
Silvester, Maj. Gen. Lindsay M.	1889-1963	Military	30				World War II U.S. general
Sim, Alastair	1900-1976	Entertainment		90		150	Br. Actor
Simenon, Georges	1903-1989	Author	65	100	275	125	Fr-Belg. Creator Inspector Maigret
Simeon II		Royalty	80				King of Bulgaria 1937
Simeon, Charles		Clergy	45		75		
Simmons, E.H.H.		Business	25	40			Pres. NY Stock Exchange
Simmons, Gene		Entertainment				70	Kiss
Simmons, Jaason		Entertainment	10			20	actor
Simmons, Jean		Entertainment	8	10	22	35	Pert Brit. Actress. Child to 'Spartacus' etc.
Simmons, Maj. Gen. Frank Keith	1888-1952	Military	25				World War II British general
Simmons, Richard		Entertainment	15			40	Actor
Simmons, Richard		Entertainment	5			15	Diet & Aerobics
Simmons, Rob S		Congress	10			15	Member U.S. Congress
Simms, Ginny		Entertainment				22	Band Vocalist
Simms, James Phillip	1837-1887	Civil War	95	150			Confederate general
Simms, William G.		Author	35	100	250		Lawyer, Pro-Slavery Editor
Simms, John Gill	1818-1898	Civil War	40	63	95		Member Conf. Congress
Simon and Garfunkel		Entertainment	40			167	
Simon, Carly		Entertainment	20			55	Singer-Composer
Simon, Claude		Author	150				Nobel Literature 1985
Simon, Herbert A.		Science	20	35	50	25	Nobel Economics
Simon, Jules	1814-1896	Head of State		45	110		Premier of France. Orator. Prof. Philosophy, Sorbonne
Simon, Neil		Author	45	75	150	75	Playwright, Screenwriter
Simon, Norton		Industrialist	15	35	65	25	Norton Simon, Inc., Philanthropy
Simon, Paul Martin		Congress	5			10	Repr., Senator IL
Simon, Paul		Composer	20	45		100	Entertainer, songwriter
Simon, Simone	1911-	Entertainment	20			56	Pouty Fr. Actress
Simon, William E.		Cabinet	5	15	25	20	Sec'y Treasury
Simon, William		Celebrity	10			15	financial expert
Simonds, Lt. Gen. Guy Granville	1903-1974	Military	20				World War II Canadian general
Simoneau, Leopold		Entertainment	5			25	Opera
Simpson, Alan		Congress	5	10		15	Senator WY
Simpson, Brian		Political	10			15	Member European Parliament
Simpson, Carole		Celebrity	10			15	media/TV personality
Simpson, Gen Sir Frank Ernest W.	1899-1986	Military	25				World War II British general
Simpson, James H.	1813-1883	Civil War	30	70			Union Gen.

NAME	DATE	CATEGORY	SIG	LS/DS	ALS	SP	COMMENTS
Simpson, James Y., Sir		Science	35	95	385		Scot.1st Obstetric Ether Use
Simpson, Junior		Celebrity	10			15	comedian
Simpson, Louis		Author	20			65	Am. Poet
Simpson, Maj. Gen. Hamilton W.	1895-1986	Military	25				World War II British general
Simpson, Maj. Gen. Noel	1907-1982	Military	25				World War II British general
Simpson, Matthew	1811-1884	Clergy	90				Methodist Bishop. Lincoln Eulogy
Simpson, Michael K. S		Congress	10			15	Member U.S. Congress
Simpson, O.J.		Celebrity				45	actor, murder suspect
Simpson, Russell		Entertainment	50			120	Grapes of Wrath, Meet John Doe
Simpson, William H.	1888-1980	Military	40	90	140	100	Gen. WW II
Sims, William S.	1858-1936	Military	30	60	85	75	Adm. USN WW I, Pulitzer Author
Sinatra, Frank	1915-1998	Entertainment	227	533		741	Actor-Singer AA, MGM DS 875.
Sinatra, Nancy		Entertainment	5	30	20	15	Pin-Up SP 25
Sinclair, Harry F.		Business	140	175	350	200	Teapot Dome
Sinclair, Maj. Gen. Sir John Alex.	1897-1977	Military	25				World War II British general
Sinclair, Upton	1878-1968	Author	58	74	152	125	Am. Writer-Socialist Politician, Novelist
Sinding, Christian A.		Composer	45	120	210		Symphonies, Concertos, Sonatas
Singer, Bryan		Celebrity	10			15	film industry
Singer, Isaac Bashevis	1904-1991	Author	40	200	300	175	Nobel Lit.'78. Polish Passport 1800, US 1000
Singer, Isaac M.	1811-1875	Inventor	575		2500		Singer Sewing Machine
Singer, Marc		Entertainment	10	12		30	
Singlaub, John K.		Military	35	50	75	50	General WW II
Singleton, Penny		Entertainment	5	20	15	25	'Blondie' (Dagwood & Blondie) Popular 40's Films
Singleton, Valerie		Celebrity	10			15	television presenter
Sinise, Gary		Entertainment	15	20	30	48	Oscar winner
Sinnhuber, Gen. of Art. Johann	1887-1979	Military	25				World War II German general
Sinopoli, Giuseppe		Conductor	5			35	
Sioli, Franco		Entertainment	5			15	Opera
Siple, Paul A.		Aviation	22	45			Explorer, Geographer
Sirhan, Sirhan		Assassin	990	1200			Assassinated Sen. Robt. Kennedy
Sirica, John J.	1904-1993	Jurist	20	35		50	Watergate Judge. Respected Federal Judge
Sirico, Tony		Entertainment				50	Pauly Walnuts, Soprano's
Siritis, Marina		Entertainment	10			20	actress
Sirk, Don		Entertainment	65				Film Director
Siroky, Villiam		Head of State	50				Premier Czech.
Sirola, Joe		Entertainment	10			20	actor
Sirtis, Marina		Entertainment	10			35	Actress. Star Trek
Siskel, Gene	1947-1999	Entertainment	12			20	Film Critic. Siskel & Ebert
Sisley, Alfred	1839-1899	Artist	150	400	1193		Fr. Impressionist.Landscape Painter
Sissle, Noble		Entertainment	25			50	Big Band Leader-Arranger
Sissons, Peter		Celebrity	10			15	news reader
Sisto, Jeremy		Entertainment				40	Billy Chenowith, Six Feet Under
Sitgreaves, John		Revolutionary War	30	75	145		Officer. Continental Congress
Sitting Bull (T. Iyotake)		Indian Leader	6817			15000	Sioux Indian Leader
Sitwell, Edith, Dame	1887-1964	Author	50	110	129	660	Br. Poet, Critic, Novelist

NAME	DATE	CATEGORY	SIG	LS/DS	ALS	SP	COMMENTS
Sitwell, Francis Osbert	1892-1969	Author	25		126		
Sitwell, Maj Gen Hervey Degge W	1896-1973	Military	25				World War II British general
Sitwell, Osbert, Sir	1892-1969	Author	35	70	148		Playwright, Novelist
Sixty Minutes (all)		Entertainment	25			45	
Sizoo, Joseph R.		Clergy	20	25	35		
Sjöstedt, Jonas		Political	10			15	Member European Parliament
Skaggs, Ricky		Country Music	10			20	
Skala, Lilia		Entertainment	10	15	25	30	
Skelly, William Grove		Business	320				Founder Skelly Oil, Financier
Skelton, Ike S		Congress	10			15	Member U.S. Congress
Skelton, Red	1913-1997	Entertainment	35	53	60	72	Film-TV Comedian.Sm.Original Clown Painting S 395
Skerrit, Tom		Entertainment	8	18	20	30	Actor.Emmy Awards. DS re 'Top Gun' 150
Skinner, B. F.		Author	20	30	44	75	Behavioral Psychology-Theorist
Skinner, Cornelia Otis	1901-1950	Entertainment	10	40	50	28	Actress, Monologuist, Author
Skinner, Cortlandt	1728-1799	Military	40	85	155		Born NJ. Loyalist General
Skinner, Frank		Celebrity	10			15	comedian
Skinner, Maj Gen Frank Hollamby	1897-1979	Military	28				World War II British general
Skinner, Otis	1858-1942	Entertainment	53	45	50	65	Vintage Stage Star
Skinner, Peter William		Political	10			15	Member European Parliament
Skinner, Samuel K.		Cabinet	10	20			Sec'y Transportation
Skinner, Stella		Artist	25	40	75		
Skipworth, Alison		Entertainment	15	15	30	25	
Skorzeny, Otto	1908-1975	Military	178	265	540	500	Nazi SS Officer & Adventurer
Skouras, Spyros	1893-1971	Business	15			175	Fndr-Pres-Chm 20th Century Fox
Skovhus, Boje		Entertainment	10			25	Opera
Slack, Freddie		Bandleader				45	
Slack, James Richard	1818-1881	Civil War	35	65			Union general
Slack, William Yarnell	1816-1862	Civil War	393	442			Confederate general
Slade, Chris		Entertainment	6			25	Music. Drummer 'AC/DC'
Slade, William	1786-1859	Congress	12				Repr. VT, Gov. VT
Slater, Christian	1969-	Entertainment	10			48	Actor
Slater, Helen		Entertainment	8	15	30	50	
Slattery, Tony		Celebrity	10			15	comedian
Slaughter, Frank G.		Author	8	15	35	10	
Slaughter, James Edwin	1827-1901	Civil War	290				Confederate general
Slaughter, Louise McIntosh S		Congress	10			15	Member U.S. Congress
Slayton, Donald K. 'Deke'		Astronaut	45	75	100	93	Mercury 7 Astro (Deceased) Flight DS 750
Sledd, Patsy		Country Music	4			12	Pin-Up SP 15
Slemmer, Adam Jacoby	1829-1868	Civil War	81	127			Union general
Slepak, Vladimir		Celebrity	10			15	motivational speaker
Slezak, Leo	1873-1946	Entertainment	45	60		125	Great Austrian Tenor, Opera. SPc 75
Slezak, Walter		Entertainment	15			35	
Slick, Gary		Celebrity	10			15	political celebrity
Slick, Gracie		Entertainment	26			48	Jefferson Airplane
Slidell, John	1793-1871	Civil War	60	130	195		Statesman, CSA Diplomat

NAME	DATE	CATEGORY	SIG	LS/DS	ALS	SP	COMMENTS
Slim, Fld. Mshl. Wm. Jos. Viscount	1891-1970	Military	40	84	120	60	World War II British general
Sliwa, Curtis		Celebrity	10			20	Founder of Guardians
Sliwa, Lisa		Celebrity	6	15		10	NY Street Protection Group
Sliwinski, Josef		Entertainment	20		100	75	Pol Pianist
Sloan, Alfred P. Jr.	1875-1966	Business	45	95	90	65	Sloan-Kettering Inst. CEO GM. Philanthropist
Sloan, John	1779-1856	Cabinet	20	45	95		Fillmore Treasurer of U.S.
Sloan, John	1871-1951	Artist	85	275	612		Am. Painter, Etcher, Illustrator. 'Ashchan School'
Sloan, Maj. Gen. John E.	1887-1972	Military	30				World War II U.S. general
Sloane, Eric	1905-1985	Artist	25	98			writer, illustrator, painter
Sloane, Everett		Entertainment	30			55	
Sloat, John Drake	1780-1867	Mexican War	45	95	130		Took California from Mexico
Slobodskaya, Olga	1888-1970	Entertainment				125	Russian soprano
Slocum, Henry Warner	1827-1894	Civil War	66	130	215		Union General, Rep. NY
Slough, John P. (WD)		Civil War	160		950		Union Gen. Killed in Gunfight 1867
Slough, John Potts	1829-1867	Civil War	95	160	225		Union general
Small, John Humphrey		Senate/Congress	5		15		Rep. NC 1899
Smallens, Alexander		Conductor	20			50	World Premiere Porgy & Bess
Smallwood, Maj. Gen. Gerard R.	1889-1977	Military	28				World War II British general
Smallwood, Norma		Entertainment	20			50	Miss America 1926
Smallwood, William	1732-1792	Rev War			483		Rev War officer
Smart, Jean		Entertainment	5			15	
Smart, Lt. Gen. Edward K.	1891-1961	Military	20				World War II Australian general
Smashing Pumpkins		Entertainment	45			142	Music. 4 Member Rock Group
Smathers, George A.		Senate/Congress	5		25	15	Rep., Senator FL 1947
Smear, Pat		Entertainment	8			55	Music. Lead Singer 'Foo Fighters'
Smedberg, William	1871-1942	Military		35		40	WW I Gen. Hero of Sp.-Am. War
Smedley, Richard		Entertainment	3	3	6	8	
Smet, Miet		Political	10			15	Member European Parliament
Smetana, Bedrich	1824-1884	Composer	1500		8750		Czech. Operas, Symphonies etc.
Smiley, Delores		Country Music	10			20	
Smilie, Carole		Celebrity	10			15	celebrity model
Smirnoff, Dimitri		Entertainment	30	55	95		Russian Tenor
Smirnoff, Yakov		Entertainment	8			15	
Smith, Adam S		Congress	10			15	Member U.S. Congress
Smith, Adam	1723-1790	Economist	3450				Architect of Br. Political Econ
Smith, Addison T.		Senate/Congress	5	10	15		Rep. ID 1913
Smith, Al*		Cartoonists	15			60	Mutt & Jeff
Smith, Alexis	1921-1993	Entertainment	15	45		35	Warner Bros. Beautiful 40'-50's Leading Lady
Smith, Alfred E.	1873-1944	Governor	40	65	75	75	Presidential Candidate, Gov NY.1st Catholic Nom.
Smith, Andrew Jackson	1815-1897	Civil War	35	70	100		Union general
Smith, Anna Nicole		Entertainment	10			45	Model-Actress.
Smith, Armistead B.		Aviation	10	22	38	28	ACE, WW II, Navy Ace
Smith, Arthur		Celebrity	10			15	comedian
Smith, Ashbel	1805-1886	Civil War	140		615		TX Patriot., Surgeon Gen. TX Rev Army
Smith, Bernie		Entertainment	6	8	15	15	

NAME	DATE	CATEGORY	SIG	LS/DS	ALS	SP	COMMENTS
Smith, Betty		Author	40	60		65	
Smith, Bob		Congress	5			15	MOC OR Agricultural Comm. Chm.
Smith, Brigadier Albert	1896-1959	Military	25				World War II British general
Smith, C. Aubrey		Entertainment	35			80	
Smith, Caleb	1808-1864	Cabinet	38	134	365		Lincoln Attorney General
Smith, Carl		Country Music	5			12	
Smith, Charles E.		Cabinet	15		25	20	P.M. General 1898
Smith, Charles Ferguson	1807-1862	Civil War	95	184			Union general
Smith, Charles M.		Entertainment	10			25	
Smith, Charles M.		Governor	5	15			Governor VT
Smith, Christopher H. S		Congress	10			15	Member U.S. Congress
Smith, Claire		Celebrity	10			15	television presenter
Smith, Connie		Country Music	5			12	
Smith, Cyrus Rowlett	1899-1990	Aviation	40	75		75	American Airlines. Aviation Hall of Fame.Cabinet
Smith, Delia		Celebrity	10			15	Cookery Writer
Smith, Edmund Kirby (WD)	1824-1893	Civil War	390	1040	1460		CSA Gen.
Smith, Edmund Kirby	1824-1893	Civil War	354	668	782		CSA Gen.
Smith, Edward K.	1850-1912	Navy			8995		Capt. Of Ill-Fated 'Titanic'
Smith, Elinor		Aviation	45	100	160	130	
Smith, Elizabeth Oakes		Reformer	90	205	385		Early Supporter Woman Suffrage
Smith, Ellison	1864-1944	Congress	5	25			Sen. SC
Smith, Elmo		Governor	10	25			Governor OR
Smith, Elton		Aviation	15	30			World Helicopter Record '52
Smith, F. E.		Celebrity	36				
Smith, Francis Hopkinson	1838-	Artist	15	20	35		Am. Engineer-Artist-Illustrator
Smith, Francis M. Borax		Business	30	65	95		Founder U.S. Borax Co.
Smith, Frank, Bishop		Clergy	15	20	25	25	
Smith, Frederick W.		Business	15	30	55	20	Fndr., Chm. Federal Express
Smith, General Albert C.	1894-1974	Military	30				World War II U.S. general
Smith, George Washington		Senate/Congress	5	15			Rep. IL 1889
Smith, Gerrit	1797-1874	Senate/Congress	45		175		Abolitionist, Reformer, Rep. NY, Philanthropist
Smith, Giles Alexander	1829-1876	Civil War	45	85			Union general
Smith, Gipsy		Clergy	25	45	75	35	
Smith, Gordon		Congress	5			15	US Senator from Oregon
Smith, Green Clay	1826-1895	Civil War	35	75	110		Union Gen., Congress KY
Smith, Gustavus Adolphus	1820-1885	Civil War	46	64	108		Union general
Smith, H. Allen		Senate/Congress	5	10		10	MOC. CA 1957
Smith, Hamilton		Science	20	30	45	25	Nobel Medicine 1978
Smith, Harry J.		Author	8			12	'World's 13th Greatest Cookbook'
Smith, Harry		Journalist	5	10		15	Broadcast Journalist
Smith, Harsen		Business	3	10	25	10	
Smith, Hedrick		Celebrity	10			15	political celebrity
Smith, Hoke	1855-1931	Cabinet	10	35	70	30	Gov., Sen.GA, Sec'y Int.1911
Smith, Holland M.	1882-1967	Military	40	95			Major General USMC
Smith, Howard K.		Journalist	15			46	TV CBS News Anchor Opposite Huntley-Brinkley

NAME	DATE	CATEGORY	SIG	LS/DS	ALS	SP	COMMENTS
Smith, Howard	1893-1968	Entertainment	25			40	Active Character Actor 40's. 'Death of a Salesman'
Smith, Ian		Head of State	10	20	50	30	South Africa
Smith, Ida B. Wise		Reformer	30	55	95		Temperance Advocate, WCTU
Smith, J. Gregory		Governor	5	15		10	Governor VT
Smith, Jaclyn		Entertainment	9	15	20	30	Actress. A 'Charlie's Angels'. Pin-Up SP 30
Smith, James Argyle	1831-1901	Civil War	95	267			Confederate general
Smith, James C., Sr.		Business	10			20	Westinghouse, Aerospace Division
Smith, James Y.		Governor	35	60			Civil War Gov. RI
Smith, James	1719-1806	Revolutionary War	175	550	3250		Signer Decl. of Indepen.
Smith, James, Jr.	1851-1927	Congress	10	15			Senator NJ 1911
Smith, Joe		Entertainment	15			45	
Smith, John Eugene	1816-1897	Civil War	30		85		Union general
Smith, John N.		Celebrity	10			15	film industry
Smith, John Pye		Clergy	20	25	35		
Smith, Joseph	180518-44	Religious Leader	675	2250			Founder Morman Church
Smith, Julia Holmes, Dr.		Science	90		425		1st Pres.Women's Med. Assoc.
Smith, Kate		Entertainment	30	65	90	75	Clear, Strong-voiced. Introduced God Bless America
Smith, Keely	1932-	Entertainment	10			30	Band Vocalist for Louis Prima. Jazz Specialist
Smith, Kent	1907-	Entertainment	6			15	Harvard Educated Actor. Atypical Hollywood Lead.
Smith, Kevin		Celebrity	10			15	film industry
Smith, L. C.		Business	50	135	240		L.C. Smith Typewriters, Business Machines etc.
Smith, Lamar S. S		Congress	10			15	Member U.S. Congress
Smith, Lt. Gen. Sir Arthur Francis	1890-1977	Military	25				World War II British general
Smith, Maggie		Entertainment	15	25	30	35	Br. AA Winner.'Prime of Miss Jean Brodie'
Smith, Maj. Gen. John P.	1883-1948	Military	30				World War II U.S. general
Smith, Maj. Gen. Sir Cecil Miller	1896-1968	Military	25				World War II British general
Smith, Margaret Chase		Senate/Congress	10	20		20	Columnist, Rep., Sen. ME
Smith, Martha		Entertainment	5			15	
Smith, Martin Luther (WD)		Civil War	130	299	1400		CSA Gen. ALS/Cont.2750
Smith, Martin Luther	1819-1866	Civil War	75	217	240		CSA General
Smith, Matthew		Revolutionary War	25	75			
Smith, Mel		Celebrity	10			15	comedian
Smith, Melancton	1744-1798	Revolutionary War	75	140			Continental Congress
Smith, Melancton	1810-1893	Civil War	58	106	152		Union Adm. Served Under Farragut
Smith, Michael J.		Astronaut	275			325	Challenger
Smith, Mike		Celebrity	10			15	television presenter
Smith, Morgan Lewis	1821-1874	Civil War	35	70	100	335	Union general
Smith, Nels H.F.		Governor	5	10		15	Governor WY
Smith, Nick S		Congress	10			15	Member U.S. Congress
Smith, Penny		Celebrity	10			15	television presenter
Smith, Preston	1823-1863	Civil War	312				Confederate general, KIA Chickamauga
Smith, Richard	1735-1803	Revolutionary War	50	130	250		Continental Congress
Smith, Robert 'Buffalo Bob'		Entertainment	16	20		102	'Howdy Doody'. Early TV Personality.
Smith, Robert H. 'Snuffy'		Aviation	15	30	50	45	ACE, WW II, Flying Tigers
Smith, Robert T.		Aviation	15	30	40	40	ACE, WW II, Flying Tigers

NAME	DATE	CATEGORY	SIG	LS/DS	ALS	SP	COMMENTS
Smith, Robert	1757-1842	Cabinet	55	170	290		Att'y Gen., Sec'y Navy, Sec'y St.
Smith, Rodney 'Gipsy'	1860-1947	Clergy	40	55	75	75	
Smith, Roger		Entertainment	5			20	Actor
Smith, Rolland		Celebrity	10			15	media/TV personality
Smith, Roy L., Bishop		Clergy	20	30	45	30	
Smith, Samuel F.	1752-1839	Revolutionary War	75	175	255		Gen'l, Rep., Sen. MD.
Smith, Samuel Francis	1808-1895	Clergy-Poet	82	396	588	1000	AQS 'America', 4 Stanzas, 1750
Smith, Shawnee		Celebrity				25	Actress
Smith, Shelley		Entertainment	5			10	Pin-Up SP 20
Smith, Stanley		Entertainment	9			25	Stage
Smith, Steve		Astronaut	5			20	
Smith, Susan M.		Playboy Ctrfold	5			10	Pin-Up SP 15
Smith, Sydney*		Cartoonist	30			150	'The Gumps'
Smith, Thomas A.		Military	95	161			Fort Smith Arkansas. General
Smith, Thomas Benton	1838-1923	Civil War	575				Confederate general
Smith, Thomas Church Haskell	1819-1897	Civil War	34	64	92		Union General
Smith, Thomas Kilby	1820-1887	Civil War	54	86	168		Union general
Smith, Tom E.		Business	5	15	30	20	Pres. Food Lion Grocery Chain
Smith, Truman	1791-1884	Senate-Cabinet	10	25	40		Rep., Sen. CT, Sec'y Interior
Smith, W. Angie, Bishop		Clergy	20	25	35	25	
Smith, W. Wallace		Clergy	40	45	60		
Smith, Walter Bedell	1895-1961	Military	45	75	125	80	Gen. WW II, Ambass., Dir. CIA
Smith, Will		Entertainment	10			50	Actor
Smith, William (WD)		Civil War	220		3475		CSA Gen.
Smith, William Duncan	1825-1862	Civil War	280				Confederate general
Smith, William Farrar	1824-1903	Civil War	34	114	188		Union Gen., ALS/cont 795
Smith, William S.	1755-1816	Revolutionary War	50	95	225		Rev. Officer. A Fndr. & Pres. Soc. Of Cincinnati
Smith, William Sidney, Sir	1764-1840	Military	50		185		Br. Adm. Napoleonic War
Smith, William Sooy	1830-1916	Civil War	50		95		Union general
Smith, William	1797-1887	Civil War	100	180	295		CSA Gen., Congress, Gov. VA.
Smith, Willie The Lion	1910-1967	Entertainment	75			125	Jazz Alto-Baritone Sax, Clarinet
Smithers, Jan		Entertainment	6	8		15	Actress
Smits, Jimmy		Entertainment	10			38	Actor. L.A. Law, NYPD Blue
Smoot, Reed	1862-1941	Congress	25	60	80	75	Senator UT. 1st Morman Sen.
Smothers Bros. (both)		Entertainment	15	50		40	Tommy and Dick
Smucker, Paul		Business	10			25	Smuckers Jams & Jellies
Smuts, Jan Christian	1870-1950	Head of State	40	130	178	250	Fld. Marshal. Pres. Un. So. Afr
Smyth, Maj. Gen. Sir John George	1893-1983	Military	25				World War II British general
Smyth, Thomas Alfred	1832-1865	Civil War	105				Last Union General Killed in War
Smythe, Reg*		Cartoonist	20	78		85	Created Andy Capp
Snell, George D., Dr.		Science	15	30	45	45	Nobel Medicine 1980
Snelling, Maj. Gen. Arthur Hugh J.	1897-1965	Military	25				World War II British general
Snipes, Wesley		Entertainment	15			40	Actor
Snodgrass, W.D.		Author	25	75		65	
Snoop Dogg		Entertainment				55	Rapper, actor 15

NAME	DATE	CATEGORY	SIG	LS/DS	ALS	SP	COMMENTS
Snow, Charles Percy	1905-1980	Author	25	55	90	75	Br. Novelist, Physicist
Snow, Hank		Country Music	25	40		50	RCA Country Music Star
Snow, John		Celebrity	10			15	news reader
Snow, Peter		Celebrity	10			15	news reader
Snow, Tony		Celebrity	10			15	media/TV personality
Snowdon, Lisa		Celebrity	10			15	celebrity model
Snowe, Olympia		Senate	10			15	United States Senate (R - ME)
Snyder, Howard		Military	10	25			
Snyder, John W.		Cabinet	15	30		25	Sec'y Treas.
Snyder, Simon		Governor	5	15	35		Governor PA
Snyder, Tom		Celebrity	10			15	media/TV personality
Snyder, Vic S		Congress	10			15	Member U.S. Congress
Snyderman, Nancy Dr.		Celebrity	10			15	media/TV personality
Soares, Mário		Political	10			15	Member European Parliament
Soarez, Alana		Entertainment	3	5	10	10	Pin-Up SP 15
Sobieski, Leelee		Entertainment				35	actress
Sobinov, Leonid	1872-1934	Entertainment	90			375	Russian Tenor
Sockman, Ralph		Clergy	15	20	25		
Soddy, Frederick, Dr.	1877-1956	Science	60	160	275	250	Nobel Chemistry 1921
Sodenstern, Gen. of Inf. Georg v.	1889-1955	Military	25				World War II German general
Soderbergh, Steven		Entertainment				60	Director/Producer/Writer
Soderstrom, Elisabeth		Entertainment				35	Opera
Sofaer, Shoshanna		Celebrity	10			15	medical expert
Soglow, Otto		Cartoonist	20			100	The Little King
Sohn, Lee		Entertainment	4			20	Singer
Sokoloff, Marla		Entertainment				35	Actress
Sokoloff, Vladimir		Entertainment	25			65	
Soles, P. J.		Entertainment	5			15	
Solis, Hilda L. S		Congress	10			15	Member U.S. Congress
Solomon, Charles		Criminal	60	300			Prohibition-Era Bootlegger. Assassinated '33
Solow, Robert M., Dr.		Economics	22	30		25	Nobel Economics 1987
Solti, Georg, Sir		Entertainment	28	45		85	Conductor. Winner of Multiple Grammys
Solzhenitsyn, Alex.	1918-	Author	92	230	648	185	Sov. Novelist. Nobel Lit. 1970
Somers, Suzanne		Entertainment	15			35	actress, business-woman
Somerset, Brigadier Nigel FitzRoy	1893-1990	Military	25				World War II British general
Somerset, Lord Fitzroy		See Raglan					SEE RAGLAN
Somervell, Arthur, Sir		Composer	20	55	85		Br. Oratorios. AMusQS 150
Somervell, Brehon B.	1892-1955	Military	35	125			Gen. WW II
Somerville, Edith Anna Oenene	1858-1949	Author			225		Writer, painter, feminist
Somerville, Julia		Celebrity	10			15	news reader
Sommer, Elke		Entertainment	9	10	20	30	pin-up
Sommer, Renate		Political	10			15	Member European Parliament
Sommers, Joannie		Entertainment	3	5		10	
Sommerville, Arthur		Author	8			12	Biblical prophecy
Somoza, Anastasio		Head of State	20	95			Nicaragua

NAME	DATE	CATEGORY	SIG	LS/DS	ALS	SP	COMMENTS
Sondergaard, Gale		Entertainment	40			75	AA
Sondheim, Stephen	b. 1930	Composer	45	90	142	140	AMusQS275- 375
Sonny & Cher		Entertainment	30			230	
Sons of the Pioneers		Country Music	100			395	Spencer, Brady, Nolan, K & H Farr, Perryman
Sontag, Henrietta Rossi		Entertainment	70		165	375	Opera
Sontag, Susan		Author	10	25	45	20	
Soo, Jack		Entertainment	30			55	
Soong, T.V. (Tzu-wen)		Diplomat	35	50			Chinese Financier, Negotiator
Sooter, Rudy		Country Music	10			20	
Soper, Donald O.		Clergy	20	25	30	30	
Soprano's		Entertainment				350	signed by 5
Sopwith, Thos. O. M., Sir		Aviation	75	115	190	125	Br. Pioneer. ALS/Content 850
Sorbo, Kevin		Entertainment	8			33	Actor. 'Hercules' SP 50
Sörensen, Patsy		Political	10			15	Member European Parliament
Sorenson, Ted		Author	6			15	JFK Aide
Sorkin, Arleen		Entertainment	4	5		10	Pin-Up SP 20
Sorma, Agnes		Entertainment	25				Opera
Sornosa Mart-nez, Marfa		Political	10			15	Member European Parliament
Sorrel, Gilbert M. (WD)	1838-1901	Civil War	295	2175	2400		CSA Gen.
Sorrel, Gilbert Moxley	1838-1901	Civil War	248	558	710		CSA General
Sorrvia, Agnes		Entertainment	20			45	Opera
Sorvino, Mira		Entertainment	15			51	AA 1996. Supporting Actress
Sorvino, Paul		Entertainment	15			40	actor
Sothern, (E)dward (A)skew	1846-1923	Entertainment	30	85	120		Actor.19th Century Romantic Idol
Sothern, Ann	1912-2001	Entertainment	15		35	44	Actress. Wisecracking 'Maizie'. 40's Star
Soto, Talisa		Entertainment	10			40	Col. Pin-Up SP 60
Soucek, Appolo, Lt .		Aviation	15	25			World Altitude Records
Souchet, Dominique F.c.		Political	10			15	Member European Parliament
Souder, Mark E. S		Congress	10			15	Member U.S. Congress
Souez, Ina		Entertainment		50			Opera. Great Mozart Soprano
Soul, David		Entertainment	5	10	20	20	
Souladakis, Ioannis		Political	10			15	Member European Parliament
Soule, Pierre		Civil War	75	170	285		Secessionist. US Sen. LA., CSA Gen.
Soult, Nicolas Jean de Dieu		Fr. Military	105	208	388		Nap. Marshal of Fr., Minister War
Soundgarden		Entertainment	35			95	Music. 4 Member Rock Group
Sousa Pinto, STrgio		Political	10			15	Member European Parliament
Sousa, John Philip	1854-1932	Composer	140	306	515	627	Bandmaster. AMuQS 600-1200
Soustelle, Jacques		Head of State	5	15	40	15	
Souter, David H.		Supreme Court	38			55	
Southampton, 1st Earl of	1505-1550	Royalty	75	215	450		Politician.Sec'y to Cromwell
Southampton, Thos. W., 4th Earl	1607-1667	Royalty	35	150			Lord Treasurer
Southcott, Joanna		Clergy	45	60	90		Br. Religious Fanatic
Southey, Robert	1774-1843	Author	95	280	450		Br. Poet Laureate 1813
Southworth, Edward		Celebrity			1950		California Gold Rush. '49er
Sovine, Red		Country Music	12			35	

NAME	DATE	CATEGORY	SIG	LS/DS	ALS	SP	COMMENTS
Soyer, Moses	1899-1974	Artist			55		Russian/American social realist painter
Soyer, Raphael	1899-1987	Artist	20	50	140	100	Signed Repro. 200-368
Soyinka, Wole (Akinwande O.)		Author	25	80			Nigerian. Nobel Literature 1986
Spaak, Paul-Henri		Head of State	15	30	50	25	Belg. Fndr. EEOC, NATO
Spaatz, Carl Tooey	1891-1974	Military-Aviation	60	144		172	Gen. WW II, AF Commander Strategic Bombing
Spacek, Sissy		Entertainment	10	15		45	AA
Spacey, Kevin		Entertainment	15			50	Actor. AA 1996
Spader, James		Entertainment	10			225	actor
Spaight, Richard Dobbs	1758-1802	Revolutionary War	92	278			Continental Congr.,Signer Constitution.Killed Duel
Spain, Fay		Entertainment	10			30	
Spalding, Albert	1888-1953	Composer	30			138	Violinist, AMQS 85-250
Spalding, J. Walter		Business	25	50	90	75	
Spall, Timothy		Entertainment	10			20	Actor
Spallanzani, Lazzaro	1729-1799	Science	120	400	1042		It. Physiologist. Artificial Insem.
Spani, Hina		Entertainment	20			110	Magnificent spinto Soprano
Spano, Joe		Entertainment	10			20	actor
Sparkman, John	1899-1985	Congress	12			25	Senator AL. VP Candidate
Sparks, Chuncey		Governor	5	20			Governor AL
Sparks, Jared	1789-1866	Author	15	35	70		US Historian, Editor, Publisher, Harvard Pres.
Sparks, Ned		Entertainment	25	30	60	70	
Sparks, William E.		Military	15	30	50		
Sparv, Camilla		Entertainment	8	9	25	20	
Spate, Wolfgang		Aviation			125		Ger. Ace WW II. Test Pilot
Spaulding, Elbridge Gerry	1809-1897	Congress	20	45			MOC NY. 'Father of the Greenback'
Spaulding, R.Z.		Business	15	40	55	25	
Speakes, Larry		Cabinet	4	10	16	10	
Speaks, Oley		Composer	38	90	125		'On The Road To Mandalay'
Spear, Ellis	1834-1917	Civil War	75	150	350	550	20th Maine General. Gettysburg.
Spears, Britney		Entertainment	18			72	singer
Spears, James Gallant	1816-1869	Civil War	40	100	140		Union general
Spears, Maj. Gen. Sir Edw. Louis	1886-1974	Military	25				World War II British general
Specter, Arlen		Senate	10			15	United States Senate (R - PA)
Spector, Phil		Entertainment	75	86		127	Rock HOF
Speed, James	1812-1887	Cabinet	62	80	300		Lincoln Att'y Gen. ALS/Cont. 995
Speed, John Gilmer		Author	5	15	25		Journalist. Biographer
Speer, Albert	1905-1981	Architect	57	109	212	222	Hitler's Architect & Nazi Leader. FDC S 55
Speer, Robert Elliott		Clergy	15	20	25		
Speer, Robert Milton		Senate/Congress	5	10	20		Rep. PA 1871
Speidel, Hans	1897-1987	Military	50	90	165	150	Nazi Gen., Rommel Chief-of Staff
Speight, John J.	1885-	Senate/Congress	10	25			Lawyer & Judge at Nurnberg War Crimes Trial
Speir, Dona		Entertainment	5			15	Pin-Up SP 20. Playboy Centerfold
Speke, John	1827-1864	Explorer			2250		Found Lake Tanganyika w/Rich. Burton
Spelling, Aaron		Entertainment	6	10		25	Film Producer, Writer
Spelling, Randy		Celebrity				20	Actor
Spelling, Tori		Entertainment	8			30	Actress

NAME	DATE	CATEGORY	SIG	LS/DS	ALS	SP	COMMENTS
Spellman, Francis, Cardinal	1889-1967	Clergy	30	48	95	45	
Spelvin, Georgina		Entertainment	5			40	Porn Queen
Spence, Jerry		Lawyer	10			15	Prominent Lawyer
Spencer, George Eliphaz	1836-1893	Civil War	25	45	65		Union General, Senator AL 1868
Spencer, Herbert, Sir	1820-1903	Author	43	102	158		Br. Philosopher
Spencer, John C.	1788-1855	Cabinet	25	60	105		Tyler Sec'y War
Spencer, John P. 5th Earl		Politician	10	15	35		Liberal Leader House of Lords
Spencer, John		Entertainment	10			45	Emmy Award winner
Spencer, Joseph	1714-1789	Revolutionary War	200	650			Am. Maj. Gen'l. Defended NY.
Spencer, Ross H.		Author	12			20	HILARIOUS mystery novels
Spencer, Susan		TV News	4			10	CBS News
Spender, Stephen	1909-1995	Author	40	85	120	90	Br. Poet, Critic. Protest Poetry
Spendlove, Rob		Entertainment	10			20	Actor
Spenser, Tim		Country Music	15			25	Fndr. Sons of the Pioneers
Speroni, Francesco Enrico		Political	10			15	Member European Parliament
Sperrle, Hugo	1885-1953	Military	40	110	160	125	German Gen. Field Marshal and Air Force Commander
Sperry, Elmer A.	1860-1930	Science	195	375	550	450	Inventor Gyroscope. Co-Founder 'Sperry-Rand'
Sperry, Roger W.		Science	22	30	35	25	Nobel Medicine 1981
Spheeris, Penelope		Celebrity	10			15	film industry
Spice Girls		Entertainment				175	Rock Group
Spielberg, David		Entertainment	5	6	15	20	
Spielberg, Steven		Entertainment	75	85	125	138	AA., Producer-Director
Spillane, Mickey		Author	35	62	110	55	Am. Detective Fiction. Created Mike Hammer
Spiner, Brent		Entertainment	15			35	Star Trek
Spinner, Francis E.	1802-1890	Cabinet	35	55	80		Treasurer for 4 Presidents. Civil War Treasurer
Spinner, Robert		Entertainment	4			25	Actor Star Trek
Spinola, Francis Barretto	1821-1891	Civil War	127	150	225		Union general
Spivak, Charlie		Entertainment	20			50	Big Band Leader-Trumpeter
Spock, Benjamin, Dr.		Science	35	57	120	50	Am. Pediatrician-Psychiatrist.
Spofford, Harriet P.	1835-	Author	10	25	40		Am. Romantic Poet, Novelist
Spohr, Louis	1784-1859	Music	45		483		Classical Violinist
Spong, Hilda		Entertainment	15			40	
Spontini, Gaspare, Count de		Composer	95		568		It. Influenced Wagner Operas
Spooner, John C.	1843-1919	Congress	5	15		10	Senator WI 1885
Spooner, Ken		Author	8			12	stock cars
Spooner, William A.		Clergy	25	35	45		Br. Creator Of The Spoonerism
Spragins, Maj. Gen. Robert L.	1890-1964	Military	30				World War II U.S. general
Sprague, Charles A.		Governor	10	20		15	Governor OR
Sprague, Frank Julian		Science	55	100	165	115	Inventor Ass't To Thos. Edison
Sprague, John Wilson	1817-1893	Civil War	40	70	95		Union general. MOH.
Sprague, William Buell		Clergy	38	58	110		
Sprague, William	1830-1915	Civil War	30	55	75	150	Union Gen., CW Gov. RI, Senate
Spratt Jr., John M. S		Congress	10			15	Member U.S. Congress
Spreckels, Claus		Business	95	325		175	Am. Sugar Manufacturer
Sprengel, Herman Johann Phil.	1834-1906	Science				180	

NAME	DATE	CATEGORY	SIG	LS/DS	ALS	SP	COMMENTS
Spring, Gardiner		Clergy	25	35	45		
Spring, Samuel		Clergy	20	25	35		
Spring, Sherwood C.		Astronaut	6			15	
Spring, Woody		Astronaut	7			25	
Springer, Jerry		Entertainment	6			28	Host of Controversial Talk Show
Springer, Robert C.		Astronaut	7			26	
Springfield, Dusty	1939-1999	Entertainment	25			45	Br. Singer
Springfield, Rick		Entertainment	14	40		25	Singer
Springfield, Sherry		Entertainment				50	Actress. E.R.
Springsteen, Bruce		Entertainment	50	75	150	217	Rock 'n Roll Superstar. S Album 'Born...USA' 250-750
Sprinkel, Beryl		Celebrity	10			15	financial expert
Sproul, William Henry	1867-1932	Congress	4	10			Repr. KS. Farmer. Oil & Gas Exploration
Sproull, Maj. Gen. Alexander W.	1892-1961	Military	25				World War II British general
Spruance, Presley	1785-1863	Congress	12	20	40		Senator DE 1847
Spruance, Raymond A.	1886-1969	Military	40	80	130	100	Am. Adm. Victor at Midway WW II
Spry, Maj. Gen. Daniel Charles	1913-1989	Military	24				World War II Canadian general
Spurgeon, Charles H.	1834-1932	Clergy	90	425	525		Br. Evangelist & Baptist Minister
Spurling, Maj Gen John Michael K	1906-1980	Military	25				World War II British general
Spurzheim, Johann Kaspar	1776-1832	Science			500		German Physician, co-founder of phrenology
Squibb, Edward R.		Business	50	84	255		Pioneer Mfg. of Pharmaceuticals
Squier, Emma		Author	5	10	15		
Squier, George O.		Military	100				General. Inventor Radio Devices
Squires, Lt. Gen. Ernest Ker	1882-1940	Military	25				World War II British general
St. Clair, Arthur	1734-1818	Military-Rev. War	142	250	786		Gen., Pres.Continental Congr.
St. Clair, Maj. Gen. Geo. Jas. Paul	1885-1955	Military	25				World War II British general
St. Clair-Ford, Maj. Gen. Sir Peter	1905-1989	Military	25				World War II British general
St. Clair-Morford, Maj. Gen. A. C.	1893-1943	Military	25				World War II British general
St. Clement, Pam		Entertainment	10			20	Actress
St. Cyr, Lili	1917-1999	Entertainment	12	15	30	40	Exotic Dancer-Actress. Pin-Up SP 50
St. Denis, Ruth	1878-1968	Entertainment	50	140	250	310	Dancer, Choreographer
St. George, T.R. 'Ozzie'		Author	5			28	Post WW II: 'C/O Postmaster'
St. Jacques, Raymond		Entertainment	15			45	African-American actor
St. James, Susan		Entertainment	10			30	Actress. 'Kate & Allie', 'McMillan & Wife'
St. John, Al Fuzzy		Entertainment	150			350	
St. John, Isaac M.	1827-1880	Civil War	125		740		CSA Gen. Sig/Rank 175
St. John, Jill		Entertainment	8	9	20	30	
St. Johns, Adela Rogers		Author	10	25	45	15	Star Hearst Reporter. Novelist
St. Laurent, Louis		Head of State	10			50	P.M. Canada
St. Patrick, Mathew		Entertainment				40	Keith Charles, Six Feet Under
St. Vincent, John Jervis	1735-1823	Military	35	65	160		Br. Adm. Of the Fleet. Earl of Vincent
Stabbing Westward		Entertainment	35			85	Music. 5 Member Rock Group
Stabenow, Debbie		Senate	10			15	United States Senate (D - MI)
Stabile, Dick		Entertainment	20			40	Big Band Leader
Stable, Maj Gen Hugh Huntington	1896-1985	Military	25				World War II British general
Stableford, Howard		Celebrity	10			15	television presenter

NAME	DATE	CATEGORY	SIG	LS/DS	ALS	SP	COMMENTS
Stacey Q		Entertainment	5			10	Rock
Stacey, John		Aviation	8	20	30	20	
Stack, Robert	d. 2003	Entertainment	10	32		37	AA. 'Most Wanted' emcee. 'Untouchables'
Stack, Rose Marie Bowe		Entertainment	4	5		9	
Stacpoole, Henry de Vere		Author	15	45	80		Writer, Publicist
Stade, Frederica von		Entertainment	15			35	Opera
Stadlman, Anthony		Aviation	10	20	30	20	
Stael, Anne-Louise, Mme. De	1766-1817	Author	65	185	675		Fr. Writer. Exiled By Napoleon
Staes, Bart		Political	10			15	Member European Parliament
Stafford, Jo		Entertainment	5			15	40's-50's Top Vocalist
Stafford, Leroy Augustus	1822-1864	Civil War	260				Confederate general
Stafford, Robert T.		Governor	8	15	20		Governor VT
Stafford, Susan		Entertainment	10				Actress
Stafford, Thomas P.		Astronaut	15			57	
Stager, Anson	1825-1885	Civil War	20	40	65		Gen. Supt. Govt. Telegraphs
Stahel, Julius	1825-1912	Civil War	40	92	141	483	Union general
Stahl, Gerald		Aviation				233	Engineer 509th Bomb Gp. (Enola Gay)
Stahl, Leslie		Journalist	5	15		25	TV. 60 Minutes
Stahl, Nick		Entertainment				30	
Stainback, Ingram M.		Governor				25	Gov. HI 1942-51
Stainer, John, Sir.	1840-1901	Entertainment	35				Composer and organist ., AMuS 400
Staley, Layne		Entertainment	8			40	Music. Lead Singer 'Alice in Chains'
Stalin, Joseph	1879-1953	Head of State	1148	3960	7550	4000	USSR Dictator. Rare WW II DS 8900
Stalin, Svetlana		Celebrity	35	80	125	75	Daughter of Stalin
Stallone, Sylvester		Entertainment	15	40	75	62	Actor. As 'Rocky' SP 75
Stamos, John		Entertainment	10			35	
Stamp, Terence		Entertainment	10			25	
Stanaland, Gene		Celebrity	10			15	media/TV personality
Stanbery, Henry		Cabinet	10	20	45		Att'y General 1866
Stander, Lionel		Entertainment	10	15	25	25	
Standing, Guy, Sir		Entertainment	25			55	
Stanford, Leland	1824-1893	Senate	200	550	975	800	RR Pres., Fndr. Stanford U., Gov. CA. Stk. S 30000
Stanford, R. C.		Governor	6	15		10	Governor AZ
Stang, Arnold		Entertainment	5			15	
Stanham, Maj Gen Sir Reginald G	1893-1957	Military	25				World War II British general
Stanhope, Edward		Military	10	20	30		
Stanhope, Hester, Lady	1776-1839	Non-Conformist	15	48	95		Adopted Eastern Ways. Prophetess
Stanhope, Phil. H., 5th Earl		Historian	10	20	25		Lord Mahon. M.P., Author
Stanhope, Phil.H., 7th Earl		Celebrity	7	20	45		
Stanhope, Philip D.	1694-1773	Author-Politician	125	420	625		4th Earl Chesterfield. Statesman, Wit, Letter-Writer
Stanislaus I Leszczynski	1677-1766	Royalty	175				Stanislaw I, King of Poland
Stanislavski, Konstantin	1863-1938	Entertainment	350	440	672	1152	Rus. Actor, Dir., Producer. Method Acting Tech.
Stanislaw II Augustus Poniatowski	1732-1798	Royalty	95	375	730		Last King of Poland
Stanley, Arthur		Business	4	6		8	Pres. Stanley Works
Stanley, David Sloane		Civil War	25	65	90		Union Gen. War dte ALS 750

NAME	DATE	CATEGORY	SIG	LS/DS	ALS	SP	COMMENTS
Stanley, Freelan O.		Inventor	325		1400		Auto. Pioneer. Stanley Steamer
Stanley, Henry M., Sir	1841-1904	Explorer	190	310	460	900	Found David Livingstone, ALS/cont 2070
Stanley, Henry, Capt.		Military	10	25	40		
Stanley, Reed	1884-1980	Supreme Court	40	90			
Stanley, Wendell M.		Science	20	25	90	30	Nobel Chemistry 1946
Stannard, George Jerrison	1820-1886	Civil War	35		80		Union general
Stans, Maurice H.	1908-1998	Cabinet	25	40		40	Nixon Sec'y Commerce. Watergate Scandal
Stansbury, Howard	1806-1863	Explorer	20	55	100		Surveyor, Military
Stanton, Benjamin		Senate/Congress	20	45	100		Rep. OH. ALS/Content 250
Stanton, Edwin M.	1814-1869	Cabinet	100	174	307	356	ALS War Dte 1,495, Sec'y War ASL/cont 805
Stanton, Elizabeth Cady	1815-1902	Women's Suffrage	168	262	428		1st Pres. National Women's Suffrage
Stanton, Frank L.		Author	5	15	25		Am. Journalist, Poet, Publ.
Stanton, Frank, Dr.		Business	15	45	80	30	Pres. CBS
Stanton, Harry Dean		Entertainment	6	8	12	20	
Stanwyck, Barbara	1907-1990	Entertainment	40	68		83	Actress. Major Film & TV Star
Stapleton, Jean		Entertainment	5	25		28	Actress. Best Known as 'Edith Bunker'
Stapleton, Maureen		Entertainment	8	10		25	
Stapp, John, Col.		Military	5	15	20	10	
Stapp, Olivia		Entertainment	10			35	Opera
Stapp, Scott		Entertainment	8			35	Music. Lead Singer 'Creed'
Star Trek (cast)		Entertainment				650	Original cast of 6
Star Wars (Cast)		Entertainment				375	SP (7)
Stark, Benjamin	1820-1898	Congress		30	70		Sen. OR, A Founder of Portland
Stark, Fortney Pete S		Congress	10			15	Member U.S. Congress
Stark, Harold R.	1880-1972	Military	35	55	80	75	Adm., Cmdr. Eur.Waters WW II
Stark, John	1728-1822	Revolutionary War	440	715	1565		War Dte LS 2500 Gen. Fr & Indian War, Bunker Hill
Starke, Peter Burwell	1815-1888	Civil War	120	225			Confederate general
Starke, William Edwin	1814-1862	Civil War	360				Confederate general, KIA Antietam
Starker, Janos		Entertainment	6	8	15	15	
Starkey, Thomas A., Bishop		Clergy	20	35	40		
Starkweather, John Converse	1830-1890	Civil War	64		110		Union general
Starr, Belle		Outlaw	2500	7625			Early West Bandit Queen
Starr, Blaze		Entertainment	15		150	90	Pin-Up SP 50. Stripper
Starr, Dixie		Entertainment	20				Western Movies. Mrs. Jack Hovie
Starr, Edwin	d. 2003	Music	10			25	'War'
Starr, Kay		Entertainment	10			65	Big Band Singer. Vocalist
Starr, Kenneth		Legal	8			29	Special Counsel Re. Clinton Investigation
Starr, Leonard*		Cartoonist	25			160	Little Orphan Annie
Starr, Michael		Entertainment	6			25	Music. Bass 'Alice in Chains'
Starr, Paul		Celebrity	10			15	medical expert
Starr, Ringo		Entertainment	80	312		184	Beatles' Drummer. Endorsed Check 350-738
Starrett, Charles Durango	1904-1988	Entertainment	25	35		68	Early Cowboy Film Star
Starry, Donald A.		Military	5	6	15	10	
Starzl, Thomas E., Dr.		Science	15	25		20	Transplant Specialist
Stasova, Helena		Celebrity			328		Famous Russian woman

NAME	DATE	CATEGORY	SIG	LS/DS	ALS	SP	COMMENTS
Stassen, Harold E.		Governor	10	15	35	20	Governor MN
Stassevitch, Paul		Entertainment	25		60		Influenced a Generation of Violinists
Statler, Ellsworth M.		Business	75	205	375	150	Statler Hotel Chain
Statlers, The		Country Music	25			50	
Stauner, Gabriele		Political	10			15	Member European Parliament
Stawell, Maj. Gen. Wm. Arthur M.	1895-1987	Military	25				World War II British general
Stead, Wm. Thomas	1849-1912	Journalist	40	75	160	100	Died On Titanic
Stearns, Cliff S		Congress	10			15	Member U.S. Congress
Stebbins, George C.		Clergy	45	70	95		
Steber, Eleanor		Entertainment	20			75	Opera, Concert
Stedman, Edmund C.	1833-1908	Author	55	90			Poet, NY Stock Broker, Publ.
Steedman, James Blair	1817-1883	Civil War	35	80			Union general
Steedman, Maj Gen John Fran. D	1897-1983	Military	25				World War II British general
Steel, Danielle		Author	10	20		25	Novelist
Steele, Barbara	1938-	Entertainment	20			35	Br. Actress. Leads in Br., Am. & Internat'l Films
Steele, Bob & Bill	1904-	Entertainment	25	30	45	50	Twins. Silent Films Age 14 to Western Starring Roles
Steele, Frederick	1819-1868	Civil War	54	95	185		Un. Gen.War Dte/Content ALS 2500
Steele, General Sir James Stuart	1894-1975	Military	28				World War II British general
Steele, Karen		Entertainment	5	5		15	Actress
Steele, Maj. Gen. Clive	1892-1955	Military	20				World War II Australian general
Steele, Richard, Sir	1672-1729	Author	200	600	1320		Essays, Drama. 'The Tatler'
Steele, Tommy	1936-	Entertainment	15		25	25	Pop Singer-Actor. Former Merchant Seaman
Steele, William	1819-1885	Civil War	110	228			Confederate general
Steely Dan		Entertainment	25			50	Rock (2)
Steenburgen, Mary		Entertainment	10			35	AA Actress
Stefansson, Vilhjalmur	1879-1962	Explorer	43	95	140	250	Arctic Explorer, Ethnologist
Stefanyshyn-Piper, Heide		Astronaut	10			30	
Steffens, Lincoln	1866-1936	Author	40	75	125	80	Journalist. Leader Muckrakers
Steger, Will		Celebrity	35	95			Arctic explorer
Stegner, Wallace		Author	20		45		Am. Novelist. Pulitzer
Steichen, Edward J.	1879-1973	Artist	68	246	375	475	Pioneer in Photgraphy as Art Form
Steig, William*		Cartoonist	20		85	100	New Yorker Cartoonist
Steiger, Rod		Entertainment	8	35		48	Oscar winner 'In The Heat of The Night'
Steimle, Edmund A.		Clergy	10	15	20		
Stein, Ben		Celebrity	10			25	media/TV personality
Stein, Gertrude	1874-1946	Author	295	535	705	795	Expatriate Am. Writer. Resided Paris From 1903
Stein, Herbert		Celebrity	10			15	financial expert
Stein, Jules		Humanitarian-Bus.	50	112			Founder MCA
Stein, Rick		Celebrity	10			15	TV Chef
Steinbeck, John	1902-1968	Author	332	1606	2232	1443	Pulitzer, Nobel Lit., DS 2,500
Steinem, Gloria		Feminist	12	25	45	25	Fndr., Editor Ms Magazine. Feminist Political Leade
Steinhoff, J. 'Mickey'		Aviation	15	25	50	30	
Steinlen, Theophile	1859-1923	Artist	35	105	250		Fr. Known For Posters, Lithography
Steinmetz, Charles P.	1865-1923	Science	40	90	175	350	Germanborn Electrical Engineer. Wizard of G. E.
Steinway, Henry Z.		Business	20	55	85	30	Steinway Piano

NAME	DATE	CATEGORY	SIG	LS/DS	ALS	SP	COMMENTS
Steinwehr, Adolph Wilhelm von	1822-1877	Civil War	45	80	120		Union Gen. Geographer, Cartographer
Steiwer, Frederick	1883-1939	Congress	5		15		Senator OR 1926
Stekel, Wilhelm		Science	65	275			Austrian Psychiatrist
Stella, Antonietta		Entertainment	25			55	Opera
Stempel, Robert		Business	25	60		35	Pres. & CEO of Gen. Motors
Sten, Anna	1908-	Entertainment	15	15	30	35	Russ. Actress. Sam Goldwyn 'Find'. Unpopular
Stendhal (Marie H. Beyle)	1783-1842	Author	350	1020	2315		19th Cent. Fr. Novelist. Served in Napoleon's Army
Stengle, Charles I.		Senate/Congress	5	15	25		Rep. NY 1923
Stenholm, Charles W. S		Congress	10			15	Member U.S. Congress
Stenmarck, Per		Political	10			15	Member European Parliament
Stennis, John C.		Senate/Congress	10	15			Sen. MS 1947. Pres. Pro Tem.
Stenzel, Ursula		Political	10			15	Member European Parliament
Stephanie, Princess		Royalty	10			25	Princess of Monaco
Stephanopoulos, George		Government	10	20		22	White House Aide. Author
Stephen, Adam	1730-1791	Revolutionary War	120	210	320		General.Trenton, Brandywine
Stephen, Phillip		Celebrity	10			15	motivational speaker
Stephens, Alexander H. (WD)		Civil War	275	525	735		V.P.CSA
Stephens, Alexander H.	1812-1883	Civil War	136	166	358	322	US MOC & Gov. GA, VP CSA. FF 190
Stephens, George F.	1859-	Artist	20		65		Sculptor, Lecturer. Single Tax Advocate
Stephens, James	1882-1950	Author				190	Irish Poet and novelist.
Stephens, William D.	1859-1944	Congress	10	30			Governor CA, Senator CA
Stephenson, George	1781-1825	Science	275	425	875		Invented 1st Practical Steam Locomotive
Stephenson, Henry	1871-1956	Entertainment	35			75	Br. Character Actor
Stephenson, Robert	1803-1859	Science	90	245	498		Br. Railroad Engineer-Devloper Steam Locomotive
Stepp, Hans		Aviation	5	15	20	20	
Steppenwolf		Entertainment	75	125		150	Rock Group (All)
Sterckx, Dirk		Political	10			15	Member European Parliament
Sterling, Andrew B.		Composer	20	50	100		
Sterling, Robert	1917-	Entertainment	5			20	Actor. Leading Man. Mostly B Films. 2nd Leads in A's
Stern, Daniel		Entertainment	10			30	actor
Stern, Henry Aaron		Clergy	20	20	25		
Stern, Howard		Celebrity	10			25	media/TV personality/radio DJ
Stern, Isaac		Entertainment	15	35	45	60	Violinist. AMQS 80, ALS/Cont. 110
Sternberg, Joseph von	1894-1969	Entertainment	100	115		75	Film Director
Sterne, Laurence	1713-1768	Author	95	375			Br. Whimsical, Eccentric Humor
Sterner, Jerry		Entertainment	10			20	actor
Sterrett, Cliff*		Cartoonist	35			225	'Polly And Her Pals'
Stettinius, Edward R., Jr.	1900-1949	Cabinet	30	70	95	75	FDR, Truman, Sec'y State
Steuart, George Hume	1828-1903	Civil War	100	156	237		Confederate general
Steuben, Friedrich von	1730-1794	Revolutionary War	883	1527			Prussian Officer. Cont'l Army. ALS/Cont 9,750-29500
Stevens, Albert W., Capt.	1846-1949	Aviation	25	50			Balloonist. Record Holder. Aerial Photographer
Stevens, Andrew		Entertainment	10	15	20	20	Actor
Stevens, Brinke		Entertainment	5			15	Actress. Scream Queen. Pin-Up SP 20
Stevens, Cat		Entertainment	30	45		65	Singer
Stevens, Clement H. (WD)	1821-1864	Civil War	375	1750	2650		CSA Gen. Died of Wounds Rec'd Atlanta

NAME	DATE	CATEGORY	SIG	LS/DS	ALS	SP	COMMENTS
Stevens, Clement Hoffman	1821-1864	Civil War	222	430			Confederate general
Stevens, Connie	1938-	Entertainment	6	8	15	20	Actress-Singer.
Stevens, Craig	1918-	Entertainment	10	15	20	20	Actor
Stevens, Dave		Artist	5			15	Rocketeer Creator
Stevens, David		Celebrity	10			15	home/gardening expert
Stevens, Ebenezer		Revolutionary War	75	195			Memb. Boston Tea Party
Stevens, George	1904-1975	Entertainment	30			60	Film Director-Major Productions. AA (2)
Stevens, Harry M.		Celebrity	25	230			Introduced Hot Dogs to the Ballpark
Stevens, Inger	1934-1970	Entertainment	75			150	Actress. Burlesque-Chorus Girl-TV-Movies-Suicide
Stevens, Isaac Ingalls	1818-1862	Civil War	164	442	747		Union general, KIA Chantilly VA
Stevens, James F.	1892-1971	Author	125	310			Paul Bunyan Stories
Stevens, John Paul, III		Supreme Court	40	85		90	
Stevens, John	1748-1838	Revolutionary War	25	50	110		Officer. Engineer. Perfected Steam Engine
Stevens, K.T.	1919-	Entertainment	5	5		10	Actress. Leads & 2nd Leads. 40's-50's Films
Stevens, Maj. Gen. Jack	1896-1969	Military	20				World War II Australian general
Stevens, Maj. Gen. William G.	1893-1975	Military	20				World War II New Zealand general
Stevens, Onslow		Entertainment	30			65	Numerous Film Leads. Ran Afoul of Wm. R. Hearst
Stevens, Ray		Country Music	5			15	Singer. Recording Artist
Stevens, Risé		Entertainment	20	25		42	Opera, Concert, Films
Stevens, Robert T.		Cabinet	10	25		20	Sec'y Army
Stevens, Stella		Entertainment	5	8		35	Actress. Pin-Up SP 35. Topless 75
Stevens, Tabitha		Entertainment	10			25	
Stevens, Ted		Senate	10			15	United States Senate (R - AK)
Stevens, Thaddeus	1792-1868	Senate/Congress	35	90	184		MOC PA 1849-68, Abolitionist
Stevens, Wallace	1879-1955	Author	288	853		2000	20th Cent. Am. Poet, Pulitzer
Stevens, Walter Husted	1827-1867	Civil War	212				Confederate general
Stevens, Warren	1919-	Entertainment	5	10	15	20	Actor
Stevenson, Adlai E.	1835-1914	Vice President	55	125	260	250	Cleveland Vice Pres., MOC, PM Gen.
Stevenson, Adlai E.	1900-1965	Governor	40	85	120	100	Gov. IL, Twice Pres. Candidate
Stevenson, Adlai E., III		Governor	5	10		15	Gov. IL
Stevenson, Andrew	1784-1857	Senate/Congress	15	20	35		MOC VA 1821. Speaker of House. Minister to Gr.Brit.
Stevenson, Carter L. (WD)		Civil War	305	740	948		CSA General. Captured & Exchanged
Stevenson, Carter L.	1817-1888	Civil War	129	399	500		CSA Gen. Vicksburg
Stevenson, Coke		Governor	5	15			Governer TX
Stevenson, John Dunlap	1821-1897	Civil War	50				Union general
Stevenson, McLean		Entertainment	35	45		64	Actor. 'Mash'
Stevenson, Rick		Celebrity	10			15	film industry
Stevenson, Robert Hooper		Civil War	25	40	75		Union Brevet Brig. General
Stevenson, Robert Louis	1850-1894	Author	335	908	2107	4370	Novelist, Poet, Essayist. 'Treasure Island' etc.
Stevenson, Sonia		Celebrity	10			15	Chef
Stevenson, Struan		Political	10			15	Member European Parliament
Stevenson, Thomas Greely	1836-1864	Civil War	95	174			Union general
Steward, Maj Gen. Reginald H. R.	1898-1975	Military	25				World War II British general
Stewart, Alexander P.	1821-1908	Civil War	208	295	380		CSA Gen.
Stewart, Alexander P. (WD)		Civil War	275	920	1200		CSA Gen.

NAME	DATE	CATEGORY	SIG	LS/DS	ALS	SP	COMMENTS
Stewart, Alexander T.	1803-1876	Business	10	25	45		Am. Merchant, Founded Garden City, L.I.
Stewart, Catherine Mary		Entertainment	5			15	Actress
Stewart, Charles	1778-1869	Military	110	275			Cmdr. USS Constitution War 1812
Stewart, Elaine		Entertainment	5			10	Actress. Pin-Up SP 15
Stewart, French		Celebrity				300	Actor
Stewart, James (Jimmy)	1908-1997	Entertainment	45	122	160	172	S 'Harvey' Original 350-800. 15 pg DS 500
Stewart, James C.		Aviation	15	25	40	30	ACE, WW II
Stewart, James S.		Clergy	30	45	60	45	
Stewart, John A.		Business	3	10	25		
Stewart, Lisa		Entertainment	5			15	
Stewart, Maj. Gen. Keith L.	1896-1972	Military	20				World War II New Zealand general
Stewart, Maj. Gen. William Ross	1889-1966	Military	25				World War II British general
Stewart, Martha		Author	5	10		20	Columnist. TV Hostess
Stewart, Nick		Entertainment	8			25	Actor. 'Brer Bear' SP 40
Stewart, Patrick		Entertainment	10			45	actor
Stewart, Paul	1908-	Entertainment	15			45	Actor-TV Dir., Radio/Orson Welles Mercury Theatre
Stewart, Peggy		Celebrity	10	20			Secretarial Science Expert
Stewart, Peggy	1923-	Entertainment	5			10	Swimmer-Rider-Actress. Films at 14. Westerns
Stewart, Potter	1915-1985	Supreme Court	35	72		95	
Stewart, Rex		Entertainment	75	95		150	Cornet
Stewart, Robert L.		Astronaut	6			25	
Stewart, Rod		Entertainment	12	50		58	Rock. 'Foolish Behavior' Alb. S 45
Stewart, Walter	1756-1796	Revolutionary War		225			Am. General. 3rd Penn. Aide de Camp to Gen. Gates
Stewart, William	1827-1909	Senate	25	45	70		Drafted US Mining Law-1872 Sen. NV
Stewart, Wynn		Country Music	10			20	Singer
Steyn, Martinus T.	1857-1916	Head of State	35				Last Pres. Orange Free State
Stiborik, Joe		Aviation	30			50	Enola Gay Radar Operator WW II
Stickney, Dorothy		Entertainment	5	7	20	25	Actress. Stage Leading Lady. Early Films
Stieglitz, Alfred	1864-1946	Artist-Photographer	200	675	810		Revolutionized Camera Technique
Stiers, David Ogden		Entertainment	35			98	Actor. 'Mash'. Reluctant Signer
Stigler, George J.		Economist	20	25	40	25	Nobel Economics 1982
Stihler, Catherine		Political	10			15	Member European Parliament
Stiles, Julia		Entertainment	6			35	Actress
Stiles, William H.	1808-1865	Congress	20		65		MOC GA, CSA Colonel
Still, William Grant	1895-1978	Composer	120	178	385	350	1st Afro-Am. Symphony Conductor
Stiller, Ben		Entertainment	8			35	Actor. 'Something About Mary' SP 45
Stiller, Jerry		Entertainment	5			37	Comic Actor. 1/2 of Stiller & Meara Team
Stills, Stephen		Entertainment	40			75	
Stilwell, Joseph W.	1883-1946	Military	120	170		412	Gen. WW II. 'Vinegar Joe'.
Stimson, Henry L.	1867-1950	Cabinet	40	74	95	80	Sec'y State 1929. Served Several Cabinets
Sting		Entertainment	42			67	Rocksinger, poet
Stirling, Brigadier James Erskine	1898-1968	Military	25				World War II British general
Stirling, Linda		Entertainment	15			35	Actress
Stirling, Wm. Alex., Lord	1726-1783	Revolutionary War	385	950	1950		General Continental Army
Stiwell, Maj. Gen. Hervey	1896-1973	Military	25				World War II British general

NAME	DATE	CATEGORY	SIG	LS/DS	ALS	SP	COMMENTS
Stnlpnagel, Gen. of Inf Karl-H. von	1886-1944	Military	25				World War II German general
Stock, Frederick A.		Composer	20	35	50	75	Dir. Chicago Symphony Orch.
Stock, Harold		Business	10	35	50	20	
Stockdale, James B.		Military	31	30		25	Adm. WW II. Perot Running Mate for V.P.
Stockmann, Ulrich		Political	10			15	Member European Parliament
Stockton, Frank R.	1834-1902	Author	25	50		50	Juvenile Fiction, Novels, Editor
Stockton, Richard	1730-1781	Revolutionary War	650	1602	3500		Declaration of Independence
Stockton, Richard	1764-1828	Senate/Congress	20	35	50		MOC, Senator NJ 1796
Stockton, Robert Field	1795-1866	Military	125	230	325		Sen. NJ. Conquered Calif. Named Stockton, CA
Stockwell, Dean	1936-	Entertainment	10			30	Child to Adult Actor. AA Nomination 'Quantum Leap'
Stockwell, Gen. Sir Hugh Charles	1903-1986	Military	25				World War II British general
Stockwell, Guy		Entertainment	10			25	Actor-Brother to Dean
Stockwell, Harry		Entertainment	50			122	
Stoddard, Richard H.	1825-1903	Author	20	30	45		Poet, Writer, Literary Critic, Novelist
Stoddart, James H.		Entertainment	20			40	Vintage Actor
Stoddert, Benjamin	1751-1813	Revolutionary War	95	270	430		1st Sec'y Navy 1798
Stoessinger, Dr. John		Celebrity	10			15	political celebrity
Stoica, Chivu		Head of State	50				Premier Roumania
Stoker, Bram	1847-1912	Author	132	325	485		Ir. Business Advisor-Sec'y Henry Irving. 'Dracula'
Stokes, Carl Burton	1927-1996	Political	20	30	40	45	1st Afr-Am Mayor of Major Am. City, Cleveland
Stokes, James Hughes	1815-1890	Civil War	35		80		Union general
Stokes, Louis	1925-	Congress	10	20		15	Afro-Am. Repr. OH
Stokes, Maj. Gen. John H. Jr.	1895-1968	Military	30				World War II U.S. general
Stokes, William	1814-1897	Civil War	25		70		Union Gen., MOC TN
Stokowski, Leopold	1882-1977	Entertainment	65	95	110	175	Br-Am. Flambouyant Conductor AMuQS 350
Stolbrand, Charles John	1821-1894	Civil War	45	57	105		Union general
Stolle, Bruno		Aviation	5	15	20	15	
Stoloff, Morris	1893-1980	Entertainment	10			30	Musical Dir.-Conductor. AA (3)
Stoltenberg, Gerhardt		Celebrity	10			15	political celebrity
Stoltz, Eric		Entertainment	9	10	20	30	actor
Stolz, Robert	1880-1975	Composer	20	75			Conductor. Composed 65 Operettas
Stolz, Teresa		Entertainment	40	75			ALS/Content 400
Stone Temple Pilots (All)		Entertainment	35			88	Rock Drumhead Signed 150
Stone, Charles Pomeroy	1824-1887	Civil War	55		140		Union general
Stone, Cliffie		Country Music	10			25	Singer, Songwriter, Record Exec.
Stone, Ezra		Entertainment	25	35		50	Vintage Radio's 'Henry Aldrich'
Stone, Fred	1973-1959	Entertainment	20		30	40	Vaudeville Star of 1st 'The Wizard of Oz' on stage
Stone, George E.	1903-1967	Entertainment	20			45	Song & Dance-Vaudeville-Stage-Character Roles
Stone, Harlan Fiske	1872-1946	Supreme Court	65	127	260	250	Chief Justice
Stone, Harold J.		Entertainment	15			30	
Stone, Irving	1903-1989	Author	20	35	60	50	Historical Biographical Novels & Successful Films
Stone, John Samuel		Clergy	20		85		
Stone, Lewis	1879-1953	Entertainment	30	40	75	65	Am. Leading Man in Silents. Later Character Actor
Stone, Lucy (Blackwell)	1818-1893	Reformer	75	180	260	1000	Suffragist, Women's Rights Pioneer.
Stone, Marcus		Artist		15	30		Illustrated for Chas. Dickens

NAME	DATE	CATEGORY	SIG	LS/DS	ALS	SP	COMMENTS
Stone, Milburn		Entertainment	55	65	100	100	Busy Character Actor Until Full Time Gunsmoke 'Doc'
Stone, Oliver	1946-	Entertainment	20			35	Oscar Winning Film Director. Writer, Producer
Stone, Paula		Entertainment	25		30	40	Western Heroine
Stone, Peter H.		Author	20		70		Playwright. Acad. Award '64, Tony '69, '81, Emmy '63
Stone, Reynolds	1909-1979	Artist			80		Designer and engraver.
Stone, Sharon		Entertainment	20	35		59	actress
Stone, Thomas	1743-1787	Revolutionary War	625	1500	3500		Signer Decl. of Indepen.
Stoneman, George	1822-1894	Civil War-Gov.	60	129	179		Union General, Gov. of CA. Sig/Rank 170
Stoney Mtn. Cloggers		Country Music	30			60	
Stooges, The Three (3)		Entertainment	1028	1600		3692	Original Stooges
Stoopnagle, Colonel Lemuel Q.		Entertainment	15	15	30	30	Vint. Radio (Fred. C. Taylor). 'Stoopnagle & Bud'
Stoops, Herbert M.		Artist	20				Illustrator, signed drwg 200
Stopes, Marie Charlotte	1880-1958	Reformer	85		250		Birth Control Pioneer
Stopford, Gen Sir Montagu Geo. N	1892-1971	Military	25				World War II British general
Stoppard, Miriam, Dr		Celebrity	10			10	health and fitness expert
Stoppard, Tom	1937-	Author	20	45	70	50	Czech Born. Br. Plays of Verbal Brilliance
Storch, Larry	1923-	Entertainment	5	8	15	18	Actor-Comedian. 'F Troop'
Storchio, Rosina	1876-1845	Entertainment	70			400	It. Soprano. Created Cio-Cio-San in Mme.Butterfly
Stordahl, Axel		Conductor-Arranger	25			65	Arranged for Major Vocalists
Storey, June		Entertainment	10			40	Actress. Western Leading Lady
Storm, Gale		Entertainment	8			25	Star of Early TV Series 'My Little Margie'
Storm, Tempest		Entertainment	10	18	28	25	Pin-Up SP 35. Stripper
Storms, Harrison A.		Business	9		25		
Storrs, Richard Salter	1821-1900	Clergy	25	35	50		Congr. Minister-Scholar-Author
Story, John P.		Military	65	125			Am. WW I Gen.
Story, Joseph	1779-1845	Supreme Court	130	225	390		ALS/Content 2,500
Stossel, John		Celebrity	10			15	media/TV personality
Stott, John		Clergy	15	25	30		
Stott, Maj. Gen. Hugh	1884-1966	Military	28				World War II British general
Stoughton, Edwin Henry		Civil War	55		120		Union General
Stoughton, William	1632-1701	Colonial America	450	1200			Gov. MA, Stoughton Hall, Harvard
Stout, Rex	1886-1975	Author	25	45	80	75	Created Detective 'Nero Wolfe'
Stovall, Marcellus Augustus	1818-1895	Civil War	110	192			Confederate general
Stowe, Harriet Beecher	1811-1896	Author	217	336	770	1610	Suffragist, Anti-Slavery. AMsS 3,850
Stowe, Madeline		Entertainment	22			43	actress
Stracciari, Riccardo	1875-1955	Entertainment	42			375	Opera. Baritone/46 Year Career
Strachen, Michaela		Celebrity	10			15	TV personality
Strachey, Lytton		Author	70	175	475		Br. Member of Bloomsbury Group
Stradlin, Izzy		Entertainment	15			40	Guns 'N Roses
Strahl, Otho French	1831-1864	Civil War	320				Confederate general, KIA Franklin TN
Straight, Beatrice		Entertainment	5	6	15	20	AA
Strait, Donald G.		Aviation	12	25	40	35	ACE, WW II
Strait, George		Country Music	10			38	
Strait, Horace Burton		Senate/Congress	10	15			Rep. MN 1873, Banker, Agri.
Stranahan, Robert A., Jr.		Business	5			10	CEO Champion Spark Plugs

NAME	DATE	CATEGORY	SIG	LS/DS	ALS	SP	COMMENTS
Strand, Paul	1890-1976	Photographer	30	85	420		Am. Known for Photo Documentaries
Strange, Glenn		Entertainment	50			150	
Strasberg, Lee	1901-1982	Entertainment	35	40	55	95	Drama Coach. Hd. Actor's Studio. Actor
Strasberg, Susan	1938-1999	Entertainment	16	25	35	35	Actress
Strassmann, Fritz	1902-1980	Science	75	270			Ger. Chemist w/Otto Hahn Worked on Nuclear Fission
Stratas, Teresa		Entertainment	25			50	Opera
Stratemeyer, George F.		Military	30	40		50	
Strathairn, David		Entertainment	10			25	actor
Strathmore, Earl of	1855-1921	Royalty	10		50		Grandfather of Queen Elizabeth II
Stratten, Dorothy		Entertainment	118	2500		889	Playboy Playmate of the year 1980
Stratton, Chas. S.		Entertainment	182		475	468	Barnum's General Tom Thumb
Stratton, Lt. Gen. Sir Wm. Henry	1903-1989	Military	25				World War II British general
Stratton, Samuel S.		Senate/Congress	5	10		10	Rep. NY. Navy Intelligence
Stratton, William G.		Gov-Congress	4	10			Rep., Gov. IL
Stratton, Winfield	1848-1902	Business	250	1300	1500		'Midas of the Rockies'., signed stock cert. 1875
Strauß, Colonel-General Adolf	1879-1973	Military	25				World War II German general
Straub, Robert W.		Governor	5	15			Gov. OR
Straube, Gen. of Infantry Erich	1887-1971	Military	25				World War II German general
Straus, Jack I.		Business	4	10	25	10	3rd Generation R.H. Macy Dept...
Straus, Nathan	1848-1931	Business	60	95	140	125	Owner R.H. Macy Co. Dept Store
Straus, Oscar	1870-1954	Composer	110	175	250	250	The Chocolate Soldier. AMusQS 250
Strause, Charles		Composer	8	15	30	25	
Strauss, Adolf		Military	10	15	35	15	
Strauss, Eduard II	1910-1969	Composer	125				Younger Brother of Johann. AMusQS 150.
Strauss, Franz Josef		Head of State	15	30	60	50	
Strauss, Johann	1804-1849	Composer	240	445	1775		Aus. Waltzes. Cond. Own Orchest
Strauss, Johann, Jr.	1825-1899	Composer	317	675	950	2500	The Waltz King. AMusQS 3000
Strauss, Peter		Entertainment	15			45	
Strauss, Richard	1864-1949	Composer	150	270	902	668	Ger. Conductor. AMuQS 700-950-1,600-2,500
Strauss, Robert		Cabinet	4	12	20	10	
Strauss, Robert		Entertainment	25			45	
Stravinsky, Igor	1882-1971	Composer	207	366	459	868	Russ-Am. AMusQS 975-2500, DS/cont 1600
Stravinsky, Sulima		Entertainment	40			120	Pianist
Straw, Ezekiel A.		Governor	5	15			Governor NH
Strawbridge, James Dale		Senate/Congress	5	15			Rep. PA. CW Brigade Surgeon
Stray Cats		Entertainment	35			100	Rock
Strayhorn, Billy		Entertainment	352				Jazz Musician
Strecker, Colonel-General Karl	1884-1973	Military	25				World War II German general
Streep, Meryl		Entertainment	20	30	45	68	Versatile AA Winning Actress
Street, Julian		Author	15			75	
Streett, St. Clair		Aviation	50	165			Alaskan Air Expedition
Streib, Werner		Aviation				60	Ger. Ace WW II. RK
Streich, Rita		Entertainment	10			25	Opera
Streicher, Julius	1885-1946	Military	126	225			Nazi War Criminal
Streight, Abel	1828-1892	Civil War	30	55	70		Union Brevet Brig. General

NAME	DATE	CATEGORY	SIG	LS/DS	ALS	SP	COMMENTS
Streisand, Barbra		Entertainment	80	230		206	AA., songstress, director
Stribling, Thomas S.		Author	12	25	60		Am. Novlist. Pulitzer
Strickland, Ted S		Congress	10			15	Member U.S. Congress
Strindberg, August	1849-1912	Author	275		872	1095	Swe. ALS's/Cont. 1,400-2,200
Stringfield, Sherry		Entertainment				40	Actress ER
Stringham, Silas Horton	1798-1876	Civil War	35	65	90		Union Adm. Led Atlantic Blockade Fleet
Stritch, Samuel, Cardinal		Clergy	40	45	75	45	
Strode, Woody		Entertainment	50				Actor-Athlete
Stroh, Maj. Gen. Donald A.	1892-1953	Military	30				World War II U.S. general
Stroheim, Eric von	1885-1957	Entertainment	160			508	Austrian.Classic Film Director-Actor
Stromberg, Hunt		Entertainment	10	15		30	Film Producer, Director
Strong, Caleb	1745-1819	Revolutionary War	78	188	338		1st U.S. Sen. & Gov. MA. Constitutional Convention
Strong, Frederick	1855-1935	Military	20		65	80	Army General. Indian Fighter. Span-Am War
Strong, George C.	1832-1863	Civil War	235	694			Union Gen. Mortally Wounded 1863
Strong, Maj. Gen. George V.	1880-1946	Military	30				World War II U.S. general
Strong, Maj Gen Sir Kenneth W.D.	1900-1982	Military	225				World War II British general
Strong, Susan		Entertainment	12			20	Vintage Actress
Strong, William	1808-1895	Supreme Court	80	170	300		
Strong, William Kerley	1805-1867	Civil War	40	75			Union general
Stroud Twins		Entertainment	18			40	
Stroud, Robert	1890-1963	Convict	82	256	637		Birdman of Alcatraz
Strouse, Charles	1928-	Composer	20	125	200	75	Broadway Composer 'Annie' AMusQS 120
Struck, Heinz		Science	10			35	Rocket Pioneer w/von Braun
Struthers, Sally		Entertainment	5	10	20	22	
Stryker (4)		Entertainment	10			20	Gospel Singers
Stuart, Alexander H. H.	1807-1891	Cabinet	25	60	95		Fillmore Sec'y Interior
Stuart, David	1816-1868	Civil War	44	80	110		Union general
Stuart, George R.		Clergy	10	15	20		
Stuart, Gilbert	1755-1828	Artist	200	500	850		Portraitist. Presidents-Royalty
Stuart, Gloria		Entertainment	5			15	
Stuart, J.E.B. (WD)	1833-1864	Civil War	4500	7958	18500		CSA Gen. ALS/Cont. 19000
Stuart, J.E.B.	1833-1864	Civil War	3222	6625	12800		CSA Gen., Calvary.
Stuart, John T.	1808-1885	History	45	264			Lincoln's law partner
Stuart, John		Entertainment	10			20	Actor
Stuart, Leslie		Composer	20				Floradora AMusQS 200
Stuart, Lt. Gen. Kenneth	1891-1945	Military	20				World War II Canadian general
Stuart, Maj. Gen. Douglas	1894-1955	Military	25				World War II British general
Stuart, March B.		Military	30	75			Supt. West Point
Stuart, Marty		Country Music	10			25	
Stuart, Randy		Entertainment	3			10	
Stuckart, Wilhelm		Military	75				Drafted the Nuremberg laws
Studdert, Maj Gen. Robert Hallam	1890-1968	Military	28				World War II British general
Studebaker, Clement	1831-1901	Business	200	500	765		Auto Pioneers.Studebaker Bros.
Studebaker, Jr., Clement		Business	40	105	195	75	Studebaker Bros. Mfg. Co.
Student, Kurt	1890-1975	Military	45	176			German general, paratroopers

NAME	DATE	CATEGORY	SIG	LS/DS	ALS	SP	COMMENTS
Studer, Cheryl		Entertainment	10			35	Opera
Stultz, Wilmer		Aviation	50	135		150	Pioneer Aviator / A. Earhart
Stumbaugh, Frederick Shearer	1817-1897	Civil War	45	70	95		Union general
Stumme, Gen. Panz. Troops Geo.	1886-1942	Military	25				World War II German general
Stump, Felix B.		Military	40	80		50	Adm.Capt. Lexington WW II
Stumpff, Hans-Juergen		Military	46				General Luftwaffe
Stupak, Bart S		Congress	10			15	Member U.S. Congress
Sturdee, Lt. Gen. Vernon A.H.	1890-1966	Military	20				World War II Australian general
Sturdy, Robert William		Political	10			15	Member European Parliament
Sturge, Joseph	1793-1859	Philanthropist	12	20	95		Quaker Pacifist, Reformer, Abolitionist
Sturgeon, Daniel		Senate-Cabinet	25	70	125		Sen. PA 1839, US Treasurer 1853
Sturges, John	1911-1992	Entertainment	30	60	75	150	Am Dir. Many Action Films Including 'Great Escape'
Sturges, Lt. Gen. Sir Robt. Grives	1891-1970	Military	25				World War II British general
Sturges, Preston		Entertainment	20			50	Film Director, Producer, Writer
Sturgis, Samuel D.		Civil War	50	105	125		Union Gen.
Sturua, Melor		Celebrity	10			15	political celebrity
Styer, Lt. Gen. Wilhelm D.	1893-1975	Military	30				World War II U.S. general
Styne, Jule		Composers	25			75	AMusQS180, 370
Styron, William		Author	20	35	80	75	'Sophie's Choice' MsS 1p 200
Styx		Entertainment	25			50	
Suarez, Ray		Celebrity	10			15	media/TV personality
Suchet, David		Entertainment	10			30	Br. Actor. Poirot
Suchet, John		Celebrity	10			15	news reader
Suchet, Louis G., Duc d'A		Napoleonic Wars	85	215	390		Marshal of Napoleon
Sucre, Antonio de	1795-1830	Military	295	1517			Liberator of Venezuela, General & 2 Bolivar's Ass't
Sudarmono, Pratiwi		Astronaut	12	25		25	
Sudre, Margie		Political	10			15	Member European Parliament
Suenens, Leo Joseph, Cardinal		Clergy	45	75	90	65	
Suetaka, General Kamezo	1884-1955	Military	27				World War II Japanese general
Sugden, Gen. Sir Cecil Stanway	1903-1963	Military	28				World War II British general
Sugiyama, Field Marshal Hajime	1880-1945	Military	27				World War II Japanese general
Suharto, General		Head of State	15	30	75	35	Indonesia
Sukarno, Achmad	1902-1970	Head of State	95				1st President (Later as Dictator) of Indonesia
Sukhoi, P.	1895-1975	Military		145			Designer of Russian aircraft
Sul, Terra		Entertainment	4			10	
Sullavan, Margaret		Entertainment	60	65		173	Retired at 33. Suicide at 49
Sullivan, Anne (Annie)		Educator	100		425		TLS/Content 1,000
Sullivan, Arthur, Sir	1842-1900	Composer	125	400	762	1000	Gilbert and Sullivan., AMuQS 1,200
Sullivan, Barry		Entertainment	10	15		25	
Sullivan, Ed	1902-1974	Entertainment	25	45	85	160	Columnist, TV Host. 'Ed Sullivan Show'
Sullivan, Francis L.		Entertainment	10	20		25	
Sullivan, James		Revolutionary War	50	95	200		Continental Congress, Gov. MA
Sullivan, Jeremiah Cutler	1830-1890	Civil War	65	85			Union general
Sullivan, John S		Congress	10			15	Member U.S. Congress
Sullivan, John	1740-1795	Revolutionary War	122	425	575		Continental Congress, General

NAME	DATE	CATEGORY	SIG	LS/DS	ALS	SP	COMMENTS
Sullivan, Kathleen		Entertainment	10			20	TV Hostess
Sullivan, Kathryn D.		Aviation-Astro.	10	25	45	30	
Sullivan, Pat*		Cartoonist	50			400	Felix The Cat
Sullivan, Peter John	1830-1890	Civil War	30	60	85		Union General
Sullivan, Susan		Entertainment	5	6	20	15	
Sullivan, Tom		Celebrity	10			15	motivational speaker
Sullivan, William	1774-1839	Author	20	40	95		Politician, Gen. Militia, Orator
Sully, Alfred		Civil War	57	80	110	150	Union General
Sully, Thomas	1783-1872	Artist	145	260	333		Lead Portrait Painter of His Day
Sully-Prudhomme, René, F.A	1839-1907	Author	30	52	90		Fr. Poet, 1st Nobel Literature
Sultan, Lt. Gen. Daniel I.	1885-1947	Military	30				World War II U.S. general
Sulzberger, Art Ochs, Jr.		Business	10	25	30	15	NY Times
Sulzer, William		Congress-Gov.	15	35		25	Rep., Gov. NY, Impeached 1913
Sumberg, David		Political	10			15	Member European Parliament
Sumi, Jo		Entertainment	5			35	Opera. Korean Coloratura
Summer, Donna		Entertainment	10	15		30	
Summerall, Charles Pelot		Military	10	20	35	25	Gen., Pres. Citadel 1931-53
Summerfield, Arthur E.		Cabinet	15	20	30	20	P.M. General, Modernized System
Summersby, Kay		Military-WWII	95	175		125	D.D. Eisenhower's WW II Aide
Summerville, Slim		Entertainment	35			75	
Summey, Jason		Author	8			12	staying in school
Sumner, Charles	1811-1874	Civil War	40	72	120		Abolitionist. Founder Rep.Party. U.S. Sen.
Sumner, Edwin Vose	1797-1863	Civil War	84		175		Union general
Sumner, Increase	1746-1799	Governor	65	170			Rev. War Jurist & Stateman
Sumner, John B.	1780-1862	Clergy	25				Archbishop Canterbury
Sumter, Thomas	1734-1832	Revolutionary War	375	864			Soldier, Rep.,Sen., SC 1789
Sun Yat-Sen	1866-1975	Head of State	700	925	3025	2500	1st Pres. Chinese Republic
Sunday, William A. 'Billy'	1862-1935	Clergy	95	146	275	453	19th Cent. Early Evangelist-Baseball Player
Sung, Kim Il		Head of State	50			150	North Viet Nam
Sununu, John		Cabinet	12	15	25	15	Chief of Staff White House
Sununu, John		Senate	10			15	United States Senate (R - NH)
Suominen, Ilkka		Political	10			15	Member European Parliament
Supertramp		Entertainment	35			130	
Supervia, Conchita	1895-1936	Entertainment	150			688	Spanish Opera Singer. Rare In Authentic SP
Suplee, Ethan		Celebrity				30	
Suppé, Franz von		Composer	110	225	450	395	Aus.Opera, Operetta,Choral
Supreme Court (Burger)		Supreme Court				3000	Burger Court
Supreme Court (Hughes)		Supreme				4900	
Supreme Court (Stone)		Supreme Court				3500	All 9 Justices. Roosevelt 1941-42
Supreme Court (Taft)		Supreme Court				5800	Wm.H. Taft Court
Supreme Court (Waite)		Supreme Court	500				Morrison R. Waite Court
Supreme Court (Warren)		Supreme Court		1400		3384	Possibly Most Influential.
Surtees, Maj. Gen. George	1895-1976	Military	25				World War II British general
Susann, Jacqueline		Author	20	35	45	40	Valley of the Dolls etc.
Susskind, David	1920-1987	Entertainment	15			25	Controversial TV Producer

NAME	DATE	CATEGORY	SIG	LS/DS	ALS	SP	COMMENTS
Sutcliffe, Stuart		Celebrity			2855		Early Beatles, signed sketch 585-2070
Sutherland, Brigadier Roy B.	1897-1943	Military	20				World War II Australian general
Sutherland, Donald		Entertainment	9	15	20	47	Actor
Sutherland, George	1862-1942	Supreme Court	50	110	225	225	Justice 1922-38. Brit. Born. Opposed FDR
Sutherland, Joan		Entertainment	25		40	40	Magnificent Australian Soprano. Opera, Concert
Sutherland, Keifer		Entertainment	10			45	
Sutherland, Lt. Gen. Richard K.	1893-1966	Military	30				World War II U.S. general
Sutherland, Thomas Dr.		Celebrity	10			15	motivational speaker
Sutro, Adolph H. J.		Business-Engineer	90	165	200		Prussian-Born Mining magnate. Sutro Tunnel
Sutter, John A.	1803-1880	CA Pioneer	900	1750	3515	3500	Sutter's Fort. ALS/Cont. 15,000
Sutton, Grady		Entertainment	8	10		15	
Sutton, John		Entertainment	5			25	Suave Br. Co-Star
Sutton, Michael		Entertainment	10			20	actor
Sutton, Willy	1901-1980	Criminal	100	210	290	300	Bank Robber. Multi Prison Escapes
Suvorov, Alexander	1729-1800	Military			414		Russian Field Marshal
Suzman, Janet	1939-	Entertainment	20			25	Oscar Nominated - 'Nicholas & Alexandra'.
Suzuki, Lt. Gen. Soroku	1865-1940	Military	25				World War II Japanese general
Suzuki, Lt. Gen. Sosaku	1891-1945	Military	25				World War II Japanese general
Suzuki, Maj. Gen. Keiji	1897-1967	Military	25				World War II Japanese general
Suzuki, Maj. Gen. Shigeji	d. 1945	Military	25				World War II Japanese general
Svanholm, Set		Entertainment	15			55	Opera
Svenson, Bo		Entertainment	4	5	9	10	
Swaggart, Jimmy		Clergy	10	30	35	30	Evangelist
Swain, Dominique		Entertainment	8			30	Actress. 'Lolita' SP 50
Swan, James	1754-1830	Revolutionary War	180	540	575		Finan'l Speculator. Scottish-Born Patriot
Swan, Paul		Music	15	60			Guitarist
Swank, Hilary		Entertainment	6			35	Actress
Swann, Thomas		Senate/Congress	5	15			Senator, Gov, MD. Pres. B & O RR
Swanson, Claude A.	1862-1939	Cabinet	18	25	60	50	Sec'y Navy 1933 FDR
Swanson, Gloria	1897-1983	Entertainment	50	110		160	Actress., Premium for 'Sunset Blvd.' SP's
Swanson, Kristy		Entertainment	15			70	Actress (See Zane, Billy)
Swart, Charles R.	1894-	Head of State	5		20	40	
Swarthout, Gladys		Entertainment	25	75		85	Opera and Film Star. 5x7 SP 50
Swasey, Ambrose		Business	40	90			
Swayne, Noah H.		Supreme Court	45	144	195		
Swayne, Wager		Civil War	45	60	105		Union General
Swayze, John Cameron		Entertainment	5			10	Radio, TV News & Commercials
Swayze, Patrick		Entertainment	20			46	Actor
Swearingen, John		Business	10	25	40	15	CEO Continental Ill. Corp.
Sweat, Lorenzo DeMedici		Senate/Congress	10	15	25		Rep. ME 1863
Swedenborg, Emanuel	1688-1772	Science	3000	4000			Swe. Science, Philosophy, Religion
Sweeney, Brian		Law Enforcement	4			10	Law Enforcement No. Ireland
Sweeney, Charles W.		Military	25	86		60	Commander, dropped Atomic bomb on Nagasaki
Sweeney, John E. S		Congress	10			15	Member U.S. Congress
Sweeney, Walter C.		Military	5	15	25	15	Gen. Tactical Air Cmd.

NAME	DATE	CATEGORY	SIG	LS/DS	ALS	SP	COMMENTS
Sweeny, Allison		Entertainment	10			20	actress
Sweeny, Thomas William	1820-1892	Civil War	40		90		Union general
Sweet, Blanche	1895-1986	Entertainment	20		30	35	Important Silent Film Star Protégé of D.W.Griffith
Sweet, John H.		Business	5	15		10	CEO US News & World Report
Swenson, Bo		Entertainment	10			30	Actor. 'Walking Tall'
Swenson, Ruth Ann		Entertainment	10			25	Opera
Swett, James E.		Aviation	15	30	50	42	ACE, WW II
Swiebel, Joke		Political	10			15	Member European Parliament
Swift, Frederick W.	1831-1916	Civil War	30	45	60		Union General, MOH
Swift, George B.		Political	10	25			Mayor of Chicago
Swift, Harold Higgins		Business	20	50	95	35	Chm. Swift & Co., Meatpackers
Swift, John W.	1750-1819	Revolutionary War	65	180			Merchant. Soldier
Swift, Jonathan	1667-1745	Author	2500	7300	13230		Satirist, Poet, Clergy, Political
Swift, Maj. Gen. Innis P.	1882-1953	Military	30				World War II U.S. general
Swift, Pat		Celebrity	10			15	motivational speaker
Swigert, John L. Jr.		Astronaut	143	282		335	Apollo 13
Swinburne, Algernon C.	1837-1909	Author	185	295	1008		Br.19th Cent. Lyric Poet
Swing, D J		Music	10			15	DJ
Swing, Philip D.	1884-1963	Congress	5	25		15	Repr. CA
Swinnerton, Frank		Author	20	55	100		Br. Novelist, Critic
Swinnerton, James*		Cartoonist	35			180	Little Jimmy
Swinton, Ernest D.	1868-1951	Military	45	110	310		British Inventor of Tank
Swit, Loretta		Entertainment	15			33	
Swithinbank, Anne		Celebrity	10			15	home/gardening expert
Switzer, Carl 'Alfalfa'	1926-1959	Entertainment	702			1198	'Our Gang' Comedies
Swoboda, Johannes (hannes)		Political	10			15	Member European Parliament
Swope, Gerard		Business	60				CEO General Electric
Swope, Herbert Bayard	1882-1958	Author	10	25	45	30	Journalist, War Corresp., Pulitz
Swope, James S.		Aviation	15	25	40	30	ACE, WW II
Swunnerton, Maj. Gen. Chas. R.A.	1901-1973	Military	25				World War II British general
Sydow, Max von	1929-	Entertainment	10	12	15	20	Swe. Character Actor
Sykes, George 'Tardy George'	1822-1880	Civil War	65	98	165		Union general
Sykes, Jerome H.		Entertainment	15			30	Light Opera
Sykes, Melanie		Celebrity	10			15	celebrity model
Sylla, Fodé		Political	10			15	Member European Parliament
Sylva, Carmen		Author	50	75			Elizabeth, Queen of Romania
Sylva, Marguerite		Entertainment	15			25	Vintage Actress
Sylvia		Entertainment	5	6	15	15	
Symes, Maj. Gen. George William	1896-1980	Military	25				World War II British general
Symington, Stuart		Cabinet	10	15	35	25	Sen. MO, Sec'y Air Force
Symmes, John Cleves		Revolutionary War	110	375	550		Patriot. Continental Congress
Szakall, S. 'Cuddles'	1884-1955	Entertainment	150			325	Character Actor
Szell, George		Entertainment	20			65	Hung. Conductor. AMusQS 125
Szent-Gyorgyi, Albert		Science	35	65	125	50	Nobel Medicine 1937
Szigeti, Joseph	1892-1973	Entertainment	40	75		239	Hung.-Am. Violinist. AMusQS 125

NAME	DATE	CATEGORY	SIG	LS/DS	ALS	SP	COMMENTS
Szilard, Leo	1898-1964	Science	47	212		68	Nuclear/Phys. TLS/Cont.2500
Szold, Henrietta	1860-1945	Zionist Leader	140	475	616		Founder, Pres. Hadassah
Szyk, Arthur		Artist	25	65	90		Highly Detailed Portaits, Manuscripts. Miniaturist
Szymanowski, Karol M.		Composer	125	235	505		AMusMsS 1250

NAME	DATE	CATEGORY	SIG	LS/DS	ALS	SP	COMMENTS
T Hooft, Visser		Author	3	5	10	10	
T., Mr.		Entertainment	8			28	Actor
Tabb, John Banister	1845-1909	Civil War Clergy	40		200		Rom. Cath. clergy, Poet. CSA
Taber, Robert		Entertainment	6	8	15	15	
Taccani, Giuseppe		Entertainment	35			225	Opera, Noted Tenor
Taft, Charles P.		Publisher	10	15	25	15	Owner-Ed. Cincinnati Times-Star
Taft, Helen Herron	1861-1943	First Lady	78	240	550	409	ALS White House 1,200
Taft, Helen Manning		First Family	40	80	120	150	First Daughter
Taft, Henry Wallace	1859-1945	Lawyer	4	10	15	15	Politician, Writer Brother of Pres. Wm. Howard Taft
Taft, Lorado	1860-1936	Artist	48	110	130	155	Influential Am. Sculptor-Author
Taft, Robert A.	1889-1953	Senate/Congress	20	35		25	S caric. 75. US Sen. OH. Taft-Hartley Amendment
Taft, Robert, Jr.	1917-	Senate/Congress	8	20		15	Rep., Senator OH.
Taft, William Howard (As Pres)		President	205	530	3081	531	White House Card S 325-375. TLS/Content 1800
Taft, William Howard	1857-1930	President	140	340	792	431	ALS/Cont. As Chief Justice 2200-4500
Tagliabue, Carlo		Entertainment	45			175	Opera
Tagliavini, Feruccio		Entertainment	35			95	Opera. 4x6 SP 50
Taglioni, Marie	1804-1884	Entertainment	300		935		It. Premier Ballerina
Tagore, Rabindranath, Sir	1861-1941	Author	100	258	350	325	Nobel Prize Lit., Indian Poet
Tait, A.C., Archbishop		Clergy	12	35	50		
Tait, Arthur Fitzwilliam		Artist	28	55	110		Landscape Artist
Tajani, Antonio		Political	10			15	Member European Parliament
Taka, Miiko		Entertainment	15			25	Japanese Actress
Takahashi, Lt. Gen. Takaatsu	1888- ?	Military	25				World War II Japanese general
Takahira, Kogoro, Baron	1854-1926	Diplomat	45				At Treaty Signing of Russo-Jap. War.
Takashima, Maj. Gen. Tatsuhiko		Military	25				World War II Japanese general
Takeda, Maj. Gen.		Military	27				World War II Japanese general
Takei, George		Entertainment	15			38	Actor. 'Star Trek'
Takeshi, Lt. Gen. Takashina	d. 1944	Military	25				World War II Japanese general
Talbert, Melvin, Bishop		Clergy	20	25	30	35	
Talbot, Fred		Celebrity	10			15	weather presenter
Talbot, Gloria		Entertainment	8			25	Actress
Talbot, Helen		Entertainment	10			25	Actress
Talbot, Lyle	1902-1996	Entertainment	8	12	20	20	Vint 'B' Movie Lead. Migrated to Westerns & Sci-Fi
Talbot, Nita		Entertainment	7	10		20	Actress
Talbot, Wm. Henry Fox	1800-1877	Science	295		1250		Br. Inventor of Photogr. Process
Talbott, Harold D.		Cabinet	10	15		20	Sec'y AF

NAME	DATE	CATEGORY	SIG	LS/DS	ALS	SP	COMMENTS
Talbott, Strobe		Celebrity	10			15	media/TV personality
Talcott, Joseph	1669-1741	Colonial America	175	525	1200		Colonial Governor CT
Talent, James		Senate	10			15	United States Senate (R - MO)
Talese, Gay		Author	10	20		20	Am. Novelist
Taliaferro, William B. (WD)		Civil War	188	422			CSA Gen.
Taliaferro, William B.	1822-1898	Civil War	95		418		CSA Gen.
Talking Heads		Entertainment	25			70	
Tallchief, Maria		Entertainment	15	20	35	45	Ballerina
Talley, Marion		Entertainment	15		45	50	Am. Soprano
Talleyrand, Charles Maurice de	1754-1838	Head of State	195	482	950		Grand Chancellor of Napoleon. Important DS 2500
Talmadge, Benjamin	1754-1835	Revolutionary War	220	475			Served Throughout War. Rep. NY
Talmadge, Constance		Entertainment	45			115	Silent Star. 'Intolerance'.
Talmadge, Eugene		Governor	20	60	95	35	Governor GA
Talmadge, Herman		Senate/Congress	10	25		20	Gov., Senator GA. Senate Watergate Committee
Talmadge, Norma		Entertainment	50			142	Beautiful Silent Screen Star
Talmage, Thomas De Witt	1832-1902	Clergy	50	70	95		America Divine, Editor
Talman, William		Entertainment	50	70	150	125	Regular on Original Perry Mason. Cancer Victim
Talvela, Marti		Entertainment	30			75	Opera. Finnish Basso
Tamblyn, Russ		Entertainment	9	12		20	Actor-Dancer
Tambor, Jeffrey		Entertainment	8	8	15	25	Actor
Tamhori, Lee		Celebrity	10			15	film industry
Tamiroff, Akim		Entertainment	30	40	75	70	Russ. Character Actor
Tamon, General Jiro	1878-1934	Military	25				World War II Japanese general
Tanaka, General Shinichi	1893- ?	Military	27				World War II Japanese general
Tanaka, General Shizuichi	1887-1945	Military	27				World War II Japanese general
Tancredo, Thomas G. T		Congress	10			15	Member U.S. Congress
Tandy, Jessica	1904-1994	Entertainment	22	39	50	60	AA & Tony Awards. Hume Cronyn & Tandy 100
Taney, Roger B.	1777-1864	Supreme Court	98	252	383		Chief Justice., Dred Scott Decision, ALS/cont 2500
Tanner, Henry Ossawa		Artist	270		750		Religious Subjects, Realistic
Tanner, Joe		Astronaut	6			20	
Tanner, John Riley		Governor	12	20			Governor IL
Tanner, John S. T		Congress	10			15	Member U.S. Congress
Tanner, Richard 'Diamond Dick'	1869-1943	Old West	200			650	Companion to Wild Bill Hickok
Tanning, Dorothea	1910-	Artist	35		200		Am. Painter
Tannock, Charles		Political	10			15	Member European Parliament
Tansman, Alexandre		Composer	40	125		240	Composer-Pianist.Operas, Symphonies, Films
Tapp, Maj. Gen. Sir Nigel Prior H.	1904-1991	Military	28				World War II British general
Tappan, Arthur	1786-1865	Abolitionist	25	65	125		Merchant, Philanthropist
Tappan, James C.	1825-1906	Civil War	80	135	245		CSA General. S/Rank 145
Tarantino, Quentin		Entertainment	20			50	AA Pulp Fiction Writer-Director
Tarbell, Ida M.	1857-1944	Author	20	45	65	75	Muckraking Journalist re Std.Oil
Tarbuck, Jimmy		Celebrity	10			15	comedian
Tarbuck, Lisa		Celebrity	10			15	television presenter
Tarkington, Booth	1869-1946	Author	38	70	85	125	Playwright, Novelist. Pulitzer. TLS/Cont 425
Tarleton, Banastre, Sir		Revolutionary War	135	365	932		Barbaric Br. General. Am. Rev.

NAME	DATE	CATEGORY	SIG	LS/DS	ALS	SP	COMMENTS
Tarnower, Herman Dr.		Medical	15	50	135	60	Murdered Diet Dr.
Tarrant, Chris		Celebrity	10			15	television presenter
Tartakov, Joakim		Entertainment			450		Opera. Imperial Russ. Baritone Star. SPc 150
Tartikoff, Brandon		Business	10			42	TV executive
Tashlin, Frank		Entertainment	15			25	Director
Tashman, Lilyan		Entertainment	30	40	75	70	Vintage Actress. Major Star in 30's
Tassigny, J.M.G. de		Military	35	90	140		Fr. Gen.
Tate, Allen	1899-1979	Author	10	30	75		Am. Poet, Critic, Biographer
Tate, Harry	1872-1940	Entertainment	10			50	Brit. Music Hall Comedian. Silent Films
Tate, Henry, Sir, 1st Baronet		Business	40	105	240		Br. Sugar Refiner Philanthropist, Art-Tate Gallery.
Tate, Jackson R.		Military	30		65	50	Adm. WW II.
Tate, Sharon	1943-1969	Entertainment	238	300	500	600	Murdered By Manson Gang. Special SP 3600
Tategawa, Lt. Gen. Yoshitsugu	1880-1945	Military	27				World War II Japanese general
Tati, Jacques	1908-1982	Entertainment	50				Fr. Actor. 'Monsieur Hulot's Holiday' SP(Pc)415
Tattersall, Richard	1724-1795	Business	20	45	105		Rendevous For Sporting-Betting
Tattnall, Joseph		Civil War			715		CSA Naval Capt.
Tatum, Edward L.	1909-1975	Science	45	70	125		Nobel 1958. Research in Molecular Genetics
Taube, Henry, Dr.		Science	25	40		30	Nobel Chemistry 1983
Tauber, Richard	1892-1948	Entertainment	50			231	Opera, Austrian-Born, British Tenor
Taufflieb, Gen.		Military	45	120	215	100	
Taurog, Norman		Entertainment	50			150	Film Director
Tauscher, Ellen O. T		Congress	10			15	Member U.S. Congress
Taussig, Frank William	1859-1940	Economist	10	25			Author.Chm. Tariff Bd.
Tauzin, W. J. (Billy) T		Congress	10			15	Member U.S. Congress
Tavare, Jim		Celebrity	10			15	comedian
Tavernier, Bertrand		Celebrity	10			15	film industry
Tawes, J. Millard		Governor	5	15			Governor MD
Tawney, James A.		Congress	7	15	25		Repr. MN 1893
Tayback, Vic		Entertainment	22			38	Character Actor. Films-TV 'Alice'
Taylor, Bayard	1825-1878	Author	20	67	135		Journalist, Traveller, Diplomat
Taylor, Brig. Gen. George A.	1899-1969	Military	30				World War II U.S. general
Taylor, Caleb Newbold	1813-1887	Congress	15		35		MOC PA. Visited Lincoln w/Recommendations
Taylor, Charles H.		Congress	5	10		15	Congressman NC
Taylor, Christine		Entertainment				38	Actress
Taylor, David		Celebrity	10			15	veterinarian expert
Taylor, Deems		Composer	35	80	90	50	Musicologist, Critic, Author
Taylor, Don		Entertainment	20			35	Actor turned Director. Star of 40's-50's Films
Taylor, Dub		Entertainment	15			40	Western Character Actor
Taylor, Elizabeth	b. 1932	Entertainment	116	548		408	AA. MGM Early Contract S 1500, DS/cont 450-750
Taylor, Estelle		Entertainment	10	25	45	45	Vintage Actress
Taylor, Gene T		Congress	10			15	Member U.S. Congress
Taylor, Gen. Sir Maurice Grove	1881-1960	Military	28				World War II British general
Taylor, George William	1808-1862	Civil War	110				Union general
Taylor, George	1716-1781	Rev. War	8000	18000	57500		Rare Signer Decl of Independence, Partial DS 6325
Taylor, Glen H.	1904-1984	Congress	10	25		25	Sen. ID, Actor, Singer

NAME	DATE	CATEGORY	SIG	LS/DS	ALS	SP	COMMENTS
Taylor, Graham		Clergy	15	25	35		
Taylor, Henry C.		Military	30	60	95		Admiral. Spanish-American War
Taylor, James Willis		Senate/Congress	4	10	20		Rep. TN 1919
Taylor, James		Composer	58	78	160	63	Singer-Guitarist
Taylor, Joan		Entertainment	7			15	Actress. Paramount Contractee. Mostly Westerns
Taylor, John W.	1784-1854	Senate/Congress	30	55	75		Speaker of U.S. House of Reps
Taylor, John		Celebrity	50	130			
Taylor, Joseph P.	1796-1864	Civil War	65	175			War 1812 & CW Union Gen.
Taylor, Karin		Celebrity	10			15	model
Taylor, Kent		Entertainment	5			15	Popular Handsome 'B' Movie Leading Man
Taylor, Laurette	1884-1946	Entertainment	32	40	50	120	Major Star of Am. Theatre. SPc 75
Taylor, Lili		Entertainment	10			20	actress
Taylor, Maj Gen. Sir Geo. Brian O.	1887-1973	Military	28				World War II British general
Taylor, Margherita		Celebrity	10			15	celebrity model
Taylor, Mary		Country Music	10			20	Singer
Taylor, Maxwell D.		Military	25	84	125	70	Gen. WW II
Taylor, Meshach		Entertainment	9			23	Afr-Am Actor. 'Designing Women', 'Dave's World'
Taylor, Nelson	1821-1894	Civil War	40		85		Union general
Taylor, Nikki		Entertainment	15			63	Actress-Model. Pin-Up 75
Taylor, Richard (WD)	1826-1879	Civil War	382	1653	3500		CSA Gen. Son of Pres. Taylor
Taylor, Richard E., Dr.		Science	20	50			Nobel Physics 1990
Taylor, Richard	1826-1879	Civil War	290	783			CSA Gen. Son of Pres. Taylor
Taylor, Robert L.	1850-1912	Congress	10	15		15	Gov., Rep. & Senator TN
Taylor, Robert	1911-1969	Entertainment	45	90	125	212	Handsome Am. Actor and Leading Man
Taylor, Rod		Entertainment	10	20		30	Actor
Taylor, Sandra		Entertainment	10			20	actress
Taylor, Thomas H. (WD)		Civil War	125	210	468		CSA Gen.
Taylor, Thomas H.	1825-1901	Civil War	80	115	275		CSA General
Taylor, Vaughn		Entertainment	20			50	
Taylor, W. Randy		Author	8			12	motivation, inspiration
Taylor, Walter H.		Civil War	50	94			CSA Col. Aide-de-camp R.E. Lee
Taylor, William, Bishop		Clergy		40	50	75	
Taylor, Zachary (As Pres.)		President	950	4650	11800		3rd Rarest in Presidentially Signed Items. FF 2500
Taylor, Zachary	1784-1850	President	744	1655	3264		General in Mexican War. ALS/Cont 8500
Taylor-Young, Leigh		Entertainment	5	8	15	15	Actress
Tazewell, Littleton		Senate/Congress	45	135	232		MOC 1800, Sen. 1824, Gov. VA
Tchaikovsky, Piotr I.	1840-1893	Composer	1731	3348	5229	5942	Rus. Opera, Symphony, Ballet, Etc.
Tchelitchew, Pavel	1898-1957	Artist	75		500		Russian-born American Painter
Tcherepnin, Alexander	1899-1977	Composer	50	125			Russian Pianist. AMuQS 350
Tchernihovsky, Saul		Author	175		550		Rus-Hebrew Dr., Poet, Translator
Te Kanawa, Kiri, Dame		Entertainment	40	55		75	New Zealand Born. Opera, Concert
Teagarden, Charlie		Entertainment	10			25	Jazz Trumpet
Teagarden, Jack		Entertainment	60	100		125	Big Band Leader-Trombonist
Teal, Ray		Entertainment	50			150	
Teale, Edwin W.	1899-1980	Nauralist			75	30	Photographer, Pulitzer Writer.

NAME	DATE	CATEGORY	SIG	LS/DS	ALS	SP	COMMENTS
Tearle, Conway		Entertainment	15			40	Vintage Br. Actor
Tearle, Godfrey, Sir		Entertainment	20			50	Br. Actor. Vintage
Teasdale, Sara	1894-1933	Author	95	160		175	Poet. Bouts of Depression. Suicide at 39
Teasdale, Veree		Entertainment	20	25	45	45	Vintage Actress 30's-40's. Wife of Adolf Menjou
Tebaldi, Renata		Entertainment	25			100	Opera. Italian Soprano
Tedder, Arthur	1890-1967	Military	46				British Chief Air Marshal
Tedrow, Irene		Entertainment	4	4		15	Character Actress 40's-50's. Mother Parts
Teissedre De Fleury, Francois		Rev War			633		
Teitjens, Therese		Entertainment	50			190	Opera
Telfair, Edward		Revolutionary War	35	95	150		Continental Congress from GA
Telford, Thomas	1757-1834	Engineer		105	330		Br. Road and Bridge Builder
Teller, Edward, Dr.	1908-1994	Science	42	90	210	110	Fermi Award. Father of 'H-Bomb'
Teller, Henry M.	1830-1914	Cabinet	30	40	50	75	Sec'y Interior 1882, Arthur
Telva, Marion		Entertainment	15			40	Opera. Noted Contralto
Temin, Howard M., Dr.		Science	20	35	55	25	Nobel Medicine 1975
Tempest, Marie		Entertainment	25	35	50	65	
Temple, Frederick	1821-1902	Clergy	22		90		Archbishop Canterbury, Educator, Author
Temple, Shirley (Agar)		Entertainment	61			350	Shirley's First Husband, John
Temple, Shirley (as a child)		Entertainment	250	414		571	As Child
Temple, Shirley (Black)		Entertainment	24	25	40	45	
Temple, Wm.		Clergy	40	45	85	65	Archbishop Canterbury
Templeton, Alec		Entertainment	10			50	Br. Blind Jazz Pianist
Templeton, Ben		Cartoonist	5			20	Motley's Crew
Templeton, Faye		Entertainment	25	30	60	65	Musical Career For Over 50 Year
Temptations (All)		Entertainment	40			125	
Ten Broeck, Abraham	1734-1810	Revolutionary War	100	160	325		Gen. Judge, Banker
Tennant, Frederick R.	1866-1957	Clergy	15	20	25		English Theologian
Tennant, Veronica		Ballet	10			25	National Ballet of Canada
Tennant, Victoria		Entertainment	5	8	25	20	
Tenniel, John, Sir	1820-1914	Artist	70	110	260		Illustr. 'Alice in Wonderland'
Tennille, Toni		Entertainment	5			15	Singer. 'The Captain & Tennille'
Tennyson, Alfred, Lord	1809-1892	Author	182	325	440	1050	Br. Poet Laureate
Tennyson, Jean		Entertainment	10			20	Am. Soprano
Terauchi, Fld Mshl Hisaichi Count	1879-1946	Military	25				World War II Japanese general
Teresa, Mother	1911-1997	Clergy	125	304	794	248	Worked w/Poorest of Poor. Nobel Peace Prize 1979
Tereshkova, Valentina		Cosmonaut	52	95		139	1st Woman in Outer Space
Terfel, Bryn		Entertainment	10			35	Welsh Operatic Baritone
Terhune, Alfred Payson	1872-1942	Author	33	75	130	50	Famous Writer of Dog Stories
Terhune, Max	1891-1973	Entertainment	100			250	Western Sidekick in Republic & Monogram Series
Terkel, Studs		Author	10	15	25	15	Columnist, Biographer, TV
Ternina, Milka		Entertainment	20		135		Opera. Croatian Soprano
Terrell, Bob		Author	10			25	Author, Newspaper Columnist
Terrell, Maj. Gen. Henry Jr.	1890-1971	Military	30				World War II U.S. general
Terrill, James Barbour	1838-1864	Civil War	260				Confederate general
Terrill, William Rufus	1834-1862	Civil War					Union general

NAME	DATE	CATEGORY	SIG	LS/DS	ALS	SP	COMMENTS
Terriss, Ellaline		Entertainment	15			48	Br. Actress. 19th Century
Terrón I Cusí, Anna		Political	10			15	Member European Parliament
Terry, Alfred Howe	1827-1890	Civil War	113	275	429		Union Gen., Cmdr. Dakota Terr.Sig/Rank 185,DS 800
Terry, Clark		Entertainment	50				Trumpet, Fluegelhorn
Terry, Ellen, Dame	1847-1928	Entertainment	35	70	135	188	Br. Actress Partner of Henry Irving. SP Pc 145
Terry, Fred	1864-1933	Entertainment	10	15	25	25	Br. Stage & Film Star
Terry, Henry D.	1812-1869	Civil War	45	65	100		Union General. Sig/Rank 65
Terry, Lee T		Congress	10			15	Member U.S. Congress
Terry, Luther, Dr.		Celebrity	3	5	10	5	
Terry, Maj. Gen. Thomas A.	1885-1963	Military	30				World War II U.S. general
Terry, Paul*		Cartoonist	50			198	Animator 'Mighty Mouse'
Terry, Phillip	1909-	Entertainment	5	6	10	15	Actor. Films from 30's. Leads-2nd Leads in B Films
Terry, Ruth	1920-	Entertainment	10			27	Actress-Singer. Films at 16. Numerous Westerns
Terry, William Richard	1827-1897	Civil War	90	195	370		CSA General. Sig/Rank 200, War Dte. DS 625
Terry, William	1814-1888	Civil War	85		270		CSA Gen. Sig/Rank 120
Tesla, Nikola, Dr.	1856-1943	Science	450	1309	2204	2075	Physicist, Electrical Genius. Power Systems
Tetard, J.		Aviation	45	60	170	100	
Tetley, Brigadier James Noel	1898-1971	Military	28				World War II British general
Tetrazzini, Luisa	1871-1940	Entertainment	50	115	200	225	It. Opera.SPc 300 as 'Lakme'
Tevis, Lloyd		Business		475			Mining & Partner of Geo. Hearst & Haggin
Teyte, Maggie		Entertainment	35			130	Opera
Thacher, James, Dr.	1754-1844	Science-Author	55		300		Revolutionary War Surgeon
Thackeray, Wm. Makepeace	1811-1863	Author	86	375	502		Br. Novelist 'Vanity Fair'
Thaden, Louise McP.		Aviation		295			Altitude, Endurance, Speed Records
Thagard, Norman E.		Astronaut	10			30	
Thalberg, Irving	1899-1936	Entertainment	167	323	525	450	MGM's Boy Genius Producer
Thant, U	1909-1974	Head of State	35	70	125	125	UN Sec'y General
Tharp, Sister Rosetta		Entertainment	65			125	Jazz Vocalist-Guitar
Tharp, Twyla		Entertainment	20	25		40	Dancer-Choreographer
Thatcher, Henry Knox	1806-1880	Civil War	55	95	155		Union Naval Commander. Sig/Rank 85
Thatcher, Margaret, Dame		Head of State	45	140	225	150	Prime Minister. Engr. P.M. Card/Addr. 175
Thatcher, Peter		Clergy	75	100	150		
Thaves, Bob		Cartoonist	5			20	'Frank & Ernest'
Thaw, Harry K.		Business	75	156	325	250	Playboy. Shot Sanford White. Major Scandal
Thaw, Russell T.		Aviation	20				Racing Pilot
Thaxter, Celia	1835-1894	Author	20	40	95	150	Am. Poet
Thaxter, Phyllis		Entertainment	10			25	Stage & Film Leading Lady
Thayer, Abbott	1849-1921	Artist	15	35	70		Am. Ideal Figures, Landscapes
Thayer, Celia		Author	5	10	15		Am. Novelist, Screenwriter
Thayer, John Milton	1820-1906	Civil War	45	70	95		Union Gen., Gov. WY Terr.
Thayer, Silvanus	1785-1872	Military	60	140	245		'Father of the Military Academy'
Thayil, Kim		Entertainment	6			25	Music. Lead Guitar 'Soundgarden'
Theato, Diemut R.		Political	10			15	Member European Parliament
Thebaw		Head of State	145				Burma
Thebom, Blanche		Entertainment	20	35		75	Am. Contralto, Opera, Concert

NAME	DATE	CATEGORY	SIG	LS/DS	ALS	SP	COMMENTS
Theißen, Gen. of Artillery Edgar	1890-1968	Military	25				World War II German general
Theiss, Ursula		Entertainment	10	15	25	25	Ger. Actress. Several Hollywood Films 50's
Theissen, Tiffany Amber		Entertainment	15			50	Actress
Thelen, Bob		Aviation	10	25	40	35	ACE, WW II, Blue Angels
Theorin, Maj Britt		Political	10			15	Member European Parliament
Theron, Charlize		Entertainment	9			48	Actress
Thesiger, Ernest		Entertainment	225			650	
Thevenot, Melchisidec	1620-1692	Traveler	20		95		French Traveler Family Introduced Coffee to France
Thewlis, David		Entertainment	10			20	actor
Thibodeaux, Keith		Entertainment	20				Child Actor. Played 'Little Ricky' on 'I Love Lucy
Thicke, Alan		Entertainment	10		25	25	Actor-Humorist. 'Growing Pains'
Thielicke, Helmut		Clergy	20	50	65	60	Germ. Evangel. Theologian
Thien, Dinh		Entertainment	10			20	actor
Thiers, Louis-Adolphe	1797-1877	Fr. Revolution	35	65	170		1st Pres. 3rd Republic
Thieu, Nguyen Van		Head of State	20	60	150	40	So. Viet Nam
Thinnis, Roy		Entertainment	5	10	20	15	Actor
Thirsk, Bob		Astronaut	5	15		15	
Thoma, Gen Panz. Wilhelm K. von	1891-1948	Military	252				World War II German general
Thomas, Allen	1830-1907	Civil War	95				Confederate general
Thomas, Ambroise	1822-1896	Music			72		Master of the French opera
Thomas, Andrew		Astronaut	6			20	
Thomas, B.J.		Entertainment	5			10	Singer-Songwriter
Thomas, Betty		Entertainment	5	6	15	10	
Thomas, Bryan Morel	1836-1905	Civil War	110				Confederate general
Thomas, C.-L.-Ambroise	1811-1896	Composer	75	120	192	250	Fr. Romantic Composer. Operas,etc. AMusQS 525
Thomas, Charles	1840-1878	Civil War	25	45	60		Union Brevet Major General
Thomas, Clarence	1948-	Supreme Court	25			35	
Thomas, Craig		Senate	10			15	United States Senate (R - WY)
Thomas, Danny	1914-1991	Entertainment	15	26		47	Comedian. 'Danny Thomas Show'
Thomas, Dave		Business	15	25		40	Founder of Wendy's. TV Spokesman. S Sketch 175
Thomas, Donald		Astronaut	8			25	
Thomas, Dylan	1914-1953	Author	510		1925	1500	Welsh Poet, Playwright, Short Stories
Thomas, E. Donnall, Dr.		Science	15	25		30	Nobel Medicine 1990
Thomas, Eddie Kaye		Celebrity				30	Actor
Thomas, Edward Lloyd	1825-1898	Civil War	100				Confederate general
Thomas, General Sir Gwilym Ivor	1893-1972	Military	25				World War II British general
Thomas, George Henry	1818-1870	Civil War	135	474	592	800	Union Gen.'Rock of Chickamauga', LS/cont 1500
Thomas, George		Celcbrity	50	55	60	70	Titanic survivor
Thomas, Heather		Entertainment	10	10	30	45	Actress
Thomas, Heck		Western Lawman		634			Special DS 2500
Thomas, Helen		Celebrity	10			15	media/TV personality
Thomas, Henry Goddard	1837-1897	Civil War	40	65			Union general
Thomas, Isaiah	1749-1831	Colonial Printer	135	380	1000		Publ.1st Eng. Bible in America
Thomas, James, Bishop		Clergy	20	25	35	30	
Thomas, Jay		Entertainment	10			20	actor

NAME	DATE	CATEGORY	SIG	LS/DS	ALS	SP	COMMENTS
Thomas, Jess		Entertainment	15			40	Opera
Thomas, John Charles	1891-1960	Entertainment	20	45	45	45	Multi-Media Am. Baritone
Thomas, John	1724-1776	Revolutionary War	510	855	1750		Am. Physician & Gen. Cont'l Army
Thomas, Jonathan Taylor	1981-	Entertainment	10			62	Talented Child-Young Actor 'Home Improvement' etc.
Thomas, Kurt		Entertainment	5	6	15	15	
Thomas, Lorenzo (WD)	1804-1975	Civil War	45	110	210		Union General. Seminole, Mexican & Civil Wars
Thomas, Lorenzo	1804-1875	Civil War	45	65	92	356	Union general
Thomas, Lowell		Entertainment	15		35	125	World Traveller. Top Radio Commentator 30's-40's
Thomas, Maj Gen. Lechmere Cay	1897-1981	Military	25				World War II British general
Thomas, Marlo		Entertainment	5	25		25	Actress & Daughter of Danny
Thomas, Michael Tilson		Conductor	15			50	Am. Conductor
Thomas, Norman	1884-1961	Socialist Leader	35	95	205	55	6 Times Presidential Candidate. Socialist Leader
Thomas, Olive		Entertainment	65	70	150	150	Actress. Jack Pickford Wife. Suicide at 36
Thomas, Philip Evan		Business	5	15	25		
Thomas, Richard		Entertainment	8	15	20	25	Actor
Thomas, Rob		Entertainment	7			30	Music. Lead Singer 'Matchbox 20'
Thomas, Robert Bailey		Author	20	45	105		Publisher, Editor 'Farmer's Almanac'
Thomas, Samuel	1840-1903	Civil War	30	55			Union General
Thomas, Seth E.	1785-1859	Business	125	250	475	315	Founder Seth Thomas Clock Co.
Thomas, Seth E., Jr.	1816-1888	Business	65	175	350		Cont'd Seth Thomas Clock Co.
Thomas, Stephen	1809-1903	Civil War	45	65	95		Union general
Thomas, Terry		Entertainment	50		100	138	Br. Comedian-Actor
Thomas, Theodore		Entertainment	15			30	Conductor. NY & Chic. Symph.
Thomas, William M. T		Congress	10			15	Member U.S. Congress
Thomas-mauro, Nicole		Political	10			15	Member European Parliament
Thomason, John	1893-1944	Art					Signed drawing 70
Thomasson, William P.	1797-1882	Congress	12	15			MOC KY, Union Officer CW
Thomberg, Kerstin		Entertainment	15			35	
Thompson Twins		Entertainment	30			75	Signed by Both
Thompson, Antony Worrall		Celebrity	10			15	TV Chef
Thompson, Benj. (Rumford)	1753-1814	Revolutionary War	275	450	1138		Count von Rumford. Br.Physicist, Inventor,Loyalist
Thompson, Benjamin	1798-1852	Senate/Congress	5	15	25		MOC MA 1845
Thompson, Bennie G. T		Congress	10			15	Member U.S. Congress
Thompson, Denman		Entertainment	10			30	Vintage Stage Actor
Thompson, Derek		Entertainment	10			20	Actor
Thompson, Dorothy	1894-1961	Author	35	55	110	80	Journalist, Correspondent, Columnist, Wit
Thompson, Emma		Entertainment	20			58	Br. Actress-Playwright AA. Pin-Up SP 75
Thompson, Fred		Celebrity	10			35	actor, Senator TN
Thompson, Gordon		Entertainment	8	9		20	
Thompson, Hank		Country Music	6			15	Singer-Songwriter
Thompson, J. Walter	1847-1928	Business	100	170		150	J. Walter Thompson Adv. Agency. Bond S 2400
Thompson, Jacob	1810-1885	Civil War-Cabinet	75	160	325		Sec'y Interior, CSA Secret Agt.
Thompson, Jim		Governor	5	10		20	Governor IL
Thompson, John P.		Business	15	30	65	20	Pres. Southland Corp.
Thompson, John T.	1860-1940	Inventor-Military	85	300			USA Officer, Inventor Thompson Submachine Gun

NAME	DATE	CATEGORY	SIG	LS/DS	ALS	SP	COMMENTS
Thompson, Lea		Entertainment	10	10		35	Actress. 'Back to the Future', 'Caroline in the City
Thompson, Linda		Entertainment	5			10	Actress. Pin-Up SP 20
Thompson, Lt. Gen. Sir Treffey O.	1888-1979	Military	25				World War II British general
Thompson, M.E.		Governor	5	15			Governor GA
Thompson, Maj. Gen. Charles F.	1882-1954	Military	30				World War II U.S. general
Thompson, Marshall		Entertainment	15		25	35	Actor. Juvenile Leads-40's. Mature Leads 50's
Thompson, Merriwether J.	1826-1876	Civil War	135	260	730		CSA General
Thompson, Merriwether J.(WD)		Civil War	212		2401	850	MO Militia General. Noted Guerrilla Fighter
Thompson, Mike T		Congress	10			15	Member U.S. Congress
Thompson, Orlo and Marvis		Country Music	20			45	(Both)
Thompson, Richard W.		Cabinet	25	45	70		Sec'y Navy 1809
Thompson, Robert E.		Clergy	10	10	15		
Thompson, Ruth Plumly	1891-1976	Author	450				Oz Books. Widow of Frank Baum
Thompson, Smith	1768-1843	Supreme Court	50	110	248		
Thompson, Sue		Country Music	10			25	Singer
Thompson, Wm. H. 'Big Bill'	1869-1944	Mayor of Chicago	125				Gangster Era Mayor. Backed by Al Capone
Thomson, Andrew		Clergy	35	65	75		
Thomson, Charles	1729-1824	Revolutionary War	140	437	625		Wealthy Merch. LS As Sec'y Cont'l Congr.1,750
Thomson, Elihu	1853-1937	Science	525	1250			Electrical Engineer-Inventor. Over 700 Patents
Thomson, Geo. Paget, Sir	1892-1975	Science	55			100	Nobel Physics 1937
Thomson, Hugh		Artist	25		100		Br. Illustrator
Thomson, James E.		Business	5	15	30	15	Pres. Merrill-Lynch.
Thomson, Joseph J., Sir	1856-1940	Science			1046		Discovered electron
Thomson, Maj. Gen. James Noel	1888-1979	Military	25				World War II British general
Thomson, Virgil	1896-1989	Composer	40	88	117	135	Conductor & Music Critic, AMusQS 125-225
Thorborg, Kerstin		Entertainment	20			75	Opera
Thorburn, Grant		Colonial Am.	40	95			Grocery, Seed Merchant. Hero
Thoreau, Henry David	1717-1862	Author	3500	6500	12500		Am. Schoolmaster-Naturalist. Retired to 'Walden Pond
Thornberry, Mac T		Congress	10			15	Member U.S. Congress
Thorndike, Sybil, Dame		Entertainment	25	52		42	Br. Preeminent Actress. Seven Decade Career
Thorne, Chas. Rob't	1814-1893	Entertainment	65	80		120	
Thorne, Paul		Celebrity	10			15	comedian
Thorne-Smith, Courtney		Entertainment	6			40	Actress
Thornhill, Claude		Entertainment	12			45	Big Band Leader
Thornhill, F.D.		Military	15	25	40		
Thorning-schmidt, Helle		Political	10			15	Member European Parliament
Thornton, Billie Bob		Entertainment	7			52	Actor. Writer-Director
Thornton, Charles Tex		Business	5	15	25	15	
Thornton, Dan		Governor	5	15		10	Governor CO
Thornton, Kate		Celebrity	10			15	television presenter
Thornton, Kathryn		Astronaut	10			27	
Thornton, Matthew	1714-1803	Revolutionary War	525	1550	3212		Signer Decl. of Indepen.
Thornton, William A.	1803-1866	Civil War	35				Union Gen. '62 DS 95
Thornton, William E., Dr.		Astronaut	10			20	
Thornton, William		Astronaut	5			20	

NAME	DATE	CATEGORY	SIG	LS/DS	ALS	SP	COMMENTS
Thornton, William	1759-1828	Revolutionary War	125	250	325		Am. Architect. Designed Capitol
Thornton, Willie Mae	1926-1984	Entertainment	90	170	275		Am. Jazz-Gospel Singer. Died of Alcoholism
Thorpe, Jeremy		Politician	10	20	45	15	Br. Parliamentarian
Thorpe, Maj. Gen. Gervase	1877-1962	Military	25				World War II British general
Thorpe, Rose Hartwick		Author	10	20	35		Am. 'Curfew Must Not Ring Tonight'
Thors, Astrid		Political	10			15	Member European Parliament
Thorson, Ralph 'Papa'		Law	10	25	45	20	Bounty Hunter
Thorvaldsen, Bertel		Artist	105	325			Dan. Sculptor 'Lion of Lucerne'
Three Suns, The		Entertainment	15			45	Pop-Jazz Musicians
Throop, Enos T.		Governor	25	55			Governor NY 1829
Thruston, Charles Mynn	1798-1873	Civil War	45	85			Union general
Thruston, Gates P.	1835-1920	Civil War	25	30	55		Union General
Thuot, Pierre		Astronaut	5			15	
Thurber, James	1894-1961	Author	105	252	419	305	Am. Humorist & Comic Artist
Thurman, Allen G.	1813-1895	Congress	10	30	45		Senator OH
Thurman, Howard		Clergy	35	40	50	50	
Thurman, Uma		Entertainment	12	30	65	58	Actress
Thurmond, J. Strom	1902-2003	Senate/Congress	10	20		15	Longest serving Senator, Governor SC
Thursby, Emma		Entertainment	30				American Soprano
Thurston, Howard	1869-1936	Entertainment	80	212	250	225	Thurston The Magician
Thurston, John M.	1847-1916	Congress	15		30		Senator NE 1895
Thurston, Lorrin A.	1858-1931	Political	35		55		Pioneer Hawaiian Political Leader
Thyssen, Marianne L.P.		Political	10			15	Member European Parliament
Tiahrt, Todd T		Congress	10			15	Member U.S. Congress
Tibbatts, John W.	1802-1852	Congress	10		55		MOC KY, Officer Mexican War
Tibbett, Lawrence	1896-1960	Entertainment	75	80		108	Opera, Concert, Films, Radio
Tibbetts, Paul W.		Aviation	30	80	130	87	Pilot of Enola Gay WW II. General.
Tibbits, William Badger	1837-1880	Civil War	40		80		Union general
Tiberi, Patrick J. T		Congress	10			15	Member U.S. Congress
Tickell, Maj. Gen. Sir Eustace F.	1898-1972	Military	25				World War II British general
Tidball, John C.	1825-1906	Civil War	25	45	60		Union Brevet Major General
Tiege, Karl		Artist	80		275		Czech. Surrealist Painter
Tiegs, Cheryl		Entertainment	8	9		25	Model. Pin-Up SP 25
Tierney, Gene	1920-1991	Entertainment	30	25	40	60	Actress. 'Laura'. Pin-Up SP 50
Tierney, Harry		Composer	40	95	195		AMusQS 350
Tierney, John F. T		Congress	10			15	Member U.S. Congress
Tietjens, Therese		Entertainment	40			135	Ger. Soprano . Opera
Tiffany, Charles Lewis	1812-1902	Business	175	500		2125	Founder Tiffany and Co. Jewelry Designer. Artist
Tiffany, Louis Comfort		Artist-Business	175	550			Stained glass artist. Spec. Ed. Book S 3200
Tiffin, Pamela		Entertainment	5	8	15	15	Actress
Tigrett, John Burton		Author	8			12	business success
Tilden, Samuel J.	1814-1886	Governor	75	160	275		Gov. NY, Presidential Cand.
Tilghman, James		Revolutionary War	25	70	165		Lawyer, Politician
Tilghman, Lloyd (WD)	1816-1863	Civil War	235		1980		CSA Gen. KIA. AES 635
Tilghman, Lloyd	1816-1863	Civil War	140	290	502		CSA General. KIA

NAME	DATE	CATEGORY	SIG	LS/DS	ALS	SP	COMMENTS
Tilghman, Matthew		Revolutionary War	200		825		Cont. Congress. ALS/Cont. 2,750
Tilghman, William M.	1755-1827	Law	200	1107	1654		Early Western Sheriff
Tilkin-Servais, Ernest		Entertainment	25			85	Opera
Tilley, Reade		Aviation	10	20	35		Am. Air Ace as Member of Royal Air Force
Tillich, Paul		Clergy	70	125	125	136	
Tillinghast, Charles C. Jr.		Business	10	20	40	15	CEO TWA. Merrill-Lynch
Tillis, Mel		Country Music	5			15	Songwriter-Singer
Tillman, Benjamin 'Pitchfork Ben'	1847-1918	Congress	25	40	55		Senator SC 1894
Tillman, Floyd		Country Music	10			25	Songwriter-Singer-Guitarist-Mandolinist
Tillotson, Johnny		Country Music	6			20	Singer
Tillson, Davis	1830-1895	Civil War	35		70		Union general
Tillstrom, Burr		Entertainment	25			50	
Tilly, Jennifer		Entertainment	8		10	43	Actress. Pin-Up SP 35-60
Tilly, Maj. Gen. Justice Crosland	1888-1941	Military	25				World War II British general
Tilly, Meg		Entertainment	10	15	20	37	Actress
Tilton, Charlene		Entertainment	25			27	
Tilton, Martha		Entertainment	12			20	Big Band Singer, Recording Artist
Tilton, Theodore	1835-1907	Journalist			90		Sued Henry Ward Beecher for Adultery
Tilton, Wm. Stowell		Civil War	25	50			Union Brevet Brig. General
Tilzer, Albert von		Composer	40	110	200	55	Founder ASCAP
Timberlake, Bob		Artist	15			20	Painter, Designer. Litho S 600+
Timberlake, Justin		Entertainment				55	Singer
Timiryazev, Kliment	1843-1920	Science	112				Botanist, physician
Timken, Henry	1831-1909	Inventor	85	140	225		Timken Tapered Roller Bearings
Timken, William Robert		Business	35	95	155	60	Pres. Timken Roller Bearings
Timothy, Christopher		Entertainment	10			20	Actor
Ting, Samuel C. C., Dr.		Science	20	35	50	25	Nobel Physics 1976
Tingey, Thomas	1750-1829	Military	140	350	525		Continental Navy
Tingley, Clyde		Governor	12	20		15	Governor NM 1935
Tinker, Grant C.		Entertainment	8	10		15	TV-Film Producer
Tinnell, Carol		Entertainment	15			45	Actress. Pin-Up 55
Tiny Tim		Entertainment	25	35		40	Singer. 'Tiptoe Through The Tulips'
Tiny, Texas		Country Music	10			20	Singer
Tiomkin, Dimitri	1894-1979	Composer	50	253	365	250	Music For Major Movie Production. AMuQS 225-675
Tippelskirch, Gen. of Inf. Kurt von	1891-1957	Military	27				World War II German general
Tippett, Michael, Sir	1905-1998	Composer	40	85		150	British Composer and Conductor
Tippit, J. D.		Celebrity	200				Dallas policeman killed November 22, 1963
Tisch, Laurence A.		Business	15			45	CEO of CBS
Tisserant, Eugene, Cardinal		Clergy	35	45	50	40	
Tissot, James	1836-1902	Artist	68	175	202		Fr. Painter, Engraver, Enameler
Titchener, Paul		Business	10	35	45	20	
Titchmarsh, Alan		Celebrity	10			15	home/gardening expert
Titford, Jeffrey William		Political	10			15	Member European Parliament
Titley, Gary		Political	10			15	Member European Parliament
Tito, Marshal (Josip Broz)	1892-1980	Head of State	85	205	280	194	Yugoslav Statesman. Communist

NAME	DATE	CATEGORY	SIG	LS/DS	ALS	SP	COMMENTS
Titov, Gherman		Cosmonaut	40			74	
Tobey, Charles W.		Senate/Congress	5	15		10	Governor, Rep., Senator NH
Tobey, Ken		Entertainment	10			25	Actor. Hundreds of Supporting Roles
Tobias, George	1901-1987	Entertainment	50			150	Actor. Stage, Films-1939-70's.
Tobin, Genevieve	1901-1975	Entertainment	15		30	35	Actress. Warner Bros. Leads-2nd Leads from 30's
Tobin, James, Dr.		Economist	22	30		25	Nobel Economics 1981
Tobin, Maurice		Cabinet	10	20	30	15	Sec'y Labor 1948, Gov. MA
Tocqueville, Alexis de	1805-1859	Author	45	150	350		Fr. Politician, Statesman, Writer
Tod, David		Governor	10	25			Governor OH
Todd, Alexander Robertus, Sir		Science	30	85		40	Nobel Chemistry 1957
Todd, Ann	1909-	Entertainment	20			40	Br. Actress. Internat'l Film Star From 30's
Todd, Charles Scott		Celebrity	5	15	40		
Todd, Henry D., Jr.	1866-	Military	15		35		WW I Genl
Todd, John Blair Smith	1814-1872	Civil War	45	75	120		Union general
Todd, Richard		Entertainment	58			100	Ir. Actor. AA Nomination for 'Hasty Heart'
Todd, Robert		Aviation	15	30	45	25	
Todd, Thelma	1905-1935	Entertainment	138	235	350	475	Actress. Mysterious Death at 30
Tognini, Michel		Astronaut	15	25		35	
Togo, Heihachiro, Marquis	1846-1934	Military	110	315	448	185	Jap. Adm. Sino-Jap. War. Small Format SP 185
Togo, Shigenori		Diplomat	250			400	Jap. Foreign Minister-Statesman
Tojo, Hideki	1884-1948	Military	250	700	1500	960	Prime Minister. Jap. Adm. Pearl Harbor.Executed
Toklas, Alice B.	1877-1967	Author	45	185	325		Companion of Gertrude Stein
Tokody, Ilona		Entertainment	5			25	Opera
Toksvig, Sandi		Celebrity	10			15	comedienne
Tokyo Rose (Iva I. Toguri)		Military	250	330	1250	950	WW II Radio Propagandist
Toledo, Francisco, Cardinal		Clergy	15000				Introduced Inquisition into Peru.
Toler, Sidney	1874-1947	Entertainment	150			362	2nd 'Charlie Chan' After Warner Oland
Tolkien, John R.R.	1892-1973	Author	400	1168	2058		Br. Writer of 'Lord of the Ring'
Tolstoy, Alexandra, Countess		Author	25		80		
Tolstoy, Leo, Count	1828-1910	Author	1200	1775	2988	2488	Rus. Novelist & Moral Philosopher
Tolvald, Linus		Science	10			30	Creator of Linux
Tomagno, Francesco		Conductor	40		250		Opera etc.
Tombaugh, Clyde W.	1906-1997	Science	25	88	158	72	Am. Astronomer, Discoverer of Planet Pluto 1930
Tomei, Marissa		Entertainment	20			57	Actress. Oscar Winner
Tomkinson, Tara Palmer		Celebrity	10			15	celebrity model
Tomlin, Lily		Entertainment	5	10	15	25	Comedienne. TV. Theatre One Woman Show
Tomlin, Pinky		Bandleader	10			35	Scat Singer
Tompkins, Angel		Entertainment	10	15	20	25	Actress
Tompkins, Daniel	1774-1825	Vice Pres.	85	129	154		Monroe VP, Governor NY
Tompkinson, Steven		Entertainment	10			20	Actor
Tompson, Alexander K.		Clergy	15	25	35		
Tonderai, Mark		Music	10			15	DJ
Tone, Franchot	1905-1968	Entertainment	22		50	73	Am. Leading Man & Later Char. Actor
Tong, Pete		Music	10			15	DJ
Tong, Shen		Celebrity	10			15	political celebrity

NAME	DATE	CATEGORY	SIG	LS/DS	ALS	SP	COMMENTS
Tony, Simon		Entertainment	6			25	Music.Guitar, Keyboard 'The Verve'
Toole, John Lawrence	1830-1906	Celebrity			75		Actor
Toombs, Robert A.	1810-1885	Civil War	87	210	304	1725	CSA General & Sec'y State. Sig/Rank 205
Toomey, Patrick J. T		Congress	10			15	Member U.S. Congress
Toomey, Regis	1902-	Entertainment	15	20		45	Actor. Familiar Face With Over 150 Film Credits
Toon, Thomas Fentress	1840-1902	Civil War	95				Confederate general
Toones, Fred Snowflake		Entertainment	150			300	
Toorop, Jan (Dutch)	1858-1928	Artist	25	100	210	125	Posters, Tiles, Stained Glass. Leader Of Luminists
Toovey, Maj. Gen. Cecil Wotton	1891-1954	Military	25				World War II British general
Topal		Entertainment	10			30	Israeli Actor. Stage, Films. AA Nominated (Fiddler)
Tope, Maj. Gen. Wilfred S.	1892-1962	Military	25				World War II British general
Toper, Justin		Celebrity	10			15	Astrologer
Topp, Erich		Military	35		175	85	Ger. U-Boat Cmdr. WW II
Topping, Dan		Business	10	15	30	20	Millionaire One Time Owner NY Yankees
Torbert, Alfred Thomas A.	1833-1880	Civil War	40	65	95		Union general
Torisu, Kennosuke		Military	60		175	150	Submarine Attack on Pearl Harbor
Tork, Peter		Entertainment	15	35		35	Singer-Actor 'The Monkees'
Torme, Mel		Entertainment	20	22		58	Vocalist, Composer. Known as 'The Velvet Fog'
Torn, Rip		Entertainment	15			38	Actor. Major Roles in Major Films-TV. Emmy Award
Torrance, Ernest	1878-1933	Entertainment	75			150	Scot. Silent Films. Ex Opera
Torrence, Ridgely	1875-1950	Author	25	30	85		Am. Poet, Editor, Dramatist
Torres Marques, Helena		Political	10			15	Member European Parliament
Torres, Jacques		Celebrity	10			15	famous chef
Torres, Raquel	1908-	Entertainment	20			45	Mex. Actress. Several Early Sound Films
Torrey, R.A.		Clergy	20	35	50		
Tors, Ivan	1916-	Entertainment	15			35	Producer-Director-Screenwriter. USAAF-OSS
Toscanini, Arturo	1867-1957	Conductor	140	221	525	557	AMusQS 750-950, AMusMs 3,750. SP Pc 625
Tosti, Paolo		Composer	25	60	155		Italian Composer
Toto	1898-1967	Entertainment	65			250	It. Comedy Star. Films From 1936
Totten, Jos. G.	1788-1864	Civil War	33	40	85		Union Gen. War dte DS 200-400, Sig/Rank 50
Totter, Audrey		Entertainment	5	15		20	Actress. Radio Dramas, TV Soaps, Films 1939
Toucey, Isaac	1792-1869	Cabinet	18	80	120		Polk Att'y Gen. 1848, Sec'y Navy '57
Touchon, Lt Gen. Robert-Auguste	1878-1960	Military	20				World War II French general
Toulouse-Lautrec, Henri	1864-1901	Artist	775	2250	4776		Fr. Parisian Nightlife. Over 300 Lithographs
Toumanova, Tamara		Entertainment	30			110	Rus-Am Ballerina
Tourel, Jennie		Entertainment	20			50	Opera
Tourgee, Albion W.	1838-1905	Author	15	20	45		Lawyer, Judge, Diplomat
Toussaint, Gen. of Infantry Rudolf	1891-1968	Military	25				World War II German general
Toussaint-L'Ouverture, Pierre	1743-1803	Statesman		2310			Haitian General. Led Haitian Slave Revolt 1791
Tower, John		Senate/Congress	5	15		25	Senator TX
Tower, Zealous B.	1819-1900	Civil War	25	41	68		Union General
Towers, Constance		Entertainment	5	6	10	10	Actress
Towery, Twyman L		Author	8			12	financial/business how-to
Towl, E. Clinton		Business	20		55		
Towne, Robert		Celebrity	10			15	film industry

NAME	DATE	CATEGORY	SIG	LS/DS	ALS	SP	COMMENTS
Townes, Charles Hanson		Science	30	40	65		Inventor. Nobel (Laser & Maser)
Townley, James		Clergy	35	50	75		
Towns, Edolphus T		Congress	10			15	Member U.S. Congress
Townsand, Colleen (Evans)		Entertainment	5	9	20	15	Actress. Short Career In Films. 50's-
Townsend, Edward D.	1817-1893	Civil War	32	50	68		Union General War date(content) 7950
Townsend, Francis Everett	1867-1960	Science	40			150	Social Reformer & Physician. Old Age Pension Plan
Townsend, Frederick	1825-1897	Civil War	30	55	90		Union Brevet Brig. General
Townsend, George A. (Gath)		Author	15		40		War Correspondent
Townsend, Lynn		Business	10	20	35	20	CEO-Pres.Chrysler Corp.
Townsend, M. Clifford		Governor	10	15			Governor IN
Townsend, Pete		Entertainment	30			70	Lead Singer 'The Who'
Townsend, Peter		Military	10	35	50	25	
Townsend, Robert		Entertainment	10	15		20	Film Director
Townsend, Washington		Senate/Congress	10	20			Rep. PA 1969
Toy Story (Cast Of)		Entertainment				275	Hanks, Varney, Potts, Rickles
Toynbee, Arnold Joseph	1889-1975	Author	20	45	84	30	Br. Historian, Prof., Paris Peace Conf.
Toynbee, Arnold	1852-1883	Author	25	105	190	80	Br. Economist, Sociologist
Tozzi, Giorgio		Entertainment	20			40	Opera
Trachte, Don*		Cartoonist	25			75	'Henry'
Tracy, Arthur		Entertainment	20			45	'The Street Singer'.
Tracy, Benjamin F.	1830-1915	Civil War	30	55	90		Union General. MOH.
Tracy, Edward Dorr (WD)	1833-1863	Civil War	475	1040			CSA Gen. KIA 5/1/63.
Tracy, Edward Dorr	1833-1863	Civil War	279	645	938		Confederate general
Tracy, Lee	1898-1968	Entertainment	10			25	Actor-Broadway '24; Screen '29. Fast-Talking Roles
Tracy, Spencer	1900-1967	Entertainment	138	250	325	348	Actor, AA
Traffic		Music					Rock group., signed album 135
Tragically Hip		Music				50	Canadian Rock Band
Train, Arthur		Author	10	15	35		
Train, George Francis	1824-1904	Author-Tycoon	36	65	116		Eccentric Financier
Trakatellis, Antonios		Political	10			15	Member European Parliament
Trapier, James H.	1815-1865	Civil War	153	299	410		CSA Gen. AES '61 575
Trapp, Maria von, Baroness		Celebrity	68	150	250	275	'Sound of Music' Fame.
Trask, Diana	1940-	Country Music	10			20	Australian Pop-Country Singer. To U.S. in 1959
Trask, Spencer		Business		950			Founder Spenser Trask & Co., Wall Street
Traubel, Helen		Entertainment	50			100	Opera. Am. Soprano. Concerts, Radio, Films
Trautloft, Hannes		Aviation	25			50	Ger. Ace WW II RK
Travalena, Fred		Entertainment	5	8	15	15	Actor-Comedy
Travanti, Daniel J.		Entertainment	6	8	15	20	Actor
Traven, Berwick (Torsvan)	1890-1969	Author	265	800	1765		Ger. Novelist, Actor, Pacifist
Travers, Henry	1974-1965	Entertainment	195			350	Mild-Mannered Character Actor. Films- Early 30's
Travers, Pamela L.		Author	25	125			'Mary Poppins' Books
Travers, Patricia		Entertainment	5		10	30	Violinist.
Traverso, Giuseppe		Entertainment	15			45	Opera
Travis, David Lee		Celebrity	10			15	BBC DJ
Travis, Kylie		Entertainment	5			20	Actress. Models, Inc. Pin-Up SP 40

NAME	DATE	CATEGORY	SIG	LS/DS	ALS	SP	COMMENTS
Travis, Merle		Country Music	20			40	Top Multi-Talented Guitarist, Singer, Songwriter.
Travis, Nancy		Entertainment	18			40	Actress
Travis, Randy		Country Music	15	32		40	Singer. Sometimes Actor
Travis, Richard	1913-	Entertainment	5			20	Actor. Became Wealthy Hollywood Realtor
Travis, William Barret	1809-1836	Military		10500	18000		Co-Cmdr. Alamo. Texas Frontier.
Travolta, John		Entertainment	25	10	20	47	Actor
Treacher, Arthur	1894-1975	Entertainment	25		40	199	Lawyer-Trained. Became Perrenial Br. Butler in 30's
Treadway, Allen Towner		Senate/Congress	4	15			MOC MA 1913
Treadwell, John		Revolutionary War	25	60	95		Del. CT. Elected to Cont.Congr.
Treas, Terri		Entertainment	5	6	8	10	
Trebek, Alex		Entertainment	10	15	20	25	Perennial Host of 'Jeopardy' TV Game Show
Trebor, Robert		Entertainment	5			20	Hercules/Xena
Tree, Herbert Beerbohm, Sir	1852-1917	Entertainment	30	85	145	75	Br. Actor-Mgr. Fndr. Royal Academy
Treen, Mary	1907-	Entertainment	5	15	30	25	Actress Comedienne. Films from 1934
Treilhard, Jean-Baptiste	1742-1810	Fr.Revolution	25	40	75		Fr. Politician. Important in Drafting Legal Codes
Trelawny, Edward	1792-1881	Author		445	750		Br. Author-Adventurer. Companion of Shelley & Byron
Tremayne, Les		Entertainment	5			20	Top Radio Actor 30's-40's—
Tremblay, Maj Gen Thomas Louis	1886-1951	Military	20				World War II Canadian general
Tremonti, Mark		Entertainment	6			25	Music. Guitar, Vocals 'Creed'
Trench, Richard C., Archbishop		Clergy	45	60	95	65	
Trenholm, George A.	1807-1876	Civil War	102	213	422		CSA Sec'y Treasury
Trent, William		Celebrity		600			
Trentin, Bruno		Political	10			15	Member European Parliament
Trettner, Henrich 'Heniz		Aviation	20	45		50	
Trevelyan, George Otto, Sir	1838-1928	Author	15	35	75		Br. Historian, Sec'y To Admiralty, Author
Treves, Frederick, Dr.	1853-1923	Science	200		462		Dr. To Elephant Man
Trevor McDonald, Sir		Celebrity	10			15	news reader
Trevor, Claire	1909-	Entertainment	20			48	AA Winning Actress. 'Key Largo', 'Stagecoach'
Trigg, Liz		Celebrity	10			15	Food Writer
Trilling, Lionel	1905-1975	Author	10	30	50	25	Am. Lit. Critic. Professor, Essayist
Trimble, Isaac R. (WD)		Civil War	393	978	1700		CSA General
Trimble, Isaac Ridgeway	1802-1888	Civil War	185	300	544		CSA General
Trimble, Lawrence	1825-1904	Congress	15		25		MOC KY
Trinh, Eugene		Astronaut	5			15	
Tripler, Charles E.		Science	75	185			Inventor Liquid Air
Tripp, Lt Gen. Wm. Henry Lainson	1881-1959	Military	25				World War II British general
Trippe, Juan T.	1899-1981	Aviation	30			55	Fndr. PanAmerican Airways. Clipper Service
Tripplehorn, Jeanne		Entertainment	15			50	Actress
Trist, Nicholas P.	1800-1874	Diplomat	75	225			Am. Negotiated Treaty of Guadaloupe
Tritt, Travis		Country Music	15			35	Singer
Tritton, William Ashbee, Sir		Science	25	70	125	40	Developed Military Tank
Trollope, Anthony	1815-1882	Author	107	145	210		Br. Novelist. 50 Novels, ALS/cont 1350
Trollope, Frances	1780-1863	Author	30	55	95		Br. Novelist. Mother of Anthony
Trollope, Thomas A.	1810-1892	Author		25	50		Novels, History. Tremendous Output
Trotsky, Leon	1879-1940	Head of State	412	1014	1750	1225	Communist Revolution leader-Assassinated

NAME	DATE	CATEGORY	SIG	LS/DS	ALS	SP	COMMENTS
Trotter, James Monroe	1842-1892	Civil War	40	250			Former Slave. Union Soldier.
Trotter, Mark C.		Clergy	15		35		
Troubridge, Thomas, Sir		Military	75		250		Br. Admiral, Battle of the Nile
Troup, Bobby	1918-1999	Entertainment	20			35	Pianist, Composer, Vocalist-Actor
Troup, Frank W.		Aviation	15			35	WW II Air Ace
Trowbridge, John T.	1827-1916	Author	15		25		
Trower, Robin		Entertainment	15			30	
Troyanos, Tatiana		Entertainment	15			40	Opera
Trudeau, Gary*		Cartoonist	40			250	1st Cartoonist Awarded Pulitzer-Editorial Cartoons
Trudeau, Pierre	1919-	Head of State	25	60	95	80	Prime Minister Canada
Trudell, John		Celebrity	10			15	political celebrity
Trueblood, D. Elton		Clergy	15	30	45	35	
Truett, George W.		Clergy	15	35	50	35	
Truex, Ernest	1890-1973	Entertainment	20			35	Character Actor From Silent Era into 50's-60's
Truffaut, Francois	1932-1984	Entertainment	83	422		402	Fr. Dir. & Critic, ALS/Content 800
Trujillo, Rafael	1891-1961	Head of State	75	95		283	Dominican Republic. Assassinated
Truly, Richard H.		Astronaut	15	25		45	
Truman, Benj. C.	1835-1916	Author	20		45		Soldier-Author
Truman, Bess W.	1885-1982	First Lady	55	84	140	136	S WH Card 85-195
Truman, Harry S. (As Pres.)		President	262	595	5088	484	ALS/TLS/Cont. 2,550-28750, S. appt. 1250-5000
Truman, Harry S.	1884-1972	President	141	285	1967	325	ALS/Content 14,000-39500
Truman, Margaret (Daniel)		First Family	25	65	80	30	Author-Daughter Of Harry S. Truman
Trumbo, Dalton	1905-1976	Author	50	200		75	Blacklisted Screenwriter. AA For 'The Brave One'
Trumbull, Annie E.	1858-1949	Author	15		25		
Trumbull, Douglas		Celebrity	10			15	film industry
Trumbull, John	1750-1831	Author-Lawyer	85	182			CT Poet & Lawyer
Trumbull, John	1756-1843	Artist	100	565	1350		ALS/Content 8,000. Engr. by R.Riker S 750
Trumbull, Jonathan Jr.	1740-1709	Military-Senate	86	180	345		Sec'y Washington's Staff
Trumbull, Jonathan	1710-1785	Revolutionary War	250	400	660		Confidant of G. Washington.ADS Special 1100
Trumbull, Lyman	1813-1896	Senate	25	80	140	200	U.S. Senator. Abolitionist.
Trump, Donald J.		Business	12	45	75	40	Entrepreneur
Trump, Ivana		Celebrity	10			40	Ex Mrs. Donald Trump
Truscott, Lucian K., Jr.	1895-1965	Military	45	125		150	TLS/Cont.225
Truth, Sojourner	1797-1883	Abolitionist	3680				Religious Missionary, RARE in any form.Only 3 Known
Truxton, William Talbot		Civil War	30	55	95		Union Naval Officer. Adm. 1882
Truxtun, Thomas	1755-1822	Revolutionary War	128	522	800		Cmdr. USS Constellation
Tryggvason, Bjarni		Astronaut	5			20	
Tryon, Tom		Entertainment	10	20	25	20	Actor-Author
Tryon, William	1728-1788	Revolutionary War	145	375	770		Colonial Gov. NC, Gov. NY
Tsatsos, Dimitris		Political	10			15	Member European Parliament
Tschernenko, Konstantin	1911-1985	Head of State	75			375	Pres. Soviet Union 1984-'85
Tshombe, Moise	1919-1969	Head of State	55	90	195	112	Prime Min.,Zaire(Congo Rep.) TLS/Cont. 795-1250
Tsiolkovsky, Konstantin	1857-1935	Science		1706	2500		Pioneer Rus. Space Program ALS/cont 6500, AMS2300
Tsongas, Paul E.		Senator	15	35	25	20	Senator MA, Pres. Hopeful 1992
Tsukata, Lt. Gen.	d. 1942	Military	27				World War II Japanese general

NAME	DATE	CATEGORY	SIG	LS/DS	ALS	SP	COMMENTS
Tubb, Ernest	1914-1984	Country Music	15			50	Country Music Hall of Fame
Tubb, Justin	1935-	Country Music	5			15	Singer-Son of Ernest Tubb
Tuchman, Barbara W.		Author	35	125	155	45	2 Time Pulitzer Pr., Historian
Tucker, Forrest	1919-	Entertainment	20	35	40	45	Actor. Husky, Blonde Bully in 40's, Hero in 50's
Tucker, John R. (WD)	1812-1883	Civil War	180	290			CSA Navy Commdr. 1812-83
Tucker, Michael		Entertainment	10			20	actor
Tucker, Orrin		Entertainment	15			25	Big Band Leader
Tucker, Richard		Entertainment	30	45		120	Opera
Tucker, Samuel	1747-1883	Revolutionary War	125	325	675		Am. Naval Hero. Commodore
Tucker, Sophie	1884-1966	Entertainment	32	40	95	67	Burlesque, Vaudeville, 'Last of the Red Hot Mamas'
Tucker, Tanya	1958-	Entertainment	10	15		28	Country Singer
Tucker, Thomas T.	1745-1848	Revolutionary War	55	105	175		Soldier, Statesman, Treasurer
Tucker, Tilghman M.		Senate/Congress	20	35	55		Senator 1838, Governor MS 1841
Tucker, Tommy		Bandleader	15			37	Big Band
Tucker, William Feimster	1827-1881	Civil War	110				Confederate general
Tudor, Anthony		Entertainment	35	45		100	Br. Dancer, Choreographer
Tuell, Jack M., Bishop		Clergy	20	25	35	30	
Tuesday, Gayle		Celebrity	10			15	comedienne
Tufts, Cotton	1734-1815	Revolutionary War	75	175	262		Highly Esteemed Physician. Patriot
Tufts, Sonny	1911-1970	Entertainment	20	25		35	1st Singer, 2nd Actor. Became Laughed-at Alchoholic
Tuker, Lt. Gen. Sir Francis Ivan S.	1894-1967	Military	25				World War II British general
Tukhachevsky, Mikhail N.	1893-1937	Military		368			Russian Revolutionary, Army Marshal
Tulford, Nellie Hughes		Astronaut	5			15	
Tully, Alice		Philanthropist	15	30		35	Lincoln Ctre. Tully Hall
Tully, Grace G.		White House	15	25	50	25	Sec'y to FDR
Tully, Susan		Entertainment	10			20	Actress
Tully, Tom		Cabinet	5	15	35	15	
Tully, Tom	1908-	Entertainment	25			45	Vet. Of US Navy, Legit. Stage, Radio & Many Films
Tulock, Art		Celebrity	10			15	motivational speaker
Tumulty, Joseph P.	1879-1954	White House	15	35	75	40	Important Aide to President Wilson
Tune, Tommy		Entertainment	10	12	15	25	Dancer, Choreographer. 'Tony' Award Winner
Tunks, Roger		Celebrity	10			15	motivational speaker
Tunnell, James M.		Senate/Congress	10	30		20	Senator DE 1940
Tunney, Jim		Celebrity	10			15	motivational speaker
Tunney, John V.		Senate/Congress	5	10		10	MOC, Senator CA
Tupper, Martin F.	1810-1889	Inventor	25		50		Brit. Author-Poet. 'Proverial Philosophy'
Turchi, Franz		Political	10			15	Member European Parliament
Turchin, John Basil (war dated)		Civil War	75	650			Union general
Turchin, John Basil	1822-1901	Civil War	40	68	130		Union general
Turco, Maurizio		Political	10			15	Member European Parliament
Turgenev, Ivan	1818-1833	Author	295	446	958	1265	Russ. Novelist, Dramatist. AQS 1450
Turkel, Ann		Entertainment	4	6		46	Model
Turkel, Studs		Author	10	20	35	20	Columnist. TV Commentator
Turlington, Christy		Entertainment	15			42	Super Model
Turmes, Claude		Political	10			15	Member European Parliament

NAME	DATE	CATEGORY	SIG	LS/DS	ALS	SP	COMMENTS
Turner, Anthea		Celebrity	10			15	television presenter
Turner, Bev		Celebrity	10			15	television presenter
Turner, Edward	1798-1837	Science	32		175		Scot. Chemist. Atomic Weights of Elements
Turner, Eva, Dame	1892-	Entertainment	40	65		75	Opera. Vocal Phenomenon
Turner, Frederick J.	1861-1932	Author	55		225		Pulitzer Prize 1932. Historian
Turner, Janine		Entertainment	20			39	Actress
Turner, Jim T		Congress	10			15	Member U.S. Congress
Turner, John Wesley	1833-1899	Civil War	143	173	361		Union General Sig/Rank 145
Turner, Joseph M. W.	1775-1851	Artist	225	605	1475		Br. Landscape Painter
Turner, Kathleen		Entertainment	10	20		40	Actress
Turner, Lana	1920-1995	Entertainment	37	73		81	Actress. Glamour StarPin-Up SP 90
Turner, Maj. Gen. Guy Roderick	1889-1963	Military	20				World War II Canadian general
Turner, Michael R. T		Congress	10			15	Member U.S. Congress
Turner, Morrie		Cartoonist	5			20	'Wee Pals'
Turner, Philip		Revolutionary War	70	135	250		Unrivalled Sugeon During War
Turner, Roscoe, Col.	1895-1970	Aviation	60	125		105	Pioneer Aviator. Early Race Pilot. Speed Records
Turner, Stansfield		Military	25			45	Admiral. Director of the CIA.
Turner, Ted		Business	20			35	Turner Broadcasting
Turner, Tina		Entertainment	20	20	40	53	Rock-Pop Singer
Turner, Wendy		Celebrity	10			15	television presenter
Turpie, David		Senator/Congress	15	25	35		Senator IN 1863
Turpin, Ben	1869-1940	Entertainment	242	325	450	379	Beloved Cross-Eyed Mack Sennett Comic. Silents
Turreau De Garambouville		Fr. Revolution	20		85		
Turtles		Entertainment	35			82	Signed by All
Turturro, Alda		Entertainment				35	Janice Soprano
Turturro, John		Entertainment	10			25	actor
Turturro, Nick		Entertainment	10			20	actor
Tusmayan, Barsag		Entertainment	5			25	Opera
Tussaud, Marie	1760-1850	Artist	200	725			Swiss Modeler in Wax. 'Madame Tussaud's Exh.'
Tuttle, James Madison	1823-1892	Civil War	35	75	120		Union general
Tuttle, Lurene		Entertainment	5	6	15	15	Top Radio Dramatic Star. Supporting Roles in Films
Tuttle, Wes & Marilyn		Country Music	15			30	Duet. Turned Evangelist. With Religious Music Only
Tutu, Desmond, Bishop		Clergy	55	95	225	155	Nobel Peace Prize
Tutwiler, Margaret D.		Cabinet	10	15		15	Ass't Sec'y State
Tuve, Merle Antony	1901-1982	Science	35	80	155	50	Neutron, Ionosphere, Radar
Twaddle, Maj. Gen. Harry L.	1888-1954	Military	30				World War II U.S. general
Twain, Mark (see Clemens)		Author					
Twain, Mark & Samuel Clemens		Author	1062	1995	5167		Both Signatures
Twain, Shania		Entertainment	12			70	Singer. Pop - Country
Tweed, Shannon		Entertainment	8	10	20	29	Actress-Model. Pin-Up SP 30, Nude SP 80
Tweed, William Marcy 'Boss'	1823-1878	Political Giant	85	171	302	750	Corrupt Politician., signed stock cert.3600
Tweedy, Jeff		Music	20			40	Rock
Twiggs, David E.	1790-1862	Civil War	140	685	1208		CSA General Sig/Rank 205
Twiggy (Nee: Leslie Hornsby)		Entertainment	15	25	25	35	60's Brit. Fashion Model. Actress
Twining, Nathan F.	1897-1982	Aviation	50	135	185	120	Gen. WW II. Commanded 15th Air Force

NAME	DATE	CATEGORY	SIG	LS/DS	ALS	SP	COMMENTS
Twiss, Peter		Aviation	10	15	30	20	
Twitty, Conway	1933-1993	Country Music	30	50		70	Early Rocker turned Country Superstar
Two Guns White Calf	1872-1934	Blackfoot Chief	650		2000	1616	Buffalo Nickel Model. SPPc 795
Tydings, Millard E.	1890-1961	Congress	20	50		30	Rep., Senator MD, Author
Tyler, Asher	1798-1875	Congress	10		35		MOC NY, Founder Elmira Rolling Mill
Tyler, Beverly		Entertainment	5			20	Actress
Tyler, Bonnie		Entertainment	15			30	
Tyler, Daniel	1799-1882	Civil War	42	85	125		Union Gen.
Tyler, Edward Burnett, Sir		Science	15	30	50		1st Prof. Anthropology Oxford
Tyler, Erastus Bernard	1822-1891	Civil War	45	68	95		Union general
Tyler, Gerald E.		Aviation	10	25	40	30	ACE, WWII
Tyler, John Jr.	1819-1895	Civil War	20	50			CSA, Acting Chief Bureau of War
Tyler, John (as President)		President	425	1285	1832		10th President of the USA, DS w/Webster 2000-2500
Tyler, John	1790-1862	President	318	846	1335		Civil War Dte ALS 4000
Tyler, Julia Gardiner	1820-1889	First Lady	150	350		650	Special DS 1,100
Tyler, Liv		Entertainment	18			55	Actress. Pin-Up 85. 'a Thing You Do' SP 65
Tyler, Moses Coit		Author	5	15	25		Historian. Am. Historical Assoc
Tyler, Robert C.	1833-1865	Civil War	220	580	850		CSA General. Killed April 16, 1865
Tyler, Robert Ogden	1831-1874	Civil War	58	90	147		Union general
Tyler, Robert	1816-1877	Civil War	40	65	150		President's Son., Confederate Register of Treasury
Tyler, Royall	1757-1826	Revolutionary War	25	50	120		Jurist, Author, Playwright
Tyler, Steven		Entertainment				55	Lead Singer Aerosmith
Tyler, T. Texas		Country Music	15			30	Singer. 'Deck o' Cards'
Tyler, Tom	1903-1954	Entertainment	68			150	Started '24 as Stuntman-Extra. Western Star 1940's
Tyndale, Hector	1821-1880	Civil War	43	75	128		Union general
Tyndale, Hector	1921-1980	Civil War	30	60	85	175	Union General Sig/Rank 45, War Dte DS 125
Tyndall, John	1820-1893	Science	44	110	182		Irish Physicist, Natural Philosopher
Tyndall, Maj. Gen. William Ernest	1891-1975	Military	28				World War II British general
Tyner, James N.		Cabinet	10	40	75		P.M. General 1876
Tyner, McCoy		Entertainment	10	20		30	Jazz Pianist-Composer
Tyson, Cathy		Entertainment	10			20	Actress
Tyson, Cicely		Entertainment	10	10	20	20	Actress.
Tyson, Don		Business	15			25	Pres., Founder, CEO Tyson's Chicken

U

NAME	DATE	CATEGORY	SIG	LS/DS	ALS	SP	COMMENTS
U-2 (All)		Entertainment	185			250	Irish Rock Group
Uca, Feleknas		Political	10			15	Member European Parliament
Udall, Mark U		Congress	10			15	Member U.S. Congress
Udall, Morris K.		Congress	4			10	Repr. AZ
Udall, Tom U		Congress	10			15	Member U.S. Congress
Udet, Ernst	1896-1941	Aviation	225	375	700	550	ACE, WWI, German Ace. 2nd Only To Richthofen
Udy, Helene		Entertainment	10			20	actress

NAME	DATE	CATEGORY	SIG	LS/DS	ALS	SP	COMMENTS
Ueberroth, Peter		Business	10	25	40	10	
Uecker, Bob		Entertainment	5	8	15	15	
Ueda, General Kenkichi	1875-1965	Military	25				World War II Japanese general
Ufford, Edward S.		Clergy	40	50	70		
Ugaki, General Kazushige	1868-1956	Military	25				World War II Japanese general
Uggams, Leslie		Entertainment	5	10	15	20	
Uhlenbroek PhD, Charlotte		Celebrity	10			15	naturalist
Ulbricht, Walter	1893-1973	Political		230			German leader 1953-1971
Ulene, Art Dr.		Celebrity	10			15	motivational speaker
Ullman, Daniel	1810-1892	Civil War	35	65	90		Union general
Ullman, Maj. Gen. Peter Alfred	1897-1972	Military	25				World War II British general
Ullman, Tracey		Entertainment	20			50	
Ullmann, Liv		Entertainment	10			20	actress
Ulmanis, Karlis		Head of State	90				1st Pres. Latvia. Fate Unknown
Ulmar, Geraldine		Entertainment	6	8	15	15	
Ulrich, Skeet		Entertainment	10			20	actor
Umberto I	1844-1900	Royalty	50	150	375		King of Italy
Umeki, Miyoshi		Entertainment	235			450	
Umezu, General Yoshijiro	1882-1949	Military	27				World War II Japanese general
Umstead, William B.		Governor	5	15	20		Governor NC
Underwood, Adin Ballou	1828-1888	Civil War	40		80		Union general
Underwood, J. T.		Inventor	25	100	200		Underwood Typewriter
Underwood, Oscar W.		Senate/Congress	4	10		10	Rep., Senator AL
Undset, Sigrid	1882-1949	Author				325	Nor. Nobel Prize Winner
Unger, Jim		Cartoonist	15	20		25	Henry
Ungher, Caroline	1803-1877	Entertainment			150		Opera. Great Contralto
Unreal, Minerva		Entertainment	25			60	
Unruh, Howard B.		Celebrity	80				
Untermeyer, Louis	1885-1971	Author	20	35	60	50	Am. Poet, Critic, Satirist, Biogr.
Untouchables (cast)		Entertainment				225	Movie cast of 4
Updike, John	1932-	Author	25	45	70	50	Am. Novelist, Poet, Short Story Writer
Upham, Charles	1802-1875	Clergy	30		95		Unitarian Minister, Author, Whig Congressman
Upham, Charles	1908-	Military	100	250			One of Only 3 Men to Win Victoria Cross Twice
Upjohn, E. Gifford, Dr.		Business	125	450			Founder Upjohn Pharmaceuticals
Upshaw, Dawn		Entertainment	10			25	Opera
Upshaw, William D.		Senate/Congress	5	15		10	Rep. GA 1919, Evangelist
Upshur, Abel Parker	1790-1844	Cabinet	30	95	110		Tyler Sec'y Navy, State
Upton, Emory	1839-1881	Civil War	32	63	135		Union Gen. War dte DS 465
Upton, Fred U		Congress	10			15	Member U.S. Congress
Urbanowicz, Witold A.		Aviation	35	70	125	60	Pol. ACE, WWII
Ure, Mary		Entertainment	5	10	20	20	
Urey, Harold C.	1893-1981	Science	78	240	433		Nobel Chemistry 1934. Disc. Heavy Hydrogen
Urich, Robert	1946-2002	Entertainment	10	15	25	38	Handsomely Rugged Actor. 'Spencer'
Uris, Leon	-2003	Author	20	65	125	65	Am. Novelist. 'Battle Cry', 'Exodus'
Uritskii, Moisei		Military		483			Russian Revolutionary

NAME	DATE	CATEGORY	SIG	LS/DS	ALS	SP	COMMENTS
Urquart, Maj. Gen. Robert Elliott	1901-1988	Military	28				World War II British general
Urso, Camilla		Entertainment	25			40	Fr. Violinist
Ursuleac, Viorica		Entertainment	30			85	Great Strauss Singer & WW II Heroine
Urvanowicz, Witold A.		Aviation	20	45	75	50	ACE, WW II, Polish Ace
Usher, John P.		Cabinet	40	110	195		Sec'y Interior 1863-65
Ushijima, Lt. Gen. Mitsuru	1887-1945	Military	25				World War II Japanese general
Ussishkin, Menachem	1863-1941	Statesman	175		625		Rus-Zionist Leader. A Founder Hebrew Univ.
Ustinov, Peter		Entertainment	30	45	60	90	And Playwright, Author, Actor. AA
Utley, Garrick		Journalist	10			35	TV Reporter & Commentator
Utrillo, Maurice	1833-1955	Artist	200	396	460	281	Fr. Montmartre, Paris Scenes
Utterson-Kelso, Maj Gen John E.	1893-1972	Military	25				World War II British general

NAME	DATE	CATEGORY	SIG	LS/DS	ALS	SP	COMMENTS
Vaccaro, Brenda		Entertainment	4	6	15	10	
Vaccaro, Tracy		Entertainment	5			15	Pin-Up SP 30
Vachetta, Roseline		Political	10			15	Member European Parliament
Vacio, Natividad		Entertainment	3	3	6	6	
Vadim, Roger		Entertainment	20			50	
Vague, Vera		Entertainment	25				SEE Barbara Jo Allen. Comedienne
Vai, Steve		Entertainment	15			35	Rock
Vairinhos, Joaquim		Political	10			15	Member European Parliament
Valdengo, Giuseppe		Entertainment	15			40	Opera
Valdivielso De Cué, Jaime		Political	10			15	Member European Parliament
Vale, Virginia		Entertainment	15				Actress
Valenciano Martínez-orozco, M E		Political	10			15	Member European Parliament
Valens, Richie	1941-1959	Music	725	725		1550	
Valenti, Jack	1921-	Entertainment	10	15		18	Pres. Motion Picture Assoc. Special Ass't LBJ
Valentine, Karen		Entertainment	4	6	10	15	
Valentine, Lewis		Law	35	105		50	Legendary NY Police Commissioner
Valentino, Rudolph	1895-1926	Entertainment	716	1275	1550	1712	Major Silent Film Star. Early Death Created Legend
Valery, Paul A.	1871-1945	Author	45	105	170		Fr. Noted Poet, Philosopher
Valette, A.J.M.		Fr. Revolution	15		75		
Valetti, Cesare		Entertainment	20			50	Opera
Vallandigham, Clement L.	1820-1871	Civil War	69		140		Civil War 'Copperhead' (Peace Democrat)
Vallee, Rudy		Entertainment	15	35	45	35	Am. Singer (Crooner). Radio-TV Personality
Vallejo, Mariano Guadalupe		Military	140	450			Early CA Official & Military Leadr
Valli, Frankie		Entertainment	15			45	Singer
Valli, Virginia		Entertainment				40	Films From 1915-1931
Vallone, Raf		Entertainment	5	6	15	15	
Vallvé, Joan		Political	10			15	Member European Parliament
Valon, Maj. Gen. Albert Robert	1885-1971	Military	25				World War II British general
Vambery, Arminius	1832-1913	Author			225		

NAME	DATE	CATEGORY	SIG	LS/DS	ALS	SP	COMMENTS
Van Alen, James Henry	1819-1886	Civil War	46	87			Union general
Van Allan, Richard		Entertainment	5			25	Opera
Van Allen, James		Science	45	70	110	80	Nobel Physics. Rocket Research. Van Allen Belt
Van Ark, Joan		Entertainment	5	8	15	15	
Van Atta, Dale		Celebrity	10			15	media/TV personality
Van Brempt, Kathleen		Political	10			15	Member European Parliament
Van Buren, Abigail		Journalist	10	18	30	20	Am. Syndicated Columnist
Van Buren, James D.		Gov't Official	5	15			Son of Pres. Van Buren
Van Buren, Martin (As Pres.)		President	275	1070	2793		Free Frank 350-475
Van Buren, Martin	1782-1862	President	217	659	819		FF 450-475 ALS/Cont 2500-5900
Van Buren, Raeburn*		Cartoonist	10			50	Abbie & Slats
Van Cleef, Lee		Entertainment	25			45	
Van Cleve, Horatio Phillips	1809-1891	Civil War	45	75	115		Union general
Van Dam, Rijk		Political	10			15	Member European Parliament
Van Dam, Rip	1662-1736	Colonial America	60	175	360		Merchant, Politics, Col. Gov. NY
Van Damme, Jean-Claude		Entertainment	20			48	Actor. Action with an Accent
Van Den Berg, Lodewik, Dr.		Astronaut	5			16	
Van Den Berg, Margrietus J.		Political	10			15	Member European Parliament
Van Den Bos, Bob		Political	10			15	Member European Parliament
Van Den Burg, Leke		Political	10			15	Member European Parliament
Van Der Beek, James		Entertainment	8			45	Young Movie/TV Star
Van Der Laan, Lousewies		Political	10			15	Member European Parliament
Van der Rohe, Ludwig Mies	1886-1969	Architect	120	350			Ger-Am. Exponent Of Glass & Steel Architecture
Van Derbur, Marilyn		Celebrity	10			15	motivational speaker
Van Derveer, Ferdinand	1823-1892	Civil War	40		85		Union general
Van Devanter, Willis	1859-1941	Supreme Court	40	86	175	150	Justice 1910-37
Van Dien, Casper		Entertainment	10			20	actor
Van Dine, S.S. (W.H.Wright)		Author	45	100	190	225	Created Philo Vance
Van Dongen, Kees	1877-1968	Artist	30	45	116		Fauvist Painter, Portraitist, signed drwg 184
Van Doren, Carl		Author	15	45	60	20	Pulitzer in Biography
Van Doren, Mamie		Entertainment	15	15	35	25	Pin-Up SP 35-45. 49'-50's Sex Symbol
Van Doren, Mark	1894-1973	Author	15	57	60	30	Critic, Editor, Pulitzer Poetry
Van Dorn, Earl (WD)		Civil War	350		5775		CSA Gen. Assassinated
Van Dorn, Earl	1820-1863	Civil War	518		1566		CSA Gen. Assassinated
Van Dresser, Marcia		Entertainment	15			40	Vintage Actress
Van Druten, John W.		Author	10	20	35	15	Playwright, Novelist
Van Dusen, Henry P.		Clergy	15	15	25	20	
Van Dyck, M. Ernest		Entertainment	15	25		40	Tenor
Van Dyke, Dick		Entertainment	8	8	15	35	
Van Dyke, Henry	1852-1933	Clergy-Author	20	40	55		Minister To Netherlands-Luxem.
Van Dyke, Jerry		Entertainment	5			20	
Van Dyke, Leroy	1919-	Country Music	5			15	Songwriter. 'The Auctioneer', 'Walk on By'
Van Dyke, Nicholas	1738-1789	Revolutionary War	110	275	625		Statesman, Continental Congress
Van Fleet, James, Gen.	1892-1992	Military	28	75	95	125	Gen. WW II. US 8th Army, Korea
Van Fleet, Jo		Entertainment	15	20	45	40	AA

NAME	DATE	CATEGORY	SIG	LS/DS	ALS	SP	COMMENTS
Van Halen (All) (4)		Entertainment	45			150	Rock LP Cover S 85, 'Women & a..1st' S 150
Van Halen (all-original)		Entertainment	88			160	Rock
Van Halen, Alex		Entertainment	20	95		50	
Van Halen, Eddie		Entertainment	25	78		58	Rock.1982 Check Signed 200
Van Hecke, Johan		Political	10			15	Member European Parliament
Van Heusen, James (Jimmy)		Composer	60	90	175	100	AMusQS 250
Van Hoften, James D.		Astronaut	6			20	
Van Horn, Burt		Senate/Congress	10	20			Rep. NY 1861, Manufacturer
Van Horne, David		Revolutionary War	10		75		
Van Hulten, Michiel		Political	10			15	Member European Parliament
Van Kirk, Theodore		Aviation	40	85		75	Enola Gay navigator
Van Lancker, Anne E.m.		Political	10			15	Member European Parliament
Van Leer, Darryl		Entertainment	10			20	actor
Van Loon, Hendrik Willem		Author	18	30	125	40	Historian, Journalist, Lecturer, Illustrator
Van Loon, William		Journalist	10		50		Lecturer
Van Ness, Cornelius P.		Governor	15	35	60		Jurist, Gov. VT, Minister Sp.
Van Nuys, Frederick	1874-1944	Congress	10			25	Senator IN 1932
Van Orden, Geoffrey		Political	10			15	Member European Parliament
Van Outen, Denise		Celebrity	10			15	celebrity model
Van Outen, Denise		Celebrity	10			15	television presenter
Van Patten, Dick		Entertainment	5	6	15	15	
Van Patten, Joyce		Entertainment	4	4	10	15	
Van Peebles, Mario		Entertainment	15			45	Actor-Dir.
Van Rensselaer, Henry	1810-1864	Civil War	75				Rep. NY 1841, Union General
Van Rensselaer, Stephen	1764-1839	Military	75	170	260		Gen'l War 1812. Helped estab. Rensselaer School
Van Sant, Gus		Celebrity	10			15	film industry
Van Schaick, Goose		Revolutionary War			2900		General Rev. War. Served Honorably Thru The War
Van Sloon, Edward		Entertainment	125			250	
Van Stade, Frederica		Entertainment	15			45	Opera
Van Straten, Michael		Celebrity	10			15	health and fitness expert
Van Sweringen, Otis P.		Business	15	40	90	35	RR Exec-Developer Shaker Height
Van Valkenburgh, Debbie		Entertainment	6	8	15	15	
Van Vechten, Carl		Author	40	75	110	75	Am. Novelist, Staff NY Times
Van Velzen, W.g.		Political	10			15	Member European Parliament
Van Vleck, John H., Dr.		Science	30	45	75		Nobel Physics 1977
Van Vliet, Stewart	1815-1901	Civil War	46		90		Union Gen. Indian Fighter
Van Vooren, Monique		Entertainment	4	6	10	15	Pin-Up SP 25
Van Voorhis, Lt. Gen. Daniel	1878-1956	Military	30				World War II U.S. general
Van Wagoner, Murray D.		Governor	5	20		15	Governor MI
Van Wyck, Charles Henry	1824-1895	Civil War	48	100	140		Union general
Van Zandt, Philip		Entertainment	50			150	
Van Zandt, Stevie		Entertainment				50	Silvio Dante, Soprano's. Member of E Street Band
Van Zant, Ronnie		Entertainment	25			100	
Van Zealand, Paul, Viscount		Head of State	15			35	Premier Belgium, Foreign Min.
Van, Bobby		Entertainment	5			20	Dancer

NAME	DATE	CATEGORY	SIG	LS/DS	ALS	SP	COMMENTS
Van, Gloria		Entertainment	5	6	15	15	
Van, Isabelle		Entertainment	5			10	Dancer
Van, Jackie		Entertainment	5			15	Dancer
Vance, A.T., Capt.		Aviation	15	25			Record Polar Flight
Vance, Cyrus		Cabinet	10	20	35	25	Sec'y State, Sec'y Army
Vance, Jack		Author	10	15	20	15	Hugo & Nebula winning SF writer
Vance, Louis Joseph		Author	15	35	90		Am. Novelist
Vance, Mike		Celebrity	10			15	motivational speaker
Vance, Robert Brank	1828-1899	Civil War	120	174	336		CSA Gen. Sig/Rank 145
Vance, Vivian	1913-1979	Entertainment	175	229		551	Actress. Lucy's TV Sidekick. Lucy SP 450
Vance, Zebulon Baird	1830-1894	Civil War	54	117	165		CSA Gov. & Sen. Of NC, Opposed J.Davis
Vandamme, Dominique Rene		Napoleonic Wars	50	150	210		Battle of Waterloo
Vandenberg, Arthur H.	1884-1951	Congress	20	70		25	Senator MI, Pres. Pro Tem.
Vandenberg, Hoyt S.	1899-1954	Military-Aviation	40	80		100	
Vander Jagt, Guy		Celebrity	10			15	motivational speaker
Vander Pyl, Jean		Entertainment	10			15	Voice Wilma-Pebbles Flintstone
Vanderbilt, Alfred Gwynn		Business	15	35	65	25	
Vanderbilt, Amy		Author	10	25	40	35	Columnist, Authority on Manners
Vanderbilt, Cornelius	1794-1877	Business	547	2487	4492	2880	The 'Commodore', ALS cont 25000
Vanderbilt, Cornelius	1843-1899	Business	250	825	1750	1250	Grandson of 'Commodore'. RRs, 'Breakers'
Vanderbilt, Cornelius, Jr.	1898-1974	Journalist	25	75	125	40	
Vanderbilt, George Washington	1862-1914	Business	250	750	1100	800	Grandson of 'Commodore'. 'Biltmore House'
Vanderbilt, Gloria		Business	25	45	80	35	Fashion Designer. Artist. Litho S 125
Vanderbilt, Harold S.	1884-1970	Business	168				Philanthropist-Businessman
Vanderbilt, Jacob H.	1807-1893	Business	500	1900	2950		Brother of 'Commodore'. RRs & Steamships
Vanderbilt, William H.	1821-1885	Business	300	1138	2225	1400	'Commodore' Son. Philanthropist. Giant RR Empire
Vanderbilt, William H., Jr.		Business	45	120	250	75	Governor RI
Vanderbilt, William K.	1849-1920	Business	250	650	1500	800	'Commodore' Gr. Son.RR Exec.,Financier-Yachtsman
Vandergrift, Alexander A.	1887-1973	Military	45	100	175	150	1st Marine Div. Gen. WW II. MOH at Guadalcanal
Vanderlyn, John	1775-1852	Artist	250	275	750		Am. Pres. Portraits, Capitol
Vandever, William	1817-1893	Civil War	35		85		Union general
Vane, Henry	1613-1662	History		690			Early Amer. Settler, 'America's 1st revolutionary'
Vane, John R., Dr.		Science	20	30	50	25	Nobel Medicine 1982
Vaness, Carol		Entertainment	10			35	Opera
Vanhecke, Frank		Political	10			15	Member European Parliament
Vanier, General Georges Philias	1888-1967	Military	20				World War II Canadian general
Vanili, Milli		Entertainment	10			50	
Vanilla Ice		Entertainment	20			40	Rock
Vanity		Entertainment	4	7		15	Pin-Up SP 25
Vanous, Lucky		Celebrity	10			15	model
Vanzetti, Bartolomeo		Political Radical	600	1800	6500		Convicted Murderer, Electrocuted
Varaut, Alexandre		Political	10			15	Member European Parliament
Vardalos, Nia		Entertainment				35	My Big Fat Greek Wedding
Varela Suanzes-Carpegna, Dan'l		Political	10			15	Member European Parliament
Varela, Leonor		Entertainment				40	

NAME	DATE	CATEGORY	SIG	LS/DS	ALS	SP	COMMENTS
Varese, Edgard	1883-1965	Composer	185	199	502		Fr.-Am. Music Pioneer
Varga, Francis		Celebrity	30				
Vargas, Alberto		Artist	135	345	575		Repro Varga Girl S 325-450
Vargas, Getuilio		Head of State	50	150		75	Revolutionary Pres. Brazil.
Varick, Richard	1753-1831	Revolutionary War	65	124	180		Soldier, Washington's Sec'y
Varley, Brigadier Arthur L.	1893-1944	Military	20				World War II Australian general
Varmus, Harold E., Dr.		Science	25	60		35	Nobel Medicine 1989
Varnay, Astrid		Entertainment	10			65	Opera
Varney, Jim		Entertainment	58			193	
Vasarely, Victor	1908-	Artist	55	130			Hungarian. Op Art Repro S 75-150-275
Vasey, Maj. Gen. Alan	1895-1945	Military	20				World War II Australian general
Vasquez, Roberta		Playboy Ctrfold	4			10	Pin-Up SP 20. Actress
Vassar, Matthew	1792-1868	Business	200	525			Founder Vassar College. ALS/Cont. 3400
Vatanen, Ari		Political	10			15	Member European Parliament
Vattimo, Gianni		Political	10			15	Member European Parliament
Vaubois, J.F.G.		Fr. Revolution	5	15	40		
Vaughan, Alfred J., Jr.	1830-1899	Civil War	80		400		CSA Gen. Sig/Rank 150
Vaughan, Brig. Charles Hilary V.	1905-1976	Military	25				World War II British general
Vaughan, Brig. Edward William D.	1894-1953	Military	25				World War II British general
Vaughan, Johnny		Celebrity	10			15	television presenter
Vaughan, Robert		Clergy	10	15	25		
Vaughan, Sarah	1924-1990	Entertainment	45	100	210	199	Am. Jazz Vocalist-Pianist
Vaughan, Stevie Ray		Music	257			371	Guitarist, signed album 283-625
Vaughan-Hughes, Brig. Gerald B.	1896-1983	Military	25				World War II British general
Vaughan-Williams, Ralph, Sir	1872-1958	Composer	97	265	371	175	Established Br. Nat'l Musical Style. SP Pc 450
Vaughn, George A.		Aviation	35	55	95	65	ACE, WW II
Vaughn, Herbert, Cardinal		Clergy	30	50	90	75	
Vaughn, John C. (WD)	1830-1899	Civil War	195	325	750		CSA Gen.
Vaughn, John Crawford	1824-1875	Civil War	110				Confederate general
Vaughn, Robert	1932-	Entertainment	6	10	15	35	Actor. Signed 'Man From Uncle' Comic Book 50
Vaughn, Vince		Entertainment	8			46	Actor
Vaughn, William S.		Business	4	10		10	Pres. Eastman Kodak
Vaux, Roberts	1786-1836	Philanthropist	110		522		Prison Reform, Houses of Refuge
Veach, Charles L.		Astronaut	5			15	
Veatch, James Clifford	1819-1895	Civil War	40		100		Union general
Vedder, Eddie		Entertainment	12			55	Music. Lead Singer 'Pearl Jam'
Vedder, Elihu		Artist	45	135	140		Drew From Dreams & Fantasy
Vedral, Joyce L.		Author	5			10	Non-Fiction
Vedrines, Jules		Aviation	200	395	650	265	
Vee, Bobby		Entertainment	8			23	Singer 14 Top-40 Hits 1960-68
Veidt, Conrad	1893-1950	Entertainment	85	90	130	175	
Veit, Stan		Author	5	10	20	20	Computer Shopper, PC historian
Vejvoda, Jarmir	1902-	Composer	70				'The Beer Barrel Polka' AMusQS 195
Velázquez, Nydia M. V		Congress	10			15	Member U.S. Congress
Velez, Lupe		Entertainment	85	95	175	188	Fiery Latin 20th Cent. Fox Musical Star. Suicide

NAME	DATE	CATEGORY	SIG	LS/DS	ALS	SP	COMMENTS
Veloz & Yolanda		Entertainment	15			35	30-40's Ballroom Dance Team
Veltroni, Walter		Political	10			15	Member European Parliament
Venable, Evelyn		Entertainment	15	20	40	35	
Venable, William Webb		Senate/Congress	5	15		10	Rep. MS 1916, Judge
Vendela		Entertainment	20			39	Model-Actress
Vendome, L.J., Duke de	1654-1712	Fr. Military	150	450			Marshal of France
Vendy, Krista		Entertainment	10			20	Tess from 'Neighbours'
Venning, General Sir Walter King	1882-1964	Military	28				World War II British general
Ventura, Charlie		Entertainment	40			150	Am. Bandleader-Saxophonist
Venture, Jesse		Political				25	Governor of Minnesota, Former Prof. wrestler
Venuta, Benay		Entertainment	7			15	
Verdi, Giuseppe	1813-1901	Composer	1175	1750	4788	4098	AMusQS 4750, 5,000, 5,700, 7,500, 12,500
Verdin, James, Lt.Cdr.		Aviation	10	25			US Navy Pilot. Record Holder
Verdon, Gwen	1925-	Entertainment	5	6	15	15	Dancer-Actress-Singer, Top Broadway Star, Films
Verdugo, Elena		Entertainment	8			15	Actress
Verdy, Violette		Entertainment	10			30	Opera
Vereen, Ben	1946-	Entertainment	8	20		20	Dancer, Singer, Actor
Vereshchagin, Vassili V.	1842-1904	Artist	35		150	500	Paintings of Russian Wars
Vergara, Sofia		Entertainment				35	
Vergennes, Chas. G., Le Comte	1717-1787	Statesman	175	375	1725		Fr. Ambass. Supported Am. Rev.
Verhoeven, Paul		Celebrity	10			15	film industry
Verlaine, Paul	1844-1896	Author	150	366	538		Fr. Symbolist Poet
Vermeer, Herman		Political	10			15	Member European Parliament
Vermehren, Werner		Aviation	15	35	55	58	Ger. Capt. WW I Zepps.
Verne, Jules	1828-1905	Author	185	615	932	1725	Fr. Sci-Fi Novelist 'Around the World in 80 Days'
Verneuil, Edouard Poulletier de	1805-1873	Science			65		Geologist and paleontologist
Verney, Maj. Gen. Gerald Lloyd	1900-1957	Military	25				World War II British general
Vernier, Theodore, Count		Fr. Revolution	35	100			
Verve, The		Entertainment	40			125	Music. 5 Member Rock Group
Vessey, John W.		Military	10			30	
Vest, George G.	1830-1904	Civil War	30	55			CSA Cong. From MO
Vetch, Samuel	1668-1732	Colonial America	250	800	2250		Colonial Military Governor
Vetri, Victoria		Entertainment	4			10	Pin-Up SP 20
Veverka, Jaroslav		Entertainment	20			45	Opera
Vezzani, Cesare		Entertainment	45			150	Opera. Corsican Dramatic Tenor
Viant, Maj. Gen. Maurice	1882-1963	Military	20				World War II French general
Viardot, Pauline		Entertainment	30		142	100	Fine Singer from Manual Garcia Musical Family
Vickers, Jon		Entertainment	15			55	Opera. Dramatic Tenor
Vickers, Lt Gen. Wilmot Gordon H.	1890-1987	Military	25				World War II British general
Vickers, Martha	1925-1971	Entertainment	4	5	6	10	Model-Actress.
Victor Amadeus III	1726-1796	Royalty	95	295			King of Sardinia
Victor Emmanuel I	1759-1824	Royalty	130	325	585		King of Sardinia
Victor Emmanuel II (It)	1820-1878	Royalty	125	320	525	500	King of Italy 1861-1878
Victor Emmanuel III & B.Mussolini		Royalty, Hd of St		250			DS by both
Victor Emmanuel III	1869-1947	Royalty	100	250			King of Italy 1900-46

NAME	DATE	CATEGORY	SIG	LS/DS	ALS	SP	COMMENTS
Victor, Claude Perrin	1766-1841	Fr. Military	75	140	210		Marshal of Napoleon
Victor, Henry	1898-1945	Entertainment	65			200	Br. Tall Leading Man of Br. Silent Movies.
Victoria, Duchess of Kent	1786-1861	Royalty	45		125		Mother of Queen Victoria
Victoria, Empress (Fred. III, Ger)	1840-1901	Royalty	85		488		Imperial Presentation Frame & SP 3700
Victoria, Mary Louisa		Royalty	40	110	136		
Victoria, Queen	1819-1901	Royalty	201	490	667	1385	Great Britain etc.DS by Victoria & Albert 575
Vidal, Gore	1925-	Author	10	20	35	20	Am. Novelist, Playwright, Critic, Screenplays
Vidal-quadras Roca, Alejo		Political	10			15	Member European Parliament
Vidocq, Francois	1775-1875	Celebrity		368			French agent, spy
Vidor, Florence	1895-1977	Entertainment	40	45	65	60	Silent Film Star. Wife of Director King Vidor
Vidor, King	1894-1982	Entertainment	30	75		89	AA Film Director. LS/Cont. 250
Viele, Egbert L.	1825-1902	Civil War	38	70	78	100	Union Gen'l, Eng'r. Sig/Rank 40, WarDte DS 150
Vietinghoff gen.Scheel, Col-Gen H	1887-1952	Military	225				World War II German general
Vigneaud, Vincent du		Science	10	25	45	15	
Vigran, Herb		Entertainment	10	15		20	Actor. Vintage Character Actor
Vila, Bob		Entertainment	5			20	TV Tool Show. 'This Old House' Host
Vila, George R.		Business	7	20	32	15	CEO Uniroyal Tire
Vilas, Jack		Aviation	6	16			
Vilas, William F.		Cabinet	30	30	45	35	P.M. Gen., Sec'y Interior 1888. Cleveland Cabinet
Viljoen, Benjamin		Celebrity	5	15	40	15	
Viljoenk, B.J.		Military	35		145		
Villa, Francesco (Pancho)	1878-1923	Military	1100	2062	5250	4000	Mexican Guerilla Leader, Revolutionary
Villa-Lobos, Heitor	1887-1959	Composer	100	262	525	333	Brazilian. AMusQS 500,AMusMsS 550-1,000
Villalpando, Catalina Vasquez		Cabinet	15			30	US Treasurer
Villechaize, Herve		Entertainment	25	30		50	Actor. 'Fantasy Island', 'Tattoo'
Villepique, John B.	1830-1862	Civil War	288	375	690		CSA Gen. Sig/Rank 350-395 Rare
Villetto, Rev. Robert		Author	8			12	religion
Villiers, Alan J.		Author	10		25		Australian. Maritime, Adventure, History
Villiers, Frederic		Artist	10	20	50	40	
Villiers, Theresa		Political	10			15	Member European Parliament
Villon, Jacques (Psued)	1875-1963	Artist	65		300		(Pseud.Gaston Duchamp) Brother Marcel Duchamp
Vinay, Ramon		Entertainment	70			200	Opera. Sang Otello Internationally
Vincent, Gene		Entertainment	175			295	Rock
Vincent, Jan-Michael	1944-	Entertainment	10		15	22	Actor. Leading Man of the 70's
Vincent, June		Entertainment	5			20	Actress. Secondary Leads & Supporting Roles
Vincent, Romo		Entertainment	5	10	20	15	Actor. Character, Supporting Player
Vincent, Stenio Joseph	1874-1959	Head of State	125				Pres. Haiti. Lawyer, Diplomat
Vincent, Strong (WD)	1837-1863	Civil War	325	3295			Union general, 3rd Brigade. KIA Gettysburg
Vincent, Thomas M.	1832-1909	Civil War	41	80	128		Union General
Vincent, Tim		Celebrity	10			15	television presenter
Vinci, Luigi		Political	10			15	Member European Parliament
Viner, Bradley		Celebrity	10			15	veterinarian expert
Vinson, Carl	1883-1991	Congress	20	40		70	Rep. GA 1914
Vinson, Frederick M.	1890-1953	Supreme Court	75	140	225	300	Chief Justice, Cabinet, Rep. KY
Vinson, Helen	1907-	Entertainment	15	20	40	35	Actress. Sophisticated Leading Lady Of 30's-40's

NAME	DATE	CATEGORY	SIG	LS/DS	ALS	SP	COMMENTS
Vinton, Bobby		Composer	5	10		15	AMusQS 40
Vinton, David	1803-1873	Civil War	30	55	80		Union Gen., 1st P.O.W.
Vinton, Francis Laurens	1835-1879	Civil War	45	60	90		Union general
Vinton, Will		Celebrity	12	25			
Virchow, Rudolf	1821-1902	Science	212	506	1188	1725	Founder Cellular Pathology
Virrankoski, Kyösti Tapio		Political	10			15	Member European Parliament
Virtanen, A. I.	1895-1973	Science	30	85	145	55	Nobel Chemistry 1945
Visclosky, Peter J. V		Congress	10			15	Member U.S. Congress
Vishinsky, Andrei		Head of State	70	230	370	120	Rus.1st Deputy Foreign Minister
Visitor, Nana		Entertainment	15			35	Actress. 'Star Trek' SP 45
Vitter, David V		Congress	10			15	Member U.S. Congress
Vittor, Frank		Artist	40		165		
Vivian, Richard H. Sir		Revolutionary War	45	125	255		
Vix, Maj. Gen. Fernand	1876- ?	Military	20				World War II French general
Vlaminck, Maurice de	1876-1958	Artist	88	235	262	312	Fr. Fauvist Painter
Vlasto, Dominique		Political	10			15	Member European Parliament
Vodges, Israel	1816-1889	Civil War	50	75	100		Union general
Voelker, John D.		Author	5	10	15	15	
Voggenhuber, Johannes		Political	10			15	Member European Parliament
Vogl, Heinrich		Entertainment	75		285		Important Early Wagnerian Tenor
Voight, Deborah		Entertainment	5			25	Opera
Voight, Jon		Entertainment	12		30	40	Oscar Winning Actor.
Voinovich, George		Senate	10			15	United States Senate (R - OH)
Voisin, Gabriel	1880-1973	Aviation	65	135	225	250	Fr. Airplane Mfg. & Pioneer Experimentor
Vokes, Christopher	1904-1985	Military	40	65	80	65	WW II Canadian General
Vokes, Rosina		Entertainment	10	15	20	15	
Volcic, Demetrio		Political	10			15	Member European Parliament
Volcker, Paul A.		Cabinet	5		10	15	Chm. Federal Reserve
Voliva, Wilbur G.	1870-1942	Clergy	30		50		
Volk, Leonard W.	1828-1895	Artist	55	350	475		Sculptor. Famed for Lincoln Works, etc.
Volkov, Vladislav	1935-1971	Cosmonaut	100			225	Russ. Astronaut Soyuz 7. Killed in Soyuz 11
Voll, John J.		Aviation	18	40	65	45	ACE, WW II
Volstead, Andrew J.	1860-1947	Congress	30	60	95	125	MOC MN 1903. Volstead Act
Volta, Alessandro	1745-1827	Science	400	2500	2917		It. Volt, Electrical Unit, For Him
Voltaire, Francois M.	1694-1778	Author	400	1938	3500		Fr. Writer-Philosopher-Satirist
Volz, Nedra		Entertainment	4			10	
Von Boetticher, Christian Ulrik		Political	10			15	Member European Parliament
Von D'niken, Erich		Author	15	30	75	30	Sci-Fi
Vonnegut, Kurt, Jr.		Author	20	45	70	50	Am. Black-Humor Novels.
Voorhees, Daniel W.		Senate/Congress	15	40			Rep., Senator IN 1861
Voorst tot Voorst, Lt. Gen. Jan J.G.	1880-1963	Military	20				Baron, World War II Dutch general
Vordaman, Carol		Celebrity	10			15	children's presenter
Vormann, General Nikolaus von	1895-1959	Military	25				World War II German general
Voronoff, Serge	1866-1951	Science	35		205		Rus. Physicist. Used Animal Glands for Rejuvenation
Vorster, Balthazar J		Head of State	25	70	165	50	Prime Minister South Afr.

NAME	DATE	CATEGORY	SIG	LS/DS	ALS	SP	COMMENTS
Voskhod 1		Astronauts				225	Crew
Voss, James		Astronaut	6			20	
Voss, Janice		Astronaut	5			22	
Vosseller, Aurelius B.		Military	35	95			
Voyant, Claire		Celebrity	10			15	Astrologer
Voysey, Charles	1828-1912	Clergy	35	50	75		Founder of the Theistic Church.
Vraciu, Alex		Aviation	15	25	50	35	ACE, WW II
Vrooman, Peter		Rev War			185		NY Colonel
VSyrynen, Paavo		Political	10			15	Member European Parliament
Vuillard, Edouard	1868-1940	Artist	140	290	367		Fr. Painter, Printmaker, Illustrator, Decorator
Vulliamy, Maj. Gen. Colwyn H. H.	1894-1972	Military	25				World War II British general
Vyshinsky, Andrei		Political		184			Soviet Deputy Foreign Minister
Vyvyan, Maj. Gen. Ralph Ernest	1891-1971	Military	25				World War II British general

NAME	DATE	CATEGORY	SIG	LS/DS	ALS	SP	COMMENTS
Wachtel. Theodor	1823-1893	Entertainment	70		195		Opera.19th Cent. Ger. Tenor
Wachtmeister, Peder		Political	10			15	Member European Parliament
Wade, Benjamin Franklin	1800-1878	Congress	40	70	95		Senator OH 1851-69
Wade, Leigh		Aviation	30	60	80	50	Pilot '24 Round The World
Wade, Maj. Gen. Douglas A. L.	1898-1996	Military	25				World War II British general
Wade, Melancthon Smith	1802-1868	Civil War	40		110		Union general
Wade. Keptha H.		Business		875			Telegraph & RR Pioneer. 'Big 3 Telegraph' 1860's
Wadopian, Eliot		Entertainment	10			25	Bassist. Paul Winter Consort. 'Grammy'
Wadsworth, James S.	1807-1864	Civil War	197	376	460		Union Gen. KIA Battle of the Wilderness
Wadsworth, James W., Jr.	1877-1952	Congress	12	30			Senator NY
Wadsworth, Jeremiah	1743-1804	Revolutionary War	145	332	384		Commissary Gen'l. Continental Army. CT. Merchant
Wadsworth, Peleg		Revolutionary War	105	315			General, Aide Artemas Ward
Waesche, Russell Randolph	1886-1946	Military	30	50			US Coast Guard Commandant
Wagener, David D.	1792-1860	Congress	12		45		MOC PA, Founder Easton Bank
Waggin, Patti		Entertainment	3	3	6	10	
Wagner, Adolf		Military/ Political		575			Nazi, Bavarian minister of Interior
Wagner, Cosima	1837-1930	Celebrity	85	150	225	400	Wife of Rich'd. Daughter of Liszt. ALS/Cont. 1850
Wagner, George Day	1829-1869	Civil War	45	95	130		Union general
Wagner, Jack		Entertainment	10			20	actor
Wagner, Jane		Author	10	15		20	Playwright. Emmy & Peabody Awards
Wagner, Lindsay		Entertainment	5	12	15	22	Actress
Wagner, Natasha Gregson		Entertainment	8			45	Actress-Daughter Natalie Wood
Wagner, Richard	1813-1883	Composer	1038	1865	2397	3325	Ger. ALS/Content 5,000, 5,500, 8500
Wagner, Robert F.	1877-1953	Senate/Congress	20	30	45	40	Senate NY 1926, Wagner Act
Wagner, Robert		Entertainment	15	25	25	32	Actor
Wagner, Siegfried	1869-1930	Music				35	Conductor, son of Richard
Wagoner, Porter	1930-	Country Music	10			25	Major Star. Duets w/Norma Jean & Dolly Parton

NAME	DATE	CATEGORY	SIG	LS/DS	ALS	SP	COMMENTS
Wagstaff, Patty		Celebrity	10			15	motivational speaker
Wahl, Ken		Entertainment	15			45	Actor
Wahl, Lutz		Military	30		75		Am. Gen. WW I
Wahlberg, Mark		Entertainment	20			61	Actor
Waigel, Theo, Dr.		Ger. Government	4	10		15	Ger. Government Official
Wainwright III, Loudon		Entertainment	10			20	actor
Wainwright, Charles S.	1826-1905	Civil War	30	75			Union General
Wainwright, James		Entertainment	5			15	Actor
Wainwright, Johathan	1864-1945	Military	20		32		MOC NY, Capt. NY Vols. Span-Am War
Wainwright, Jonathan M.	1883-1953	Military	75	170	250	225	Am. Gen. WW II. MOH. 'Death March'. SP/Mac. 995
Wainwright, Maj. Gen. Charles B.	1893-1961	Military	252				World War II British general
Waite, H. Roy		Aviation	15	25	40		
Waite, Morrison R.	1816-1888	Supreme Court	60	130	225	250	ALS as Chief Justice Supreme Court 435
Waite, Ralph		Entertainment	5	10	15	25	Actor. 'Walton's Mountain'
Waite, Terry		Hostage	30		40	35	Also Hostage Negotiator
Waitley, Dennis		Celebrity	10			15	motivational speaker
Wakely, Jimmy	1914-	Country Music	30			100	Major Country Star During 40's & Early 50's
Wakely, Maj. Gen. Arthur Victor T.	1886-1959	Military	25				World War II British general
Wakeman, Rick		Entertainment	15			30	
Waksman, Selman A.	1888-1978	Science	45	75	95	82	Nobel Medicine 1952
Walburn, Raymond		Entertainment	10	15	40	35	Vintage Buggy-Eyed Comedic Character Actor
Walch, Brigadier Gordon		Military	28				World War II British general
Walcott, Fred C.	1869-1949	Congress	10	30			Senator CT 1929. Mfg., Banker
Walcutt, Charles C.	1838-1898	Civil War	52	70	80		Union General Sig/Rank 45, War Dte DS175
Wald, George		Science	15	30	50	25	Nobel Medicine 1967
Wald, Jerry		Bandleader	10			40	Big Band
Wald, Lillian D.	1867-1940	Reformer	30	90	175	50	1st City School Nurse Service
Walden, Greg		Congress	5			15	MOC from Oregon
Waldheim, Kurt	1918-	Head of State	30	55	75	60	P.M. Austria. Sec'y Gen'l U.N. WW II War Criminal
Waldo, Anna Lee		Author	15			20	
Waldo, Janet		Entertainment	4			15	Major Radio Actress. Judy Jetson Voice
Waldren & Kreitlow		Music	7				folk music
Waldron, Hicks B.		Business	5			10	CEO Heublein Inc.
Waldron, Maj. Gen. Albert W.	1892-1961	Military	30				World War II U.S. general
Walesa, Lech		Head of State	35	65		110	Nobel Peace Pr., Pres. Poland. FDC S 30
Walford, Maj. Gen. Alfred Ernest	1896-1990	Military	24				World War II Canadian general
Walgreen, Charles Rudolph	1873-1939	Business	35	70	145		Pharmacist Fndr. of Walgreen Drugs
Walke, Henry	1809-1896	Civil War	35		90		Rear Admiral
Walken, Christopher		Entertainment	15		30	45	Actor. 'Deer Hunter'
Walker, Alice	1944-	Author	23			45	Novelist. 'Color Purple' etc.
Walker, Benjamin	1753-1818	Revolutionary War	50	125			Rev. Army Officer. Rep. NY
Walker, Bree		Journalist	5			10	TV News
Walker, Charles		Astronaut	5			15	
Walker, Clint		Entertainment	33	48	100	62	Top Western Actor-Cowboy
Walker, David M.		Astronaut	5			30	

NAME	DATE	CATEGORY	SIG	LS/DS	ALS	SP	COMMENTS
Walker, Francis Amasa	1840-1897	Civil War	60	116	172		Union Gen. Rose From Private. Sig/Rank 75
Walker, Frank B.		Celebrity	10			15	medical expert
Walker, Frank C.		Cabinet	5	15		10	P.M. General 1940
Walker, Fred L.		Military	10	35	50		
Walker, Gilbert C.		Governor	15	20	25		Gov. VA 1869, Rep. VA 1875
Walker, Henry Harrison	1832-1912	Civil War	100	140	206		Confederate general
Walker, James Alexander	1832-1901	Civil War	95				Confederate general
Walker, James J. 'Jimmie'	1881-1946	Politician	25	40	60	50	Flamboyant Mayor NYC. Corruption Charges
Walker, James	1794-1874	Clergy	15	25	44		Pres. Harvard
Walker, Jerry Jeff		Entertainment	10	15	30	35	
Walker, Jimmy		Entertainment	5			15	Afr.-Am. Actor-Comedian. 'Good Times'
Walker, John Brisben		Journalist	10	30			Editor 'Cosmopolitan Magazine'
Walker, John George	1822-1893	Civil War	110	229	283		CSA General. Sig/Rank 195
Walker, Justin		Entertainment	10			20	actor
Walker, Leroy Pope (WD)	1817-1884	Civil War	265	440	640		CSA Gen.-1st CS Sec'y of War
Walker, Leroy Pope	1817-1884	Civil War	117	187	220		Confederate general
Walker, Lt. Gen. Walton H.	1889-1950	Military	30				World War II U.S. general
Walker, Lucius Marshall	1829-1863	Civil War	280				Confederate general
Walker, Maj. Gen. Fred L.	1887-1969	Military	30				World War II U.S. general
Walker, Mary E.	1832-1919	Civil War	225	632	751	1500	Union Nurse & Surgeon, MOH, ALS/Cont.10,000
Walker, Meriwether L.		Military	40		125		Am. WW I Gen. Panama Canal Zone Gov.
Walker, Mort*		Cartoonist	15			80	'Beetle Bailey'
Walker, Nancy	1921-1992	Entertainment	20			30	Comedienne-Actress. Broadway, Films
Walker, Paul		Entertainment	5			38	Actor. Co-Star 'Varsity Blues'
Walker, Percy	1812-1880	Congress	15	35			MOC AL, Medicine, Soldier
Walker, Reuben Lindsay	1827-1890	Civil War	80		285		CSA Gen. Comdr. Artillery in 64 Battles
Walker, Robert J.	1801-1869	Cabinet	25	55	80		Polk Sec'y Treasury. Largely Created US Dept. Int.
Walker, Robert Jarvis C.		Senate/Congress	12	20			MOC PA. 1881.
Walker, Robert, Jr.		Entertainment	10			25	Actor son of Rob't Walker & Jennifer Jones
Walker, Robert, Sr.	1918-1951	Entertainment	50		150	155	Actor Leading-Man-Husband of Jennifer Jones
Walker, Roy		Celebrity	10			15	impressionist
Walker, T. Bone		Entertainment	30			85	Jazz Guitar-Vocalist
Walker, Walton H.	1898-1950	Military	30	55	102	75	General. Killed in Korea 1950
Walker, William S.	1822-1899	Civil War	85		305		CSA Gen. Sig/Rank 150-200
Walker, Wm Henry T.	1816-1864	Civil War	233	342	575		CSA Gen. KIA
Walker, Wm. Henry T. (WD)	1816-1864	Civil War	205	1350	1742		CSA Gen. KIA 1864
Wallace, Alfred R.	1823-1913	Science	75	160	372		Developed Theory of Evolution Same Time As Darwin
Wallace, Chris		Celebrity	10			15	media/TV personality
Wallace, Dee		Entertainment	5	6	15	18	Actress. 'E.T.' DS 125
Wallace, Dewitt	1889-1981	Publisher	30			85	Founder Readers Digest
Wallace, Dillon		Author	5	15	30	10	
Wallace, Edgar	1875-1932	Author	75	270	345	370	Popular Thriller Writer
Wallace, George C.		Governor	25	50	95	80	4 Term AL Governor. Pres. Candidate
Wallace, Henry A.	1888-1965	Vice President	30	75	148	125	FDR V.P., Sec'y Agr., Sec'y Commerce
Wallace, Henry C.	1866-1924	Cabinet	15	25	50	20	Sec'y Agriculture 1921

NAME	DATE	CATEGORY	SIG	LS/DS	ALS	SP	COMMENTS
Wallace, Irving		Author	20	45	75	75	Am. Novelist
Wallace, Jean	1923-	Entertainment	10	15	20	25	Blonde Leading Lady From Early 40's
Wallace, John		Civil War	100	300			Black Leader 1860's
Wallace, Lewis 'Lew'	1827-1904	Civil War, Author	95	360	398		Union Gen.-Statesman-Author 'Ben Hur'
Wallace, Lila Acheson		Business	10	25	35	20	
Wallace, Lurleen B.		Governor	20	30		25	Governor AL. Replaced Husband
Wallace, Maj. Gen. Charles John	1886-1943	Military	25				World War II British general
Wallace, Maj. Gen. Fred C.	1887-1959	Military	30				World War II U.S. general
Wallace, Marcia		Entertainment	10			20	actress
Wallace, Marjorie		Entertainment	4			20	Miss USA, Actress
Wallace, Mike		Journalist	18	15	25	30	News Journalist. '60 Minutes'
Wallace, Vincent	1812-1865	Music					Composer AMQS 80
Wallace, William H. (WD)	1827-1901	Cicil War	140	425			CSA general
Wallace, William H. L.	1827-1901	Civil War	85	258			CSA Gen. Sig/Rank 210, War Dte DS 425
Wallach, Eli		Entertainment	5	6	22	30	Stage-Film Character Actor
Wallburg, Donnie		Entertainment	10			45	Marky Mark
Wallenberg, Knut	1853-1938	Financier	60	155			Swe. Enskilda Bank, Statesman
Wallenberg, Raoul	1912-?	History		10925			Righteous Gentile WWII, Swedish Diplomat
Wallenda, Debbie		Entertainment	20			40	Trapeze Artist. 'Flying Wallendas'
Wallenda, Karl	1905-1978	Entertainment	100			450	Trapeze Artist. 'Flying Wallendas'. Killed High Wire
Wallenstein, Alfred, Dr.		Conductor	20			75	Am. Cellist/Conductor
Waller, Littleton		Military	100				Marine General 1880-1920
Waller, Robert James		Author	5			10	Novelist
Waller, Thomas 'Fats'	1904-1943	Composer	206	387	525	764	Jazz Pianist. AMusQS 900
Waller, Thomas M.		Governor	15	25	40		Governor CT 1883
Walley, Deborah		Entertainment	5	10	15	30	Actress
Wallin, Florence		Author	8			12	novelist
Wallington, Jimmy	1907-1972	Entertainment	15	25		20	Radio, TV Announcer-Actor 'Burns & Allen' Show
Wallis, Barnes, Sir		Aviation	30	75			Br. Aircraft Designer. Inventor
Wallis, Brigadier C.		Military	28				World War II British general
Wallis, Diana		Political	10			15	Member European Parliament
Wallis, Hal	1898-1986	Entertainment	15	20		50	Major Film Producer & Exec.
Wallis, Ruth		Entertainment	10			25	
Wallis, Shani		Entertainment	5	5	10	10	
Wallmann, Jeff		Author	5	10	15	10	
Walmsley, John		Entertainment	5			10	Actor
Walpole, Horace	1717-1797	Author	150	450	1160		Br. Wit, Letter Writer, Novelist
Walpole, Hugh Seymour, Sir	1884-1941	Author	30	105	120		Novelist, Playwright, Biographer
Walpole, Robert, Sir	1676-1745	Head of State	96	225	575		First Recognized Prime Minister of England
Walpole, Spencer H.		Celebrity	5	15	25		
Walsh, Blanche		Entertainment	15			35	Vintage Actress
Walsh, Brigadier A.P.		Military	25				World War II British general
Walsh, Brigadier G.		Military	20				World War II Canadian general
Walsh, David I.	1872-1947	Congress	10	15			Governor MA 1914, Senator 1919
Walsh, Dylan		Entertainment	10			20	actor

NAME	DATE	CATEGORY	SIG	LS/DS	ALS	SP	COMMENTS
Walsh, James T. W		Congress	10			15	Member U.S. Congress
Walsh, John		Entertainment	5	5		10	Fox TV Host
Walsh, Kenneth		Aviation	15	25	50	35	ACE, WW II, CMH
Walsh, M. Emmet		Entertainment	5	6	15	15	Character Actor
Walsh, Maj. Gen. Francis James	1900-1987	Military	25				World War II British general
Walsh, Maj. Gen. Geo. Peregrine	1899-1972	Military	25				World War II British general
Walsh, Raoul	1887-1980	Entertainment	35			75	Film Director-Actor From 1912. Dir. 1914-1964
Walsh, Thomas J.	1859-1933	Cabinet	15	40		25	Senator MT 1912. FDR Att'y Gen.
Walsh, Tommy		Celebrity	10			15	home/gardening expert
Walston, Ray		Entertainment	10	15	20	45	Actor. Vet. Character Comedian Stage, TV, Films
Walt, Lewis W.		Military	20			75	Korea. Sr. Marine General Vietnam
Walter, Bruno	1876-1962	Conductor	62		118	291	Ger. Conductor. AmusQS 200. SP Pc 100-275
Walter, Gustav		Entertainment	65		160		Wagnerian Tenor, Famous Lieder Singer
Walter, Jessica	1940-	Entertainment	6	8	15	22	Actress
Walter, Ralf		Political	10			15	Member European Parliament
Walter, Richard		Celebrity	10			15	film industry
Walters, Barbara	1931-	Entertainment	10	15	20	25	TV Anchor
Walters, Julie		Entertainment	5	6	15	15	
Walters, Vernon A.		Military	5		10		
Walthall, Edward C. (WD)		Civil War	190	1272			CSA Gen.
Walthall, Edward C.	1831-1898	Civil War	121	210	361		CSA Gen.
Walthall, Henry B.	1878-1936	Entertainment	30		55	65	Stage Actor. Joined Griffith for 'Birth of a Nation
Walton, Ernest T. S., Dr.		Science	75				Nobel Physics 1951
Walton, George	1741-1804	Rev. War	282	700	1518		Signer, Cont'l Congr, Gov. GA., ADS/Content 2,500
Walton, Gladys		Entertainment	5	6	15	15	
Walton, Jayne		Entertainment	5	6	15	10	
Walton, Sam M.		Business	58	145		75	Founder Wal-Mart. Deceased
Walton, William, Sir	1902-1983	Composer	70	90	195	150	AMusQS 375-500-700
Walz, Carl		Astronaut	5			20	
Wambaugh, Joseph		Author	12	25	40	20	Am. Novelist re Law Enforcement
Wamp, Zach W		Congress	10			15	Member U.S. Congress
Wanamaker, John	1838-1922	Business-Cabinet	40	75	110	225	Dept. Store Pioneer of Money Back Guarantee Fame
Wanamaker, Zoe		Entertainment	4			25	Actress. Stage
Wang, Cheng-T'ing		Diplomat	20	60	90		Chin. Political Leader, Ambass.
Wang, Taylor		Astronaut	7			20	
Wanger, Walter	1894-1968	Entertainment	30	40		45	Am. Film Producer. Served Time For Shooting Agent
Wapner, Jos. A., Judge		Jurist	5			15	TV Judge
War		Entertainment	35			70	Rock Group (All)
Warburton, Irvine 'Cotton'		Entertainment	30		45		AA Film Editor, Football Star
Ward, A. S.							See Rohmer, Sax
Ward, Aaron	1790-1867	Military	15	35	50		General and Politician
Ward, Artemas	1727-1800	Revolutionary War	375	1495	1800		Revolutionary War Commander
Ward, Artemas	1834-1867	Author	20	35	60		(Pseud.Of C.F. Browne) Humorist. Vanity Fair Staff
Ward, Burt		Entertainment	15			29	Actor. TV 'Bat Man's' Robin
Ward, David		Entertainment	10			35	Opera

NAME	DATE	CATEGORY	SIG	LS/DS	ALS	SP	COMMENTS
Ward, General Sir Alfred Dudley	1905-1991	Military	25				World War II British general
Ward, Genevieve		Entertainment	4	5		10	
Ward, Henry A.	1835-	Merchant	40		150		1st White Child Born on Site of Chicago
Ward, Henry	1732-1797	Revolutionary War	150	430	870		Colonial Congr. Pro Independence
Ward, J.H. Hobart	1823-1903	Civil War	35	77	101		Union General. Sig/Rank 50
Ward, John Q. Adams	1830-1910	Artist	25	80	118	80	Am. Sculptor
Ward, Joseph, Sir		Head of State	15	25	60		PM New Zealand
Ward, Maj. Gen. Orlando	1891-1972	Military	30				World War II U.S. general
Ward, Marcus L.		Congress	15	25			MOC NJ 1873
Ward, Mary A. (Mrs. Humphrey)		Author	10	30	60		Br. Moral, Reforming Novels
Ward, Rachel		Entertainment	9	10	20	25	Aus. Actress. Pin-Up SP 30
Ward, Richard	1689-1763	Colonial Am.	150	425			Colon'l Gov. RI
Ward, Samuel	1725-1776	Am. Revolution		625	775		Patriot, Farmer, Merchant, Colon'l Legislator
Ward, Sela		Entertainment	12			30	Actress
Ward, William Thomas	1808-1878	Civil War	34	64	85		Union general
Warden, Jack		Entertainment	6	8	15	15	Durable Character Actor
Wardlaw, Ralph W.		Clergy	30	35	45		
Ware, Eugene F.	1841-1911	Author-Lawyer	15	30			
Ware, Henry	1764-1845	Clergy	15	25	55		Led Unitarian Separation
Ware, Linda		Entertainment	4	5		15	40's Teen Singing Star in Films
Warfield, David	1866-	Entertainment	35	40	75	75	Am. Stage Actor for Belasco Prod.
Warfield, Marsha		Entertainment	5			20	Actress. 'Night Court'
Warfield, William		Entertainment	10	15	20	40	Afr-Am Singer-Actor. 'Ol' Man River' Baritone
Warhol, Andy	1930-1987	Artist	174	260	450	347	Am. Pop Artist. Celebrity Repros S 450-4600
Waring, Fred		Entertainment	15	20	25	30	Big Band & Chorus. Waring Blender
Wark, Kirsty		Celebrity	10			15	news reader
Warlimont, Gen. of Artillery Walter	1894-1976	Military	25				World War II German general
Warner, A.P. (Borg-Warner)		Business	45	145		75	Fndr. Stewart-Warner. Speedometer
Warner, Adoniram J.	1834-1910	Civil War	35		115		Union Gen., MOC OH 1879
Warner, Charles Dudley	1829-1900	Author	20	65	115		Am. Man of Letters, Editor, Essays
Warner, Harry M.		Business	95	245	395	300	Fndr. Warner Bros.(One of Four)
Warner, Henry B.	1876-1958	Entertainment	25			65	Br. Actor. Am. Films 1914. Christ in 'King of Kings'
Warner, Jack L.	1891-1978	Business	72	206	300	270	Fndr. Warner Bros.(1 of Four)DS re MGM 900
Warner, James Meech	1836-1897	Civil War	45	65	108		Union general
Warner, James		Aviation	25		40		
Warner, John		Senate	10			15	United States Senate (R - VA)
Warner, Malcolm Jamal		Entertainment	10	30		25	Actor. 'Cosby Show'
Warner, Seth	1743-1784	Revolutionary War	200	575	1200		Officer. Leader w/Ethan Allen. Fndr.Green Mt. Boys
Warner, Ty		Business	10			25	Beanie Babies
Warnow, Mark		Entertainment	10			25	Big Band Leader
Warrant		Entertainment	45			72	Rock Group (All)
Warren Commission		Kennedy Assass.				975	Photograph of Entire Comm. Signed
Warren, Chas. Marquis	1912-	Author	10	15	25	30	Screenwriter, Prod, Dir, Novelist. Films & TV
Warren, Earl	1891-1974	Supreme Court	70	160	200	150	Chief Justice, Governor CA
Warren, Fitz-Henry	1816-1878	Civil War	38	84	138		Union general

NAME	DATE	CATEGORY	SIG	LS/DS	ALS	SP	COMMENTS
Warren, Francis	1844-1929	Congress	40	65	80		CW MOH, Gov., Senator WY
Warren, Gouverneur (WD)		Civil War	190	917			Union General
Warren, Gouverneur K.	1830-1882	Civil War	122	241	456	1438	Union Gen., ALS/Cont. 1,250
Warren, Harry	1893-1981	Composer	30	45		60	Over 300 Songs. 3 Oscars. AMusQS 275-450
Warren, James	1726-1808	Revolutionary War	119	200	540		Patriot, Merchant, Colon'l Assembly
Warren, Jennifer		Entertainment	5		10	15	Actress
Warren, Joseph	1741-1775	Rev. War	6875	24000			Physician, General. KIA. Bunker Hill
Warren, Joseph, Sr.		Colonial America	45	135	175		
Warren, Lavinia	1841-1919	Entertainment	60			295	Mrs. Tom Thumb, Charles Stratton
Warren, Leonard		Entertainment	75			175	Opera. Am. Baritone
Warren, Leslie Ann		Entertainment	10	15	20	30	Actress
Warren, Maj. Gen. Dermot F.W.	1895-1945	Military	25				World War II British general
Warren, Michael		Entertainment	5	8	10	15	
Warren, Robert Penn	1905-1989	Author	35	50	75	85	Am. Poet, Novelist. Pulitzers 1st US Poet Laureate
Warren, Russell	1783-1860	Architect	25		165		RI Designer of Many Early Banks, Churches
Warren, William	1812-1888	Entertainment	5		25		Am. Character Actor
Warrick, Ruth	1915-	Entertainment	9	10	20	38	40's Leading Lady. 'Citizen Kane'. Singer, Soaps
Warsitz, Erich		Aviation	15	35	65	40	
Warwick, Evelyn F., Countess		Celebrity	35	125			Mistress of Edward VII
Warwick, Robert R.	1587-1658	Parlementarian		475			2nd Earl. Gov. Eng. Plantation Owners in America
Washburn, Bryant	1889-1963	Entertainment	5	9	15	20	Actor. Star of Silents. Character Actor Till 40's
Washburn, Cadwallader C.	1818-1882	Civil War	37	60	80	150	Union Gen., Gov. WI 1855. War Dte. DS 225
Washburn, Israel, Jr.	1813-1883	Governor	20	40	65		Civil War Gov. ME
Washburn, W. D.		Senate/Congress	4	15			MOC MN 1879, Senator 1889
Washburne, Elihu B.	1816-1887	Cabinet	20	40	75		Sec'y State 1869, Minister Fr.
Washington, Booker T.	1856-1915	Author-Educator	282	476	747	1495	Afro-Am. Built Tuskegee, AMS 1840
Washington, Bushrod	1762-1829	Supreme Court	108	350	662		
Washington, Denzel		Entertainment	20	40		63	AA Actor
Washington, Dinah	1924-1963	Entertainment	125			200	Extraordinary Vocalist. Late 40's to Early 60's
Washington, George Augustine		Presidential Relative			900		
Washington, George C.		Senate/Congress	15	35	55		MOC MD 1827
Washington, George	1732-1799	President	5721	14630	25830		G. Washington & T. Jefferson DS 12,000-20,000
Washington, Harold		Senate/Congress	10	15	35	20	MOC IL 1981, Mayor Chicago 1983
Washington, John A.	1821-1861	Civil War	155		788		CSA Lt.Col., G. Washington Nephew. Killed 1861
Washington, Martha	1732-1801	First Lady	6392		22500		
Washington, Ned		Composer	45			100	
Washington, William	1752-1810	Military	65	165	315		Patriot. General
Wason, Lt. Gen. Sydney Rigby	1887-1969	Military	25				World War II British general
Wassel, Corydon M., Dr.		Military	45	85	150	50	Med. Missionary China. WW II Hero
Wasserman, Dale		Composer	15		35	30	'Man of LaMancha'
Wassermann, August von	1866-1925	Science	360				Ger. Bacteriologist. Blood Test for Syphilis. RARE
Watanabe, Gedde		Entertainment	9	10	20	25	
Watanabe, General Jotaro	? -1936	Military	25				World War II Japanese general
Watanabe, Maj. Gen. Nobuyoshi		Military	25				World War II Japanese general
Watari, Lt. Gen. Hisao	? -1939	Military	25				World War II Japanese general

NAME	DATE	CATEGORY	SIG	LS/DS	ALS	SP	COMMENTS
Waterhouse, Benjamin	1754-1846	Science	255	765	2750		Pioneer in Small Pox Vaccination
Waterhouse, J. W.		Artist	12		50		
Waterhouse, Maj. Gen. Geo. Guy	1886-1975	Military	25				World War II British general
Waterhouse, Richard	1832-1876	Civil War	148	388	833		CSA General. War Dte. ALS 1050
Waterloo, Stanley		Author	10	20	35		
Waterman, Denise		Celebrity	10			15	television presenter
Waterman, F.D.		Business	75	195			Waterman Pen
Waterman, Robert		Celebrity	10			15	motivational speaker
Waterman, W.		Aviation	15		25		
Waters, Ethel	1896-1977	Entertainment	50	115	128	180	Prominent Black Actress-Singer. Stage-Films
Waters, Lesley		Celebrity	10			15	TV Chef
Waters, Maxine W		Congress	10			15	Member U.S. Congress
Waters, Muddy		Entertainment	110	188		248	Jazz Musician
Waterston, Robert Classie		Clergy	10	15	30		
Waterston, Sam	1940-	Entertainment	10	12	15	38	Actor
Watie, Stand	1806-1871	Civil War	212	446			Confederate general
Watkins, Henry George Gino		Explorer	125		450		Youngest Arctic Expl. Died at 25
Watkins, Louis Douglass	1833-1868	Civil War	48		78		Union general
Watkinson, William L.		Clergy	15	20	35		
Watson, Barry		Entertainment				35	
Watson, Diane E. W		Congress	10			15	Member U.S. Congress
Watson, Elkanah	1758-1842	History			90		Helped est. NY canals, father of 'Country Fairs'
Watson, Emily		Entertainment	10			45	Actress
Watson, Emma		Entertainment				65	Actress
Watson, General Sir Daril G.	1888-1967	Military	25				World War II British general
Watson, Graham R.		Political	10			15	Member European Parliament
Watson, Harold F.		Aviation	10	30	45	25	
Watson, J. Crittenden	1842-1923	Military	25	60	105		Union Naval Officer. Admiral.
Watson, James D., Dr.		Science	35	70	60	85	Nobel Medicine 1962. Genetics, DNA
Watson, James E.	1863-1948	Congress				40	Senator IN. Majority Leader
Watson, John	1850-1907	Clergy	15		35		Presbyterian Minister-Author
Watson, Maj. Gen. Edwin M.	1883-1945	Military	30				World War II U.S. general
Watson, Maj. Gen. Leroy H.	1893-1975	Military	30				World War II U.S. general
Watson, Maj. Gen. Norman V.	1898-1974	Military	25				World War II British general
Watson, Minor		Entertainment	5	6		15	Fine Stage-Film Character Actor
Watson, R.J. Doc		Aviation	10	22	38	30	ACE, WW II, USAAF Ace
Watson, Thomas A.	1854-1934	Science	65	275	315	450	Ass't To A.G. Bell. Teleph. Pioneer
Watson, Thomas E.	1856-1922	Congress	15	35			US Sen. GA, 1904 President'l Cand.
Watson, Thomas J., Jr.	1914-1993	Business	75	126	225	175	Developed IBM. Chmn. in Productive Growth Years
Watson, Thomas J., Sr.	1874-1956	Business	80	210		250	Founder IBM
Watt, James		Cabinet	7	10	20	20	Controversial Sec'y Interior 1981
Watt, James	1736-1819	Science	400	895	2250		Scottish Inventor. Steam Engine
Watt, James, Jr.	1769-1848	Science	45	85	185		Marine Engineer. Son of Inventor
Watt, Melvin L. W		Congress	10			15	Member U.S. Congress
Wattenberg, Ben		Celebrity	10			15	financial expert

NAME	DATE	CATEGORY	SIG	LS/DS	ALS	SP	COMMENTS
Watterson, Bill*		Cartoonists	25			165	'Calvin & Hobbes'
Watterson, Henry	1840-1921	Journalist-Congress	15	50	90	95	CSA Army. Editor, Pulitzer
Watts, Charlie		Entertainment	45			75	Rolling Stones drummer
Watts, George Frederick	1817-1904	Artist	75	150	255		Br. Painter & Sculptor
Watts, Mark Francis		Political	10			15	Member European Parliament
Watts, Rolonda		Celebrity	10			15	media/TV personality
Watts, Thomas H.	1819-1892	Civil War	60		460		CSA Att'y Gen.,Gov. AL. Sig/Rank 60, War DS 270
Waugh, Evelyn	1903-1966	Author	40	75	130	90	'Brideshead Revisited'. ALS/Cont.1350
Waul, Thomas Neville	1813-1903	Civil War	95	168	368		Confederate general
Wavell, Archibald, Sir	1883-1950	Military	50	158	175	65	Br. Field Marshal, Viceroy India
Wax, Ruby		Celebrity	10			15	comedienne
Waxman, Henry A. W		Congress	10			15	Member U.S. Congress
Wayans, Damon		Entertainment	7			42	actor
Wayans, Keenen Ivory		Entertainment	7			42	Actor
Wayne, Anthony	1745-1796	Rev. War Military	428	1588	1764		'Mad Anthony' ADS 4500
Wayne, Carol		Entertainment		55	130	137	
Wayne, David	1914-1996	Entertainment	15	30	45	45	Broadway Since '38. Wide Variety Films Roles-40's
Wayne, Henry C. (WD)		Civil War	175	336			CSA Gen.
Wayne, Henry C.	1815-1883	Civil War	117	265	563	250	CSA General
Wayne, James M.	1790-1867	Supreme Court	85	200	350		
Wayne, John	1907-1979	Entertainment	474	650	850	1012	Actor, DS Wayne & John Ford 1,500-2500
Wayne, Michael		Celebrity	10			15	media/TV personality
Wayne, Pat		Entertainment	10			20	Actor-Son of John
Wazniak, Steve		Business	15			70	Co-founder of Apple Computer
Weare, Meshech	1713-1786	Revolutionary War	50	250			Pres. of New Hampshire Council DS 2500
Weatherhead, Leslie D.		Clergy	30	35	60	40	
Weathers, Carl		Entertainment	6	8	15	30	Actor
Weaver, Dennis	1924-	Entertainment	9	15	20	33	Actor. Supporting Roles From Early 50's. TV Star
Weaver, Doodles		Entertainment	15			30	Rather Eccentric Comedy Act. Films, Night Clubs
Weaver, Erasmus		Military	35		125		Am. WW I Gen.
Weaver, James B.	1833-1912	Civil War	30		65		Union Gen., Pres. Candidate
Weaver, Maj. Gen. William G.	1888-1970	Military	30				World War II U.S. general
Weaver, Robert C.		Cabinet	20	45		30	1st Afro-Am. Cabinet Member. Sec'y HUD
Weaver, Sigourney		Entertainment	12			44	Actor
Weaver, Walter Reed	1885-1944	Military	45	150			Extensive Aviation Career
Webb, Alexander S.	1835-1911	Civil War	58	90	153		Union General. Sig/Rank 140. War Dte DS 255
Webb, Beatrice Potter	1858-1943	Reformer	45	130			Member Fabian Society. SP Pc/ Matthew Webb 375
Webb, Charles Henry		Author	5	15	30		
Webb, Clifton	1891-1966	Entertainment	30	35		65	Dancer-Actor. Silents in 20's-To Villain in 'Laura'
Webb, Del		Business	5	15	25	25	'Desert Inn Casino', Las Vegas
Webb, Jack	1920-1982	Entertainment	56	84	110	142	Radio-TV Actor. 'Dragnet' SP 125
Webb, James E.		Astronaut	10			25	Admiral
Webb, Jimmy		Composer	20	35		65	Singer-Songwriter
Webb, Marti		Music	10			15	performing musical artist
Webb, Matthew	1848-1883	Channel Swimmer			250		'Captain Webb'. 1st Man to Swim English Channel

NAME	DATE	CATEGORY	SIG	LS/DS	ALS	SP	COMMENTS
Webb, Richard		Entertainment	15			35	'Capt. Midnight'
Webb, Samuel B.		Revolutionary War	105	324	645		Fndr. Soc. of Cincinnati
Webb, Sidney	1859-1947	Reformer	40		125	150	Br Economist, Fabian Society. SP Pc/Beatrice 375
Webb, U.S.		Political	6		25		California Official
Webb, W.R. 'Spider'		Aviation	15	30	45	35	ACE, WW II, Ace in a Day
Webber, Andrew Lloyd	1948-	Composer	82	250		250	Br. Musical Theatre. 'Cats', 'Phantom of the Opera'
Webber, Robert		Entertainment	15	20		35	Actor. Versatile Lead, 2nd Lead & Character
Weber (Joe)& Fields (Lew)		Entertainment	85			175	Pioneer Vaudeville Comedians
Weber, Joe	1867-1942	Entertainment	25	35	45	45	Vintage Comedian w/Lew Fields
Weber, Karl Maria von	1786-1826	Composer	375	1035	1320		9 Operas. Leader Ger. Romantic & Nationalist Music
Weber, Max	1824-1901	Civil War	45	56	90		Union general
Weber, Steven		Entertainment	10			20	actor
Weber, Walt		Author	8			12	Mountains to Sea trail, mountain hiking
Webster, Ben		Entertainment	125				Tenor Sax-Arranger
Webster, Daniel	1782-1852	Cabinet-Senate	100	328	500		NH Statesman, LS/cont.1750., ALS/cont.2500-5000
Webster, Harold T.*	1885-1952	Cartoonist	20	45		125	'TheTimid Soul'. 'Caspar Milquetoast'
Webster, Jean	1876-1916	Author	15	45	135		Am. Novelist. 'Daddy-Long-Legs'
Webster, Joseph Dana	1811-1876	Civil War	35	60	95		Union general
Webster, Noah	1758-1843	Author	460	616	1446		Am. Lexicographer. Editor. Dictionary Eng. Language
Webster, Paul Francis		Composer	20	50	70	45	
Webster, William		Cabinet	10			40	Director FBI
Wedd, Brigadier William Basil	1890-1966	Military	20				World War II Canadian general
Wedekind, Erika		Entertainment	10		50		Opera. Legendary 19th Cent. Soprano
Wedell, Jimmie		Aviation	12	30	40	35	
Wedemeyer, General Albert C.	1896-1960	Military	35	78	110	100	World War II U.S. general
Wedgwood, John H., Sir		Business	15	25	40	35	Decorative Ceramics. One of World's Major Producers
Wedgwood, Josiah	1730-1795	Potter	450		1980		Fndr. World Famous Wedgwood Pottery. Rare Sig.
Weed, Marian		Entertainment	15			50	Opera
Weed, Stephen Hinsdale	1831-1863	Civil War	150				Union Brig. General, KIA Gettysburg.
Weed, Thurlow	1797-1882	Politician	15	30	62		Influential Political Leader NY, Journalist
Weede, Robert		Entertainment	10			35	Opera, Concert, Operetta
Weedon, George		Revolutionary War	220	245	1900		Gen'l Cont'l Army. ALS/Content 2500
Weeks, Lt. Gen. Ronald Morce	1890-1960	Military	25				World War II British general, Baron of Ryton
Weeks, Anson		Entertainment	15			45	Dancin' with Anson. Big Bandleader
Weeks, John W.	1860-1926	Cabinet	15	35	70		Sec'y War 1921. US Sen. MA
Weeks, Maj. Gen. Ernest Geoffrey	1896-1987	Military	20				World War II Canadian general
Weeks, Sinclair	1893-1972	Cabinet	5	15	35	20	Sec'y Commerce 1953. US Senator
Weems, Ted		Bandleader	20	20	62	45	Big Band Leader-Trombone. Vocalist-Perry Como
Weiß, Colonel-General Walter	1890-1967	Military	25				World War II German general
Weicker, Lowell Jr.		Congress	10	20		15	Repr. CT 1969, Senator 1971. Watergate Committee
Weidenbaum, Murray Dr.		Celebrity	10			15	financial expert
Weidler, Virginia	1927-1968	Entertainment	12	15	20	25	Actress
Weidman, Jerome		Author	5	10	20	10	
Weikl, Bernd		Entertainment	5			20	Opera
Weil, Andrew		Celebrity	10			15	medical expert

NAME	DATE	CATEGORY	SIG	LS/DS	ALS	SP	COMMENTS
Weiler, Barbara		Political	10			15	Member European Parliament
Weill, Kurt	1900-1950	Composer	250	460	750	750	Ger.-Am. Opera, Ballet, Musical Comedy, Films
Weinberg, Steven, Dr.		Science	25	35		30	Nobel Physics 1979
Weinberger, Casper		Cabinet	10	10	30	40	Sec'y HEW, Sec'y Defense, Sec'y State
Weiner, Anthony D. W		Congress	10			15	Member U.S. Congress
Weingartner, Felix von	1863-1942	Composer	90	125	180	150	Austrian Conductor & Writer on Music
Weir, Benjamin M.		Celebrity	12	15	25	20	
Weir, Julian Alden		Artist	40	135	250		Early Am. Impressionist
Weir, Maj. Gen. Stephen	1905-1969	Military	20				World War II New Zealand general
Weir, Peter		Entertainment	5			25	Movie Director
Weir, Robert Walter	1803-1889	Artist	50	135	288		Prof. Drawing At West Point. Taught R.E. Lee
Weisbart, David		Entertainment	15			25	Director-Producer
Weiser, Jan Conrad	1696-1760	Indian Agent	290	950	1600		Helped Form Iroquois-Eng. Alliance Against French
Weisiger, David A.	1818-1899	Civil War	80	282			CSA Gen. ALS/Cont. 1045, Sig/Rank 175
Weiss, John	1818-1879	Clergy	10	15	28		Unitarian Author, Abolitionist
Weiss, Michael T.		Entertainment	9			52	Actor. 'The Pretender'
Weissmuller, Johnny	1904-1979	Entertainment	109	338		350	SP As Tarzan 325-695. Olympic Gold Swimmer
Weitz, John	d. 2002	Author				35	
Weitz, Paul J.		Astronaut	10			25	
Weitzel, Godfrey (WD)		Civil War	45	130	250		Union Gen. 1835-84
Weitzel, Godfrey	1835-1884	Civil War	30	99	146		Union general
Weiz, Paul		Astronaut	8			37	
Weizman, Vera		First Lady	25	80		35	Widow of 1st Pres. Israel
Weizmann, Chaim	1874-1952	Head of State	445	1316	1650	1500	1st Pres. Israel., LS/cont. 3950
Weizmann, Ezer		Head of State	25	65			Israeli AF Gen. Pres. of Israel
Welby, Amelia		Author	450		2900		Poet. Appreciated by E.A.Poe
Welch, Herbert, Bishop		Clergy	15	25	30	35	
Welch, Jack		Business				20	Ex-CEO of GE
Welch, Raquel		Entertainment	10	20	30	45	Actress
Welch, Robert A.		Business	25	40	82	35	Batchelor Oil Multi-Millionaire
Welch, Tawnee		Entertainment	10			20	actress
Weld, Maj. Gen. Charles Joseph	1893-1962	Military	25				World War II British general
Weld, Tuesday	1943-	Entertainment	10	15	30	30	Actress
Welden, Ben		Entertainment	10			25	Actor
Weldon, Curt W		Congress	10			15	Member U.S. Congress
Weldon, Dave W		Congress	10			15	Member U.S. Congress
Weldon, Felix de		Artist	60	85			Iwo Jima Memorial Statue
Welensky, Roy, Sir		Head of State	20	55	115		
Welk, Lawrence		Entertainment	10	20	35	38	Big Bandleader-TV Variety Show. 50's Most Popular
Weller, Jerry W		Congress	10			15	Member U.S. Congress
Weller, Peter		Entertainment	10	15	25	20	Actor
Weller, Thomas H., Dr.		Science	25	35	50	30	Nobel Medicine 1954
Welles, Gideon	1802-1878	Cabinet-CW	87	180	292	675	Lincoln Sec'y of Navy, LS War Dte 775-850
Welles, Orson	1915-1985	Entertainment	124	232		467	AA. Actor-Dir.-Prod-Writer. Special DS 650
Welles, Sumner	1892-1961	Diplomat	25	75	150	55	State Dept., Ambassador

NAME	DATE	CATEGORY	SIG	LS/DS	ALS	SP	COMMENTS
Wellington, 1st Duke of	1769-1852	Head of State	150	200	276		Arthur Wellesley, LS/cont. 700, ALS/cont 1750
Wellington, George Louis	1852-1927	Congress	12	20			MOC 1895, Senator MD
Wellman, Manly Wade		Author	35	100		60	North Carolina Literary Figure
Wellman, Walter	1858-1934	Aviation-Explorer	60	145	230	175	Aviator-Explorer. Dirigible Time Distance Record
Wells, B. H.		Military	30	75			Am. WW I Gen.
Wells, Carolyn		Author	10	25	40	15	Sketches, Parodies,Detective
Wells, Carveth		Author	20	45	110	60	Explorer, Author, Lecturer
Wells, Claudia		Entertainment	10			20	actress
Wells, Dawn		Entertainment	5	10	20	47	Actress. Gilligan's Island
Wells, H(erbert) G(eorge)	1866-1946	Author	133	295	416	1268	Br. Sci-Fi Novelist, ALS/Cont.6000
Wells, Henry & Fargo, James		Business	850	1082			Wells-Fargo, American Express
Wells, Henry & Fargo, William G.		Business		1475			Wells-Fargo. American Express Stk. Cert. S 800
Wells, Henry	1805-1878	Business	258	963	2325		Wells-Fargo, Founder American Express
Wells, James M.		Governor	15	40			Governor LA 1865
Wells, Junior		Entertainment	4			10	
Wells, Kitty	1918-	Country Music	10			30	Onetime 'Queen of Country Music'. Country HOF
Wells, William (WD)		Civil War	155	240			Union General
Wells, William	1837-1892	Civil War	50	75	140		Union General. MOH.
Wellstone, Paul	d. 2002	Political				35	Senator MN
Welsh, Thomas	1824-1863	Civil War	84	155			Union general
Welstein (Wells), Harvey		Celebrity	10			15	General Manager of Radio Stations
Welty, Eudora		Author	35	100	225	100	Am. Short Stories, Novelist.
Welty, Ron		Entertainment	6			25	Music. Drummer 'Offspring'
Welvert, Brig. Gen. Marie-Jos.-Ed.	1884-1943	Military	20				World War II French general
Wemyss, Gen Sir Henry Colville B	1891-1959	Military	25				World War II British general
Wenck, Walter	1900-1982	Military	40	75	120	230	WWI I German General
Wendelin, Rudolph*		Cartoonist	32			125	'Smokey the Bear'. FDC 250, signed drwg 150-200
Wendorf, E.G. Wendy		Aviation	10	25	40	30	ACE, WW II, Navy Ace
Wendt, George		Entertainment	15	35		35	Actor. 'Cheers'
Wenrich, Percy		Composer	55	125			AMusQS 175, 350
Wentworth, Benning	1696-1770	Colonial America	140	470	850		Col. Gov. NH. Bennington, VT
Wentworth, John	1737-1820	Revolutionary War	125	425	700		Colonial Governor of N.H.
Wentworth, Joshua	1742-1809	Revolutionary War		320	975		Soldier, State Sen. NH, Declined Cont'l Congr.Appt.
Wentz, Carol		Entertainment	7	12	30	30	Actress. Pin-Up 75
Wenzel-Perillo, Brigitte		Political	10			15	Member European Parliament
Werfel, Franz	1890-1945	Author	100			350	Aus. '40 Days of Musa Dagh', 'Song of Bernadette'
Wermuth, Arthur W.		Military	20	35	50	35	WW II Hero
Werner, Oskar	1922-	Entertainment	25		45	60	Intelligent, Sensitive Actor. AA Nom. 'Ship of Fools'
Wernher, Maj Gen Sir Harold Aug	1893-1973	Military	25				World War II British general
Werrenrath, Reinald	1883-	Opera	15		23	50	Am. Baritone. Met.Debut 1919
Wert, Richard L.		Military	5	15	25	20	
Wesley, Charles	1707-1788	Clergy	188		1035		Methodist Divine. Authored Several Thousand Hymns
Wesley, John	1704-1791	Clergy	438	650	2000		Methodist Fndr, ALS/Cont.3000
Wesley, Samuel	1663-1735	Clergy	50				Father of John & Charles Wesley. AQS 580
Wessell, Vivian		Entertainment	10		40	35	

NAME	DATE	CATEGORY	SIG	LS/DS	ALS	SP	COMMENTS
Wessells, Henry Walton	1809-1889	Civil War	40	56	105		Union general
Wesselowsky, Alessandro		Entertainment	40			160	Opera
Wesson, Daniel B.	1825-1906	Inventor	488		875		Inventor, Mfg., Gunsmith (Smith & Wesson)
Wesson, Edwin		Inventor			150		Gunsmith, Smith & Wesson
West, Adam		Entertainment	10	25		34	Actor. 'Batman' TV Series
West, Benjamin	1738-1820	Artist	240	779	1683		Am. Born Historical Painter, signed drwg 2070
West, Dottie	1932-	Country Music	15			40	Singer. Many Awards, a Few Movies, 400 Songs
West, Francis Henry	1825-1896	Civil War	30	46	75		Union Gen. War Dte LS 250
West, Jessamyn		Author	12	30	35	20	Popular Novelist
West, Joseph R.	1822-1898	Civil War	38	88			Union Gen.
West, Mae	1892-1980	Entertainment	73	177	300	182	Provocative Seductress. S Chk 175
West, Maj. Gen. Clement Arthur	1892-1972	Military	25				World War II British general
West, Morris L.		Author	15	45	80	30	'Shoes Of The Fisherman'
West, Rebecca, Dame	1892-1983	Author	20	45	102	50	Br. Novelist, Critic, Historian
West, Richard L.		Aviation	10			30	ACE WW II
West, Roy O.		Cabinet	25	40			Sec'y Interior 1928
West, Timothy		Entertainment	10			20	Actor
Westall, William		Artist	15	40	95		
Westendorp Y Cabeza, Carlos		Political	10			15	Member European Parliament
Westheimer, Ruth, Dr.		Medical	5	15	25	20	Sex Therapist. Radio-TV Personality
Westinghouse, George	1846-1914	Business	125	588	788	350	Fndr. Westinghouse Corp. Over 400 Patents
Westlife		Entertainment				75	Band of 5
Westman, Nidia	1902-1970	Entertainment	15	15	35	30	1sta s Child Stage Actress. From '32 Comic Support
Westminster, 2nd Earl		Royalty	15	50			Robert Grosvenor
Westmore, Wally		Entertainment	15			50	Hollywood Makeup Director
Westmoreland, Wm. C.	1914-1993	Military	30	136	167	74	Gen. WW II, Korean & Viet Nam War
Weston, Logan Colonel		Military	8			12	Author, served WW II, Korea, Vietnam
Weston, Agnes, Dame		Celebrity	6	20	40	25	
Weston, Diane		Entertainment	10			20	Actress
Weston, Edward	1850-1936	Business	40	125	315	75	Weston Electrical Instruments.
Weston, Edward	1886-1958	Artist	35		600		Am. Western Photographer. ALS/Cont. 600
Weston, Lt. Gen. Eric Culpeper	1888-1950	Military	25				World War II British general
Weston, Paul	1912-1996	Entertainment	18			35	Composer-Arranger-Conductor-Pianist For Top Stars
Westover, Russ*	1887-1966	Cartoonist	25		45	75	'Tillie The Toiler'
Westphal, Gen. of Cav. Siegfried	1902-1982	Military	25				World War II German general
Westropp, Maj Gen. Victor John E	1897-1964	Military	25				World War II British general
Westwood, Vivienne		Celebrity	10			15	Designer
Wetherbee, James D.		Astronaut	6			20	
Wettig, Patricia		Entertainment	6			32	Award Winning Actress- TV
Wexler, Robert W		Congress	10			15	Member U.S. Congress
Weyer, Kurt		Military	15			60	
Weygand, Maxime	1867-1965	Military	40	75	110	150	Fr. Gen. Foch's Chief of Staff. WW I, WW II
Weyman, Stanley J.	1855-1928	Author	25	35	75		Brit. Novelist
Whale, James		Celebrity	10			15	television presenter
Whalen, Grover		NYC Official	10	30		15	Merchant-NYC Official Greeter

NAME	DATE	CATEGORY	SIG	LS/DS	ALS	SP	COMMENTS
Whalen, Michael	1902-1974	Entertainment	10	15	20	30	Leading Man of Many 'B' Movies. 30's-40's
Wharton, Edith N.	1862-1937	Author	205	475	1600		Pulitzer, 'Age of Innocence', 'Ethan Frome'
Wharton, Gabriel C.	1824-1906	Civil War	80		294		CSA Gen. DS '64 470, Sig/Rank 125
Wharton, John A. (WD)		Civil War	700	900	2042		CSA general
Wharton, John A.	1828-1865	Civil War	181	564	1100		CSA Gen. Killed in Feud 4/6/1865.
Wharton, Thomas	1735-1778	Revolutionary War	132	1068	1482		Gov. PA, Patriot. Pres. PA 1777. Wealthy Merchant
Whately, Kevin		Entertainment	10			20	Actor
Wheatley, Edward Jacob		Celebrity	10	20			Autograph Expert
Wheatley, Melvin E., Bishop		Clergy	20	25	35	30	
Wheaton, Frank	1833-1903	Civil War	50	74	104		Union general
Wheaton, Nathaniel S.	1792-1862	Clergy	10		36		Founder Trinity College, Hartford, Washington Coll
Wheaton, Will		Entertainment	20			45	Actor. 'Star Trek', 'Westley'
Wheatstone, Charles, Sir	1802-1875	Science	100	320	565		Br. Physicist, Inventor
Wheeler, Bert	1895-1968	Entertainment	25			75	Comedy Team Wheeler & Woolsey. Vaudeville, Films
Wheeler, Burton K.	1882-1975	Congress	25	70		35	Senator MT 1922. Progressive Party V.P. Candidate
Wheeler, Caron		Music	10			15	performing musical artist
Wheeler, Charles B.		Military	35	125			Am. WW I Gen.
Wheeler, Earle G.		Military	15			50	
Wheeler, Ellie		Entertainment	10	15	25	25	
Wheeler, Joseph (WD)	1836-1906	Civil War	295	1375	1525		CSA Gen.
Wheeler, Joseph	1836-1906	Civil War	104	235	244	950	CSA Gen. 'Fightin Joe'
Wheeler, Lt. Gen. Raymod A.	1885-1974	Military	30				World War II U.S. general
Wheeler, Lyle	1905-	Entertainment	15			30	Film Art Director. AA 'Gone With the Wind' & 3 More
Wheeler, William A.	1819-1887	Vice President	67	140	200		Hayes VP
Whelan, Arleen	1916-	Entertainment	10		25	20	Actress. Redheaded Leading Lady. Late 30's-50's
Whelchel, Lisa		Entertainment	8			18	Actress. 'Facts of Life'
Wherry, William M.	1836-1918	Civil War	25	55			Union Gen. MOH
Whewell, William	1794-1866	Science		90			1st to Measure Tides in S. Pac. To Learn of Forces
Whicker, Alan		Celebrity	10			15	television presenter
Whiley, Jo		Music	10			15	DJ
Whipple, Abraham	1733-1819	Revolutionary War	250	750			Fired 1st Gun of Rev. on Water
Whipple, Amiel Weeks	1816-1863	Civil War	115	235	539		Union Major Gen.
Whipple, Edwin Percy	1819-1886	Author	15		30		Essayist, Critic, Lecturer
Whipple, Fred L.	1906-	Author-Science	10	25		18	Astronomer. Rocket Research
Whipple, George H.	1878-1976	Science	45	75	150		Nobel Medicine 1934
Whipple, Henry B.	1822-1901	Clergy	50	100	200		Episcopal Bishop. Reforms re Cruelty to Indians
Whipple, William D.	1826-1902	Civil War	28	49	58		Union Gen'l. Sherman Aide-de-Camp. Sig/Rank 40
Whipple, William	1730-1785	Revolutionary War	622	1250	4200		Signer Decl. of Ind.
Whirry, Shannon		Entertainment	8			25	Actress. 'Exit'
Whisner, William T.		Aviation	20	45	75	50	ACE, WW II
Whistler, Gen. Sir Lashmer G.	1898-1963	Military	25				World War II British general
Whistler, James McNeill	1834-1903	Artist	288	525	787	1150	Am. Painter, Etcher. Lived Abroad Never to Return
Whitaker, Forest		Entertainment	10			30	Actor
Whitaker, Johnnie		Entertainment	10			22	Actor
Whitaker, Maj. Gen. Sir John A. C.	1897-1957	Military	25				World War II British general

NAME	DATE	CATEGORY	SIG	LS/DS	ALS	SP	COMMENTS
Whitaker, Walter Chiles	1823-1887	Civil War	45	68	98		Union general
Whitcombe, Maj. Gen. Philip S.	1893-1989	Military	25				World War II British general
White, Alice	1907-1983	Entertainment	30	45		75	Vintage Actress. Late Silents & Early Sound Films
White, Andrew Dickson	1832-1918	Educator-Diplomat	20	75	85	50	Co-Fndr. Cornell University
White, Anthony Walton	1750-1803	Revolutionary War	55	165	250		Washington Aide-de-Camp. General
White, Betty		Entertainment	9	15	20	20	'Golden Girls', 'Mary Tyler Moore Show'. Emmy Wins
White, Byron R.		Supreme Court	40	80	125	90	
White, Dan		Celebrity	10			15	motivational speaker
White, E.B.		Author	30	118			'Charlotte's Web'
White, Edw.H. & McDivitt, J.		Astronauts				1148	
White, Edward D.	1845-1921	Supreme Court	50	127	225	299	Chief Justice
White, Edward H. II	1930-1967	Astronaut	292	419	696	842	1st Am. To Walk In Space
White, General Brudenell	1876-1940	Military	20				World War II Australian general
White, General Isaac D.	1901-1990	Military	30				World War II U.S. general
White, George Stuart	1835-1912	Military	40		65		Br. Fld. Marshal. Ladysmith Seige
White, George		Entertainment	40	60	75	100	Founder-Producer 'George White's Scandals'
White, Horace	1865-1943	Governor	10	25			Gov. NY
White, Horace	b. 1834	Journalist	25		75		Editor NY Evening Post. Corresponded w/Lincoln
White, Hugh		Governor	5	20		15	Governor MS 1936
White, I.D.		Military	10			25	
White, Jacqueline		Entertainment	5			15	Actress
White, Jesse	1919-	Entertainment	25	40		40	Character Actor. TV 'Maytag' Spokesman
White, Jim		Explorer	40		175		Discover Carlsbad Caverns
White, Josh		Entertainment	60			225	Am. Folk Singer
White, Julius	1816-1890	Civil War	30	55	85		Union General
White, Lee 'Lasses'		Entertainment	25				Minstrel
White, Maj. Gen. Arthur A.	1889-1981	Military	30				World War II U.S. general
White, Maj Gen. Cecil Meadows F	1897-1985	Military	25				World War II British general
White, Maj. Gen. John B.	1874-1945	Military	20				World War II Canadian general
White, Paul Dudley, Dr.	1886-1973	Science	30	60		80	Heart Specialist
White, Pearl	1889-1938	Entertainment	150		290	285	Queen of the Silent Serials
White, Robert, Maj.		Aviation	10	25		30	'60 Speed & Altitude Records
White, Sanford	1853-1906	Architect	100	268	525	450	Murdered By Harry K. Thaw. TLS/Content 1,600-5,500
White, Somers		Celebrity	10			15	motivational speaker
White, Stewart E.	1873-1946	Author	10	20	40	30	Am. Western Adventure Stories
White, Theodore		Author	9	15	25	20	Detailed Presidential Campaigns
White, Vanna & Pat Sajak		Entertainment	15			37	'Wheelof Fortune'
White, Vanna		Entertainment	5	10		25	TV Personality. 'Wheel of Fortune'
White, Wallace H., Jr.	1877-1952	Congress	5	15			MOC ME 1917, Senator 1930
White, William Allen	1868-1944	Author	25	45	85	60	Pulitzer Journalist. 'Sage of Emporia'
White, William	1748-1836	Clergy	130	210	250		1st Protestant Episcopal Bishop
White, Windsor T.		Business	110		550		Pioneer Auto-Truck Mfg.
Whitefoord, Maj. Gen. Philip G.	1894-1975	Military	25				World War II British general
Whitehead, Phillip		Political	10			15	Member European Parliament
Whitehouse, James	1833-	Artist	25		75		Tiffany Designer-Engraver of Many Major Pieces

NAME	DATE	CATEGORY	SIG	LS/DS	ALS	SP	COMMENTS
Whitelaw, Billie	1932-	Entertainment	15			30	Br. Actress. Stage 50s. Leading Lady TV, Films 60s
Whiteley, Gen Sir John Francis M.	1896-1970	Military	25				World War II British general
Whiteman, Paul	1890-1967	Entertainment	45	85	120	155	King of Jazz. Introduced Gershwin Rhaposdy in Blue
Whitestone, Heather		Entertainment	15			40	Miss America 1995. Hearing impaired
Whitfield, Ed W.		Congress	10			15	Member U.S. Congress
Whitfield, John Wilkins	1818-1879	Civil War	72	144	220		Confederate general
Whitfield, June		Entertainment	10			20	Actress
Whitfield, Maj Gen John Yeldham	1899-1971	Military	25				World War II British general
Whitford, Bradley		Entertainment	10			40	The West Wing
Whiting, Jack		Entertainment	5	8	10	10	Actor
Whiting, John D.		Diplomat	5		20		Jerusalem
Whiting, Margaret		Entertainment	10			15	Pop Vocalist
Whiting, Richard		Composer	50		135	100	Top Pop & Standards. AMusQS 150
Whiting, William Henry (WD)	1824-1865	Civil War	235		1923		CSA General
Whiting, William Henry	1824-1865	Civil War	155		250		Confederate general
Whitlam, Gough		Head of State	10			20	Prime Minister Australia
Whitley, Ray	1901-	Country Music	10			35	Singing Cowboy. Movies from '38. Major Sidekick
Whitman, Charles S.		Governor	10	25		15	Governor NY 1915
Whitman, Slim	1924-	Country Music	5			15	Singer. Slips in a Yodel or Two. London Palladium
Whitman, Walt	1819-1892	Author	760	2500	2978	2484	Am. Poet. Self-Educated. 'Leaves of Grass'
Whitmore, James	1921-	Entertainment	5		15	15	Actor. Excellent Character Actor
Whitney, Adeline D.	1824-1906	Author	20		35		
Whitney, Asa	1797-1872	Merchant	30		100		Promoter of Transcontinental RR
Whitney, C.V.		Business	15	35	70	25	
Whitney, Casper		Publisher	10	25	35		Publisher
Whitney, Courtney		Military	15	40	75	35	General WW II. MacArthur Aide
Whitney, Eli	1765-1825	Science	650	2100	3250		Am. Inventor Cotton Gin
Whitney, Grace Lee		Entertainment	15	30	35	45	Actress. 'Star Trek'
Whitney, Josiah D.	1819-1896	Science	65		275		CA State Geologist. Mt. Whitney in His Honor
Whitney, Richard		Business	35	50			Pres. NY Stock Exchange
Whitney, William Collins	1841-1904	Cabinet	25	45	82	35	Financier, Cleveland Sec'y Navy
Whitson, Peggy		Astronaut	7			25	
Whittaker, Charles E.	1901-1973	Supreme Court	50	84	175	125	
Whittaker, Sally		Entertainment	10			20	Actress
Whitten-Brown, Arthur, Sir		Aviation	250	375			Pioneer Aviator w/John Alcock
Whittier, John Greenleaf	1807-1892	Author	48	120	210		Quaker Poet. Abolitionist
Whittle, Frank, Sir		Aviation	20	50		45	Invented jet engine
Whittle, Josephine		Entertainment	5	6	15	15	
Whittlesey, Elisha	1783-1863	Statesman	20		55		Founder of Whig Party
Whitty, Maj. Gen. Henry Martin	1896-1961	Military	25				World War II British general
Whitty, May, Dame	1865-1948	Entertainment	35	45	85	75	Grand Old Brit. Character Actress. 2x Nominated AA
Who, The (All 4)		Entertainment	412			710	Rock. DS 2050
Whorf, Richard	1906-1966	Entertainment	10			20	Actor-Producer-Director
Wickard, Claude		Cabinet	15	25			Sec'y Agriculture 1940
Wicke, Lloyd C., Bishop		Clergy	15	25	35	30	

NAME	DATE	CATEGORY	SIG	LS/DS	ALS	SP	COMMENTS
Wicker, Irene		Entertainment	10			25	Vintage Radio's 'Singing Lady'
Wicker, Roger F. W		Congress	10			15	Member U.S. Congress
Wicker, Tom		Celebrity	10			15	media/TV personality
Wickersham, George W.	1858-1936	Cabinet	15	45	75	45	Taft Att'y Gen. 1909
Wickes, Mary	1916-	Entertainment	18			30	Lanky, Gawky, Character Comedienne. Films 40s-70s
Wickham, William C. (WD)	1820-1888	Civil War	145	395			CSA Gen.
Wickham, William C.	1820-1888	Civil War	110	290			CSA Gen.
Wickliffe, Charles A.		Cabinet	30	60	95		P.M.Gen. 1841
Widmark, Richard	1914-	Entertainment	15	10	25	65	Actor
Widor, Charles Marie		Composer	30		165		Fr. Organist, Teacher
Wieck, Dorothea	1908-	Entertainment	15	15	35	30	Max Reinhardt Protégé. German Star. 2 Am. Films
Wieghorst, Olaf		Artist	60	225	350	180	Dean of Western Art
Wieland, Rainer		Political	10			15	Member European Parliament
Wiemann, Ernst		Entertainment	5			20	Opera
Wien, Noel		Aviation	25	55	105	65	
Wiere Brothers		Entertainment	15			25	
Wiersma, Jan Marinus		Political	10			15	Member European Parliament
Wiese, Gen. of Infantry Friedrich	1892-1975	Military	25				World War II German general
Wiesel, Elie		Author	20	45	55	25	Nobel Peace Prize 1986. Holocaust Authority
Wiesel, Torsten S., Dr.		Science	22	30	45	25	Nobel Medicine 1981
Wiesenthal, Simon		Activist	20	45	90	35	Famed Nazi Hunter
Wiest, Diane		Entertainment	20		35	45	Actress. AA Winner
Wietersheim, Gen. Inf. Gustav A.	1884-1974	Military	25				World War II German general
Wigfall, Louis T.	1816-1874	Civil War	175	242	632	278	CSA Gen. CSA Senator. Sig/Rank 210
Wiggin, Kate Douglas	1856-1923	Author	60		140	125	Author of Popular Children's Books.
Wigglesworth, Edward	1804-1876	Editor	5		30		Harvard Law Grad. Mercantile Business.Charities
Wigglesworth, Frank		Composer					AMusQS 100
Wigglesworth, Richard B		Congress	5	10			MOC MA 1928, Diplomat
Wigner, Eugene P. Dr.		Science	30	40	70	30	Nobel Physics 1963. Atomic Nuclei.Typescript S 150
Wihan, Hanus		Entertainment	30		120		Czech Viol-Cellist. AMusQs 85
Wijkman, Anders		Political	10			15	Member European Parliament
Wiktorin, Gen. of Inf. Mauritz von	1883-1956	Military	25				World War II German general
Wilberforce, Samuel, Bishop	1805-1873	Clergy	30	45	60		'Soapy' Wilberforce. Evolution Controversy w/T.Huxley
Wilberforce, William	1759-1833	Abolitionist	50	145	300		Br. Anti-Slavery Politician, Philanthropist
Wilbur, Curtis D.		Cabinet	10	25	35	25	Sec'y Navy 1924
Wilbur, Ray Lyman		Cabinet	15	25	55	20	Sec'y Interior 1929
Wilbur, Richard		Author	5		35	10	U.S. Poet Laureate. Pulitzer. LS/Cont. 135
Wilbur, W.H.		Military	5	15	25	10	
Wilburn Bros.		Country Western	10			35	Teddy & Doyle
Wilby, Maj. Gen. Francis B.	1883-1965	Military	30				World War II U.S. general
Wilcox, Cadmus M. (WD)	1824-1890	Civil War	190	400			CSA Gen.
Wilcox, Cadmus M.	1824-1890	Civil War	108	234	320		CSA Gen.
Wilcox, Ella Wheeler	1850-1919	Author	20	35	73		Journalist, Poet, Essayist, Daily Syndicated Poem
Wilcoxon, Henry	1905-	Entertainment	20		35	45	Actor. Important Roles w/DeMille. Supporting in Bs
Wilcutt, Terry		Astronaut	5			20	

NAME	DATE	CATEGORY	SIG	LS/DS	ALS	SP	COMMENTS
Wild Choir		Entertainment	15			35	Rock
Wild, Edward A.	1825-1891	Civil War	88	171	236		Union General Sig/Rank 95, War Dte DS 175
Wild, Jack		Entertainment	5			15	Actor. 'The Artful Dodger' in 'Oliver'
Wilde, Cornel	1915-1989	Entertainment	10	22	40	31	Handsome Leading Man. Played Variety of Roles
Wilde, Oscar	1856-1900	Author	842	1550	3865	3000	Ir.-Born Eng. Poet, Playwright, Wit. AQS 2000- 3200
Wilde, Percival		Author	20	55	110		Playwright, Novelist
Wilder, Billy	1906-	Entertainment	20	50		57	Multiple AA Film Dir. Producer. Content DS 285
Wilder, Douglas		Celebrity	10			15	motivational speaker
Wilder, Gene	1935-	Entertainment	10	33		40	Actor-Comedian. 'Young Frankenstein'
Wilder, Marshall P.		Entertainment	15	20	30	35	Vintage Reciter, Imitator.
Wilder, Thornton	1897-1975	Author	50	110	262	150	Playwright, Novelist. 3 Pulitzers, ALS/Content 675
Wilding, Michael	1912-1979	Entertainment	30			55	Br. Actor. Ex Leading-Man Husband Eliz. Taylor
Wilentz, David T.		Celebrity	25				
Wiley, Alexander	1884-1967	Congress	15	40			Senator WI 1938
Wiley, Harvey W., Dr.	1844-1930	Science	80	195			Created FDA. Chemist Investigated Food Adulteration
Wilhelm I (Ger)	1787-1888	Royalty	110	245	378		King of Prussia, Emperor Ger.
Wilhelm II, Kaiser	1859-1941	Royalty	120	292	510	350	Official DS 8500. Last Emperor of Ger.
Wilhelm, August	1882-1951	Military	50			150	Son of Kaiser. WW I General
Wilhelmina, Queen	1880-1962	Royalty	110		400		Netherlands. Abdicated in Favor of Juliana
Wilhelmj, August	1845-1908	Entertainment	25			75	Ger. Violinist
Wilk, Brad		Entertainment	6			25	Music. Drummer 'Rage Against the Machine'
Wilke, Robert J.		Entertainment	10			25	
Wilkerson, Guy		Entertainment	25			65	
Wilkes, Charles	1798-1877	Civil War	60	121	184		Union Adm., Explorer. Sig/Rank 70, War Dte. DS 180
Wilkes, Earle		Military	10			50	
Wilkie, David, Sir	1785-1841	Artist	60	88	137		Br. Genre Paintings, Portraits
Wilkins, Geo. Hubert, Sir	1888-1958	Explorer	30	55	110	55	Led Arctic & Antarctic Exped.
Wilkins, Hans		Aviation	10	25	45	30	
Wilkins, Roy		Activist	15	35	70	25	Sr. Statesman of Civil Rights
Wilkins, T. H.		Science	15	25	40	20	
Wilkinson, Geoffrey		Science	15	25	40	25	Nobel Chemistry 1985
Wilkinson, James	1757-1825	Revolutionary War	125	342	430		General, Implicated In Aaron Burr Conspiracy
Wilkinson, June		Entertainment	6	10	18	20	Actress. Pin-Up SP 30
Wilkinson, Raven		Dance	4			12	Ballerina
Wilks, Matthew		Clergy	15		25	50	
Will, George		Celebrity	10			15	political celebrity
Willard, Charles		Aviation	15			35	
Willard, Edward S.		Entertainment	15		35	30	Vintage
Willard, Frances E.	1839-1898	Temperance	50	216	259		Pres. W.C.T.U. Prof. At Northwestern U.
Willard, Frank*		Cartoonist	35			182	'Moon Mullins'
Willard, Fred		Entertainment	10	6	12	35	Actor
Willard, John		Entertainment	10			25	Playwright
Willcox, Lt. Gen. Sir Henry B. D.	1889-1968	Military	25				World War II British general
Willcox, Orlando B.	1823-1907	Civil War	48	130	227		Union Gen. Sig/Rank 60
Willcox, Toyah		Celebrity	10			15	television presenter

NAME	DATE	CATEGORY	SIG	LS/DS	ALS	SP	COMMENTS
Willebrands, John, Cardinal		Clergy	30	45	65	40	
Willem VI & I,	1772-1848	Royalty		692			Prince of Orange, King Netherlands
Willett, Marinus	1740-1830	Revolutionary War	52	91	252		Officer Cont. Army. Mayor NYC
William III (Eng)	1650-1702	Royalty	605	1609	2500		Wm. III & Mary II DS 2195. Jointly Ruled
William IV (Eng)	1765-1837	Royalty	112	226	322		The Sailor King, DS 995, ALS/cont 1750
William, Warren	1894-1948	Entertainment	10	15	40	45	Am. Film Leading Man & Character Actor
Williams, Alford J., Jr.		Aviation	25	45	95	125	
Williams, Alpheus Starkey	1810-1878	Civil War	40	65	90		Union general, War date AES 184
Williams, Andy		Entertainment	20	35		41	Major 50's-70's Pop Singer. TV, Records, Vegas
Williams, Barry		Entertainment	10	16	20	27	Actor. 'Brady Bunch'
Williams, Bart		Entertainment	5			15	
Williams, Ben Ames	1889-1953	Author	15	25	40	25	Am. Novelist
Williams, Betty		Celebrity	10			15	political celebrity
Williams, Bill	1916-	Entertainment	10	15		25	Nice Guy Leading Man-Husband of Barbara Hale
Williams, Billy Dee	1937-	Entertainment	10	25		48	Actor. 'Empire Strikes Back'
Williams, Brian		Journalist	4			22	Broadcast News TV
Williams, Brig. Edward Steven B.	1892-1977	Military	25				World War II British general
Williams, Brigadier Kenneth	1896- ?	Military	20				World War II Australian general
Williams, Cindy		Entertainment	5	6	15	27	Actress. 'American Graffiti', 'Laverne & Shirley'
Williams, Cliff		Entertainment	6			25	Music. Bass Guitar 'AC/DC'
Williams, Clifton C.		Astronaut	6			25	
Williams, David Henry	1819-1891	Civil War	40		105		Union general
Williams, Donald E.		Astronaut	6			20	
Williams, Edward B.		Law	5	15	40	15	Top Criminal Lawyer
Williams, Edward F.		Author	8			12	Civil War & Tennessee history
Williams, Edward M.		Business	35	90	155		
Williams, Edy		Entertainment	5			20	Actress. Pin-Up SP 30
Williams, Eleazer	1787-1858	Clergy	45	115	160		Am. Missionary.Louis XVII 'Lost Dauphin' Author
Williams, Esther	1923-	Entertainment	8	10	20	46	Actress-Swimmer-Part-Time Model. Major Star
Williams, G. Mennan	1911-	Political	5	20		35	5 Times MI Gov., Ambass. Philippines. 'Soapy'
Williams, Gen. Sir Guy Charles	1881-1959	Military	25				World War II British general
Williams, Geoffrey		Science	10	20	35	20	
Williams, George H.		Cabinet	10	25	40		Att'y Gen. 1872, Senator OR
Williams, Gluyas*	1888-1982	Cartoonist	10		45	75	New Yorker Cartoonist
Williams, Grant		Entertainment	45			125	Actor
Williams, Gregalan		Celebrity	10			15	media/TV personality
Williams, Griff		Bandleader	25				Big Band
Williams, Guinn 'Big Boy'	1899-1962	Entertainment	75			150	Actor. Starred in Many Westerns.
Williams, Gus		Entertainment	10			25	Showman
Williams, Guy	1924-1989	Entertainment	130	200		375	Actor. 'Lost in Space', 'Zorro'. SP as Zorro 695
Williams, Hal		Entertainment	5			15	Afro-Am Actor
Williams, Hank Jr.		Country Music	20	30		38	
Williams, Hank	1923-1953	Country Music	536	1200		1250	Major Country Singing Star
Williams, Harland		Entertainment				30	
Williams, Harrison A., Jr.	1919-	Congress	15	35		20	Rep.1953, Senator NJ

NAME	DATE	CATEGORY	SIG	LS/DS	ALS	SP	COMMENTS
Williams, J.R.*		Cartoonist	18	25		85	'Way Out West'
Williams, JoBeth		Entertainment	10	15		28	Actress
Williams, Joe		Entertainment	15			45	Jazz Vocalist
Williams, John Sharp		Congress	10	20		20	MOC MS 1893, Senator 1910
Williams, John Stuart	1818-1898	Civil War	102	252			Confederate general
Williams, John		Composer	20	65	75	62	Conductor. AMusQS 225, 100
Williams, Jonathan		Author	5	15	25		
Williams, Kellie Shanygne		Entertainment	10			20	actress
Williams, Kimberly		Entertainment	10			20	actress
Williams, Maj. Gen. Aubrey Ellis	1888-1977	Military	25				World War II British general
Williams, Maj. Gen. Sir Leslie H.	1892-1956	Military	25				World War II British general
Williams, Maj Gen Walter David A	1897-1973	Military	25				World War II British general
Williams, Mary Alice		Journalist	10			20	TV News Journalist
Williams, Mary Lou		Music				230	Jazz singer
Williams, Mason		Entertainment	10			20	Singer-Guitar Soloist-Composer
Williams, Michelle		Entertainment	12			40	Actress
Williams, Montel		Entertainment	4			15	Talk Show Host-TV
Williams, Nelson Grosvenor	1823-1897	Civil War	40	80			Union general
Williams, Olivia		Entertainment	10			20	actress
Williams, Otho	1749-1800	Revolutionary War	140	420	735		Officer. Fought w/Gates & Greene
Williams, Paul		Composer	5	7	15	20	Actor-Singer
Williams, Robbie		Music	10			25	performing musical artist
Williams, Robin		Entertainment	17			45	Actor-Comedian. AA
Williams, Roger		Entertainment	5		20	32	Pianist-Arranger
Williams, Russ		Music	10			15	DJ
Williams, Seth	1822-1866	Civil War	25	67	74		Union Gen. War Dte. LS 175, Sig/Rank 55
Williams, Tennessee (Thos L.)	1914-1983	Author	127	298	600	395	Pulitzer. 'Cat on a Hot Tin Roof' & 'Streetcar'
Williams, Tex		Country Music	10			20	Big Band-Singer-Leader
Williams, Thomas	1815-1862	Civil War	352				Union general. KIA Baton Rouge, LA
Williams, Treat		Entertainment	5	10	12	25	Actor
Williams, Van		Entertainment	25			43	TV's 'Green Hornet'
Williams, Vanessa		Entertainment	20			42	Miss America, singer, actress
Williams, Vaughan R.	1872-1958	Composer					SEE VAUGHAN-WILLIAMS
Williams, Warrene		Author	8			12	financial, nonprofits
Williams, William Carlos	1883-1963	Author	275	374	775	525	Am. Poet, Novelist, Physician
Williams, William	1731-1811	Revolutionary War	197	394	753		Signer Decl. of Indepen. Statesman
Williams, Willie, Chief		Law Enforcement	5			25	Los Angeles Chief of Police
Williamson, Fred		Entertainment	8			20	Afro-Am. Actor
Williamson, Gordon K.		Celebrity	10			15	financial expert
Williamson, Hugh	1735-1819	Revolutionary War		2000			Continental Congress. Signer of the Constitution. Rare.
Williamson, James A.	1829-1902	Law	5		20		
Williamson, James Alexander	1829-1902	Civil War	36	57	80		Union general
Williamson, Marianne		Author	5			10	Non-Fiction
Williamson, Nicol		Entertainment	10			20	actor
Willich, August von	1810-1878	Civil War	40		100		Union general

NAME	DATE	CATEGORY	SIG	LS/DS	ALS	SP	COMMENTS
Willie Wonka (cast)		Entertainment				200	Cast of 5
Willie, David		Author	8			12	poetry
Williiams, Roger Q.		Aviation	10		20		'29 Record Non-Stop Flight
Willing, Foy	1915-	Country Music	10			25	And The Riders of the Purple Sage
Willing, Thomas		Revolutionary War	75	250			Banker, Continental Congress
Willis, Bruce		Entertainment	20	25		70	Actor. Mega Action & Straight Leads
Willis, Nathaniel P.	1806-1867	Author	20	40	118		Major Editor Poetry Mags. Playwright, Critic
Willis, Richard S.		Clergy	20	25	35		
Willison, Brigadier Arthur Cecil	1896-1966	Military	25				World War II British general
Willkie, Wendell	1892-1944	Politician	25	45	60	50	Pres. Candidate
Wills, Bob	1905-1975	Country Music	75			200	Bob Wills and His Texas Playboys
Wills, Brigadier Kenneth A.	1896-1977	Military	20				World War II Australian general
Wills, Chill	1903-1978	Entertainment	55			85	Actor. Character Actor. Many Western & Other Genre
Wills, Wincey		Celebrity	10			15	weather presenter
Willson, Meredith	1902-1984	Composer	25	45	75	80	'The Music Man'
Willson, Quentin		Celebrity	10			15	television presenter
Willys, John North		Business	60	110	245	90	Auto Pioneer, Diplomat. (Originally 'Willys Jeep')
Wilmer, Richard Hooker, Bishop		Clergy	8	25	40		
Wilmot, David	1814-1868	Congress	40	75	90		Repr. & Senator PA. 'Wilmot Proviso'
Wilson, August		Author	10	30	45	20	Dramatist, Dir., Pulitzer, Tony
Wilson, Bill W.		Celebrity			2500		Founder AA
Wilson, Bob		Celebrity	10			15	television presenter
Wilson, Brian		Entertainment	50	75		100	Singer-Songwriter-Record Producer 'Beach Boys'
Wilson, Bridget		Entertainment	8			32	Actress.
Wilson, Carnie		Celebrity	10			15	media/TV personality
Wilson, Charles Edward	1886-1972	Business	20	75			Pres. General Electric
Wilson, Charles Erwin	1890-1961	Business-Cabinet	20	35	70	30	Pres. GM., Sec'y Defense 1953
Wilson, Claudius Charles	1831-1863	Civil War	338				Confederate general, KIA Ringgold, GA
Wilson, Demond		Entertainment	10			35	Actor. 'Sanford & Son'
Wilson, Dennis		Entertainment	62			129	'Beach Boys' 95
Wilson, Dick		Entertainment	10			20	actor
Wilson, Don 'The Dragon'		Entertainment	10			20	actor
Wilson, Don		Entertainment	5			25	Jack Benny Announcer & Sidekick
Wilson, Dooley	1894-1953	Entertainment	432			900	Supporting Player 'Casablanca'
Wilson, E. Willis		Governor	12	25			Governor WV 1885
Wilson, Earl		Journalist	10	15	25	15	Powerful Synd. Columnist
Wilson, Edith Bolling	1872-1961	First Lady	75	160	250	250	ALS as 1st Lady 500-805
Wilson, Edmund Beecher	1856-1939	Author-Science	350	450			Am. Biologist. Morphology, Cytology, Heredity
Wilson, Edmund	1895-1972	Author	25	85	130		Am. Critic. ALS/Content 650
Wilson, Ellen Louise		First Lady	100	345	590		1st Wife - Pres. Wilson
Wilson, Flip	1934-1998	Entertainment	20	30		52	Afr-Am. Comedian. 'Flip Wilson Show'. 'Geraldine'
Wilson, Francis	1854-1935	Entertainment	12		15	25	Vintage Actor
Wilson, Gahan*		Cartoonist	20		125	62	Mag. Cartoonist for Playboy, New Yorker etc.
Wilson, Gen. Sir Roger Cochrane	1882-1966	Military	25				World War II British general
Wilson, George W. Lt.		Celebrity	15	35	120		

NAME	DATE	CATEGORY	SIG	LS/DS	ALS	SP	COMMENTS
Wilson, Harold, Sir	1916-1995	Head of State	38	65	110	75	Br. Prime Minister
Wilson, Heather W		Congress	10			15	Member U.S. Congress
Wilson, Henry	1812-1875	Vice President	66	110	175	350	Grant VP. Died in Office.Started Career as Cobbler
Wilson, Jackie		Entertainment	242	598		450	Singer
Wilson, James G.	1833-1914	Civil War	30		80		Union Gen. Led 4th U.S. Colored Cavalry
Wilson, James H.	1837-1925	Civil War	72	100	160		Union Gen. Cavalry. Captured Jefferson Davis
Wilson, James	1742-1798	Supreme Court	300	800	1450		Scottish Born Signer. ALS/Content 4,000. SB 2250
Wilson, James	1835-1920	Cabinet	25	50	95		Sec'y Agriculture 1897
Wilson, Joe W		Congress	10			15	Member U.S. Congress
Wilson, John Lockwood	1850-1912	Congress	15	30	40		MOC 1889, Senator WA 1895
Wilson, Joseph R.		Celebrity	40		175		Father of Woodrow Wilson
Wilson, Julie		Entertainment	10			35	
Wilson, Kemmons		Business	20	60	80	70	Founder 'Holiday Inn' Chain Hotels-Motels
Wilson, Lois	1896-	Entertainment	15	15	35	40	Starred in Many Paramount Silents. Talkies to 1949
Wilson, Luke		Entertainment	10			35	Actor. Brother to Owen
Wilson, Maj. Gen. Bevil Thomson	1885-1975	Military	25				World War II British general
Wilson, Maj. Gen. Durward S.	1886-1970	Military	30				World War II U.S. general
Wilson, Maj. Gen. Nigel Maitland	1884-1950	Military	25				World War II British general
Wilson, Maj. Gen. Thos. Arthur A.	1882-1958	Military	25				World War II British general
Wilson, Maj. Gen. T.H.F.	1896-1961	Military	25				World War II British general
Wilson, Maj. Gen. Walter K.	1880-1954	Military	30				World War II U.S. general
Wilson, Marie	1916-1972	Entertainment	25	35	65	59	'My Friend Irma' Early TV. Years Wiith Ken Murray
Wilson, Mary		Entertainment	10			20	Rock, 'The Supremes'
Wilson, Owen		Entertainment	10			35	Actor. Brother to Luke
Wilson, Peta		Entertainment	7			32	Actress. Pin-Up 55
Wilson, Pete		Governor	10	20		20	Governor CA
Wilson, Richard		Entertainment	10			20	Actor
Wilson, Robert, Dr.		Science	15	25	35	25	Nobel Physics 1978
Wilson, Sloan		Author	15	35	58	25	'Man in the Grey Flannel Suit'
Wilson, Stephanie			8			25	
Wilson, Teddy	1912-1986	Entertainment	40		75	95	Pianist-Arranger. Big Band
Wilson, Tom*		Cartoonist	20			50	'Ziggy'
Wilson, William B.	1862-1934	Cabinet	10	25	50	40	Organized United Mine Workers. Sec'y Labor 1913
Wilson, William Sydney	1816-1862	Civil War	35	85	98		Member of CSA Congress
Wilson, Woodrow & FDR		Presidents		3167			DS by both
Wilson, Woodrow (As Pres.)		President	325	618	5089	592	LS/Cont 2500- 9500, DS/cont 4600-18400
Wilson, Woodrow	1856-1924	President	185	415	870	448	AQS 2950, ALS/cont 3000-5000
Wilson-Haffenden, Maj. Gen. D.J.	1900-1986	Military	25				World War II British general
Wiman, Dwight Deere		Business	15	25			John Deere Farm Implements
Wimberley, Maj Gen Douglas Neil	1896-1983	Military	28				World War II British general
Winans, Ross		Inventor	85	250			Railroad Equipment
Winant, John	1889-1947	Governor	25			40	Gov. NH, WW II Ambassador to Britain. Suicide
Wincer, Simon		Celebrity	10			15	film industry
Winchell, Paul		Entertainment	10	25	35	78	Talented Ventriloquist
Winchell, Walter	1897-1972	Journalist	30	38	45	35	Powerful Radio-Newspaper Columnist

NAME	DATE	CATEGORY	SIG	LS/DS	ALS	SP	COMMENTS
Winchester, Oliver F.	1810-1880	Industrialist	338	850	1500		Winchester Repeating Arms, Inc. LS on Lttrhd 5850
Winchester, Wm.P.Sir,1st Marquis		Statesman	275	955			Elizabeth I. Lord Treasurer Eng. 1485-1572
Wincot, Jeff		Entertainment	10			20	actor
Winder, Charles S. (WD)	1829-1862	Civil War			6335		CSA Gen. 1829-62 KIA
Winder, Charles Sidney	1829-1862	Civil War	428	640			Confederate general, KIA Cedar Mt, VA
Winder, John Henry (WD)	1800-1865	Civil War	160	506	680		CSA Gen. Commandant Libby & Andersonville
Winder, John Henry	1800-1865	Civil War	112	304	411		Confederate general
Winder, Levin		Rev. War-Gov.	15		55		Gov. MD 1812
Windeyer, Maj. Gen. Victor	1900-1987	Military	20				World War II Australian general
Windgassen, Wolfgang		Entertainment	15			45	Opera
Windom, William		Cabinet	20	35	60	40	Sec'y Treasury 1881
Windsor, Barbara		Entertainment	10			20	Actress
Windsor, Claire	1897-1972	Entertainment	10	15		25	Blonde-Blue-eyed 20's Silent Star.
Windsor, Duke & Duchess of		Royalty	445			967	Edward & Wallis
Windsor, Marie	1922-	Entertainment	5	8	15	15	Actress. Many 2nd Leads & Westerns. Pin-Up SP 30
Windsor, Wallis, Duchess of		Royalty	110	180	350	300	1896-1986. Content ALS 775, FDC S 150
Winfield, Paul		Entertainment	5	15	15	28	Actor
Winfrey, Oprah		Entertainment	18			42	Actress-TV Host. Award Winner. Producer
Wing, Maj. Gen. Leonard F.	1893-1945	Military	30				World War II U.S. general
Wing, Toby		Entertainment	10	15	25	25	Vintage Film Actress
Wingate, Francis R., Sir	1861-1953	Military	35	75	140	75	Gen. Succeeded Kitchener. Gov.-Gen. Of Sudan
Wingate, Maj. Gen. Orde Charles	1903-1944	Military	25				World War II British general
Winger, Debra		Entertainment	10	32	42	38	Actress
Winget, Larry		Celebrity	10			15	motivational speaker
Winick, Judd		Celebrity	10			15	media/TV personality
Winkelman, General Henri	1876-1952	Military	20				World War II Dutch general
Winkler, Betty		Entertainment	5	6	15	15	Top Radio Performer-40's
Winkler, Henry	1945-	Entertainment	5	15	20	30	Actor. 'The Fonz' on 'Happy Days'
Winkler, K.C.		Entertainment	4			10	Pin-Up SP 20
Winner, Septimus	1827-1902	Composer	92	205	350		Wrote Many Pop Songs. AMusQS 495-1,000
Winning, Brigadier Robert E.	1906- ?	Military	20				World War II Australian general
Winninger, Charles	1884-1969	Entertainment	25		50	60	Much Seen Character Actor 30's-50's. 'Cap'n Andy'
Winninger, Tom		Celebrity	10			15	motivational speaker
Winningham, Mare		Entertainment	10			25	Actress. AA Nominee
Winokur, Marissa		Entertainment				35	Actress
Winship, Blanton	1809-1894	Politician	30			75	Orator, Philanthropist
Winship, Blanton	1869-1947	Military	40			125	General. Sp-Am & Phil.Insurrection. Billy Mitchell
Winslet, Kate		Entertainment	14			67	Br. Actress. 'Titanic'
Winslow, Edward	1699-1753	Colonial America	225	675			Silversmith. Government Official
Winslow, Edward	1714-1784	Revolutionary War	25	50	90		Loyalist. Port Plymouth Collector
Winslow, John Ancrum	1811-1873	Civil War	141	242	355	506	Union Naval Cmmdr. Kersage. ALS/cont 2415
Winslow, John F.		Civil War	65	162	225		Builder of the 'Monitor'
Winslow, John	1753-1819	Revolutionary War	20	65	110		Soldier, Hero, Patriot, General
Winsor, Kathleen		Author	15	35	90	30	Novelist 'Forever Amber'
Winter, Gen of Mtn Troops August	1897-1979	Military	25				World War II German general

NAME	DATE	CATEGORY	SIG	LS/DS	ALS	SP	COMMENTS
Winter, William	1836-1913	Author	20	30	34		Drama Critic, Poet, Biographer
Winters, Jonathan		Entertainment	10	15	22	30	Comedian. Standup-TV-Films
Winters, Roland	1904-1989	Entertainment	30	45	85	110	Actor 'Charlie Chan'. Third And Last
Winters, Shelley		Entertainment	8		25	32	Actress. Oscar Winner.
Winterton, Maj. Gen. Sir Thos J W	1898-1987	Military	25				World War II British general
Winthrop, John	1714-1779	Revolutionary War	200	685			Physicist-Astron. Science Leader
Winthrop, John, The Younger	1638-1707	Colonial America	800	1900	4750		Col. Gov. CT.
Winthrop, Robert C.	1809-1894	Congress	21	40	41		Served out Daniel Webster's Term. Speaker
Winthrop, Theodore	1828-1861	Author	75		450		Soldier. Killed CW. Heroic CW Death. AMsS 950
Winthrop, Thomas L.	1760-1841	Revolutionary War	35	55	100		Merchant. Widely Esteemed
Winwood, Estelle	b. 1883	Entertainment	25	35		45	Br. Character Actress. Often Eccentric Parts
Winwood, Steve		Entertainment				65	Rock Singer
Wire, Calvin C.		Aviation	10	15	30	25	ACE, WW II
Wirt, William	1772-1834	Cabinet	40	100	155		Att'y General 1817. Author
Wirth, Don		Author	8			12	fishing
Wirtz, Willard		Cabinet	5	10	20	15	Sec'y Labor 1962
Wirz, Henry Hartmann		Civil War	603	3850	5400		CSA Comdr. Andersonville. HUNG for WAR CRIMES
Wisch, Theodor		Military	110		165		
Wise, Henry A. (WD)	1806-1876	Civil War	130	240	377		CSA Gen., DS/cont 3750
Wise, Henry A.	1806-1876	Civil War	78	160	240		CSA General. Gov.,Senator VA
Wise, Robert	b 1914	Entertainment	15	38		30	Film Dir. 2 AA. 'Sound of Music' & 'West Side Story
Wise, Stephen S.	1874-1949	Clergy	32	70	110	125	Jewish Leader, TLS/cont 1100
Wiseman, L.H.		Clergy	10	15	25	20	
Wiseman, Nicholas	1802-1865	Clergy	25	45	74		Br. Cardinal of Catholic Church. Author
Wiseman, Rosalind		Celebrity	10			15	motivational speaker
Wisliceny, Gunther-Ehrhardt		Military	25			55	Ger. SS-Panzer Div. RK
Wisoff. Peter		Astronaut	5			20	
Wistar, Isaac Jones	1827-1905	Civil War	35	65	90		Union general
Wister, Owen	1860-1938	Author	50	110	225	150	Am. Novelist, 'The Virginian'
Witchell, Nicholas		Celebrity	10			15	news reader
Withers, Jane		Entertainment	10	10	25	25	Shirley Temple Sidekick
Withers, Jones Mitchell	1814-1890	Civil War	110				Confederate general
Withers, Robert W	1835-1896.	Civil War	32	45	75		CSA Colonel, US Sen. VA. War Dte.S 70, DS 105
Witherspoon, Jimmy		Entertainment	14			30	Jazz Musician
Witherspoon, John	1723-1794	Rev. War-Clergy	712	3100	7500		Signer Decl. of Indepen., Active Clergy When Signed
Witherspoon, Reese		Entertainment	10			53	Actress. Pin-Up 75
Witkin, Georgia		Celebrity	10			15	medical expert
Witt, Alicia		Entertainment	10			38	Actress. Pin-Up 65
Wittber, Bill		Aviation	20	50	75	80	
Witte, Serge	1849-1915	Head of State	25	50	95	340	1st Constitutional Russian Prime Minister. SP Rare
Wittig, Georg F.K.		Science	25	50		40	Nobel Chemistry 1979
Witts, Lt. Gen. Fred. Vavasour B.	1889-1969	Military	25				World War II British general
Witzleben, Field Mrshl. Erwin von	1881-1944	Military	25				World War II German general
Wixell, Ingvar		Entertainment	20			45	Opera
Wodehouse, P. G.	1881-1875	Author	75	180	325	550	Br. Novelist Creator of 'Jeeves'. TMS 10,000

NAME	DATE	CATEGORY	SIG	LS/DS	ALS	SP	COMMENTS
Wodrig, General of Artillery Albert	1883-1972	Military	25				World War II German general
Wofford, William Tatum	1824-1884	Civil War	85	250			Confederate general
Wogan, Maj. Gen. John B.	1890-1968	Military	30				World War II U.S. general
Wogan, Terry		Celebrity	10			15	television presenter
Wogau, Karl von		Political	10			15	Member European Parliament
Woggon, Elmer*		Cartoonist	5			35	'Big Chief Wahoo'
Woidick, Franz		Aviation	15	25	45	35	
Wolcott, Derek		Author	15	25		25	Poet. Nobel Literature
Wolcott, Edward O.	1848-1905	Congress	10	25			Senator CO 1889
Wolcott, Oliver	1726-1797	Rev. War	247	406	1875		Signer Decl. of Ind. Gov. CT. FF Addr. Leaf 875
Wolcott, Oliver, Jr.	1760-1833	Cabinet	50	134	200		Washington & Adams Sec'y Treas. FF 350
Wolf, David		Astronaut	8			25	
Wolf, Frank R.		Congress	10			15	Member U.S. Congress
Wolf, Gary		Entertainment	5			15	Voice of Roger Rabbitt
Wolf, George (Wolfe)	1777-1840	Governor	35	90	185		Gov. PA 1829, Statesman
Wolf, Hugo	1860-1903	Composer	175		1500		Austrian. RARE ALS/Cont.3500
Wolf, Scott		Entertainment	8			28	Actor. 'Party of Five'
Wolfe, Ian	1896-	Entertainment	10			25	Stage Vet. Hollywood Films Mid-30s. Shady Charact's
Wolfe, James	1727-1759	Military	1550		8250		Br. Gen. French & Indian War
Wolfe, Thomas	1900-1938	Author	525	1431	2500		Early Death For Gifted Writer 'Look Homeward Angel'
Wolfe, Tom		Author	15	40	70	35	Am. Novelist
Wolfe-Barry, John, Sir	1836-1918	Civil Engineer	15	30	45		London Electr. RR, Docks, Bridges
Wolff, Amalie		Entertainment	15	15	30	25	
Wolff, Joseph		Clergy	35	40	50		
Wolff, Karl		Military	100	275			Ger. Gen. SS
Woll, Matthew		Labor	10	30	80		Lux.-Am. Labor Leader
Wollin, Gary		Celebrity	10			15	financial expert
Wolper, David	1928-	Entertainment	12	15	20	20	Film Producer, Executive
Wolseley, Garnet J., Viscount	1833-1913	Military	25	60	105	90	Br. Field Marshal; Crimean War. Led Nile Expedition
Wolsey, Thomas	1475-1530	Statesman		7800			Influential Cardinal, Statesman.
Womack, Lee Ann		Music				40	Singer
Wonder, George*		Cartoonist	20			95	'Terry & The Pirates'
Wonder, Stevie		Entertainment	232			99	Blind Pianist-Composer. Thumbprint Subs for Sig.
Wonders, Whitney		Entertainment	10			35	Porn Queen
Wong, Anna May	1907-1961	Entertainment	81	150	165	185	1st Major Chinese Film Star
Woo, John		Entertainment	10			35	Actor. 'Face Off' SP 65
Wood, Edward F.L.	1881-1959	Statesman	15	35	50	25	Diplomat, Ambassador to U.S.
Wood, Elijah		Entertainment	10			20	actor
Wood, Evelyn, Sir.		Military	20		55		Br. Fld. Marshal (Boer War)
Wood, F. Derwent		Artist	10	25	60		
Wood, Fernando	1812-1881	Civil War	20	45	60		Civil War Mayor NYC. Tammany MOC 'Copperhead'
Wood, Garfield 'Gar'		Science	60		80	75	Boat Designer, Builder, Racer
Wood, Grant	1891-1942	Artist	150	338	575		'American Gothic'
Wood, Haydn	1882-1959	Composer	20	55	85	60	AMusQS 100-150
Wood, Henry J.	1869-1944	Composer	35	60		60	Br. Conductor. Founder of the 'Proms'

NAME	DATE	CATEGORY	SIG	LS/DS	ALS	SP	COMMENTS
Wood, James	1750-1813	Revolutionary War	50	82	132		House of Burgesses; Gov. VA
Wood, John Taylor	1830-1904	Civil War	86	189	322		Confederate Commander Navy
Wood, Lana		Entertainment	12	15	20	25	Actress. 'James Bond'.
Wood, Leonard, Dr.	1860-1927	Military	35	75	82	250	Gen'l T. Roosevelt's Rough Riders.
Wood, Lt. Gen. Sir Ernest	1894-1971	Military	25				World War II British general
Wood, Maj. Gen. George Neville	1898-1982	Military	25				World War II British general
Wood, Maj. Gen. John E.	1891-1963	Military	30				World War II U.S. general
Wood, Maj. Gen. John S.	1888-1966	Military	30				World War II U.S. general
Wood, Murray		Entertainment	20	80		85	Actor. Munchkin. 'Wizard of Oz'
Wood, Natalie	1938-1981	Entertainment	170	272		401	Am. Child & Top Adult Actress. SP/R. Wagner 524
Wood, Nigel		Astronaut	8			25	
Wood, Peggy	1892-1978	Entertainment	20	35		35	Theatre & TV Award Winner. 'I Remember Mama'
Wood, Robert E.		Military	20	70		25	Business (Sears), Gen. WW II
Wood, Robert W.	1868-1955	Science	10	25		20	Physicist. Manhattan Project
Wood, Robert		Astronaut	7			18	
Wood, Sam	1883-1949	Entertainment	40			90	Dir.-Producer. 'GoodbyMr. Chips', 'Night at Opera'
Wood, Sharon		Celebrity	10			15	motivational speaker
Wood, Sterling Alex. M. (WD)		Civil War	150	534	1541		1823-91. CSA General. Wounded. Resigned 1863
Wood, Sterling Alexander Martin	1823-1891	Civil War	128	334	550		Confederate general
Wood, Thomas J.	1823-1906	Civil War	45	76	95		Union Gen. Sig/Rank 60
Wood, Thomas Waterman	b. 1823	Artist	10	20	55		Pres. Am. Water-Color Society
Wood, Victoria		Celebrity	10			15	comedienne
Woodard, Alfre		Entertainment	10			20	actress
Woodburn Kirby, Maj Gen Stanley	1895-1968	Military	28				World War II British general
Woodbury, Daniel Phineas	1812-1864	Civil War	80	134			Union general
Woodbury, Levi	1789-1851	Supreme Court	50	110	175		Gov., Sen., Sec'y Navy & Treas. (Busy Politician)
Woodcock, Amos Walter, Gen.		Military	10	20		25	War Crimes Prosecution Staff. WW II
Woodfill, Samuel		Military	10	30	50	50	Major WW I, MOH Winner
Woodford, Brig Edw. Cecil James	1901-1988	Military	25				World War II British general
Woodford, Kevin		Celebrity	10			15	TV Chef
Woodford, Stewart L.	1835-1913	Civil War	55	85	120		Union Gen., Led 103rd Colored Troops. Gov. NY
Woodhouse, Brigadier L.J.		Military	28				World War II British general
Woodhouse, Henry		Financier-Explorer	65	265			Turned Forger
Woodhull, Nathaniel	1722-1776	Rev War		750			'Godsave us all', American gen.
Woodhull, Victoria C.	1838-1927	Reformer	115	240	510		1870's Feminist. Legalized Prostitution.
Woodring, Henry H.	1890-1967	Cabinet	21	45	70	50	FDR Sec'y War. TLS/Cont. 300
Woodruff, Judy		Celebrity	10			20	media/TV personality
Woodruff, Maj. Gen. Roscoe B	1891-1975	Military	30				World War II U.S. general
Woodruff, Wilford	1807-1898	Religion	25	65	130		Morman Religious Leader. In 1st Group to Salt Lake
Woods, Charles Robert	1827-1885	Civil War	34	60	92		Union General. Sig/Rank 55-75
Woods, Donald	1904-	Entertainment	15	20	30	30	Actor. Leading Man 30's-40's. Mostly Stage 50's on
Woods, James		Entertainment	15	15	30	45	Actor. Versatile Leads. Controversial Personality
Woods, Maj. Gen. Edw. Ambrose	1891-1957	Military	25				World War II British general
Woods, Maj. Gen. Ernest	1894-1971	Military	25				World War II British general
Woods, Phil		Entertainment	15			45	Jazz Alto Sax-Clarinet

NAME	DATE	CATEGORY	SIG	LS/DS	ALS	SP	COMMENTS
Woods, Rose Mary		White House	15		35	75	Nixon Sec'y. Watergate
Woods, William B.	1824-1887	Supreme Court	75	140	225	250	Also a Civil War General
Woodward, Bob		Author, Journalist	10	25	40	28	Uncovered Watergate w/C.Bernstein
Woodward, Edward		Entertainment	10	15	25	20	Br. Actor. Active in TV Series'
Woodward, George W.	1809-1875	Congress	15		25		MOC PA, Attorney, Judge
Woodward, Joanne		Entertainment	15	20		52	Oscar Winning Actress. SP with Paul Newman 187
Woodward, Lt. Gen. Eric W.	1899- ?	Military	20				World War II Australian general
Woodward, Marjorie		Entertainment	4	6	10	15	Actress. 40's Glamour Girl
Woodward, Robert Burns	1917-1979	Science	20	40	78	35	Nobel Chemistry 1965
Woodworth, Samuel		Author-Composer	45	140	350		Wrote 'The Old Oaken Bucket'
Wool, John E. (WD)	1784-1869	Civil War	100	260	635		Union general
Wool, John E.	1784-1869	Civil War	240	65	112		Union Gen., 1812 Vet., ALS '47 2000
Wooley, Sheb	1921-	Country Music	12			26	Very Versatile Actor-Singer. Co-Star 'Rawhide'
Woolf, Virginia	1882-1944	Author	450	1650	4567	4500	Br. Novelist, Essayist
Woollard, William		Celebrity	10			15	television presenter
Woollcott, Alexander		Journalist	30	95		150	Drama Critic, Actor Essayist. Algonquin Round Table
Woolley, Mary E.	1863-1947	Educator	30	50	75		1st Woman Grad. Brown U. Pres. Mt. Holyoke
Woolley, Monty	1888-1963	Entertainment	25	35		50	Character Actor Star of 'Man Who Came To Dinner'
Woolner, Maj Gen Chris. Geoffrey	1893-1984	Military	25				World War II British general
Woolrich, Cornell		Author	150	550			Am. Writer of Detective Fiction
Woolsey, Lynn C. W		Congress	10			15	Member U.S. Congress
Woolsey, Theodore D.	1801-1889	Educator		38	75		Pres. Yale 186-1871
Woolson, Albert	1846-1956	Civil War	100		295		Last Surviving Union Soldier
Woolworth, Charles S.		Business	250	1250			F.W. Woolworth's Brother-Partner. Stk.Proxy S 1650
Woolworth, Frank W.	1852-1919	Business	450	950	1550		Fndr. F.W. Woolworth Co. TLS/Cont 9500
Woorinen, Charles		Composer	10	20	40	40	Pulitzer, AMusQS 100
Wooster, David	1710-1777	Revolutionary War	235	875	2638		General; Continental Army. Mortally Wounded
Wootten, Maj. Gen. George	1893-1970	Military	20				World War II Australian general
Wootten, Maj. Gen. Richard M.	1889-1979	Military	25				World War II British general
Wootton, Percy		Celebrity	10			15	medical expert
Wopat, Tom		Entertainment	10	12	15	20	Actor. 'Dukes of Hazzard'
Worden, Al M.		Astronaut	15			50	
Worden, Hank		Entertainment	10			20	
Worden, John L.	1818-1897	Civil War	196	253	412		Union Navy, Comdr. Monitor.
Wordsworth, Christopher		Clergy	20	30	35	35	
Wordsworth, Maj. Gen. Robert H.	1894-1984	Military	25				World War II British general
Wordsworth, William	1770-1850	Author	339	729	1450		Br. Romantic Poet Laureate. AQS 2500
Work, Hubert	1860-1942	Cabinet	15	30	45	50	Sec'y Interior 1923
Worley, Jo Ann		Entertainment	5			18	'Laugh-In' Comedienne
Worth, Irene		Entertainment	10			25	Actress
Worth, William J.	1794-1849	Military	30	75	125		General; Mexican War
Wouk, Herman		Author	30	45	70	50	Am. Novelist; 'Caine Mutiny' Pulitzer
Woulfe, Michael		Fashion Designer	5			30	Film
Wozniak, Steve		Inventor	42		295	68	Co-Inventor of 1st Apple Computer, signed drwg 1207
Wray, Fay	1907-1998	Entertainment	45			85	1st King Kong Heroine. 'King Kong' SP 150

NAME	DATE	CATEGORY	SIG	LS/DS	ALS	SP	COMMENTS
Wren, Christopher	1632-1723	Architect-Science	1250	2750	3600		St. Paul's Cathedral, London. Last Recorded Prices
Wren, Percival Christopher	1885-1941	Author			135		
Wright, Ambrose Ransom	1826-1872	Civil War	90	140			Confederate general
Wright, Bobby	1942-	Country Music	7			15	Actor-Singer. 'McHale's Navy'
Wright, C.S.		Celebrity	15	35			
Wright, Cobina Sr. & Jr.		Entertainment	5			10	Socialite-Actresses of the 40's
Wright, Edyth		Entertainment	15			25	Band Vocalist
Wright, Frank Lloyd	1867-1959	Architect	748	1407	3100	3811	ALS/Content 4,000, 4,750
Wright, George	1803-1865	Civil War	40		90		Union general
Wright, Harold Bell	1872-1944	Author	10	20	35	25	Am. Novelist & Minister. 'Shepherd of the Hills'
Wright, Henry C.	1797-1870	Reformer	10	20	35		Anti-Slavery Reformer-Lecturer
Wright, Horatio G.	1820-1899	Civil War	48	75	120	460	Union General. Sig/Rank 65
Wright, Jerauld		Military	10	35		30	
Wright, Jim (James Claude)		Senate/Congress	10	30		20	Rep. TX 1955, Speaker
Wright, John J., Cardinal	1909-1979	Clergy	40	75	90	65	
Wright, Luke E.	1846-1922	Cabinet	15	45	90	35	Sec'y War 1908, Ambass. Japan
Wright, Marcus J. (WD)	1831-1922	Civil War	140	260	358		Confederate general
Wright, Marcus J.	1831-1922	Civil War	88	160	260		CSA Gen. Sig/Rank 175-250
Wright, Orville & Wright, Wilbur		Aviation		8500		12500	First Flight Pioneers
Wright, Orville	1871-1948	Aviation	461	971	2625	2318	TLS/Historical Content 15,000, S Chk 500-750
Wright, Richard	1908-1960	Author	70	225		375	Afro-Am. Wrote of Suffering, Prejudice
Wright, Robin Penn		Entertainment	10			40	Actress. 'Jenny' in Forrrest Gump
Wright, Silas, Jr.	1795-1847	Senate/Congress	20		75		Gen'l, Statesman, Gov. & Sen. NY
Wright, Teresa	1918-	Entertainment	30			60	AA for 'Mrs. Miniver'
Wright, Turbutt	1741-1783	Revolutionary War	35	60	95		Continental Congress
Wright, Wilbur	1867-1912	Aviation	900	2865	10250	6423	Historic SP 12,500, TLS 15,000, check 1898-1955
Wright, William		Military	25		125		Am. WW I General
Wrigley, Philip K.	1894-1977	Business	80	120	200	125	Wrigley Gum; Chicago Cubs
Wrigley, William, Jr.	1861-1932	Business	128	240	387	315	Founder Wrigley Gum Mfg.
Wrisberg, Lt Gen. Sir Frederick G.	1895-1982	Military	25				World War II British general
Wu, David W.	b. 1955	Senate	10			15	Member U.S. Congress, Oregon
Wuermeling, Joachim		Political	10			15	Member European Parliament
Wunderlich, Fritz		Entertainment	75			500	Opera
Wunsche, Max		Military	50			125	Hitler's Adj. WW II
Wuori, Matti		Political	10			15	Member European Parliament
Wurtz, Francis		Political	10			15	Member European Parliament
Wyant, Alexander Helwig	1836-1892	Artist	85		350		Of Hudson River School. Landscapes. ALS/Cont.750
Wyatt, Jane	1911-	Entertainment	5			30	Actress. Broadway. Film Leading Lady From 1934
Wyatt, Wendell		Congress	5	10		15	MOC OR 1964
Wyche, General Ira T.	1887-1981	Military	30				World War II U.S. general
Wyden, Ron		Senate	10			15	United States Senate (D - OR)
Wyeth, Andrew	1917-	Artist	170	375	700	750	Eminent Am. Painter.
Wyeth, Henriette		Artist	75	225			Artist in Her Own Right. Sister of Andrew Wyeth
Wyeth, Jamie		Artist	80	170	225	250	Orig. Ink Sketch Pig 550-950-1275 Signed
Wyeth, John A.		Medical Author	65		250		Noted Surgeon

NAME	DATE	CATEGORY	SIG	LS/DS	ALS	SP	COMMENTS
Wyeth, N. C.	1882-1945	Artist	140	470	766	875	Am. Painter-Illustrator of Classic Children's Books
Wÿhler, Otto	1894-1987	Military	25				World War II German general
Wyle, Noah		Entertainment	10			40	actor
Wyler, Gretchen		Entertainment	5	6	15	15	Actress
Wyler, William	1902-1981	Entertainment	30			100	3 Best Picture Acad. Awards
Wylie, Elinor	1885-1928	Author	60	95	285		Am. Poet, Novelist
Wylie, Philip	1902-1971	Author	15	30	60	50	Iconoclastic Author. 'Generation of Vipers'
Wylie, Robert	1839-1877	Artist	45	150			
Wyllys, Samuel	1739-1823	Revolutionary War	15	35	45		Military. Sec'y State of CT
Wyman, Bill		Entertainment	40		495	136	Rolling Stones Bass Guiitar
Wyman, Jane		Entertainment	14	25	40	50	AA Actress
Wyman, Willard G.	1898-1969	Military	40	65	90	75	4 Star General WW II
Wymore, Patrice		Entertainment	5	9	15	15	Actress-Model-Singer. Married Errol Flynn 1950
Wyn, Eurig		Political	10			15	Member European Parliament
Wyndham, Charles, Sir	1837-1919	Entertainment	15	32	45	58	Br. Actor-Mgr, Physician, Civil War Surgeon
Wyndham, Mary, Lady		Entertainment	5	6	10	18	
Wyndorf, Dave		Entertainment	18			35	Music. Lead Singer 'Monster Magnet'
Wynette, Tammy	1942-1998	Country Music	15			45	Singer-Actress. Queen of Country. 50 Albums
Wynn, Albert Russell W		Congress	10			15	Member U.S. Congress
Wynn, Ed	1886-1966	Entertainment	50	92	100	108	Vaudeville Comic. Ziegfield Follies Spec'l DS 350
Wynn, Keenan	1916-1986	Entertainment	25	30		45	Actor-Son of Ed Wynn. Dependable Supporting Actor
Wynn, Terence		Political	10			15	Member European Parliament
Wynter, Dana	1930-	Entertainment	5			15	Br. Actress. Elegant, Reserved Leading Lady
Wynter, Lt. Gen. Henry D.	1886-1945	Military	20				World War II Australian general
Wynyard, Dianna	1906-1964	Entertainment	5	6	15	25	Br. Charming, Graceful Leading Lady 30's-40's
Wysong, Forrest R.		Aviation	10	15	30	20	
Wyszynski, Stefan, Cardinal	1901-1981	Clergy	50	65	100	75	Defied Communist Government
Wythe, George	1726-1806	Rev. War	550	1296	3750		Signer. ALS/War Dte. 7,500. Historic DS 7900

Xarchakos, Stavros		Political	10			15	Member European Parliament
Xenakis, Iannis	1922-	Composer	75			175	Greek Composer
Xenia, Alexandrova	1875-1960	Head of State	75		412		Russia. Grand Duchess. Sister of Nicholas II
X-Files		Entertainment				100	Cast signed photo

Yadin, Yigael		Science		55		85	War Hero. World Famous Archaelogist
Yale, Brian		Entertainment	5			22	Music. Bass Guitar 'Matchbox 20'
Yale, Elihu	1648-1721	Statesman			5000		Benefactor of Yale University

NAME	DATE	CATEGORY	SIG	LS/DS	ALS	SP	COMMENTS
Yalow, Rosalyn S.		Science	15	25	40	20	Nobel Medicine 1972
Yamada, General Otozo	1881-1965	Military	25				World War II Japanese general
Yamaguchi, Maj. Gen. Takeo		Military	25				World War II Japanese general
Yamamoto, Isoroku, Adm.		Military	150	295	625	475	Pearl Harbor Attack, 12/7/1941
Yamamura, Maj. Gen. H.		Military	27				World War II Japanese general
Yamanashi, Hanzo		Military	95	265			
Yamaoka, Maj. Gen. Shigeatsu	1884- ?	Military	27				World War II Japanese general
Yamasaki, Minoru		Celebrity	10	25	60	20	
Yamashiro, Katsumari		Military	100			300	
Yamashita, Tomoyuki	1883-1946	Military	150	375	460	450	Jap. General. Hanged
Yamazaki, Lt. Gen. Yasuo	d.1942	Military	27				World War II Japanese general
Yanagawa, Lt. Gen.	1879-1945	Military	27				World War II Japanese general
Yang, Chen N.		Science	15	20	35	20	Nobel Physics 1957
Yang, Y. C.		Diplomat	10			20	Ambassador to Republic of Korea
Yankovic, Frank		Entertainment	4	4	9	10	
Yankovic, Weird Al		Celebrity	10			25	Comedian
Yardbirds		Entertainment	322			528	Rock Group. Special SP 2171
Yarnell, Harry E.	1875-1959	Military	40	75		60	Adm. Fleet Commander
Yarnell, Lorine		Entertainment	3	3	6	6	Shields & Yarnell
Yarrow, Ernest A.		Clergy	15	20	25		
Yarwood, Mike		Celebrity	10			15	impressionist
Yates, Edmund	1831-1894	Author	15	25	40		Br. Journalist-Novelist, Editor
Yates, Peter W.	1747-1826	Revolutionary War	30	120	175		Continental Congress
Yates, Richard	1815-1873	Civil War	25	40	60		Civil War Governor IL 1861
Yaw, Ellen Beach		Entertainment	30			200	Am. Soprano
Yeager, Chuck	1923-	Aviation	45	50	85	110	Ace, WW II, Pioneer, Test Pilot, Broke Sound
Yeager, Jeana & Dick Rutan		Aviaton	75	100		105	Voyager
Yeager, Jeana		Aviation	15	30		35	
Yearwood, Trisha		Country Music	10			35	Singer
Yeates, Jasper	1745-1817	Revolutionary War	15	35	60		Jurist
Yeats, Jack Butler		Artist	25	60	150		Brother of Wm. Butler Yeats
Yeats, Wm. Butler	1865-1939	Author	162	360	632		Nobel Poet, Dramatist; Abbey Theatre
Yeh, Emerald		Celebrity	10			15	media/TV personality
Yeltsin, Boris		Head of State	255	454		470	Russia
Yen, C.K.		Head of State	50	175			Pres. Republic China
Yeoh, Michelle		Entertainment	10			20	actress
Yerby, Frank G.	1916-1991	Author	35	60	80	70	Afro-Am. Novelist
Yerkes, Charles T.		Business	35	100			Capitalist. TLS/Content 450
Yes		Entertainment	45			85	Rock DS 125. Signed by all 5 1984
Ying, Ye		Celebrity	10			15	film industry
Yoakam, Dwight		Entertainment				45	CW Singer
Yogananda, Paramhansa		Religious (Yoga)			495		
Yokoyama, Lt. Gen. Shizuo	1890-1961	Military	25				World War II Japanese general
Yokum, Dwight		Country Music	10			35	
Yon, Pietro A.	1886-1943	Composer	25				Ital-Am. 'Gesu Bambino' AMusQS 195

NAME	DATE	CATEGORY	SIG	LS/DS	ALS	SP	COMMENTS
Yorath, Gabby		Celebrity	10			15	television presenter
Yorgesson, Yogi		Country Music	10			20	
York, Alvin, Sgt.	1887-1964	Military	232	382	575	522	MOH WW I
York, Dick	d. 1992	Entertainment	45			80	Darrin on Bewitched 1964-69
York, Michael		Entertainment	8	10	20	20	
York, Susanna		Entertainment	6	8	15	20	
York, Zebulon	1819-1900	Civil War	110				Confederate general
Yorty, Sam	1909-1998	Political	15	20		15	MOC CA, Mayor L.A.Unsuccessful Pres. Candidate
Youdale, Diane		Celebrity	10			15	television presenter
Youmans, Vincent		Composer	55	165	255	150	Tea for Two. MusMsS 800
Young, Alan	1919-	Entertainment	10	15	20	32	Early TV Comedian. 'Mr Ed' etc.'Alan Young Show'
Young, Andrew		Political	10	20	35	25	Afro-Am. Mayor Atlanta
Young, Angus		Entertainment	6			25	Music. Lead Guitar 'AC/DC'
Young, Ann Elizabeth		Celebrity	125				One of Brigham Young's Plural Wives
Young, Art*		Cartoonist	20			125	Political Cartoonist
Young, Brigham	1801-1877	Clergy	516	1778	4450	3738	Morman Leader. Rare DS 8500
Young, Burt		Entertainment	6			20	
Young, Charles Augustus		Science	35	140	225		Am. Astronomer, Author
Young, Charles William (Bill)		Congress	10			15	Member U.S. Congress
Young, Chic*	1901-1973	Cartoonist	35	55		100	5 Original Pieces S for WW II Cartoons. 2000
Young, Clara Kimball		Entertainment	45			75	Vintage Stage Actress
Young, Coleman		Political	5	15		20	Afro-Am. Mayor of Detroit
Young, David H.		Aviation	10	25		30	
Young, Dean		Cartoonist	25				'Dagwood'. Orig. Strip 275
Young, Don Y		Congress	10			15	Member U.S. Congress
Young, Faron		Country Music	10			30	Deceased
Young, Gig		Entertainment	30	38	70	67	Oscar Winner
Young, Henry E.		Civil War	25	45	70		CSA Major, Judge Advocate
Young, John		Astronaut	62	126		144	Moonwalker. Apollo 16, Shuttle Cmdr.
Young, John		Senate/Congress	15	25	45		Rep. NY 1836
Young, Kirsty		Celebrity	10			15	television presenter
Young, Lester		Entertainment	70	75	145	150	Jazz, Tenor Saxophone
Young, Loretta		Entertainment	20	25	35	66	Actress., AA & Emmy
Young, Lyman*		Cartoonist	10			50	Tim Tyler's Luck
Young, Maj. Gen. Bernard Keith	1892-1969	Military	25				World War II British general
Young, Maj. Gen. Hugh A.	1898-1982	Military	20				World War II Canadian general
Young, Maj. Gen. James V.	1891-1961	Military	20				World War II Canadian general
Young, Malcolm		Entertainment	6			25	Music. Rhythm Guitar 'AC/DC
Young, Neil		Entertainment	20			71	Crosby Stills Nash and Young, solo artist
Young, Owen D.	1874-1962	Business	15	25	50	20	CEO GE, Financier, Law, Advisor to Pres.
Young, Paul		Music	10			15	performing musical artist
Young, Pierce Manning Butler	1836-1896	Civil War	133	156	300		CSA Gen. S War Dte. 155, DS 350
Young, Richard		Celebrity	10			15	photographer
Young, Robert		Entertainment	15	25	35	55	Actor. Films-TV 'Father Knows Best','Marcus Welby'
Young, Roland		Entertainment	50			75	Droll Br. Actor. Remembered for 'Topper'

NAME	DATE	CATEGORY	SIG	LS/DS	ALS	SP	COMMENTS
Young, Samuel B.M.	1840-1924	Civil War	46	65	91		Union General Bvt.
Young, Sean		Entertainment	15	20		35	Actress
Young, Thomas L.	1832-1888	Civil War	30		65		Union Brevet Brig. General
Young, Trummy		Entertainment	15			45	Jazz Musician
Young, Whitney		Activist	5	20	45	15	Am. Civil Rights Leader. Author
Young, William Hugh	1838-1901	Civil War	90				Confederate general
Youngdahl, Luther		Governor	5	15		10	Governor MN 1947
Younger, Bob		Outlaw	2500				Fought w/Quantrill. Died in Prison
Younger, Maj. Gen. John Edw. T.	1888-1974	Military	25				World War II British general
Younger, Maj. Gen. Ralph	1904-1985	Military	25				World War II British general
Younger, Thomas C. (Cole)	1844-1946	Outlaw	3750	5750	16500		Bank Robber. Jesse James Gang.
Youngman, Henny	1906-1998	Entertainment	20	25	30	30	Club & TV Comedian.
Ysaye, Eugene-Auguste	1858-1931	Composer	80			225	Belg. Violin Virtuoso,Conductor. AMusQS 120
Yudenich, Nikolay N.		Military	95			175	Rus. Gen. Russo-Jap.& WW I
Yukawa, Hideki		Science	35	45	70		Nobel Physics 1949
Yulee, David Levy	1810-1886	Civil War	45		140		CSA Congress
Yun Fat, Chow		Entertainment	10			20	actor
Yun, Isang	1917-	Composer		80		150	Korean Born. Kidnapped by S. Korean Agents
Yung, Carl Gustav	1875-1961	Science	375	1250			Swiss Founder Analytical Psychology.
Yung, Victor Sen		Entertainment	35			65	
Yunge, Traudl		Military	35			55	Hitler's Pers'l Sec'y End of WW II
Yurka, Blanche	1886-1974	Entertainment	30		40	45	Hamlet/Barrymore
Yutang, Lin		Author	50	165			Chin. Novels, Philosophy, Plays
Yvon, Adolphe	1817-1893	Artist			92		Painter

Z

Zabach, Florian		Entertainment	5			20	
Zabeleta, Nicanor		Entertainment	40			150	Opera
Zabell, Theresa		Political	10			15	Member European Parliament
Zablocki, Clement John		Senate/Congress	5			20	Rep.WI 1949
Zabriskie, Andrew C.		Business	35		140		Capitalist, Financier
Zach, David		Celebrity	10			15	financial expert
Zacharakis, Christos		Political	10			15	Member European Parliament
Zackerly		Entertainment	3			10	TV Horror Host
Zadora, Pia		Entertainment	5			20	
Zaharoff, Basil	1850-1936	Manufacturer				1495	Mystery Munitions Mfg. A Cause of WW I
Zahn, Timothy		Author	10			35	Star Wars Trilogy
Zais, Melvin		Military	10	20	35	15	
Zajic, Dolora		Entertainment	5			25	Opera
Zamboni, Maria		Entertainment	40			200	Opera
Zancanaro, Giorgio		Entertainment	10			30	Opera
Zandonai, Riccardo	1883-1944	Composer			60	195	Opera

NAME	DATE	CATEGORY	SIG	LS/DS	ALS	SP	COMMENTS
Zane, Billy		Entertainment	15			40	'Phantom' Cast of 100+. 'Titanic'
Zangen, Gen. Inf. Gustav-Adolf v.	1892-1964	Military	25				World War II German general
Zangwill, Israel	1864-1926	Author	40	75	95	125	Br. Playwright, Novelist, Poet, Journalist
Zanuck, Darryl F.	1902-1979	Entertainment	50	120		125	Producer. Co-Founder 20th Century Fox
Zanuck, Richard Darryl		Entertainment	8	8	20	25	Film Producer, Exec.
Zapata, Emiliano	1879-1919	Revolutionary	500	1100	1625		Mex. Guerilla Leader
Zappa, Frank	1940-1993	Entertainment	35	100		175	Composer, Guitarist, Mothers of Invention
Zappala, Stefano		Political	10			15	Member European Parliament
Zapruder, Abraham		Celebrity	40				Filmed JFK Assassination in 8mm
Zaslow, Jeffery		Celebrity	10			15	media/TV personality
Zavodszky, Zoltan		Entertainment	30			85	Opera
Zeani, Virginia		Entertainment	15			45	Opera
Zeeman, Pieter	1865-1943	Science	200		975		Nobel for Physics 1902. Dutch Physicist
Zefferelli, Franco		Entertainment	12			35	Film Director
Zeitzler, Colonel-General Kurt	1895-1963	Military	27				World War II German general
Zelenski, Wladyslaw		Composer	50		150		Polish Music Teacher
Zell, Harry von		Entertainment	10	15	25	25	Radio Announcer-Comedian, Jack Benny Sidekick
Zeller, General André-Marie	1898- ?	Military	20				World War II French general
Zeller, General Henri	1896-1971	Military	20				World War II French general
Zellerbach, James D		Business	15	40	85	35	US Ambassador, Industrialist
Zellweger, Renee		Entertainment	10			55	actress
Zelnick, Bob		Celebrity	10			15	media/TV personality
Zeman, Jacklyn		Author-Actress	5	8	10	10	
Zemekis, Robert		Entertainment	5	15		20	Film Director
Zemke, Hubert 'Hub'		Aviation	15	35	65	40	ACE, WW II, Triple Ace
Zemlinsky, Alexander		Composer	90	265			Aus. Conductor
Zenatello, Giovanni		Entertainment	45		65	125	Opera
Zeppelin, Ferdinand, Graf von	1838-1917	Aviation	225	650	888	1250	Inventor Dirigible Air Ship
Zerbe, Anthony		Entertainment	10		25	25	
Zeta-Jones, Catherine		Entertainment				55	AA winner
Zetterling, Mai		Entertainment	15			35	Actress
Zhukov, Georgi K.	1896-1974	Military	85	383	492	450	Rus. Marshal. Soviet Hero WW II., DS/cont 1207
Ziegfeld, Florenz	1869-1931	Entertainment	150	374	512	550	Am. Vaud. Prod. Famous 'Follies', ALS/Content 950
Ziegler, General of Artillery Heinz	1894-1972	Military	25				World War II German general
Ziegler, George M.	1834-1912	Civil War	25	40	60		Union General, Bvt.
Ziegler, Karl		Science	45	65	70	55	Nobel Chemistry 1969
Ziegler, Ronald L.	d. 2002	White House	10	20	25	20	White House Aide. Nixon Press Sec'y
Ziegler, Vincent C.		Business	5			10	CEO Gillette Safety Razor Co.
Ziering, Ian		Entertainment	5			25	Actor. 'Beverly Hills 90210'
Zilli, Aldo		Celebrity	10			15	Chef
Zimbalist, Efrem, Jr.		Entertainment	5	8		20	Popular Actor. Leading Man Films. Early TV Leads
Zimbalist, Efrem, Sr.		Entertainment	45			265	Violinist, Composer
Zimbalist, Stephanie		Entertainment	6	10	15	20	Actress. Pin-Up SP 30
Zimeray, Frantois		Political	10			15	Member European Parliament
Zimmer, Norma		Entertainment	3	5		10	Early TV Vocalist for Lawrence Welk

NAME	DATE	CATEGORY	SIG	LS/DS	ALS	SP	COMMENTS
Zimmerling, Jürgen		Political	10			15	Member European Parliament
Zimmerman, Laura		Celebrity	10			15	media/TV personality
Zindel, Paul		Author	10	20		25	Playwright
Zinnemann, Fred		Entertainment	20		35	60	AA Film Director
Zinoviev, Grigori E.	1883-1936	Political			575		Soviet Communist leader, purged by Stalin
Ziolkowski, Korczak		Artist	15	35	65	40	
Zissener, Sabine		Political	10			15	Member European Parliament
Zmed, Adrian		Entertainment	5	6	15	15	
Zog I		Royalty	40			85	King Albania
Zola, Emile	1840-1902	Author	145	350	559	2070	Fr. Novelist & Social Reformer
Zollicoffer, Felix K.	1812-1862	Civil War	270	382	561		CSA General
Zollicoffer, Felix K. (WD)	1812-1862	Civil War	575	1750			CSA Gen. KIA
Zombie, Rob		Entertainment	10			50	White Zombie Lead Singer
Zook, Samuel Kosciusko	1821-1863	Civil War	188	1859	4250		Union general, KIA Gettysburg
Zorba, Myrsini		Political	10			15	Member European Parliament
Zorina, Vera		Entertainment	20			35	Ballerina, Films, Stage
Zorn, Gen. of Infantry Hans	1891-1943	Military	25				World War II German general
Zrihen, Olga		Political	10			15	Member European Parliament
Zuazo, Hernan Siles		Head of State	10	15	25	15	
Zucco, George		Entertainment	85			250	
Zucherman, Pinchas		Entertainment	10			65	Violinist
Zukoffsky, Louis		Author	25		80	50	Am. Poet
Zukor, Adolph	1873-1976	Entertainment	50	145	200	120	Founder Paramount.Pioneer Film Producer
Zuloaga, Ignacio		Artist	25	75			Sp. Painter
Zumwalt, Elmo R., Jr. 'Bud'	1920-2000	Military	20	30	55	65	Adm. WW II
Zuniga, Daphne		Entertainment	10			20	actress
Zweig, Arnold		Author	25	65		50	Ger. Novelist, Playwright
Zweig, Martin		Celebrity	10			15	financial expert
Zweig, Stefan	1881-1942	Author	30	65	120	80	Aus. Psychoanalytical Biogr.
Zweigert, Eugen, Lt.		Aviation	100			300	Ger. ACE WW II
Zwicky, Fritz		Science	20	35		45	Am. Astronomer. Jet Propulsion
Zworykin, Vladimir		Science	70	260	350	95	Am. Inventor TV System. Father of Am. TV
ZZ Top		Entertainment				150	Rock Band, signed album 152

The faces behind the prices: While *many* people contributed to the pricing in this book, the final checking was done by Dr. Richard Saffro (above left) and Jim Smith (above right). Left, Dick and Jim in the offices of Alexander Books correcting the final galleys just before this book went to press. They truly learned the meaning of the old publishing term, "galley slaves."

The **SANDERS** Price Guide to **Autographs**

6

Sixth Edition

Section 3:

FACSIMILES

Being depictions of authentic autographs for your handy comparison as to authenticity.

The late George R. Sanders and Helen Sanders (cofounders of this price guide with Ralph Roberts) during a visit to the offices of Alexander Books in 1997.

Chapter 16

Facsimiles

Anyone can sign John Wayne's name, and many do! A person of low morals might invest $2 in an 8x10 glossy of Wayne, sign it as Wayne, and sell it at a collectibles show for $35 or $40. If this unprincipled thief got a good deal on an assortment of Hollywood stars, he might come away with several hundred dollars from the pockets of unsuspecting autograph collectors. The trash they've bought is, of course, worthless!

Our best advice is to buy autographs only from reputable dealers (such as the ones advertising in this book). Yet, we all dream of finding that signed Greta Garbo photograph at the flea market for $5. It's good to dream but, how do you know what's authentic and what's just so much ink on paper? The answer is having known authentic examples of signatures available. These are called *facsimile signatures*. They are simply copies of real signatures of the celebrity. Compare your "find" to a known good sig and, if it matches, you're much more likely to have an authentic autograph!

The following pages are a good start to developing your own reference library of facsimiles. This book presents you with several thousand facsimiles known to be good. While our attorney screams if we try to say anything absolute (i.e. we make no warranties either express or implied), the sigs in this book are good to the best of our knowledge.

Use this book as a start in amassing a reference library of facsimiles. Enlarge the library with other facsimile books (we have a few of those in the works ourselves) and by keeping (*never* throwing away!) all the dealer catalogs you can find. Please write the dealers advertising in these pages, many of them put out most useful and interesting catalogs, chock full of facsimiles. Then when you come across a questionable signature, a few minutes of browsing through your facsimile library can answer the question of authenticity by simple comparison with a known good example.

Which is not to say all of this is easy. Over the course of years, a person's signature changes with age and through other factors such as injury or just the technology of writing instruments. You'll want to accumulate, wherever possible, the facsimiles of an individual's autograph at differing ages.

There is no such thing as having too many facsimiles!

We hope these that follow prove helpful.

Ronald Reagan happily signs for George Sanders. George's long stint in broadcasting and the entertainment business means that he was able to meet and personally obtain the autographs of thousands of celebrities. This "in-person" knowledge is the basis of the authentic facsimiles in this book.

A

Bud Abbott

Red Adair

Ansel Adams

President John Adams

President John Quincy Adams

Maude Adams

Charles Addams

Jane Addams

Richard Adler

Louis Agassiz

Edward Albee

Jack Albertson

Buzz Aldrin

Horatio Alger

Fred Allen

Roald Amundsen

Wally "Famous" Amos

Roscoe "Fatty" Arbuckle

General Robert Anderson

Sir William Armstrong

Jack Anderson

President Chester A. Arthur

Marian Anderson

Isaac Asimov

Maxwell Anderson

Nils Asther

Maxine & Patty Andrews

Lady Astor

Norman Angell

Waldorf Astor

Walter H. Annenberg

William Backhouse Astor

President David R. Atchison

Clement Attlee

Jacqueline Auriol

Gene Autry

B

Leo Hendriik Baekeland

F. Lee Bailey

Theodorus Bailey

Bernt Balchen

James Baldwin

Stanley Baldwin

Tallulah Bankhead

Michael A. Banks

John Bardeen

Vice President Alben William Barkley

Christian Barnard

P. T. Barnum

J. M. Barrie

Mona Barrie

Ethel Barrymore

Lionel Barrymore

Frederic Auguste Bartholdi

Freddie Bartholomew

Clara Barton

Bernard M. Baruch

P. G. T. Beauregard

Noah N. Beery

Menachem Begin

S. N. Behrman

Alexander Graham Bell

Ralph Bellamy

Saul Bellow

Peter Benchley

Your obedient servant,

Stephen Vincent Benet

Joan Bennett

Jack Benny

Ezra Taft Benson

Most sincerely,

Gertrude Berg

Gertrude Berg

Elizabeth Bergner

Irving Berlin

Sarah Bernhardt

Father Daniel Berrigan

Ken Berry

Josh Billings

Clarence Birdeye

Jussi Bjoerling

Hugo L. Black

Patrick M. S. Blackett

Harry A. Blackmun

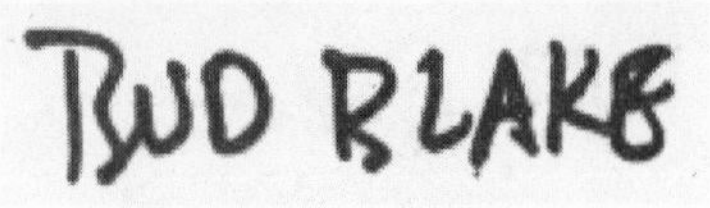

Bud Blake

Eubie Blake

Mel Blanc

Major General Zenas Bliss

Herb Block

Guion S. Bluford Jr.

Eleanor Boardman

Niels Bohr

Ray Bolger

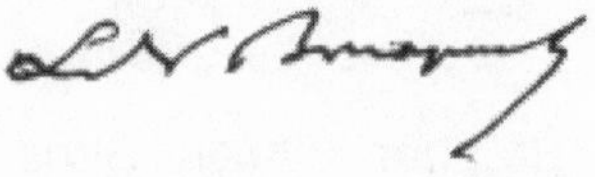

Louis Napoleon Bonaparte

Julian Bond

Pat Boone

Edwin Booth

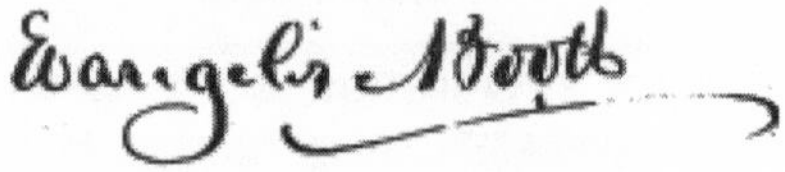

Evangeline Booth

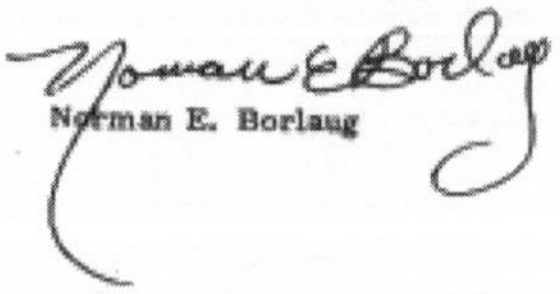

Norman E. Borlaug

Frank Borman

Major Edward Bowes

Bill "Hopalong Cassidy" Boyd

Ray Bradbury

General of the Army

Omar Bradley

Louis D. Brandeis

Dan Brandenstein

Willy Brandt

Karl Branting

Bertolt Brecht

John Cabell Breckinridge

Justice William J. Brennan, Jr.

Leonid I. Brezhnev

David Brinkley

W. E. Brock

Clive Brook

Rand Brooks

Joe E. Brown

Johnny Mack Brown

Dik Browne

Robert Browning

President James Buchanan

Pearl S. Buck

General D. C. Buell

David D. Buick

Ned Buntline

Luther Burbank

Justice Warren E. Burger

Billie Burke

William John Burns

General Ambrose E. Burnside

David Burpee

Aaron Burr

President George Bush

Vannever Bush

Francis Bushman

Major General Benjamin F. Butler

James Branch Cabell

James Cagney

Sammy Cahn

Erskine Caldwell

John Caldwell Calhoun

Melvin Calvin

Rod Cameron

Albert Camus

Milton Caniff

Yakima Canutt

Truman Capote

Al Capp

Mary Carlisle

King Juan Carlos

Hoagy Carmichael

Andrew Carnegie

Dale Carnegie

Scott Carpenter

John Carradine

Dr. Alexis Carrel

Sunset Carson

Enrico Caruso

George Washington Carver

Pablo Casals

Kellye Cash

Catherine II (The Great)

Bruce Catton

Whittaker Chambers

Coco Chanel

John Charles XIV

Cesar Chavez

Paddy Chayefsky

Gilbert Keith Chesterton

Maurice Chevalier

Walter P. Chrysler

Lady Clementine Churchill

Andre Citroen

Joe Clark

Mae Clarke

President Grover Cleveland

President Bill Clinton

Dewitt Clinton

Irvin S. Cobb

Major General Howell Cobb

Jacqueline Cochran

William F. "Buffalo Bill" Cody

Ronald Coleman

Vice President Schuyler Colfax

P. T. Collins

Jerry Colonna

Jerry Colonna

Jackie Coogan

President Calvin Coolidge

Peter Cooper

General Samuel Cooper

Aaron Copeland

Jean Baptiste Camille Coret

"Wrong Way" Corrigan

Jacques Cousteau

Joan Crawford

Michael Crichton

Dr. A. J. Cronin

Bing Crosby

E. E. Cummings

Sir Samuel Cunard

Charles Curtis

Harvey W. Cushing

Richard Cardinal Cushing

D

Idi Amin Dada

Richard J. Daley

Vice President George M. Dallas

Charles Darwin

Marion Davies

Richard Harding Davis

Sir Humphry Davy

Charles G. Dawes

Dr. Lee de Forest

Charles de Gaulle

Geoffrey de Havilland

Alexander P. de Seversky

Dr. William DeVries

Dr. Michael DeBakey

John Deere

Delores Del Rio

Cecil B. de Mille

Thomas Dewey

Benjamin Disraeli

Dorothea Dix

James D. Dole

Abner Doubleday

Cordially yours,

Donald W. Douglas

Lloyd C. Douglas

William O. Douglas

Sir Arthur Conan Doyle

W. E. B. DuBois

Pierre S. Du Pont

Love 'n kisses,
JIMMY DURANTE

Jimmy Durante

E

Amelia Earhart

Jubal Early

George Eastman

Kevin Eastman

Abba Eban

Hugo Eckener

Mary Baker Eddy

Sir Anthony Eden

Thomas A. Edison

Albert Einstein

Julie Nixon Eisenhower

Mamie Doud Eisenhower

T. S. Eliot

Queen Elizabeth II

Ralph Waldo Emerson

Charles Evers

F

John Eberhard Faber

Vice President Charles Fairbanks

Michael Faraday

Diane Feinstein

Edna Ferber

Cyrus W. Field

Eugene Field

Marshall Field, Jr.

President Millard Fillmore

James Montgomery Flagg

Father Flanagan

Sir Alexander Fleming

Errol Flynn

Anthony Fokker

Henry Fonda

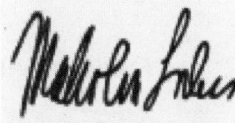

Malcolm Forbes

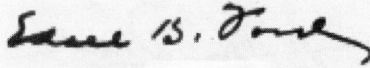

Benson Ford

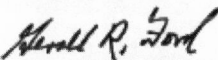

Edsel B. Ford

President Gerald R. Ford

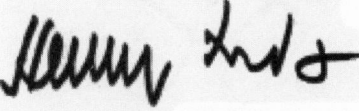

Henry Ford II

Henry Ford

E. M. Forster

Justice Felix Frankfurter

King Frederick VII

John Charles Fremont

Milton Friedman

David Frost

G

R. Buckminster Fuller

John Galsworthy

Indira Gandhi

Mahatma Gandhi

Greta Garbo

Ava Gardner

Erle Stanley Gardner

President James A. Garfield

Guiseppe Garibaldi

Vice President John Nance Garner

William Lloyd Garrison

Richard Gatling

King George I

Henry George

Elbridge Gerry

Ira Gershwin

J. Paul Getty

Charles Dana Gibson

A. C. Gilbert

John Gilbert

Allen Ginsberg

Lillian Gish

John A. Glenn, Jr.

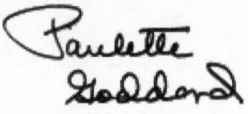

Paulette Goddard

Arthur Godfrey

George W. Goethals

William Golding

Samuel Goldwyn

Samuel Gompers

Benny Goodman

Charles Goodyear, Jr.

Mikhail S. Gorbachev

Chester Gould

Betty Grable

Cary Grant

Ulysses S. Grant

Dave Graue

Horace Greeley

John Green

Zane Grey

David W. Griffith

Gus Grissom

Gilbert Grosvenor

Edgar Guest

Daniel Guggenheim

Peggy Guggenheim

Charles Guiteau

H. Rider Haggard

Josephine Hall

Dr. Armand Hammer

Oscar Hammerstein

E. Y. "Yip" Harburg

President Warren G. Harding

Oliver Hardy

Thomas Hardy

W. Averell Harriman

Joel Chandler Harris

President Benjamin Harrison

President William Henry Harrison

Johnny Hart

Moss Hart

William S. Hart

Paul Harvey

Prince Hassam

Brig General Joseph R. Hawley

Helen Hayes

President Rutherford B. Hayes

Susan Hayward

William Randolph Hearst

Edward Heath

Christie Hefner

Joseph Heller

Lillian Hellman

Henry III (old age)

Henry III (young)

Katharine Hepburn

Frank Herbert

Victor Herbert

Thor Heyerdahl

Sir Edmund Hillary

Alfred Hitchcock

Vice president Garret A. Hobart

William Holder

Oliver Wendell Holmes

Winslow Homer

Herbert Hoover

J. Edgar Hoover

Hedda Hopper

Harry Houdini

Major General Oliver Otis Howard

Julia Ward Howe

Victor Hugo

Hubert H. Humphrey

King Hussein

Will Hutchins

Aldous Huxley

I

Lee Iacocca

Henrik Ibsen

James B. Irwin

J

Andrew Jackson

Jesse Jackson

Andrew Johnson

Lyndon Baines Johnson

Richard Mentor Johnson

Quincy Jones

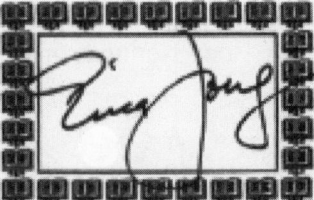

Erica Jong

Janis Joplin

Jim Jordan "Fibber McGee"

C. G. Jung

K

Henry J. Kaiser

Chiang Kai-Shek

Madame Chiang Kai-Shek

Bob Kane

Boris Karloff

Bill Keane

Major General Philip Kearny

Buster Keaton

Carolyn Keene

Helen Keller

W. K. Kellogg

Emmett Kelly, Sr.

Grace Kelly

Arthur Kennedy

Ethel Kennedy

John F. Kennedy

Joseph P. Kennedy

Rose Kennedy

Hank Ketcham

Cammie King

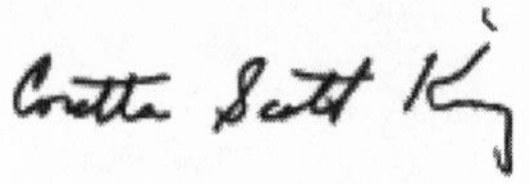

Coretta Scott King

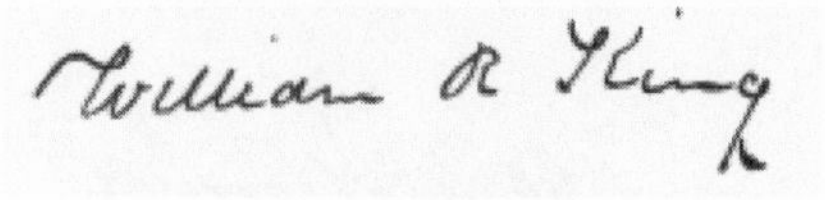

William R. King

Lane Kirkland

Calvin Klein

Werner Klemperer

Evel Knievel

Henry Thatcher Knox

Edward I Koch

Christopher Kraft

Eugene Kranz

Paul Kruger

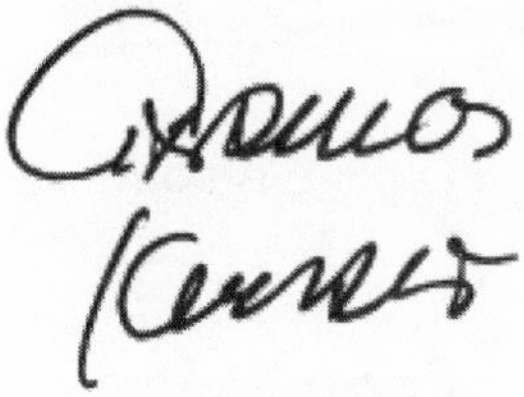

Charles Kuralt

L

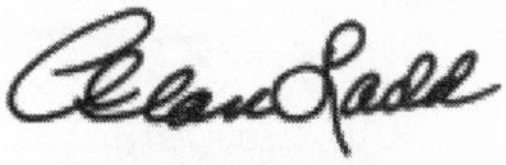

Alan Ladd

Fiorello LaGuardia

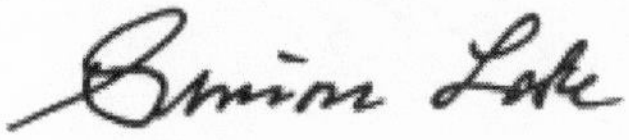

Simon Lake

Veronica Lake

Dorothy Lamour

Louis L'Amour

Bert Lance

Edwin Land

Ann Landers

Carole Landis

Alf Landon

Samuel Pierpont Langley

Lillie Langtry

Walter Lantz

Ring Lardner

Lash LaRue

Stan Laurel

Yves Saint Laurent

Ernest Lawrence

Gertrude Lawrence

Mary D. Leakey

Norman Lear

John leCarre

Anna Lee

Gypsy Rose Lee

Robert E. Lee

Dr. Willy Ley

Liberace

Trygve Lie

Beatrice Lillie

Abraham Lincoln

Robert Todd Lincoln

Jenny Lind

Charles Lindbergh

Joseph Lister

Franz Liszt

David Livingstone

Harold Lloyd

David Lloyd-George

Allan Lockheed

Gina Lollobrigida

Alice Roosevelt Longworth

King Louis VIII

King Louis Philippe

Bernard Lovell

James Russell Lowell

Clare Booth Luce

Henry R. Luce

Allen Ludden

Robert Ludlum

Marion Mack

Ted Mack

Archibald MacLeish

Dolley Madison

President James Madison

Ramon Magaysay

Norman Mailer

Bernard Malamud

Henry Mancini

Edouard Manet

Horace Mann

Thomas Mann

Mantovani

Gugelielmo Marconi

Ferdinand Marcos

Johnny Marks

Justice Thurgood Marshall

Glenn L. Martin

Groucho Marx

Harpo Marx

Zeppo Marx

Raymond Massey

Henri Matisse

W. Somerset Maugham

Hiram Percy Maxim

Louis B. Mayer

Dr. Charles W. Mayo

Dr. William Mayo

Frederick L. Maytag

General George McClellan

Cyrus McCormick

Colonel Tim McCoy

President William McKinley

Ray Milland

Aimee Semple McPherson

Arthur Miller

Margaret Mead

Henry Miller

General George Meade

Newton Minow

George Meany

Ed Mitchell

Adolphe Menjou

Tom Mix

Burgess Meredith

Walter F. Mondale

Ethel Merman

President James Monroe

Robert Moog

Christopher Morley

Samuel F. B. Morse

Major John "the Gray Ghost" Mosby

Grandma Moses

R.G. Mugabe

Rupert Murdock

Edward R. Murrow

Story Musgrove

Russell Myers

N

Napoleon

Ogden Nash

Poli Neri

Edwin Newman

Brigitte Nielsen

John Ringling North

Lord North

Alfred Noyes

O

Hermann Oberth

Edmond O'Brien

Sandra Day O'Connor

Clifford Odets

Ransom E. Olds

Eugene O'Neill

Robert Oppenheimer

Baroness Orczy

P

David Packard

William S. Paley

John Dos Passos

Lester B. Pearson

Sir Robert Peel

J.C. Penney

George Plimpton

Svetlana Peters

President James K. Polk

Eugene Peugeot

Lily Pons

Slim Pickens

Admiral David Porter

Mary Pickford

Cole Porter

President Franklin Pierce

Katherine Anne Porter

J.S. Pillsbury

Marina Oswald Porter

ZaSu Pitts

Emily Post

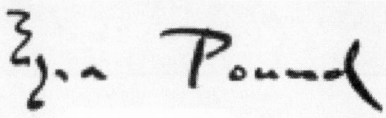

Ezra Pound

Dick Powell

Lewis Powell

Tyrone Power

Francis Gary Powers

Otto Preminger

Jackie Presser

Robert Preston

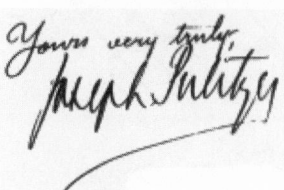

Andre Previn

John Profumo

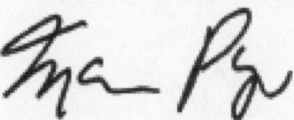

Joseph Pulitzer

Melvin Purvis

Mario Puzo

Ernie Pyle

Howard Pyle

Q

Col. Muammar el-Qaddfi

Dan Quayle

Ellery Queen

Vidkun Quisling

R

Prince Ranier

Sally Rand

James Earl Ray

Ronald Reagan

William Rehnquist

Renek

Duncan Renaldo

Pierre Auguste Renoir

Judith A. Resnick

James B. Reston

Jason Robards

Robert Reud

Kenneth Roberts

Walter Reuther

Oral Roberts

Yours very truly,

President.

Richard Reynolds

Ralph Roberts

Captain Eddie Rickenbacker

Happy Rockefeller

Leni Riefenstahl

John D. Rockefeller, Jr.

James Whitcomb Riley

Nelson Aldritch Rockefeller

"BELIEVE IT OR NOT"

Robert Ripley

Norman Rockwell

Richard Rodgers

August Rodin

Ginger Rogers

Charles S. Rolls

Sigmund Romberg

Stu Roosa

Franklin Roosevelt

Theodore Roosevelt

General William S. Rosecrans

Jerry Rubin

Arthur Rubenstein

Helena Rubenstein

Charlie Ruggles

Damon Runyon

Bertrand Russell

Lillian Russell

S

Dick Rutan

Carl Sandberg

David Sarnoff

Rafael Sabatini

Vidal Sassoon

Dr. Albert B. Sabin

Arthur Schlesinger

Pierre Salinger

Charles Schulz

Dr. Jonas Salk

Charles Schwab

Randolph Scott

George Sand

Sir Walter Scott

General Winfield Scott

Glenn Seaborg

Jean Seberg

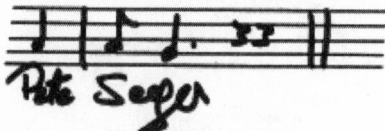

Pete Seeger

Andres Segovia

David O. Selznick

Mack Sennett

Rod Serling

Dr. Seuss

Sir Ernest Shackleton

George Bernard Shaw

Alan B. Shepard Jr.

Ann Sheridan

General Philip Sheridan

General W. T. Sherman

William Shockley

Maria Shriver

Phil Silvers

Georges Simenon

Neil Simon

Frank Sinatra

Harry F. Sinclair

Upton Sinclair

Isaac B. Singer

B. T. Skinner

Alfred P. Sloan

Alfred Smith

Kate Smith

Kingford Smith

Sir Thomas Sopwith

Ann Souther

John Philip Sousa

Francis Cardinal Spellman

Elmer A. Sperry

Mickey Spillane

Dr. Benjamin Spock

Edward Robinson Squibb

Lili St. Cyr

Sir Henry Stanley

Frank Stanton

Harold Stassen

John Steinbeck

Charles P. Steinmetz

Inger Stevens

Adlai E. Stevenson

James Stewart

Jimmy Stewart

Tempest Storm

Rex Stout

Igor Stravinsky

Ed Sullivan

Arthur Sullivan

T

William Howard Taft

Booth Tarkington

Zachary Taylor

Edward Teller

God bless you

Mother Teresa

Valentina Tereshkova

Studs Terkel

Nikola Tesla

Margaret Thatcher

Jeremy Thorpe

Tito

Arnold J. Toynbee

George A. Trenholm

Gary Trudeau

Pierre Trudeau

Harry S. Truman

Donald Trump

Forest Tucker

Ted Turner

U

John Updike

Leon Uris

V

Rudy Vallee

James Van Allen

Martin Van Buren

S. S. Van Dine

Carl Van Doren

Mark Van Doren

Amy Vanderbilt

Cornelius Vanderbilt

George W. Vanderbilt

Jules Verne

Queen Victoria

Wernher von Braun

Erich Von Daniken

Alexander von Humboldt

Maria Von Trapp

Terry Waite

Kurt Waldheim

Lech Walesa

Agard Henry Wallace

Irving Wallace

Barbara Walters

Andy Warhol

Robert Penn Warren

Jessamyn West

George Washington

George Westinghouse

Harold Washington

James McNeil Whistler

Thomas Watson

Byron White

James Watt

Edward H. White

John Wayne

Theodore H. White

Charlie Weaver "Cliff Arquette"

Walt Whitman

Daniel Webster

Eli Whitney

Charles E. Whitaker

John Greenleaf Whittaker

Oscar Wilde

Thornton Wilder

Sincerely yours,

Wendell Wilkie

King WIlliam IV

Ben Ames Williams

Esther WIlliams

John Williams

Mason Williams

Paul Williams

Tennessee Williams

Meredith Willson

Henry Wilson

Woodrow Wilson

Walter Winchell

Owen Wister

Thomas Wolfe

Grant Wood

Natalie Wood

Orville Wright

Andrew Wyeth

Y

Charles E. "Chuck" Yeager

Jeana Yeager

Frank Yerby

Sgt. Alvin E. York

Brigham Young

Z

Ferdinand von Zeppelin

Dream Autographs by Ralph Roberts

We are often asked, "What is the *most* valuable autograph?" Our stock answer for the past fifteen years that we have been doing autograph price guides has consistently been, "Button Gwinnett"—that being the highest valued autograph outside of a museum that a private collector might reasonably hope to acquire. Gwinnett was a Signer of the Declaration of Independence and the first governor of Georgia. Gwinnett County, where a great deal of Atlanta lies, was named after him. He had a brief moment of glory, then promptly got himself killed in a duel. Hence, his very rare signature is valued at (as of this edition) $150,000 just for his sig.

The above answer, however, begs the question. Handwriting, after all, has been around something like 5,000 years. The authentic handwriting of truly great historic figures would certainly soar into the millions of dollars. The signature of Our Lord, Jesus Christ (with provenance) would be incalculable. Moses, Alexander the Great, Hamurabi, Socrates, Julius Caesar, Buddha, Cleopatra, Helen of Troy, a signed poem by Homer—all would grace any collection and be worth millions, even billions.

Well, dream on. No one has found a signed Julius Caesar in a yard sale yet. But, following are some you *might* find. (Well... maybe... Let's dream, huh?)

First, the bad news—no known signatures by famed persons of classic antiquity exist. The earliest attributable autographs (i.e. *handwriting* instead of actual signatures) belong to clerics during the early Middle Ages, literacy being pretty much their sole province in those generally illiterate times. It was mostly—says the *Encyclopedia Britannica*—"an age of anonymity rather than individuality and works such as chronicles are often of unknown authorship."

The earliest known "lay" autograph is that of the Spanish captain, El Cid, dating from the year 1096. (Remember Charlton Heston in the movie *El Cid?*—that's the guy!)

Early English kings usually signed with an "X." While Edward III (1327-1377) was not the first literate English monarch, he is the first whose writing survives. And there are examples in museums of all following English kings and queens. So, yes, you could dream about finding one of those. Don't hold your breath, but at least those are not totally impossible.

Most of the big names of the Renaissance—Leonardo of *Mona Lisa* fame, Michaelangleo, and so forth—have their autographs preserved in national libraries. It is possible you *could* run across one out there somewhere but—I remind you again—this section *is* entitled "Dream Autographs."

Still, just in case, following are some facsimilies of highly collectible names to dream about. Enjoy. And please let us know if you find any. And *where* you found them. Thanks.

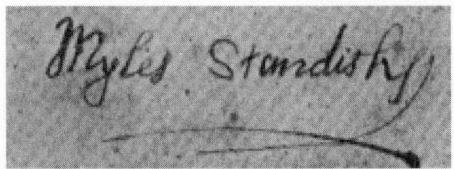

Myles (or Miles) Standish (1584?-1656), Pilgrim military hero and assistant governor of Plymouth Colony.

Charles I (1600-1649) was dethroned and beheaded by Oliver Cromwell.

John Calvin (1509-1564), one of the leaders of the Protestant Reformation.

Juan Ponce de Léon (c 1460-1521) Spanish explorer—discovered Florida.

Hernando de Soto (1500-1542), Spanish explorer and the first white man to cross the Mississippi River.

Sir Frances Drake (c 1540-1596) was the first Englishman to sail around the world.

Sir John Hawkins (1532-1595), first English slave trader and Elizabethian naval hero.

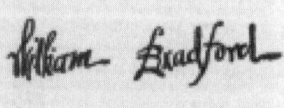

William Bradford (1590-1657), second governor of Plymouth Colony and author. Called "the father of American History."

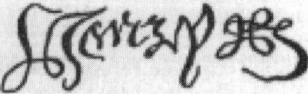

Henry VIII (1491-1547) of England, whose marital problems put those of the current English royal family to shame.

Elizabeth I (1533-1603), queen of England and Ireland, only child of Henry VIII.

The SANDERS
Price Guide
to
Autographs

Sixth Edition

Section 4:

DEALERS

Being a guide to some recommended dealers in autographs and historic documents.

Chapter 17

Autograph Dealers

This section contains a **Buyer's Guide** representing many of the major dealers in the autograph world. While inclusion here does not *per se* mean we endorse a particular dealer over one not participating in this guide, it *does* mean we believe the dealers here to be reputable experts in their various areas of expertise. And—on the other hand—just because a dealer elected not to participate does not necessarily mean that he or she should be avoided.

However, we hasten to point out that the kind folks who *are* in this book deserve a great vote of thanks (and even a little business, perhaps) from all of us, authors and readers alike. They made this huge book practical and allowed us to both add much more than otherwise would have been possible, and to keep the retail price down to a most reasonable $29.95. Believe us, the printing bill on this tome is immense—please at least say a hearty "thank you" to our wonderful advertisers.

Dealer Index

University Archives .... One of the World's Leading Buyers & Sellers of Autographs .... Back Cover

R&R Enterprises .... Leading Autograph Auction with Extensive Monthly Catalog .... Inside Front Cover
Todd Mueller .... "Highest Prices and Fastest Cash Payout" .... Inside Back Cover

A. Lovell Elliott Autographs .... All sorts in nearly every category 706
Abraham Lincoln Book Shop, Inc. .... Lincolniana, Civil War, US Presidents, American & Military History 730
Alexander Autographs .... Auctioneers of quality autographs 711
American Historical Guild .... Historic Autographs, Letters, & Documents 722
American Memorabilia .... Over 100 years of combined experience 713
Autograph Pros .... World's Largest Autographed Guitar Dealer 712
Benedikt & Salmon .... Music & Performing Arts Memorabilia 716
Catherine Barnes .... Quality Autographs in American & European History, Science, Finance, & Arts 715
Christophe Stickel Autographs .... Monthly bargain autograph auctions 708
Collectibles Insurance Agency .... Insurance for Autographs 714
David M. Beach .... Buying Letters, Stocks, and Documents of Important Businessmen and Inventors 718
EAC Gallery .... Autographs, books, manuscripts, documents, presidential, sports, fine art 707
Early American History Auctions, Inc. .... Autographs, Americana, Civil War, Maps, Coins, Currency, more 733
Edward N. Bomsey Autographs, Inc. .... Quality Autographs Bought and Sold 712
Elmer's Autographs & Nostalgia .... Entertainment, Political, Historical, Literary, Military, Space & Pop Culture 730
Estoric.com .... Specialize in Revolutionary War & Presidential manuscripts 716
Fred Senese Autographs .... Buying and Selling Autographs Since 1991 724
Gerard A.J. Stodolski, Inc. .... Historic Autographs, Letters, Manuscripts, & Documents 720
Heroes & Legends .... Rock & Roll and Hollywood Autographs 732
Historical Rarities .... Dealing in Rare and Unusual Finds 732
History Emporium .... Specialize in Colonial America, Political Documents, & Early American Ephemera 718
Howard Hurwitz Autographs .... Vintage Hollywood and Big Band Era Autographed Photos 714
I.A.C.C./I.A.D.A. .... International Autograph Collectors Club / Dealers Alliance 728

Jack Bacon & Company	Fine Historical Autographs since 1977	724
Kaller Historical Documents, Inc.	Major Historical Documents and Letters	727
Keya Gallery	Specializing in Signed Historical Documents, Letters, Photographs.	726
Larry's Books & Autographs	Specializing in Jazz, Blues, Big Band, Movie Directors	720
Lewis Leigh, Jr.	Confederate & Union Memorabilia, Uniforms, Weapons, Letters & Diaries	730
Lone Star Autographs	All Fields, Free Catalog on Request	728
MastroNet ,Inc.	Consignment Auction House	736
Michael J. Masters, M.D.	Buying Quality Signed Documents, Letters, & Photographs for Personal Collection	706
Mitchell Marketing	Autographed Memorabilia	729
PADA	The Professional Autograph Dealers Association	723
Pages of History—Jerry Docteur	Buying and Selling in all Fields since 1983	712
Provenance Collectibles Inc.	Americana, Historical, Presidential, Militaria, & Supreme Court	732
Roger Gross, Ltd.	Musical Autographs Bought and Sold	724
Scott J. Winslow Associates, Inc.	Autographs, documents, Americana, ephemera, stock certificates & bonds	708
Showcase Portfolios	Fine Preservation Framing	710
Signature House	A Quality Auction House	717
Signatures in Time	Photos, Documents, Letters, Books—vintage to modern	714
Smythe Autograph Auctions	Let Smythe's Experts Work for You	708
Sterncastle Collectibles	Vintage Hollywood Autographs & Photos, Classic Television Autographs	719
Steven L. Hoskin Historical Autographs	Quality American Historical Autographs, Documents, and Letters	710
Steven S. Raab Autographs	A Reputation for Integrity Built Over a Decade, Earned Day by Day	722
Stuart Lutz Historic Documents Inc.	Letters and Groupings with Important and Interesting Historical Content	705
The Inkwell Autograph Gallery	Gettysbutrg's Largest Selection of Civil War Era Autographs	730
The Manuscript Society	For Dealers, Collectors, Scholars, Authors, Caretakers of Public Collections	734
Treasures for a Lifetime	Autographed First Edition Books	709
Treasures—The Brams Collection	Every facet of the Autograph Market	721
U.A.C.C.	An Organization for Collectors Run by Collectors	735
University Archives	One of the World's Leading Buyers & Sellers of Autographs	704
University Archives	One of the World's Leading Buyers & Sellers of Autographs	731
Visible ink, Inc.	Specializing in cultural, scientific, & fine arts of all ages, in all languages	725

Still the Best.

As one of the world's premier auctioneers of quality autographs, Alexander Autographs offers the finest material available in all areas of collecting. Every one of our catalogs offers an extensive selection including Presidents, Revolutionary and Civil War, Americana, artists, authors, scientists, vintage sports and Hollywood, and much more.

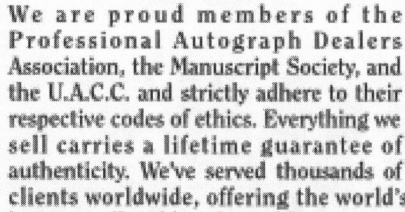

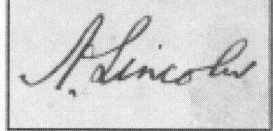

We are proud members of the Professional Autograph Dealers Association, the Manuscript Society, and the U.A.C.C. and strictly adhere to their respective codes of ethics. Everything we sell carries a lifetime guarantee of authenticity. We've served thousands of clients worldwide, offering the world's finest and most important historic collectibles obtainable. Let us serve you!

Catalogs for upcoming auctions are available for a nominal charge. Should you be interested in consigning or selling outright, please contact our Senior Vice President Peter Klarnet at (203) 622-8444.

BEST IN QUALITY • BEST IN SELECTION • BEST IN PRICE

Alexander Autographs

**100 Melrose Avenue, Suite 100
Greenwich, Connecticut 06830
203-622-8444 • Fax 203-622-8765
http://www.alexautographs.com**

HOWARD HURWITZ AUTOGRAPHS

VINTAGE HOLLYWOOD AND BIG BAND ERA AUTOGRAPHED PHOTOS BOUGHT AND SOLD

UACC REGISTERED DEALER RD067

WEBSITE: **W W W**
SILVERSCREENAUTOGRAPHS.COM

VIEW 500 SCANS ONLINE

FULL LISTING OF INVENTORY

SENT UPON REQUEST

32 SKYLINE DRIVE
MECHANICSBURG, PA 17050

PHONE (717) 691-7776

E-MAIL - info@silverscreenautographs.com

SIGNATURES IN TIME

Randy Thern

Serving Autograph Collectors for 15 Years

Photos * Documents * Letters * Books

Vintage to Modern

Find me on the **Net**

Watch for my frequent auctions on *EBAY*

Send for a **free list**

I also **buy** individual pieces to large collections – contact me anytime for terms.

P. O. Box 180

Scandinavia, WI 54977

Ph: 715-445-3251, Fax: 715-445-4691

Email: **randy@signaturesintime.com**

On the Web: **www.signaturesintime.com**

Member: UACC, IADA & Manuscript Society

INSURANCE FOR AUTOGRAPHS

Your homeowners insurance is rarely enough to cover your collectible treasures. We have provided economical, dependable collectibles insurance since 1966.

• **Sample collector rates:** $3,000 for $14, $10,000 for $38, $25,000 for $95, $50,000 for $190, $100,000 for $278, $200,000 for $418. Above $200,000, rate is $1.40 per $1,000.

• **Our insurance carrier** is AM Best's rated A+ (Superior).

• **We insure autographs and well over 100 other kinds of collectibles** from antiques, stamps, paper ephemera, manuscripts, and books, to sports cards, china, glass, and limited editions—**plus scores of other collectibles.** "One-stop" service for practically everything you collect.

• **Replacement value.** We use expert/professional help valuing collectible losses. Consumer friendly service: Our office handles your loss—you won't deal with a big insurer who doesn't know collectibles.

• **Detailed inventory** and/or professional appraisal not required. Collectors list items over $5,000, dealers no listing required.

• **See our website** (or call, fax, e-mail us) for full information, including standard exclusions.

Collectibles Insurance Agency

P.O. Box 1200-SPG • Westminster MD 21158
E-Mail: info@insurecollectibles.com

See the online application and rate quote forms on our website!

Call Toll Free:1-888-837-9537 • Fax: (410) 876-9233

Need A Rate Quote?
Visit: www.collectinsure.com

CATHERINE BARNES
HISTORICAL AUTOGRAPHS

Please visit us at
www.BarnesAutographs.com
for
Quality Autographs in American & European History,
Science, Finance, & the Arts

AUTOGRAPHS WANTED!
We are always buying autographs,
ranging from single items to partial or whole collections

AUTOGRAPHS FOR SALE
Sample catalogue sent on request

P.O. Box 27782-G, Philadelphia, PA 19118
Phone: 215-247-9240
Fax: 215-247-4645
E-mail: mail@barnesautographs.com

Established 1985
Member: Professional Autograph Dealers Association;
Antiquarian Booksellers Association of America; Manuscript Society; UACC

Signature House

Since 1994

A company is only as good as its guarantee.
Signature House is the only company that offers a Golden Guarantee.

NOW OFFERING FREE APPRAISALS

We have the expertise to advise you whether to sell or hold on
to your autographs, how you can realize the best price, whether
to take to auction or sell outright.

OVERNIGHT PAYMENT IF WE BUY YOUR AUTOGRAPHS

Contact
Gil & Karen Griggs
Signature House
407 Liberty Avenue
Bridgeport, WV 26330
Phone: 304-842-3386
Email: editor@signaturehouse.net
Website: www.signaturehouse.net

Members: IADA   Manuscript Society   UACC

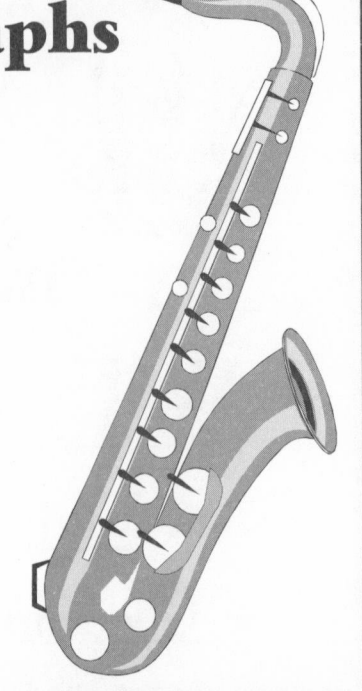

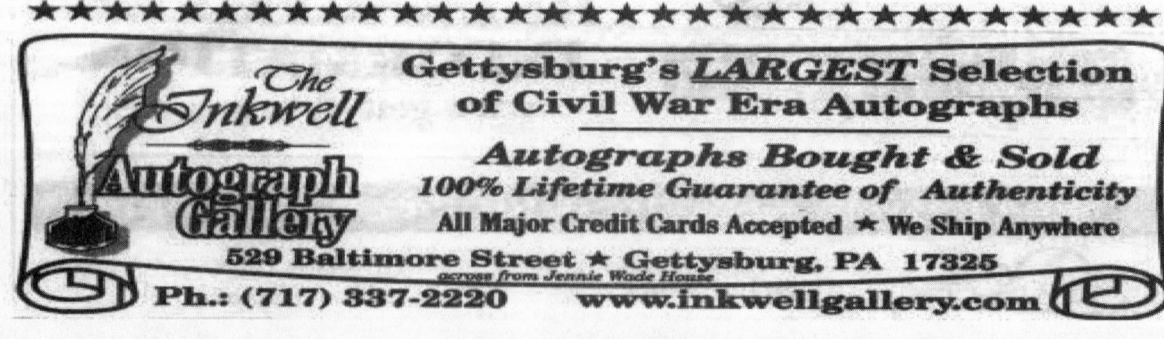

The Manuscript Society

THE MANUSCRIPT SOCIETY (_www.manuscript.org_), founded in 1948 as the National Society of Autograph Collectors, has grown to an international membership of approximately 1,500 encompassing the spectrum of private collectors, manuscript professionals (curators, archivists, and librarians), and dealers. Many historical societies, museums, special collections and academic libraries are valued institutional members as well.

The Manuscript Society welcomes new members. The annual individual or institutional membership fee is $45. Contributing memberships at $100, sustaining memberships at $250, benefactor memberships at $500, and patron memberships at $1000 help in furthering Society interests. Memberships are on a calendar year basis; new members joining after July 1 may pay half the annual rate. Your dues support the following: our publication program; scholarships for individuals interested in the use of manuscripts (e.g. Richie Maass Memorial Grant); the defense of individuals in appropriate replevin suits; and the expenses of managing the Society's programs and activities.

To join, the society, contact:

Edward C. Oetting
Executive Director
The Manuscript Society
1960 E. Fairmont Dr.,
Tempe, AZ 85282-2844
www.manuscript.org
manuscrip@cox.net

UNIVERSAL AUTOGRAPH COLLECTORS CLUB

an invitation to join the U.A.C.C.

The Universal Autograph Collectors Club, Inc. is a federally approved nonprofit organization dedicated to the **education** of the autograph collector. Founded in 1965, the **U.A.C.C.** is known as "**The Collectors Advocate.**" The organization sponsors shows worldwide and publishes its journal the *Pen and Quill* bi-monthly. The U.A.C.C. is an organization for collectors, run by collectors.

The U.A.C.C. sponsors autograph shows in major U.S. cities and London, England featuring educational displays, autograph dealers who abide by the U.A.C.C. Code of Ethics, and celebrity guests. Seminars are occasionally held in conjunction with the shows to educate our members and the public on all aspects of collection and preservation, and identification of non-authentic (bogus or forged) material.

Finally, the U.A.C.C. sponsors mail auctions through *The Pen and Quill* as well as an annual live floor auction near Washington, DC. These auctions are another avenue to assist our members who buy and sell autographs.

To learn more about the U.A.C.C., send your request for a brochure and membership application to the address below. You can also get membership information and an application by visiting our Internet web site at **http://www.uacc.org**. We hope you will join our universe of fellow collectors soon.

For membership information, please write:

UACC
Dept. SPG
P.O. Box 5262
Clinton, N.J. 08809

Check out the UACC's newest venture on
www.uaccauction.com
The finest authentic autographs auctioned by
UACC Registered Dealers only.

Look for UACC Registered Dealer logo when you make your next
autograph addition to your collection.

Visit our website at: **http://www.uacc.org**
The UACC now accepts Visa/MasterCard